$55.05

ENVIRONMENTAL STUDIES
Earth as a Living Planet

ENVIRONMENTAL STUDIES
Earth as a Living Planet

Second Edition

Daniel B. Botkin
Edward A. Keller
University of California, Santa Barbara

Merrill Publishing Company
A Bell & Howell Information Company
Columbus   Toronto   London   Melbourne

Cover Photo: Robert Llewellen

Published by Merrill Publishing Company
A Bell & Howell Information Company
Columbus, Ohio 43216

This book was set in Leawood

Administrative Editor: David C. Gordon
Production Coordinator: Mary Harlan
Art Coordinator: Lorraine Woost
Cover Designer: Cathy Watterson
Text Designer: Cynthia Brunk

"Agroforestry: Production and Protection for the Tropics" adapted from *Garden* magazine, January 1986, published by the New York Botanical Garden.

Acknowledgments for figures and photographs appear on pages 667–75.

Library of Congress Catalog Card Number: 86-63814
International Standard Book Number: 0-675-20462-3
Printed in the United States of America
1 2 3 4 5 6 7 8 9—91 90 89 88 87

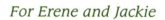

For Erene and Jackie

Preface

The study and management of our environment have undergone great change in the last two decades. In the 1960s, enthusiasm for protection of the environment and recognition of the effects of modern civilization on our surroundings became popular. Views were more polarized then. Some people argued that everything about the environment was good and·should be protected without change—and that all development of natural resources was bad. Opponents argued that these extreme "environmentalists" were opposed to progress and possibly to everything good about civilization and technology—and, therefore, that a concern with the environment was bad.

In the 1970s, progress was made in dealing with environmental issues and enthusiasm remained high. A number of nations enacted their first environmental laws. Agencies were established to manage pollution and conserve endangered species.

Environmentalism in the 1980s is characterized in part by a more concentrated shift from enthusiastic rhetoric to development of alternative ways to solve environmental problems associated with such local, regional, and global issues as overpopulation, hazardous waste, acid precipitation, nuclear power, the increase of carbon dioxide in the atmosphere, and the management of resources. This energy in problem solving is evident at both individual and institutional levels. While some activists put Earth first in a quasi-militant, nonyielding position, most strive for change by affecting the bureaucratic system, influencing people's values and priorities, and learning more about the workings of Earth as an ecosystem.

Today, the field of environmental studies emphasizes the role of environmental concerns in all our activities. A concern with the environment is viewed as part of economic development, and the great majority of the people want to live in a clean, pleasing, and productive environment. The enthusiasts of the 1960s have matured into today's environmental professionals: executives in alternative energy corporations, applied scientists who work in international projects to spread appropriate technologies to our inner cities and to developing nations, economists who calculate the costs and benefits of pollution controls, environmental lawyers who help write laws to promote wise use of our resources, and other people in many fields.

In recent years our understanding of many aspects of the environment has greatly increased, ranging from our knowledge of the transport and fate of pollutants in air and water to an appreciation of what is really necessary to save endangered species. The second edition of *Environmental Studies: Earth as a Living Planet* reflects these changes. It is an up-to-date introduction to the most important and useful concepts in the study and management of the environment presented from a contemporary perspective. It provides the interdisciplinary perspective within which we must view environmental issues in order to deal successfully with them; it provides an introduction to the ideas and approaches important to modern environmental management.

INTERDISCIPLINARY APPROACH

The field of environmental studies integrates many disciplines and includes some of the most important applied topics of modern civilization as well as one of the oldest philosophical concerns of human beings—that of the nature of our relationship with our surroundings. Both applied and basic aspects of environmental studies require a solid foundation in the natural sciences, in addition to a foundation in anthropology, economics, history, and philosophy of the environment. Not only do we need the best ideas and information to deal successfully with our environmental problems, but also we must be aware of the cultural and historical context in which we make decisions about our environment and understand the ways in which choices are made and implemented. Thus, the field of environmental studies integrates the natural sciences with environmental ethics, environmental economics, environmental law, and planning. *Environmental Studies: Earth as a Living Planet* provides an introduction to the entire spectrum of relationships between people and the environment.

ORGANIZATION

The text is divided into five parts. Part I provides a broad overview of the ethical and historical background to environmental studies and an introduction to the nature of life and the environment on Earth. Part II discusses the ecological concepts that are basic to environmental studies—the fundamental properties of populations, ecological communities, ecosystems, and biological geography. A separate chapter is devoted to human population dynamics, because human population growth underlies essentially all of our environmental issues. Part III discusses renewable biological resources, the management of which is based on the ecological concepts of Part II.

Part IV discusses our physical resources—air, water, minerals, and energy—and introduces basic concepts concerning the nonbiological environment, with special emphasis on natural hazards and hazardous wastes. In Part V, important applications of all the concepts are discussed: planning, environmental economics, environmental laws, and the urban environment. In keeping with contemporary concerns are the special chapter on cities (most of us live in cities, and a concern with city environments is growing), and the general emphasis throughout on global and international topics, reflecting the growing recognition of the international and planetary aspects of environmental issues.

Although *Environmental Studies: Earth as a Living Planet* is organized to provide a progression from one topic to another, it is also designed to be used with a variety of courses of different lengths. We recommend that each section be read in turn, but we have written each chapter to stand alone, so that the book can be used also as a reference or refresher. Because this text is an introduction to environmental studies, college-level prerequisites in the sciences or humanities are not necessary to read and understand this book.

FEATURES

Considerable changes in organization and content appear in the second edition, with expanded coverage on a number of topics. New chapters have been added on World Food Supply (Ch. 10), Waste Disposal (Ch. 16), and Citizens, Laws, and Agencies (Ch. 21). Material on the basic physical and biological processes of Earth has been integrated into a single chapter (Ch. 2), while material on Ecosystems and Communities has been reorganized, expanded, and divided into two chapters (Ch. 4 and 5).

Among the features new to this edition are

☐ *Key Concepts* The list of significant concepts that appears at the beginning of each chapter provides an overview of important topics and also serves as an aid for review.

☐ *Case Studies* The case study examples that show the impact of environmental processes, their causes and solutions, have been expanded and now introduce each chapter and appear throughout the text.

☐ *Career Profiles* Interviews with professionals from widely varying backgrounds demonstrate how environmental concerns affect their lives and careers.

☐ *Feature Essays* The text discussion is supplemented by brief essays on current topics of concern in the field of environmental studies.

Other pedagogical features in each chapter include key terms boldfaced in the text, a chapter summary, study questions, and a list of suggestions for further reading. At the end of the book are conversion charts, a geologic time scale and biologic evolution chart, and glossary, along with text references for each chapter.

Most of all, we have designed *Environmental Studies: Earth as a Living Planet* to help you, the reader, think through environmental issues for yourself. We have provided the concepts and the information to help you evaluate environmental issues as they develop in the world around you, or as they take focus in your line of work.

ACKNOWLEDGMENTS

Successful completion of this text would not have been possible without the cooperation of many people. To all those who so freely offered their help in this endeavor, we offer our sincere appreciation. We wish to thank the following people for their constructive comments in reviewing the manuscript: Stanley Awramik, University of California, Santa Barbara; Margriet Caswell, University of California, Santa Barbara; Roderick Nash, University of California, Santa Barbara; Sally Holbrook, University of California, Santa Barbara; Dorothy A. Rosenthal, University of Rochester. *For pre-revision reviews:* David Egloff, Oberlin; Robert Walker, University of Massachusetts; Jeff White, Indiana University; Hubert Yammamoto, Minneapolis Community College. *For chapter-by-chapter reviews:* Clyde W. Hibbs, Ball State; Donald L. Rice, University of Maryland; Ruth F. Weiner, Western Washington University. *For specialist reviews:* Henry W. Art, Williams College; Garrett Hardin, Santa Barbara; Oscar Soule, Evergreen State College. *Art review:* Wakefield Dort, Jr., University of Kansas. *Final review:* Susan W. Beatty, University of California at Los Angeles.

We would like to thank Harold Morowitz, Yale University, for his helpful suggestions about the introduction of energy concepts; Harold Ward, Brown University, who contributed Chapter 21, "Citizens, Laws, and Agencies"; John Disinger, Ohio State University, who compiled the lists of Key Concepts; all those featured as Career Profiles, for allowing us to interview them; and the more than one hundred national environmental agencies and organizations that responded to a survey on current topics essential to address in an environmental studies text.

We are indebted to Jennifer Knerr at Merrill, without whom this second edition would not have been possible, for her help with extensive revisions, in editing, overall organization, and planning of the text. Our thanks also to Mary Harlan, production coordinator; Jean Simmons Brown, copy editor; Lorraine Woost, art coordinator; Terry Tietz, photo editor; Michele Davis, photo researcher; Dan Duffee, for help with manuscript organization; and the Merrill College Division WP Group, for processing the text.

The Environmental Studies Program and the Departments of Biological Sciences and Geological Sciences at the University of California, Santa Barbara, provided the stimulating atmosphere necessary for writing. Fellowships to D. B. Botkin from the East-West Center, Honolulu, the Rockefeller Bellagio Study and Conference Center, Bellagio, Italy, and from the Woodrow Wilson International Center for Scholars, Washington, D.C., provided time and stimulating environments in which ideas in the text underwent growth and enrichment.

Contents

CONTENTS

I
Ethics and Science

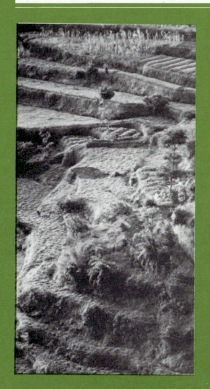

1
Environmental Ethics

- [ ] A proper environment is essential to sustain all renewable resources, including ourselves.
- [ ] To consider the people-nature relationship, three questions must be addressed: (1) What is the condition of nature when undisturbed by human influences? (2) What is the influence of nature on people and human society? (3) What is humanity's effect on nature, and what should it be?
- [ ] Nature undisturbed by human beings has been regarded at various times as perfectly ordered, or dangerous, chaotic, or capricious; to be valued as beautiful or machinelike; and to be treated either as a commodity to be used or as a system necessary for our survival and therefore to be protected and sustained.
- [ ] Ideas about nature must be reinterpreted and reexamined in every age.
- [ ] Throughout most of our time on Earth, people have been important ecological factors, creating major changes in the environment and having major effects on the rest of life.
- [ ] All technology, from primitive to advanced, causes some changes in the environment.

- [ ] Increasing human populations and technological expansion create increased demands on the environment.
- [ ] Environmental ethics is concerned with the value of the physical and biological environment, whereas classical ethical concerns had to do with the relationships among people.
- [ ] There are practical and moral reasons for placing a value on the environment. The practical reasons include utilitarian and ecological ones, and the moral reasons include aesthetics, the rights of nonhuman living things, and our obligations to future human generations.
- [ ] Environmentalism became popular during the 1960s and 1970s but was seen by many as strident and opposed to progress and technology. Today, there is a recognition that a concern with the environment is part of economic development.
- [ ] Environmental studies is a broad, interdisciplinary area; dealing with environmental problems demands competence in many disciplines and creates a need for interdisciplinary teams.

PLACING VALUE ON THE ENVIRONMENT

More people are alive today than have ever lived on Earth at one time, and we are using more resources and producing more wastes than any previous civilization. When there were few people on Earth, our planet's ability to provide resources and absorb wastes appeared infinite. Today, our rapidly expanding technological civilization creates new demands on all aspects of our environment. We can no longer avoid the question: How valuable is our environment?

How valuable is it? The simplest answer is that a proper environment is essential in order to sustain all renewable resources—food, fibers, wood, air, water, and even ourselves and our own health. But people have placed many other kinds of values on the environment, and the debate over its ethical value is as old as civilization.

Although our modern civilization has had many negative effects, we recognize that modern civilization has also made the environment more livable in many ways. With modern medicine and technological advances, we have better health care, better control of parasites, and better ability to protect ourselves from natural hazards. We are able to feed more people better than ever before. In recent years, we have learned to live in closer harmony with our environment; for example, we control pests in a more benign manner, using natural, biological control. We are finding new ways to use renewable, nonpolluting sources of energy. We are learning to choose carefully among alternate technologies. At the heart of these new developments is a change in how we perceive our natural environment and how we define our roles and responsibilities.

Whether the benefits of technology will outweigh negative effects in the long run is an open question. The choices we make now will lead us in one of two directions. We can move forward to a future in which we live in harmony with our environment, maintaining our renewable resources and conserving and reusing our nonrenewable ones. Or we can act in ways that will lead to an impoverished and highly polluted landscape, depleted of resources, with our soils, forests, and fisheries exhausted and many important species extinct. Our choices will depend in part on our knowledge of the environment and in part on our values.

A fundamental principle of environmental studies is that an understanding of complex environmental problems requires a team approach involving several disciplines. The serious student of the environment must be aware of the contributions to environmental research from biology, conservation, atmospheric science, chemistry, environmental law, architecture, engineering, and geology as well as from physical, cultural, economic, and urban geography and philosophy and history. Environmental studies, by its very nature, must be seen as a broad and interdisciplinary subject.

THE CHANGING AMERICAN VIEW

Arriving late in the fall of 1620, after two months on the stormy north Atlantic, the 73 men and 29 women on the *Mayflower* confronted what they considered a wild and savage land. Although these first colonists did not adapt quickly to their new environment, they and their successors had a great effect on the New World, largely because of three factors. First, they brought a new technology: The axe, the gun, and the wheel enabled them to conquer the land and its earliest inhabitants, the native Americans. Second, the colonists planned to remake the New World through organized work and the use of work animals, and they had a European market for their surplus productions. Finally, their concept of land ownership was completely alien to that of the native Americans, whose bonds to the land were more religious and involved kinship with nature rather than exclusive possession. The colonists' idea was that ownership involved absolute title, regardless of who worked the land or how far away the owner was. After the native Americans were displaced, therefore, land use or abuse depended entirely on the attitude of the owner [1].

America today suffers from the effects of the "myth of superabundance," which was widely held in the early years and is prevalent still. The myth assumed that land and resources in America were inexhaustible and therefore management of resources was not nearly as important as locating and using resources. Stuart Udall writes that the land myth was instrumental in environmental degradation from the "birth of land policy" in the eighteenth century through the "raid on resources" that continued well into the twentieth century. Thomas Jefferson, who in later life did become aware of the value of conservation, stated in his younger years that there was such an abundance of farmland that he could waste it as he pleased [1].

The westward migration in the United States was led by the mountain men, an adventurous lot who were financed by companies interested in the huge profits to be made in selling furs, such as beaver skins that were used for fashionable hats in Europe. The trapping of the beaver and other fur-bearing animals in the 1820s began the raid on resources in western North America. This beginning was followed by machines that, for the first time, were capable of large-scale removal of resources and alteration of the landscape. Sawmills facilitated the destruction of the American forest, and on the west coast the "Little Giant" hose nozzle produced water pressure sufficient to tear up entire hillsides in the search for California gold.

Accompanying the raid on resources was the "great giveaway" of land, which hastened the destruction of forests and the erosion of soil. Although this phase of American history closed toward the end of the nineteenth century, when hydraulic mining was outlawed, the effects of these land-use practices can still be viewed from the forests of New England to the gold fields of California. Other notable casualties of this period were the buffalo, passenger pigeon, and grizzly bear.

Modern warnings of environmental problems began in the United States in the mid-nineteenth century, with the publication of *Man and Nature* by George Perkins Marsh and with the writings of Thoreau and others who saw the infringement of civilization on nature. Relatively little attention, however, was paid to the warnings of these pioneer thinkers.

The dust bowl of the 1930s raised a new concern for what we were doing to our land. Paul Sears eloquently stated the issues for his time in *Deserts on the March*. Mother Nature, said Sears, cannot be conquered except on her own terms [2]. We must learn how nature works so that we can live in harmony with our environment. Meanwhile, geologists and geographers studying the materials processes and form of the terrain, biologists studying ecology, and oceanographers and atmospheric scientists studying regional and global change were gathering disturbing facts that suggested we were changing not just local environments but the entire environment of our planet. But the flowering of technology after World War II made a widespread concern with the environment inevitable. We, as a civilization, were doing too much in too many places to avoid seeing the changes.

Environmentalism—a movement concerned with protecting the environment and using its resources wisely—developed in the 1960s in response to a growing awareness of our effects on the environment. This movement was at first strident and negative. With the publication of Rachael Carson's *Silent Spring*[3] (a book suggesting that the widespread use of DDT would lead to the extinction of songbirds) and with the knowledge that fallout from atomic tests (among other events) was polluting the entire Earth, some began to believe that all of technology and most of civilization was bad for the environment. The extremists wanted to reject all modern technology and knowledge on the grounds that the scientific method had gotten us into this trouble. The more moderate wanted to halt all technological progress. Opposing them were those who believed that continuous exploitation of the environment, regardless of the consequences, was necessary to the very survival of civilization. Our society seemed ready to divide into two camps: those who saw themselves as the saviors of the environment and those who saw themselves as the saviors of civilization.

In spite of these extreme tendencies, the environmentalism of the 1960s and 1970s had many positive effects, especially in developing social mechanisms to help ensure a healthful environment. For example, establishment of the Environmental Protection Agency in the United States and passage of laws to control pollution and to protect wilderness, endangered species, and marine mammals in many nations. International accords have led to better protection of those endangered species dispersed across national boundaries. Many educational programs have been established to teach the interdisciplinary approach to environmental studies.

Today, there is general acknowledgment that a proper environment is necessary to sustain civilization. There is a recognition that technology is not only part of the problem with the environment, but part of the solution and the benefits. Large industries hire graduates of environmental studies programs to help them comply with environmental regulations and concerns. Local groups are involved in using appropriate technology and alternative energy sources to rebuild inner cities and establish suburban gardens. Large farms are beginning to use non-till and low-till agriculture to reduce soil erosion. Satellite remote sensing is improving our knowledge of the current state of the environment. Once the concern of an activist minority, environmentalism has become an international concern.

NATURE AS AN IDEA

Although environmentalism may seem a relatively recent interest, its roots, in fact, lie deep within human history, society, and psychology. Every human society has had a set of beliefs about nature, the effects of nature on human beings, and the effects of human beings on their natural surroundings. These beliefs have reflected attempts to find order and harmony in nature, to discern a design and purpose for this natural order, and to define the role of humanity in nature. Environmental studies unite these traditional concerns with modern scientific and technological knowledge and principles.

Throughout Western civilization, three central questions have been asked about people and nature:

1 What is the condition of nature when undisturbed by human influences?
2 What is the influence of nature on people?

3 What is the effect of humanity on nature, and what is humanity's role within nature [4]?

These are social and personal issues of moral, ethical, religious, and metaphysical importance, and they must be interpreted and reexamined in every age. At many times in history these three questions have aroused controversy. In this section we will discuss the history of each of these questions and the various answers that have been given to them (see color photo galleries for historical paintings that illustrate these ideas).

Wilderness as a Concept and a Reality

To put a value on what we are doing to our environment, we must first understand what it is we are doing to that environment. To understand this, we must know what nature is like without human influence. Thus one of our first tasks in environmental studies is to establish what nature is when undisturbed, i.e., What is **wilderness**? Wilderness as a concept is important to all aspects of environmental studies. In addition, wilderness has taken on significance as a reality, having intrinsic value.

Today it is popular to think of wilderness in a positive way, as something to be valued and preserved. But this was not always so. In some nontechnological societies, there was no concept of wilderness as separate from one's immediate surroundings—everything was habitat [5]. As one native American, Chief Luther Standing Bear, said, "We did not think of the great open plain, the beautiful rolling hills and the winding streams with their tangled growth as 'wild.' Only to the white man was nature a wilderness and . . . the land infested with wild animals and savage people" [5].

Nature as Dangerous The idea of wilderness as separate from people and their habitats can be found rather early in European civilization. The word itself is derived from the Anglo-Saxon word *wild(d)ēor* (wild beast) and means literally the place of wild creatures. In the great Anglo-Saxon epic poem *Beowulf*, wilderness was viewed as a place of danger and discomfort [6]. It was the home of strange and terrible creatures like the monster Grendel and a place where a brave man could prove himself a hero, as did Beowulf when he ventured from the warm hearth of the king's castle to slay the evil Grendel and the monster's mother. In many primitive societies, when civilization had yet to develop much control over the environment, this is the way uninhabited nature was seen: as a wild and dangerous place where a person could test himself against the challenges of nature.

Nature as Chaotic   A related view of wilderness is common in Western civilization and appears even in eighteenth-century Europe. In a classical work of that century, *Natural History, General and Particular*, Count de Buffon described nature untouched by human beings as "melancholy deserts" that are "overrun with briars, thorns and trees which are deformed, broken and corrupted" or wetlands "occupied with putrid and stagnating water . . . covered with stinking aquatic plants" that "serve only to nourish venomous insects, and to harbour impure animals." A person in a wilderness has to "watch perpetually lest he should fall victim to [wild animals'] rage, terrified by the occasional roarings and even struck with the awful silence of those profound solitudes" [7].

To those who see wilderness in this sense—as chaotic and uncontrolled—the role of people is to tame, manage, and order it. It is a human being who "cuts down the thistle and the bramble, and he multiplies the vine and the rose" [7]. From this point of view, nature is disordered, and the role and purpose of people is to add the order, harmony, and balance that are lacking.

Nature as Ordered   The idea that people are needed to control and order nature contrasts with another view that runs throughout Western civilization and is particularly common in our own time. This is the view that nature undisturbed is perfectly ordered, balanced, and harmonious [4]. According to this belief, human beings upset the order and are the great destroyers of nature's balance. This viewpoint is evident in the writings of many classical Greek and Roman philosophers, suggesting a belief that physical and biological nature have a perfect order, balance, and harmony. Perfect order seemed to imply that there was a pur-

pose behind the order, that the purpose was divine, and that the object of this purpose was humanity. Aristotle, who some call the grandfather of the study of ecology, perceived this order in many aspects of biology as he observed it [8]. Cicero summarized many of the classical beliefs in *The Nature of the Gods*. He saw order in the food habits of animals and wrote of the amazing adaptations of living creatures for their needs. Lacking a theory of biological evolution, Cicero and other classical writers believed these adaptations were part of a divinely clever and purposeful plan. Even the elephant, Cicero observed, "has a trunk, as otherwise the size of his body would make it difficult for him to reach his food" [9]. Order in nature was seen in the interactions among species, as in symbiotic relationships. Cicero describes a shellfish that "by entering into an alliance" with a small fish obtains its food: "When a small fish swims inside the gaping shell, the [fish] with a bite signals it to close it. So two very different creatures combine to seek their food together." Cicero marveled at these adaptations and asked, "What power is it which preserves them all according to their kind," adding, "Who cannot wonder at this harmony of things, at this symphony of nature which seems to will the well-being of the world?"

Assuming a purpose behind the order in nature, the next question was, for whom was the world so well ordered? The answer naturally enough had to be human beings, who alone among all living things were intelligent enough to appreciate it. This interpretation of nature, then, is that nature is ordered, balanced, and harmonious; human beings, like all living things, have a place and purpose in this order; and the divine purpose of nature's order is for human benefit.

Nature as Capricious   Among the Greek and Roman writers, Lucretius was one of the strongest opponents of the view of nature as ordered. He argued the opposite: Nature was not made for human benefit; nature gave human beings only a hard life; and one must struggle to survive and obtain the necessities of life against the natural workings of things. He saw nature as capricious. "How many a time the produce of great agonies of toil burgeons and flourishes," wrote Lucretius in *De Rerum Natura*, "and then the sun is much too hot and burns it to a crisp; or sudden cloudbursts, zero frosts, or winds of hurricane force are, all of them, destroyers'' [10]. While nature provides for every need of other creatures, human beings alone must struggle for their existence. This view characterizes nature as unpredictable and uncaring, and sees the role of human beings as struggling for survival against the capriciousness of Mother Nature. Human influence on nature is small and affects only those living things that bear directly on human life.

It has been argued that people in hunting and gathering societies do not make a distinction between human beings, their habitat, and a separate wilderness. With the development of agriculture and herding, wilderness was seen as separate from home and human habitat [11,12]. The less control one has over nature, the more likely that one would view nature undisturbed by human influence as dangerous, capricious, and an obstacle to survival. Thus it is not surprising to find such views among societies with less technological control over their environment—and therefore less assurance about the production of the necessities of life—than our own.

Nature as Machine During the European Renaissance the ideas for and against order in nature were reexamined and the controversy over the balance and harmony of nature was renewed. Exploration and the discovery of strange creatures, the development of science and an increased understanding of the processes involved in nature, and an increase in technology and civilization versus. power over the environment all promoted such a reexamination. The same issues were restated, and the same arguments presented, with new pieces of evidence [4,13].

With the development of the new physics of Newton, Galileo, and others, many people optimistically believed that the workings of the world could be understood from physical laws—that the world and the creatures who lived in it could be understood like a mechanical device. They believed nature was a system following inexorable laws of the universe and they could learn to understand and control it. Their view was that nature is like a machine, and human beings can learn to

be nature's engineers—captains of the great Earth ship [13].

Nature as Beautiful In the nineteenth century, another great change in ideas took place, best known to us through the writings of the English Romantic poets. Part of this view is that wildness is to be appreciated and that the power and unpredictable grandeur of nature is beautiful, sublime, and a demonstration of the power and glory of God. The change from the belief that wilderness was dangerous, and therefore bad, to a belief that wilderness was wonderful and magnificent can be traced in the reports of British travelers through the Alps in the eighteenth and nineteenth centuries [13]. At first, those who traveled through the Alps saw them as places of horrible disorder and danger to be passed through quickly. Soon after, travelers began to talk of the Alps as having a ''terrible joy.'' Finally, Percy Bysshe Shelley saw in the Alps' Mont Blanc the ultimate in powerful sublimity. ''Mont Blanc yet gleams on high; /The power is there,'' he wrote. ''Power dwells apart in its tranquillity,/ Remote, serene, and inaccessible.'' In viewing the mountain, Shelley found ''The secret strength of things,/ Which governs thought, and to the infinite dome of heaven as a law'' (Fig. 1.1) [14]. The Romantic view was that nature's wild power was grand and that the experience of wild nature was of great significance, a source of inspiration, peace, and beauty. This is a view of nature as beautiful in its wildness, and a key for an individual to discover himself and the meaning for existence.

Nature as Commodity With the discovery of the Americas, the largest wilderness ever known to Western civilization was opened to exploration. Early explorers and settlers saw wilderness as a commodity or a resource to mold into something usable to improve their economic well-being. Progress, as seen in a nineteenth-century American painting (see color photo galleries), was a grand lady subduing the wilderness, driving away the wild animals and primitive Indians, and bringing with her the wondrous new inventions of technology.

In early New England, for example, the wilderness was forest to be cleared—to be burnt up or

FIGURE 1.1
The rugged scenery of the Alps illustrates the "remote, serene, and inaccessible" quality of wild nature, as interpreted by the Romantic poets of the nineteenth centruy.

cut down and transformed into farms (Fig. 1.2). In the Big Woods of Michigan, wilderness was 8 million hectares* of white pine, a commodity to be cut to build houses across the eastern and midwestern United States. Today a single preserve of less than 25 ha of white pine exists in central Michigan. The American wilderness was Buffalo Bill killing Indians; it was Daniel Boone; it was the big sky. It was "The People, Yes" country of Carl Sandburg's poem [15]—a place for optimism, of big things to conquer. The American western wilderness was the land of the strange and the big, and the land of the tall tale, where the wind blew so strong you had to make a kite of an iron shutter and a chain [16]; where fog was so thick you could put shingles on it; where plants grew so fast that "the boy who climbed a cornstalk . . . would have starved to death if they hadn't shot biscuits up to him;" and where a herd of cattle got lost in a hollow redwood tree [16].

Nature as Necessary for Survival Following not far behind the belief in progress and subduing the wilderness for personal benefit was the recognition that industry might kill the soil that grew the

*1 hectare = approximately 2.5 acres and is abbreviated ha.

FIGURE 1.2
The summit of New Hampshire's Mt. Monadnock, once forested to the top, was burned in nineteenth-century fires lit to clear lands in the valleys. Trees and soils were removed by the fires, leaving a barren, rocky summit which has not revegetated, except in drainages and lower areas where soil can accumulate.

golden corn and ruin the streams that were full of trout and salmon. At first the wilderness seemed too big for anyone to destroy. The early loggers in Michigan are said to have believed they would never run out of wood; by the time the last of the virgin forests were cut, the first ones would have grown back and could be cut again.

The view that wilderness was a commodity conflicted with a new belief that wilderness and human beings were somehow intimately tied together and that the preservation of the latter required the preservation of the former. In 1864 the first important American statement of these concerns appeared in *Man and Nature* by George Perkins Marsh, native of Vermont and U.S. ambassador to Italy and Egypt [17]. Struck by the differences between the soils, forests, and general appearance of the landscape in Europe and North Africa, which had been used by civilized human beings for thousands of years, and those of the still barely touched wilderness of Vermont and New Hampshire, Marsh proposed that the rise and fall of civilizations were linked to the use and misuse of nature. He suggested that the misuse of farmland contributed to the fall of Rome; as the Romans exhausted the soil near the city, they were forced to expand their empire to obtain new sources of food. Repetition of this process led to an ever-increasing network of transportation and government. The empire finally collapsed when the distances required to transport the food exceeded the technological capabilities of the period.

While modern historians may argue that such a view is oversimplified, Marsh was the first to state the possibility that sustaining human life depends on nature's balance. He became the mid-nineteenth century's classic proponent of the idea that nature undisturbed achieves a permanency of form and substance, a harmony that only human beings destroy. Thus the view that in wilderness is one of the mechanisms for the survival of human beings began in the United States with George Perkins Marsh.

Nature as Scenic Wonder The opening of the American West led to the discoveries of scenic grandeur in Yosemite (Fig. 1.3), Yellowstone, and the Grand Canyon, which were eventually set aside as national parks—monuments of nature's freaks, curiosities, and grandeur. As historian Alfred Runte has made clear, monumental scenery was the United States' answer to the architectural and sculptural wonders of the older civilizations in Europe [18]. The national parks were seen not as biological or ecological units to be preserved as natural living systems, but as places where the

FIGURE 1.3
Yosemite Valley, a place of scenic grandeur, illustrates the American view of wilderness as a curiosity of nature, like a national sculpture, to be seen and set aside for the future.

average citizen could view the peculiar (geysers, rock formations, and so forth) and gain a sense of peace, beauty, or even religious experience, such as Shelley had found in the Alps. In the late nineteenth century, then, developed the idea of wilderness as a place of the strange and monumental. In this view, wilderness is beyond practical concerns; it provides pleasure and entertainment, as a circus does for some, or spiritual inspiration, as a church for others [18].

The first major conservation movement in the United States began in the late nineteenth and early twentieth centuries, stimulated by the nineteenth-century writings of Henry David Thoreau, Ralph Waldo Emerson, and Marsh; by the ideas of the founders of the national parks and forests, such as John Wesley Powell, who in 1869 was first to travel down the Grand Canyon's Colorado River; and by the deep reverence for nature found in the writings of John Muir.

Put in the most general terms, the change in the last two centuries regarding ethics about nature is an expansion of the idea of who or what has intrinsic rights (Fig. 1.4). In *The Descent of Man,*

Charles Darwin wrote that the history of human moral development has involved a continued extension of those objects that received our "social instincts and sympathies" [19]. In the simplest, most primitive pre-ethical past, one's view of who had rights might have extended only to one's self. But since the beginning of written history, that view has expanded. In the twentieth century, the right to vote was extended from men to women. Similarly, with the development of the new environmentalism after World War II, the concept of rights has expanded.

EARLY HUMANS AS ECOLOGICAL FACTORS

For most of our presence on Earth, people have been important ecological factors, creating major changes in the environment and having major effects on the rest of life on our planet. The industrial and scientific revolutions have led to rapid changes in our environment, but all technology, from the most primitive to the most advanced, causes some changes in the environment.

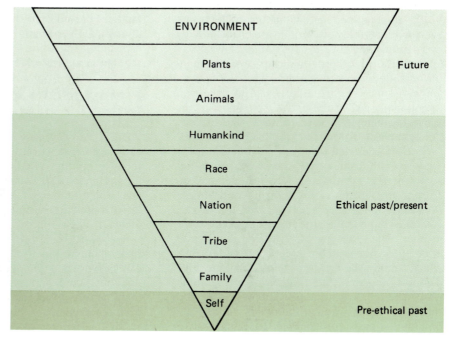

FIGURE 1.4
The evolution of ethics (after Nash). Only in this century has the relationship between people, civilization, and the environment emerged as a relationship with moral considerations. Earliest in human history, we can imagine that people valued only themselves, but some valued themselves and their families. This expanded to include the tribe, then one's nation and race. Even more recently, values expanded to include all humankind. In Western civilization an ethical value for nonhuman animals has been extended to other forms of life and, recently, to some nonliving aspects of the environment and the systems that include and sustain life.

Our ancestors greatly affected the environment even when the number of people on Earth was small. Prehistoric people changed the environment by burning, by decreasing the abundance of some animals through hunting, by increasing the abundance of others when they altered habitats and made them more favorable to those species, by domesticating plants and animals, by changing erosion rates by agricultural and other land-clearing practices and thus altering soils as well as vegetation, and by transporting organisms into new areas from which they had been isolated by geographical boundaries.

Fire

Fire was one of the first major ecological tools used by human beings to change the environment for their own benefit. Indeed, fire has been used around the world by early peoples to clear the land for improved travel and hunting or for farming. In Africa the persistence of the great open plains and savannas is believed to depend in large part on annual or almost annual fires. It is also believed that, for perhaps tens of thousands of years, many of these fires were set by people.

The ability of people to affect the environment, even without the power of modern technology, was demonstrated by the native Americans, as various historical records indicate. For example, throughout the colonial period, reports of fires are common, and fires are usually said to have been intentionally set by the native Americans to improve the habitat in various ways. The explorer Verrazano sailed along the Carolina coast in North America in 1582 and saw "veri great fiers," and in 1610 Henry Hudson's crew also saw "a great fire" somewhere in what is now New Jersey, along the coast south of Sandy Hook. William Wood wrote in *New England's Prospect* in 1634 that it was "the custome of the Indians to burne the wood in November, when the grass is withered, and leaves dried. It consumes all the underwood, and rubbish, which would over grow the country, making it impassable, and spoil their much affected hunting" [20]. Where fires were not lit, the woods were so thick that riding through them was difficult and getting lost easy. For example, one historical record states that "in some places where the Indians

dyed of the Plague some foureteene years agoe, is much underwood . . . because it hath not been burned'' [21].

As further evidence, in 1701 a Dutch family, the Mettlers, obtained rights to a large area of land near the present city of New Brunswick, New Jersey. Much of the land was cleared for farming, but some was left as woodlots. One small stand of this woodlot, about 30 ha, was never burned or cut after 1701 and is the only known virgin stand along the New Jersey Piedmont. Known today as the William L. Hutcheson Memorial Forest, this stand is a nature preserve administered by Rutgers University and is one of the few remaining links with the forests Verrazano and Hudson saw.

Today Hutcheson Forest has a dense underbrush that is almost impossible to walk through and is not penetrable on horseback. As late as 1749, however, this same area was described by the Swedish naturalist Peter Kalm as so open a woods that one could ride a horse and carriage through it [22]. A study of the oldest trees in Hutcheson Forest reveals that fire scars, which are the result of fire injury to the trees and which remain visible in the wood afterward, occurred approximately every 10 years until 1701, the year the Mettlers moved onto the land; no fire scars occur afterward. The burning not only opened up the forests, but changed the species, favoring those trees that better withstand fires.

Prehistoric People and the Extinction of Species

There is growing evidence that prehistoric people caused the extinction of many species, either directly by hunting or indirectly by changing the habitats of species so that they could no longer survive. The fossil record shows that many species of large mammals became extinct during the last great ice age.

For example, in Scotland many species of animals, including the lynx, brown bear, wolf, wildcat, beaver, and reindeer, lived in the Neolithic Age, but then disappeared. Hunting and replacement by domestic animals are believed to have been responsible for their disappearance [23].

Similar extinctions occurred in North America. Some experts believe these were the result of climate change, but Paul Martin, an American anthropologist, has proposed that these extinctions could have been caused by the native Americans when they first arrived in North America via a land bridge from Asia. Martin suggested that the native Americans could have acted as a newly introduced predator confronting a prey with no prior experience or adaptation to the predator. Even a small number of people, concentrated along a thin but densely populated line and migrating southward and eastward from Alaska down through North America, could have extinguished entire species with available techniques, including fire, he suggested [24]. Others believe that climatic changes must have played an important or causal role. Most likely a number of factors operated together to cause the extinctions.

Prehistoric People and Wilderness

This great impact of early people on the landscape further alters our ideas about wilderness. Indeed, by the time the wilderness concept arose as a part of conservation or even became a part of "nature to be admired," as in the early nineteenth century, there were few areas of Earth that had not been strongly affected by people for a long time. True wilderness—nature unaffected now or in the past by human beings—is a rarity.

In the conterminous United States, the fraction of land that meets the criterion of true wilderness is very small. Parts of the Rocky Mountains, some of the more inhospitable parts of our national parks, and parts of the deserts would seem to be true wilderness. East of the Rockies there are even fewer wilderness areas. Isle Royale National Park, Michigan, may be the only true wilderness in the North Woods east of the Rocky Mountains of the United States. In New Hampshire, a U.S. Forest Service study revealed only two small forested areas in the entire state that had not been logged, cleared, farmed, or settled.

Antarctica and the deep sea are true wilderness, as are parts of the higher Himalayas. But most of Africa, India (outside of the highest mountains), Europe (except for the snow-covered peaks of the Alps), and North and South America (except for the Amazon basin, the higher Andes, and parts of

Tierra del Fuego) have all been modified by human beings. In Central and South America the practice of shifting, or *milpa*, agriculture, has caused changes in forest composition over large areas [23].

In Europe, Neolithic people cleared forests in Denmark and other areas of northern Europe. Pollen deposits in lakes in Denmark show that tree species were removed between 2500 and 2300 B.C. Tree pollen is replaced by pollen from weedy plants and then by pollen from species like birch, which regenerates after fire. Replicas of Neolithic axes with flint blades and ash handles were used by two archeologists, Jorgen Traelssmith and Sven Jorgensen, to show that forests could indeed be cleared effectively with them [25]. The evidence suggests that cutting and burning were used together to first clear and then maintain open land.

The following is an ecological picture of *Homo sapiens* in Europe since the end of the last ice age. As the ice retreated northward, tundralike, open areas appeared where Neolithic people hunted; as the climate warmed further, forests developed, and for a while people moved away or became less abundant. Then around 4000–5000 years ago, Neolithic people began to clear land and move into large areas of former forests, where they grazed cattle and grew crops. Thus the impact of *Homo sapiens* on northern Europe was widespread long before the beginning of the modern era [26].

RECENT HUMANS AS ECOLOGICAL FACTORS

The story of the rise of civilization and its many direct influences on the landscape is well known from history books and need not be repeated here. Recent studies suggest that these influences may have been greater than was formerly believed, strongly affecting population growth and the development—the rises and falls—of human cultures and civilizations.

For example, the medieval period in Europe was formerly pictured as comparatively static, with little expansion in development of the land. The environment, however, underwent great change through human activities. In A.D. 900 a large part of what is now modern Germany was forested

FIGURE 1.5
(a) About A.D. 900 most of
central Europe was in forest. (b) By 1900, owing to
the activities of human
beings, all but a small fraction of this area had been
cleared. (From Thomas;
after Schlüter.)

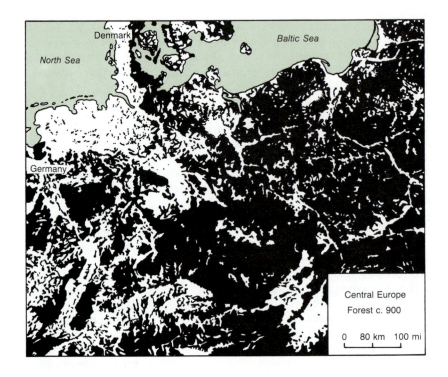

Central Europe

Forest c. 900

0   80 km   100 mi

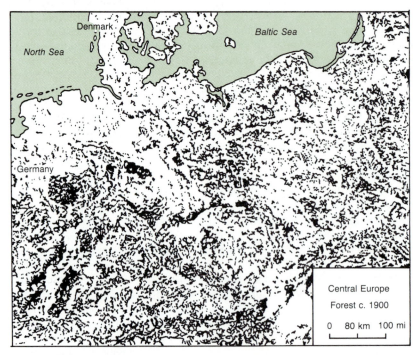

Central Europe

Forest c. 1900

0   80 km   100 mi

(Fig. 1.5a); settlement of these forests began about that time, and the land was steadily cleared. By 1900 only a small fraction of the original forested area remained (Fig. 1.5b).

Technological advances during the medieval period, including the invention of the modern horse collar, accelerated land clearing. Prior to this, horses were collared with modified oxbows, which, because horses lacked oxlike shoulders, choked them and prevented them from pulling with their entire strength. The new collar allowed plowing of rougher land and increased the rate of land clearing [27]. Much land that was abandoned during the Black Death was repopulated. By the time of the great era of exploration, much of England's forests had been cleared. Some historians suggest that the need for timber, particularly for the British navy, was an important factor in the British colonization of North America [27].

Thus, through history, our species has greatly modified Earth's surface. In succeeding chapters we will examine current environmental issues so that we learn to manage our environment wisely.

ENVIRONMENTAL ETHICS

The **land ethic** put forward by Aldo Leopold in 1949 affirms the right of all resources, including plants, animals, and earth materials, to continued existence and, at least in certain locations, to continued existence in a natural state [28]. This ethic effectively changes our role from conqueror of the land to citizen and protector of the environment. This new role requires that we revere and love our land and not see it solely as an economic commodity to be used up and thrown away.

Leopold emphasized our changing sense of ethics through the story of Odysseus, who, upon returning from Troy, hanged a dozen slave women for suspected misbehavior during his absence. His right to do this was unquestioned; the women were property, and the disposal of property was a matter of expediency. Although since that time ethical values have been extended so that humans are no longer considered the personal property of others, only within this century have moral considerations been extended to include our physical environment (Fig. 1.4).

Ecological ethics limit social as well as individual freedom of action in the struggle for existence [12]. A land ethic assumes that we are ethically responsible not only to other individuals and society, but also to that larger community of plants, animals, soils, atmosphere, and water—that is, the environment.

There is a potential source of confusion in distinguishing between an ideal and a realistic land ethic. Giving rights to plants and animals and landscape might be interpreted as granting to individual plants and animals the fundamental right to live, as in the Eastern Indian religion called Jainism. However, we must eat to live; not being able to make our own food from sunlight and minerals, as do trees and flowers, we must consume other organisms. Therefore, although the land ethic assigns rights for animals to survive as species, it does not necessarily assign rights to an individual deer, cow, or chicken for that survival. The same argument may be given to justify using stream gravel for construction material or mining other resources necessary for our well-being. However, unique landscapes with high aesthetic value, or ecosystems that sustain endangered species, need to be protected within this ethical framework.

The land ethic places us in the role of husbanders of nature, with a moral responsibility to sustain nature for ourselves and for future generations. According to this view, wilderness has intrinsic value to be maintained for itself and because our own survival depends upon it.

In the 1970s, philosophers began to formulate what they called **environmental ethics.** Environmental ethics is concerned with the value of the physical and biological environment, whereas classical ethical concerns had to do with social factors (the relationships among people) [29]. There are both practical and moral reasons for placing a value on the environment.

Practical reasons have to do with our own survival or economic benefit, from our need for individual animals and plants as sources of food to the need to preserve the life-support system of our whole planet. It is now customary to categorize the practical reasons into two groups: utilitarian, which either provide an individual with economic benefit or are necessary to an individual's survival (for example, I need to maintain a pasture so my cows can eat); and ecological, which have to do with the life-support functions of large portions of the environment (for example, polluting a stream ruins my source of drinking water; burning coal and oil is leading to a change in climate that will affect the entire Earth). These practical reasons form a basis for the conservation of nature that is essentially enlightened self-interest.

Moral reasons include aesthetic arguments (for example, you might say that wilderness is beautiful and you would rather live in a world with wilderness than without it) as well as direct moral arguments (for example, that nonhuman organisms have certain moral rights, which we have an obligation to protect). While such opinions have often been viewed as merely emotional, philosophers in recent years have begun to examine the arguments for and against these principles [30].

Why do we need a new set of ethics for the environment? The answers include (1) new effects on nature: because our modern technological civilization affects nature, we must examine the ethical consequences; (2) new knowledge about nature: modern science demonstrates to us ways, which we did not know about before, in which we have changed and are now changing our environment; and (3) expanding moral concerns: some argue that it is a natural extension of civilization to begin including the environment in ethics.

A concern with environmental ethics leads to a discussion of the rights of animals and plants, the rights of nonliving structures, and the rights of large systems that are important to our life support. Because our effects on the environment today have consequences for the future, discussions of environmental ethics also involve the rights of future generations. The arguments for and against various principles in environmental ethics are made more complex because of conflicting values. For example, some people believe that protecting the environment is an economic drain rather than an economic benefit; others believe the opposite. Still other people believe that only the rich benefit from protection of the environment and that the poor will only become poorer as the environment becomes better protected. The resolution of these conflicts requires a basic scientific knowledge about the environment as well as the ability to clearly formulate a logical argument.

Does Nature Have Rights?

One of the growing concerns of those interested in environmental ethics is with the question: Does nature have rights? This question arose in the 1970s in a case over the proposed development of Mineral King Valley, a wilderness area in the Sierra Nevada Mountains of California. Christopher D. Stone, a lawyer, discussed this idea in his article *Should Trees Have Standing? Toward Legal Rights for Natural Objects* [19].

Disney Enterprises, Inc., proposed to develop this valley into a ski resort with a multimillion-dollar complex of recreational facilities. The Sierra Club, arguing that this development would adversely affect the aesthetics of this wilderness as well as its ecological balance, brought a suit against the government. But the case brought up a curious question: If a wrong was being done, who was wronged? The California courts decided that the Sierra Club itself could not claim direct harm from the development. Moreover, because the land was government owned and the government represented the people, it was difficult to argue that the people in general were wronged. Stone suggested that the Sierra Club's case might be based, by common-law analogy, on the idea that in some cases inanimate objects have been treated as having legal standing, as, for example, in a precedent involving ships. Stone suggested that trees also should have legal standing. The Sierra Club was not able to claim direct damage to itself, but instead argued on behalf of the nonhuman wilderness.

The case was taken to the U.S. Supreme Court, which concluded that the Sierra Club itself did not have sufficient "personal stake in the outcome of the controversy" to bring the case to court. But in a famous dissenting statement, Justice William O. Douglas addressed the question of legal standing. Douglas proposed the establishment of a new federal rule that would allow "environmental issues to be litigated before federal agencies or federal courts in the name of the inanimate object about to be despoiled, defaced, or invaded by roads and bulldozers and where injury is the subject of public outrage." In other words, trees would have legal standing. While trees did not achieve legal standing in that case, it was a landmark in that legal rights and ethical values were explicitly discussed for wilderness and natural systems. This subject in ethics is still a lively, controversial one. Should our ethical values be extended to nonhuman, biological communities and even to the life-support system of Earth? What position you, as reader of this book, take will depend in part on your understanding of the characteristics of wilderness, natural systems, and other environmental factors and features.

Obligations to the Future

Another major development in environmental ethics has been a concern with the question of what we owe future generations. While most of us think at one time or another about the future and our descendants, this question has become of more than personal concern because we know that our modern technology is affecting the environment in ways that will last hundreds and thousands of years and that we are producing chemicals that can remain active even longer. Of special concern are (1) radioactive wastes from nuclear power plants, (2) environmental effects of thermonuclear war, (3) long-term climatic change resulting from land-use changes and technological activities, (4) worldwide spread of nonradioactive toxic chemicals, (5) extinctions of large numbers of species as a result of human activities, (6) direct effects of rapid increases in human population, (7) destruction of forests and fertile soils that will impoverish them for agricultural production for very long periods, and (8) long-term impacts of apparently short-term technological benefits, such as the impact on natural systems of the current rapid advances in genetic engineering. As with other aspects of environmental ethics, what we know about these effects influences the value judgments we make. As Ernest Partridge, a philosopher of environmental ethics, has written, "Our moral responsibility grows with foresight " [31].

For example, in 1983, a meeting of scientists in the United States determined that a major thermonuclear war could lead to a "nuclear winter." Because of extensive fires and the transport of dust into the high atmosphere, the sky might be darkened for months or years, possibly leading to freezing temperatures over much of Earth and putting a halt to the growth of green plants. This new information (based on mathematical and computer analysis and projections) puts the concern with thermonuclear war in a new ethical light, suggesting that the chances that such a war would end much of life on Earth are even greater than previously believed. This new information deepens the ethical quandary that faces all of us. One hundred years ago no one could imagine that a device made by humans could end all of life. But today we realize that our power over the environment could make us or our children the last generation.

Philosophers in the 1970s began to grapple with the complex issues that arise out of a concern with the rights of future generations and the idea of "stewardship" of Earth. At the heart of this ethical viewpoint is the belief that we do not really possess Earth during our lifetime, but that we are merely another group in the line of human beings who are the "shepherds" or "stewards" of Earth while we are here.

The overwhelming impact of these issues has led some people to reject all science, technology, and progress and to seek to return to a simpler age. But this head-in-the-sand approach can only be a short-term answer. The long-term solution, if there is to be one, will come from the best use of science and technology within the framework of an evolving ethic. To quote Partridge, "It is a fundamental paradox of our age that scientific knowledge and discipline, supplemented by critical moral sense and passionate moral purpose, will be needed to save the future" [31].

Critical Thinking and Environmental Ethics

Perhaps the most important thing you can get from this book is to learn how to think through for yourself what viewpoint you want to take in regard to environmental issues. To do this, you have to know the facts, understand the concepts, and be able to construct a logical argument and analyze someone else's argument for logical consistency. The process of constructing and analyzing arguments is called critical thinking.

Two classic types of disagreement that can arise over an environmental issue are a disagreement about facts (or, more generally, the nature of the

Career Profile: Charles Harper

I claim to be the only wildlife artist in America who has never been compared to Audubon," laughs Charles Harper. Harper prefers to be called a nature illustrator rather than a wildlife artist. He likes to believe he shows people an alternative way of looking at nature. His artistic style is a unique combination of straight/ curved line drawing, caricature, and a touch of whimsy.

His career began in commercial art, doing what he calls "happy housewife" ads. He hated the work and decided, "I had to create a new style that I liked and was salable." He concentrated on simplicity. Rather than destroying the two-dimensional plane of paper with the illusion of three dimensions, he used the two-dimensional plane as a tool.

His career turned toward wildlife art while he was working for *Ford Times* magazine. The art director was an amateur naturalist who gave Harper opportunities to illustrate travel and nature subjects in his own style. Harper calls his style minimal realism. "I try to reduce animals to their simplest visual terms without losing their identity." He compares it to using symbols for complex ideas.

Later, Harper illustrated books about nature subjects for Golden Press. "Then came the ecological crisis of the 1960s and everyone wanted nature art," he recalls. He joined the

Frame House Gallery, a publisher of wildlife prints. For 20 years, they have been producing limited edition prints of his serigraphs, which are prints made with a silkscreen technique.

The prints are satisfying to Harper because he can illustrate any animal in any situation and express his own ideas. Each of his serigraphs is accompanied by a brief text. Harper explains, "You can do delicate coloring and subtle shading with words that you cannot do with pictures." He sums up his feelings about nature with a quote from one of his prints, "Can a nature lover ever find true happiness at the top of the food chain?"

Harper believes that nature is not for people to exploit. "I disagree with the Biblical implication that nature was created for man. Man is an integral part of it all."

Some of his most personally satisfying projects are posters he has painted for conservation and wildlife agencies and organizations. He is completing a series of posters for the National Park Service. He visits the parks, then represents as much of the ecological situation there as he can. Harper's environmental concern is also apparent in his support of local nature organizations, such as the Cincinnati Nature Center. Posters that he has done for no charge have been used to raise money for such organizations.

Harper is quick to point out that his formal education is in art and not in science. Indeed, he describes his nature education as spotty and largely experiential. "I know a lot about certain things and how to find out what I don't know. I guess that is what education is supposed to teach you—how to find out what you don't know." He learns as much as he can about the creatures he illustrates, which includes observing them when he can. He does consider himself an amateur naturalist, but distinguishes himself as the world's worst birdwatcher, saying he has a hard time identifying birds in the field.

Harper feels our lives depend on our environmental awareness. To him, no area of knowledge is more important. It is not only important to our survival but has spiritual rewards as well. His work is a self-expression of his own environmental awareness.

Michele Wigginton

environment and of life) and a disagreement over values.

As an example of the first type, suppose you and a friend are discussing the problem of the American bald eagle, which is said to be endangered. Both of you agree that the eagle should be saved from extinction. Your friend says, "Nature can take care of itself and so can the eagle. There are plenty of eagles. I was just camping and saw eagles nesting. I read that they are breeding successfully and there are more young born than old dying. I think they will survive if we just leave them alone." You reply, "I'll bet that the death rate of eagles is greater than the birth rate, and that the population is declining; we must do something immediately to change this trend."

Your disagreement in this case revolves around facts about the eagle, about its birth and death rates. You believe deaths exceed births, and your friend believes the opposite. You can resolve your disagreement by obtaining more information—by studying the eagle population in North America.

Any logical argument about environmental issues involves premises or assumptions (those things or concepts accepted to be true), a set of facts, and a method of arriving at a logical conclusion. Almost every argument, in addition, involves hidden assumptions—unstated (and often unrecognized) assumptions.

The case of the Furbish lousewort illustrates the need for critical thinking. In the 1970s, the U.S. Army Corps of Engineers proposed building a $1.2 billion dam on the St. Johns River in Maine. Although this area had been logged since the 1840s and therefore was not an undisturbed wilderness, it did contain an endangered species—the Furbish lousewort, a small flowering plant growing along the steep banks of the St. Johns River. If the dam were built, the lousewort would probably become extinct. Under the U.S. Endangered Species Act of 1973, this would be illegal, so work on the dam was halted. The question arose: Should a $1.2 billion project be halted to avoid the extinction of a rare plant that hardly anyone ever sees? This case illustrates both disagreements about facts and disagreements over values.

First, opposing parties can disagree about the ecological importance of the Furbish lousewort—a disagreement over facts. Proponents of the dam could argue that this species is so rare and unimportant that the world could get along easily without it. Protectors of the lousewort took another point of view, arguing that (1) natural ecosystems have a built-in stability and a resiliency against disturbances that have evolved over millions of years and are a key to the survival of life on Earth; (2) plants like the Furbish lousewort play some essential role important to the long-term stability of life in the Maine forests; and (3) by extension, the Furbish lousewort is important to the long-term persistence of life on Earth. From this point of view, the forest is a complex system, and all of its existing parts must be preserved for it to function in its highly stable way. If the facts about the Furbish lousewort were all correct, one would conclude that the plant should be saved. The two sides in this argument disagreed about facts, but in a more complex way than in the example of the bald eagle. In this case, the disagreement had to do with the nature of the complex system that includes and supports life on Earth. Such systems are poorly understood, and it is very difficult to predict what would happen to such systems if a small component were removed. To resolve this disagreement, simple facts are not enough; what is needed is an understanding of the operation of complex natural systems. In this case, the information needed to resolve the disagreement does not yet exist, and the decision about what our society should do must be based on hypotheses.

The case of the Furbish lousewort also illustrates a disagreement over values. Suppose it were known that this small plant did play a small role in the long-term stability of the forest. Proponents of the dam could still argue that the short-term gains over the 10- to 20-year lifetime of the dam were much more important than the very long-term effect on the stability of the natural system. On the other side, protectors of the lousewort could argue that our obligation to future generations outweighed the short-term gain to ourselves and that we had a moral obligation to preserve this species.

These two examples illustrate in a comparatively simple form the problems that we face in trying to construct a logical argument about an environmental issue. Most actual cases are as complex as these or more complex.

In our discussion, we have assumed that the scientific method is valid and useful. While a complete analysis of the scientific method is beyond the intent of this book, the simple, general characteristic of all science is that it allows a way to reject a hypothesis. If a statement cannot be open to such a test, then it is not a statement that is part of the scientific method.

Earlier in this chapter we said that ideas about nature must be reinterpreted and reexamined in every age. Having seen the development of these ideas throughout Western history, we can ask: What is the truth about nature for our times?

From the viewpoint of the individual, wild nature—nature undisturbed by human influence—means many different things. In our age wilderness represents unfettered power to be watched in awe or to serve as a place to test one's self. It is also seen as a place of sublime peace and beauty or as a reservoir of mineral and biological resources to be used for our economic betterment. Although we have changed much of Earth, at the end of the twentieth century, wilderness can still be found in some places. As Roderick Nash, one of this century's historians of wilderness, has written, wilderness is in the end a state of mind—wilderness is where you find it [11,12]. The wilderness that is a source of peace or a place to test one's self might be found by a city dweller in an urban park or at a seashore much altered by civilization. Recent incidents of mountain climbers scaling city skyscrapers may be seen as one illustration of this viewpoint. For someone familiar with backcountry, only the most pristine areas distant from all sounds of modern civilization might serve that same purpose.

From a societal point of view, mounting scientific evidence tells us that we indeed depend on the living processes of nature; ours is a living planet, and its atmosphere, oceans, and sediments are biological products. Two modern scientists, J. E. Lovelock and L. Margulis, have argued that we should return to the ancient Greek idea of *Gaia*—of Mother Earth as the sustainer [32]. This idea recognizes that in the end our survival depends on the persistence of natural systems and processes that our civilization has already begun to change. The moral and ethical implication of this view is that human beings must husband or manage wisely the natural environment and its rare and endangered species. Thus, wilderness and human beings are indivisible; the persistence of each depends on the other. Nature is still seen as strongly influencing individuals, but each person in his own way detects this influence to a greater or lesser degree. The characteristics of nature remain an area of intensive scientific inquiry—a subject with many questions but few answers—and one important for us to study.

SUMMARY

Every human society has a set of beliefs about nature, the effects of nature on human beings, and the effects of human beings on their natural surroundings. In the history of Western civilization, these beliefs have included the following.

1 Nature is wild, dangerous, and horrible; a place where an individual can test himself against its challenges.
2 Nature is disordered without human beings, and humanity's role is to create the final order, harmony, and balance.
3 Nature is perfectly harmonious, ordered, and in balance without human beings; it is disrupted and made unharmonious and imbalanced by people's poor actions. The purpose of nature's order is human benefit. Human beings can learn to act in the right way by understanding the natural order.
4 Nature is unpredictable and capricious, so people must struggle to survive against natural hazards of all kinds. People create a small amount of order and regularity and predictableness in a chaotic world.
5 Nature resembles a machine whose workings are exact and predictable. People are nature's engineers and can modify nature's operations to their own ends.
6 Nature is magnificent and beautiful in its wildness, power, and unpredictability; a key for individual discovery of the self and the meaning of existence; an expression of divine power.
7 Nature is a commodity to use up, and people are the marketers of the commodity.

8 Nature is a life-support system that must be maintained in its wild state for the survival of human beings.

9 Nature is a place of the strange, monumental, and peculiar. People are entertained or inspired by nature.

10 Nature has an intrinsic value in and of itself. People have a moral obligation to preserve it. (This belief is related to belief 2 above.)

11 Nature cannot be separated from human beings; the persistence of each depends on the other.

During recent years, a rapid growth in the concern with the environment has raised philosophical, social, and scientific issues. The philosophical issues include questions of what values we should attach to the environment and how we should determine these values and evaluate their relative importance. A new field of philosophy called environmental ethics has developed; it involves the study of ethical principles concerning the natural and nonhuman biological environment, as contrasted with the social concern (the ethics of relationships among people) that has been a primary focus of traditional ethics.

The two basic kinds of reasons for placing a value on the environment are practical and moral. Moral reasons include aesthetic ones (for example, one might argue that wilderness is beautiful, therefore it should be preserved), as well as the moral rights of natural objects, of nonhuman life, and of the future generations who will be affected by our present actions. The practical reasons concern our survival and our economic benefit. They can involve such simple units of our environment as individual plants or animals or even single landforms, but they extend to include the complex natural systems that support life. The recognition of the importance of these large systems is a new development that forces us to ask new questions about the values we attach to our environment. In this chapter we have introduced the basic value issues. In the next section of this book we begin to explore the basic scientific knowledge that provides the necessary basis for all our choices about the environment.

STUDY QUESTIONS

1 What is meant by the statement, "Wilderness is a state of mind?"

2 Why might a society that changed from hunting to agriculture also change its view of wilderness?

3 How might the following inventions alter a society's views of wilderness: (a) the magnet compass; (b) the sailing ship; (c) the steam engine?

4 Is the surface of the moon a wildnerness? Explain your answer in terms of the different concepts of nature: nature as dangerous, chaotic, ordered, capricious, and beautiful.

5 It has been said that national parks are the United States' answer to the great sculptures and paintings of Europe. Explain this idea, which is known as "monumentalism."

6 Should cities have national parks? Explain your answer.

7 What are the three central questions that have been asked about people and nature?

8 What is meant by the statement that nature is a commodity?

9 What are the major ways that people have been ecological factors (a) in prehistory and (b) since the industrial revolution?

10 Explain the difference between a disagreement about facts and a disagreement about values, with reference to environmental ethics.

FURTHER READING

COUNCIL ON ENVIRONMENTAL QUALITY. 1976. *Environmental quality.*

EGERTON, F. N. 1973. Changing concepts of the balance of nature. *Quarterly Review of Biology* 48: 322–50.

GLACKEN, C. J. 1967. *Traces on the Rhodian shore: Nature and culture in Western thought from ancient times to the end of the eighteenth century.* Berkeley: University of California Press.

LEOPOLD, A. 1949. *A Sand County almanac.* New York: Oxford University Press.

LITTON, R. B. 1973. Aesthetic dimensions of the landscape. In *Natural Environments,* ed. J. V. Kantilla. pp. 262–91. Baltimore, Md.: Johns Hopkins University Press.

MARSH, G. P. 1967. *Man and nature.* Cambridge, Mass.: Belknap Press. (Originally published in 1864, ed. D. Lowenthal, by Charles Scribner's Sons, New York.)

NASH, R. 1967. *Wilderness and the American mind.* New Haven, Conn.: Yale University Press.

NICHOLSON, M. H. 1959. *Mountain gloom and mountain glory.* Ithaca, N. Y.: Cornell University Press.

PARTRIDGE, E., ed. 1981. *Responsibilities to future generations.* Buffalo, N. Y.: Prometheus Books.

SHADER-FRECHETTE, K. S., ed. 1981. *Environmental Ethics.* Pacific Grove, Calif.: Boxwood Press.

2
Physical and Biological Processes on Earth

- ☐ The ultimate fate of every species is extinction. Human activities increase or decrease the time required for extinction to occur for any species, including its own.
- ☐ Sustained life is a characteristic of an ecosystem, the smallest unit of the biosphere with the inputs, outputs, and cycles necessary to keep life going.
- ☐ Ecosystems can be natural or managed; unplanned human activity is a type of management.
- ☐ Present natural processes are the same as those of the past and will continue into the future. Human activity influences the rates at which these processes operate.
- ☐ All natural systems involve feedback. Negative feedback is stabilizing; positive feedback is destabilizing.
- ☐ Systems involve cycles; subcycles of the geologic cycle include the tectonic cycle, the hydrologic cycle, the biogeochemical cycles, and the rock cycle.

AMBOSELI NATIONAL PARK

Amboseli National Park is located in southern Kenya at the foot of the northern slope of Mt. Kilimanjaro. The park is a game reserve and in the past has supported a tourist industry amounting to several million dollars per year. The long-term management of the park and its resources is dependent upon understanding of the physical, biological, and human-use linkages that characterize this interesting landscape. Figure 2.1a shows the boundary of the park as well as the major geologic units. Particularly important is the fact that the park is centered on an ancient lake bed, remnants of which include the seasonally flooded lake, Amboseli, and some swampland. Mt. Kilimanjaro is a famous volcano, composed of alternating layers of volcanic rock and ash deposits. To the north of the lake the bedrock consists of granite. Precipitation that falls on the slopes of Kilimanjaro infiltrates into the volcanic material and moves slowly down the slopes to saturate some of the ancient lake beds, eventually emerging at springs located in the swampy, seasonally flooded land. The groundwa-

FIGURE 2.1
(a) Generalized geologic map of the Amboseli National
Park and surrounding area. (After Dunne and Leopold.) (b)
Aerial view of swamp and lake bed with dead, dying, and
live fever trees.

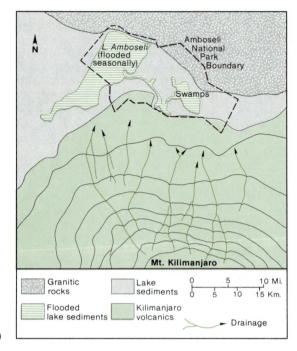

(a)

(b)

24

ter becomes very saline as it percolates through the lake beds.

The climate of the park area is arid, with 350–400 mm of rainfall per year, sufficient to support dry savannah grasslands and brush (Fig. 2.1b). Prior to the mid-1950s, the park area was characterized by fever tree woodlands that supported mammal species such as kudu, baboon, vervet monkey, leopard, and impala. Starting in the 1950s, and particularly during the 1960s, the fever tree woodlands rapidly disappeared and were replaced by short grass and brush with an accompanying change to typical plains animals such as zebra, wildebeest, and kongoni. Loss of the woodland habitat was prematurely blamed on overgrazing of cattle by the Masai people and damage to the trees from elephants. Of course, overgrazing can cause serious erosion problems and change of vegetation, and it is well known that herds of elephants can and do damage woodlands in their feeding behavior. In the case of Amboseli National Park, however, careful work showed that a change in climatic variables and soils were the culprits rather than people and elephants, which were shown to be of only secondary importance in the loss of the woodland habitat [1,2]. Most dead trees were located in an area that had been stock-free since 1961, which predated the major decline in the woodland environment. Furthermore, it was noted that some of the woodlands that suffered the least decline were those that had some of the highest density of people and cattle. These observations suggest that livestock and overgrazing were not responsible for loss of the trees [1]. Damage to trees from elephants was noted; over 83% of trees in some areas showed some debarking. Some trees were pushed over, but these tended to be the younger, smaller trees. Careful research concluded that elephants apparently played a catalytic role in causing habitat change; as the density of woodland species decreased, the incidence of damage due to elephants increased.

Research that examined the groundwater conditions (rainfall, history, and soils) suggested that Amboseli National Park area is very sensitive to changing climatic conditions. During dry periods the groundwater table lowers and soils are leached of salts. These conditions favor the development of woodland environments. During wet periods the groundwater table rises, bringing with it salt that invades the root zones of trees. Loss of the trees is due then to "physiological drought," and as the woodlands dwindle they are replaced by salt-tolerant grasses and low brush. During the most recent loss of woodland environment, the groundwater level rose as much 3.5 m in response to unusually wet years in the 1960s. Analysis of the soils confirmed that the tree stands that were the most damaged were those associated with highly saline soils [1,2].

Evaluation of the historic record from early European explorers, the Masai herdsmen, and fluctuating lake levels in other East African lakes such as Victoria and Rudolf suggested that prior to 1890 there was another period of above-normal rainfall and sparse woodland environment. Thus we conclude that the climatic cycles have a pronounced effect on the East African soils, vegetation pattern, and assemblage of animals present [1].

The Amboseli case history has important implications concerning long-term resource planning in East Africa. It can be expected that there will be continued cycles of wet and dry periods and that associated with these will be changes in the soils, distribution of plants, and abundance and type of animals present. Furthermore, if during wet periods groundwater tables rise close to the surface, then this may affect planning for development of tourist facilities such as roads and sewage systems that may be adversely affected by high groundwater levels and accompanying swampy conditions [1,2]. The case history emphasizes that careful, detailed work is necessary to understand the natural environment. Human use—such as overgrazing by Masai herdsmen—while being an attractive culprit was in this case a hasty conclusion refuted by better understanding the effects of long-term climatic cycles on the ecosystem.

THE EARTH AND LIFE

Earth was formed approximately 4.6 billion years ago when a cloud of interstellar gas known as a solar nebula collapsed, forming protostars and planetary systems. Life on Earth began approximately two billion years later and since that time has profoundly affected our planet. Since the evolution of first life, many kinds of organisms have evolved, flourished, and died, leaving only their fossils to record their place in history.

Several million years ago, our ancestors set the stage for the eventual dominance of the human race on Earth. Because our sun will eventually die, we too will disappear and the impact of humanity on Earth history may not be particularly significant. However, to us living now and to our children and theirs, how we affect our environment is very important.

Human activities increase and decrease the magnitude and frequency of natural Earth processes. For example, rivers will rise periodically and flood the surrounding countryside regardless of human activities, but the magnitude and frequency of flooding may be greatly increased or decreased by human activity. Therefore, in order to predict the long-range effects of such processes as flooding, we must be able to determine how our future activities will change the rate of a geological process.

From a biological point of view, we know that the ultimate fate of every species is extinction. However, Figure 2.2 shows that as the human population has increased, there has been a parallel increase in the extinction of species. These extinctions are closely related to land-use change—to

agricultural and urban uses that influence the ecological conditions of an area. While some species are domesticated or cultivated, others are removed as pests.

Human activities now also affect Earth on a global scale, and these effects are increasing with technological advances. Our civilization has the potential to greatly alter our climate; the chemistry of our atmosphere, soil, and water; and even the chances that life will continue to persist on Earth. In this chapter we will discuss the interaction of life with its environment and selected aspects of the major Earth systems and physical cycles.

LIFE AND ITS ENVIRONMENT

Earth as a planet has been profoundly altered by life. Earth's air, oceans, soils, and sedimentary rocks are very different from what they would be on a lifeless planet. In some ways, life controls the makeup of the air, oceans, and sediments. It has greatly changed Earth's surface during the last three billion years and continues to control and to modify it.

The influence of life on global Earth processes is illustrated by the story of the source of phosphorus for agricultural fertilizer. Historically, major sources of phosphorus for fertilizer have been deposits on certain peculiar islands found only in dry regions and in low latitudes, such as off the coast of Africa, in the Caribbean, in the middle and western Pacific, and along the coast of Peru. The deposits, as much as 40 m deep, lie on otherwise flat-topped islands. Valuable and plentiful, the fertilizer is part of an international trade, which began in earnest in Peru about 1840 when ships carried the material to London—as much as 9 million tons per year—where it was sold for 28 British pounds per ton.

What is the source of the fertilizer, and why does it occur only on certain kinds of islands in certain climates and latitudes? The fertilizer is guano, the excrement of birds who nest on the islands in thousands and have done so for thousands of years. The three principal species—the guanay, the piquero, and the Chilean pelican—feed on anchovy, a schooling fish that lives in re-

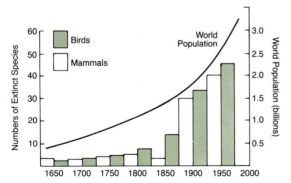

FIGURE 2.2
Increase in human population paralleled by an increase in the extinction of birds and animals. (From Ziswiler.)

gions rich in tiny, floating organisms called plankton. The plankton, in turn, thrive where nutritionally essential chemical elements like nitrogen and phosphorus occur. These nutrients are abundant near certain islands where ocean currents rise and carry elements to the surface.

Thus one of the world's major sources of phosphorus depends on a peculiar combination of biological and geological processes. The guano is deposited in great amounts only where there are large colonies of nesting, colonial birds. The birds nest on islands free from predators and near a vast source of food. The guano hardens into a rocklike mass only in a relatively dry climate [3]. Without the plankton, fish, and colonial birds, the phosphorus would have remained in the oceans, and the world's agricultural production would have been significantly reduced. In this way, living organisms have had important effects on the global cycle of an important element.

The Biosphere

Life interacts with its environment on many scales. A single bacterium in the soil interacts with the air, water, and particles of soil around it, within the space of a fraction of a cubic centimeter. A forest extending hundreds of square kilometers interacts with large volumes of air, water, and soil. All of the oceans, all of the lower atmosphere, and in fact all of the near-surface part of the solid Earth are affected by life as a whole.

A general term, **biota,** is used to refer to all living things (animals and plants, including microorganisms) within a given area, from an aquarium to a continent or Earth as a whole. The region of Earth where life exists is known as the **biosphere.** It extends from the depths of the oceans to the summits of mountains, but most life exists within a few meters of Earth's surface. The biosphere includes all of life, the lower atmosphere, and the oceans, rivers, lakes, soils, and solid sediments that are in active interchange of materials with life (Fig. 2.3). All living things require energy and materials. In the biosphere, energy is received from the sun and the interior of Earth, and is used and given off while materials are recycled.

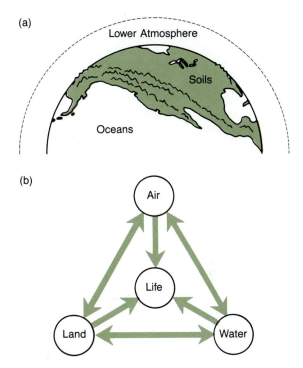

FIGURE 2.3
The biosphere. (a) The biosphere includes the lower atmosphere, all Earth's life, the oceans, soils, and the solid sediments that exchange elements actively with the rest of the biosphere. (b) The biosphere is a linked system; all its parts are connected.

To understand what is required to sustain life, consider the following question: How small a part of the biosphere could be isolated from the rest and still sustain life? Suppose you took a glass container and put parts of the biosphere into it and sealed it. What minimum set of contents would sustain life? If you placed a single green plant in the container along with air, water, and some soil, the plant could make sugars from water and from carbon dioxide in the air and could make many organic compounds, including proteins and woody tissue, from these sugars and from inorganic compounds in the soil. But no green plant can decompose its own products and recycle the materials. Eventually, your green plant would die. We know of no single organism, population, or species that both produces all of its own food and completely recycles all of its own metabolic products. For life to persist, there must be several species within an environment that includes fluid media—air and water—to transport materials and energy.

Ecosystems

The smallest unit of the biosphere that can sustain life is called an ecosystem. An **ecosystem** consists of a community of organisms and its local nonliving environment. It is a fundamental principle that sustained life on Earth is a characteristic of ecosystems, not of individual organisms or populations or single species.

The smallest ecosystems that have been known to sustain life over a long period of time are Folsom bottles. These are materially closed ecosystems that Professor Claire Folsom of the University of Hawaii made by placing water, algae, bacteria, and sediment from Honolulu Bay into a liter flask and then sealing the top. Some of these have sustained life for almost twenty years, sitting on a shelf facing out the north window of his laboratory. Folsom's bottles contain what is needed to sustain life and not much extra: air, energy exchanged through the glass, materials recycled by the algae and bacteria through the water. You could easily make one of these simple systems from local materials.

The term ecosystem is applied to areas of all sizes, from the smallest puddle of water to a large forest. Ecosystems also differ greatly in composition, that is, in the number and kinds of species, in the kinds and relative proportions of nonbiological constituents, and in the degree of variation in time and space. Sometimes the borders of an ecosystem are well defined, as in the transition from a rocky ocean coast to a forest or from a pond to the surrounding woods. Sometimes the borders are vague, as in the subtle gradation of forest to prairie in Minnesota and the Dakotas in the United States, or from grasslands to savannahs or forests in East Africa. What is common to all ecosystems is not physical structure—size, shape, variations of borders—but the existence of the processes we have mentioned: the flow of energy and the cycling of chemical elements.

Ecosystems can be natural or artificial. A pond constructed as part of a waste treatment plant is an artificial ecosystem. Ecosystems can be natural or managed, and the management can vary over a wide range of actions. Agriculture can be thought of as partial management of certain kinds of ecosystems.

Natural ecosystems carry out many "public service" functions for us. Waste water from houses and industries is often converted to drinkable water by passage through natural ecosystems, and pollutants, like those in the smoke from industrial plants or in the exhaust from automobiles, are often converted to harmless compounds by forests.

UNIFORMITARIANISM

Earth and its life forms have changed many times, but certain processes necessary to sustain life and a livable environment have occurred throughout much of history.

The principle that present physical and biological processes that are forming and modifying our Earth can help explain the geologic and evolutionary history of Earth is known as the doctrine of **uniformitarianism.** Simply stated as "the present is the key to the past," uniformitarianism was first suggested by James Hutton in 1785. Because Charles Darwin was impressed by the concept of uniformitarianism, it pervades his ideas on biological evolution. Today this doctrine is considered one of the fundamental principles of the biological and earth sciences.

Uniformitarianism does not demand or even suggest that the magnitude and frequency of natural processes remain constant with time. Obviously, some processes do not extend back through all of geological time. For example, some of the processes operating in the oxygen-free environment of the first billion years or so of Earth's history must have been quite different from processes we observe today. However, for as long as the early continents, oceans, and atmosphere have been like modern ones, and as long as the basic factors that rule biological evolution have not changed, we can infer that present processes also operated in the past. If we study present-day stream channels and learn something about the types of deposits associated with streams, then we can infer that similar-looking deposits in ancient rocks are most likely stream deposits. Similarly, we can study modern organisms and the relationships between their forms and biologic functions to theorize how organisms known only through fossils might have functioned. For example, the bone structure of dinosaurs, along with other information, has been used to argue that dinosaurs, rather than being cold-blooded and close relatives of reptiles, may have been warm-blooded animals more closely related to birds.

To be useful from an environmental standpoint, the doctrine of uniformitarianism will have to be more than a key to the past. We must turn it around and say that a study of past and present processes may be the key to the future. That is, we can assume that in the future the same physical and biological processes will operate, but the rates will vary as the environment is influenced by human activity. Geologically ephemeral landforms, such as beaches and lakes, will continue to appear and disappear in response to moderate and catastrophic natural processes; extinctions of animals and birds will also continue to some extent in spite of people's activities.

SYSTEMS AND CHANGES

Solutions to environmental problems often involve an understanding of systems and rates of change. A system is a set of components or parts functioning together to act as a whole. In environmental studies, at every level, we deal with complex systems; thus it is important to understand certain basic characteristics of every system. A single organism is a system. A sewage treatment plant is a system. A city can be a system. Earth is a system.

Systems may be open or closed. A system that is open in regard to some factor exchanges that factor with other systems. The ocean is an open system in regard to water, which it exchanges with the atmosphere. A system that is closed in regard to some factor does not exchange that factor with other systems. Earth is an open system in regard to energy and a closed system (for all practical purposes) in regard to material.

Systems respond to inputs and have outputs. Your body, for example, is a complex system. If you are hiking and see a grizzly bear, the sight of the bear is an input. Your body reacts to that input—the adrenalin level of your blood goes up, your heart rate increases, and so on. Your response—perhaps moving away from the bear—is an output.

Feedback

Feedback, a special kind of system response, occurs when the output of the system also serves as an input and leads to changes in the state of the system. A classic example of feedback is human temperature regulation. If you go out in the sun and get hot, the increase in temperature affects your sensory perceptions (input). If you stay in the sun, your body responds physiologically: your skin pores open and you are cooled by evaporating water. You may also respond behaviorally: because you feel hot (input), you walk into the shade and your temperature returns to normal. This is an example of negative feedback because the system's response is in the opposite direction to the output (an increase in temperature leads to a later decrease in temperature). With positive feedback, an increase in output leads to a further increase in the output. A fire starting in a forest provides an example of positive feedback. The wood may be slightly damp at the beginning and not burn well, but once a fire starts, wood near the flame dries out and begins to burn, which in turn dries out a greater quantity of wood and leads to a larger fire. The larger the fire, the more wood is dried, and the more rapidly the fire increases.

Negative feedback is generally desirable because it is stabilizing—it leads to a system that remains in a constant condition. Positive feedback, sometimes called the "vicious circle," is destabilizing. A serious situation can occur when our use of the environment leads to a positive feedback. Off-road vehicle use, for example, may cause a positive feedback in erosion. As vehicle use increases, more plants are uprooted, increasing erosion. As this occurs, a defined path is established, and more vehicles use it. The resulting increase in erosion damages more plants, which die and lead to a greater increase in erosion and death of plants.

Environmental Unity

The discussion of positive and negative feedbacks introduces a fundamental concept in environmental studies—that of environmental unity. Simply stated, environmental unity means that it is impossible to do only one thing; that is, everything affects everything else. Of course, this cannot be absolutely true. The extinction of a species of snails in North America is hardly likely to change the flow characteristics of the Amazon River. On the other hand, many aspects of the natural environment are closely related. Disruptions or changes in one part of the system will often have secondary and tertiary effects within the system or will even affect adjacent systems. Earth and its ecosystems are complex entities in which any action has several or many effects.

Consider, for example, a major change in land use from forests and grassland to a large urban complex. Clearing the land for urban use will change the amount of sediment eroded from the land, which will affect the form and shape of the channel. Eventually, as more land becomes paved or otherwise made impervious, the amount of sediment eroded from the land will decrease, and the streams will readjust to this lesser sediment load. The urbanization process is also likely to pollute the streams or otherwise change water quality, which will affect the biological systems in the stream and adjacent banks. If skyscrapers are constructed, they may form local rain shadows that modify the climate of the immediate area by affecting both the amount and pattern of precipitation. Furthermore, if the city's power plants burn fossil fuels, certain contaminants will enter the atmosphere, and along with those produced by au-

tomobiles and industries, will cause air pollution that could change the air quality for the entire region around the urban center. Acid rain might also result in adjacent areas. Thus land-use conversion can set off a whole series of changes in the local and regional environment, and each change is likely to precipitate still others.

Exponential Growth

A particularly important example of positive feedback occurs in the **exponential growth** of a population; in such growth the increase is a constant rate of the current amount. The greater the amount (output), the greater the number added, and so the population grows faster and faster. This results in a growth curve shaped like the letter J, thus often referred to as the J-curve. Figure 2.4 shows a typical J-curve for a 7%/yr growth. Many systems, both human-induced and natural, may approach the J-curve for some lengths of time.

Exponential growth involves two important factors: the rate of growth measured as a percentage and the doubling time in years, which is the time necessary for the quantity of whatever is being measured to double. A general rule of thumb is that the doubling time is approximately equal to 70

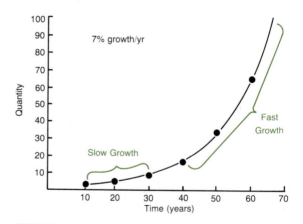

FIGURE 2.4
The J-curve for exponential growth. Notice that in the lower part of the J the growth is slow, but past the bend, growth becomes extremely rapid.

divided by the growth rate. This rule applies to growth rates up to approximately 10%; beyond that, the errors may become quite large.

Exponential growth has some interesting consequences, as illustrated in a story by Albert Bartlett [4]. Imagine a hypothetical strain of bacteria that has a division time of 1 minute (the doubling time is 1 minute). Assume that our hypothetical bacterium is put in a bottle at 11:00 A.M., and it is observed that the bottle is full at 12:00 noon. An important question is, When was the bottle half-full? The answer is 11:59 A.M. If you were an average bacterium in the bottle, at what time would you realize you were running out of space? There is no single answer to this question, but at 11:58 the bottle was 75% empty, and at 11:57 it was 88% empty. Now assume that at 11:58 some farsighted bacteria realized that they were running out of space and started looking around for new bottles. Let's suppose that they were able to find three more bottles. How much time did they buy? Two additional minutes. They will run out of space at 12:02 P.M.

The preceding example, while hypothetical, illustrates the power of exponential growth. Many systems in nature display exponential growth for some periods of time, so it is important that we be able to recognize it. In particular, it is important to recognize exponential growth in a positive feedback cycle, as it may be very difficult to stop. Negative feedback, on the other hand, tends toward an equilibrium and thus is easier to control.

Changes in Systems

Changes in natural systems may be predictable and should be recognized by anyone looking for solutions to environmental problems. Where the input into the system is equal to the output (Fig. 2.5a), there is no net change and the system is said to be in a **steady state.** An approximate steady state may occur on a global scale, such as in the balance between incoming solar radiation and outgoing radiation from Earth, or on the smaller scale of a university in which new students are brought in and seniors graduate at a constant rate. When the input into the system is less than the output (Fig.

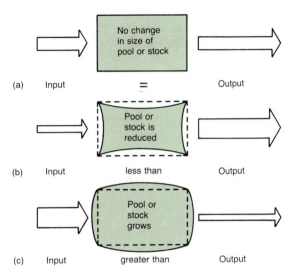

FIGURE 2.5
Major ways that a pool or stock of some material may change. (Modified from Ehrlich, Ehrlich, and Holdren.)

2.5b), change occurs, as can happen with the use of resources such as groundwater or the harvest of certain plants or animals. If the input is much less than the output, the groundwater may be completely used up or the plants and animals may die out. In a system where input exceeds output (Fig. 2.5c), positive feedback may occur, and the stock of whatever is being measured will increase. Examples are the buildup of heavy metals in lakes or the pollution of soil water. By using rates of change or input/output analysis of systems, we can derive an average residence time for such factors. The average residence time is a measure of the time it takes for the total stock or supply of a particular material, such as a resource, to be cycled through the pool. To compute the average residence time, take the total size of the stock or pool and divide it by the average rate of transfer through that pool or stock.

An understanding of changes in systems is primary in many problems in environmental studies. In some cases, very small growth rates may yield incredibly large numbers in modest periods of time. With other systems, however, it may be possible to compute an average residence time for a particular resource and use this information to develop sound management principles. Recognizing positive and negative feedback systems and calculating growth rates and residence times, then, enable us to make predictions concerning resource management. We also need, however, to understand the ways in which physical and biological processes, with or without human interference, may modify Earth.

EARTH'S ENERGY BUDGET

As a planet, Earth is part of an energy system, receiving energy from the sun. This energy undergoes changes; affects life, oceans, atmosphere, and sediments; and is eventually emitted as heat back into the depths of space. In this energy system, Earth is an intermediate part between the source (the sun) and the sink (space). Energy flows continuously from the source to Earth to the sink.

Solar Radiation

Essentially all the energy available at Earth's surface comes from the sun; a small additional amount is generated at Earth's core, produced by radioactive processes that heat up the center of Earth (Fig. 2.6). Although Earth intercepts only a very tiny fraction of the total energy emitted by the sun, solar energy sustains life on Earth and creates the movement of air in the atmosphere, generating

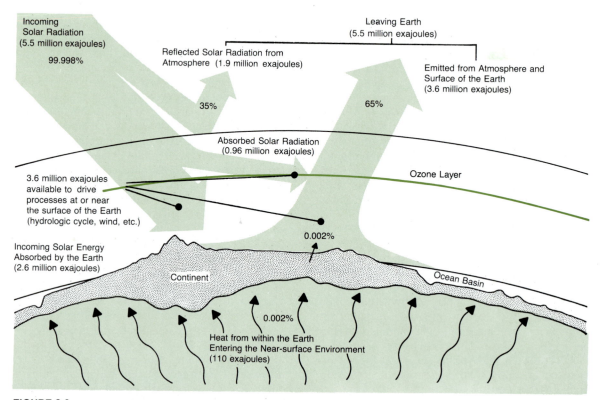

Incoming Solar Radiation (5.5 million exajoules)
99.998%

Leaving Earth (5.5 million exajoules)

Reflected Solar Radiation from Atmosphere (1.9 million exajoules)

Emitted from Atmosphere and Surface of the Earth (3.6 million exajoules)

35%
65%

Absorbed Solar Radiation (0.96 million exajoules)

Ozone Layer

3.6 million exajoules available to drive processes at or near the surface of the Earth (hydrologic cycle, wind, etc.)

0.002%

Incoming Solar Energy Absorbed by the Earth (2.6 million exajoules)

Continent
Ocean Basin

0.002%

Heat from within the Earth Entering the Near-surface Environment (110 exajoules)

FIGURE 2.6
Annual energy flow to Earth from the sun and the relatively small component of heat from Earth's interior to the near-surface environment, measured in exajoules. An exajoule (10^{18} joules) is a convenient measure to express large amounts of energy. (Modified from Marsh and Dozier.)

climate and weather and creating the circulation of waters in the oceans.

Energy is emitted from the sun in the form of electromagnetic radiation. Different forms of electromagnetic energy may be distinguished by their wavelengths; the collection of all the possible wavelengths of electromagnetic energy, considered as a continuous range, is known as the **electromagnetic spectrum** (Fig. 2.7). A modest appreciation of the spectrum is fundamental to understanding many environmental problems.

The amount of energy radiated from a body such as the sun or Earth varies with the fourth power of the temperature of the body. Thus, if a body's temperature doubles, the energy radiated increases by 16 times. This explains why the sun, with a temperature of 5800°C, radiates a tremendously greater amount of energy than Earth at 15°C (Fig. 2.8). Figure 2.8 illustrates another important point: The sun emits relatively short-wave radiation, whereas Earth emits relatively long-wave radiation. The hotter an object is, the more rapidly it radiates heat and the shorter the wavelength of the predominant radiation. That is, a blue flame is hotter than a red flame. Earth's surface and the surfaces of animals, plants, clouds, water, rocks, and so on, are so cool that heat is radiated predominantly in the infrared, which is invisible to us [5].

Energy from the sun travels to Earth at the speed of light through the vacuum of space. Of the solar energy that reaches our atmosphere, only about half ever arrives at Earth's surface. The rest is either absorbed by the atmosphere or reflected back into space. Much of the harmful radiation, such as X-rays and ultraviolet radiation, is filtered out by the upper atmosphere. The ozone layer, extending from approximately 15 to 45 km above Earth's surface, is particularly important in absorbing ultraviolet radiation, which is potentially hazardous to all living things. The small amount of ultraviolet radiation that manages to get through the ozone layer causes sunburns and some skin cancers.

Absorption and Reflection

The rate at which solar energy is absorbed and reflected at different parts of Earth's surface, as well as for Earth as a whole, depends upon surface temperature and color.

If an object is cold and gives off less heat than it receives, it will warm up, but as it warms up it will also radiate heat more rapidly. As a result, for any constant input of energy, a physical object will eventually reach a temperature that will allow it to radiate heat energy at the same rate that it receives energy. In addition, differences in the colors of different parts of Earth result in differences in the amount of solar energy absorbed and reflected.

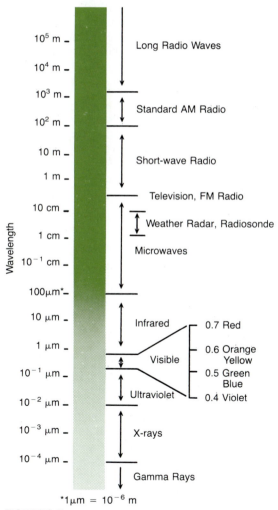

FIGURE 2.7
The electromagnetic spectrum.

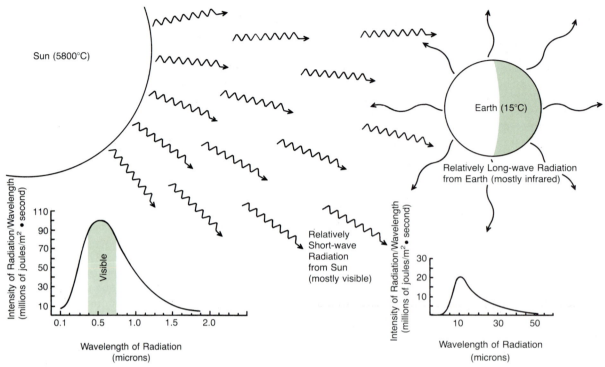

FIGURE 2.8
Emission of energy from the sun compared with that from Earth. Notice that the solar emissions have a relatively short wavelength, whereas those from Earth have a relatively long wavelength. (Modified from Marsh and Dozier.)

Black surfaces radiate heat much more readily than white surfaces, which tend to reflect light rather than absorbing and radiating heat. For example, ice reflects 80–95% of light, a dry grassland 30–40%, and a conifer forest 10–15%.

The temperature of Earth's surface, therefore, is a result of energy exchange and of physical characteristics of the surface. It is the differences in temperature that drive the circulation of the atmosphere and the oceans and produce weather and climate. In addition, the temperature within the biosphere is crucial for continuation of life because living things can exist only within a narrow range of temperatures. Most organisms can be active only between 0°C and 50°C, but a few can survive temperatures close to boiling (100°C). Any significant change in Earth's temperature could have dramatic effects on life.

It has been estimated that under present atmospheric conditions, a 1% change in the amount of sunlight reflected by Earth would cause approximately a 1.7°C change in the surface temperature. Changes in the absorption of energy can be due to changes in the cloud cover or in the amount of ice on Earth's land surfaces. Organisms, particularly grasses, trees, and algae, can also change the absorption rate. Such biological changes occur seasonally. Marine algal mats can change from light and highly reflective in one season to nearly black and highly emitting in another. Algae can also produce sediments such as calcium carbonate, which when pure are chalky white and have a different reflective characteristic than the sediments produced from a lifeless surface. Because the surface characteristics of any physical object determine its emission of heat energy, a very thin surface—even a single-cell layer of algae—over a large area of water could greatly alter the rate of emission of energy and therefore the temperature of Earth's surface.

The energy exchanged by Earth's surface is affected also by the chemical composition of the atmosphere. Certain compounds absorb more strongly in some wavelengths of light energy than others. The infrared wavelengths radiated from Earth's surface are strongly absorbed by water and carbon dioxide. If the water content or the carbon dioxide content of the atmosphere changes, so does the reabsorption of the energy released from Earth's surface.

If carbon dioxide had been removed from Earth's early atmosphere, Earth's surface would have cooled, as if a window in a greenhouse had been opened. According to some scientists, the sun may have become hotter since the ancient times in which life originated; this would have counteracted the cooling process. A lifeless Earth would have a much higher surface temperature than the present Earth or than the ancient Earth when life first evolved.

To summarize, a fundamental characteristic of our planet is its flow of energy, received from the sun, transformed on Earth, and emitted back into space. The differences in the surface characteristics of parts of Earth lead to differences in the amount of energy absorbed and reflected. At any one time, parts of Earth are hotter than others, and these temperature differences drive the circulation of the atmosphere and the oceans, which in turn greatly affect life. Because life, in turn, affects how the solid surfaces, atmosphere, and oceans absorb and reflect energy, it can influence atmospheric and oceanic circulation, weather, and climate. As life became abundant, it changed the atmosphere's chemistry and the characteristics of Earth's surface, particularly as to the reflection and absorption of radiant energy. Both of these changes, chemical and physical, affect the energy budget of Earth. Any major change in the abundance and distribution of life on Earth's surface, today or in the future, will affect the reflection and absorption of light and infrared radiant energy and therefore change Earth's heat budget. Moreover, human activities, particularly those of a technological civilization, change Earth's energy budget by introduc-

ing into the atmosphere carbon dioxide and pollutants like dust, smoke, haze, or small compounds that absorb infrared radiation. Modern civilization is changing drastically the distribution and abundance of life forms on Earth, and this may have concomitant effects on Earth's energy budget. Those effects will be discussed in later chapters.

THE ATMOSPHERE, CLIMATE, AND CLIMATIC CHANGE

Atmosphere

The **atmosphere,** the layer of gases that envelops Earth, is composed of gas molecules held close to Earth's surface by gravitation. The major gases in the atmosphere are nitrogen (78%), oxygen (21%), argon (0.9%), and carbon dioxide (0.03%). The atmosphere also contains minor or trace amounts of numerous elements in compounds, including methane, ozone, hydrogen sulfide, carbon monoxide, oxides of nitrogen and sulfur, hydrocarbons, and various dust particles called particulates. In addition, water vapor in the atmosphere varies from zero to approximately 4% by volume.

The atmosphere is a dynamic system, changing continuously. The physical movement of air masses, each with a different temperature and moisture content, produces weather and climate. The atmosphere is a vast chemical-reacting system, fueled by sunlight, by high-energy compounds emitted by living things, and by human industry. Many complex chemical reactions take place in the atmosphere; these reactions change from day to night and with the chemical elements available in any given part of the atmosphere.

Two important properties of the atmosphere at any particular elevation above sea level are pressure and temperature. Pressure is a force per unit area; atmospheric pressure increases as altitude decreases because there is a greater weight from the overlying air.

Winds, the movement of clouds, and the passing from stormy to clear skies show us that the atmosphere changes rapidly and continually. This atmospheric circulation takes place at a variety of scales. The lower atmosphere is heated by the surface of Earth. Energy is also transferred from the land and bodies of water by the evaporation of water. As warm air rises, it cools by expansion; winds are produced as cooler surface air is drawn in to replace rising warm air. The lower atmosphere is therefore said to be "unstable" because it tends to circulate and mix, particularly in the lowest 4 km or so.

On a global scale, atmospheric circulation results primarily from Earth's rotation and the differential heating of the atmosphere. These processes produce global patterns that include prevailing winds and latitudinal belts of low or high air pressure from the equator to the poles (Fig. 2.9). In general, belts of low pressure develop at the equator and 50°–60° north and south latitude as a result of rising columns of air; belts of high pressure due to descending air develop at 25°–30° north and south latitude. These belts have been romanticized by names such as doldrums—areas at the equator with little air movement; trade winds—northeast and southeast winds important in the early days of international trade when clipper ships moved the world's goods; and horse latitudes—two belts centered at about 30° north and south of the equator. Earth's major deserts occur in the horse latitudes as a result of pervasive high pressure sandwiched between the equatorial and mid-latitudinal lows.

Climate

Climate refers to the representative or characteristic atmospheric conditions at particular places on Earth. Because the climate of a particular location may depend upon extreme or infrequent conditions, it is more than a simple average temperature and precipitation regime. Thus, while the simplest classification is characterization of climate by latitude as tropical, subtropical, mid-latitudinal (continental), subarctic (continental), and arctic, several other categories are necessary. These include humid continental, mediterranean, monsoon, desert, and tropical wet-dry, among others (Fig.2.10). Precipitation and temperature

FIGURE 2.9
Generalized circulation of the atmosphere. (From Williamson, *Fundamentals of air pollution,* © 1973, Figure 5.5. Reprinted with permission of Addison-Wesley, Reading, MA.)

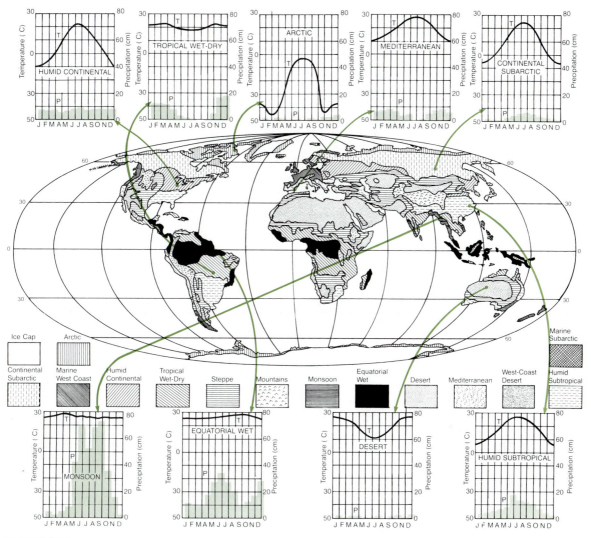

FIGURE 2.10
The climates of the world and some of the major climate types in terms of characteristic precipitation and temperature conditions. (Modified from Marsh and Dozier, *Landscape*, © 1981, John Wiley & Sons. Reprinted with permission of John Wiley & Sons, Inc.)

show tremendous variability on a global scale. Although detailed discussion of climatic types is beyond our scope here, it is important to recognize the importance of potential climatic variability in determining what kinds of organisms live where. Like climates produce like kinds of ecosystems. This concept is important and useful for environmental studies. Knowing the climate, we can predict a great deal about what kinds of life we will find in an area and what kinds could survive there if introduced.

On a regional scale, air masses that cross oceans and continents may have a profound influence on seasonal patterns of precipitation and temperature. On a local scale, climatic conditions can also vary considerably and produce a local effect referred to as a **microclimate.** Microclimate may vary even from one side of a small rock to another or from one side of a tree to another. Organisms often take advantage of these different conditions. Furthermore, as we shall discuss later, urban areas produce a characteristic microclimate with important environmental consequences.

Climatic Change

Another important aspect of climate is climatic change. During the last million years there have been major climatic changes involving swings in the world's mean annual temperature of several

degrees centigrade. The present ice age began approximately two million years ago. Since then there have been numerous changes in Earth's mean annual temperature (Fig. 2.11). On a scale of change over one million years, the times of high temperature reflect ice-free periods (interglacial periods) over much of Earth, whereas the low-temperature points reflect the glacial events. As one goes to a scale of 150,000 years, minor glacial and interglacial events are more prominent. Finally, the change over the last 1500 years reflects several warming and cooling trends that have greatly affected people. For example, during the major warming trend, from A.D. 800 to 1200 (Fig. 2.11d),

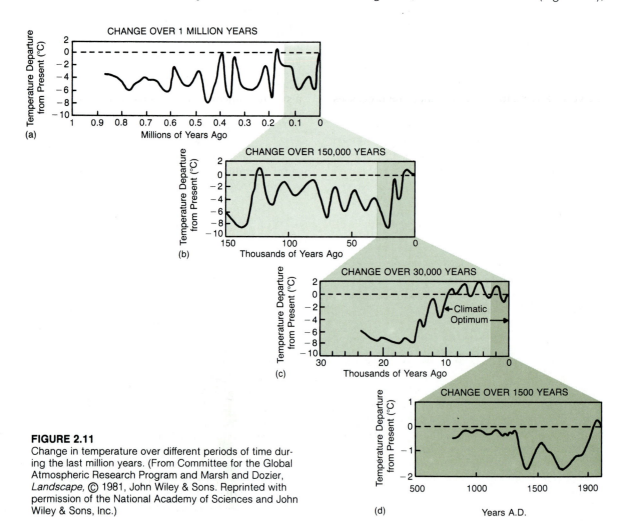

FIGURE 2.11
Change in temperature over different periods of time during the last million years. (From Committee for the Global Atmospheric Research Program and Marsh and Dozier, *Landscape,* © 1981, John Wiley & Sons. Reprinted with permission of the National Academy of Sciences and John Wiley & Sons, Inc.)

the Vikings colonized Iceland, Greenland, and North America. When glaciers advanced during the cold period, around A.D. 1400, the Viking settlements in North America and parts of Greenland were abandoned. Since approximately 1750 a warming trend has been apparent, lasting until the 1940s, when temperatures again began to cool [6]. These major changes in climate are complex, and their causes are not well understood. Nevertheless, the consequences of climatic change are important from an environmental standpoint and will influence future conditions for people on Earth.

THE GEOLOGIC CYCLE

Throughout the nearly five billion years of Earth's history, the materials at or near its surface have been more or less continuously created, maintained, and destroyed by numerous physical, chemical, and biological processes. Except during the very early history of our planet, the processes that produced many earth materials necessary for life have recurred periodically. Collectively, the processes responsible for the formation and destruction of earth materials are referred to as the **geologic cycle** (Fig. 2.12), which is actually a group of subcycles: the tectonic cycle, the hydrologic cycle, the biogeochemical cycles, and the rock cycle.

The Tectonic Cycle

The **tectonic cycle** is driven by forces originating deep within Earth. It deforms Earth's crust, producing external forms such as ocean basins, continents, and mountains. We now know that Earth's outer layer, containing the continents and oceans, is about 100 km thick. This layer, known as the **lithosphere,** is not a continuous, uniform layer. Rather, the lithosphere is broken into several large segments called plates, which are moving relative to one another (Fig. 2.13). According to the theory of **plate tectonics,** the continents float on the tectonic plates. Thus, as the lithospheric plates move over the **asthenosphere,** thought to be a more or less continuous layer of little strength below the lithosphere, the continents also move. This movement of continents is known as **continental drift.** It is believed that the most recent episode of drift started approximately 200 million years ago when a supercontinent known as Pangaea broke up. The movement of the continents throughout Earth history has greatly affected life. Closely related forms have been isolated by continental drift for millions of years, leading to the evolution of new species.

The boundaries between plates are geologically active areas; most volcanic activity and earthquakes occur there. Three main types of boundaries are known: divergent, convergent, and trans-

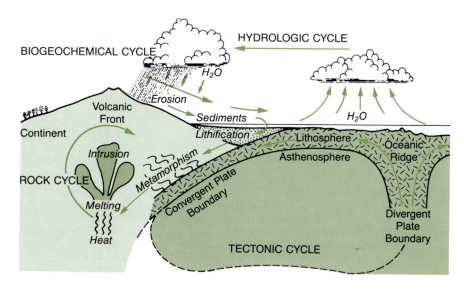

FIGURE 2.12
The geologic cycle and its subcycles, including the tectonic, hydrologic, rock, and biogeochemical cycles.

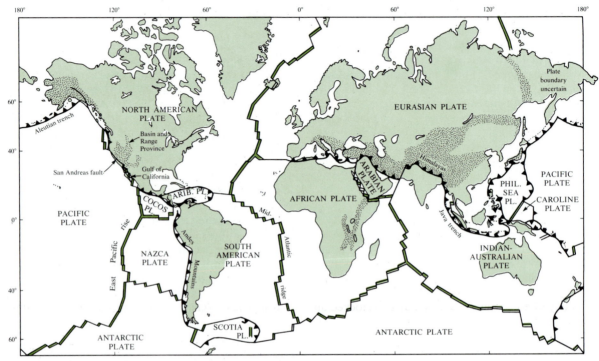

FIGURE 2.13
Generalized map of Earth's lithospheric plates. Divergent plate boundaries are shown as
double lines, convergent boundaries are shown as barbed lines, and transform boundaries
are shown as single lines. Also shown (by stipple pattern) are areas of active deformation
located away from plate boundaries. (From Burchfiel et al.)

form fault. A **divergent plate boundary** occurs at
oceanic ridges where plates are moving away from
one another and new lithosphere is produced. A
convergent plate boundary (subduction zone)
occurs when one plate dives or moves beneath the
leading edge of another plate. However, if both
leading edges are composed of relatively light continental material rather than heavier oceanic crust,
it is more difficult for subduction to start, and a
special type of convergent plate boundary known
as a collision boundary may develop. Collision
boundaries may produce linear mountain systems,
such as the Alps and the Himalayas. Because
mountain ranges affect climate locally and regionally, the mountain-building processes are very important in the long run to life on Earth. A **transform fault boundary** occurs where one plate
slides past another. A good example of this type of

boundary occurs in California where, for several
hundred kilometers, the San Andreas fault (a
transform fault) is the boundary between the North
American and Pacific plates. There is a very close
relationship between the tectonic cycle and the
other cycles. The tectonic cycle provides water
from volcanic processes as well as energy to form
and change many earth materials.

The Hydrologic Cycle

The **hydrologic cycle** (Fig. 2.14), which is driven
by solar energy, encompasses the movement of
water from the oceans to the atmosphere and back
to the oceans by way of evaporation, runoff from
streams and rivers, and groundwater flow. The hydrologic cycle supplies nearly all of our water resources. Of the total supply of water, approxi-

FIGURE 2.14
The hydrologic cycle.

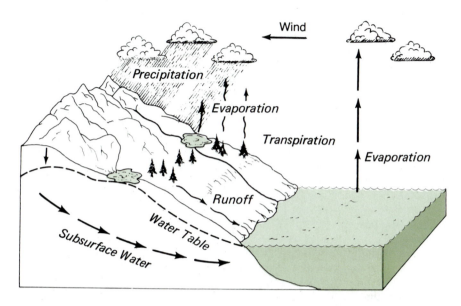

mately 97% is in the oceans, about 2% is locked up in glaciers and the icecaps, and only a small fraction of 1% is in the entire atmosphere. Nevertheless, the freshwater phase of the hydrologic cycle is dependent upon the atmospheric portion of Earth's water. Although only a very small amount of water is active in the hydrologic cycle at any one time, it is very important in moving chemical elements, sculpturing the landscape, weathering rocks, transporting and depositing sediments, and providing our water resources. Knowing how the hydrologic cycle operates will help us better understand and utilize our water resources.

Oceans Water in the oceans of the world has been slowly released to the surface by volcanic activity through geologic time. The present positions of the ocean basins are due to plate tectonics and continental drift.

Oceanic circulation (Fig. 2.15) is driven by prevailing winds (trade winds, westerlies, and polar easterlies) in conjunction with earth's rotation.

FIGURE 2.15
Oceanic surface water circulation. (From Foster.)

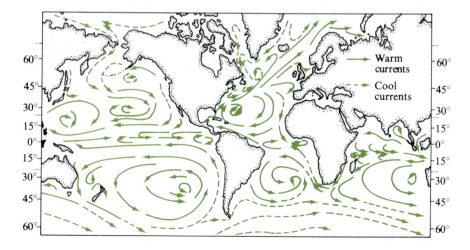

Ocean currents rotate clockwise in the Northern Hemisphere and counterclockwise in the Southern Hemisphere. This is due to the fact that, as a result of Earth's rotation, oceanic currents veer to the right in the Northern Hemisphere and left in the Southern Hemisphere, a phenomenon known as the Coriolis effect after the French scientist who first explained it.

Prevailing easterly winds (trade winds) cause the water in the equatorial Pacific to generally move to the west, delivering warm water and precipitation to the western Pacific while keeping parts of Peru, Ecuador, and Bolivia a desert. As the Pacific water moves westward away from the coast of South America, changes called upwellings occur at the equator and on the coasts. As the cold nutrient-rich bottom waters rise to the surface to replace the water that has moved to the north and west, biologic productivity greatly increases. This dominant pattern of oceanic circulation and upwelling has been disrupted seven times in the last 100 years by the El Niño phenomenon, in which the trade winds weaken or even reverse, the eastern equatorial Pacific becomes anomalously warm, and the equatorial ocean current that usually moves west weakens or even reverses. In addition to disrupting the upwelling of nutrients, El Niño can have global consequences, as illustrated by the 1982–83 event that caused droughts in Australia, Africa, and India, and flooding in China, California, northern Peru, and Ecuador. This aspect of El Niño will be discussed in greater detail with other natural hazards in Chapter 17. Although we know that El Niño conditions will occasionally occur, there is no consensus about their cause.

Groundwater   Rain that falls on the land either evaporates, runs off along the surface, or moves below the surface and is transported underground. Locations where surface waters infiltrate the groundwater system are known as recharge zones. In the conterminous United States, approximately 30% of the rainfall enters the surface-subsurface flow system. Of this, approximately 1% reaches the ocean by way of groundwater flow. Water that moves into the ground first enters a belt of soil moisture known as the **zone of aeration** (Fig. 2.16). It may then move through the intermediate belt, which is seldom saturated, and enter the

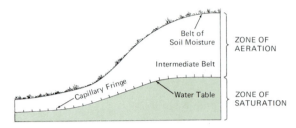

FIGURE 2.16
Zones in which groundwater occurs.

groundwater system in the **zone of saturation.** The upper surface of this zone is called the **water table.** The area just above the water table is a narrow belt called the capillary fringe, where water is drawn up by capillary action, caused by surface tension. The rate of movement of groundwater depends upon the permeability of the soil or rock and upon the hydraulic gradient, which is related to the slope of the water table.

Groundwater is an important source of useful water for drinking, industry, and irrigation. An **aquifer** is a zone of earth material containing sufficient groundwater that the water can be pumped from a well at a useful rate. Unconsolidated gravel and sand, as well as sandstone, granite, and metamorphic rocks with high porosity or open fractures, generally make good aquifers.

Water pumped from a well may produce a **cone of depression** in the water table, caused by withdrawing water at a faster rate than it can be replenished by natural groundwater flow. Overpumping an aquifer may lower the water level dangerously. Possible solutions include lowering the pump setting or drilling deeper wells; possible risks include exhausting the available water supply.

Groundwater provides the drinking water for about 50% of the people in the United States today. Protection of our groundwater resource is one of the major environmental problems of the 1980s and 1990s. Pollution of groundwater can be caused by such activities as improper disposal of hazardous waste; infiltration of mining, agricultural, and urban industrial runoff; and accidental spills of toxic liquids. We need to develop methods to monitor the zone of aeration because once a pollutant reaches the groundwater, correction of the problem becomes very difficult and expensive. Billions of dollars will be spent in the next 10 years to identify potential problems before the groundwater resource is damaged.

Streams and Rivers   There are two types of streams: effluent and influent. An **effluent stream** tends to be perennial; stream flow is maintained during the dry season by groundwater seepage into the channel. On the other hand, an **influent stream** is entirely above the groundwater table and flows only in direct response to precipitation. Water from an influent stream seeps down to the water table, forming a recharge mound—an elevated groundwater level located over a recharge zone. These streams may flow only a part of the year.

Streams and rivers form the basic transportation systems in the erosion and deposition of sediment. The amount and kind of sediment moved by a stream or river depend on the velocity and amount of water. Because there is a delicate balance between the flow of water and the movement of sediment, changes in the sediment load entering a stream lead to changes in the shape of the stream channel—its slope and cross-sectional shape—that effectively change the velocity of the water. Changes in velocity may increase or decrease the amount of sediment carried. Any change in the sediment load or rate of flow will initiate slope changes to bring the system into balance again.

For example, when farmland is converted back to forest, the sediment load tends to decrease, and the stream reacts by eroding the channel to lower the slope, which in turn lowers the velocity of the water. This process continues until an equilibrium is reestablished between the load imposed and the work done. In parts of the Piedmont of the southeastern United States, this change has been observed and recorded. Some once-muddy streams choked with sediment are now clearing slightly and eroding their channels. Whether this trend continues depends upon continuing land-use change and conservation measures. This example illustrates the important effect living things can have on geologic and hydrologic processes.

Local stream conditions may have environmental significance. For example, stream and river channels often contain a series of regularly spaced pools and riffles. **Pools** at low flow are deep areas with slow-moving water; they are produced by scour at high flow. **Riffles** at low flow are shallow areas with fast-moving water; they are produced by depositional processes at high flow. Streams with well-developed pools and riffles provide a variety of flow conditions and are characterized by deep, slow-moving water alternating with shallow, fast-moving water. These conditions foster desirable biological activity. Such streams also produce visually pleasing landscape variations, which have become known as the "aesthetic amenity," and increase recreational potential by providing better fishing and boating conditions. Unfortunately, land-use changes such as urbanization or timber harvesting, which increase sediment input to streams, may degrade a stream's pool-riffle environment.

The Biogeochemical Cycles

A **biogeochemical cycle** is the cycling of a chemical element through Earth's atmosphere, oceans, sediments, and lithosphere as it is affected by the geological and biological cycles. It can be described as a series of compartments, or storage reservoirs, and pathways between these reservoirs. The factors that control the flow between compartments must be understood for scientific and managerial purposes. The storage reservoirs in biogeochemical cycles are large units of the earth, such as the atmosphere or all terrestrial vegetation (Fig. 2.17).

Of the elements that circulate in the biogeochemical cycles, many are required for life (Table 2.1). We can divide these into three groups: (1) the "big six" that form the major building blocks of organic compounds: carbon, hydrogen, oxygen, nitrogen, phosphorus, and sulfur; (2) the other **macronutrients,** required in large amounts by most forms of life (this group includes potassium, calcium, iron, and magnesium); and (3) **micronutrients,** those required in very small amounts by at least some organisms (this group includes boron, used by green plants; copper, used in some enzymes; and molybdenum, used by nitrogen-fixing bacteria).

TABLE 2.1
Periodic table of the elements.

1 H Hydrogen																	2 He Helium
3 Li Lithium	4 Be Beryllium											5 B Boron	6 C Carbon	7 N Nitrogen	8 O Oxygen	9 F Fluorine	10 Ne Neon
11 Na Sodium	12 Mg Magnesium											13 Al Aluminum	14 Si Silicon	15 P Phosphorus	16 S Sulfur	17 Cl Chlorine	18 Ar Argon
19 K Potassium	20 Ca Calcium	21 Sc Scandium	22 Ti Titanium	23 V Vanadium	24 Cr Chromium	25 Mn Manganese	26 Fe Iron	27 Co Cobalt	28 Ni Nickel	29 Cu Copper	30 Zn Zinc	31 Ga Gallium	32 Ge Germanium	33 As Arsenic	34 Se Selenium	35 Br Bromine	36 Kr Krypton
37 Rb Rubidium	38 Sr Strontium	39 Y Yttrium	40 Zr Zirconium	41 Nb Niobium	42 Mo Molybdenum	43 Tc Technetium	44 Ru Ruthenium	45 Rh Rhodium	46 Pd Palladium	47 Ag Silver	48 Cd Cadmium	49 In Indium	50 Sn Tin	51 Sb Antimony	52 Te Tellurium	53 I Iodine	54 Xe Xenon
55 Cs Cesium	56 Ba Barium	57 La Lanthanum	72 Hf Hafnium	73 Ta Tantalum	74 W Wolfram	75 Re Rhenium	76 Os Osmium	77 Ir Iridium	78 Pt Platinum	79 Au Gold	80 Hg Mercury	81 Tl Thallium	82 Pb Lead	83 Bi Bismuth	84 Po Polonium	85 At Astatine	86 Rn Radon
87 Fr Francium	88 Ra Radium	89 Ac Actinium															

58 Ce Cerium	59 Pr Praseodymium	60 Nd Neodymium	61 Pm Promethium	62 Sm Samarium	63 Eu Europium	64 Gd Gadolinium	65 Tb Terbium	66 Dy Dysprosium	67 Ho Holmium	68 Er Erbium	69 Tm Thulium	70 Yb Ytterbium	71 Lu Lutetium
90 Th Thorium	91 Pa Protactinium	92 U Uranium	93 Np Neptunium	94 Pu Plutonium	95 Am Americium	96 Cm Curium	97 Bk Berkelium	98 Cf Californium	99 Es Einsteinium	100 Fm Fermium	101 Md Mendelevium	102 No Nobelium	103 Lw Lawrencium

Atomic Number → 20

Element Relatively Abundant in Earth's Crust → **

Environmentally Important Trace Elements → **

Ca Calcium

← Biological Role

← Name

● = Required for all life

◊ = Required for some life forms

\ = Moderately toxic; either slightly toxic to all life or highly toxic to a few forms

× = Highly toxic to all organisms, even in low concentrations

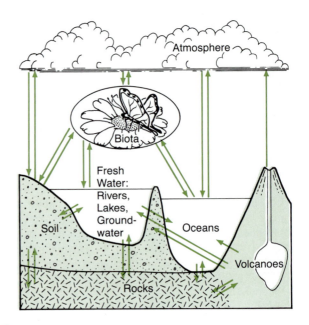

FIGURE 2.17
Generalized biogeochemical cycle. The major parts of the biosphere are connected by the flow of chemical elements and compounds. In many of these cycles, the biota play an important role. Matter from Earth's interior is released by volcanoes. The atmosphere exchanges some compounds and elements rapidly with the biota and oceans. Rock exchanges materials more closely with soils and the oceans.

Although there are as many biogeochemical cycles as there are chemical elements necessary for life, there are certain general rules for these cycles:

1   Some chemical elements cycle quickly and are readily regenerated for biological activity. Oxygen and nitrogen are among these. Others are easily tied up in relatively immobile forms and are returned only slowly, by geological processes, to locations where they can be reused by the biota. Phosphorus is involved in this kind of cycle.
2   Biogeochemical cycles that include a gaseous phase (a residence time in the atmosphere) tend to have more rapid recycling. Those without an atmospheric phase, like phosphorus, are more likely to end up as deep-ocean sediments and to be relatively slow to recycle. We are most concerned with this type of cycle.

3   Earth's biota have greatly altered the cycling of chemicals among the air, waters, and soils and have greatly changed our planet. The continuation of these processes is essential to the long-term maintenance of life on Earth.
4   Through modern technology, we have begun to alter the transfer of chemical elements among the air, waters, and soils at rates comparable to natural biological ones. These activities benefit society, but also pose great dangers. To wisely manage our environment, we must recognize both the positive and negative consequences of these activities, attempt to accentuate the first and minimize the second.

The Carbon Cycle   The major aspects of the carbon cycle, which involves a gaseous phase, are shown in Figure 2.18. Carbon exists in the atmosphere in several compounds; the primary one is

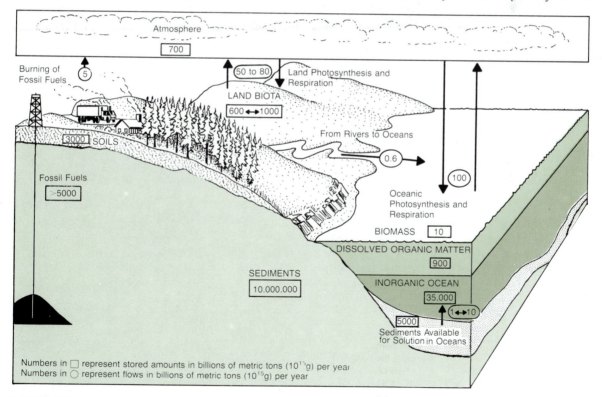

FIGURE 2.18
The global carbon cycle. (From Bolin et al.)

Career Profile: Gerald Livingston

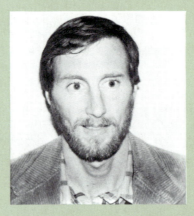

Gerald Livingston says he knows it sounds like motherhood, but he really hopes to make a significant contribution to understanding interactions in our environment. He and other scientists are working to set up a program to look at the global biogeochemical budget. The project is funded by NASA, which has contracted with a private company for research services.

Right now, the project's focus is on the nitrogen cycle. Field measurements are being compared with remote-sensing satellite data in an attempt to correlate them.

Livingston describes remote sensing as a "surrogate" for an actual person making measurements everywhere. Using a familiar example, he says that field measurements may tell you the temperatures in New York City and Baltimore, but you won't know what is happening in between. With remote-sensing data, you can figure out what is happening without actually being there.

Remote sensing lets you back off and see the big picture so you can compare what is happening across large areas, he says. "The purpose of remote sensing is to give you a unique vantage point above Earth and the atmosphere. You get a small-scale view of a large area."

Livingston says by far most of his work is in the lab, although some fieldwork is involved. At specific sites, gas chromatography is used to measure gases coming from the ground and soil samples are taken to be chemically analyzed in the lab. Livingston makes trips to the field to verify the data from time to time. In the lab, he also develops field techniques and plans ways to make the experiments as successful as possible. A major task is converting remote-sensing data into a usable form. To do this, Livingston spends a lot of time working at a computer terminal.

As an undergraduate in college, Livingston was interested in science. He majored in biology with heavy emphasis in chemistry. Some environmental courses he took helped him focus his interests. He went to graduate school to study marine ecology. His long-term goal was to become a college professor and do research.

The further he went in graduate school, he says, the more his environmental interests "snowballed." After receiving his master's degree and Ph.D., he got a job that involved him in remote-sensing work.

For Livingston that was a big change in direction—from marine studies to ecosystem studies. He compares it to going from working in your backyard to working in regional experiments. "The basics are all the same, but the details are so much different," he says. Whether on a local or global scale, Livingston says, everything influences all the rest of Earth. He believes that people need to understand how interrelated the entire Earth is. Everything that humans do has influence on the environment, and the environment will in turn influence people, he says.

To Livingston, remote sensing is "like putting on a whole new set of glasses. You see the world in a new way." The global biogeochemical budget project is in its early stages, but he hopes it will have an impact on how people use the environment.

Michele Wigginton

carbon dioxide, but organic compounds like methane and ethylene occur in lesser amounts. Certain parts of the carbon cycle are inorganic; that is, they do not depend on biological activities. Carbon dioxide is soluble in water and is exchanged between the atmosphere and ocean or freshwater lakes by the physical process of diffusion (Fig. 2.19). Other things being equal and lacking any living systems or source of external energy, the diffusion of carbon dioxide gas will continue in one direction or the other until a steady state is reached between the carbon dioxide in the atmosphere above water and the dissolved carbon dioxide in the water. When carbon dioxide is dissolved in water, a mild acid is formed, which in turn changes the amount of carbon dioxide that can be subsequently dissolved. Dissolved carbon dioxide forms carbonate and bicarbonate in the water. When a great deal of carbonate is formed, the water becomes saturated, and the carbonate will combine with metallic elements like calcium and be deposited as salt, in which calcium carbonate

predominates. These sediments exist in a dynamic steady state with the water and can redissolve when the carbonate concentration in the water decreases. Thus a solution of water over a calcium carbonate rock will eventually come into a steady state just as an air and water solution will come into a steady state.

Carbon dioxide enters the biological cycles through **photosynthesis**—the synthesis of sugars from carbon dioxide and water by living organisms using light as energy—in which carbon, hydrogen, and oxygen are combined to form organic compounds. The rate of carbon dioxide uptake depends on the number and the activity of photosynthetic plants, on the concentration of carbon dioxide in the atmosphere, and on other environmental conditions. Plants grow faster when the carbon dioxide concentration of the air is increased, as long as their other needs for light, water, nutrients, and so on, are met. Most of the carbon in living tissue is stored in the woody tissue of vegetation, particularly in forests.

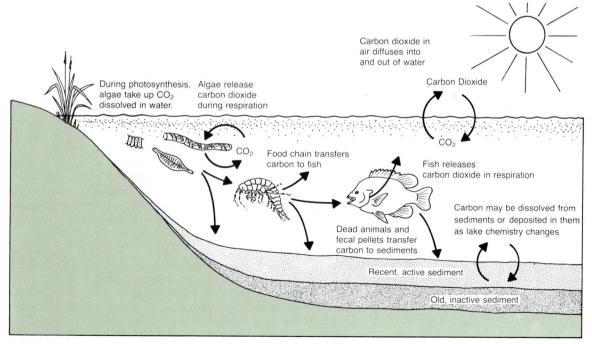

FIGURE 2.19
The carbon cycle in a lake.

Carbon leaves the living biota through **respiration,** the process by which organic compounds are transformed into gaseous carbon dioxide. The carbon dioxide is released to the atmosphere either directly or by way of fresh or marine waters. When living tissue dies, some of the dead organic matter may be stored (in some cases for a considerable length of time) in soil or in deep-sea sediments. Other dead organic matter is food for bacteria and fungi, and through the respiration of these organisms, carbon returns to the atmosphere as methane and carbon dioxide.

Terrestrial organic matter can be transported by the geological cycles to the ocean, transported by rivers and streams as dissolved or particulate organic matter, or carried by wind. Some of this organic material is added to deposits that eventually convert to rock, and thus the carbon enters the rock cycle. As we can see in Figure 2.18, most of the carbon in Earth's surface exists as rock, particularly as carbonates. Shells of many marine organisms are composed of calcium carbonate that the organisms take from seawater. The next largest storage reservoirs in the carbon cycle are the oceans, where the dissolved carbon is 50 times the amount in the atmosphere.

The cycle of carbon dioxide between land organisms and the atmosphere represents a large flux, with approximately 10% of the total amount of carbon in the atmosphere being taken up by photosynthesis and released as respiration annually.

The Phosphorus Cycle Phosphorus is one of the essential elements for life. Although it is in relatively short supply, it is a major nutrient for all living things. Phosphorus does not have a major gaseous phase in its biogeochemical cycle; it exists in the atmosphere only as small particles of dust. In contrast to the carbon cycle, the phosphorus cycle is slow, and much of it proceeds one way—from the lands to the oceans (Fig. 2.20). Phosphorus enters living things from the soil, where it exists as phosphate and in minerals combined with calcium, potassium, magnesium, and iron. Because these minerals are relatively insoluble in water, phosphorus becomes available very slowly

through the weathering of rocks or rock particles in the soil. In a relatively stable terrestrial ecosystem much of the phosphorus that is taken up by vegetation will be returned to the soil. Some of the phosphorus, however, is inevitably lost to the ecosystem. It moves out of the soils in a water-soluble form and is transported by waters through rivers and streams to the oceans. Thus the phosphorus cycle is a gradual flow, from the removal of phosphorus from the land to its deposition in the oceans. Because phosphorus is one of the major constituents of agricultural fertilizers, sources of phosphorus, such as the guano deposits on oceanic islands, are extremely important to us.

The return of phosphorus to the land is also a slow process. We have already learned that ocean-feeding birds provide one pathway to return phosphorus from the ocean to the land. Another major source of phosphorus fertilizers is sedimentary rocks made up of the fossils of marine animals. The richest such mine in the world is "Bone Valley," 40 km east of Tampa, Florida. Between 15 and 10 million years ago, Bone Valley was the bottom of a shallow sea where marine invertebrates lived and died [7]. Through geological processes, Bone Valley was uplifted. In the 1880s and 1890s, the discovery of its phosphate ore led to a "phosphate rush," and now the valley provides more than one-third of the world's entire phosphate production and three-fourths of U.S. production. Bone Valley represents a very slow return of phosphate to the land; redistribution over wide areas occurred only when people used technology to mine, transport, and spread the fertilizer.

Perhaps the most important point about the phosphorus cycle is the slowness of the return from ocean to land. Because it is a crucial macronutrient for all life and because many of its compounds are relatively water-insoluble, phosphorus is likely to be one of the most difficult to get, most subject to competition, and most limiting of all the chemical elements necessary for life.

The mining of phosphorus ores poses several environmental issues. First, Bone Valley, for example, has become an environmental problem. Mined of much of its ore, it consists of several hundred square kilometers of strip mine with huge slime ponds—a scar on the landscape. Second,

Numbers in ☐ represent stored amounts in millions of metric tons (10^{12}g) per year

Numbers in ◯ represent flows in millions of metric tons (10^{12}g) per year

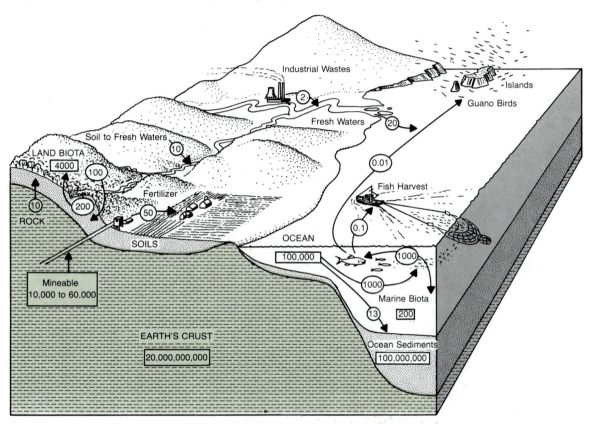

FIGURE 2.20
The global phosphorus cycle. Phosphorus is recycled to soil and land biota by geological uplifting processes, by birds producing guano, and by human beings. Although Earth's crust contains a very large amount of phosphorus, only a small fraction of it is mineable by conventional techniques. Phosphorus is therefore one of our most precious resources. (Values are compiled from various sources. The estimates are approximate and are given here to the approximate order of magnitude. Based primarily on Delwiche and Likens, and Pierrou.)

what will we do when the Peruvian Islands and mines like Bone Valley are exhausted?

Some experts believe that, if the current mining costs of $15 per ton are maintained, the total U.S. reserves of phosphorus are about 2.2 billion metric tons, a quantity estimated to supply our needs for several decades. However, for a higher price per ton, more phosphorus is available. Florida is thought to have 8.1 billion metric tons of phosphorus recoverable with existing methods, and there

are large deposits elsewhere [7]. However, the mining processes have negative effects on the landscapes. How to balance the need for phosphorus with the environmental impact of the mining is a major environmental issue.

The Nitrogen Cycle The nitrogen cycle, one of the most important and most complex cycles, is most likely to cause environmental problems for us. One of the "big six" elements, nitrogen is required by all living things as an essential part of amino acids that make up proteins. Earlier in this chapter we learned that the biota have greatly changed the nitrogen content of the atmosphere. Life maintains nitrogen in the molecular form (N_2) in the atmosphere, rather than in ammonia (NH_3) or nitrogen oxides, as would occur on a lifeless planet. Nitrogen exists in our atmosphere in seven forms: molecular nitrogen (N_2), oxides of nitrogen (N_2O, NO, and NO_2), and hydrogen-nitrogen compounds (NH, NH_3, and HNO_2).

In contrast to hydrogen, oxygen, and carbon, nitrogen is comparatively unreactive and tends to remain in small inorganic compounds. Considerable energy is required to connect molecular nitrogen to some other compounds, and most organisms cannot use molecular nitrogen directly. It must be converted to ammonia (NH_3), nitrate ion (NO_3^-), or amino acids. There are only two major natural pathways for this conversion: lightning and life. By far the greater amount is converted by biological activity.

The major pathways of the nitrogen cycle are shown in Figure 2.21. One of the more curious and important points we should keep in mind about the nitrogen cycle is that the conversion of molecular nitrogen to ammonia or nitrate, and other chemical transformations of inorganic forms of nitrogen, can be done only by cyanobacteria, members of the **prokaryotes** which are primitive forms that lack a membrane-bounded cell nucleus. Only these microorganisms carry out certain chemical reactions without which all life would stop.

So important are these conversions of nitrogen that many major higher organisms called **eukaryotes** (with a membrane-bounded cell nucleus) have evolved symbiotic relationships with some nitrogen-transforming microbes. These include many flowering plants, particularly the legume family, having nodules on the roots that support nitrogen-fixing bacteria, which convert N_2 to ammonia. The acacia trees, very important in the African savannahs, are also part of such a symbiotic relationship. The trees provide carbohydrates for, and an environment conducive to, bacterial growth. Nitrogen-fixing bacteria also are symbionts in the stomachs of some animals, particularly ruminants—cud-chewing, herbivorous mam-

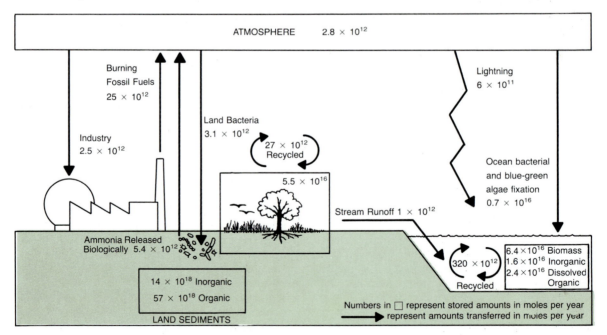

FIGURE 2.21
The nitrogen cycle. (From Garrels et al)

mals with specialized four-chambered stomachs—like cows, deer, moose, and giraffes. The ruminant bacteria provide as much as half of the total nitrogen for the ruminants, with the rest being provided by protein in green plants. The ruminants provide food for the bacteria, which not only enrich the food with nitrogen (by growing, incorporating nitrogen, and being digested themselves by the ruminants), but also digest plant material that would otherwise not be usable by the mammals.

Ammonia is released into the atmosphere by bacterial decomposition; it is very soluble in water and is returned to the oceans and land in rain as salts of ammonia (ammonium sulfate and ammonium nitrate).

If bacteria only fixed nitrogen, molecular nitrogen would slowly be removed from the atmosphere. But bacteria also carry out **denitrification,** releasing the molecular nitrogen as a gas back into the atmosphere. Thus the removal from and addition to the atmosphere of nitrogen are primarily controlled by bacterial activity. Nitrogen enters the ocean through the fixation of atmospheric nitrogen by planktonic cyanobacteria, which live in the ocean. Nitrogen compounds also are carried into the ocean by freshwater runoff from rivers and streams.

In contrast to phosphorus, nitrogen has a major gaseous phase, is highly mobile, and is rapidly recycled. Like phosphorus, nitrogen is a major agricultural fertilizer and pollutant of groundwater. Only natural sources provided nitrogen for fertilizers until World War I, when German scientists discovered that electrical discharges could be used to fix nitrogen industrially. Industrial fixation today is a major source of commercial nitrogen fertilizer.

Nitrogen oxides are formed by a high-temperature chemical reaction where nitrogen and oxygen are present. Oxides of nitrogen not only are a major pollutant from automobiles but are the most difficult to eliminate because they are formed by the high temperature in the cylinders when ordinary air is used.

Nitrogen compounds are thus a bane and a boon for modern technological society. Nitrogen is required for all life, and its compounds are used in many technological processes and devices, including explosives and fuels.

The Rock Cycle

The **rock cycle,** the largest of the Earth cycles, consists of a group of processes that produce rocks and soil. The rock cycle depends on the tectonic cycle for energy, the hydrologic cycle for water, and the biogeochemical cycle for materials. As shown in Figure 2.22, there are three classifications of rock—igneous, sedimentary, and metamorphic—involved in a worldwide recycling process. Internal heat from the tectonic cycle drives the rock cycle and produces igneous rocks from molten material crystallizing on or beneath Earth's surface. Rocks located at or near the surface break down chemically and physically by weathering processes, forming sediments that are transported by wind, water, or ice. The sediments accumulate in depositional basins, such as the ocean, where they are eventually transformed into sedimentary rocks. After the sedimentary rocks are buried to sufficient depth, they may be altered by heat, pressure, or chemically active fluids to produce metamorphic rocks, which may then melt to start the cycle again. Possible variations of this idealized cycle are indicated by the arrows in Figure 2.22.

Recycling of rock and mineral material is the most important aspect of the rock cycle. Our interest in this cycle is more than academic because it is upon these earth materials that we build our homes, industries, roads, and other structures, and it is from them that we obtain many mineral resources. Furthermore, because all life is greatly affected by the characteristics of rock substrate, understanding the various aspects of the rock cycle will facilitate the best use of those resources produced by the cycle.

Life interacts with the rock cycle. On the land, what lives where depends in part on the kind of rock base and its chemical characteristics. In turn, life affects what kinds of minerals are formed. For example, the economically valuable iron-rich rocks—the rocks that form the major iron ranges where iron is mined—were laid down more than two billion years ago. It is believed that iron in solution in the ancient oceans formed sediments when it combined with the oxygen produced by early organisms. These sediments eventually became the rocks that provide our iron ore. When most of the dissolved iron had been oxidized and

FIGURE 2.22
The rock cycle and major paths of material transfer from the solid earth to the atmosphere as modulated by life. (From Foster.)

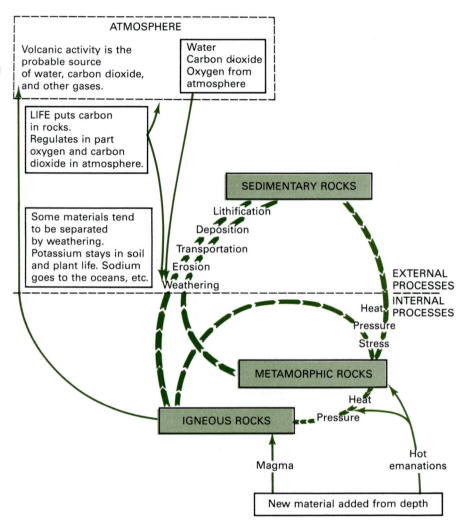

ATMOSPHERE

Volcanic activity is the probable source of water, carbon dioxide, and other gases.

Water
Carbon dioxide
Oxygen from atmosphere

LIFE puts carbon in rocks. Regulates in part oxygen and carbon dioxide in atmosphere.

Some materials tend to be separated by weathering. Potassium stays in soil and plant life. Sodium goes to the oceans, etc.

SEDIMENTARY ROCKS

Lithification
Deposition
Transportation
Erosion
Weathering

EXTERNAL PROCESSES
INTERNAL PROCESSES

Heat
Pressure
Stress

METAMORPHIC ROCKS

Heat
Pressure

IGNEOUS ROCKS

Magma

Hot emanations

New material added from depth

deposited, then the oxygen produced by organisms began to build up in the atmosphere. Thus our major iron ore deposits, as well as free oxygen in the atmosphere, are a result of life's influence on the biosphere.

The rock cycle concentrates as well as disperses materials—a process extremely important for the mining and use of minerals. We take resources that are concentrated by one aspect of the rock cycle, transform these resources through industrial activity, and then return them to the geologic cycle in a diluted form, where they are further dispersed by earth processes. Once this dispersion process has

taken place, the resource may not be concentrated again within a useful period of time. For example, the lead in automobile fuel is mined in a concentrated form, transformed and diluted in fuel, and further dispersed by traffic patterns, air currents, and other processes. Eventually, it may become sufficiently abundant to contaminate soil and water but it can never be efficiently recycled. Similar situations apply to other resources used in paints, solvents, and other industrial products.

Minerals and Rocks   A **mineral** is a naturally occurring inorganic crystalline substance with physical and chemical properties that vary within prescribed limits. A **rock** is an aggregate of a mineral or minerals. Although there are over 2000 minerals, only a few are necessary to identify most rocks. Nearly 75% by weight of Earth's crust is oxygen and silicon; these two elements in combination with aluminum, iron, calcium, sodium, potassium, and magnesium compose the minerals that make up about 95% of Earth's crust. These minerals, called the **silicates,** are the most important rock-forming minerals. The physical and chemical properties of the major minerals affect soil fertility, ability to hold water, engineering uses, and potential as a resource or a pollutant.

The strength of rocks, and thus their ability to form mountains and their utility for building sites and other human uses, is affected by their composition, texture, and structure. Composition refers to the minerals in a rock; texture describes the size, shape, and arrangement of the mineral grains; and structure refers to such aspects as the nature of the forces holding the mineral grains together or the size and number of fractures.

All rocks are fractured, and fractures affect the strength of a rock. For example, water may concentrate and move along fractures, facilitating weathering and reducing rock strength. Furthermore, rocks tend to move along fractures, thereby creating geological faults. The movement may cause earthquakes or may grind or pulverize the rocks, producing zones of weak rocks. The orientation of fractures is especially important, as fractures that dip down a slope may form potential slip planes, along which landslides might occur.

Types of Rocks In discussing the generalized rock cycle, we mentioned that there are three rock families: igneous, sedimentary, and metamorphic. Table 2.2 lists the common rock types by family. Although rocks are primarily classified according to both mineral makeup and texture, it is texture—the size, shape, and arrangement of mineral grains—that is most significant in environmental studies. Rock texture, along with discontinuities such as fractures, determines the strength and utility of a particular rock.

Igneous rocks are rocks that have crystallized from a naturally occurring mobile mass of quasi-liquid earth material known as **magma.** If magma crystallizes below Earth's surface, the resulting igneous rock is called intrusive. One of the most common of the intrusive rocks is granite, which is generally a strong rock suitable for many engineering purposes.

Extrusive igneous rock forms when magma reaches the surface and is blown out of a volcano as pyroclastic debris or flows out as lava. One of the more common extrusive igneous rocks is basalt, which often forms extensive flows. Extrusive igneous rocks vary considerably in composition as well as in texture and structure; therefore, they have to be carefully evaluated as to suitability for a specific purpose. This was tragically emphasized on June 5, 1976, when the Teton Dam in Idaho failed, killing 14 and inflicting approximately $1 billion in property damage. The causes of the failure had strong geologic aspects, including highly fractured volcanic rocks over which the dam was constructed and highly erodable wind-deposited clay-silts used in the construction of the dam interior, or core. Open fractures in the volcanic rocks were probably not completely filled with a cement slurry (grout) in construction, and while the reservoir was filling, the water began moving under the foundation area of the dam. When the water came in contact with the highly erodable material of the core, it quickly tunneled through the base of the dam, which explains the whirlpool, several meters across, that was observed in the reservoir just prior to failure. In other words, the development of a vortex of water draining out of the reservoir near the dam strongly suggested the presence of a subsurface tunnel of free-flowing water below the dam. Minutes later, the final failure of the dam sent a wall of water up to 20 m high downstream, destroying homes, farms, equipment, animals, and crops along a 160 km reach of the Teton and Snake rivers.

Sedimentary rocks form when sediments are weathered, transported, deposited, and then formed into rock by natural cement, compression, or other mechanism. Physical processes are obviously important in forming sedimentary rocks. Perhaps less well known is that Earth's biota also play an important role in all stages of sedimentary rock formation. Biological processes are especially significant in weathering, depositing, and cement-

TABLE 2.2

Common rocks (engineering geology terminology).

Type	Texture	Materials
Igneous		
Intrusive		
Granitic[a]	Coarse[b]	Feldspar, quartz
Ultrabasic	Coarse	Ferromagnesians, ± quartz
Extrusive		
Basaltic[c]	Fine[d]	Feldspar, ± ferromagnesians, ± quartz
Volcanic breccia	Mixed—coarse and fine	Feldspar, ± ferromagnesians, ± quartz
Welded tuff	Fine volcanic ash	Glass, feldspar, ± quartz
Metamorphic		*Parent material*
Foliated		
Slate	Fine	Shale or basalt
Schist	Coarse	
Gneiss	Coarse	Shale, basalt, or granite
Nonfoliated		
Quartzite	Coarse	Sandstone
Marble	Coarse	Limestone
Sedimentary		*Materials*
Detrital		
Shale	Fine	Clay
Sandstone	Coarse	Quartz, feldspar, rock fragments
Conglomerate	Mixed—very coarse and fine	Quartz, feldspar, rock fragments
Chemical		
Limestone	Coarse to fine	Calcite, shells, calcareous algae
Rock salt	Coarse to fine	Halite

[a]Textural name for a group of coarse-grained, intrusive igneous rocks, including granite, diorite, and gabbro.
[b]Individual mineral grains can be seen with naked eye.
[c]Textural name for a group of fine-grained, extrusive igneous rocks, including rhyolite, andesite, and basalt.
[d]Individual mineral grains cannot be seen with naked eye.

ing sediment, but also may be directly involved in the transport of sediment on a variety of scales. For example, many substances carried in chemical solution in river water are taken up by marine organisms and thus end up in sedimentary rocks when the organisms die and become part of the sedimentary record. As another example, kelp beds along the California coast are responsible for the transport of large (several centimeters in diameter) blocks of rock. Each main strand of kelp is attached by a holdfast to one or several rocks on the bottom. In storms the kelp bed may be torn up, and as the kelp stems drift they move the rocks. In one instance near Santa Barbara, California, a substantial pad of gravel constructed to support an offshore sewage pipe was eroded in this manner.

The two major types of sedimentary rocks are detrital sedimentary rocks, which form from broken parts of previously existing rocks, and chemical sedimentary rocks, which form from chemical or biochemical processes that remove material carried in chemical solution. The detrital sedimentary rocks include shale, sandstone, and conglomerate. Of these, shale is by far the most abundant and causes most of the environmental problems associated with sedimentary rocks. Two types of shale are generally recognized: compaction shale and cementation shale. Compaction shale is an extremely weak rock, often characterized by a propensity to expand and contract on wetting and drying and by a high erosion potential. On the other hand, cementation shale can be a very hard rock, depending on the cementing agent. The presence of shale rock indicates the need for detailed evaluation before any land use is planned.

Sandstones and conglomerates are coarse grained and make up about 25% of all sedimentary rocks. Depending upon the type of cementing material, these rocks may be very strong and suitable for many engineering purposes. However, because of variations in chemistry, they vary considerably in their fertility as a base for soils.

Limestone makes up about 25% of all sedimentary rock and is by far the most abundant of the chemical sedimentary rocks. Limestone is composed almost entirely of the mineral calcite, which weathers readily in the presence of water, forming open cavities or caverns within the limestone. In addition, large surface pits known as **sinkholes** may form. Limestone tends to form highly fertile soils, as shown by adjacent valleys in Virginia near the North Carolina border. One, known as Rich Valley, has good soils and prosperous farms—the bedrock is limestone. The other, where the soils are less productive and the farms less prosperous, is called Poor Valley—the bedrock is shale.

Another important chemical sedimentary rock is salt, which is composed primarily of the mineral halite (sodium chloride, or common table salt). Rock salt forms when shallow seas or lakes dry up. As water evaporates, a series of salts, one of which is halite, is precipitated. The salts may later be covered by other types of sedimentary rocks as the area again becomes a center of sediment deposition. It is from these sedimentary basins that salt is often mined. Rock salt is of particular environmental significance because it is one of the rock types being seriously considered as a storage medium for high-level radioactive waste.

Metamorphic rocks are changed rocks. Heat, pressure, and chemically active fluids produced in the tectonic cycle may change the mineralogy and texture of rocks. This, in effect, produces new rocks. Two types of metamorphic rocks are recognized: foliated (that is, occurring in layers like pages in a book), formed of elongated or flat mineral grains having a preferential alignment and forming parallel layers; and nonfoliated, without preferential alignment or segregation of the mineral grains. Foliated metamorphic rocks such as slate, schist, and gneiss have a variety of physical and chemical properties; it is therefore difficult to generalize about their usefulness for engineering purposes or their qualities as a base for soils. Foliation planes in metamorphic rocks, however, are potential planes of weakness affecting the strength of the rock, in particular its potential to slide, because the rock is less strong along the foliation planes than across them. Nonfoliated metamorphic rocks include quartzite and marble. Quartzite, a metamorphosed sandstone, is generally a hard, durable rock suitable for many engineering purposes. Marble, formed from the metamorphism of limestone, consists of recrystallized calcite. Marbles have many of the problems associated with limestones, namely, the development of solution pits, caverns, or sinkholes.

Soils **Soils** are made of weathered rock material and organic matter and thus are produced by interactions between geologic (rock and hydrologic cycles) and biologic processes. **Weathering**—the physical, chemical, and biological breakdown of rocks—is the first step in the soil-forming process. The more insoluble weathered material may remain essentially in place and be further modified by organic processes to form a residual soil, such as the red soils of the Piedmont in the southeastern United States. Weathered material that is transported by water, wind, or ice and then deposited and further modified by organic processes forms a transported soil. The exceptionally fertile soils formed from the glacial deposits in the midwestern United States are an example.

Soils may be defined in two ways in environmental studies. A soil scientist defines soil as a solid earth material that has been altered by physical, chemical, and organic processes so that it can support rooted plant life. An engineer, on the other hand, defines soil as any solid earth material that can be removed without blasting.

The formation of soil is affected by climate, topography, parent material (material from which the soil is formed), maturity (age), and biological activity. Most of the differences we observe in soils are due to the effects of climate and topography. The type of parent rock, the organic process, and the length of time soil-forming processes have operated are of secondary importance. Given enough time, similar soils may develop from different parent materials if climate and topography are the same.

The vertical and horizontal movement of material in soils often produces a distinctive soil layering, or soil profile, divided into zones, or **soil horizons** (Fig. 2.23). An important process is **leaching** (downward movement of soluble material) from the upper zone, called the A-horizon, to the intermediate zone, known as the B-horizon, where the leached material is deposited. Depending upon climate and other variables, the B-horizon may contain a "hardpan" layer of compacted clay or calcium carbonate-cemented materials known as caliche. In addition, materials may also move upward in the soil in response to a natural rise of the water table or in response to human use, such as extensive irrigation or removal of vegetation (timber harvesting) that induces a rise in the level of groundwater. When accompanied by extensive evaporation, this upward movement may cause salts to move up and be deposited in the upper soil layers or even on the ground surface. This happened in the Indus River valley in Pakistan, where approximately 93,000 km² were irri-

gated. The water table rose and extensive evaporation deposited salts, making the soils unsuitable for crops. The problem can be, and in some places has been, corrected by installing drainage systems for the land and then providing an abundance of water to leach out the salts. A careful analysis and a special system of wells to lower the water table were used with success in Pakistan to reclaim soils damaged by salts. In the Great Valley of California, salts deposited on the surface by evaporation of irrigation water are regularly leached out of the soil by periodic applications of a large amount of water. Nevertheless, salt buildup in soils is becoming a serious problem there also.

Soil Classification Soil scientists have developed a comprehensive and systematic classification of soils known as soil taxonomy (informally called "the Seventh Approximation"), based on physical and chemical properties of the soils. The major kinds of soil in this classification, which is especially useful for agriculture, are given in Table 2.3.

Another soil classification, known as the **unified soil classification system** (Table 2.4), has been devised for engineering purposes. In this system, soils are divided according to the predominant particle size or the abundance of organic material. A useful way of estimating the size of soil particles in the field is as follows: It is **sand** or larger (coarse soil) if you can see the individual grains, **silt** (fine soil) if you can see the grains with a 10–power hand lens, and **clay** (fine soil) if you cannot see the grains with such a hand lens.

Because soils greatly affect the best use of the land, a soil survey to identify and map soils is an important part of environmental planning. The physical structure, fertility, and organic content of soil all affect the movement of water and nutrients. The more important properties of soils for planning are strength, sensitivity, compressibility, erodibility, permeability or drainage potential, corrosion potential, ease of excavation, and shrink/swell potential.

The strength of a soil depends upon cohesive and frictional forces within the soil itself. In general, cohesion is most important in the fine-

A HORIZON (topsoil): Upper part is often rich in organic material; lower portion is the zone of leaching

B HORIZON (subsoil) Zone of accumulation

C HORIZON (subsoil) Partially altered parent material

Unaltered parent material

FIGURE 2.23
Soil profile showing the A, B, and C horizons.

TABLE 2.3
General properties of soil orders used with the Seventh Approximation.

Order	General Properties
Entisols	No horizon development (azonal); many are recent alluvium; synthetic soils are included; are often young soils.
Vertisols	Include swelling clays (greater than 35%) that expand and contract with changing moisture content. Generally form in regions with a pronounced wet and dry season.
Inceptisols	One or more of horizons have developed quickly; horizons are often difficult to differentiate; most often found in young but not recent land surfaces, have appreciable accumulation of organic material; most common in humid climates but range from the Arctic to tropics; native vegetation is most often forest.
Aridisols	Desert soils; soils of dry places; low organic accumulation; have subsoil horizon where gypsum, caliche (calcium carbonate), salt, or other materials may accumulate.
Mollisols	Soils characterized by black, organic rich "A" horizon (prairie soils); surface horizons are also rich in bases. Commonly found in semiarid or subhumid regions.
Spodosols	Soils characterized by ash-colored sands over subsoil, accumulations of amorphous iron-aluminum sesquioxides and humus. They are acid soils that commonly form in sandy parent materials. Are found principally under forests in humid regions.
Alfisols	Soils characterized by: a brown or gray-brown surface horizon, an argillic (clay-rich) subsoil accumulation with an intermediate to high base saturation (greater than 35% as measured by the sum of cations, such as calcium, sodium, magnesium, etc.). Commonly form under forests in humid regions of the mid-latitudes.
Ulfisols	Soils characterized by an argillic horizon with low base saturation (less than 35% as measured by the sum of cations); often have a red-yellow or reddish-brown color; restricted to humid climates and generally form on older landforms or younger, highly weathered parent materials.
Oxisols	Relatively featureless, often deep soils, leached of bases, hydrated, containing oxides of iron and aluminum (laterite) as well as kaolinite clay. Primarily restricted to tropical and subtropical regions.
Histosols	Organic soils (peat, muck, bog).

Source: Soil Conservation Service, Soil Survey Staff.

grained soils, where soil particles are held together by molecular and electrostatic forces. Tree roots or moisture films between coarse grains may provide some apparent cohesion, explaining the ability of wet sand (which is cohesionless when dry) to stand in vertical walls in children's sand castles on the beach [8]. For important projects the strength of a soil may be measured in the laboratory.

A soil's sensitivity reflects changes in its strength due to such disturbances as vibration or excavation. Fine-grained soils may lose up to 75% or more of their strength following disturbance and thus are considered quite sensitive. Coarser soils of sand and gravel, with little or no clay, are the least sensitive [9].

The compressibility of a soil is a measure of its tendency to consolidate or decrease in volume. It is partly a function of the elastic nature of the soil particles. Excessive compression may crack foundations and walls. In general, finer soils have a high compressibility.

Erodibility is another important property of soils. Generally, soils that are easily eroded include unprotected silts, sands, and other loosely consolidated materials. Cohesive soils with a relatively high clay content, or naturally cemented soils, are not easily moved and therefore have a low erosion factor.

Permeability is the measure of the ease with which water can move through a material. The per-

TABLE 2.4
Unified soil classification system.

Major Divisions				Group Symbols	Soil Group Name
COARSE-GRAINED SOILS Over half of material larger than 0.074 mm	GRAVELS	CLEAN GRAVELS	Less than 5% fines	GW	Well-graded gravel
				GP	Poorly graded gravel
		DIRTY GRAVELS	More than 12% fines	GM	Silty gravel
				GC	Clayey gravel
	SANDS	CLEAN SANDS	Less than 5% fines	SW	Well-graded sand
				SP	Poorly graded sand
		DIRTY SANDS	More than 12% fines	SM	Silty sand
				SC	Clayey sand
FINE-GRAINED SOILS Over half of material smaller than 0.074 mm		SILTS Nonplastic		ML	Silt
				MH	Micaceous silt
				OL	Organic silt
		CLAYS Plastic		CL	Silty clay
				CH	High-plastic clay
				OH	Organic clay
Predominantly organics				PT	Peat and muck

centage of void or empty space in a soil or rock is known as the porosity. As the size of the material decreases, the permeability generally decreases. Clean gravels or sands have the highest permeabilities, transmitting several hundred cubic meters of water per day through a cross-sectional area of one square meter. Some of the most porous materials, such as clay, have a very low permeability; although small, flat clay particles can have a good deal of pore space, the individual small openings tenaciously hold the water. A typical cross-sectional area of one square meter of clay may transmit only one-tenth or less of a cubic meter of water per day.

The shrink/swell potential reflects the tendency of a soil to gain or lose water. Soils that tend to increase or decrease in volume with water content are called expansive. The swelling is caused by the chemical attraction and addition of layers of water molecules between the flat submicroscopic clay plates of certain clay minerals. Expansive soils cause significant environmental problems (Fig. 2.24) and in terms of total property damage to structures are one of our most costly natural hazards [10].

Differences in soil properties mean that certain materials are more suitable than others for particular types of land uses. Properties such as strength, sensitivity, compressibility, erodibility, and permeability should be carefully considered before beginning a project involving the use of soils.

Soil Fertility A single cubic meter of soil may contain millions of living things, including small rodents, insects, worms, algae, fungi, and bacteria. These animals and plants are important in releasing and converting nutrients in soils into forms that are useful to plants and in mixing and aerating soil materials and particles [11]. Soil fertility, then, refers to the capacity of a soil to supply nutrients, such as nitrogen, phosphorus, and potassium,

FIGURE 2.24
Expansive soils: (a) idealized diagram showing an expansive clay as layers of water molecules are incorporated between clay plates; (b) effects of a soil's shrinking and swelling at a home site. (After Mathewson and Castleberry.) (c) Cracked wall resulting from expansion of clay soil under the foundation.

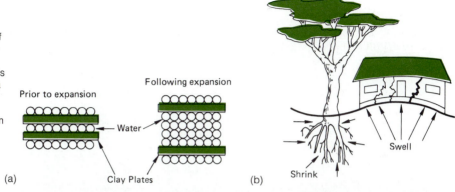

(a)

(b)

(c)

needed for plant growth when other factors are favorable [12]. Soils developed on some floodplains and glacial deposits contain sufficient nutrients and organic material to be naturally fertile. Soils developed on highly leached bedrock or loose sand deposits with little organic material may be nutrient-poor and have low fertility. Soil fertility can be and often is manipulated to increase agricultural plant yield by application of nutrients (fertilizers) or material to improve soil texture and retention of moisture. It is important to recognize that soil fertility can be reduced by soil erosion or leaching that removes nutrients; by the interruption of natural processes, such as flooding, that supply nutrients; or by continuous use of pesticides that alter or damage those organisms in the soil that render nutrients into forms available to plants.

LANDFORMS

Landforms, the natural features of land surfaces, are very important to us. Every human activity on the surface of Earth, whether it be agriculture or

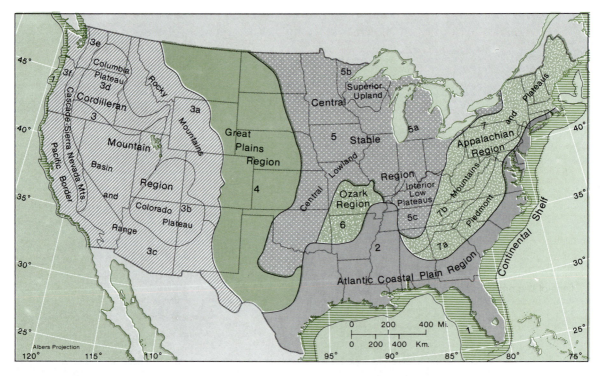

FIGURE 2.25
Physiographic regions and landforms of the conterminous United States.

land development for urban or industrial uses, involves the use of landforms. Geological processes create and change the shape and makeup of the land surface. Biological processes, by changing and modifying erosion and depositional patterns, also influence the development of landforms. The kind of landform found in any particular area, therefore, depends not only on the underlying material but on geological and biological processes. The particular set of landforms associated with river and stream processes, for example, is distinctly different from that produced by volcanic processes or coastal processes.

Because each combination of geological and biological processes produces rather distinctive landforms, it is possible to make a genetic classification of landform assemblages and, on a larger scale, to outline physiographic regions and provinces. For example, Figure 2.25 shows the physiographic regions for the conterminous United States. An understanding of these regions and the

types of landforms found in each is essential in environmental planning. The characteristic assemblages of plants and animals in these physiographic regions are also important in planning. The plants affect the soil, the erosion potential, and other factors, which eventually feed back to change the landform assemblages themselves.

Wind and ice-related processes are responsible for the erosion, transport, and deposition of vast quantities of material on Earth's surface. These processes create and modify a substantial number of landforms in such environmentally sensitive areas as coasts, deserts, and arctic and subarctic terrains.

Windblown Deposits

Windblown deposits are generally divided into two major groups: sand deposits, mainly dunes; and loess, or windblown silt. Extensive deposits of windblown sand and silt cover thousands of

Physiographic Regions of the Conterminous United States

(Figure 2.25, opposite)

1 *Continental Shelf:* Shallow sloping submarine plain with water depths of less than a few hundred meters. Major environmental problems include management of resources such as oil, gas, and marine mammals. This part of the marine environment is the most susceptible to ocean pollution.

2 *Atlantic Coastal Plain Region:* Low hills to nearly flat plains adjacent to the coast. Of particular importance here are the Mississippi Delta, the Coastal Wetlands, Barrier Islands, and the Everglades in Florida. These areas all are relatively fragile and may be damaged by unwise development. Coastal areas along the plain are vulnerable to storm damage.

3 *Cordilleran Mountain Region:* This region comprises six physiographic provinces.

    3a *Rocky Mountains:* Rugged, complex mountains, plateaus, and intermontane basins. Some sections of this province are experiencing population explosion. Land-use planning is thus a major environmental issue, as is development of mineral and water resources.

    3b *Colorado Plateau:* Series of high plateaus cut by deep canyons, including the Grand Canyon of the Colorado. Environmental problems relate to development of mineral and energy resources as well as to management of important recreational areas, including the Colorado River.

    3c *Basin and Range:* Series of isolated mountain ranges separated by wide desert plains or basins. The province has been described by some as resembling an army of caterpillars marching north out of Mexico. Contained within the province are many ancient lake beds as well as active alluvial fans and other desert landforms. Environmental problems here relate to energy and mineral resource management as well as disposal of radioactive waste.

    3d *Columbia Plateau:* High plateaus underlain by extensive lava flows and cut by canyons. In this province, not far from the Columbia River, a site is being evaluated for potential disposal of radioactive waste.

    3e *Cascade-Sierra Nevada Mountains:* Extensive mountain system stretching from California to Washington, characterized by active earthquake activity and volcanism. Management of recreational resources is important in many areas. Because water from the eastern Sierra is transported by means of an aquaduct to the Los Angeles area, water rights have become an important environmental issue.

    3f *Pacific Border:* A complex area of valleys, mountains, and narrow coastal plains. The southern part includes southern California with a myriad of environmental problems related to air and water pollution resulting from an ever-increasing population. The area is characterized by numerous geologic hazards, including earthquakes, landslides, and flooding.

4 *Great Plains Region:* Large area characterized by broad river plains and low plateaus. The region rises toward the Rocky Mountains and in some locations has altitudes greater than 2000 m. Management of water resources is a primary environmental concern in much of the Great Plains region, which is characterized by high-intensity agriculture practices. Of particular concern is the overdrafting of the High Plains aquifer.

5 *Central Stable Region:* This region comprises three physiographic provinces.

    5a *Central Lowland:* Landscape characterized by low rolling or nearly level plains, mostly covered by a thin layer of glacial deposits with scattered lakes and morains. This area is a major agricultural belt in the United States. Environmental problems relate to the variety of materials found in glaciated areas, including windblown deposits and high-organic soils. Around the Great Lakes, environmental problems relate to high population density as well as to shoreline erosion of the lakes.

    5b *Superior Upland:* A hilly area of topography developed on ancient granitic rocks. Major environmental problems include susceptibility to acid precipitation and management of scenic and other resources.

    5c *Interior Low Plateaus:* Low plateaus developed on sedimentary rocks. Environmental problems related to land uses on various rock types. Of particular importance here are the limestone areas characterized by numerous subsurface void and sinkholes.

6 *Ozark Region:* This region consists of the Ozark Plateaus to the northern part and ridges and valleys in the southern part. Management of recreational resources and water resources is important.

7 *Appalachian Region:* This region includes two major physiographic provinces.

    7a *Piedmont:* Rolling hills developed mostly on granitic and metamorphic rocks. A large number of eastern cities are developed on the Piedmont, and land-use issues are important.

    7b *Mountains and Plateaus:* These are the high Appalachian Mountains, consisting of a variety of rock types. Environmental problems are related to management of recreational resources, acid precipitation, and coal mining, as well as water resource development.

square kilometers in the United States. Sand deposits are found along the coasts of the Atlantic and Pacific oceans and the Great Lakes. Inland bodies of sand are found in areas of Nebraska, southern Oregon, southern California, Nevada, and northern Indiana, and along large rivers flowing through semiarid regions—for example, the Columbia and Snake rivers in Oregon and Washington. The majority of loess is located adjacent to the Mississippi Valley, but it is also found in the Pacific Northwest and Idaho.

Sand dunes are ridges or hills of sand formed by winds moving sand close to the ground. They are of many sizes and shapes and develop under a variety of conditions. Regardless of where they are located or how they form, actively advancing sand dunes cause environmental problems. Stabilization of sand dunes is a major problem in the construction and maintenance of highways and railroads that cross sandy areas of deserts. Building and maintaining reservoirs in sand-dune terrain are even more troublesome and are extremely expensive. Such reservoirs can be constructed only if a very high water loss can be tolerated. Canals in sandy areas should be lined to hold water while controlling erosion.

In contrast to sand, which seldom moves more than a meter or so off the ground, windblown silt and dust can be carried in huge clouds thousands of meters in the air (Fig. 2.26). A dust storm may be 500–600 km in diameter and carry over 100 million tons of silt and dust, sufficient to form a pile 30 m high and 3 km in diameter. The huge dust storms in the 1930s in Oklahoma and nearby areas exceeded these figures, perhaps carrying over 58,000 tons of dust/km^2. It is important to recognize, however, that the extreme damage caused by those dust storms and the drought was directly related to poor conservation practices and the poor weather conditions of the period. Furthermore, the heat and dryness accelerated the hatching of grasshoppers, which from 1934 to 1938 destroyed crops worth several hundred million dollars.

Glacial Topography

Only a few thousand years ago, the most recent continental glaciers retreated from northern Indiana, Michigan, and Minnesota. Figure 2.27 shows the maximum extent of these ice sheets. In the last two to three million years the ice advanced southward numerous times; we are still speculating whether it will advance again.

Glacial ice today still covers about 10% of the land area on Earth, and individual glaciers can cause rapid environmental change. For example, the 1986 surge of Alaska's Hubbard Glacier blocked Russel Fjord, forming a lake behind the ice dam. The event was so rapid that it trapped seals, porpoises, and other marine animals in the new lake. There was concern that the lake would spill into the Situk River, damaging its important fish-

FIGURE 2.26
Dust storm caused by cold front at Manter, Kansas, in 1935.)

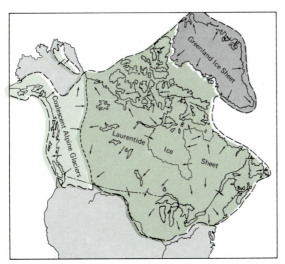

FIGURE 2.27
Maximum extent of ice sheets during the Pleistocene glaciation. (From Foster.)

ery. In the fall of 1986, the ice dam ruptured, releasing the marine animals, but the future is uncertain—the ice may again advance!

The effects of recent glacial events are easily seen in the landscape. The flat, nearly featureless ground moraine, or till plains, of central Indiana are composed of material called till, carried and deposited by continental glaciers. The till buried preglacial river valleys, so beneath the glacial deposits is topography much like the hills and valleys of southern Indiana, which the glaciers did not reach. The deposits of till and other material associated with glaciers create a varied landscape. Small lakes called kettle lakes, formed where ice blocks remained and melted, may fill up rather quickly with sediment and organic material and thus are different from the surrounding glacial deposits. Furthermore, sands and gravels from streams in, on, under, or in front of the ice provide further diversity in materials. Because of the wide variety of deposits, a glaciated area's physical properties must be evaluated in detail for planning, designing, and constructing large structures such as dams, highways, and buildings.

Glacial topography also affects natural ecosystems. For example, glaciated areas have many lakes and bogs, which provide habitat for fish and wildlife. Glacial till often supports rich soil that provides a good foundation for the development of forests.

Permafrost

In the higher latitudes permanently frozen ground, called **permafrost,** is a widespread natural phenomenon underlying about 20% of the world's area. Special environmental problems are associated with the design, construction, and maintenance of such structures as roads, railroads, pipelines, airfields, and buildings in permafrost areas. Lack of knowledge about permafrost has led to very high maintenance costs and relocation or abandonment of highways, railroads, and other structures. In general, most problems are encountered where permafrost occurs in fine-grained, poorly drained, frost-susceptible materials such as silt. These generally contain a lot of ice, which melts if the temperature increases. Melting produces unstable materials, resulting in settling, subsidence, and downslope flow of saturated sediment. It is the thawing of permafrost and subsequent frost heaving and subsidence caused by freezing and thawing of the upper layer that are responsible for most of the environmental problems in the permafrost areas of the arctic and subarctic regions.

SUMMARY

Life on Earth began about 2 billion years ago and since that time has profoundly affected our planet.

Sustained life on Earth is a characteristic of ecosystems—local communities of interacting populations and their local nonbiological environment—not of individual organisms or populations.

Earth and its life forms have changed many times, but certain processes necessary to sustain life and a livable environment have occurred throughout much of the Earth's history. This is the concept of uniformitarianism. Solutions to most environmental problems involve an understanding of open and closed systems and rates of change. Of particular importance are feedback mechanisms that may regulate or destroy components of a system; exponential growth; and average residence time for materials and/or life forms in a system. Finally, everything affects everything else and it is impossible to do only one thing—this is the principle of environmental unity.

Although Earth intercepts only a very tiny fraction of the energy emitted from the sun, it is solar energy that sustains life and drives two of Earth's physical systems—the hydrologic cycle and atmospheric circulation—and ultimately drives Earth's climate.

Climate and climatic change are important topics in environmental studies for two main reasons. First, many human endeavors are dependent on favorable climatic conditions. Second, human-induced processes are now capable of modifying local, if not global, climate.

Processes that create, maintain, change, or destroy earth materials—minerals, rocks, soil, and water, as well as entire landforms—are collectively referred to as the geologic cycle. More correctly, the geologic cycle is a set of subcycles that include the tectonic, hydrologic, rock, and biogeo-

chemical cycles. Earth materials found in different parts of the cycle are initially uncontaminated or in a concentrated state. Once dispersed or used, these materials may not be so available for human use.

Hydrologic systems tend to establish a rough steady state in which various parts of a system adjust to one another. Changes, whether artificial or natural, cause readjustments and produce a new steady state. These readjustments may have adverse impacts on human systems.

The physical properties of earth materials are important to recognize in environmental studies. These materials behave predictably but differently for various land uses.

Each chemical element necessary for life is transformed by life, and its global cycle is greatly affected by Earth's biota. In this chapter we have considered the complexities of a few of the global cycles, the ways in which life affects them, and the impact of our modern technological society on them. The wise use of our resources and management of our environment depend on our understanding of each of these cycles.

STUDY QUESTIONS

1 Describe how Earth's energy exchange is influenced by life.
2 How do living things influence global chemical cycles?
3 Discuss the importance of the geological cycle to the maintenance of the biosphere.
4 Distinguish between climate and weather. Which is most influenced by a major city?
5 How can the tectonic cycle influence the pattern of rainfall on Earth's surface?
6 Why is a city sidewalk built over a clay soil more likely to crack and break than a sidewalk built over a sandy soil?
7 Why does groundwater move more slowly than surface water in streams? What is the implication of this for the management of water pollution?
8 What were the causes of the dust bowl in the United States in the 1930s? What is the likelihood of this phenomenon occurring again?
9 Why is it difficult to build a city on permafrost?
10 Your neighbor contends that glaciers could return quickly—in 10 years. Would you agree or disagree? Explain.

11 Discuss the difference between positive and negative feedback cycles. Provide one example of each that has environmental significance.

12 Why is the J-curve so important in understanding environmental problems?

13 Input/output analysis of systems is important in evaluating many environmental problems. Discuss potential problems where input is less than output. Provide two examples, one each from biological and physical systems.

14 Discuss how natural ecosystems perform "public service" functions for us. Which functions are most important? Why?

FURTHER READING

BOLIN, B.; DEGENS, E. T.; KEMPE, S.; and KETNER, P., eds. 1979. *The global carbon cycle.* New York: Wiley.

BOWEN, H. J. M. 1979. *Environmental chemistry of the elements.* New York: Academic Press.

CLOUD, P. 1978. *Cosmos, Earth, and man.* New Haven, Conn.: Yale University Press.

DASMANN, R. F. 1976. *Environmental conservation.* 4th ed. New York: Wiley.

DAY, J. A.; FOST, F. F.; and ROSE, P., eds. 1971. *Dimensions of the environmental crisis.* New York: Wiley.

FORTESCUE, J. A. C. 1980. *Environmental geochemistry: A holistic approach.* New York: Springer-Verlag.

GARRELS, R. M.; MACKENZIE, F. T.; and HUNT, C. 1975. *Chemical cycles and the global environment.* Los Altos, Calif.; William Kaufmann.

GATES, D. M. 1972. *Man and his environment: Climate.* New York: Harper & Row.

GEIGER, R. 1965. *The climate near the ground.* Cambridge, Mass.: Harvard University Press. (English translation by Scripla Technica, Inc.)

GREGORY, K. J., and WALLING, D. E., eds. 1979. *Man and environmental processes.* London: William Dawson.

GRIBBEN, J., ed. 1978. *Climatic change.* Cambridge, England: Cambridge University Press.

HENDERSON, L. J. 1913. *The fitness of the environment.* New York: Macmillan.

HOLLAND, H. D. 1978. *The chemistry of the atmosphere and oceans.* New York: Wiley-Interscience.

HUTCHINSON, G. E. 1954. The biochemistry of the terrestrial atmosphere. In *The Earth as a planet,* ed. G. P. Kuiper, pp. 371–433. Chicago: The University of Chicago Press.

KELLER, E. A. 1985. *Environmental geology.* 4th ed. Columbus, Ohio: Charles E. Merrill.

LE ROY LADURIE, E. 1971. *Times of feast, times of famine: A history of climate since the year 1000.* Garden City, N.Y.: Doubleday.

LOVELOCK, J. E. 1979. *Gaia, a new look at life on Earth.* New York: Oxford University Press.

MARSH, W. M., and DOZIER, J. 1981. *Landscape.* Reading, Mass.: Addison-Wesley.

MATHEWSON, C. C. 1981. *Engineering geology.* Columbus, Ohio: Charles E. Merrill.

SELLERS, W. D. 1965. *Physical climatology.* Chicago: The University of Chicago Press.

SHORT, N. M.; LOWMAN, P. D., Jr.; FREEMAN, S. C.; and FINCH, W. A., Jr. 1976. *Mission to Earth: LandSat views the world.* Washington, D.C.: U.S. Government Printing Office.

SKINNER, B. J., ed. 1981. *Use and misuse of the Earth's surface.* Los Altos, Calif.: William Kaufmann.

UTGARD, R. O.; McKENZIE, G. D.; and FOLEY, D., eds. 1978. *Geology in the urban environment.* Minneapolis: Burgess.

WALKER, J. C. G. 1977. *Evolution of the atmosphere.* New York: Macmillan.

II
The Living Environment

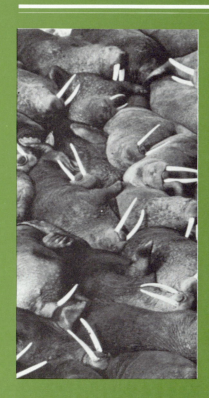

3

The Ecology Of Populations

- Populations have a great capacity for rapid growth under appropriate environmental conditions, but this rarely occurs in nature.
- A population growing exponentially has a constant percent rate of increase; populations are capable of exponential growth, but this is rarely achieved in nature and can never be sustained indefinitely.
- The abundance and distribution of a species is ultimately limited by the availability of required resources. When a resource is in such short supply that it can limit population growth, it is called a limiting factor.
- The carrying capacity is the maximum population that can exist in a habitat or ecosystem over a long time without detrimental effects to either that population or to the habitat or ecosystem.
- A population has five major characteristics: a size; rates of birth, death, and growth; and an age structure.
- The age structure of a population is the num-

ber of individuals of each age. The age structure can have a great effect on rates of birth, death, and population growth. Changes in the age structure can lead to changes in the impact of a population on its environment.

- There are often delays in the responses of populations to changes in the environment. These delays can lead to major environmental effects.
- No species can exist alone—each requires other species for its persistence.
- Species interact in five ways: commensalism, symbiosis, parasitism-predation, competition, and inhibition.
- Two species that have exactly the same requirements cannot coexist in a uniform environment. This is known as the competitive exclusion principle. Competing species coexist by using different aspects of a heterogeneous habitat.
- Where an organism lives is its habitat; what it does is its niche.

PRIBILOF ISLANDS REINDEER

In 1911 the U.S. government introduced small groups of reindeer on two of the Pribilof Islands that lie in the cold Bering Sea between Alaska and Siberia: 4 bucks and 21 does on St. Paul, the largest of the islands, covering 12,000 ha; 3 bucks and 12 does on St. George, the second largest island [1]. The reindeer were introduced to provide a much needed source of food for the islands' inhabitants, a group of Aleuts who had been settled there in 1787 by Gerasim Pribilof, the Russian explorer for whom the islands are named.

When the United States purchased Alaska from Russia in 1867, the Pribilof Islands and their inhabitants came under U.S. jurisdiction. The Aleuts had survived primarily on what the sea offered, but to those concerned with management of the islands, some additional source of protein seemed necessary. The islands had abundant vegetation and no wolves or other predators large enough to affect reindeer. In 1922 G. D. Hanna, a wildlife expert, wrote in an article in *Scientific Monthly*, "It would seem that here is the place to maintain model reindeer herds and to determine many of the needed facts for the propagation of these animals on a large scale. At no other place are conditions so favorable" [2].

In spite of favorable conditions, something went very wrong with the Pribilof Islands reindeer. At first, the introductions seemed a success; in the spring of 1912, 17 fawns were born on St. Paul and 11 on St. George (Fig. 3.1). But, ironically, in the year that Hanna wrote his enthusiastic report, the population on St. George had reached a peak of 222 individuals, from which it declined, never to return. By the 1940s the reindeer herd on St. George numbered between 40 and 60, but in the 1950s the herd became extinct. On St. Paul the herd reached a peak of 2000 animals in 1938, when there was 1 deer for every 6 ha of the island and 1 for every 5 ha of rangeland. Soon after, the reindeer herd rapidly declined, and the St. Paul population numbered only 8 in 1950 and 2 in 1951.

Throughout this time, the herds were monitored and attempts were made to manage them so that they would provide a sustained food supply for the inhabitants. Why did this management go wrong?

What happened to the reindeer herds that, in spite of efforts to the contrary, brought them to decline and essentially to extinction? Was their fate inevitable, the result of unassailable laws of nature? And, if so, could we discover these laws and use them in the wise management of our living resources? To answer these questions, we must understand the principles of population dynamics.

Understanding populations is necessary to many issues in environmental studies, especially the management and conservation of our living resources—endangered species, fisheries, forests, agriculture. It is also essential to understanding human population growth and the effects of future human population increases on our environment.

POPULATION DYNAMICS

People have long been interested in understanding what controls the growth of populations of living

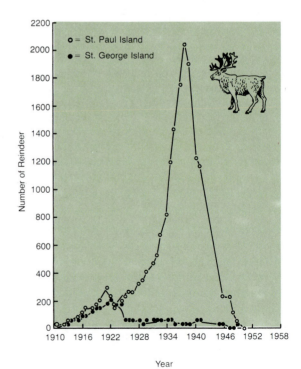

FIGURE 3.1
The population growth of the Pribilof Islands reindeer. (Modified from Sheffer.)

things. A **population** is a group of individuals of the same species living in the same area or inter-breeding and sharing genetic information. A **species** is all individuals that are capable of inter-breeding. A species is made up of populations. Many environmental issues require that we under-stand the basic concepts of population growth. If a population is endangered, we must try to under-stand why it is not growing. If a pest population threatens an important resource (for example, the Mediterranean fruit fly threatening the California citrus industry), a knowledge of population growth may help us find the best way to control the pop-ulation. Farmers, wildlife managers, foresters, managers of fisheries—all must understand these concepts. The study of population dynamics also gives us insight into more philosophical questions, such as the character of nature unaffected by human beings. The concepts of population growth also help us understand our choices in dealing with human population growth and the impact of this growth on the environment.

Individual populations are capable of rapid growth, but this is rarely achieved in nature: con-trol of populations is the norm. Rapid growth in nature is demonstrated by the northern elephant seal, which lives in the Pacific Ocean and breeds on islands along the coast of California and Mex-ico. Hunting by commercial sealers reduced this species to fewer than 100 individuals in the 1800s, at which time hunting ceased. Although people be-lieved that the elephant seal was doomed to ex-tinction, this did not happen. The population has regrown rapidly, reaching 60,000 (Fig. 3.2). No other large mammal has a recorded history of such a rapid recovery [3]. The annual rate of increase (the growth rate) has been 9%, which means that the population doubles in less than 8 years. The population has grown exponentially, meaning that the percentage increase is constant.

The great capacity for population growth has been known since Aristotle, whose writings con-tain some of the oldest existing discussions in western culture of the fundamental characteristics

FIGURE 3.2
History of the elephant seal population. Exponential growth of northern ele-phant seals since the nadir of the population in 1890.

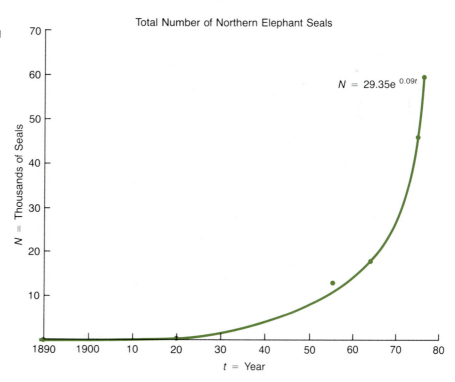

Total Number of Northern Elephant Seals

$N = 29.35e^{0.09t}$

N = Thousands of Seals

t = Year

of populations. Aristotle wrote about a pregnant female mouse that was shut up in a jar filled with millet seed and "after a short while," when the jar was opened, "120 mice came to light" [4].

Although all biological populations have the capacity for exponential growth, few achieve it. Charles Darwin's recognition of this led him to perceive that there would be competition for survival and to propose his theory of biological evolution. Since the industrial revolution, Earth's human population has increased at a rate more rapid than an exponential increase: that is, the annual increase in the total number of people has been an increasingly larger fraction of the current population.

Clearly, no population can sustain an exponential rate of growth indefinitely—eventually it would run out of food and space. For example, some bacteria cells can divide rapidly. Suppose a cell divided every 2 hours. If there were 2 cells at the beginning, there would be 4 cells after 2 hours, 8 cells after 4, 16 after 6, and 4096 after 1 day. In a matter of weeks the number of cells would require all the matter in the universe.

In some countries the human population is growing at 5%/yr, which means the population doubles in 14 years. A population of 100 increasing at 5%/yr would grow to 1 billion in less than 325 years. If the human population had increased at this rate since the beginning of recorded history, it too would now exceed the matter available in the universe.

If no real population can grow exponentially, what kind of growth can we expect? The study of changes in population sizes and the causes of these changes is called **population dynamics.** To understand population dynamics, we must first know the primary characteristics that describe a population. Any population has a size, which is its total number of individuals. A population is also characterized by its **birth rate, death rate,** and **growth rate.** When we are interested only in the total number of individuals in a population, these three rates can be related to each other simply: the growth rate equals the birth rate minus the death rate.

Sometimes we are interested not only in the number of individuals, but in the amount of living matter (or organic material contained in living or-

ganisms), called **biomass.** Whether we want to measure population growth by the number of individuals or by the biomass depends on the question to be answered. If we are trying to determine whether a species is endangered, then the number of individuals is the measure of interest. When the question concerns one population that is a food source for another, then the appropriate measure is often the biomass.

The Logistic Growth Curve

In 1838 a European scientist, P. F. Verhulst, suggested that a real population would grow according to an S-shaped curve, called the **logistic** (Fig. 3.3). The logistic adds to an exponential growth curve the concept that any real population must be limited eventually by some resource in its environment [5]. A **resource** is something an organism requires or uses and obtains from its environment. This limitation is represented in the simplest possible way by the population's **carrying capacity,** which is the maximum population size that can exist in a habitat or ecosystem over a long period of time without detrimental effects to either that population or to the habitat or ecosystem. Detrimental effects are any population effects that would result in a decrease in the carrying capacity.

In the logistic growth curve it is assumed that each individual has some negative effect, however small, on the others, either by decreasing the population's reproductive rates or by increasing mortality rates. When a population growing according to the logistic is small, its growth is very close to exponential (the "exponential" phase in Fig. 3.3). At every population level, however, the competition for some resource diminishes the population growth rate. The growth limitation is proportional to the population size, so the rate of growth decreases as the population size increases. After an initial, almost exponential, rate of growth, a logistic population passes into a second phase, in which limited resources cause the population to increase along an almost straight line. The absolute numbers added to the population in each time period are constant, and the growth rate declines (the "linear phase" in Fig. 3.3). Finally, as resources become even more limiting, the growth

FIGURE 3.3
Exponential and logistic growth. An exponentially growing population increases by a constant percentage every time period. A logistic population initially grows at almost an exponential rate, then slows down and stops growing at its carrying capacity.

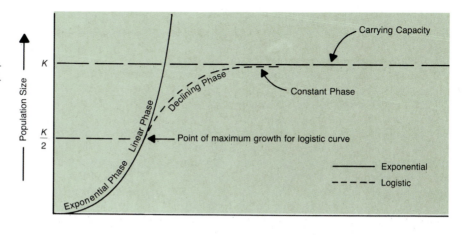

slows still more until the population reaches a final size in which births equal deaths, and the population is said to be at its carrying capacity [5].

If the population becomes larger than the carrying capacity, deaths exceed births, the growth is negative, and the population declines back to the carrying capacity. If the population is reduced below the carrying capacity, births once again exceed deaths, and the population grows back to the carrying capacity.

Does logistic growth ever actually take place? In laboratories, the answer is yes. For example, the logistic has been found to fit the growth of fruit flies confined in a laboratory container and fed a constant supply of food under constant environmental conditions.

Under what conditions could we expect the logistic growth curve to be found? Suppose, in studying ways to control Mediterranean fruit flies that were attacking oranges in California, you needed a constant supply of the flies. You could set up a cage, put a few flies in it, add a constant amount of food every day (say, one orange), and keep the environment in the cage constant.

At first, when there was much more food per fly than any one could eat, the population would grow rapidly. The birth rate would be greater than the death rate. Then as the number of flies increased, the food per fly would lessen and the death rate would increase. Eventually a point would be reached where there was exactly enough food for every fly. If the population exceeded this amount,

more flies would die and the death rate would exceed the birth rate. Thus the population would tend to stay at this constant amount—its carrying capacity. When flies were removed for studies, the population would be reduced below its carrying capacity, the growth rate would again become positive, and the population would increase back to the carrying capacity.

If logistic growth can be made to occur in a laboratory, why did it not occur for the reindeer on the Pribilof Islands? Had it occurred, the reindeer population on each island would have remained at the maximum level observed rather than undergoing a rapid and extreme decline to extinction. A review of the history of Pribilof Islands reindeer herds by Victor Sheffer sheds some light on what might have caused the decline [1]. Grasses and small flowering plants and shrubs found in the interiors of the islands are the main foods for the reindeer population during the spring, summer, and fall. These plants remained abundant, however, throughout the entire period of the rise and fall of the reindeer population, so the decline was not caused by a lack of the grasses and herbs that provided the bulk of their diet.

The key to the population decline appears to lie in the winter—the time of greatest stress for the reindeer—when they paw through the snow to feed on lichens called reindeer moss. Because lichens are very slow growing, they were rapidly depleted by the reindeer. A particularly cold winter in 1940 worsened matters. Island records indicate that in that year a crust of glare ice remained on the snow for weeks. Although reindeer can paw through as much as a meter of soft snow, they had difficulty digging through this crust. In early spring 150 dead reindeer, primarily females, were found on St. Paul Island.

The reindeer ran out of their crucial food during the most stressful time of year, and more females died because they were carrying calves and required additional nutrition. In contrast to a hypothetical logistic population, the reindeer did not adjust instantaneously to changes in their food supply.

Reindeer live a relatively long time, and they starve to death slowly—slowly enough that a large population can have a great effect on future food supplies. The Pribilof Islands reindeer herds grew rapidly when all their food was in great abundance, but the population rapidly outstripped the capacity of the reindeer moss to sustain the reindeer over a long time. However, the decline of the reindeer took a number of years; during these years the supply of slow-growing lichens was further reduced, so that the supply of winter food continued to be less than that required by the reindeer population, even though that population grew smaller and smaller.

The history of the Pribilof Islands reindeer illustrates several concepts: (1) there was a lag effect in the population's response to changes in its habitat (the number of reindeer continued for several years to exceed that which could be supported by the lichens in winter); (2) the death rate was higher for certain parts of the population (after a particularly hard winter in 1940, deaths occurred mainly among females); and (3) the population was controlled by an aspect of its life that occupied a crucial but comparatively short period of time (the food available late in winter).

The logistic equation does not take these concepts into account; it does not include time lags or distinguish among the kinds of individuals in a population or the kinds of food. Both the exponential equation and the logistic equation assume that all individuals in a population are equivalent—in both equations the population is described only by its total number and its three population rates. However, we know that many populations have

complicated life histories and are made up of individuals in many different stages in their lives.

In spite of potential and real limitations, the logistic curve has been important in the management of populations, as well as in the study of population dynamics. For many years the logistic has been the basis for management of many biological resources, especially oceanic fisheries, endangered species like the great whales, and game populations like the large grazing mammals of the great African savannahs.

The logistic is very appealing to those of us who want to believe in a nice balance of nature—in a nature that sustains itself in a constant and desirable condition and returns to this condition after being disturbed. Because a logistic population always returns to its carrying capacity (as long as it does not become extinct), the logistic has this kind of balance, which is called **stable equilibrium.** The carrying capacity is in **equilibrium** because, when undisturbed, the population remains at this size. Thus the logistic population is constant and stable, suggesting that it is balanced and in harmony with its environment. Many champions of the environment have argued that the logistic provides a basis for us to believe in a harmonious, balanced nature. Although the logistic growth curve is therefore appealing, actual populations, in general, do not follow this curve. Knowing this, we must search for another basis for our view of what undisturbed populations in nature are really like.

When managers of biologic resources first began to use a scientific basis, earlier in this century, the logistic was not a bad place to start. Today we understand a great deal more about populations and their environment, and if we hope to manage these resources successfully, we must move past this approach.

A More Realistic Population Growth Curve

How do real populations grow? According to the Australian ecologist Graeme Caughley, populations of large herbivorous mammals introduced into new habitats undergo a pattern of growth involving three phases: an eruptive phase, a declining phase, and an adjusted phase (Fig. 3.4) [6]. In the eruptive phase, the population "explodes," undergoing an increase similar to that shown by an exponential curve until the population reaches a peak, the maximum that it ever attains. In the declining phase, the population "crashes," decreasing rapidly to a low value. Sometimes, as with the Pribilof Islands reindeer, a population may go extinct during this phase. If it does not, it enters the third phase, the adjusted phase, in which the population fluctuates over time in a more or less random way but does not increase or decrease greatly in comparison to its initial growth.

What accounts for this pattern? The Pribilof Islands reindeer give us insight into the answers. The population initially has abundant resources. Births increase rapidly, and the population outstrips the available food supply. By the time negative factors take effect, the population is very large, and the impact is dramatic. Finally, the population comes into a kind of adjustment with its new environment. Having permanently decreased the food supply, it fluctuates in response to changes in climate, changes in food supply, changes in other populations, and other environmental factors.

Population Cycles

Some populations vary over time in a way that appears to follow a cycle. In a population cycle, the population increases and decreases in size within a more or less regular time period. The most famous cases of population cycles are those of arctic mammals hunted for their fur. The arctic lynx and arctic hare have been known to undergo dramatic changes in population abundance ever since the seventeenth century, when fur traders began hunting them. The famous British ecologist of our century, Charles Elton, studied the records of the Hudson's Bay Company, long the dominant company in the Canadian fur trade, and other sources [7]. The Hudson's Bay Company provided us with recent data, so that we could graph the population of the arctic lynx through the 1970s (Fig. 3.5). The number of lynx caught in traps indicates that the lynx population undergoes a complete cycle of increase and decrease about every 10 years. Smaller animals, like the arctic hare, appear to cycle over shorter periods of about 4 years.

Whether these cycles are very regular, and what causes them, has been a long-standing contro-

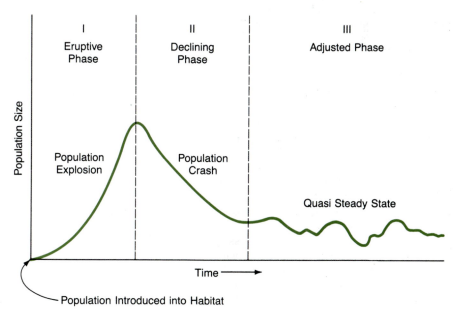

FIGURE 3.4
A more realistic population growth curve for a wild population introduced into a new habitat. The population "explodes" because resources greatly exceed requirements (phase I). Once the population size exceeds resource supply, the population "crashes" (II). Finally, the population reaches an "adjusted phase" (III), where it and its resources vary over time

FIGURE 3.5
Number of Arctic lynx caught in traps per year in the North American Arctic. The number varies greatly, with the time between peaks and troughs occurring at roughly regular intervals.

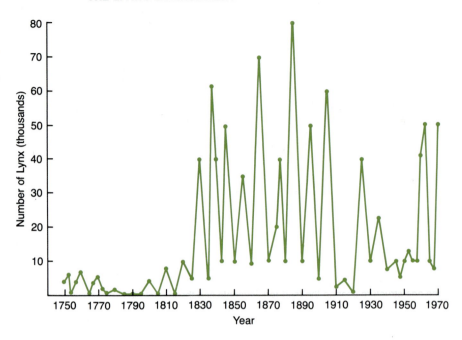

Age, Size, And Sex: The Structure of Populations

versy. If these cycles are natural, then those who want to preserve truly natural populations must allow these fluctuations to continue. However, such large changes in populations can have undesirable effects. Suppose, for example, you operate a national park famous for its wildlife, but the wildlife populations cycle. During peak periods, visitors would be pleased to see many animals, but the populations would damage their habitat, decreasing the aesthetics of the scenery. During periods of decline, visitors would see less wildlife. Especially in the management of economically valuable populations, such population cycles can be undesirable, and one would want to prevent them. But if we do not understand their causes, we may not be able either to prevent them or to help them continue.

Such population cycles have been recognized for a wide variety of animals, from salmon to elephants. Evidence suggests that length of a cycle may be related to the average generation time of the species: populations of long-lived animals have longer cycles than short-lived ones, with the average period of a cycle being four or five times the generation length [8]. The generation length is the time from an individual's birth to the attainment of reproductive maturity.

To this point, we have said that a population has four characteristics important to us: size, and the rates of birth, death, and growth. To these we must add a fifth: **age structure.** The age structure of a population is the number of individuals of each age in the population. The age structure of a population can have a great effect on birth rates, death rates, and growth rates. A change in the age structure can alter how a population affects its habitat and how it affects other populations. Age structure is especially important in human population growth and, therefore, to attempts to project the size of human populations and the effects of human populations on the environment.

To understand the importance of age structures, consider, for example, a herd of elephants (Fig. 3.6). A young elephant weighs 225 kg, less than one-tenth of adult weight. Its food requirements, and thus its effects on the food supply, are very different from those of an adult. So too is its ability to resist predators and disease and to survive on its own. With elephants, the three population rates (birth, growth, and death) will vary with the proportion of the population that is immature and

(a)

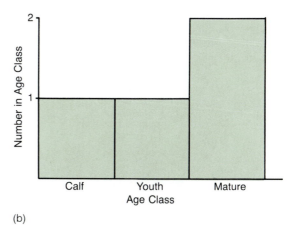

(b)

FIGURE 3.6

Age structure in an elephant herd. Elephant herds vary greatly in size, from as few as 4 to more than 60 animals. (a) In this small herd, the age structure consists of 2 adults, a teen-aged youth, and a calf. (b) The herd's age structure is represented by a graph. Changes in the age structure change the food requirements and the impact elephants have on their environment.

mature; that is, these rates will vary with the population's age structure.

The introduction of ten immature elephants into a small park habitat would have very different effects from the introduction of five pregnant females and five mature bulls. The birth rate of the population of ten immature animals would be zero for a number of years, but the mortality rate could be greater than zero. In the population of immature animals one would expect an initial decrease in the number of living elephants, with the possibility that all might die before they reproduce. In contrast, the population of five bulls and five pregnant females would most likely increase in the following year. Moreover, the rate of mortality would be smaller among these mature individuals than among the ten immature, so the population as a whole would grow much faster. In addition, because the food requirements of the large animals would be much greater, the habitat would be changed more rapidly. Thus, for any population made up of individuals with a complex life cycle and a long lifetime, it is important that we consider how the individuals are divided among ages, or at least among the important stages in the life cycle. Because the logistic and exponential curves do not take age structure into account, this is another rea-

son why they are inadequate to predict accurately the fate of many populations.

For most higher organisms there is a stage of immaturity that can make up a large fraction of the life cycle. In addition, some organisms have very complex life cycles, with the young having different habitats than the adults.

Our view of a life cycle is affected very much by our own cycle and those of domestic mammals. For us and our cats, dogs, horses, and cows there is clearly a difference between young, mature, and old, but kittens look like little cats and babies are clearly humans. For much of the plant and animal kingdom, however, the stages in the life cycle differ much more from one another.

For example, parasites have some of the most complex life cycles, which we must understand if we are to control certain human diseases. Schistosomiasis, one of the world's major health problems (Fig. 3.7), is caused by a waterborne parasite. In its free-swimming stage the parasite lives in freshwater ponds and rice paddies, where it penetrates human skin, often through the feet of rice farmers wading in the water, and finds its way to the veins and to organs, particularly the liver and bladder but including many tissues. A severe case can cause coughs, fever, enlarged liver and spleen,

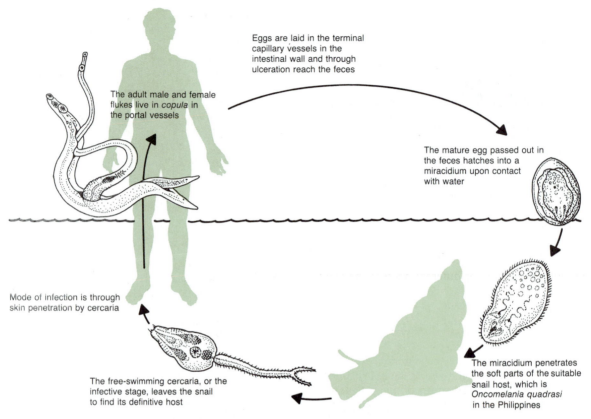

Eggs are laid in the terminal capillary vessels in the intestinal wall and through ulceration reach the feces

The adult male and female flukes live in *copula* in the portal vessels

The mature egg passed out in the feces hatches into a miracidium upon contact with water

Mode of infection is through skin penetration by cercaria

The miracidium penetrates the soft parts of the suitable snail host, which is *Oncomelania quadrasi* in the Philippines

The free-swimming cercaria, or the infective stage, leaves the snail to find its definitive host

FIGURE 3.7
The complex life cycle of *Schistosoma japonicum,* the parasite that causes schistosomiasis, a sometimes fatal disease in humans. Many organisms have complex life histories, which make their management, control, or protection a difficult task. (From Noble and Noble.)

and even death. Eggs laid in the human host are eliminated with feces. If the feces contaminate fresh water, the eggs produce another stage in the life cycle—a parasite of a freshwater snail. The snail parasite then produces the free-swimming form, which penetrates human skin and repeats the cycle. It would be difficult to represent the complex natural history of this parasite with a simple logistic curve; the representation needs to include some aspects of age structure.

Understanding Age Structures The easiest way to understand age structures is to learn about cohorts and cohort survivorship curves. A **cohort** is all the individuals in a population that are the same age and therefore were born during the same

time period. The number of the cohort alive each year can be plotted on a "cohort survivorship curve," as shown in Figure 3.8 for a cohort of trout.

Imagine that every year in the same part of a stream five trout eggs hatch and one of each cohort dies. Figure 3.8 shows the number alive for each cohort as the cohort ages for 5 years. Figure 3.9 shows the age structure of this population (a snapshot at one time of all the cohorts), while the cohort survivorship curve shows the history of one cohort. If birth and death continue to be exactly the same for each cohort, the age structure will always look the same. This is called a stationary age structure.

If the birth rate varies each year, the curve for the age structure no longer smoothly decreases to

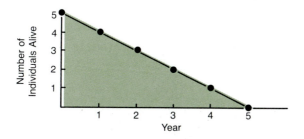

FIGURE 3.8

Cohort survivorship curve and age structure. In a part of a stream, five trout hatch each year. The trout born in the same year form a cohort. Each year thereafter, one individual of the cohort dies, so the cohort decreases by one each year. The resulting cohort survivorship curve is shown.

the right but has a saw-toothed shape (Fig. 3.10). Variation in deaths for different ages of the trout would also make the curve saw-toothed. Such a curve is called a nonstationary age structure.

An age structure is sometimes represented as an age structure pyramid (Fig. 3.11). Age struc-

tures of wild animals are usually drawn as in Figure 3.9, while human age structures are usually drawn as in Figure 3.11.

Whether an age structure is stationary or nonstationary is very important. Only a population with a stationary age structure can be constant over time. A graph of a stationary age structure always decreases to the right. A nonstationary age structure may increase to the right (meaning that some older age classes have more members than some younger ones)[9].

We can learn a lot about a population by examining its age structure. For example, Figure 3.12 shows four idealized stationary age structures. In type I, there is a very high survival rate (low mortality rate) in the young, and therefore the number of individuals decreases very slowly from one cohort to another. The mortality is very high in older age classes, so that the size of cohorts decreases abruptly among the older cohorts. Type IV is an age structure for a very different kind of population—one with low juvenile survival (high mortality) and higher adult survival. In type III survival, a

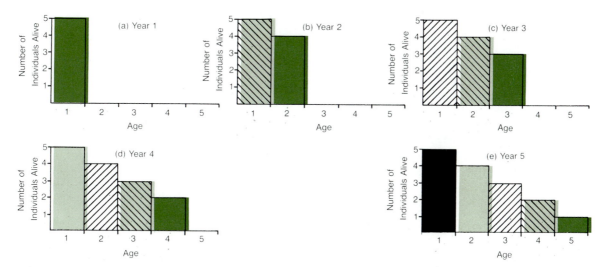

FIGURE 3.9

Stationary age structure. Every year another five trout hatch, and the death rate follows the same pattern for each new cohort. The number of trout of each age in this part of the stream is shown for five years in (a) through (e), with each cohort shown by a different shading. At the end of five years, there is a cohort for each age class (e). Because there will be no six-year-olds, the age structure for future years will look like (e). In this case, the age structure is stationary because the death rate is constant.

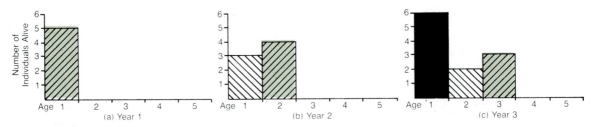

FIGURE 3.10
A nonstationary age structure. In another part of the same stream, the number of trout hatching each year varies, and even though the death rate is constant, the resulting survivorship curve, shown for three years (a,b,c), changes over time and is called non-stationary. It has a characteristic saw-toothed shape.

constant percentage of the population survives each time period, so that the survivorship curve forms a negative exponential. In type II, a constant number of individuals survive in each cohort, so that the graph of the age structure is a straight line.

These four types of stationary age structures are useful concepts, even though they are rarely found in nature. If a population, such as an elephant group in Africa or the Pribilof Islands reindeer, grew exactly according to a logistic and remained at a constant steady-state population size for a long time, the age structure eventually would become stationary. Because a population's age structure greatly affects the fate of the population and the impact of the population on the habitat, it is important for us to consider what kinds of age structures actually occur in nature.

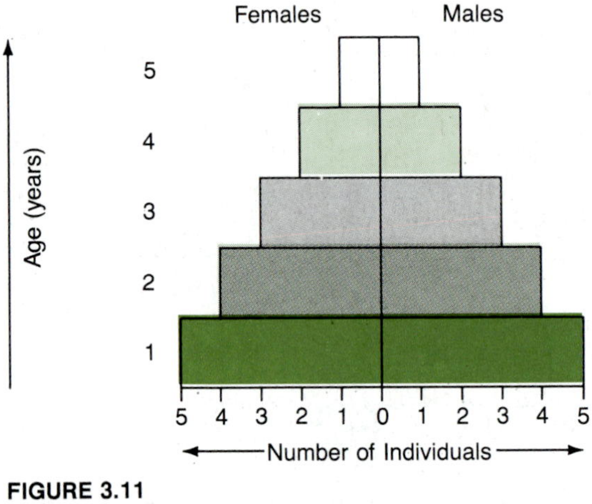

It is very difficult to obtain data for age structures of wild animal populations—the kind of census taken for people, with questionnaires, is obviously impossible. Fortunately, with many large

FIGURE 3.11
In an age structure pyramid, the numbers of individuals are graphed along the horizontal axis and the age is graphed vertically. Human age structures are often graphed this way. Usually males and females are graphed separately, one on each side of the pyramid. In this figure, there are five individuals of each sex in the one-year-old age class, four two-year-olds of each sex, and so forth. If you turn the graph clockwise, you will see that the graph of the females looks just like the age structure of trout in Figure 3.9e. They are exactly the same; the only difference is that the axes have been reversed. This way of graphing age structure is used commonly for human populations.

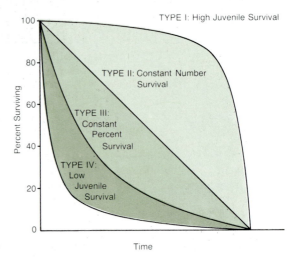

FIGURE 3.12
Idealized stationary age structure graphs. (From Slobodkin.)

mammals, age can be determined from teeth. In a study of moose at Isle Royale National Park, in Lake Superior, the age structure of the population was determined by collecting the jaws of the animals at death [10]. The teeth of moose have layers, one for each year; careful cutting, polishing, and observation of a cross section of a tooth can be used to calculate age. Isle Royale is an undisturbed wilderness area in which there is human recreation but no hunting, and the primary cause of moose mortality is predation by wolves. Thus the age structure of the moose population at Isle Royale provides one of the few examples of such a structure in a true wilderness area.

As shown in Figure 3.13, the age structure of the Isle Royale moose population does not fit neatly with any of the four patterns described. Instead, this age structure has a more complex shape, with three main sections. The number of individuals

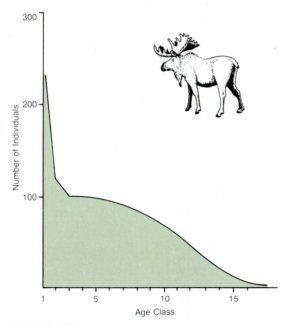

FIGURE 3.13
Age structure of the moose herd at Isle Royale National Park. This age structure, which could be stationary, has three sections: the number of individuals decreases rapidly in early age classes, then decreases slowly among mature animals older than 3, and finally decreases more rapidly in animals older than 14. (From Jordan, Botkin, and Wolf.)

falls off rapidly in the early ages, indicating that mortality is high among the young. Then there is a small decrease in the numbers until age 15, suggesting that the mature adults have a very low death rate. Finally, as the animals grow old, their death rate increases. This three-stage survivorship curve is characteristic of many mammals, including many human populations; it is an important curve for us to remember in the management of biological resources.

In summary, populations of many species must be characterized by an age structure. A population in steady state has a stationary age structure, meaning that the proportion of individuals in each class remains constant in time, and the change from one age class to another is the same in each unit of time. There are four types of idealized age structures, but real populations of many species have more complex age structures that appear to be changing, rather than constant, in time.

The age structure of a population affects its reproduction, mortality, and its effects on other species and on its habitat. When we manage a population of wild creatures, we must remember that our management affects not only total numbers but the distribution of these numbers among ages.

THE REGULATION OF POPULATIONS

If a population cannot grow forever, some thing or process must limit the growth. The limitation might be nonbiological (a windstorm), or biological but external to a population (a predator), or due to a process that occurs within the population itself. In the last case, a population might be self-regulating. Most populations are partially limited by many factors at the same time.

For example, in the north woods of Michigan, it is spring. The male red-winged blackbird sings to establish his territory and displays his bright reddish-orange shoulder patch. In the early morning another male flies nearby and sits on an exposed branch. The first male continues to call and the second approaches. There is a flurry in the air and the males separate. This is repeated several times; at last the intruder, threatened with a real attack, flees. The red-winged blackbird has defended his territory. He has limited the density of the population of his own species within a specific area and, because such a territory is required for breeding, has affected the reproduction of the population. The population of blackbirds in this breeding territory is therefore controlled by the activities of the individuals themselves.

A population that is self-regulating is said to have **density-dependent population regulation.** Under density-dependent population regulation, the rate of population growth is inversely related to population size: the larger the population, the smaller the growth rate. Density-dependent population regulation implies that there is a feedback; that is, the population in some way responds to its own size or density, bringing about changes in its birth and death rates.

A population that is not self-regulating may be subject to **density-independent population regulation.** In density-independent control, the mechanism of control has no relationship to population size. For example, given the death of insects in a forest subject to hurricanes, the population size of the insects would have no effect on the frequency or path of hurricanes. Moreover, if all the trees were knocked down by the hurricane and all the insects were killed, the mortality rate would be 100% regardless of population density.

Both density-dependent and density-independent population regulation seem possible in nature. Which is more important? What causes either kind? There has been a long-standing controversy in the study of populations as to the relative importance of these regulatory mechanisms. Density-dependent population regulation has been shown to occur for a few species. In some cases this has been demonstrated by experimentation, in others by observation.

An experimental study was done with the freshwater snail. Three fenced areas were set up in a pond, and the densities of the snails were changed by moving snails from one area to another. If the population sizes converged (that is, if each population eventually reached almost the same abundance), one could infer that a density-dependent mechanism must exist. In the first generation the snails survived equally well in all areas, but in the next generation the effects of population density

became visible. The number of offspring per adult was inversely proportional to the population density [11]. Density-dependent population regulation occurred, but it took two generations to be expressed.

Some observational studies show that density-dependent population regulation takes place for some large mammals. One of the best studies is of a population of wild Soay sheep living on St. Kilda Island north of Scotland [12]. The survival of lambs and adults was studied over a number of years as the total population of sheep changed. Graphs of lamb survival and adult survival compared to population size show that survival decreased as population size increased (Fig. 3.14). Stated more formally, there is a strong negative correlation that is statistically significant [13]. Why

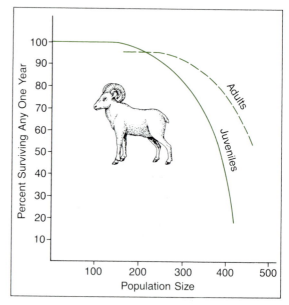

FIGURE 3.14
Do animals regulate their own abundance? Soay sheep on St. Kilda Island off the coast of Scotland in the north Atlantic appear to do so. The sheep graze widely on the island's rugged terrain. The survival rates of lambs and adults decrease as the population increases. However, the effect is more pronounced with the lambs. Their survival is nearly 100% at low population levels, but falls off to near zero at higher levels. In contrast, some adults die even at low densities, but at high densities adult survival is higher than that of the lambs.

did this occur? Like reindeer on the Pribilof Islands, the sheep lost weight in the winter. Those who lost the most weight tended to have the highest mortality. When ewes were undernourished, they gave less milk and the lambs lost weight and were more likely to die. The less winter food, the higher the death rate. Thus population size affects the food available per individual, which leads to a density-dependent control.

It is generally believed that density-dependent population regulation does occur for many populations, but it is very difficult to prove its existence for any specific population. A population that is not self-regulating would seem to be more prone to great fluctuations and to have a greater chance of extinction than a self-regulating one. Although the idea is appealing—and density-dependent population regulation is often said to occur—few data demonstrate clearly that this kind of regulation exists in nature. Either observations must be carried out over many years, as with the Soay sheep, or clever experiments must be conducted over several generations, as with the freshwater snails. More evidence is accumulating that suggests the existence of such regulation, long argued by all who have thought carefully about the control of wild populations.

The Logistic and Density-dependent Growth

Perhaps by now you can see a connection between density-dependent population growth and the logistic growth curve. Remember that in a logistic population the growth rate decreases as the population size increases; thus our hypothetical logistic population has density-dependent regulation. This is another reason why the logistic has been so appealing to people who have been interested in conservation and the wise management of our living resources.

In the management of wild animals and plants, it is often important to know whether there are natural density-dependent population mechanisms. If they exist, managers may be able to use them to achieve their goals. The stronger the natural density-dependent regulation, the less intense must be the control mechanisms by the manager.

In the past, wildlife has been managed as if density-dependent population regulation existed and could be relied on, often with poor results [14,15].

The Balance of Nature and Population Regulation

Density-dependent population regulation suggests a world that is well balanced and well controlled—a world where life hums along like a well-running automobile engine, responding smoothly to changes in population size. On the other hand, a population that is regulated only by density-independent mechanisms seems destined to undergo abrupt changes in size, to be the slave of unpredictable forces of the physical environment. The eruptive growth that we said was more realistic, at least for large mammals, is not as pleasing in this sense as the logistic, because the eruptive growth curve implies that a population will go through at least one phase when it is out of balance with its environment and that it will fluctuate indefinitely, perhaps in an unharmonious, unbalanced way.

Most of us would prefer to live in a well-balanced, harmonious world, and most of us would like to believe that most of life was self-regulating. In the history of the study of the environment, many people have tended to believe in density-dependent regulation despite insufficient evidence. Unfortunately, many failures in the management of our biological resources can be traced, at least in part, to this unjustified assumption, especially to assuming that the density-dependency was expressed as the logistic. One of the hardest but most important tasks that confronts us in environmental studies is going beyond what we wish were true to discover what is actually true, for only in this way can we manage our living resources wisely and achieve a true harmony with our surroundings.

POPULATION INTERACTIONS

No individual or population exists alone; the essence of sustained life is the interaction of species. It is possible that one population might regulate another, or that two populations, through their interactions, might regulate each other, even if neither could regulate itself. Population interactions therefore could lead to density-dependent regulation.

Populations of different species interact in many ways. The interactions are intricate, elaborate, sometimes amazing. For example, consider the interactions among some tropical hummingbirds, flowers, and certain species of mites. Hummingbirds have elongated beaks, well suited to extracting nectar from certain flowers (Fig. 3.15). The hummingbirds obtain nectar (a sugar solution) from the flower and spread pollen from flower to flower, fertilizing the flowers. The flowers they feed on are typically shaped like a cone or funnel with a long tube called a corolla; the nectar can be reached only by the kind of beak the hummingbirds have. The bird and flower seem uniquely suited to one another. The plants require that pollen from one flower be transported to other flowers of the same species; the more specific the transporting agent, the more likely the fertilization of flowers. Thus birds that move the pollen between flowers of only one species assure a greater chance of seed production than wind dispersal or birds that feed on many species.

The flowers that hummingbirds visit are the homes of several species of mites [16,17], which are small arthropods related to spiders. The mites travel from one flower to another by riding on the beak (in the nasal passage) of a hummingbird. Individual mites compete with each other and are territorial about their flowers. When a hummingbird arrives at a flower, a mite has only a few seconds to decide whether to get off—if the flower is unoccupied—or continue. Experimental observations show that the mite must make a dash down the beak of the hummingbird—equivalent, for its size, to the dash of a cheetah chasing its prey.

When mites of each species were experimentally introduced into the flowers where they were not found normally, the mites survived and reproduced. This suggests that the exclusion of the mites from certain species of flowers is the result not of some characteristic of the flower but of the interaction between species of mites. Adult male mites are very aggressive and appear to restrict the use of flowers to their own species by killing males of other species. Thus the adult male mites protect a territory.

These mites, birds, and flowers interact in many ways, some of which are beneficial to several species, some of which are detrimental to one and beneficial to another. The plants compete for pollinators; the pollinating birds compete for nectar; the mites compete among themselves. The birds and flowers benefit each other; the mites benefit from the birds; but the birds do not appear to benefit or suffer from the mites. Each of these inter-

FIGURE 3.15
A tropical hummingbird obtaining nectar from a flower.

actions could affect the population dynamics of each species.

Thus some living things form an important part of the environment of other living things. For the mites, the flowers are habitat and food, the hummingbirds are transportation. Without the flowers and the hummingbirds, that group of species of mites could not exist. In this case, the importance of other species to the mites is obvious, but in other cases the importance and effects of one species on another are not so clear. For example, if a gardener is not attentive, weeds will appear in a lawn. Do these occasional weeds have an effect on the persistence or abundance of the lawn grass?

Interactions such as these have long fascinated people. Philosophers have speculated about the origins of and reasons for such interactions since the time of the classical Greek and Roman civilizations. Ecologists pursue some of the same questions scientifically. They ask whether these interactions tend to increase the chances that certain forms of life will persist in a local area or on Earth. What are the pressures on populations that led to the evolution of such elaborate and intricate relationships? What is their advantage to individual organisms and species? Are the interactions needed or optional for each species? How important are interactions in the distribution and abundance of living things?

The Basic Kinds of Interactions between Species

A reindeer on the northern wastes of the Pribilof Islands may appear to be alone but carries with it many companions. Like domestic cattle, the reindeer is a ruminant, with a four-chambered stomach (Fig. 3.16) teeming with microbes—a billion per cubic centimeter. Some of these digest cellulose, take nitrogen from the air in the stomach, and make proteins. The bacterial species that digest the parts of the vegetation that the reindeer cannot digest itself—in particular, the cellulose and lignins of cell walls in woody tissue—require a peculiar environment. They can survive only in an environment without oxygen. One of the few places on Earth's surface where such an environment exists is the inside of a ruminant's stomach

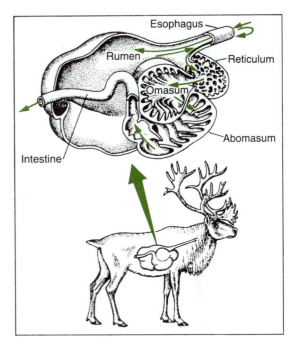

FIGURE 3.16
The microbes in the stomach of a ruminant (such as a cow, deer, moose, or giraffe) illustrate many kinds of population interactions. Microbes in the rumen digest plant tissue that the mammal cannot digest alone; both benefit from this relationship. The elaborate structures of the ruminant's stomach benefit the animal and its microbes.

[18]. In this partially closed environment, the respiration of the microorganisms uses up the oxygen.

Inside the rumen are other species of bacteria, some neither helping nor hurting the reindeer. There are also single-celled, ciliated microbes that feed on the bacteria. Elsewhere in the body of the reindeer, perhaps in its lungs or liver or even in the heart muscle, are parasitic worms. These also require the reindeer to survive, but they slowly weaken the animal, making it easier prey to large predators like wolves.

The examples of reindeer and hummingbirds suggest that there are several kinds of interactions between species. In fact there are five: competition, inhibition, predation-parasitism, commensalism, and symbiosis (Table 3.1). An important point is that species do not just interact occasionally

TABLE 3.1
Kinds of interactions among species.

	Interaction	Effect[a]		Result	Example
		Species A	Species B		
0	Neutralism	0	0	Neither affects the other.	
1	Competition	−	−	A and B compete for the same resource; each has a negative effect on the other.	Two hummingbird species competing for the same flower nectar
2	Inhibition	0	−	A inhibits B; A is unaffected.	One species of bacteria in a cow's rumen releases a chemical that inhibits another bacterium
3	Parasitism-predation	+	−	A, the parasite or predator, benefits. A feeds on B, the host or prey, who thereby suffers a direct negative effect.	Heartworm in a reindeer
4	Symbiosis	+	+	A and B require each other to survive.	Hummingbirds and hummingbird flowers; some bacteria and reindeer
5	Commensalism	+	0	A requires B to survive; B is not affected significantly.	Mites and hummingbird flowers

[a]0 = no effect
+ = positive effect on birth, growth, or survival
− = negative effect on birth, growth, or survival

with one another. No species exists alone; every species interacts with others through one of these five ways.

We will now consider some of the major kinds of interactions separately. We will focus first on competition, then predation-parasitism, then symbiosis.

Competition

In its most general form, **competition** can be defined as any interaction between individuals, populations, or species that has negative effects on birth, growth, or survival (Fig.3.17). Competition occurs when a number of organisms use common resources that are in short supply. If the resources are not in short supply, then competition can occur if the organisms interfere or harm each other in the process of obtaining the resources.

Populations that require the same resources from a limited supply and have access to the same reserves will compete. For example, different spe-

cies of trees in a forest compete for light, for water, for the chemical elements in the soil, and for a space to grow. In the southern oceans near Antarctica, whales, penguins, seals, and various fish and invertebrate animals compete for krill, small shrimplike crustaceans that grow there in great abundance.

An individual competes for resources with others of its own species and with individuals of other species who need the same resources.

Limiting Factors Individuals and populations compete for resources. When a resource is in such short supply that it can limit growth, it is called a limiting factor. If you walk from a desert up into mountains where the annual rainfall is much higher, there is a great increase in vegetation. In this case, water is a limiting factor for the growth of vegetation. Some soils lack small amounts of certain chemical elements that are required in very small amounts by living things. For example, in Australia there are many old soils from which nu-

FIGURE 3.17
A cougar snarls to defend its elk kill from an intruding grizzly bear; these large carnivores compete within and between species.

trients have been leached by water over long periods of time. In some of the areas, pasture grass sown to feed sheep grew very poorly because the soils were deficient in certain métals. Some soils were found to have insufficient amounts of molybdenum, an essential nutrient for all living things. The addition of only 140 g over an entire hectare, applied once every five or ten years, increased the yield of pasture grass sixfold [19]. An ounce of molybdenum produced a ton of pasture grass. The concept of limiting factors is important not only for crop production but also for the management of all renewable resources, including human populations.

The idea that some single factor determines the growth, and therefore the presence, of a species is known as **Liebeg's Law of the Minimum.** Justus von Liebeg was a nineteenth-century agriculturalist. He knew that crops required a number of nutrients in the soil and that crop yields could be increased by adding these as fertilizers. But the factor that caused an increase varied. Liebeg wrote in 1840 that the yield of a crop was limited by the single nutrient that was in the shortest supply. Since then, ecologists have generalized Liebeg's law beyond soil nutrients to include all life requirements. A general statement of this law is: The abundance and distribution of a species is limited by the single factor in shortest supply or having the greatest impact.

If Liebeg's law were always true, then environmental factors would always act one by one to limit the distribution of living things. For example, commercial fertilizers commonly contain nitrogen, phosphorus, and potassium. If a particular soil had nitrogen in least supply, phosphorus second, and potassium third, then, if Liebeg's law were correct, the growth of plants would be increased by adding nitrogen up to some maximum amount. Adding phosphorus or potassium before adding nitrogen would have no effect. However, once the nitrogen content of the soil reached the maximum a particular plant requires, then the plant's growth would be limited by phosphorus. Because phosphorus would now be the limiting factor, adding it would increase the yield. We could add phosphorus until the maximum was reached, at which point potassium would become the limiting factor. And so forth, until we fertilize the soil to the point that the plant has all the nutrients it can use. Its growth might then be limited by water and light, which we could increase to a maximum. When all life requirements are available at a maximum amount, the yield of the plant is restricted by its own genetic characteristics and by the constraints imposed by fundamental laws of energy, which we discuss later.

All this seems very reasonable, and Liebeg's law seems to be true for the Australian soil that lacked molybdenum. But Liebeg's Law of the Minimum is too restrictive as stated, and we must expand it. It implies that there is no interaction between environmental factors; each operates independently. But this may not always be true. For example, nitrogen is a necessary part of every protein, and proteins are essential building blocks of cells. It might be that a plant limited by nitrogen could lack sufficient proteins to make it efficient in taking up and using phosphorus. Increasing nitrogen supply to the plant might therefore increase its ability to use phosphorus and consequently increase its growth response to an addition of phosphorus. If this were the case, the two elements would have a synergistic effect. Such synergy enhances the growth response and thus the competitiveness of the plant even more than does overcoming successive limiting factors.

The Competitive Exclusion Principle An important idea in the study of competition is the **competitive exclusion principle.** According to this principle, two species that have exactly the same requirements cannot coexist in exactly the same habitat. Instead, one species will always win out over the other. This species will be the one that is somewhat more efficient in the use of any or all of the resources.

If the competitive exclusion principle is correct, how do species coexist? Some classic studies of the competitive exclusion principle used flour beetles *(Tribolium)* that live on wheat flour (Fig. 3.18). They make good subjects because the exper-

FIGURE 3.18
The competitive exclusion principle. When two competing species of beetles are introduced into the same jar of flour, one persists and the other dies out. Which species wins depends on the flour's temperature and moisture content.

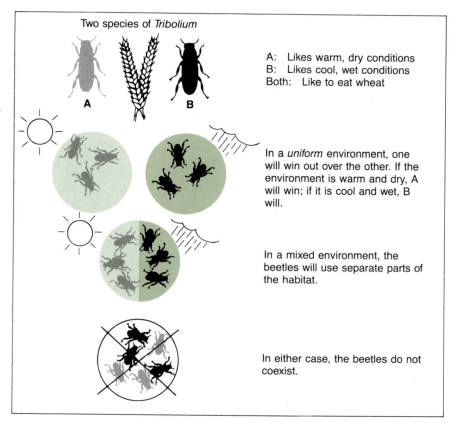

Two species of *Tribolium*

A
B

A: Likes warm, dry conditions
B: Likes cool, wet conditions
Both: Like to eat wheat

In a *uniform* environment, one will win out over the other. If the environment is warm and dry, A will win; if it is cool and wet, B will.

In a mixed environment, the beetles will use separate parts of the habitat.

In either case, the beetles do not coexist.

iments require only containers of wheat flour and the beetles.

Experiments show that, although two species are unlikely to coexist indefinitely in a uniform habitat, they coexist by utilizing different parts of a variable or heterogeneous habitat [20]. Sometimes a habitat can be divided in time rather than in space. For example, some tree species are adapted to the conditions that occur soon after a catastrophic clearing in a forest. At such a time the resources are all available in great abundance; there is much light, chemical elements necessary for life tend to be available in easily used forms, and therefore trees can grow rapidly. Other tree species are adapted to old-age forest conditions, when resources are tied up in living and dead trees and are relatively unavailable. In northeastern North America, birch trees are characteristic of early stages in forest development, and spruce are characteristic of late stages. This partitioning of time following a disturbance will be explored further in our discussion of communities and ecosystems in Chapters 4 and 5.

The Ecological Niche   From the previous discussions, we can see that each species has a unique role. If it uses the same resources as its competitors, it uses them best under a unique set of environmental conditions. We can think of the individuals of a species as having a unique job, or "profession." This profession is called the ecological niche. Where an organism lives is its **habitat**; what it does is its **niche.** Suppose you have a neighbor, Mr. Jones, who is a bus driver. Where he lives and works is your town; what he does is drive a bus. Similarly, if someone says, "Here comes a wolf," you think not only of a creature who inhabits the northern forests but of a predator who feeds on large mammals.

Understanding the niche of a species is useful in assessing the impact of development or changes in land use. Will the change remove an essential requirement for some species' niche? A new highway that makes car travel easier might eliminate Mr. Jones' bus route and his niche. In the same way, cutting a forest may drive away prey and eliminate the niche requirements of the wolf.

We can determine the niche of a species by finding out all of the environmental conditions under which it persists. The set of conditions under which it can persist without competitors from other species is called the fundamental niche. The set of conditions under which it persists in the presence of natural competitors is called its realized niche. We can picture parts of a niche in diagrams like Figure 3.19, which shows aspects of the niches of trees and of warblers. In general, the function of the tree niche is to carry out photosynthesis, grow tall above many competitors, obtain water and nutrients from the soil, obtain energy and carbon dioxide from the air, and so on. In regard to temperature and light, we can see that tree species in forests of New England have different niche requirements. White birch grows under cool conditions and bright light; sugar maple grows under warmer conditions and less light.

Predators, Parasites, and Prey

Most organisms are predator, parasite, prey, or host. In common usage, a predator is an organism that eats others and usually (but not always) kills the prey. A parasite is an organism that lives by feeding on (and usually living within or on) a prey and does not usually kill the host, at least not immediately. Any or all of the basic population rates—birth, survival, and growth—will be less for the prey or host in the presence of the predator or parasite than without it. A predator or parasite population will become extinct in the absence of the prey, if that prey is its only food; if it has other foods, the predator may have lower birth, growth or survival rates.

The predator-prey, parasite-host interactions include many different kinds of organisms. In the broadest sense, herbivory, the feeding on plants by animals, is a predator-prey interaction.

Predation and parasitism are linked—parasitism can influence the outcome of predation. For example, North American white-tailed deer have many parasitic worms in their lungs, livers, and even in their hearts. A deer with a large number of these parasites will be considerably weakened and relatively easy prey to a mountain lion.

Although predators cause the extinction of prey in laboratory experiments, rarely in nature does a predator cause extinction of its prey. Extinction sometimes occurs when new predators or para-

FIGURE 3.19

The niche concept. (a) Spruce, sugar maple, and pin cherry all grow in the northeastern United States. Spruce grows well in temperatures cooler than maple or cherry can tolerate; cherry requires bright light, while spruce and maple can persist in the shade. These qualities determine where we will find the different species. Spruce is found in cool areas like the tops of mountains or along cool lakeshores. Cherry and sugar maple are found in warmer places, such as the valleys below mountains or the protected interiors of islands. (b) Warblers are small birds that feed in flocks of several species. Why are not all but one species eliminated by competition? Each species feeds in a different region of a tree: bay-breasted warblers feed at the upper, outermost branches; Cape May feed in the central branches; and myrtle feed on the lower branches. The flocks include other species not shown. ((b) after MacArthur.)

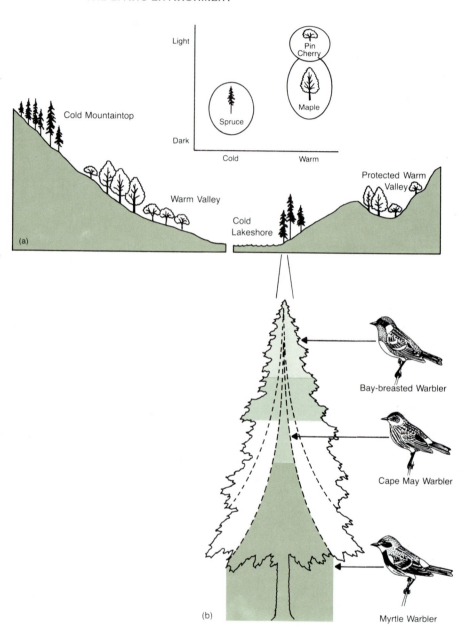

sites are introduced into a habitat that has a susceptible prey.

It is often speculated that predators regulate the population of their prey by reducing the degree of variation in the prey population, perhaps even keeping the prey population constant. Regulation can also be viewed as a negative feedback relationship between predator and prey: if the prey population increases above a certain level, the predator kills prey at a greater rate and decreases the prey abundance; if the prey population decreases below that level, the predator pressure lessens, allowing

FIGURE 3.20
Gause's predator-prey experiments. Gause studied predator-prey interactions with simple experiments using microorganisms: one single-celled organism fed on another, which in turn was fed bacteria at a constant rate. (a) The experiments were conducted in laboratory test tubes. (b) When the habitat (the water inside the test tube) was uniform, the predator caused extinction of the prey, and then, lacking food, also became extinct. (c) In another experiment, a refuge for the prey was added in the form of sediment. The prey could hide, so eventually the predators became extinct; the prey, fed at regular intervals, persisted.

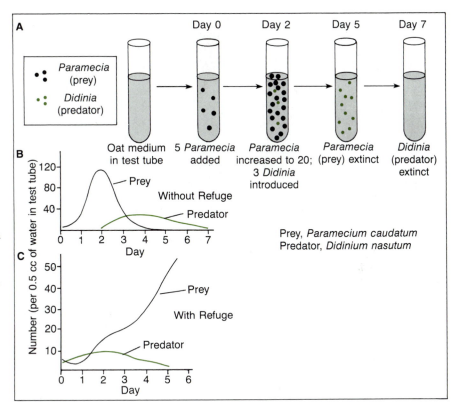

the prey to increase. Regulating prey is thus quite different from simply causing a decrease in the prey population. Although predators are often assumed to play the role of regulator of prey abundance, the evidence for this is thin and incomplete; this topic requires more research.

How can we determine the importance of predator-prey interactions? The ability of predators to affect prey was demonstrated in an experiment by Gause [21] using two single-celled protists: *Paramecium caudatum* as the prey and *Didinium nasutum* as the predator (Fig. 3.20).

The experiments were conducted in small test tubes to which a nutrient solution containing bacteria *(Bacillus subtilis)*, a food for the paramecia, was added at a constant rate. In one set of experiments, five paramecia were introduced into each tube; two days later three *Didinium* were added. The paramecia increased in abundance, reaching 120 individuals by the second day, and then declined rapidly when the predators were introduced. The predators, *Didinium*, increased to about 20 individuals. By the fifth day, the paramecia were completely eliminated by the predators, after which the predators died of starvation (Fig. 3.20b).

This simple experiment demonstrates that under certain circumstances a predator can cause the extinction of its prey, after which the predator also suffers extinction. If this occurred consistently in nature, there would be few living predators and prey. If a predator can completely eliminate its prey in a laboratory experiment, how can predator and prey coexist in nature? Gause conducted another experiment in which he provided the paramecia with a refuge consisting of sediment containing food (Fig. 3.20c). With the refuge, the outcome was quite different. The predator declined and became extinct, after which the prey continued to increase, undergoing an exponential rise until the end of the experiment. The refuge provided protection for the prey but did not lead to coexistence of both predator and prey. The second experiment suggests that complexity in the environment may increase the chance of persistence of the prey.

Predator-Prey Utility in Environmental Management Some populations of predators greatly affect populations of prey. An understanding of parasite-host relationships is essential to our control of diseases, both human diseases and those of animals and plants of economic value. Thus the study of predator-prey and parasite-host interactions has great practical importance. Predation and parasitism are particularly important in the management of renewable resources, including forests, crops, wildlife, fisheries, and endangered species, as demonstrated by the practice of biological control of pests. For example, mosquito fish are introduced into rice fields in many parts of the world to control mosquitoes. In the United States, this practice is used in the large rice fields of the great Central Valley of California, in southern Nevada, in Louisiana and Alabama, and elsewhere. Mosquitoes lay eggs in fresh water, and the larval stages live in the water. Mosquito fish— predators that feed on mosquito larvae as well as other small animals—can be quite effective. In an experimental study at the Rice Experiment Station, Crowley, Louisiana, mosquito fish at a density of 49 kg/ha (43.6 lb/acre) reduced the mosquito larvae population 96%.

Parasites can be used to control economically important pests. In the olive tree groves in California, an insect pest called the olive scale has been controlled by the introduction of two insect parasites that lay eggs in the larvae of the scale. When the eggs hatch, the parasite larvae feed on the scale larvae and kill them [22,23].

The use of predators and parasites to control pests is an old practice. Records going back to A.D. 400 show that farmers in China placed nests of a certain ant in citrus trees. The ant killed several insect pests of the trees, including the citrus stink bug. This method of pest control is still used in China [24].

How can we predict whether the use of a parasite or predator will be successful as a method to control a pest? Will the parasites and their prey be self-regulating so that neither gets out of hand? To answer these questions, we must understand the basic principles of predator-prey and parasite-host population interactions.

In the wild, predators such as the mountain lion kill herbivores such as the mule deer. For a long time, conservation and wildlife managers have asked several questions about the effects of mountain lion predation: Will the lions kill just enough deer so that both predator and prey will persist indefinitely in a "balance of nature" and provide a free managerial service for us? Will the lions kill so many deer that both species become either extinct or so rare that hikers or hunters will rarely see them? Or will the lions kill so few deer that there will be no noticeable impact on the size of the deer population? An understanding of the principles of predator-prey population interactions is necessary to answer these questions.

Symbiosis

Symbiosis, derived from the Greek for "living together," means a relationship between two organisms that is beneficial to both. Each partner in symbiosis is called a symbiont. The widespread occurrence of symbiosis is illustrated by our own bodies. Microbiologists tell us that 10% of a person's body weight is actually the weight of symbiotic microorganisms in his intestines. We become very aware of this intestinal community when it changes—for example, when we travel to a strange country and ingest new strains of bacteria. Then we suffer the well-known traveler's malady: a short-term (or not so short-term) stomach upset. The resident bacteria help us in our digestion; we provide a habitat that supplies all their needs, both we and they benefit, hence the relationship is symbiotic. We have many other symbionts. Our skin, for example, harbors a rich community of small organisms, some of which are beneficial to us.

There are two kinds of symbiosis. One, called **mutualism,** is a necessary relationship—each organism dies without the other. The second, called **protocooperation,** is not necessary to either organism, in the sense that each can survive without the other, but the interaction is beneficial to both. Both kinds of symbiosis are extremely important in nature. Most organisms live in a symbiotic relationship with other organisms, and it is not an understatement to say that life as we know it could not take place without symbiosis. Symbiosis is a dynamic relationship that can change, sometimes rapidly, over time. As an example, in many cases parasitism is a symbiosis that has become unstable. In other cases, parasitism evolves gradually into symbiosis.

There is a great range of symbiosis in nature. At one extreme the partners are intimately involved, and one organism lives within another. It may even be difficult to distinguish the internal symbiont from an organ of the host, as, for example, in the case of bacteria that form nodules on the roots of soybeans (and all other members of the legume family) within which nitrogen fixation takes place.

At the other extreme of symbiosis two organisms live separately and only occasionally benefit one another. As an example, baboons often accompany impala as both feed in the grasslands and savannahs of eastern and southern Africa. Each can live without the other, but both appear to benefit from the other's presence, especially in warning each other of predators. The baboon has good eyesight and the impala has a good sense of smell; together they appear to have a better chance of becoming aware of a predator. The baboons may also be aided in their search for food; they feed on animals in the soil, and as the impala graze, their hooves break open the soil.

In some forms of symbiosis, one animal cleans another; the cleaner obtains food, and the cleaned animal has parasites removed. This is especially common among marine organisms. More than 40 species of fish are known to clean other fish; hermit crabs and shrimp clean fish; even sea gulls have been seen to clean parasites from sunfish in Monterey Bay, California. Small coral reef fish set up a ''cleaning station'' in a sheltered area of a reef. When other fish come to these stations, the cleaning fish not only remove parasites from the skin but also enter the mouths and gill cavities of fish that prey on other small fish [25]. The cleaning fish obtains food, and the cleaned fish is relieved of parasites.

The cleaning activities of fish and shrimp are very important. Experimental removal of all cleaning organisms on coral reefs in the Bahamas led in a few days to a great decrease in the number of fish found on the reef. Only territorial fish remained, and after two weeks these had many swellings, sores, and frayed fins [26].

Another striking and ecologically important symbiosis is the relationship between termites and bacteria. Termites eat wood, but few organisms can digest woody tissue. Only certain bacteria have evolved enzymes that can break down wood. All higher organisms that eat woody tissue have bacterial symbionts.

One of the most important symbiotic relationships allows land plants to take up nutrients. This relationship is between a fungus and a green plant but may include a whole community of organisms, including bacteria. The roots of green plants are leaky, oozing sugars and starches and perhaps other compounds; these are food for the fungi. The fungi emit digestive enzymes into the soil to convert insoluble soil compounds to soluble ones. The nutrients are thus transferred from the soil to the fungus and then to the plant roots. Most families of higher plants from the Arctic to the tropics form such symbiotic relationships in order to obtain necessary nutrients from the soil.

SUMMARY

Every population has certain characteristics that describe its current condition and may be used to project its future. These include total size; rates of birth, growth, and death; and structure as to age, size, and sex. Because nothing can achieve an infinite size, every real population must have some upper limit. Biological populations have a great capacity to grow rapidly under the appropriate environmental conditions; thus, there must be factors that limit the size of populations.

The factors that regulate populations are divided into two groups: density-dependent and density-independent. When there is density-dependent regulation, the growth rate of the population decreases as the size increases. In density-independent regulation, there is no relation between population size and birth, growth, or death. Density-independent mechanisms include climatic catastrophes, such as hurricanes, tornadoes, and fire. Some species seem to have their own density-dependent mechanisms, like the territorial behavior of red-winged blackbirds. Other species may be subjected to a density-dependent regulation because of their interactions with other species. Density-dependent regulation has, at least theoretically, the potential to lead to greater stability and the appearance of harmony and constancy in populations or groups of populations of different species.

Populations of different species interact; these interactions are an essential part of life on Earth. There are five kinds of interactions: competition, inhibition, predation-parasitism, commensalism, and symbiosis. The competitive exclusion principle tells us that complete competitors cannot coexist. If two competitors require exactly the same resources under exactly the same conditions, one will win out, and the other will become extinct. This principle leads to the idea of the ecological niche—a species' profession. Competing species tend, over time, to divide a habitat so that each uses the resources under slightly different conditions than the others—the species specialize. Populations are limited by resources such as water, nutrients, light, and a place to grow and reproduce. When a resource is in such short supply that it can limit population growth, it is called a limiting factor. Liebeg's Law of the Minimum states that a population will be limited by the single factor in shortest supply, and therefore increasing that factor will increase the growth and size of that population. The law implies that increasing any other factor will not increase population growth. Although Liebeg's law is a useful concept for use in the management of the living resources, it is too restrictive; sometimes resources interact (are synergistic) in their effects on populations.

The management of populations requires that we understand and measure their important attributes. A careful manager of a natural population will keep track of the population size, the rates of birth, growth, and death, and the population structure. He will understand its habitat and niche requirements. The rapid growth of human populations underlies many of our environmental problems. To understand and deal with human populations, we must apply the concepts of population dynamics we have studied in this chapter. The taking of a census is the way that we obtain the basic human population characteristics. Projections about future human population trends are then made from these measurements (see Chapter 7).

The concept of population dynamics is also important in agriculture, especially in the control of pests (see Chapter 10).

Although these attributes are important in the management of populations, few real populations can be understood or managed if they are considered in isolation from their environment or from other species. A more complete view of the dynamics of populations takes into account an ecosystem perspective, which is the topic of our next chapter.

STUDY QUESTIONS

1 Explain the difference between *habitat* and *niche*.

2 What could have been done to improve the management of the Pribilof Islands reindeer?

3 You are asked to plan a preserve for the North American wild turkey. What factors would you take into account in planning this preserve? How would you prevent overpopulation?

4 Debate the statement, ''Predators are necessary to control the population of prey.''

5 It has been said that in nature herbivores are never limited by food supply. What are the arguments for and against this statement?

6 Which of the following is most likely to maintain a constant number over time: (a) silkworms in a terrarium given the same amount of food every day; (b) a European species of snail introduced into southern California, where the climate is similar to the snails' place of origin; (c) goats introduced on an island off the coast of Maine that has a small grassy clearing but is otherwise densely wooded?

7 How can the age structures of a population affect the overall (a) birth rate and (b) death rate? Consider an example of a common and familar species.

8 It has been said that a "prudent predator" would feed mainly on the very young and very old. Making use of the information you have read on birth rates, death rates, and age structure, explain what advantages this would have for a predator population.

9 Explain how the average age at which women give birth affects the growth rate of the population.

10 It has been suggested that the solution to human population problems is to colonize other planets. Consider the annual increase in the world's population. Do you think this is a practical solution? Explain your answer.

11 Compare and contrast the effect of weather on two of the following: (a) tuna in the open ocean; (b) trout in a freshwater stream; (c) earthworms in the forest near the trout stream; (d) a species of insect that the trout eat (the immature stages of this insect are caterpillars feeding on tree leaves; the mature stage lives only long enough to mate).

FURTHER READING

Important historical references:

DARWIN, C. A. 1859. *The origin of species by means of natural selection, or the preservation of proved races in the struggle for life.* London: Murray. (Reprinted variously.)

ELTON, C. 1942. *Voles, mice and lemmings: Problems in population dynamics.* Oxford: Clarendon Press.

LACK, D. 1967. *The natural regulation of animal numbers.* Oxford: Clarendon Press.

MALTHUS, T. R. 1798. *An essay on the principle of population, as it affects the future improvement of society, with remarks on the speculations of Mr. Godwin, M. Condorcet, and other writers.* London: J. Johnson.

References that provide good summaries and introductions to basic topics beyond what is covered in this text:

HUTCHINSON, G. E. 1978. *An introduction to population ecology.* New Haven, Conn.: Yale University Press.

KORMONDY, E. J. 1984. *Concepts of ecology.* Englewood Cliffs, N.J.: Prentice-Hall.

KREBS, C. 1978. *Ecology: The experimental analysis of distribution and abundance.* 2nd ed. New York: Harper & Row.

MAY, R. M. 1981. *Theoretical ecology, principles and applications.* Sunderland, Mass.: Sinauer.

ORGANIZATION FOR ECONOMIC CO-OPERATION AND DEVELOPMENT. 1985. *The state of the environment.* Paris: OECD.

PIANKA, E. R. 1982. *Evolutionary ecology.* New York: Harper & Row.

SLOBODKIN, L. B. 1980. *Growth and regulation of animal populations.* New York: Dover.

4

Ecosystems and Communities I: Physical Properties

- [ ] An ecological community is a set of interacting populations of different species: an ecosystem is an ecological community and its local, nonliving environment.
- [ ] Sustained life on Earth is a characteristic of ecosystems, not of individual organisms, populations, or species.
- [ ] The ecosystem concept is at the heart of the management of natural resources.
- [ ] An ecosystem must lie between an energy source and an energy sink; these comprise a thermodynamic system. An ecosystem must be an open system with respect to energy; the net flow of energy is one way through the ecosystem.
- [ ] A community contains food webs, which can be viewed as a diagram of who feeds on whom.
- [ ] A community can also be divided into trophic levels. A trophic level consists of all the organisms the same number of food web steps away from the original source of energy.
- [ ] A basic quality of life is its ability to create order on a local scale; this is one quality that distinguishes life from its nonliving environment.
- [ ] Biomass is the quantity of organic matter; ecological production is the change in organic matter.
- [ ] Respiration is the process by which organisms use energy. Gross production is the production of new organic matter before any is used. Net production is the net amount remaining after use.
- [ ] Autotrophs produce their own food from energy and inorganic material; this is called primary production. Heterotrophs feed on other organisms; their new organic matter is called secondary production.
- [ ] Every individual requires a number of chemical elements, and these must be available in the right forms, at the right times, and in the right ratios to one another.
- [ ] Chemical elements cycle within ecosystems; in theory the cycling could be complete but in reality there is always some loss. However, many biological processes tend to conserve chemical elements within the ecosystem.

LAGO DI MONTEROSI AND MEDICAL LAKE

In 171 B.C. the Romans constructed Via Cassia, a road that led north from Rome through what was then an uninhabited forest. About 40 km north of the city the construction passed Lago di Monterosi, a small roughly circular body of water, no more than six m deep, that had a closed drainage basin.

More than two thousand years later, in the 1960s, the lake lay in the midst of settled and long-used land (Fig. 4.1). Scientists from Italy and the United States began a study of Lago di Monterosi, removing from the lake's bottom a long cylinder of deposits called a core, which they then studied to reconstruct the history of the lake [1]. This core, a sample of the deposits transported to the lake through the hydrologic cycle (see Chapter 2) was made of mud, sand, shells of small freshwater animals, plants, and bits of leaves, twigs, and pollen from the trees around the lake. Modern scientific instruments enable researchers to read the core like a book. Radioactive carbon in the sediments dates the book's "pages," which are sometimes visible in the deposits as annual cycles, known as varves. The bits and pieces of the organisms tell a biologist what creatures lived in and around the lake. The thickness of a year's deposit tells a hydrologist the rate of erosion from the surrounding watershed.

An examination of the core shows that the lake sediments changed abruptly approximately two thousand years ago, around the time that the Romans built Via Cassia. The amount of nitrogen deposited suddenly increased (Fig. 4.2). **Phytoplankton**—microscopic algae and photosynthetic bacteria that floated in the lake—increased. In particular, a photosynthetic blue-green bacteria called *Aphanizomenon* bloomed. In addition, the rate of sediment flow increased. The concentration of alkaline earths (calcium, magnesium, and potassium) and organic production increased.

The changes in Lago di Monterosi in 171 B.C. closely resemble changes in lakes of North America in the 1960s and 1970s. For example, in the summer of 1971, the waters of Medical Lake in the state of Washington became clogged with algae and bacteria and turned a dark, turbid green; fish,

algae, and bacteria died and the wind blew them into masses of stinking algae, bacteria, and fish windrows on the lee shore (Fig. 4.3). Once clear, Medical Lake had become dark and dying [2]. These two lakes, Lago di Monterosi and Medical Lake, were connected across two thousand years and thousands of kilometers—they shared an intricate set of causes and effects that resulted from the actions of humans. The changes in the lake core indicate that soon after the Roman road had been built, Lago di Monterosi underwent changes like those observed in 1971 in Medical Lake. In both, some processes had caused a great increase in photosynthetic blue-green bacteria—a population explosion reminiscent of that of the reindeer on the Pribilof Islands discussed in Chapter 3.

Why did this occur? What are the underlying rules and principles that govern these events, connecting them over time and space? Those who have understood the causes and effects have used their knowledge to clean up lakes, so that some lakes that were once dark and dying are now clear and living [3]. The cause of fish deaths in Medical Lake cannot be determined by examining any population alone. It can be explained only by understanding the interrelationships among the entire community of organisms in the lake and their local nonbiological environment, which together form the lake ecosystem [4].

As we learned in Chapter 3, all biological populations have the potential for exponential growth, but this potential is always restricted by the limitation of resources necessary for growth. Ordinarily, the growth of any algae or bacteria population in a lake is limited by the supply of energy and necessary chemical elements. Any increase in algae is countered by the death of individuals, through grazing by herbivorous animals, the starvation of those who do not obtain enough resources, and the sinking of the algae or bacteria to the bottom of the lake.

Sewage or runoff from fertilized agricultural areas can pollute a lake, leading to such population explosions as that observed in Medical Lake. What factors in the waters entering a lake produce increases in the algae and bacteria populations? A group of scientists at the Canadian Freshwater Institute in Manitoba studied factors yielding such

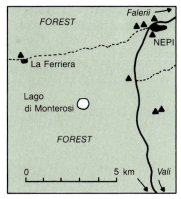

(a) Pre-Roman (Estruscan) Period (before the Roman road)

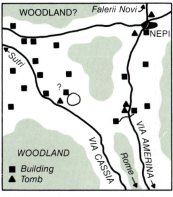

(b) Roman Period (when the Roman road was new)

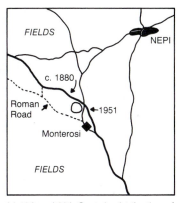

(c) 19th and 20th Centuries (at the time of 20th-century scientific studies)

FIGURE 4.1

The history of Lago di Monterosi. (a) Before the Roman period, the lake was surrounded by forests. (b) The Romans built Via Cassia and cleared land around the lake. Land clearing and development have continued until today, as shown in the map (c) and aerial photo (d). (From Hutchinson, 1970.)

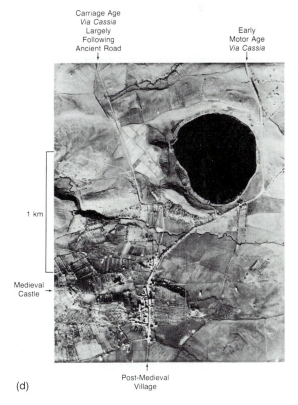

(d)

increases [5]. They divided a lake into two ecologically similar parts by putting a plastic sheet down the middle of it (Fig. 4.4). Fertilizers were added to one side; nothing was done to the other. Of the various chemical fertilizers, only phosphorus produced population explosions like those observed in Medical Lake. The researchers concluded that phosphorus is a primary cause of pollution problems and is a limiting factor for the growth of algae and photosynthetic bacteria.

The fish death in Medical Lake resulted from changes in the lake's entire ecosystem. Phosphorus causes a population explosion of photosynthetic blue-green bacteria. They become so thick that those at the top shade those at the bottom. Those at the bottom do not receive enough light and begin to die. The dead bacteria become food for other bacteria, which use oxygen as they feed on the dead cells (Fig 4.3). This process depletes the supply of oxygen in the water. Because fish require more oxygen than bacteria, the fish die.

Thus the fish did not die in Medical Lake from phosphorus poisoning; they died from a lack of oxygen that was the result of the response of an entire system to the input of phosphorus. The unpleasant effects resulted from the interactions among different species, the effects of the species on chemical elements in their environment, and the condition of the environment (the lake and the air above it). This is what is meant by calling the effect of phosphorus on the lake an "ecosystem effect."

An understanding of the lake as a biological community and as an ecosystem is necessary to understand why fish died when phosphorus was added to Medical Lake. Such a perspective is necessary for many environmental issues [6]. To ob-

tain this perspective, we must understand the basic characteristics of communities and ecosystems.

Today, the ecosystem concept has become a central theme in the management of our natural resources. In this chapter we will consider the nature of an ecosystem, community structure and trophic levels, ecosystem production, energy and ecosystems, and ecosystem mineral cycling.

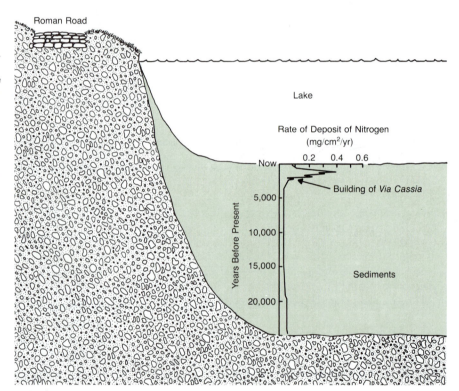

FIGURE 4.2
The effect of Roman road building about 2000 years ago is seen in the lake sediments of Lago di Monterosi. Eroded soil entered the lake, increasing the growth of algae and the rate of sediment deposition. One change that occurred was increased nitrogen deposition in the sediments, shown in this greatly simplified cross-sectional view of the lake (vertical view greatly exaggerated). (From Hutchinson, 1970.)

FIGURE 4.3 (opposite)
The eutrophication of a lake. (a) In a lake low in nutrients (called an oligotrophic lake), there is little algae, the water is relatively clear, and there is enough dissolved oxygen for the fish. (b) When phosphorus is added to a stream, it enters the lake and stimulates the growth of algae. The algae become so abundant that a dense layer is formed, cutting off the sunlight and killing the algae on the bottom. (c) The dead algae are fed upon by bacteria, which use up the oxygen in the water so the fish die from lack of oxygen. Dead fish and algae are blown to the shore. The lake is divided into two major zones. The upper zone, the epilimnion, is mixed by the wind and receives much light. The lower zone, the hypolimnion, is not mixed by the winds and receives less light. The floating algae grow in the upper layer. Dead algae and other sediments pass through the hypolimnion to the lake bottom. In many lakes, the entire lake mixes, or "turns over," in the spring and fall with changes in the temperature.

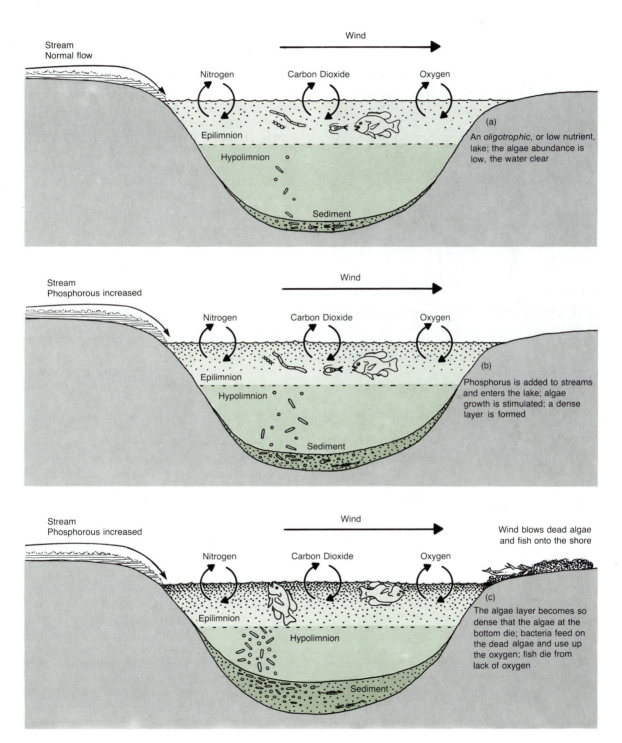

Stream
Normal flow

Wind

Nitrogen   Carbon Dioxide   Oxygen

Epilimnion

Hypolimnion

Sediment

(a)

An *oligotrophic*, or low nutrient, lake; the algae abundance is low, the water clear

Stream
Phosphorous increased

Wind

Nitrogen   Carbon Dioxide   Oxygen

Epilimnion

Hypolimnion

Sediment

(b)

Phosphorus is added to streams and enters the lake; algae growth is stimulated; a dense layer is formed

Stream
Phosphorous increased

Wind

Wind blows dead algae and fish onto the shore

Nitrogen   Carbon Dioxide   Oxygen

Epilimnion

Hypolimnion

Sediment

(c)

The algae layer becomes so dense that the algae at the bottom die; bacteria feed on the dead algae and use up the oxygen; fish die from lack of oxygen

FIGURE 4.4
Aerial photograph of a lake divided into two parts by a large plastic sheet. The Canadian Freshwater Institute added chemical elements to one side only. The results of this experiment demonstrated that phosphorus produced algae blooms and was an important limiting nutrient.

THE NATURE OF AN ECOSYSTEM

Ecosystems have several fundamental characteristics. First, an ecosystem has structure—nonliving and living parts; the living part is the **community,** which is a set of species connected by food webs and trophic levels. Second, an ecosystem has processes: energy flows through it and chemical elements cycle within it. Third, an ecosystem changes over time, through a process called succession.

Sustained life on Earth is a characteristic of ecosystems, not of individual organisms or populations [7]. Any entity that sustains life over long time periods must have two characteristics. There must be a flow of energy through the living system

and a complete cycling of all the chemical elements necessary for life. That is, each element required for growth and reproduction must be made available in a reusable form by that system: wastes converted into food, converted into waste, converted into food. No individual cells, populations, or communities of populations form a sufficient system. No single organism, population, or species produces all of its own food and completely recycles all of its own metabolic products. Green plants in light produce sugar from carbon dioxide and water, and from sugar and inorganic compounds they make many other organic compounds, including protein and woody tissue. But no green plant can degrade woody tissue back to its original inorganic compounds.

Those living things, such as bacteria and fungi, that degrade living tissue do not produce their own food, but instead obtain their energy and chemical nutrition from the dead tissues they feed on. Thus, for complete recycling of chemical elements to take place, there must be several species. But, in addition, the recycling of chemical elements and the flow of energy require a nonliving transport and storage medium: water, air, soil, rock, or a combination of these.

The minimal systems that can maintain the required flow of energy and complete chemical cycling are composed of at least several interacting populations of different species and their nonbiological environment. The smallest candidates for such minimal systems are ecosystems. An **ecosystem** is a local community of interacting populations of different species and their local, nonbiological environment. An ecological community is the living part of an ecosystem—it is the set of interacting populations of many species.

We can see now that life involves a hierarchy of different entities, extending from individual organisms to populations, communities, ecosystems, and the biosphere (Fig. 4.5).

The term "ecosystem" is applied to areas of Earth that differ greatly in size, from the smallest puddle of water to a large forest. Ecosystems differ greatly in composition: in the number and kinds of species, in the kinds of and relative proportions of nonbiological constitutents, in the degree of variation in time and space. Sometimes the borders of

FIGURE 4.5

Life involves a hierarchy of entities, from cells through organisms, and from organisms to populations, communities, ecosystems, and the biosphere. These in turn lie between other hierarchies, from molecules down to subatomic particles and from Earth to the universe. (After *Living in the Environment: An Introduction to Environmental Science*, 4th edition, by G. Tyler Miller, Jr. © 1985 by Wadsworth, Inc. Reprinted by permission of the author and the publisher.)

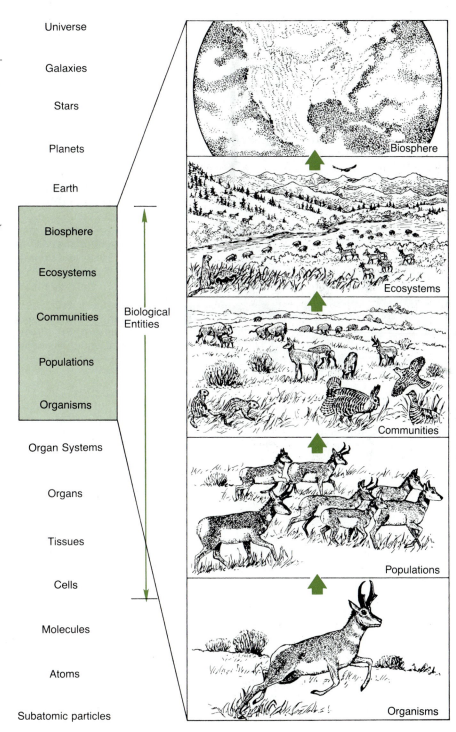

Universe

Galaxies

Stars

Planets

Earth

Biosphere

Ecosystems

Communities

Populations

Organisms

Organ Systems

Organs

Tissues

Cells

Molecules

Atoms

Subatomic particles

Biological Entities

Biosphere

Ecosystems

Communities

Populations

Organisms

the ecosystem are well-defined, as between the border of Lago di Monterosi and the surrounding countryside, or in the transition from desert to forest on the slopes of the San Francisco Mountains in Arizona, or in the transitions from forest to tundra that occur near the summits of many mountains. Sometimes the borders are vague, as in the subtle gradations of forest into prairie in Minnesota and the Dakotas in the United States or in the transition from grasslands to savannahs and forests in East Africa.

What is shared in common by all ecosystems is not physical size or sharp boundaries, but the existence of the processes we have mentioned—the flow of energy and the cycling of chemical elements. Ecosystems also share the pathways for these flows and cycles, which follow along food webs from trophic level to trophic level (terms which we will define later in this chapter).

Ecosystems can be natural or artificial. A forested watershed is often studied as a single ecosystem, as has been done in the Hubbard Brook ecosystem study in New Hampshire and the Andrews Experimental Forest in Oregon. Lakes, ponds, and bogs, such as those that are common in Minnesota, Wisconsin, and southern Canada, are often studied as individual ecosystems. An artificial pond that is a part of a waste treatment plant is an example of an artificial ecosystem.

Ecosystems can be natural or managed, and the management can vary over a large range of actions. Agriculture can be thought of as partial management of certain kinds of ecosystems. So can many forests managed for timber production. Wildlife preserves also are examples of partially managed ecosystems. Sewage treatment plants are examples of highly managed ecosystems.

Ecosystem and Community Structure

An ecosystem has living and nonliving parts. An ecological community is the living part of an ecosystem—a set of interacting species.

One way individuals in a community interact is by feeding on one another. Energy, chemical elements, and some compounds are thus transferred from creature to creature along **food chains**, which in more complex cases are called **food webs.** Ecologists group the organisms in a food web into trophic levels. A **trophic level** consists of all those organisms in a food web that are the same number of feeding levels away from the original source of energy. The original source of energy in most ecosystems is the sun. Green plants can make food by directly interacting with sunlight, so they are grouped into what is called the first trophic level. Herbivores, which feed on plants, are members of the second trophic level; carnivores that feed directly on herbivores are in the third trophic level; carnivores feeding on third-level carnivores are in the fourth trophic level; and so on.

For example, in the oceans (Fig. 4.6) tiny single-celled planktonic algae are in the first trophic level. Small invertebrates called zooplankton and some fish feed on them, forming the second trophic level. Other fish and invertebrates that feed on these herbivores form the third trophic level. The great baleen whales, which filter the seawater for food, feed primarily on small herbivorous crustaceans, and thus the baleen whales are also in the third level. Some fish and marine mammals, like the killer whale, feed on the predatory fish and form higher trophic levels. A terrestrial example of food chain trophic levels is shown in Figure 4.7.

In the abstract a trophic-level diagram seems simple and neat, but in reality food webs are complex because most creatures feed on several trophic levels. The harp seal is at the fifth level [8]. It feeds on flatfish, which feed on sand lances, which feed on euphausids, which feed on phytoplankton (Fig. 4.8). The harp seal itself feeds at several trophic levels, from the second through the fourth, and it feeds on predators of some of its prey [8]. A species that feeds on several trophic levels typically is classified as belonging to the trophic level above the highest from which it feeds.

ECOSYSTEM PROCESSES I: ENERGY FLOW, BIOMASS, AND ECOLOGICAL PRODUCTION

Energy Flow and Biomass All life requires energy. Energy is the ability to do work, to move matter. As anyone who has dieted knows, we obtain

Career Profile: Karen O'Neil

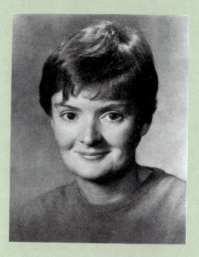

At Monument Mountain Regional High School in Massachusetts, students are learning about the laws of thermodynamics and about ATP, a molecule that stores energy in the body. Not particularly unusual, except that when science teacher Karen O'Neil presents traditional energy concepts such as these, she includes current issues of renewable and nonrenewable resources, population growth, and environmental pollution.

O'Neil teaches biology and physical science. She has also taught a combination science and social studies course called 21st Century. She incorporates environmental issues in her curriculum in two ways. Sometimes she uses them to illustrate traditional concepts of biology or physical science. The loss of energy between levels in a food pyramid is one example. To demonstrate the magnitude of the loss, O'Neil has students pour out nine-tenths of the contents of a soft drink bottle to represent the loss of energy from the first to the second trophic level. Nine-tenths of the remainder is then poured out to represent the loss from the second to the third level, and so on. "Most students can easily see why some people choose a vegetarian lifestyle to make more food available," she points out.

O'Neil also develops special environmental units. In one such unit, she has students research and present proposals about energy alternatives, such as fossil fuels, nuclear fission and fusion, solar energy, and biomass, in a simulated budget hearing.

School administrators are supportive of her. "It is not difficult to justify activities such as these in science classes," she says. "If it's meaningful to students and gets them excited, most administrators think it's wonderful. Of course, you can't throw out the traditional curriculum," she explains. "Many people say, 'Where am I going to fit this in?' With energy, so many areas relate to science, social studies, . . . and everything else. It's not something you 'cover.' It's part of the whole."

O'Neil observes, "Students like the variety. They find the activities meaningful and their reactions to the material are good." She gauges student reaction in part by what former students recall from her classes.

O'Neil has a degree in biology. But in her last year of college she realized, "I wasn't into lab work that much. I liked working with people." She graduated, then went back to school to become a teacher. She began teaching in 1973, the year of the oil embargo, when the energy crisis hit home. She enrolled in a college course called Energy and Man that helped her focus on the need for energy education. "I think we're very vulnerable," O'Neil states with concern. "We have to look forward—not just one year or ten years from now, but 30 to 40 years. Everybody needs to be aware of the problem—it's long term."

O'Neil develops some of her own teaching materials. At conventions, she trades materials with other people. She finds newsletters and journals are good resources, too. Industry publications are useful sometimes. "There is a lot of information about energy out there. Whenever you get information, you have to consider the source," she cautions. "What's the motivation for writing this? Think critically." O'Neil hopes her students learn at least that—to be critical thinkers.

Michele Wigginton

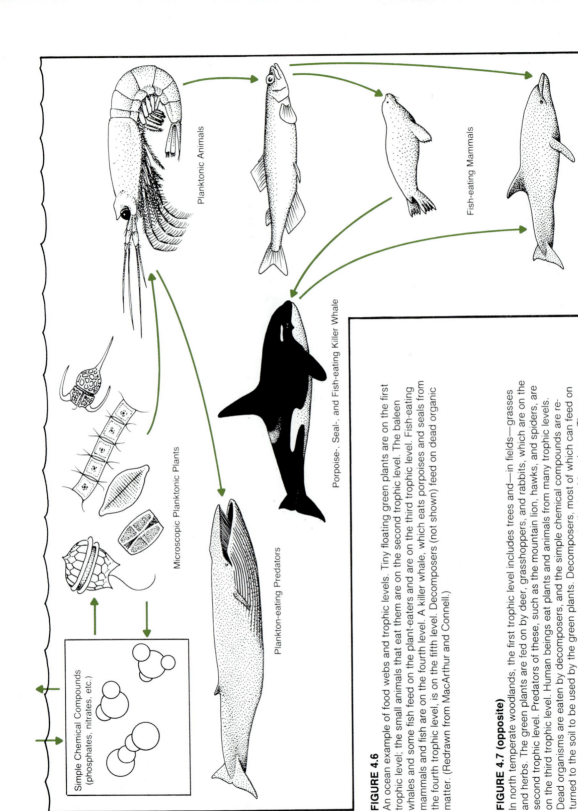

FIGURE 4.6
An ocean example of food webs and trophic levels. Tiny floating green plants are on the first trophic level; the small animals that eat them are on the second trophic level. The baleen whales and some fish feed on the plant-eaters and are on the third trophic level. Fish-eating mammals and fish are on the fourth level. A killer whale, which eats porpoises and seals from the fourth trophic level, is on the fifth level. Decomposers (not shown) feed on dead organic matter. (Redrawn from MacArthur and Connell.)

FIGURE 4.7 (opposite)
In north temperate woodlands, the first trophic level includes trees and—in fields—grasses and herbs. The green plants are fed on by deer, grasshoppers, and rabbits, which are on the second trophic level. Predators of these, such as the mountain lion, hawks, and spiders, are on the third trophic level. Human beings eat plants and animals from many trophic levels. Dead organisms are eaten by decomposers, and the simple chemical compounds are returned to the soil to be used by the green plants. Decomposers, most of which can feed on many kinds of dead tissue, are usually separated as shown in the trophic scheme. These diagrams are greatly simplified. In reality, many organisms feed on several different trophic levels, as shown in Figure 4.8.

Labels within figure:
Planktonic Animals
Fish-eating Mammals
Porpoise-, Seal-, and Fish-eating Killer Whale
Microscopic Planktonic Plants
Plankton-eating Predators
Simple Chemical Compounds (phosphates, nitrates, etc.)

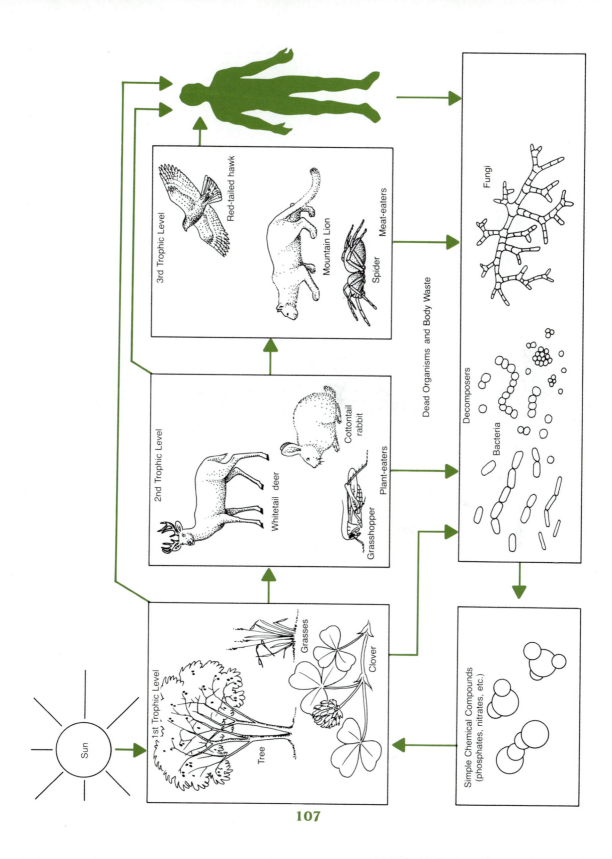

Sun

1st Trophic Level

Tree

Grasses

Clover

2nd Trophic Level

Whitetail deer

Cottontail rabbit

Grasshopper

Plant-eaters

3rd Trophic Level

Red-tailed hawk

Mountain Lion

Spider

Meat-eaters

Dead Organisms and Body Waste

Decomposers

Fungi

Bacteria

Simple Chemical Compounds (phosphates, nitrates, etc.)

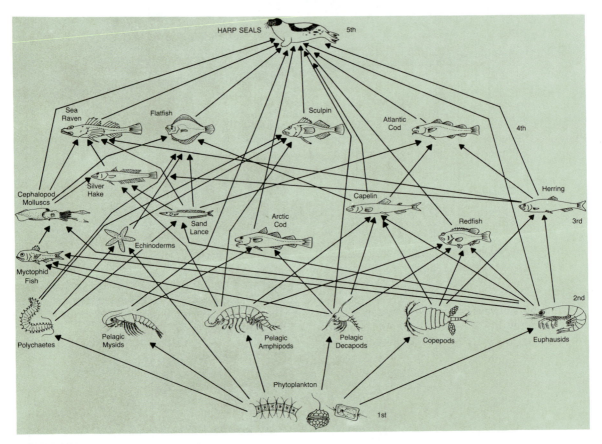

FIGURE 4.8
The food levels of the harp seal. In contrast to the idealized diagrams in Figures 4.6 and 4.7, the actual food web of the harp seal has many connections at several trophic levels. The number of steps in the food chain between the harp seal and sunlight is five, so we say that the harp seal is on the fifth trophic level. But the harp seal also feeds on intermediate trophic levels. For example, it feeds on amphipods at the third trophic level and on capelin at the fourth level. The harp seal thus competes with its own prey (capelin) for its food (amphipods). Because the harp seal competes with other species, including other marine mammals and humans, the entire food chain is very complex. (Modified from Lavigne et al.)

energy from our food. Our weight is a delicate balance between the energy we take in and the energy we use. What we don't use and don't pass on, we store. Our use of energy, and whether we gain or lose weight, follows the laws of physics. So it is with entire ecosystems. At first glance this may seem simple enough: we take energy in and use it, just like a machine. But if we dig a little deeper into this subject, we discover it is one of the most philosophical aspects of environmental studies. When

we consider the role of energy in an ecosystem, we consider the heart of the matter of what it is that distinguishes life and life-containing systems from the rest of the universe. As you recall from Chapter 3, organic matter is called biomass. Ecological production is the change in organic matter. Because there is a close relationship between the amount of organic matter and the amount of stored energy, ecological production is measured both ways—as amounts of matter (for example, tons per square meter) or as energy (for example, calories per square meter). Energy enters an ecosystem, is used, stored, and eventually given off (Fig. 4.9). Matter and energy are both subject to laws of conservation. The kind of laws we are referring to here are laws of physics; the kind of conservation we are talking about may be explained this way:

☐ In any physical or chemical change, matter is neither created nor destroyed, but merely changed from one form to another.
☐ In any physical or chemical process, energy is neither created nor destroyed, but merely changed from one form to another.

The law of conservation of energy is also called the **first law of thermodynamics.** It addresses the observation that energy changes form, not amount.

If energy is always conserved, why can't we just recycle energy inside our bodies? And similarly, why can't energy be recycled in ecosystems and in the biosphere? We are often told we eat to get particular chemical elements: calcium from milk, nitrogen from meat. But, if all matter must be conserved and one atom of an element is indistinguishable from another, why can't we recycle all our elements and only add new elements to replace those lost by accident or required for growth [9]?

As an example, frogs eat insects, including mosquitoes. Mosquitoes in turn, as we know, suck blood from vertebrates, including frogs. Consider an imaginary closed ecosystem consisting of water, air, a rock for frogs to sit on, frogs, and mosquitoes. In this system, the frogs eat the mosquitoes and the mosquitoes provide energy for frogs (Fig. 4.10). Why can't this system maintain itself indefinitely? Such a closed system would be a biological perpetual motion machine—it could continue indefinitely without an input of any new material or energy. This sounds nice, but unfortunately it is impossible.

The general answer as to why this system could not persist lies with the **second law of thermodynamics,** which addresses the kind of change in form that energy undergoes:

☐ Energy always changes from a more useful, more highly organized form to a less useful, disorganized form. Energy cannot be completely recycled to its original state of organized, high-quality usefulness.

For this reason, the mosquito-frog system will eventually stop—there will not be enough useful energy left.

To understand why we cannot recycle energy, imagine a closed system containing a pile of coal, a tank of water, air, a steam engine, and an engineer (Fig. 4.11). Suppose the engine runs a lathe that makes furniture. The engineer lights a fire to boil the water, creating steam to run the engine. As the engine runs, the heat from the fire gradually warms the entire system. When all the coal is completely burned, the engineer will not be able to boil any more water and the engine will stop. The average temperature of the system is now higher than the starting temperature. The energy that was in the coal is now dispersed throughout the entire system, much of it as heat in the air. Why can't the engineer recover all that energy, recompact it, put it under the boiler, and run the engine? This is where the second law of thermodynamics applies. Physicists have discovered that no real use of energy can ever be 100% efficient. Whenever useful work is done, some energy is inevitably converted to heat. Collecting all the energy dispersed in this closed system would require more energy than could be recovered.

Our imaginary system began in a highly organized state, with energy compacted in the coal. It ended in a less organized state, with the energy dispersed throughout the system as heat. The energy has been degraded, and the system is said to have undergone a decrease in order. The measure of the decrease in order (the disorganization of energy) is called **entropy.** The engineer did produce some furniture, converting a pile of lumber into nicely ordered tables and chairs. The system had a local increase of order (the furniture) at the cost of a general increase in disorder (the state of the entire system). All energy of all systems tends to flow toward states of increasing entropy.

From this discussion we achieve a new view of a basic quality of life [9]. It is the ability to create

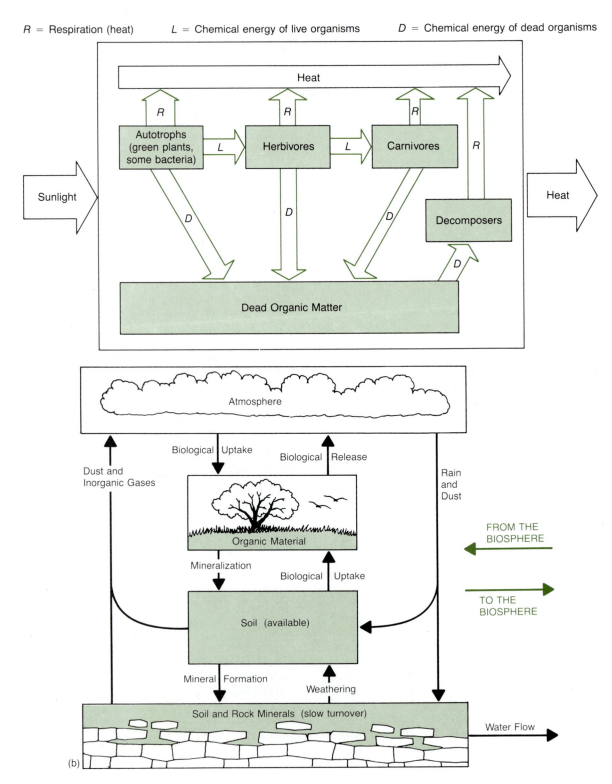

R = Respiration (heat) L = Chemical energy of live organisms D = Chemical energy of dead organisms

Heat

R R R

Autotrophs (green plants, some bacteria) L Herbivores L Carnivores

R

Sunlight

D D D Decomposers

Heat

D

Dead Organic Matter

Atmosphere

Biological Uptake   Biological Release

Dust and Inorganic Gases   Rain and Dust

Organic Material

FROM THE BIOSPHERE

Mineralization   Biological Uptake

TO THE BIOSPHERE

Soil (available)

Mineral Formation   Weathering

Soil and Rock Minerals (slow turnover)   Water Flow

(b)

110

FIGURE 4.9 (opposite)

Energy flows through an ecosystem; chemical elements cycle. (a) The pathway of usable energy is from an external source through the ecosystem's food chain, and to an external sink as heat energy. Some stored energy may be cycled temporarily in chemical bonds of compounds that are transferred from one organism to another, but the predominant flow is one way. At each trophic level, some energy is released as heat by respiration (R), some is transferred to the next trophic level (L), and some is transferred to the decomposers through death and excrement (D). (After Bowen.) (b) Generalized ecosystem mineral cycling. Chemical elements cycle *within* an ecosystem and are exchanged *between* an ecosystem and the biosphere. Organisms exchange elements with the nonliving environment; some elements are taken up from and released to the atmosphere, while others are exchanged with water and soil or sediments. The parts of an ecosystem can be thought of as storage pools for an element. The elements move among pools at different transfer rates and remain within different pools for different average lengths of time called residence times. For example, the soil in a forest has an active part, which rapidly exchanges elements with living organisms, and an inactive part, which exchanges elements slowly. Generally, life benefits if elements are kept within the ecosystem and are not lost by erosional processes.

FIGURE 4.10

An impossible ecosystem: Frogs and mosquitoes and nothing else. Frogs eat insects, such as mosquitoes. Mosquitoes also feed on the blood of frogs. Why is it not possible to have an ecosystem made up only of frogs and mosquitoes, each feeding on the other? As the text explains, the laws of thermodynamics tell us that such a biological perpetual motion machine is impossible.

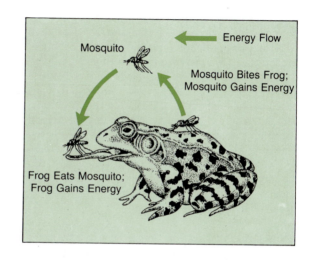

FIGURE 4.11

An imaginary closed thermodynamic system, with a steam engine running a lathe. An engineer puts coal and water into the engine, which runs the lathe to make furniture. When the coal has all burned, the energy it contained is dispersed as heat throughout the system.

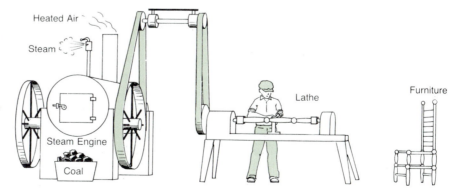

order in a local scale that distinguishes life from its nonliving environment. Obtaining this ability requires energy in a usable form, and this is the essence of what we eat. This is true for every ecological level: individual, population, community, ecosystem, and biosphere. Thus energy must continually be added to an ecological system in a usable form. Energy is inevitably degraded into heat and thus heat must be released from the system. (If it is not released, the temperature of the system would increase indefinitely.) This is what is meant by the statement that the net flow of energy is one way through an ecosystem.

Now we have explained the general reason why the frog-mosquito system could not persist indefinitely without another source of energy. (There is also a particular reason—only female mosquitoes require blood and then only in order to reproduce. Mosquitoes are otherwise herbivorous.)

From what we have just discussed, it is clear that an ecosystem must lie between a source of usable energy and a sink for degraded (heat) energy. The ecosystem is said to be intermediate between the energy source and the energy sink. The energy source, ecosystem, and energy sink form a thermodynamic system. The ecosystem can undergo an increase in order (called a local increase) as long as the entire system undergoes a decrease in order (called a global decrease).

Ecological Production   Regardless of what level we are looking at, creating local order involves the production of organic matter. Producing organic matter requires energy, and organic matter stores energy.

Production of organic matter can be measured at individual trophic levels as well as for entire ecosystems. To measure production at the individual trophic level, we must first divide organisms according to their energy roles. Organisms may be considered either producers or consumers. The producers are the **autotrophs,**—those organisms at the first trophic level that can manufacture food for themselves and for the consumers directly from the primary source of the ecosystem's energy, which is either light or energy stored in certain inorganic compounds. When light is the source, this fixation of energy is carried out by plants or certain

bacteria through **photosynthesis.** When certain inorganic chemicals are the source, the fixation of energy is carried out by bacteria. This is called **chemosynthesis.** This occurs in certain special environments, including warm deep-sea vents and the muds of ponds and marshes. When the energy is fixed in photosynthesis, the process is called a photochemical one. Simple sugars are produced from carbon dioxide and oxygen in the presence of sunlight. The autotrophs that produce these sugars then convert them to other kinds of organic compounds: carbohydrates, oils, proteins. As energy is passed from one organism to another, it is used in many different steps. The consumers are called **heterotrophs**—organisms that feed on other organisms and make up all other trophic levels in the ecosystem.

The production of the first trophic level is called primary production (Fig. 4.12). In a forest this would include the addition of new biomass of trees, shrubs, and herbs. In the ocean, it is the production of algae, including the tiny floating phytoplankton and large multicellular algae such as kelp along the shores. In a pond, primary production is the production of phytoplankton and aquatic flowering plants, such as water lilies.

Production of the heterotrophs is called secondary production. To understand and measure ecological production, we must make a few other distinctions. First we must distinguish between gross production and net production. Gross production is the increase in biomass or energy content before any is used.

For example, in a forest it is all the sugars produced by all the green plants before any is used—even by the leaves. Net production is what remains after energy is used. Respiration is the process by which energy is used. Living things use energy through the process of respiration for new tissues, repair, movement, and so forth. Gross production, net production, and respiration are connected by a simple relationship: net production equals gross production minus respiration.

Consider the flow of energy in a forest (see Plate 2, a and b). Photosynthesis in a tree leaf fixes energy, some of which the leaf uses immediately to maintain its own life processes. Energy not used in this way is transported to roots, stems, flowers,

FIGURE 4.12
Ecological production. This figure illustrates the major differences between gross and net production and between primary and secondary production. Primary production is the production of new organic matter by organisms that make their own food from inorganic compounds and a source of energy. Primary producers are plants and some bacteria. Secondary production is the production of new organic matter by organisms that must feed on other organisms. Animals, protists, fungi, viruses, and many bacteria are secondary producers. Gross production is the amount of organic matter added before any is used. Gross and net production are illustrated here for a tree and for rabbits. For rabbits, the organic matter in newborns plus the permanent weight increase in the previously living rabbits make up net production.

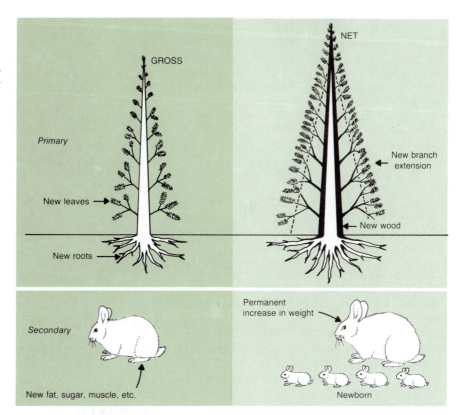

and fruits or stored within the leaf cell. Some energy is lost as heat in the transfer; other energy is used to make other organic compounds—cell walls, proteins, and so forth. The feeding of herbivores requires energy. A caterpillar feeding on the leaves, stems, flowers, and fruits requires energy. Its digestive system uses energy, as does the process of building new tissue from the digested food. Each step uses energy. At some steps some energy is stored; in others, it is dissipated (as when the caterpillar moves and the friction produces heat energy). The caterpillar, like other herbivores, stores some of the energy as fat for future growth and movement.

In most ecosystems, energy is fixed first within the ecosystem; however, freshwater streams are an exception. Heterotrophs have two major sources of vegetation in freshwater streams: the photosynthesis of the stream algae and the input of dead vegetation from the surrounding land ecosystems (dead leaves and twigs fall into the stream or are washed into it during storms). Typically, the second is the larger source, and a food chain is based on it. Of the numerous herbivorous animals it supports, some are "shredders," who tear up leaves; others feed on the smaller pieces. Grazers move along the surface of rocks and scrape off attached algae. Many stream predators are larvae of land-dwelling insects. Some stream carnivores also capture prey from the land, as in the case of trout that catch flying insects.

An extreme case of a food chain based on external food input occurs in the floodplain of the Amazon River basin, in which fish feed on fruits and nuts carried into the streams during the rainy season. Here, the production of herbivorous fish exceeds what would be possible from the aquatic primary production alone, yielding an abundant food supply for the human populations of the region.

Large areas of the ocean have low productivity per unit of surface area; combined, however, they account for a major portion of the total energy fixed. Highly productive areas of the oceans occur in coastal areas and in areas of upwelling water. These account for about 10% of the ocean area, but about 25% of the ocean's total primary productivity. Of practical importance, these coastal and upwelling regions supply more than 95% of the estimated fishery yield.

In the open ocean, the base of the food chain is the production of organic matter by many species of floating algae, collectively called phytoplankton. In one major pathway of energy flow, energy moves among the planktonic food chains in the upper waters, from algae to zooplankton to fish. The second is based on dead organic material that is produced at the surface and sinks toward the ocean floor; this material includes cells of algae, the dead bodies and excrement of heterotrophs, and some material, such as logs, transported from the land. These form the energy base for two groups of carnivores and detritivores—those that swim at depth and catch the material as it sinks and those that live on the ocean bottom and hunt for material once it has been deposited. These food chains thus depend on an external input of energy as the base of energy flow.

Chemosynthetic Energy Flow in the Oceans
Another class of oceanic food chains has recently been discovered in the depths of the oceans. These food chains support previously unknown life forms. The basis of the food chain is chemosynthesis, in which the source of energy is not sunlight but hot inorganic sulfur compounds emitted from vents in the ocean floor. The sulfur-laden water is emitted from hot-water vents, occurring at depths of 2500–2700 m, associated with areas where flowing lava causes sea-floor spreading. A rich biological community exists in and around the vents, including large white clams up to 20 cm in diameter, brown mussels, and white crabs (Fig. 4.13). The clams and mussels filter bacteria and particles of dead organic matter from the water. Some vents have limpets, pink fish, white tube worms, and octopi. Among the most curious creatures found in the vents were giant worms, some 3

FIGURE 4.13
Artist's drawing of the recently discovered type of biological community that forms around hot-water vents on the ocean floor. The food chain is based on chemosynthesis.

m long; they also live on organic matter dissolved in the water [10].

In every ecosystem, the energy flow provides a foundation for life and thus imposes a limit on the abundance and richness of life. The amount of energy available to each trophic level in a food chain depends not only on the richness of the energy source, but on the efficiency with which the energy is transferred along the food chain.

Energy Efficiency and Transfer

Efficiency is the ratio of output to input. How efficiently do living things use energy? The laws of physics and chemistry state that no system can be 100% efficient. As energy flows through a food web it is degraded and less and less is usable. Other things being equal, the more energy an individual gets, the more it has for its own use. But organisms differ in how efficiently they use the energy they obtain. A more efficient organism has an advantage over a less efficient one. Generally, energy efficiency is defined as the amount of useful work obtained from some amount of available energy. Efficiency can therefore be defined for artificial and natural systems: machines, individual organisms, populations, trophic levels, ecosystems, and the biosphere [11].

Efficiency has different meanings to different users. A farmer thinks of an efficient corn crop as one that converts a great deal of solar energy to sugar and uses little of that sugar to produce stems, roots, and leaves. In other words, the most efficient crop is the one that has the most harvestable energy left over at the end of the season.

A truck driver views an efficient truck as one that uses as much energy as possible from its fuel and leaves as little energy in the exhaust as possible. When we view organisms as food, we define efficiency as the farmer does—in terms of energy storage (net production/available energy); when we are the users, we define efficiency as the truck driver does—in terms of how much useful work we accomplish with the available energy.

A common ecological measure of energy efficiency is called trophic-level efficiency, which is the ratio of production of one trophic level to the production of the next lower trophic level. This efficiency is never very high. Green plants convert only 1–3% of the energy received from the sun during the year to new plant tissue.

The efficiency with which herbivores convert plant energy into herbivorous energy or the efficiency with which carnivores convert herbivores into carnivorous energy is usually less than 1%. It is frequently written in popular literature that the transfer is 10%, for example, that 10% of the energy in corn can be converted into energy in a cow. In natural ecosystems, however, the organisms in one trophic level tend to utilize more energy than they store for the next trophic level. At Isle Royale National Park the trophic-level efficiency of wolves is about 0.01% because they use most of the energy they take in for themselves [12]. From the wolves' point of view, they are very efficient, but from the point of view of someone who wants to feed on wolves, they appear very inefficient (Fig. 4.14).

The rule of thumb for ecological trophic energy efficiencies is that more than 90% (usually much more) of all energy transferred between trophic levels is lost as heat. Less than 10% (approximately 1% in natural ecosystems) is fixed as new tissue. In highly managed ecosystems such as ranches, however, the efficiencies might be greater.

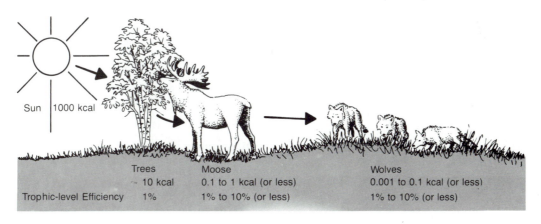

	Trees	Moose	Wolves
	~ 10 kcal	0.1 to 1 kcal (or less)	0.001 to 0.1 kcal (or less)
Trophic-level Efficiency	1%	1% to 10% (or less)	1% to 10% (or less)

FIGURE 4.14
An example of ecological efficiency. Trophic-level efficiency is the ratio of net production of one trophic level to the net production of its energy source. With autotrophs, this ratio is their net production compared with the source energy available. Trophic-level efficiency, rarely more than a percent or two, is sometimes much less and probably never more than 10%.

ECOSYSTEM PROCESSES II: ECOSYSTEM CHEMICAL CYCLING

Many factors can limit or reduce the efficiency of energy flow and the production of organic matter. One of the most important factors is the availability of chemical elements necessary for life. If some element or group of chemical elements is not available in sufficient amounts, then energy cannot be fixed or transferred at maximum rates (Table 4.1).

Chemical elements cycle within ecosystems, sometimes more, sometimes less, completely. This cycling of chemical elements within an ecosystem and into and out of an ecosystem is called ecosystem mineral cycling or ecosystem chemical cycling. Every individual requires a number of chem-

ical elements, and these must be available in the right forms, at the right time, and in the right ratios. Chemical elements can be reused—they can be recycled. If there were no erosion, and if each individual were 100% efficient in recycling, there would be no environmental issues related to chemical cycling. However, the nonbiological forces of the environment, both chemical and physical, tend to erode the land surface and to move chemical elements from the upper parts of bodies of waters to solid sediments or to the deeper waters. Slowly, over time, elements can become unavailable, or poorly available, in an ecosystem.

Chemical elements cycle within an ecosystem from organism to organism through nonliving fluid media (water and air) and sediments (soil and

TABLE 4.1
The macronutrients and their functions. These chemical elements are required by all life forms in large amounts.

Element	Function
Carbon	The primary building block for large organic compounds; forms long chains and combines with many other elements
Calcium	The beam and girder element, important in strong structures—shells, bones, teeth of animals, and cell walls of plants; also involved in nerve impulse transmission and muscle contraction
Hydrogen	The lightest element, a constituent of water and of all organic molecules
Iron	Various functions in enzymes and some respiratory compounds (hemoglobin)
Magnesium	Along with calcium, has structural functions (e.g., in bones and shells); also important in some electrochemical and catalytic roles
Nitrogen	The protein element, occurs in cell proteins, genetic compounds, and all chlorophylls; occurs in very large compounds, but also important in small compounds, including nitrate (an oxide of nitrogen) and ammonia; as ammonia and nitrate, can be taken up by green plants from soils as a nitrogen source
Oxygen	The respiration element, required in aerobic respiration; one of the major (or big six) elements of organic compounds and a constituent of water
Phosphorus	The energy element, important in energy transfer as the compounds ATP and ADP; also a constituent of nucleic acids; along with calcium and magnesium, important in vertebrate teeth and bones and in some shells of invertebrates
Potassium	Required for certain enzymes; important in nerve cell transmission
Sodium	Essential to animals but not to most plants; important in nerve impulse transmission and in salt balance of vertebrate blood
Sulfur	Required for many proteins; an essential constituent of some enzymes

rocks) and cycle between an ecosystem and the rest of the biosphere. Ecosystem chemical cycling can be viewed as a system, with the parts of an ecosystem serving as storage pools for each element (see Fig.4.9b). The elements move among the pools at different transfer rates. The cycling of different elements varies considerably, as illustrated in Figure 4.15 (sulfur) and Figure 4.16 (calcium). The calcium cycle is representative of a metallic element cycle and the sulfur cycle of a nonmetal. Another difference between the two cycles is storage and flow through the atmosphere. Calcium does not form a gas and has no major phase in the atmosphere, where it occurs only as dust particles in compounds. Sulfur forms several gases, including sulfur dioxide (important in acid rain) and hydrogen sulfide ("swamp" or "rotten egg" gas). Because sulfur has a gaseous phase, it can be returned to an ecosystem from the rest of the biosphere much more rapidly than calcium can. The annual input of sulfur from the atmo-

sphere to a forest ecosystem is almost 10 times that of calcium. Calcium is very soluble in water in its inorganic form and is readily lost to a land ecosystem in water transport, both in the flow of streams above ground and in groundwater.

There are many biological aspects to chemical cycling. Many of the biological processes involved in cycling tend to conserve chemical elements within an ecosystem. Dead organic matter in soils, for instance, helps retain many elements in land ecosystems. Because highly organic soils store large amounts of elements, an ecosystem with highly organic soils will remain fertile for a longer period than an ecosystem without such a soil.

To sustain life indefinitely within an ecosystem, energy must be continuously added (as we've discussed) and the storage of essential chemical elements must not decline. It is a common belief that, without human influence, life will be sustained in a constant condition indefinitely. It is also common to believe that life tends to function to pre-

FIGURE 4.15
Annual sulfur cycle in a forest ecosystem. In the circles are the amounts transferred per unit time (the flux rates) (kg/ha/yr). The other numbers are amounts stored (kg/ha). Sulfur has a gaseous phase as H_2S and SO_2. The information in this diagram was obtained from the Hubbard Brook ecosystem. (After Likens et al.)

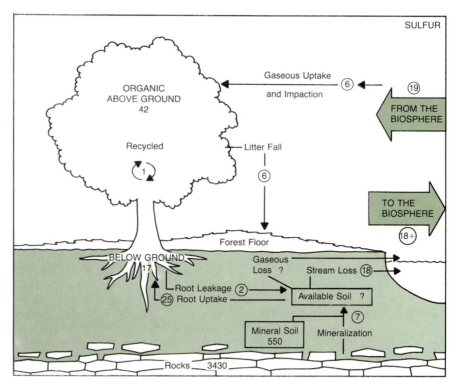

FIGURE 4.16
Annual calcium cycle in a
forest ecosystem. In the
circles are the amounts
transferred per unit time
(the flux rates) (kg/ha/
yr).The other numbers are
amounts stored (kg/ha).
Unlike sulfur (Fig. 4.15),
calcium does not have a
gaseous phase. The infor-
mation in this diagram was
obtained from the Hubbard
Brook ecosystem. (After
Likens et al.)

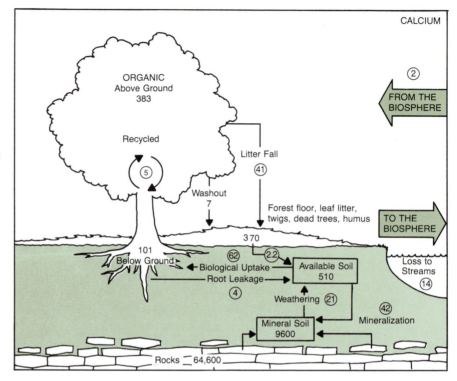

serve an environment beneficial to itself. Both
these beliefs presume that the chemical elements
necessary for life exist in a steady state within an
ecosystem. But are ecosystems in a steady state
with regard to chemical cycling? If not, what natural (biological as well as nonbiological) influences disturb the steady state and how do they interact with human influences to affect the cycling
of chemicals within and outside of ecosystems?

To answer these questions requires measuring
(1) the uptake of a chemical element by the ecosystem, (2) the loss of that element from the ecosystem, (3) the amount stored within each compartment within the ecosystem, and (4) the rate of
flow along each pathway.

In accomplishing these measurements, we must
be able to define an ecosystem as a unit on the
landscape, with defined boundaries so that flows
into and out of the boundaries can be measured.
Two American ecologists, Bormann and Likens, realized that for forested ecosystems a natural unit
was the watershed. A **watershed** is an area of land

drained by a single stream or river; thus any drop
of rain that falls into a watershed will leave
through one stream (Fig. 4.17).

An Experiment in Ecosystem Chemical Cycling

Several experiments have been conducted in forested watersheds to study the effects of natural
and human disturbances on ecosystem chemical
cycling. The first of these experiments was the
Hubbard Brook Ecosystem Study in the White
Mountains National Forest, New Hampshire [13].
At Hubbard Brook and other U.S. Forest Service research areas in the United States, watersheds were
subjected to different kinds of logging. The logged
watersheds (called "treatments") were compared
to unlogged watersheds (called "controls").

The inputs to the system are from rain, atmospheric dust (called "dry fallout"), and rock weathering. Outputs are dissolved and suspended parti-

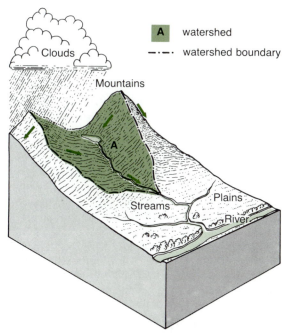

FIGURE 4.17
Diagram of a watershed. A watershed is a land area in which any drop of water that falls as rain will flow out through the same stream system. A watershed makes a good experimental ecosystem because of these natural boundaries.

cles in the stream water, gases to the atmosphere, and chemicals returned to rocks or to the deep soil (beyond the reach of plant roots).

In both the logged and the uncut control watershed there was an annual loss of some of the elements required by life. In the uncut control watershed, for example, there was a net annual loss of calcium. Other elements such as sulfur showed a net gain within the ecosystem (the inputs were greater than the outputs). The uncut control ecosystem showed a net annual gain in sulfur, nitrogen, phosphorus, chlorine, and hydrogen and a net loss in aluminum, calcium, magnesium, potassium, and sodium [13].

The Hubbard Brook control forest was young as forests are concerned, because it had been previously logged earlier in the century; however, the last logging occurred about 55 years before the study. This forest showed a net gain in some elements and a net loss in others, so that the forest was not in a chemical steady state. The forest ecosystem was slowly "running down." If these trends continue, eventually the ecosystem might have too little of some chemical elements to sustain an abundance of trees. For example, calcium is a macronutrient, used by green plants in cell walls, in the bones of mammals, and in the nerve transmissions of all animals. If observed trends were to continue, calcium would eventually reach a concentration that would lead to a decrease in the growth and biomass of most organisms, but this condition would not be reached for a long time.

What determined rates of input and output of the major chemical element? The acidity of the water was a major factor. An increase in acidity would make some chemical elements more soluble in the water and would lead to greater loss to the watershed.

The clearcut watershed had a much greater flow of stream water throughout most of the year and lost much more of its chemical elements. Thus life in the forest slowed down the loss of most chemical elements and led to a net increase in some. Life does tend to work against the forces of erosion and in this way appears to act to promote more life in the future. The process is not perfect, however; some loss of some elements occurs, and over a very long time even forest ecosystems appear to be running down, like a clock unwinding.

SUMMARY

The ecosystem is a central concept in the study of the environment and in the management of our landscapes. An ecosystem is made up of an ecological community—the living part—and its local, nonliving environment. An ecosystem is the smallest unit capable of sustaining life over long periods of time. It is the smallest unit that can maintain the essential characteristics of energy flow and chemical cycling, so that all living things can obtain their requirements.

Today, the ecosystem concept has become a central theme in the management of our natural resources. Just as experiments were done on forest watershed ecosystems at Hubbard Brook, so now there is a movement to managing forests, grasslands, and other types of vegetation in an ecosystem context, taking account of what might be limiting factors and whether the ecosystem is in a steady state in regard to energy flow or cycling of crucial elements. At another level, ecosystem concepts provide us with crucial insights into the old and still important questions about the character of nature with and without human influence.

In this chapter we learned that an ecosystem has structure and processes. The structural characteristics include the food chains, trophic levels, and species diversity and dominance. The processes include production, energy flow, chemical cycling, and ecological succession.

Chemical cycling determines much of the actual condition of ecosystems. An ecosystem that has very little loss of chemical elements can sustain life in its current condition for longer periods than a "leaky" ecosystem. All ecosystems, however, eventually "leak" and thus require disturbances over time to renew the stock of chemical elements.

The ecosystem concept is therefore central to management of our environment and to the point of view with which we think about our environment.

All of these concepts were illustrated by Lago di Monterosi. Today that lake is a small, peaceful, almost unknown body of water, appearing constant and changed only by people. But like all else on Earth's surface, it has experienced many changes over many scales of time. Disrupted by glaciers and by the action of Roman road builders, it has responded not merely as a collection of individual species and water, sediments, and air, but as a unit. Only by understanding this unit—this ecosystem—can we understand its responses and predict and manage it and other bodies of water and areas of land of Earth's surface.

That small lake is a unit of processes—of a flow of energy and the cycling of chemical elements. It has a community of organisms related to each other by a food web made up of trophic levels. The flux of energy and the cycling of elements affect which species dominate the waters at any one time. They affect the total biomass and production. A lake undergoes changes in time, called succession, and given enough time may disappear from the landscape as it finally becomes filled in with sediments. For short periods of time, that lake will appear stable.

Terrestrial, freshwater, and marine ecosystems have the major characteristics we have just discussed: (1) a set of species that interact as a living community and change over time, (2) an amount of biomass, (3) production of new biomass and loss of existing biomass, (4) a flow of energy, and (5) cycling of chemical elements. Ecosystems are linked through the biosphere.

Some ecosystems exist in regions of frequent variation and disturbances (like fire and storms). Such ecosystems usually require these disturbances to retain the characteristics we desire in them. In ecosystems biological processes tend to build, and physical processes of erosion tend to tear down; the state of an ecosystem is the result of the interplay between these. Without disturbances, at least some ecosystems seem to degrade—that is, they slowly lose nutrients, become less productive, and have fewer species and smaller biomass.

STUDY QUESTIONS

1 What are the major actions that can be taken to reduce the undesirable effects of *eutrophication*?

2 Why is the pollution of a lake likely to be an *ecosystem* problem?

3 Distinguish among *ecosystem, community,* and *habitat.*

4 Long space voyages would require the production of food—a biological life-support system. Describe the major features necessary for such a life-support system.

5   Some experimental sewage treatment facilities make use of ponds in which aquatic animals and plants are allowed to grow. What processes would take place to change raw sewage into drinkable water?

6   You are asked to be the manager of one of two preserves for the Indian lion, an endangered species. In the first preserve there are 200 lions on a heavily eroded landscape. Vegetation and animals are generally sparse. In the second, there are 10 lions, the soil is fertile, and the vegetation is abundant. Which would you choose to manage? Why?

7   It has been said that in conserving endangered species it is better to have a few individuals in a healthy ecosystem than a large number in a poor ecosystem. Explain this statement.

8   Distinguish between *trophic level* and *food chain*.

9   Why is it unlikely that there would be a species on the twentieth trophic level? (Consider the net production of various trophic levels.)

10   Describe a forest that is efficient from the point of view of (a) a forester, (b) an earthworm, (c) a bird that feeds on leaf-eating caterpillars.

11   What is a limiting factor? Can there be more than one in the same ecosystem?

FURTHER READING

BLUM. H. F. 1962. *Time's arrow and evolution*. New York: Harper & Row.

BORMANN, F. H., and LIKENS, G. E. 1981. *Pattern and process in a forested ecosystem*. New York: Springer-Verlag.

BROECKER, W. S. 1974. *Chemical oceanography*. San Francisco: Harcourt, Brace, Jovanovich.

GATES, D. M. *Biophysical ecology*. New York: Springer-Verlag.

MALONE, T. F., and ROEDERER, J. G., eds. 1985. *Global change*. Cambridge, England: Cambridge University Press.

McINTOSH, R. P. 1976. Ecology since 1900. In *Issues and ideas in America*, pp. 353–372. Norman: University of Oklahoma Press.

McNAUGHTON, S. J., and WOLF, L. L. 1979. *General ecology*. New York: Holt, Rinehart and Winston.

MOROWITZ, H. J. 1979. *Energy flow in biology*. Woodbridge, Conn.: Oxbow Press.

WARING, R. A., and SCHLESINGER, W. S. 1986. *Forest ecology*. New York: Springer-Verlag (in press).

WEST, D. A.; SHUGART, H.; and BOTKIN, D. B. 1981. *Forest succession: Concerns and applications*. New York: Springer-Verlag.

5

Ecosystems and Communities II: Biological Properties

- In most communities, a few species in each tropical level are very abundant and the rest are uncommon or rare. The very abundant species are called the dominants.
- Within an ecological community, some species play crucial nonreplaceable roles. These are called keystone species.
- Species diversity includes two concepts: the number of species present in an area and the relative abundances of the species. The relative abundance is also referred to as the evenness with which the individuals in that area are divided among the species.
- Ecosystems are characterized by change, not constancy.
- Ecosystems and communities develop and change over time, following a sequence called succession.
- Primary succession is the initial establishment and development of an ecosystem: secondary succession is reestablishment of an ecosystem.
- The final stage of succession was once thought to be a steady state that remained constant unless subject to new disturbance, but we know now that these last stages are also subject to change over time.
- Biomass and species diversity reach a maximum in the middle or late successional stages, and then decrease.
- Succession can be viewed as an interplay between biological and physical processes, with the biological processes building up organic matter and the storage of chemical elements, and physical processes eroding and degrading organic matter and chemical elements.
- If the physical processes are too harsh, or disturbance too frequent, succession does not occur.
- Because species have adapted to each successional stage, it may not be desirable to disrupt or halt the successional process.
- For management purposes, we need to think in terms of persistence of ecosystems within acceptable ranges of conditions, resistance to change, ability to recover following disturbance, and recurrence of an ecosystem's desirable states.

PACIFIC SEA OTTERS

The biological part of an ecosystem is called the ecological community, which is a set of interacting species. The species interact in a variety of ways (Chapter 3) including feeding on one another in food chains (Chapter 4). Communities differ in the complexity of their food chains and in the overall diversity of species. Communities also form spatial patterns and differ one from another in the complexity and size of these patterns. Communities change over time, sometimes in response to the physical environment and sometimes in response to biological factors. It is an old belief that life influences its own survival and that ecological communities tend to function in ways that increase the storage of energy and chemical elements and thus increase the likelihood of the persistence of life in the future. In this chapter we will discuss two basic properties of communities—diversity and succession—and the ways that these influence energy flow, chemical cycling, and the persistence of life.

Interactions at the community level can affect individual populations. This is illustrated by the sea otters of the Pacific Ocean. Sea otters feed on shellfish, including sea urchins and abalone [Fig. 5.1]. Sea otters originally occurred throughout a large area of the Pacific Ocean coasts, from northern Japan, northeastward along the Russian and Alaskan coast, and southward along the coast of North America to Morro Hermoso in Baja California, Mexico [1]. The otters were brought almost to extinction by commercial hunting for their fur during the eighteenth and nineteenth centuries—sea otters have one of the finest furs in the world. By the end of the nineteenth century there were too few otters left to sustain commercial exploitation, and there was concern that the species would become extinct. A small population survived and has increased since. Now sea otters occur in just two areas: in the Aleutian Islands of Alaska and along the California coast from Monterey Bay south to Point Conception.

Legal protection of the sea otter by the U.S. government began in 1911 and continues under the U.S. Marine Mammal Protection Act of 1972 and the Endangered Species Act of 1973. This animal has been a focus of controversy and research. On the one hand, fishermen argue that there are too many sea otters today because they take large amounts of abalone and compete with commercial fishing [2].

On the other hand, conservationists argue that sea otters have an important community role, necessary for the persistence of many oceanic species. What is this important role? One of the preferred foods of sea otters is the sea urchin. Sea urchins feed on kelp, the large brown algae that form undersea "forests." Kelp beds are an important habitat for many species and are the location for reproduction of some of these species. Sea urchins do not eat entire kelp. Instead, they graze along the bottoms of the beds, feeding on the base of the kelp, called holdfasts. When the holdfasts, which attach the kelp to the bottom, are eaten through, the kelp float free and die.

Where sea otters are abundant, as on Amchitka Island in the Aleutian Islands of Alaska, kelp beds are also abundant and there are few sea urchins. At nearby Shemya Island, which lacks sea otters, sea urchins were abundant and there is little kelp (Fig. 5.1b, c) [1]. Experimental removal of sea urchins led to an increase in kelp [3].

The otters affect the abundance of kelp, but the influence is indirect. Sea otters do not feed on kelp, nor do they protect individual kelp plants from attack by sea urchins. The sea otters reduce the number of sea urchins. With fewer sea urchins, there is less destruction of the kelp. With more kelp there is more habitat for many other species—so indirectly, sea otters increase the diversity of species [3]. This is a **community effect.**

This example shows us that there are community level effects that occur through food chains. These community level effects can alter the distribution and abundance of individual species. When a species such as the sea otter has a large effect on its community or ecosystem, it is called a keystone species or a "key" or "nonreplaceable species."

DIVERSITY

There are somewhere between 3 and 30 million species on Earth; that is a great diversity of life, and that diversity has always fascinated people.

FIGURE 5.1

The sea otter food chain (a) includes kelp—the large brown algae that grow along the shores—and other algae. These produce their own food from sunlight and inorganic chemicals in the ocean. Sea urchins, a kind of shellfish, feed on the holdfast, the part of the kelp that holds it to the bottom. Other shellfish are filter-feeders and scrapers. The sea otters feed on the shellfish. (b) Sea otters have a significant effect on their community. Shemya Island, without sea otters, had a high abundance of sea urchins near the surface, while Amchitka Island, which had sea otters, had a low abundance of urchins. (c) The island without sea otters had a much lower cover of kelp than the island with sea otters. The otters remove urchins, allowing the kelp to grow. Without otters, urchins remove the kelp. The otters have a community effect.

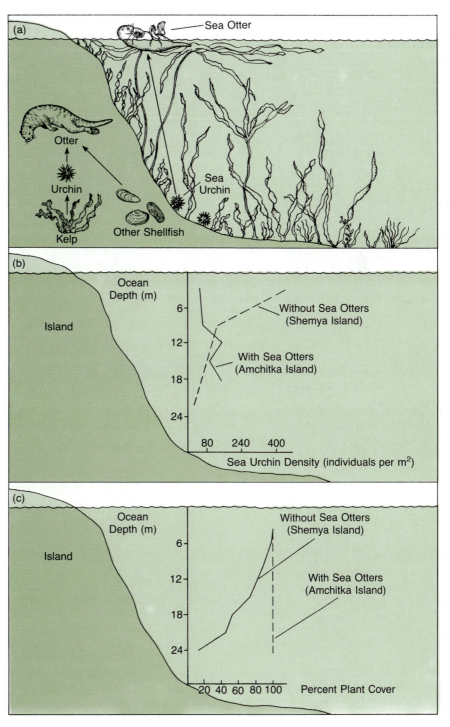

125

Diversity is important in regard to how people perceive the environment. For example, a day's walk in the country is more pleasant if there are many kinds of flowers and trees and animals, and a seashore where one can see crabs, sea otters, sea lions, and many kinds of shellfish and shore birds is more interesting and fun than is a beach without any life or with just one kind. On the other hand, visits to the country or beach would be less pleasant if the environmental diversity included swarms of mosquitoes or other biting or stinging insects.

There are many more important questions that have to do with diversity. These include: What accounts for this difference in the number of species in any area? Does this diversity of life tend to increase the likelihood of life's persistence? And how can we maintain the diversity of life on Earth?

Species diversity is important in the conservation of endangered species. If you are trying to save a species from extinction, you are trying to maintain a higher species diversity. In that case, you must understand what factors tend to increase diversity and what tend to decrease it. These are major considerations in the management and conservation of our living resources.

The following factors tend to increase diversity (Fig. 5.2):

1   a physically diverse habitat
2   moderate amounts of disturbance (such as fire or storm in a forest or a sudden storm-flow of water into a pond)
3   a small variation in environmental conditions (temperature, precipitation, nutrient supply, etc.) during nondisturbance times
4   a high diversity at one trophic level, increasing the diversity at another
5   an environment highly modified by life (for example, a rich organic soil)
6   middle stages of succession (which we will discuss later)
7   evolution

The following factors tend to decrease diversity:

1   environmental stress
2   extreme environments (conditions near to the limit of what living things can withstand)

3   a severe limitation in the supply of an essential resource
4   extreme amounts of disturbance
5   at nondisturbance times, a wide variation in environmental conditions
6   recent introduction of exotic species (species from other areas)
7   geographic isolation (being on a real or ecological island)

In general, the activities of people in urbanization, industrialization, and agriculture decrease diversity because such activities decrease the physical variability of the environment and because we purposefully favor specific species, manipulating populations to make our life more pleasant, to increase economic productivity, and so forth.

Diversity varies greatly from place to place. Suppose you were to count all the species in a field or any open space near where you are reading this book. The number of species would differ greatly depending on where on Earth you were. If you live in northern Alaska or northern Canada, the number of species you would find would, in general, be many fewer than if you lived in the tropical areas of Brazil, New Guinea, or Central Africa.

Changes in diversity are in some ways related to the environment. For example, in eastern and southern Africa, the well-drained sandy soils have a diverse vegetation, including many species of *Acacia* and *Combretum* trees, as well as many grasses (Fig. 5.3). In contrast, on very heavy clay soils of wet areas near rivers, such as occur along the Sengwa River in Zimbabwe, the woodlands are composed almost exclusively of a single species called *Mopane*. In this case, the very heavy clay soils impose a stress on plants; these soils hold water and allow little oxygen to reach plant roots. Trees are restricted to those with very shallow roots, and only a few can grow tall and survive under those conditions. In contrast, the well-drained soil is not stressful.

As another example, on the island of Hawaii there are rain forests with many species (Fig. 5.4), while on the new volcanic areas at high elevations, such as occur in Volcano National Park and on the slopes of Mauna Loa and Mauna Kea, there is only one species of tree, the 'Ohi'a tree (see Plate 3, a

FIGURE 5.2
Three important factors that influence biological diversity are disturbance, habitat diversity, and the amount of organic matter. (a) In general, biological diversity is highest when disturbances occur with moderate frequency. (b) Biological diversity tends to increase with the habitat diversity up to a maximum; beyond that maximum there is a decrease. (c) Biological diversity tends to increase with the amount of organic matter.

A Disturbance

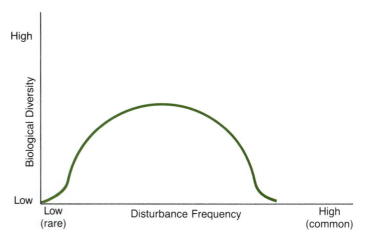

B Habitat

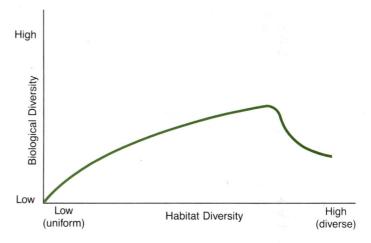

C Biological Influence

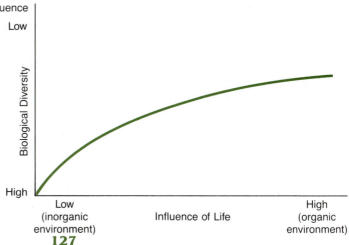

FIGURE 5.3
An acacia-combretum savannah in Zimbabwe. The local environmental conditions encourage species diversity.

FIGURE 5.4
Forests differ greatly in the number of species present; tropical rain forests have the greatest species diversity.

and b). The new lava flows on the slopes of these volcanoes have little or no soil, so that seedlings are easily washed away, and it is difficult for plants to obtain chemical elements from the soil. Water is not retained by the bare rock, and the sunlight is intense. Temperatures vary greatly from day to night. Few plants can persist under these conditions, and on an island like Hawaii, there are few species of trees to begin with.

In your own area, the number of species you could find per unit of area would be different in an abandoned city lot and in an old, long undisturbed forest.

Not only do the number of species per unit area vary in space, there are also changes in the number of species with time. Variations occur within all kinds of time periods, from the very short (a year in a single pond), to moderate (years, decades), and long (centuries or more in a forest), and over very long geological periods. For example, the diversity of animals in the early Paleozoic (beginning about 500 million years ago) was much lower than in the late Mesozoic (beginning about 130 million years ago) and Cenozoic (beginning about 75 million years ago) [4].

Career Profile: Jan Hall

On weekdays, Jan Hall is a production manager for a publishing company in Columbus, Ohio. Several weekends a year, she is an "atlaser" for the Ohio Department of Natural Resources (ODNR). ODNR is about mid-way through a five-year breeding bird survey of all 88 counties in the state. Volunteer atlasers throughout Ohio are doing the survey according to ODNR guidelines.

Hall defines surveying as finding out all of the bird species that will nest in a particular area. "I have been assigned a five square mile plot in Madison County," she says. The plot is about 20 minutes from her home. Within her plot, Hall has selected several subplots, including a wooded area and field, a swampy area, a culvert, and a woodlot. She carefully surveys these places whenever she visits the plot. She tries to go to the plot four or six times a year, especially during May and June when many birds are breeding.

Hall carries binoculars and several field guides with her when she surveys. During her first year as an atlaser, she noted all the birds she heard or saw. She also looked for nesting evidence. Several levels of nesting evidence are used to establish that a bird species breeds in an area. Males singing or defending their territory, pairs of birds, courtship displays, and nest construction are examples. Each level is assigned a point value. The maximum number of points is allotted for juveniles hatching or being fed by parents. Hall looks for higher levels of nesting evidence each year.

Better wildlife management is one goal of the breeding bird survey. In addition, Hall feels the survey is important in keeping track of environmental quality. "Birds in an area are indicative of quality," she says. In terms of environmental quality, differences in bird populations 10 or 15 years from now may indicate habitat destruction or pollution. For example, Hall has been told by farmers living within her survey plot that barn owls were present 15 years ago, but they no longer are.

Some volunteers who began the survey three years ago have since dropped out, according to Hall. She stays with it because it helps her keep in touch with other people who are interested in birding. ODNR puts out a newsletter for atlasers, and occasionally an intensive survey of a county is done. Then, atlasers can volunteer for a weekend outing and work together to survey an area.

She traces her birding interest to her childhood, remembering that her mother gave her a field guide when she was in first or second grade. She liked to learn the names of the birds in the book and what they looked like. She may be passing her interest on to her own three-year-old daughter who often accompanies her to the Madison County plot. "You can't get a babysitter at 6 A.M.," she smiles.

During college, Hall joined the Audubon Society partly because she enjoyed the social aspects of field trips and projects. Later, she became part of a splinter group called the Avid Birders' Club. When the Audubon Society asked for volunteers to participate in ODNR's breeding bird survey, Hall accepted. "First, I thought I could be helpful. Second, my interest goes beyond the sport of listing birds," she says. (She has about 300 birds on her life list.) "I want to know about their behavior," she continues. "Being an atlaser gives me an opportunity to have to sit and watch a bird—what it does, where it goes. I have to be all-around more observant and patient."

Michele Wigginton

Dominance and Diversity

Imagine two communities, each with 10 species and 100 individuals (Fig. 5.5). In the first community 82 individuals belong to one species, and the remaining 9 species are represented by 2 individuals each. In the second community all the species are equally abundant and each therefore accounts for 10% of the individuals. Which community is more diverse? The second would appear more diverse. If you walked through the first community, most of the time you would see individuals only of the predominant species, and there would be many species you probably would not see at all. In the second community, even a casual visitor would see many of the species in a short time. The first community would appear relatively low in diversity until it was subject to extremely careful study.

This example suggests that merely counting the number of species is not enough to describe ecological diversity. Diversity has to do with the appearances—the relative chance of seeing species—as much as it has to do with the actual number present. A community in which each species had the same number of individuals as all others would appear to be the most diverse, whereas a community with one species making up most of the individuals would seem the least diverse. It is unusual to find a community with all species of about the same number of individuals.

Usually a few species are very abundant and the rest are rare. The most abundant species are called **dominant.** For example, in the kelp beds where sea otters are found, two species of kelp, *Hedophyllum sessile* and *Laminaria longipes,* are typically dominant plants, while the sea otter is the dominant carnivore, and abalone and urchins might be the dominant herbivores. Typically, there are several dominant species at each trophic level in a community.

We know from the competitive exclusion principle (Chapter 3) that if environmental conditions were constant over time and uniform spatially the dominants would tend to increase at the expense of the rare species. A habitat that has a variety of local environments can offer refuges to the rarer species and thus leads to greater species diversity.

Predation can increase the diversity of the prey trophic level. Some studies have shown that a moderately grazed pasture has more species of plants than an ungrazed one. The same thing seems to be true about natural grasslands and savannahs. Without grazers and browsers, there are fewer species of plants in African grasslands and savannahs. This is because the herbivores reduce the abundance of the dominant plants and prevent competitive exclusion from reaching its final stage among the vegetation species.

Moderate environmental disturbance works in a similar way to increase diversity. For example, fire is a common disturbance in many forests and grasslands. Occasional light fires produce a mosaic of recently burned and unburned areas; these patches favor different kinds of species and increase the overall diversity.

Other factors that influence diversity are related to large-scale events—events that occur over broad areas and long periods of time. These topics fall under a category of study called biogeography (Chapter 6).

The Importance of Diversity

Many practical issues in the management of the environment concern diversity. Is it necessary to promote a high diversity everywhere, or just to maintain the existing diversity? This is a controversial topic. Let us consider the two sides of this controversy. Arguments in favor of maintaining a high diversity are of two kinds: (1) those having to do with individual species and (2) those having to do with ecosystems and communities as systems.

As an example of the first, many conservationists have worked to protect the blue whale, for its own sake, because it is the largest creature ever to live on Earth (an aesthetic argument) and because some people believe that whales have a moral right to persistence (an ethical argument). Opponents to the aesthetic position argue that blue whales are not aesthetic, or not sufficiently important aesthetically, to justify much effort on our part to support them. Opponents to the moral position argue that whales, because they are not people, do not have moral rights.

Other arguments for diversity are utilitarian. We obtain many useful products from organisms. For example, many plants are the original sources of

FIGURE 5.5
Diversity includes two concepts: (1) the number of species and (2) the evenness with which they are represented in the community. Both community (a) and community (b) have 10 species and 100 individuals. In (a), species 1 has 82 individuals and each of the rest has 2; in (b), all species have 10 individuals. (b) appears more diverse than (a)—it is easier to see more species in (b) than in (a).

(A)

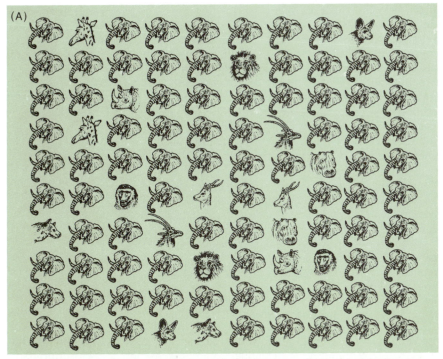

(B)

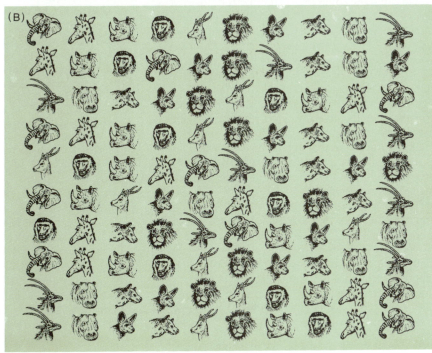

medicines, and there are many species that produce compounds that might be useful to treat other diseases if we only had time to discover these compounds. Supporters of a utilitarian view argue that it would be unfortunate if a species that produced an anticancer chemical went extinct before that compound were discovered. Opponents of this view could argue that only a few of the Earth's millions of species could provide such useful chemicals and the risk of losing a precious chemical from any one extinction is small.

Another argument for diversity is ecological. For example, one can argue that the sea otter must be protected because of its role in maintaining kelp beds, which are in turn breeding grounds for other species. In this case, the sea otter is seen as playing a crucial role—as a necessary part of the ecological machinery. Some extend this second kind of argument to all organisms, suggesting that each has an essential role and that therefore all species must be protected. Opponents could argue that most species are redundant from an ecosystem perspective and that rarely is a single species absolutely necessary for the persistence of life.

We can think about these arguments by an analogy with an automobile. If we remove a spark plug, the other spark plugs will function and the car will still run on its remaining cylinders, although poorly. If we remove a hose from the oil pump, the car will lose all of its oil and the engine will be ruined. If we remove a knob on the cigarette lighter, the car still runs, and we have lost a small convenience. The hose is obviously absolutely necessary, more so than a single spark plug, and both are more important than the lighter. In a car, some parts are essential and have no redundancy, others are redundant but play an essential role, and others are not necessary.

So it is with life as we understand it. The niche concept (Chapter 3) tells us that there are specific jobs that must be done if life is to persist on Earth. Often there are competitors that provide redundancy and therefore provide a kind of safety. Where there is a lot of redundancy, the risk may be low that the entire system will cease to function if one part is lost. However, it is prudent, where we know so little about life, not to throw away any

part before its function is thoroughly understood. It is also prudent to maintain as much redundancy as possible.

ECOSYSTEM AND COMMUNITY PATTERNS

Ecosystems and communities change over time, undergoing patterns of development called **ecological succession.** The two kinds of succession are primary and secondary. Primary succession is the initial establishment and development of an ecosystem; secondary succession is a reestablishment of an ecosystem. Forests that develop at the edge of a retreating glacier or on a new lava flow near a volcano are examples of primary succession. A forest that develops on an abandoned pasture is an example of secondary succession, as is a forest that grows after a hurricane, flood, fire, or clearcutting. In secondary succession, remnants of the previous biological community are present—such as organic matter and seeds in the soil of a forest—but in primary succession such remnants do not exist or are negligible. Examples of succession are all around us. When a city lot is abandoned, weeds and eventually trees will grow—secondary succession is taking place. Farmers weeding crops or homeowners weeding lawns are fighting secondary succession.

Forest Succession

Succession involves recognizable, repeated patterns of change [5], such as have occurred in many part of New England, where a hurricane knocked down many trees in 1938. The following year in the new forest clearings seeds of short-lived weedy plants and some trees sprouted (Fig. 5.6a). Some time later young trees became established, including white pine (Fig. 5.6b), pin cherry, and white and yellow birch—species that have widely distributed seeds and are fast growing, particularly in bright light. After several decades the pioneer species formed a dense stand of small trees. Once this forest was established, other species began to

(a)

(b)

(c)

FIGURE 5.6
Succession in a New England forest. (a) Some time after a farm field is abandoned, it is occupied by short-lived weeds and annual and perennial plants. During this time seedlings of
pioneer trees sprout. (b) After a decade, small trees like the white pines are abundant and
are replacing the herbs. After 30 years, the pine trees grow into a fairly uniform, dense
stand. (c) After half a century, many other species of trees have become established. These
include late successional species that sprout and grow well in the shade of the forest as well
as the older remaining pioneer trees. Given enough time (several centuries) without disturbances, the pioneer species will become rare and the forest will be dominated by sugar maples, beech, and other species that grow well in shade.

133

grow, including sugar maple and beech in the lower, warmer areas and red spruce and balsam fir in the higher, cooler locations (Fig. 5.6c). Although these trees grow more slowly than the pioneer species, they have other capabilities. Called "shade-tolerant" by foresters, they grow relatively well in the deep shade of a redeveloped forest. After 30 years, most of the short-lived pin cherry had matured, borne fruit, and died; these trees cannot grow in forest shade and do not regenerate in a re-established forest. After 50 years, the forest has a rich mixture of birches, maples, beech, and other species. The trees are generally taller, but the forest has many sizes of trees in it. After one or two centuries, these forests will be composed mainly of the shade-tolerant species—beech, sugar maple, fir, and spruce. From this pattern, we can abstract several general features of succession. (Fig. 5.7)

The assortment of species present changes during succession (Fig. 5.8a). Plants that grow rapidly and are short-lived, that do well in the bright light and high-nutrient conditions that often occur after disturbances, and that have widely and rapidly dispersed seeds tend to dominate the early stages of succession. These are called **pioneer species.** Plants that are slow-growing and long-lived do well in the shade of the forest; they have seeds that can persist but may not be widely dispersed. These species dominate later stages and are called late successional species.

The biological community changes during succession (Fig. 5.8b). In early stages, the amount of living organic matter—the biomass—increases. The diversity of life forms also increases. In the middle stages of succession, there are many species and sizes of trees.

Finally, the forest ecosystem changes during succession (Fig. 5.8c). Organic material accumulates in the soil, and the amount of chemical elements stored in the soils and the trees increases. If the forest remains undisturbed for a very long period—hundreds of years or more—it may achieve a temporary steady state, known as the **climax**

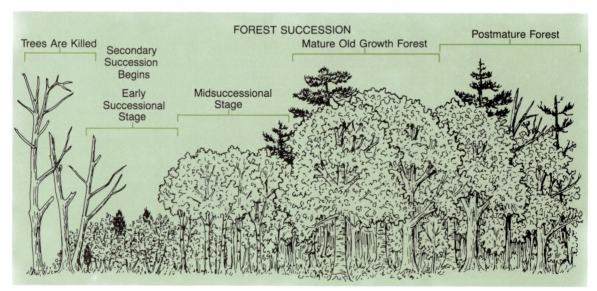

FIGURE 5.7
Forest succession. Secondary succession in a forest begins after a forested area is cleared by some disturbance such as a fire, storm, or logging. Plants dominant in early stages tend to grow rapidly in the open conditions. They tend to have seeds that are spread easily and rapidly by wind or animals. Plants dominant in later stages grow well in the deep shade of the older forest.

stage, or the mature stage. Then the forest will slowly change again: diversity will decrease (only the most shade-tolerant species will persist), the amount of live organic matter will decrease, and the soil may lose some of its chemical elements. Such very old ecosystems are called **senescent.** This general pattern of succession occurs in many kinds of ecosystems.

In primary succession, the earliest stages involve hardy species, such as lichens and mosses, that can persist on bare rock or inorganic soil.

These may help retard erosion and allow the development of soil on which trees and shrubs may grow.

Pond and Bog Succession

Ponds and bogs also undergo succession. From a geological point of view, a pond is a temporary landscape feature, which eventually fills in with sediments. Ponds are therefore common in areas with large-scale geological disturbances that shift

FIGURE 5.8
Species, communities, and the ecosystem change during succession. (a) Vegetation changes from short-lived pioneer weeds (herbaceous plants) to early successional, relatively short-lived trees and finally to long-lived tree species that can regenerate in the deep forest shade. (b) The community changes; biomass and diversity increase, then decrease somewhat. (c) The ecosystem changes; soil organic matter and the total storage of chemical elements increase to a peak in late succession, decreasing somewhat afterwards. The patterns shown are idealized; real patterns differ depending on local conditions.

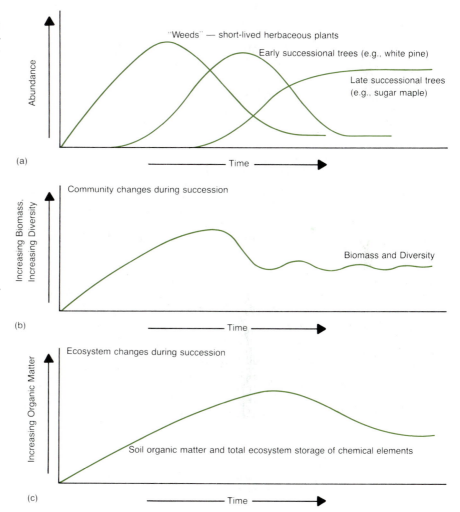

drainage patterns of streams and create depressions and dams. These phenomena occur in areas subject to glaciation. Minnesota, which lies within the heavily glaciated area of North America, is therefore called the "Land of 10,000 Lakes," whereas Oklahoma, in the southern Great Plains, south of the glacial moraines, has few natural ponds.

When a pond is first created, it tends to have clear water with little sediment, low concentra-tions of chemical elements, and little organic mat-ter (Fig. 5.9a). Over time, streams deposit sedi-ments and bring to the pond chemical elements suspended in the particles and dissolved in their waters. These enrich the pond, adding the nu-trients necessary for life. This increase in chemical elements is called the eutrophication of the pond (Chapter 4). The young, nutrient-poor pond is called **oligotrophic,** and the old, nutrient-rich pond is called **eutrophic.** The input of sediments

FIGURE 5.9
Bog succession. Ponds and bogs of northern gla-ciated areas gradually fill in and disappear. (a) The pond begins as open water with water plants such as the pondweed *(Potamoge-ton)*. A floating mat of sedge forms, gradually thickening as it accumu-lates organic matter and soil particulates. (b) Sedi-ments also accumulate in the center of the bog. As the sedge thickens, other plants are able to grow in it, including bog plants like cranberries and young trees like balsam fir and white cedar. (c) The sedi-ments at the bottom of the lake and the floating mat meet at the edges of the pond and finally the entire bog fills in. The soil forms a slightly raised hummock in the center. The floating sedge disappears and is replaced by trees adapted to wet ground, such as firs and cedars. Eventually, these are replaced by tree species from the surround-ing forest that are adapted to drier soils.

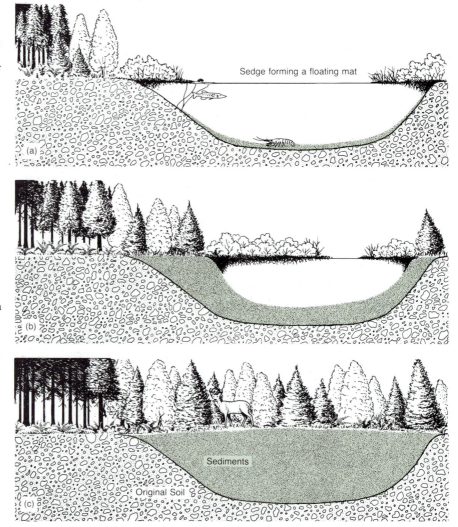

and nutrients is sometimes referred to as a "nutrient loading" of the pond.

The increase in a pond's chemical elements allows a greater production of plants and animals, leading to an increase both in live organic matter and in organic content of the sediments. In a natural pond this process is usually very gradual; over a long period the pond may even shift back and forth, from oligotrophic to eutrophic to oligotrophic, with changes in the climate and land vegetation in the watershed supplying the pond's waters.

A bog is a body of fresh water with inlets but no surface outlets. The succession of a bog (Fig. 5.9, Plate 4c) proceeds inward toward the center. In the quiet waters, plants that form floating mats grow out over the water surface. These pioneers are short-lived shrubs with mats of thick, organic matter that form a primitive soil which can be used by other plant species, allowing taller and longer-lived species to grow. As the bog slowly fills, the floating mats and sediments eventually meet to form a firmer base that can support trees. The first trees are those adapted to wet ground and include such species as cedars and larch, found commonly in the northern forests of Minnesota, Michigan, and New England. But if the process continues undisturbed, the entire bog fills with a raised, heavily organic soil in which other kinds of trees can survive. In some cases, the bog may disappear and be replaced by the tree species characteristic of the mature forests of the well-drained soils of the region.

Sand Dune Succession

Succession occurs in sand dunes along beaches (see Plate 3c). The dunes along the shores of Lake Michigan were among the first sites where this phenomenon was studied, early in the twentieth century. Sand dunes are unstable and are continually formed, destroyed, and reformed by the action of winds, tides, and storms. Along the east coast of North America, dune grass is the earliest pioneer plant that survives on a newly formed dune. It has long runners that anchor the plant in the sand and soil. The sharp ends of these runners

force their way through the sand and help stabilize the dune, which in turn allows other plants, including shrubs, to establish themselves. Shrubs are followed by small trees, and eventually a small forest develops, including pines and oaks. A major storm can force the ocean to break through the dune, redistribute the sand, and start the process over again.

In some places, like the shores of Lake Michigan or the coast of Australia, series of dunes extend a considerable distance inland. The interior dunes were deposited earlier and have an older forest.

From these examples we see the general pattern of change in the growth form of plants of each stage of succession. Generally, succession begins with small plants (the dune's grasses and the bog's floating mats) and progresses to larger plants. The species of animals also change during succession.

Succession and Wilderness

The succession on dunes and in forests leads to one of the oldest and most intriguing questions in environmental studies: What is nature undisturbed? What is the state of nature when it is unaffected by human beings? In other words, what is a true wilderness?

There has long been a common belief that an undisturbed ecosystem has a kind of constancy and permanency.

In the nineteenth century, George Perkins Marsh wrote in *Man and Nature* [6] that "nature left undisturbed" achieves "a permanency of form, outline and proportion," and that when disturbed, natural processes repair the "superficial damage" and restore the "former aspect." These natural processes, he wrote, lead to "a condition of equilibrium" that remains "with little fluctuations, for countless ages."

In the twentieth century, ecological theory developed around this idea that succession leads inevitably to an essentially constant state—the climax stage that would reproduce itself over time because it was composed of species of trees whose seeds could germinate and seedlings grow and mature in the shade of the parent trees. It was believed that all the desirable characteristics of a forest—the amount of timber, the total biomass, the fertility of the soil (both in total organic matter and content of chemical elements), and the diversity of species—increased during succession to a maximum at the climax stage [7].

Recent studies of very long successional patterns cast doubt on these ideas, however. For example, a sequence of dunes in eastern Australia provides information for more than 100,000 years of succession. The patterns observed are surprising. At first, the pattern of succession follows the classic idea; as one walks inland to progressively older dunes, the stature of the forest increases, as does the total soil organic matter and the richness of the species. But then these factors decrease, and the very oldest dunes are poor in vegetation. Gone are the large trees and the great diversity of species. On the oldest dunes one finds low shrubs and a comparatively barren landscape. Nutrients have been leached from the soil and washed so far below the surface that tree roots can no longer reach them. The ecosystem has become senescent [8].

Other evidence suggests that mature forests in North America are also "leaky"; that is, they lose chemical elements. A forest in steady state by definition must have a zero net production—no organic matter can be added. Such a forest can lose nutrients through geological processes but has little means to gain them, in contrast to an earlier successional forest, which accumulates organic matter and stores chemical elements. Thus a forest that has never been disturbed will ultimately go downhill biologically [9].

Natural areas are subject to disturbances of many kinds, regardless of whether people are involved. Furthermore, such disturbances have existed as part of the environment for so long that animals and plants have adapted to them [10].

One of the best examples of this point is the role of fire in the North Woods of North America. The Boundary Waters Canoe Area, a million-acre international recreational area lying in northern Minnesota and southern Ontario, is one of the best examples of nature relatively undisturbed by people. The native Americans who lived there had relatively little impact, as did the French voyageurs who traveled through the region hunting and trading for furs. Although some logging and farming were done in the nineteenth and early twentieth centuries, for the most part the land has been relatively untouched. And yet fires occur somewhere in this forest almost every year; on the average the entire area is burned at least once in a century. In areas set aside as preserves that have been prevented from burning, the main species change, sometimes from desirable to less desirable ones. In addition, unburned forests appear more subject to insect outbreaks and disease [11].

Thus recent ecological research suggests that change is a part of wilderness and that succession and disturbance are continual processes.

Because species have adapted to each stage in succession, it is not always desirable to manage an ecosystem so that it progresses totally to the mature state. A good case in point is the history of an endangered species, a small bird of the North Woods called the Kirtland's warbler (Fig. 5.10a). This bird lives in jack pine forests of Michigan (Fig. 5.10b). The jack pine is an early successional species during post-fire regeneration. When fires were suppressed in Michigan during the first part of the twentieth century, jack pine began to disappear, as did the Kirtland's warbler. Ornithologists wanting to preserve this species recognized that fire and fire-generated succession were needed to save the warbler, so now management practices have changed to promote light fires.

Similarly, the redwood forests of California also appear to require fires. Redwood trees do not regenerate—seeds do not sprout and survive—without the disturbances of light fires. Although not damaged by moderate fires, they may be by severe ones. The importance of fire is even more striking in the savannahs and grasslands of eastern and southern Africa (Fig. 5.10c), where fires are almost an annual event. These fires are very important in maintaining the production of early successional vegetation, which provides most of the food for the vast herds of animals. Because fires in Africa appear to have been set for a very long period, some ecologists speculate that the persistence of the African savannahs and grasslands and their great abundance of wildlife are in fact due to human actions.

FIGURE 5.10
Fire and ecosystems. Fire is important in maintaining many ecosystems. (a) The Kirtland's warbler, an endangered bird, lives in jack pine forests. (b) Jack pine regenerates only after fires and is short-lived; without fire at intervals of 50 years or less, jack pine is replaced by other species and the warbler's habitat is lost. Only through intentionally managed fires has this species been protected. (c) The savannahs and grasslands of Africa burn frequently, and the new vegetation growth following fire is an important food source for many species.

(a)

(b)

(c)

Until recently succession was believed to be an inevitable one-way process—that is, each stage had to occur in a fixed sequence, and succession could progress only from small plants to large or from low organic matter to high. Recent studies, however, suggest much more complicated patterns (see Plate 4, a and b). For example, a study of bogs in Great Britain shows that, although patterns of succession tend to proceed along a certain vegetation sequence, they can undergo variations of this pattern and even move "backward" [12].

From our modern perspective, we see succession as part of a dynamic change of the landscape. Succession is the biological process of building up life's effects on the landscape. It is continually countered by physical processes that tend to degrade, such as the slow process of erosion by water or the faster processes of hurricanes, tornadoes, or fires. Without disturbances, the building-up process eventually slows down, but degradation continues. With too much disturbance, the biological processes do not lead to a significant accumulation of organic material.

The kind of community that develops in any area depends on this interaction of biological and physical processes. In deserts the rates of growth are so slow that there is no appearance of succession. The kinds of plants that grow on a recently disturbed area are the ones that can be found there long afterward. In an area heavily disturbed by people, like an abandoned city lot or the edge of a highway, the rate of disturbance exceeds the ability of the ecological processes to develop any but the earliest succession stages.

In the ocean, succession occurs where there is relative constancy, such as in a coral reef or along the shore in rocky areas between the tides. In the open waters, continually stirred by winds, waves, and currents, there is no perceptible succession.

The examples of succession we have considered provide important lessons for our management of the landscape. First, there is rarely just one desirable state for an ecosystem; rather, there is a series of desirable conditions, which vary with particular social goals. Second, change is sometimes desirable or necessary. Third, a natural ecosystem is a mosaic of patches, each subject to a slightly different history. These provide a pattern in space that results in part from the temporal patterns of succession.

ECOSYSTEM STABILITY

Ecosystems are characterized by change, not constancy. Formerly, however, an ecosystem was believed to have an equilibrium condition—its climax condition—to which it would return after a disturbance, like a clock's pendulum. When pushed, a pendulum will move back and forth until friction slows it. Eventually, the pendulum will stop at its vertical rest point, called a point of stable equilibrium (Fig. 5.11). In contrast, an ecosystem maintains certain processes (the flow of en-

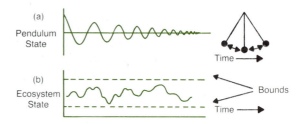

FIGURE 5.11
Ecological stability. (a) A pendulum has a stable equilibrium. When disturbed from that rest point, it moves back and forth until friction causes it to slow down. It stops at its original rest point. The idea that an undisturbed wilderness will remain in a constant state and will return to it when disturbed is a similar concept of ecological stability. However, ecosystems rarely show the stability of a pendulum. (b) Ecosystem characteristics, such as biomass, the stored amount of an element or compound, or the abundances of species, change over time within some bounds. The bounds vary with many factors, including human influence. Ecosystems have a certain resistance to change during a disturbance and a certain ability for recovery afterward, sometimes referred to as resilience.

ergy and cycling of chemical elements), but its species composition can change over time. In some cases, the more we attempt to maintain an ecosystem in a static, constant condition, as in the attempt to suppress fires in wilderness areas, the less likely we are to achieve what we want. The only way to manage an ecosystem in which disturbance has been a long-term characteristic is to allow natural disturbances to occur.

Thus the pendulum concept is inadequate for the management and wise use of ecological communities and ecosystems. We need to think in terms of the persistence of ecosystems, resistance to change, resilience or the ability to recover rapidly following a change, and recurrence of an ecosystem's desirable conditions [12,13,14]. Many of our actions can affect whether an ecosystem will persist, how resistant it will be to undesirable or desirable changes, how resilient it may be in returning to a desirable state following a disturbance, and under what conditions desirable states of the ecosystem will recur or can be made to recur. Later in this book we will find that we must use these concepts to discover a proper relationship between ourselves and our environment.

SUMMARY

In this chapter we discussed the biological component of an ecosystem—the ecological community—which is the set of interacting populations within the ecosystem. We focused on two of the essential qualities of ecological communities: species diversity and ecological succession. Both are very important in the management and conservation of our living resources.

Within an ecological community, some species, like the sea otter, play crucial, nonreplaceable roles. When such a species is removed, the community and the ecosystem are greatly changed. Such species are sometimes called key species. Other species have competitors that can carry out the same "job," but do that job best under slightly different environmental conditions. Such a pair of species is redundant, and when one is eliminated, the other can carry on its ecosystem and community functions. Such species redundancy provides a kind of insurance policy of the ecosystem.

If there are many species in a community, then the community is called diverse. The concept of species diversity includes two ideas: the total number of species in a community and the evenness—the distribution of individuals among the species. If most of the individuals in a community belong to a single species, that species is called dominant, and the community is less diverse than another in which all the species are of equal abundance.

People interested in conservation of our living resources often argue that maintaining a high species diversity is important. There are two major bases for such a position: (1) the value of certain individual species and (2) the role of species, especially key species, in ecosystems and communities.

Ecosystems change over time, following sequences of changes called succession. Primary succession is the succession that takes place where there is no previous remnant of life; secondary succession is the re-establishment of a community and ecosystem following a disturbance. Ecosystems are characterized by change, not constancy, and some ecosystems require change at rather frequent intervals. The concept of succession suggests that we must revise the old notions of the constancy of nature undisturbed by human influence—even natural ecosystems do and must change.

STUDY QUESTIONS

1 Farming has been described as managing land to keep it in an early stage of succession. Explain this statement.

2 A city park manager has run out of money to buy new plants. What might he do to increase the diversity of (a) trees and (b) birds in his parks, making use only of the labor force he has working for him?

3 Redwood trees reproduce successfully only after disturbances (including fire and floods), yet individual redwood trees may live more than 1000 years. Is redwood an early or late successional species?

4 A plague of locusts visits a farm field. Soon after, many kinds of birds arrive to feed on the locusts. Describe the changes that occur in animal dominance and diversity. Begin with the time before the locusts arrive and end with the time after the birds have been present for several days.

5 Compare dominance and diversity in (a) a zoo and (b) a natural wildlife preserve.

6 Other things being equal, how would fishing affect diversity of fish? Compare the following: (a) very low amount of fishing; (b) moderate level of fishing; and (c) intensive overfishing.

7 As a general rule, would pollution tend to favor early or late successional species? Why?

8 What is meant by the statement, Succession does not take place in a desert shrubland (an area where rainfall is very low and the only plants are certain drought-adapted shrubs)?

FURTHER READING

BENTON, A. T., and WERNER, W., Jr. 1983. *Manual of field biology and ecology.* 6th ed. New York: Burgess.

EGERTON, F. N. 1978. *History of American ecology: An original anthology.* Salem, N.H.: Ayer.

GOLLEY, F. B. 1977. *Ecological succession.* New York: Hutchinson and Ross.

HUTCHINSON, G. E. 1965. *The ecological theater and the evolutionary play.* New Haven, Conn.: Yale University Press.

KORMONDY, E. J. 1984. *Concepts of ecology.* 3rd ed. Englewood Cliffs, N.J.: Prentice-Hall.

KORMONDY, E. J., and McCormick, J. F., 1981. *Handbook of contemporary developments in world ecology.* Westport, Conn.: Greenwood.

MAY, R. M., ed. 1981. *Theoretical ecology.* Sunderland, Mass.: Sinauer.

MUELLER-DOMBOIS, D., and ELLENBERG, H. 1974. *Aims and methods of vegetation ecology.* New York: Wiley.

PATRICK, R. ed. *Diversity.* New York: Hutchinson and Ross.

WHITTAKER, R. H. 1970. *Communities and ecosystems.* London, England: MacMillan.

6

Biogeography

- [ ] Generally, organisms have evolved together so that predator, parasite, prey, competitors, and symbionts have adjusted to one another. Human interventions frequently upset these adjustments.
- [ ] Successful introduction of new species requires careful selection, initial isolation to eliminate parasites, and study of niche and population dynamics.
- [ ] A biotic province is a region inhabited by organisms sharing a related ancestry, bound by barriers that prevent their spread and the immigration of foreign species.
- [ ] Similar environments lead to the evolution of organisms with similar form and function and to similar ecosystems.
- [ ] A biome is a class of ecosystems that occur in a certain range of environmental conditions. Parts of a biome can be completely isolated geographically from others, and the organisms in one part can differ in genetic heritage from those in another part.
- [ ] Potential biome is based on climate; actual biome is the potential biome affected by soils and history, including recent weather patterns, natural disturbances, and human land-use activities.
- [ ] On land, what lives where depends on climate, geologic substrate, ecological attributes of the species, biological interactions, and changes over time.
- [ ] Changes in elevation lead to the same biogeographic effects as do changes in latitude.
- [ ] The number of species decreases as the environment becomes more stressful.
- [ ] When populations are separated, the separated subspecies evolve separately.
- [ ] Over a long time, an island tends to maintain a rather constant number of species; this number is influenced by its size and distance from the mainland.
- [ ] An ecological island is an area of one kind of habitat isolated by topography, climate, human activities, or other environmental factors. Ecological islands function like real islands in terms of species diversity and evolution.

AMERICAN CHESTNUT BLIGHT

People have greatly changed the geographic distribution of many species. Even accidental introductions of species can have serious effects, as illustrated by the history of the American chestnut (Fig. 6.1). The American chestnut was once a major tree of the Atlantic coastal states of the United States. Forests of chestnuts, oaks, and hickories stretched for hundreds of kilometers, from Connecticut to Georgia. Chestnut was important economically as a source of tannin and as a decay-resistant wood for fence posts, telephone poles, and railroad ties. The nuts were a major food for wildlife and a commercial feed for hogs.

About the turn of the century a shipload of wood from Europe accidentally carried to North America a fungus parasite of European chestnut, a relative of the American species. Because the European chestnut and the fungus had long coexisted, the European tree was resistent to the disease. Never having been exposed to the fungus, the American chestnut had no resistance and succumbed rapidly. The disease was first noticed in 1904 in the New York City Zoo. It spread quickly, reaching Connecticut, Massachusetts, Vermont, New Jersey, and Pennsylvania in 4 years, covering all of New England in 20 years, and then crossing Virginia at the rate of 40 km/yr [1].

Large sums were spent to prevent the spread of the disease. Between 1911 and 1913, Pennsylvania alone spent more than $250,000 (an amount exceeding $10 million 1986 dollars) to remove a line of chestnut trees from the middle of the state to provide a barrier to the fungus [1]. The efforts were ineffective because the fungus could survive on other tree species to which it was not fatal. By the 1930s the chestnut had disappeared as a major tree of the vast forests of the eastern United States. Today chestnut sprouts continue to appear in the New England and Atlantic coastal states, but they die before they reach 10 m in height, killed by the fungus that persists in oaks and other trees.

Although a chestnut breeding program was begun in 1931 to cross American trees with Japanese and Chinese chestnuts, no breeding trees have yet been produced. Recently a viruslike agent that appears to control the fungus disease has been found in Italy. Tests are now being made to determine whether this agent should be introduced into North America, this time with the hope of allowing the return of chestnuts to North American forests [2].

The story of the American chestnut is a story of ecological patterns in space, of biogeography—the study of the geographic distribution of living things, including the causes of the distribution, and the origin, history, and migration of species. American and European chestnuts evolved from a common ancestor. The two populations were subsequently isolated from each other so that they evolved along slightly different lines. One evolved in the presence of the fungus and developed resistance to it, while the other had no chance to develop immunity.

The distribution of life everywhere is affected by Earth's geological and climatological processes (see Plate 5). This effect occurs on many scales—local, regional, and global. At the local level, a subtle change in elevation—a few inches in a salt marsh along the ocean shore—can change the life forms that live there. At regional levels, the presence of major mountain ranges, lakes, and islands affects the patterns of life. At the global level, plate tectonics, ocean currents, and the circulation of the atmosphere affect the species population of an area. Thus the geography of life integrates many of the concepts discussed in Chapters 2 through 5.

At the local level, the number of individuals, populations, and species within an ecosystem is affected by biogeographical factors—by where the species came from, what species were there before, and so forth.

Just as geographical factors were important to the chestnut and those who used it, so is biogeography important in considering many environmental issues, from local issues to global, biospheric issues. At the global level, any major change in the abundance or distribution of land vegetation could change Earth's reflection and absorption of light and infrared radiant energy and therefore change the global energy budget. Such a major change would also affect the global cycling of chemical elements.

The geography of life is important to the conservation of endangered species. The number of

FIGURE 6.1
(a) The American chestnut was once a major tree of the forests of the eastern United States; it was a large and pleasant tree often planted for decorative purposes. (b) Its nut was an important food for wildlife and an economically valuable product. (c) An introduced disease removed it from its original large range, which is shown in the map. [(c) Adapted from Little.]

(a)

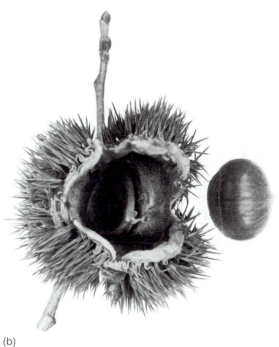

(b)

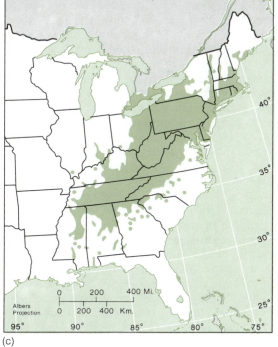

(c)

145

species on Earth is estimated at from 3 to 30 million; the range is large because parts of Earth are relatively unexplored for many kinds of species [3]. If we are to conserve species, we must understand how so many can coexist on our planet.

REALMS AND BIOMES

Major global patterns in the distribution of species have long been recognized. Aristotle established some of the first principles of biogeography; he wrote about boreal, temperate, and tropical life zones. During the nineteenth century, global patterns became a subject of intense study, partly because of explorations of the New World tropics, South America, the South Pacific, Australia, and parts of Asia.

Wallace's Realms

In 1876, A. R. Wallace suggested that the world could be divided into six biogeographic regions on the basis of fundamental features of the animals found in them [4]. Wallace referred to these regions as "realms" and named them Nearctic (North America), Neotropical (Central and South America), Palaearctic (Europe, northern Asia, and northern Africa), Ethiopian (central and southern Africa), Oriental (the Indian subcontinent and Malaysia), and Australian. These have become known as "Wallace's realms" (Fig. 6.2a). In each realm, certain families or orders of animals are dominant. In each realm the animals filling ecological niches are of different genetic stock. For example, bison and pronghorn antelope are among the large mammalian herbivores in North America; rodents such as the agouti fill those niches in South America as do kangaroos in Australia; and in central and southern Africa large herbivores include many species of ruminants such as giraffes and antelopes.

The basic concept of Wallace's realms is still considered valid and has been extended to all life forms, including plants (Fig. 6.2b) and invertebrates. These regions are now referred to as biotic provinces. A **biotic province** is a region inhabited by a characteristic set of taxa (species, families, orders), bound by barriers that prevent the spread of

the distinctive kinds of life to other regions and prevent the immigration of foreign species [5]. In a biotic province, organisms share a common genetic heritage but may live in a variety of environments, as long as they are genetically isolated from other regions.

Wallace did not have our modern understanding of geological processes to explain how distinct biological groups could have evolved in major habitat regions. The modern explanation for the origin of Wallace's realms is that continental drift, caused by plate tectonics, has resulted in the periodic unification and separation of the continents (Fig. 6.3). Unification resulted in genetic mixing, whereas separation imposed geographic isolation. Continental unification and land bridges spread genetic stock, which provided organisms with the potential to exploit new habitats; continental separation led to genetic isolation and the evolution of new species.

Local Patterns

The geographical distribution of organisms is controlled in large part by climate and soils but is influenced also by biological interactions (see Chapters 3 and 4) and by history, including human actions and natural disturbances. On land, what lives where depends on climate, geologic substrate (rock and soil), ecological attributes of the species, biological interactions, and history (changes in time). Some of the possible interrelationships are illustrated in Figure 6.4.

On a local scale on the land, the kinds of species and ecosystems that occur change with soils and with changes in the topographic characteristics of slope, aspect (in which direction the slope faces), elevation, and relation to a drainage basin. Change in the relative abundance of a species over an area is referred to as an **ecological gradient.**

In mountainous areas, changes in elevation lead to the same biogeographic changes that occur with changes in latitude, as shown for the Grand Canyon and vicinity of Arizona in Figure 6.5. Such patterns are most easily seen in vegetation, but they occur for all organisms; the pattern of distribution of representative African mammals on Mt. Kilimanjaro is shown in Figure 6.6.

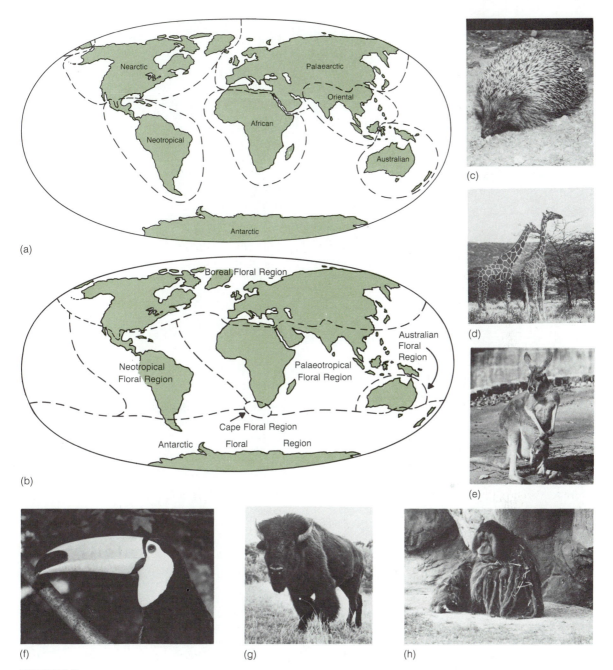

FIGURE 6.2

(a) The main biogeographic realms for animals are based on genetic factors. Within each realm the mammals are in general more closely related to each other than to mammals of other realms. (b) The major vegetation realms are also based on genetic factors. Flowering plants within a realm are more closely related to each other than they are to flowering plants of other realms. (c–h) Animals of different biogeographic realms: (c) European hedgehog; (d) reticulated giraffe (Africa); (e) kangaroo (Australia); (f) toucan (South America); (g) bison (North America); (h) orangutan (Indonesia). [(a) from A. R. Wallace; (b) from Cox et al.]

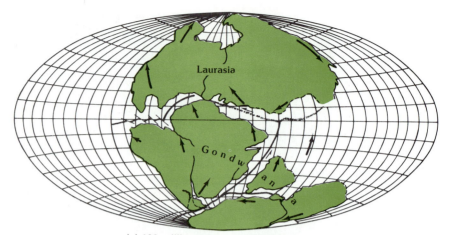

(a) 180 million years ago (Triassic Period)

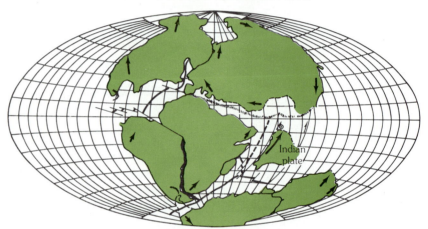

(b) 135 million years ago (Jurassic Period)

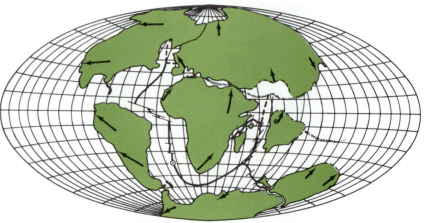

(c) 65 million years ago (Cretaceous Period)

148

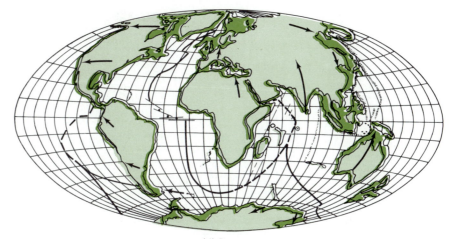

(d) Present

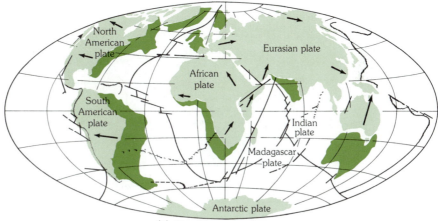

(e) 50 million years from now

FIGURE 6.4
Interrelationships among climate, geology, soil, vegetation, and animals. What lives where depends on many factors. Climate, geological features (bedrock type, topographic features), and soils influence vegetation. Vegetation in turn influences soils and the kinds of animals that will be present. Animals in turn affect the vegetation. Arrows represent a causal relationship; the direction is from cause to effect. A dashed arrow indicates a weak influence and a solid arrow a strong influence. (From Miller et al.)

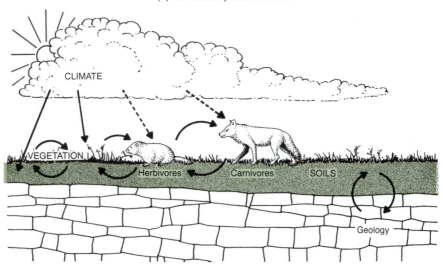

149

FIGURE 6.5
Changes in elevation lead to biogeographic changes similar to those that occur with latitude. As elevation above sea level increases, the climate becomes colder and wetter, creating a pattern in the distribution of life up a mountaintop that parallels changes that occur from equator to pole. The altitudinal zones of vegetation in the Grand Canyon of Arizona and in the nearby San Francisco Mountains are shown. (From *Natural regions of the United States and Canada* by Charles B. Hunt, W.H. Freeman and Company. Copyright © 1974.)

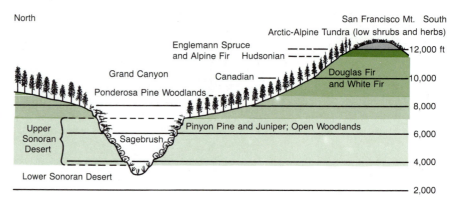

FIGURE 6.6
Changes in the distribution of animals with elevation on a typical mountain in Kenya. (From Cox et al.)

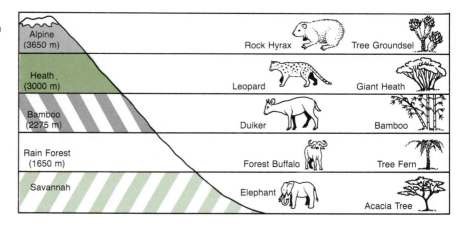

Regional Patterns

The concept of continental drift leaves us with a picture of huge land masses moving ponderously over Earth's surface, periodically isolating and remixing groups of organisms and leading to an increase in the diversity of species. If each continent were a uniform plot of land in a uniform climate, then biological diversity within a continent would be low.

Important patterns of distribution occur regionally and across continents, as illustrated by those that occur from west to east across North America. A generalized cross section of the United States shows the relationships among weather patterns, topography, and biota (Fig. 6.7).

Off the West Coast of the United States in the Pacific basin occur the pelagic ecosystems: "euphotic" zones, with sufficient light for photosynthesis and occupied by small, mainly single-celled algae, and other zones with too little light for photosynthesis, occupied by animals that depend for food on dead organisms that sink from above. Near the shore, particularly in areas of upwelling such

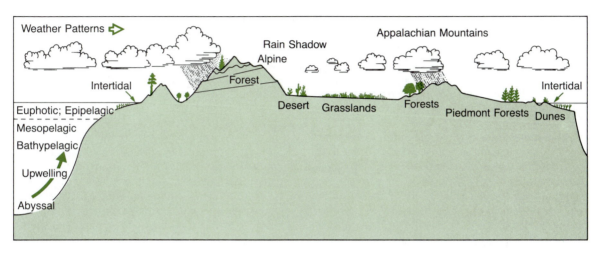

FIGURE 6.7
Generalized cross section of North America showing weather, landforms, and the geography
of life. The weather patterns move from west to east.

as occur in the Santa Barbara channel, there is an abundance of algae, fish, birds, shellfish, and marine mammals. Where the tides and waves alternatively cover and uncover the shore, a long, thin line of intertidal ecosystems is found, dominated by kelp and other large algae that are attached to the ocean bottom; by shellfish like mussels, barnacles, and abalone; by crabs and other invertebrates; and by shore birds like the sandpiper.

Weather—storms, low- and high-pressure systems—moves from west to east in the Northern Hemisphere. As air masses are forced up over the coastal and Rocky Mountains, they are cooled, and the moisture in them condenses. The West Coast is an area of moderate temperature because water has a high capacity to store heat and the Pacific Ocean modulates the temperature. Annual amounts of rainfall increase with elevation on the west slopes of the mountains. In the south, along the southern California coast, rainfall remains low until the mountains force the air high enough to condense much of its moisture. In general, the colder, wetter heights of the mountains support coniferous forests.

In the north, along the coasts of Washington and Oregon, cool temperatures year-round lead to heavy rains near the shore, producing an unusual temperate-climate rain forest. The most famous example of these forests occurs in Olympia National Park on the northwestern edge of the state of Washington.

The eastern slopes of the coastal ranges form a rain shadow: First, the air that passes over these eastern slopes has given up most of its moisture to the mountains; that is, it is dry as it passes to the east. Then, as the air sinks to lower elevations, it is warmed and can hold more moisture. This dry air tends to take up moisture from the ground, producing the deserts of Utah, California, Arizona, and New Mexico. Whereas annual rainfall in the Olympic peninsula of Washington reaches 375 cm (150 in.)/yr., east of the Cascades it falls to 20 cm (8 in.)/yr.

The same effect occurs in the Rockies. Less than 160 km west of Denver, in the Rocky Mountains, the annual rainfall is 100 cm (40 in.) One hundred and sixty km east of Denver in the Great Plains the rainfall is 30–40 cm (12–16 in.)/yr. Average annual rainfall increases steadily eastward: 50 cm at Dodge City, Kansas; 70 cm near Lincoln, Nebraska; and 90 cm near Kansas City, Missouri [6].

The biomes reflect these changes in rainfall. Just east of Denver are short-grass prairies, which are replaced by what is known as a mixed-grass prairie (meaning a mixture of short- and tall-grass prairie) and then by tall-grass prairies eastward. Farther east, rainfall reaches levels sufficient to support forests. This occurs near the South Dakota-Minnesota border in the north (where the annual rainfall reaches 50–64 cm). From there to the East Coast the deciduous and boreal forest of eastern North America predominates.

Sometimes these ecological borders, as that between the short- and tall-grass prairies, are said to be subtle, but they were quite striking and visible to some of the early travelers in the West. One such traveler, Josiah Gregg, wrote in his journal in 1831 that to the west of Council Grove, Missouri, at the border of the tall- and short-grass prairies, the "vegetation of every kind is more stinted—the gay flowers more scarce, and the scant timber of a very inferior quality," while to the east of that place he found the prairies to have "a fine and productive appearance . . . truly rich and beautiful" [6].

The patterns described for the United States occur worldwide. Changes with elevation from warm, dry-adapted woodlands to moist, cool-adapted woodlands are found in Spain, where beech and birch, characteristic of middle and northern Europe (Germany, Scandinavia, etc.) are found at high elevations, and alpine tundra is found at the summits. Similar patterns are found in Venezuela, where a change in elevation from sea level to 5000 m at the summits of the Andes is equivalent to a latitudinal change from the Amazon basin to the southern tip of the South American continent. The seasonality of rainfall as well as the total amount often determine which ecosystems occur in an area.

Two other general concepts of biogeography, illustrated by both the latitudinal patterns from the arctic to the tropics and the altitudinal patterns from mountain tops to valleys, are (1) the number of species declines as the environment becomes more stressful and (2) on land the stature of vegetation decreases as the environment becomes more stressful (Fig. 6.8). These concepts apply to most stresses, including those that human beings impose by adding pollutants to the environment, by decreasing the fertility of soils or otherwise im-

poverishing habitats, and by increasing the rate of environmental disturbance. From these concepts we can predict that highly polluted and disturbed landscapes and seascapes will have few species and that, on the land, the dominant species of plants will be of small stature.

Biomes

Similar environments lead to the evolution of organisms with similar form and function (but not in genetic heritage or internal makeup) and to similar ecosystems. This is known as the rule of climatic similarity. This rule leads to the concept of the biome. A biome is a kind of ecosystem, and similar kinds of ecosystems occur in similar environments.

As a result, it is common and convenient to divide the biosphere into biomes. Parts of a biome can be completely isolated geographically from other parts.

Potential and Actual Biomes The strong relationship between climate and life suggests that if we know the climate of an area, we can predict what biome will be found there, what its biomass and production are, and what the dominant kinds of organisms will be if the environment remains constant. The biome that would be found in an area if the environment were constant for a long time is called the potential biome. What is actually found in an area, as affected by soils and by history, including the recent history of weather patterns, recent natural disturbances such as fires and storms, and recent human land-use activities, is called the actual biome. The potential condition is what would be there, given the climate, if there had been no disturbance and if recent weather conditions were the same as long-term average climatic conditions. The actual condition of the biome is what really is there now. Most maps of biomes show the potential condition.

Diagrams showing the relationships between biomes and climate serve many purposes. The general relationship between biome type and the two most important climate factors—rainfall and temperature—are diagrammed in Fig. 6.9.

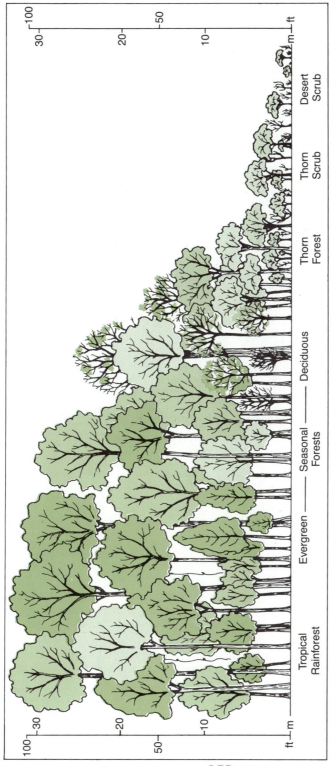

FIGURE 6.8
Environmental stress and biogeography. Certain general patterns can be found as an environment becomes more stressful. In this diagram, the effect of increasing water stress is shown. Where rainfall is plentiful, vegetation is abundant, and there are forests of tall trees of many species. As rainfall becomes less, the size of the plants decreases to small trees, then shrubs and grasses, then scattered plants. The total biomass decreases and in general the number of species decreases. Similar changes accompany increases in other kinds of stress, including the stress of certain pollutants. (Adapted from Whittaker.)

FIGURE 6.9
A pattern of vegetation types in relation to humidity and temperature. Boundaries between types are approximate. For example, tropical rain forests occur in areas with an approximate annual rainfall range of 250–450 cm and an approximate temperature range of 18–20°C. Note that deserts occur over a wide range of annual temperatures, from 20° to −5°C, as long as rainfall is less than 50 cm/yr. The warmer the climate, the more rainfall is required to move from desert to another biome. (Redrawn with permission of Macmillan Publishing Company from *Communities and Ecosystems* by Robert H. Whittaker. Copyright © 1970 by Robert H. Whittaker.)

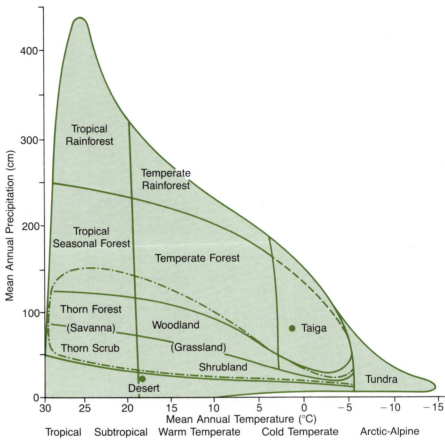

Biomass and the Geography of Net Primary Production   Biomass and net primary productivity follow geographic patterns. In general, on land both biomass and net primary production rise with rainfall and temperature. Net primary production is lowest for deserts and tundra, highest for tropical rain forests. The biomass per unit area stored on the land is much greater than in the oceans because woody plants maintain a large amount of woody tissue. Per unit area, the open ocean has a net primary production similar to that of deserts. Areas of the oceans that have higher nutrient concentrations—the upwelling zones, continental shelves, reefs, and estuaries—have net primary production per unit area similar to that of the more productive land biomes. Using correlations between net primary production and temperature

and rainfall, it is possible to project average net primary production for the major land areas.

Biogeography and Glaciation   The species composition of biomes and ecosystems is not constant over time. It changes over long periods of time in response to changes in climate associated with advances and retreats of continental glaciers, the most recent of which occurred only about 10,000 years ago. Deposits of pollen in lakes and ponds indicate that chestnut reached the area of Connecticut and New Jersey only about 2000 years ago (Fig. 6.10a). Oaks returned much faster after the retreat of the glaciers, reaching this area 8000 years earlier, about 10,000 years ago (Fig. 6.10b). Thus the oaks and chestnuts seen by the first European settlers in the seventeenth century had,

FIGURE 6.10
Changes in distribution of tree species during the last 10,000 years in North America. At the end of the last glacial period, as the climate warmed, tree species began to migrate northward. The history of their migration can be traced by studying pollen deposits in lakes. These graphs show the time (in thousands of years before present) that the pollen of (a) chestnut, (b) oak, (c) maple, and (d) white pine first appears in records from different areas of North America. From this information, one can reconstruct the general path of migration (shown by the arrows). Chestnut, oak, and maple migrated from a refuge in the south-central United States; white pine migrated from the southeast, from a refuge now offshore and under water. From a geological perspective, these species have been together in the mid-Atlantic states for a relatively short time. Chestnut reached the vicinity of what is now New York City about 2000 years ago, but oak arrived there 8000 years earlier. The forests seen by the early European explorers (and thought to be relatively permanent associations of species) had changed in the preceding several thousand years. (From M. B. Davis.)

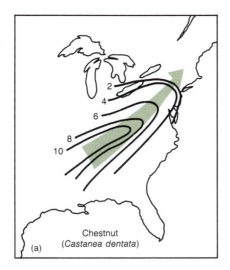

(a) Chestnut *(Castanea dentata)*

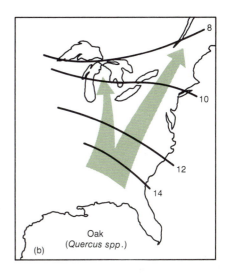

(b) Oak *(Quercus spp.)*

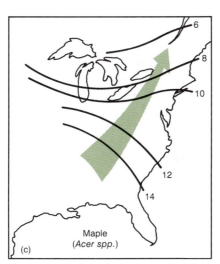

(c) Maple *(Acer spp.)*

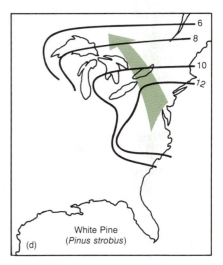

(d) White Pine *(Pinus strobus)*

from a geological time scale, only recently come together [7].

Farther north in New England, the early settlers found maple and white pine growing in the same general areas. At the height of the glaciations, however, these species occurred in places hundreds of kilometers apart. Maple grew in what is now Louisiana and Mississippi and returned northeastward from this southwestern refuge (Fig. 6.10c). White pine moved northwestward from a southeastern refuge, which was then dry land but is now under water offshore (Fig. 6.10d).

Records of pollen in lakes and ponds give important insights into the true character of wilderness uninfluenced by human beings. Chestnuts and oaks were thought to be members of the same cli-

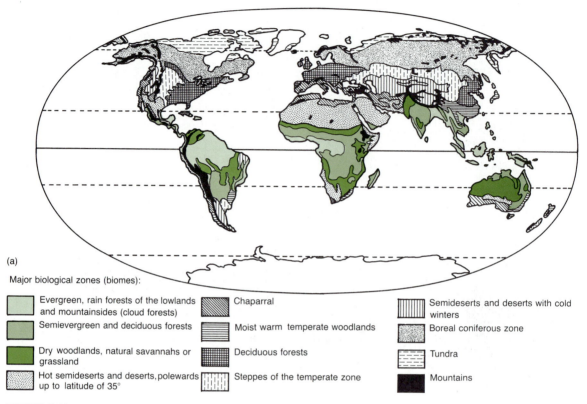

(a)

Major biological zones (biomes):

- Evergreen, rain forests of the lowlands and mountainsides (cloud forests)
- Semievergreen and deciduous forests
- Dry woodlands, natural savannahs or grassland
- Hot semideserts and deserts, polewards up to latitude of 35°
- Chaparral
- Moist warm temperate woodlands
- Deciduous forests
- Steppes of the temperate zone
- Semideserts and deserts with cold winters
- Boreal coniferous zone
- Tundra
- Mountains

FIGURE 6.11
(a) Distribution of Earth's major terrestrial biological zones (biomes). The major biomes are distinguished from one another by the dominant kinds of vegetation as well as by certain effects of climate and substrate: (b) tundra (Rocky Mountains, Colorado); (c) chaparral (California); (d) saltwater marsh (Florida); (e) rocky intertidal (Galápagos Islands). Other types are illustrated in Plate 6. [(a) from Walter.]

max forest, a forest that would persist indefinitely in an area as long as the climate remained the same. Before pollen records became available, the species were believed to have migrated as a unit and could have been found together, although much farther south, at any time during the glacial periods. Similarly, northern forests of maples and white pines were commonly thought to have moved across the landscape to the same refuges. Now we know that the concurrences of such groups of species depend in part upon historical events. Wilderness has changed greatly over the last several thousand years even without human influence. Ecological communities, at least as far as tree species are concerned, seem to be relatively loosely coupled groupings.

EARTH'S MAJOR BIOMES

Knowing the basic characteristics of the world's major biomes and the features of life within each is important for planning, for dealing with environmental issues, and for determining beneficial introductions of new species.

The number of classes of biomes and the boundaries between biomes vary from one expert's

(b)

(c)

(d)

(e)

table or diagram to another's. Biomes are named for either the dominant organisms (for example, forests of conifers as opposed to grasslands), or the dominant shape and form of the dominant organisms (called the physiognomy) (forest versus shrub land), or the dominant climatic conditions (cold desert versus warm desert). A world map of the major terrestrial biomes is shown in Figure 6.11a.

Tundra

Tundras are treeless plains that occur under the harsh climates of low rainfall and low average temperatures (Fig. 6.11b). The dominant vegetation includes grasses and their relatives (sedges), mosses, lichens, low flowering dwarf shrubs, and mat-forming plants.

There are two kinds of tundra—arctic, which occurs at high latitudes, and alpine, which occurs at high elevations. The vegetation of both is similar but the dominant animals are different. Arctic tundras typically have important large mammals, as well as important small mammals, birds, and insects; in alpine tundras, the dominant animals are small rodents and insects. Alpine tundras occupy comparatively small isolated areas, while populations of large mammals require large territories, such as are found in arctic tundras.

Parts of tundra have **permafrost,** which is permanently frozen ground. Such areas are extremely fragile ecologically; when disturbed by such activities as the development of roads, permafrost areas may be permanently changed or may take a very long time to recover. As the environment becomes more harsh, the vegetation grades from dwarf shrubs and grasslike plants to mosses and lichens, and finally to bare rock surfaces with occasional lichens. The extreme tundra occurs in Antarctica, where the major land organism in some areas is a lichen that grows within rocks, just below the surface.

Taiga, or Boreal Forests

The taiga biome includes the forests of the cold climates of high latitudes and high altitudes (see Plate 6b). Taiga forests are dominated by conifers, especially spruce, fir, and larch, and certain kinds of pines. Aspen and birch are important flowering trees. Boreal forests are characterized by dense stands of relatively small trees, typically under 30 m, which form dense shade and make walking difficult. Although boreal forests cover very large areas, relatively few important species of trees occur. There are only about 20 major tree species in North American boreal forests, for example. Boreal forests are among the most economically important biomes as they are the source of much lumber and paper pulp.

The dominant animals of boreal forests include a few large mammals (moose, deer, wolf, and bear), small rodents (squirrels and rabbits), small carnivores (foxes), many insects, and migratory birds, especially waterfowl and carnivorous land birds such as owls and eagles.

Disturbances—especially fires, storms, and outbreaks of insects—are common in the boreal forests. For example, the entire million acres of the Boundary Waters Canoe Area of Minnesota burns over (through numerous small fires) an average of once each century, and individual forest stands are rarely more than 90 years old.

Temperate Forests

Temperate forests occur in climates slightly warmer than those of the boreal forest. These forests occur throughout North America, Eurasia, and Japan, with many genera in common. Dominant vegetation includes tall deciduous trees; typical species are maple, beech, oak, hickory, and chestnut, typically larger in stature than trees of the boreal forest. These forests are important economically for the hardwood trees used for furniture. Temperate deciduous forests are among the biomes most changed by human beings, because they occur in regions long dominated by civilization.

In the temperate deciduous forest, large mammals are less common than in the taiga; herbivores include deer. The low density of large mammals results in part from the deep shade of the forest interior; there is less for ground-dwelling mammals to feed on. The dominant animals are small mammals, including those that live in trees (such as squirrels) and those that feed on soil organisms and small plants (such as mice). Birds and insects are abundant.

Temperate Rain Forests

Temperate rain forests occur under moderate temperature regimes where the rainfall exceeds 250 cm/yr. Such rain forests are rare but spectacular; these are the giant forests. The dominant trees are evergreen conifers. This biome includes the redwood forests of California and Oregon, where the tallest trees in the world exist. It also includes forests of the state of Washington and adjacent Canada, dominated by such large trees as Douglas fir and western cedar. Trees are taller than 70 m and are long lived, with the Douglas fir living more than 400 years.

Temperate rain forests have low diversity of plants and animals, in part because the climatic conditions tend to favor specialized species, in part because the abundant growth of the dominants produces a very deep shade in which few other plants can grow to provide food for herbivores.

This biome is also important economically; redwood, Douglas fir, and western cedar are major North American timber crops.

Temperate Woodlands

With temperate temperature regimes but slightly drier climates than required by the temperate deciduous forests, temperate woodlands occur. Temperate woodlands are dominated by small trees such as pinyon pines and evergreen oaks. The stands tend to be open, with considerable light reaching the ground. Generally pleasant, they are often used for recreation. Small pines are typical of many temperate woodlands and occur from New England south to Georgia and to the Caribbean islands. In these dry woodlands, fires are a common disturbance, to which many species are adapted.

Temperate Shrublands

Under still drier climates temperate shrublands occur. A distinctive feature of this biome is **chaparral**, a miniature woodland dominated by dense stands of shrubs that rarely exceed a few meters in height (Fig. 6.11c). Chaparral occurs in Mediterranean climates—climates with low rainfall that is concentrated in the cool season. Chaparrals are found along the coast of California, in Chile, in South Africa, and in the Mediterranean. There are few large mammals; reptiles and small mammals are characteristic.

The vegetation typically is distinctively aromatic, with pleasant scents of sage; some scientists believe the aromatic compounds are means of competition among the plants. The animals and plants have little economic value at present, but this local biome is important for watersheds and erosion control. Because of the desirable climate for settlement, chaparrals are undergoing rapid change by human activities. The vegetation is adapted to fires; many species regenerate rapidly, and some promote fires by producing abundant fuel in the form of dead twigs and branches. As a result, stands are rarely more than 50 years old. When intense precipitation follows fire, erosion rates can increase to some of the highest known until renewed vegetation again protects the slopes. Managing fires in chaparral is especially important because housing is often near the fire-prone vegetation.

Temperate Grasslands

Temperate grasslands occur in regions too dry for forests and too moist for deserts. A major biome in terms of area covered, these grasslands include the great North American prairies, the steppes of Eurasia, the plains of eastern and southern Africa, and the pampas of South America. Dominant species are grasses and other flowering plants, many of which are perennials with extensively developed roots.

Soils often have a deep organic layer. The highest abundance and the greatest diversity of large mammals are found in grasslands: the wild horses, asses, and antelopes of Eurasia; the once-huge herds of bison that roamed the American western prairies; the kangaroos of Australia; and the antelopes and other large herbivores of Africa. Temperatures are moderate, similar to those of the temperate deciduous forests, and rainfall is usually seasonal.

Tropical Rain Forests

When the average annual temperature exceeds 18°C, tropical biomes occur. In the wettest climates, and those with rainfall well distributed throughout the year, are found the tropical rain forests of South and Central America, northeastern Australia, Indonesia, the Philippines, Borneo, Hawaii, and parts of Malaysia. Species diversity is very high, with hundreds of species of trees within a few square kilometers. Trees are generally very tall, and a distinct layering of vegetation is found. Many species of animals occur; mammals tend to be tree-living but some are ground-dwelling. Insects and other invertebrates are abundant and show a high diversity. Rain forests remain poorly known and many undiscovered species are believed to exist there.

Except for dead organic matter at the surface, soils tend to be very low in nutrients. Most chemical elements (nutrients) are held in the living vegetation, which has evolved to survive in this environment; otherwise rainfall would rapidly remove many chemical elements necessary for life.

Tropical rain forests exist in regions of low disturbances. Despite their great diversity and abundance, tropical rain forests appear to be quite fragile under disturbances.

Tropical Seasonal Forests and Savannahs

Where rainfall is high but very seasonal, tropical seasonal forests occur, as found in India and Southeast Asia, in Africa, and in South and Central America. In areas of even lower rainfall, tropical savannahs—grasslands with scattered trees—are found. These include the savannahs of Africa, which, along with the grasslands, have the greatest abundance of large mammals remaining anywhere in the world. The number of plant species is high.

Tropical Rain Forests—Nature at Its Finest

Earth's tropical rain forests straddle the equator in Africa, Asia, and Latin America, extending roughly 10° latitude on either side. By far the richest, most diverse, and most complex biome on the planet, they are also the least understood by science.

Compared to temperate forests, the number of species in the tropics is astounding. The continental United States has roughly 750 tree species; Costa Rica, half the size of Ohio, has 1200. The entire state of Michigan has 12 species of frogs; one national park in Costa Rica, Corcovado, has 42 species.

The abundance of heat and moisture, two essentials for plant growth, account for the exuberant vegetation in the humid tropics (Fig. A). Enormous trees, many supported by buttressed roots, rise to heights over two hundred feet, spreading branches into lofty canopies. Second and third understories of trees are formed by smaller species and immature individuals of larger species. Woody vines, called lianas, are abundant, some climbing from the dark forest floor up to the sunlight in the upper canopy. Shade-tolerant herbaceous plants form the forest floor, and light-loving epiphytes perched high on tree branches fill ecological niches in an ecosystem where little space is forsaken.

The lush vegetation of a tropical rain forest belies the in-

FIGURE A Tropical rain forest, Costa Rica.

fertility of the soil that lies beneath it. The nutrient base of the forest is in the biomass. Dead plants fall to the forest floor and rapidly decompose, releasing nutrients that are quickly absorbed by living plants, in a closed cycle in which very little is lost.

This botanical backdrop is inhabited by a great diversity of members of the animal kingdom, ranging in size from large mammals such as tapirs and jaguars down to minute insects and microscopic invertebrates. The tropical rain forest, as biologist Marston Bates points out in his book *The Forest and The Sea*, is inhabited by different life forms at successive levels, just as occurs in the ocean. Some mammals, such as deer, peccaries, tapirs, and armadillos are confined to the forest floor, while others such as coatimundis and opossums are at home

on the ground or in the trees. Monkeys, and notably sloths, rarely, if ever, descend from the heights of the forest canopy. This same phenomenon occurs with different species of birds, insects, reptiles, and amphibians.

The plants and animals of the tropical rain forest interact in an infinitely intricate pattern of interrelationships. Animals seek plants for food; in turn insects, birds, and even some mice and bats are pollinators of plants. Some plants depend on birds, mammals, and even fish for seed dispersal.

Because of their complexity, tropical rain forests are very fragile ecosystems, easily disrupted by man. As the biological storehouses of many of Earth's species, they should be treated with the utmost care.

David Perry

Ethnobotany: Linking the Past to the Future

A mong the herbal remedies in the Indian "Witches' Market" in La Paz, Bolivia, may be the raw material from which a valuable Western medicine could someday be made (Fig. A). The knowledge of local plants that indigenous peoples have developed over centuries can be useful to Western scientists in search of new industrial, agricultural, and medicinal products.

This situation has led to the evolution of a relatively new branch of science: ethnobotany, the synthesis of ethnology (the study of cultures) and botany. The new science's most important endeavors are being made in tropical rain forest regions, such as the Amazon Basin, where a vast portion of the world's plant species are found. South American tribes possess a valuable storehouse of knowledge about the multitude of plants in their environment, but both tribes and forests are disappearing so quickly that the need for ethnobotanical research has become urgent.

Examples abound of contributions made to modern society by tribal cultures. Rubber was used extensively by South and Mesoamerican Indians years before Europeans adopted it. Malaria, the most common disease in developing countries, is controlled with quinine, extracted from the bark of a tree first used by Andean Indians. Serpentwood, the root of which has

FIGURE A The "Witches' Market," La Paz, Bolivia.

been used in Hindu medicine for 4000 years, is now used by Western medicine to combat hypertension. Reserpine, one of the active ingredients, is the main source material for tranquilizers. In recent years, the rosy periwinkle of Madagascar has yielded two drugs, vincristine and vinblastine, that are highly effective in the treatment of leukemia and several other forms of cancer. The U.S. National Cancer Institute and the World Health Organization have joined in the search for other tropical plants that could yield similar "miracle drugs."

Ethnobotanist Brian M. Bloom of New York Botanical Garden recently conducted a study of the Chacobo tribe in the Amazon rain forest of Bolivia. To his surprise, he found that the tribe used 90% of the plant species in the surrounding forest for food, fuel, medicine,

construction, and crafts. Although Dr. Bloom catalogued hundreds of ethnobotanical uses of plants, he feels that the same study couldn't be conducted ten years from now. The younger generation of the 280–member tribe is undergoing rapid acculturation and, as tribe elders die off, so does botanical knowledge acquired over a millennium.

As tropical forests and tribal cultures continue to disappear at an accelerating pace, it is at least heartening that some tropical countries are attempting to preserve both. Late twentieth-century ethnobotany may well prove to be an invaluable link between ancient and future knowledge—or in the words of Brian M. Bloom, "the most worthwhile effort for this generation of field botanists."

David Perry

Disturbance, including fires and the impact of herbivory on the vegetation, is common, but may be necessary to maintain these areas as savannahs; otherwise they would revert to woodlands in wetter areas or to shrublands in drier areas. Under still drier climates, the savannahs are replaced by shrublands, characterized by small shrubs, a generally low abundance of vegetation, and a low density of vertebrate animals.

Deserts

Deserts occur where the rainfall is less than 50 cm/yr (see Plate 6a). Although most deserts occur at low latitudes, as the Sahara of North Africa, the southwestern United States and Mexico, and Australia, cold deserts occur in the basin and range area of Utah and Nevada and in parts of western Asia. Most deserts have a considerable amount of specialized vegetation, as well as specialized vertebrate and invertebrate animals. Soils often have abundant nutrients but little or no organic matter and need only water to be very productive. Disturbance is common in the form of occasional fires, occasional cold weather, and sudden, infrequent, and intense rains that cause flooding.

There are relatively few large mammals in deserts. The dominant animals of warm deserts are nonmammalian vertebrates—snakes and reptiles. Mammals are usually small, like the kangaroo mice of North American deserts.

Wetland Biomes

Wetlands include freshwater swamps, marshes, and bogs and saltwater marshes (Fig. 6.11d). All have standing water—the water table is at the surface, and the ground is saturated with water. This creates a special soil environment with very little oxygen, so decay takes place very slowly, and only plants with specialized roots can survive. Bogs— wetlands with a stream input but no surface water outlet—are characterized by floating mats of vegetation. Swamps and marshes are wetlands with surface inlets and outlets.

Dominant plants are small, ranging from small trees, such as the mangoes of warm swamps to black spruce and larch of the north, to shrubs, sedges, and mosses. Small changes in elevation make a very great difference; on slight rises, roots can obtain oxygen and small trees can grow; in lower areas are patches of open water with algae and mosses.

Although wetlands occupy only a small portion of earth's land area, they are very important in the biosphere. In the oxygenless soils, bacteria survive that cannot live in high-oxygen atmospheres. These bacteria carry out important chemical reactions such as production of methane and hydrogen sulfide, which have important effects in the biosphere. Over geologic time, wetland environments produced the vegetation that today is coal. Saltwater marshes are important breeding areas for many oceanic animals and contain many invertebrates. The dominant animals include crabs and such shellfish as clams. Saltwater marshes are therefore an important economic resource.

Dominant animals in freshwater wetlands are many species of insects, birds, and amphibians; few mammals are exclusive inhabitants of this biome. The larger swamps of warm regions are famous for large reptiles and snakes, as well as for a relatively high diversity of mammals where topographic variation allows small upland areas.

Freshwater Biomes

Although freshwater lakes, ponds, rivers, and streams make up a very small portion of Earth's surface, they are critical for our water supply for homes, industry, and agriculture. They are major recreational resources but are easily polluted. Dominant plants are floating algae, referred to as a group as phytoplankton. Along the shores and in shallow areas are rooted flowering plants like water lilies. Animal life is often abundant. The open waters have many small invertebrate animals (collectively called zooplankton)—both herbivores, which feed on the floating algae, and carnivores. Many species of finfish and shellfish are found. Rivers and streams are important in the biosphere as major transporters of materials from the land to the ocean. Freshwaters are economically important to people for their fish, for their often abundant bird life, and for recreation and transportation.

Estuaries—areas at the mouths of rivers where river water mixes with the ocean waters—are rich in nutrients and usually support an abundance of fish. They are important as breeding sites for many commercially important fish and as fishing areas.

Marine Biomes

Intertidal   The intertidal biome includes areas exposed alternately to the air during low tide and to ocean waters during high tide (Fig. 6.11e). The constant movement of waters transports nutrients into and out of these areas, which are usually rich in life and are major economic resources. Large algae are found here, from the giant kelp of temperate and cold waters to the algae of coral reefs in the tropics. Attached shellfish are typically abundant and form a major part of the economic resources. Birds are usually abundant. The nearshore areas are often important breeding grounds for many species of fish and shellfish, often of economic significance. This nearshore part of the oceanic environment is most susceptible to pollution from land sources and, as a major recreational area, is subject to considerable alteration by people who build near it, walk on it, and regularly harvest it. Some of the oldest environmental laws concern the rights to use the resources of this biome, and today some major legal conflicts continue about access to intertidal areas and the harvesting of biological resources.

Open Ocean   Called the pelagic region, the open ocean biome includes the open waters of much of the oceans. These vast areas, generally, are very low in nitrogen and phosphorus—"chemical deserts" with low productivity and a low diversity of algae. Many species of large animals occur, but at low density.

The Benthos   The benthos—"deeps"—is the bottom portion of the oceans. The primary input of food is dead organic matter that falls from above; the waters are too dark for photosynthesis, so no plants grow there.

Upwellings   In upwelling regions the upward flow of waters brings nutrients to the surface, allowing abundant growth of algae and animals that depend on the algae. Upwellings are found at high latitudes, near the Arctic and Antarctic ice sheets, and under certain conditions along the shores of continents.

Hydrothermal Vents   These recently discovered biomes (see Chapter 4) occur in the deep ocean where plate tectonic processes create vents of hot water with a high concentration of sulfur compounds. These sulfur compounds provide an energy basis for chemosynthetic bacteria, which grow in great abundance and support giant clams, worms, and other unusual life forms. Pressures are very high, and temperatures range from the boiling point in the waters of the vents to the frigid (about 4°C) waters of the deep ocean.

SPECIES AND PLACE

One of the questions that is most often discussed is Why are there so many species on Earth? We can provide various explanations, though not a complete answer [8]. According to the competitive exclusion principle, complete competitors cannot coexist; one will always exclude the other. Over a very long period of time, one would expect this exclusion to operate over a large area. Taken to its logical extreme, we could imagine an Earth with very few species—perhaps one green plant on the land, one herbivore to eat it, one carnivore, and one decomposer. If we added four species for the ocean and four for fresh waters, we would have only twelve species on our planet.

Being a little more realistic, we would allow for the necessity of adaptations to major differences in climate and other environmental aspects. Perhaps we could specify 100 major climatic or environmental categories—cold and dry, cold and wet, warm and dry, warm and wet, and so forth. Even so, we would still expect that within each environmental category competitive exclusion would result in few species. Allowing four species per major environmental category gives only 400 species. Yet there are between 3 and 30 million species on Earth. The number is so great, we do not have even a good estimate of it. How can they all coexist?

First, diversity in the environment leads to diversity in species or, put another way, habitat diversity increases species diversity. This diversity can be in space or in time, and can occur at all scales from the global to the local.

Moderate levels of disturbance in an area increase the number of species that can coexist. If the environment is constant, certain species will be favored over all others as a direct consequence of the competitive exclusion principle. Under extreme disturbance, only specialized species can persist. Under moderate environmental disturbance, a greater range of environmental conditions will exist over time and space, allowing a greater number of species to persist per unit area. Studies of tropical rain forests and tropical coral reefs, both noted for high species diversity, show this trend [10].

If competing species evolve to avoid competition and to exploit different niches, those species can divide the resources more finely and more species will be able to coexist. This can occur where, over very long periods of time, environments are relatively constant or follow regular patterns and vary little over time.

Moreover, the presence of one species affects another, so that as the number of species at one trophic level grows, more kinds of species can exist at other trophic levels. For example, ten species of trees will allow more species of herbivores, parasites, tree diseases, soil symbionts, and so forth, than will a single species.

Other reasons for diversity are the effects of plate tectonics, ecological islands, and some consequences of evolution. These are discussed in the next section.

Geology and Diversity

Continental drift provides one of the explanations as to why there are so many species [9]. If Earth had only one continent that had never divided, there would be fewer species.

In each biological realm, evolution is restricted by the available genetic stock; the species that evolved in one realm may have different competitive abilities than those in another. In an area or region with a history of high species diversity, the surviving species have won out over intense competition (Fig. 6.12).

When a land bridge is open, a new round of competition takes place and the best adapted survive. A land bridge is a connection that develops between two previously separated bodies of land. It allows interaction between two biotic provinces. As an example, on the African continent large mammals from Europe and India had mixed and competed with those previously native to Africa, and only certain species have survived. In Australia the marsupials had exploited similar niches but had not been subject to repeated competition from genetically different species. One would, therefore, expect that African mammals could generally outcompete Australian ones, and this has proved true.

Human introductions of species from one realm to another create artificial land bridges that have led to sudden competition between previously isolated species, resulting in endangerment or extinction of native species.

A species introduced into a new geographical area is called an **exotic species.** A species that is native to a particular area and not native elsewhere is called **endemic.** For example, Monterey pine is endemic to the California coast and exotic in New Zealand. A species with a broad distribution, occurring all over the world wherever the environment is appropriate, is called a cosmopolitan species. The moose is a cosmopolitan species of the northern boreal forests and is found in both North America and Europe. The house mouse is cosmopolitan because it occurs many places where people provide a habitat for it. Species that are found almost anywhere are called ubiquitous. Humans are ubiquitous, as are some of our symbionts and parasites; for example *Escherichia coli*, the common bacterium of human intestines, can probably be found almost anywhere on the land and in fresh waters.

Evolution and Diversity

Similar environments eventually lead to the evolution of species with similar adaptations and to

FIGURE 6.12
Development of biogeo-
graphical realms.

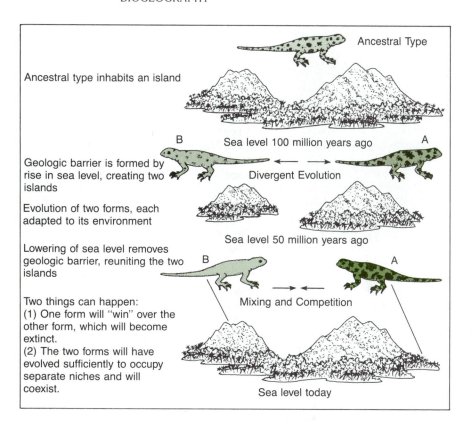

Ancestral Type

Ancestral type inhabits an island

B   Sea level 100 million years ago   A

Geologic barrier is formed by
rise in sea level, creating two
islands

Divergent Evolution

Evolution of two forms, each
adapted to its environment

Sea level 50 million years ago

Lowering of sea level removes
geologic barrier, reuniting the two
islands

B   A

Two things can happen:
(1) One form will "win" over the
other form, which will become
extinct.
(2) The two forms will have
evolved sufficiently to occupy
separate niches and will
coexist.

Mixing and Competition

Sea level today

similar ecosystems. This phenomenon ultimately explains the existence of biomes.

For example, certain plants of the American and African deserts that look similar are not closely related, belonging to different biological families (Fig. 6.13). Although geographically isolated for 180 million years, they have been subjected to similar climates, which imposed similar stresses and opened up similar ecological opportunities. The plants evolved to adapt to these stresses and potentials and have come to look alike and prevail in like habitats—a process known as **convergent evolution.** The ancestral differences between these look-alike plants can be found in their flowers, fruits, and seeds, which are evolutionarily the most conservative (least changing) organs and provide the best clues as to the genetic history of species.

People make use of convergent evolution when they move decorative and useful plants around the world. Cities around the world that lie in similar climates now share many of the same decorative plants (Fig. 6.14). Bougainvillea, a spectacular bright flowering shrub originally native to Southeast Asia, decorates cities as distant as Los Angeles and the capital of Zimbabwe. In New York City and its outlying suburbs, one can find the Norway maple from Europe, the tree of heaven and the gingko tree from China, and such native species as sweetgum, sugar maple, and pin oak.

Another important concept is **divergent evolution.** In divergent evolution, a population is separated, usually by geographic barriers; the separated subpopulations evolve separately but retain some common characteristics. It is now believed that the ostrich, the rhea, and the emu have a common ancestor but evolved separately (Fig. 6.15). In open savannahs and grasslands, a large bird that can run quickly but feed efficiently on small seeds and insects has certain advantages over other or-

(a)

(b)

(c)

FIGURE 6.13
An illustration of the rule of climatic similarity. Given sufficient time and similar climates in two different areas, similar kinds of species and biological communities will tend to occur. (a) The Joshua tree (a) and sahuaro cactus (b) of North America look like the giant euphorbia (c) of East Africa. All three are tall, have green succulent stems that replace the leaves as the major sites of photosynthesis, and have spiny projections, but they are not closely related. The Joshua tree is a member of the agave family, the sahuaro is a member of the cactus family, and the euphorbia is a member of the spurge family. Their similar shapes are a result of evolution under similar desert climates—a process known as convergent evolution.

FIGURE 6.14
A positive effect of introductions of exotic species. Trees from around the world add beauty to many cities. For example, the county courthouse in Santa Barbara, California, is landscaped with trees from five continents. In this photograph, the two tall trees in left center, Norfolk Island pine (left) and bunya bunya trees (center), are native to Australia. The tall palms on the right are native to North America. Smaller trees represent Asia, Africa, and South America.

(a)

(b)

FIGURE 6.15
Divergent evolution. These three large flightless birds evolved from a common ancestor, but are now in widely separated regions of the Earth: (a) the ostrich in Africa, (b) the rhea in South America, and (c) the emu in Australia.

ganisms seeking the same food. Thus these species maintained the same characteristics in widely separated areas.

Island Biogeography

Islands have a special fascination for naturalists. Darwin's visit to the Galapagos Islands gave him his most powerful insight into biological evolution [11]. There he found many species of finches that were related to a single species found elsewhere. On the Galapagos, each species was adapted to a different niche. Darwin suggested that the finches, isolated from other species that filled these niches

(c)

on the continents, eventually separated into a number of groups, each adapted to a more specialized role to exploit unused resources. This process is called **adaptive radiation.** As another example, on the Hawaiian Islands, a finchlike ancestor evolved into several species, including fruit and seed eaters, insect eaters, and nectar eat-

FIGURE 6.16
Evolutionary divergence among honeycreepers in Hawaii. Sixteen species of birds, each with a beak specialized for its food, evolved from a single ancestor to fit ecological niches, which, on the North American continent, were previously filled by other species not closely related to the ancestor. The sixteen species, plus the ancestor, are 1, unknown finchlike colonist from North America; 2–5, *Psittacirostra psittacea, P. kona, P. bailleui, P. cantans;* 6, *Pseudonestor xanthophrys;* 7–9, *Hemignathus wilsoni, H. lucidus, H. procerus;* 10–12, *Loxops parva, L. virens, L. coccines;* 13, *Drepanidis pacifica;* 14, *Vestiana coccinea;* 15, *Himatione sanguinea;* 16, Palmeria dolei; and 17, *Ciridops anna.* (From Cox et al.)

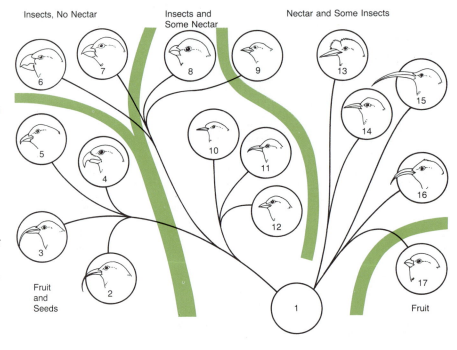

Insects, No Nectar
Insects and Some Nectar
Nectar and Some Insects
Fruit and Seeds
Fruit

ers, each with a beak adapted for its food (Fig. 6.16) [12].

Islands have fewer species than continents. The smaller the island, the fewer the species, as can be seen for the number of reptiles and amphibians in various West Indian islands (Fig. 6.17). The farther the island from the mainland, the fewer are the species [13].

The two sources of new species on an island are migrants from the mainland and the evolution of new species (as with Darwin's finches on the Galapagos). Every species is subject to some risk of extinction. Extinctions can be caused by random fluctuations, predation, disease (parasitism), competition, climatic change, or habitat alteration. The smaller the island, the smaller the population of a particular species that can be supported. Other things being equal, the smaller the population, the greater its risk of extinction.

Thus, over a long time, an island tends to maintain a rather constant number of species—the re-

sult of the rate at which species are added minus the rate at which they become extinct. These numbers follow the curves shown in Figure 6.18. For any island, the number of species of a particular life form (such as birds, mammals, herbivorous insects, or trees) can be predicted from the island's size and distance from the mainland [13].

Ecological Islands Insights gained from studies of real islands have important implications for environmental studies, particularly for the management of any population, species, or ecosystem that is partially or wholly isolated. Almost every park is a biological island for some species. A small city park, occupying a square between streets, may be an island for trees and squirrels. Even a large national park is an island. For example, the great wildlife parks of eastern and southern Africa are becoming islands of natural landscape surrounded by human settlements. Lions and other great cats exist in the parks as isolated populations, no

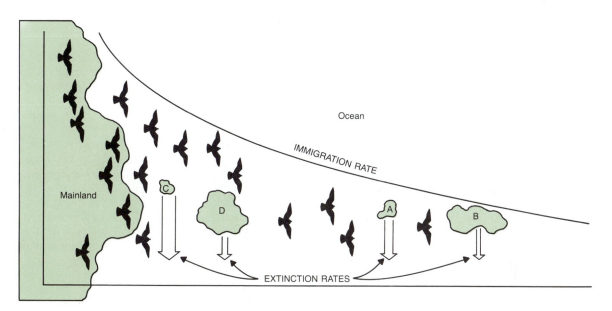

FIGURE 6.17

Idealized relation between an island's size, its distance from the mainland, and its number of species. The nearer to the mainland an island is, the more likely it is to be found by an individual. Thus, the nearer an island to the mainland, the higher the rate of immigration. The larger the island, the larger the population it can support, and the chance of persistence of a species increases. Small islands have a higher rate of extinction. The average number of species, therefore, depends on the rate of immigration and the rate of extinction. Thus, a small island near the mainland may have the same number of species as a large island far from the mainland. The thickness of the arrow represents the magnitude of the rate. (Modified from MacArthur and Wilson.)

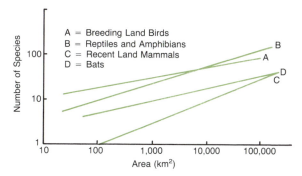

FIGURE 6.18

Islands have fewer species than mainlands, and the larger the island, the greater the number of species. This general rule is shown by a graph of the number of species of birds, reptiles and amphibians, land mammals, and bats for islands in the Caribbean. (Modified from Wilcox.)

longer able to roam freely and mix over large areas. Other examples are islands of uncut forests created by logging operations, and oceanic islands, where intense fishing has isolated parts of fish populations.

Our management of endangered species and of forests, fisheries, and wildlife can benefit by the study of island biogeography. The knowledge gained in such study is being put to use in a Brazilian project originated by the U.S. World Wildlife Fund. Logging operations in the Brazilian Amazon are being carried out so as to leave uncut islands of many sizes, from a few hectares to hundreds of square kilometers. The intent of the experiment is to learn the minimum size of forest island that is adequate to protect the forest's species [14].

Size and Survival What is a sufficiently large ecological island to guarantee the survival of a species? The size varies with the species, but can be estimated. Some islands that seem large to us are too small for species we wish to preserve. For example, a preserve was set aside in India in an attempt to reintroduce the Indian lion into an area where it had been eliminated by hunting and changing patterns of land use. In 1957, a male and two females were introduced into a 95 km^2 preserve in the Chakia forest—the Chandraprabha Sanctuary [15]. The introduction was carried out carefully and the population counted annually. There were 4 lions in 1958, 5 in 1960, 7 in 1962, and 11 in 1965, after which they disappeared and were never seen again. Why? Although 95 km^2 seems large to us, male Indian lions have territories of 130 km^2. Within such a territory, females and young also live. A population that would persist for a long time would have a number of such territories, and an adequate preserve would require 640–1300 km^2. Various reasons were suggested for the disappearance of the lions, including poisoning and shooting by villagers, but regardless of the immediate cause, a much larger area than was set aside was required for long-term persistence of the lions.

Using genetic factors, it has been estimated that for a specific population at least 50 breeding adults of any animal should be maintained even for a small number of years if genetic problems of small populations are to be avoided and the chance of extinction kept acceptably low [16, 17]. A population with 50 breeding adults will have many non-breeding individuals, including newborn, young and premature, and old post-breeding. Thus several hundred individuals are, as a rule of thumb, a minimum safe number for a population. To maintain a population for a long period of time, 500 or more individuals are preferable in order to avoid problems of low genetic variability [17].

The size of parks and preserves for rare predatory birds and mammals is a particularly difficult issue because these populations require large areas. Can we ever set aside enough space for our endangered species? We will return to this question when we discuss natural resource management in Chapter 8.

HOW PEOPLE AFFECT BIOGEOGRAPHY

Since the beginning of the age of exploration, human beings have been conducting a gigantic experiment in biogeography, intentionally and unintentionally moving many species of animals and plants around the world.

The geography of life is important to people. The spread of disease by the introduction of new species by people is not limited to the chestnut. After the arrival of Europeans in North and South America, European diseases, particularly smallpox and chicken pox, caused fatal epidemics among native Americans. As Lewis and Clark traveled by boat up the Mississippi and Missouri rivers in 1806, they passed many abandoned villages; their native guides told them the inhabitants had died from these new diseases [18].

Changing the geography of life is one of the major ways we are changing the world. Since the beginning of agriculture, people have carried with them their favorite crops and domestic animals as they settled new territories. In Great Britain, for example, the only native foods—things that Great Britain's first people would have found there—are nuts, berries, and wild game. Every other food grown in Britain has come from other parts of the world. The discovery of new foods, including the New World's maize and potato, led to intentional introductions that greatly benefited human beings and were an important factor in nineteenth-century human population growth in parts of Europe.

Many major crops have been transported wherever they would grow. For example, citrus fruits, such as oranges, originated in southern China, but are now grown in mediterranean climates worldwide. Wheat's wild relatives are from the Middle East and northern Africa; corn's wild relatives are from Mexico and South America. Corn and wheat are now grown on every continent except Antarctica and in all temperate climates where people live. Barley, a native of North Africa, is a $100 million a year crop in California. Coffee, a native of the Middle East, is a major export from 40 countries as widely separated as Kenya and Brazil [19].

Humans continue the process of introductions today. A recent example is the introduction of live turkeys from North America (where they are native) to mainland China. In 1979 several hundred fertile turkey eggs were sent from Canada to the Peking Animal Husbandry Bureau, and by 1984 turkeys had become a significant food item.

While many of these intentional introductions have been of great benefit to human beings, others have had disastrous effects. When introductions are successful, they are often extremely successful, as with many crops, but it is probably not an exaggeration to say that most of the species artificially introduced into new areas by human beings have had negative effects.

People have transported pests worldwide—usually unintentionally. Mice, rats, and many weeds have come along for the ride whenever people have migrated to new areas. Since the Renaissance the great human migrations have brought European rats (known as the Norway rat) to every continent and many islands. Many of the familiar roadside flowers and weeds in North America were transported as seeds mixed in with crop seeds or carried in the mud on the hooves of cows and horses.

Intentional introductions of animals as pets or for economic benefit or visual pleasure have often had disastrous consequences. The Asian walking catfish was recently introduced as a pet in Florida; now it has become wild, spread widely, been impossible to eradicate or control, and is becoming so abundant as to threaten with extinction many native freshwater fish species in Florida.

The gypsy moth is another example of a well-intentioned introduction that has undesirable effects. The moth was introduced into Cape Cod, Massachusetts, at the turn of the twentieth century, in order to serve as a basis of an American silk industry, but it escaped and is now a major pest of eastern U.S. forests.

Why do some introduced species seem to become very abundant pests? In general, organisms in nature have persisted together for a long time and have evolved together so that predator, parasite, prey, competitors, and symbionts have had time to adjust to one another. An introduced species rarely brings its own predators and usually brings some of its parasites. If it is a successful competitor, it typically undergoes a population explosion free from its natural enemies; therefore the population increase is more rapid and lasts longer than would ordinarily occur. For example, in 1839 the Asian water buffalo was introduced as a beast of burden into northern Australia, an area with no native grazers on floodplain vegetation and no major predators of large mammals. The water buffalo arrived with only a few of its natural parasites. For example, only 11 species of parasitic worms occur in the Australian water buffalo instead of the 77 species found in Asia. Lacking major disease or predation, and in a suitable climate with suitable food, the water buffalo underwent a population explosion that seriously affected the vegetation. The population increased beyond the capacity of its food resources, resulting in several large die-offs, during which many animals died from slow starvation. In Asia, death would have come more quickly, as weakened individuals would have been easy targets for predators and parasites. This slow form of death is much worse for the population's habitat, because slowly starving animals continue to eat all possible vegetation. The vegetation was greatly affected; in some areas only bare soil is found in the dry season [20]. The Australian water buffalo population persists today but is less stable, fluctuating widely over time, in comparison to the populations of its native Asia.

Often the parasites brought by an introduced species attack native species, as the fungal parasite of the European chestnut attacked the American chestnut and more recently, as an Asian fungus disease of elm trees (called Dutch elm disease because the introductions came via Europe) was introduced into North America and has destroyed the American elm over most of its range.

If an introduced species is successful, it is a superior competitor, and the competitive exclusion principle begins to operate. The introduced species increases rapidly and as a secondary consequence threatens native competitors with extinction.

How can introductions be done successfully, avoiding the negative effects? First, introduce only those species that are truly useful or important. Second, isolate a population and keep it isolated for several generations to eliminate undesirable parasites. Third, study the species's niche and its population dynamics.

An example of a careful and (so far) successful introduction is that of dung beetles into Australia. Domestic cattle and sheep were brought to Australia by the early British settlers, and large areas are devoted to grazing. There is no native equivalent of the dung beetle, which buries cattle droppings in the soil, speeding up their decomposition. A serious problem developed in Australia because cattle dung was not decaying rapidly enough and was accumulating over the pasturelands. Here was an unoccupied niche.

The Australian government scientists obtained dung beetles from Africa and brought them to an intermediate location where they were raised through several generations to eliminate parasites that could spread to other animals. Only after several generations were the beetles introduced. The care taken in this case should be used with all introductions.

If we are to shepherd our planet successfully in the future, we must choose our introductions of new species much more carefully than we have in the past, and we must learn to reduce, if not eliminate, our unintentional transportation of organisms.

SUMMARY

Biogeography is the study of the spatial patterns of life. Knowledge of these patterns and their causes is very important to issues concerning the biosphere, to the management of our living resources—especially endangered species, agriculture and forest management, management of wildlife—and to ourselves, especially for our health but also to maintain a functioning and pleasing environment. Changing the geography of life is one of the major ways we are changing the world. There are millions of species on Earth, and it is an old question why there are so many. We gain insight into this question by study of life's geography.

The geography of life—the distribution of living things on Earth—has an important role in the global cycling of chemical elements and in Earth's pattern of energy exchange with the solar system. The geography of life is a consequence of several factors, including the history of the continents (plate tectonics); the origin of species; the creation and destruction of "bridges" between geographically isolated areas; local climate, topography, and substrate; and ecological interactions among species (competition, predation, and parasitism).

The large-scale changes in the environment have created biotic provinces, where one set of organisms has been genetically isolated from others for a very long period.

Similar environments lead to the evolution of similar kinds (in external form and function, but not in genetic heritage or internal makeup) of biota and biological communities. This is known as the rule of climatic similarity. When this occurs in several biotic provinces, the result is known as convergent evolution.

The rule of climatic similarity also leads to the concept of the biome. A biome is a kind of ecosystem; similar kinds of ecosystems occur in similar environments. Organisms in one geographic region of a biome may not be closely related genetically to those in another region of the same biome.

The geography of edible and otherwise useful plants and animals has affected every human culture and society. Since domestication of plants and animals began, human beings have transported and introduced exotic species into new areas.

The study of the geography of life can help us to decide which transplants of species will be beneficial and which may be disastrous. Unfortunately, this knowledge has been little used in the past in planning introductions of exotic species.

When we introduce species into new locations, we alter relationships among organisms—predation, parasitism, competition, symbiosis—that have evolved over very long periods, and this sudden alteration has great effects. As a result, most introductions of species into new areas have negative effects. Sometimes the species fails to survive (it becomes locally extinct); sometimes it becomes so abundant it becomes a pest and may cause the extinction or loss in abundance of desirable native species.

To be successful, introductions must be done carefully, making use of our knowledge of ecology and biogeography, and the process should include temporary isolation and study of the species to be introduced.

What lives where depends on climate, substrate, ecological attributes of a species, biological interactions, and history.

Biogeography affects the environment; the geographic patterns of life can influence Earth's energy exchange, its climate, and its chemical cycles.

Islands have special biogeographic features; we can use the insights gained from studying real islands to manage ecological islands. An ecological island is an area genetically isolated from other islands containing closely related species. Commonly, climate causes ecological islands, but many environmental factors, including artificial ones, can create ecological islands.

Islands have fewer species than mainlands. The smaller the island, the fewer the number of species. The farther an island is from the mainland, the fewer the species. There is a tendency for the number of species on an island to become more or less constant over time. The number of species depends both on the island size and on its distance from the mainland. Species may come and go, but the total number tends to remain constant. These insights are especially helpful in management.

STUDY QUESTIONS

1 Why are introductions of species so often unsuccessful?

2 What is a geological barrier, and why is this concept important in the geography of living things?

3 Other things being equal, on which kind of planet would you expect a greater diversity of species: (a) a planet with intense tectonic activities or (b) a tectonically dead planet? (Remember that tectonics refers to the geological processes that involve the movement of tectonic plates and continents, processes that lead to mountain building, and so forth.)

4 You conduct a survey of city parks. What relationship would you expect to find between the number of species of trees and the size of the parks?

5 What is meant by the statement "Every nature preserve must be managed as if it were an island"?

6 Why are no land mammals native to New Zealand?

7 What are the major factors that determine which species live in a particular location on a continent?

8 Riding in a balloon, you become lost in the clouds and eventually land on an island. The island is characterized by rolling hills with low, dense vegetation. The plants have thick leaves that give off strong, pleasant smells. Are you sorry that you forgot to take your umbrella?

9 What are the consequences of geographical isolation?

10 In Jules Verne's classic novel *The Mysterious Island*, a group of Americans find themselves on an isolated volcanic island inhabited by kangaroos and large rodents closely related to the agoutis of South America. Why is this situation unrealistic? What would make this co-occurrence possible?

11 Why does desert occur *west* of the Andes in Chile when the desert is *east* of the Rocky Mountains in North America?

12 Why is tundra found both in the far north and on mountaintops? What differences, if any, would you expect to find between those two kinds of tundra, *arctic* and *alpine*?

13 What is the difference between a biome and a biotic province?

14 List three ways that people have altered the distribution of living things.

15 From the perspective of biogeography, why do people attach so much importance to conservation of tropical rain forests?

FURTHER READING

AGENCY FOR INTERNATIONAL DEVELOPMENT. 1985. *U. S. strategy on the conservation of biological diversity: An interagency task force report to Congress.* Washington, D. C.

HUNT, C. B. 1967. *The physiography of the United States.* San Francisco: W. H. Freeman.

MacARTHUR, R. H. 1972. *Geographical ecology.* New York: Harper & Row.

MacARTHUR, R. H., and WILSON, E. O. 1967. *The theory of island biogeography.* Princeton, N.J.: Princeton University Press.

MYERS, N. 1983. *A wealth of wild species.* Boulder, Colo.: Westview Press.

NITECKI, M. H., ed. 1984. *Extinctions.* Chicago: University of Chicago Press.

OLDFIELD, M. L. 1984. *The value of conserving genetic resources.* Washington, D. C.: U. S. Department of Interior.

PIELOU, E. C. 1979. *Biogeography.* New York: Wiley.

WILSON, E. O. 1985. The biological diversity crisis. *BioScience* 35: 700–706.

7

Human Populations

- [ ] The human population issue is the fundamental environmental issue because most current environmental damages result directly or indirectly from the very great number of people.
- [ ] The age structure of a population affects its birth, death, and growth rates, its impact on environment, and its social and economic status.
- [ ] All the growth in human populations has occurred with little or no change in the maximum lifetime.
- [ ] Death rate increases with crowding; the greater the population density, the greater the crowding effects.
- [ ] The current average rate of growth of Earth's human population is approximately 1.7%/yr., which translates to a 41–year population doubling time.
- [ ] The current human population represents something unprecedented in the history of the world: never before has one species had such a great impact on the environment in such a short time and continued to increase at as rapid a rate.
- [ ] Countries with a high standard of living move more quickly to a lower birth rate than countries with a low standard of living.
- [ ] One of the remarkable things about our species is that our technology keeps increasing the carrying capacity of the environment for us. Because we cannot predict the impact of future technologies, we cannot be certain what the future carrying capacity of Earth for people will be.
- [ ] Considerable lags in the responses of human populations to changes in birth and death rates occur because of age structure of the population.
- [ ] Modern medical practices and improved supplies of necessities have decreased death rates and accelerated the net rate of human population growth.
- [ ] The demographic transition is a three-stage pattern of change in birth and death rates as a country is transformed from underdeveloped to developed.

JOHN ELI MILLER FAMILY

When John Eli Miller died on his farm in Middle-field, Ohio, in 1961, he was the head of the largest family in the United States. He was survived by 5 children, 61 grandchildren, 338 great-grandchildren, and 6 great-great grandchildren. Within his lifetime, John Miller had witnessed a population explosion. Glenn D. Everett noted in the *Population Bulletin* that it was remarkable that the explosion started with a family of just 7 children—not all that unusual for nineteenth-century America. During most of his long life, John Miller's family was not unusually large. It is just that he lived long enough to find out what simple multiplication can do, wrote Everett [1]. While the number of children born to John Miller or each of his descendants was not unusually large, the death rate among infants, children, and young adults was very small compared with the history of most human populations. Of 7 children born to John Miller, 5 survived him; of 63 grandchildren, 61 survived him; and of 341 great-grandchildren (born to 55 married grandchildren—an average of slightly more than 6 children per parent), only 3 had died. All 6 great-great grandchildren were healthy (Fig. 7.1).

THE PROPHECY OF MALTHUS

John Miller's family illustrates a major factor in our modern population explosion: Modern technology and its medical practices and the supply of food, clothing, and shelter have decreased death rates and accelerated the net rate of growth [1].

Almost 200 years ago Thomas Malthus wrote the following key phrases: "I think I may fairly make two postulates. . . . First, that food is necessary to the existence of man. . . . Second, that the passion between the sexes is necessary and will remain nearly in its present state" [2]. The problem as Malthus saw it was that, assuming his two postulates, "the power of population is indefinitely greater than the power in the Earth to produce subsistence for man. Population, when unchecked, increases in a geometric ratio. Subsistence increases only in an arithmetical ratio." Malthus' *geometric* growth is the same as exponential growth (Chapter 3), which is a constant percentage increase in the population.

Malthus' projections of the ultimate fate of humankind were dire—as pessimistic a picture as that painted by the most extreme environmentalists of our own time. The power of population

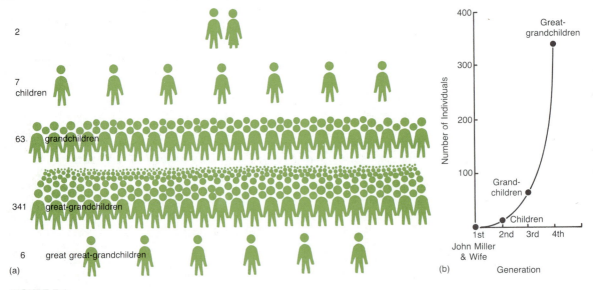

FIGURE 7.1
(a) A simplified family tree of the John Eli Miller family. (b) The population explosion of the John Eli Miller family shown in graphic form.

growth is so great, he wrote, that "premature death must in some shape or other visit the human race. The vices of mankind are active and able ministers of depopulation . . . but should they fail . . . sickly seasons, epidemics, pestilence and plague, advance in terrific array, and sweep off their thousands and ten thousands." And worst of all, should these fail, "gigantic famine stalks in the rear, and with one mighty blow, levels the population with the food of the world" [2].

Critics of Malthus have continued to point out that his predictions have yet to come true; whenever things have looked bleak, our technological society has found a way out. They have argued that in the future our technologies will continue to save us from a Malthusian fate. Who is correct? While some believe Earth can support many more people than it does now, in the long run there must be an upper limit. The basic issue that confronts us is, How can we achieve a constant world population, or at least halt the increase in the population, in a way that is most beneficial to most people? This is undoubtedly one of the most important questions that faces—or has ever faced—humanity. To find the answer, we must apply the basic principles of environmental studies discussed in earlier chapters. Like every other biological species, humans can be characterized as a group of populations, each with rates of birth, death, and growth and with a population structure, which is the relative proportion or the number of individuals of each age and sex. Furthermore, we as a species depend on the biosphere and ecosystems for our existence. We cannot escape these constraints; we are part of the biosphere and must live within its laws.

Indeed, the story of John Eli Miller's family is our story. In the third quarter of the twentieth century the most dramatic increase in the history of the human population has occurred. In merely 25 years the human population of the world increased from 2.5 billion to over 4.5 billion (Fig. 7.2) [3] . Although the average rate of growth was only 2%/ yr., when applied to a very large number it led to huge increases in a short time. It has not always been this way for our species, however. Although new fossil finds continue to push back the dates for the origin of *Homo sapiens*, it is clear that for most of human history the total population was small and had an extremely low long-term rate of increase compared with today's population.

In some ways, the human population issue is *the* issue of the environment, because most current environmental damages result from the very high number of people. When there were few people on Earth and technology was limited, human impact was local. In that situation, the overuse of a local resource had little or no large or long-lasting effects. Human effects were like those of the herds of grazing mammals in the African plains and savannahs. The herds seek out the richest, most nutritious vegetation in a local area and devour it all. When they are done the ground looks devastated; no live vegetation can be seen above the trampled soil. But the animals move on to a new patch, and the old one recovers. Roots send up new shoots. Runners grow in from adjacent areas.

As long as people were few, we could treat our environment in this way, and we did. The fundamental problem now is that there are so many people that we can no longer treat our impacts as local and isolated. Our old habits, however, do not change quickly.

The fact there are so many of us means that we affect the environment in old ways, but with quantitatively greater effects. In addition, we are so inventive with our technology that we change Earth in new ways; and each of us has potentially much more power over the environment than people did before. Thus any of us can create a change that only a large population could have created before, and we can do this in new ways, such as adding novel chemicals to the environment.

As we discussed in Chapter 1, disagreements can center about what *is* or about what we *should* do—what value we attach to what is and what actions we will accept. Both kinds of disagreements are involved in the human population issues. In this chapter we will present the current situation about the human population and the environment and what our choices are. With this information, each of us must decide what we believe should be done. This is a matter beyond science, involving religious, ethical, philosophical, aesthetic, and cultural beliefs. Let no one minimize or disparage the importance of either part of the human population dilemma.

BASIC CONCEPTS

To understand the severity of the population problem, one must understand certain basic concepts. These include how age structure changes as population changes and how changes in an age structure affect the future of a population; what has happened to birth and death rates, what is the demographic transition, and what is total fertility; how our population has grown although maximum human lifetime has not increased; how average life expectancy is changing. We will learn that it is not merely how many of us there are, but what fraction of us are men or women; what fraction of us are young, adult, and old; and what fraction of us are working and what fraction are dependents, not working.

The study of these concepts is called human demography. **Demography** means the study of populations. Demographers count a population (determine the actual size at some time) and attempt to project changes into the future.

We will also consider relationships between human population and the environment, including why death rate increases with crowding; why death rates will increase if we do not decrease birth rates, and what kinds of causes of death can be expected; what simple ways can decrease birth rates; and how improved economy is correlated with decreased birth, death, and growth rates.

From all of these, we will get a sense of the dynamics of our own population—how it changes with time and has never been stagnant in recent history. We will learn where our population has been, what its geographic patterns are today, where it can go in the future, and what are and are not solutions to our human population dilemma.

In discussing what *is*, we will attempt to answer the questions: How many people are there? How rapidly is the human population growing? How much more can we expect it to grow in the next 5, 10, 50, 100 years? What impact does the current population have and what impact will future populations have? The most controversial question is, Is there an environmental "carrying capacity" for our population, and if so, what is it?

The answer is clouded by lag effects (what we do now may not show up for many years), by incomplete understanding of ecosystems and the biosphere, and by our inability to project how future changes in technology might alter our answers.

Growth Rate

All the growth in human populations has occurred with little or no change in the maximum lifetime. What has changed are birth rates, death rates, growth rates, age structure, and life expectancy.

How rapidly a population changes depends on the growth rate, which, as we learned in Chapter 3, is the difference between the birth rate and death rate. Rates for human populations are often stated as a crude rate—the rate per 1000 individuals—rather than as a percent—the rate per 100 individuals. The base of 1000 is used for convenience. For example, in 1981 in the United States the crude death rate was 9, meaning that 9 of every 1000 people died; as a percent, the rate was 0.9. The crude birth rate is the number of births per 1000 individuals in a population. In 1981, the crude

FIGURE 7.2
Growth in the world's human population from A.D. 1000 to A.D. 2000. The total population is given below each date; the pie charts show the approximate percentage of total population in major geographic areas (1960 and earlier are shown with fewer geographic categories). The increases in the sizes of the pies illustrate the increases in total population. Asia provided about the same percentage of the population in A.D. 1000 (60%) that it did in 1975 (58%) and that it is estimated it will provide in A.D. 2000 (60%). Europe and Russia contained approximately 17% in A.D. 1000 and 18% in 1975, but it is estimated that this will drop to 13% by A.D. 2000. (Data for 1975 and 2000 from Council on Environmental Quality and the Department of State and Haub; remaining data from Desmond.)

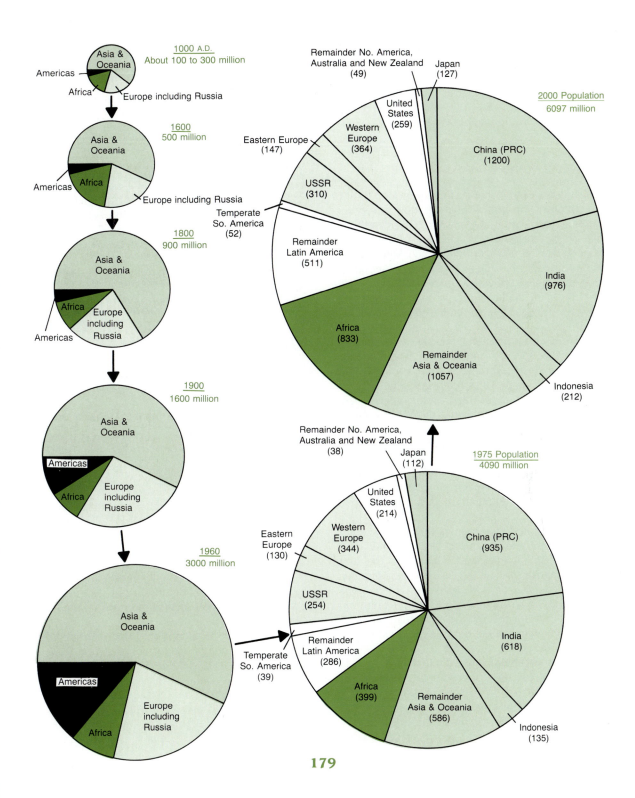

1000 A.D.
About 100 to 300 million

Asia & Oceania
Americas
Africa
Europe including Russia

1600
500 million

Asia & Oceania
Americas
Africa
Europe including Russia

1800
900 million

Asia & Oceania
Africa
Americas
Europe including Russia

1900
1600 million

Asia & Oceania
Americas
Africa
Europe including Russia

1960
3000 million

Asia & Oceania
Americas
Africa
Temperate So. America (39)
Europe including Russia

2000 Population
6097 million

Remainder No. America, Australia and New Zealand (49)
Japan (127)
United States (259)
Western Europe (364)
Eastern Europe (147)
USSR (310)
Temperate So. America (52)
Remainder Latin America (511)
Africa (833)
Remainder Asia & Oceania (1057)
China (PRC) (1200)
India (976)
Indonesia (212)

1975 Population
4090 million

Remainder No. America, Australia and New Zealand (38)
Japan (112)
United States (214)
Western Europe (344)
Eastern Europe (130)
USSR (254)
Remainder Latin America (286)
Africa (399)
Remainder Asia & Oceania (586)
China (PRC) (935)
India (618)
Indonesia (135)

179

birth rate in the United States was 16, that is, the average for the entire population was 16 births per 1000 individuals [3]. The crude growth rate in 1981 for the United States was therefore 16 minus 9, or 7; so that for every 1000 people at the beginning of 1981, there were 1007 at the end of the year.

Death Rate

The first important change in human population growth since the industrial revolution was a decrease in the death rate. We can get an idea of the change by comparing a modern industrialized country such as Switzerland, which has a crude death rate of 9 per 1000, with a developing nation such as Bangladesh, which has a crude death rate of 17. Modern medicine, agriculture and technology have decreased early death rates.

Epidemic and Chronic Diseases Human diseases can be grouped into chronic and epidemic diseases. A chronic disease is always present in a population; it occurs in a relatively small but relatively constant percentage. Some cancers are chronic diseases. An epidemic disease is usually rare but undergoes outbreaks during which a large fraction of the population is infected. The plague, measles, mumps, and cholera are examples of epidemic diseases. One of the major successes of modern sanitation and medicine has been the control and essential elimination of some epidemic diseases.

One of the first to recognize the difference between epidemic and chronic diseases was John Graunt, a British merchant who made the first modern English study of the causes of death. In his work titled *Natural and Political Observations Made Upon the Bill of Mortality* (1662), Graunt examined the death records for more than 20 years in several parishes of London. He observed that of the 229,250 deaths, "there died of acute diseases (the plague excepted) about 50,000 or 1/9 parts ... about 70,000 died of chronical diseases" [4] (Fig. 7.3).

Deaths caused by a particular disease are often expressed by a cause-specific death rate, which is the number of deaths from a specific cause divided

(9)

The Diseases, and Casualties this year being 1632.

Cause	Number	Cause	Number
Abortive, and Stilborn	445	Jaundies	43
Affrighted	1	Jawfaln	8
Aged	628	Impostume	74
Ague	43	Kil'd by several accidents	46
Apoplex, and Meagrom	17	King's Evil	38
Bit with a mad dog	1	Lethargie	2
Bleeding	3	Livergrown	87
Bloody flux, scowring, and flux	348	Lunatique	5
Brused, Issues, sores, and ulcers,	28	Made away themselves	15
Burnt, and Scalded	5	Measles	80
Burst, and Rupture	9	Murthered	7
Cancer, and Wolf	10	Over-laid, and starved at nurse	7
Canker	1	Pallie	25
Childbed	171	Piles	1
Chrisomes, and Infants	2268	Plague	8
Cold, and Cough	55	Planet	13
Colick, Stone, and Strangury	56	Pleurisie, and Spleen	36
Consumption	1797	Purples, and spotted Feaver	38
Convulsion	241	Quinsie	7
Cut of the Stone	5	Rising of the Lights	98
Dead in the street, and starved	6	Sciatica	1
Dropsie, and Swelling	267	Scurvey, and Itch	9
Drowned	34	Suddenly	62
Executed, and prest to death	18	Surfet	86
Falling Sickness	7	Swine Pox	6
Fever	1108	Teeth	470
Fistula	13	Thrush, and Sore mouth	40
Flocks, and small Pox	531	Tympany	13
French Pox	12	Tissick	34
Gangrene	5	Vomiting	1
Gout	4	Worms	27
Grief	11		

Christened { Males—4994 / Females—4590 / In all —9584 } Buried { Males —4932 / Females—4603 / In all —9535 } Whereof, of the Plague-8

Increased in the Burials in the 122 Parishes, and at the Pesthouse this year 993
Decreased of the Plague in the 122 Parishes, and at the Pesthouse this year, 266

C   7 In

FIGURE 7.3
John Graunt's summary of the number of people dying of various causes in parishes near London in 1632. He studied similar records for a 20-year period. (From Graunt.)

by the total number of deaths, usually expressed as deaths per 100,000 deaths. For example, John Graunt found that out of 229,250 deaths, 1797 people died of consumption (tuberculosis). The cause-specific death rate for consumption (tuberculosis) was 1797 divided by 229,250 times 100,000, or 784. (This is the same as saying that 0.78% of deaths were due to tuberculosis.)

Although the causes of death in modern societies have changed dramatically, nations vary considerably in the relative importance of causes of death. The death rate decrease that occurred in the first industrialized countries was due first to the control of epidemic or acute disease; only more recently did the death rate from chronic infectious diseases begin to decrease, and only in the last few decades have significant strides been made in decreasing deaths due to chronic noninfectious ailments, such as heart disease. According to the Population Reference Bureau, in 1900 the cause-specific death rate for pneumonia-bronchitis-influenza in the United States was 17,200 (17.2% of all deaths) while the rate for heart disease was 7,100 (7.1%). In 1976, the rate for pneumonia-bronchitis-influenza was 3,600 (3.6%) while the rate for heart disease was 38,000 (38%) [5].

Other terms used in reference to disease are: *incidence rate, prevalence rate,* and *case fatality rate.* The incidence rate is the number of people contracting a disease during a time period, usually measured per 100 people. The prevalence rate is the number of people afflicted by a disease at a particular time. The case fatality rate is the percentage of people who die once they contract a disease. All of these have to do with morbidity, which is a general term meaning the occurrence of disease and illness in a population [5].

Crowding   The number of human deaths and the death rate increase with crowding. This is as true today as in the past; the greater the population, the more important crowding effects will become. There are several reasons for this. First, the greater the population density, the more deaths per unit area will occur with a natural disaster that devastates an area. For example, in 1972 and 1974, major floods occurred in Bangladesh, which occupies floodplains and coastal plains and coastal regions that flood naturally. With a population density of 645 persons per square kilometer, for each kilometer flooded a high number of people died. By contrast, a similar flood on the almost uninhabited desert coast of Chile would kill few persons.

Second, the greater the population density, the fewer refuges from disasters there will be, and the smaller the fraction of the population that find safety. Again using Bangladesh as an example, when floods threaten there is little room for people to move inland. In contrast, floods in the early 1980s from summer hurricanes along the Gulf coast of the United States resulted in relatively few deaths. People from Galveston and Houston, Texas, were able to find shelter several hundred kilometers to the interior. In this case, population density was not the only factor: The means and funds for transportation were more readily available in Texas than in Bangladesh.

Third, under crowded conditions, the chance of an outbreak of an epidemic disease increases, disease spreads more rapidly, and the mortality from disease increases. The chance that a carrier of a disease will be present is greater. As crowding occurs, the limit of sanitation facilities is reached; eventually there is insufficient clean water for drinking and washing and for toilets. Because groundwater and soil are the ultimate sink for human wastes, they may reach the limit of their ability to take hazardous wastes.

Furthermore, people living in crowded conditions tend to be in poorer health and succumb more readily to epidemic diseases, increasing the percentages that contract disease and that die from it. Cholera, for example, produces extreme vomiting and diarrhea for several days. A person who is healthy and does not become dehydrated can survive, although modern medical aids, including intravenous injections of saline solution, are sometimes necessary. If a person who is already sick or malnourished contracts cholera, however, cholera could kill that person. Or a previously unhealthy person may die at a level of dehydration lower than that which would kill a previously healthy person.

Famine   Famine has been a major cause of death throughout human history. For example, an estimated one-sixth of the people in Sweden died during the 1690s after several years of poor crops. The Irish potato famine (1845–49), brought on by a potato disease, caused more than 800,000 deaths in Ireland and led to a large emigration to North America. Some estimate that 19 million died in India between 1890 and 1910 as the result of famines [6]. In the 1970s and 1980s a major famine occurred in Ethiopia and other areas of Africa near the Sahel. This famine and its causes will be discussed in more detail in Chapter 10.

Birth Rates

There are a number of terms and concepts used to describe fertility and births. *Fertility* refers to pregnancy; *birth rate* refers to the number actually born. The *general fertility rate* is the number of live births expected in a year per 1000 women aged 15 to 44 years, which are considered to be the childbearing years. The *age-specific fertility rate* is the number of births expected per year among a specific age group of women in a population.

One of the most important concerns about fertility and birth is the average number of children expected to be born to a woman during her lifetime; this is known as the total fertility rate. The TFR is calculated from current conditions, using the age-specific fertility rates for the current year. For example, the TFR for 1995 will be calculated by assuming that as a woman ages from 15 to 44, she would first have the 1995 15–year-old fertility rate, then the 1995 16–year-old fertility rate, then the 1995 17–year-old fertility rate, and so on. The TFR is important in population projections. Figure 7.4 shows the TFRs in the United States from 1930 to 1980. The TFR peaked at about 3.8 in the late 1950s and by 1980 was about 1.8. This means that

a woman who was 15 in the late 1950s would have been expected to have about four children by the time she reached 44, while a 15–year-old woman in 1980 will be expected to have only about two children in her lifetime. A population that maintained a TFR of 3.8 over a long time would increase rapidly, while a population that had a TFR of 1.8 over a long time would decline. One of the problems in making population projections is that the birth and fertility rates vary over time in ways that are only partially predictable.

Replacement level fertility is the TFR required for a population to remain constant. A population that achieves replacement level fertility will continue to grow for several generations—about 50 to 200 years. This is called population momentum or population lag effect and is important in discussing zero population growth. How does this momentum occur? On the day that women currently alive reach replacement level fertility, the age structure is still weighted toward the young. Because previous fertility has been greater than required for replacement levels, there are more women of child-bearing age than would occur in a completely constant population. These women continue to bear children throughout their child-

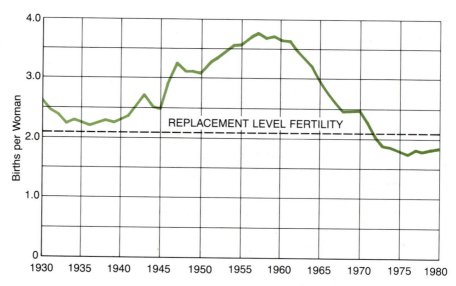

FIGURE 7.4
Total fertility rate in the United States from 1930 to 1980. This rate peaked in the 1950s and has declined below the replacement level in recent years. (From Haupt and Kane.)

bearing years. Because there are more of these women than necessary to replace the population, the population continues to grow.

Eventually, if the population maintains replacement level fertility, the population size will become constant, but the final size will be larger than the present size. Even though the United States TFR is below replacement level, the total population is still growing.

The Demographic Transition

The demographic transition is a three-stage pattern of change in birth and death rates as a nation is transformed from undeveloped to developed. In stage I, in an undeveloped country, birth and death rates are high and the growth rate low (Fig. 7.5) [7]. The first step in development is typically an improvement in health and sanitation. As a nation achieves better medical care and sanitation, the death rate drops. The birth rate remains high, however, and the population enters stage II, a period where growth rate is high. Many African nations are in this stage. As education and the standard of living increase, and as family planning methods become more widely used, stage III is reached: the birth rate drops toward the death rate and the growth rate therefore also decreases, eventually to a low or zero growth rate. The problem many nations face is making the transition from stage II to stage III, especially if the growth rate is so high as to outpace increases in economic development. The developed countries are approaching stage III, but it is an open question whether some developing nations will make the transition before a serious population crash occurs.

Although the demographic transition is traditionally defined as consisting of three stages, it is

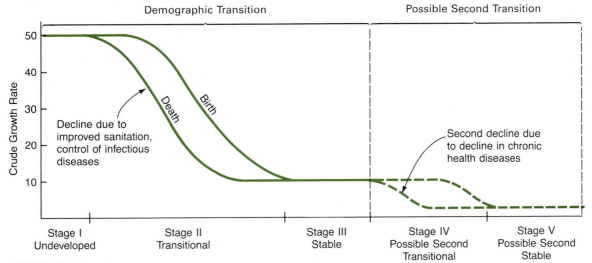

FIGURE 7.5
The demographic transition is the term used to refer to the changes that take place in birth and death rates as a country undergoes economic development and there is a trend toward a zero growth rate. In stage I, as in present-day subsahara Africa, modern medicine and health practices reduce death rates, while birth rates remain high. As a result growth rates increase. In stage II, as in present-day Latin America and the Caribbean, the birth rate begins to decline, but the death rate also continues to decline. In stage III, as in present-day China and for the industrialized nations, the birth rate declines rapidly to approach zero. An important modern issue is whether the poorer developing nations will be able to decrease the birth rate so that this demographic transition takes place. Because advances in treating chronic health problems are leading to a further decline in the death rate, a second transition (stage IV) may occur. To achieve a second stable phase (stage V), the birth rate would have to decline to match the death rate.

possible—with advances in treating chronic health problems—that a stage III country would experience an additional decline in the death rate. This could bring about a second transitional phase of population growth (stage IV). A second stable phase of low or zero growth (stage V) would be achieved only when the birth rate declined to match the decline in the death rate.

Doubling Time

Doubling time, a concept used frequently in discussing human population growth, is the time required for a population to double in size. The standard way to calculate doubling time is to assume that the population is growing exponentially (has a constant growth rate).

The doubling time based on an exponential is very sensitive to growth rate (Fig. 7.6). A simple way to estimate doubling time is to divide 70 by the annual growth rate stated as a percent. The U.S. population grew approximately 1%/yr during the 1970s; at this rate it would double in 70 years. During the same period, the Ivory Coast population grew at 4.9%/yr and would double in a little more than 14 years, while populations of Switzerland, Austria, Great Britain, and West Germany were growing at an annual rate of 0.1% and would require 700 years to double. The world's most populous country, China, grew at an annual rate of 1.4%; its population would double in 50 years. In 1981 the world population growth rate was 1.7%, which would lead to a doubling in 41 years [7].

Age Structure

As was discussed in Chapter 3, the age structure of a population greatly affects its current and future birth, death, and growth rates, as well as its effect on the environment. In addition, the age structure in a human population affects its current and future social and economic status. While the precise age structure varies by nation, the general types are illustrated in Fig. 7.7.

FIGURE 7.6
Doubling time changes rapidly with the population growth rate. The doubling time can be estimated simply by dividing the number 70 by the growth rate expressed as a percent. Because the world's population is increasing at a rate between 1% and 2%, we expect it to double within the next 35–70 years.

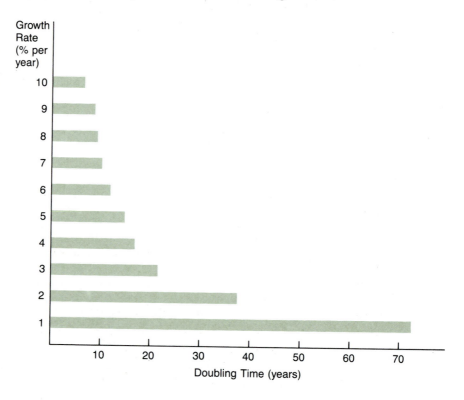

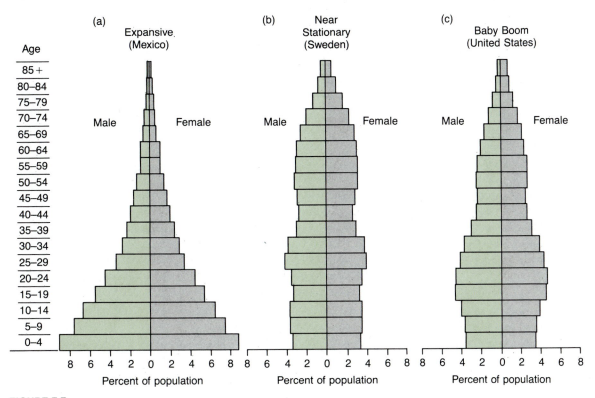

FIGURE 7.7
Major types of age structures of importance in the human population dilemma. (a) An age structure weighted toward youth; (b) an age structure nearing a stationary (unchanging) condition; (c) the baby boom in the United States. Baby boom refers to the great increase in births that occurred just following World War II, which shows up as a pulse in the pyramid age structure. Also apparent is a decrease in births during the great economic depression of the 1930s, when couples tended to have fewer children. Another event visible in this chart is the baby boom from World War I, evident in the age class born around 1915. [(a) and (b) from World Bank; (c) from U.S. Bureau of the Census]

Figure 7.7a shows the age structure in a rapidly growing population heavily weighted toward youth; Figure 7.7b shows a population approaching stability in which the average age is much older. Although population B is tending toward a no-growth condition and thus may avoid a Malthusian fate, population A may seem more pleasant to some. The high proportion of young people and the larger average family size of population A are especially desirable in nontechnological, agrarian societies that depend on the physical strength of young people. A greater proportion of older people in population B would, in many societies, be dependent on a smaller percentage of active younger people for food, clothing, and shelter. In addition, a stable society like population B offers relatively few opportunities for a young person. Many of the desirable jobs are filled, and when the population is in a steady state the replacement rate for these jobs is small. No modern society has achieved a true steady state but some nations that have begun to approach it by encouraging birth control have found the decreasing pool of young people to be an extremely serious problem. Partly for this reason, some countries have even begun to advocate an increase in births.

What is good for a population may not be pleasant (or good) for the individual. Conversely, what is pleasant for an individual may be detrimental to the population. Among the most important problems facing the next few generations are how to deal with a steady-state population and how to maintain a satisfying lifestyle for the individual while maintaining a constant population.

In a developing nation with a high birth rate, low life expectancy, high death rate, and a short generation time, the population is weighted toward the young (Figure 7.7a). In developing countries today, about 40% of the populations are under 16 years [7]. Such an age structure indicates the population will grow very rapidly and will have a long lag effect.

The age structures of Kenya and Mexico, typical of most developing nations, have a high age dependency ratio—the ratio of dependent-age people to working-age people. It is customary to define dependent-age people as those under 15 and over 65 and working-age people as all the rest. The age dependency ratio is the sum of the number of people under 15 and over 65 divided by the number between 15 and 64. For example, in 1976 in the United States there were 52,507,000 under 15 and 22,934,000 over 65, for a total of 75,441,000 dependent-age people. There were 139,677,000 working-age people, so that the dependent-age ratio was 0.54 (75,441,000 divided by 139,677,000) or 54 dependent-age people for every 100 working-age people.

The age dependency ratio of a population affects economic conditions. The larger this ratio, the lower the present and near-future living standards. As an example, in 1976 Libya had a ratio of 113, Japan 47 [5], meaning that in Libya every productive person had to support more than twice as many dependents as in Japan.

An age structure weighted toward older age classes (Fig. 7.7b) will lead to a low growth rate. The problem with such an age structure is that the dependency ratio is high and will remain high.

After a population has been subjected to famine, to other catastrophes such as an outbreak of an epidemic disease or a period of harsh weather, or to other sources of mortality that fall especially heavily on the young and the old, the age structure will change over time (it is nonstationary) (Fig. 7.7c).

To make accurate projections about a population and its effects on its environment, we must know its age structure. The age structure also provides insight into a population's history and its current status. For example, the "baby boom" that occurred after World War II in the United States (leading to a great increase in births from 1946 through 1964) formed a pulse in the population of several cohorts. This pulse is moving through the age structure. At each life stage, the baby boom has stressed social and economic resources; for example, schools were crowded when the baby boomers were of primary and secondary school age, after which the schools had an overcapacity. The baby boomers will in turn have a disproportionate number of offspring and create another pulse, smaller, one generation later (Fig. 7.7c).

Life Expectancy

The human population's great rate of increase has occurred despite the fact that many aspects of individual biological life have remained unchanged. We began this chapter by pointing out that John Eli Miller's original family of seven children was not especially large in the history of human beings. Nor has the longevity of individuals changed very much. In fact, the chances of a person 75 years old living to be 90 were considerably greater in ancient Rome than they are today (Fig. 7.8).

Life expectancy is the estimated average number of years a person of a specific age can expect to live. It is an age-specific number; each age class within a population has its own life expectancy figure. For general comparison, however, the life expectancy at birth is used, thus life expectancy is often used loosely to mean life expectancy at birth.

Life expectancy differs by nation and by sex, age, and other factors and has changed greatly in human history, as shown in Figure 7.9. By studying the dates on tombstones, the life expectancy of other periods can be reconstructed (Fig. 7.9a). The age at death can also be used to infer the survivorship curve of the population (Fig. 7.9b). These reconstructions suggest that death rates were much higher among young people in Rome and medieval

FIGURE 7.8
Mortality in ancient Rome, medieval England, and the modern U.S. This graph shows the chance of dying during the next year for various ages. The chances of dying in York, England, and in Rome were reconstructed from the ages of death given on tombstones. Of the three, the chance of young people dying is lowest in the modern United States; in contrast, for people older than 70 the chance of dying during the next year is highest in the United States. A considerably smaller fraction of the population reached 75 in Rome. In technical terms, the chance of dying given here is called the age-specific mortality rate. (Modified from Hutchinson, 1978. Reprinted by permission of Yale University Press from *An Introduction to Population Ecology*, copyright 1978.)

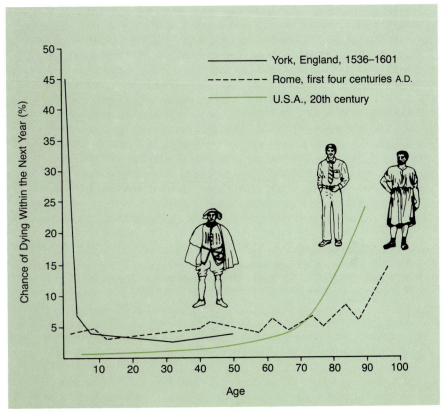

Europe than they are now. In ancient Rome, the life expectancy of a 1–year-old was about 22, while in twentieth-century England it has been about 50 years. The life expectancy in a primitive hunter-gatherer society is short; among the !Kung bushmen of Botswana, life expectancy at birth is 33 years [8]. Life expectancy in modern England is greater than it was in ancient Rome for all ages until about age 55, when the life expectancy values appear higher for ancient Romans than for a modern Britisher, suggesting that the hazards of modern life may be concentrated more on the aged than in earlier times. Pollution-induced diseases are one factor in this change.

Carrying Capacity

When we talk about the limits to human populations, we are talking about the carrying capacity of the environment for human beings. Speaking generally, **carrying capacity** means the maximum population size that can be sustained indefinitely by the environment. A population that exceeds the carrying capacity will change the environment in a way that will decrease the future carrying capacity. This is the meaning of carrying capacity we will use in this chapter. As discussed in Chapter 3, carrying capacity is sometimes used to mean the final equilibrium value of a logistic population—the size that such a population attains, maintains indefinitely, and returns to after a disturbance. This concept of carrying capacity assumes that the environment remains constant and that a population has a constant relationship to the environment. Neither is true for human populations.

How can we determine the carrying capacity for human beings on a national basis? This is difficult, but several simple indices are used to provide a general idea of a nation's carrying capacity, including the gross national product (GNP) per capita

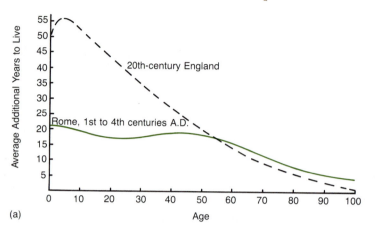

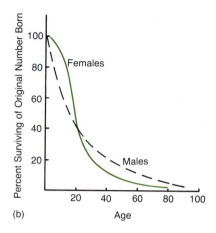

FIGURE 7.9

(a) Life expectancy in ancient Rome and modern England. This graph shows the average additional number of years one could expect to live having reached a given age. For example, a 10–year-old in England could expect to live about 55 more years; a 10–year-old in Rome could expect to live about 20 more years. Among the young, life expectancy is greater in modern England than it was in ancient Rome. However, the graphs cross at about age 60. An 80–year-old Roman could expect to live longer than an 80-year-old modern Englishman. The graph for Romans is reconstructed from ages given on tombstones. (b) Approximate survivorship curve for Rome for the first four centuries A.D. The percent surviving decreases rapidly in the early years, reflecting the high mortality rates for children in ancient Rome. Females had a slightly higher survivorship rate until age 20, after which males had a slightly higher rate. (Modified from Hutchinson, 1978. Reprinted by permission of Yale University Press from *An Introduction to Population Ecology*, copyright 1978.)

and the calories of food per capita. These indices vary considerably among nations.

Calories Per Capita Ratio The estimated average daily calorie requirement per person is about 2600. This value varies with climate, average body size, and activities. And one can calculate a value for each country. In the United States, the number of calories used per capita is about 3600, or 138% of the estimated daily requirement, meaning that there is 38% more food available than the population requires. The average for industrialized nations is 3400. By contrast, the lowest values are for Mali and Afghanistan—1758, or 68% of what is required. Relatively few of the African and Asian developing countries have a calories per capita ratio of 100% or more. If the calories per capita ratio falls below 100,% the death rate should rise and the birth rate decrease. The value of this ratio is therefore an indicator of future population growth [7].

GNP Per Capita Ratio The GNP per capita ratio indicates the economic status of a country in relation to its population size. The higher this ratio, the better off the country is today, and the better off it is likely to be in the near future. The GNP per capita ratio also has an inverse relationship to birth rates (Fig. 7.10). The higher the GNP per capita, the lower the birth rate and the higher the average education level.

Nations vary considerably in their GNP per capita ratio. The GNP per capita in the United States is about $13,000, and the average for all industrialized countries, given as U.S. dollars, is $11,000. In contrast, the value for Ethiopia is $140; India's is $260 and China's is $310 [7].

Limiting Factors

Eventually human populations will be limited by some factor or combination of factors, as discussed in Chapter 3 for other populations. The cal-

FIGURE 7.10
Total fertility rate decreases as income increases. Average curves are shown for developing nations in 1972 and 1982. Some specific values for selected countries are also shown. (Modified from World Bank.)

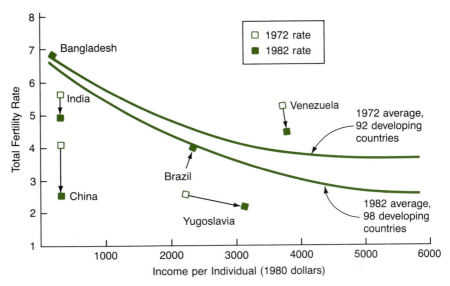

ories per capita ratio and the GNP per capita ratio give us a rough idea of the status of a population in relation to its resources. But what can we say beyond this—what specific factors are likely to limit a human population or cause it to decrease? We can group the limiting factors into those that could affect a population during the year in which they became limiting (short-term factors), those whose effects would be apparent no sooner than 1 year but before 10 years (intermediate-term factors), and those whose effects would not be apparent for 10 years after they became limiting (long-term factors). These are convenient categories, but you should be aware that there is considerable spillover from one to another.

The most important short-term factor is something that disrupts the distribution of food within a country. This disruption could be the result of political events, including wars, or of a shortage of energy to transport food coupled with a local loss of current crops. Abrupt changes in weather, such as a drought, can cause such a disruption. Other short-term factors include major world catastrophes, such as thermonuclear war; the worldwide spread of a major toxic chemical; and the outbreak of a new disease or a new strain of a previously controlled disease.

Intermediate-term factors include certain climatic changes; energy shortages that affect food

production and distribution; desertification; wide dispersal of certain pollutants, such as the spread of certain metals into waters and fisheries; disruption in the supply of certain nonrenewable resources, such as rare metals used in making steel alloys for transportation machinery; and decrease in the supply of firewood or other fuels for heating and cooking.

Long-term factors include soil erosion; decline in groundwater supplies; disruption in the supply of nonrenewable resources, similar to those listed as intermediate-term factors; climatic change such as a warming resulting from changes in atmospheric chemistry; and wide dispersal of certain pollutants, such as acid rain.

HUMAN POPULATION HISTORY: THE PAST

How many people have lived on Earth? Of course, before written history there were no censuses. The first estimates of population in Western civilization were attempted in the Roman era. During the Middle Ages and the Renaissance, scholars occasionally estimated the number of people. The first modern census, however, was made in 1655 in the Canadian colonies by the French and the British [10]. The first series of regular censuses taken by a country began in Sweden in 1750. The United States has taken a census every decade since 1790, but most countries began much later. The first Russian census, for example, was made in 1870. Even today, many countries do not take censuses or do not do so regularly. The population of China has only recently begun to be known with any accuracy. By studying modern primitive peoples and applying principles of ecology, however, we can gain a rough idea of the total number of people who might have lived on Earth [9].

Growth through History

Early human beings were hunters and gatherers, and people who follow this way of life live at a density of about 1 person/130–260 km^2 in the most habitable areas [10]. Given the area where these people probably lived, the average early Stone Age population could have been as low as one-quarter of a million [11]—less than the population of modern small cities like Hartford, Connecticut.

The total human population was very low for a long time—certainly less than a few million, which is fewer than live now in many of our cities. Many authorities have assumed that the number was fairly constant, but there were undoubtedly fluctuations that accompanied changes in climate, the gradual discovery of new habitable areas, or sporadic outbreaks of epidemic diseases. Whatever the short-term changes, the average rate of increase for most of human history—from the beginning of our species until the beginning of domestic agriculture—was extremely low. The average annual rate of increase over the entire history of human population is less than 0.00011%/yr, although in recent decades the rate has approached 2% [10]. With the domestication of plants and animals and the rise of settled villages, the population density increased greatly, beginning the second great period in human population history. We know this because primitive peoples who practice agriculture have population densities greatly exceeding those of hunters and gatherers. Although this second phase saw a general increase in the total number of people, the average rate of growth remained low by modern standards. An increase of

0.03% would have brought the population from 5 million in 10,000 B.C. to about 100 million in A.D. 1, with the Roman Empire accounting for about 54 million [12].

From A.D. 1 to 1000, the population increased to between 200 and 300 million (see Fig. 7.2), then reached about 500 million in 1600. During this period, Western civilization experienced a great disaster, the Black Death (Fig. 7.11). This epidemic disease, caused by the bacteria *Bacillus pestis* and spread by fleas that live on rodents, was first recorded in Western history as a major human problem when it occurred in the seventh century in the Roman Empire and in North Africa. The plague probably first appeared in India in the seventh century [13] and spread rapidly northward and westward. After that, however, it did not cause another major widespread epidemic until the fourteenth century. Like a true epidemic, it spread rapidly, reaching Italy in 1348 and Spain, France, Scandinavia, and central Europe within two years (Fig. 7.11). In England one-fourth to one-third of the

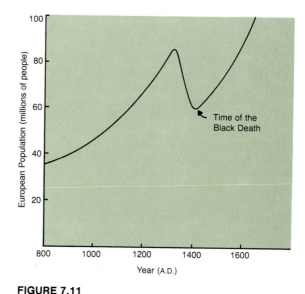

FIGURE 7.11

European population in general increased exponentially from the ninth through the seventeenth centuries but total population dropped drastically during the fourteenth century as a result of the Black Death and remained low for 200 years. (Data from Langer and from Matras.)

population died within a single decade. Entire towns were abandoned, and the production of food for the remaining population was jeopardized [14].

The third period of human population growth began about 1600 with the Renaissance in Europe. Some experts say that this time marked the transition from agricultural to literate societies, with a literate society's greater ability to reduce the death rate. By 1600, the rate of increase was on the order of 0.1%/yr, a rate that increased about one-tenth of a percent every 50 years until 1950 [10]. After recovering from the Black Death, the human population underwent another rapid increase with discovery of the causes of diseases, invention of vaccines, improvements in sanitation, other advances in medicine and health, and great increase in the production of food, shelter, and clothing [9].

As the growth rate increased, the population grew to about 900 million in 1800, almost doubled in the next century, and almost doubled again (to 3 billion) by 1960.

The rapid increase during the second half of the twentieth century marks the beginning of the fourth period in human population history. Today the population is more than 4.5 billion.

Summing all these values, the estimate is that about 50 billion people have lived on Earth [15]. The 4.5 billion people alive today represent about 9% of all of the people who have ever lived.

Current Trends

In addition to the great overall increase in the total human population, the geography of human population is changing greatly.

With economic development comes urbanization, although this process is reversing to a certain extent in the United States and some other industrialized countries, where there has been a recent movement from inner cities to suburbs. In the developed countries, 70% of the people live in urban areas, while in the developing countries only 28% are urban. It is projected that by the end of the century the urban population will increase to about 40% in the developing countries and to more than 80% in the developed countries [7].

Within nations there is considerable migration from one region to another. For example, in the United States there has been a general trend of population concentration westward and, more recently, to the southwest [5, 16].

Geographic differences in growth rates also occur. The nations of the world can be divided into three groups in regard to growth rates: (1) industrialized (developed) nations with crude growth rates below 1%, (2) developing countries with growth rates between 2 and 4.5%, and (3) developing countries with rates between 1 and 2%. The second group includes most of the countries of Africa, Asia, and South America. China is the most important of the third group [7].

As an example of geographic patterns in human populations, consider Africa. The area of this continent south of the Sahara has a population of 400 million [17], with an average growth rate of 3%/yr. The population densities vary from a low of 7.6 people per km^2 in the Sudan (19 million in an area of 2.5 million km^2) to a high of 92 people/km^2 in Nigeria (85 million in 924,000 km^2). The population growth rate varies from 1.5% in Gabon to 4% in Kenya. The birth rates for those countries vary from 4% to 5.2%; the death rates from 1% to 1.8%. Much of the population increase results from a lowered death rate resulting from disease control [17]. The potential future increase is very great for some of these countries.

To put the current African growth in perspective, when European population growth was most rapid, the growth rate never exceeded 1.6% and was accompanied by high agricultural production and high health standards. In contrast, African agriculture is low in productivity and subject to droughts, and per capita production decreased 10% between 1970 and 1980. In the last decade, concern with population regulation has grown, and 25 African countries now have national family planning organizations [17].

In contrast to the African nations, a few nations—Austria, Belgium, East and West Germany, Luxembourg, Sweden, and Great Britain—have essentially reached a no-growth state. These countries have a growth rate below 1%, and some are even declining in population [18]. These countries account, however, for only 4% of the world's population. Several other developed countries, including France, Italy, Japan, the U.S., the U.S.S.R., the

Netherlands, Denmark, and Norway, are near a no-growth condition[18].

The ten most populous countries—China, India, Indonesia, Brazil, Pakistan, Nigeria, Bangladesh, the U.S., the U.S.S.R., and Japan—account for about 62% of the world's total population; China alone accounts for almost one-quarter (Table 7.1). The fertility rates in all but Nigeria have begun to drop, and in all but Nigeria, Pakistan, and Bangladesh are dropping rapidly [7]. Nevertheless, the ten largest countries will continue to have major impacts on the biosphere; their human populations affect all of us wherever we live.

The ten countries with the greatest growth rates between 1970 and 1982 were United Arab Emirates (16%) Kuwait (6%), Ivory Coast (4.9%), Saudi Arabia (4.8%), Mozambique (4.3%), Oman (4.3%), Libya (4.1%), Kenya (4%), Nicaragua (3.9%) and Iraq (3.5%), with several other countries close behind, including Tanzania (3.5%) and Uganda and Honduras (3.4% each). Such rapid growth rates have typically led to social, if not economic, stresses. Where growth rates of about 3%/yr are coupled with a low standard of living, great problems lie ahead [7]. Because some of these countries contain important resources, a population increase can have global repercussions. For example, Tanzania contains the Serengeti Plains, one of the world's greatest remaining areas of wildlife; growing national human population will put greater and greater pressure on this world treasure.

The countries with the greatest annual increase in numbers tend to be those with the largest populations rather than the highest growth rates, because of the great effect of the huge current population size. The annual increase in the number of people in each of the ten most populous countries exceeds the total population of the country with the greatest percent increase, the United Arab Emirates, which has a population of 2 million.

FACING THE FUTURE

Human beings cannot escape the laws of population growth. As we learned in Chapter 3, individual populations are capable of rapid exponential growth, but this is rarely achieved in nature; control of populations is the norm. The degree of control and the causes of control determine many features of ecosystems and the life around us. Although the overall rate of growth is a small percentage (approximately 2%/yr), the number of individuals added to the world population is huge and beyond our ability to imagine.

Population Projections

What projections we make about the human population depend in part on what kind of curve the

TABLE 7.1

Population features of the ten most populous countries

Country	Population (millions)	Growth Rate (% per year)	Annual Increase (numbers)
China	1,008	1.4	14,000,000
India	717	2.3	16,500,000
USSR	270	0.9	2,400,000
United States	232	1.0	2,300,000
Indonesia	153	2.3	3,500,000
Brazil	127	2.4	3,000,000
Japan	118	1.1	1,300,000
Nigeria	91	2.6	2,370,000
Bangladesh	93	2.6	2,420,000
Pakistan	87	3.0	2,600,000
Total	2786		

Source: World Bank.

population will follow. It is customary among demographers to use the logistic growth curve (Chapter 3), which assumes that the population will grow smoothly to a constant carrying capacity, to estimate long-term trends (Fig. 7.12). Among various problems with using this curve, a particularly difficult problem for our own population has to do with what is called the inflection point in the logistic curve. This curve is S-shaped, curving upward at first and then changing slope and curving toward the horizontal. The point at which the curve changes is the inflection point. Until a population has reached the inflection point, we cannot project the final size. The human population has not made the bend around the inflection point. The typical way this has been dealt with is to assume that today's population is just reaching the inflection point. This standard practice, however, leads invariably to a great underestimate of the maximum number of people that will occur. For example, one of the first projections of the upper limit of the United States population, made in the 1930s, assumed that the inflection point occurred then. That resulted in an estimate that the final population of the United States would be about 200 million, a number that has already been exceeded.

As discussed in Chapter 3, the logistic involves other assumptions that are as unrealistic for human populations as for other mammals. These assumptions include a constant carrying capacity, no lag effects, and a population that is homogeneous (all individuals identical in their effects on each other). These are additional reasons that the logistic is not a good basis upon which to make human population projections.

Various Approaches Short-term (10–50-year) projections of human populations are made from the current demography by using the current age structure, birth rate, and death rate. These give an estimate of what size the population will reach as long as current conditions hold. This information is useful in showing us the implications of our cur-

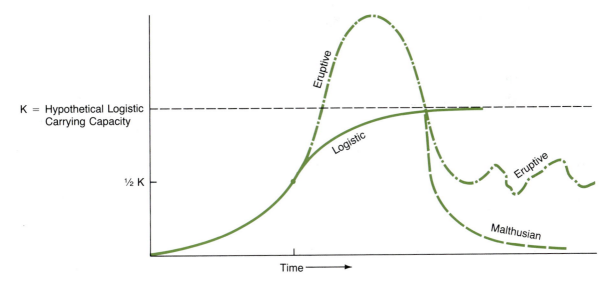

FIGURE 7.12
Hypothetical growth curves for human populations. Most projections use the logistic, which assumes a constant carrying capacity, a measured inflection point, and no time lag. Here the logistic is compared to the eruptive and the Malthusian growth curves. The eruptive growth curve, found among wild populations of large mammal herbivores, is more typical of populations that become "out of control." The Malthusian curve shows a population growing rapidly at first and then crashing to a low level that continues.

rent situation, even though we cannot take such projections as true, necessary, or accurate. The U.S. Census Bureau has used such a method to estimate that the world population in year 2000 will be between 5.9 and 6.8 billion (varying with the choice of birth and death rates) [19].

Another approach is to assume that current levels of birth and death rates will change so that replacement level fertility (RLF) is achieved. The final world population size then would depend on the length of time required to reach RLF. If the RLF were achieved in 2020–25, the population would level off at about 11 billion; if RLF were not achieved until 2045–50, the population would level off at 16 billion. These projections show that the population level is very sensitive to small changes in the timing of RLF [20].

The World Bank has made a series of projections based on current birth and death rates and assumptions about how these will change. Their critical assumptions are (1) mortality will fall everywhere and level off when female life expectancy reaches 82; (2) fertility will reach replacement levels everywhere between 2005 and 2025; and (3) there will be no major worldwide catastrophe. Even assuming a rapid achievement of replacement fertility, this approach projects an equilibrium world population of 11 billion (Fig. 7.13) [7]. Developed countries would increase only from 1.2 billion today to 1.4, but developing countries would increase from 3.6 billion to 8.4. Bangladesh would reach 450 million (in an area the size of Wisconsin); Nigeria 650 million; India 1.7 billion. In these projections, the developing countries con-

FIGURE 7.13
Three possible paths of future world population growth, as projected by the World Population Bureau. The constant path assumes that the 1978 growth rate will continue unchanged. The slow fertility reduction path assumes that the world's fertility will decline to reach replacement level by the year 2040. Under this assumption the world's population would stabilize at about 15 billion by the twenty-second century. The rapid fertility reduction path assumes that the world's fertility will rapidly decline to reach replacement level by the year 2000. Under this assumption the world's population could stabilize at about 8 billion sometime during the twenty-first century. The world's actual growth curve should come somewhere between the slow and rapid curves. (From Haupt and Kane).

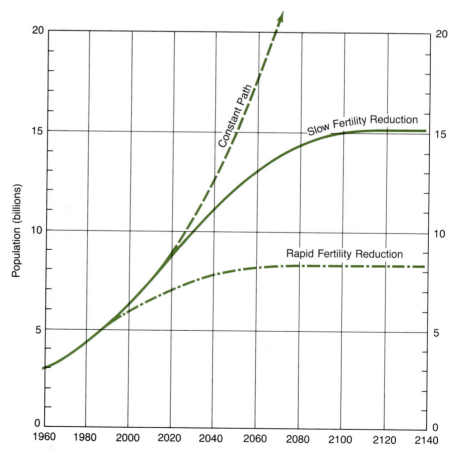

tribute 90% of the increase [20]. As noted earlier, if we do not control the birth rate, the death rate will increase and human catastrophes would increase; this might actually lead to a decline in total world population. We may be already witnessing catastrophic declines, which began with the floods in Bangladesh in 1972 and 1974. Since the late 1970s, dry weather in Northern and Central Africa has led to a major famine. In 1974, 300,000 died of starvation in Ethiopia. In 1984 continued famine in Ethiopia led to a mass migration of people from rural areas to cities. Those of a more pessimistic viewpoint argue that these incidents are merely the tip of the iceberg and that major catastrophic decline from natural hazards, pollution, famine, and disease are just around the corner. Optimists argue that we still have great technological potential to increase all resource production. We will examine many of these issues in more detail in later chapters.

Influence of Resources An analysis of the change in per capita resources suggests that we have already passed the peak in amount of biological resources available per person: some argue, therefore, that we have exceeded the long-term carrying capacity of Earth for people. According to United Nations FAO and USDA figures, the per capita production of wood peaked at 0.67 m^3/person in 1967, fisheries peaked at 19.5 kg/person in 1970, beef at 11.81 kg/person in 1977, mutton at 1.92 in 1972, wool at 0.86 in 1960, cereal crops at 342 in 1977 [9]. Prior to these peaks, the production had grown rapidly. Although part of the decline may be due to short-term economic forces, part is the result of our nearing the limit of capacity with existing technology. This is certainly the case with fisheries, as we will discuss in Chapter 8.

Energy resources are also a key to living standards. Between 1950 and 1978, world oil production increased from 3.8 billion barrels to 22 billion barrels per year [18]. Countries with high oil production have a high standard of living; United Arab Emirates, the country with the highest per capita GNP, has undergone a dramatic demographic change: the crude birth rate dropped from 46 in 1960 to 28 in 1982, and the crude death rate dropped during the same period from 19 to 3. The growth rate thus changed from 2.8% to 1.6%; the United Arab Emirates is in the middle of the demographic transition [7].

Potential Medical Advances A second medical revolution appears to be at hand. The first involved the control of infectious disease. The second will involve genetic engineering, preventive medicine, and results from research on aging and on chronic noninfectious ailments like heart disease. Genetic engineering can provide new chemicals to cure diseases or greatly reduce the cost of medicines (by developing new bacteria strains that produce these chemicals). And genetic engineering may lead to correction of some genetic defects and new approaches to cancer treatment.

Preventive medicine and improved nutrition appear already to have led to a significant decline in deaths from heart attacks in the United States. Research on aging, including the use of transplants and artificial organs, will allow more people to live longer. Thus we can expect a second decline in mortality rates (see Fig. 7.5). This will lead to another increase in growth and require an even greater decrease in birth rates. The longer each of us lives, the fewer children there can be.

Other medical advances, however, are leading to increases in fertility and birth rates. These consist primarily of techniques to counter infertility by such means as artificial insemination (to overcome infertility of the male partner), surrogate mothers (to overcome infertility in the female partner), and"test-tube babies"—a term used for artificial fertilization of a human egg and sperm outside of the body and subsequent implantation of the fertilized egg within the uterus of the mother. Other techniques to increase fertility tend to increase the frequency of multiple births, thus also increasing the total fertility rate in a population. There are strong personal pressures to use such techniques—an inability to have children often causes stress between a couple, and there are strong family pressures to have children.

Cultural Factors Most human cultures have put a strong positive value on large families and high birth rates. In a society without life insurance, disability, and retirement programs, a large family provides a kind of insurance for retirement. When one is too old to care for one's self, one's children could. Also, a large family provides a greater chance of leaving descendants. Moreover, a large family affords protection from enemies. As a result of these and other factors, having a large family is pragmatic in a primitive society. These attitudes have carried over into our modern world. Of course there are other cultural, religious, and moral arguments for large families, discussions of which go beyond the scope of this book.

As long as increasing fertility is desirable to too many individuals, it will have inevitable negative effects on the world human population and the environment.

The increase in birth rates and decrease in mortality resulting from medical advances has not been entered into population projections. Such changes will greatly tax Earth's resources and probably lead to great catastrophic die-offs from famines and natural hazards. Current and potential alterations of birth and death rates make clear that what is pleasant and desirable for each of us is not always best for our population.

Accuracy of Projections We cannot predict with any accuracy what the maximum human population size of Earth might be. This is in part because technology is changing rapidly and it is difficult to predict the ways it will change and the effects it will have on population. It is also difficult to predict the maximum population size because we do not know with any certainty how much crowding each of the peoples of Earth will stand. Third, we do not know accurately how the environment will change. For example, we live now in a fortunate time in North America because good rainfall occurs over areas of good soil. But the changes we ourselves are inducing in global climate might shift these patterns and decrease total world food production, negatively affecting populations.

Controlling Growth

The ways we can control our population all involve affecting one or two rates—the birth rate and the death rate. If we don't decrease the birth rate,

eventually the death rate will increase on its own. Because artificially increasing the death rate is morally repugnant and rejected by all civilizations, we can act directly only by decreasing the birth rate. If we do not act in a positive way to decrease birth rates, we will find more and more cases of starvation, malnutrition, and deaths from natural hazards, pollution, and disease.

We are forced to confront a dilemma that everyone would just as soon avoid. The dilemma is that we must decrease birth rates or accept increases in suffering and death among the living. Neither choice is desirable, but in the past people could defer the dilemma to the future. Now the dilemma is at hand; it must be confronted by this or the next generation.

The simplest and one of the most effective means of slowing population growth is to delay the age of first child-bearing by women [21]. As more women enter the working force and as education levels and standards of living increase, this tends to occur naturally. Social pressures that lead to deferred marriage and child-bearing can be very effective.

Countries with high growth rates have early marriages. In South Asia and Africa south of the Sahara, about 50% of women marry between the ages of 15 and 19. In Bangladesh women marry at 16 on the average, while in Sri Lanka the average age is 25. The World Bank estimates that if Bangladesh adopted Sri Lanka's marriage pattern, families could average 2.2 fewer children [7]. Increases in the marriage age could account for 40–50% of the required drop in fertility to achieve a zero population growth for many countries [7]. Age at marriage has increased in some countries, especially in Asia. For example, in Korea the average marriage age changed from 17 in 1925 to 24 in 1975 [7]. China passed laws fixing minimum marriage ages, first at 18 for women and 20 for men in 1950, then 20 for women and 22 for men in 1980.

Another simple means of decreasing birth rates is breast-feeding, which can delay resumption of ovulation; this is used consciously as a birth control method by women in a number of countries and in the mid-1970s provided more protection against conception in developing countries than family planning programs, according to the World Bank [7].

The details of current birth control methods are beyond the scope of this book; here we consider these only in terms of their consequences for the environment. Traditional methods range from simple abstinence to induction of sterility with natural agents. Modern methods include "the pill," artificial hormone control for preventing ovulation, surgical techniques for permanent sterility, and mechanical devices. The method of last resort is abortion, which is both one of the most controversial from a moral perspective (although now safe medically, in most cases, when done properly) and one of the most important in terms of its effects on birth rates.

The abortion ratio is the estimated number of abortions per 1000 live births in a given year [5]. The abortion rate is the estimated number of abortions per 1000 women aged 15–44 years in a given year [5]. For example, in 1975 in the District of Columbia, the abortion ratio was 1007 while the abortion rate was 124. That is, for every 1000 live births, there were 1007 abortions, and out of 1000 women of child-bearing age, 124 had an abortion.

Another change in our current situation has to do with migration. In the past, if the population of one area or one country exceeded the current resources, people would emigrate from their homeland and immigrate into a new area. Of course the story of America is the story of immigration, as are the stories of Australia and New Zealand, but people have always migrated. Migration is still an important movement of people in response to political situations, natural disasters, or other compelling factors, but the relief it provides to population problems is temporary and finite. Today we have run out of new territories on Earth. Some believe that our technologies will allow us to colonize previously unused areas, such as the Antarctic and even the deep sea; this may be possible to a limited extent. Others suggest that we can take care of the Earth's population problems by creating space stations or migrating to other planets. We may be able to inhabit other planets, but this is not a solution for our problems.

National Programs

Reduction in birth rates requires a change in attitude, knowledge of the means to control birth, and the availability of these means. The change in attitude can come about simply as changes in viewpoint that may accompany an increase in a standard of living. Many countries, however, have found it necessary to provide formal family planning programs to explain the problems arising from rapid population growth, the benefits to individuals of reduced population growth, and information about birth control methods, as well as to provide access to the methods. As discussed earlier, the choice of population control methods is an issue that involves social, moral, and religious beliefs, which vary from country to country as to what methods are acceptable. It is thus difficult to generalize about what approach to use throughout the world.

In 1974, a World Population Conference in Bucharest, Romania, was attended by 136 countries. They approved a world population plan which recognized that individuals have the right to decide freely the number and spacing of their children and to have access to information telling how to achieve their goals [5].

Before 1965, few developing countries had official family planning programs; from 1965 to 1975 there was widespread introduction of such plans; by 1976 only Burma, North Korea, and Peru did not provide some support for family planning [20]. The first country to adopt an official population policy was India, whose program was initiated in 1952. Although most countries now have some kind of program, the effectiveness varies greatly. International aid for family planning reached $260 million by 1977 [7].

A wide variety of approaches have been used, from simply providing more information, to promoting and providing some of the means for birth control, to offering rewards and extending penalties. Penalties are usually in the form of taxes. For example, Ghana, Malaysia, Pakistan, Singapore, and the Philippines have used one or a combination of a limit to maternity benefits, tax allowances for children, and tax deductions after one or two children [7]. Tanzania has taken another approach: restricting paid maternity leave to women to once in three years [7]. Singapore does not take family size into account in allocating government-built housing, so larger families are more crowded. As an example of the use of rewards, Singapore increased the priority of school admission to children from smaller families [7].

China has one of the oldest and most effective family planning programs. In 1978 China adopted an official policy to reduce the country's human population growth from 1.2% in that year to zero by 2000. An emphasis was placed on single-children families. The government uses education, a network of family planning that provides information and means for birth control, and a system of rewards and penalties. Women are given paid leave for abortions and for sterilization operations. While there are benefits to families with a single child, including financial subsidies in some areas, in some parts of China families that have a second child must give up or even return the bonuses received for the first. Other rewards and penalties vary from province to province [7]. Other countries, including Bangladesh, India, and Sri Lanka, have paid people who have been sterilized. In Sri Lanka, this has applied only to families with two children, and a voluntary statement of consent must be signed [7].

The major means by which countries are actually reducing their population growth is an increase in the age of marriage, which accounts for as much as 35–45% of the growth reduction in some developing countries. Increases in living standards have had a major effect in leading to a change in attitudes, as has the considerable emphasis placed on family planning centers.

The evidence suggests that the use of contraceptive devices is widespread in many parts of the world, especially in Eastern Asia, where surveys have suggested that about two-thirds of women use contraceptive devices; in Africa the percentage is below 10%, and in central and south America about 40% [7]. Abortion is also widespread; according to the World Development Report [7], between 30 and 50 million abortions are performed each year.

SUMMARY

The current human population represents something unprecedented in the history of the world: never before has one species had such a great impact on the environment in such a short time and continued to increase at as rapid a rate. These qualities make the human population issue *the* environmental issue, because most current environmental damages result from the very high number of people and our great power to change the environment.

Throughout most of our history, the human population and its average growth rate have been small. It has been estimated that a total of 50 billion people have lived on Earth, and the present population of more than 4.5 billion represents 9% of all the people who have ever lived on our planet. The growth of the human population can be divided into three major phases. In the early hunter-gatherer phase, the average growth rate was very small. The second period, beginning about 10,000 years ago, experienced more rapid growth. The third era, which began about 1600, continues to the present day. Except for the great plagues of the fourteenth century, the population has grown rapidly and its rate of increase has become greater over time. Like other biological populations, humans are capable of a geometric increase—in fact, in recent decades the rate of growth of the human population has been faster than exponential.

This rapid increase has occurred without much increase in longevity, but through an increase in early survival. As mentioned, once one reached 75 years or older in ancient Rome, one's chances of living another year were greater than in the modern United States. Much of the increase in the rate of growth can be attributed to a decrease in the death rate.

There are two kinds of disagreements about human population control: the first about what the current situation is and what can be done and the second about what we ought to do. In this chapter we have discussed the first set of issues: the current situation and our options about it. The second set of issues—how we use this information and what we choose to do—is a matter that extends beyond science to social, political, moral, and religious beliefs. It is clear, however, that if we do not succeed in decreasing the birth rate, eventually environmental catastrophes will lead to great increases in death rates.

Countries that have undergone a decrease in

birth rates have experienced a demographic transition marked first by a decrease in death rates due to modern sanitation, nutrition, and medicine, followed by a later decrease in birth rates. Most developed nations have followed this pattern and are at one stage or another in the demographic transition. Many developing nations have experienced a great decrease in the death rate but still have a very high birth rate. It remains an open question whether some of these nations will be able to achieve a lower birth rate before reaching disastrously high population levels that will be subject to catastrophic causes of mortality. Already, recent droughts, famines, and natural hazards have caused large numbers of deaths in Asia and Africa.

Countries with a high standard of living move more quickly to a lower birth rate. Thus, countries with a low dependency ratio (a low number of young and old dependent on those in the work force) and with a high gross national product ratio (a high GNP per capita) tend to have lower birth rates and lower net growth rates. The growth rates vary from 0.1% for Switzerland, Austria, Great Britain, and Germany to 4.9% for Mozambique. The doubling times of the populations range from 700 years for Switzerland to about 14 for Mozambique.

The maximum population Earth can sustain and what population will be attained by human beings are controversial questions. Most projections assume that current rates of births and deaths will continue for some time and that birth rates will gradually decrease until replacement level fertility is reached; projections differ as to when such a level will be reached. Standard estimates suggest that the human population will reach somewhere between 10 and 16 billion before stabilizing. However, these projections assume that resources will be adequate to support all of these people and that no catastrophic events will lead to sudden decreases. On the other hand, some believe we have already exceeded the carrying capacity of Earth and that the future population will be less than at present. One of the remarkable things about our species is that our technology keeps increasing the carrying capacity of the environment for us. Because we cannot predict the impact of future technologies, we cannot be certain what the future carrying capacity of Earth for people will be. An important part of the human population dilemma is how to maintain a high quality of life and an environment that is beautiful, healthy, and pleasing to us, as well as one that sustains our physical needs.

Considerable lags in the responses of human populations to changes in birth and death rates occur because of the age structure of the population. A population that achieves replacement level fertility will continue to grow for several generations. Projections of the growth of the human population involve a consideration of the age structure. A population's age structure has important environmental, social, and economic effects. A human population with zero growth will have a greater proportion of older people; this in itself is an adjustment our societies will have to make in the future.

Our population is increasing so rapidly that we must confront the problems caused by decreasing the growth rate, must deal with changes in age structure, and must live within our resources. An understanding of human population processes is essential for wise solutions to these problems.

STUDY QUESTIONS

1 What are the principal reasons that the human population has grown so rapidly in the twentieth century?

2 What is meant by the statement, ''Technology continues to prove Malthus wrong''?

3 Why is the density of people who live by hunting and gathering lower than the density of people who practice agriculture?

4 Why is it important to consider the age structure of a human population?

5 Three characteristics of a population are birth rate, growth rate, and death rate. How has each been affected by (a) modern medicine, (b) modern agriculture, (c) modern industry?

6 What is meant by the statement, "What is good for an individual is not always good for a population"?

7 Strictly from a biological point of view, why is it difficult for a human population to achieve a constant size?

8 What environmental factors are likely to increase the chance of epidemic disease outbreaks?

9 Why is it so difficult to predict the growth of Earth's human population?

10 Before the beginning of the scientific and industrial revolutions, what factors tended to decrease the size of the human population?

11 To which of the following can we attribute the great increase in human population since the beginning of the industrial revolution? Changes in human (a) birth rates, (b) death rates, (c) longevity, (d) death rates among the very old. Explain.

12 What is meant by the demographic transition? When would one expect replacement level fertility to be achieved—before, during, or after the demographic transition?

13 Explain what is meant by doubling time. If the doubling time of the human population is decreasing, can the human population be growing strictly according to an exponential curve? Explain.

14 Present arguments for or against the following statement: "With proper planning, we can achieve a constant carrying capacity for human beings on Earth."

15 On the basis of the history of human populations in various countries, how would you expect the following to change as per capita income increased: (a) birth rates, (b) death rates, (c) average family size, and (d) age structure of the population? Explain.

FURTHER READING

CHAPMAN, W. B., JR. 1981. *Human ecosystem.* New York: Macmillan.

DUMOND, D. E. 1975. The limitation of human population: A natural history. *Science,* 187: 713–721.

KEYFITZ, N. 1968. *Introduction to the mathematics of population.* Reading, Mass.: Addison-Wesley.

MALTHUS, T. R. 1817. *An essay on the principle of population.* London: Murray.

MAULDIN, W. P. 1980. Population trends and prospects. *Science* 209: 148–157.

ROBINSON, H. 1981. *Population and resources.* New York: St. Martin's Press.

STOCKWELL, E. G., and GROAT, H. T. 1984. *World population: An introduction to demography.* New York: Franklin Watts.

WEEKS, J. R. 1981. *Population: An introduction to concepts and issues.* Belmont, Calif.: Wadsworth.

WORLD BANK. 1985. *Population change and economic development.* Oxford, England: Oxford University Press.

YUKEY, D. 1985. *Demography: The study of human populations.* New York: St. Martin's Press.

III
Renewable Biological Resources

8

Managing Wildlife

- Biological resources are renewable in the sense that populations can regrow, but these resources are vulnerable and must be managed carefully.
- Biological resource management involves the concept of multipile use.
- There are utilitarian, ecological, aesthetic, and moral reasons to conserve wildlife and endangered species.
- Recent wildlife management goals have shifted from maximum sustainable yield to optimum sustainable yield and optimum sustainable populations.
- Maximum sustainable yield of a population means the maximum production per unit time that can be sustained indefinitely. Optimum sustainable yield means the maximum production that can be maintained without detriment to the population or its ecosystem.
- Important considerations in the conservation of endangered species are the minimum viable population size and the habitat that such a population requires.
- Conservation of endangered species in the wild can be accomplished only through conservation of ecosystems and habitats.
- Causes of extinction include population risk, environmental risk, natural catastrophe, genetic risk, and human actions.
- Throughout human history, people have been an important cause of extinctions, but modern technological civilization and the large number of people have greatly increased the rate of extinction.
- Species that are likely to become endangered through human activities tend to share certain traits; especially vulnerable are large, long-lived species with low reproductive rates.
- Fisheries have been actively managed for decades, but the results have not often been successful. The failures are in part the result of the emphasis on maximum sustainable yields, and the lack of attention to community and ecosystem responses.
- Human actions are the primary reasons that marine mammals are endangered.

AMERICAN WHOOPING CRANE AND CALIFORNIA CONDOR

The American whooping crane and the California condor are two of North America's largest birds (Fig. 8.1). The whooping crane is the tallest, measuring more than 1.5 m, or approximately 5 ft. The condor has the greatest wing span—almost 3 m, or 9 ft. Although both are rare and endangered, both are protected and have large preserves set aside for them. The two species, however, seem to be suffering different fates. In 1937 the whooping crane population was reduced to 14 individuals; it has since recovered and now numbers more than 100. In the preservation of endangered species, the whooping crane is a success story [1]. The California condor population, on the other hand, is declining. Historical records suggest that after 1840 its numbers rapidly diminished; the population declined to about 60 in the 1940s and about 25 in the mid-1970s [2]. At that time, the U.S. Fish and Wildlife Service and the American Audubon Society began a condor recovery program involving the removal of birds and eggs from the wild and hatching and rearing chicks in zoos, with the hope of eventually returning them to the wild.

By the mid-1980s, the condor recovery program had established more than 15 birds in captivity. Only a handful remained in the wild and there was a controversial plan to remove them all to controlled environments.

The extinction of species is not new; in a world of chance, the eventual fate of every species is extinction. Nor is the extinction of "the biggest" new. As early as 1876, Alfred Wallace, an English biological geographer, noted that "we live in a zoologically impoverished world, from which all of the hugest, and fiercest, and strangest forms have recently disappeared"[3]. Given that history, why is the whooping crane recovering while the California condor has not? The explanations can be found in the principles of environmental studies. Briefly, the differences are ecological, as affected by human history. Although the whooping crane and California condor are both large and long-lived, they differ greatly in habitat and food. Unlike the crane, which migrates thousands of miles, the condor lives year-round in the Sierra foothills and coastal ranges of southern and central California.

The crane feeds in wetlands on small aquatic animals; the condor, a member of the vulture family, feeds on carrion, primarily of large mammals.

The recovery of the crane is possible because its habitat is in good condition; food and nesting sites are still sufficient and plentiful. The condor, on the other hand, exists in a greatly altered habitat. Food is scarce—the number of big game mammals such as deer and elk is greatly reduced in the mountains. What food exists is harder for the condor to find—some areas that once burned often and were relatively open grasslands have become more heavily grown with dense chaparral and woodlands. Few active nest sites are found, even far from human disturbance. Thus, although the condor was more abundant than the crane in the 1940s, the future is brighter for the crane than for the condor.

There is a lesson in this comparison: For an endangered species, it is better to have an ecosystem in good condition and a small population than to have an abundant population in an ecosystem in poor condition. The histories of the condor and crane also illustrate that the successful management of endangered species requires the application of the principles of environmental studies. This is true for all biological resources.

In this chapter we will explore the management of wildlife (including marine mammals), fisheries, and endangered species. We will discover, however, that there is no such thing as the conservation of an endangered species, only the conservation of endangered habitats and ecosystems. We must view an individual species within its environmental context. For the management of wildlife and fisheries, we will review the basic principles and practices that have developed in each area.

WILDLIFE

Why Conserve or Manage Wildlife?

The profession of wildlife management has traditionally focused on terrestrial wild animals that were hunted for food, commercial products, or sport, that is, large mammals and birds. Aldo Leopold, the father of modern wildlife management,

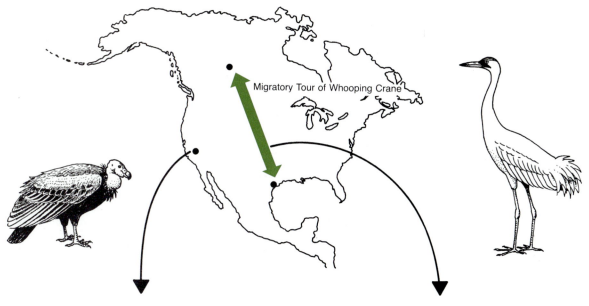

Migratory Tour of Whooping Crane

(a)

(b)

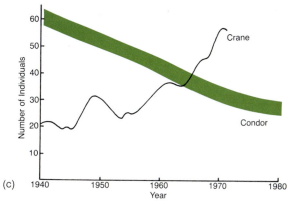

(c)

FIGURE 8.1
(a) The California condor. (b) The whooping crane in its habitat. (c) While the condor population has been decreasing, the whooping crane population has been increasing generally along an exponential curve.

defined game (or wildlife) management as "the art of making land produce sustained annual crops of wild game for recreational use" [4].

Reasons for conservation of wildlife can be grouped into utilitarian, aesthetic, ethical, and ecological. An example of an aesthetic reason is that they add beauty to a landscape. Utilitarian reasons include: wildlife can provide important, vital needs for people (food, leather, materials for medicine and jewelry); money can be made from harvesting wildlife and from tourism. Ethical reasons include: wildlife species have a moral "right" to exist, and it is our moral obligation to assist wildlife in their survival, especially because wildlife is so often threatened by our activities. By an ecological reason we mean that a species of wildlife plays an important role in an ecological community, ecosystem, or the biosphere, and we believe that role must be maintained. (See Chapter 1 for additional discussions of the reasons for conservation.)

Wildlife management can be traced back to ancient times, when Egyptians tamed and kept wild cheetahs and birds, as shown in Egyptian murals. Restrictions on the taking of game can be found in the Bible in Deuteronomy 22:6. Many wildlife preserves began in medieval times as private, protected hunting preserves owned by nobility. The story of Robin Hood can be viewed as the story of a twelfth-century noble's private game reserve and the irritation that it caused to others. In the thirteenth century, Marco Polo described the earliest known system of game management for conservation. He observed during his travels in the Mongol Empire, "There is an order which prohibits every person throughout all the countries subject to the Great Khan from daring to kill hares, roebucks, fallow deer, stags or other animals of that kind, or any large bird, between the months of March and October. This is that they may increase and multiply."

In England, laws establishing closed seasons can be traced back to Henry VIII. Early laws protected game for royalty. In the United States, the management of wildlife began as the control of hunting. In 1776, 12 of the original 13 colonies had closed seasons on certain species to allow these species to breed.

In the United States, much of the management is carried out by state fish and game departments and by the Fish and Wildlife Service of the Department of the Interior.

The economic value of wildlife should not be underestimated. In the United States, wildlife means big business, with more than $10 billion spent annually on hunting, fishing, bird watching, hiking, and other activities [5].

Every nation has wildlife enthusiasts, both those who hunt and those who look. In more densely populated areas, the manipulation of habitat is intense. In New Jersey, for example, fields are planted with nutritious plants liked by deer; hunters sometimes shoot the deer in or near these fields.

In one year in the United States more than 18 million hunters spent more than $1 billion on 2.25 million big game animals yielding about 225,000 metric tons (500 million pounds) of meat [6]. By 1981 there were almost 29 million hunting licenses, permits, tags, and stamps issued at a cost of $242 million. That same year almost 38 million paid individual sport fishing licenses, permits, tags, and stamps were obtained, costing $213 million [5]. There are about 7 million bird watchers and 4.5 million wildlife photographers; hikers, bird watchers, and photographers spend more than 786 million days in the field (Table 8.1). Bird watchers spend more than $500 million per year in the United States [5]. By 1980 there were 37.5 million acres of land in wildlife management areas and wildlife refuges in the United States, and $236 million was spent on wildlife and freshwater sport fishing management, surveys, and management research. [7].

The pursuit of furbearing animals, a major activity in the eighteenth and nineteenth centuries, played an important role in the exploration of North America. In recent years, annual income from furs in the United States was $100 to $125 million [8]. Beaver, muskrat, opossum, mink, weasel, and otter are among the major sources of fur. Large mammals managed for hunting include deer, caribou, moose, sheep, bison, and elk. The principal birds include geese, duck, and quail.

In addition to recreation, wildlife and plants have other uses. Some people depend on wildlife

TABLE 8.1
Outdoor recreation in the United States.

Activity	Numbers (millions)	Percentage of U.S. Population
Camping		
Developed areas	51.8	30
Undeveloped areas	36.0	21
Hiking and backpacking	48.1	28
Rock climbing	0.2	—
Hunting	32.6	19
Fishing	91.0	53
Off-road vehicles	43.6	25
Water activities		
Sailing	19.1	11
Canoeing, kayaking, etc.	26.9	15
Other boating	57.3	33
Scuba diving	0.2	—
Winter activities		
Skiing	11.9	7
Snowmobiling	13.8	8

Source: Based on U.S. Bureau of the Census, 1979.

Note: Data for persons 12 years and older participating from June 1970 to June 1977.

for some of their essential foods, clothing, and materials. In some parts of the world, especially eastern Africa, wildlife tourism is a major industry. In the 1960s, wildlife tourism was the second or third largest income-producing industry in Kenya, Tanzania, and Uganda [9]. This tourism declined dramatically in Uganda following the dictatorship of Idi Amin, but continues to be important in Kenya.

During the last 20 years, a controversy has developed over the commercial exploitation of wildlife products, including meat, leather, bone, and ivory. Conservationists have argued both sides of this issue. Conservationists in favor of the commercial exploitation of wildlife often argue that a commercially important species is safer from extinction than a noncommercial species: If a species makes money for people who live in an area, those people will have an interest in maintaining that species. If wildlife is not commercially useful, the local people will favor using the wildlife habitat for commercial development, such as agriculture, forestry, urbanization, or industrialization. Those favoring the use of wildlife also argue that the world's peoples need protein and that it is immoral to deny the local people access to the protein in wildlife. Furthermore, these proponents of commercial exploitation give an ecosystem argument:

In areas where domestic species of cattle are not native, wildlife ranching is less harmful to the land than traditional cattle ranching (Fig. 8.2) [9].

Those opposed argue that it is unethical or immoral to exploit wildlife commercially and, in direct contradiction to the proponents, they argue that commercial exploitation will lead to extinction.

The Goals of Wildlife Management The traditional goal of wildlife management was the maintenance of large numbers of individuals of an age, size, and vigor most desired by hunters. Recently, wildlife management has broadened to include the management of endangered animals or those, like many kinds of antelopes in the national parks of Kenya and other African nations, that are naturally abundant but are managed to maintain large populations for viewing in national parks and preserves.

Goals have changed and been modified over time. Earlier in the twentieth century, a primary goal was achievement of a **maximum sustainable yield** (MSY) of a specific species—the maximum increase per time unit in either the number of individuals or the total biomass of a desired bio-

FIGURE 8.2
Animals of the African plains and savannahs that have been used in African game ranching. Wild game are maintained on native habitat and harvested for meat, leather, and other products. Some evidence suggests that wild game ranching results in less damage to the vegetation and soils than does cattle ranching.

logical resource, usually a single population such as anchovies or white pine trees. Maximum sustainable yield is a goal sought when a consistent harvest is desired for economic return or for use as food or fuel. A consistent predictable harvest is important so that from year to year the number of jobs does not vary widely and the amount of food and fuel per household remains fairly constant.

Although the goal of MSY was common in past decades for the management of wildlife, including management of fisheries, it became clear in recent years that the MSY for a single species could have detrimental effects on other species, on the ecosystem, and for other uses of the landscape. It was also recognized that the estimation of maximum yield was based on relatively short-term measurements and might be in error. Thus, this goal has been modified to that of seeking an **optimum sustainable yield** (OSY)—as large a yield as possible that will not reduce the capacity of the population or its ecosystem to support that yield in the future or interfere with any other management goal for that ecosystem or habitat.

The goals of both MSY and OSY focus on economic production. When the purpose is simply the conservation of wildlife, as in the management of endangered species, the goal is maintaining as large a population as possible, consistent with the ability of the population and its ecosystem to sustain that size population indefinitely. This has become known as the goal of **optimum sustainable population** (OSP).

For endangered species, the minimum goal is to prevent the population from becoming extinct during some specified time period. This goal is humbler than that of optimum sustainable population; it does not attempt to maximize any number or quantity but merely to increase the length of time that a species persists on Earth.

A management goal must be defined for some specified time period (such as 1 year or 10 years). In formal management, one speaks of a planning time horizon, which is the time during which one hopes to achieve and sustain the goals. To some people, the notion that we would limit our view to some finite time period seems unfair and unethical. To formulate a clear operational policy, however, a management period must be established. We could say that the management time horizon is forever, but few societies ever consciously plan for very long periods, and history makes clear that over decades changes occur that lead to alterations in policy. Thus, it is reasonable in many ways to limit our view and set down relatively short time periods for our goals—a decade or two is usually called long-term for management.

The Practice of Wildlife Management Modern wildlife management is based on the principles and concepts of ecology, including an ecosystem perspective which assumes that the entire ecosystem and habitat of wildlife, rather than a single species, are managed. Indeed, it is now becoming widely recognized that there is no such thing as conserving an endangered species alone; there is only the conservation of endangered habitats and ecosystems that contain endangered species.

Wildlife management techniques include direct regulation of the number of animals by setting limits on the sex, size, or age of individuals killed or removed from a habitat, and indirect methods to manipulate the habitat and ecosystem, including changing the abundance of food supply, water, or physical shelter, changing the abundances of predators, and controlling parasites. As an example of direct population management, for many species the annual allowable take is varied so that the population is not allowed to fall below a certain size. In the state of Maine, for example, wildlife managers count moose each year from aircraft to determine how many licenses will be issued to moose hunters. As an example of habitat management, in Wankie National Park, Zimbabwe, artesian wells were dug to increase water supply and thus increase the abundance of wildlife. As an example of ecosystem management, in a number of parks, fires are allowed to burn or controlled fires are started; in some cases this is done to provide new forage for grazing animals.

Laws and Wildlife Management Most countries have laws governing the hunting and capture of wildlife and the management of wildlife habitats and preserves. In the United States, state laws and regulations differ markedly although wildlife does not obey state boundaries. Most states issue licenses allowing hunters a fixed take, which must be recorded. The scientific data thus provided are used to set subsequent levels for hunting. Some migratory birds are also regulated by state laws, even though they cross many states during their annual migrations.

U.S. government programs for the management of wildlife and freshwater sport fishing are administered under the Pittman-Roberson Act of 1937, which provides federal aid for fish and wildlife restoration programs carried out by the U.S. Fish and Wildlife Service. The funds are provided by taxes on the sale of hunting equipment. Another act, the Dingell-Johnson Act, passed in 1950 to aid sport fishing management, is funded by taxes on fishing equipment [6].

Despite legal protection in many countries, products from endangered species are widely traded within and between nations. The wildlife trade, both legal and illegal, is large. In Argentina alone, 5.4 million vertebrates from 25 species are exported each year, mostly as skins and leather. Although three-fourths of the more than $150 million produced by this trade comes from introduced species, native species are also threatened [10]. The guanaco, a native wild relative of the llama, is one of the species exploited; of an estimated 500,000 remaining, about 10%, or 50,000, are exported each year [10].

Wildlife is sold for fur, skin (for leather), and other products such as ivory, antlers, and horns; some are used for meat. Live animals are sold for medical and scientific research and as pets. For example, more than 400,000 animals were legally exported from the Philippines during the 1960s and 1970s, with an estimated value of more than $2 million. Most of these were monkeys used in medical research. There is legal trade in horn from nonendangered species such as the red deer from New Zealand and illegal trade from endangered species such as the rhinoceros.

Ivory is a unique product. Elephant ivory stands alone among wildlife products in that its trade resembles the trade in gold, silver, and diamonds more than it resembles trade in other commercial products. Like other precious commodities, ivory is valued regardless of whether it has been carved or formed into a useful product. Although all trade in ivory (except that taken in the past and resold) is illegal in many countries, there is a worldwide, active market in this commodity.

More than 780 species of animals and higher plants throughout the world are listed as threatened or endangered. [11]. These include 59 species of deer, antelope, and their relatives that are hunted as game; 45 species of carnivores, predators thought to be harmful; 35 species of primates, mostly used in medical research; and 33 marsupi-

Career Profile: Pieter de Marez Oyens

When Pieter de Marez Oyens was 16, he vacationed in Antarctica. The trip was a dream come true. When Oyens was 9, his father promised to take him to Antarctica some day. At age 16, the promise was fulfilled.

Oyens says, "In Antarctica, I felt a real sense of the diversity of our planet and the importance of maintaining samples of those ecosystems for future generations." The trip was a turning point in Oyens' life—it led him to a career in international conservation.

Oyens grew up in South America. Most of his existence has been urban. "I developed a personal commitment to preserve nature from my own need to experience it," he says. "I was always very moved when I spent time in nature. The experience was very rewarding to me and made me feel the importance of having a natural environment, a natural heritage."

After two years of liberal arts education, including "lots of biology," Oyens decided to tailor a major in environmental studies to his international interests. Today Oyens is Senior Program Officer for Brazil and the Guianas with the World Wildlife Fund-U.S. (WWF).

WWF is a private, nonprofit, international organization that works to establish protected

areas and to preserve biological diversity. The organization's purpose is to achieve a balance between environmental protection and development.

"I am involved in developing projects, by working directly with Brazilians, to establish research priorities and provide information for conservation action," he said. He works with scientists and private organizations to develop proposals for projects. He reviews the proposals with WWF staff—experts in wildlife management, parks, conservation, the sciences, and other areas—to determine whether the projects should be funded by WWF. When a project is funded, Oyens works to see that the objectives of the projet are accomplished.

Oyens believes that Brazil is beginning to set regional, national, and international exam-

ples of conservation action in South America. Private companies in Brazil are beginning to pay more attention to their role in environmental degradation and how to minimize it, he says. The goal is that development practices be established to ensure that renewable resources will be sustained and that biologically important areas always be protected from human impact.

"I think that there are many ways in which we can coexist with the natural environment—utilize its wealth of resources and maintain the biological diversity that guarantees the survival of nature and of our own human species," Oyens says.

When he chose to prepare for an environmental career, Oyens had to convince his father, a banker, that such an idealistic career was worthwhile. Today, his father sees how important his son's work in environmental conservation is to his own work in banking. For example, he now agrees that the long-term environmental costs of a development project can limit economic success. And the long-term success of a project is an important consideration in the decision to lend money.

Michele Wigginton

als, some killed for hides and some unsuccessful in competing with introduced mammals. This list does not include the endangered marine mammal species described elsewhere in this chapter. In the United States alone, more than 270 species are listed as endangered or threatened by the U.S. Council on Environmental Quality (Fig. 8.3).

As noted before, between 3 and 30 million species exist, most of which are insects. Most species are found in tropical areas on the land. Species in each of the five kingdoms of life (protists, monerans, fungi, plants, and animals) are endangered, but most of the past interest in endangered species has focused on mammals and birds, secondarily on

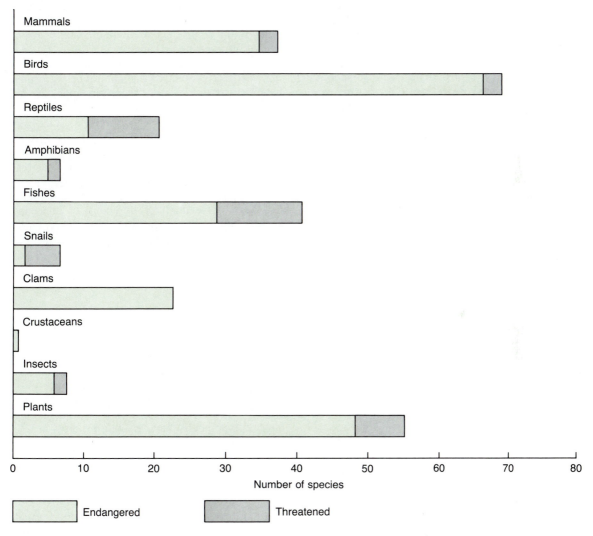

FIGURE 8.3
Threatened and endangered animal and plant species in the United States. Species are classified as endangered by the Secretary of the Interior, under the 1973 Endangered Species Act. Other organizations and agencies have classified additional species as threatened, rare, or sensitive. (From Council on Environmental Quality.)

higher plants. More recently, there has been a widened recognition that we must be concerned about the endangered species of all the kingdoms of life.

Why Save Endangered Species?

As mentioned, there are utilitarian, aesthetic, ethical and ecological reasons to save endangered species. One utilitarian reason is the need to maintain genetic variation. For example, modern agricultural production of such crops as wheat and corn depends on the continued production of genetic hybrids and the introduction of fresh genetic characteristics from wild strains of these crops. According to the U.S. Department of Agriculture, this continued introduction increases farm production by $1 billion per year. Why is this important? One reason is that disease organisms keep changing their genetic characteristics; as new disease strains develop, the crops become vulnerable. By introducing fresh genetic characteristics from the wild, researchers can develop hybrid strains with resistance to the new disease strains.

In addition, many important chemical compounds come from, or were first discovered in, wild organisms. Digitalis, an important drug in the treatment of certain heart ailments, comes from the purple foxglove, a small flowering plant native to Europe and Morocco.

Other organisms may produce useful medical compounds that are as yet unknown and untested. For example, scientists are now testing marine organisms for pharmaceutical drugs. Coral reefs offer a particularly promising area of study for such compounds, because many coral reef species produce toxins for defense [7, 12]. If we cause the extinction of species before we have a chance to test their compounds, we have lost an opportunity forever.

Many wild species might be useful to us, and it is imprudent to destroy them before we have a chance to test their uses. Many plants, for example, might have potential as food crops. Thus there are strong practical reasons to conserve as many species as possible; it is simply in our own best interest—it can save our lives and make us money.

The ecological arguments for conserving endangered species have grown stronger in recent years. As we learn more about the biosphere, we begin to understand how species affect one another around the world. Bacteria, for example, carry out chemical reactions that affect the chemical makeup of the atmosphere. Some bacteria convert molecular nitrogen in the atmosphere to chemical compounds that can then be used by other living things. The relatively few species of bacteria that can fix nitrogen are important to all of us. In the central ocean, there are very few species of nitrogen-fixing bacteria, but these few species are very important. Keystone species—those that carry out a function that cannot be performed by any other species—are especially important for us to conserve.

Aesthetic arguments for the conservation of endangered species are important to many people, especially as some of the most beautiful and appealing life forms on Earth become rarer. The presence of endangered species adds considerably to the diversity of landscapes and seascapes (Fig. 8.4). Diversity is an important quality of landscape beauty, and many organisms—especially birds, large land mammals, and flowering plants, but also many insects and ocean animals—are considered beautiful by many people.

Extinction

Extinction is the rule of nature. Although extinction is a species' ultimate fate, the rate of extinctions has varied greatly over geologic time and has increased rapidly since the industrial revolution. On the average, from 580 million years ago until the beginning of the industrial revolution, about one species per year became extinct. An estimated 500 million species have existed on Earth at one time or another [13].

Natural extinctions often appear to follow understandable patterns, with the replacement of one form by a more successful one. This was not the case, however, about 10,000 years ago at the end of the last great continental glaciation. At that time, massive extinctions of large birds and mammals occurred for no obvious reason.

During that time in North America, there was a loss of 33 genera of large mammals (those weighing 50 kg or more), while only 13 genera had be-

FIGURE 8.4
Among the many species considered endangered in the United States are (a) the ocelot, hunted for its fur; (b) the manzanita, a shrub of the heath family, photographed at Natural Bridges National Monument, Utah; and (c) the desert tortoise.

(a)

(b)

(c)

come extinct in the preceding 1 or 2 million years. Smaller mammals were not so affected, nor were marine mammals. It has also been observed that these sudden extinctions did not seem to be correlated with major environmental change [3]. Instead, they seemed to coincide with the arrival, on different continents, at different times, of Stone Age people.

The Causes of Extinction   Five causes of extinction are population risk, environmental risk, natural catastrophe, genetic risk, and human actions. Population risk refers to random variations in population rates—in birth and death rates—that could cause a species of low abundance to become extinct. For example, blue whales swim over vast areas of ocean. Because the total population is only several hundred, there are year-to-year variations in the success of individual blue whales in finding mates. If one year most whales were unsuccessful in finding a mate, births could be dangerously low. Such random variation in populations, typical among many species, can occur without any change in the environment. It is a risk especially to species that consist of only a single population in one habitat.

Environmental risk refers to random changes in the environment that occur from day to day, month to month, and year to year, but are not severe enough to be considered catastrophes. The environmental variation could be either in the environment or biological (variations in predator, prey, symbiotic species, or competitor species).

Paul and Anne Ehrlich described the local extinction of a population of butterflies in the Colorado mountains [11]. These butterflies lay their eggs in the unopened buds of a single plant species of the legume family—the lupine. When the caterpillars hatch they feed on the flowers. In one year, a very late snow and freeze killed all the lupine buds and caused the local extinction of the butterflies (the plants survived, and their roots produced new stems and leaves and then flowers in the next year). Had this been the only population of that butterfly, the entire species would have gone extinct. In some cases, species are sufficiently rare and isolated that such normal variations can lead to their extinction. In other cases, species succumb to catastrophic variation in the environment.

A natural catastrophe is a sudden change in the environment not due to human action. Generally, fire, major storms, earthquakes, floods, and meteorite impacts are natural catastrophes on the land; changes in currents and upwellings are major catastrophes in the ocean.

The explosion of the volcano on the island of Krakatoa in Indonesia in 1883 caused the extinction of most forms of life found there. Many of these were local extinctions, in that the species continued to exist elsewhere and recolonized the island later, but the event could have caused the complete extinction of any species found only on that island.

To explain the difference between environmental risk and natural catastrophe, consider the heath hen, once a common bird of the eastern United States, but reduced to very low numbers by habitat change and hunting. By the last quarter of the nineteenth century, the heath hen existed only on the island of Martha's Vineyard, off Cape Cod, Massachusetts. In 1907, a part of the island was made into a preserve for this bird, whose numbers had been reduced to about 100. The predators of the bird were controlled and the population increased to 800 by 1916, when two things happened: A fire destroyed most of the nesting areas (a catastrophe), and the next winter an unusually heavy concentration of goshawks on the island (environmental risk) caused high mortality. The population was reduced to less than 200 and was extinct by 1932 [14].

Genetic risk refers to changes in genetic characteristics that can occur in small populations from a variety of effects, excluding external environmental changes [14].

Human actions cause extinction of species through (1) disruption or elimination of habitats; (2) introduction of new parasites, predators, or competitors of a species; and (3) hunting for commercial purposes, for sport, or through the belief that the species is a pest (see Plate 7).

People have caused extinctions over a long time, not just in recent years; New Zealand provides a good example. Because New Zealand was isolated from the continents for a long period that included the rise of mammals, the native land vertebrates of New Zealand consist almost entirely of birds. Fossils suggest that more than 150 species of large, flightless, grazing birds lived there when the first Polynesians arrived about A.D. 950 [15]. By the time Captain Cook reached New Zealand in 1769, 20 species of moas and several other birds had been driven to extinction. European settlers increased the extinction rate even further; the last of the world's moas were killed in the late eighteenth century, as well as 2 species of flightless geese, a great swan, a great eagle, and all of the flightless rails [15].

Modern civilization has greatly increased the rate of extinction. The current rate of extinction among most groups of mammals is estimated to be 1000 times greater than the "high" extinction rate at the end of the Pleistocene [16]. The International Union for the Conservation of Nature estimates that three-fourths of the extinctions since 1600 of birds and mammals were caused by human beings. Hunting is estimated to have caused 42% of the extinctions of birds and one-third of the extinctions of mammals. In the United States, 47 species of wildlife became extinct between 1700 and 1970, but 25 of these were lost in the last 50 years (Fig. 8.5).

Species that are likely to become endangered through human activities tend to share certain traits. Knowledge of these common traits helps us protect and manage such species. Easily endangered species, particularly vertebrates, are generally long-lived and large. Such species tend to have low reproductive rates and recover slowly from lowered population levels. The potential growth rate of a pair of rats, for example, who may have several litters of several offspring each year, is markedly different from that of a pair of condors, who raise one offspring once in several years. The biggest and largest also require the largest territories and the most food per individual.

Carnivores are particularly subject to extinction because they are higher on food chains and require a larger base in the net primary production of veg-

etation than do herbivores; thus they require large home ranges or habitats to maintain a viable population. Carnivores are also vulnerable because they are usually viewed as dangerous to domestic animals.

The Conservation of Endangered Species

Knowledge of environmental studies provides us with basic tools to promote the conservation and wise management of endangered species. The needs, however, exceed our capacities; the choices are ours. We cannot rely on nature to protect the endangered species or to provide all the answers as to which we should save. We must choose to save those species most important to our survival according to our sense of right and wrong and according to our sense of what is desirable in nature.

Minimum Safe Population Sizes The minimum population that can be sustained for a long period with low risk of genetic problems resulting from a small gene pool is approximately 500 individuals or more [14].

FIGURE 8.5
Extinct vertebrate species and subspecies, 1760–1979. The number of species becoming extinct increased rapidly after 1860. Note that most of the increase is due to the extinction of birds. (From Council on Environmental Quality.)

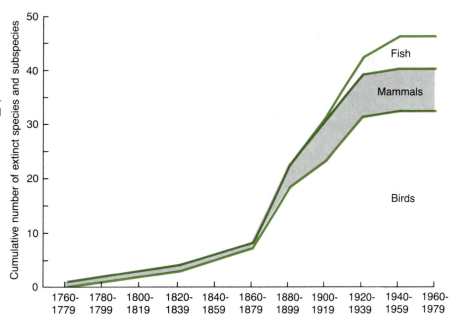

Because few nature preserves can be large enough for the persistence of some of the large animals without active management, the future survival of such species requires active human manipulation. For example, because wolves require about 26 km^2 each, a preserve that could maintain this minimum population would have to be approximately 13,000 km^2. In contrast, 500 field mice could persist in a preserve that is a fraction of 1 km^2.

In small populations, genes that carry harmful characteristics can become dominant simply because there is little other genetic material in the population. This is called **genetic drift.** Genetic drift can be avoided by occasionally moving individuals from one preserve to another.

Because larger organisms are more subject to extinction, we must be particularly careful in our management of them. Undoubtedly, choices will have to be made. One leading conservationist, Norman Myers, urges that we adopt a "triage strategy," taken from the French medical practice in World War I. In that war, doctors found that there were more wounded than they could care for, so they assigned each wounded soldier to one of three categories: those who would be helped by medical attention and might not survive without it; those who would survive without medical attention; and those who would die regardless. The doctors concentrated on the first, and Myers suggests that we apply the same strategy to endangered species [12].

Endangered Pests and Dangerous Wildlife
Thus far we have considered wildlife and endangered species mainly from the point of view of their benefits, but in some cases wildlife and endangered species are pests. In such cases, controversies arise over whether the endangered species should be moved from the location where it is a pest or whether it should be allowed to go extinct. If suitable habitat elsewhere is lacking, a transfer of the species is difficult. Important cases of this kind in recent years include burros in the Grand Canyon of Arizona, grizzly bears in Yellowstone National Park, feral goats and sheep on islands off the California coast, and tigers in regions of India.

Endangered Species and Society People can aid in the conservation of endangered species through a wide range of activities and methods. During the last 20 years, many countries have enacted laws protecting endangered species, and international legal agreements among nations have increased. One of the most successful international efforts has been the International Whaling Commission, which is discussed later. Efforts to increase public awareness have had considerable effect.

Legal protection for endangered species has increased in many countries. In the late 1960s and early 1970s several landmark acts, including the 1969 Endangered Species Conservation Act, the 1972 Marine Mammal Protection Act, and the 1973 Endangered Species Act, were passed in the United States. These acts define when a species is legally endangered.

The Endangered Species Act of 1973 represented a major change in the federal government's role in the protection of endangered species, in the legal attitude toward endangered species, and in the legal position of endangered species. This act declares that endangered species of wildlife and plants "are of aesthetic, ecological, educational, historical, recreational, and scientific value to the nation and its people." The act provides a means to conserve ecosystems on which endangered species depend. Thus the act established the need for an ecosystem approach to the management of endangered species. The act states that all federal departments and agencies should seek to conserve endangered species and use their authorities to further the purpose of the act. The act recognizes two groups of protected species: endangered and threatened. As defined by the act, an endangered species is one in danger of extinction through all or a significant portion of its range. A threatened species is one likely to become endangered within the foreseeable future through all or a significant portion of its range.

The Endangered Species Act of 1973 made it unlawful for any person in the United States to import, export, or sell in interstate or international commerce any endangered species or any product of an endangered species. The law also made it illegal to harass, harm, or capture any such species within the United States or on the high seas.

Another important activity is habitat conservation and preservation, which is carried out by both private organizations and governments.

A third group of activities concerns attempts to affect the birth and death rates of species by direct action, including stopping human harvest of the species. In eastern and southern Africa, for example, the black rhinoceros is seriously endangered because its horn, believed to have medicinal properties, is very valuable—a single horn can be worth a year's income to some of the local inhabitants.

In other cases, increasing the birth rates in populations has been attempted. The program of the U.S. Audubon Society and the U.S. Fish and Wildlife Service to aid the California condor by taking eggs from nests in the wild and incubating them in captivity is an example of this approach.

A more extreme approach is the increasingly important use of zoos to breed and maintain populations of endangered species. When wild habitats are completely destroyed or seriously decreased and threatened, zoos provide the only remaining places where species can persist. In many cases, zoos are seen as holding areas where a species may be maintained for decades until suitable habitats can be restored and the species returned to the wild. For example, the only remaining truly wild horses live in zoos. The conservation of species within zoos has led to international programs to maintain proper genetic diversity in zoo populations by exchanging individuals of endangered species. Some zoos, such as the Jersey Island Trust, a zoo on the Isle of Jersey, Great Britain, are primarily devoted to the conservation of endangered species.

More radical approaches to the conservation of endangered species include political activism. Members of the Canadian organization called Greenpeace have put themselves in small boats between whaling ships and whales, in a direct attempt to prevent the killing of the whales. This political radicalism for the conservation of endangered species is a novel development in the modern world, and shows the great importance some people attach to conservation.

Earlier in this century, the approach to conservation was a hands-off attitude; that is, because human activities have increased extinctions, we should remove all human interference. More knowledge, however, has given us a new perspective: Only by active management can we prevent the extinction of some species. Active management varies from studying the endangered species to establishing preserves, improving their habitats, providing new sources of food and other resources, and even captive breeding.

On the one hand, we face a sad truth: The wilderness—in the sense of nature untouched by civilization—is passing away. Even areas once believed pristine we now recognize to have been affected by people for many centuries. On the other hand, our knowledge gives us great opportunities and great choices. Only with the perspective of environmental studies—the interrelated functions of the earth's geology, climatology, oceanography, and biology—and an understanding of human history and values, can we learn to choose and act wisely. In the end, we are the primary biological resource.

FISHERIES

Fisheries are a major source of the world's food, particularly protein sources. Many species of fish and shellfish are caught, but fewer than 20 species provide two-thirds of the catch and 90% of the value. The worldwide annual harvest of fish is slightly more than 70 million metric tons per year (60 from marine fisheries, 10 from fresh water) [17]. Approximately 6 million metric tons comes from aquaculture—the farming of fish in artificial ponds and tanks. Directly edible fish and shellfish provide about 5% of the world's protein—8% when adjusted for quality. Fish are used also as feed for poultry and pigs, which supply another 5% or 6% of the world's protein. Thus fish may provide 10–13% of the world's protein [18], but they provide only 0.6% of the world's human food calories.

In Japan, Iceland, and Scandinavian countries, fish provide 25% of the protein. In the United States the percentage is much less; the annual per capita intake of fish is 5 kg. Moreover, in the United States the use of fish as food decreases with the distance from the shore; people in coastal areas consume 83% more fish than those in other areas. For Peru, Iceland, Japan, Canada, and Denmark, fish are a major export [18].

Between 1950 and 1970, the world fishery catch expanded from 24 million to 66 million metric tons, or about 12%/yr, but since 1970 the catch has increased more slowly, remaining between 70 and 75 million metric tons (Fig. 8.6). The value of the world's fisheries increased between 1963 and 1973 from $6.3 billion to $18 billion. Fish vary greatly in value, from tens of dollars to a thousand dollars per ton depending on the species and port.

Fishing is international, but a few countries dominate. Four countries—Japan, China, Russia, and the United States—caught 51% of all the world's catch in 1973 [18].

We tend to think of the oceans as a vast, inexhaustible resource. However, from the viewpoint of fisheries management, most of the ocean is a desert. Commercial fisheries are concentrated in relatively few areas of the world's oceans (Fig. 8.7). Ten percent of the oceans—the continental shelves—provides more than 90% of the fishery harvest. Fish are abundant where their food is abundant and, ultimately, where there is a high production of algae. Algae are most abundant in areas with relatively high concentrations of the chemical elements necessary for life, particularly nitrogen and phosphorus. These areas occur most commonly along the continental shelf, particularly in regions of upwelling and sometimes quite close to shore. Upwelling areas are rich in chemical elements necessary for life because the rising currents carry these elements from the deep ocean to the surface.

The Management of Fisheries

A fish population is referred to as a stock. A stock of fish has traditionally been managed as if it grew

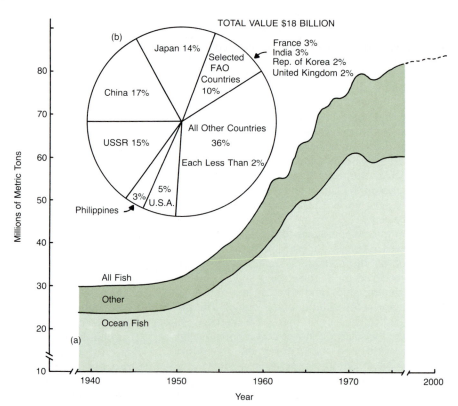

FIGURE 8.6
(a) Annual catch of oceanic fish (lower line) and all marine animals. The graph shows a downward trend for the catch of oceanic fish right after 1970. Catch is estimated for the period shown by a dashed line. (b) The catch by major fishing countries. [(a) From Council on Environmental Quality and the Department of State; (b) modified from Bell.]

TOTAL VALUE $18 BILLION

(b)
Japan 14%
Selected FAO Countries 10%
France 3%
India 3%
Rep. of Korea 2%
United Kingdom 2%
China 17%
All Other Countries 36%
USSR 15%
Each Less Than 2%
3%
5%
U.S.A.
Philippines

(a)
All Fish
Other
Ocean Fish

Millions of Metric Tons

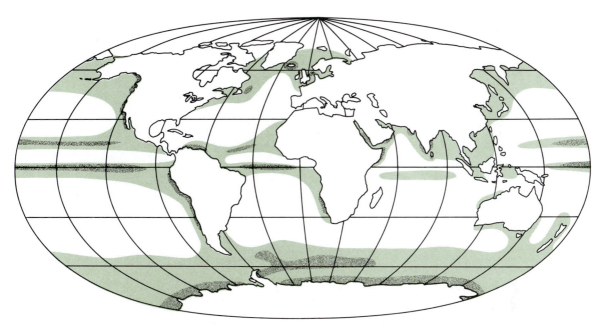

FIGURE 8.7
Earth's major fishery regions. Heavier shading indicates regions of upwelling or high productivity. The major fisheries occur wherever the productivity of marine algae is high: near continents, in areas of upwelling, near estuaries, and along the continental shelves. The central ocean, which occupies the largest area, is relatively a desert in terms of economically valuable fish. (From Mackintosh, 1965. Reproduced by permission of the Buckland Foundation from *The stocks of whales*, published by Fishing News Books Ltd.)

independently of other species and as if it were supplied with a constant amount of food. In the past, fish stock was generally assumed to grow in accordance with the logistic growth curve (Fig. 8.8).

Fishermen are interested in obtaining as large a catch as possible, but the fisheries manager wants to keep the annual net growth rate of a fish stock as large as possible without adversely affecting the population or its environment. Overfishing can lead, in subsequent years, to a decrease in the rate of growth.

How rapidly can a fish stock grow? If we assume that a fish stock grows according to the logistic curve, we can estimate the population size that gives the maximum rate of growth. In Figure 8.8a the logistic growth curve for a fish population shows the change in the number of fish over time. We can regraph this relation to show the rate of growth plotted against the population size (Fig. 8.8b). In this graph we see that when the number of fish is small, the total number added is also small. We also see that at the logistic carrying capacity the net growth is zero. This must be true by definition; if the net growth were not zero, the population would be changing and thus would not be at its carrying capacity. The rate of growth increases between the smallest population and the carrying capacity. For a population growing according to the logistic curve, the maximum rate of growth occurs when the population is exactly one-half its carrying capacity.

If a fish population really did grow according to this curve, then the management strategy would be to harvest enough fish every year to bring the population to one-half its carrying capacity. Then the amount added the next year would be the maximum that could be added by that species. The

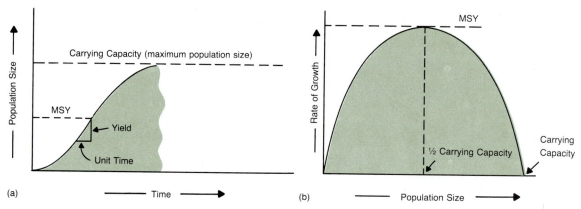

FIGURE 8.8
Idealized growth of a fish population. (a) Growth over time. (b) Growth rate at different population sizes. A logistic population grows to a maximum size, called the carrying capacity. The
growth curve is steepest when the population is one-half the maximum, called the point of
maximum sustainable yield (MSY). Growth of real populations may differ considerably from
that shown in this idealized graph.

point on the logistic growth curve where the maximum growth rate is obtained has become known
as the point of maximum sustainable yield (MSY).

For the MSY concept to be true, so management
can be based on it, three things must hold:

1 The population must have an exact and single
   carrying capacity, and its growth must be determined exactly by the classical logistic curve.
2 It must be possible to know precisely both the
   carrying capacity and the present population
   size.
3 It must be possible to obtain complete cooperation from all fishermen of all countries so
   that they manage their individual catches to
   make the sum add up exactly to the amount
   required.

In reality, none of these conditions is met.
Rarely do we know the true carrying capacity, and
therefore estimates of one-half the carrying capacity are subject to great error. Because we cannot
very well count all the fish of a species in the
ocean, elaborate international sampling schemes
are used to estimate the populations and determine annual allowed catches on some fishing
grounds.

Furthermore, many factors interact to cause
population size changes over time. This is just as
true for fish as it is for other organisms, and in

reality we can expect the carrying capacity and the
actual size of a population to vary over time
whether or not people are catching fish. We cannot
expect to harvest the same amount every year and
maintain a population at exactly its point of maximum growth.

Suppose we assume a fish stock is at MSY and
proceed to harvest it at the MSY level every year. If
we follow the logistic exactly, we can get into a disastrous situation. Even the slightest mistake in
overestimating the MSY will push the population
to a smaller size the second year. If we continue to
maintain the same harvest levels, expecting the
population to be at MSY, then we will drive the
population to lower and lower levels and finally to
extinction, unless we recognize our error.

In reality, we rarely fish a species to complete
extinction because it is not worthwhile or practical
economically to maintain fishing until the last fish
is caught. Extinction of fish species occurs when
one population is taken fortuitously—that is,
whenever it happens to be found with another species being fished—or when a population is driven
to such a low point that other events, including
random variations, force the remaining small population to decline even after fishing has ceased.

Because it is not possible to know the exact size
of a fish population, fishing limits cannot be set at
exactly the right number to obtain maximum yield.

Nor is it possible to set up a cooperative agreement in which fishermen hunt exactly to the right level, although in certain cases, as in the tuna fisheries of the United States, there has been considerable cooperation among the fishermen. Some variations in the population and in the fishing effort always exist.

For all of these reasons, the logistic equation and the point of MSY cannot be taken exactly and literally. In an attempt to avoid the pitfalls of this approach, fisheries managers have defined an optimum sustainable yield (OSY). In current practice, OSY is defined as 10% more than the population size that provides maximum yield. This OSY is thought to provide some cushion against errors in estimating the carrying capacity, the point of MSY, and the current population size. Although not really optimum in any sense, the OSY provides a certain amount of protection against our lack of information. OSY deals with only one of the three classes of problems in fisheries management— that of the error in the estimate of population levels and other data.

During the last 200 years, one fishery after another has been developed and has crashed. The failure of the world's fisheries continues today, even in those areas with the most conscientious and active management [18, 19].

A classic case of a managed failure is the history of the Peruvian anchovy fishery, once the world's largest commercial fishery. In 1970 7.3 million metric tons were caught, but by 1972 only 1.8 million metric tons were caught—15% of the 1970 peak. Anchovy are found in the upwelling regions, where nutrient-rich waters move upward. As we discussed in Chapter 2, they are one of the principal foods of the birds that produce guano and thus are an important link in the global phosphorus cycle.

Why did the Peruvian anchovy fishery crash? Some claim that overfishing was responsible. The real cause is not known, but the failure of this major fishery is a blow to the world's protein supply and to the management of fisheries. The fishery was actively managed by the Peruvian government with assistance from the U. N. Food and Agriculture Organization (FAO). They tried to manage the anchovies to keep the population at the level that would provide the MSY. Unintentionally, the population may have been brought to a level below MSY, and as long as the catch was kept at the MSY level, the anchovy could only decrease.

Others blamed the decrease on long-term environmental fluctuations, which have been known for centuries to occur, particularly the condition called El Niño. When the winds change, the upwelling ceases, there is less algal production, and the fish become uncommon. Historical records of the guano deposits from birds that eat anchovies show that these failures in upwelling have occurred repeatedly in the past. Therefore, management policies based on MSY were bound to fail because they assumed a constant environment.

In the last 20 years, a number of other major fisheries, including salmon fisheries off the California coast, have experienced similar crashes under intentional management regimes (Table 8.2).

TABLE 8.2
Problems of some major fisheries.

Anchovy:
  Reached peak in 1970 (10,000,000 tons), then declined.

Atlantic herring:
  Exploitation so high that recruitment was decreased.

Arctonorwegian cod:
  High fishing level followed by 4 years of poor recruitment.

Downs' stock of herring in the North Sea:
  Managers failed to grasp stock and recruitment problems.

North Atlantic haddock:
  Catch averaged 50,000 tons for many years; increased to 155,000 in 1965, 127,000 in 1966, then fell off to 12,000 in 1971–74. In 1973, the International Commission for the Northwest Atlantic Fisheries (ICNAF) established a quota of 6000 tons. Apparently, haddock could sustain a 50,000-ton catch, but when this was tripled, the population was so decreased that only a smaller catch could be sustained.

Atlantic menhaden:
  Peak catch was 712,000 metric tons in 1956; in 1969, it was 161,400. Fisheries experts believe the drop was due to overfishing.

Pacific sardines:
  Declined catastrophically in the 1950s through the 1970s.

Source: Cushing.

The U.S. National Marine Fisheries defines the status of a fish stock in terms of MSY. A stock is called "depleted" if it has been so reduced through overfishing or any other human activity or natural cause that fishing effort must be substantially curtailed to allow the stock to replenish itself. A stock is called "in imminent danger" when it has been reduced to MSY, and the available fleet has the capability to catch enough fish to reduce the population below MSY. A stock is "in intensive use" when the population is being reduced to the estimated MSY.

Some marine resources are abundant and relatively unexploited. One of the most important occurs in the ocean waters surrounding Antarctica. This area is well known for the abundance of krill, a small shrimplike crustacean, and other animal life—birds, penguins, and marine mammals, including many of the great whales and seals. All of the vertebrates depend either directly or indirectly on krill; we described this food chain in Chapter 4. The production of krill is estimated to be on the order of 100 or more million metric tons per year, a production considerably larger than the yield from all other commercial fisheries.

The krill provide food for some species of the great baleen whales. Krill occur in large, dense patches. When the great baleen whales find one of these patches (which may be one or more kilometers in diameter), they swim back and forth, leaving a row of cleared water much like a farmer plowing a hayfield. In fact, the nineteenth-century whalers were able to pursue whales by following these trails through the "whale feed."

Some countries, including the Soviet Union, have in recent years begun sending trawlers down to the Antarctic waters to harvest krill as a protein source. In the next decades we will see other attempts to exploit relatively unused oceanic areas as the better known fisheries become less productive.

Although the history of commercial fisheries and their management is mainly one of failure, there is a bright side. No other area of natural resource management has exceeded fisheries in the attempt to use formal mathematics, statistics, economic theory, and scientific methods to formulate appropriate policies. This conscientious scientific attempt has provided a new dimension in resource management. Managers trained in economics, mathematics, statistics, and biology will be in demand for careers associated with fisheries. As in other areas of environmental studies, the management of fisheries must also take into account culture and human history as they affect peoples' appreciation of and desire to use fisheries as a resource.

The Future of Fisheries

Although optimistic projections suggest that the world's fisheries may provide greater yields in the future, this is doubtful. Many fisheries have declined in yield in this century, and the harvest of most kinds of fish appears near or beyond a maximum sustainable level. Not only are many fisheries overharvested, but the world's fisheries are subject to pollutants of many kinds that, in the long run, may decrease the productivity of the fish and the organisms that provide their food.

Aquaculture could provide additional sources of fish. At the World Conference on Aquaculture held by the U. N. Food and Agriculture Organization in 1976, it was concluded that the harvest from this method could increase 5 to 10 times in the next several decades if sufficient money and resources were available [17].

Several challenges face the managers of fisheries. The primary ones are to prevent further crashes in major fisheries and to protect the world's oceans as living systems. Because fisheries are generally international, the management of fish populations requires an unusually high degree of cooperation among countries.

WHALES AND OTHER MARINE MAMMALS

Marine mammals have long fascinated people. Drawings dated to 2200 B.C. show whales [20], and there is evidence that Eskimos used whales for food and clothing as long ago as 1500 B.C. In the ninth century A.D., whaling by Norwegians was reported by travelers whose accounts were written down in the court of the English King Alfred.

During the last 80 million years, several separate groups of mammals have undergone adaptations to marine life. All originally inhabitants of the land, each group today shows a different degree of transition to ocean life. Some, such as dolphins, porpoises, and great whales, complete their entire life cycle in the oceans and have organs and limbs that are highly adapted to life in the water. The seals and their relatives, called the pinnipeds (literally, fin-foot), breed on the land and can move about in both water and land environments. The sea otter appears to be a more recent addition to marine environments, living near shore and having legs that seem still relatively adapted to land.

Because of the great interest these animals evoke, and because of their past economic utility, marine mammals have been the focus of a number of classic conflicts in the conservation of endangered species. In the following section we will review some of these major cases; they are important in themselves, but they also illustrate many of the issues that focus on endangered species.

The Great Whales

In recent history, the great whales have been a food and economic resource and a major concern in conservation. Whales are said to be used for subsistence when they form part of the basic food or materials of a culture, as with present-day Eskimos, Japanese, and inhabitants of Tonga and Greenland. Other uses of whales are called commercial. By tradition, whaling grounds are referred to as fisheries, even though whales are mammals.

The earliest hunters killed whales from the shore or from small boats near shore, but gradually whale hunters ventured farther out. In the eleventh and twelfth centuries, the Basques hunted the Atlantic right whale from open boats in the Bay of Biscay, off the western coast of France. Medieval whaling was still shore-based; the whales were hunted from open boats and brought ashore for processing.

Whaling became pelagic—that is, took to the open ocean—with the invention of furnaces and boilers (tryworks) for extracting whale oil at sea. With this invention, whaling grew as an industry.

The English and the Dutch sought right and bowhead whales in the Atlantic in the seventeenth and eighteenth centuries, sailing from Spain to Hudson Bay. American fleets developed in the eighteenth century in New England, and in the next century the United States dominated the industry, providing most of the ships and even more of the crews for whaling [21, 22].

The pelagic whaling ships at first sought whales that were large, slow moving, and easy to process. The right whale got its name because it was the "right" whale to catch; that is, it floated rather than sank after dying, yielded great quantities of oil, and was relatively docile and easy to catch. Bowhead, gray, and sperm whales were the other species sought in the nineteenth century (Fig. 8.9).

Whales provided many nineteenth-century products. The oil was used for cooking, lubrication, and lamps, and whales provided the main ingredients for the base of perfumes. The elongated teeth (whalebone, or baleen), which enable baleen whales to strain the ocean waters for food, are flexible and springy and were used for corset stays and other products before the invention of inexpensive steel springs. Whaling actually increased in the twentieth century. Although the nineteenth-century whaling ships are more famous, made popular by such novels as *Moby Dick*, more whales have been killed in the twentieth century (Fig. 8.10).

Whaling was never a major world industry in terms of gross or net economic return. In 1959, the gross value of whaling production was approximately $500 million, while in the same year the gross value of all other fisheries was approximately $4 to $5 billion.

Attempts to control whaling by international agreements began with the League of Nations in 1924. The first agreement, the "Convention for the Regulation of Whaling," was signed by 21 countries in 1931. In 1946 a conference in Washington, D.C., initiated the International Whaling Commission (IWC), which has since regulated the take of whales by voluntary agreement among countries [20, 21].

Whatever its success or failure, the IWC was a major landmark in wildlife conservation and the management of biological resources. It repre-

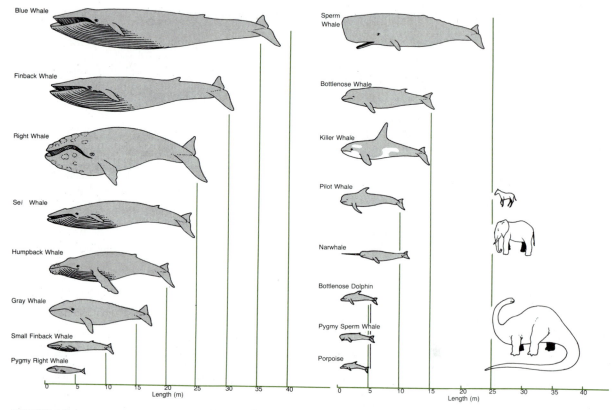

FIGURE 8.9
The two major groups of whales are baleen whales, which have large, comblike teeth used
to filter small food items out of sea water, and toothed whales. Except for the sperm whale,
all of the great whales are baleen whales. (From U. N. Food and Agriculture Organization.)

sented a major attempt by nations to agree on a reasonable annual catch of whales. The annual meeting of the IWC has become a forum to discuss international conservation, to work out basic concepts of maximum and optimum sustainable yields, and to formulate a scientific basis for commercial harvesting. The IWC has played a major role in the overall reduction—almost elimination—of the commercial harvest of whales.

The Management of Whales and Other Marine Mammals

The basis for the management of whales and other marine mammals has been similar to that for fisheries management. As with fish populations, each marine mammal population has been treated as if it were isolated, had a constant supply of food, and was subject only to the effects of human harvesting. It was assumed that the growth of a marine mammal population followed the logistic curve, and that the point of MSY occurred when the population size was equal to one-half the carrying capacity. It is realized now that management policies must be expanded to include ecosystem concepts and the understanding that populations interact in complex ways.

Whales The goal of whaling management, however, is different from that of fisheries. The international agreements about whaling are concerned with preventing extinction and maintaining large

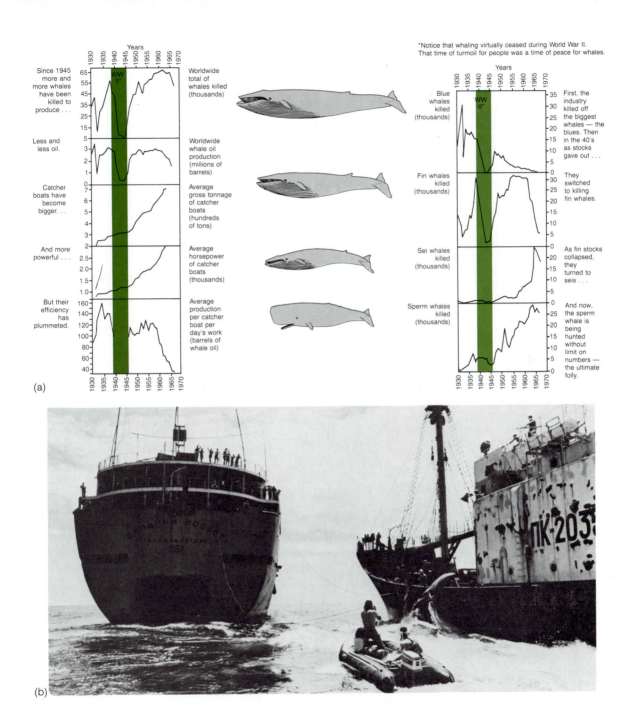

FIGURE 8.10

(a) The history of the whaling industry in modern times. (b) In an ongoing effort to prevent commercial whaling, members of the Greenpeace organization confront Soviet whalers from the factory ship *Vladivostok* and its companion ship. [(a) After Payne, 1968, in Bell, 1978. Reprinted by permission of Westview Press from *Food from the sea: The economics and politics of ocean fisheries* by Frederick W. Bell. Copyright © 1978 by Westview Press, Boulder, Colorado.]

population sizes rather than maximizing production. For this reason, the Marine Mammal Protection Act enacted by the United States in 1972 defines an optimum sustainable population (OSP) as its goal rather than a maximum or optimum sustainable yield (MSY or OSY).

Since the formation of the IWC, no species has gone extinct, the total take of whales has decreased, and harvesting of species considered endangered has been halted. The endangered species protected from hunting have had a mixed history (Table 8.3). The blue whale appears to have recovered little and remains rare and endangered. The gray whale, however, appears to have increased and is now relatively abundant, numbering 11,000.

Sea Otters The case of the sea otter illustrates conflicts among competing interests. It became endangered because it was hunted almost to extinction in the nineteenth century. In the twentieth century the otter has been protected and its numbers have increased; now it competes with fishermen for valuable shellfish. This conflict is particularly significant because the otter plays an important role in its marine ecosystems; that is, ecosystems with sea otters are quite different from those without them (see Chapter 5).

The sea otter inhabits the shallow nearshore areas of the cold northern Pacific where it feeds on shellfish, sometimes using one shell as a tool to break open another. Before commercial exploita-

tion, the otter was found from the northern islands of Japan through the Aleutians and south along the coast of North America to Baja California. The story is told that about 1870 a group of shipwrecked Russian sailors survived by eating sea otters and using their skins as protection from the cold. When the sailors returned, the sea otter pelts they brought with them were recognized as extremely valuable, and commercial exploitation began. The species was rapidly depleted and by the beginning of the twentieth century had declined from several hundred thousand to a few thousand.

Protection of sea otters began in 1911, and since then the species has begun to occupy about 30–40% of its original range and now numbers more than 100,000. Sea otters are found along the coast of North America as far south as central California, near San Simeon [21].

Although sea otters represent an aesthetic resource for people and they are important in their ecosystems, the catch of abalone and clams has been reduced in areas where sea otters are present. Commercial fishermen claim that the otters are a major cause in the reduction of abalone; others argue that the fishermen are the major cause of this reduction and that the otters play a lesser role.

The conflict illustrates the problem of multiple use of a natural renewable resource—one in which any management policy will have several effects. Some suggest moving otters to areas where they do not compete directly with commercial fishermen. If we learn how to balance all the conflicting interests in the sea otter situation, we may find a

TABLE 8.3
Whale abundances: past and present.[a]

Species	Before Commercial Whaling (number of individuals)	Recent Estimates (number of individuals)
Blue	200,000	<1,000[d]
Bowhead	30,000[b]	2,400+[b]
Humpback	100,000+	5,000
Fin	450,000	102,000
Right	50,000[c]	4,000[c]
Gray	15,000[c]	11,000[c]
Sperm	950,000	+600,000+
Sei	200,000	74,000
Minke	250,000	+200,000+

[a]All values from Australia, 1979, unless otherwise noted.
[b]Bockstoce and Botkin.
[c]Sheffer.   [d]Various sources

key to managing other natural renewable resources with multiple uses.

Dolphins and Other Small Cetaceans Among the many species of small "whales" or cetaceans are dolphins and porpoises. More than 40 of these species have been hunted commercially or have been killed inadvertently as a part of other fishing efforts [21]. A classic case in this regard is that of the spinner, spotted, and common dolphins of the eastern Pacific. Because these carnivorous, fish-eating mammals often feed with yellowfin tuna, a major commercial fish, commercial tuna fishing has inadvertently netted and killed large numbers of these marine mammals. More than 100,000 of these dolphins have been killed in recent years [21].

The attempt to reduce dolphin mortality illustrates cooperation among fishermen, conservationists, and government agencies and the role of scientific research in the management of renewable resources. The U.S. Marine Mammal Commission and commercial fishermen have cooperated in seeking methods to reduce the dolphin mortality. Research conducted on dolphin behavior helped in the design of new netting procedures that would be less likely to trap the mammals. These new procedures have been adopted by the fishermen and have greatly reduced the trapping of dolphins in the tuna nets. This demonstrated that cooperation among apparently competing interests is possible and that scientific research can help balance the multiple uses of our renewable biological resources.

The Manatee The manatee and its relatives, known as the sirenians, are the only herbivorous marine mammals; they are all relatively rare. In North America, the manatee is one of the rarest and most endangered large mammals; only a few hundred remain in Florida. While these docile creatures were once caught and eaten by people, they are now protected. Even so, they still suffer from destruction of their habitat and inadvertent killing. Manatees feed on aquatic plants that grow in shallow streams and brackish inlets. These areas have been greatly altered by channelization and other development; water pollution and the use of herbicides to clear channels for boats have killed the aquatic plants in many areas. Thus there are few remaining places where the manatee can feed and reproduce. In addition, the animals are occasionally cut by propellers from motorboats. Although these accidents are relatively rare, the reproductive rate of manatees is so low that a few additional deaths a year could cause an overall decline. Although much is being done to protect these animals, including the posting and patrolling of waterways, the future of this species is in doubt. The case of the manatee illustrates that it is important to have a habitat in a good condition in order to help save an endangered species.

These examples are only a few of the many cases involving the management and conservation of marine mammals. It is clear that many people attach great significance to marine mammals compared with other wildlife. In the United States, whale watching, particularly of the grey whale off the southern California coast and of sperm, fin, and other whales off Cape Cod, Massachusetts, has become quite popular. Few other issues in environmental studies have raised as much public attention and debate as the harvesting of marine mammals [22].

SUMMARY

Biological resources are renewable because populations and communities can be regrown, but biological resources are vulnerable. They provide food and many kinds of economically useful materials; they are important in recreation and have aesthetic, religious, and cultural value for every human society.

Every biological resource has at least one factor that we would like to be as abundant or as productive as possible; usually we can identify more than one such factor. Biological resource management, therefore, involves the concept of multiple use.

In discussing the modern management of wildlife and fisheries and the conservation of endangered species, we have adopted an ecosystem perspective, viewing the species of interest within its ecosystem. We have emphasized that in the end there is no such thing as conserving an endangered species, only conserving its endangered ecosystem and habitat.

Managers have believed that an ecosystem or habitat has a certain carrying capacity for any species. In the past, managers have often sought to maximize the production of a useful resource (managing for maximum sustainable yield), but the uncertainties of our knowledge, the inevitable changes that occur over time, and the requirement for multiple use have led to a goal of optimum sustainable yields and optimum sustainable populations. In most cases wise management of biological resources requires us to view the resource from an ecosystem perspective, often from a global perspective.

STUDY QUESTIONS

1 Why are we so unsuccessful in making rats an endangered species?

2 Debate the following issue: The failure of the sardine fisheries along the California coast was due not to overfishing but to environmental changes.

3 Distinguish between an *optimum* and a *maximum* yield of a biological resource. Why is it likely that a manager would never achieve a maximum yield for a long time?

4 What is meant by an optimum abundance of a biological resource such as trees or fish?

5 What is meant by multiple use of a biological resource? How would you apply this concept to (a) whales and (b) Douglas fir trees on U. S. Forest Service land?

6 In the next 50 years, are fish likely to provide a greater or lesser percentage of the human protein requirement?

7 What are the major causes of extinction (a) in recent times and (b) before people existed on Earth?

8 Make a plan to save the California condor for one of the two following goals: (a) to maintain a wild species in the wilderness; (b) to save the genetic characteristics of the condor.

9 Present arguments for and against the following statement: Eating meat helps preserve endangered species.

10 What are the differences between game ranching and traditional cattle ranching?

FURTHER READING

BELL, F. W. 1978. *Food from the sea: The economics and politics of ocean fisheries.* Boulder, Colo.: Westview Press.

BROKAW, H. P., ed. 1979. *Wildlife and America.* Washington, D. C.: U. S. Government Printing Office.

DASMANN, R. 1981. *Wildlife biology.* 2nd ed. New York: Wiley.

EHRLICH, P. R., and EHRLICH, A. 1981. *Extinction: The causes and consequences of the disappearance of species.* New York: Random House.

HOLT, S. J., and TALBOT, L. M. 1978. *New principles for the conservation of wild living resources.* Wildlife Monographs No. 59. Washington, D. C.: The Wildlife Society.

McNEELY, J. A., and MILLER, K. R., eds. 1984. *National parks, conservation and development.* Washington, D. C.: The Smithsonian Press.

MYERS, N. 1979. *The sinking ark.* Oxford, England: Pergamon Press.

STODDARD, C. H. 1978. *Essentials of forestry practice.* 3rd ed. New York: Wiley.

THIBODEAU, F., and FIELD, H., eds. 1984. *Sustaining tomorrow: A strategy for world conservation and development.* Hanover, N. H.: University Press of New England.

U. N. FOOD AND AGRICULTURE ORGANIZATION. 1978. *Mammals in the seas.* Report of the FAO Advisory Committee on Marine Resources Research, Working Party on Marine Mammals. FAO Fisheries Series 5, Vol. 1. Rome: U.N. Food and Agriculture Organization.

9

Managing Landscapes

- Modern management of landscapes has a scientific basis in our understanding of ecosystems, island biogeography, and landscape ecology.
- Forests are among our most important renewable resources; they are one of our most abundant resources but are being rapidly depleted.
- Deforestation occurred in prehistory and throughout the history of civilization; whenever people have lived near or in forested areas, the forests have been cut.
- Most forests are managed for multiple use, including the supply of timber for wood, paper, and fuel; the supply of water; the retardation of erosion; as a habitat for wildlife, including endangered species; for various forms of recreation; and for scientific research.
- A classic goal in forestry is sustainable yield, meaning that a forest can be cut periodically for an indefinite period without decreasing the ability of the trees or their ecosystem to sustain future harvest.
- The goals of park management include preservation of unique natural scenery; conservation of wilderness, of representative natural areas, and of wildlife habitat; and maintenance of areas for outdoor recreation and scientific research.
- A park or preserve is an ecological island, and the management of such areas benefits from the concepts of island biogeography.
- The size and shape of a park greatly affects its ability to sustain natural ecosystems and conserve biological resources.
- Managing wilderness is a relatively new idea that appears to involve a paradox: A true wilderness would seem to need no management, but in modern life even wilderness must be defined and managed.

THE GIR FOREST OF INDIA

The Gir Forest of India is the last preserve of the Indian lion. This forest represents, in one small area, most of the issues that face us in the management of conservation of landscapes and ecosystems. There are many uses of this area, and the conflicts that arise can be resolved only by active management and trade-off. In addition to serving as a preserve for the Indian lion, the Gir Forest serves as a watershed, supplying water for downstream farms, and is a place where teak is logged, firewood is collected, and cattle are grazed. There are many conflicting goals for the management of the Gir: as a preserve for rare and endangered species considered treasures for the entire world (Fig. 9.1), as a site for tourism, and as a source of food for local cattle and wood for local homes [1].

Underlying the Gir's problem is the human population issue. The Gir is an island of a natural ecosystem in the midst of a human-dominated landscape. It lies in northeastern India, in the state of Gujarat, about 320 km northwest of Bombay. The Gir is the largest nature preserve in India, covering 1200 km^2. As an ecological island, it is no longer self-sufficient and cannot persist without help by people from outside.

Maldhari herdsmen who live nearby graze 25,000 cattle in the forest. During dry seasons, other herders from farther away bring another 25,000–75,000 domestic cattle and buffalo to the Gir. The domestic cattle trample the soil, compacting it and affecting the regrowth of shrubs and trees [1].

The forest's trees and shrubs provide food for several species of large animals, including the spotted deer, sambar deer, Indian gazelle, nilgai antelope, wild boar, and the four-horned antelope, now rare animals. These in turn are prey to the Indian lion. Tourists come to see these lions and watch them feed on bait put out for them by employees of the preserve.

Another problem is that, as the use of the Gir by cattle and the encroachment of crops decrease the area available for lion habitat, the lions feed on domestic cattle (in fact these are now the lions'

FIGURE 9.1
Gir Forest woodlands. A nilgai antelope pauses in the broken woodland that forms a transition between the forests of the western Gir and the open savannah woodlands of the eastern third of the sanctuary.

major food source). As a result, most of the resources of the Gir have been in decline. For example, the number of lions decreased from 250 in 1965 to 177 in 1968. The combination of native wildlife crowded into a small preserve and domestic cattle was leading to overgrazing, which was causing a decrease in the vegetation available to feed the herbivores [1].

The Maldhari also cut wood from the forest to build their houses and fences to protect their cattle at night. They plant some crops within the preserve's boundaries, decreasing the habitat for the wild animals in the forest. These people also take topsoil, which they mix with buffalo dung and sell as fertilizer, further decreasing the soil fertility in the Gir. The Maldhari live close to a level of malnutrition and bare subsistence, and the Gir Forest makes the difference for them between life and death.

Destruction of the natural vegetation and the soil decreases the ability of the forest to act as a natural watershed; there will be less water storage capacity, increased seasonal runoff and flooding, and a decline in the total water available for crops.

Managing the Gir poses problems in multiple land use. If these people and their cattle were removed, the forest could be saved, but then the major current source of food for the lions would also be removed. Moving the Maldhari means that they may have to take up new livelihoods and change their traditional way of life. A study of this forest by the wildlife expert Stephen Berwick led to a suggested solution: Reduce the domestic cattle and introduce some other species that are adapted to that kind of woodland, could live within it without causing serious damage, and provide sufficient food for the lions. Members of one such species are the zebu cattle, which evolved in this region.

In this chapter we will explore the problems that face us today, just as they exist in the Gir Forest in India, in managing landscapes, including forests, parks, and wilderness. The major terms and concepts we will discuss include optimum sustained yield and multiple use; forestry, including rotation time, clearcutting, and the world firewood crisis; wilderness; the reasons for parks; and island biogeography applied to diversity in parks [1].

FORESTRY

The Resources and Importance of Forests

Forests are areas of the land where trees are the dominant vegetation. There are **closed canopy forests**, where leaves and twigs of adjacent trees touch, and **open woodlands,** where only some leaves and twigs of adjacent trees overlap. Estimates of forest land usually include the sum of closed forest plus open woodland, including scrub and brushland areas that are neither forest nor open woodland, and some deforested areas where forest regeneration is not taking place. Forests grade into **savannahs,** which are grasslands with many scattered trees.

Forests have always been important to people, and there is a link between forests and civilization. Wood provided one of the major building materials and the major source of fuel for early towns and cities and helped pave the way for the rise of civilization. Forests provided the materials for our first boats and first wagons. Forests are now and always have been a major economic resource. It is estimated that nearly half the people in the world depend on wood for cooking; in colder areas in the developing nations wood remains the primary source of heating fuel.

Forests and individual trees have also had much symbolic meaning for people, being seen both as places of beauty and grandeur and fearsome dark wildernesses. Forests are important for recreation—for hiking, hunting, and bird and wildlife viewing.

Forests also have many indirect uses for people. They often cover major watersheds that provide water for cities, preventing erosion and moderating the availability of water. Forests are habitats for endangered species and wildlife. At regional and global levels, forests may be important climate factors and may be important in other global biospheric processes, such as the storage of carbon.

Although the forests are subject to change, the pace of that change is long compared with our lives—forests seem to us relatively permanent aspects of the landscape. Early travelers to North

America noted impressive stands of large trees. For example, the coastal forests of New England in 1634 were described by William Wood in *New England's Prospect*, where he wrote, "The timber of the country grows straight and tall, some trees being twenty, some thirty foot high before they spread for their branches" [2]. There is a tendency to believe that forests are constant in time when undisturbed by people. In reality, however, the North American forests that the European colonists found in the seventeenth century were "in a state of constant change wrought by forest succession, climatic change, fire, wind, insects, fungi, browsing animals and Indian activity" [3].

Countries differ greatly in the amount of forest resources that they have, depending first on the potential of the land and climate for tree growth and second on the history of land use and deforestation. About 50% of Indonesia is forest, 40% of Brazil, 18% of India, and less than 13% of China [4]. The USSR has the largest closed forest land resource (785 million ha) in the world—one-third more than the United States and Canada combined. Europe has 135 million ha (Table 9.1).

The United States has approximately 340 million ha of commercial-grade forest, which is defined as forest land believed or known to be an economically profitable source of timber and capable of producing at least 1.4 m³/ha/yr of wood. In addition, the United States has about 300 mil-lion ha forested to the extent that it is 10% stocked with trees and another 340 million ha in rangeland, which includes natural grasslands, shrubland, most deserts, tundra, coastal marshes, and meadows (Fig. 9.2) [5].

Commercial timberland occurs in many parts of the United States: nearly 75% in the eastern half (about equally divided north and south), the rest in the west (Oregon, Washington, California, Montana, Idaho, and Colorado) and in Alaska and the other Rocky Mountain states.

In the United States, 62% of forest land is privately owned, 19% is on U.S. Forest Service lands, and 19% is on other federal lands. The publicly owned forests are primarily in the Rocky Mountain and Pacific Coast states on sites of poor quality and high elevation. Because there has never been much harvesting from these areas, they hold a large part of the nation's timber.

Forestry is big business. The worldwide harvest of forest products, including that used in firewood, construction, paper, and industrial processes, is more than 3 billion m³ [6]. Canada, the largest net exporter, sells about $5 billion worth of forest products. Sweden, the second largest, has a net export of $3.6 billion. The United States, although a large producer of timber, imports about $700 million more than it exports. Japan, the world's largest importer, buys about $4.4 billion more than it exports.

TABLE 9.1
World forested area (millions of hectares) by region.

	Forest Land	Closed Forest	Open Woodland	Total Land Area	Closed Forest (% of land area)
North America	630	470	(176)	1,841	25
Central America	65	60	(2)	272	22
South America	730	530	(150)	1,760	30
Africa	800	190	(570)	2,970	6
Europe	170	140	29	474	30
USSR	915	785	115	2,144	35
Asia	530	400	(60)	2,700	15
Pacific area	190	80	105	842	10
World	4030	2655	(1200)	13,003	20

Source: Council on Environmental Quality and the Department of State, 1980.
Notes: Data on North American forests represent a mid-1970s estimate. Data on USSR forests are a 1973 survey by the Soviet government. Other data are from Persson (1974); they represent an early-1970s estimate. Forest land is not always the sum of closed forest plus open woodland, as it includes scrub and brushland areas which are neither forest nor open woodland, and because it includes deforested areas where forest regeneration is not taking place. In computation of total land area, Antarctica, Greenland, and Svalbard are not included; 19 percent of arctic regions are included.

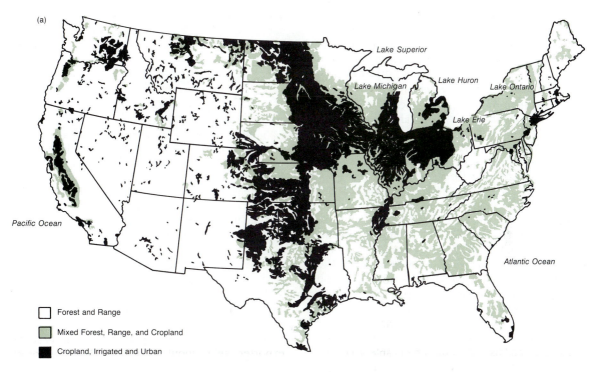

(a)

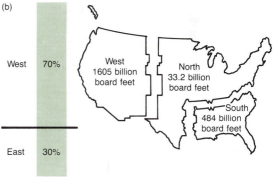

(b)

FIGURE 9.2
Forest and range land in the conterminous United States.
(a) Land use by area. (b) Sawtimber volume. Three fourths
of this country's commercial forest land is in the east.
However, in terms of sawtimber volume, almost the reverse is true: 70% in the west and 30% in the east. [Part
(a) from U.S. Forest Service, 1980; part (b) from U.S. Forest Service and Stoddard, 1978.]

DEFORESTATION: A GLOBAL DILEMMA

Forests are one of the world's most abundant resources, but they are rapidly being depleted. It is
estimated that forests covered one-quarter of
Earth's entire land area in 1950 and one-fifth in
1980 [6]. There are approximately 2.5 billion ha of
closed forest and 1.2 billion ha of open woodlands
and savannahs [6].

The decline in forested area due to cutting is occurring worldwide and has occurred throughout
the history of civilization and in prehistory; whenever people have lived near or in forested areas,
the forests have been cut. Forests were cut in the
Near East, in Greece, and in Rome and the Roman
empire before the modern era. The removal of forests continued northward in Europe with civilization. There is evidence in the fossil record that prehistoric farmers in Denmark cleared forests to the

extent that early successional weeds occupied the open fields. Great Britain was cut over and many forested areas removed in medieval times. With the colonization of the New World, much of North America was cleared.

Today deforestation continues in areas where forests remain; many of these forests are in the tropics, in mountain regions, or in high latitudes— places that were difficult to exploit before [7]. The problem is especially severe in the tropics because the countries with very rapid human population growth are situated in these regions. For example, in 1961 Thailand was 57% forests, but this decreased to 37% in 1974; the rate of deforestation in the mid-1980s was estimated to be 7,600 ha annually [8]. The United Nations Food and Agricultural Organization (FAO) estimates that half of the forests that existed in 1950 were cut by 1984. The major regions where deforestation is occurring rapidly include the Amazon basin, especially in Brazil; the tropical forests of western and central Africa and of southeast Asia and the Pacific regions, including Borneo, Indonesia, the Philippines, and Malaysia. The United Nations FAO estimates that Central America has lost more than two-thirds of its forests, central Africa more than half of its forests, and Southeast Asia and Latin America more than a third. The FAO's estimates are, if anything, underestimates, because that organization has to rely primarily on official statements from member nations. Losses due to illegal cutting or other unstated cutting would not necessarily be included. The U. S. Office of Technology Assessment estimates that every year an area the size of the state of Pennsylvania is deforested in the tropics [9].

Forests are a global resource, and cutting forests in one country affects other countries. For example, Nepal, one of the most mountainous countries in the world, lost more than half of its forest cover between 1950 and 1980, and the estimates are that if present trends continue little forest land will remain in that country by the year 2000. This cutting is leading to increases in runoff and in the sediment load in streams and, once the ground has lost the stabilizing influence of the trees, to landslides. Many of the streams from Nepal feed rivers that run into India and form some of that country's major water courses. The deforestation in Nepal is causing flooding and has done an estimated $2 billion in property damage.

The Causes of Deforestation

The simplest reason people are cutting forests is to sell and use the timber for lumber and paper products. Both logging by large commercial timber companies and local cutting by rural villagers are major causes of deforestation. Another important cause is the clearing of forest land for use in agriculture. For example, it is one of the principal causes of deforestation in countries such as Nepal and Brazil [9]. Another reason forests are cut is to convert them to pasture and cropland [7].

The World Firewood Shortage One of the most important causes of land clearing is the need for firewood. There is a world firewood shortage causing a world firewood crisis. In many parts of the world wood is a major energy source. As the human population grows, the amount of firewood used increases. For example, in Kenya, where the human population is growing at a rate of 4%/yr, even if use per person remains constant, the need for firewood will double in less than 20 years. In Kenya there is already a firewood crisis, and the amount of forested area is decreasing. Thus there is little hope that the production of wood can double in 20 years. In this case, alternative fuels must be found, or people will have no fuel for cooking.

Throughout much of human history, firewood was *the* energy source. In the United States, the homes of colonial New England were heated by firewood. Before 1900, wood provided more energy than any other source in the United States. Although its use decreased in the United States in the first part of the twentieth century, there has been a resurgence in the use of firewood since the 1970s, in part following the energy crisis of 1973 and in part the result of the back-to-nature movement that began to develop in the 1960s.

Slightly more than half of all wood used in the world is used for firewood. The developed countries used slightly less than half of this fuel wood. In developed countries, firewood provides less than 1% of total commercial energy, but it provides one-quarter of the energy in developing countries and more than half of the energy in Africa [10].

The firewood crisis is especially serious in the poor nations of the humid tropics. In rural areas of such countries, fuel is primarily biological and includes animal dung, waste from crops, plant crops themselves, and wood gathered from trees and shrubs. More than 80% of this energy, on average, is supplied by wood [10].

The firewood crisis is most severe in India, central Africa, the Caribbean, and the Andean region of South America. Erik Eckholm describes people stripping bark off trees in Pakistan for firewood and a steady stream of people carrying firewood on their backs into Kathmandu, Nepal [11].

There is a vicious circle in the use of firewood in poor countries. As population increases in a small village, locally available wood is cut. The people begin to travel farther to cut wood, but as the population continues to increase, this nearby source is also exhausted, and wood must be sought from even farther away. Transportation of fuel wood becomes a major factor in everyday life. Eventually the land suffers the effects of deforestation, becomes poorer both for forests and crops, and there is a general impoverishment of the land.

In such a situation intentional management practices need to be introduced, including management of woodland stands to improve growth. However, well-planned management of firewood stands has been the exception rather than the rule.

Good management practices would include limiting access and cutting; cutting first slower growing and poorer burning species and promoting the growth of the better firewood species; making use of plantations; and supplementing firewood with other fuels, such as solar heat for cooking ovens. However, such practices are often in conflict with cultural traditions and are introduced with great difficulty. At this time it is not clear whether, in many of the developing nations, a successful management policy can be developed in time to prevent serious damage to the forests and land.

Indirect Deforestation Another, more subtle source of the loss of forests is indirect deforestation—the death of trees from pollution or disease.

Acid rain and other pollutants are killing trees in many areas, especially those near industrial countries. This is a particularly serious problem in West Germany, where there is talk of *Waldsterben*—forest death; the government have estimated that one-third of the country's forests has suffered damage in the form of the death of standing trees, yellowing of needles, and poorly formed shoots. The causes are unclear, but appear to be the result of a number of influences, including acid rain, ozone, and other air pollutants that tend to weaken the trees and make them more likely to become diseased. This problem extends throughout central Europe. A similar curious damage to red spruce is occurring in the United States in New England. (The effects of acid rain are discussed in greater detail in the chapter on air resources.)

FOREST MANAGEMENT

The wise management of forests of the world is a major environmental priority. Many new plans and programs have been proposed, especially for tropical forests. *Tropical Forests: A Call to Action* puts forth a plan for 56 countries [12].

The management of forests is called **silviculture.** Silviculture has a long history, and forestry is a profession with its own schools and undergraduate and graduate degrees. A goal of forest management is sustained yield, which is defined as an indefinitely repeatable harvest without damage to the land or the trees. This goal is similar to the fishery manager's concept of optimum sustainable yield, which was discussed in the previous chapter. Some forests are managed like mechanized farms; a single species is planted in straight rows, and the land is fertilized, sometimes by helicopter. Modern machines make harvesting rapid and some remove the entire tree, root and all. Intensive management is characteristic of Europe and parts of the northwestern United States, particularly in Washington and Oregon. In forests that are managed less actively, such as those of New England, forests are allowed to reseed naturally and little is done to the forest except to cut trees. Which approach works best depends on the forests, the environment, and

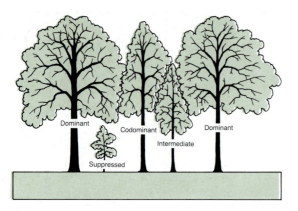

FIGURE 9.3
Tree crown classes. Foresters divide a forest stand into
the dominant trees—the most vigorous and the best timber trees; the codominant trees—slightly less vigorous,
but with some branches in the top of the forest; intermediate trees, and suppressed trees.

the characteristics of the commercially valuable
species.

Foresters call an area of forest a stand, and they
classify stands on the basis of tree composition.
The two major kinds of commercial stands are
even-aged stands, where all live trees began
growth from seeds or root sprouts in about the
same year, and uneven-aged stands, which have at
least three distinct age classes. Even in even-aged
stands, trees differ in height, girth, and vigor. A forest that has never been cut is called a virgin forest;
one that is cut and has regrown is called second
growth, no matter how many times it has been cut
and regrown. Another important management
term is rotation time, which is the time between
cuts of a stand. Trees are divided into the dominants (tallest, most vigorous), codominants, intermediate, and suppressed trees (Fig. 9.3).

Management and Productivity

How productive a forest is depends on the fertility
of the soil, the supply of water, and the local climate. Foresters classify sites by site quality, which
is the maximum timber crop the land can produce
in a given time. Site quality can decrease with poor

management. For example, too frequent burning
of forests decreases the potential for tree growth
by lowering soil fertility. Foresters develop site indices for forested areas and derive yield tables to
estimate future production. The management of
forests also involves thinning to remove poorly
formed and unproductive trees and to permit the
larger trees to grow more rapidly, planting genetically controlled seedlings, and fertilizing.

Managers attempt to protect trees from disease
and insect infestations. Insect outbreaks tend to
occur infrequently, but when they do occur, they
have devastating results. Some insect problems
are due to introductions. The gypsy moth, for example, was introduced intentionally into New
England around the turn of the century as a source
of silk, but it escaped and has spread through many
eastern states. Other insect outbreaks appear to be
naturally recurrent and to have existed for a long
time. For example, a nineteenth-century gazetteer
for Cheshire County in New Hampshire refers to a
"plague of loathesome worms" that removed all
the leaves from large areas of forest. Herbicides are
sometimes used to combat these insects. Insects affect trees by defoliating them (removing the
leaves), by eating the buds at the tops of the trees
and destroying a straight form, by eating fruits, and
by serving as carriers of diseases.

Tree diseases are primarily fungal ones. Often,
as with the Dutch elm disease, an insect spreads
the fungus from tree to tree. There has been relatively little success in controlling diseases in
forests.

Forests are much easier to manage than fisheries for obvious reasons. Trees stay in one place and
can be easily counted and measured, and the factors that make them grow are relatively easy to
study. In addition, the age and growth rate of trees
can be measured from tree rings (Fig. 9.4). In temperate and boreal forests, trees produce one
growth ring per year, and a tree can be aged by
counting the number of rings. As a result, forestry
science has proceeded in general beyond that of
the study of fisheries and marine mammals. Forest
geneticists breed new strains of trees like agricultural geneticists have bred new strains of corn,
wheat, tomatoes, and most other crop plants. New
"super trees" are supposed to be able to maintain

FIGURE 9.4
How a tree grows. (From Stoddard.)

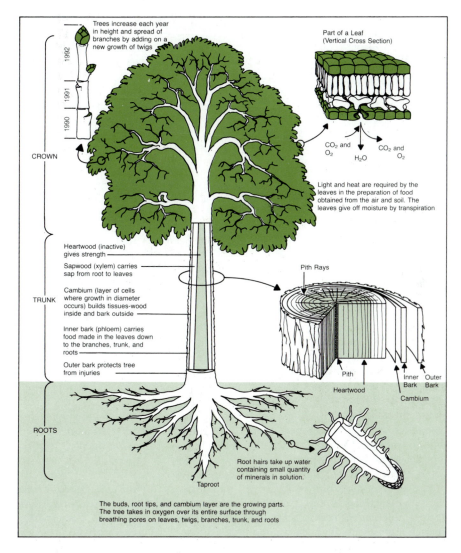

Trees increase each year in height and spread of branches by adding on a new growth of twigs

1992
1991
1990

CROWN

Part of a Leaf
(Vertical Cross Section)

CO_2 and O_2 CO_2 and O_2
H_2O

Light and heat are required by the leaves in the preparation of food obtained from the air and soil. The leaves give off moisture by transpiration

Heartwood (inactive) gives strength

Sapwood (xylem) carries sap from root to leaves

Cambium (layer of cells where growth in diameter occurs) builds tissues-wood inside and bark outside

TRUNK

Inner bark (phloem) carries food made in the leaves down to the branches, trunk, and roots

Outer bark protects tree from injuries

Pith Rays

Pith
Heartwood
Inner Bark
Outer Bark
Cambium

ROOTS

Root hairs take up water containing small quantity of minerals in solution.

Taproot

The buds, root tips, and cambium layer are the growing parts. The tree takes in oxygen over its entire surface through breathing pores on leaves, twigs, branches, trunk, and roots

a high rate of growth and increase the total production of forests.

Modern forestry tends to take an ecosystem approach to management. It must, because the success of trees depends on soils, climates, competition, and the abundance of parasites and herbivores—in short, on the ecosystem.

One way that an ecosystem approach is taken in forest management is in the use of the concept of **ecological succession,** which is the process of development of an ecosystem over time [see Chap-

ter 5]. The process of succession involves several stages, and species tend to be adapted to specific stages. Early in the development of a forest an area is relatively open and sunlight penetrates to the ground. Later in succession, trees cast considerable shade and the trees are taller. Some forests are managed for early successional species, others are managed for late successional species (Fig. 9.5). For example, in northern forests such as found in Canada, some of the useful trees are aspen, birch, and pines, all of which are early

FIGURE 9.5
The use of an ecosystem approach in modern forestry. Forest options for harvest, shown in relation to forest succession.

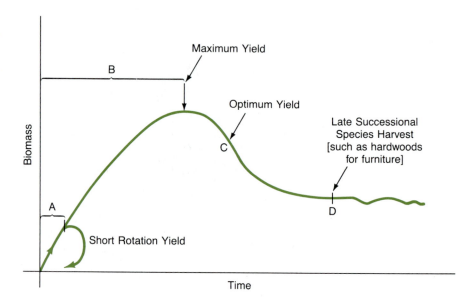

The Clearcutting Controversy

successional species. For these, the rotation times are comparatively short—less than a century. In contrast, forests that are managed for hardwoods used in furniture, such as oaks in Germany or maples in the eastern United States, are late successional species, and those forests, if the yield is to be maintained, must be managed for long rotation time, or cutting must be done very selectively so that the forest is never opened up greatly.

Another important concept in the management of forests is multiple use, which means that a forest is managed for several uses at the same time. For example, in addition to timber, the U.S. Forest Service manages its lands for the purposes of recreation, wildlife, and water supply. It also maintains research stations from which some of the major research in ecology has been conducted during the last several decades. Because it is not possible to manage a resource so that more than one thing is maximized at any time, multiple use involves compromises and tradeoffs. If there is logging and hiking, some balance must be arrived at between cutting for the most efficient production of trees and cutting so that the forest contains a mixture of stands of different ages that are pleasant for hikers to walk through.

Clearcutting is the practice of cutting all trees in a stand at the same time. Alternatives to clearcutting are selective cutting and strip cutting. In selective cutting, individual trees are marked and cut. In strip cutting, narrow rows of forests are cut, leaving wooded corridors. Because clearcuts often looked like disaster areas, those wanting to use forests for recreation have opposed this practice (Fig. 9.6). Others criticize clearcutting as harmful to the forest ecosystem and merely economically expedient. These critics claim that clearcutting increases erosion; increases the frequency of landslides; and causes loss of soil and soil fertility, degradation of drainage patterns, and permanent decreases in site quality. Clearcutting has been defended as necessary for the regeneration of some desirable species, especially when those species require large open areas to reproduce and abundant light for growth.

Scientists have tested the effects of clearcutting (Fig. 9.7) [13]. For example, in the U. S. Forest Service Hubbard Brook Experimental Forest, New Hampshire, an entire watershed was clearcut and herbicides were applied to prevent regrowth for

FIGURE 9.6
Clearcutting is a controversial method of logging. On this steep slope, serious erosion has occured.

two years. The results were dramatic. Erosion increased and the pattern of water runoff changed substantially. The exposed soil decayed more rapidly, and the concentrations of nitrates in the stream water exceeded public health standards so that the waters in this forest stream were no longer drinkable. Defenders of clearcutting pointed out that water flow increased during August, the low point of flow; because these forests served as sources of water, the defenders claimed the clearcutting had at least one beneficial effect.

In another experiment carried out by the U.S. Forest Service at the H. J. Andrews Experimental Forest in Oregon, clearcutting greatly increased the frequency of landslides, as did the construction of logging roads. In this forest, the rainfall is very high (about 240 cm/yr) and the trees—mainly Douglas fir, western hemlock, and Pacific silver fir—grow very tall and live a long time [14].

Clearcutting also changes chemical cycling in forests and results in the loss of chemical elements necessary for life from the soil. When the forest is clearcut, trees are no longer available to take up nutrients. The ground, opened to the sun and rain, becomes warmer and the process of decay is speeded up; chemical elements such as nitrogen are converted more rapidly to forms that are water soluble and can be readily lost in runoff during rains (Fig. 9.7) [15].

Such experiments show that clearcutting can be a poor practice on steep slopes in areas of moderate to heavy rainfall. However, where there is little slope and less rainfall and where the desirable species require open areas for growth, clearcutting may be desirable.

Harvesting All of the Trees The technology used in cutting trees greatly affects the ecosystem.

FIGURE 9.7
Effects of clearcutting on forest chemical cycling. Chemical cycling (a) in an old growth forest and (b) after clearcutting. (c) Increase in nitrate concentration in streams following logging and the burning of "slash"—leaves, branches, and other such tree debris. [(a) and (c) modified from Fredriksen.]

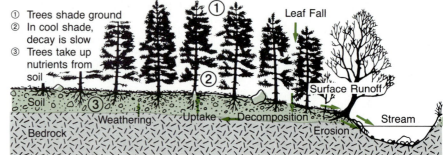

(a) Chemical Cycling in Old Growth Forest

① Trees shade ground
② In cool shade, decay is slow
③ Trees take up nutrients from soil

Leaf Fall

Surface Runoff

Soil

Weathering   Uptake   Decomposition   Stream

Bedrock   Erosion

(b) Chemical Cycling after Clearcutting

① Branches, etc., decay rapidly in open warm area
② Soil is more easily eroded without tree roots
③ Runoff is greater without evaporation by trees

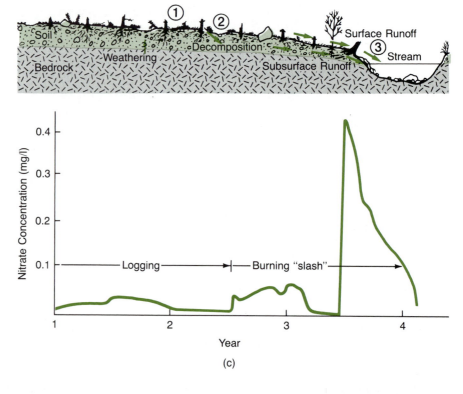

Soil

Weathering   Decomposition   Surface Runoff

Bedrock   Subsurface Runoff   Stream

(c)

Logging   Burning "slash"

Nitrate Concentration (mg/l)

Year

Traditional timber harvesting removes only the main stems and largest branches of the trees—those parts with the straightest, most valuable tim-ber. The stem wood is composed mainly of carbon, hydrogen, and oxygen, all readily available to the forest even when the timber is harvested. The remaining parts—leaves, bark, small stems, and roots—stay behind in the forest and contain the bulk of other chemical elements.

Newer practices, with modern machinery, remove all of the above-ground parts of the tree, much of which is chipped into small fragments for making paper. This is called whole-tree harvesting. Other machines remove roots and, thus, even more of the valuable nutrients from the forest. This technique can produce more wood fiber per unit area, but the benefit is short-term. In the long run, these practices are detrimental to the forest [16]. Whole or complete tree harvesting over long periods of time will require the addition of considerable amounts of fertilizers to replace the chemicals lost. Forests subject to these kinds of harvests will be run much like the large "agrobusiness" farms, with highly mechanized and energy-consuming operations. As the shortage of wood and paper becomes more intense worldwide, the pressure to use these techniques will grow and major conflicts will develop among the various users of forest lands.

Shorter Rotation Times

In older, traditional forests, rotation times were long—a century or more. In recent years, however, there has been an increasing emphasis on shorter and shorter rotation times. In some cases, where saplings are harvested for paper pulp, the rotation time is as short as ten years. Such very short rotations can be hard on the soil and the forest ecosystem. Each cut results in some erosion and soil loss, especially when heavy machinery is used. Artificial fertilization becomes necessary.

Managing with and for Fire

For much of the twentieth century, it was the practice to try to suppress all fires. As we discussed earlier, some tree species and some forest animals depend on fire and grow only in areas that have burned. Areas with very high forest fire danger, like the chaparral areas of California, may best be managed through the intentional introduction of frequent light fires, which clear the ground of fuel and prevent conditions that lead to fires that destroy

homes, property, and life. Because burned-over areas are usually not pleasant to look at, and because occasionally controlled fires become uncontrolled, the use of fire as a management tool will continue to be controversial.

However, prescribed fire, also called controlled burning, is becoming increasingly common. In the southeastern United States, prescribed burning is used on about one million hectares annually. Study of this practice suggests that it has no significant effect on soils, nutrient cycling, or waterflow from the forests; prescribed fires reduce risk from wildfire, control certain tree diseases, increase food and habitat for wildlife, and can be used to manage the forests for greater production of desirable tree species [17].

REFORESTATION

As the original forests of the world are cut and the need for timber increases, it is important to plant new trees and develop programs in reforestation. There are international and national efforts for reforestation; most countries with a significant amount of economic forestry have such programs, at least on paper, and many private forestry corporations plant trees and reforest areas they have cut. Internationally, the World Bank has a reforestation program with 48 projects in different nations. In China, 700,000 farmers cooperated to plant a 100-m wide and 2400-km long shelterbelt of trees to protect crops. While impressive, such programs are small compared to the rate of forest cutting.

Community Forestry

In many parts of the world, as we have learned, the cutting of forests is the result of local needs of people in small communities. This is particularly true in the developing nations, where the use of firewood for fuel constitutes up to half or more of all energy used (Fig. 9.8).

In the past, most government forestry departments concentrated their efforts on government-owned forest land or else acted merely to police a country's forests. Now there is a realization that

FIGURE 9.8
Firewood use.

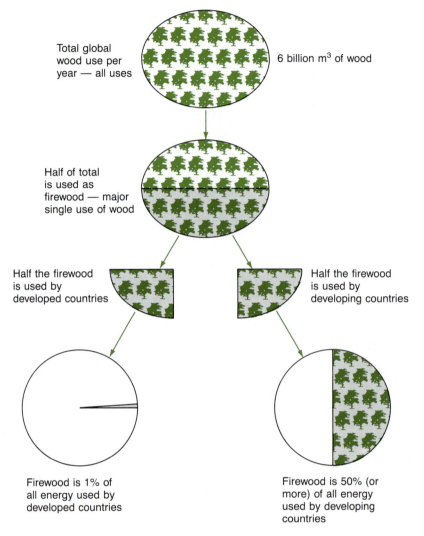

Total global wood use per year — all uses

6 billion m³ of wood

Half of total is used as firewood — major single use of wood

Half the firewood is used by developed countries

Half the firewood is used by developing countries

Firewood is 1% of all energy used by developed countries

Firewood is 50% (or more) of all energy used by developing countries

this approach must change. In some countries, there is a new emphasis on community forestry, where professional foresters help villagers to develop woodlots with the goal of achieving some kind of sustainable local harvest to meet local needs. The United Nations FAO and the World Bank are supporting these programs. For example, in Malawi, Africa, there is a World Bank and UN FAO project in reforestation in which almost 40% of the households in that country have planted trees. In South Korea, villagers have been reforesting the country at the rate of 40,000 ha/yr.

Such community efforts are impressive and yet make a small impact on the large problem of worldwide shortage of firewood. Community forestry, focusing on the local needs of people in small communities, stands in sharp contrast to the use of forests as cash crops. Such commercial use is only one of several factors feeding into the worldwide firewood shortage, which takes its heaviest toll in the areas most dependent on firewood as a primary fuel source. Community forestry could help ease the shortage.

Good management practices would include

limiting access and cutting; cutting first the slower growing and poorer burning species; promoting the growth of the better firewood species; making use of plantations; and supplementing firewood with other, more easily renewable fuels. Although we can list several ideas for effective local forestry management, some of these practices are in conflict with local traditional activities or are difficult to implement for other reasons.

It is not clear whether the developing nations can implement a successful management policy in time to prevent serious damage to their forests and the land. In countries where population, and thus demand for firewood, doubles every 20 years, production of forests cannot possibly keep pace. If alternate fuels cannot be found, the effects will be severe, not only to the land, but to the people. In some cases, like the Gir Forest in India, a short-term action may require the protection of the land from exploitation by people.

PARKS AND PRESERVES

The park is as old as civilization, and the city park is as old as cities. The original country parks were part of the estates of nobility and the rich. The word *parc,* from old French, referred to an enclosed area for keeping wildlife to be hunted; these were set aside for nobility, excluding the public. The first major public park of the modern era was Victoria Park in Great Britain, authorized in 1842. But the national park is a new idea, originating in North America, that includes protection of nature as well as public access [18]. The first national park was Yosemite Valley in California, which was made a park by passage of a bill signed by President Lincoln in 1864 (Fig. 9.9a). The name "national park," however, was first used with the establishment of Yellowstone in 1872 (Fig. 9.9b).

In recent years there has been a rapid growth of national parks throughout the world. For example, Taiwan had no national parks prior to 1980, but there are now four national parks that include within their boundaries representative areas of most natural ecosystems of the nation. In the United States, the area in national and state parks has increased. The national parks have grown from less than 30 million acres in 1950 to almost 80 million today, much of the increase resulting from the establishment of parks in Alaska.

The Goals of Park Management

The goals of managing parks are many but we can group them into the following: (1) preservation of unique "wonders" of nature such as Niagara Falls and the Grand Canyon; (2) preservation of nature without human interference (preserving wilderness for its own sake); (3) preservation of nature in a condition thought to be representative of some prior time period as, for example, the United States prior to European settlement; (4) wildlife conservation, as discussed in the previous chapter, and therefore conservation of the required habitat and ecosystem of the wildlife; (5) maintenance of wildlife for hunting; (6) maintenance of uniquely or unusually beautiful landscapes for aesthetic reasons; (7) maintenance of representative natural areas for an entire country; (8) maintenance for outdoor recreation, including a range of activities from viewing scenery to wilderness recreation (hiking, cross-country skiing, rock climbing) to intense use in tourism (car and bus tours, swimming, downhill skiing, camping, etc.); and (9) maintenance of areas set aside for scientific research, both as a basis for park management and for the pursuit of answers to fundamental scientific questions.

The purpose of the earliest national parks established in America was to preserve the unique, awesome, and grand landscapes of the country—a purpose the historian Alford Runte refers to as "monumentalism." In the nineteenth century, Americans saw their national parks as a contribution to civilization equivalent to the architectural treasures of the Old World and sought to preserve them as a basis of their pride in their country [18].

In the twentieth century, there was a great increase in the establishment of parks as wildlife viewing areas. This led to the development of many of the national parks in the countries of eastern and southern Africa, including those of Kenya, Uganda, Tanzania, Zimbabwe, and South Africa.

In the second half of the twentieth century, the emphasis has become more ecological, with parks

FIGURE 9.9
The first national parks. (a)
Yosemite, (b) Yellowstone.

(a)

(b)

established both for scientific research and to maintain examples of representative natural areas. For example, Zimbabwe has established Sengwa National Park solely for scientific research; there are no tourist areas and tourists are not generally allowed. The purpose is to study the natural ecosystems with as little human interference as possible so that the principles of wildlife and wilderness management can be better formulated and understood.

Another increasingly common goal of national parks is to conserve representative natural areas of a country. A representative natural area is an area set aside for conservation—an area that represents a specific type of ecosystem of that country.

In New Zealand, current park planning has as a goal to set aside, in a national park or preserve, at least one area representing every major ecosystem of the nation, from seacoast to mountain peak. In this case, the goal is quite different from the original United States idea of preserving only the curious and awesome. In the United States, the idea of conserving natural areas is also increasing in popularity. The current U. S. national park system includes about one-half of the major ecosystems.

LANDSCAPE ECOLOGY

Parks and Preserves as Islands

A park is an area set aside for some kind of use by people, a preserve may be used directly, but its primary purpose is to conserve some resource, typically a biological one. Every park or preserve is an island—an island of one kind of landscape surrounded by a different kind of land use. Islands have special ecological qualities, and concepts of island biogeography are used in the design and management of parks [see Chapter 6]. Islands have fewer species than a mainland, and the smaller the island, the fewer the species that can be sustained. Also, the farther the island is from a mainland (that is, from a source of species), the fewer species will be found on the island. Planning the use of landscapes makes use of a branch of ecology called landscape ecology and of the concepts of island biogeography.

One of the important differences between a park and a truly natural wilderness area is that a park has definite boundaries. These boundaries are usually arbitrary from an ecological viewpoint, established for political, economic, or historical reasons not related to the natural ecosystem. Many parks have been developed on what are otherwise considered waste lands, useless for any other purposes. When national parks were first established in the United States as preserves of natural mon-

uments, there was little concern for the natural ecological requirements of the boundaries.

Even where parks or preserves have been set aside specifically with some species or group of species in mind, the boundaries are usually arbitrary. There are cases where the arbitrariness of park boundaries has caused problems and attempts have been made to modify the park area. For example, several preserves for redwood trees in California have been established according to the availability of land and the availability of areas from which redwood had not been cut. In recent years, logging in the upper watershed areas adjacent to such parks has led to erosion and sedimentation in the redwood preserves, threatening the continuation of the trees and the pleasing nature of the landscapes.

The Size and Shape of Parks

Other things being equal, a larger park will sustain more species. Of two parks with the same area, the one with a greater diversity of habitats can support more species (Fig. 9.10).

The shape of a park can determine what species can survive within it. For example, Lake Manyara National Park, Tanzania, is famous for its elephants, but was originally established with boundaries incorrect for the elephant habits. Prior to the establishment of this national park, the elephants would spend part of the year feeding along a steep escarpment above the lake, while at other times of the year they would migrate down to the valley floor, depending on the availability of food and water. The annual movements of the elephants were necessary so that they could obtain food of sufficient nutritional quality throughout the year.

When the park was originally established, farms were laid out along its northern border. These farms crossed the traditional pathways of the elephants and had two negative effects. First, it brought the elephants into direct conflict with the farmers and led to numerous incidents of the elephants crashing through farm fences, eating corn and other crops, and disrupting the farmers. Second, whenever the farmers were successful in preventing the movement of the elephants, the animals were cut off from reaching the escarpment and obtaining some of the necessary food.

FIGURE 9.10
Park shapes and island biogeography. A large park (a) can maintain more species, but several small parks (b) provide a kind of insurance against catastrophe. For example, if a storm struck one park and killed all individuals of one species in it, other populations of that species could survive in the other parks. (c) A combination that provides the benefits of both a single large park and several small ones. Here the small parks are connected by corridors that allow occasional migration among the parks; the total area is equal to that of (a), and the distribution over the landscape provides greater insurance.

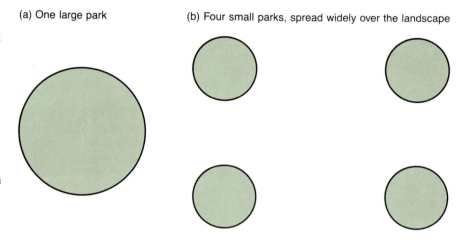

(a) One large park

(b) Four small parks, spread widely over the landscape

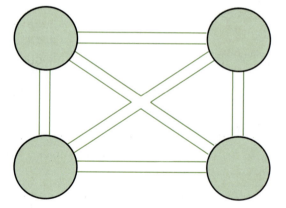

(c) Four small parks connected by narrow corridors

In this case, the arbitrariness and inappropriateness of the park boundaries were clear and adjustments were made so that the park boundaries were extended to cover those traditional migratory routes. This reduced the conflicts between elephants and farmers as well.

Parks isolate populations genetically and may provide too small a habitat for the maintenance of a minimum safe population size. For example, an attempt was made to reestablish approximately ten lions in a preserve of 150 km² in India. At first the introduction seemed a success. For several years lions persisted and some cubs were born. After a few years, however, the population dec-

lined rapidly and disappeared. Many reasons were put forward to explain this, including intentional shooting of the lions by the local farmers and a temporary lack of sufficient food. However, a general analysis of the habitat requirements of Indian lions suggests a deeper explanation. Lions are highly territorial and, because they are large and eat large prey, require a considerable amount of land. Thus, an area much larger than 150 km² is needed to sustain a viable lion population. In fact, approximately 25 km² are needed to support a single large lion [19].

If parks are to function as biological preserves, then they must be adequate to maintain a minimum population that will not undergo the serious genetic difficulties that can occur in small populations. A small population can suffer from the founder effect and undergo genetic drift. In the founder effect, the inherited traits of the individuals that by chance form the park population become more common and important than such traits would be in a wild, large population. For example, the individuals who form the park population might by chance have a high susceptibility to certain diseases. Such inherited characteristics, which are bad for survival and reproduction, may become predominant because of inbreeding (genetic drift), while in a larger population natural selection would lead to the disappearance of such genes or, at least, keep them at a low frequency in the population. Geneticists believe that genetic drift in small populations can place the population in jeopardy. Thus, a park-island must be large enough to maintain a genetically viable population.

A park manager must be concerned about an endangered species going through a "genetic bottleneck," which means that the population is suddenly reduced to a very low number and then increases. When a genetic bottleneck occurs, the genetic diversity is greatly reduced, and undesirable inherited characteristics may become fixed in the population. For example, populations of the bighorn sheep have been limited to small isolated groups in one or a few valleys, cut off from other populations by mountains and by ranches. A number of such populations are known which, while remaining isolated, have gone through a series of bottlenecks when their numbers dropped below 15. In the case of the sheep, no serious genetic problems have appeared.

If a park is too small, a manager can move individuals of a species from one park to another, or between the park and zoos, so that genetic diversity is maintained. For example, lions in Africa can be found in many parks. Once a decade several lions could be moved from one of these parks to another to maintain genetic diversity (Fig. 9.11).

The smaller the park-island, the more intense must be the actions of the manager. At the extreme case is a zoo where the manager provides for all the needs of an animal, bringing in food and water

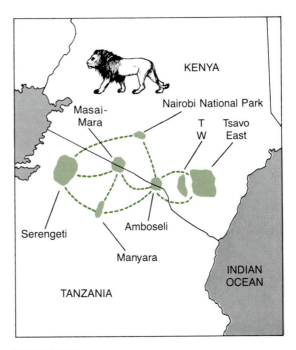

FIGURE 9.11
A plan to move lions among major parks in Kenya and Tanzania could maintain genetic diversity of this species if the numbers fell too low in each park. This map shows the location of six major parks. The plan is strictly hypothetical.

and removing wastes, providing shelter and the proper temperature, humidity, and so forth. At the other extreme is the natural world, before civilization, where the ecosystem maintained itself. In between are many choices. In some new zoos, the landscape is managed to look wild and the animals appear to roam about freely, but are fed and maintained, and the visitors are kept in vehicles and do not mix with the animals. The step from this to some national parks is surprisingly small. For example, a visitor today to Amboseli or Masai Mara parks in Kenya, wonderful for viewing Africa's great wildlife, may be taken in a small vehicle to view and photograph the animals. He will probably stay in the vehicle and will see the animals only from a distance. His experience is not very different from that of the visitor to a wildlife park in the United States to which the African animals have been transported.

When a park is first established and cut off from the surroundings, there is a rapid and immediate loss of some species; in addition, there is an edge effect, which means that many species escape from the cut area and seek refuge in the border of the forest. This may result in a short-term increase in the number of species. In the long-term, there is an exponential decline in the number of species following the initial creation of the island [20]. This is shown in a study of forest preserves left as islands as the tropical forests in the Amazon Basin of Brazil are being cut for timber. The study is a cooperative venture of the Brazilian government and the World Wildlife Fund.

CONSERVING WILDERNESS

Wilderness is, most simply, in its modern legal concept, an area untrammeled by people, where people are visitors who do not remain. The conservation of such an area is a new idea of the second half of the twentieth century but one that will become more important as the human population increases and the effects of civilization become more pervasive throughout the world. The idea of wilderness preservation is, in legal origin, an American one.

The United States Wilderness Act of 1964 was a landmark piece of legislation, marking the first time anywhere in the world that wilderness was recognized by national law as a national treasure to be preserved. That purpose of the act is to assure that some lands be preserved and protected in their natural condition. The policy of Congress was ''to secure for the American people of present and future generations the benefits of an enduring resource of wilderness.''

Under this law, wilderness included ''an area of undeveloped Federal land retaining its primeval character and influence, without permanent improvements or human habitation, which is protected and managed so as to preserve its natural conditions.'' Such lands were those in which (1) the ''imprint'' of human work is ''unnoticeable;''

(2) there were opportunities for solitude and for primitive and unconfined recreation; and (3) there were at least 5000 acres. The law also recognized that these areas could have value for ecology, geology, education, scenery, or history.

The Wilderness Act required certain maps and descriptions of wilderness areas which resulted in the development of the U.S. Forest Service *Roadless Area Review and Evaluation (RARE I and RARE II)*, which is an evaluation of lands that should be included in legally designated wilderness.

Only some countries can manage wilderness because only some countries have any wilderness left to preserve. As Roderick Nash, an American historian of wilderness, has written, many countries have no wilderness to protect. Switzerland is a country in which wilderness is not a part of preservation. And in the Danish language even the word ''wilderness'' has disappeared, although that word was an important one in the ancestral languages of modern Danish [21]. Nash contrasts a national park in Switzerland with a wilderness preserve. The Swiss park lies in the awesome scenery of the Alps—the scenery that inspired the English Romantic poets of the early nineteenth century to begin to praise what they saw as wilderness. But the park is situated in an area that has been heavily exploited for such activities as mining and foundries since the Middle Ages. The purpose of the park is for protection from human influences rather than for people to experience solitude and nature untrammeled by human beings. This makes the park a biological sanctuary and a research area rather than a wilderness preserve [21].

In another, perhaps deeper, sense, wilderness is an idea and an ideal that can be experienced by some people in many places, as in Japanese gardens. In Japan, there are roadless recreation areas but these are filled with people. In one high-altitude marsh there is a two-day hiking circuit with huts from which trash is removed by helicopters. Countries with a significant amount of wilderness include New Zealand, Canada, Sweden, Norway, Finland, the USSR, and Australia; some countries of eastern and southern Africa; many countries of South America, including parts of the Brazilian and Peruvian Amazon Basin; the mountainous high-altitude areas of Chile and Argentina; some of the remaining interior forests of Southeast Asia; and the Pacific-rim countries—parts of Borneo, the Philippines, Papua New Guinea, Taiwan and Indonesia. In addition, wilderness can be found in the polar regions, including Antarctica, Greenland, and Iceland.

The legal definition of wilderness has led to a number of controversies. On the one hand, those interested in developing the natural resources of an area, including forest and mineral ores, have argued that the rules are unnecessarily stringent and that there is plenty of wilderness elsewhere. On the other hand, those who wish to conserve more wild areas have argued that the interpretation of the U.S. Wilderness Act is also too stringent because the requirement of purity of the land from human influence has been taken too narrowly. The wilderness system in the United States began in 1964 with 9.2 million acres in U.S. Forest Service control and by 1979 had grown to include 19 million acres. There are 75 million acres proposed, including 42 million in Alaska.

Managing Wilderness

The management of wilderness is a paradox. A true wilderness would seem to need no management but, in fact, in modern life, with the great numbers of people in the world, even wilderness must be defined, legally set aside, and controlled. There are two distinct ways to view the goal of managing wilderness—one in terms of the wilderness itself and the other in terms of people. In the first, the goal is to preserve nature untrammeled by human beings. In the second, the purpose is to provide people with a wilderness experience, whatever is necessary to achieve that. The management of wilderness areas has matured to include management plans. Following from the first goal, wilderness can be seen as one extreme in a spectrum of environments to manage [22]. A manager of wilderness would strive to use as little action as possible in his management so as to minimize any human influence. One of the necessities, ironically, is to control human access and, therefore, to impose a carrying capacity for visitors so that any visitor has little, if any, sense that there are other people present. This also means restricting access to wilderness for various kinds of activities such as operation of motor vehicles, snowmobiles, and off-road vehicles (see Plate 15). As an example, in one year the Desolation Wilderness area in California, an area of more than 60,000 acres, had more than 250,000 visitors [22]. Could each visitor really have a wilderness experience in that area or was the human carrying capacity exceeded? This is a subjective judgment; if every visitor saw only his own companions and believed he was alone, then the actual number of visitors did not matter for the wilderness experience. If every visitor found his solitude ruined by strangers, then the management had failed.

Wilderness must be managed with a knowledge of adjacent lands. A wilderness next to a garbage dump or a power plant emitting smoke into it is a contradiction. Whether a wilderness can be adjacent to high-intensity campgrounds, or near a city, is a more subtle question that must be resolved by citizens.

Modern wilderness management recognizes that wild areas change over time and that these changes should be allowed to occur as long as they are natural. This is a change from earlier views that nature undisturbed was unchanging and should be managed so that it did not change. Finally, in choosing what activities can be allowed in a wilderness, emphasis should be given to those activities that depend on wilderness—experience of solitude or the observation of shy and elusive wildlife—rather than to those that can be carried out elsewhere, such as downhill skiing.

Wilderness Conflicts and Solutions

To summarize the major conflicts and their solutions that we have discussed, we can say the following. Wilderness areas frequently contain resources of economic importance, including timber, mineral ores, and sources of energy. One conflict is between those who want to conserve the wilderness and believe it is morally right that wilderness be protected for future generations and those who believe it is important and morally right that our society has access to the resources. Solutions to these conflicts generally require specific litigation

Agroforestry: Production and Protection for the Tropics

Although it may look more like a forest than the work of a farmer, the conglomeration of plants illustrated in Figure A is actually a combination of both. It's an example of an agroforestry system, a traditional land management technique often employed in the humid tropics, in which trees are incorporated with agricultural crops and/or animals. Among the many benefits of agroforestry are a diversity of food and forest products, sustained production from infertile rain forest soils, and environmental protection.

The Ecuadorian farmer who manages the system illustrated has four main crops. The lower strata consist of two subsistence crops—cassava and plantains. Cacao trees, from which the farmer harvests his main cash crop, form the third stra-

FIGURE A
Agroforestry in the lowlands of Ecuador.

tum. Towering over everything are fast-growing *Schizolobium* trees, which will eventually be

harvested for timber. Avocado, mango, and citrus trees scattered randomly about the plantation supply fruit and firewood for the farmer and his family.

Like most small landholders who practice agroforestry, this farmer has little money to invest in fertilizers or pesticides and must work the land intensively without benefit of machinery. His agroforestry system is one of many variations developed by agrarian peoples in Latin America, Africa, and Asia over centuries in response to their particular needs and environments.

Fruit and timber trees are frequently used as cover for shade crops such as cacao, coffee, or tea or are interspersed with light-demanding crops such as corn, tomatoes, or pineapple. Windbreaks and borders of trees planted around fields

and a decision about the relative value of the specific resource relative to the specific wilderness. Is a wilderness downwind from a major power plant really a wilderness? If not, should the power plant emissions be controlled just to preserve the wilderness? Those opposed to such an action argue that the conservation of the wilderness serves a few, while the production of energy (or some other industrial product) or the activities of a nearby heavily used recreational area or city serve many. Those favoring the wilderness argue also that beyond satisfying current needs, the conservation of

wilderness is a moral responsibility to future generations.

Another conflict is between user access to wilderness and conservation of the wilderness. In a democracy, there is on the one hand a belief that everyone should have access to the wilderness. On the other hand, such open access will ruin the wilderness. The solution in this case is to provide an equal opportunity to all for a limited number of user-days in the wilderness. This approach is taken, for example, in raft trips down the Colorado River through the Grand Canyon.

produce large amounts of fruit, firewood, and timber in a space that might otherwise be wasted. Trees are also combined with pastures; some species provide nutritious forage for cattle.

Even though agroforestry systems are used in many parts of the world, the practice is not as common as it could be. However, as vast areas of tropical rain forests are cut to make room for conventional agriculture and grazing operations, and as these ventures fail due to rapid deterioration of soil fertility, scientists have become interested in traditional agroforestry techniques. By approximating the structure and ecology of a tropical forest, agroforestry systems maintain ecosystem functions better than conventional agriculture. Multistrata systems protect fragile soils from eroding under torrential rains; organic matter from trees and crops maintains soil fertility; the diversity of plant species inhibits pests and diseases; and the microclimate created by the vegetation is beneficial to both the soil and the regulation of the water cycle. Well-managed agroforestry systems reduce pressures to cut existing forests by allowing sustained production from deforested lands, in addition to a steady supply of forest products.

Although agroforestry has been practiced for centuries, scientific investigation in the discipline is still in its infancy. In recent years, however, interest in agroforestry has gained momentum. Two international organizations that are actively promoting studies in agroforestry are the Tropical Agronomic Center of Investigation and Teaching (CATIE) in Turrialba, Costa Rica, and the International Council for Research in Agroforestry (ICRAF) in Nairobi, Kenya. Owing to the complex nature of agroforestry, interdisciplinary studies are almost imperative, opening the field to people in areas as diverse as agronomy, forestry, ecology, economics, and anthropology.

Agroforestry is not a panacea for the problems of either deforestation or world hunger. But as the expanding world population makes ever-increasing demands for food and forest products from an increasingly strained environment, the wider implementation of agroforestry systems holds great promise to increase agricultural and forestry production while minimizing environmental damage [9].

David Perry

A fourth controversy is between the need to study wilderness—to understand wilderness so that it can be better conserved—and the desire to leave the wilderness undisturbed. Those in favor of scientific research in the wilderness argue that it is necessary for the conservation of the wilderness. Those opposed argue that scientific research is contradictory to the purpose of a designated wilderness as an area untrammeled by man and where the presence of people is not visible. One solution is to establish separate research preserves.

SUMMARY

In this chapter we have discussed the conservation and management of forests, parks, and wilderness: ecosystems that can be renewable if managed properly but which can also become endangered and extinct. Modern management of renewable resources emphasizes scientifically based management, which includes the concepts of ecosystems and island biogeography.

Forests are among civilization's most important renewable resources and forests have always had special meaning for people. In managing a forest, one seeks a sustainable harvest that allows multiple use of the landscape. The best practices vary with the kind of forest, with the terrain and soil, and with climate. There are a number of important controversies surrounding the management of forests, including questions about clearcutting, the use of firewood as a fuel, and rotation times.

The management of parks for biological conservation is a relatively new idea that began in the nineteenth century. There are nine major reasons that people establish parks, ranging from preservation of curious works of nature to maintenance of representative natural areas to scientific research. A manager of a park must be concerned with its shape and size. Parks that are too small, or of the wrong shape, may not be able to sustain the species for which the park was established. Today, parks share individuals of endangered species and exchange these with zoos, which also function as preserves for endangered species. The study of island biogeography provides us with insight into the appropriate size and shape of parks.

A special extreme in conservation of natural areas is the management of wilderness. In the United States, the 1964 Wilderness Act provided a legal basis for this conservation. The management of wilderness involves a basic contradiction: trying to preserve an area untrammeled by people requires the interference of the manager to limit user access and to maintain the wilderness in a natural-like state.

The quality of our lives and our access to important biological resources requires that we conserve forests, parks and wilderness. The problems are complex but the principles of environmental studies provide us with an approach to successful management and conservation.

STUDY QUESTIONS

1 Discuss how the concept of ecological succession can help us manage forests.

2 What environmental conflicts might arise when a forest is managed for the multiple uses of (a) commercial timber, (b) wildlife conservation, and (c) as a watershed for a reservoir? In what ways would management for one use benefit another?

3 Give arguments for and against the following statement: Clearcutting is natural and necessary for forest management.

4 Can a wilderness park be managed to supply water to a city? Discuss.

5 What is meant by the statement, "There is a world firewood crisis"? How might that crisis in one country affect the environment in another?

6 Compare the important environmental considerations in planning (a) a park to preserve a rare species of deer, and (b) a park in the same area for recreation, including hiking and hunting. The park will be established in rugged mountains where there is a high rainfall.

7 What changes in our environment are leading us to try to manage wilderness?

8 What are the environmental effects of decreasing the rotation time in forests from an average of 60 years to 10 years? Compare these effects for (a) a woodland in a dry climate on a sandy soil and (b) a rain forest.

9 Present arguments for and against the following statement: Fire is necessary in forest management.

10 What environmental factors have contributed to the world firewood shortage?

11 How might a gradual warming of the climate affect most parks established for (a) conservation of endangered species or (b) scenic beauty?

FURTHER READING

CAMPOS-LOPEZ, E., ed. 1980. Renewable resources: A systematic approach. New York: Academic Press.

CARPENTER, R. A., ed. 1983. *Natural systems for development: What planners need to know.* New York: Macmillan.

ECKHOLM, E. P. 1975. The firewood crisis. *Natural History* 84: 7–22.

RUNTE, A. 1979. National parks: The American experience. Lincoln: University of Nebraska.

SEARS, P. 1935. *Deserts on the march.* Norman: University of Oklahoma Press.

SEDJO, R. A., and CLAWSON, M. 1984. Global forests. In *The resourceful Earth,* eds. J. L. SIMON and H. KAHN. New York: Blackwell.

SOULE, M. E. 1980. Thresholds for survival: Maintaining fitness and evolutionary potential. In *Conservation biology,* eds. M. E. Soule and B. A. Wilcox, pp. 151–69. Sunderland, Mass.: Sinauer.

SPURR, S. H., and BARNES, B. V. 1973. *Forest ecology.* New York: Ronald Press.

STODDARD, C. H. 1978. *Essentials of forestry practice.* 3rd ed. New York: Wiley.

SUTTON, S. L.; WHITMORE, T. C.; and CHADWICK, A. C., eds. 1983. Tropical rainforest: Ecology and management. Oxford, England: Blackwell.

SYNGE, H. 1980. *The biological aspects of rare plant conservation.* New York: Wiley.

U.S. FOREST SERVICE. 1980. *An assessment of the forest and range land situation in the United States.*

10
World Food Supply

- [ ] Agriculture changes the environment by attempting to stop natural succession, promoting monocultures, attempting to eliminate predators and parasites, and plowing the soil.
- [ ] Today there is enough food produced in the world to feed all of the people. The main food problem worldwide is distribution.
- [ ] Sustainable agriculture in most cases requires the use of fertilizers. Chemical elements removed from the soil by crops must be replaced. They can be replaced slowly by natural processes, but in most cases the natural rate is less than the rate of removal.
- [ ] Promoting increases in local food production is the best solution to current food distribution problems. Food aid among nations is less satisfactory but has been repeatedly practiced.
- [ ] The balance between population growth and increased food production is an uncertain one; in the long run, there are limits to both.
- [ ] The world's best agricultural land is already in production; portions of it are being constantly lost to urbanization, highways, and soil erosion.
- [ ] Only a small fraction of the land can support crop production; poorer land can be used as range or pasture.
- [ ] Water will become the major limiting factor for crop growth; thus impacts on the water supply (e.g., irrigation, overdraft) carry serious environmental implications.
- [ ] Soil is continuously formed, but slowly; good management can improve the formation rate dramatically while reducing the rate of erosion.
- [ ] Farming produces conditions tending to promote pest species. Broad-spectrum chemical pesticides affect many organisms, including beneficial ones.
- [ ] Integrated pest management involves a variety of techniques used in a coordinated fashion that recognizes ecological communities. Its goal is control, not extinction.
- [ ] Global effects of agriculture include climatic effects, addition of particulates and CO_2 to the atmosphere, and changes in biogeochemical cycles.

1980s AFRICAN FAMINE

In the mid 1980s, starvation due to drought in Africa gained worldwide attention and brought world food problems and their relationship to the environment to the front pages of newspapers. In one year, as many as 22 African nations suffered catastrophic food shortages, and 150 million Africans faced starvation. Four million tons of emergency food per year were needed. Five million refugees sought food and shelter.

The year 1983 was especially bad—it was called the drought of the century. The first warnings of widespread starvation surfaced in September 1982. By May 1983, the United Nations Food and Agricultural Organization telegraphed 27 nations asking for emergency food assistance.

Ten years earlier, a similar catastrophic situation had developed following the 1973–74 drought in the Sahel in Africa. At that time 500,000 Africans starved to death, and several million more were permanently affected by malnutrition. The most severely hit countries were Chad, Ethiopia, Ghana, São Tomé, and Mozambique [1].

Drought is not new to Africa, but the huge populations the drought affects are new. Human population growth in Africa has exceeded the increase in food production. The average population growth has been 3.2%/yr. At this rate, by 1990 64% more agricultural land will be needed in Africa than exists at present. In 1962, the African nations produced 98% of their food, but this has decreased steadily. Between 1961 and 1980 the production of food in Africa dropped 14%; today the decline is 2%/yr. Imports increased 9.5% annually between 1961 and 1980. In 1981 the countries south of the Sahara needed 2.7 million tons annually of food aid. By 1990 they will need 17 million tons/yr [2]. It is not clear how this need could ever be met. Deserts seem to be spreading—in part the result of changing climate, but in part the result of human activities: poor farming practices have increased erosion; deforestation may be helping to make the environment drier. Thus environment affects agriculture, but agriculture also affects environment.

Africa is not alone in suffering recently from catastrophic food shortage. In 1982, for example, many other areas suffered serious droughts and re-duction in crop growth. Australia experienced the worst drought in 50 years, affecting 80,000 farms. Nicaragua lost $72 million in crop production. Spain experienced the worst drought of a century [2]. Food has become a major global concern.

A severe famine developed in recent years in the Brazilian state of Ceará in the northeastern part of that country. The starvation caused social disruption. About two million people, called the *flagelados* ("scourged ones"), many near starvation, fled the rural countryside for the cities along the coasts. There, lacking food, they broke into markets and warehouses and caused riots in their search for food. No rain fell in five years over a large area. In 1984, 87% of the northeast was involved and 24 million people were affected [3].

FOOD AND FAMINE

There is more food per person today than at any time in history, and more food is produced on Earth every year than is eaten, yet it is estimated that 500 million people are malnourished (Fig. 10.1) [4, 5].

Food problems are typically the result of many factors and of many complex interrelations. Many of the factors that led to the recent famines were environmental. In addition to the drought, the contributing factors were desertification, human population growth, livestock population growth, inefficient agricultural production, low use of fertilizers (Africa has the lowest fertilizer consumption of all populated continents), poor transportation facilities (poor roads and poor storage facilities), and social disruptions.

The famines in Africa and elsewhere illustrate many of the environmental issues that concern food. There are three major aspects to the relation between world food supply and the environment. First, food production depends on the environment. When there is a drought, or a lack of any crucial resource, food production decreases. Because the environment is always varying, there will be good years and bad years, and farmers must continually adjust to these environmental variations.

Second, agriculture changes the environment. When these changes are detrimental, large num-

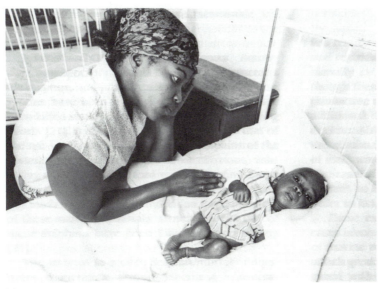

(a)

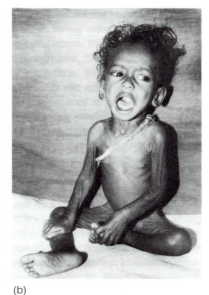

(b)

FIGURE 10.1
Effects of malnutrition. (a) A Swaziland mother tends her baby, who has kwashiorkor—an
often-fatal condition resulting from a protein-deficient diet. (b) A 13–month-old Indian child
with marasmus—progressive emaciation caused by a lack of protein and calories.

bers of people can suffer. The history of agriculture can be viewed as a series of attempts to overcome environmental limitations and problems. But each new solution has created new environmental problems, which have in turn required their own solutions. In seeking to improve our agriculture, we must expect these undesirable side effects and be ready to cope with them.

Third, our modern food problem is the result of the great increase in human population growth, which outstrips local food production in many areas, and an inadequate food distribution system for this growing population.

In addition to the role that environment plays in food production, the world food supply is also greatly affected by social disruptions and social attitudes, which affect the environment and in turn affect agriculture. While these social aspects are not the subject of this text, we must see the interplay between environment and agriculture as affected by society and against a background of social change. In Africa, social disruptions since 1960 have included 12 wars, 50 coups, and 13 assassi-

nations. This social instability makes sustained agriculture yield difficult.

Not long ago, people in the developed nations believed that famine was a thing of the past, but today we know that famine is a major global issue and will be so for some time into the future. The reasons for this are in part environmental; because agriculture has a major impact on the environment, changes in food production and supply have major environmental effects [1].

THE SOURCES OF FOOD

Some primitive societies obtain food through hunting and gathering, but the great majority of people obtain food through the cultivation of plants and the domestication of animals. The sources of food are primarily three: the products of traditional agriculture, the new strains produced by modern techniques, and the products of aquaculture.

Products of Traditional Agriculture

People obtain food from the land, fresh waters, and oceans, but 95% of the protein and most of the calories are obtained from the land production of traditional agriculture. These products include both crops and livestock [5, 6].

Crops Although there are 350,000 species of plants, only about 3000 have been tried as agricultural crops, only 300 species of plants are used for food, and only 100 are used on a large scale. Some crops provide food; others provide commercial products, including oils. Most of the world's food is provided by only 20 crop species. These are, in approximate order of importance: wheat, rice, corn, potatoes, barley, sweet potatoes, cassava, soybeans, oats, sorghum, millet, sugarcane, sugarbeets, rye, peanuts, field beans, chick peas, pigeon peas, bananas, and coconuts. Other crops are important food for domestic animals; these include alfalfa, sorghum, and various species of grasses grown as hay. Alfalfa is the most important such crop in the United States, where 30 million acres are planted in alfalfa—one-half of the world's total.

The bulk of the food of the world is provided by grains: wheat, rice, corn, barley, oats, sorghum, millet, and rye. Grains are the major sources of calories and proteins for most of the world.

There is a large world trade in small grains, with only North America, Australia, and New Zealand as major exporters. The world's annual grain production is about 1.5 billion tons, but of this, developing countries, with one-half of the world's population, produce only 400 million tons. There has been a very great increase in grain production—more than a doubling between 1950 and 1971 (from 631 million metric tons to 1237), but the increase in production is slowing down.

It is useful to group farming into cash crops and subsistence crops. Cash crops are grown to be sold or traded in a large market. Subsistence crops or food crops are used directly for food by the farmer, or sold locally where the food is used directly. Some cash crops may not provide a food at all. For example, rubber plantations produce latex from the sap of rubber trees; the latex is then sold to make rubber products. Other cash crops, such as coffee or tea, do not provide primary nutrition and are not necessary for survival, but in many countries such cash crops are a major source of international trade and foreign "hard" currencies, so that there is governmental and economic pressure to grow these cash crops instead of food crops.

Livestock Domesticated animals are an important food source and have a major impact on the land. The major domesticated animals used as food are ruminants—animals that have a four-chambered stomach in which bacteria convert woody tissue to proteins and fats that can be digested by the animal. In this way, ruminants convert cellulose, Earth's most abundant organic compound, to human food. The major livestock are cattle, sheep, and goats, but there are other important species, including the water buffalo common in Southeast Asia, the camel of North Africa, and the llama of the South American Andes. There are more than 1.5 billion sheep and goats and 1.2 billion cattle; estimates suggest that these will increase to about 1.8 billion sheep and goats and 1.6 billion cattle by the end of the century.

Domestic grazing and browsing animals are maintained on pasture and range. Range is land that provides or can provide food for grazing and browsing animals without plowing and planting; pasture is land that is plowed and planted to provide forage for the animals.

New Strains

From the beginning, farming has affected the genetics of domesticated animals and plants. The act of farming makes certain species abundant where they were rare before. Features that would make a species, or a population with a certain genetic strain, called a genotype, a less strong competitor under natural conditions sometimes make it more desirable as a crop. The features that make a plant easy to grow and harvest may make it a poor competitor in the wild. For example, wild relatives of wheat lose their seeds when the seeds are ripened and gently shaken by wind or animals. If you try to cut wild wheat stems and bring them home, most of the seeds will be shaken off and you will have few left. Some individuals of wild wheat have a mutation that makes the seeds remain on the stalk. In the wild these mutants leave fewer offspring and do not persist in the population; this means that in the wild the mutants are less fit genetically. Early farmers would have naturally selected these mutants because they were easier to collect. In this way, people have changed the selective pressures on wheat and changed and hastened the evolution of wheat strains that are useful to us, but which could not survive on their own. People also domesticated wheat by moving it to habitats to which it was not originally adapted, developing new strains, and changing the environmental conditions of that habitat [7]. In this sense the relationship between ourselves and wheat is a form of symbiosis—we eat the domestic wheat, and make it possible for such strains of wheat to survive.

Corn (maize) went through a similar process of domestication. Its ancestral wild relatives had very small, irregular heads. Ancient deposits of Indian corn found in burials or in very dry areas show a change over the centuries to a larger and larger head with more even kernels. Similarly, domestic animals have also been bred to make them more docile and better producers of those kinds of meat or dairy products that we most prefer. For example, chickens and turkeys have been selected to produce a high percentage of white meat. Domestic turkeys, however, are comparatively helpless and have little chance of survival in the wild.

The **green revolution** is the name attached to programs that have led to the breeding of new strains of crops that had higher yield or better resistance to disease or could grow under less optimal conditions (Fig. 10.2). These programs gained momentum after World War II. A spectacular success of the green revolution was the development of super strains of rice at the International Rice Research Institute in the Philippines. These strains had a much higher yield per acre, but also required a greater use of fertilizers and in some cases produced a rice that was not considered as desirable to eat. Another success in the green revolution has been the development at the International Maize and Wheat Improvement Center in Mexico of strains of corn with improved disease resistance.

FIGURE 10.2
A regular variety of wheat (left) compared to giant wheat developed by crossing a genetic strain from Mexico with new genetic material.

Genetic Engineering There is considerable interest in the potential for genetic engineering to develop strains of crops with entirely new characteristics. One focus of this research is development of new crops that fix nitrogen, creating the same symbiotic relationship found in legumes (members of the pea family). Legumes have bacteria that grow in root nodules, where they live on products made by the legumes and where the bacteria fix nitrogen (meaning that they convert atmospheric gaseous nitrogen to a form that can be used by green plants; see Chapter 4). Legumes are often rotated with other crops so that the soil is enriched in nitrogen [8].

It may be possible to develop new strains of corn and other crops that, along with new strains of bacteria, can form a symbiotic nitrogen-fixing relationship. If this were accomplished, it would lead to an increase in production of these crops and a reduction in costs of buying fertilizers.

Another goal of the genetic manipulation approach to increasing crop production is development of strains with tolerance to drought, cold, heat, and toxic chemical elements. For example,

Vanishing Genetic Resources

Corn was, quite literally, the staff of life in the Americas in prehistoric times. From Colorado to South America, civilizations rose and fell on the stable nutritional base that the grain provided formerly nomadic groups.

Today corn, along with wheat, rice, and other major food crops, is still very important to modern civilization. Without a steady agricultural base, the industrial and technological revolutions would never have occurred. Modern society cannot ignore the fact that if the agricultural base were to disappear, so would modern society.

The green revolution has done much to secure the world food supply. Use of fertilizers and pesticides has greatly increased crop production. However, by far the most important component of the green revolution is the development of high-yielding hybrids by plant geneticists.

Among the individuals of a plant species, there is usually a great amount of genetic variety. One crop can have thousands of genetic variations, the majority in its area of geographic origin. Different varieties of corn, for example, have short or long stalks, tolerance for cold, heat, or drought, or resistance to specific pests and diseases. By using the different wild and primitive varieties of crops as raw material, plant geneticists have produced high-yielding hybrid varieties.

Modern hybrids, however, have been inbred to the point that they are now very vulnerable to disease and pests. In 1970, 70% of the corn planted in the United States was derived from only five inbred lines. Facilitated by the genetically identical plants and vast areas of contiguous corn monoculture, a fungus disease swept through the corn belt, destroying 15% of the crop.

With great effort, plant geneticists developed a new hybrid resistant to the disease before planting time the following year. However, a disease needs only 5 to 15 years to evolve to the point that it can attack a new hybrid. For this reason, plant geneticists need a steady supply of fresh genetic material to keep one step ahead of the plant diseases.

But the genetic resources needed to do this are disappearing very rapidly. The wild and primitive varieties of crops are becoming extinct at a rapid pace for three principal reasons: the destruction of natural ecosystems; the change of subsistence agriculture to commercial agriculture; and the natural inclination of farmers to plant hybrid varieties instead of the traditional primitive varieties.

This transition from genetic diversity to genetic uniformity in food crops creates a situation that invites massive crop failures similar to the one that decimated Ireland's potato production in the 1840s.

Efforts have begun, however, to protect the world's gene pool of cultivated plants. The International Board for Plant and Genetic Resources in Rome is encouraging seed collection and storage. Some organizations are more local, such as Seed Search in Tucson, Arizona, which is dedicated to preserving native American crops adapted to the arid Southwest.

Meanwhile, the genetic erosion continues. A mountainous region in Mexico that harbors the few remaining wild stands of teosinte, a wild perennial variety of corn potentially worth billions of dollars, is subjected to massive deforestation. A Peruvian farmer chooses to replace his traditional cornfield with a coffee grove. A Guatemalan makes tortillas from his seed corn of a unique local variety handed down by his Mayan ancestors and plants a higher yielding hybrid in its place. Ironically, he may have just eaten the last living vestige of the raw material from which the hybrid he plants was developed.

David Perry

there is currently an attempt to develop wheat that is resistant to high levels of aluminum, an element that has negative effects on the growth of many plants [9].

While genetic modifications have proven to have great benefit, there are limitations. Proponents of the approach argue that world food production must double or triple in the next several decades if all the people of the world are to be fed and that, if distribution of food is the real problem, then one solution is to increase local production.

Opponents argue that (1) the approach relies too heavily on mechanized agriculture, which is too costly for the developing nations where the increase is most needed and has too many environmental drawbacks; (2) the approach does not pay enough attention to methods of natural pest control and other factors that lead to a loss in harvests; (3) some of the new strains require high amounts of certain fertilizers, straining resources; and (4) the high production of certain crops requires intense cultivation methods, which may lead to greater erosion and to greater dependence on artificial chemical pest control. As with all other forms of agriculture, the major challenge facing genetic engineering of crops is development of sustainable agriculture.

Crop Domestication   There is considerable potential for developing new crops by domesticating species that are currently wild. Although new crops are unlikely to replace current crop species as major food sources in this century, there is great interest in new crops to increase production in marginal areas and to increase the production of nonfood products such as oils.

The development of new crops has been a continuing process in the history of agriculture. As people spread around the world, new crops were discovered and transported from one area to another. The process of introduction and increase in production of crops continues today. For example, in the United States, the area devoted to the production of sunflowers, once a minor crop, has increased to 3 million acres.

Among the likely candidates for new crops are amaranth for seeds and leaves; *Leucaena*, a legume useful for animal feed; and triticale, a synthetic hybrid of wheat and rye. A promising source of new crops is the desert; none of the 20 major crops are plants of arid or semiarid regions, yet there are vast areas of desert and semidesert. In the United States there are 200,000 million ha of arid and semiarid rangeland. Africa, Australia, and South America have even greater areas. There are several species of plants that can be grown commercially under arid conditions, thus allowing us to exploit a biome that has been little used in the past; examples are guayule (a source of rubber), jojoba (for oil), bladderpod (for oil from seeds), and gumweed (for resin). Jojoba is a native shrub of the American Sonoran desert. It produces an extremely fine oil, remarkably resistant to bacterial degradation, and useful in cosmetics and as a fine lubricant. Jojoba is now grown commercially in Australia, Egypt, Ghana, Iran, Israel, Jordan, Mexico, Saudi Arabia, and the United States [10].

Aquaculture

Aquaculture is the production of food from aquatic habitats—marine and freshwater (Fig. 10.3). Although aquaculture provides only a small amount of the world's food at present, it is important in certain areas of the world for the supply of protein and it offers a potentially important cash crop in other parts of the world. For example, in China, growing fish in rice fields is an ancient practice that can be traced back to a treatise on fish culture written by Fan Li in 475 B.C. [11]. In the Sichuan area alone there are more than 100,000 ha of ricefields; fish are farmed in the flooded fields along with the rice.

Animals grown in aquaculture include oysters (in many countries); shrimp (in China and Japan); herbaceous fish such as the carp (grown widely) and *Tilapia* (in Africa, Israel, the United States, and many other countries); eels (China); catfish (grown in the southern United States and sold in fast food outlets); minnows (in China); trout such as the rainbow salmon, the southeast Asian milkfish, plaice and sole of Great Britain, and sturgeon in the Ukraine. Only a few species—trout and carp—have been subject to genetic breeding programs [11].

FIGURE 10.3
Aquaculture. At an oyster
farm in Japan, the oysters
are placed in wire cages
that are suspended from
rafts. Eventually the oysters will be harvested for
food.

Freshwater Aquaculture Some fish growers in
China and other Asian countries make use of the
different ecological niches of various species to
grow them together in the same pond. For example, ponds developed mainly for carp, a bottom-
feeding fish, also contain minnows, which feed at
the surface on higher plant leaves that are added
to the pond [11].

An interesting example of an ecosystem approach to aquaculture occurs in China, where the
production of freshwater fish and silkworms is
combined. The silkworms feed on mulberry leaves,
and the mulberry trees are planted around fish
ponds. The leaves and the droppings from the silkworms are added to the ponds to provide fertilizers
for the growth of algae, which in turn provide food
for the fish. The sediment from the pond is used to
fertilize the trees. In this way the chemical elements are recycled. In China, aquaculture includes
a wide variety of organisms, from 50 species of
fish, shrimp, crab, and shellfish to marine algae,

sea turtles, sea cucumbers (a marine animal), and
water chestnuts [12].

In the United States, aquaculture has grown
rapidly as a producer of cash crops, especially in
southern states where catfish and crawfish (freshwater relatives of lobsters) are fast becoming important cash crops, providing incomes that greatly
exceed those of traditional farming.

In some cases, fish ponds are designed to use
otherwise wasted resources. Some make use of the
fertilized water available from treated sewage (this
has been done in countries as far apart as West
Germany and Indonesia); other fish ponds make
use of natural hot springs (as in Idaho) and of the
warmed water used in cooling electric power
plants in Long Island, New York, and in Great Britain [11].

Aquaculture can be extremely productive on a
per area basis, especially because flowing water
brings food into the pond or enclosure from outside. While the area of Earth that can support

freshwater aquaculture is small, we can expect that this kind of aquaculture will increase in the future and become a more important source of protein.

Mariculture Mariculture—the production of food from marine habitats—is part of aquaculture. This too has grown rapidly in the last decade, and can be expected to increase in the future. Although mariculture provides only a small fraction of the world's protein, it can be important in certain countries and can provide valuable cash crops. The great difference between mariculture and traditional agriculture is that in regard to the sea we are still only hunters and gatherers, not farmers. This is now changing rapidly, but because it is so much harder for us to learn about ocean life than about land life, the methods for farming ocean organisms are more difficult to learn. Such delicacies as abalone and oysters, whose natural production is limited, are undergoing increased production as part of mariculture. In the United States and Canada, for example, there is research to learn how to attract the young, swimming stages of these shellfish to areas in which they will settle on surfaces where they can be conveniently grown and harvested.

Oysters and mussels are typically grown on rafts that are lowered and raised in the ocean. These animals are filter feeders and obtain food from the water that is moved by them in the currents. A small area of a raft is therefore exposed to a large volume of water and the food it contains, so that rafts can be extremely productive. For example, mussels grown on rafts in the bays of Galicia, Spain, produce 300 metric tons/ha, while public harvesting grounds of wild shellfish in the United States yield only about 10 kg/ha [11].

MODERN AGRICULTURE

There are two major approaches to agriculture: (1) production based on highly mechanized technology, with a high demand for resources, including land, water, and fuel, and with little use of biologically based technologies; (2) production based on biological technology, with conservation of land, water, and energy. The first kind is demand-based

agriculture—production is determined by economic demand and limited by such demands and not by resources. The second kind is resource-based agriculture—the production is limited by the availability of resources—economic demand usually exceeds production (Fig. 10.4) [6]. The world as a whole is moving from the first to the second approach. The history of agriculture might be summarized most simply as (1) the introduction of resource-based agriculture about 10,000 years ago; (2) a shift to mechanized, demand-based agriculture during the industrial revolution of the last two centuries; and (3) a modern return to resource-based agriculture. The new resource-based agriculture, however, includes many modern approaches and uses all forms of technology where these are appropriate.

An Ecological Perspective

When we farm, we create abnormal ecological conditions and novel ecosystems. These novel ecosystems are called agro-ecosystems. When we farm, we attempt to keep the agro-ecosystem in a constant condition—freezing it in time, trying to prevent natural changes from occurring. Most crops are planted on cleared land, which is then kept clear. This is different from a natural clearing; when an area is cleared of vegetation following a natural disturbance such as a fire or storm, the vegetation returns. There is a predictable, repeatable pattern to this return, called ecological succession (see Chapter 5). Some species are adapted to the early stages in succession, some to later ones. Most crops are early successional species, which means that they do best in bright sunlight and when water and the chemical nutrients in the soil are abundant. Under natural conditions, crop species would be replaced in a sequence with other plants. Farming is an attempt to stop this natural succession (Fig. 10.5).

A second way that agriculture creates an abnormal ecosystem is that large areas are planted to a single species, or even to a single strain or subspecies, such as a hybrid corn. This is called monoculture. Moreover, in most cases crops are planted in neat, regular rows. In most natural ecosystems there are many species of plants in the same area,

FIGURE 10.4
Agricultural technologies.
(a) Demand-based agricul-
ture; (b) resource-based
agriculture.

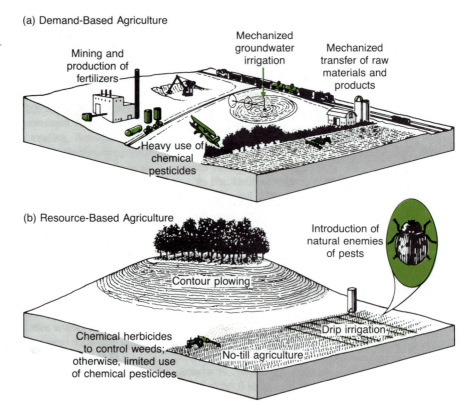

(a) Demand-Based Agriculture

Mining and
production of
fertilizers

Mechanized
groundwater
irrigation

Mechanized
transfer of raw
materials and
products

Heavy use of
chemical
pesticides

(b) Resource-Based Agriculture

Introduction of
natural enemies
of pests

Contour plowing

Drip irrigation

Chemical herbicides
to control weeds;
otherwise, limited use
of chemical pesticides

No-till agriculture

mixed together in complex patterns, rarely forming regular rows. The complex patterns are important to many ecological factors; the complexity tends to decrease the abundance of pest animals that feed on the crops.

Because any single species of plants has its own set of requirements for chemical elements in the soil, the repeated planting of a single species over a large field can reduce the availability of essential chemical elements. This can be counteracted to a certain extent by crop rotation. In crop rotation, a series of different crops are planted in turn in the same field, with the field occasionally left without any planting for one season (left fallow). The use of artificial fertilizers can counter some of these effects also.

A third way that agriculture creates an abnormal ecosystem is that natural predators and parasites are greatly reduced or eliminated. We try to eliminate these organisms because we want all of the production of the crop saved for one species—ourselves. But the reduction in the number of species tends to make the ecosystem more susceptible to undesirable changes.

A fourth way that agriculture creates an abnormal ecosystem is by plowing, which is unlike any natural disturbance in the way that the soil is repeatedly and regularly turned over to a specific depth. Plowing exposes the soil to erosion and can affect the physical structure and chemical makeup of the soil in ways that may be bad for future, long-term food production.

Any attempt to prevent natural processes from occurring requires actions on our part and input of energy and our own time and effort. To manage agriculture successfully, in a way that will allow for long, sustained use, we must take an ecosystem perspective.

FIGURE 10.5
How farming changes an ecosystem.

A farm keeps the land in a stage of early succession.

Natural landscape has many species of animals and plants.

A farm is simplified in number of species.

A farm has few species.

Herbivores and parasites are reduced or eliminated.

Plowing causes unique changes in soils.

Chemicals used in pesticides have new ecological effects

The Effect of the Environment on Agriculture

Agriculture depends on the environment in many ways, and any area has a certain potential, determined by the environment, for the production of crops. The goal of a farmer, from an environmental standpoint, is to obtain yields as close to this potential as possible, without endangering his future level of production or causing undesirable environmental effects elsewhere. This leads us to the concepts of sustainable yields and optimum sustainable yields.

Sustainable Yields A maximum sustainable agricultural yield is an amount produced per unit area that can be continued indefinitely without decreasing the ability of that crop species to sustain that yield, regardless of the effect on the environment or the ecosystem. An optimum sustainable yield of a crop is the largest yield that can be obtained on a unit area without decreasing the ability of the agro-ecosystem to sustain that yield in the future. Little of modern agriculture is sustainable, and one of the major challenges in the future will be to create a sustainable agriculture.

In terms of human beings and world food production, the major question is: How many people can be fed on a sustainable basis? In ecological terms, this translates into: What is the optimum sustainable population (or the optimum sustainable carrying capacity) of Earth for human beings? The challenge before us is to produce adequate food to meet the demands of improved diets for an expanding world population and an increasingly affluent human population.

A major obstacle to obtaining an answer to this question is that technology for food production, processing, and distribution keeps changing faster than we can understand the effects of these changes, and these changes have both positive and negative impacts on the environment. With our modern technology, given enough energy and materials, we can grow food in a completely artificial environment; we might even do this someday on a spacecraft, but this is too expensive a solution, in terms of money, resources, and effects on the environment in general, to be a large-scale solution to food production.

Optimum Environmental Conditions The concept of sustainable yield leads us to the concept of optimum environmental conditions for the growth of any single crop. Every crop species has its own set of optimum environmental conditions for growth, and therefore crops differ in where they will grow best. Some crops, such as rye, grow best under relatively cool, moist conditions and are important in higher latitudes; other crops, such as maize, do better in warmer, dryer climates.

Regions of Earth differ greatly in their capacity for crop production. As an example, in the United States, the states differ greatly in their crop production (Fig. 10.6). California has the greatest value of crop production of any state in the United States, exceeding $20 billion per year. East of the Rockies in the western states are grazing lands and irrigated farmlands, mainly planted in grains—corn, wheat, and so forth. Farther east in Nebraska are areas of winter wheat, with spring wheat planted in the Dakotas to the north. The Midwest is the corn belt, with dairy and hay for cattle produced in the northern states from Minnesota east to Maine. In the Southeast, major crops include cotton and tobacco, as well as vegetables and fruits.

High crop production requires a good fertile soil, a moderate rainfall well distributed throughout the growing season, and moderate to warm temperatures during the growing season, but with the proper seasonal variations for the crops to be planted—most crops require a definite seasonal pattern. Some areas, such as the poles, are unsuited to any agriculture because of temperature. Other areas lack water or crucial chemical elements.

Only 11% of Earth's land surface is considered arable, which means that it is suitable for plant crops [5]; about 25% of the land (about 470 million acres, or 190 million ha) in the United States is arable; 80% was in production in the mid-1970s. There is an additional 740 million acres (300 million ha) in pasture and rangeland. Draining swamps and irrigating deserts could add an additional 75 million acres (30 million ha). The best agricultural land is already in production. It is, however, being lost constantly to urbanization, highways, and soil erosion (about 2.5 million acres

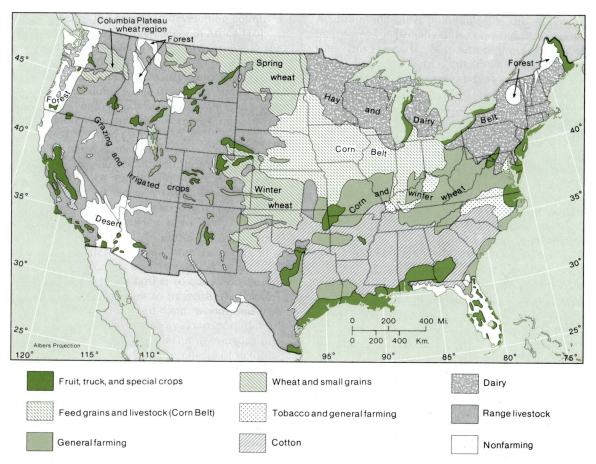

FIGURE 10.6
Major types of land use in the United States. (U.S. Department of Agriculture data.)

or 1 million ha/yr). Because irrigation and drainage add about 1.25 million acres/yr (500,000 ha/yr), the net loss is 1.25 million acres/yr (500,000 ha/yr).

Limiting Factors Agriculture also depends heavily on soil quality. A high-quality soil for agriculture has all the chemical elements required for plant growth and has a physical structure that lets both air and water move freely through the soil, while retaining water reasonably well. Such a soil will have a high organic content, which helps retain chemical elements, and a mixture of particle

sizes (some of which help retain moisture and chemical elements, others of which help the flow of water). The physical qualities required vary with the crop; for example, lowland rice that grows in flooded ponds requires a heavy, water-saturated soil, while watermelons grow best in very sandy soil.

In many areas of the world, soils lack one or more of the chemical elements required by crops. Such an element is called a limiting factor. An agricultural limiting factor is a single requirement for growth that is available in the least supply in comparison to the need of the crop. In most cases, this lack is one of the macronutrients—a chemical element required in large amounts by all living things. In other cases, soils are lacking in micronutrients, which are specific trace elements—typically some metal required only in small amounts. The older a soil, the more likely it is to lack trace elements. This is because, as a soil ages, its supply of chemical elements tends to be leached by water from the upper layers to deeper layers. When crucial chemical elements are leached below the reach of crop roots, then the soil becomes infertile (Fig. 10.7).

Some of the most striking cases of soil nutrient limitations have been found in Australia, which has some of the oldest soils in the world. The Australian soils occur on land that has been above sea level for many millions of years, during which time severe leaching has taken place. Sometimes trace elements are required in extremely small amounts; for example, crops require very small amounts of

molybdenum, and the addition of very small amounts has very great effects; it is estimated that adding an ounce of molybdenum increased the yield of grass in sheep pastures by one ton.

Because of the geographic variation in the quality of environments for crops, some countries are net exporters of crops and others are net importers. Among leading food exporters are Argentina, Australia, Brazil, Colombia, Cuba, Denmark, Netherlands, New Zealand, Malaysia, the Philippines, and the United States. Food is one of the major exports of the United States. Agricultural exports were valued at about $22 billion in the mid-1970s [5]. Of the African nations, only the Ivory Coast exports crops worth more than $1 billion/yr.

Fertilization

Fertilizers play an important role in modern agriculture. A fertilizer is any material added to the soil

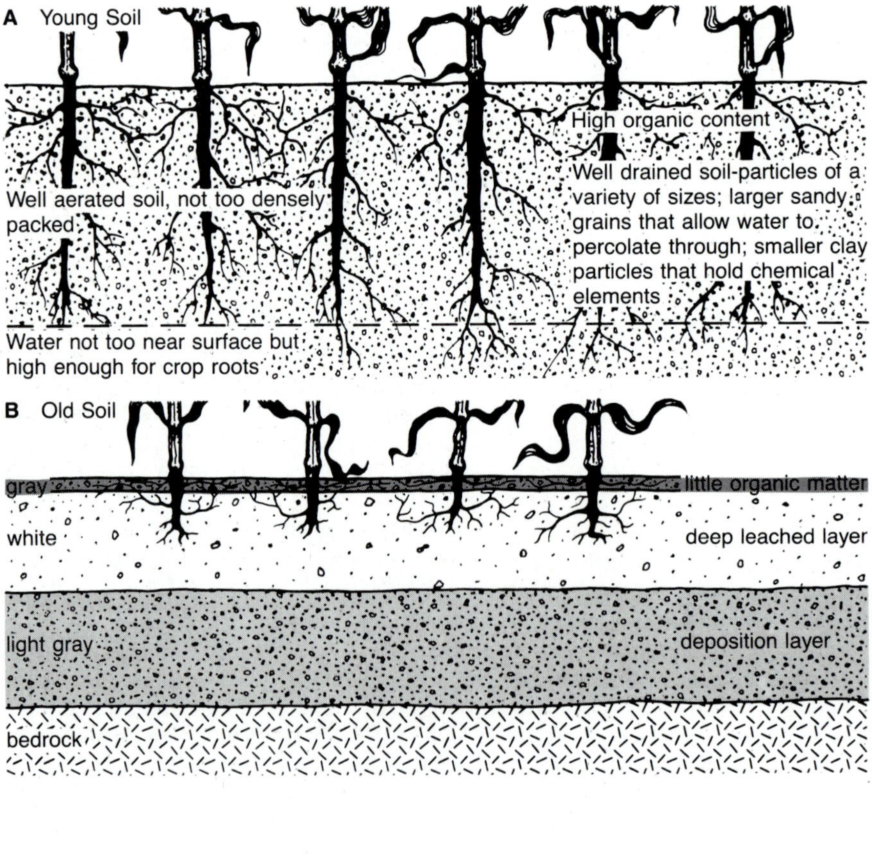

FIGURE 10.7
Aging of soil. (a) A young soil that will support most crops. (b) An old soil in which crucial chemical elements have been leached beyond the reach of crop roots.

A Young Soil

High organic content

Well aerated soil, not too densely packed

Well drained soil-particles of a variety of sizes; larger sandy grains that allow water to percolate through; smaller clay particles that hold chemical elements

Water not too near surface but high enough for crop roots

B Old Soil

gray   little organic matter

white   deep leached layer

light gray   deposition layer

bedrock

to improve the soil and increase crop production. Fertilizers improve either the chemical or physical characteristics of a soil. Chemical improvements include the addition of elements that are limiting factors and the alteration of the soil acidity. Physical factors include the improvement of drainage and the water-holding capacity of soils. Some fertilizers are derived from waste material from living things, such as ground-up plant bark and leaves, or partially decayed vegetation, or manure. Other fertilizers are derived from rock, especially from limestone, which in turn may have an organic origin as the shells or deposits of marine organisms.

The major chemical elements in fertilizers are nitrogen, phosphorus, potassium, and sulfur. Iron is also common in fertilizer. Phosphorus is obtained from rocks or from the deposits of guano from fish-eating birds that nest on islands off the coasts of South America and Africa. Nitrogen is obtained from manure and other organic sources or by artificial production from nitrogen gas in the atmosphere. The invention of the technology to produce nitrogen fertilizer from nitrogen gas in the atmosphere was one of the most important twentieth-century advances in agriculture.

Fertilizers have played an important role throughout the history of agriculture; adding fertilizer to a soil is one of the principal ways that people have made local agriculture less dependent on the local production. Because crops remove chemical elements from the soil, it is necessary that the elements be replaced. They can be replaced slowly by natural processes, but in most cases the natural rate is less than the rate of removal. Sustainable agriculture in most cases requires the use of fertilizers.

There is a tendency to depend on chemical fertilizers and ignore fertilizers that improve the physical properties of a soil. Over the long run, however, both kinds are needed. One of the direct environmental problems with modern agriculture is that it emphasizes chemical fertilizers and leads to a decline in the physical properties of the soil, which are harder to maintain and slower to restore.

There are important indirect environmental effects of the use of fertilizers. Invariably some of the fertilizers added to a soil are lost by erosion and are carried downstream. These fertilize streams, rivers, lakes, and reservoirs, a process known as eutrophication, which leads to many undesirable effects, including the buildup of undesirable algae and the death of fish (see Chapter 4).

Fertilizers should be specific to a particular soil, especially when the soil is lacking in a trace element. The best fertilizers will improve the physical and chemical properties of the soil and will minimize the loss of chemical elements to stream runoff.

Irrigation

Plants require water, and much of modern agriculture involves the artificial addition of water which is known as irrigation. With the increased use of fertilizers, water will become the major limiting factor for crop growth in the future. Soil moisture in the spring is now the major determinant for agricultural production in the corn and wheat belts of the United States.

Like the use of fertilizers, techniques to add water to cropland are as old as agriculture (Fig. 10.8). The sources of irrigation water include groundwater; nearby water courses such as rivers and streams; and natural lakes, rivers, and artificial reservoirs upstream. The importance of water for agriculture has led to a long history of water rights for farmers and to many controversies over water use. There is frequently a conflict between those whose farms are upstream and who want to remove water for their own use and those whose farms are downstream and want water left for their use.

Canals and aqueducts—artificial water courses to bring water from a distant source—were important in ancient times and are important today. For example, canals carry water from the north of California to the farms in the Great Central Valley and to southern California. California's great central valley is now one of the world's major areas for growing vegetables. Rainfall in this valley is too low to support the growth of commercial vegetable crops, but major irrigation projects make the farming possible.

These large-scale irrigation projects cause environmental problems that are important through-

FIGURE 10.8
Irrigation. (a) In 1946 this American sugar beet farmer used a shovel and a canvas check with sock outlet to control the flow of water. (b) At a modern agricultural research station in Saudi Arabia, a gated pipe irrigation system brings water to a corn field.

(a)

(b)

out the world, especially as such projects become more important in developing nations. The construction of reservoirs changes the local environment; some habitats are destroyed, stream patterns changed, and erosion rates increased in the watershed of the reservoir (Fig. 10.9).

Modern agriculture mines water just as surely as we mine the land for oil and iron. There are two important sources of water: (1) annual rainfall, which is used immediately and which is renewable, and (2) fossil deposits of water, accumulated deep in the Earth over thousands or millions of years,

and representing a nonrenewable resource. Unfortunately, too much of our modern agriculture depends on the nonrenewable sources. Overdraft is the amount by which water use exceeds the input from rainfall. In the United States, the overdraft is 20 to 25 million acre-feet/yr, much of it from the Ogallala aquifer—a huge water resource underlying parts of eight western states from South Dakota to Texas.

Solutions to the present overdraft problems include an increased use of techniques to conserve water, including soil mulches that help the soil re-

High elevation natural
forest "islands" to be
maintained as representative
ecological types

Slopes too
steep for
intensive use

Upstream areas
acceptable for
intensive use

Former farmland
flooded

Area subject
to salinization

Area subject
to sedimentation

FIGURE 10.9
Some ecological considerations in watershed development. (Redrawn from computer graphic by R. A. Carpenter.)

tain water; plastics for greenhouses, solar stills, soil mulches, tubing, and piping; techniques to improve the efficiency of water use, such as drip irrigation which decreases water evaporation; and new sources of water, which might be obtained by the use of solar stills. There is considerable use of these techniques around the world. For example, in China in 1981 there were 25,000 ha of plastic mulches and 9,000 ha of plastic greenhouses.

Slash and Burn

In the industrialized countries of temperate zones, there is a history of agriculture with plowing, while in the less industrialized tropical areas there is a history of agricultural methods that depend on clearing the vegetation without plowing. Where the loss of nutrients from the soil occurs rapidly following a clearing (Fig. 10.10), the traditional practice among people using nonmechanized farming is to cut the forest in small patches, but not cut it completely (some shrubs, or other small plants, are left). The land is planted with several crops, used for a few years, and then allowed to grow back to a natural forest stand. The natural process of secondary succession—the redevelopment of the ecosystem—is allowed to occur; in fact, the farming practices promote this redevelopment and increase the conservation of chemical elements in the ecosystem. After the forest has grown back, the process is repeated. In theory, this method could be sustainable.

This kind of agriculture has many names around the world. It is sometimes called "slash and burn," in reference to the methods used for clearing, or "cultivation with forest" or "bush fallow." In Latin America, it is called "milpas" agriculture; in England, it is called "swidden" agriculture; in West Africa, it is called "Fang" agriculture.

For many years agricultural experts from developed nations viewed slash and burn agriculture as a poor method used only by primitive peoples, with low, short-term production. Now it is understood that this kind of agriculture is much better suited to high-rainfall lands, where erosion and the loss of chemical elements necessary for crop growth is rapid once the land has been cut. Allow-

ing some natural vegetation to stay reduces erosion.

In this kind of agriculture, there is typically a mixture of crops, including root, stem, or fruit crops. For example, in western Africa, Fang agriculture includes yams (a root crop) plus maize; in Southeast Asia, there are root crops with rice and millet or rice and maize [13]. The mixture of crops allows different species to contribute soil fertility in different ways. Some perennial plants slow physical erosion; native legumes add nitrogen to the soil; and so forth.

MANAGING PESTS

All agriculture suffers from pests. Even today, with our modern technology, the total losses from all pests are estimated to be one-third of the potential harvest and another 10% after harvest. The preharvest losses include reduction in the growth of crops due to competition from weeds, as well as losses to disease and herbivores [14].

From an ecological point of view, pests are undesirable competitors, parasites, or predators. The major agricultural pests are insects (mainly feeding on the live parts of plants, especially leaves and stems); nematode worms (small worms that live mainly in the soil and feed on roots and other plant tissues); bacterial and virus diseases; weeds (flowering plants that compete with the crops); and vertebrates, mainly rodents and birds that feed on the grain or fruit. Although we tend to think that the major pests are insects, in fact, weeds are the major problem in terms of the loss in potential crop production.

Farming produces special environmental and ecological conditions that tend to promote pests. To understand these, we must remind ourselves that the process of farming is an attempt to (1) hold back the natural processes of ecological succession, (2) prevent the normal entrance of migrating organisms into an area, and (3) prevent natural interactions—including competition, predation, and parasitism—among populations of different species.

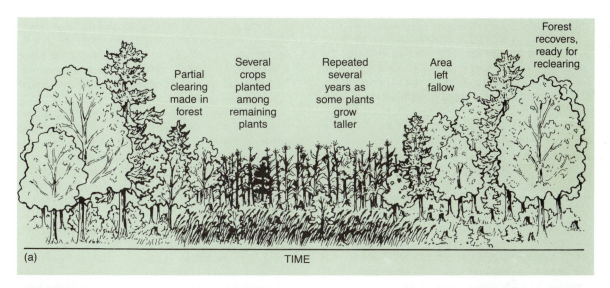

Partial clearing made in forest

Several crops planted among remaining plants

Repeated several years as some plants grow taller

Area left fallow

Forest recovers, ready for reclearing

(a)   TIME

(b)

FIGURE 10.10
Slash and burn agriculture. (a) Over time, secondary succession will take place on land partially cleared by slash and burn. (b) A Honduran farmer clears a hillside for planting crops.

A farm is in a very early stage in ecological succession and, with the addition of fertilizers and water, a very good place for early successional plants to grow. These early successional plants tend to be short-lived but very fast growing and have adaptations that make it possible for them to be transported widely and to enter a new area rapidly. Some of these plants have seeds that are very light and are blown readily by the wind. Others, just like many crops that we grow and eat, produce large, edible fruits, which are eaten by animals; the seeds are spread as the animals travel. Thus the very nature of cropland opens it to the introduction of weeds and provides a good habitat for them to grow.

There are about 30,000 species of weeds, and in any year a typical farm field is infested with between 10 and 50 weed species. Weeds compete with crops for all resources—light, water, and nutrients. The more weeds, the less crop. The agricultural losses in the United States due to weeds exceed $16 billion/yr, and about $3.6 billion is spent annually for chemical weed control; this amounts to 60% of all pesticide sales in the United States. As an example of the effect of weeds, the production of soybeans can be reduced 60% if there is just one individual of the weed called cocklebur per row [15].

Control Techniques

Before the industrial revolution there was little that farmers could do to prevent pests except to remove them when they appeared or to use farming methods that tended to decrease the density of pests, such as the slash and burn agriculture of the tropics, in which the presence of noncrops and a diversity of crops in a single field reduced the density of pests.

With the rise of modern agricultural sciences, chemical pesticides were developed. The use of these has grown greatly, reaching more than 300 million kg/yr in the United States alone. The ultimate, most desirable pesticide is a "magic bullet"—a chemical that is lethal to a single pest species and rapidly seeks out individuals of that species and kills them, with no effect on any other form of life. No pesticide has reached that perfection.

The earlier chemical pesticides were broad spectrum pesticides, meaning that they affected a wide range of organisms. One of the earliest pesticides used was arsenic, a chemical element toxic to all life, including people. It was certainly effective in killing pests, but it was also dangerous and killed beneficial organisms as well.

The second stage in the development of pesticides, which began in the 1930s, was the development of oil sprays and the use of natural plant chemicals. Many plants produce natural chemicals as a defense against disease and herbivores; many of these natural chemicals are effective pesticides. Some of these insecticides (including some still in wide use today) use nicotine as the primary active agent. While natural plant pesticides are comparatively safe, they are also relatively broad spectrum and are not as effective as desired.

The real revolution in chemical pesticides—the development of more sophisticated pesticides—began with the end of World War II and the discovery of DDT and other chlorinated hydrocarbons, including aldrin and dieldrin. At first, DDT was thought to be the long sought "magic bullet"—it appeared to have no short-term effect on people and seemed to kill only insects. DDT was not very soluble in water and therefore DDT did not appear to pose an environmental hazard—at that time scientists believed that a chemical could not be readily transported from its original site of application unless it was water soluble.

DDT was used very widely until three things were discovered: (1) it has longer term effects on other, desirable organisms, especially affecting the ability of birds to produce eggs and possibly increasing the chance of cancer in other organisms; (2) it is stored in oils and fats and is concentrated as it is passed up food chains, so that the higher an organism is on a food chain the higher the concentration of DDT it contains; and (3) the storage of DDT in fats and oils allows the chemical to be transferred biologically even though it is not very soluble in water.

In birds, intake of DDT and the products of its natural breakdown (known as DDD and DDE) resulted in thin shells that broke easily, so that the birds could not reproduce successfully. This problem was especially severe in birds that were high on the food chain—predators that feed on other predators, such as the bald eagle, osprey, and pelicans that feed on fish, many of which are also predators.

As a result of these problems, DDT was banned in most developed nations. Since its banning in the United States in 1971, there has been a dramatic recovery in the population of affected birds. For example, the brown pelican of the California coast, which had become rare and endangered and whose reproduction had been restricted to offshore islands where DDT had not been used, is now common again.

Although DDT was banned in most developed nations, it has continued to be used in developing and less developed nations, especially as a control for mosquitoes, because it is cheap, because it has been effective, and because people have become accustomed to using it. According to the United Nations World Health Organization, more than 30 thousand metric tons are used a year.

Although people in developed nations believe they are free from the effects of DDT, in fact the chemical is transported to industrial nations in agricultural products from nations using the chemical. Also, migrating birds that spend part of the year in malaria regions are still subject to the effects of DDT on egg shells. DDT remains an important world issue in pest control, in spite of its banning from the developed nations. The use in developing nations of pesticides banned in other nations extends to other chemicals.

With the banning of DDT in many nations, other chemicals became more prominent. Newer chemicals were sought that were less persistent. Among the next generation of insecticides were organophosphates—nerve chemicals involving phosphorus. These are toxic to people and must be handled extremely carefully by those who apply them. However, these chemicals are more specific and decay rapidly in the soil; they therefore do not have the same persistence as DDT.

While chemical pesticides have created a revolution in agriculture, there are major drawbacks to their use in addition to the negative environmental effects of individual chemicals, such as those we have discussed for DDT. One of these drawbacks is secondary pest outbreaks, which can occur in several ways: (1) reduction in one target species reduces competition with a second, which then increases and becomes a pest; (2) the pest develops resistance to the pesticides through evolution and natural selection, which favor those in the population with a greater immunity to the chemical [16].

Developed resistance has occurred with many pesticides. For example, Dasanit, an organophosphate, was first introduced in 1970 to control maggots that attack onions in Michigan; while it originally gave high control, it is now so ineffective that it can no longer be used for that crop.

Integrated Pest Management

Modern approaches to pest control involve integrated pest management (IPM), which is an ecosystem approach to pest management and integrates a variety of techniques: the use of natural enemies of pests, including parasites, diseases, and predators; the use of a greater diversity of crops to reduce the chance that pests will find a host plant; the use of no-till or low-till agriculture, which helps natural enemies of some pests to build up in the soil; and the application of a set of highly specific chemicals, which are used much more sparingly than in earlier approaches. IPM is an approach that recognizes ecological communities and ecosystems; IPM takes into account the effect of one species on others—a decrease in one species may lead to an increase in another, and decreases in still others.

There are four principles of IPM: (1) the goal is control, not extinction; pests will continue to exist at a low, tolerable level; (2) the use of natural control agents is maximized; (3) the ecosystem is the management unit; and (4) any control action can have unexpected and unwanted effects [17].

The components of integrated pest management include chemicals; culture (meaning how the land is physically managed, including whether and how it is plowed, what kind of crop rotation is used, the dates of planting, and basic means of handling crop harvests to reduce the presence of pests in residues and products sold); the development of genetically resistant stock; and biological control.

Biological control includes the intentional introduction of predators, diseases, or other parasites of a pest. For example, ladybugs are common predators of many plant-eating pests; it is possible to buy quantities of ladybugs for release in home gardens or farms, with the hope that these will feed on the pests and reduce their abundance.

There are more specialized and more effective biological controls. One of the most effective is a bacterial disease, *Bacillus thuringiensis,* which kills larval forms of many insect pests, including many caterpillars.

The control of the oriental fruit moth that attacks a number of fruit crops is an example of IPM. The moth was found to be a prey of a wasp, whose introduction into fields helped control the moth. The effectiveness of the wasp in peach groves was increased when there were nearby strawberry fields. These strawberry fields provided an alternative habitat for the wasp, especially important for overwintering [17].

Other effective biological control agents are small wasps that are parasites of caterpillars. The wasps lay their eggs in the caterpillars, and the larval wasps feed on the caterpillar and kill it. These wasps tend to have very specific relationships—one species of wasps will be a parasite of one species of pest—and so are both effective and narrow spectrum (Fig. 10.11).

A study of integrated pest management by the U.S. Office of Technology Assessment concluded that integrated pest management could reduce the use of pesticides by as much as 75 %, while at the same time reducing the large preharvest pest-caused losses by 50%. This would also reduce the costs to the farmers for pest control by a great amount [14].

Current agricultural practices in the United States involve a combination of approaches, but in most cases, these are more restricted than an IPM strategy. Biological control methods are used to a comparatively small extent; they are the primary tactic for the control of vertebrate pests (mice, voles, and birds) of lettuce, tomatoes, and strawberries in California, but not a major technique for grains, cotton, potatoes, apples, or melons. For insect pests the principal control methods are chem-

FIGURE 10.11
Integrated pest management, the biological control of insect pests.

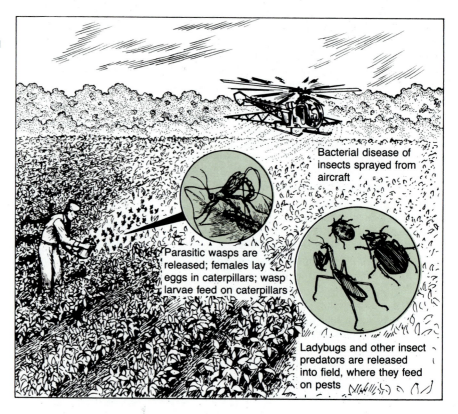

Bacterial disease of insects sprayed from aircraft

Parasitic wasps are released; females lay eggs in caterpillars; wasp larvae feed on caterpillars

Ladybugs and other insect predators are released into field, where they feed on pests

icals, but cultural methods are important in weed control, and the use of genetically resistant stock is important for disease control for wheat, corn, cotton, and some vegetable crops such as lettuce and tomatoes.

ENVIRONMENTAL EFFECTS OF AGRICULTURAL PRODUCTION

The production, processing, and distribution of food alter the environment. Agriculture is the world's oldest and largest industry; more than one-half of all the people of the world still live on farms, and thus large effects on the environment are unavoidable. These effects can be seen as both positive and negative. For example, pesticides created a revolution in agriculture in the short term, but their long-term effects could prove extremely undesirable.

Agriculture has both primary and secondary environmental effects, also known as on-site and off-site effects. A primary effect is an effect on the area where the agriculture takes place (an on-site effect). A secondary effect is an effect on an environment not used in agriculture (an off-site effect).

Major environmental problems that result from agriculture include deforestation, desertification, soil erosion, overgrazing, degradation of water resources, salinization, toxic metal accumulation, local overcapacity and overproduction, and water pollution, including eutrophication.

The effects of agriculture on the environment can be divided into three groups: local, regional, and global. Local effects include erosion and the loss of soils and increases in sedimentation downstream. Regional effects include the creation of deserts. The global effects include climatic and other far-reaching changes.

Soil Erosion and Other Local Effects

The type of local environmental effect depends upon the type of agriculture practiced in the area. The effects are clearly different for crop production and livestock production.

Crops and Soil Erosion   When land is cleared of its natural vegetation, such as forest or grassland, the soil begins to lose its fertility. Some of this occurs by physical erosion—water and wind remove the loosened soil, which is more vulnerable because it lacks the protective vegetation cover. Chemical elements required for life are lost to this physical erosion and are dissolved in water and transported away. About one-half of the amount of an element such as nitrogen can be lost. The time over which a soil loses one-half of a chemical element varies; it is much faster in warmer and wetter climates, like those where the natural vegetation is a tropical rain forest, than it is in colder or dryer climates, such as those where the natural vegetation is a temperate-zone grassland or forest [18].

In temperate climatic zones, there is a strong change in seasons and a long history of use of the plow. The land is plowed in the spring, turning over the soil completely. The same land is planted year after year, with some years allowed for fields to lie fallow without plowing or harvesting. The practice of annual plowing and planting makes possible intense use of the land and high production of crops. On the negative side, these practices open the land to erosion in two ways: soil loosened by plowing can (1) blow away when it is dry and (2) wash away with rain water. Plowed lands lose their most fertile upper soils where the organic matter is found, making the addition of fertilizers necessary. The less organic matter in the soil, the more vulnerable the soil is to further erosion (Fig. 10.12).

Since the founding of the United States, about one-third of the country's topsoil has been lost [5]. In the United States, even today, 90% of the land used for row crops and small grains is used without soil conservation practices. Erosion is estimated to be worse now than during the great dust bowl of the 1930s, when an estimated 100 million acres were ruined for agriculture because of soil erosion.

Rivers carry about 4 billion tons/yr of sediment in the United States, 75% of which is from agricultural lands. Of this total, 3 billion tons/yr is deposited in reservoirs, rivers, and lakes. The sediments affect ecosystems downstream. They can cause eutrophication, reduce fish production,

FIGURE 10.12
Erosion of a cultivated bean field resulting from runoff of rainwater.

transport toxins, and, where the sediment load enters the ocean in the tropics, destroy coral reefs that are near shore. Sediment damage costs the United States about $500 million/yr, including reduction in the useful life of reservoirs, and costs of dredging.

Soil is lost from all forms of agriculture, but the rate of loss varies with the crop and methods of agriculture. In the United States, about 80 million ha have been either totally ruined by soil erosion or made only marginally productive. Yet, soil is continuously formed, typically on good lands at a rate of about 1 mm/decade to 1 mm/40 yr; with good management, however, the rate can be improved to 1 mm/yr. Ideal farming would result in soil loss no greater than the production of new soil.

To counter erosion from plowing, there has been an emphasis in the twentieth century on contour plowing and more recently a new emphasis on no-till agriculture (Fig. 10.13). In contour plowing, the land is plowed along the contours (perpendicular to the slope, therefore as much in the horizontal plane as possible). In traditional plowing, the plowed furrows make a path for water to flow, and if the furrows go downhill, then the water moves rapidly along them, increasing the erosion rate. Plowing along the contours can greatly reduce erosion loss due to water runoff.

In the recent past, contour plowing has been the most effective single method to reduce soil erosion. In an experiment, land planted in potatoes in rows that were plowed up and down hill lost 14.4 tons/acre while contour-plowed rows lost only 0.1 ton/acre. In addition, contour plowing used less fuel and time. But only a small fraction of the land receives this treatment. For example, of Minnesota's 10.3 million acres of cropland, only 1.3 million are contour plowed.

Other solutions to soil erosion include reduced-tillage and no-tillage agriculture. The tendency to use these techniques is driven not merely by good will or the desire to prevent further soil loss, but by the increasing high costs of energy to run tractors (Fig. 10.14).

In no-till agriculture the land is not plowed

FIGURE 10.13
Alternate agricultural methods. (a) Contour strip crops in Wisconsin; (b) no-till soybean crop planted in wheat stubble on a Kansas farm.

(a)

(b)

every year and the stems and roots that are not harvested are allowed to decay in place; weeds are controlled by other means, including the use of herbicides. This practice can greatly reduce soil loss, although it may result in much greater use of chemical pesticides. The use of such techniques, known generally as conservation tillage, increased from 4 million acres in 1962 to 100 million acres in 1982 in the United States.

Overgrazing and Other Livestock-related Effects Much of the grazing of domestic animals results in a nonsustainable agriculture. Traditional herding practices and industrialized agriculture have different effects on the environment. In modern industrialized agriculture, cattle are initially raised on open range, and then transported to feedlots. Overgrazing on the open range reduces the diversity of plant species, leads to reduction in

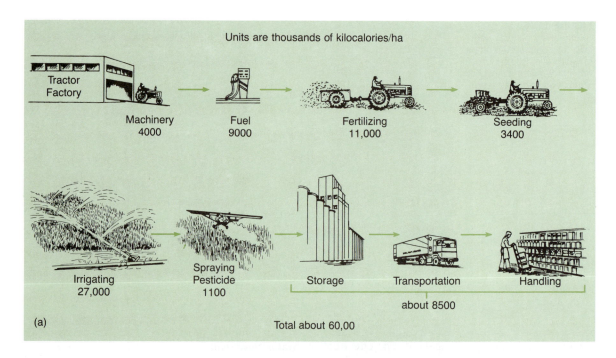

Units are thousands of kilocalories/ha

Tractor Factory

Machinery
4000

Fuel
9000

Fertilizing
11,000

Seeding
3400

Irrigating
27,000

Spraying Pesticide
1100

Storage

Transportation

Handling

about 8500

(a)   Total about 60,00

FIGURE 10.14
Energy-intensive agriculture. (a) Energy required by demand-based agriculture. (b) U.S. wheat harvest with nineteen combines in one field.

(b)

vegetation growth and dominance of plant species that are relatively undesirable to the cattle, increases the loss of soil by erosion as the plant cover is reduced, and causes damage through the mechanical action of the cattle on the land. For example, in rugged countryside, paths made as the cattle travel to the same water hole or streamside develop into gullies, which erode rapidly in the rain.

The carrying capacity of land for cattle varies with the rainfall and the fertility of the soil. In areas with moderate to high rainfall evenly distributed throughout the year, cattle can be maintained at high densities, but in arid and semiarid regions the density drops greatly. For example, in Arizona cattle are ranched at a density of one head of cattle for 7–10 ha. Near Paso Robles, California, in an area where the rainfall is about 25 cm/yr, a ranch where cattle are grazed without artificial irrigation or fertilization supports about 1 head for 6 ha (Fig. 10.15).

Feedlots are used to fatten cattle for market. These have become widely known in recent years as sources of local pollution. The cattle are kept at extremely high densities and fed grain; the grain is transported to the feedlot, and manure builds up in large mounds. When there is rain, the manure pollutes local streams. Feedlots are popular with producers of meat because they are, under current conditions, economic for the rapid production of good-quality meat; however, the feedlots require intense use of energy and other resources and have negative environmental effects.

Traditional herding practices affect the environment especially through overgrazing. Goats are especially damaging to vegetation, but all domestic herbivores can destroy a rangeland. The effect of domestic herbivores on the land varies greatly with the density. At low to moderate densities, the animals may actually stimulate the growth of above-ground vegetation, while at high densities the vegetation is eaten faster than it can grow, some spe-

TABLE 10.1
Condition of rangeland

Condition	Soils and Vegetation (percent of potential[a])
Good	61–100
Fair	41–60
Poor	21–41
Very poor	0–20

[a]Estimated percentage quality of the soils and vegetation compared to the best conditions.
Source: U.S. Forest Service.

cies are lost, and the growth of others is greatly reduced.

People have distributed cattle, sheep, goats, and horses, as well as other domestic animals, around the world and then promoted the growth of these animals to densities high enough to change the landscape; this is one of the most important ways that agriculture has affected the environment. Domestic animals have been introduced into Australia, New Zealand, and North and South America. The horse, cow, sheep, and goat were brought to North America after the sixteenth century. The spread of cattle brought new animal diseases and new weeds, which arrived on the hooves and in the manure of the cattle.

Much of the rangeland in the world is in poor condition from overgrazing. The condition of rangeland is measured in terms of the vegetation cover and the soil and is a comparison between the believed potential condition and the actual condition (Table 10.1) [19]. For example, in the United States, there are 370 million ha of rangeland, out of 910 million ha of total land, or 40% of the land. Of this rangeland, less than one-half is rated in good to fair condition.

A recent important issue in cattle production is the opening up of tropical forest areas and their conversion to rangeland. This has occurred in South America, where the land is economically productive for cattle production generally for only a few years. In such areas, the land's capabilities for many uses, including forest growth, are greatly reduced by the grazing [20].

The spread of domestic herbivores around the world is one of the major ways that human beings

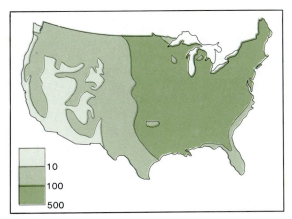

FIGURE 10.15
Carrying capacity of pasture and rangeland in the United States, in average number of cows per square mile. (U.S. Department of Agriculture statistics.)

10
100
500

have changed the environment through agriculture. As human population increases, and when income and expectation rise, the demand for meat will increase and there will be an increased demand for rangeland and pasture land in the next decades. A major challenge in agriculture is to develop ways to make the production of domestic animals a sustainable agriculture.

Desertification: A Regional Effect

Deserts occur where there is too little water for substantial plant growth; the plants that do grow are too sparse and unproductive to create a soil rich in organic matter. Desert soils are mainly inorganic, and the soils are coarse and typically sandy. When rain does come, it often is heavy, and erosion is rapid and severe. The climatic conditions that lead to a desert are a combination of low rainfall and high temperatures. The warmer the climate, the greater the rainfall required to convert an area from desert to a more productive area, such as a grassland. The crucial factor in all of this is the amount of water in the soil available for plants to take up and use and then to evaporate through their leaves. Thus factors that destroy the ability of a soil to store water can create a new desert.

Earth has five main natural, warm desert regions, all of which lie between latitudes 15° and 30° north and south of the equator. These are the deserts of the southwestern United States and Mexico; the Pacific coast deserts of Chile and southern Ecuador; the Kalahari desert of southern Africa and its extensions into South Africa; the Australian deserts (most of that continent); and the greatest desert region of them all—the desert that extends from the Atlantic coast of north Africa (the Sahara) eastward to the Arabian deserts, the deserts of Iran and Russia, Pakistan, India, and then into China [2]. Only Europe lacks a major warm desert—since it lies north of the desert latitudinal band.

On the basis of climate, about one-third of Earth's land area should be desert, but estimates from the condition of soils and vegetation suggest that much more of the land is actually desert—about 43% of the total land area. This additional desert area is believed to be manmade; such deserts occupy about 9 million km^2, an area greater than the size of Brazil [21].

The spread of deserts is called **desertification.** This is a serious modern problem [22]. About 20% of Earth, involving 100 nations and 80 million people, is threatened with desertification. Every year, an area equal to the size of Senegal (200,000 km^2) is lost to economically productive agriculture, and the losses in agricultural production are about $26 billion/yr, more than the entire value of California's crops or of Thailand's Gross Domestic Product [2].

Some areas of Earth are marginal lands, which might become deserts or might not. In these areas, the rainfall is enough, but just barely enough, to make the area more productive of vegetation than a desert, but only if the soils are maintained within a certain range of conditions.

Causes of Desertification Deserts are created in marginal areas (also known as arid lands) when the vegetation and soil are destroyed in ways so that neither recovers. The leading causes are bad farming or just plain too much farming; overgrazing; the conversion of rangelands in marginal areas to croplands, where rainfall is not sufficient to support crops for a long time; and bad forestry practices, including cutting all of the trees in an area marginal for tree growth.

For example, in northern China, areas that were grasslands have been overgrazed, and some of these rangelands were converted to croplands. Between 1949 and 1980 an area of 65,000 km^2 (an area larger than Denmark) became deserts. Then sandstorm occurrence increased from about 3 days/yr in the early 1950s to an average of 17 in the next decade and more than 25/yr at present. An additional 160,000 km^2 is in danger of becoming deserts [12].

Deserts can be created anywhere by poisoning of soils, which can occur from the application of persistent pesticides or other toxic organic chemicals. Industrial processes that lead to improper disposal of toxic chemicals can also create deserts.

Irrigation of soils in arid areas can lead to a desert. When irrigation water evaporates, a residue of salts is left behind. Although these may have been

FIGURE 10.16
Salinization resulting from repeated irrigation has severely reduced this alfalfa crop in California.

in very low concentrations in the irrigation water, over time the salts build up in the soil to the point that they can become toxic (Fig. 10.16). This effect can be reversed in some cases if irrigation is increased greatly so that the water redissolves the salts, percolates down into the water table in large amounts, and carries the salts down with it.

Kesterson Refuge   An important example is the area near the Kesterson National Wildlife Refuge in California. In spring of 1985, the U. S. Bureau of Reclamation announced that it was closing the Kesterson National Wildlife Refuge, a 42,000–acre preserve in the San Joaquin Valley of California and, at the same time, that it was closing an 82–mile long irrigation drainage canal. The closing of the canal would take about 50,000 acres of farm-

land out of production, with the loss of $45 million annually and 1200 jobs. The canal drained water that had been used in farm irrigation into the refuge, where it provided water for a wetland habitat for birds.

Why were the wildlife refuge and the canal closed? In 1983, biologists began to discover birth defects in water birds born in the refuge. These defects were due to a high concentration of the chemical element selenium, an element harmless in the natural, small concentrations normally found in soils and waters, but which causes gene changes when it is present in high concentrations. The selenium was carried into the refuge in the irrigation water. Selenium was not high in the original irrigation water, but in the dry California valley, water used in irrigation evaporated quickly from the soil, concentrating the selenium. In order to prevent severe buildup of salts within the soils, the farmers periodically had to use enough water to leach the soil of the salts. The water dissolved the salts, carried them down into the soil below the reach of the roots, and then drained from the farmland with subsurface water flow. This drainage water was high in many chemical elements, of which selenium is one. The heavily saline water was carried by the canal into the wildlife refuge, with the intention of serving two purposes: providing wetland habitat for waterfowl and disposing of the water. Unfortunately this led to the buildup in selenium.

The toxic levels of selenium in the refuge threaten life beyond the wildlife refuge. There is concern that selenium pollution might spread to thousands of acres in nearby marsh and farmlands, where it could poison livestock and enter the water used for home water supply.

Preventing Desertification   The major symptoms of desertification are lowering of the water table (wells have to be dug deeper and deeper); increase in salt content of the soil; reduced surface water (streams and ponds dry up); increased soil erosion (the dry soil, losing its organic matter too, begins simply to blow away and to be washed away in heavy rains); and loss of natural native vegetation (the native vegetation, not adapted to desert conditions, can no longer survive) [23].

The most important local factors in preventing the spread of deserts are (1) good soil conservation, (2) good management of forests and grasslands, and (3) proper irrigation. Good soil conservation includes contour plowing; reducing plowing where possible and using no-till agriculture; rotating crops; and using windbreaks, terracing, and other structures to hold the soil. A landscape with trees is a landscape with a good chance to prevent the creation of deserts. Therefore practices that lead to deforestation in marginal areas should be avoided, including cutting timber for firewood and for lumber. Reforestation must be encouraged, including the planting of windbreaks—narrow lines of trees that help slow down the wind and prevent wind erosion of the soil and sandstorms.

Global Effects

Local and regional effects of agriculture on the environment are easily identified. Global effects are not as obvious, though they are potentially as serious. First, agriculture induces changes in land cover and therefore changes in reflection of light by the land surface and in evaporation of water. These changes can have regional and global climatic effects. Since the beginning of agriculture, the changes in the reflection of light by Earth's surface solely due to land clearing by people could have had a significant effect on climate. Second, as a major user of fossil fuels, agriculture contributes to the increase in carbon dioxide concentration in the atmosphere. Land clearing for agriculture, which converts carbon in live organic matter and in dead organic matter in soils, also increases the CO_2 concentration in the atmosphere, contributing to global changes. Third, fires associated with land clearing for agriculture, especially in tropical countries, may have significant effects on the climate by adding small particulates to the atmosphere. Fourth, artificial production of nitrogen compounds for use in agriculture may be leading to significant changes in global biogeochemical cycles. And fifth, the loss of natural ecosystems (because of agricultural land use) increases the number of endangered species.

FOOD NEEDS AND EXPECTATIONS

There are two kinds of starvation: undernourishment (including lack of enough energy in food to keep one's body running, so that one has little or no ability to move or work), and malnourishment, the lack of specific aspects of food, such as lack of protein or of a vitamin or an essential chemical element. Both are global problems; the first is obvious and dramatic and fast acting when it happens. The second is long-term and insidious; people may not die outright, but they are less productive than normal and can suffer brain damage so that they have a permanent loss in capabilities.

To determine our food security and the chances of famine in the future, we need a measure of the world's food status. How do we measure the world's food situation? A measure of the world's ability to deal with famine is the days supply of grain on hand. This has decreased during the last decades, dropping from a 100 day supply in 1960 to 40 days in 1980, and the famines since then have decreased the supply even more. This can be taken as a measure of the food reserves available to prevent undernourishment.

The United States stores more than one-half of the world's surplus grains and has four million tons of grain for emergency relief. Since World War II, the United States has been the leading food donor in the world.

Because weather uncertainties cause strong fluctuations in food production, a system of stocks (preserves of food) and transportation to guard against these fluctuations is important. For the entire world, such a system would require a standing stock of 10 to 20 million tons; at a price of $137/ton, this would be about $2 billion worth of crops; maintenance of this stock would require only $200 million per year [24].

In considering the availability of food, we need to focus on per capita food production as well as total production. The per capita food production is the amount of food produced per person. Between 1960 and 1980, world food production grew faster than world population; by the end of the 1970s total production was more than 40% greater than in 1960 and per capita production was about 25% greater.

There were important geographic variations in total and per capita production [22]. Per capita production decreased in many developing nations in the 1960s and 1970s. Today, population growth and food production are in a "tug of war," and it is unclear in the short run which will increase faster, although we know in the long run there are limits to both. For example, the relation between population growth and food production is shown in Figure 10.17. Both population and food supply have increased, but food production has varied more; on the average there is no gain in the food available per person.

The demand for food is the amount of food that would be bought at a given price if it were available. The demand increases with population and with per capita income. Growth in per capita demand is the increase in economic demand per person. The per capita demand increases as the standard of living and average income increase. The per capita demand also increases with rising expectations—when people become aware of the possibilities that they could have more to eat and could have a greater variety of food. Modern communication has led to rising expectations.

A number of ways have been put forward to meet the increase in food needs caused by a growing world population and by some people's growing expectations. Three ways that have gained some prominence in the discussion are (1) an increase in food production, especially in local production in areas of great need, (2) a change in consumption to a lower level on the food chain, and (3) a modification of the distribution of food. For reasons to be explained, the first and last are most likely to make a major difference.

Limits to Food Production

Even given great strides that can take place in food production from the use of new crops, genetic engineering, more fertilizer and more water, there is eventually a limit to the production of food on

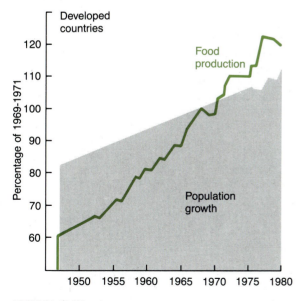
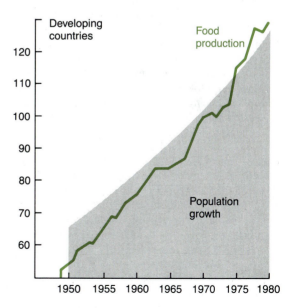

FIGURE 10.17
Relationship between population growth and food production in (a) developed and (b) developing countries. (Modified from Barr.)

Earth. There have been great increases in world food production. The production of wheat doubled between 1935 and 1975, keeping pace with world population during that period [25]. It is estimated that, for all people to be adequately fed, the production of food must double or triple by the first decade of the next century. There are obstacles to this increase. First of all, we appear to have reached the limit with many crops when it comes to increasing fertilizer application as a way of increasing the yield per unit area. In the future, increases in yield per unit area must come from the development of new, higher-producing crops or new superstrains of existing ones (as in the superstrains of rice). Another possible means to increase yield is with better irrigation techniques, which can improve yield and reduce overall water use. Drip irrigation—the application of water to the soil from tubes that drip water slowly—greatly reduces the loss of water from direct evaporation and increases yield. However, this is an expensive approach, most likely to be applied in developed nations or those nations with a large surplus of hard currency—in other words, in few of the countries where hunger is most severe.

Climatic change is more likely to decrease yield than increase it because at the present time areas with the best soils in the world also happen to have climates well suited to agriculture. Thus most climatic changes are likely to make things worse, although a general warming accompanied by consistent rains could increase yields.

Widespread erosion and poor agricultural practices are leading to a general loss of soil fertility and will decrease yield. Only a widespread application of strict soil conservation measures will counter this. Overgrazing of lands that could be used for crops or that would otherwise provide good rangeland and grazing of marginal areas are also decreasing the area in agricultural production.

Finally, the use of groundwater from deep aquifers to irrigate land is only a short-term solution to agricultural production. When the groundwater is exhausted, the area is lost to agriculture. This has already occurred in parts of the western United States. In addition, the use of groundwater and transported irrigated water leads to the buildup of salts in the soils, poisoning the soil and ending its

use for agriculture. The Central Valley of California, one of the world's major agricultural areas, may suffer this fate. Thus there are many reasons that the production of agriculture may decrease in many areas in the future; this makes the task of increasing production even more difficult.

Increasing the Area in Agriculture What are the opportunities to add new lands to agriculture? Most of the best land for agriculture is already so used; this means that more and more marginal lands will be farmed. These lands are considered marginal because of lack of water (only desalination is a long term solution, but mining groundwater is the common approach) or poor soil quality or because of too steep slopes or too heavy rainfall (these lands will fail in a short time).

Some suggest that in the future we will rely more and more on artificial agriculture, such as hydroponics, the growing of plants in a water solution on a completely artificial substrate in an artificial environment, such as a greenhouse. This approach is capital intensive and unlikely to be effective in the developing nations, where hunger is the greatest.

Eating Lower on the Food Chain

Some people believe that it is ecologically unsound to use domestic animals as food, on the grounds that each step farther up a food chain leaves much less food to eat per acre. This argument is as follows. No organism is 100% efficient. Of the energy in food taken in, only a fraction is converted to new organic matter. Crop plants may convert 1–10% of sunlight to edible food while cows may convert only 1–10% of hay and grain to meat. Thus, other things being equal, the same area could produce 10 to 100 times as much vegetation per year as meat.

There are three reasons why this argument is not sound. First, other things are not equal. The argument can be applied only to land that can sustain vegetable crop production, but only a small fraction of the land can support vegetable crop production on a sustainable basis. Poorer land— land on steeper slopes, or with thinner soils, or

FIGURE 10.18
Land unsuitable for crop production on a sustainable basis can be used for other purposes.

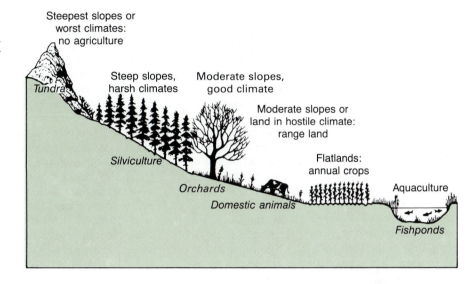

Steepest slopes or worst climates: no agriculture

Tundra

Steep slopes, harsh climates

Moderate slopes, good climate

Moderate slopes or land in hostile climate: range land

Silviculture

Flatlands: annual crops

Orchards

Aquaculture

Domestic animals

Fishponds

with lower rainfall—can be used as range or pasture. Land too poor for crops can be excellent rangeland (Fig. 10.18). If we could eat grass and hay, then the comparison would be valid. Many lands have been ruined when they have been converted unwisely from range to croplands. Similarly, many marginal rangelands have been ruined by overgrazing.

Second, food is more than calories, and animals are important sources of proteins and minerals. Animals provide the major source of protein in human diets—56 million tons of edible protein per year. In the United States, 75% of the protein, 33% of the energy, and most of the calcium and phosphorus in human nutrition comes from animal products.

Third, domestic animals are often used for other purposes—as beasts of burden; for plowing, carrying loads, and transportation; or as sources of clothing material (wool and leather). The use of such animals for food represents an increase in efficiency.

Eating lower on the food chain makes sense from an ecological perspective only for prime agricultural land. Of course, some people maintain vegetarian diets for religious or moral reasons or because of specific dietary problems, but these are independent of ecological arguments.

Modification of Food Distribution

If present trends continue, eventually human population growth will outstrip growth in world food production, and there will not be enough food to feed all the people of the world. But the primary world food problem today is poor distribution, not production. Today there is enough food produced in the world to feed all of the people. Starvation and malnutrition occur because this food is not distributed as needed to all people. The distribution problem is clearly illustrated by the recent famines. Food distribution fails because poor people cannot buy the food and pay for its delivery or because of the lack of proper means of transportation or the expense of the transportation. Although there is considerable international trade in food, most of the trade is among the rich nations.

As long as food distribution is the primary problem, the best solution is to increase local production; truly useful aid efforts will focus on the longer term and try to help people develop their own means of food production, improve the environment for agriculture, and make sure that agriculture is not destructive to the landscape in a way that will decrease or end future production.

But another solution, one that is commonly used, is food aid among nations—where one nation gives food and ships it to another or gives or loans money that is then used to purchase food and pay for its transportation. This has become highly publicized in recent years, especially with the interest of pop music stars in the African famine. A peak in international food aid occurred in the 1960s when 12 million tons/yr (about 3% of the world's total consumption) were given by one nation to another. Except for episodes of famine, the amount of food distributed in aid programs has been decreasing. In 1975 food aid had decreased to between 8 to 9 million tons, or 2% of consumption. The United States is and has been the main supplier of food aid.

When a group of people starve, the world sorrows for them, and there has been much recent activity to provide them with food. These humanitarian gestures are important and well meaning, but in themselves cannot provide a solution to the world food problem. Food aid is only a short-term answer. In the longer run, where there is starvation there must be an increase in local food production. In fact, in the longer run, food aid can work against an increase in the availability of food in a location. Free food undercuts the local farmers; they cannot compete with free food, and local production of food decreases.

SUMMARY

There are three major aspects to an environmental perspective on agriculture: (1) agriculture depends on the environment, and good agricultural practices require an understanding of the relationships between crop growth and the environment; (2) agriculture changes the environment, and the more agriculture the greater the changes; and (3) as human population increases, there is a need to conserve our agricultural resources and to increase production while decreasing the negative effects of agriculture on the environment.

The industrial revolution and the rise of agricultural sciences have led to a revolution in agriculture, with many great benefits and with some serious drawbacks. Modern fertilizers have greatly increased the yield per unit area. Plant breeding has led to the green revolution, with more productive strains, more disease-resistant strains, and strains that can be grown under less optimal conditions. Modern chemistry has led to the development of a wide variety of pesticides that have reduced, but not eliminated, the loss of production to weeds, diseases, and herbivores.

Most twentieth-century agriculture has relied on machinery and the use of abundant energy, with relatively little attention paid to the loss of soils, the limit to groundwater, and the negative effects of chemical pesticides. The next revolution in agriculture will be an ecological one; this revolution has begun. In the next phase, pest control will be dominated by integrated pest management, combining a knowledge of agricultural lands as ecosystems with a careful use of artificial chemicals. This phase will emphasize soil conservation through no-till agriculture and contour plowing; it will emphasize water conservation through drip irrigation and the development of drought resistant plant strains.

Only by farming with an appreciation of the environment and of the long-term requirements of croplands can we hope to sustain the production of food required by the world's growing population. While the human population is in a sense *the* environmental problem, in the same sense an appropriate agriculture is one of the necessary solutions. Whether all of the world's nations can move toward a sustainable agriculture is an open question.

Today the major cause of hunger and starvation is the failure of distribution of food; the total current food production in the world is adequate for the world's current human population. This will change in the future, however, unless there is a doubling or tripling of food production.

**STUDY
QUESTIONS**

1. Explain the difference between demand-based and resource-based agriculture. Which of these characterizes traditional slash and burn agriculture?

2. A city garbage dump is filled; it is suggested that the area be turned into a farm. What factors in the dump might make it a good area to farm, and what might make it a poor area to farm?

3. Explain how an insect pest species can become resistant to a pesticide.

4. Most crops are characteristic of what stages in ecological succession? How might we use our knowledge of succession to make agriculture sustainable?

5. What is meant by a pesticide "magic bullet"? What would be its characteristics?

6. Ranching of wild animals—animals that are fenced but never tamed—has been suggested as a way to increase food production in Africa, where there is a great abundance of wildlife. On the basis of your reading in this chapter, discuss the environmental advantages and disadvantages of such game ranching.

7. What is meant by the statement, "The world food problem is one of distribution, not of production"? What are the major solutions to this world food problem?

8. You are sent into the Amazon rain forest to look for new crop species. In what kinds of habitats would you look? What kinds of plants would you look for?

9. How might farming lead to the spread of deserts? What might be done to stop this desertification?

10. It has been said that farming can never be sustainable. What is meant by this statement? Do you agree or disagree? List your reasons.

**FURTHER
READING**

CURRY, B., and HUGO, G. 1984. *Famine as a geographical phenomenon*. Boston: D. Reidel.

GRAINGER, A. 1982. *Desertification: How people make deserts, how people can stop and why they don't*. Earthscan Books, 2nd ed. London: Russell Press Ltd., Nottingham.

LASHOF, J. C., ed. 1979. *Pest management strategies in crop protection*. Vol I. Washington, D.C.: Office of Technology Assessment. U.S. Congress.

MURDOCK, W. E. 1980. *The poverty of nations: The political economy of hunger and population*. Baltimore, Md.: Johns Hopkins University Press.

SHERIDAN, D. 1981. *Desertification of the United States*. Washington, D. C.: Council on Environmental Quality.

WITTWER, S. (in press). *Feeding a billion: Agriculture in China*.

IV
Physical Resources

11
Pollutants

- Categories of environmental pollutants include toxic chemical elements, radioisotopes, organic compounds, heat, particulates, and noise.
- Pollutants may be eliminated or reduced by stopping their production, transforming or degrading them to harmless substances, or placing them in safe depositories.
- The effect of any toxic factor depends on its dose, or concentration. The extent to which thresholds can be found for environmental toxins is currently being debated.
- Tolerance to pollutants may result from behavioral, physiological, or genetic adaptation.
- Acute effects of pollutants often lead to death, while chronic effects may cause mutations, lead to cancer, or affect offspring.
- Thermonuclear war is our potential ultimate global pollutant. Environmental effects of nuclear war could include extinction of the human species!
- Prevention of a nuclear war must be considered top priority over all other potential environmental problems.

MINAMATA, JAPAN

In the Japanese coastal town called Minamata, on the island of Kyushu, a strange illness began to occur in the 1950s. It was first recognized in birds that lost their coordination and fell to the ground or flew into buildings and in cats that went mad, running in circles and foaming at the mouth [1]. The affliction, known by local fishermen as the "disease of the dancing cats," spread to the people, particularly families of fishermen. The first symptoms were subtle and included fatigue, irritability, headaches, numbness in arms and legs, and difficulty in swallowing. More severe symptoms involved the sensory organs; vision was blurred and the visual field was restricted. Afflicted people became hard of hearing and lost muscular coordination. Some complained of a metallic taste in their mouths; their gums became inflamed and they suffered from diarrhea. Eventually, 43 people died and 111 were severely disabled; in addition, 19 babies were born with congenital defects. Those affected lived in a small area, and much of their protein came from fish from the Minamata Bay.

A plastics factory on the bay used mercury in an inorganic form in its production processes. The mercury was released in water effluent that flowed into the bay. What was not realized was that the industrial processes converted inorganic mercury into a much more toxic organic form. Inorganic mercury does not pass through cell membranes readily; it damages the intestines, liver, and kidneys. Organic methyl mercury, however, readily passes through cell membranes, is transported by the red blood cells throughout the body, and enters and damages brain cells [2]. Moreover, the organic form is rapidly incorporated into food chains. For example, fish absorb methyl mercury from water 100 times faster than they absorb inorganic mercury. Once absorbed, methyl mercury is retained 2–5 times longer than inorganic mercury is retained [2]. The effects of the mercury are delayed from 3 weeks to 2 months. If mercury intake ceases, symptoms may gradually disappear [2].

The mercury episode at Minamata illustrates five major factors that must be considered in evaluating and treating environmental pollutants. First, individuals vary in their response to exposure to the same dose, or amount, of a pollutant. Not everyone in Minamata responded in the same way; there was variation even among those most heavily exposed. Because we cannot predict exactly how any single individual will respond, we need to find a way to state an average expected response of individuals in a population. Second, some pollutants may have a threshold—that is, a level below which the effects are not observable and above which effects become apparent. Symptoms appeared in individuals with 500 parts per billion of mercury; no measurable symptoms appeared in individuals with significantly lower concentrations in their bodies. Third, some effects are reversible. Some people recovered when the mercury-filled seafood was eliminated from their diet. Fourth, the chemical form of the pollutant has a great effect on its toxicity. Fifth, the pollutant and its activity are changed markedly by ecological and biological processes. In the case of mercury, its chemical form and concentration changed as the mercury moved along the food webs.

In addition to disease-carrying organisms, there are several major categories of environmental pollutants: toxic chemical elements (particularly heavy metals), ionizing radiation, organic compounds, heat, particulates, noise, personal pollutants such as drugs, and occupational pollutants.

To understand the problems posed by these pollutants, we must understand how they are produced; how they affect individuals, populations, ecosystems, the biosphere, and human health; and how they are transported (and what changes they undergo as they are transported through the environment).

In this chapter we will discuss some basic concepts concerning pollutants, each of the major categories of pollutants, general effects of pollutants, dose-response curves, tolerance, acute and chronic effects, ecological gradients, and pollution control. We will also consider the ultimate global pollution—the environmental effects of thermonuclear war.

POLLUTION: SOME BASICS

The soil in which we cultivate plants for food, the rock on which we build our homes and industries, the water we drink, and the air we breathe all may influence our chances of developing serious health problems. On the other hand, the same factors can also influence our chances of living a longer, more productive life. Surprisingly, many people still believe that soil, water, or air in a "natural," "pure," or "virgin" state must be "good" and that if human activities have changed or modified them, they have become "contaminated," "polluted," and therefore "bad" [3]. This belief is by no means the entire story—many natural processes, including dust storms, floods, and volcanic processes, can introduce materials harmful to humans and other living things into the soil, water, and air. This was tragically shown on the night of August 21, 1986, when Lake Nios in Cameroon, Africa, vented a poisonous gas, probably consisting mostly of CO_2. The gas was heavier than air and settled in villages, killing about 2000 people by asphyxiation. Likewise, activities of people may release into the environment materials that have a positive effect on living things. Application of fertilizers to crops is a common example.

A polluted state is a state of being impure, defiled, dirty, or otherwise unclean. The process of producing that state is known as **pollution**, and a **pollutant** refers to chemicals, radiation, or noise producing the pollution [1]. **Contamination** has a meaning close to that of pollution and implies making something unfit for a particular use through introduction of undesirable materials; for example, contamination of water by hazardous waste. The term **toxic** refers to materials that are poisonous to people and other living things. Toxicology is the science that studies poisons (or toxins) and their effects as well as clinical, industrial, economic, or legal problems associated with toxic materials. A **carcinogen** is a particular kind of toxin, one that causes cancer. Because cancer seems to be increasing and has traditionally been fatal, carcinogens are among the most feared and regulated toxins in our society.

A concept important in looking at pollution problems is **synergism**, which refers to cooperative actions of different substances such that the combined effect is greater than that of any of the substances taken separately. For example, sulfur dioxide and particulates are both air pollutants. Either one taken separately may cause adverse health effects, but when they combine, as when sulfur dioxide is adsorbed onto small particles, they may be inhaled deeper than sulfur dioxide alone and cause greater damage to lungs.

Pollutants are commonly introduced into the environment by way of point sources, such as smokestacks or pipes, or by way of more diffused area sources, such as urban runoff or automobile exhaust. Area sources are difficult to isolate and correct because the problem is often very dispersed over a region, as is runoff from an agricultural area that contains pesticides.

Concentration of Pollutants

How we measure the amount of a pollutant that is introduced into the environment or the concentration of that pollutant varies widely, depending upon the substance involved. For example, the amount of sewage that enters Santa Monica Bay in the Los Angeles area is measured in millions of gallons per day, whereas the emission of nitrogen and sulfur oxides into the environment is often reported in millions of tons per year. When extremely toxic materials (such as dioxin) are re-

leased to soil or water, even in very small amounts, they may cause big problems.

The concentration of pollutants in the environment is often measured in units such as parts per million (ppm), or parts per billion (ppb). It is important to keep in mind that the concentration in parts per million or parts per billion may be by either volume or weight. Parts per million may also be recorded as percent concentrations (100 ppm is equal to 0.01%).

When dealing with water pollution the units of concentration for a pollutant may be milligrams per liter (mg/L) or micrograms per liter (μg/L). A milligram is one-thousandth of a gram and a microgram is one-millionth of a gram. Air pollutants are commonly measured in units such as micrograms of pollutant per cubic meter of air (μg/m^3).

Units such as parts per million, parts per billion, or micrograms per cubic meter reflect very small concentrations. For example, if you were to use one-tenth of an ounce (about 3 g) of salt to season popcorn then to have that salt at a concentration of 1 ppm by weight would require you to pop approximately 3 metric tons of popcorn! Other pollutants, such as radioactivity, noise, and thermal pollution, have different units of measurement of concentration, which will be discussed in this chapter.

TOXIC HEAVY ELEMENTS

Among the major heavy elements that pose hazards are mercury, lead, cadmium, nickel, gold, platinum, silver, bismuth, arsenic, selenium, vanadium, chromium, and thallium. Each of these has uses in our modern industrial society, and each is also a byproduct of the mining, refining, and use of other elements. Heavy elements often have direct physiological toxic effects. Some are stored or incorporated in living tissue, sometimes permanently. The content of heavy metals in our bodies is referred to as the **body burden.** Figure 11.1 shows the average human body burden of some toxic heavy elements.

Mercury, thallium, and lead are very toxic to humans. They have long been mined and used, and their toxic properties are well known. Mercury, for

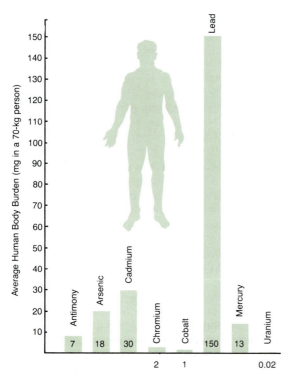

FIGURE 11.1
Average human body burden of major toxic heavy metals. (Data based on Lippmann and Schlesinger.)

North America. Strict regulation of emissions has reduced them by 40% since 1969, but they still produce about 2,000 tons per day.

Nickel has been found contaminating soils 50 km from the stacks, and over the last 50 years the combination of the acid rain from the sulfur dioxide and the particulates containing heavy metals has devastated forests that once surrounded Sudbury. An area of approximately 250 km² is nearly devoid of vegetation, and damage to forests in the region is visible over an area of approximately 3500 km².

Attempts to minimize the pollution problem close to the smelting operation by increasing the smokestack height have spread the problem even more widely. Acid rain, once local, is now widespread. For example, in 1977, rainfall several kilometers east of the Sudbury stacks was often highly acid and thus potentially harmful to people and other living things, especially plants. Secondary effects, in addition to loss of vegetation, include soil erosion and drastic changes in soil chemistry due to the influx of the heavy metals. More about acid rain, as well as the effects of heavy toxic elements such as lead and cadmium, is presented in Chapter 12.

example, is the "Mad Hatter" element. At one time, mercury was used in making hats; because mercury damages the brain, hatters were known to act peculiarly in Victorian England. Thus, the Mad Hatter in Lewis Carroll's *Alice in Wonderland* had a real antecedent in history.

A famous example of a point source of pollution is provided by the smelters for the refining of nickel and copper ores at Sudbury, Ontario. Sudbury contains one of the world's major nickel and copper ore deposits. Within a few kilometers of each other, there are 3 smelters, 13 mines, 1 open-pit mine, 6 concentrators, 2 iron-ore recovery plants, and 1 copper refinery. The ores contain a high percentage of sulfur, and the smelter stacks emit large amounts of sulfur dioxide as well as particulates containing nickel, copper, and other metals toxic to living things. The complex is the largest single source of sulfur dioxide emissions in

RADIATION AND RADIOISOTOPES

A **radioisotope** is a form of a chemical element that spontaneously undergoes radioactive decay. It changes from one isotope to another and during the process emits one or more forms of radiation. Isotopes are atoms of an element that have the same atomic number (the number of protons in the nucleus) but which vary in atomic mass number (the number of protons plus neutrons in the nucleus). For example, two isotopes of uranium are $_{92}U^{235}$ and $_{92}U^{238}$. The atomic number for both atoms of uranium is 92, whereas the atomic mass numbers are 235 and 238, respectively. The two different isotopes may be written as uranium-235 and uranium-238, or U-235 and U-238. Each radioisotope has its own characteristic emissions; some isotopes emit only one kind of radiation, and some emit a mixture.

There are three major kinds of radiation: alpha particles, beta particles, and gamma rays. Alpha particles (the nuclei of helium atoms) have the most mass and generally travel the shortest distance before being stopped by other matter. Alpha particles may be stopped by very thin material. Gamma rays are very similar to X-rays but may be more energetic and penetrating. They travel the longest average distance of all radiation and can penetrate thick shielding. Beta particles (electrons) are intermediate in mass and are stopped by moderate shielding.

An important characteristic of a radioisotope is its **half-life,** which is the time required for one-half of a given amount of the isotope to decay to another form. Every radioisotope has a unique characteristic half-life. Radioactive iodine, for example, has a short half-life of 8 days. Radioactive carbon-14 has an intermediate half-life of 5570 years. Uranium-235 has a half-life of 700 million years.

Some radioisotopes, particularly those of very heavy elements, undergo a series of radioactive decay steps, finally reaching a stable, nonradioactive isotope. For example, uranium decays through a series of steps and ends up as a stable isotope of lead. There are three naturally occurring chains or series: the uranium, actinium, and thorium chains.

The three kinds of radiation have different toxicities. In terms of human health, or the health of any organism, alpha radiation is most dangerous when ingested. All of its radiation is stopped within a short distance by the body's tissues, and therefore all the damaging radiation is absorbed by the body. On the other hand, when an alpha-emitting isotope is stored in a container outside the body, it is relatively harmless. A gamma emitter can be dangerous outside or inside the body, but when ingested, some of the radiation emitted passes outside the body. Beta radiation is intermediate in its effects, although most beta radiation will be absorbed by the body when a beta-emitter is ingested.

Tritium, the radioactive isotope of hydrogen that occurs in heavy water, is dangerous to ingest but may be stored safely in containers. Carbon-14, the radioactive isotope of carbon that occurs naturally in the form of carbon dioxide, is a beta-emitter; it is dangerous to ingest but may be stored relatively safely. Uranium emits gamma rays, which may be dangerous even from a long distance away. Uranium can be dangerous inside or outside the body and must be stored under heavy shielding.

A radioisotope's degree of dangerousness, either to the environment or to human health, depends on several factors: the kind of energy of the radiation emitted, the half-life, and the ordinary chemical activity of the isotope. Other things being equal, low-energy, short half-lived isotopes are less dangerous than high-energy, long half-lived isotopes. However, isotopes that readily enter a gaseous phase and are released into the atmosphere where they can be inhaled may be extremely dangerous even with low energies and short half-lives. Tritium and carbon-14 are examples of such dangerous isotopes.

Radiation Units

The commonly used unit for radioactive decay is the curie,* which is the amount of radioactivity from 1 g of radium-226 that undergoes about 37 billion nuclear transformations per second. Radium-226 has a half-life of 1622 years; by the end of that time the initial gram of radium will be reduced to 0.5, the nuclear transformations will be reduced to about 18.5 billion/sec, and the amount of radioactivity present will be 0.5 curies [1].

The actual dose of radiation that is delivered by radioactivity is commonly measured in terms of rads and rems. The energy retained by living tissue that has been exposed to radiation is called the radiation adsorbed dose (rad). However, because different types of radiation have different penetration and therefore do variable damage to living tissue, the rad is multiplied by a factor known as the relative biological effectiveness to produce rem units. The rem is thus an empirically derived unit. When small doses of radioactivity are being considered, the millirem (mrem), which is one thousandth of a rem, is used [1, 2, 4]. When measuring

*The International System (SI) of measurements uses metric units. In that system, curies are converted to becquerels, rads to grays, rems to sieverts, and roentgens to coulombs per kilogram.

X-rays or gamma radiation, the commonly used unit is the roentgen.

Radiation Doses

The natural background radiation received by Americans averages about 150 mrem/yr. The range, however, is from about 100 to 250 mrem/yr [1]. In general, the highest levels of radiation are in the mountain states and the lowest level is in Florida. The differences are due to elevation and geology. More cosmic radiation is received at higher elevations, and granitic rocks that contain radioactive minerals are more common in mountain areas. Florida, with a basic limestone geology and low elevation, has a relatively low level of background radiation [4]. The precise amount and sources of low-level background radiation received by people are not completely agreed upon. However, some of the major sources include potassium-40 and carbon-14, which are present in our bodies and probably deliver between 20 and 25 mrem/yr; cosmic rays, which deliver between 35 and about 150 mrem/yr, depending upon elevation; and radioactive materials in rocks and soils, which deliver about 35 mrem/yr (this number may be much larger in tightly sealed homes where radon gas seeps in). Anthropogenic sources of low-level radiation include X-rays for medical and dental purposes, which may deliver an average of 70–80 mrem/yr; nuclear weapons testing and nuclear power plants that may be responsible for approximately 4 mrem/yr; and burning of fossil fuels such as coal and oil and natural gas, which may add another 3 mrem/yr [1, 4]. A person's occupation and lifestyle can also affect the annual dose of radiation. Every time you fly at high altitudes you receive an additional few millirems of radiation. If you work at a nuclear power plant or conventional coal-fired plant or in a number of industrial positions, you may also be exposed to additional low-level radiation. Precisely how much radiation is received on job sites is closely monitored at obvious sites such as nuclear power plants and laboratories where X-rays are produced; personnel must wear badges that reflect the dose of radiation received. In recent years there has been a move toward conservation of energy, with the result that our homes

are becoming tighter and tighter. This is becoming a problem in some areas where natural radioactive gas (radon) accumulates and is producing a health hazard. This will be discussed following our treatment of general health problems related to radiation.

Radiation Doses and Health   A major question concerning radiation exposure to people is, When does the exposure or dose become a hazard to health? There are not a lot of easy answers to this question. A dose of about 500,000 mrem (500 rem) is considered lethal to 50% of all people exposed to it; 100,000–200,000 mrem (100–200 rem) is sufficient to cause serious health problems, including vomiting, fatigue, potential abortion of pregnancies of less than two-months duration, and temporary sterility in males; 50,000 mrem (50 rem) is the dose where physiological damage is recorded; and the maximum allowable dose of radiation per year for workers in industry is 5,000 mrem (5 rem), which is approximately 30 times the average whole-body natural background radiation received by people [1, 4]. The maximum permissible annual dose for the general public in the United States is 500 mrem, or about three times the average annual background [1]. Although a good deal of information is known about the effects of high doses of radiation on people, most of the information comes from study of people who survived the atomic bomb detonations in Japan at the end of World War II, people exposed to high levels of radiation in uranium mines, workers painting watch dials with luminous paint containing radium, and people treated with radiation therapy for diseases [5]. Workers in mines that are exposed to high levels of radiation have been shown to suffer a significantly higher rate of lung cancer than the general population. Study of mortality rates suggests there is a delay of 10–25 years between the time of exposure and onset of the disease. There is debate about the nature of the relationship between radiation exposure and cancer mortality. Some scientists believe there is a linear relationship such that any increase in radiation will produce an additional hazard (Fig. 11.2). Other workers believe that the body is able to handle and recover from very low levels of increased radiation, but that be-

FIGURE 11.2
Possible relations between radiation exposure and cancer mortality. We know that high exposures increase cancer mortality; the colored area in the figure indicates this. The path there may be linear or nonlinear. (After University of Maine and the Maine Department of Human Services.)

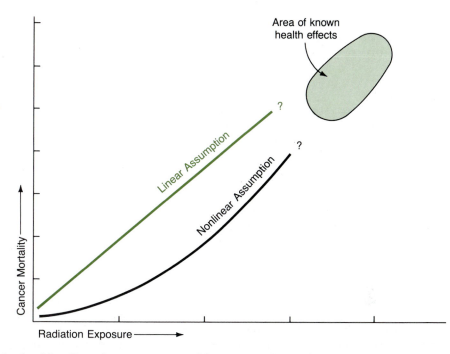

Environmental Effects of Radioisotopes

Radioisotopes affect the environment in two ways: by emitting radiation that affects other materials and by entering the normal pathways of mineral cycling and ecological food chains. The explosion of an atomic weapon does damage in both ways. At the time of the explosion, intense radiation of many kinds and energies is sent out, killing organisms directly. The explosion generates large amounts of radioactive isotopes, which are dispersed into the environment. Nuclear bombs exploded in the atmosphere produce a huge cloud that sends radioisotopes directly into the stratosphere, where the radioactive particles may be widely dispersed by winds. Atomic "fallout"—the deposit of these radioactive materials around the world—was a major environmental problem in the 1950s and 1960s when the United States, the Soviet Union, China, France, and Great Britain were testing and exploding nuclear weapons in the atmosphere.

yond some threshold the health effects become more apparent. The verdict is still out on this subject but it seems prudent to take a conservative stand and accept that there may be a linear relationship. That is, any increase in radiation is likely to be accompanied by an increase in adverse health effects.

The pathways of some of these isotopes illustrate the second way that radioactive materials can be dangerous in the environment. One of the radioisotopes emitted and sent into the stratosphere by atomic explosions was cesium-137. This radioisotope was deposited in relatively small concentrations but widely dispersed in the Arctic region of North America. It fell on reindeer moss, a lichen that is a primary winter food of the caribou. A strong seasonal trend was found in the levels of cesium-137 in caribou; the level was highest in the winter, when reindeer moss was the principal food, and lowest in the summer. Eskimos who obtained a high percentage of their protein from caribou ingested the radioisotope by eating the meat, and their bodies concentrated the cesium. The more that members of a group depended on caribou as their primary source of food, the higher was the level of the isotope in their bodies.

The cesium was moved long distances by biospheric phenomena. After entering specific ecosystems through the vegetation, it underwent **biomagnification**, or ecological food-chain concentration. That is, at each trophic level the concentration of the toxic material, relative to concentrations of other materials in the bodies of organisms, increased. Cesium-137 concentrations approximately doubled with each trophic level. This biomagnification was unknown until radioisotopes and toxic organic compounds were found to be occurring at higher and higher concentra-

tions at higher and higher trophic levels. Food-chain or trophic-level concentration is one of the major ecological factors in environmental toxicology.

The actual body burden of cesium varied within the Eskimo population. Adult males between the ages of 20 and 50 had the highest levels, apparently because their diet contained the most caribou meat. Concentration varied seasonally and increased over the years of intensive atmospheric bomb testing (Fig. 11.3) [6].

FIGURE 11.3
Cesium-137, released into the atmosphere by atomic bomb tests, was part of the fallout deposited on the soil and plants. (a) The cesium fell on lichens, which were eaten by caribou. The caribou were in turn eaten by the Eskimo. Measurements of cesium in the lichens, caribou, and Eskimo in the Anaktuvuk Pass of Alaska (b) show that the cesium was concentrated by the food chain. (c) Peaks in concentrations occurred first in the lichens, then in the caribou, and last in the Eskimo. [(c) Reprinted with permission from W. G. Hanson, Cesium-137 in Alaskan lichens, caribou, and Eskimos, *Health Physics* 13: 383–89. Copyright 1967, Pergamon Press, Ltd.]

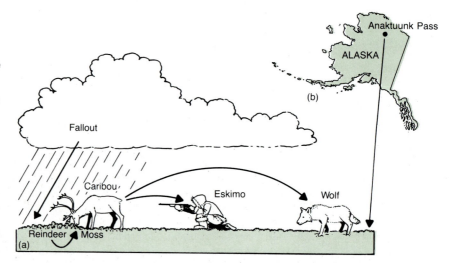

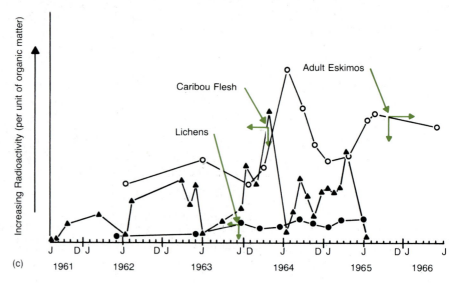

PLATE 1
Views of nature and wilderness.

(a) *The Unicorn in Captivity,* a medieval tapestry, shows the mythical creature amid detailed representations of actual plants. This mixture of the imagined and the real is found throughout the history of human thoughts about nature. (b) The view that nature is a useful commodity or a raw resource is illustrated in the 1872 painting *American Progress* by John Gast. The role of people as adding order to a disordered nature is also implied.

A

B

C

(c) Nature as harmonious, ordered, and complete without human influence is illustrated in *Autumn on the Hudson River* by Jaspar Francis Cropsey. The nineteenth-century painting can also be seen as depicting nature as beautiful and as a key to self-discovery.

[(a) Courtesy of Metropolitan Museum of Art, New York; (b) Harry T. Peters, Windholm Farm, Orange, Virginia; (c) National Gallery of Art, Washington, D.C. From Sweeney.]

A

PLATE 2
Energy in the environment.

Energy is required for all life activities.
(a) The energy exchange between plants and the environment is normally invisible to us.
(b) With infrared photgraphy, the hotter leaves appear deep red, the cooler bark still looks white.
(c) Human requirements for energy have led to alternative technologies to provide renewable, less polluting energy sources, such as this wind power farm in the Altamont Pass, 45 miles east of San Francisco.

B

C

A

B

C

PLATE 3
Ecological succession.

(a) At Volcano National Park, Hawaii, early successional species grow on a patch of older lava, paler than the surrounding new lava due to weathering and the action of small plants and microbes. Eventually a soil forms that can support trees and shrubs.

(b) 'Ohi'a is the only tree that grows in Volcano National Park; when they mature and die, the forest declines but may develop again. (c) In this sand dune near Lake Michigan, pioneering species include grasses (foreground) whose runners and stems help stabilize the sand. Succession then proceeds to shrubs and trees (background). Sometimes sand is blown inland, covering a forest; when the sand is blown further inland, the dead tree stems are exposed (center).

PLATE 4
Ecological succession.

In the rain forests of New Zealand, succession begins with lichens growing on bare rock exposed by a receding glacier.
(a) Eventually a mature forest of many species develops, but the heavy rains slowly leach the soil of its nutrients.
(b) Most chemical elements required for life have been transported to the lower layer. The gray, leached layer above supports only grasses and shrubs that can survive on poor soils or whose roots can penetrate deep enough to tap the deposition layer.

A

PLATE 5 (opposite)
Biogeography.

The strong influence of climate on life processes is indicated in these satellite images.
(a) In August, when it is summer in the northern hemisphere and winter in the southern, the green leaf density is high, even into Alaska and Siberia.
(b) In February, green leaf density increases in the southern hemisphere and becomes low in much of the northern.

B

C

(c) At Livingston Bog, Michigan, the remaining open water is surrounded by a floating mat of sedges; as a soil develops, shrubs will grow in this mat. Eventually the floating mat and solid bottom meet, and on this solid surface a forest develops (background).

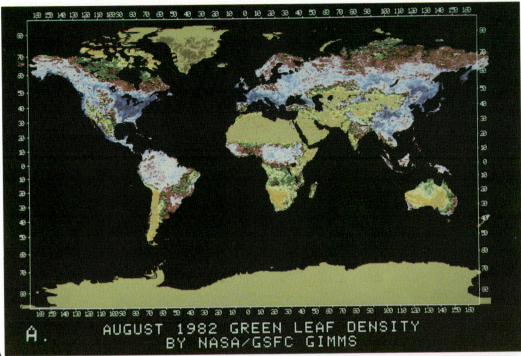

AUGUST 1982 GREEN LEAF DENSITY
BY NASA/GSFC GIMMS

A.

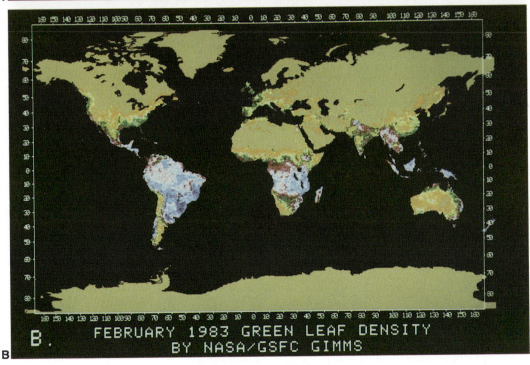

FEBRUARY 1983 GREEN LEAF DENSITY
BY NASA/GSFC GIMMS

B.

A

C

B

PLATE 6
Biomes.

(a) Warm-climate deserts, like the Mojave of California, occur also in South America, Europe, Asia, Africa, and Australia. (b) The transition from boreal forest to tundra is visible in this view of Lake O'Hara in the Canadian Rockies. (c) Mud flats, such as that at Laguna Figueron of Baja California, represent perhaps the most ancient of biomes, made up of microorganisms that emit gases, causing the bubbles visible here.

A

B

C

PLATE 7
Endangered species.

(a) The nene bird of Hawaii was brought close to extinction by habitat destruction and hunting; it is now protected. (b) The sea otter was hunted almost to extinction because of its valuable fur. Although some people work to increase its numbers, others want the population controlled because sea otters compete with us for abalone.

(c) The cougar (puma or mountain lion) once roamed widely through U.S. and Canadian forests. Regarded as a pest by ranchers, the cougar has been eliminated or endangered in many parts of the United States.

A

PLATE 8
Managing living resources.

(a) In Tsavo National Park, Kenya, the elephant population increased greatly, then suffered a major die-off during a two-year drought in the late 1960s. (b) Searching for food, the elephants destroyed so much of the park's vegetation that the park is denuded (left), while the unmanaged area outside retains its vegetation (right). (c) In a Landsat satellite image, the park shows as a brown, denuded area distinct from the reddish color representing vegetation. (The black area within the park is a large grassland fire.)

B

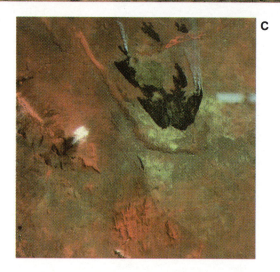

C

A

B

PLATE 9
Life and toxic substances.

At Brookhaven National Laboratory, Long Island, New York, the forest ecosystem was exposed to a source of gamma rays 20 hours a day for many years.
(a) Near the source, all living things were killed. This dead area formed a roughly circular patch, visible from the air. (b) Some plants survived in the shadow of standing dead tree stems, which shielded them from the radiation. Small early successional species were the most resistant to the radiation and survived nearest to the source. (c) Ten years after the radiation source was removed from the cement box, the forest shows some recovery.

C

A

PLATE 10
Sediment pollution.

Erosion of soil from urban sites during construction (a) often produces a pollution problem for nearby areas (b). Sediment control ordinances in many areas now minimize such problems.

PLATE 11 (opposite)

Two extremes of channelization. (a) Concrete ditch, Carpinteria Creek, California, and (b) channel restoration of Briar Creek near Charlotte, North Carolina.

B

A

B

1. Bingham copper mine
2. Great Salt Lake
3. Lake Utah
4. Tailing pond from copper smelters
5. Commercial salt evaporating pond
6. Wasatch front along Wasatch fault that uplifts snow-covered Mts.

N

0   20 km

Salt Lake City, Utah. This area contains the Bingham copper mine as well as evaporite resources associated with the Great Salt Lake, which is only a remnant of the once much larger Lake Bonneville. (ERTS photo)

Lavendar Pit copper mine, Bisbee, Arizona, (Photo courtesy of Peter L. Kresan)

PLATE 13

Land failure resulting in property damage.

(a) Winter Park, Florida, sinkhole that developed in May 1981. The subsidence caused $2 million in damages and swallowed part of the community swimming pool, parts of two businesses, a house and several expensive sports cars, trailers, and other vehicles.

(b) The large complex landslides in Santa Barbara, California, which destroyed two homes, involved reactivation of an older slide in part because of urban runoff and erosion of the toe of the slope by waves.

A

B

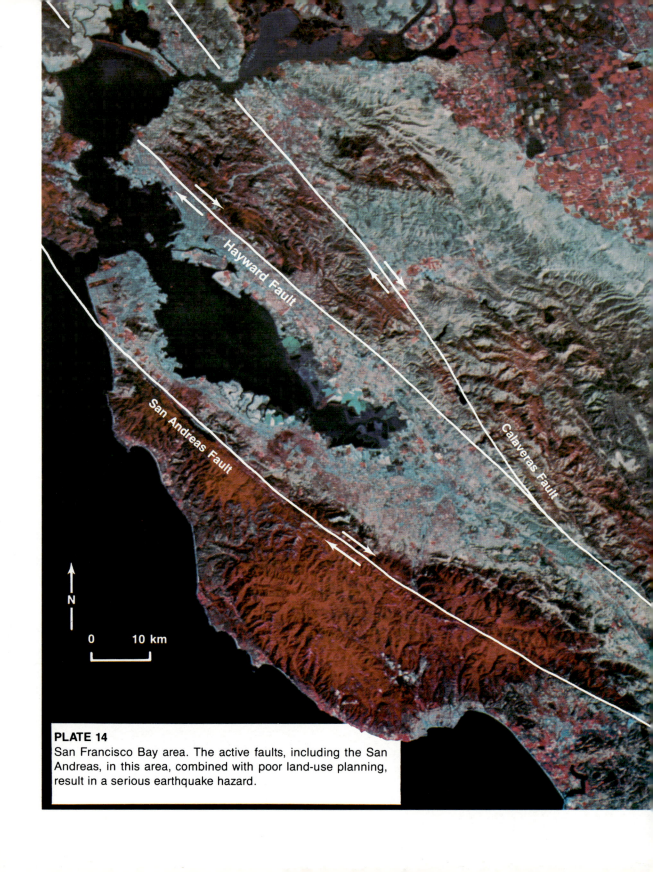

PLATE 14
San Francisco Bay area. The active faults, including the San Andreas, in this area, combined with poor land-use planning, result in a serious earthquake hazard.

PLATE 15
Pismo Dunes State Vehicular Recreation Area, south of Pismo Beach, California. Use of off-road vehicles in this area has created controversy. ORV use is incompatible with most other land uses and is destructive in environmentally sensitive areas.

· RARE ·
PLANTS
LITTLE
COREOPSIS HILL
DUNE 2 - USGS

PLATE 16
This flood channel was constructed in the small village of Lynmouth, England, after a flash flood killed 34 people and destroyed 93 houses in August, 1952. A flood wall protects the village on the left bank of the Lyn River and a rock berm with steps to the river protects the right bank. Tourists seeking recreation use the flat berm. A repeat of the damage is unlikely due to the new protective structures.

Another important factor in the toxicity of cesium-137 from fallout is the length of time the isotope remains in the body. This is measured by the biological half-life—the time for one-half the concentration to be lost. In the caribou, the average biological half-life was 15 days. The biological half-life in the Eskimos, however, was approximately 65 days.

It is possible to predict the environmental pathways that radioisotopes will follow because we know the normal pathways of nonradioactive isotopes with the same chemical characteristics. Our knowledge of biomagnification and of large-scale air and oceanic movements that transport radioisotopes throughout the biosphere will also help us to understand the effects of radioisotopes.

Nuclear Power Plants

One of the most dramatic events in the history of radiation pollution occurred on March 28, 1979, at the Three Mile Island nuclear power plant near Harrisburg, Pennsylvania. Malfunctions in the nuclear plant resulted in a release of radioisotopes into the environment as well as intense radiation release within one of the nuclear facilities. The actual release into the environment was at a low level per person exposed. Exposure from the plume emitted into the atmosphere has been estimated at 100 mrem, which is low in terms of the amount of radiation required to cause acute toxic effects. However, radiation levels were much higher near the site. On the third day after the accident, 1200 mrem/hr were measured at ground level near the site.

The Three Mile Island incident made clear that there are many problems with the way our society has dealt with nuclear power. Historically, nuclear power has been relatively safe, and the state of Pennsylvania was somewhat unprepared to deal with the accident. For example, there was no state bureau for radiation health, and the State Department of Health did not have a single book on radiation medicine (the medical library had been dismantled two years before for budgetary reasons). One of the major impacts of the incident was fear, yet there was no state office of mental health or any authority to allow anyone from the Department of Health to sit in on briefing sessions.

Because the long-term chronic effects of exposure to low levels of radiation are not well understood, the effects of the Three Mile Island exposure—although apparently small—are difficult to estimate. This case illustrates that our society needs to improve its ability to handle the crises that could arise from sudden releases of pollutants from our modern technology. It also shows our lack of preparedness and apparent readiness to treat a nuclear power plant as an acceptable risk [7].

Lack of preparedness to deal with a serious nuclear power plant accident was dramatically illustrated by events that began unfolding on the morning of Monday, April 28, 1986. Workers at a nuclear power plant in Sweden, frantically searching for the source of high levels of radiation near the plant, concluded that it was not their installation that was leaking radiation but that the radioactivity was coming from their Soviet neighbors by way of prevailing winds. Confronted, the Soviets on late Monday announced that there had been an accident at their nuclear power plant at Chernobyl. This was the first notice to the world that the worst accident in the history of nuclear power generation had occurred.

It is speculated that the system that supplies cooling waters for the reactor failed, causing the temperature in the reactor core to rise to over 3000°C, melting the uranium fuel. Explosions occurred that removed the top of the building over the reactor, and graphite surrounding the fuel rods used to moderate the nuclear reactions in the core ignited. The fires produced a cloud of radioactive particles that rose high into the atmosphere. Radiation killed about twenty people at and near the plant site in the days following the accident, and millions of other people were exposed to potentially harmful radiation as the cloud in the days after the start of the accident drifted first over parts of the Soviet Union, then north to Scandinavia, and then to eastern Europe.

During the next 25–30 years an increase in cancers will document the impact on humans from the accident. Beyond that, it is estimated that as much as 150 km^2 of valuable farmland in the USSR may be contaminated with radiation for decades [8].

One of the avoidable tragedies in the accident was the way the Soviet government handled the accident. Delays in warning people in their own country and outside resulted in unnecessary exposure to radiation. Although the Soviets have been accused of not giving attention to reactor safety and of using outdated equipment, people are now wondering if such an event could happen again. With about 400 reactors producing power in the world today, the answer has to be yes. In fact, the Chernobyl accident follows a history marked by about ten accidents that have released radioactive particles during the past 34 years. Therefore, while Chernobyl is the most serious nuclear accident to date, it certainly wasn't the first. Many countries such as Japan, Britain, and France that depend heavily on nuclear power plants for generating electric power are rethinking the risks of siting power plants close to high densities of people. While the probability of a serious accident is very small at a particular site, the consequences of the event may be great, perhaps resulting in an unacceptable risk. As a result of Chernobyl, risk analysis in nuclear power is now a real-life experience rather than a computer simulation.

As long as people build nuclear power plants and manage them, there will be the possibility of accidents. It's as much a problem of human nature as anything else. Considering the potential tremendous consequences of serious accidents like that at Chernobyl, we may have to recognize that we may not be ready as a people to handle nuclear power.

Radon Gas and Indoor Air Pollution

Radon is a naturally occurring radioactive gas that is colorless, odorless, and tasteless. It may be found in low concentrations almost everywhere on Earth. It is soluble in water and so commonly is found in well water. Radon is the intermediate product resulting from radioactive decay of radium and is approximately midway in a chain of radioactive transformations that begins with uranium-238 and eventually ends with lead-210. The half-life of radon gas is 3.8 days and, as radioactive decay occurs, other isotopes with shorter half-lives are produced until stable lead-210 is reached [5].

People are worried about radon gas because today in the United States 20% of all deaths are due to cancer and approximately 25% of these, or 100,000/yr, are due to lung cancer. Although there are as yet no direct studies and evidence linking radon gas exposure in houses to increased incidence of cancer, estimates of such linkage come from studies of people who have experienced high exposure to radiation through such activities as mining uranium. The health risk from radon gas is related primarily to alpha radiation, particles of which may adhere to dust and be inhaled into the lungs or be dissolved in water and ingested through drinking.

The natural concentration of radon gas varies with geology. In general, areas underlain by granitic rocks have a higher content of uranium and thus of radon gas. Three major sources or pathways have been identified by which radon gas may enter homes (Fig. 11.4). These are (1) groundwater pumped into homes through wells, (2) gas that mi-

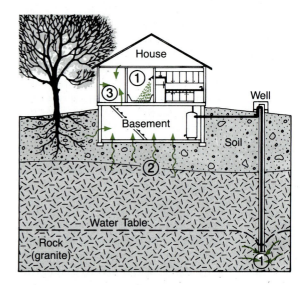

FIGURE 11.4
How radon may enter homes. (1) Radon in groundwater enters well and goes to house where it is used for water supply, dishwashing, showers, and other purposes. (2) Radon gas in rock and soil migrates into basement through cracks in foundation and pores in construction. (3) Radon gas is emitted from construction materials used in building the house.

grates upward from soil and rock into basements and other parts of houses, and (3) construction materials such as building blocks made of substances that emit radon gas [5].

In recent years there has been a move to make houses tighter to better conserve energy. In doing this we have also inadvertently increased indoor air pollution. In areas where natural concentrations of radon gas are high, radon may be concentrated in homes to a level that is considered dangerous. It was recently reported in Pennsylvania that some homes built there on granite bedrock had concentrations of radon gas several hundred times that considered to be acceptable. In the Pennsylvania case, the radon in homes was discovered accidentally because a worker in a nuclear power plant was continually tripping radiation alarms at work. In looking for the cause, it was discovered that the source of radiation was the worker's home! Since that first discovery, health officials have identified hundreds of Pennsylvania homes with potentially hazardous concentrations of radon gas. Other areas, such as Colorado and Maine, have also been identified as having high concentrations of radon gas in homes. Correction of the problem in homes may be very costly; certainly property values have dropped in those areas following identification of the radon gas problem.

Methods to control radon gas in homes are coupled to the sources [5]. Radon in well water may be removed by several methods related to filtering the water, boiling it, and letting it stand for a period of time. Radon that enters a home from soil and rock may be removed through proper ventilation and perhaps filters. Radon gas in construction materials may be avoided if the materials are identified. Surface sealants may also be used, and if radon is discovered in existing materials, those materials may be removed from the home. Of course, if the levels of radon gas are very high and the sources difficult to control, then homes will need to be abandoned. We are only beginning to understand the nature and extent of the radon gas problem in the United States. As more areas and potential sources are identified, we should gain additional experience in dealing with the problem. The work is necessary, however, because health officials believe that several thousands of deaths per year from lung cancer may be related to the radon gas problem.

ORGANIC COMPOUNDS

Organic compounds are compounds of carbon produced either by living organisms or artificially. It is difficult to generalize about the environmental and health effects of artificially produced organic compounds because there are so many of them, because they have so many uses, and because they have a potential for so many different kinds of effects. Artificial organic compounds are used primarily in industrial processes, pest control, pharmaceuticals, food additives, and other consumer products. A computer registry of chemicals, maintained by the American Chemical Society, has more than 4 million entries, and there are about 6000 additions per week. About 33,000 chemicals are in common use; this figure does not include pesticides, pharmaceuticals, or food additives. According to the U.S. Food and Drug Administration, there are about 4000 active and 2000 inert ingredients in drugs. There are 2500 nutritional additives and 3000 additives to promote the life of products [6]. The production of artificial organic compounds has grown rapidly in the twentieth century (Fig. 11.5).

Organic compounds can have physiological, genetic, or ecological effects. Because artificial organic compounds are new and organisms have had little time to adjust to them, they are more likely to be toxic to living organisms than are natural organic compounds. Some organic compounds are potentially more hazardous than others. For example, rapidly degrading substances are less likely to cause problems as chronic hazards than slowly degrading ones. Fat-soluble compounds are likely to undergo biomagnification.

The problems likely to be posed by an organic compound depend on the pathways it will follow through the environment. We can determine the likely path for a chemical by testing its solubility in water, absorption by natural solids, leaching rates, volatility, and oil or fat solubility [6]. Artificial organic compounds are spread widely throughout the biosphere and can be found in many species.

FIGURE 11.5
The production of artificial organic compounds has increased rapidly during the twentieth century. Current production exceeds 100 billion kg/yr. (From G. F. White.)

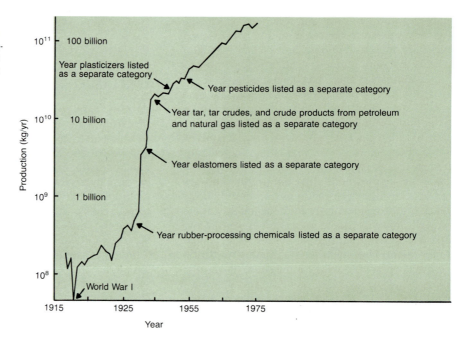

Oil Spills

Oil spills—one of the most spectacular forms of pollution—have attracted great attention. However, the primary effects of oil pollution appear to be short-term. When an oil well blew out in the Santa Barbara Channel, California, in 1969, the beaches of the city were blackened with 4500 tons of crude oil and approximately 3600 birds were killed. Public concern culminated in the establishment of an organization whose sole aim was to combat the oil pollution.

Major oil spills in the last several decades have resulted from ship accidents, such as the collision between the *Fort Mercer* and the *Pendleton* near Chatham, Massachusetts, in 1952, as well as from blowouts like the Santa Barbara incident. Although ship spills are highly publicized, they are by no means the only source of pollution of waters by oil. Oil released by automobiles on roadways is transported by surface water runoff to rivers, which contribute the greatest amount of oil to the

ocean of all land sources. Municipal wastes and coastal refineries also contribute a significant amount. Of the marine sources, tanker spillage contributes the most oil, but offshore seeps, the clearing of ships' bilges, and dry-docking procedures also contribute large amounts.

Oil's acute effects on the ocean are perhaps more well known than its chronic effects. Oil is a particular problem for commercially valuable ocean life because most major oil spills have occurred near shore, where there is an abundance of shellfish and finfish. Oil is a mixture of hydrocarbons, some of which are light and float and others which are heavy and sink. Generally, chronic effects are most pronounced from the heavier compounds. For example, gasoline evaporates quickly and is less of a chronic problem than crude oil.

Oil is directly toxic to some organisms when it is ingested, and it reduces the insulating properties of fur and feathers. When birds are covered with oil, their feathers no longer provide insulation against the cold water and air and the birds cannot fly. Because they cannot feed, they die of cold shock and starvation. Similarly, sea otters lose the insulating properties of their fur.

A layer of oil floating on the ocean surface can

In fact, such compounds are found in nontarget marine animals far from the sources of production of the synthetic chemicals (Table 11.1).

TABLE 11.1
Some synthetic organic compounds in marine animals.

Species	Source	Chemical (mg/kg fresh tissue)		
		Dieldrin	DDT	PCB
Shellfish				
Mussel	Mediterranean	0.001–0.030	0.01–0.65	0.08–0.18
	Baltic	—	0.005–0.07	0.01–0.33
Fish (mg/kg muscle)				
Herring	North Sea	<0.001–0.034	0.035–0.17	<0.001–0.48
Sardine	Mediterranean	<0.001–0.14	0.001–0.63	0.03–6.9
Cod	North Sea	<0.001–0.023	<0.003–0.052	<0.001–0.099
Cod	Newfoundland	—	0.011	0.038
(liver)		—	2.7	22.
Haddock	Newfoundland	—	0.002	0.030
Shark (liver)	North Atlantic	—	4.8	5.8
Mammals (mg/kg blubber)				
Grey seal	Scotland	0.46–1.7	8.5–36.3	12–88
Common seal	Netherlands	<0.02–0.09	9.5	385–2530
Porpoise	Scotland	3.1–4.5	16.8–37.4	31–68
Sea lion	California	—	41–2678	—
Various cetaceans	Atlantic Ocean	<0.1–3.0	1.1–268	0.7–114
Birds				
White-tailed eagle				
(muscle)	Baltic Sea	—	290–400	150–240
Cormorant (fat tissue)	Arctic Ocean	—	6.5–15	14–47
Various (liver)	North Atlantic	—	—	0.02–311

Source: Compiled from Whittle et al., 1977, in *Chemical contamination in the human environment* by Morton Lippman and Richard Schlesinger. Copyright © 1979 by Oxford University Press, Inc. Reprinted by permission.

Note: Some areas are considered particularly heavily contaminated with DDT and/or PCB. These are the Baltic, western Mediterranean, southern area of the North Sea, west coast of the United Kingdom, and coast of California.

interfere with the exchange of oxygen and carbon dioxide and reduce the rate of photosynthesis of marine plankton and the respiration of marine animals. Fuel oil added to sea water in very low concentration (199 ppb) depresses photosynthesis.

The death of birds from oil spills has attracted much attention. In the *Torrey Canyon* incident in 1967, an estimated 40,000–100,000 birds died. The *Fort Mercer* and *Pendleton* collision in 1952 reduced the wintering population of eider ducks from 500,000 to 150,000 [9]. Some believe that the jackass penguin, which lives in South Africa, is endangered because floating oil from tankers rounding the Cape of Good Hope is killing hundreds of thousands of these birds each year.

Surprisingly, in spite of the great amount of publicity that surrounds oil spills, little is known about their long-term effects. Immediately after the spill, there is a great effort to save the lives of oil-soaked birds and to clean up the oil on beaches

(Fig. 11.6). In fact, special techniques have been developed solely for these purposes. However, once the initial problem has been dealt with, there has been little follow-up study. Only a few oil spills have been subject to long-term studies. The spill of No. 2 fuel oil off West Falmouth, Cape Cod, Massachusetts, in 1969 occurred near the Woods Hole Oceanographic Institute, whose scientists began a study that continued for several years. In that spill, benthic (ocean-bottom dwelling) organisms, including valuable shellfish, died rapidly and in great numbers. The *Torrey Canyon* spill, which took place near the Marine Biological Association Laboratories in Milford Haven, England, was also well studied. In that incident, larval fish concentrated near the ocean surface came in direct contact with the oil and were killed in massive numbers.

The chronic effects of oil spills appear less serious than the acute effects. Oil, a natural hydro-

FIGURE 11.6
Oil-soaked western grebe, San Francisco Bay, following an oil spill.

carbon, is food for some marine microorganisms and is degraded by them. When the oil spills are localized, marine organisms can migrate back into the destroyed area once the oil has been degraded.

Perhaps the most serious long-term problem may be the slow, widespread leakage of oil at many points all over the oceans. The oil may contain chemicals that have specific toxic effects on certain species. If the chemicals are sufficiently widespread, they may be able to affect an entire species. Although the tanker oil spills and drilling rig blowouts are spectacular, their limited effects may cause less of a problem than more persistent sources such as the ships that navigate the world's oceans and slowly leak oil.

Pesticides

Few issues in environmental studies are simple; most involve a complex balancing of difficult and conflicting choices. This is nowhere better illustrated than by pesticides.

The conflicts were vividly brought to public attention by the medfly problem in California in 1981. The medfly, a pest that destroys fruits, was accidentally introduced into the state's fruit-growing areas in 1981, and its population grew rapidly. The misuse of one kind of biological control—the release of supposedly sterile male flies, which turned out not to be sterile—made the problem worse. The fly population expanded so rapidly that local spraying from the ground of chemical pesticides did not work. The state government had to weigh the positive effects of aerial spraying (possible control of the medfly) against its negative effects, which ranged from damage to automobile paint to potential, unknown, long-term health hazards. Fortunately, timely technical advances allowed the pesticide to be sprayed in sugary droplets that attracted the fly but relatively few other species. Thus, unable to control the fly in any other way and facing a billion-dollar effect on the state's agricultural industry, the state government opted for aerial spraying of the pesticide.

Ever since the beginnings of agriculture, pests have been the bane of farmers. In the United States, pests consume about one-third of the total potential crop before harvest and 10% after harvest [10]. Pesticides have been used in one form or another for more than 2000 years, but pesticide use became widespread only in the last century.

The ideal pesticide would be a "magic bullet"—a chemical that affected only the pest and no other living thing or aspect of the environment. The history of pesticide development can be seen as an attempt to find chemicals that have more and more specific effects and that are effective in controlling pests.

The first modern chemical pesticides were arsenic compounds used on potatoes, cotton, and apples. Although these are effective on the insect pests of those crops, the compounds are also highly toxic to human beings and many other forms of life. Green plants produce some natural pesticides—nicotine, for example—that were used in some of the earlier compounds. Inorganic chemicals were most important until DDT and other chlorinated hydrocarbons were developed in the 1940s, leading to a revolution in pesticides. In the last 30 years, U.S. agriculture has come to depend more and more on chemical pesticides. During the last decade the use of pesticides has increased by a factor of 12 [11], and millions of kilograms of various chemicals are produced every year.

Like their precursors, modern pesticides have been a mixed blessing and the center of major environmental controversies. Although it is commonly believed that pesticides are used primarily against insects, particularly those that eat leaves and fruits of crop plants, only about one-third of pesticide sales in the United States in recent years are for this purpose. Almost 60% are herbicides (chemicals to control weed competitors of crops), and slightly less than 10% are fungicides (chemicals to control fungal plant diseases). The herbicides 2,4–D and 2,4,5–T and a contaminant from them, dioxin, are among the pesticides currently causing the most environmental concern.

Pesticides help to reduce some human diseases that are spread by insects. Prior to the use of modern insecticides, there were approximately 300 million cases and 3 million deaths annually worldwide from insect-borne diseases (primarily malaria). These figures have been reduced to 120 million cases and 1 million deaths, in spite of the great increase in the world's human population [12].

The primary problem with pesticides is that they are intentionally toxic, and if they are toxic to undesirable organisms, they may be toxic also to desirable ones, including ourselves. This danger was brought to public attention in 1962 with the publication of Rachel Carson's *Silent Spring*, a book that brought to public attention the possibility that DDT and other chemicals might be affecting the reproduction of birds [13].

DDT is a classic case of a pesticide thought to be safe and effective. Paul Muller, the discoverer of its use as an insecticide, was awarded a Nobel Prize. DDT came into widespread use after World War II and first appeared to be an amazing chemical. It contributed to the control of at least 27 diseases, and by 1953 it was credited with saving 5 million lives and preventing 100 million illnesses [12]. Early experiments, including those with human volunteers, indicated that DDT had little direct (i.e., acute) toxic effect on people, although it was recognized by 1948 that the compound was stored in body fat. DDT and other chlorinated hydrocarbons are persistent. At first, this appeared to be an advantage; for example, they could be sprayed on the walls of a house and kill mosquitoes for a long time afterward. However, their persistence in the environment became a problem.

The drainage of DDT into rivers, swamps, and coastal waters killed crabs; fish were killed in streams that drained forests where DDT had been sprayed to control the spruce budworm. Its wide distribution in the biosphere was evident when it was detected in Antarctic penguins at very low levels (1 ppb) and in canned milk, fresh cow's milk, and human milk. In high concentrations, DDT has been found to injure the livers of animals, and there is some controversial evidence that it might cause cancer.

In the 1960s, scientists recognized that widespread and rapid decrease in the weight of eggs and thickness of eggshells of birds had been occurring for the previous several decades in Britain and North America (Fig. 11.7). Both effects appeared to correlate with the use of DDT and other persistent pesticides. The eggshell thinning was found in more than 20 species, and a decrease in shell weight of 20% or more was found in 9, including the peregrine falcon, the bald eagle, and the osprey [14]. Experiments on mallard ducks verified that DDT and its chemical derivatives, particularly DDE, caused eggshell thinning.

DDT is poorly soluble in water, but quite soluble in fats and organic oils. DDT was taken up by aquatic organisms and stored in their fatty tissues or, in the case of vegetation, in oils. When these aquatic organisms or plants were eaten, the metabolism of the predators tended to favor the retention of DDT in body fat, and the predators con-

FIGURE 11.7
The egg at left will never hatch; the shell was too thin for the embryo to survive. Such eggshell thinning has been linked to the use of DDT and other pesticides.

centrated it in their own bodies. Each step in the food chain resulted in an increased concentration of DDT. Finally, the carnivorous birds at the top of the food chain seem to have built up concentrations sufficient to cause toxic effects.

As the history of DDT illustrates, fat-soluble organic compounds can have subtle, hidden, but important environmental effects. Because the compounds, poorly soluble in water, appear rare in the nonbiological environment, they are easily ignored. However, they do undergo trophic-level concentration or biomagnification, and thus negative effects can take place when the compound appears to be only a trace substance in the environment. The discovery of biomagnification has led to a better understanding of the pathways of pollutants through the environment.

In the 1960s, DDT fell from its earlier status as a miraculous saver of lives and crops to a symbol of all that was bad in our misuse of the environment. After decades of discussion, DDT still remains controversial. There is no agreement about its actual effects on human health or on the extent to which it has caused environmental damage compared with other artificial organic compounds and other forms of pollutants. Defenders of the use of DDT have pointed out that PCBs, chemicals used in the plastics industry, have similar effects and are difficult to distinguish from DDT.

Although banned in the United States, DDT is still used in other countries. Birds migrating to the United States from areas where DDT is in use may become prey for North American hawks and other birds of prey. Thus DDT may still pose an environmental problem for North America.

In recent years, there has been an attempt to develop alternative methods of pest control. Because of the problems caused by the persistence of chlorinated hydrocarbons such as DDT, shorter-lived chemicals such as organic phosphates have been used more widely. These, however, tend to have a higher acute toxicity in people and must be handled carefully. As an alternative to these toxic compounds, chemical sex attractants have been used to attract one sex of an insect into a trap, thus limiting the reproduction of more pests. This method has been used to control the bollworm in cotton.

Alternative pest control strategies, generally lumped under the name of integrated pest management (IPM), include chemical, cultural (mechanical cultivation of the soil, crop rotation, etc.), and biological (the use of predators and parasites of the pests) pest control as well as the development of pest-resistant plants. IPM has a number of advantages. In addition to reducing the use of dangerous chemicals, IPM can be used where pests have built up a resistance or tolerance to a chemical pesticide.

The use of parasites and predators of pests has proven effective. For example, the bacterium *Bacillus thuringiensis,* which causes diseases in many pests but is harmless to human beings or other mammals and birds, is now used extensively.

Industrial Chemicals

Among the artificial organic compounds similar to DDT is a group used in the production of plastic-polychlorinated biphenyls, or PCBs. PCBs are toxic to people and other organisms. An example of their effects involves an industrial plant near the

Hudson River. This plant used the chemical in producing electrical capacitors and released the wastes into the river. In 1971 striped bass in the Hudson River were found to have 11 ppm PCB in their eggs and 4 ppm in their flesh. Fish with PCB concentrations above 5 ppm exceed health safety levels; all fish in the lower Hudson River exceeded this value except shad, large sturgeon, and goldfish. The shellfish industry in the Hudson estuary, worth million of dollars, was closed. The manufacturers of PCBs voluntarily restricted production as a result of these problems. Although PCBs are no longer released into the river, cleaning up the sediments remains an important issue. Dredging may do more harm than good by dispersing the chemical more widely.

PCBs are an example of a useful chemical thought to be safe but found to be toxic and harmful to the environment. Voluntary action has reduced its production, but the chemical remains in the environment [15].

Dioxin: The Big Unknown   Dioxin is a colorless crystal made up of the elements oxygen, hydrogen, carbon, and chlorine. There are about 75 known types of dioxin that are distinguished from each other by arrangement and number of chlorine atoms in the molecule. In environmental toxicology, " dioxin " is the name given to the most poisonous of the 75, a chemical known as 2,3,7,8,-TCDD [16]. Dioxin is not normally manufactured intentionally but is a byproduct resulting from chemical reactions in the production of herbicides [17]. It is the dioxin in " agent orange, " used during the Vietnam War, that is considered to be the most toxic component of the herbicides used to defoliate large areas in the war zone. Lawsuits are still pending concerning military personnel exposed to agent orange and its dioxin.

The big unknown with dioxin is that, while the chemical is known to be extremely toxic to mammals, its actions on the human body are not well known. No one has proven that dioxin has ever killed any person, and the smallest amount that can make a person sick is not known. What is known is that sufficient exposure to dioxin produces a condition called chloracne, which is a severe form of acne that may be accompanied by loss of appetite and weight, liver disorders, and nerve damage [18]. Dioxin is also suspected to be a carcinogen.

The problem is that dioxin is a stable, long-lived chemical that is accumulating in the environment. As yet we have not been able to determine a safe, reliable, and economically feasible way to clean up areas contaminated by dioxin (Fig. 11.8). Many old waste disposal sites are contaminated by dioxin; that dioxin may be found in the soil and streams for several kilometers around the sites. The dioxin problem became well known in 1983 when the town of Times Beach, Missouri, with a population of 2400, was evacuated and purchased for $36 million by the government. The evacuation and purchase occurred after it was discovered that oil sprayed on the town's roads to control dust contained dioxin that contaminated the entire area. Since that time Times Beach has been referred to as a dioxin ghost town, and about 100 other sites in Missouri alone have been identified as having some degree of dioxin contamination present!

THERMAL POLLUTION

When heat released into water or air produces undesirable effects, thermal or heat pollution occurs. Heat pollution can occur as a sudden, acute event or as a long-term, chronic release. Sudden heat releases may emanate from natural events such as brush or forest fires and volcanoes or from anthropogenically induced events such as the firestorms during World War II or the fires following the bombing of Hiroshima. The major sources of chronic heat pollution are electric power plants that produce electricity in steam generators.

The release of large amounts of heated water into a river changes the average water temperature and thus changes the river's species composition. Every species has both a range of temperature within which it can survive and an optimal temperature. For some species of fish, this range is small, and a slight change in water temperature can disturb them. Lake fish move away when the water temperature rises more than 1.5°C above normal; river fish can withstand a rise of 3°C (Fig. 11.9) [19]. Thus heating the water can change

FIGURE 11.8
Removal of soil at a site contaminated with dioxin.

original conditions and disturb the river ecosystem.

There are several solutions to thermal discharge into bodies of water. The heat can be released into the air by cooling towers, or the heated water can be temporarily stored in artificial lagoons until it is cooled to normal temperatures. Some attempts have been made to use the heated water to grow organisms of commercial value that require warmer water temperatures.

PARTICULATES

Particulates are small particles of dust that are released into the atmosphere by many activities. Modern farming adds considerable amounts of particulates to the atmosphere, as do dust storms, fires, and volcanic eruptions [2].

Many chemical toxins, like sulfur oxides and heavy metals, enter the biosphere as particulates. However, some particulates can cause environ-

FIGURE 11.9
Acceptable temperatures for various species of fish. Trout require colder water than perch and bass, which require colder water than catfish. Heat pollution can change the species of fish that occur in a river, stream, or lake. (From Chanlett.)

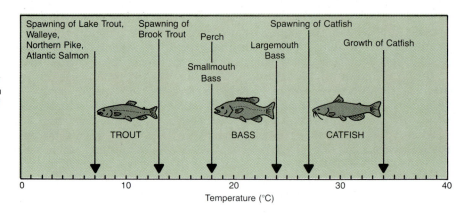

mental problems, not because of specific toxic effects of the elements or compounds that compose them, but merely because they are small particles of solids suspended in the air. In addition, some nontoxic particulates can join forces with toxic substances and thus create a dual threat.

Particulates have effects on human health, ecosystems, and the biosphere. Dust that enters the lungs may lodge there and have chronic effects on respiration. Certain materials, such as asbestos, are particularly dangerous in this way. Dust raised by road building and plowing and deposited on the surfaces of green plants may interfere with their absorption of carbon dioxide and oxygen and their release of water, and heavy dust may affect the breathing of animals. Dust associated with large construction projects may therefore kill organisms and damage large areas, changing species composition, altering food chains, and generally affecting ecosystems.

During the twentieth century, our modern industrial society has added more and more dust to the atmosphere. Dust reflects the sunlight and, when present in sufficient amounts, may thereby cool Earth's surface. In fact, the increase in atmospheric dust from human activities may offset the warming effects that may be occurring from the burning of fossil fuel and the addition of carbon dioxide to the atmosphere. Whether the cooling of the atmosphere from particulates will have a greater effect than the warming trends caused by carbon dioxide is unknown. More about toxic and toxin-joining particulates is presented in Chapter 12.

NOISE POLLUTION

Noise pollution is unwanted sound. Sound, a form of energy, is measured in units of decibels (dB). The threshold for human hearing is 1 dB, homes have an average of about 45, automobiles 70, and jet aircraft taking off about 120. A ten-fold increase in the strength of a particular sound adds 10 dB units on the scale. An increase of 100 times would add 20 units [1].

Environmental effects of noise depend not only on the total energy, but also on the sound's pitch, frequency, and time pattern. Very loud noises (more than 140 dB) cause pain, and high levels can cause permanent loss of hearing. Lower levels of noise may interfere with human communication, cause annoyance, and certainly be unpleasant. In recent years, there has been concern for teenagers (and for older people for that matter) who have suffered some permanent loss of hearing following extended exposure to amplified hard rock music. Noise in the 50–60 dB area is sufficient to interfere with sleep and produce a feeling of fatigue upon awakening. Finally, noise in the 90 dB range may cause irreversible changes in the autonomic nervous system [1].

PERSONAL POLLUTANTS

Personal pollutants are those that we ingest voluntarily for a variety of reasons. The most common are tobacco, alcohol, and other drugs. Use and abuse of these substances has led to a myriad of human ills ranging from suffering and/or dying from chronic disease, criminal activity such as reckless driving or manslaughter, street crime, loss of careers, and straining of human relations at all levels.

Tobacco

From a scientific basis there seems little doubt that cigarettes have conclusively been shown to be harmful to human health. Cigarette smoke contains a variety of components that are either toxic, carcinogenic, or radioactive.

The primary effect of smoking that people are most aware of is lung cancer. Smoking has also been suggested as a potential cause of cancers of the mouth, larynx, esophagus, pancreas, and bladder. Some authorities have gone so far as to say that smoking-related disorders may account for as many as 30% of all cancers in the United States. The American Cancer Society has stated that cigarette smoking is responsible for 85% of lung cancer in men and 75% in women. Probably not all of the potential carcinogenic material in cigarette smoke is recognized; about one half of the lung cancers attributed to smoking may be due to radioactivity in cigarette smoke. Tobacco plants are commonly fertilized with phosphates that contain uranium, which is taken up by the plants and absorbed by leaves. Radioactive materials deposited in the lungs may reside there for months or years, damaging tissue through emission of both alpha and beta radiation. Cigarette smoke also contains many other materials that are known or thought to be cocarcinogens (substances that interact or combine with other materials to cause cancer). In addition to the cancers, smoking is also related to heart disease and chronic diseases such as asthma, bronchitis, and emphysema. Finally, very young children with parents who smoke heavily at home suffer a higher incidence of diseases related to the heart and lung systems [20].

Recent studies suggest that the percentage of people who smoke in the United States is decreasing. In some circles, particularly among more educated people, the drop has been dramatic. In fact, it is becoming socially unacceptable to smoke in many locations and in many different circumstances. People are also becoming concerned about second-hand smoke. Certainly cigarette smoke is irritating to many people. Given the available evidence concerning cigarette smoking, it would seem prudent that the thinking adult would choose to not start smoking and, if addicted to cigarettes, make every effort to terminate the habit.

So-called "smokeless tobacco" products, such as chewing tobacco and snuff, are also considered dangerous. Young people who use these products may increase their risks of contracting cancer.

Alcohol

A very large portion of people in our society use alcohol at social gatherings and celebrations. Something like 70% of all American adults drink some alcohol. Moderate use of alcohol is legal and accepted in our society for the most part. However, when alcohol is abused it can become a very serious problem. It is a fairly widely quoted statistic that approximately one-half of all deaths in automobile accidents are related to drinking drivers. Furthermore, a good portion of violent criminal activity is committed by people under the influence

of alcohol. Finally, millions of people in the United States today live with alcoholic parents, brothers or sisters, or spouses, and stories of personal tragedies related to abuse of alcohol are very common indeed. In fact, it has been stated that alcohol is the most abused drug in our society [20].

Abuse of alcohol has many strong and significant effects on the human body. First of all, alcohol is a depressant, even though some people think it to be a stimulant because it tends to reduce anxiety and inhibitions in some situations. If alcohol is consumed quickly in large quantities, its depressant effects on the brain can cause death. First, the cortex of the brain stops functioning, producing a state of unconsciousness. Skin may become pale, cold, and clammy, and the cardiovascular system may slow down to a point at which the person may die from suffocation. Breathing is slowed to a point that it is no longer automatic, and because a person cannot will the lungs to breathe further, death may result. Such deaths are rare; it is much more common for alcoholics to die slowly from nutrient starvation, liver failure, and/or heart failure. In fact, the most important muscle that is affected directly by alcohol is the heart. The alcohol tends to lead to fat being deposited in the heart muscle, and as a result it becomes weaker and less able to work effectively, resulting in fatigue and shortness of breath [2].

Treatment for alcoholism involves a variety of methods, ranging from psychotherapy to use of drugs that help eliminate some of the symptoms of withdrawal, to drugs that make the individual uncomfortable if alcohol is used. Certainly one of the most effective approaches has been through the group interactions that involve active alcoholics with previous users of the drug. Although there have been tremendous strides in the identification and correction of alcoholism, the problem is going to be with society for a long time to come.

Other Drugs

There are a variety of illegal drugs commonly used in the United States and other parts of the world. These drugs have a variety of effects on their users but the end result is often the degradation of the mind and/or body. Illegal drugs, because there is often little quality control concerning their strength, composition, and other chemical characteristics, are particularly dangerous to people. It is difficult to pick up the newspaper or listen to local news without hearing of drug-related problems. Of particular concern is the rapid development of synthetic (designer) drugs that seem to be proliferating. The evidence seems all too clear that consumption of illegal drugs is one of the most serious assaults that an individual can make on his mind and body. Today there is a lot of education starting at a relatively young age concerning potential dangers of drug use. In spite of this, problems related to drug abuse are all too common, with resulting degradation to our social environment and stressing of individuals, families, institutions, and agencies connected with the problem. Finally, perhaps as much as one-third of all crime is related to drugs, involving those maintaining the drug supply systems as well as drug users desperate to obtain their supply.

OCCUPATIONAL POLLUTANTS

The history of occupational pollutants extends back at least as far as the time people began to experiment with fire, mine the minerals of the earth, and experiment with a wide variety of natural materials that might be used to make life more comfortable or the hunt easier. Today in our urban society, people spend approximately 90% of their time indoors, and a good deal of this is at the workplace, where people may come into contact with a variety of substances that are potentially harmful to their health.

Occupational and health standards at workplaces in the United States have made enormous progress during the last 100 years. Early factories were sweat shops where chemicals were freely used and people exposed to hazardous materials either knew little about them or had little recourse. Now, U.S. companies are beginning to open factories outside the country and there is some concern that we are merely exporting some of the problems to nations where standards are not so

strictly enforced and labor costs are cheap. This practice tends to move occupational pollution problems around, but not necessarily to solve them.

People in virtually all types of occupations have the potential to be exposed to harmful chemicals, dust, or other hazardous material as part of their regular work assignments. This exposure varies from well-known occupational pollutants such as radiation, coal dust, asbestos, microbes, formaldehyde, carbon monoxide, and nitrogen dioxide to a variety of materials contained in solvents and other products commonly used in the workplace by a variety of people.

In the United States today it is certainly in the best interest of employers to ensure that employees have a safe workplace. Liability issues are of such magnitude that few employers are willing to take risks with hazardous materials. On the other hand, we are working today with such a wide variety of potentially hazardous chemicals that, even if care is taken, some exposure is bound to result; effects of this will continue to range from chronic problems to acute toxicity. Furthermore, some types of employment are always going to be hazardous. Firemen will continue to be exposed to hazardous chemicals in smoke even if they are well prepared to fight fires, and personnel involved in the cleaning up of hazardous waste sites will occasionally be exposed to hazardous materials even if extreme care is taken.

GENERAL EFFECTS OF POLLUTANTS

Although there are many kinds of pollutants, each with its own method of action and environmental pathways, there are certain features that are characteristic of most environmental toxins.

Almost every part of the human body is affected by one pollutant or another (Fig. 11.10a). For example, lead and mercury affect the brain, arsenic the skin, carbon monoxide the lungs, and chlorinated hydrocarbons concentrate in the fat. Similarly, the effects of pollutants on wildlife have been documented for many organs and aspects of the life cycle (Table 11.2 and Fig. 11.10b).

FIGURE 11.10
(a) The site of effects of some major pollutants in human beings. (b) Known sites of effects of some major pollutants in wildlife. [(a) From Waldbott, G. L., *Health effects of environmental pollutants*, 2nd ed. Copyright 1978 by C. V. Mosby, St. Louis. Part (b) from Newman.]

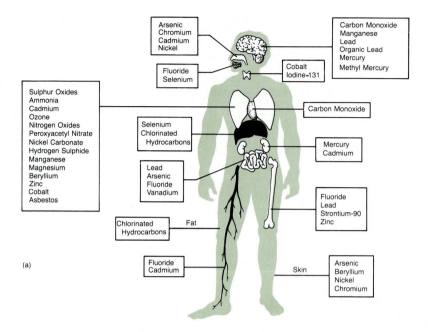

(a)

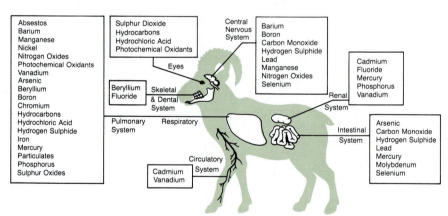

Dose-Response Curves and Threshold Effects

Five centuries ago, Paracelsus wrote that "everything is poisonous, yet nothing is poisonous." That is, essentially anything in too great amounts can be dangerous, yet anything in extremely small amounts can be relatively harmless. Every chemical element has a spectrum of possible effects on a particular organism. For example, selenium is required in small amounts by living things, but may be toxic to or cause cancer in cattle when it is in high concentrations in soil. Copper, chromium, and manganese are other examples of chemical elements that are required in small amounts but are toxic in higher amounts.

It was recognized many years ago that the effect of a certain chemical or any toxic factor on an individual depends on the dose or concentration of the toxic factor. This **dose dependency** can be represented by a generalized dose-response curve (Fig. 11.11).

TABLE 11.2
Effects of pollutants on wildlife.

Effect on Population	Pollutants
Changes in abundance	Arsenic, asbestos, cadmium, fluoride, hydrogen sulfide, nitrogen oxides, particulates, sulfur oxides, vanadium
Changes in distribution	Fluoride, particulates, sulfur oxides
Changes in birth rates	Arsenic, lead, photochemicals, oxidants
Changes in death rates	Arsenic, asbestos, beryllium, boron, cadmium, fluoride, hydrogen sulfide, lead, particulates, photochemicals, oxidants, selenium, sulfur oxides
Changes in growth rate	Borium, fluoride, hydrochloric acid, lead, nitrogen oxides, sulfur oxides

Source: From Newman.

When various concentrations of a chemical or toxic factor present in a biological system are plotted against the effects on the organism, three things are apparent. First, while relatively large concentrations are toxic, injurious, and even lethal (*D-E-F* in Fig. 11.11), trace concentrations may be beneficial or necessary for life (*A-B*). Second, the dose-response curve has two maxima (*B-C*), forming a plateau of optimal concentration and maximum benefit. Third, the threshold concentration, where harmful effects to life start, is not at the origin (zero concentration) but varies with concentrations less than at point *A* (where there is too little of the factor) and greater than at point *D* (where there is too much of the factor) in Figure 11.11.

Points *A, B, C, D, E,* and *F* in Figure 11.11 are significant threshold concentrations. Unfortunately, points *E* and *F* are known only for a few substances for a few organisms, including people, and the very important point, *D,* is all but unknown. The width of the maximum benefit plateau (points *B* and *C*) for a particular form of life depends on the organism's particular physiological

FIGURE 11.11
Generalized dose-response curve.

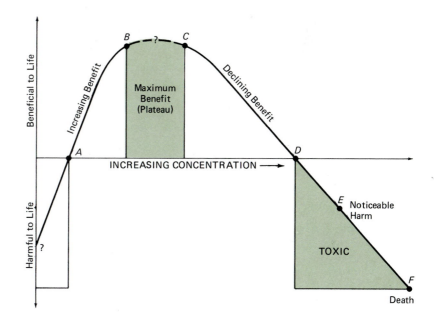

state. The levels that are beneficial, harmful, or lethal may differ widely quantitatively and qualitatively and therefore are difficult to characterize.

Fluorine in rocks and soils illustrates this general dose-response curve. Fluorine is fairly abundant in rocks and soil, and industrial activity and application of fertilizers have also, on a limited basis, contributed locally to an increase in the concentration of fluorine in soils. An important trace element, fluorine forms fluoride compounds, which prevent tooth decay. The same processes occur in bones, where fluorine promotes the development of a more perfect bone structure.

Relationships between the concentration of fluoride (in a compound of fluorine such as sodium fluoride, NaF) and health indicate a specific dose-response curve, as shown in Figure 11.12. The plateau for optimal fluoride concentration (point B to point C) for reduction of dental caries is from about 1 ppm (100 ppm = 0.01%) to just less than 5 ppm. Fluoride levels greater than 1.5 ppm do not significantly decrease tooth decay but do increase the occurrence of mottling (discoloration) of teeth. Concentrations of 4–6 ppm reduce prevalence of osteoporosis, a disease characterized by loss of bone mass. Toxic effects begin between 6 and 7 ppm (point D in Fig. 11.12).

The Toxic Dose-Response Curve   The effect of an environmental pollutant is often described by a slightly different dose-response curve, which is actually a more detailed view of the generalized curve from point D to point F in Figure 11.11. Toxic dose-response curves show a negative response, either death or injury, plotted against the increasing intensity of exposure to a pollutant. The upper limit of such curves represents 100% of the population affected. The general dose-response curve suggests there is a threshold for negative effects.

A controversy exists over whether and when thresholds can be found for environmental toxins. A threshold is a level below which no effect occurs and above which effects begin to occur. If a threshold exists, then any level in the environment below that threshold would be safe. Alternatively, it is possible that even the smallest amount of toxin has some negative effect (Fig. 11.13). Some data suggest the existence of a threshold and of a toxic dose-response curve.

For example, Figure 11.14 shows the dose-response curves for three species of trees exposed to chronic (long-term) radioactivity. These trees were in a forest that was part of an experiment at Brookhaven National Laboratory on Long Island, New

FIGURE 11.12
Dose-response curve for fluoride.

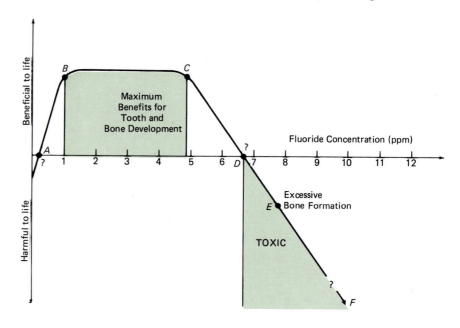

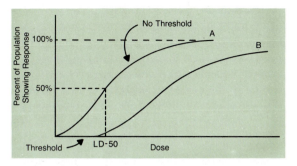

FIGURE 11.13
In this hypothetical toxic dose-response curve, toxin A has no threshold; even the smallest amount has some measurable effect on the population. The LD-50 for toxin A is the dose required to produce a response in 50% of the population.

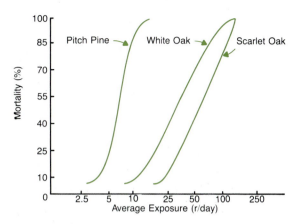

FIGURE 11.14
Dose-response curves for three species of trees exposed to gamma radiation for 32 months at Brookhaven National Laboratory. The experiment indicates that pitch pine is much more sensitive to radiation than oaks, and that scarlet oak is the least sensitive of the three species. The oaks appear to have a threshold level of about 10 roentgens/day before any mortality above that occurring in the normal forest can be measured. (From Woodwell and Rebuck.)

York, to test the effects of radioactivity on a natural ecosystem (see Plate 9). In this experiment, a source of gamma radiation, cesium-134, was placed in the center of an oak-pine forest. The cesium source was placed on a vertical shaft that could be lowered into a lead shield. The forest was irradiated for 20 hours every day for many years; during the 4 hours per day that the source was shielded, scientists could enter the forest to examine the site.

The damage to the forest by the gamma radiation varied with the species and among individuals within species. There were several clearly distinguishable zones of effects. Nearest the source, where radiation was the most intense, a completely devastated zone was produced in which all woody plants were killed. This occurred at dosages of 200 roentgens or greater per day.

The dose-response curves (Fig. 11.14) show the percentage of tree mortality as a function of the amount of radiation they received. According to the graph, essentially 100% of pitch pines were killed at an exposure of 10 roentgens/day, the level at which mortality is first measurable for white oak. Both scarlet oak and white oak can withstand ten times more radiation (100 roentgens/day) than the pine before suffering 100% mortality, suggesting that oaks have a higher threshold in regard to radiation than pitch pine.

LD-50 A concept closely linked to the dose-response curve is the amount of exposure required for 50% of the population to show a response. For death, this concept is known as the **LD-50,** the lethal dose, or the amount of exposure to a toxin that results in the death of one-half of the exposed population (see Fig. 11.13). A similar concept can be used for the exposure required to produce any nonlethal symptom in 50% of the population. The LD-50 is useful because individuals differ in their responses, and it is difficult to estimate the exact dose that will cause a response in a particular individual.

Tolerance The determination of dose-response curves may be made more difficult because of the development of tolerance in individuals and in populations. Tolerance is an increase in resistance that results from exposure. It can develop for some pollutants in some populations, but not for all pollutants in all populations.

Tolerance may result from behavioral, physiological, or genetic adaptation. As an example of behavioral response, mice learn to avoid traps. Physiological tolerance means that the body of an individual adjusts to tolerate a higher level of a pollutant. For example, people become tolerant of low oxygen at high altitudes over a period of days because the body increases the number of red blood cells. Mice and rats exposed to small doses of lead show increased resistance to death from lead, but not to all injury [21]. There are many mechanisms for physiological tolerance, including detoxification, or the internal transport of the toxin to a part of the body where it is not harmful. Genetic adaptation results when those individuals who are more resistant survive an exposure to a toxin and have more offspring than others. These resistant individuals will prevail in later generations, as has been observed among some insect pests following exposure to some chemical pesticides. For example, certain strains of malaria-causing mosquitoes are now resistant to DDT.

Acute and Chronic Effects

Pollutants can have both acute and chronic effects. An acute effect is one that occurs soon after exposure, usually to large amounts of a pollutant. A chronic effect is one that takes place over a long period, often due to exposure to low levels of a pollutant. For example, a person exposed to a high dose of radiation at one time may be killed (an acute effect), but that same total dose received slowly, in small amounts over an entire lifetime, may instead cause mutations, lead to cancer, or affect the person's offspring.

Ecological Gradients

The experiment to determine the effects of radiation on a forest at Brookhaven National Laboratory illustrates another general effect of pollutants. The species differences in dose-response effects produce a curious ecological result. The kinds of vegetation that persist nearest to the radiation source are small plants with relatively short lifetimes (grasses, sedges, and weedy species usually regarded as pests) and which are adapted to harsh and highly variable environments. Near the radiation source, a sedge persisted under radiation lev-

els of 300 roentgens/day (400–450 roentgens is enough in a single dose to kill 50% of the human beings exposed to it). Farther from the source, trees were able to survive. The changes in vegetation with distance from the radioactive cesium are similar to the kinds of changes one finds in walking down a mountain from the summit—the harshest environment—to the valley floor—the most benign environment.

The radiation also simplified the forest, decreasing the total number of species represented in the area. The nearer to the radiation source, the fewer species remained. A similar effect occurred in old fields exposed to radiation, where the diversity of vegetation was reduced 50% at radiation levels of 1000 roentgens/day [22].

The same patterns of disturbance are found around smelters and other industrial plants that discharge pollutants to the atmosphere from stacks. These patterns can be seen in the area around Sudbury, Ontario, where, as mentioned, one of the largest metal smelters in the world is located. Tall smokestacks emit toxic metals and sulfur oxides into the air. Near the smelters, an area that was once forest is now a patchwork of bare rock and soil occupied by small plants. Vegetation characteristic of disturbed areas occurs nearer to the smelters than do forest trees.

THE ULTIMATE GLOBAL POLLUTION: THERMONUCLEAR WARFARE

Increased population with continued stress on global resources in developing countries, along with industrialization and the arms race in others, is increasing the potential for a global catastrophe induced by humans. On one front are problems of desertification, deforestation, and global air and water pollution. However, the expected magnitude of disruption from these processes, while large, seems nearly insignificant compared to projected environmental consequences of a large-scale thermonuclear war. The potential effect of multiple nuclear explosions is the production of a new ''Dark Age'' in human history. It has been projected that over one billion deaths from the effects of the

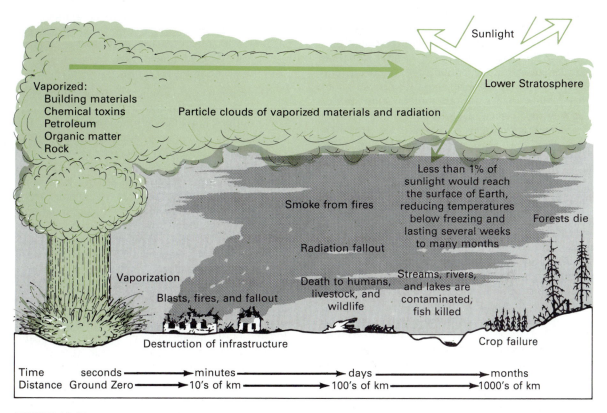

Vaporized:
Building materials
Chemical toxins
Petroleum
Organic matter
Rock

Particle clouds of vaporized materials and radiation

Sunlight

Lower Stratosphere

Less than 1% of sunlight would reach the surface of Earth, reducing temperatures below freezing and lasting several weeks to many months

Smoke from fires

Forests die

Radiation fallout

Vaporization

Blasts, fires, and fallout

Death to humans, livestock, and wildlife

Streams, rivers, and lakes are contaminated, fish killed

Destruction of infrastructure

Crop failure

Time	seconds → minutes →	days →	months
Distance	Ground Zero → 10's of km →	100's of km →	1000's of km

FIGURE 11.15
Artist's conception of the effects of thermonuclear warfare. Effects vary with distance from the blast center and over time following the event. Radiation may spread over vast areas, for example, and crop failure may occur from weeks to months later. Not to scale.

blasts, fire, and radiation would occur, and about that many people would require urgent medical care, which generally would not be available. Thus the immediate impact of such a war could kill up to 50% of all people living on Earth today.

That, however, would be only the beginning of the environmental disruption. Consideration of climatic models suggests that even a moderate nuclear war would probably plunge the earth into a "nuclear winter" characterized by extreme cold and darkness lasting several weeks to several months or more (Fig. 11.15). The nuclear winter would severely alter global ecosystems for years and render recovery by human survivors of the war very difficult indeed [23, 24]. In fact, projections of the biological effects of thermonuclear war sug-

gest that the structure and function of the biosphere would be at considerable risk [25].

Projections about the effects of thermonuclear warfare are based on model studies that predict atmospheric and biological changes as the result of large nuclear explosions that would loft tremendous amounts of gas, soot, smoke, and particles into the upper atmosphere. Temperatures resulting from the blast and fireball would be sufficient to vaporize everything close to the center of the blast. This would include all sorts of human debris—building materials, petroleum products, hazardous chemicals, organic material (including people, plants and animals)—and even nonhuman material such as bedrock. Because a fireball is less dense than the surrounding air, it would rise high into the atmosphere until a balance was achieved between the density of the fireball and that of the surrounding atmosphere. This would occur somewhere in the lower stratosphere. Assuming that the particulates would eventually be relatively uniformly spread over the Northern Hemisphere, they then would reduce the amount of sunlight that reaches the surface of Earth by a factor of more than one hundred. This effect could last anywhere from several weeks to several months and would produce sufficient darkness to inhibit photosynthesis [26]. Along with this would be freezing temperatures caused by the fact that most of the sunlight would be absorbed in the upper atmosphere, producing a tremendous temperature inversion (see Chapter 12 for more on temperature inversion). It is the development of that inversion that would cause the extreme cold at the surface of Earth, producing the "nuclear winter." Effects of the nuclear winter would impact people and nations at great distances from the nuclear conflict. Thus, in summary, the model studies have suggested that, for as long as several months following a thermonuclear war, freezing temperatures, drastically reduced sunlight reaching Earth's surface, and potentially high doses of radiation could destroy the global ecosystem structure to such an extent that extinction of the human species is a real possibility [23].

It is estimated that the world's nuclear arsenal is about 18,000 megatons (Mt) contained in 37,000–50,000 warheads. This is equivalent to 18 billion tons of trinitrotoluene (TNT), which works out to be approximately three to four tons of this explosive for every single person on earth [27]! The anticipated effects of exploding even a small portion of this arsenal are so terrible that its prevention must be given top priority over all other potential environmental problems.

POLLUTION CONTROL

If we decide that a certain substance is toxic and must be eliminated or reduced, we have the following choices:

1 Stop its production (either find a substitute or

stop using the process and products that led to the toxin's production).
2 Learn to transform it or degrade it to a harmless material at a faster rate.
3 Find a safe repository for it.

There seems little doubt that an environmental ethic is becoming an important part of our personal outlook and of government institutions. The ethic is being incorporated into our legal, political, and economic principles to such an extent that no longer is the best use of land or other resources that which returns the greatest and quickest profit. This new ethic establishes that the human race is a part of the entire land community or global ecosystem that includes soil, rocks, trees, animals, and scenery. The ethic affirms the belief that Earth is our only suitable habitat and dictates that we are morally bound to assure communities and thus, peoples, of continued existence. The right to continued existence is paramount in the issues concerning thermonuclear warfare but also figures in the consideration of a variety of pollutants in the general environment, the home, and the workplace. The ethic essentially recognizes the rights of people to breathe clean air, drink unspoiled water, and generally exist in a quality environment.

In the past, we have often taken for granted the air, water, and other resources necessary for our survival. Particularly in America we have tended to suffer and in some cases still suffer from the myth of superabundance and think of our resources as inexhaustible. In the large cities of the world, with accompanying large populations and numerous cars and industrial sites, resources are deteriorating and, as a result, regulations and laws are necessary to control pollution. This certainly is not a new trend. For example, as early as the year 1306, London's air contained large amounts of smoke from burning coal. The smoke polluted the air to such an extent that a royal proclamation was issued to curtail the use of coal. Violations of the law were reportedly punishable by death.

The most common method of controlling pollutants today is through passing laws or punishing polluters through legal action. Although scientists and other concerned people are beginning to view Earth as a closed system and a single ecosystem, we do not yet have the global legal framework nec-

The Trashing of Low Earth Orbit

The word "space" conjures up in our minds oceans of nothing between stars and planets. Yet space is far from empty: it contains high-energy radiation particles, gas clouds, dust meteorites and, since 1957, a growing array of human-made objects and debris (old rockets, payloads, fuel tanks, and remnants of previous explosions and collisions).

Although most of our space junk burns up in Earth's atmosphere, enough of our high-tech sky has fallen since the 1960s to cause concern for human safety. A chunk of *Sputnik IV* landed at an intersection in Manitowoc, Wisconsin. Pieces of the skin of John Glenn's *Atlas* booster were recovered in Africa with inspectors' hand-stamps still visible. *Skylab* dribbled a 3000–mile (4800 km) "footprint" across the Indian Ocean before the last piece fell on Australia. A section of *Cosmos 954* containing its nuclear power source landed in northern Canada.

Were we just lucky they didn't hit a large population center? Not according to a NASA study. Because so little of Earth is inhabited compared to the amount covered by water, the hazard posed by these reentries is lower than the hazard posed by entering meteorites. And because there have been few verified injuries due to meteorites over the last 200 years, the study concluded that injury or significant damage from space junk would be rare.

But in low Earth orbit—the 300–1200 nautical mile strip where most human activity takes place—the risk picture is reversed. It is more likely that spacecraft or satellites will collide with artificial debris, which orbits permanently in this narrow band, than with a meteorite, which travels through it. Although it is now possible to track more than 5000 artificial objects that are baseball-sized and larger, a more serious threat comes from the golfball-sized junk and billions of explosion fragments that cannot be tracked. The space shuttle *Challenger* returned from one flight with a crack on its windshield, and parts retrieved from the *Solar Maximum* satellite were peppered with holes. The prime suspects in both cases are tiny flakes of metal or paint propelled through space, by an explosion, at speeds as high as 18,000 mph (29,000 k/hr).

It is increasingly possible that many useful regions of low Earth orbit could inadvertently be made extremely hazardous for space operations. This "on-orbit" hazard is self-perpetuating because each launch adds more debris to the buildup that has no "natural enemies." Decay times are very long and there is little atmospheric drag to scrub it away. Also, because these terrestrial contaminants disperse randomly and at high speeds, chasing them down with an orbital "vacuum cleaner" would take too much fuel for such a procedure to be a practical solution. These two characteristics (persistence and random dispersal) also make collisions with spacecraft and other chunks of debris more likely to occur. Researchers speculate that collisions among orbital debris could breed further debris, and a runaway buildup could occur.

This low Earth orbit region could also be made deliberately hazardous. Tests of antisatellite weapons are already a major source of debris: The Soviets have already carried out a number of these tests. It is also conceivable that if "star wars" policies evolve further, the superpowers could create "minefields" of debris in regions deemed more valuable to their enemies than themselves.

These considerations and the limits we are now placing on future uses of low Earth orbit should be compelling enough to spark national and international agreements to curb space waste. If we don't do it soon, the word "space" may conjure up in our minds old rockets, payloads, fuel tanks, and explosion fragments permanently littering our cosmic doorstep.

Mary Kuhner

essary to attack pollution problems effectively at the global level. This is unfortunate because many of the pollution problems are becoming global in nature. However, as thoughts concerning this evolve, we may yet develop what is becoming known as the "global trust," which involves obligation of the present generation to future generations.

Emergence in recent years of ideas associated with a land ethic and global trust reflects our concern for future generations and our environment. As population continues to grow and demand on resources increases it will become even more important that we develop safe ways to deal with pollution problems through the variety of mechanisms at our disposal. These will continue to include laws at the federal, state, and local levels as well as, in the future, at the global level. In addition, people will have to take a stronger personal stand concerning these issues at all levels, from the home to the workplace to the entire global environment.

SUMMARY

Pollution produces an impure, defiled, dirty, or otherwise unclean state. Contamination has a meaning close to that of pollution and implies making something unfit for a particular use through introduction of undesirable materials. The term toxic refers to materials that are poisonous to people and other living things, and toxicology is the study of toxic materials, including the clinical, industrial, economic, and legal problems associated with them. A concept important in studying pollution problems is synergism, which refers to cooperative actions of different substances such that the combined effect is greater than the effect of any taken separately.

How we measure the amount of a particular pollutant introduced into the environment or the concentration of that pollutant varies widely depending upon the substance involved. Common units for the concentration of pollutants are parts per million (ppm), or parts per billion (ppb). Air pollutants are commonly measured in units such as micrograms of pollutant per cubic meter of air ($\mu g/m^3$).

Categories of environmental pollutants include toxic chemical elements (particularly heavy metals), radiation, organic compounds, heat, particulates, noise, personal pollutants such as drugs, and occupational pollutants.

Among the major elements that present hazards to the environment are mercury, lead, cadmium, nickel, arsenic, selenium, and chromium, among others. Each of these has uses in modern society and most are by-products of mining, refining, and other uses of resources. Heavy metals often have direct physiological toxic effects, and some are permanently stored or incorporated in living tissue. Heavy metals often undergo biological concentration or biomagnification as they move up the trophic levels through food chains.

The three major kinds of radiation are alpha particles, beta particles, and gamma rays. Each type of radiation has a different effect and toxicity. A particular radioisotope's degree of hazard depends on several factors, including the kind of radiation emitted, the half-life, and the chemical activity. In general, low-energy, short half-lived isotopes are less dangerous than high-energy, long half-lived isotopes. However, isotopes such as radon that readily enter a gaseous phase or are readily absorbed in water become extremely dangerous when concentrated. In the United States today, it is hypothesized that several thousand deaths per year from lung cancer are related to the radon gas problem.

A major question concerning radiation exposure to people is, When does the exposure or dose become a hazard? There are no easy answers to this question, but two hypotheses are being tested. The first is that there is a direct linear relationship between exposure and hazard, and the second is that there is some threshold of radiation which, if exceeded, will cause damage to people and other living things. Certainly for higher levels of radiation, thresholds apparently exist. The controversy is about lower doses, where effects must be measured in terms of statistics concerning health problems.

Organic compounds of carbon are produced either by living organisms or artificially. Organic compounds that are artificially produced may have physiological, genetic, or ecological effects when introduced into the environment. Some organic compounds are potentially more hazardous than others and some are more readily degraded in the environment than others. In particular, fat-soluble compounds are likely to undergo biomagnification and others are extremely toxic even at very small concentrations. Some of the organic compounds that are causing serious concern include petroleum, pesticides, and dioxin.

Heat released into water or air may produce undesirable effects known as thermopollution. The major source of such pollution is electric power plants that use water for cooling.

Particulates are small particles of dust released into the atmosphere by a variety of activities. Particulates have effects on human health, ecosystems, and the biosphere.

Noise is essentially unwanted sound. Loud noises may cause pain, disrupt people, and cause permanent hearing loss. Lower levels interfere with human communication and are annoying or unpleasant.

Personal pollutants, taken voluntarily for a variety of reasons, include tobacco, alcohol, and other drugs. Use and abuse of these substances have led to a great variety of human suffering ranging from death from chronic disease to criminal activity, loss of careers, and strain of human relations at all levels.

Occupational pollutants are those that people are exposed to as the result of their work. People in virtually all types of occupations face potential exposure to harmful chemicals, dust, or other hazardous materials as part of their regular work assignments.

Almost every part of the human body is affected by one pollutant or another. For example, lead and mercury affect the brain, arsenic the skin, carbon monoxide the lungs, and chlorinated hydrocarbons concentrate in the fat. Furthermore, effects of pollutants on wildlife have been documented for many organisms.

The effect of certain chemicals or toxic materials on an individual depends upon the dose or concentration of that material. Toxic dose-response curves show a negative response, either death or injury, plotted against increasing intensity or exposure to a pollutant. Closely linked is the amount of exposure required for 50% of the population to show a response. For death, this concept is known as the LD-50—the lethal dose or amount of exposure that results in death of one-half of the exposed population.

With respect to pollutants and toxins, it is also important to determine potential tolerances of individuals as well as acute and chronic effects.

Pollution control begins with the individual in the home or workplace. Many laws and ordinances have been passed by state and local governments, as well as by the federal government, to improve quality of life and reduce threats of environmental pollution.

The ultimate global pollution comes from the threat of thermonuclear warfare. The global effect of such a war would be to produce a new "Dark Age" in human history that could destroy a significant part, if not all, of the biological support system necessary to support human life, perhaps causing extinction of the human species. Model studies suggest that the huge quantities of dust, soot, and particles that would be blown into the upper atmosphere would cause a "nuclear winter" that would last from several weeks to several months. Subfreezing temperatures and lack of light would result. Anticipated effects of nuclear war are so terrible and so widespread that its prevention must be given top priority over all other potential environmental problems.

STUDY QUESTIONS

1 What kind of life forms would most likely survive in a highly polluted world? After a nuclear war? What would their general ecological characteristics be?

2 Some environmentalists argue that there is no such thing as a "threshold" for pollution effects. What is meant by this statement? How would you de-

termine if it were true for a specific chemical and its effects on a specific species?

3 What is a "reversible" effect of a pollutant?

4 What is biomagnification?

5 You are lost in Transylvania while trying to locate Dracula's castle. Your only clue is that the soil around the castle has an unusually high concentration of the heavy metal arsenic. You wander in a dense fog, only able to see the ground a few meters in front of you. What changes in vegetation warn you that you are nearing the castle?

6 Distinguish between acute and chronic effects of pollutants.

7 Design an experiment to test whether tomatoes or cucumbers are more sensitive to lead pollution.

8 Why is it difficult to establish standards for acceptable levels of pollution? In giving your answer, distinguish among the geological, climatological, biological, and social reasons.

9 You are hiking in the Blue Ridge Mountains of Virginia. You notice a blue haze on the hills in the distance. Your companion says, "That haze is produced by trees. If trees pollute the air, so can we—it's perfectly natural." Would you agree or disagree? State your reasons.

10 In what ways is controlling pollution from solid wastes easier than controlling air pollution?

11 A new highway is built through a pine forest. Driving along the highway, you notice that the pines nearest the road have turned brown and are dying. You stop at a rest area and walk into the woods. One hundred meters away from the highway the trees seem undamaged. How could you make a crude dose-response curve from direct observations of the pine forest? What else would be necessary to devise a dose-response curve from direct observation of the pine forest? What else would be necessary to devise a dose-response curve that could be used in planning the route of another highway?

12 Why is arsenic a poor choice as a pesticide?

FURTHER READING

ALEXANDER, M. 1981. Biodegradation of chemicals of environmental concern. *Science* 211: 132–38.

BOND, R. G., and STRAUB, C. P. 1973–74. *CRC handbook of environmental control.* Cleveland: CRC Press.

BUTLER, G. C. 1978. *Principles of ecotoxicology.* (SCOPE Report No. 12.) New York: Wiley.

CHANLETT, E. T. 1979. *Environmental protection.* 2nd ed. New York: McGraw-Hill.

GROVER, H. D., and HARWELL, M. A. 1985. Biological effects of nuclear war II: Impact on the biosphere. *BioScience* 35: 576–83.

GROVER, H. D., and WHITE, G. F. 1985. Toward understanding the effects of nuclear war. *BioScience* 35: 552–56.

EHRLICH, P. R.; HARTE, J.; HARWELL, M. A.; RAVEN, P. H.; SAGAN, C.; WOOD-WELL, G. M.; AYENSU, E. S.; EHRLICH, A. H.; EISNER, T.; GOULD, S. J.; GROVER, H. D.; HERRARA, R.; MAY, R. M.; MAYR, E.; McKAY, C. P.; MOONEY, H. A.; MYERS, N.; PIMENTAL, D.; and TEAL, J. M. 1983. Long-term biological consequences of nuclear war. *Science* 222: 1293–1300.

HOLDGATE, M. D. 1979. *A perspective of environmental pollution.* Cambridge, England: Cambridge University Press.

HORNE, R. A. 1978. *The chemistry of our environment.* New York: Wiley.

MUDD, J. B., and KOZLOWSKI, T. T. 1975. *Responses of plants to air pollution.* New York: Academic Press.

NATIONAL ACADEMY OF SCIENCES. 1981. *Testing for effects of chemicals on ecosystems.* Washington, D.C.: National Academy of Sciences.

OFFICE OF TECHNOLOGY ASSESSMENT. 1979. *Pest management strategies in crop protection.* Vol. 1.

SCHLESINGER, W.; REINERS, W.; and KNOPMAN, D. 1974. Heavy metal concentrations and deposition in bulk precipitation in montane ecosystems of New Hampshire, U. S. A. *Environmental Pollution* 6: 39–47.

STEPHENS, S. L., and BIRKS, J. W. 1985. After nuclear war: Perturbations in atmospheric chemistry. *BioScience* 35: 557–62.

STOKER, H. S., and SEAGER, S. L. 1976. *Environmental chemistry: Air and water pollution.* 2nd ed. Glenview, Ill.: Scott Foresman.

WALDBOTT, G. L. 1978. *Health effects of environmental pollutants.* 2nd ed. St. Louis: C. V. Mosby.

12

Air Pollution

- If human activities that pollute the air exceed the natural abilities of the atmosphere to remove wastes, then acute or chronic conditions that affect human health and well-being may result.
- Air pollution created by humans has been recognized for more than 700 years. Recent efforts to control air quality have been in response to increased health problems and economic loss resulting from air pollution.
- Meteorological conditions and atmospheric chemical interactions can determine whether polluted air is only a nuisance or a major health problem.
- Pollution problems are different in different regions: contributing factors include patterns of urbanization, population concentration, industry, and transportation facilities as well as climate factors and local to regional geography.
- Acidic deposition occurs near and far downwind of places where fossil fuels are burned. Areas particularly sensitive to acid rain include those in which the bedrock and soils cannot buffer the acid input.
- The best strategies for controlling air pollutants include those that collect, capture, or retain pollutants before they enter the atmosphere.
- Air pollutants affect many aspects of the environment, including visual aesthetics, vegetation, animals, soils, water quality, natural and artificial structures, and human health.

LONDON SMOG OF THE 1950s

In London, during the first week of December 1952, the air became stagnant and the cloud cover did not allow much of the incoming solar radiation to penetrate. The humidity climbed to 80%, and the temperature dropped rapidly until the noontime temperature was about −1°C. A very thick fog developed, and the cold and dampness increased the demand for home heating. Because the primary fuel used in homes was coal, emissions of ash, sulfur oxides, and soot increased rapidly. The stagnant air became filled with pollutants, not only from home heating fuels but from automobile exhaust. At the height of the crisis, visibility was greatly reduced and automobiles had to use their headlights at midday. Between December 4 and 10, an estimated 4000 people died from the pollution. Figure 12.1 shows the increase in sulfur dioxide and smoke and the accompanying deaths during this period. The siege of smog finally ended when the weather changed and the air pollution was dispersed. The environment, not human activities, finally solved this problem. Since the beginning of the industrial revolution and before, people had survived in London and other major cities in spite of the weather and of pollution. What had finally gone wrong?

During the London smog crisis, the stagnant weather conditions together with the number of homes burning coal and cars burning gasoline exceeded the atmosphere's ability to remove or transform the pollutants; even the usually rapid natural mechanisms for removing sulfur dioxide were saturated. As a result, sulfur dioxide remained in the air and the fog became acid, adversely affecting people and other organisms, particularly vegetation. The health effects on people were especially destructive because small acid droplets became fixed on larger particulates, facilitating their being drawn deep into the lungs.

The 1952 London smog crisis was a landmark event. Finally, human activities had exceeded the natural abilities of the atmosphere to serve as a sink for the removal of wastes. The crisis was due in part to a positive, or reinforcing, feedback situation. Burning fossil fuels added particulates to the air, increasing the formation of fog and decreasing

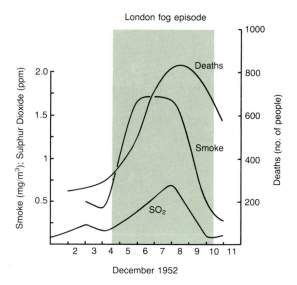

FIGURE 12.1
The relationship between the number of deaths and the London fog of 1952. (Modified from Williamson.)

visibility and light transmission; the dense, smoggy layer increased the dampness and cold and accelerated the use of home heating fuels. The worse the weather and the pollution, the more people acted so as to further worsen the weather and the pollution.

Before 1952, London was well known for its fogs; what was relatively little known was the role of coal burning in the accentuation of fog conditions. Since 1952, London fogs have been greatly reduced because coal has been replaced to a large extent by much cleaner gas as the primary home heating fuel. A foggy day in London is now not so common and no longer seems quite so romantic.

THE ATMOSPHERE

The atmosphere is a great resource. The movement of air across Earth's surface, as local winds or as weather fronts, continually renews the air around us. The atmosphere is a complex chemical factory, with many little-understood reactions taking place within it. Many of these reactions are strongly influenced by sunlight and by compounds produced by life.

The air is a mixture of nitrogen (78%), oxygen (21%), argon (0.9%), carbon dioxide (0.03%), and other trace elements and compounds, including methane, ozone, hydrogen sulfide, carbon monoxide, oxides of nitrogen and sulfur, hydrocarbons, and various particulates. The atmosphere's most variable component is water vapor (H_2O), which can range from 0 to 4% by volume in the lower troposphere (the portion of the atmosphere below the stratosphere—11–16 km from Earth's surface). The maximum amount of water vapor that can be held in the air is temperature dependent—warmer air can potentially hold more water than cooler air. It is this small variable amount of water vapor in the atmosphere that supplies the precipitation in the hydrologic cycle that is necessary for survival of most of the biosphere [1].

Except for molecular argon and other noble or inert gases, all the compounds in Earth's atmosphere are either produced primarily by biological activity or greatly affected by the biota. Although the atmosphere has been greatly modulated by life during the last 3.5 billion years, we consider most of these alterations to be natural; that is, they have produced an atmosphere whose makeup is relatively constant and essential to our own survival.

Ever since life began on Earth, the atmosphere has been an important resource for chemical elements and a medium for the deposition of wastes. The earliest plants that carried out photosynthesis dumped oxygen—the element that was their waste—into the atmosphere. The long-term increase in atmospheric oxygen, in turn, made possible the development and survival of higher life forms that required high rates of metabolism and rapid use of energy. For our biological ancestors and for ourselves, oxygen became a necessary resource for respiration, the process by which we burn our internal biological fuels and provide the energy to sustain our life processes.

As the fastest moving fluid medium in the environment, the atmosphere has always been one of the most convenient places to dispose of unwanted materials. Ever since fire was first used by people, the atmosphere has all too often been a sink for waste disposal.

POLLUTION OF THE ATMOSPHERE

Chemical pollutants can be thought of as compounds that are in the wrong place or in the wrong concentrations at the wrong time. As long as a chemical is transported away or degraded rapidly relative to its rate of production, there is no pollution problem. Pollutants that enter the atmosphere through natural or artificial emissions may be degraded not only within the atmosphere but also by natural processes in the hydrologic and geochemical cycles; on the other hand, pollutants that leave the atmosphere may become pollutants of water and of geological cycles.

People have long recognized the existence of atmospheric pollutants, both natural pollutants and those induced by humans. Perhaps one of the first laws attempting to control air pollution was enacted in 1273, when the king of England convinced Parliament to pass an act that prohibited the burning of soft coal in London. Enforcement evidently was strict; one man reportedly was executed for burning forbidden coal. Leonardo da Vinci wrote in 1550 that a blue haze formed from materials emitted into the atmosphere from plants—he had observed a natural photochemical smog whose cause is still not completely understood.

Acid rain was first described in the seventeenth century, and by the eighteenth century it was known that smog and acid rain damaged plants in London. Beginning with the industrial revolution in the eighteenth century, air pollution became more noticeable; by the middle of the nineteenth century, particularly following the American Civil War, concern with air pollution increased. The word ''smog'' was probably introduced by a physician at a public health conference in 1905 to denote poor air quality resulting from a mixture of smoke and fog.

Two major pollution events, one in the Meuse Valley in Belgium in 1930 and the other in Donora, Pennsylvania, in 1948, were responsible for raising the level of scientific research about air pollution. The Meuse Valley event lasted approximately one week and caused 60 deaths and numerous illnesses. The Donora event caused 20 deaths and

14,000 illnesses. By the time of the Donora event, people recognized that meteorological conditions were an integral part of the production of dangerous smog events. This view was reinforced by the 1952 London smog crisis, after which regulations to control air quality began to be formulated. Today, in the United States and in many other countries, legislation to reduce emission of air pollutants has been successful, but much more needs to be done in many areas.

General Effects of Air Pollution

The effects of air pollution are considerable and impact many aspects of our environment: visually aesthetic resources, vegetation, animals, soils, water quality, natural and artificial structures, and human health. Air pollutants affect visual resources by discoloring the atmosphere, reducing visual range and atmospheric clarity so that the visual contrast of distant objects is decreased. We can't see as far in polluted air, and what we do see has less color contrast. These effects were once limited to cities, but they now extend even to the wide open spaces of the United States. For example, emissions from the Four Corners fossil fuel-burning power plant, near the area where the borders of New Mexico, Arizona, Colorado, and Utah meet, is altering the visibility in a region where one has been able to see 80 km from a mountain top on a normally clear day [2].

Effects of air pollution on vegetation include damage to leaf tissue, needles, or fruit; reduction in growth rates or suppression of growth; increased susceptibility to a variety of diseases, pests, and adverse weather; and the disruption of reproductive processes. Damage to entire terrestrial or aquatic ecosystems in turn can affect the vegetation [2].

Effects of air pollutants on vertebrate animals include impairment of the respiratory system; damage to eyes, teeth, and bones; increased susceptibility to disease, pests, or other stress-related environmental hazards; decrease in availability of food sources such as vegetation impacted by air pollutants; and reduction in ability to reproduce [2].

Air pollution can affect soil and water when the pollutants in the air are deposited in soil and water. Soils and water may become toxic from the deposition of various pollutants. Soils may also be leached of nutrients by pollutants that form acids.

Air pollutants can greatly affect human health. Some of the primary effects include toxic poisoning, eye irritation, and irritation of the respiratory system. In urban areas people suffering from respiratory diseases are likely to be affected by air pollutants. Healthy people tend to acclimate to pollutants in a relatively short period of time. Nevertheless, urban air can be a serious health problem. Many of the pollutants have synergistic effects; for example, sulfate and nitrate may attach to particles in the air, facilitating their inhalation deep into lung tissue.

Effects of air pollution on artificial structures include discoloration, erosion, and decomposition of building materials, as discussed in the section on acid rain.

Sources of Air Pollution

Many of the pollutants in our atmosphere have natural as well as human-related origins. Examples of natural emissions of air pollutants include release of gases such as sulfur dioxide through volcanic eruptions; release of hydrogen sulfide from geyser and hot spring activities and by biological decay from bogs and marshes; increased concentration of ozone in the lower atmosphere as a result of unstable meteorological conditions, including violent thunderstorms; and emission of a variety of particles from wildfires and windstorms [2].

Major natural and human-produced air pollutants and sources are shown in Table 12.1. These data suggest that, with the exception of sulfur and nitrogen oxides, natural emissions of air pollutants exceed human-produced input. Nevertheless, it is the human component that is most abundant in urban areas and leads to the most severe air pollution events for human health.

The two major kinds of air pollution sources are stationary and mobile. Stationary sources are those that have a relatively fixed location. These include point sources, fugitive sources, and area sources. Point sources are those stationary sources that emit air pollutants from one or more discrete controllable sites such as smokestacks of power

TABLE 12.1
Major natural and human-produced components of air pollutants.

Air Pollutant	Emissions (% of total)		Human-produced Component Major Sources	%
	Natural	Human-produced		
Particulates	89	11	Industrial processes	51
			Combustion of fuels (stationary sources)	26
Sulfur oxides (SO_x)	55	45	Combustion of fuels: (stationary sources, mostly coal)	78
			Industrial processes	18
Carbon monoxide (CO)	91	9	Transportation (mostly automobiles)	75
			Agricultural burning	9
Nitrogen dioxide (NO_2)		Nearly all	Transportation (mostly automobiles)	52
			Combustion of fuels (stationary sources, mostly natural gas and coal)	44
Ozone (O_3)	A secondary pollutant derived from reactions with sunlight, NO_2 and oxygen (O_2)		Concentration that is present depends on reaction in lower atmosphere involving hydrocarbons and thus automobile exhaust	
Hydrocarbons (HC)	84	16	Transportation (mostly automobiles)	56
			Industrial processes	16
			Evaporation of organic solvents	9
			Agricultural burning	8

plants at industrial sites. Fugitive sources are types of stationary sources that generate air pollutants from open areas exposed to wind processes. Examples include dirt roads, construction sites, farmlands, storage piles, surface mines, and other exposed areas from which particulates may be removed by wind. Area sources are the final type of stationary sources and are locations from which air pollutants are emitted from a well-defined area within which are several sources, as, for example, small urban communities or areas of intense industrialization within urban complexes. Mobile sources are those emitters of air pollutants that move from place to place while actually in the process of yielding emissions. These include automobiles, aircraft, ships, and trains [2].

AIR POLLUTANTS*

There are two main groups of air pollutants: primary and secondary. Primary pollutants are those that are emitted directly into the air and include

*This section is summarized from *Air Resources Management Manual,* National Park Service, 1984.

particulates, sulfur oxides, carbon monoxide, nitrogen oxides, and hydrocarbons. Secondary pollutants are those produced through reactions among primary pollutants and normal atmospheric compounds. As an example, over urban areas ozone forms through reactions among primary pollutants, sunlight, and natural atmospheric gases. Thus ozone becomes a serious pollution problem on bright, sunny days in areas where there is much primary pollution. This has been particularly well documented for southern California cities like Los Angeles, but occurs worldwide under appropriate conditions.

The primary pollutants that account for nearly all air pollution problems are particulates, hydrocarbons, carbon monoxide, nitrogen oxides, and sulfur oxides. Each year well over a billion metric tons of these materials enter the atmosphere from human-related processes. About half of this is carbon monoxide, and the other four each account for a few percent. At first glance this amount of pollutants appears to be very large. However, if the pollutants were uniformly distributed in the atmosphere, it would amount to only a few parts per million by weight. Unfortunately, pollutants are not uniformly distributed, but tend to be released, produced, and concentrated locally or regionally as a function of variable rates of input, storage, and output of potential pollutants in the lower atmosphere. For example, in large cities weather and climatic conditions along with urbanization-industrialization combine to produce air pollution problems that exist primarily over large urban centers.

The major air pollutants occur either in a gaseous form or as particulate matter (PM). The gaseous pollutants include sulfur dioxide (SO_2), nitrogen oxides (NO_x), carbon monoxide (CO), ozone (O_3), hydrocarbons (HC), hydrogen sulfide (H_2S), and hydrogen fluoride (HF). Particulate-matter pollutants are particles of solid or liquid substances and may be either organic or inorganic.

Sulfur Dioxide

Sulfur dioxide (SO_2) is a colorless and odorless gas under normal conditions at Earth's surface. One of the significant aspects concerning SO_2 is that once it is emitted into the atmosphere it may be converted through complex reactions to fine particulate sulfate (SO_4). The major source for the anthropogenic component of sulfur dioxide is burning of fossil fuels, mostly coal in power plants. Another major source is a variety of industrial processes ranging from refining of petroleum to production of paper, cement, and aluminum.

Destructive effects associated with sulfur dioxide include corrosion of paint and metals and injury or death to plants and animals, especially to crops such as alfalfa, cotton, and barley. Sulfur dioxide is capable of causing severe damage to human and other animal lungs, particularly in the sulfate form.

Nitrogen Oxides (NO_x)

Nitrogen oxides are emitted in several forms. The most important of these is nitrogen dioxide (NO_2), which is a visible yellow-brown to reddish-brown gas. A major concern with nitrogen dioxide is that it may be converted by complex reactions in the atmosphere to fine particulate nitrate (NO_3). Additionally, nitrogen dioxide is one of the main pollutants that contribute to the development of photochemical smog. Nearly all nitrogen dioxide is emitted from anthropogenic sources; the two major contributors are automobiles and power plants that burn fossil fuels such as coal and oil.

Environmental effects of nitrogen oxides are variable but include irritation of eyes, nose, and throat; increased susceptibility of animals and humans to infections; suppression of plant growth and damage to leaf tissue; and impaired visibility when the oxides are converted to their nitrate form in the atmosphere. On the other hand, when nitrate is deposited on the soil, it can act to promote plant growth.

Carbon Monoxide

Carbon monoxide (CO) is a colorless, odorless gas that at very low concentrations is extremely toxic to humans and other animals. The toxicity of carbon monoxide to animals results because of a striking physiological effect—namely, that carbon monoxide and hemoglobin naturally have a strong attraction for one another. Hemoglobin in our blood will take up carbon monoxide nearly 250 times more rapidly than it will oxygen. Therefore if there is any carbon monoxide in the vicinity, a person will take it in very readily, with potential dire effects. Many people have been unintentionally asphyxiated by carbon monoxide produced from incomplete combustion of fuels in campers, tents, and houses. Actual effects may range from dizziness and headaches to death. Carbon monoxide is particularly hazardous to people with known heart disease, anemia, or respiratory disease. Finally, the effects of carbon monoxide tend to be worse in the higher altitudes, where oxygen levels are naturally lower.

Approximately 90% of the carbon monoxide in the atmosphere comes from natural sources and the other 10% comes mainly from sources such as fires, automobiles, and other sources of incomplete burning of organic compounds. The problem is that local concentrations of carbon monoxide can build up and cause serious health effects in a localized area.

Ozone

Photochemical oxidants result from atmospheric interactions of pollutants (such as nitrogen dioxide) and sunlight. The most common photochemical oxidant is ozone (O_3), which is a colorless, unstable gas with a slightly sweet odor.

Ozone is a form of oxygen in which three atoms of oxygen occur together rather than the normal two. Ozone is relatively unstable and releases its third oxygen atom readily, so that it oxidizes or burns things more readily and at lower concentrations than does normal oxygen. Ozone is sometimes used to sterilize; for example, bubbling ozone gas through water is a method used to purify water. However, when it is released into the air or produced in the air, ozone injures things that we wish to have unharmed, including ourselves.

Ozone is so active chemically that it has a very short average lifetime in the air. Its production is often the result of complex chemical reactions involving sunlight and several chemical compounds. As we discussed in Chapter 2, ozone, owing to the effect of sunlight on normal oxygen, forms a natural layer high in the atmosphere (stratosphere). This ozone layer is very beneficial, protecting us from harmful ultraviolet light from the sun. Thus, ozone is a pollutant when present in the lower atmosphere at high concentrations but is beneficial in the stratosphere (Fig. 12.2).

The major sources of oxidants, and particularly ozone, are automobiles and burning of fossil fuels as well as industrial processes that produce nitrogen dioxide. Effects of oxidants, primarily ozone, are well known and include, among others, damage to rubber, paint, and textiles as well as a variety of biological effects, including damage to plants and animals.

The effects of ozone on plants can be subtle. At very low concentrations, ozone can reduce growth rates while not producing any visible injury. At higher concentrations, ozone kills leaf tissue, eventually killing entire leaves and, if the pollutant levels remain high, killing whole plants. The death of white pine trees planted along highways in New England is believed due to ozone from automobiles. Ozone also affects animals, including people, causing a variety of damage, especially to the eyes and the respiratory system.

Hydrocarbons

Hydrocarbons are compounds composed of hydrogen and carbon. There are thousands of such compounds, including natural gas or methane (CH_4), butane (C_4H_{10}), and propane (C_3H_8). Analysis of urban air has identified many different hydrocarbons, some of which are much more reactive with sunlight to produce photochemical smog than others. Potential adverse effects of hydrocarbons are numerous because many are toxic to plants and animals or may be converted to harmful compounds through complex chemical changes that occur in the atmosphere. Approximately 85% of hydrocarbons (which are primary pollutants) that enter the atmosphere are emitted from natural sources. The most important anthropogenic source is the automobile (see Table 12.1).

Hydrogen Sulfide

Hydrogen sulfide (H_2S) is a highly toxic corrosive gas easily identified by its rotten egg odor. Hydrogen sulfide is produced from natural sources such as geysers, swamps, and bogs, as well as from human sources such as plants that produce petroleum and that smelt metals. Potential effects of hydrogen sulfide include functional damage to plants

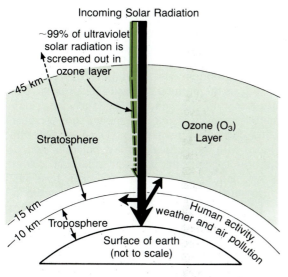

FIGURE 12.2
Structure of the atmosphere.

and health problems ranging from toxicity to death for humans and other animals.

Hydrogen Fluoride

Hydrogen fluoride (HF) is a gaseous pollutant that is released primarily by industrial activities such as production of aluminum, coal gasification, and burning of coal in power plants. Hydrogen fluoride is a very toxic gas and even a small concentration (as low as 1 ppb) may cause problems for plants and animals. Hydrogen fluoride is particularly dangerous to grazing animals because some plants that the animals eat can be very toxic.

Other Hazardous Gases

It's a rare month when the newspapers don't carry a story of a truck or train accident that releases toxic chemicals in a gaseous form into the atmosphere. As a result people are often evacuated until the leak is stopped or the gas dispersed to a non-toxic level. Chlorine gases are often involved, but a variety of other materials used in chemical and agricultural processes may be involved.

Another source of air pollution is sewage treatment plants. Urban areas deliver a tremendous variety of organic chemicals, including paint thinner, industrial solvents, chloroform, and methyl chloride to treatment plants by way of sewers. These materials are not removed in the treatment plants; in fact, the treatment processes facilitate the evaporation of the chemicals into the atmosphere, where they may be inhaled by people. Many of the chemicals are toxic and/or are suspected of causing cancers. It is a cruel twist of fate that the treatment plants designed to control water pollution are becoming sources of air pollution. This is leading to the understanding that while some pollutants can be moved from one location to another and even change form, as from liquid to gas, we really can't as easily get rid of them as we once thought.

Some chemicals are so toxic that extreme care must be taken to ensure that they don't enter the environment. This was tragically learned again on December 3, 1984, when toxic gas (stored in liquid form) from a pesticide plant leaked, vaporized, and formed a toxic cloud that settled over a 64-km² area of Bhopal, India. The gas leak lasted less than one hour—yet over 2000 people were killed and more than 15,000 were injured by the gas, which causes severe irritation (burns on contact) to eyes, nose, throat, and lungs. Breathing the gas in large quantities, in concentrations of only a few parts per million, causes violent coughing, swelling of the lungs, bleeding, and death. Less exposure can cause a variety of problems, including loss of sight.

The colorless gas, called methyl isocyanate, is an ingredient of the common pesticide known in the United States as Sevin and of at least two other insecticides used in India. Another plant located in West Virginia also makes the chemical; small leaks have evidently occurred there as they did prior to the catastrophic accident in Bhopal. The accident clearly suggests that hazardous chemicals that can cause catastrophic injuries and death should not be stored close to large populations of people. Furthermore, more reliable accident-prevention equipment and personnel trained to control leaks or other problems at chemical plants are needed as well.

Particulate Matter

Particulate matter encompasses the small particles of solid or liquid substances that are released into the atmosphere by many activities. Modern farming adds considerable amounts of particulate matter to the atmosphere, as do desertification and volcanic eruptions. Nearly all industrial processes, as well as the burning of fossil fuels, release particulates into the atmosphere. Much particulate matter is easily visible as smoke, soot, or dust; other particulate matter is not easily visible. Included with the particulates are materials such as airborne asbestos particles and small particles of heavy metals such as arsenic, copper, lead, and zinc, which are usually emitted from industrial facilities such as smelters. Of particular importance with reference to particulates are the very fine particle pollutants less than $2.5\mu m$ in diameter (2.5 millionths of a meter—a very small distance indeed). Among the most significant of the fine particulate pollutants are sulfates and nitrates. These are primarily secondary pollutants produced in the atmosphere through chemical reactions between normal atmospheric constituents and sulfur dioxide and nitrogen oxides. These reactions are particularly important in the formation of sulfuric and nitric acids in the atmosphere and will be discussed further in the section on acid rain [2]. When measured, particulate matter is often referred to as total suspended particulates (TSP).

Particulates have effects on human health, ecosystems, and the biosphere. Particulates that enter the lungs may lodge there and have chronic effects on respiration. Certain materials, such as asbestos, are particularly dangerous in this way. Dust raised by road building and plowing and deposited on the surfaces of green plants may interfere with their absorption of carbon dioxide and oxygen and their release of water; heavy dust may affect the breathing of animals. Particulates associated with large construction projects may therefore kill organisms and damage large areas, changing species composition, altering food chains, and generally affecting ecosystems. In addition, modern industrial processes have greatly increased the total suspended particulates in Earth's atmosphere. Particulates block sunlight and thus cause changes in climate. Such changes have lasting effects on the biosphere.

Asbestos Asbestos particles have only recently been recognized as a significant hazard. In the past, asbestos was treated rather casually, and people working in asbestos plants were not protected from dust. Asbestos was used in building insulation and in brake pads for automobiles. As a result, a considerable amount of asbestos fibers have been spread throughout industrialized countries, especially those of Europe and North America, and especially within urban environments. In one case, the products of asbestos were sold in burlap bags that eventually were used in nurseries and other secondary businesses, thus further spreading the pollutant. Asbestos particles are believed to be carcinogenic, or to carry with them carcinogenic materials, and so must be carefully controlled.

Lead Lead is an important constituent of automobile batteries and other industrial products. When lead is added to gasolines, automobile engines burn more evenly. The lead in gasoline is emitted into the environment in the exhaust. In this way, lead has been spread widely around the world and has reached high levels in soils and waters along roadways.

Once released, lead can be transported through the air as particulates to be taken up by plants through the soil or deposited directly on plant leaves. Thus it enters terrestrial food chains.

When lead is carried by streams and rivers, deposited in quiet waters, or transported to the ocean or lakes, it is taken up by aquatic organisms and thus enters aquatic food chains.

The concentration of lead in Greenland glaciers (Fig. 12.3) shows that lead was essentially at zero concentration in the ice around A.D. 800 and reached measurable levels with the beginning of the industrial revolution in Europe. The lead content of the glacial ice increased steadily from 1750 until the mid-twentieth century, when the rate of accumulation by the glaciers increased rapidly. This increase reflects the rapid growth in the use of the internal combustion engine in automobiles and trucks and the use of lead additives in gasoline. Lead reaches the Greenland glaciers as air-

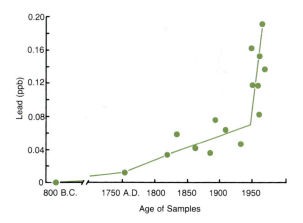

FIGURE 12.3
Concentration of lead in Greenland glaciers. In the Middle Ages, essentially no lead fell on Greenland glaciers. With the beginning of the industrial revolution, the amount of lead reaching Greenland began to increase. The steep rise after 1940 reflects the increasing use of automobiles and lead additives to gasoline. (From Murozimi et al.)

borne particulates and by sea water. The accumulation of lead in these glaciers demonstrates that our use of heavy metals in this century has reached a point where the entire biosphere is affected. The reduction and eventual elimination of lead in gasoline will, we hope, reverse this.

Cadmium Cadmium may enter the environment in part in the ash from burned coal. Cadmium, a trace element in the coal, exists in a very low concentration of 0.05 ppm. The ash is spread widely from stacks and chimneys and falls on plants, where the cadmium is incorporated into plant tissue and concentrated three to seven times. As the cadmium moves up the trophic levels through the food chains, each trophic level concentrates it approximately three times over what it was in the next lower trophic level. Herbivores have approximately three times the concentration of green plants, and carnivores approximately three times the concentration of herbivores.

URBAN AREAS AND AIR POLLUTION

Wherever there are many sources producing air pollutants over a wide area—automobile emissions in Los Angeles or smoke from wood-burning stoves in Vermont—there is potential for the development of smog. Whether air pollution develops depends on the topography and weather conditions, because these factors determine the rate at which pollutants are transported away from their sources and converted to harmless compounds in the air. When the rate of production exceeds the rate of chemical transformations and of transport, dangerous conditions may develop.

Influence of Meteorology and Topography

Meteorological conditions can determine whether air pollution is only a nuisance or is a major health problem. The primary adverse effects of air pollution are damage to green plants and aggravation of chronic illnesses in people. Most of these effects are due to relatively low-level concentrations of toxins over a long period of time. Pollution periods in the Los Angeles basin or other areas generally do not cause large numbers of deaths. However, as with the London, Belgium, and Pennsylvania cases mentioned, serious pollution events can develop over a period of days and lead to an increase in deaths and illnesses.

In the lower atmosphere, restricted circulation associated with inversion layers may lead to pollution events. An **atmospheric inversion** occurs when warmer air is found above cooler air and is particularly a problem when there is a stagnated air mass. Figure 12.4 shows two types of developing inversions that may worsen air pollution problems. In the upper diagram, which is somewhat analogous to the situation in the Los Angeles area, descending warm air forms a semipermanent inversion layer. Because the mountains act as a barrier to the pollution, polluted air moving in response to the sea breeze and other processes tends to move up canyons, where it is trapped. The air pollution that develops occurs primarily during the summer and fall.

The lower part of Figure 12.4 shows a valley with relatively cool air overlain by warm air. This type of situation can occur in several ways, one of which we will explain here. When cloud cover associated with a stagnant air mass develops over an urban area, the incoming solar radiation is blocked by the clouds, which absorb some of the energy and thus heat up. On the ground, or near Earth's surface, the air cools. If there has been a fair amount of humidity, then as the air cools the dewpoint is reached and a thick fog may form. Because the air is cold, people living in the city burn more fuel to heat their homes and factories, and more pollutants are delivered into the atmosphere. As long as the stagnant conditions exist, the pollutants will build up. This sort of scenario has led to very serious smog problems, as in the London crisis of 1952.

Evaluating meteorologic conditions can be extremely helpful in predicting which areas will have potential smog problems. Figure 12.5 shows the number of days in a 5–year period for which conditions were favorable for reduced dispersion of air pollution for at least a 48–hour period. This illus-

FIGURE 12.4
Two causes for the development of a temperature inversion, which may aggravate air pollution problems.

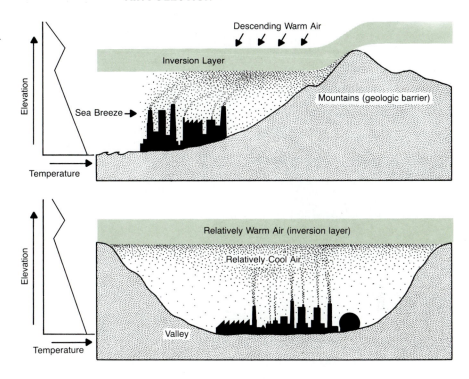

Potential for Urban Air Pollution

tration clearly shows where most of the problems have been located in the western United States. Of particular interest is that the San Diego area in southern California may eventually have a very serious pollution problem because the number of days with reduced dispersion of pollutants is greater there than in Los Angeles. This may also show why areas such as Denver, Colorado, and Phoenix, Arizona, have pollution problems.

Cities that are situated in a topographic "bowl" surrounded by mountains are more susceptible to smog problems than cities in open plains. Cities where certain kinds of weather conditions, such as temperature inversions, occur are also particularly susceptible. Both the surrounding mountains and the temperature inversions prevent the pollutants from being transported by the winds and weather systems. The production of air pollution is particularly well documented for Los Angeles, which has mountains surrounding the urban area and lies within a region that tends to have stagnating air conditions that promote air pollution (Fig 12.6).

The potential for air pollution in urban areas is determined by the following factors: the rate of emission of pollutants per unit area; the distance downwind that a mass of air may move through an urban area; the average speed of wind; and, finally, the height to which potential pollutants may be thoroughly mixed in the lower atmosphere (Fig. 12.7) [3]. The concentration of pollutants in the air is directly proportional to the first two factors. That is, as either the emission rate or downwind travel distance increases, so will the concentration of pollutants in the air. On the other hand, city air pollution decreases with increases in two meteorological factors: the wind velocity and the height of mixing. The stronger the wind and the higher the mixing layer, the lower the pollution. Assuming a constant rate of emission of air pollutants as the column of air moves through the urban area, it will collect more and more pollutants. The inversion layer acts as a lid for the pollutants, but near

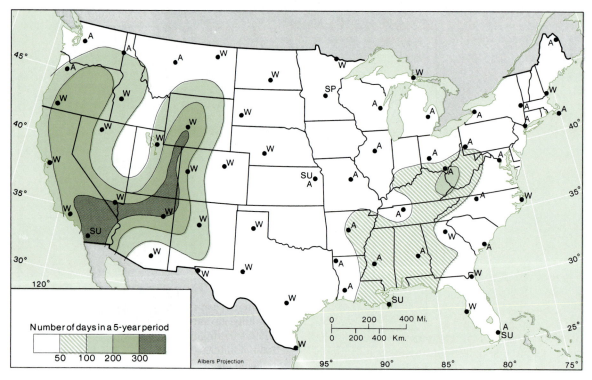

FIGURE 12.5
Number of days in a 5–year period characterized by conditions favorable for reduced disper-
sion and local buildups of air pollutants which existed for at least a 48–hour (2–day) period.
The time of year when most of these periods occurred is shown by the season: SP (spring),
A (autumn), W (winter), or SU (summer). (Modified after Holzworth, as presented in Neibur-
ger, Edinger, and Bonner.)

a geologic barrier such as a mountain, there may
be a "chimney effect," in which the pollutants spill
over the top of the mountain (see Fig. 12.6). This
effect has been noticed particularly in the Los Angeles basin, where pollutants may climb several
thousand meters, damaging mountain pine trees
and other vegetation and spoiling the air of mountain valleys.

The Urban Microclimate

The very presence of a city affects the local climate
(Table 12.2), and as the city changes, so does its
climate. For example, in the middle of the eighteenth century, Manhattan Island was "generally

reckoned very healthy" [4], perhaps because of its
nearness to the ocean and its relatively unob-
structed ocean breezes. Today, the air pollution
and the effects of tall buildings on air flow lead the
average visitor to Manhattan to a quite different
conclusion.

Although air quality in urban areas is in part a
function of the amount of pollutants present or
produced, it is affected also by the city's ability to
ventilate and thus flush out pollutants. The
amount of ventilation depends on several aspects
of the urban microclimate.

Cities are warmer than surrounding areas. The
observed increase in temperature in urban areas is
approximately 1–2°C in the winter and 0.5–1.0°C

FIGURE 12.6
Part of southern California showing the Los Angeles basin (south coast air basin). (Modified after Williamson, *Fundamentals of air pollution,* © 1973. Reprinted with permission of Addison-Wesley, Reading, MA.)

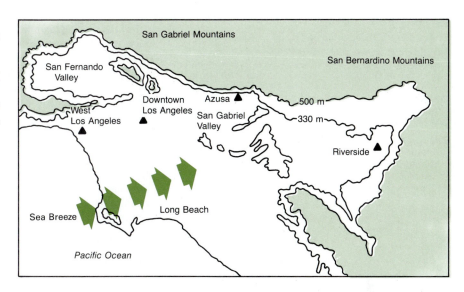

in the summer for mid-latitude areas. The temperature increase results from increased production of heat energy; the heat emitted from the burning of fossil fuels and other industrial, commercial, and residential sources; and the decreased rate of heat loss—the dust in the urban air traps and reflects back into the city long-wave (infrared) radiation emitted from city surfaces. In the winter, space heating from the city is primarily responsible for heating the local air environment. For example, in Manhattan, the input of heat from industrial, commercial, and residential space heating in the

winter has been measured to be about 2.5 times the solar energy that reaches the surface of the city; the annual average, however, is closer to 33% of the solar input. In large urban areas characterized by warmer winters, the heat input from artificial sources is much less [4]. Concrete, asphalt, and roofs also tend to act as solar collectors and quickly emit heat, helping to increase the sensible heat in cities [1].

Cities are in general less windy than nonurban areas. Air over cities tends to move more slowly than in surrounding areas because buildings and

FIGURE 12.7
The higher the wind velocity and the thicker the mixing layer (shown here as H), the less is the potential air pollution. The greater the emission rate and the longer the downwind length of the city, the greater the air pollution. The "chimney effect" allows polluted air to move over a mountain down into an adjacent valley.

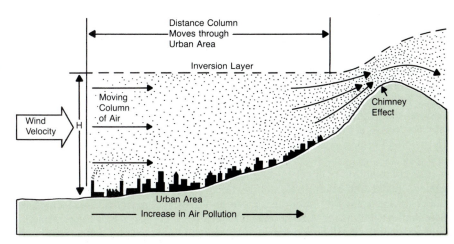

TABLE 12.2
Typical climate changes caused by urbanization.

Type of Change	Comparison with Rural Environs
Temperature	
Annual mean	0.5–1.0C° higher
Winter minima	1.0–3.0C° higher
Relative Humidity	
Annual mean	6% lower
Winter	2% lower
Summer	8% lower
Dust Particles	10 times more
Cloudiness	
Cloud cover	5–10% more
Fog, winter	100% more frequent
Fog, summer	30% more frequent
Radiation	
Total on horizontal surface	15–20% less
Ultraviolet, winter	30% less
Ultraviolet, summer	5% less
Wind Speed	
Annual mean	20–30% lower
Extreme gusts	10–20% lower
Calms	5–20% more
Precipitation[a]	
Amounts	5–10% more
Days with 0.2 in.	10% more

Source: After Landsberg in Matthews et al. From Council on Environmental Quality and the Department of State.
[a]Precipitation effects are relatively uncertain.

other structures obstruct the flow of air. Thus, it is not uncommon that wind velocities are reduced by 20–30% and calm days are 20% more abundant in urban areas than in nearby rural areas [5].

Particulates in the atmosphere over a city are often 10 times or more as high as in surrounding areas. Although the particulates tend to reduce incoming solar radiation by up to 30% and thus cool the city, the effect of particulates is small relative to the effect of processes that produce heat in the city [5].

The combination of lingering air and abundance of particulates and other pollutants in the air produces the well-known urban dust dome and heat island effect (Fig. 12.8). Also shown in Figure 12.8 is the general circulation pattern of air moving from the rural or suburban areas toward the inner city, where it flows up and then laterally out near the top of the dust dome. This circulation of air often occurs when a strong heat island develops over the city. For example, when the dust dome and heat island have developed during a calm period in New York City, there is an upward flow of air over the heavily developed Manhattan Island, accompanied by a downward flow over the nearby Hudson and East rivers, which are green belts and thus are characterized by cooler air temperatures [1]. Figure 12.8 also shows the air-temperature profile, which delineates the heat island. The dust dome effect explains why air pollution often tends to be most intense at city centers.

Particulates in the dust dome provide condensation nuclei, and thus urban areas experience 5–10% more precipitation and considerably more cloud cover and fog than surrounding areas. The formation of fog is particularly troublesome in the winter and may impede air traffic into and out of airports. If the pollution dome moves downwind, then increased precipitation may be reported outside of the urban area. For example, in the mid-1960s, effluent from the southern Chicago–northern Indiana industrial complex apparently caused a 30% increase in precipitation at La Porte, Indiana, 48 km downwind to the south. La Porte also has almost 2.5 times as many hailstorms, 38% more thunderstorms, and less sunshine than the countryside not directly downwind [6]. The La Porte case is extreme, but it is not unique. There is little doubt that atmospheric particulate matter from urban sources has altered local weather at numerous locations.

In summary, cities are cloudier, warmer, rainier, and less humid than their surroundings. Cities in middle latitudes receive about 15% less sunshine and 5% less ultraviolet light during the summer and 30% less ultraviolet light during the winter than nonurban areas. They are 10% rainier and 10% cloudier and have a 25% lower average wind speed, 30% more summer fog, and 100% more winter fog than nonurban areas. Average relative humidity is 6% less in cities than in their environs, partly because cities have large, impervious surfaces and little surface water to exchange by evaporation with the atmosphere. The average maxi-

FIGURE 12.8
Lingering air, an abundance of particulates, and the flow of air over heavily built-up areas create an urban dust dome and a heat island.

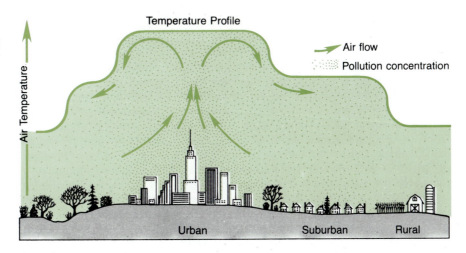

mum temperature difference between a city and its surroundings is about 3°C [7].

Smog

There are three major types of smog: photochemical smog, which is sometimes called L.A.-type smog or brown air; sulfurous smog, which is sometimes referred to as London-type smog or gray air; and the recently identified particulate smog. Solar radiation is particularly important in the formation of photochemical smog (Fig. 12.9). The reactions that occur in the development of photochemical smog are complex and involve both nitrogen oxides (NO_x) and organic compounds (hydrocarbons).

The development of photochemical smog is directly related to automobile use. Figure 12.10 shows a characteristic pattern in terms of how the nitrogen oxides, hydrocarbons, and oxidants (mostly ozone) vary throughout a typically smoggy

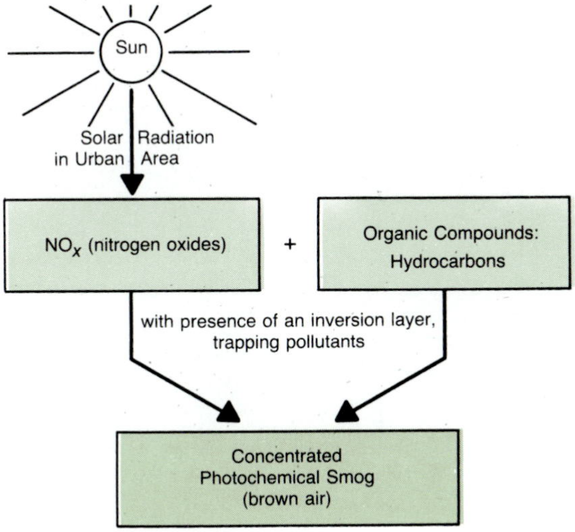

FIGURE 12.9
How photochemical smog may be produced.

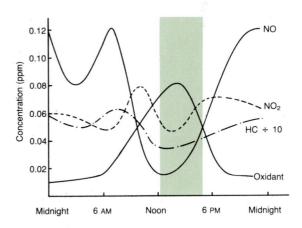

FIGURE 12.10
Development of photochemical smog over the Los Angeles area on a typical warm day.

day in southern California. Early in the morning, when commuter traffic begins to build up, the concentrations of nitrogen oxide (NO) and hydrocarbons begin to increase. At the same time, the amount of nitrogen dioxide NO_2 may decrease owing to the sunlight's action on NO_2 to produce NO plus atomic oxygen. The atomic oxygen is then free to combine with molecular oxygen to form ozone, so after sunrise the concentration of ozone also increases. Shortly thereafter, oxidized hydrocarbons react with NO to increase the concentration of NO_2 by midmorning. This reaction causes the NO concentration to decrease and allows ozone to build up, producing the midday peak in ozone and minimum in NO. As the smog matures, visibility may be greatly reduced (Fig. 12.11) owing to light scattering by aerosols.

Sulfurous smog is produced primarily by burning coal or oil at large power plants. Sulfur oxides and particulates combine under certain meteorological conditions to produce a concentrated sulfurous smog (Fig. 12.12).

The importance of particulate smog is just beginning to be appreciated. Several cities, including San Francisco, have an air-quality problem even though the sunlight necessary for the development of true photochemical smog is at a minimum (this problem is observed only in the winter in San Francisco). Sources that burn fossil fuel—automobiles, home gas heaters, and power plants—produce

(a)

(b)

FIGURE 12.11
Smog. Downtown Los Angeles photographed (a) on a relatively clear day and (b) on a smoggy day.

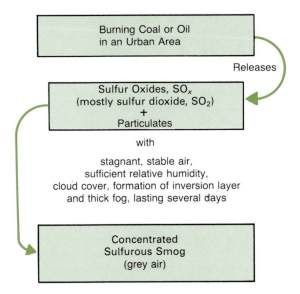

FIGURE 12.12
How concentrated sulfurous smog and smoke might develop.

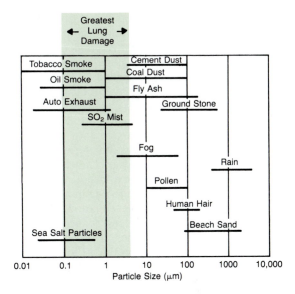

FIGURE 12.13
Size of selected particulates. Shaded area shows size range that produces the greatest lung damage. (Modified from Giddings, and Hidy and Brock.)

very small primary particulates. When these particulates are exhausted from their sources, they have a diameter of about $0.1\mu m$. These particulates can grow under certain situations (such as in a photochemical smog atmosphere) and inhibit visibility. Thus strategies worked out in the Los Angeles basin to control ozone may not be applicable to San Francisco and other cities plagued by small-particulate smog.

The importance of these very small particles has not been recognized until very recently as a source of primary pollutants. Figure 12.13 shows the sizes of several particles, including those from automobile exhaust, dust, and smoke.

Future Trends for Urban Areas

Air pollution levels in cities in developed countries have steadily improved, owing to increases in regulation of pollution during the last several decades. For example, sulfur oxide concentrations in New York and Chicago decreased markedly from the late 1960s to the early 1970s, and from 1980 to 1985 air pollution in the Los Angeles area has been reduced by about 18%. Improvements in Los

Angeles are due in part to regulatory efforts to control primary pollutants from automobiles, and the result has been a reduction in the number of pollution episodes. Although air pollution has improved, the outlook may not be bright. As oil and gas become scarce and industrialized societies return to a dependency on coal, air quality in cities is projected to decline [8]. In the United States, if emission standards remain constant but energy production begins to emphasize coal, urban air quality could begin to deteriorate before the end of the century.

Exposure to air pollutants decreases with increased income; the city's poor often live where there is more pollution. For example, in St. Louis, Missouri, those with low income were subject in recent years to suspended particulates of 91.3 $\mu g/ml$ of air; those with higher incomes lived where the air had a concentration of 64.9. Those who can afford it move away from pollution!

Cities in less developed countries with burgeoning populations are particularly susceptible to air pollution now and in the future; they don't have the financial base necessary to fight air pollution.

They tend to be more concerned with basic survival and finding ways to house and feed their growing urban populations. A good example is Mexico City, with a present population of 18 million people—projected to expand to 26 million by the end of the century, making it the largest urban area in the world. Industry and power plants in Mexico City emit hundreds of thousands of tons of particulates and sulfur dioxide into the atmosphere. The city is at an elevation of about 7400 ft. (2255 m) in a natural basin surrounded by mountains—a perfect situation for a severe air pollution problem. It is becoming a rare day in Mexico City when the mountains can be seen, and physicians report that there has been a steady increase in respiratory diseases. Headaches, irritated eyes, and sore throats are common on the all too common days when the pollution settles in.

INDOOR AIR POLLUTION

In recent years buildings have been constructed more and more tightly for purposes of energy conservation. As a result, air is filtered through rather extensive systems in many buildings. Unless filters are maintained properly, indoor air can become polluted with a variety of substances, including smoke, chemicals, and disease-carrying organisms. For example, some investigators believe the virus responsible for Legionnaires' disease, a respiratory infection, multiplies and is transported through buildings by way of the air filters and the ventilation systems. There has also been a great deal of concern over the slow release of asbestos fibers from insulation and other fixtures common in some buildings. People exposed to asbestos fibers may develop a rare form of lung cancer. Two gases that have potential to cause harm are carbon monoxide and nitrogen dioxide. Both may be released in homes from unvented or poorly vented gas stoves, furnaces, or water heaters. As final examples, consider formaldehyde, which is present in some insulation materials and wood products used in home construction, and the radioactive gas radon, which is present in some well water and building materials, such as concrete block and bricks if they are made from materials with a high radon concentration. Formaldehyde is known to cause irritation to ears, nose, and throat, and radon is suspected of causing lung and other cancers.

Modern urban structures are built of many substances, some of which release minute amounts of chemicals and other material into the nearby air. Buildings that lack a good system to recirculate the air with clean air are likely to have indoor pollution problems. Recommendations on how to improve indoor air quality will undoubtedly be forthcoming. It is interesting to note that people who lived centuries ago also suffered from indoor air pollution. In 1972 the body of a fourth-century Eskimo woman was discovered on St. Lawrence Island in the Bering Sea. The woman evidently was killed during an earthquake or landslide and her body frozen soon after death. Detailed autopsies showed that the woman suffered from black lung disease, which coal miners occasionally suffer from today. Anthropologists and medical personnel who studied the case concluded that the woman breathed very polluted air for a number of years. They speculate that the air she breathed included hazardous fumes from lamps that burned seal and whale blubber, causing the black lung disease. There is a long history of indoor air pollution [9].

ACID RAIN

Acid rain encompasses both wet and dry acidic deposits that occur near and downwind of areas where major emission of sulfur dioxide (SO_2) and nitrogen oxides (NO_x) occur as a result of burning fossil fuels. Although the oxides (sulfur and nitrogen) are the primary contributors, other acids also are involved in the acid rain problem. For example, hydrochloric acid is emitted from coal-fired power plants.

The term **acid rain** is a fairly recent one, even though the problem probably extends back at least as far as the beginning of the industrial revolution. In recent decades the problem of acid rain has gained more and more attention; today it is considered one of the major global environmental problems facing industrialized society.

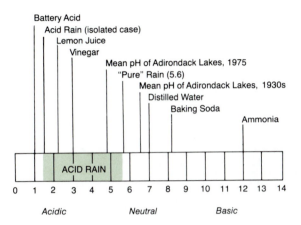

FIGURE 12.14
pH scale. (Modified after U.S. Environmental Protection Agency, 1980b.)

Causes of Acid Rain

During the last eighty years the amounts of sulfur dioxide and nitrogen oxides released into the environment have been steadily increasing (Fig. 12.15). Today more than 20 million tons per year each of nitrogen oxide and sulfur dioxide are released into the atmosphere. Following emission of sulfur dioxide and nitrogen oxide into the atmosphere, they are transformed into sulfate (SO_4) or nitrate (NO_3) particles, which may combine with water vapor to form sulfuric and nitric acids. These acids may travel long distances with prevailing winds to be deposited as acid precipitation (Fig. 12.16). Such precipitation may be in the form of rainfall, snow, or fog. Sulfate and nitrate particles may also be deposited directly on the surface of the land as dry deposition. These particles may later be activated by moisture to become sulfuric and nitric acids.

Sulfur dioxide is emitted primarily from stationary sources such as power plants that burn fossil fuels, whereas nitrogen oxides are emitted from both stationary and transport-related sources such as automobiles. During 1980 approximately 27 million tons of sulfur dioxide and 21 million tons of nitrogen oxides were emitted in the United States. Of these totals, approximately 80% of the sulfur dioxide and 65% of the nitrogen oxides came from within states east of the Mississippi River. During the last 45 years sulfur dioxide emissions have increased approximately 50% while nitrogen oxides have increased by as much as 300%, probably reflecting the increased utilization of automobiles in urban areas (Fig. 12.15). Throughout that same period, emission stacks have become taller and taller. Taller stacks have reduced local concentrations of air pollutants, but have increased regional effects by spreading the pollution more widely. In this case, dumping waste into someone else's back yard has created more rather than fewer problems. For example, Swedish scientists have traced acid precipitation problems in Scandinavian lakes to airborne pollutants from Germany, France, and Great Britain; similarly, problems associated with acid precipitation in Canada may be traced to the emission of sulfur dioxide and other pollutants in the Ohio Valley.

Many people are surprised to learn that all rainfall is slightly acidic: water reacts with atmospheric carbon dioxide to produce carbonic acid. Thus pure rainfall has a pH (a numerical value to describe the strength of an acid) of about 5.6. Acid rain is defined as precipitation in which the pH is below 5.6 (Fig. 12.14). Because the pH scale is logarithmic, a pH value of 3 is 10 times more acidic than a pH value of 4 and 100 times more acidic than a pH value of 5. Automobile battery acid has a pH value of 1. It is alarming to learn that in Wheeling, West Virginia, rainfall has been measured with a pH value of 1.5, nearly as acidic as stomach acid and far more acidic than lemon juice or vinegar.

Perhaps more important than isolated cases of very acid rain (Fig. 12.14) is the apparent growth of the problem. Until quite recently it was believed that acid rain was primarily a European problem. It is now recognized that acid rain affects all industrial countries. In the United States it was believed that acid rain affected only a relatively small area in the northeastern United States. Now it is believed to affect nearly all of eastern North America, and West Coast urban centers such as Seattle, San Francisco, and Los Angeles are now beginning to record acid rainfall and acid fog events. The problem is also of great concern in Canada.

FIGURE 12.15
Trends in U.S. emissions of sulfur dioxide and nitrogen oxides from 1900 to 2023. Estimates for 1900–1940 and projections for 1990–2030 are uncertain. Projections involve assumptions concerning energy use and production and economics with no change in current air pollution laws and regulations. (After Office of Technology Assessment.)

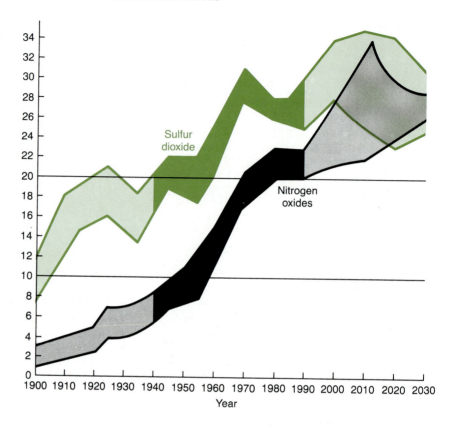

Effects of Acid Rain

The length of time that pollutants remain in the atmosphere depends upon weather patterns and the pollutants' chemical interactions with the atmosphere. Typically, the pollutants may return to Earth very quickly or may remain in the atmosphere for a week or longer. Prevailing winds in the eastern United States, particularly in the Ohio Valley where most of the sulfur dioxide is produced, tend to push the pollutants to the northwest and northeast. This accounts for the observation that acid precipitation problems are most prevalent in the northeastern United States and parts of Canada.

Analysis of the distances that sulfur compounds may be transported before deposition suggests that approximately one-third of the total amount deposited over the eastern United States originates from sources greater than 500 km away. Another one-third comes from sources between 200 and 500 km away, and the remainder comes from sources less than 200 km away [10].

Geology and climatic patterns as well as types of vegetation and soil composition all affect the potential impacts of acid rain. Figure 12.17, showing areas of the United States and Canada sensitive to acid rain, is based on some of these factors. Particularly sensitive areas are those in which the bedrock cannot buffer the acid input; such areas include terrain dominated by granitic rocks, as well as those in which the soils have little buffering action. Areas least likely to suffer damages are those in which the bedrock contains an abundance of limestone or other carbonate material or in which the soils contain a horizon rich in calcium carbonate. Soils in sensitive areas may be damaged from a fertility standpoint, either because nutrients are leached out by the acid or because the acid releases into the soil elements that are toxic to plants.

It has long been suspected that acid precipita-

FIGURE 12.16
Paths and processes associated with acid rain. (Modified after D. L. Albritton, as presented in J. M. Miller.)

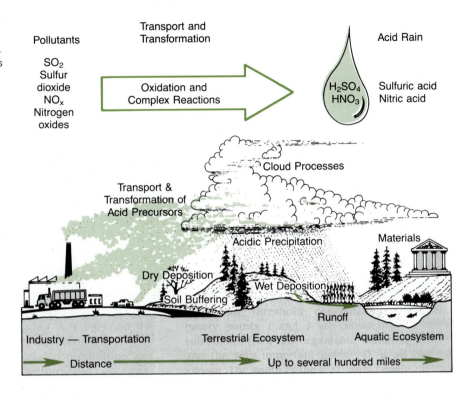

tion, whether in the form of snow, rain, fog, or dry deposition, adversely affects trees. Studies in West Germany have led scientists to blame acid rain and other air pollution for the death of thousands of hectares of evergreen trees in Bavaria. Similar studies in the Appalachian Mountains of Vermont suggest that in some locations half of the red spruce trees have died in recent years. The damage is attributed to acid rain and fog with pH levels of 4.1 and 3.1, respectively. Acid solutions enter the soil and free toxic metals such as aluminum and cadmium from the minerals found there. These toxic metals may then move into the roots of plants and trees and weaken them.

Effect on Lake Ecosystems In recent years fish that were once abundant and were used for food and recreation have disappeared from lakes in Sweden. Records of fifteen years or more from Scandinavian lakes show an increase in acidity accompanied by a decrease in fish (Fig. 12.18). The death of the fish has been traced to acid rain—the result of industrial processes far away in other

countries, particularly in West Germany and Great Britain.

Acid rain affects a lake ecosystem by dissolving chemical elements necessary for life and keeping them in solution so that they leave the lake with the water outflow. Elements that once cycled within the lake are thus lost from the system. Without these nutrients, the lake algae do not grow, and the small animals that feed on the algae have little to eat. The fish that are typically predators on the small invertebrate animals also lack food. The acid water has other adverse effects on living organisms and their reproduction. For example, crayfish produce fewer eggs in acid water, and those eggs produced often have malformed larvae.

To better study the effects of acidification on lakes, scientists in Canada added sulfuric acid to a lake in northwest Ontario over a period of years and observed the effects. When the experiment started, the pH of the lake was 6.8. The following year, owing to addition of the acid, the pH had dropped to 6.1. The initial drop in pH was not harmful to the lake, but as more and more acid was

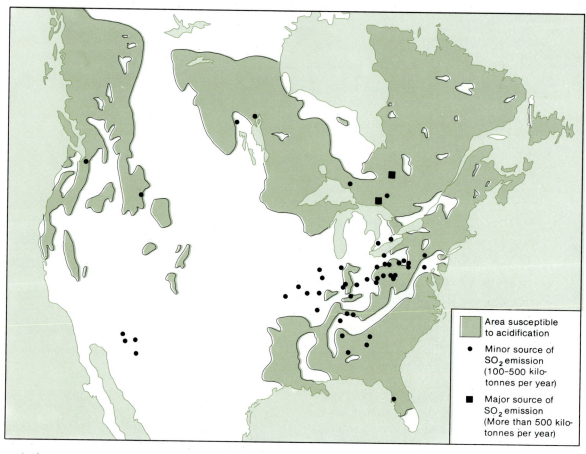

FIGURE 12.17
Areas in Canada and the United States that are sensitive to acid rain. (After *Canada Today.*)

added the pH dropped first to 5.8 then to 5.6, 5.4, and finally, five years after the project started, to 5.1. The problems started when the pH was lowered to 5.8; some species disappeared and others experienced reproductive failure. At a pH of 5.8, the death rate among lake trout embryos increased. When the pH was lowered to 5.4, lake trout reproduction failed [11].

Those experiments proved valuable in pointing out what might be expected in thousands of other lakes that are now becoming acidified. The precise processes involved in the toxicity and damage to the lakes are poorly understood. However, it is known that acid rain leaches metals such as aluminum, lead, mercury, and calcium from the soils and rocks in a drainage basin and discharges them into rivers and lakes. Elevated concentrations of aluminum are particularly damaging to fish because the metal can cause clogging of the gills and suffocate the fish. The heavy metals may pose human health hazards because they may become concentrated in fish and be passed on to people, mammals, and birds when the fish are eaten. Of course, drinking water taken from acidic lakes and water may also have high concentrations of toxic metals.

Not all lakes are as vulnerable to acidification as the Ontario lakes. The acid is neutralized in wa-

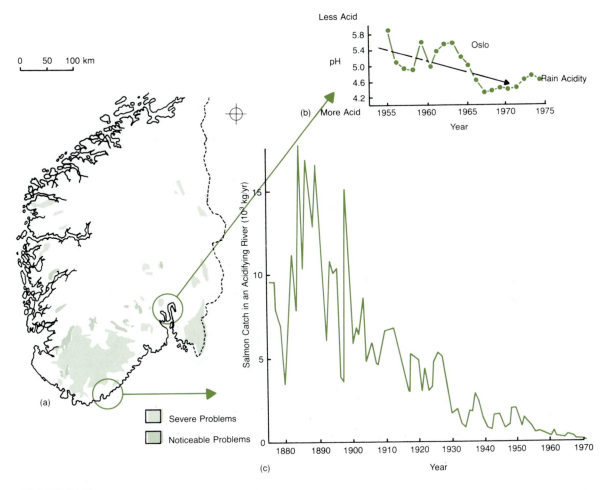

FIGURE 12.18

(a) In Norway, many lakes in the south have severe problems with acid rain. (b) The rain has become more acidic during the last 20 years, as measured at Oslo. Measurements at five other sites in southern Norway show the same trend. (c) The catch of fish, as illustrated by the catch of salmon in the Tovdalselva River of southern Norway, has decreased dramatically. [(a), (c) from Wright et al., 1976; data for (a) from Muniz et al. and data for (c) from Snekvik, 1970. (b) from Odén.]

ters with a high calcium or magnesium content— lakes on limestone or other rocks rich in calcium or magnesium carbonates can readily release the calcium and magnesium. This buffers the lakes against the addition of acids. Lakes with high concentrations of such elements are called hard-water lakes, whereas lakes on sand or igneous rocks such as granite tend to lack sufficient buffering to neutralize the acid and thus are more susceptible

to acidification. In practice a simple and fast index of a lake's hardness or buffering capacity is its electrical conductivity. Pure water is a poor conductor of electricity; water high in dissolved elements is a good conductor [12].

Figure 12.17 shows parts of the United States and Canada that are particularly susceptible to acid rain. Within these regions thousands of kilometers of rivers and thousands of lakes are currently in various stages of acidification. In Nova Scotia, for example, at least a dozen rivers have acid contents sufficiently high that they no longer support healthy populations of Atlantic salmon. In the northeastern United States about 200 lakes in the Adirondacks are no longer able to support fish, and thousands more are slowly losing the battle with acid rain.

One solution to lake acidification is rehabilitation by the periodic addition of lime. This has been done in New York state as well as in Sweden and Ontario, Canada. This solution is not satisfactory over a long period, however, because it is expensive and requires a continuing effort. The only practical long-term solution to the acid rain problem is to ensure that the production of acid-forming components in the atmosphere is minimized.

Effect on Human Society   Acid rain affects not only forests and lakes; it is capable also of damaging many building materials, including steel, paint, plastics, cement, masonry, galvanized steel, and several types of rock, especially limestone, sandstone, and marble (Fig. 12.19). Classical buildings on the Acropolis in Athens, Greece, and other cities show considerable decay that has accelerated in this century as a result of air pollution. The problem has grown to such an extent that statues and other monuments need to have new protective coating replaced quite frequently, resulting in costs that reach billions of dollars a year [11].

In the United States, cities along the eastern seaboard are more susceptible to acid rain today because emissions of sulfur dioxide and nitrogen oxide are more abundant there. However, the problem is moving westward—acid precipitation has been recorded in California. Even more alarming is the discovery that acid fog events in Los Angeles, California, may have a pH as low as 3, which is over ten times as acidic as the average acid rain in the eastern United States. In contrast to acid rain that may form relatively high in the atmosphere and travel long distances, acid fog forms when water vapor near the ground mixes with pollutants and turns into an acid. The acid evidently condenses around very fine particles of smog and, if the air is sufficiently humid, a fog may form. When the fog eventually burns off, nearly pure drops of sul-

FIGURE 12.19
Detail of damage attributed to acid rain, Parliament Building, Ottawa, Ontario, Canada.

furic acid may be left behind. These acid fogs may be considerable health hazards because the tiny particles containing the acid may be inhaled deeply into people's lungs.

It is interesting that the geologic aspect of acid rain problems may help predict future effects and potential solutions. Since 1875 the Veteran's Administration in the United States has provided over 2.5 million tombstones to national cemeteries. These tombstones have come from only three rock quarries and have a standard size and shape. These stones, now located in various parts of the country, are being evaluated to assess damages caused by acid rainfall because they provide a variety of dates and locations to work from. Research will provide valuable data on air pollution and the meteorological patterns that contribute to acid rain [13].

A GLOBAL PERSPECTIVE

Air pollutants affect not only local areas or regions—they affect the entire biosphere. The fundamental problem is that people of the world are collectively responsible for emitting materials into the atmosphere at amounts and rates similar to those of natural processes. For example, the annual production of carbon dioxide from the burning of fossil fuels is approximately one-tenth the amount emitted by the respiration of all living things.

Pollution of the biosphere has two kinds of effects: climate alterations and chemical changes in the atmosphere that may be hazardous to living things. Particulates and carbon dioxide may be instrumental in climatic change, and chemicals that alter the atmosphere's ozone layer are direct hazards to life.

Carbon Dioxide and Climate

Life continues today to affect the characteristics of Earth's surface, even those areas we think are far removed from living things. This was shown to be true by samples of the air taken near the summit of Mauna Loa, Hawaii, one of the largest active volcanoes in the world [14]. These samples, used to measure the carbon dioxide concentration of Earth's atmosphere, were taken on Mauna Loa because it was far from any local, direct effects of human or other biological activity. Because carbon dioxide is taken up by green plants during photosynthesis and released in the respiration of all oxygen-breathing organisms, a measure of the carbon dioxide in the atmosphere is like a measure of the breathings in and out of all life on Earth.

The Mauna Loa measurements are remarkable observations. Two important aspects of this record are clearly evident in Figure 12.20a. An annual cycle is extremely regular—a peak is reached in the winter, a trough in the summer. The curve is indeed a measure of life activities, including human activities, of the entire Northern Hemisphere. In the summer green plants are most active, and the total amount of photosynthesis exceeds the total amount of respiration; thus carbon dioxide is removed from the atmosphere, and the

concentration, as measured on Mauna Loa, decreases. In the winter, photosynthesis decreases greatly and becomes less than total respiration, so the carbon dioxide concentration of the atmosphere increases [15].

Similar observations have been made in Antarctica for the same period. (Because Antarctica is so inaccessible, measurements are much more sporadic.) The same trends are observed: an annual cycle and a strong upward trend (Fig. 12.20b). The annual cycle is smaller in amplitude than the Mauna Loa cycle because of the relatively smaller land area in the Southern Hemisphere and the smaller amount of woody vegetation that stores carbon and exchanges carbon dioxide with the atmosphere [15]. More recently, observations at many locations around the world confirm these trends.

The upward trend in both the Mauna Loa and Antarctica curves for carbon dioxide is thought to be due to the addition of carbon dioxide from the burning of fossil fuels and other human activities, such as the cutting of forests and the burning of wood. These curves show that life touches the entire Earth and that human activities have begun to affect Earth's entire atmosphere. More importantly, an increase in carbon dioxide may change the climate.

The Greenhouse (Atmospheric) Effect The mechanism by which carbon dioxide heats the atmosphere is referred to as the **greenhouse,** or atmospheric, **effect.** When incoming, relatively short-wavelength, visible radiation from the sun is absorbed by Earth, it is ultimately reradiated as long-wave radiation. In the atmosphere, carbon dioxide effectively traps or absorbs long-wave radiation emitted from Earth, and this trapped radiation heats up the atmosphere (Fig. 12.21). Another way to say this is that incoming solar radiation is transparent to carbon dioxide but outgoing radiation ("earthshine") is more opaque to carbon dioxide and is trapped.

Thus, as the amount of carbon dioxide in the atmosphere increases, the atmosphere has a corresponding increase in temperature. Actually, a greenhouse heats up because the air inside is retarded from circulating with outside air, but the ef-

FIGURE 12.20
Changes in carbon dioxide concentration in the atmosphere at (a) Mauna Loa, Hawaii, and (b) the South Pole. The concentration is small and is measured in parts per million (ppm). (From Ekdahl and Keeling.)

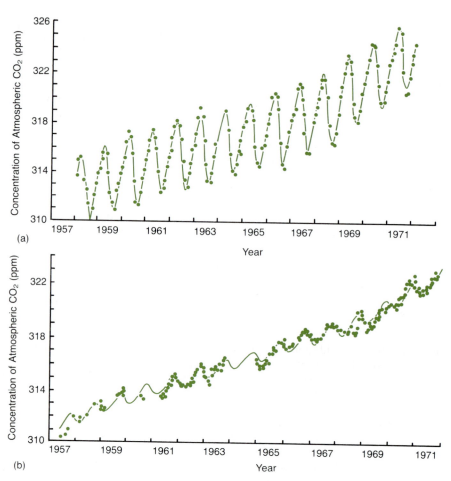

(a)

(b)

fect of trapping long-wave radiation is still known as the greenhouse effect. Water vapor and liquid water droplets contribute to the greenhouse effect. Fluorocarbons in the atmosphere may also cause a greenhouse effect.

Today there is a major controversy over the possible effects of increasing carbon dioxide in Earth's atmosphere. It is generally accepted that around the turn of the century the concentration of carbon dioxide in the atmosphere was about 290 ppm (0.029%) and that since that time there has been a steady increase to the present level of approximately 330 ppm (0.033%). The projected value for the year 2000 is 380 ppm (0.038%)—almost 20% higher than the present concentration. This increase, however, is only half that expected

if all of the carbon dioxide from the burning of fossil fuels had remained in the atmosphere. The fate of the rest of the carbon dioxide is the subject of a major scientific debate. Some scientists argue that it is being absorbed by the oceans; others argue that land plants—particularly trees in forests—are growing faster and taking up the additional carbon dioxide.

The extrapolation of increase in carbon dioxide until the year 2000 is based on several assumptions that may not be entirely correct. First, it is assumed that the ocean will continue to absorb about 50% of the carbon dioxide emitted. Second, it is assumed that large-scale and significant atmospheric circulation changes will not take place. Given these assumptions, the temperature increase

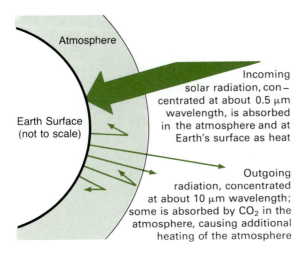

Atmosphere

Incoming
solar radiation, con-
centrated at about 0.5 μm
wavelength, is absorbed
in the atmosphere and at
Earth's surface as heat

Earth Surface
(not to scale)

Outgoing
radiation, concentrated
at about 10 μm wavelength;
some is absorbed by CO_2 in the
atmosphere, causing additional
heating of the atmosphere

FIGURE 12.21
The greenhouse effect.

due to atmospheric carbon dioxide should be approximately 0.5°C by the year 2000. This temperature increase in unlikely to create major problems, but if the carbon dioxide content continues to build for several hundred more years, then a temperature rise of 2–3°C may be possible and would cause major problems. A change of a few degrees Centigrade in the mean annual temperature might be sufficient to melt a significant part of the Antarctic ice sheet, raising sea levels around the world by several meters and flooding major cities. Another concern is that the global warming will cause thermal expansion of the upper ocean. This effect may cause a rise of sea level of about 15 cm during the next 50 years. This rise would be in addition to the rise caused by melting glacial ice—predicted to be as much as 20 cm during the next 50 years. This would cause a serious global coastal erosion hazard. For this reason and others, carbon dioxide in the atmosphere is being very carefully monitored. What happens in the next few thousand years may be affected significantly by human-induced changes in the composition of the atmosphere.

Effects on the Global Ecology An increase in the atmosphere's carbon dioxide concentration can greatly affect living things at local, regional, and global levels. At the local level, green plants grow better when the air around them is enriched with carbon dioxide. This has been known since the eighteenth century, when Joseph Priestley discovered that a green plant grew better in a bell jar in which a mouse had lived and died (and therefore added carbon dioxide from its own respiration and from the respiration accompanying its decay) than a plant did in another bell jar. Thus, if no other environmental factor interfered to limit growth, a worldwide increase in carbon dioxide might increase annual net vegetation production. On the other hand, the complex interactions among species in a natural ecosystem might tend to stabilize the net production and prevent such increases.

The increasing carbon dioxide concentration in the atmosphere could have other, indirect effects. If the climate were to warm, some kinds of vegetation would increase and others would decrease. The effects of changes in weather patterns, including rainfall, could be complicated and cannot be predicted at this time.

The problem of increasing atmospheric carbon dioxide due to burning of fossil fuels is still unresolved. There is no general agreement on what the effects are, primarily because we are not certain of the effects resulting from interaction between the chemical and biological worlds.

Particulates in the Atmosphere

How particulate material in the atmosphere will affect global changes in the atmosphere's mean annual temperature is being debated. What is certain is that particulates are being added to the atmosphere through human activity. Today about 20% of all the particles are from human sources, and this may increase to approximately 50% by the year 2000. Particulates come from primary sources, as from burning of coal and other fossil fuels, or from secondary sources, as from reactions involving photochemical smog. Secondary particles may result from primary particulates, which grow larger as photochemical smog develops and matures.

Regardless of how they are produced, particulates have two important effects. First, they act as condensation nuclei and therefore cause an increase in precipitation or fog. Second, they affect the amount of sunlight reaching Earth. As the total amount of particulates in the atmosphere increases, a larger percentage of incoming solar radiation may be reflected away from Earth, causing mean annual temperature to decrease. On the other hand, some particles may absorb incoming solar radiation, causing an increase in the atmospheric and land-surface temperature. This second effect is observed in urban areas, where particulates are concentrated. Furthermore, if particles filter out of the atmosphere and are deposited on snow, then a greater portion of the solar radiation will be absorbed, making available more radiation to heat the atmosphere. There seems little doubt that particulates in the atmosphere can interfere with incoming solar radiation.

Volcanic eruptions have caused slight global cooling and spectacular sunsets for up to a year or so following an eruption that blasts volcanic ash and other material into the atmosphere. The eruption in 1883 of the volcano Krakatoa, a small island in the East Indies, is a spectacular example. The eruption, which is the largest in historic time, was explosive, blowing about 2.6 km^3 of volcanic ash and other material as high as 27 km into the atmosphere. The hole left in the ocean floor was 300 m deep and the blast could be heard 5,000 km away! Dust in the stratosphere circled Earth for months before it settled out, causing a slight lowering in the mean temperature of the lower atmosphere. Recent research suggests that it is not so much the amount of ash that reaches the stratosphere as the composition that is important in determining climatic effects. For example the eruptions of Mount St. Helens in 1980 and of El Chicón in southern Mexico in 1982 both ejected volcanic debris into the stratosphere. Mount St. Helens caused little or no climatic disturbance, whereas El Chicón caused a measurable, significant effect, even though both events were of similar magnitude (both were much smaller than Krakatoa). The stratospheric cloud from El Chicón was sulfur rich and formed a cloud of aerosol sulfuric acid droplets that were about 100 times as dense as the stratospheric cloud from the Mount St. Helens eruption, which had little sulfur in it. While fine volcanic ash settles out in a few weeks, an aerosol of sulfuric acid droplets may circle Earth for several years before it settles out. It is hypothesized

that the El Chicón eruption caused a drop in mean annual temperature of about 0.3–0.5°C during a three-year period following the eruption. The eruption also may have contributed to the formation of the strong 1982–83 El Niño by disrupting (weakening) atmospheric circulation that drives oceanic circulation [16]. That is, the sulfurous cloud caused a warming in the stratosphere because of the absorption by the cloud of incoming solar radiation. Less radiation reached Earth—this cooled the lower atmosphere. These processes reduced normal atmospheric circulation, making it easier for oceanic currents to move west near the equator off South America rather than east as they normally do, helping produce the El Niño event.

Yet it is not the particulate matter from volcanic eruptions that causes concern. During the twentieth century, modern industrial society has added more and more particulate matter to the atmosphere. Particulates reflect sunlight and, when present in sufficient amounts, may thereby cool Earth's surface. In fact, the increase in atmospheric dust from human activities may offset the warming effects that may be occurring from the burning of fossil fuels and the addition of carbon dioxide to the atmosphere. Whether the cooling of the atmosphere from particulates will have a greater effect than the warming trends caused by carbon dioxide is unknown.

Threats to Stratospheric Ozone

Ozone (O_3) is produced in the stratosphere at altitudes of 16–60 km above Earth when two reactions take place. The first reaction is the splitting of an oxygen molecule into atomic oxygen by sunlight. The second reaction, involving a union of a molecule of oxygen (O_2) with an atom of oxygen (O) to make ozone (O_3), takes place only when a third molecule (a catalyst) is present.

Ozone is destroyed naturally by ultraviolet radiation. As the ozone is destroyed, it performs a service function for organisms at Earth's surface by greatly reducing the amount of ultraviolet radiation that reaches Earth. In the stratosphere, ozone is constantly being formed and destroyed and therefore is maintained in a rough steady state. Any reduction in ozone is potentially dangerous because more ultraviolet light would reach Earth and possibly cause an increase in skin cancer. The relationship between ultraviolet radiation and skin cancer is estimated to be such that a 1% depletion in ozone would result in a 2% increase in skin cancer.

Another aspect of the ozone depletion problem involves potential heating or cooling in various parts of the atmosphere. If there were less ozone, more radiation would reach Earth and would heat up the lower atmosphere. On the other hand, as ozone is depleted in the stratosphere, the upper atmosphere cools and hence less thermal radiation from the stratosphere reaches Earth's surface. This tends to cool the lower atmosphere.

Human-induced change in the amount of ozone in the stratosphere is a subject of considerable controversy. It has been suggested that aerosols, particularly fluorocarbons, will destroy some ozone. Others have suggested that nitrous oxide emitted by industrial fertilizers through interactions with the biosphere may rise and eventually destroy stratospheric ozone. As is the case with carbon dioxide and particulates in the atmosphere, the potential effects of ozone depletion and the processes involved are not completely understood. For instance, ten years ago it was believed that the proposed supersonic transport (SST) would release into the stratosphere materials that would deplete ozone, but now that work is overturned.

CONTROL OF AIR POLLUTION

Reducing air pollution requires a variety of strategies tailored to specific sources and type of pollutants. The two major types of sources are stationary and mobile, and for both of these the only reasonable strategies (with an exception for indoor pollution) have been to collect, capture, or retain pollutants before they enter the atmosphere. Other strategies may only exacerbate the problem. Consider the case of Sudbury, Ontario, Canada. The ores contain a high percentage of sulfur, and the smelter stacks emit large amounts of sulfur dioxide as well as particulates containing nickel, copper, and other metals toxic to living things. Attempts to minimize the pollution problem close to the smelters by increasing the height of the smoke-stacks have backfired by spreading the pollution over a larger area.

Pollution problems vary in different regions of the world. There is great variance even within the United States. For example, in the Los Angeles basin, nitrogen oxides and hydrocarbons are particularly troublesome because they combine in the presence of sunlight to form photochemical smog. Furthermore, in Los Angeles most of the nitrogen oxides and hydrocarbons are emitted from automobiles—a nonpoint source [6]. In other urban areas, such as in Ohio and the Great Lakes region in general, air-quality problems result from emissions of sulfur dioxide and particulates from industry and coal-burning power plants, which are point sources. This is not to say that automobiles are not a problem in areas outside of Los Angeles, but rather to emphasize contrasting conditions. It is important also to keep in mind that automobiles produce many small particulates, whose pollution potential is only beginning to be understood. Thus areas such as San Francisco, with a relatively cool climate, have a serious air pollution problem from automobile exhaust, which resembles photochemical smog. However, such areas lack the necessary sunlight to produce that type of smog. Of course, the small particulates are also abundant in Los Angeles, where the problem is more pronounced because of the photochemical smog.

In the United States, nitrogen dioxide is primarily a southern California problem and is related to automobiles. Oxidants (mostly ozone), however, are a problem in both the southwestern and northeastern United States, as are particulates. Thus oxidants and particulates may be related to factors such as general atmospheric circulation that favors reduced dispersion of pollutants[4].

Because the problems vary so greatly from country to country and from region to region, it is often difficult to obtain both the monies and the political consensus for effective control. Nevertheless, effective control strategies do exist for many air pollution problems.

Control of Particulates

Particulates emitted from fugitive, point, or area stationary sources are much easier to control than

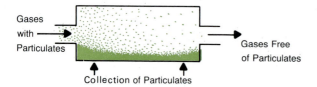

Gases with Particulates → → Gases Free of Particulates

Collection of Particulates

Gases Free of Particulates

Gases with Particulates →

Collection of Particulates →

(b)

FIGURE 12.22
Devices being used to control emissions of particulates before they enter the atmosphere: (a) a simple settling chamber that collects particulates by gravity settling; (b) centrifugal collector, in which particulates are forced to the outside of the chamber by centrifugal force and then fall to the collection site.

are the very small particulates of primary or secondary origin released from mobile sources such as automobiles. As we learn more about these very small particles new methods will have to be devised to control them.

Control of coarse particulates from power plants and industrial sites (point or area sources) utilizes a variety of settling chambers or collectors, some of which are generalized in Figure 12.22. These methods are effective because they provide a mechanism that induces particles to settle out in a location where they may be collected for disposal in landfills.

Particulates from fugitive sources (such as a waste pile) must be controlled on-site before they are removed (eroded) and enter the atmosphere by wind action. This may be done by protecting open areas, by dust control, or by reducing the effect of wind. For example, waste piles may be covered by plastic or other material and soil piles may be vegetated to inhibit wind erosion; water or a combination of water and chemicals may be spread to hold dust down; and structures or vegetation may be placed to lessen wind velocity near the ground, thus retarding wind erosion of particles.

Control of Automobile Pollution

Control of pollutants such as carbon monoxide, nitrogen oxides, and hydrocarbons in urban areas is best achieved through pollution control measures

for automobiles, because most of the anthropogenic portion of these pollutants comes from transportation. Furthermore, control of these materials will also regulate the ozone in the lower atmosphere, where it forms from by reactions with nitrogen oxides and hydrocarbons in the presence of sunlight.

The control of nitrogen oxides from automobile exhausts is accomplished by recirculating exhaust gas, which dilutes the air-to-fuel mixture being burned. The dilution reduces the temperature of combustion and decreases the oxygen concentration in the burning mixture (that is, it makes a richer fuel). This method produces fewer nitrogen oxides. Unfortunately, the effect is just the opposite for hydrocarbon emissions, which are greater for rich fuels (those with a low air-to-fuel ratio). Nevertheless, exhaust recirculation to reduce nitrogen oxide emissions has been in common practice in the United States since 1975 [17].

The two most common devices used to remove carbon monoxide and hydrocarbon emissions from automobiles are the catalytic converter and the thermal exhaust reactor [17]. In both devices carbon monoxide is converted to carbon dioxide and the hydrocarbons to carbon dioxide and water. In the high-temperature, or thermal exhaust, reactor, the addition of outside air (oxygen) assists in the more complete combustion of exhaust fumes in the high-temperature chamber. The catalytic converter works at a lower temperature and involves a metal catalyst material over which the exhaust gases are circulated with air. Oxidation then occurs, removing carbon monoxide and hydrocarbons from the exhaust. Catalytic converters have one major problem—the catalyst bed may be rendered ineffective by a number of substances, including lead additives in gasoline. As a result, there has been a tremendous shift to nonleaded gasoline in recent years.

It has been argued that the automobile emission regulation plan in the United States has not been very effective in reducing pollutants. The pollutants may be reduced while a car is relatively new, but many people simply do not take care of their automobiles well enough to ensure that the emission control devices work over the life of the automobile. Also, some people disconnect smog control devices. The evidence suggests that these devices tend to become less efficient every year following purchase. Because of these adverse aspects of emission control, it has been suggested that effluent fees replace automobile controls as the primary method of regulating air pollution in the United States [18]. Under this scheme, vehicles would be tested each year for emission control, and fees would then be assessed of the owners on the basis of the test results. The fees would provide a positive incentive for the purchase of automobiles that pollute less, and the annual inspections would insure that pollution control devices are properly maintained. Although there is considerable controversy at this time over enforced pollution inspections, such inspections are common in a number of areas and are expected to increase as air pollution abatement becomes imperative.

Control of Acid Rain

Acid rain is a particularly troublesome problem because the pollutants may be emitted long distances, sometimes across national boundaries, from where the actual acid rain falls. For example, the trees that are dying in West Germany are receiving acid precipitation that results from power plants that emit sulfur dioxide and nitrogen oxide in both West Germany and eastern Europe. Similarly, problems in Scandinavian lakes result from pollutants emitted from a variety of locations, including Great Britain and Germany. Canada and the United States also have air pollution problems that cross back and forth across the international border.

The cause of acid precipitation is fairly well known. We also know that the only long-term solution involves lowering of emissions of sulfur dioxide and nitrogen oxides. However, getting countries to cooperate with research and emission controls has proved difficult. This results because the equipment that must be added to power plants to control pollutants is expensive and this adds a significant cost to the production of energy. Furthermore, countries that cause the pollution may have difficulty raising funds for effects across their borders. In spite of these potential problems Canada and the United States are working on the problem; many millions of dollars are being spent on acid rain research projects aimed at eventually controlling the problem.

Control of Sulfur Dioxide

Sulfur dioxide emissions can be reduced by abatement measures performed before, during, or after combustion. The technology to clean up coal so that it will burn cleanly is already available, although the cost of removing the sulfur does make the fuel more expensive. However, if nothing is done, the consequences of burning sulfur-rich coal in the next decade or so will be very expensive indeed to us in future generations.

Changing from high-sulfur coal to low-sulfur coal seems an obvious solution to reducing emission of sulfur dioxide into the atmosphere. In some regions this will work. Unfortunately, most of the low-sulfur coal in the United States is located in the western part of the country, whereas most of the coal is actually burned in the eastern part. Therefore, the use of low-sulfur coal is a solution only in cases where it is economically feasible. Another possibility is cleaning up relatively high-sulfur coal by washing it to remove the sulfur. In the washing process finely ground coal is washed with water, and the iron sulfide (the mineral pyrite) settles out because of its relatively high density compared with that of coal. The washing process removes some of the sulfur, but it is an expensive procedure. Another option is coal gasification, which converts coal that is relatively high in sulfur

Acid Politics

It will take more than laws to get rid of acid rain. The Clean Air Act (CAA) of 1970 has apparently made SO_2-caused acid rain a more widespread and a more difficult political problem. Since the law required polluters to meet state public health standards, tall stacks have become more numerous. Instead of investing in scrubbers to neutralize the sulfur dioxide, utilities opted for "dilution as the solution to pollution": they raised the stack height and superheated emissions to send them farther from the source. As a result local air got cleaner, but the air downwind—across state and national borders—got dirtier and the rain more acidic. When it became clear that long-range transport was causing problems for areas downwind, the act was amended in 1977 to limit emissions. But the law has not been enforced by the Environmental Protection Agency (EPA), which has been operating in an antiregulatory political climate. The agency has been effectively "leashed" until scientists can provide a "comprehensive" study of the problem and a direct link between power plant emissions and acid rain.

But scientists insist that we know enough now to take action. The National Academy of Sciences found that the circumstantial evidence of power plants' role in acid rain production "overwhelming." Other studies have concluded that if we do not act now to reduce the pollutants that cause acid rain, we risk widespread, irreversible damage to the ecosystems upon which our well-being and our economy depend.

Those who would label such concern alarmist have only to consider what these studies have uncovered. Ten years ago there were only a few lakes in the Adirondacks too acid to sustain life. Now there are thousands of sterile lakes and more are acidifying as far east as Maine and as far west as the Colorado Rockies and southern Arizona. Evergreens, shrouded regularly in vinegar-strength fogs, are dying on high-altitude slopes in the Appalachians. Not only are trees in these areas dying but their growth rates are declining and their reproductive capacity is also becoming severely impaired. Acid rain has also been eating away at the copper skin of the Statue of Liberty and the marbles and sandstones of other priceless historic structures at such an alarming rate that it has been called the number one threat to the national parks that house them. Acid rain is also a threat to human health. Not only do the air pollutants worsen respiratory and cardiac problems, they also leach heavy metals into public water supplies.

Despite all these consequences, shortsighted policy makers still equate pollution controls with bad economics. Also, in the case of Midwest polluters, federal and state officials are particularly reluctant to place additional financial burdens on the "rust belt" economy shaken by obsolescence and foreign competition. They claim the region's remaining advantage is abundant, cheap electricity from burning local high-sulfur coal. So an advantage for one region is gradually disadvantaging other regions.

What may tip the balance? Failing to control pollution is bad economics. The cost of acid rain now outstrips the cost of controlling it: visible damage has been loosely estimated at $5 billion annually. Even conservative Wall Street analysts warn that acid rain is bad for business. A Standard and Poor's report cautions that it presents a clear danger to the $49 billion forestry and forest products industry. They argue that if acid rain eats into enough timber, "the stock prices will fall faster than the trees." It is hoped that this concern from the business sector about the impact of pollution will provide the necessary push to get pollution controls in place. If it does not, our political system may undermine its economic foundations by its very stability. The checks and balances that make our system resist sudden change may, in this instance, resist too long.

Mary Kuhner

to a gas in order to remove the sulfur. The gas obtained from coal is quite clean and can be transported relatively easily, augmenting supplies of natural gas. The synthetic gas produced from coal is now fairly expensive compared to gas from other sources, but may become more competitive in the future [4].

During combustion of coal a process known as fluidized-bed combustion can be utilized to eliminate sulfur oxides. The process involves mixing finely ground limestone with coal and burning it in suspension. Sulfur may also be removed by a process known as limestone injection in multistage burners; this involves injecting ground limestone into a special burner. Both of these processes work because the sulfur oxides combine with the calcium in the limestone to form calcium sulfides and sulfates, which may be collected.

Sulfur oxide emissions from stationary sources such as power plants can also be reduced by removing the oxides from the gases in the stack before they reach the atmosphere. Perhaps the most highly developed technology for the cleaning of gases in tall stacks is scrubbing (Fig. 12.23). In this method the gases are treated with a slurry of lime (calcium oxide, CaO) or limestone (calcium carbonate, $CaCO_3$). The sulfur oxides react with the calcium to form insoluble calcium sulfides and sulfates, which are collected and then disposed of. A major problem with this method is that the residue containing the calcium sulfides and sulfates is a sludge that must be disposed of at a land disposal site. Because the sludge can cause serious water pollution if it interacts with the hydrologic cycle, it must be treated carefully [4]. Furthermore, scrubbers are expensive and add significantly (10–15%) to the total cost of electricity produced by burning coal.

Finally, an innovative approach has been taken at a large coal burning power plant near Mannheim, West Germany, to remove sulfur before it enters the atmosphere. Smoke from combustion is treated with liquid ammonia (NH_3), which reacts with the sulfur to produce ammonium sulfate. The sulfur-contaminated smoke is cooled by outgoing clean smoke to a temperature that favors the reaction; then outgoing clean smoke is heated by incoming dirty smoke to force it out the vent. Waste heat from the cooling towers also heats nearby buildings, and the plant sells the ammonium sul-

FIGURE 12.23
A scrubber, used to remove sulfur oxides from the gases emitted by tall stacks.

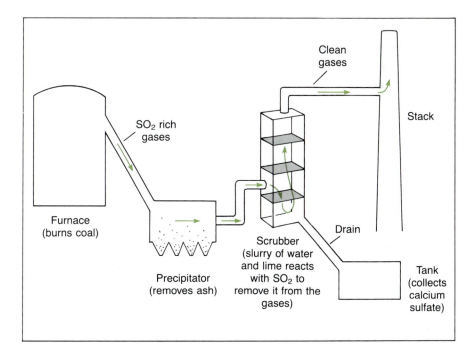

fate to farmers as fertilizer in a solid granular form. The plant was finished in 1984 and was built in response to tough pollution control regulations in West Germany that resulted from the recognition that sulfur oxides were important in causing acid precipitation that is killing forests there.

That pollution abatement can be successful is illustrated by the Japanese example. Japan had what was considered the most severe sulfur pollution problem in the world, and the health of the Japanese people was being directly affected. It was not uncommon to see residents of Yokohama and other areas forced to wear masks when out on the streets. The Japanese government in 1967 issued control standards, and between 1970 and 1975 the sulfur dioxide level was reduced by 50%, while the level of energy consumption increased by over 100%. New goals were set in 1973 and emission levels have steadily decreased. The Japanese have also begun to control nitrogen oxides as well. Power plants have met requirements for the most part by installing scrubbers known as flue gas desulfurization systems. These are capable of removing over 95% of the sulfur from smokestacks before the smoke is emitted into the atmosphere. In Japan today there are over 1000 of these in use [19].

Air Quality Standards

Air quality standards are important because they are tied to emission standards that attempt to control air pollution. Many countries have developed air quality standards. France, Japan, Israel, Italy, Canada, the Soviet Union, West Germany, Yugoslavia, Norway, and the United States, among others, have taken this first step. However, examination of the standards for different countries shows there is a good deal of variability concerning acceptable levels of pollution over a particular time period. For example the standard for sulfur oxides varies from 0.05/24 hr in the USSR to 0.15/24 hr in Yugoslavia to 0.2/24 hr in Norway to 0.38/24 hr in Italy. The units are thousandths of a gram per cubic meter of air over a 24–hour period, and the large range in the standards suggests there is a big difference in opinion concerning acceptable levels of sulfur oxide in the atmosphere. One of the prob-

lems in establishing air quality standards is that there is not general agreement concerning what concentrations of pollutants cause environmental problems [18].

U.S. Standards National Ambient Air Quality Standards (NAAQS) for the United States reflect the U.S. Clean Air Amendments of 1977, which define two levels or types of air quality standards. Primary standards are levels that are set to protect the health of people, but may not protect against damaging effects of air pollution to structures, paint, and plants. Secondary standards are designed to protect from other environmental degradation resulting from air pollution; however, most secondary levels are the same, or nearly so, as the primary levels [18].

The 1977 amendments also set air quality standards for particular areas or land uses to prevent significant deterioration of air quality beyond baseline measurements (air quality before significant pollution is present). This was done for three classes: national parks and wilderness areas (Class I); areas where moderate deterioration is allowed (Class II); and industrial areas (Class III). In practice all areas are considered Class II unless they are designated as Class I or III [18].

In order to enforce air quality standards in the United States, states are required to submit to the Environmental Protection Agency (EPA) State Implementation Plans that state how and when they expect to conform to the standards. Revised plans may be submitted for areas where nonattainment of standards occurs, and the EPA designates Air Quality Maintenance Areas for locations that may have problems maintaining air quality standards if potential new sources of air pollutants are not strictly regulated [18].

In the United States, air quality in urban areas is often reported as good, moderate, unhealthy, very unhealthy, or hazardous (Table 12.3). These levels, or stages, are derived from monitoring the concentration of five major pollutants: total suspended particulates, sulfur dioxide, carbon monoxide, ozone, and nitrogen dioxide. During a pollution episode in Los Angeles, hourly ozone levels are reported and a first-stage smog episode begins if the primary National Ambient Air Quality Standard (NAAQS) (0.12 ppm) is exceeded. This corresponds to unhealthy air with a Pollutant Standard Index (PSI) between 100 and 300. A second-stage smog episode is declared if the PSI exceeds 300, a point at which the air quality is hazardous to all people. As the air quality decreases during a pollution episode, people are requested to remain indoors, minimize physical exertion, and avoid driving automobiles. Industry also may be requested to reduce emissions to a minimum during the episode.

Data from major metropolitan areas in recent years suggest that the total number of unhealthful and very unhealthful days has declined. Although these data do not mean that air pollution has been eliminated, they do indicate that the nation's air quality is improving. However, most urban areas such as New York and Los Angeles still have unhealthful air much of the time.

Cost of Controls

In the United States today over $25 billion per year is spent on air pollution controls, and of this about 40% is for facilities to reduce emissions from stationary sources. The nonfarm private-business sector alone spends about $5 billion/yr on capital outlays to support pollution control [17]. This is a great deal of money!

The cost and benefits of air pollution control are controversial subjects. It has been argued that the present system of setting air quality standards is inefficient and unfair. This results because regulations are tougher for new sources than for existing sources, and even if benefits of pollution control exceed total costs, there is tremendous variability in the cost of air pollution control from one industry to another. For example, consider the incremental control costs (cost to remove an additional unit of pollution beyond what is presently required) for utilities burning fossil fuels and for an aluminum plant. The utilities cost for incremental control in a fossil fuel-burning utility is a few hundred dollars per additional ton of particulates removed compared to as much as several thousand dollars per ton for the aluminum plant to remove an additional ton of particulates [14]. Some economists would argue that it is wise to increase the standards for utilities and relax or at least not increase them for aluminum plants. This would lead to more cost-efficient pollution control while maintaining good air quality. However, the geographic distribution of various facilities will obviously determine the amount of prospective trade-offs that might be possible [14].

Another economic consideration is that, as the degree of control of a pollutant increases, eventually a point is reached where the cost of incremental control (reducing additional pollution) is greater than additional benefits of the increased control. Because of this and other economic factors, it has been argued that fees and taxes for emitting pollutants might be a better way to go than attempting to evaluate uncertain costs and benefits. The argument is that it makes more economic sense to enforce fees rather than enforce standards. This debate is likely to go on for some time before any change is made in the present system. Some of the variables that must be considered are shown in Figure 12.24. Notice on this idealized graph that with increasing air pollution controls the capital cost to control air pollution increases, and as the controls for air pollution increase the loss from pollution damages decreases. The total cost is thus the sum of these two items, and the minimum is well defined in terms of a particular average pollution level. This graph shows also that if the desired pollution level is lower than that level at which the minimum total cost occurs, then additional costs to obtain the desired pollution level will be necessary. This type of diagram, while valuable in looking at some of the major variables, does not consider adequately all of the loss from pollution damages. For example, long-term exposure to air pollution may aggravate or lead to chronic diseases in human beings, with a very high cost. How do we determine what portion of the cost is due to air pollution? In spite of these drawbacks, it seems worthwhile to reduce the air pollution level below some particular standard. Thus, in the United States, the ambient air quality standards have been developed as a minimum acceptable pollution level. However, as discussed, it is also a good idea to consider alternatives such as charging fees or taxes for emissions. If such charges are determined carefully and emissions

TABLE 12.3
Pollutant Standards Index[a]

PSI Index Value	Air Quality Level	Cautionary Statements	Health Effect Label	Pollutant level					
				TSP (24-hour) $\mu g/m^3$	SO$_2$ (24-hour) $\mu g/m^3$	CO (8-hour) $\mu g/m^3$	O$_3$ (1-hour) $\mu g/m^3$	NO$_2$ (1-hour) $\mu g/m^3$	
500	Significant harm	All persons should remain indoors, keeping windows and doors closed. All persons should minimize physical exertion and avoid traffic.		1000	2620	57.5	1200	3750	Premature death of ill and elderly. Healthy people will experience adverse symptoms that affect their normal activity
400	Emergency	Elderly and persons with diseases should stay indoors and avoid physical exertion. General population should avoid outdoor activity.	Hazardous (PSI > 300)	875	2100	46.0	1000	3000	Premature onset of some diseases in addition to significant aggravation of symptoms and decreased exercise tolerance in healthy persons.
300	Warning	Elderly and persons with existing heart and lung disease should stay indoors and reduce physical activity.	Very unhealthful (PSI = 200 to 300)	625	1600	34.0	800	2260	Significant aggravation of symptoms and decreased exercise tolerance in persons with heart or lung disease, with widespread symptoms in the healthy population.

TABLE 12.3
(*Continued*)

PSI Index Value	Air Quality Level	Cautionary Statements	Health Effect Label	TSP (24-hour) $\mu g/m^3$	SO$_2$ (24-hour) $\mu g/m^3$	CO (8-hour) $\mu g/m^3$	O$_3$ (1-hour) $\mu g/m^3$	NO$_2$ (1-hour) $\mu g/m^3$	General Health Effects
200	Alert	Persons with existing heart or respiratory ailments should reduce physical exertion and outdoor activity.	Unhealthful (PSI = 100 to 200)	375	800	17.0	400	1130	Mild aggravation of symptoms in susceptible persons, with irritation symptoms in the healthy population.
100	NAAQS[b]			260	365	10.0	240	(c)	
50	50% of NAAQS[b]		Moderate (PSI = 50 to 100)	75[c]	80[d]	5.0	120	(c)	
0			Good (PSI = 0 to 50)	0	0	0	0	(c)	

Source: Council on Environmental Quality.

[a]One measure of air quality is the Pollutant Standards Index. It is a highly summarized health-related index based on five of the criteria pollutants: carbon monoxide, ozone, sulfur dioxide, total suspended particulates, and nitrogen dioxide. The PSI for one day will rise above 100 in a Standard Metropolitan Statistical Area when one of the five pollutants at one station reaches a level judged to have adverse short-term effects on human health.

[b]NAAQS = National Ambient/Air Quality Standard.

[c]There are no index values reported at concentrations below those specified by Alert criteria.

[d]Annual primary NAAQS.

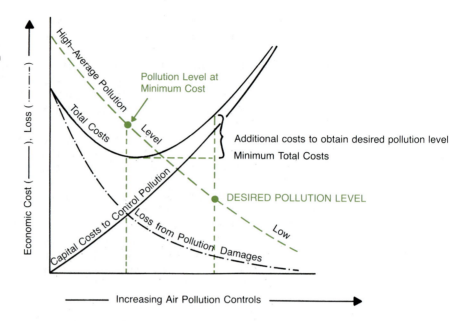

FIGURE 12.24
Some of the relationships between economic cost and increasing air pollution controls. (Modified after Williamson.)

are carefully monitored, then the charges would be an incentive for installation of control measures to avoid or lower fees or taxes. The end result would, we hope, be the same for both—better air quality.

SUMMARY

Every year approximately 250–300 million metric tons of primary pollutants enter the atmosphere above the United States from processes related to human activity. Considering the enormous volume of the atmosphere, this is a relatively small amount of material. If it were distributed uniformly, there would be little problem with air pollution. Unfortunately, the pollutants are not generally evenly distributed but rather are concentrated in urban areas or in other areas where the air naturally lingers.

The two major types of pollution sources are stationary and mobile. Stationary sources have a relatively fixed position and include point sources and area sources.

There are two main groups of air pollutants: primary and secondary. Primary pollutants are those emitted directly into the air: particulates, sulfur ox-

ides, carbon monoxide, nitrogen oxides, and hydrocarbons. Secondary pollutants are those produced through reactions among primary pollutants and other atmospheric compounds. A good example of a secondary pollutant is ozone, which forms over urban areas through photochemical reactions among primary pollutants and natural atmospheric gases.

The major air pollutants are sulfur dioxide, nitrogen oxides, carbon monoxide, ozone, and particulates. Each pollutant has characteristic properties and environmental effects.

Effects of the major air pollutants are considerable and include effects on visual resources, vegetation, animals, soil, water quality, natural and artificial structures, and human health.

There are three major types of smog: photochemical, sulfurous, and particulate smog. Each type of smog has particular environmental problems that vary with geographic region, time of year, and local urban conditions.

Meteorological conditions greatly affect whether or not polluted air is a problem in a particular urban area. In particular, restricted lower-atmosphere circulation atmosphere associated with temperature inversion layers may lead to pollution events.

A city creates an environment that is different from that of its surrounding areas. Cities change the local climate and, in general, are cloudier, warmer, rainier, and less humid than their surroundings. A growing problem in urban areas is indoor air pollution.

Combustion of large quantities of fossil fuels results in emission of sulfur and nitrogen oxides into the atmosphere, resulting in a problem known as acid rain. Environmental degradations associated with acid rain include loss of fish and other life in lakes, damage to trees and other plants, leaching of nutrients from soils, and damage to stone statues and buildings in urban areas. During the next decade or so, the acid rain problem is likely to remain as one of the most serious environmental problems facing the United States and other industrialized nations.

Air pollutants and modification of the land associated with civilization affect local, regional, and even global climates. Problems of particular concern include the increase in atmospheric carbon dioxide, which may eventually cause a global warming; the increase in particulates emitted into the atmosphere, which may locally or over a short period affect atmospheric conditions; and the increase in fluorocarbon and nitrous oxide (from fertilizers) emissions, which may eventually reduce stratospheric ozone. There is currently considerable debate over the magnitude and extent of climatic problems resulting from air pollution. We do know, however, that the effects are measurable and may be increasing.

Methods to control air pollution are tailored to specific sources and types of pollutants. These methods vary from settling chambers for particulates to catalytic converters to remove carbon monoxide and hydrocarbons from automobile exhaust to scrubbers or combustion processors that use lime to remove sulfur before it enters the atmosphere.

Air quality in urban areas is usually reported in terms of whether the quality is good, moderate, unhealthy, very unhealthy, or hazardous. These levels or stages are defined in terms of the Pollution Standard Index (PSI) and National Ambient Air Quality Standard (NAAQS). There is some indication that the nation's air quality has improved in recent years; however, there are still numerous areas where urban air quality is unhealthful a good deal of the year.

The relationships between emission control and environmental cost are complex. The minimum total cost is a compromise between capital costs to control pollutant and losses or damages resulting from such pollution. If additional controls are necessary to lower the pollution to a more acceptable level, then additional costs are incurred. These costs can increase quite rapidly beyond a certain level of pollution abatement. People believe that our present system of setting air quality standards is inefficient and unfair and that we should change to a system that charges fees or taxes for emissions.

STUDY QUESTIONS

1 Compare and contrast the London 1952 fog event with smog problems in the Los Angeles basin.

2 Why do we have air pollution problems when the amount of pollution emitted into the air is a very small fraction of the total material in the atmosphere?

3 What is the difference between point and nonpoint sources of air pollution? Which is easier to manage?

4 Distinguish between primary and secondary pollutants.

5 We know that natural rainfall is slightly acidic. Why then are we concerned about acid rain?

6 What is particulate smog? How does it differ from other smog? What problems does it pose for the future?

7 Why is it so difficult to establish national air quality standards?

8 In a highly technological society, is it possible to have 100% clean air? Is it feasible or likely?

9 Carbon dioxide is a nutrient as well as a pollutant. Explain this paradox.

FURTHER READING

ANTHES, R. A.; CAHIR, J. J.; FRASER, A. B.; and PANOFSKY, H. A. 1981. *The atmosphere*. 3rd ed. Columbus, Ohio: Charles E. Merrill.

BATTAN, L. J. 1974. *Weather*. Englewood Cliffs, N.J.: Prentice-Hall.

BRODINE, V. 1973. *Air pollution*. New York: Harcourt, Brace, Jovanovich.

CLAIRBORNE, R. 1970. *Man and history*. New York: Norton Press.

GATES, D. M. 1972. *Man and his environment: Climate*. New York: Harper & Row.

HODGES, L. 1973. *Environmental pollution*. New York: Holt, Rinehart and Winston.

NEIBURGER, M.; EDINGER, J. G.; and BONNER, W. D. 1973. *Understanding our atmospheric environment*. San Francisco: W. H. Freeman.

TORIBARA, T. Y.; MILLER, M. W.; and MORROW, P. E., eds. 1980. *Polluted rain*. New York: Plenum Press.

WILLIAMSON, S. J. 1973. *Fundamentals of air pollution*. Reading, Mass.: Addison-Wesley.

13

The Waters

- Total abundance of water on Earth is not a problem; there is plenty of it. The problem is its availability where and when it is needed, in the appropriate form.
- Water has unique characteristics that together make it critical for the existence of life and an important factor in many physical and biochemical processes.
- The residence times of water in various parts of the hydrologic cycle are critical to water use and pollution potential.
- Sediment pollution is a critical environmental problem that depletes soil resources and degrades water quality.
- A water budget summarizing inputs and outputs is useful in analyzing water supply problems and potential solutions.
- Groundwater is a particularly useful resource, though it is not often perceived as such. Problems associated with groundwater pollution are fast becoming recognized as one of our most significant environmental problems.
- Water resource management will become more difficult as demand for water increases. Management strategies must include use of data concerning the natural flux of water resources.
- Pollution of waters occurs when too much of an unwanted substance enters a body of water. Reduction of pollution sources, removal of pollutants from problem locations, and conversion of pollutants to harmless forms before they enter surface or ground waters are ways of dealing with water pollution problems.
- Wastewater treatment is increasingly expensive; innovative approaches are needed.
- Emerging water quality problem areas include oceans, coastal and freshwater wetlands, and tropical rain forests.

SEATTLE, PUGET SOUND, AND LAKE WASHINGTON*

The city of Seattle, Washington, lies between two major bodies of water—saltwater Puget Sound to the west and freshwater Lake Washington to the east. Beginning in the 1930s, the freshwater lake was used for disposal of sewage. By 1954, 10 sewage treatment plants that removed disease organisms and much of the organic matter had been built along the lake. With an additional treatment plant added in 1959, 76,000 m³ of effluent flowed per day from the treatment plants into the lake. Smaller streams that fed the lake brought in additional untreated sewage.

The lake's response to these effluents was a major bloom of undesirable algae in 1955, affecting fishing and the general aesthetics of the lake. Public concern increased immediately, and the city's mayor that year appointed an advisory committee to determine what might be done. Some of the committee members were scientists connected with the University of Washington in Seattle. These members had studied changes in the lake for years and knew the lake's biota well.

The committee advised the city to change its sewage treatment methods and to divert the sewage effluents from the lake into Puget Sound. The sound was much larger, and its waters were flushed rapidly and exchanged with waters of the open ocean because of the strong currents and tides that flowed in and out of the sound. A sewage diversion project began in 1963 and was completed in 1968. Sewage that had polluted the lake was taken by pipes to a very deep point far offshore in the sound.

By 1969 changes were noticeable in the lake. The unpleasant algae decreased in abundance, and the surface waters became two and one-half times clearer than they had been five years before. Oxygen concentrations in deep water increased immediately to levels above those observed in the 1930s, favoring an increase in the fish population.

*This case history is based on J. T. Lehman, 1986, Control of eutrophication in Lake Washington. In *Ecological knowledge and environmental problem solving*, ed. G. H. Orians, pp. 302–16. Washington, D. C.: National Academy of Science.

Phosphorus in the sewage effluent had been the major stimulant of the algal growth and was the major limiting factor for living things in the lake. With the elimination of sewage flow into the lake, the amount of phosphorus decreased and the undesirable algae decreased in response. Since then the lake has continued to improve and to return to conditions that are considered desirable by the city residents.

The story of the restoration of Lake Washington represents many important aspects of the relationship between human beings, the biosphere, and our water resources. Most importantly, Lake Washington is a success story and shows that public concern, long-term and accurate scientific information, and an understanding of ecosystem processes combined with appropriate policies, laws, and regulations can improve our environment without detriment to other social, economic, or aesthetic factors.

Water is a basic resource necessary for all life on Earth. Our discussion of this important resource will center on several aspects including, among others, properties of water that make it a unique liquid; selected aspects of the water cycle; water supply, use, and management; water quality; surface and groundwater pollution; land use, hydrology, and soil erosion; sediment pollution; wastewater treatment; and potential ecological problems related to extensive changes in patterns of water use, pollution, and management of fragile areas such as tropical forests and wetlands.

WATER: A BRIEF GLOBAL PERSPECTIVE

On a global scale, total water abundance is not the problem; the problem is water's availability in the right place at the right time in the right form. Water is a heterogeneous resource that can be found in either liquid, solid, or gaseous form at a number of locations at or near Earth's surface. Depending upon the specific location of water, the residence time may vary from a few days to many thousands of years (Table 13.1). Furthermore, more than 99% of Earth's water is unavailable or unsuitable for beneficial human use because of its salinity (sea water) or form and location (ice caps and glaciers).

TABLE 13.1
The world's water supply
(selected examples).

Location	Surface Area (km²)	Water Volume (km³)	Percentage of Total Water	Estimated Average Residence Time of Water
Oceans	361,000,000	1,230,000,000	97.2	Thousands of years
Atmosphere	510,000,000	12,700	0.001	9 days
Rivers and streams	—	1,200	0.0001	2 weeks
Groundwater: shallow, to depth of 0.8 km	130,000,000	4,000,000	0.31	Hundreds to many thousands of years
Lakes (freshwater)	855,000	123,000	0.009	Tens of years
Ice caps and glaciers	28,200,000	28,600,000	2.15	Up to tens of thousands of years and longer

Source: Data from U.S. Geological Survey.

Thus the amount of water for which all the people on Earth compete is much less than 1% of the total.

As the world's population and the industrial production of many goods increase, the use of water will also accelerate. Today, world per capita use of water is 710 m³/yr, and the total human use of water is 2600 km³/yr. It is estimated that by the year 2000 world use of water will more than double to 6000 km³/yr—a significant fraction of the naturally available fresh water.

The total average annual water yield (runoff) from Earth's rivers is approximately 48,000 km³ (Table 13.2), but its distribution is far from uniform. Some occurs in relatively uninhabited regions, such as Antarctica, which produces 2300 km³, or about 5%, of Earth's total runoff. South America, which includes the relatively uninhabited Amazon basin, provides 16,660 km³ or about one-third of total runoff; and in North America, total

runoff is about one-half of that for South America, or 8100 km³/yr. Unfortunately, much of the North American runoff occurs in sparsely settled or uninhabited regions, particularly in the northern parts of Canada and Alaska.

Compared with other resources, water is used in tremendous quantities. In recent years the total amount of water used on Earth per year is approximately 1000 times the world's total production of minerals, including petroleum, coal, metal ores, and nonmetals [1]. Because of its great abundance, water is generally a very inexpensive resource. But, because the quantity and quality of water available at any particular time are highly variable, statistical statements about the cost of water on a global basis are not particularly useful. Shortages of water have occurred and will continue to occur with increasing frequency. Such shortages lead to serious economic disruption and suffering by people [2].

TABLE 13.2
Water budgets for the continents.

Continent	Precipitation (cm/yr)	Evaporation (cm/yr)	Runoff (cm/yr)	Runoff (km³/yr)
Africa	69	43	26	7,700
Asia[a]	60	31	29	13,000
Australia	47	42	5	380
Europe	64	39	25	2,200
North America	66	32	34	8,100
South America	163	70	93	16,600
All continents	469	257	212	47,980

Source: Modified after Budyko.
[a]Includes the USSR.

The U.S. Water Resources Council has estimated that water use in the United States by the year 2020 may exceed surface water resources by 13%. As early as 1965, 100 million people in the United States used water that had already been used once before, and by the end of the century most of us will be using recycled water. How can we manage our water supply, use, and treatment to maintain adequate supplies?

WATER AS A UNIQUE LIQUID

To understand water as a necessity, as a resource, and as part of the pollution problem, we must understand its characteristics, its role in the biosphere, and its role in living things. Water is a unique liquid; without it, life as we know it is impossible. Compared with most other common liquids, water has the greatest capacity to absorb or store heat and is a good liquid solvent. Because many natural waters are slightly acidic, they can dissolve a great variety of compounds, from simple salts to minerals, including sodium chloride (common table salt) and calcium carbonate (calcite) in limestone rock. Water also reacts with complex organic compounds, including many amino acids that are found in the human body. Compared with other common liquids, water has a high surface tension—a property that is extremely important in many physical and biological processes that involve moving water through or storing water in small openings or pore spaces. Among common compounds and molecules, water is the only one whose solid form is lighter than its liquid form, which is why ice floats. If ice were heavier than liquid water and were to sink to the bottom of water bodies, the biosphere would be greatly different from what it is, and life—if it existed at all—would be greatly altered [3].

A peculiar feature of the biosphere is that the temperatures at Earth's surface are near what is known as the triple point of water. The triple point is the temperature and pressure of water vapor in the atmosphere at which the three phases of water—solid (ice), liquid, and gas (water vapor)—can exist together.

These qualities of water led L. J. Henderson to write early in the twentieth century that our planet was peculiarly and amazingly "fit" to support life. For the support of life, he wrote, "there are no other compounds which share more than a small part of the qualities of fitness of water" [3].

THE WATER CYCLE

As with all geochemical cycles, the cycle of water involves its flow from one storage "compartment" to another. In its simplest form, the global water cycles can be viewed as water flowing from the oceans to the atmosphere, falling from the atmosphere as rain onto the ocean, land, or fresh water, and then returning to the oceans as runoff or to the atmosphere by evaporation.

The problems and potentials of water differ with the uses and needs on the land, the fresh waters, and the oceans. Of particular significance are the residence times of water in the various parts of the cycle (see Table 13.1). This results because the residence times are related to pollution potential. For example, water in rivers has a short average residence time of about two weeks. Therefore, a one-time pollution event (one that does not involve the pollutant's attaching to sediment on the river bed, which would result in a much longer residence time) will be relatively short-lived because the water will soon leave the river environment. Many circumstances, such as sewage spills or pollutant-carrying truck or train crashes, can produce one-time point source events. News of such events is frequent these days. However, pollution is more likely to result from chronic processes, which discharge pollutants directly into rivers. Groundwaters, unlike river waters, have long residence times (from hundreds to thousands of years). Therefore natural removal of pollutants is a very slow process, and correction of groundwater pollution is very costly and difficult.

Surface Runoff

Surface runoff is important because of its effect on erosion and the transport of materials. Water moves materials either in a dissolved state or as suspended particles, and surface water can dislodge soil and rock particles on impact (Fig. 13.1). The size of particles and the amount of suspended

FIGURE 13.1
Raindrops strike the earth with enough force to tear apart unprotected soil and separate particles from one another. They wash the soil and generally move soil particles downslope.

particles moved by surface waters depend in part on the volume and depth of the water and the velocity of flow. That is, the faster a stream or river flows, the larger the particles it can move and the more material is transported.

The flow of water on the land is divided into watersheds. A watershed, or drainage basin (Fig. 13.2), is an area of ground in which any drop of water falling anywhere in it will leave in the same stream or river (assuming, that is, that the drop is not consumed by the biosphere, evaporated, stored, or transported out of the watershed by subsurface flow). Two drops of rain separated by only centimeters along the boundary of a major continental divide may end up a few weeks later in different oceans thousands of kilometers away. The amount of surface-water runoff from a watershed or drainage basin and the amount of sediment carried vary significantly. The variation results from biologic, climatic, geologic, physiographic, and land-use characteristics of the particular drainage basin together with variations of these factors with

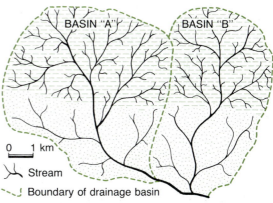

BASIN "A"   BASIN "B"

0   1 km

⅄ Stream

╌╌╌╌ Boundary of drainage basin

▭ Part of basin underlain by shale with high runoff potential and greater drainage density

▭ Part of basin underlain by sandstone with lower runoff potential and lower drainage density

FIGURE 13.2
Two drainage basins. Water falling on one side of the central boundary will drain into Basin A; on the other side, water will drain into Basin B. In this case, the streams from both basins eventually converge.

time. For instance, even the most casual observer is aware of the difference in the amount of sediment carried by streams in flood state (they are often more muddy) compared with what appears to be carried at low-flow conditions.

The principal geologic factors affecting surface-water runoff and sedimentation include rock and soil type, mineralogy, degree of weathering, and structural characteristics of the soil and rock. Fine-grained, dense, clay soils and exposed rock types with few fractures generally allow little water to move downward and become part of the subsurface flows. The runoff from precipitation falling on such materials is comparatively rapid. Conversely, sandy and gravelly soils, well-fractured rocks, and soluble rocks absorb a larger amount of precipitation and have less surface runoff. These principles are illustrated in Figure 13.2. The upper parts of basins A and B are underlain by shale and the lower parts are underlain by sandstone. The shale has a greater potential to produce runoff than the more porous sandstone. Therefore the drainage density (length of channel per unit area) is much greater in the shale areas than for sandstone areas.

Life affects stream flow in several ways. Vegetation decreases runoff by increasing the amount of rainfall intercepted and removed by evaporation. An experimental clear-cutting of an entire forested watershed at Hubbard Brook, New Hampshire, increased the stream flow in midsummer, when the flow was lowest [4]. The clear-cutting reduced evapotranspiration (water used by the trees and released to the atmosphere), making more water available for subsurface runoff. Runoff eventually diminished as the forest became reestablished following timber harvesting. Vegetation also retards erosion by roots binding or holding soil particles in place and by intercepting the rain and reducing its impact on the soil surface. In southern California, where fires are common and the soils highly erodible, areas that burn during a dry season frequently are subject to hazardous mudslides the next rainy season.

Animals may affect surface water runoff by removing vegetation; in fact, large mammals create paths that can turn into small channels during intense precipitation. Soil organisms alter the soil's physical structure, sometimes allowing greater

percolation into the soil and reducing runoff and erosion. Because it is cohesive (its particles stick together) and tends to hold water, a highly organic soil will tend to erode less rapidly than a sandy soil with low cohesion, high porosity, and high permeability.

The above principles and processes suggest that runoff can be variable depending upon geologic, climatic, and biologic conditions. For example, under natural conditions with continuous forest cover, direct surface runoff as shown in Figure 13.1 is unusual because trees and lower vegetation intercept the precipitation and the potential for water to infiltrate the soil is high. In such cases the runoff is subsurface by way of shallow throughflow confined to the soil above the groundwater (Fig. 13.3a). An exception to this may occur near

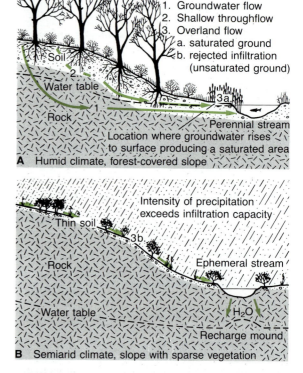

FIGURE 13.3
Paths of water from slopes to streams. (a) On a humid, forest-covered slope and (b) in a semiarid climate on a slope with sparse vegetation.

streams and in hillslope depressions if the ground-water table rises to the surface. Such saturated areas can produce surface runoff even in humid climates with good vegetation cover (point 3a, Fig. 13.3a). Areas that are saturated tend to expand and contract, being more abundant during the time of spring snow melt than in the late summer or fall, when precipitation is less. In disturbed areas, areas with sparse vegetation cover, semiarid lands, and areas with land uses such as row crops or urbanization, overland flow is often produced because the intensity of precipitation is greater than the potential for the water to infiltrate the ground (Fig. 13.3b).

Thus we can identify three major paths by which water on slopes can be transported to the stream environment and exported from the drainage basin: overland flow, throughflow (a type of shallow subsurface flow above the groundwater table), and groundwater flow (Fig. 13.3). Understanding potential paths of runoff for a particular site or area is critical in evaluating hydrologic impacts of projects that involve land-use changes. Loss of vegetation and soil compaction during urbanization, for example, will produce more overland flow (point 3b, Fig. 13.3b), as will land-use change from forest to row crops.

Groundwater

Groundwater is the water that penetrates the soil and reaches the water table. Some groundwater is derived directly from precipitation. Other sources of groundwater include water that infiltrates from surface waters, including lakes and rivers; stormwater retention or recharge ponds; and wastewater treatment systems such as cesspools and septic-tank drain fields.

The soil and rocks that groundwater passes through act as natural filters. Under the right conditions, this filtering system cleanses the water, trapping disease-causing microorganisms and particulates that contain toxic compounds. The water actually exchanges materials with the soil and rocks. If the soil or rock surface is already highly contaminated or contains naturally toxic elements, the water may be rendered toxic by these natural processes. For instance, water may become toxic by dissolving sufficient amounts of a toxic element or mineral, such as arsenic. An interesting example with serious environmental implications comes from the western San Joaquin Valley in California, where selenium (a very toxic heavy metal) in the natural soils is released by application of irrigation waters. Subsurface drainage of the selenium-rich water from fields enters the surface waters and has caused birth defects in waterfowl. The extent of the problem is only now being learned. Selenium is also toxic to people. Like many trace metals, selenium has a dual character: it is necessary for life processes at trace concentrations, but toxic at some higher concentrations. Most often, the groundwaters dissolve a mixture of minerals and some gases that can be nuisances to some human uses. Some examples are iron as ferrous hydroxide, which colors the water brown and leaves a brown discoloration on porcelain; calcium carbonate, which creates the so-called hardness of water; and hydrogen sulfide, which produces a "rotten egg" odor.

People's perceptions about groundwater affect the way they view our water resources. First, people tend to assume that water is available when, where, and in the amounts they want. We turn on a faucet and expect water—it is somebody else's responsibility to see that we have it. Second, because groundwater is out of sight, it is out of mind and/or mysterious. Third, groundwater is not as easily measured quantitatively as surface water. Therefore, precise quantitative values of groundwater reserves are not available, and we rely on estimates of the probable reserves.

WATER SUPPLY: U.S. EXAMPLE*

The water supply at any particular point on the land surface depends upon several factors in the hydrologic cycle, including the rates of precipitation, evaporation, stream flow, and subsurface flow. The various uses of water by people also significantly affect water supply. A concept useful in

---

*Much of the discussion concerning water supply and use is summarized from U.S. Water Resources Council, 1978, *The nation's water resources, 1975–2000*, Vol. 1.

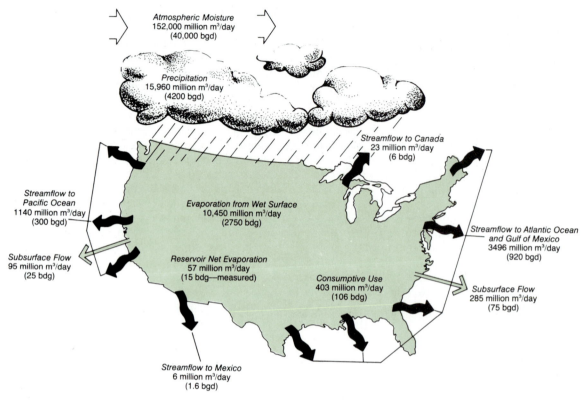

FIGURE 13.4
Water budget for the United States. (From Water Resources Council, 1978.)

understanding water supply is the **water budget,** or the inputs and outputs of water in a system. On a continental scale, the water budget for the conterminous United States is shown in Figure 13.4. The amount of water vapor passing over the United States every day is approximately 152,000 million m³ (40,000 billion gallons), and of this approximately 10% falls as precipitation in the form of rain, snow, hail, or sleet. Approximately two-thirds of the precipitation evaporates quickly or is transpired by vegetation. The remaining one-third, or about 5510 million m³ (1450 billion gallons) per day, enters the surface or groundwater storage systems, flows to the oceans or across the nation's boundaries, is used by consumption, or evaporates from reservoirs. Unfortunately, owing to natural variations in precipitation that cause either floods or droughts, only a portion of this water can be de-

veloped for intensive uses. Thus only about 2565 million m³ (675 billion gallons) per day are considered to be available 95% of the time [2].

On a regional scale, it is critical to consider annual precipitation and runoff patterns in order to develop water budgets. Figures 13.5 and 13.6 illustrate the variability of precipitation and runoff for the conterminous United States. Potential problems with water supply can be predicted in areas where average precipitation and runoff are relatively low, such as in the southwestern and Great Plains regions of the United States as well as in some of the intermontane valleys in the Rocky Mountain area. The theoretical upper limit of surface water supplies is the mean annual runoff, assuming it could be successfully stored. Unfortunately, storage of all the runoff is not possible because of evaporative losses from large reservoirs

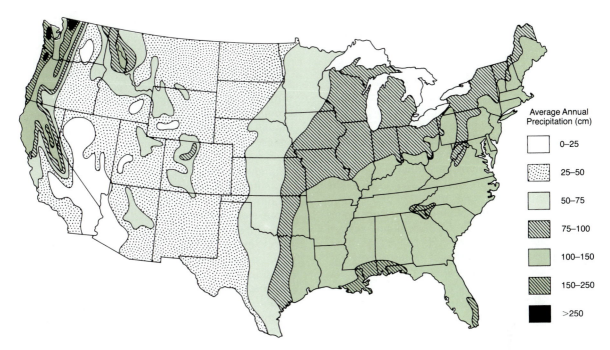

FIGURE 13.5
Average annual precipitation for the conterminous United States. (From Water Resources Council, 1978.)

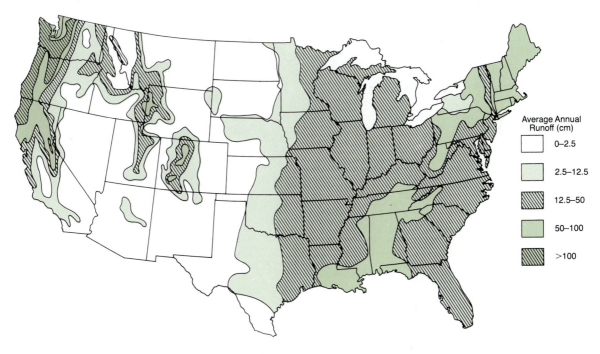

FIGURE 13.6
Average annual runoff for the conterminous United States. (From Water Resources Council, 1978.)

and a limited number of suitable sites for reservoirs. As a result, there are bound to be shortages in water supply in areas with low precipitation and runoff. Strong conservation practices are necessary to ensure an adequate supply [2].

Because there are large annual variations in stream flow, even areas with high precipitation and runoff may periodically suffer from droughts. For example, the dry years of 1961 and 1966 in the northeastern United States and 1976 and 1977 in the western United States produced serious water shortages. Fortunately, in the more humid eastern United States stream flow tends to vary less than in other regions, and drought is less likely [2]. Nevertheless, the drought of summer 1986 in the southeastern United States caused tremendous hardships and inflicted several billions of dollars in damage.

Nearly one-half of the population of the United States uses groundwater as a primary source for drinking water. Fortunately, the total amount of groundwater available in the United States is enormous, accounting for approximately 20% of all water withdrawn for consumptive uses. Within the conterminous United States the amount of groundwater within 0.8 km of the land surface is estimated to be between 125,000 and 224,000 km^3. To put this in perspective, the lower estimate is about equal to the total discharge of the Mississippi River during the last 200 years. Unfortunately, owing to the cost of pumping and exploration, much less than the total quantity of groundwater is available. Figure 13.7 shows the major aquifers in the conterminous United States capable of yielding more than 0.2 m^3 (50 gallons) per minute [2].

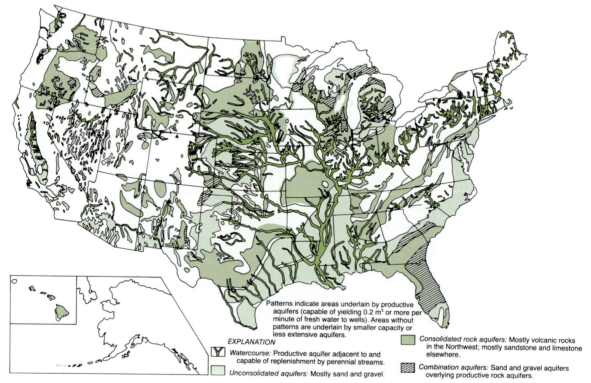

Patterns indicate areas underlain by productive aquifers (capable of yielding 0.2 m^3 or more per minute of fresh water to wells). Areas without patterns are underlain by smaller capacity or less extensive aquifers.

EXPLANATION

Watercourse: Productive aquifer adjacent to and capable of replenishment by perennial streams.

Unconsolidated aquifers: Mostly sand and gravel.

Consolidated rock aquifers: Mostly volcanic rocks in the Northwest; mostly sandstone and limestone elsewhere.

Combination aquifers: Sand and gravel aquifers overlying productive rock aquifers.

FIGURE 13.7
Groundwater resources for the conterminous United States. Shown are major aquifers that are capable of yielding more than 0.2 m^3/min of groundwater. (From Water Resources Council, 1978.)

In many parts of the country, groundwater withdrawal from wells exceeds natural inflow. In such cases, water is being mined and can be considered a nonrenewable resource. Groundwater overdraft is a serious problem in the Texas-Oklahoma-High Plains area, California, Arizona, Nevada, New Mexico, and isolated areas of Louisiana, Mississippi, Arkansas, and the south Atlantic-Gulf region (Fig. 13.8a). In the Texas-Oklahoma-High Plains area alone, the overdraft amount is approximately equal to the natural flow of the Colorado River (Fig. 13.8b) [2]. In this area lies the Ogallala aquifer, which is composed of water-bearing sands and gravels that underlie an area of about 400,000 km^2 from South Dakota into Texas. Although the aquifer holds a tremendous amount of groundwater, it is being used in some areas at a rate that is up to 20 times that of natural recharge by infiltration of precipitation. The water level in many parts of the aquifer has declined in recent years (see Fig. 13.8) and there is concern that eventually a significant portion of land now being irrigated will return to dry farming as the resource is used up.

To date only about 5% of the total groundwater resource has been depleted but water levels have declined as much as 30–60 m in parts of Kansas, Oklahoma, New Mexico, and Texas. As the water table becomes lower, yields from wells decrease and energy costs to pump the water increase. The most severe problems in the High Plains and of the Ogallala aquifer today are in those locations where irrigation was first started in the 1940s.

In many areas, pumping of groundwater has forever changed the character of the land. For example, rivers in the Tucson, Arizona, area, prior to lowering of the water table through pumping, were perennial, with healthy populations of trout, beaver, and other animals. Today the native riparian trees have died and the rivers are dry much of the year. Ironically, these processes also increased the flood hazard in Tucson, which currently gets its entire water supply from groundwater sources! Loss of riparian trees and the root strength they provided to stream banks render the channels much more vulnerable to lateral bank erosion. During the 1983 floods in Tucson this became very apparent as roads, bridges, and buildings were damaged by the shifting channels. Tree-lined channels are much more stable, but riparian trees need a groundwater table sufficiently close to the surface for healthy growth. Unfortunately, mining of groundwater in the Tucson area has precluded restoration of trees.

WATER USE

In order to discuss water use, it is important to distinguish between instream and offstream uses. Offstream uses remove water from its source— water is taken for drinking, for washing and sewage, and for agricultural irrigation. Consumptive use is an offstream use in which water does not return to the stream or groundwater resource immediately after use [2].

Instream water use includes the use of rivers for navigation, hydroelectric power generation, fish and wildlife habitat, and recreation. These multiple uses usually create controversy because each instream use requires different conditions to prevent damage or detrimental effects. Fish and wildlife require certain water levels and flow rates for maximum biological productivity; these levels and rates may differ from the requirements for hydroelectric power generation, which requires large fluctuations in discharges to match power needs. Similarly, both of these may conflict with requirements for shipping and boating. The discharge necessary to move the sediment load in a river may require yet another pattern of flow. Figure 13.9 shows some of these conflicting demands. A major problem concerns how much water may be removed from a stream or river and transported to another location without damaging the stream system. This is a problem in the Pacific Northwest, where certain fish like the steelhead trout and salmon are on the decline partly because humans have induced alterations in land use and stream flows that have degraded fish habitats.

In California, demands are being made on northern rivers for reservoir systems to feed the cities of southern California. In our modern civilization, water is often moved vast distances from areas with abundant rainfall to areas of high usage. In California two-thirds of the state's runoff occurs north of San Francisco, where there is a surplus of

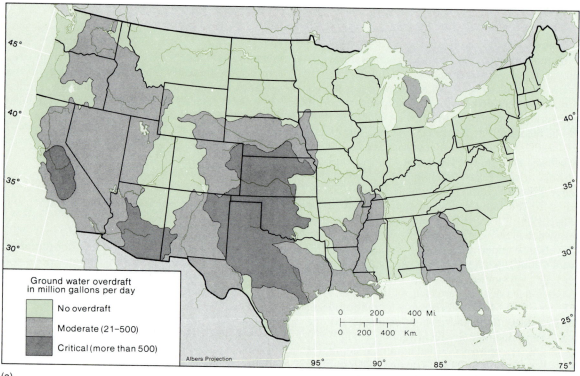

(a)

FIGURE 13.8
(a) Groundwater overdraft,
1975, for the conterminous
United States. (b) A detail
of water level changes in
the Texas-Oklahoma-High
Plains area. (From U.S.
Geological Survey.)

Ground water overdraft
in million gallons per day

No overdraft

Moderate (21–500)

Critical (more than 500)

Albers Projection

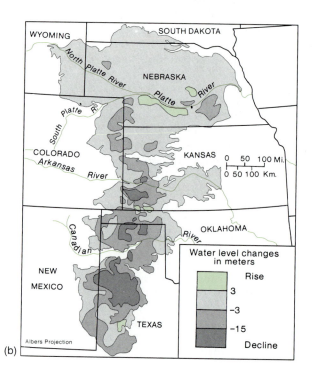

(b)

Water level changes
in meters

Rise

3

-3

-15

Decline

Irrigating the Desert: A Temporary Eden?

Since the dawn of civilization in Mesopotamia and Egypt, people have diverted water from rivers and streams to irrigate parched, unproductive deserts and make them blossom. Although irrigated lands comprise only about 13% of all the world's arable land, they are by far the most productive. Irrigated fields in Arizona produce over 2½ times more wheat per hectare than the national average; cotton yields are almost ten times higher.

Despite obvious advantages, irrigation does have its problems. It is by far the major consumer of water withdrawals—70% worldwide. Overappropriation of water in some areas has reduced raging rivers to mere trickles or even to cracked mud flats. Other regions that irrigate with groundwater are in danger of rapidly depleting the aquifers on which they depend.

The most widespread detrimental effects of irrigation are salinization, alkalinization, and waterlogging of soils, already affecting half of the world's irrigated lands to some degree. These problems occur where water is applied to the soil faster than drainage can remove it. The level of the water table rises to within reach of plant roots, depriving them of oxygen. The water table often carries high levels of soluble salts accumulated over time from irrigation water. The saline water and salt deposits formed on the soil surface inhibit the growth of crops or kill them outright. Irrigation waters passing through extensive areas of affected fields return to streams and rivers with salt levels that may impair or prohibit irrigation projects downstream. Large areas of irrigated lands have already been abandoned for these reasons.

Prevention is the best way to deal with these problems. Proper drainage systems, although initially expensive, prevent waterlogging and salinization from occurring. Methods that use water more efficiently, such as drip irrigation, reduce both problems and conserve precious water from rivers and aquifers.

Reclamation of fields already affected is costly and can be time consuming. Waterlogged fields can be drained and the accumulated salts washed out, but these efforts often require major hydraulic engineering. This tends to move the problem rather than solve it, however, as the saline waters drained cause repercussions downstream.

Rather than meeting the problems associated with irrigation head-on, there are ways to sidestep them. Genetic engineering could produce crop varieties that require much less water than those planted today. In Arizona, the Hopi Indians grow a strain of corn that requires as little as five inches of rainfall annually. Researchers at the University of California have successfully raised special varieties of barley, wheat, and tomatoes irrigated with sea water. Such strains may eventually be cultivated in soils affected by salinization.

The idea of sea-water-tolerant crops could be taken literally one step farther—from coastline to ocean. The Seri Indians of western Mexico harvest a protein-rich grain from a flowering marine plant, *Zostera marin*, which merits scientific investigation.

Lessons being learned today in arid zones around the world are the same as those learned in ancient times on the banks of the Tigris, Euphrates, and upper Nile rivers: Irrigation can turn the desert green, but if applied incorrectly will eventually cause a farmer's crops to wither and die, like a leaf of summer in the cold winds of autumn.

David Perry

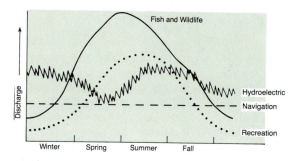

FIGURE 13.9
Instream water uses and the varying discharges for each use. Discharge is the amount of water passing by a particular location and is measured in cubic meters per second.

water, while two-thirds of the water use occurs south of San Francisco, where there is a deficit. In recent years, canals constructed by the California Water Project and the Central Valley Project have moved tremendous amounts of water from the northern to the southern part of the state.

The major water projects in California are shown in Figure 13.10a. Of particular interest is the long-standing dispute between the city of Los Angeles and the people in Owens Valley on the eastern side of the Sierra Nevada. Los Angeles near the end of the nineteenth century had a drought and, after looking for a potential additional new supply, settled on the Owens Valley. By various means (some of which were controversial to say the least) the city purchased most of the water rights and constructed the Owens River Aqueduct,

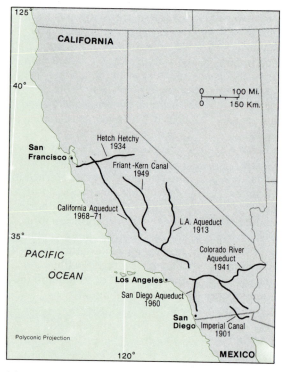

(a)

(b)

FIGURE 13.10
(a) California aqueducts and irrigation canals; (b) view of the Los Angeles Owens River Aqueduct in the Owens Valley.

which was completed in 1913 (Fig. 13.10b). Since that time groundwater has also been taken. As a result of the tremendous exportation of surface water and groundwater, the Owens Valley has suffered from desertification. Protests that were more violent in the early 1900s are now court battles, and only recently have both parties come closer to a settlement that will include limits on the amount of water taken by Los Angeles and projects to halt environmental degradation.

Many large cities in the world must seek water from areas farther and farther away. For example, New York City has imported water from nearby areas for over 100 years. Water use and supply in New York City represent a repeating pattern. Originally, local groundwater, streams, and the Hudson River itself were used. However, water needs exceeded local supply, so in 1842 the first large dam was built more than 48 km north of the city. As the city expanded rapidly from Manhattan to Long Island, water needs again increased. The sandy soils of Long Island were at first a source of drinking water, but this water was removed faster than rainfall replenished it. Local cesspools contaminated the groundwater, and salty ocean water intruded. A larger dam was built at Croton in 1900. Further expansion of the population created the same pattern: initial use of groundwater; pollution, salinification, and exhaustion of this resource; and subsequent building of new, larger dams farther and farther upstate in forested areas. The pattern continues with development of tract housing in eastern Long Island, where there are now problems of pollution, salinification, and exhaustion of the resource. Eventually, the cost of obtaining water from long distances and competition for the available water will place an upper limit on the water supply of the city and its environs.

As more and more water is needed for cities and agriculture, conflicts will increase and intensive argument will center on instream water use. An important, fruitful area of research is more careful evaluation of what flows are necessary to maintain a natural river system.

Offstream water-use withdrawals in the United States today amount to more than 1700 million m³/day (450 billion gallons/day)—considerably more than one-half the average flow of the Missis-

sippi River, which drains approximately 40% of the conterminous United States. Consumption of water amounts to approximately 22% of that withdrawn or 379 million m³/day (100 billion gallons/day). Figure 13.11 lists present sources and disposition of offstream water withdrawals, amount of withdrawals by the major users (self-supplied industry, agriculture, public supply, and rural), and consumptive use of fresh water. Figure 13.12 shows recent trends in water withdrawals, consumptive use, and population. Examination of the information in these figures reveals that industry (self-supplied, including thermoelectric power) and agriculture (irrigation) withdraw 58% and 34%, respectively, while public supply (domestic, public, commercial, and industrial uses) and rural (domestic and livestock uses) withdraw much less [5]. In terms of consumption, agriculture (irrigation) consumes about 80% of the total fresh water used [5]. Trends in withdrawals and consumption (Fig. 13.12) suggest that self-supplied industry (especially power plants) has been responsible for much of the recent growth in water resource utilization. It is expected that withdrawals will decrease by the year 2000 while water consumption will increase slightly. It is hoped that projected reductions in offstream withdrawals will be realized from conservation endeavors, improved technology, and recycling of water. Increases in consumption from the present level will most likely reflect growth and greater water demand for industries, manufacturing, agriculture, and steam generation of electricity [2].

What can be done to use water more efficiently and reduce withdrawal and consumption? Improved agricultural irrigation could reduce withdrawals by between 20% and 30%. Such improvements include lined and covered canals that reduce seepage and evaporation; computer monitoring and scheduling of water releases from canals; a more integrated use of surface waters and groundwaters; night irrigation; improved irrigation systems (sprinklers, drip irrigation); and better land preparation for water application.

Domestic use of water accounts for only about 6% of the total national withdrawals. Because this use is concentrated, it poses major local problems. Withdrawal of water for domestic use may be sub-

FIGURE 13.11
Water use in the United States, 1980: (a) sources, (b) disposition, (c) off-stream withdrawals, (d) consumptive use; "bgd" = billions of gallons per-day. (Data from Solley et al.)

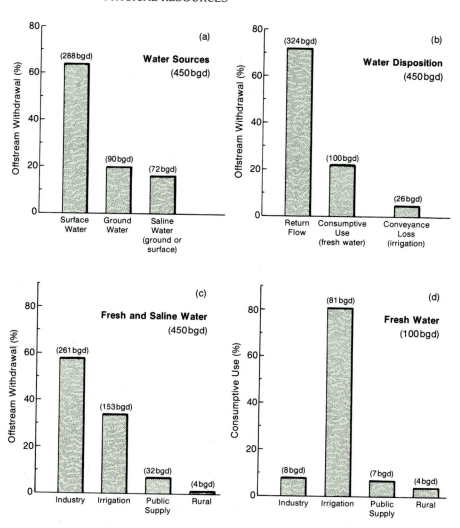

stantially reduced at a relatively small cost with more efficient bathroom and sink fixtures, night irrigation, and drip irrigation systems for domestic plants.

How water supply is perceived by people is also important in determining how much water is used. For example, people in Tucson, Arizona, perceive the area as a desert (which it is) and one sees a lot of native plants (cactus and other desert plants) in yards and gardens around homes and buildings. Tucson's water supply is all from groundwater, which is being mined (used faster than it is being naturally replenished), and the water use is about 605 liters (160 gallons) per person per day. Not far away the people of Phoenix, Arizona, use about 983 liters (260 gallons) of water per person per day. Parts of Phoenix use as much as 3780 liters (1000 gallons) per person per day to water mulberry trees and high hedges! Phoenix has been accused of having an "oasis mentality," concerning water use. Water rates also make a difference. The people in Tucson pay about 75% more for water than the people in Phoenix, where the water supply is drawn from the Salt River rather than from groundwater. Water rates in Tucson are structured to encourage conservation, and some industries

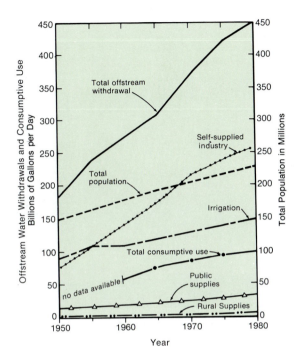

FIGURE 13.12
Offstream water withdrawals and consumptive use, 1950–1980. (After Solley et al.)

DAMS, RESERVOIRS, AND CANALS

Our discussion of water supply established that many agricultural and urban areas require water delivered from nearby, and in some cases not so nearby, sources. To accomplish this a system of water storage and routing by way of canals and aqueducts from reservoirs is needed. The parties interested in water and water development range from government agencies to local water boards and conservation groups. There often is a good deal of controversy concerning water development, and the day of development of large projects in the United States without careful environmental review has passed. The resolution of development issues now involves input from a variety of groups that may have very different needs and concerns. These range from agricultural groups who see water development as critical for their livelihood to groups of people whose primary concerns are with wildlife and wilderness preservation. It is a positive sign that the various parties on water issues are now at least able to meet and communicate their desires and concerns.

consider water as a cost control measure [6]. The message here is that water in the southwestern United States and other locations will be in short supply in the future and we could all do with a little of Tucson's "desert mentality," particularly large urban areas such as Los Angeles and San Diego. Whether Tucson can maintain its desert mentality following importation of Colorado River water remains to be seen.

Considering steam generation of electricity, water removal could be reduced as much as 25–30% by different types of cooling towers that use less or no water. Manufacturing and industry might curb water withdrawals by increasing in-plant treatment and recycling of water or by developing new equipment and processes that require less water [2]. Because the field of water conservation is changing so rapidly, it is expected that a number of innovations will reduce the total withdrawals of water for various purposes, even though consumption will continue to increase [2].

Dams and Reservoirs

Dams and their accompanying reservoirs are generally designed to be multifunction structures. That is, those that propose the construction of dams and reservoirs point out that reservoirs may be used for activities such as recreation, as well as providing flood control and assuring a more stable water supply. It is important to recognize that it is often difficult to reconcile these various uses at a given site. For instance, water demands for agriculture might be high during the summer, resulting in a drawdown of the reservoir and the production of extensive mud flats (Fig. 13.13). Those interested in recreation find the low water level and the mud flats to be aesthetically degrading, and these effects of high water demand may also interfere with wildlife (particularly fish) by damaging or limiting spawning opportunities. Finally, dams and reservoirs tend to provide a false sense of security to those living below the water retention structures, because dams cannot fully protect us against great floods.

FIGURE 13.13
Reservoirs provide water for many purposes, including agriculture and recreation. High water demand can lead to a drawdown and produce mud flats, as shown here.

There is little doubt that we will need additional dams and reservoirs if our present practices of water use are continued. Some existing structures will even need to be heightened. As more people flock to urban areas, water demands there are going to increase and additional water storage will be required. This is particularly true in the more arid parts of the country (including the southern California belt extending eastward into Arizona), where populations are growing rapidly.

Conflicts over construction of additional dams and reservoirs are bound to occur—water developers may view a canyon dam site as a resource for water storage, while other people view it as a wilderness area and recreation site for future generations. The conflict is particularly pointed because good dam sites are often sites of high-quality scenic landscape. Unless water-use patterns change in agricultural and urban areas, however, additional water supply facilities will be a high priority for rapidly growing urban areas, perhaps taking precedence over aesthetic environmental concerns.

Whenever a dam and reservoir are constructed on a river system, that system is changed forever. The flow of water and sediment is changed, as are the physical and biological habitats and land uses

below the dam. Effects of constructing dams and reservoirs are discussed further in Chapter 17, where we consider the subject of flood control.

Canals

Water from upstream reservoirs may be routed to downstream needs by way of natural watercourses or by canals and aqueducts.

Canals, whether lined or unlined, are often attractive nuisances to people and animals. Where they flow through urban areas, drownings are an ever-present threat. When they are unlined, canals may lose a good deal of water to the subsurface flow system. While it may be argued that this is a form of artificial groundwater recharge, it may be an inefficient one because canals may cross areas with little potential for groundwater development or areas of poor groundwater quality. In these cases, water seeping from unlined canals is essentially lost water (Fig. 13.14).

The construction of canal systems, especially in developing countries, has led to serious environmental problems. For example, when the High Dam at Aswan was completed in 1964, a series of canals was needed to convey the water to agricul-

FIGURE 13.14
Lining the East Bench Canal, Montana, with a 63–foot wide sheet of polyvinyl chloride to reduce water loss from the canal.

tural sites. The canals became infested with snails that carry the dreaded disease schistosomiasis (snail fever). This disease has always been a problem in Egypt but the swift currents of Nile flood waters flushed the snails out each year. The tremendous expanse of waters in irrigation canals now provides happy homes for these snails. The disease is debilitating and so prevalent in parts of Egypt that virtually the entire population of some areas may be affected by it. The Egyptian canals are also a home for mosquitoes, one particular variety of which carries a form of malaria that killed 100,000 Egyptians in 1942.

Reservoirs and canal systems are being planned in a variety of environments around the world today. Environmental concern in the United States ensures that important environmental review will take place. This may not be true in many developing countries, where attention to environmental concerns is not as high a priority as, for instance, the production of food. In such areas construction of large, long canals may considerably alter land use and the biologic environment by producing new and different water systems and barriers to migration of wildlife. This is not meant to say that water development in developing countries is not necessary, but it does emphasize the need for environmental concern at the ecosystem level when planning and developing water resources. At the very least, we can share with developing countries the mistakes we have made in the past so that they need not be repeated in the future. Water development and environmental concern are not necessarily incompatible. However, tradeoffs must be made if a quality environment is to be preserved.

WATER MANAGEMENT

Management of water resources is a complex issue that will become more difficult in coming years as the demand for water increases. This will be especially true in the southwestern United States and other semiarid and arid parts of the world where water is or soon will be in short supply. Options open to people who plan on minimizing potential water supply problems include location of alternative supplies and better management of existing supplies. In some areas location of new supplies is unlikely, and serious consideration is being given to ideas as original as towing icebergs to coastal areas where fresh water is needed. It seems apparent that water will become much more expensive in the future and, if the price is right, many innovative programs are possible. Recently one city in southern California began to consider a plan to import Colorado water via a private company that owns water rights there. Such thoughts and plans are causing concern among government people who manage water resources through regulations that control allocation and price. Cities in need of water are beginning to treat water like a commodity that can be bought and sold on the open market. If cities are willing to pay for water and are allowed to somehow avoid current water regulation, then allocation and pricing as it is now known will change; if the price is right, "new water" from a variety of sources may become available. For example, irrigation districts (water managers for an agricultural area) may contract with cities to supply water to urban areas. They could do this without any less water being available for crops by using conservation measures to minimize present water loss through evaporation and seepage from unlined canals. Currently most irrigation districts do not have the capital to finance expensive conservation methods, but money from cities for water could finance the projects. It's a new ball game if water does become a free-market commodity sold like oil and gas.

Luna Leopold recently suggested that a new philosophy of water management is needed—one based on geologic, geographic, and climatic factors as well as on the traditional economic, social, and political factors. He argues that the management of water resources cannot be successful so long as it is naively perceived primarily from an economic and political standpoint. However, this is how water use is approached. The term "water use" is appropriate because we seldom really "manage" water [7]. The essence of Leopold's water management philosophy is summarized in this section.

Surface water and groundwater are both subject to natural flux with time. In wet years there is plenty of surface water and the near-surface groundwater resources are replenished. During these years we hope that our flood-control structures, bridges, and storm drains will withstand the excess water. Each of these structures is designed to withstand a particular flow (for example, the 20–year flood), which, if exceeded, may cause damage or flooding.

All in all, we are much better prepared to handle floods than water deficiencies. During dry years, which must be expected even though they may not be accurately predicted, we should have specific strategies to minimize hardships. For example, there are subsurface waters in various locations in the western United States that are either too deep to be economically extracted or have marginal water quality. These waters may be isolated from the present hydrologic cycle and therefore are not subject to natural recharge. Such water might be used when the need is great. However, advance planning to drill the wells and connect them to existing water lines is necessary if they are to be ready when the need arises. Another possible emergency plan might involve the treatment of wastewater. Reuse of water on a regular basis might be too expensive, but advance planning to reuse treated water during emergencies might be a wise decision [7].

When dealing with groundwater that is naturally replenished in wet years, we should develop plans to use surface water when available and not be afraid to use groundwater in dry years; that is, the groundwater might be pumped out at a rate exceeding the replenishment rate in dry years. During wet years natural recharge and artificial recharge (pumping excess surface water into the ground) will replenish the groundwater resources. This water management plan recognizes that excesses and deficiencies in water are natural and can be planned for.

WATER POLLUTION

Water pollution refers to degradation of water quality as measured by biological, chemical, or physical criteria. Degradation of water is generally judged in terms of the intended use of the water, departure from norm, effects on public health, or ecologic impacts. From a public health or ecologic view, a pollutant is any biological, physical, or chemical substance in which an identifiable excess is known to be harmful to other desirable living organisms. Thus excessive amounts of heavy metals, certain radioactive isotopes, fecal coliform bacteria, phosphorus, nitrogen, sodium, and other useful (even necessary) elements, as well as certain pathogenic bacteria and viruses, are all pollutants. In some instances, a material may be considered a pollutant to a particular segment of the population although not harmful to other segments. For example, excessive sodium as a salt is not generally harmful, but it is to some people on diets restricting intake of salt for medical purposes.

There are many different materials that may pollute surface water or groundwater. Our discussion here will focus on selected aspects of biochemical oxygen demand, fecal coliform bacteria, nutrients, hazardous chemicals, oil, heavy metals, radioactive materials, and sediment. Several of these pollutants have been introduced in Chapter 11 in considerable detail that will not be repeated here. Discussion of others such as hazardous chemicals will be discussed again when we consider waste disposal in Chapter 16.

SELECTED WATER POLLUTANTS

Biochemical Oxygen Demand (BOD)

Dead organic matter in streams decays. Bacteria carrying out this decay require oxygen. If there is enough bacterial activity, the oxygen in the water can be reduced to levels so low that fish and other organisms die. A stream without oxygen is a dead stream for fish and many organisms we value. The amount of oxygen required for such biochemical decomposition is called the **biochemical oxygen demand (BOD),** a commonly used measure in water quality management. BOD is measured as milligrams per liter (mg/L) of oxygen consumed over five days at 20°C. Dead organic matter is contributed to streams and rivers from natural sources (such as dead leaves from a forest) as well as from agriculture and urban sewage. Approximately 33%

of all BOD in streams results from agricultural activities, but urban areas, particularly those with combined sewer systems, also add considerable BOD to streams.

The Council on Environmental Quality defines the threshold for a water pollution alert as a dissolved oxygen content of less than 5 mg/L of water. The diagram in Figure 13.15 illustrates the effect of BOD on dissolved oxygen content in a stream when raw sewage is introduced as a result of an accidental spill. Three zones are recognized: (1) the pollution zone, with a high BOD and reduced dissolved oxygen content as initial decomposition of the waste begins; (2) an active decomposition zone, where the dissolved oxygen content is at a minimum owing to biochemical decomposition as the organic waste is transported downstream; and (3) a recovery zone, in which the dissolved oxygen increases and the BOD is reduced because most oxygen-demanding organic waste from the input of sewage has decomposed and natural stream processes replenish the water with dissolved oxygen. All streams have some capability to degrade organic waste after it enters the stream. Problems result when the stream is overloaded with biochemical oxygen-demanding waste, overpowering the stream's natural cleansing function.

Fecal Coliform Bacteria

Disease-carrying microorganisms are important biological pollutants. Among the major waterborne human diseases are cholera and typhoid. Because it is often difficult to monitor the disease-carrying organisms directly, we use the count of human fecal coliform bacteria as a common measure of biological pollution and a standard measure of microbial pollution. These common, harmless forms of bacteria are normal constituents of human intestines and are found in all human waste. The threshold used by the Council of Environmental Quality for pollution is 200 cells of fecal coliform bacteria per 100 mL of water.

Nutrients

As we saw in the case of Lake Washington, nutrients released by human activity lead to lake eutrophication and a form of water pollution. Two

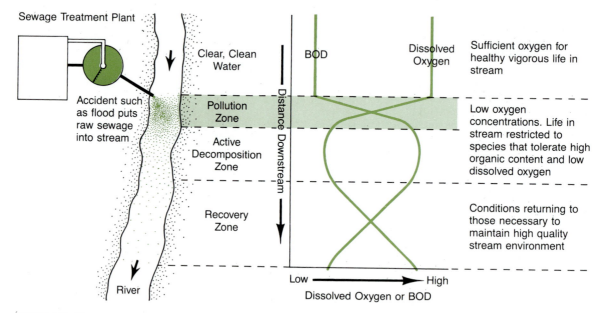

FIGURE 13.15
Relationship between dissolved oxygen and biochemical oxygen demand (BOD) for a stream following the input of sewage.

important nutrients that can cause pollution problems are phosphorus and nitrogen, both of which are released from a variety of sources related to land use (Fig. 13.16). Forested land has the lowest concentrations of phosphorus and nitrogen in stream waters. Increase in these nutrients is observed in urban streams because of the introduction of fertilizers, detergents, and the products of sewage treatment plants. The highest concentrations of phosphorus and nitrogen are found in agricultural areas—sites of sources such as fertilized farm fields and feedlots [2].

Oil

Oil discharged into surface water (usually the ocean) has caused major pollution problems. Several large oil spills from submarine oil drilling operations have occurred in recent years, such as the 1969 oil spill in the Santa Barbara Channel and the 1979 Yucatan Peninsula spill in Mexico. The latter is the world's largest spill to date, spewing out about 3 million barrels of oil before being capped in 1980. Both spills were caused by an oil well blowing out, and both caused damage to beaches

and marine life when the oil drifted ashore. Favorable winds averted a major disaster on Texan beaches and inland wetlands, as the oil only touched the shore briefly. Santa Barbara was not so lucky. Beaches were covered with oil and waterfowl were killed. Oil is also released into the ocean from oil tankers. A recent example was the July 29, 1979, collision 80 km northwest of Tobago in the Caribbean of the *Atlantic Empress,* loaded with 276,000 metric tons of crude oil, with the *Aegean Captain,* carrying 200,000 metric tons of crude. The total amount of oil entering the sea exceeded 216,000 metric tons, making this incident the largest spill from an oil tanker to date. The *Atlantic Empress* sunk, losing or burning its cargo, while the *Aegean Captain* spilled about 20,000 metric tons.

Heavy Metals

Heavy metals such as mercury, zinc, and cadmium are dangerous pollutants and are often deposited with natural sediment in the bottoms of stream channels. If these metals are deposited on floodplains, then the heavy metals may become incor-

FIGURE 13.16
Relationship between land use and average nitrogen and phosphorus concentration in streams (in milligrams per liter). (From Council on Environmental Quality, 1978.)

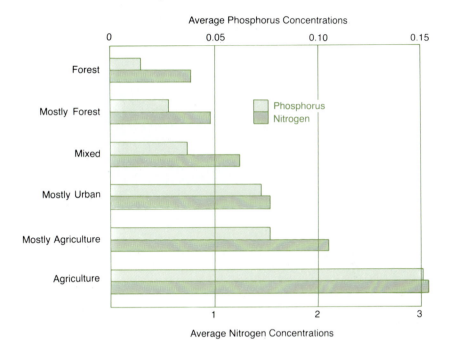

porated in plants, food crops, and animals. If they are dissolved and the water is withdrawn for agriculture or human use, heavy-metal poisoning can result.

Thermal Pollution

A heating of waters, primarily from hot-water emission from industrial and power plants, causes thermal pollution. There are several problems with heated water. Even water several degrees warmer than the surrounding water holds less oxygen. Warmer water favors different species than cooler water and may increase growth rates of undesirable organisms, including certain water plants and fish. On the other hand, the warm water may attract and allow better survival of certain desirable fish species, particularly during the winter.

Hazardous Chemicals

Many synthetic organic and inorganic compounds are toxic to people and other living things. When these materials are accidentally introduced into surface or subsurface waters, serious pollution may result. The complex problem of hazardous chemicals and their management is discussed in detail in Chapter 16.

Radioactive Materials

Radioactive materials in water may be dangerous pollutants. Of particular concern are possible effects to people, other animals, and plants of long-term exposure to low doses of radioactivity. Chapters 11 and 16 discuss radiation in terms of environmental effects and waste disposal.

SEDIMENT AND SEDIMENT POLLUTION

Sediment consists of rock and mineral fragments ranging in size from sand particles less than 2 mm in diameter to silt, clay, and even finer colloidal particles. By volume, it is our greatest water pollutant. In many areas sediment is choking streams; filling lakes, reservoirs, ponds, canals, drainage

FIGURE 13.17
Severe soil erosion and
loss of a valuable resource.

ditches, and harbors; burying vegetation; and generally creating a nuisance that is difficult to remove. It is truly a resource out of place. It depletes a land resource (soil) at its site of origin (Fig. 13.17), reduces the quality of the water resource it enters, and may deposit sterile materials on productive croplands or other useful land (Fig. 13.18) [8].

FIGURE 13.18
Sediment pollution damaging productive farmland.

Sediment in Rivers

The amount of sediment carried by rivers varies with geology, climate, topography, vegetation, and land use. Hence, some rivers are consistently and noticeably different in their clarity and appearance, as can be inferred from Table 13.3. This table reflects varying degrees of human influence as well as sizeable differences in the sediment load per unit area in various parts of the world. For instance, on the average, the Lo River of China carries nearly 200 times more suspended load than does the Nile River of Egypt. Within the United States, the Mississippi is not as "muddy" as the Missouri and the Colorado rivers. Notice that the data in Table 13.3 suggest that, as the size of the drainage basin increases, the sediment yield per unit area decreases. Although there are notable exceptions to this relation, it generally holds because smaller basins tend to be at higher elevations that have steeper topography and receive greater precipitation. The greater precipitation and steep topography combine to produce a greater amount of sediment. The data from basins with areas less than 260 km² for the major water resources regions of the United States tend to confirm this. No-

TABLE 13.3
Some major rivers of the world ranked by sediment yield per unit area.

River	Drainage Basin (10³ km²)	Sediment Load per Year (tons/km²)
Amazon	5776	63
Mississippi	3222	97
Nile	2978	37
Yangtze	1942	257
Missouri	1370	159
Indus	969	449
Ganges	956	1518
Mekong	795	214
Yellow	673	2804
Brahmaputra	666	1090
Colorado	637	212
Irrawaddy	430	695
Red	119	1092
Kosi	62	2774
Ching	57	7158
Lo	26	7308

Source: Data from Holman, 1968.

tice, for example, that the average sediment yields for the midwestern United States (Fig. 13.19) are all considerably greater than for the Mississippi River as a whole, even though the Mississippi

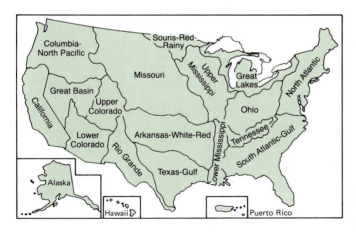

Region	Estimated Sediment Yield (metric tons/km²/yr)		
	High	Low	Average
North Atlantic	4240	110	880
South Atlantic-Gulf	6480	350	2800
Great Lakes	2800	40	350
Ohio	7391	560	2780
Tennessee	5460	1610	2450
Upper Mississippi	13,660	40	2800
Lower Mississippi	28,760	5460	18,220
Souris-Red-Rainy	1650	40	175
Missouri	23,470	40	5250
Arkansas-White-Red	25,760	910	7710
Texas-Gulf	8140	320	6310
Rio Grande	11,700	530	4550
Upper Colorado	11,700	530	6310
Lower Colorado	5670	530	2100
Great Basin	6240	350	1400
Columbia-North Pacific	3850	120	1400
California	19,510	280	4550

FIGURE 13.19
Water resource regions of the United States and estimated ranges in sediment yield from drainage areas (within these regions) of 260 km² or less. (From Water Resources Council, 1978.)

drains nearly the entire region. Thus we conclude that most of the sediment production is from the smaller drainage basins in a region. This has important implications for plans to control sediment production, suggesting we need to concentrate soil conservation efforts on the smaller drainage basins. These effects will be discussed in detail later in this chapter when sediment pollution is considered.

The difference between the sediment loads carried by major rivers is so great that it is part of American folklore. A story is told about a man who claimed that the muddier Mississippi water was more wholesome to drink than the clear waters of the Ohio. He said, ''You look at the graveyards, that tells the tale. Trees won't grow worth shucks in a Cincinnati graveyard, but in a St. Louis graveyard they grow upwards of eight hundred foot high. It's all on account of the water the people drunk before they laid up. A Cincinnati corpse don't richen a soil any'' [9].

Rivers and lakes have been major resources throughout human history. They provided the first major means for transporting large quantities of goods and people, and rivers, lakes, and ocean harbors are the sites of major cities. This is no ac-

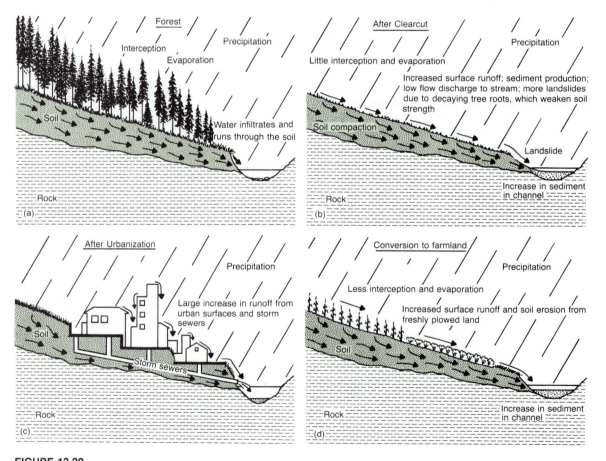

FIGURE 13.20
(a) Water relations for a natural forested slope. Following several land-use changes, the water relations change: (b) after clearcut, (c) after urbanization, and (d) after conversion to farmland.

cident. Not only do rivers, lakes, and oceans provide transportation, but rivers have provided a major source of energy as water power. Ever since the rise of Egyptian civilization, the fertile soils deposited on floodplains have been a major agricultural resource.

Land Use and Sediment

Many human activities affect the pattern, amount, and intensity of surface-water runoff, erosion, and sedimentation. Sediment production for possible land-use changes (timber harvesting, urbanization, and conversion to farmland) is idealized in Figure 13.20, and Figure 13.21 summarizes estimated and observed variations in sediment yield under various historical changes in land use.

Figures 13.20 and 13.21 suggest that the effects of land-use change on the drainage basin and its streams may be quite dramatic. Streams in naturally forested or wooded areas may be nearly stable; that is, there is no excessive erosion or deposition. Converting forested land to agriculture generally increases the runoff and sediment yield or erosion of the land. As a result, streams become muddy and may not be able to transport all of the sediment delivered to their channels. Therefore, the channels will partially fill with sediment, possibly increasing the magnitude and frequency of flooding.

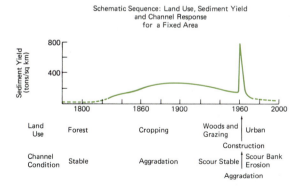

Schematic Sequence: Land Use, Sediment Yield
and Channel Response
for a Fixed Area

FIGURE 13.21
The effect of land-use change on sediment yield in the Piedmont region of the United States before the beginning of extensive farming and continuing through a period of construction and urbanization. (After Wolman.)

The change from agricultural, forested, or rural land to highly urbanized land is even more dramatic. First, during the construction phase, there is a tremendous increase in sediment production, which may be accompanied by a moderate increase in runoff. The response of streams in the area is complex and may include both channel erosion and aggradation, resulting in wide, shallow channels. The combination of increased runoff and shallow channels increases the flood hazard.

Following the construction phase, much of the land is covered with buildings, parking lots, and streets, and sediment yield drops to a low level. However, the large impervious areas and use of storm sewers increase runoff, which increases the magnitude and frequency of flooding. The streams may respond to the lower sediment yield and higher runoff by eroding (deepening) their channels.

Sediment Pollution Control

Some polluting sediments are debris from the disposal of industrial, manufacturing, and public wastes. Such sediments include trash directly or indirectly discharged into surface waters. Most of these sediments are very fine grained and difficult to distinguish from naturally occurring sediments unless they contain unusual minerals or other unique characteristics.

Artificially induced polluting sediments come from disruption of the land surface for construction, farming, deforestation, off-road vehicle use, and channelization. In short, a great deal of sediment pollution is the result of human use of the environment and of civilization's continued change of plans and direction. It cannot be eliminated, only ameliorated.

The solution to sediment pollution requires sound conservation practices, especially in areas where tremendous quantities of sediment are produced and during urbanization (see Plate 10). Figure 13.22 shows a typical sediment and erosion control plan for a commercial development. The plan calls for diversions to collect runoff and a sediment basin to collect sediment and keep it on the site, thus preventing stream pollution.

That sediment control measures can reduce sediment pollution in an urbanizing area is dem-

FIGURE 13.22
Example of a sediment-
and erosion-control plan for
a commercial development.
(Courtesy of Braxton Wil-
liams, U.S. Soil Conservation Service.)

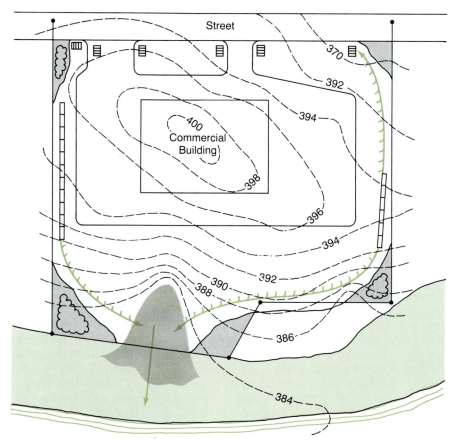

Commercial Sediment and Erosion Control Plan

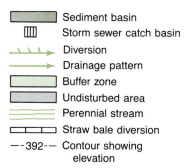

onstrated by a study in Maryland [10]. The suspended sediment transported by the northwest
branch of the Anacostia River near Colesville,
Maryland, with a drainage area of 54.6 km², was
measured over a 10-year period (1962–1972).
During that time, urban construction within the
basin involved about 3% of the area each year. The
total urban land area in the basin was about 20%
at the end of the 10-year study. Sediment pollution was a problem because the soils are highly

susceptible to erosion and there is sufficient precipitation to ensure their erosion when not protected by a vegetative cover. Most of the sediment was transported during spring and summer rainstorms. A sediment-control program initiated between 1965 and 1971 reduced sediment yield by an estimated 35%. The basic sediment control principles were to tailor the development to the natural topography, expose a minimum amount of land, provide protection for exposed soil, minimize surface runoff from critical areas, and trap eroded sediment on the construction site [10].

The above discussion of potential pollutants in water certainly is not complete. For some of the pollutants we have discussed, Table 13.4 lists the thresholds used by the Council on Environmental Quality as indicators of water quality. As we learn more about water pollution and its effect on the environment, threshold concentrations and the list of potential pollutants will certainly change.

SURFACE WATER POLLUTION

Pollution of surface waters occurs when too much of an undesirable or harmful substance flows into a body of water, exceeding the natural ability of that water body to remove the undesirable material or convert it to a harmless form.

As with atmospheric pollutants, water pollutants are categorized as emitted from point or non-point sources. Point sources are discrete and confined, such as pipes that empty into streams or rivers from industrial or municipal sites. In general, point-source pollutants from industries are controlled through on-site treatment or disposal and are regulated by permit. Municipal point sources are also regulated by permit. In older cities in the northeastern and Great Lakes areas of the United States, most point sources are outflows from combined sewer systems. These sewer systems combine storm-water flow with municipal waste. During heavy rains, urban storm runoff may exceed the capacity of the sewer system, causing it to back up and overflow, delivering pollutants to nearby surface waters.

Nonpoint sources are diffused and intermittent and are influenced by factors such as land use, climate, hydrology, topography, native vegetation, and geology. Common urban nonpoint sources include urban runoff from streets or fields; such runoff contains all sorts of pollutants, from heavy metals to chemicals and sediment. Rural sources of nonpoint pollution are generally associated with agriculture, mining, or forestry. Nonpoint sources are difficult to control.

Consider again the Seattle, Washington, case history discussed at the beginning of this chapter. When Seattle was a small city, the pollution of streams flowing into Lake Washington had little noticeable effect. Natural biological degradation and inorganic processes were sufficient to take

TABLE 13.4
Thresholds used by the Council on Environmental Quality in analyzing the nation's water quality.

Indicator	Abbreviation	Threshold Level
Fecal coliform bacteria	FC	200 cells/100 mL[a]
Dissolved oxygen	DO	5.0 mg/L[b]
Total phosphorus	TP	0.1 mg/L[c]
Total mercury	Hg	2.0 μg/L[d]
Total lead	Pb	50.0 μg/L[d]
Biochemical oxygen demand	BOD	5.0 mg/L[e]

Source: From Council on Environmental Quality, 1979.

L = liter; mL = milliliter; mg = milligram; μg = microgram.

[a]Criteria level for ''bathing waters'' from EPA ''Redbook.''

[b]Criteria level for ''good fish populations'' from EPA ''Redbook.''

[c]Value discussed for ''prevention of plant nuisances in streams or other flowing waters not discharging directly to lakes or impoundments'' in EPA ''Redbook.''

[d]Criteria level for ''domestic water supply (health)'' from EPA ''Redbook.'' Criteria level for preservation of aquatic life is much lower.

[e]Value chosen by CEQ.

care of the effluents. By the 1950s, however, the city had become so large that the rate at which effluents were being dumped into the lake greatly exceeded the lake's capacity to remove them or transform them into harmless forms.

As in the case of Lake Washington, we have three ways to deal with water pollution: reduce the sources; transport the pollutants to some place where they will not do damage; or convert the pollutants to harmless forms. In the Lake Washington case, the second method was the easiest and most practical because of a unique situation—that is, the nearness of Puget Sound with its rapid rate of flushing with the Pacific Ocean. This method was less expensive than adding improved treatment processes to remove the phosphorus. The effluent flowing from the city sewage to the lake had already been subjected to secondary treatment, meaning that it was free of disease-causing organisms and major organic compounds.

Few other cities are as fortunate as Seattle, but there are other success stories in the treatment of water pollution. One of the most notable is the cleanup of the Thames River in England. For centuries London's sewage had been dumped into that river, and there were few fish to be found downstream in the estuary. In recent decades, however, improvement in water treatment has led to the return of a great number of species of fish—some not seen in the river in centuries.

Since the 1960s there has been a serious attempt in the United States to reduce water pollution and thereby increase water quality. The basic assumption is that people have a real desire for safe water to drink, to swim in, and to use in agriculture and industry. At one time water quality near major urban centers was considerably worse than it is today, and there was at least one instance in which a river was inadvertently set on fire. In recent years there have been a number of very encouraging success stories; perhaps the best known is the Detroit River. In the 1950s and the early 1960s the Detroit River was considered a dead river, having been an open dump for sewage, chemicals, garbage, and urban trash. Tons of phosphorus were discharged each day into the river, and a film of oil up to 0.5 cm thick was often present. Aquatic life was damaged considerably, and

thousands of ducks and fish were killed. Although today the Detroit River is not a pristine stream, the improvement resulting from industrial and municipal pollution control has been considerable. Oil and grease emissions were reduced by 82% between 1963 and 1975, and the shoreline is usually clean. Phosphorus and sewage discharges have also been greatly reduced. Fish once again are found in the Detroit River. Other success stories include New Hampshire's Pemigewasset River, North Carolina's French Broad River, and the Savannah River in the southeastern United States. These examples are evidence that water pollution abatement has positive results [11].

The Hudson River assessment and cleanup of PCBs (polychlorinated biphenyls, with chemical structure similar to DDT and dioxin) is another good example of the determination of people to clean up our rivers. PCBs were used mainly in electrical capacitors and transformers; discharge of the chemicals from two outfalls on the Hudson River started about 1950 and terminated in 1977. Approximately 295,000 kg of PCBs are believed to be present in Hudson River sediments. Concentrations in the sediment are as high as 1000 ppm near the outfalls compared to less than 10 ppm several hundred kilometers downstream at New York City [12]. The U.S. Food and Drug Administration permits less than 2.5 ppm PCBs in dairy products and the New York State limit for drinking water is 0.1 ppb. PCBs are carcinogenic and are known to cause disturbances of the liver, nervous system, blood, and immune response system in people. Furthermore, they are nearly indestructible in the natural environment and become concentrated in the higher parts of the food chain—thus the concern! Water samples in the 240–km tidal reach of the Hudson River have yielded average PCB concentrations ranging from 0.1 to 0.4 ppb, but PCBs are concentrated to much higher levels in some fish. As a result fishermen on the lower Hudson have suffered a significant economic impact from the contamination because nearly all commercial fishing was banned, and sport fishing was greatly reduced [12, 13].

The cleanup plan for the Hudson River will cost nearly $30 million and involves removing and treating contaminated river sediment. Dredging will be done in "hot spots" where the concentration of PCBs is greater than 50 ppm and should be completed in the mid-1980s. The dredging will greatly reduce the time necessary for the river to clean itself by the natural process of sediment transport to the ocean.

GROUNDWATER POLLUTION

Approximately one-half of all people in the United States today depend on groundwater as their source of drinking water, and we have long believed that groundwater is in general quite pure and safe to drink. Therefore, it may be alarming for some people to learn that groundwater may in fact be quite easily polluted by any one of several sources (Table 13.5) and that the pollutants, even though they are very toxic, may be difficult to recognize. One of the best known examples is the Love Canal near Niagara Falls, New York, where burial of chemical wastes has caused serious water pollution and health problems.

Unfortunately, Love Canal is not an isolated case of groundwater pollution. Hazardous chemicals have been found or are suspected to be in groundwater supplies in nearly all parts of the world, developed and developing countries alike. Developed industrial countries produce thousands of chemicals and many of these, particularly pesticides, are exported to developing countries, where they protect crops that eventually are imported by the same industrial countries, completing a circle. For example, Costa Rica imports several pesticides, including DDT, aldrin, endrin, and chlordane, that are banned or heavily restricted in the United States. Most of these pesticides are used on crops destined for export to richer nations [14].

In the United States today, only a small portion of the groundwater is known to be contaminated. Nevertheless, several million people have used that water, and the problem is growing as testing of groundwater becomes more common. For example, Atlantic City, New Jersey, and Miami, Florida, are two eastern cities threatened by polluted groundwater that is slowly migrating toward their wells, and it is estimated that 75% of the 175,000 known waste disposal sites in the country may be producing plumes of hazardous chemicals that are migrating into groundwater resources. Because many of the chemicals are toxic and/or known as suspected carcinogens, it appears that we have been conducting a large-scale experiment on the effects of chronic low-level exposure of people to potentially harmful chemicals. Unfortunately the final results of the experiments won't be known for many years [15]. Preliminary results suggest we had better act now before a hidden time bomb of health problems explodes.

TABLE 13.5
Classification of sources of groundwater pollution and/or contamination.

Wastes		Nonwastes
Sources designed to discharge waste to the land and/or groundwater	Sources that may discharge waste to the land and groundwater unintentionally	Sources that may discharge a contaminant (not a waste) to the land and groundwater
Spray irrigation	Surface impoundments	Buried product storage tanks and pipelines
Septic systems, cesspools, etc.	Landfills	Accidental spills
Land disposal of sludge	Animal feedlots	Highway deicing salt stockpiles
Infiltration or percolation basins	Acid water from mines	Ore stockpiles
Disposal wells	Mine spoil piles and tailings	Application of highway salt
Brine injection wells	Waste disposal sites for hazardous chemicals	Product storage ponds
		Agricultural activities

Source: Modified after U.S. Environmental Protection Agency and Lindorff.

The hazard presented by a particular groundwater pollutant depends upon several factors such as volume of pollutant discharged, concentration or toxicity of the pollutant in the environment, and degree of exposure of people or other organisms [16]. Table 13.6 summarizes 118 cases of groundwater pollution in terms of type of contaminant, areas of detection, and direct or indirect remedial actions that were taken.

Groundwater pollution differs in several ways from surface water pollution. Groundwater often lacks oxygen—a situation that is helpful in killing aerobic types of microorganisms but which may provide a "happy home" for anaerobic varieties. Bacterial degradation of pollutants, generally confined to the soil or to material a meter or so below the surface, does not occur readily in groundwater. Furthermore, the channels through which groundwater moves are often very small and variable. Thus, the rate of movement is much reduced (except, perhaps, in large solution channels in rocks such as limestone), and the opportunity for dispersion and dilution is very limited.

Most soils and rocks can filter out solids, including pollution solids. However, this ability varies with different sizes, shapes, and arrangements

TABLE 13.6
Summary of case histories of groundwater contamination.

Contaminant	Total	Cases Affecting or Threatening Water Supplies	Cases Causing or Threatening Fire or Explosion
Industrial wastes	40	26	2
Landfill leachate	32	7	0
Petroleum products	18	10	8
Chlorides (road salt and oil field brine)	11	9	0
Organic wastes	11	9	0
Pesticides	3	2	0
Radioactive wastes	1	0	0
Mine wastes	2	1	0
Totals	118	64	10

Means of Detection

Well contamination	58	Not mentioned	4
Investigation	32	Fumes in basement	1
Stream contamination	9	Fumes in ground	1
Spill on ground	5	Fumes in sewer line	1
Leak discovered	4	Animal deaths	1

Total 116

Remedial Action

Direct		Indirect	
Gound water pumped and treated	27	Extent of groundwater	
Contaminated soil removed	8	contamination determined:	44
Trench installed	8	Leading to remedial action 25	
Artificial recharge employed	4	No further action 19	
Nutrients added	2	New water supply provided	16
Source of contamination eliminated	26	Action being considered	9
Surface water collected and		Monitoring begun	2
treated	7	Damages awarded	4
Landfill site closed	9	Charcoal filters installed	2
Site regraded	3	None mentioned	12
Total	94	Total	89

Source: Lindor and Cartwright.

of filtering particles. Clays and other selected minerals capture and exchange some elements and compounds when they are in solution. Such exchanges are important in the capture of pollutants like heavy metals.

Overpumping of groundwater may lead to infiltration of salt water from the ocean (Fig. 13.23). The intrusion of salt water into freshwater supplies has caused serious problems in coastal areas of New York, Florida, and California.

Long Island, New York, is a good example of an area with groundwater problems. Two counties on the island, Nassau and Suffolk, with a population of several million people, are entirely dependent on groundwater for their water supply. Two major problems associated with groundwater in Nassau County are intrusion of salt water and shallow-aquifer contamination [17]. Figure 13.24 shows the general movement of groundwater under natural conditions for Nassau County. Salty groundwater is restricted from inland migration by the

large wedge of fresh water moving beneath the island.

In spite of the huge quantities of water in Nassau County's groundwater system, intensive pumping in recent years has caused water levels to decline as much as 15 m in some areas. As groundwater is removed near coastal areas, the subsurface outflow to the ocean decreases, allowing salt water to migrate inland. Some saltwater intrusion has occurred in Nassau County but is not yet a serious problem.

The most serious groundwater problem on Long Island is shallow-aquifer pollution associated with urbanization. Sources of pollution in Nassau County include urban runoff, household sewage from cesspools and septic tanks, salt used to deice highways, and industrial and solid waste. These pollutants enter surface waters and then migrate downward, especially in areas of intensive pumping and declining groundwater levels [17].

Drilling of deep wells, such as those for petroleum exploration, also can cause degradation of freshwater aquifers. Some wells allow considerable material to enter freshwater aquifers. This was particularly a problem during the early phases of petroleum and other well drilling (especially for salt), when little was known about the depths at which fresh waters could occur in many parts of the United States and throughout the world.

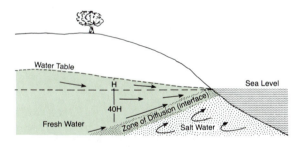

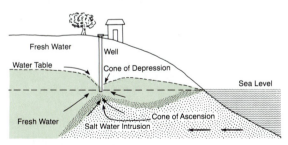

FIGURE 13.23
How saltwater intrusion might occur: (a) the groundwater system near the coast under natural conditions, and (b) well with both a cone of depression and a cone of ascension. If pumping is intensive, the cone of ascension may be drawn upward, delivering salt water to the well. The H and 40H represent the height of the freshwater table above sea level and the depth of salt water below sea level, respectively.

WASTEWATER TREATMENT

The quality of water used for industrial and municipal purposes is often degraded by addition of suspended solids, salts, bacteria, and oxygen-demanding material. By law, these waters must be treated before being released back into the environment. Such treatment in the United States now costs approximately $12 billion/yr, and the price is expected to double during the next 10 years (Fig. 13.25). Therefore, we can see that wastewater treatment is big business. Conventional methods include disposal and treatment of household wastewater by way of septic-tank disposal systems in rural areas and centralized water treatment plants that collect wastewater in cities from sewer systems. Recently, innovative approaches to

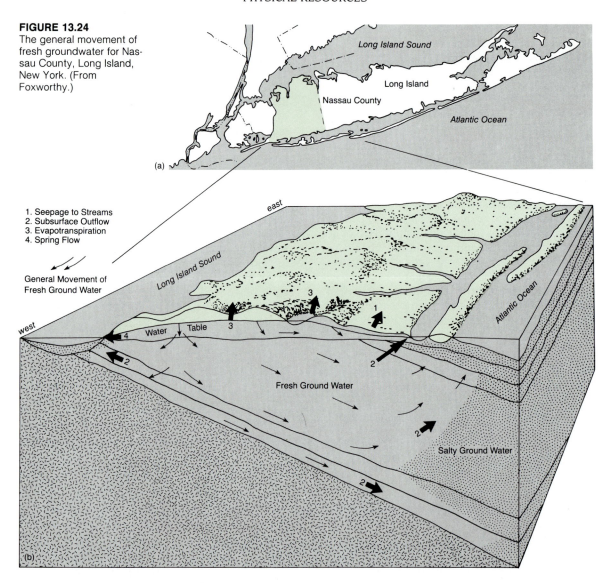

FIGURE 13.24
The general movement of fresh groundwater for Nassau County, Long Island, New York. (From Foxworthy.)

1. Seepage to Streams
2. Subsurface Outflow
3. Evapotranspiration
4. Spring Flow

General Movement of Fresh Ground Water

Septic-Tank Disposal System

In recent years in the United States, people have been moving in great numbers from rural to urban or urbanizing areas. In many instances, a city's

wastewater treatment have been application of wastewater to the land, aquaculture, and wastewater renovation and reuse.

sewage system and wastewater treatment facilities have not been able to keep pace with the growth. As a result, the individual septic-tank disposal system continues to be an important method of sewage disposal. Unfortunately, not all land is suitable for installation of a septic-tank disposal system, so evaluation of individual sites is usually required by law before a permit can be issued. An alert buyer will check to make sure that the site is satisfactory

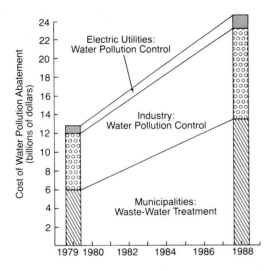

FIGURE 13.25
Cost of water pollution abatement for U.S. municipalities, industry, and electrical utilities from 1979 to 1988. (Data from Council on Environmental Quality and the Department of State.)

for septic-tank disposal before purchasing property on the fringe of an urban area where such a system is necessary. Failure to do so has made many buyers unhappy, and they may pass the property on to another unsuspecting person.

The basic parts of a septic-tank disposal system are shown in Figure 13.26. The sewer line from the house leads to an underground septic tank in the yard. The tank is designed to separate solids from liquid, digest and store organic matter through a period of detention, and allow the clarified liquid to discharge into the seepage bed, or absorption field, which is a system of piping through which the treated sewage may seep into the surrounding soil. As the wastewater moves through the soil, it is further treated by the natural processes of oxidation and filtering. By the time the water reaches any freshwater supply, it should be safe for other uses.

Sewage absorption fields may fail for several reasons. The most common cause is poor soil drainage (Fig. 13.27), which allows the effluent to rise to the surface in wet weather. Poor drainage can be expected in areas with clay or compacted soil with low permeability, a high water table, im-

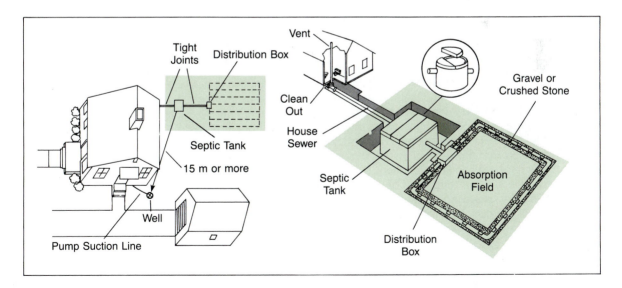

FIGURE 13.26
Septic-tank sewage disposal system (right) and location of the absorption field with respect to the house and well. (After Indiana State Board of Health.)

FIGURE 13.27
Effluent from a septic-tank sewage disposal system rising to the surface in a backyard. Septic systems in poorly drained soils will not function well during wet weather.

permeable rock near the surface, or frequent flooding. When a septic-tank absorption field does fail, serious pollution of ground and surface waters may result.

Wastewater Treatment Plants

Conventional wastewater treatment falls into two broad classes: **primary treatment,** which involves the mechanical removal of solid material in the water, and **secondary treatment,** which involves biological oxidation of dissolved organic material (Fig. 13.28). Primary treatment lowers the biochemical oxygen demand (BOD) to some extent, but it is during secondary treatment that the BOD is greatly reduced. A third class of treatment, known as **tertiary treatment,** removes remaining solids, particularly dissolved minerals or organic compounds. Probably the most common type of tertiary treatment is chlorination, which removes disease-causing organisms. Other advanced tertiary treatment processes that remove undesirable chemicals (e.g., phosphorus) that promote unpleasant algae growth in streams and lakes or dis-

solved organic compounds or inorganic minerals are not yet in widespread use. However, tertiary treatment will become more common in the future as more stringent water-quality standards are enforced.

Land Application of Wastewater

The innovative practice of applying wastewater to the land involves the fundamental belief that waste is simply a resource out of place. The idea is sometimes expressed as the wastewater renovation and conservation cycle, as shown schematically in Figure 13.29. The major processes in the cycle are as follows: return of treated wastewater by a sprinkler or other irrigation system to crops; renovation, or natural purification by slow percolation of the wastewater through the soil, to eventually recharge the groundwater resource with clean water; and reuse of the water by pumping it out of the ground for municipal, industrial, institutional, or agricultural purposes [18].

Recycling of wastewater is now being practiced at a number of sites around the United States. In a

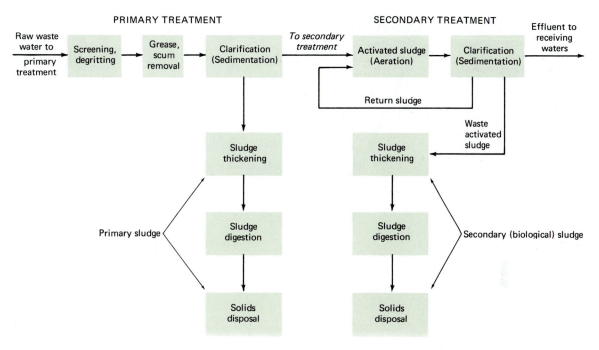

FIGURE 13.28
Flow chart showing various procedures in primary and secondary treatment of wastewater.
(From American Chemical Society.)

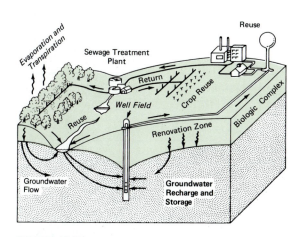

FIGURE 13.29
The wastewater renovation and conservation cycle. (After
Parizek and Myers.)

large-scale wastewater recycling program near
Muskegon and Whitehall, Michigan (Fig. 13.30),
raw sewage from homes and industry is transported by sewers to the treatment plant, where it
receives primary and secondary treatment. The
wastes are then chlorinated and pumped into a
network that transports the effluent to a series of
spray irrigation rigs. After the wastewater trickles
down through the soil, it is collected in a network
of tile drains and transported to the Muskegon
River for final disposal. This last step is an indirect
tertiary treatment using the natural physical and
biological environment as a filter. To date, this excellent system removes most of the potential pollutants as well as heavy metals, color, and viruses.

Wastewater is also being applied experimentally to freshwater marshes and forest lands. In the
future we can expect more tertiary treatment of
wastewater by use of biological systems.

FIGURE 13.30

(a) Two effluent-application areas near Muskegon and Whitehall, Michigan, will eliminate the necessity to discharge inadequately treated industrial and municipal waste into surface waters. The two subsystems are designed to replace four municipal treatment facilities. The effluent-on-land system is designed to handle the 1992 requirements of the county, which at present has a population of about 170,000. (b) Raw sewage from the sewers of Muskegon is transported by way of a pressure main to the Muskegon-Mona Lake reclamation site. There the effluent flows through three aerated treatment lagoons (1, 2, and 3) and then is diverted either to a large storage basin or into the settling lagoon (4) before going into the outlet lagoon (5). Wastewater leaving the outlet lagoon is chlorinated and then pumped through a piping system that carries it to spray irrigation rigs. Circles on the diagram indicate the radius sweep by the spray rigs. After the effluent trickles down through the soil, it is collected by a network of underground pipes and pumped to surface waters. (From Chaiken, Poloncsik, and Wilson.)

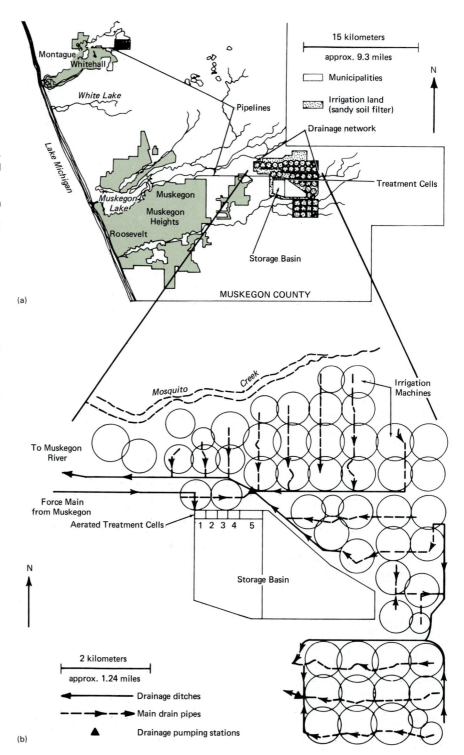

Aquaculture and Wastewater Treatment

Use of municipal sewage in fish ponds is evidently a very old practice. For example, in China, where aquaculture started, waste disposal in fish ponds was quite common; in fact, it is reported that latrines were even built directly over the ponds. This method had two benefits: First, it solved a waste disposal problem; and second, the addition of waste caused an increase in the fish yield. Of course, adding waste to the water may have also created a health hazard to the people working in the ponds or eating the fish, but this potential hazard was evidently not recognized [19]. Today aquaculture is teamed up with waste-disposal systems at several sites. Two examples, one from northern California and the other from Israel, will emphasize the spectrum of relationships between aquaculture and wastewater treatment.

The wastewater treatment system utilized by the city of Arcata in northern California services approximately 20,000 people. The wastewater comes mostly from homes, with minor inputs from lumber and plywood plants, and is treated by standard primary and secondary methods. It is then chlorinated and dechlorinated before being discharged into Humboldt Bay.

Oxidation ponds—part of the secondary treatment—are where aquaculture begins. Pacific salmon fingerlings are raised in water drawn from the oxidation ponds. During the winter the water is aerated so that it is not toxic to the fish, and during the summer the pond water is diluted slightly with sea water from the bay to provide a better habitat for the young fish.

Using wastewater for aquaculture comes from the philosophy that our domestic sewage is really water plus fertilizer. That is, wastewater is a resource that may actually grow fish. In the Arcata example, the young fish are released into the ocean by way of streams and Humboldt Bay, where presumably they will return a few years later as mature salmon. Thus the wastewater is not directly used to feed fish that people consume. Rather, the fish enter the natural environment for some period before returning to local streams to spawn. In some respects, aquaculture may be thought of as an advanced biological tertiary treatment; because

the fish and other living things in the pond utilize the waste, there is no reason to chlorinate and dechlorinate the water. Thus no chlorinated hydrocarbons are produced from the chlorination, and no costly dechlorination units need to be installed [20].

The experiments at Arcata, California, certainly indicate that further research to meld aquaculture with wastewater treatment is a worthwhile endeavor. There have been problems with the fish being killed either by the water or by predation by birds, but overall the survival rate has improved with experience. The Coho salmon and trout have a better survival rate than do the Chinook salmon, suggesting that some fish species adapt better to these specialized ponds.

There is little doubt that organic waste, when added to ponds, increases the supply of food available, and that these ponds produce higher yields of fish. The organic waste from sewage carries nutrients (nitrogen and phosphorus, as well as trace elements) that are important for phytoplankton, which are a significant link in the food chain of fish ponds. In commercial fish ponds supplemental fertilization has increased the biomass of plants and other organisms that are natural food for the fish. Data from a commercial fish farm in Israel clearly illustrate the benefits of applying wastewater to fish ponds. The entire sewage from a community of approximately 500 people is treated by primary methods, diluted with fresh water, and then spread among three fish ponds with a combined area of 2.7 ha. A fourth pond receives the flow of manure and wash water from a dairy serving the community. Data suggest that these ponds produce high-quality fish that have experienced no major health problems. The fat content of the fish in the wastewater ponds is lower than for fish that receive supplemental rations of pelletized food. The lower fat content is probably the result of eating more natural food [19].

The consumption of fish raised in wastewater ponds presents cultural problems. People are not generally willing to buy and eat such fish even though they may be of high quality. Fish produced in the Arcata experiment may be more palatable because they are released into the natural environment and return with the natural stock to local streams, where they are harvested. Thus the systems most likely to succeed will be those that use biological systems for advanced tertiary treatment and include natural ecosystems for at least part of the life cycle of the fish involved.

Water Reuse

Water reuse generally refers to the use of wastewater following some sort of treatment and is often discussed in terms of an emergency water supply, a long-term solution to a local water shortage, or a fringe benefit to water pollution abatement. Data have been or are being collected in many locations in the United States as part of water reuse research or implementation [21].

Water reuse can be inadvertent, indirect, or direct (Fig. 13.31). Inadvertent reuse of water results when water is withdrawn, used, treated, and re-

FIGURE 13.31
Three types of water reuse.(Modified from Symons, by Kasperson.)

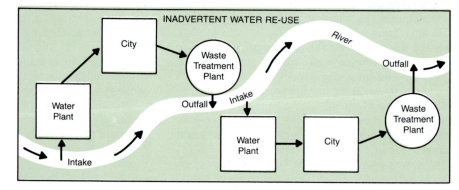

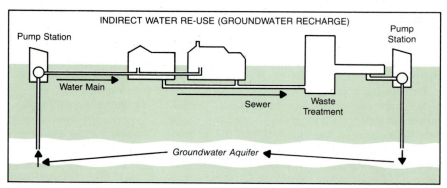

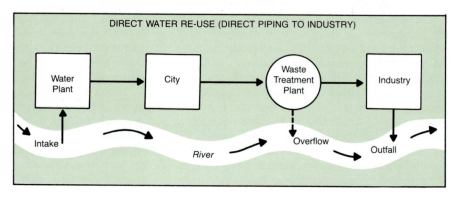

turned to the environment without specific plans for further withdrawals and use, which nevertheless occur (Fig. 13.31a). Such use patterns occur along many rivers and, in fact, are accepted as a common and necessary procedure for obtaining a water supply. There are several risks associated with inadvertent reuse. Inadequate treatment facilities may deliver contaminated or poor-quality water to users. Because the fate of disease-causing viruses during and after treatment is not completely known, we are uncertain about the environmental health hazards of treated water. In addition, each year many new chemicals, some of which cause birth defects, genetic damage, or cancer in humans, are introduced into the environment. Unfortunately, harmful chemicals are often difficult to detect, and their effects on humans may be hidden if the chemicals are ingested in low concentrations over many years [21]. In spite of these problems, inadvertent reuse of water will by necessity remain a common pattern. If we recognize the potential risks, we can plan to minimize them by using the best possible water treatment available.

Indirect water reuse (Fig. 13.31b) is a planned endeavor, one example of which is the wastewater reclamation cycle shown in Figure 13.29. Similar plans have been used in southern California, where several thousand cubic meters of treated wastewater per day have been applied to surface recharge areas. The treated water eventually enters into groundwater storage to be reused for agricultural and municipal purposes.

Direct water reuse refers to treated water that is piped directly to the next user (Fig. 13.31c). In most cases the "user" will be industry or agricultural activity. Very little direct use of water is planned (except in emergencies) for human consumption because of cultural attitudes. Figure 13.32 summarizes these attitudes: Direct ingestion is accepted least, whereas uses in which there is no body contact are generally much more acceptable.

Desalination

Desalination of sea water, which contains about 3.5% salt (each cubic meter of sea water contains about 40 kg of salt), is an expensive form of water

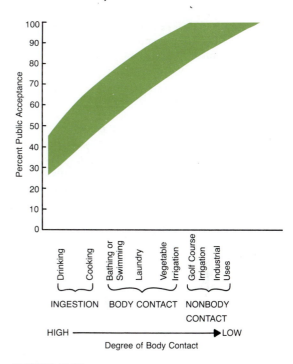

FIGURE 13.32
Public acceptance of use of treated wastewater. In general, people have a negative attitude toward direct reuse, that is, drinking of treated wastewater. (Modified after Kasperson.)

treatment practiced at several hundred plants around the world. The salt content must be reduced to about 0.05%. Large desalination plants produce 20,000–30,000 m^3 of water per day at a cost of about 10 times that paid for traditional water supplies in the United States. Desalinated water has a "place value," which means that the price increases quickly with the transport distance and elevation increase from the plant at sea level. Because the various processes that actually remove the salt require energy, the cost of the water is tied to ever-increasing energy costs. For these reasons, desalination will remain an expensive process that will be used only when alternative water sources are not available.

Middle Eastern countries in particular will continue to use desalination. In many arid regions, including the Middle East, there are brackish ground and surface waters with a salinity of about 0.5%

(one-seventh that of sea water). Obviously, desalination of this water is less expensive and plants may be located at inland sites.

WATER AND ECOSYSTEMS

The major ecosystems of the world have evolved in response to physical conditions that include, among others, climate, nutrient input, soils, and hydrology. Changes in these factors will affect ecosystems; in particular, changes induced by humans may cause far-reaching changes. Throughout the world today, with few exceptions, people are assaulting natural ecosystems on a regional and global scale. Hydrologic conditions, particularly surface water processes and quality, are becoming limiting factors in many systems. Even the ultimate global hydrologic system, the oceans, is experiencing pollution problems. Figure 13.33 shows parts of the oceans and large lakes that are currently accumulating pollutants or have the potential for intermittent pollution. These areas often coincide with the near-shore productive areas of the marine environment and clearly suggest that despite their great size oceans can become polluted. The major pollutants are oil, synthetic chemicals, solid waste, liquid waste (sewage), radioactive particles, and heavy metals.

Pollution of the oceans is most severe near large urban coastal areas and along major shipping lanes. Many pollutants discharged into the oceans through outfalls, spills, deliberate dumping accidents, or rivers are cycled in the oceans, degraded there, or deposited with sediment. Some, however, do not decompose easily and accumulate in the living tissue of ocean organisms. These include heavy metals such as mercury and synthetic chemicals such as DDT. Mercury is known to accumulate through the food chain to large commercial fish such as swordfish and tuna. DDT also accumulates, and fish-eating birds including the California brown pelican, have had poor nesting success because DDT caused the females to lay soft eggs. Their plight helped lead to the ban on DDT in the United States. However, the chemical is still used in other parts of the world. This brings up an interesting point—there is very little international

cooperation in ocean pollution problems. If we are to maintain a quality marine environment we will eventually have to deal with pollution on a global scale and it will have to be done with international cooperation [22].

Protection of coastal wetlands, which serve as nursery areas for a high percentage of marine fish resources sought after by people, is also a high priority. It is estimated that as much as 60% of the United States' commercial fish catch depends on estuaries and adjacent wetlands [23]. Pollution of coastal wetlands has caused major problems for shellfish industries in several locations along the East Coast. Shellfish are particularly susceptible to pollution because they are filter feeders and collectors of heavy metals and synthetic chemicals.

While most coastal salt marshes are now protected in the United States, freshwater wetlands are still threatened in many areas. One percent of the nation's total wetlands is lost every two years—freshwater wetlands account for 95% of that loss, ranging from swamps in North Carolina to prairie potholes in the Midwest to vernal pools in California. Everyone knows wetlands are highly productive for fish and wildlife. What is needed are incentives for private land owners to preserve wetlands rather than fill them to develop the land [23].

Water resource development may be important to people but it can also adversely effect ecosystems. Construction of large dams permanently changes rivers. For example, construction of the High Dam at Aswan on the Nile River in Egypt deprived the eastern Mediterranean Sea of nutrients delivered from the river, causing a one-third reduction in plankton production. As a result sardine, mackerel, lobster, and shrimp fishing have declined because these species depend on plankton for a food base. The dam, Lake Nasser, and associated canals also made a happy home for snails and mosquitoes. The former carry the disease schistosomiasis (snail fever) and the latter malaria.

The Amazon River basin in South America has an average flow that amounts to 20% of the fresh water in the world's rivers. The river has many large tributaries, several of which surpass the Mississippi in size. This resource constitutes an immense energy potential and Brazil hopes to de-

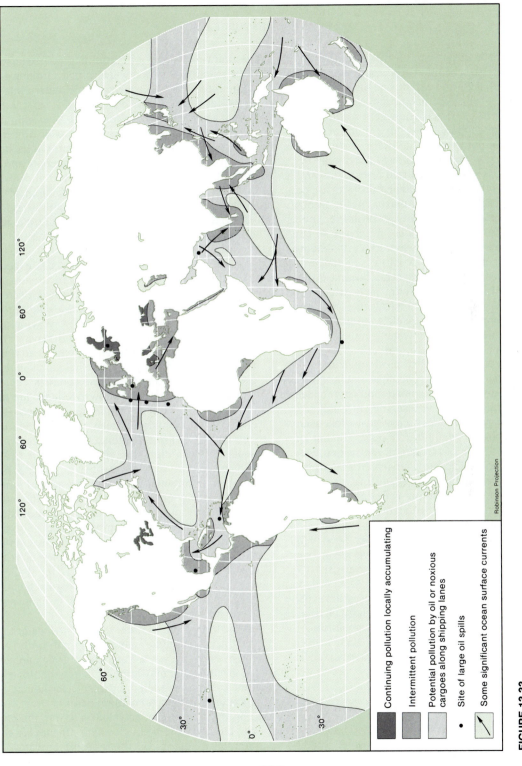

120°   60°   0°   60°   120°

Robinson Projection

Continuing pollution locally accumulating

Intermittent pollution

Potential pollution by oil or noxious
cargoes along shipping lanes

• Site of large oil spills

Some significant ocean surface currents

FIGURE 13.33
Sites of ocean pollution throughout the world.

413

velop it. The Tucurui Dam on the Tocantins River in the basin is scheduled for completion by the mid- to late 1980s and will be one of the largest in the world. It will eventually produce about 8000 MW of electricity. This is equivalent to the energy produced by about eight large nuclear power plants. Total power potential in the basin is close to 100,000 MW! The reservoir will flood more than 2000 km^2 of virgin tropical rain forest. This and a number of other similar planned projects are certain to impact upon the Amazon Basin through downstream effects on plants and wildlife. This is especially true if herbicides are necessary to control aquatic weeds such as water hyacinth that provide a good environment for carriers of dangerous diseases such as malaria and schistosomiasis. Herbicides used in the past include 2,4–D, which contains Agent Orange, a chemical that has been linked to cancers and birth defects. Aquatic mammals (manatees) that eat water plants are being imported and this may help [24].

Newly created lakes in tropical areas have historically been beset with problems—including anaerobic decay of organic materials in the deep water and filling in of the reservoir with sediment. Decay of plants produces a more acidic lake water that may corrode equipment, and sediment decreases useful life of a reservoir for storing water and producing electricity. It is feared that continued timber harvesting upslope and upstream of the Tucurui Dam and reservoir will significantly increase soil erosion and sediment production, thus reducing the useful life of the reservoir [24].

Tropical rain forests contain over 50% of all species on Earth. Most species have never been studied; some may contain chemicals useful in fighting disease, be useful for food crops, or have other potential utilitarian value. Large-scale experiments to change the basic hydrology in these areas should be done cautiously to avoid unnecessary ecologic damage. However, such caution seems unlikely considering the potential short-term benefits from development.

SUMMARY

An obvious and well-known detrimental aspect of human use of surface water, groundwater, and atmospheric water is the pollution of rivers and

groundwaters. We are beginning to understand that solutions to many hydrologic problems require integrating all aspects of the water cycle.

Water is one of the most abundant and important renewable resources on Earth. However, more than 99% of Earth's water is unavailable or unsuitable for beneficial human use because of its salinity or location. The pattern of water supply and use on Earth at any particular point on the land surface involves interactions between the biological, hydrologic, and rock cycles. To evaluate a region's water sources and use patterns, a water budget is developed to define the natural variability and availability of water.

During the next several decades it is expected that the total water withdrawn from streams and groundwater in the United States will decrease slightly, but that the consumptive use will increase because of greater demands from a growing population and industry. Water withdrawn from streams competes with other instream needs, such as maintaining fish and wildlife habitats and navigation, and may therefore cause conflicts.

Water pollution specifically refers to degradation of water quality as measured by physical, chemical, or biological criteria. These criteria take into consideration the intended use for the water, departure from the norm, effects on public health, and ecological impacts. Water pollutants have point or nonpoint sources, as do air pollutants. The major water pollutants are oxygen-demanding waste (BOD), pathogens and fecal coliform bacteria, nutrients, synthetic organic and inorganic compounds, oil, heavy metals, radioactive materials, heat, and sediment. Since the 1960s there has been a serious attempt to improve water quality in the United States. Although the program seems to have been successful, water quality in many areas is still substandard.

The movement of water down to the water table and through aquifers is an integral part of the rock and hydrologic cycles. In moving through an aquifer, groundwater may improve in quality. However, it may also be rendered unsuitable for human use by natural or artificial contaminants.

In the case of groundwater pollution, the physical, biologic, and geologic environments are considerably different from those of surface water. The ability of many soils and rocks to physically or otherwise degrade pollutants is well known, but not so generally known is the ability of clays and other earth materials to capture and exchange certain elements and compounds.

Pollution of an aquifer may result from disposal of wastes on the land surface or in the ground. It can also result from overpumping of groundwater in coastal areas, leading to intrusion of salt water into freshwater aquifers.

Principal human influences affecting runoff and sediment production include varied land uses (especially urban) and use of off-road vehicles.

Sediment pollution, natural or artificial, is certainly one of the most significant pollution problems. A great deal of sediment pollution is a result of human activity, particularly construction, agriculture, and urbanization. Although the problem cannot be completely eliminated, it can be minimized.

Wastewater treatment in the United States costs about $12 billion/yr, and the cost is expected to double in the next 10 years. Conventional methods of water treatment include large central treatment plants. Application of wastewater to farm or forest land, use of wastewater in aquaculture, and wastewater renovation for direct and indirect reuse are recent innovations.

Desalination of sea water in specific instances will continue, but large-scale desalination is not likely because of increasing costs of the energy used in the treatment process and in transporting the water to use sites.

Water resource management is in need of a new philosophy that considers geologic, geographic, and climatic factors and utilizes creative alternatives.

Water is an integral part of ecosystems, and it is possible to pollute even the world's largest hydrologic system, the oceans, especially near large coastal urban areas and along major ship lanes.

Construction of dams and reservoirs on major rivers such as the Mississippi, Nile, and Amazon has caused or will cause significant environmental change to important regional ecosystems.

Water resources in the wetlands of the world are very important for biological productivity, especially of fish that are an important food source to people. Shellfish are particularly vulnerable to water pollution and millions of dollars have been lost to pollution of shellfish beds in the nation's wetlands.

STUDY QUESTIONS

1 Would the strategy used to deal with water pollution in Seattle, Washington, have worked in Santa Fe, New Mexico? Why or why not?

2 If water is one of our most abundant resources, why are we concerned about its availability in the future?

3 How does clearcut logging affect surface runoff?

4 Why did fish in streams decrease in abundance following logging in New England?

5 Which is more important from a national point of view: conservation of water use in agriculture or in urban areas?

6 Distinguish between instream and offstream uses of water. Why is instream water use so controversial?

7 Compare and contrast surface water pollution with groundwater pollution. Which is easier to treat and why?

8 Why is sediment pollution considered to be one of the major pollution problems?

9 In the summer you buy a house with a septic system which appears to function properly. In the winter, effluent discharges at the surface. What could be the possible environmental causes of the problem?

10 What are possible socially acceptable, beneficial uses of wastewater?

11 In a city along an ocean coast, rare water birds are found to inhabit a pond that is part of a sewage treatment plant. How could this have happened? Is the water in the sewage pond polluted? Consider this question from the birds' and your point of view.

12 When and where is desalination the answer to water supply problems?

FURTHER READING

CANFIELD, C. 1985. *In the rainforest.* New York: Alfred A. Knopf.

DUNNE, T., and LEOPOLD, L. B. 1978. *Water in environmental planning.* San Francisco: W. H. Freeman.

LEOPOLD, L. B. 1974. *Water: A primer.* San Francisco: W. H. Freeman.

MILLS, D. H. 1972. *An introduction to freshwater ecology.* Edinburgh: Oliver and Boyd.

MORISAWA, M. 1968. *Streams.* New York: McGraw-Hill.

SCHUMM, S. A. 1977. *The fluvial system.* New York: Wiley.

STOKER, H. S., and SEAGER, S. L. 1976. *Environmental chemistry: Air and water pollution.* 2nd ed. Dallas: Scott, Foresman.

UNESCO. 1978. *World water balance and water resources of the Earth.* New York: Unipub.

WATER RESOURCES COUNCIL. 1978. *The nation's water resources, 1975–2000.* Vol. 1. Washington, D.C.

14

Energy Resources

- [ ] It is not energy that becomes in short supply, but preferred sources for particular uses.
- [ ] Energy is never created nor destroyed; it can be transformed from one kind to another.
- [ ] In any real process, energy tends to go from a more usable to a less usable form.
- [ ] Energy efficiency is always appreciably less than 100%.
- [ ] People in industrialized countries consume a disproportionate share of the world's total energy consumption. There is a direct relationship between a country's standard of living and its per capita energy consumption.
- [ ] All fossil fuels are forms of stored solar energy. The fossil fuel resource is being rapidly depleted.
- [ ] The use of fission-produced nuclear energy is decreasing because of costs, environmental concerns, and political decisions. The energy potential of nuclear fusion is nearly inexhaustible, but many problems need to be solved before it is practical on a large scale.
- [ ] Renewable energy sources (solar, wind, water, biomass) again are receiving consideration; technological problems exist for each of them.
- [ ] Due to uncertainties regarding continuing flow of energy, measures such as conservation, increased efficiency, and cogeneration are being promoted.
- [ ] Some energy planners propose a ''hard path'' approach to energy provision; others a ''soft path.'' Both of these extremes have positive and negative points.
- [ ] The next 30 years will be crucial in terms of energy decisions made.

ENERGY CRISES IN ANCIENT GREECE AND ROME

It is fashionable today to think that an energy shortage is something new. In fact, people for thousands of years have had to deal with different types of energy shortages, going back at least to the early Greek and Roman cultures. The climate in coastal areas of Greece today is characterized by warm summers and cool winters, much as it was 2500 years ago. However, at that time the Greeks did not have any artificial method of cooling their houses during the summer, and their small charcoal-burning heaters were undoubtedly not very efficient in warming their homes during the winter. Wood was their primary source of energy, as it is today for approximately half the world's people.

By the fifth century B.C. fuel shortages had become common, and much of the forest in many parts of Greece was destroyed for firewood. As local supplies were depleted, it became necessary to import wood from farther and farther away. Olive groves became sources of wood to be made into charcoal for burning, reducing a valuable resource. By the fourth century B.C. the city of Athens had banned the use of olive wood for fuel.

About this time the Greeks began to build their houses to face the south so that the low winter sun penetrated areas to be heated and the high summer sun shaded areas to be cooled. Recent excavations of ancient Greek cities suggest that large areas were planned so that individual homes could take maximum advantage of passive solar energy. Thus the Greeks' use of solar energy to assist in heating homes was a logical answer to their energy problem [1].

The use of wood in ancient Rome is somewhat analogous to the use of oil and gas in the United States today. Wealthy Roman citizens about 2000 years ago had central heating in their large homes, burning as much as 125 kg of wood every hour. Not surprisingly, local wood supplies were exhausted quickly, and the Romans had to import wood from outlying areas, as had the Greeks. Eventually wood had to be imported from as far away as 1600 km.

Thus, for the same reasons that the Greeks eventually sought out solar energy, so did the Romans. However, in the Roman era solar technology became advanced. The Romans used windows to increase the effectiveness of solar heating, developed greenhouses to raise food during the winter, and oriented large public bathhouses (some of which accommodated up to 2000 people) to use passive solar energy (Fig. 14.1). The Romans believed that sunlight in bathhouses was healthy, and it also saved greatly on fuel costs, allowing more wood to be available for heating the bath waters and steam rooms. The use of solar energy in ancient Rome was evidently quite widespread and resulted in the establishment of laws to protect a person's right to solar energy. As evidence of this, in some areas it was illegal for one person to construct a building that shaded another's [1].

The energy situation facing the United States and the world today is much like that faced by the early Greeks and Romans. The use of wood in the United States peaked in the 1880s when coal became abundant. The use of coal in turn began to decline after 1920, when oil and gas started to become available. Today we are facing the peak of oil and gas utilization. Fossil fuel resources, which took millions of years to form, may be essentially exhausted in just several hundred years. The decisions we make today will affect energy use for generations. Should we choose complex, centralized energy production methods, or use simpler, widely dispersed energy production methods? Which renewable sources of energy should be emphasized? How can we rely on nonrenewable energy sources? There are no easy answers.

The only thing very certain about the energy picture for tomorrow is that it will involve living with a good deal of uncertainty concerning energy availability, cost of energy, and environmental effects of energy use. The sources and patterns of energy utilization will undoubtedly change. It can be expected that supplies will continue to be regulated, and there is a good deal of potential for disruption of supplies. In recent years the Organization of Petroleum-Exporting Countries (OPEC) has attempted to control the flow of crude oil. In some instances this has been successful, but not nearly as successful as the exporting countries would have liked. Environmental effects of energy use at local, regional, and global scales will continue to be a topic of particular public concern. Finally, it

FIGURE 14.1
The Baths of Diocletian, circa A.D. 305, from a nineteenth-century engraving by Edmund Pau-
lin. Enormous windows facing the south and southwest, as well as a sand floor in the sweat
room, trapped solar heat so that Roman baths were quite warm late on a winter afternoon.

can be expected that serious "shocks" will occur
in the future as they have in the past. For example,
the 1973–74 Arab oil embargo caused significant
economic impact in the United States and other
countries and in 1979–80 the Iranian revolution
caused exports of petroleum to drop significantly.
Although in the 1980s there is a glut of petroleum
on the world market, this situation may be short-
lived because petroleum is a nonrenewable energy
source [2].

ENERGY BASICS

When we buy electricity by the kilowatt-hour, what
are we buying? We say we are buying energy, but
what does that mean? Energy is an abstract con-

cept. You can't see it or feel it, even if you have to
pay for it.*

To understand the concept of energy, it is easiest to begin with the idea of a **force.** We all have
had the experience of exerting force—of pushing
or pulling. The strength of a force can be measured
by how much it accelerates an object. Suppose
your car stalls while you are going up a hill, and
you get out and push it to the side of the road (Fig.
14.2). You apply a force against gravity. If the
brake is left on, the brakes, tires, and bearings
might heat up from friction. The longer the distance over which you exert the same force, the
greater is the change in the car's speed, position

*The following discussion is based on H. J. Morowitz,
1979, *Energy Flow in Biology,* Oxbow Press, New Haven,
Conn.

FIGURE 14.2
Some basic energy concepts, including force, potential energy, kinetic energy, and heat energy.

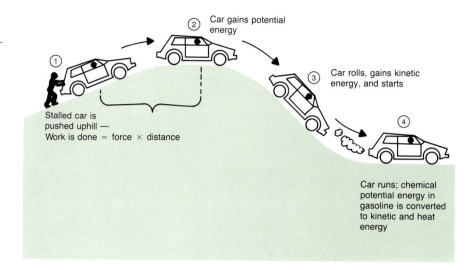

① Stalled car is pushed uphill —
Work is done = force × distance

② Car gains potential energy

③ Car rolls, gains kinetic energy, and starts

④ Car runs; chemical potential energy in gasoline is converted to kinetic and heat energy

uphill, or the heat in the brakes, tires, and bearings—that, in a physicist's terms, is the work done. **Work** is exerting a force over a distance; that is, work is the product of force times distance. If you push hard, but the car doesn't move at all, you have not done any work (according to the definition), even if you feel tired and sweaty.

In pushing your stalled car, you have done three things: changed its speed, moved it against gravity, and heated parts of it. These three things have something in common: they are all forms of **energy.** You have converted chemical energy in your body to the energy of motion of the car (kinetic energy), the gravitational (or potential) energy of the car, and heat energy. Energy is never created or destroyed; it is always conserved. It can be transformed from one kind to another. The principle of the conservation of energy is known as the **first law of thermodynamics.**

The conservation and conversion of energy can be illustrated by the example of a clock pendulum. When the pendulum is held in its highest position, it is neither moving nor getting hotter. It does, however, contain energy (owing to its position). We refer to the stored energy as **potential energy,** which is converted to other forms when it is released. Other examples of potential energy are the gravitational energy in water behind a dam; chemical energy in coal, fuel oil, and gasoline, as well as in the fat in your body; and nuclear energy, which is related to the forces binding the nuclei of atoms.

When the pendulum is released, it moves downward. At the bottom of the swing the speed is greatest, and there is no potential energy. At this point all of its energy is in the energy of motion, which is called **kinetic energy.** As the pendulum swings back and forth, the energy continually changes between the two forms, potential and kinetic. But at each cycle the pendulum slows down because of the friction of the pendulum moving through air and the friction at its pivot. The friction generates heat. Eventually all the energy is converted to heat and the pendulum stops.

This example illustrates another property of energy—its tendency to dissipate and end up as heat. It is relatively easy to transform various forms of energy into low-grade heat, but difficult to change heat into energy with high efficiency. Physicists have found that we can change all of the gravitational energy in a pendulum to heat, but we cannot change all the heat energy thus generated back into potential energy.

Heat energy is the energy of the random motion of atoms and molecules, and there is something special about it. The tendency of energy to become randomly distributed as the kinetic energy of molecules forms the basis of the second law of thermodynamics. The **second law of thermody-namics** states that, in any real process, energy always tends to go from a more usable form to a less usable form.

Let us return to the example of your stalled car, which you have now pushed to the side of the road. Having pushed the car a little way uphill, you have increased its potential energy. You can convert this to kinetic energy by letting it roll back downhill. You engage the gears to restart the car. As the car idles, the potential chemical energy to move the car is converted to waste heat energy and various amounts of other energy forms, including electricity to charge the battery and play the radio. According to the first law of thermodynamics, the total amount of energy is always conserved. If this is true, why should there ever be any energy problem? Why could we not collect that wasted heat and use it to run the engine? Here we discover the importance of the second law of thermodynamics. According to that law, energy is always degraded to heat, which can never with 100% efficiency be reconverted to useful work. When we refer to low-temperature heat energy as "low grade," we mean that relatively little of it is available to do useful work. High-grade energy, such as gasoline or sunlight, is largely available to do useful work. The biosphere continuously receives high-grade energy from the sun and radiates heat to the depths of space [3].

The unit of work used in the metric system is the joule. In talking about energy used, we use the unit exajoule, which is equivalent to 10^{18} (a billion billion) joules. The exajoule is roughly equivalent to one quadrillion, or 10^{15}, British thermal units (Btu). To put this in perspective, the United States now consumes about 80 exajoules of energy per year, and world consumption is about 250 exajoules.

In many instances, we are particularly interested in the rate of doing work, which is known as **power.** In the metric system, power is defined as joules per second, which is called a watt. When larger units of power are needed, we may use the kilowatt-hour, the unit by which we pay an electric bill. This unit is 1000 watts applied for 1 hour (3600 seconds), which is equivalent to 3,600,000 joules.

Table 14.1 lists average estimated electrical power used for typical household appliances over a period of one year. The total power used in a year is a function of the power required to run the appliance and the time it is actually used. Appliances that use the most power are clothes dryers, washing machines, refrigerators, and water heaters (assuming they are electrical). A list of electrical power used by typical household appliances is useful in identifying areas where power may be saved through conservation or efficiency. For example, a typical refrigerator uses approximately the same amount of power required for twenty 100–watt bulbs. Considerable electricity could be saved by designing refrigerators that operate more efficiently.

TABLE 14.1
Average estimated electrical power used for typical household appliances in a year.

Appliance	Power (watts)	Av. Hours Used per Year	Approximate Power Used per Year (kilowatt-hours)
Clock	2	8760	17
Clothes dryer	4600	228	1049
Hand-held hair dryer	1000	60	60
Hi-fi	30		43
Light bulbs	100	1080	108
Television	350	1440	504
Washing machine	700	144	1008
Toaster	1150	48	552
Refrigerator (frost free, 14 ft³)	360	6000	2160
Water heater (40 gal)	4500	1044	4698
Vacuum cleaner	750	120	90

Source: Data from U.S. Department of Energy.

ENERGY CONSUMPTION AND SCARCITY

People in industrialized countries, while a relatively small percentage of the world's population, consume a disproportionate share of the total energy produced in the world. In fact, there is a direct relationship between a country's standard of living (as measured by the gross national product) and the energy consumption per capita. In the next several decades, as petroleum and natural gas become more scarce and expensive, developing and developed countries are going to have to find innovative ways to obtain energy.

For the last 30 years most of the energy consumed in the United States has come from natural gas and petroleum (Fig. 14.3), with moderate amounts from coal and small amounts from water power and nuclear power. The United States has huge reserves of coal, but major new sources of natural gas and petroleum are becoming scarcer and few new large hydropower plants can be expected. Planning and construction of a large number of new nuclear power plants in the next few years have become uncertain for a variety of economic, social, political, and environmental reasons.

There is little doubt that the beginning of the energy transition from nonrenewable to renewable energy sources has begun. Although all resources are renewable as long as Earth processes are op-erating, we classify resources such as oil, natural gas, and minerals as nonrenewable resources because the time required for renewal is too long to be of use to humans. Other resources such as air, water, timber, and wildlife are classified as renewable resources because they are regenerated at a rate useful to humans. It is important to remember that renewable resources are renewable only as long as processes favorable to replenishment are operating. Pollution or extinction may render certain renewable resources much less renewable than we presume or desire.

In the United States today, oil and gas still supply approximately three-fourths of our energy needs; but as oil and gas become scarce or more costly, we will slowly change to other energy sources. The three major sources of energy likely to be used are such fossil fuels as coal and oil shale, nuclear energy, and the various renewable energy sources. In many parts of the world, renewable energy sources may be the only energy sources indigenous to a given region.

FOSSIL FUELS

The fossil fuels (crude oil, natural gas, coal, oil shales, and tar sands) are all forms of stored solar energy. They were created from incomplete biologic decomposition of dead organic matter; some organic material was buried, escaped oxidation,

FIGURE 14.3
United States consumption of energy, 1949 to 1982. (Data from U.S. Department of Energy.)

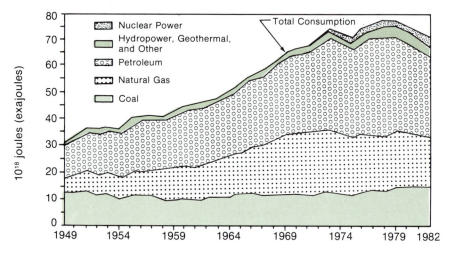

Career Profile: Robert Lucacher

Robert Lucacher wanted to make the world a better place to live. With that noble goal, he decided to major in environmental studies at college. Now, with a graduate degree in environmental management, he is a safety specialist with an oil company in California.

He has also worked as an environmental coordinator and analyst. "Safety and environmental regulations have a tendency to overlap to some extent," he says. "Although I'm in safety today, I may get put back in environmental, depending on where the need is in the company."

The oil company's main objective is to find and produce petroleum reserves. Various local, state, and federal government agenices regulate and direct how oil companies will conduct their businesses. "My job is to make sure my company finds and produces oil according to the regulations," Lucacher says. "I have to know what the regulations are and then make sure the company is carrying them out."

Occasionally, Lucacher lectures in local college classes about offshore petroleum exploration and production. Some students find the idea of an environmentalist working for an oil company to be a paradox. But Lucacher firmly believes that oil can be extracted in an

environmentally safe manner if the operating company has the proper attitude and commitment. "The oil company is just as concerned about doing the job correctly as I am. They do not want oil anywhere but in the pipelines. It doesn't make money if it is anywhere else," he points out.

Lucacher finds very few people in the oil industry who do not care. "Everybody likes clean water and beaches. So, everybody does as much as they can to do a good job," he says. Lucacher does not find it difficult to be objective in his position. As a responsible individual, he feels it is his job to correct the problems that he finds. "The day I get overly compromised—and we all compomise—is the day I resign," he says. So far he does not feel he has been. "Most people are willing to listen," he explains.

Although pro-alternative energy, Lucacher describes himself

as realistic, too. He believes oil and natural gas will continue to be predominant fuels in the United States for economic reasons. In his opinion, the public is a "fickle animal, depending on whether they are lined up for gasoline or prices are going down." In other words, what the public wants one day is different from what it wants the next. He feels the public interest as a whole in the long term is being served quite responsibly by the oil industry. He describes the people in his company as "sharp enough to comply with the spirit of the law and maximize profit."

Lucacher hopes that students today understand the coordination and effort required by engineers, managers, truckers, and others to get crude oil out of the ground, to a refinery, and to market. He also hopes they have a sense of how petroleum is used—for medicines, plastics, lubricants, fuels—and how dependent we are on it. He hopes the students are not like a child in a supermarket who sees only hamburger without recognizing that it came from a cow.

As far as making the world a better place, Lucacher is not yet satisfied with his contribution. He says, "There is so much more I want to do. There *is* so much more to do."

Michele Wigginton

and was converted by complex chemical reactions in the geologic cycle to fossil fuels. The biologic and geologic processes in the part of the geologic cycle that produces sedimentary rocks are responsible for the formation of fossil fuels. The fossil fuel resource is finite, taking millions of years of Earth history to form and a few hundred years of human history to burn. Using even the most optimistic predictions, we can expect the total fossil fuel epoch in human history to be only about 500 years. Thus, while fossil fuels were extremely significant to the development of modern civilization, they must be an ephemeral event in the span of human history.

Environmental impacts of fossil fuel exploration and development range from negligible for remote-sensing techniques in exploration, to significant, unavoidable impacts for projects such as the Trans-Alaska Pipeline. Exploration for energy often involves building roads, exploratory drilling, and constructing supply lines (for camps, airfields, and other facilities) to remote areas. These activities, except in sensitive areas such as some semi-arid to arid environments and some permafrost areas, generally have few adverse effects on the landscape and resources compared with development and consumption activities.

Crude Oil and Natural Gas

Crude oil and natural gas are found primarily along young tectonic belts at plate boundaries. Most of the known reserves (that amount of the total resource that is identified and can be extracted at a profit—about 600 billion barrels) are located in a few fields (65% of the reserves are in 1% of the fields), the largest of which are in the Middle East. Although new oil and gas fields have recently been and are still being discovered in the United States, Mexico, Alaska, South America, and other areas, it is apparent that the present world reserves will be depleted in the next few decades. On the other hand, these numbers suggest that we are not soon going to run out of crude oil. At the present world-wide rate of consumption we have at least 70 years if our estimates of the resource and potential resource base are correct. It is, however, important to understand that there is a good deal of uncer-

TABLE 14.2
Crude oil: resources, reserves, and consumption.

	Billions of Barrels
World resources (ultimate production)	2000
World reserves	646
U.S. reserves	30
Already consumed	340
Expected future discoveries	1014
Annual world consumption	22
Depletion of present reserves (assuming constant consumption)	Year 2010
Peak in world production	1985–2000

Source: Council on Environmental Quality and the Department of State.

tainty concerning the estimated size of the petroleum reserves and potential resources. The total resource always exceeds known reserves; it includes petroleum that can't be extracted at a profit and petroleum that is suspected of being present but which hasn't been proven. Only 40 years ago the size of the total resource was estimated to be about 400 billion barrels. Today that estimate is closer to 2,000 billion barrels (Table 14.2) [2].

Worldwide estimates of recoverable natural gas range from approximately 6000 to 10,000 trillion cubic feet, which at the present rate of world consumption is sufficient to last approximately 100 years. In the United States, there have recently been considerable discoveries of natural gas and at present consumption the resource is expected to last at least 20–30 years. Only recently have we begun to really look hard for natural gas and utilize the resource to its potential. One reason for this is that natural gas is transported primarily by pipelines and only in the last few decades have these been constructed in large numbers. In fact, until recently, natural gas found with petroleum was often (and still is) simply burned off as waste [2].

In spite of the new discoveries and construction of pipelines and so forth, the long-term projections for a steady supply of crude oil and natural gas have a great number of uncertainties surrounding them. Everyone agrees that the supply is finite and at present rates of consumption it is only a matter of time until the resource is depleted. Of course we will never really run out of all crude oil and natural gas, but the price will rise appreciably as the resource becomes scarcer.

Development of oil and gas fields involves drilling wells on land or beneath the sea. Removing oil or gas may cause a surface subsidence hazard and requires the disposal of wastewaters. But the most extensive environmental problems associated with oil and gas occur when fuel is delivered and consumed. Crude oil is mostly transported on land in pipelines or across the ocean by tankers, and both methods have the potential to produce oil spills. Marine oil spills are best known and, although the effects are relatively short-lived, have killed thousands of sea birds, temporarily spoiled beaches, and caused loss of tourist revenue.

The Trans-Alaska Pipeline, completed in 1977, provides a good example of the possible spectrum of effects of an oil transport system on a sensitive environment. Main unavoidable impacts include disturbance of land and of fish and wildlife habitats; human use of the land during construction, operation, and maintenance of the pipeline itself, access roads, and other support facilities; discharge of oil and other effluents at Valdez, Alaska (the shipping point), from the tanker system; and increased pressure on services, utilities, and the culture of the native population [3].

Coal

Partially decomposed vegetation deeply buried in sedimentary environments may be slowly transformed into solid, brittle carbonaceous rock coal

as idealized in Figure 14.4. Coal is by far the world's most abundant fossil fuel, with a total recoverable resource of about 6000 billion tons. Because the annual world consumption is about 4 billion tons, the resource should last many hundreds of years.

Coal is classified according to its carbon and sulfur content (Table 14.3). Energy content is greatest in bituminous coal, which has relatively few volatiles (oxygen, hydrogen, and nitrogen) and low moisture content, and least in lignite, which has a high moisture content.

The distribution of the common coals (bitumi-

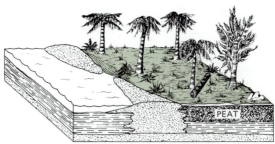

(a) *Coal swamp forms.*

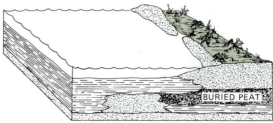

(b) *Rise in sea level buries swamp in sediment.*

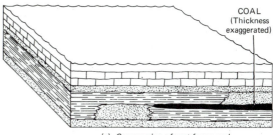

(c) *Compression of peat forms coal.*

FIGURE 14.4
Processes by which buried plant debris (peat) is transformed into coal.

TABLE 14.3
Distribution of U.S. coal resources according to their rank and sulfur content.

Rank	Sulfur Content (percent)		
	Low 0–1	Medium 1.1–3.0	High 3+
Anthracite	97.1	2.9	—
Bituminous coal	29.8	26.8	43.4
Subbituminous coal	99.6	0.4	—
Lignite	90.7	9.3	—
All ranks	65.0	15.0	20.0

Source: Murphy.

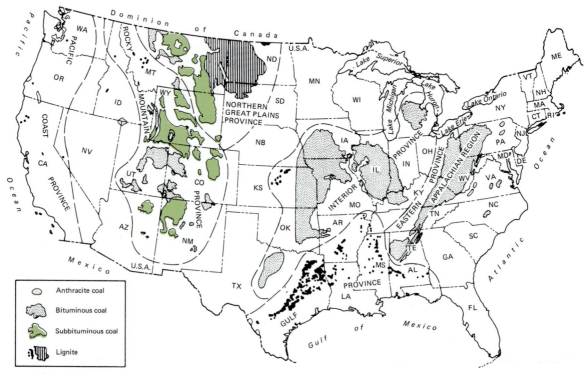

FIGURE 14.5
Coal fields of the conterminous United States. (After U.S. Bureau of Mines, 1971.)

nous, subbituminous, and lignite) in the conterminous United States is shown in Figure 14.5. Most of the low-sulfur coal in the United States is relatively low-grade, low-energy lignite and subbituminous coal found west of the Mississippi River. The location of low-sulfur coal has environmental significance because low-sulfur coal causes less air pollution and therefore is more desirable as a fuel for power plants. Therefore, to avoid air pollution, thermal power plants on the East Coast will have to continue to treat some of the local coal to lower its sulfur content. Although it is expensive, treating the coal may be more economical than transporting low-sulfur coal from the western states.

Most coal mining in the United States is done underground, but strip mining, which started in the late nineteenth century, has steadily increased because it tends to be cheaper and easier than un-

derground mining. The increased demand for coal will lead to more and larger strip mines. There are 40 billion metric tons of coal reserves that are now accessible to surface-mining techniques. In addition, approximately another 90 billion metric tons of coal within 50 m of the surface is potentially available for strip mining.

Strip Mines The impact of large strip mines for fossil fuels varies from region to region, depending upon topography, climate, and reclamation practices. In humid areas of the eastern United States with abundant rainfall, mine drainage of acid water is a serious problem. Surface water infiltrates the spoil banks (material left after the coal or other minerals are removed), where it reacts with sulfide minerals such as pyrite (FeS_2) to produce sulfuric acid, which then runs into and pollutes streams and groundwater resources. Acid water also drains from underground mines and roadcuts in areas where coal and pyrite are abundant, but the problem is magnified when large areas of disturbed material remain exposed to surface waters. Acid drainage can be minimized by channeling surface runoff and groundwater before they enter a mined area and diverting them around the potentially polluting materials [4].

In arid and semiarid regions, water problems associated with mining are not as pronounced as in wetter regions, but the land may be more sensitive to mining activities such as exploration and road building. In some areas in arid environments of the western and southwestern United States, the land is so sensitive that even tire tracks across the land survive for years. Reportedly, wagon tracks from the early days of the westward migration of settlers have survived in some locations. Furthermore, soils are often thin, water is scarce, and reclamation work is difficult.

All strip mining has the potential to pollute or destroy scenic, water, biologic, or other land resources. However, good reclamation practices can minimize the damage (Fig. 14.6). Although reclamation is often site-specific, a case history of a modern coal mine in Colorado emphasizes the important principles of modern reclamation practices.

The Trapper Mine on the western slope of the Rocky Mountains in northern Colorado is a good example of a new generation of large coal strip mines. The main operation is designed to minimize environmental degradation during the mining and reclaim the land for dry-land farming and grazing of livestock and big game without artificial application of water.

Over a 35–year period the mine will produce 68 million metric tons of coal from 20–24 km^3 to be delivered to a 800 MW power plant located adjacent to the mine. Four coal seams, varying from about 1 to 4 m thick, each separated by various depths of overburden, will be mined. Depth of overburden to the coal varies from zero to about 50 m.

A number of steps are involved in the actual mining. Vegetation and topsoil are removed by bulldozers and scrapers, and the soil is stockpiled for reuse. The overburden along a cut up to 1.6 km long and 53 m wide is removed with a 23–m^3 dragline bucket. The exposed coal beds are then drilled and blasted to fracture the coal, which is removed with a backhoe and loaded into trucks. Finally, the cut is filled, the topsoil replaced, and the land is either planted in a crop or returned to rangeland.

At the Trapper Mine the land is reclaimed without artificially applying water. The precipitation (mostly snow) is about 35 cm/yr, which is sufficient to reestablish vegetation provided there is adequate topsoil. This emphasizes an important point—namely, that reclamation is site-specific. What works at one location may not be applicable to other areas.

Water and air quality are closely monitored at the Trapper Mine. Surface water is diverted around mine pits and groundwater intercepted while pits are open. Settling basins, constructed downslope from the pit, trap suspended solids prior to discharging water into local streams. Air quality at the mine is degraded by dust produced from blasting, hauling, and grading of the coal. Dust is minimized by regularly watering or otherwise treating roads and other surfaces.

Reclamation at the Trapper Mine has been successful during the first years of operation. Although reclamation increases the cost of the coal by as much as 50%, it will pay off in the long-range productivity of the land as the land is returned to farming and grazing uses. It might be argued that the Trapper Mine is unique in its combination of geology, hydrology, and topography, allowing for successful reclamation. On the other hand, the success of the mine operation demonstrates that, with careful site selection and planning, the development of energy resources is not incompatible with other land uses.

Federal guidelines governing strip mining of coal in the United States require that mined land be restored to support its premining use. The new regulations also prohibit mining on prime agricultural land and give farmers and ranchers the opportunity to restrict or stop mining on their land, even if they do not own the mineral rights. Reclamation includes disposing of wastes, contouring the land, and replanting vegetation. Unfortunately, reclamation is difficult, and it is unlikely that it will be completely successful.

FIGURE 14.6
A small open-pit mine (a) before and (b) after reclamation.

(a)

(b)

Transport of Coal The transport of large amounts of coal, or energy derived from coal, from production areas with low energy demand to large population centers is a significant environmental issue. Coal may be converted on-site to electricity, synthetic oil, or synthetic gas, which are relatively easy to transport, but with a few exceptions these alternatives all have problems. Transmission of electricity over long distances is expensive, and there may not be sufficient water for cooling in

FIGURE 14.7
A coal slurry pipeline system. Locations of existing or planned pipelines in the United States are shown on the map. (From Council on Environmental Quality, 1979.)

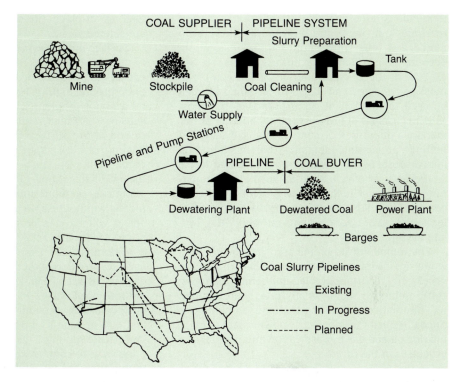

power plants in semiarid, coal-rich regions. Conversion of coal to synthetic oil or gas, while possible, is expensive, and the technology is primitive. Furthermore, the conversion requires a tremendous amount of water, placing a significant demand on local water supplies in the coal regions of the western United States [5].

Methods of transporting large volumes of coal for long distances include freight trains and coal slurry pipelines. Trains will continue to be used because of relatively low costs for new capital expenses. Coal slurry pipelines, designed to use water to transport pulverized coal, have an economic advantage over trains provided that

1 transport distance is long and the volume of coal shipped is large,
2 rates of inflation are high and interest rates are low,
3 mines are large and have customers that will purchase large volumes of coal over a long period of time, and
4 sufficient, low-cost water is available.

The economic advantages of the slurry pipeline are therefore rather tenuous, especially in the western United States, where large volumes of water will be difficult to obtain [5]. For example, a pipeline transporting 30 million tons of coal requires about 20 million m^3 of water per year—an amount sufficient to meet the water needs for a city of about 85,000 people or irrigate up to 40 km^2 of farmland. In spite of these problems, some pipelines will probably be constructed. Figure 14.7 shows an idealized slurry pipeline system and locations of existing, in progress, and planned pipelines in the United States. At present there is considerable public opposition to slurry pipelines, and the future prospects are uncertain.

Future of Coal The real shortages of oil and gas are still a few years away, but when they do come, they will put tremendous pressure on the coal industry to open more and larger mines in both the eastern and the western coal beds of the United States. An increased number of mines may have tremendous environmental impacts for several reasons. First, more and more land will be strip mined and thus will require careful restoration. Second, unlike oil and gas, burned coal leaves ash (5–20% of the original amount of the coal) that must be collected and disposed of. Some ash can be used for landfill or other purposes, but most (85%) is useless at present. Third, handling of tremendous quantities of coal through all stages— mining, processing, shipping, combustion, and final disposal of ash—will have potentially adverse environmental effects such as aesthetic degradation, noise, dust pollution, and, most significant, because it is likely to cause serious health problems, release of trace elements into the water, soil, and air [6].

Environmental problems associated with coal, while significant enough to cause concern, are not necessarily insurmountable, and careful planning could minimize them. At any rate, there may be few alternatives to mining tremendous quantities of coal to feed thermoelectric power plants and to provide oil and gas by gasification and liquefaction processes in the future.

Oil Shale

Oil shale is a fine-grained sedimentary rock containing organic matter. Upon heating (destructive distillation), oil shale yields significant amounts of hydrocarbons that are otherwise relatively insoluble. The best known oil shales in the United States are those in the Green River Formation, which underlies approximately 44,000 km^2 of Colorado, Utah, and Wyoming.

Total identified world shale-oil resources are estimated to be about 3 trillion barrels of oil. However, evaluation of the oil grade and the feasibility of economic recovery with today's technology is not completed. Shale-oil resources in the United States amount to about 2 trillion barrels of oil, or two-thirds of the total identified in the world; of this, 90%, or 1.8 trillion barrels, is located in the Green River oil shales [7].

The environmental impact of developing oil-shale resources varies with the recovery technique used. At present, surface and subsurface mining as well as in-place (in situ) techniques are being considered.

Surface mining, whether open pit or strip mine, is attractive because nearly 90% of the shale-oil can be recovered compared with less than 60% for underground mining. However, waste disposal will be a major problem with any mining, surface or subsurface, which requires that oil shale be processed at the surface for retorting (crushing and heating raw oil shale to about 540°C to obtain crude shale oil). The volume of waste will exceed the original volume of shale mined by 20–30%. Therefore, the mine from which the shale was removed will not be able to accommodate the waste, and it will have to be piled up or otherwise disposed of. The impact of the waste disposal can be considerable. For example, if surface mining is used to produce 100,000 barrels of shale oil per day for 20 years, the operation will produce 570 million m^3 of waste. If 50% of this is disposed of on the surface, it could fill an area 8–16 km long and 600 m wide to a depth of 60 m. Therefore, if large-scale mining is used, we will have to determine ways to contour and vegetate oil-shale waste to minimize the visual and pollutional impacts [8, 9]. Experiments to learn more about how to accomplish this are now being conducted.

A process of oil-shale recovery being very seriously tested is known as modified in situ, or MIS, in which part of the oil shale (about 20%) is mined and the remainder is highly fractured or rubbled to increase permeability. A block of shale so treated, known as the retort block, is then ignited, and released oil and gas are recovered through wells.

Tar Sands

Tar sands are sedimentary rocks or sands impregnated with tar oil, asphalt, or bitumen. Petroleum cannot be recovered from them by usual commercial methods such as wells because the oil is too viscous to flow easily. Seventy-five percent of the world's known tar sand deposits are in Canada. The total resource is about 1000 billion barrels, but it is not known how much of this will eventually be recovered.

NUCLEAR ENERGY

Nuclear energy is energy of the atomic nucleus. Two reactions have been used to release that energy to do work: fission and fusion. Nuclear **fission** is the splitting of an atom into smaller fragments. Nuclear **fusion** is the combining of atoms to form heavier atoms. A byproduct of both reactions is the release of nuclear energy. For the production of electricity, controlled nuclear reactions take place within commercial nuclear reactors.

Fission

The first controlled nuclear fission, demonstrated in 1942, led to the development of the primary uses of uranium—that is, in explosives and as a heat source to provide steam for generation of electricity. One kilogram of uranium oxide produces a heat equivalent of approximately 16 metric tons of coal, making uranium an important source of energy in the United States and the world for at least a few more years [10].

Three types of uranium occur in nature: uranium-238, which accounts for approximately 99.3% of all natural uranium; uranium-235, which makes up about 0.7%; and uranium-234, which makes up about 0.005%. Uranium-235 is the only naturally occurring fissionable material and therefore is essential to production of nuclear energy. Processing uranium to increase the amount of uranium-235 from 0.7% to about 3% produces enriched uranium, which is used as fuel for the fission reaction.

Fission reactors split uranium-235 by neutron bombardment (Fig. 14.8). The reaction produces three more neutrons released from uranium, fission fragments, and heat. The released neutrons each strike other uranium-235 atoms, releasing more neutrons, fission products, and heat. As the process continues, a chain reaction develops as more and more uranium is split, releasing more neutrons.

Most reactors now in use consume more fissionable material than they produce and are known as burner reactors. The reactor itself is part of the nuclear steam supply system, which produces the steam to run the turbine generators that

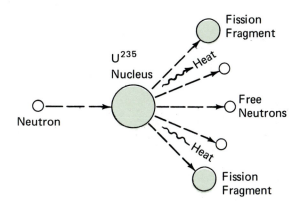

FIGURE 14.8
Fission of uranium-235. A neutron strikes the uranium-235 nucleus, producing fission fragments and free neutrons and releasing heat. The released neutrons may then each strike another uranium-235 atom, releasing more neutrons, fission fragments, and energy. As the process continues, a chain reaction develops.

produce the electricity [11]. Therefore, the reactor has the same function as the boiler that produces the heat in coal- or oil-burning power plants (Fig. 14.9).

The main components of the reactor shown in Figure 14.10 are the core, control rods, coolant, and reactor vessel. The core of the reactor is enclosed in a heavy stainless steel reactor vessel. Then, for extra safety and security, the entire reactor is contained in a reinforced concrete building [10].

Fuel pins, consisting of enriched uranium pellets placed into hollow tubes with a diameter less than 1 cm, are packed together (40,000 or more in a reactor) into fuel subassemblies in the core. A stable fission chain reaction in the core is maintained by controlling the number of neutrons that cause fission as well as the fuel concentration. A minimum fuel concentration is necessary to keep the reactor critical—that is, to achieve a self-sustaining chain reaction. The control rods, which contain materials that capture neutrons, are used to regulate the chain reaction. If the rods are pulled out, the chain reaction speeds up; if they are inserted into the core, the reaction slows down [11].

FOSSIL FUEL POWER PLANT

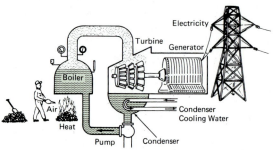

NUCLEAR POWER PLANT
Boiling Water Reactor (BWR)

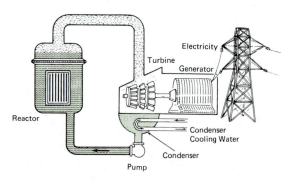

FIGURE 14.9
Comparison of a fossil fuel power plant and a nuclear power plant. Notice that the nuclear reactor has exactly the same function as the boiler in the fossil fuel power plant. (From American Nuclear Society.)

The function of the coolant is to remove the heat produced by the fission reactions. When water is used as the coolant, it acts also as a moderator, slowing the neutrons down and facilitating efficient fission of uranium-235 [10].

Other parts of the nuclear steam supply system are the primary coolant loops and pumps, which circulate a coolant (usually water) through the reactor, extracting heat produced by fission, and heat exchangers or steam generators, which use the fission-heated coolant to make steam.

In recent years there has been a sharp decline in the nuclear industry in the United States, where over 100 nuclear projects have been cancelled since the mid-1970s [12]. At the global scale the amount of electricity generated from nuclear reactors is 50% in France, 17% in Japan, 13% in the United States, and 6% in the Soviet Union [12]. This is considerably less than projected only a few years ago. The move away from nuclear energy results from a complex set of circumstances, including increased cost, environmental concerns, and political decisions. Some energy experts believe that the problem with nuclear energy is that the industry has not matured as rapidly as expected and that the plants have not operated as safely and smoothly as hoped for. On economic grounds alone, since 1970 the cost for new nuclear power plants has gone from being lower than that for coal to considerably higher. Therefore, the full impact of what began in 1942 is still to be determined.

The adequacy of the supply of natural uranium-235 was hotly debated in the 1970s. Apparently there is no problem with supply of uranium today owing to the slowdown in the growth of the nuclear industry. In fact, the real price of uranium has dropped to approximately one-half of what it was only a few years ago [2].

Fusion

In contrast to fission, which involves splitting heavy atoms such as uranium, fusion involves combining light elements such as hydrogen to form a heavier element such as helium. As fusion occurs, heat energy is released (Fig. 14.11). Similar reactions are the source of energy in our sun and other stars. In a hypothetical fusion reactor, two isotopes of hydrogen (atoms with variable mass due to a different number of neutrons in the nucleus)—deuterium (D) and tritium (T)—are injected into the reactor chamber where the necessary conditions for fusion are maintained. Products of the D-T fusion include helium, carrying 20% of the energy released, and neutrons, carrying 80% of the energy released (Fig. 14.11) [13].

Several conditions are necessary for fusion to take place. First, there must be an extremely high temperature (approximately 100 million°C for D-T fusion). Second, the density of the fuel elements must be sufficiently high. At the necessary temperature for fusion, nearly all atoms are stripped of their electrons, forming a plasma. Plasma is an

FIGURE 14.10
(a) Main components of a nuclear reactor; (b) inspecting the fuel element.

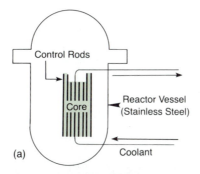

Control Rods

Reactor Vessel
(Stainless Steel)

Core

Coolant

(a)

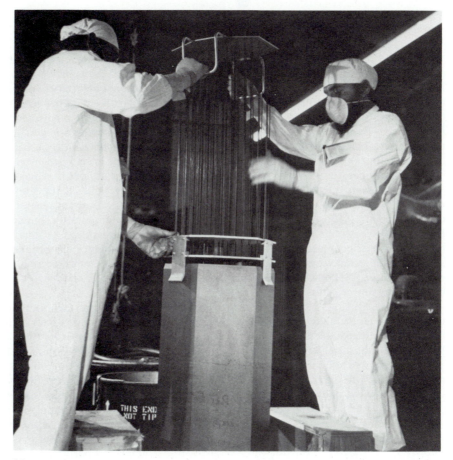

(b)

electrically neutral material consisting of positively charged nuclei, ions, and negatively charged electrons. Third, the plasma must be confined for a sufficient time to ensure that the energy released by the fusion reactions exceeds the energy supplied to maintain the plasma [13, 14].

FIGURE 14.11
Deuterium-tritium (D-T) fusion reaction. (Modified from U.S. Department of Energy, 1980.)

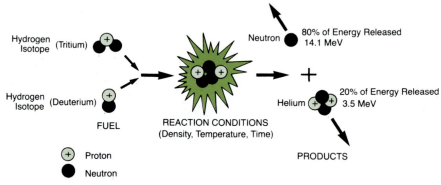

Hydrogen Isotope (Tritium)

Hydrogen Isotope (Deuterium)

FUEL

REACTION CONDITIONS
(Density, Temperature, Time)

Neutron — 80% of Energy Released 14.1 MeV

Helium — 20% of Energy Released 3.5 MeV

PRODUCTS

(+) Proton

● Neutron

MeV Million electron Volts (measure of energy)

The potential energy available when and if fusion-reactor power plants are developed is nearly inexhaustible. One gram of D-T fuel (from a water and lithium fuel supply) has the energy equivalent of 45 barrels of oil. Deuterium can be extracted economically from ocean water, and tritium can be produced in a reaction with lithium in a fusion reactor. Lithium can be extracted economically from abundant supplies.

Many problems remain to be solved before nuclear fusion can be used on a large scale. Research is still in the first stage, which involves basic physics, testing possible fuels (mostly D-T), and magnetic confinement of plasma. Progress in fusion research has, in recent years, been steady, so there is optimism that useful power will eventually be produced from controlled fusion.

Energy from fusion, once released, has a variety of applications, including heating and cooling of buildings and production of synthetic fuels, but production of electricity is probably the most important. It is expected (but not proven) that fusion power plants will be competitive economically with other sources of electrical energy.

Nuclear Energy and the Environment

Throughout the entire nuclear cycle—from mining and processing of uranium to controlled fission, reprocessing of spent nuclear fuel, and final disposal of radioactive waste—various amounts of radiation enter and affect the environment.

The chance of a disastrous nuclear accident is estimated to be very low. Nevertheless, the probability of an accident occurring increases with every reactor put into operation. The 1979 accident at Three Mile Island nuclear power plant near Middletown, Pennsylvania, involved a chain of what were believed to be highly improbable events resulting from both mechanical failure and human error. Although a major disaster was avoided at Three Mile Island, the incident raised important questions about reactor safety; five other reactors were temporarily shut down as a result of potential design-safety problems, reducing the total amount of nuclear power produced in the United States for the first time since 1960. Concern for reactor safety is now at a new high since the serious accident at Chernobyl, USSR, in 1986. See Chapter 11 for information concerning this incident, which has been responsible for rethinking risk analysis and reactor safety.

There are potential hazards associated with transporting and disposing nuclear material as well as supplying other nations with reactors. Terrorist activity and the possibility of irresponsible persons in governments add a risk that is present in no other form of energy production. Nuclear energy may indeed be an answer to our energy problems and perhaps someday it will provide unlimited cheap energy. However, with nuclear power must come an increased responsibility to ensure that nuclear power is used for, not against, people and that future generations inherit a quality environment and are free from worrying about hazardous nuclear waste.

Fusion appears attractive from an environmental point of view. First, land-use and transportation impacts are small compared with those associated with fossil fuel or fission energy sources. Second, compared with fission breeders, fusion reactors produce no fission products and little radioactive waste and are less likely to be involved in an accident [15]. On the other hand, fusion power plants probably will use materials that are toxic to people; lithium, for example, is toxic when inhaled or ingested. Other potential hazards include strong magnetic fields and microwaves used in confining and heating plasma and short-lived radiation emitted from the reactor vessel [13]. The problems associated with disposal of nuclear waste are discussed in Chapter 16. The hazards associated with radiation are discussed in Chapter 11.

GEOTHERMAL ENERGY

The useful conversion of natural heat from the interior of Earth to heat buildings and generate electricity is an exciting application of geologic knowledge and engineering technology. The idea of harnessing Earth's internal heat is not new. As early as 1904, geothermal power utilizing dry steam was developed in Italy, and natural internal heat is now being used to generate electricity in the USSR, Japan, New Zealand, Iceland, Mexico, and California. Yet existing geothermal facilities constitute only a small portion of the total energy that might eventually be tapped from Earth's reservoir of internal heat. Geothermal energy is sometimes considered a renewable resource because in specific instances the natural heat flow may be sufficiently high that it may be replenished relatively quickly. But in most instances it is better thought of as a nonrenewable resource.

Natural heat production within Earth is only partly understood. We do know that some areas have a higher flow of heat from below than others and that for the most part these locations are associated with the tectonic cycle. Oceanic ridge systems (divergent plate boundaries) and convergent plate boundaries, where mountains are being uplifted and volcanic island arcs are forming, are areas where this natural heat flow is anomalously high.

The relative distribution of heat flow from within Earth for the United States has been mapped in a generalized way, but the map has limited value for locating specific sites where geothermal energy resources could be developed [16]. It is interesting to note that the region of high heat flow is concentrated in the western United States, where tectonic activity and volcanic activity have been recent.

Types of Geothermal Systems

On the basis of geologic criteria, several geothermal systems may be defined: hydrothermal convection systems, hot igneous systems, and geopressured systems [17, 18]. Each of these systems has a different origin and different potential as an energy source, but the total resource base is very large (Table 14.4).

Hydrothermal convection systems are characterized by the circulation of steam and/or hot water that transfers heat at depths to the surface. An example is The Geysers, 145 km north of San Francisco, California, where several hundred megawatts of electrical energy are produced.

Hot igneous systems involve hot, dry rocks with or without the presence of near-surface molten rock (**magma**). These systems contain a tremendous amount of stored heat (Table 14.4), and recent experiments in New Mexico are investigating the scientific feasibility of extracting energy from them.

Geopressured systems exist where the normal heat flow from Earth is trapped by impermeable

TABLE 14.4
U.S. geothermal resources.

Type	Quantity of Energy[a] (exajoules)
Hydrothermal convection systems	12,000
Hot igneous systems (dry rock)	13,000,000
Geopressurized	190,000

Source: Data from Los Alamos Scientific Laboratory.
[a]The present total energy used in the United States is about 80 exajoules/yr.

clay layers that act as an effective insulator. Perhaps the best known regions where geopressurized systems develop are along the Gulf Coast of the United States. These systems have the potential to produce large quantities of electricity for three reasons. First, they contain hot-water thermal energy that could be extracted. Second, mechanical energy from the high-pressure water could be used to turn hydraulic turbines to produce electricity. Third, the waters contain considerable amounts of dissolved methane gas (up to 1 m^3 per barrel of water) that could be extracted and used to generate electricity [18, 19].

Use of Geothermal Energy

Although the potentially adverse environmental impact of intensive geothermal energy development is perhaps not as extensive as that of other sources of energy, it is nevertheless considerable. Geothermal energy is developed at a particular site, and environmental problems include on-site noise, emissions of gas, and industrial scars. Fortunately, development of geothermal energy does not require the extensive transportation of raw materials or refining typical of the fossil fuels. Furthermore, geothermal energy does not produce the atmospheric particulate pollutants associated with burning fossil fuels, nor does it produce radioactive waste. However, geothermal development, except for the vapor-dominated systems, does produce considerable thermal pollution from hot waste waters, which may be saline or highly corrosive. These waters can be disposed of by reinjecting them into the geothermal reservoir, but injection of fluids may activate fracture systems in the rocks and cause earthquakes. In addition, the original withdrawal of fluids may compact the reservoir, causing surface subsidence. It is also feared that subsidence might occur when the heat in the system is extracted and the cooling rocks contract [18].

At present, geothermal energy supplies only a small fraction of 1% of electrical energy produced in the United States. With the exception of unusual vapor-dominated systems such as The Geysers in California, the production of electricity from geothermal reservoirs is still rather expensive, gener-

ally more so than from other sources of energy. For this reason, commercial development of geothermal energy will not take place rapidly until the economic picture improves. Even if commercially available, geothermal sources would supply only 10% of the total electrical energy output in the near future, even in states like California, where it has been produced and where expanding facilities are likely [19].

RENEWABLE ENERGY SOURCES

The renewable energy sources—direct solar, water, wind, and biomass—are often discussed as a group because they are all functions of the sun's energy. That is, solar energy, broadly defined, comprises all the renewable energy sources, as shown in Figure 14.12. They are renewable precisely because they can be regenerated (renewed) by the sun within a time useful to humans.

These sources have the advantage of being inexhaustible and are generally associated with minimal environmental degradation. With the exception of burning biomass or its derivative, urban waste, solar energy sources do not pose a threat of increasing atmospheric carbon dioxide and thus modifying the climate. One major disadvantage is that many forms of solar energy are intermittent and spatially variable. Furthermore, some of these sources (solar cells, in particular) are currently much more expensive than fossil fuel or nuclear energy.

Another important aspect of renewable sources is the lead time necessary to implement the technology. The construction lead time is often quite short relative to development of new sources or construction of power plants to utilize fossil or nuclear fuels.

Direct Solar Energy

The total amount of solar energy reaching Earth's surface is tremendous. For example, on a global scale, two weeks of solar energy is roughly equivalent to the energy stored in all known reserves of coal, oil, and natural gas on Earth. In the United States, on the average, 13% of the sun's original

FIGURE 14.12
Routes of the various types
of renewable solar energy.

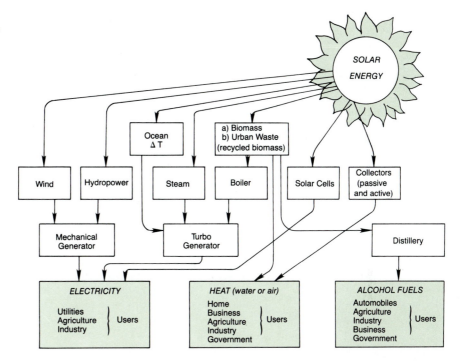

energy entering the atmosphere arrives at the ground. However, the actual amount at a particular site is quite variable, depending upon the time of the year and the cloud cover. The average value of 13% is equivalent to approximately 177 watts/m^2 on a continuous basis [20].

Direct use of solar energy may be through either passive solar systems or active solar systems. **Passive solar energy systems** often involve architectural design to enhance and take advantage, without requiring mechanical power, of natural changes in solar energy that occur throughout the year. Many homes and other buildings in the southwestern United States as well as other parts of the country now use passive solar systems for at least part of their energy needs. **Active solar energy systems** require mechanical power, usually pumps and other apparatus, to circulate air, water, or other fluids from solar collectors to a heat sink, where the heat is stored until used.

Solar Collectors Solar collectors are usually flat panels consisting of a glass cover plate over a

black background upon which water is circulated through tubes. Short-wave solar radiation enters the glass and is absorbed by the black background. As longer-wave radiation is emitted from the black material, it cannot escape through the glass, so it heats the water in the circulating tubes to 38°–93°C (100–200°F) [20]. Thus, solar collectors act as greenhouses. The number of systems using these collectors in the United States exceeds 100,000 and is rapidly growing.

Figure 14.13 shows a schematic of a flat plate collector, in which the heating fluid is water, and the basic plumbing to run a solar water heater. Recent tax advantages in the United States have made systems such as this attractive to many people who live in areas with consistent sunshine. Without such incentives there is little doubt that the interest in solar energy would be much lower. This results because present systems are still quite expensive relative to the amount of hot water they produce. In other words, more traditional methods of heating water are still preferred by most of the general public.

Career Profile: Phil Bell

I have seen the results of what solar energy can do for people—it helps people," says Phil Bell. He is General Manager of the Oklahoma City Division of Sunbelt Energy Corporation, a national company headquartered in Denver. Sunbelt Energy Corporation builds, sells, and services silicon closed-loop systems, an active method of solar space and water heating.

Bell sold sewing machines, life insurance, and cemetery plots before becoming a salesman for Solar Unlimited, Inc. That company later became consolidated with Sunbelt Energy Corporation. Bell was sales manager, then national sales manager and marketing director before assuming his present position. The Oklahoma City Division, which serves the western two-thirds of Oklahoma, is the largest division in the company. Bell oversees all functions of the division, which employs about 60 people, including salespeople, engineers, managers, and office help. In addition, he is a member of the Board of Directors of the Oklahoma Solar Energy Industries Association. The trade association develops a code of ethics for solar development in the state, suggests legislation, and lobbies for it.

Bell is personally as well as professionally committed to solar energy. He has a Sunbelt solar energy system in his home and matter-of-factly states that he would not have anything else. According to Bell, the Sunbelt energy systems are known as the "Mercedes of the industry."

The company does new installations as well as retrofitting in commercial and residential settings. Preliminary site evaluation is done by salespeople to assess building measurements, energy use, and what Bell terms the "solar window." For example, in some locations trees or tall buildings may obstruct the sun and limit the usefulness of solar energy. When a sale is made, engineers do pre-installation surveys to make sure the company can do the job as the salesperson described it.

"We sell about one out of every three people we visit with," Bell says. A major advantage of solar energy is saving money. Whether people understand the energy tax credits is a key factor in sales.

Oklahoma is usually considered oil country, but Bell thinks that may be an advantage for his salespeople. "People who understand what's going to happen in the oil and gas situation know they better find some energy alternatives. They know prices are going up. The question is how fast and how much," Bell says.

He acknowledges other energy alternatives, but explains that passive solar, while advantageous for new construction, is difficult in terms of retrofitting. Some areas do not have sufficient winds to make wind energy viable. Traditional sources are much less expensive than photovoltaics for electricity generation, he continues. Bell feels active solar is the most cost-effective and viable energy alternative.

Bell predicts that every home in the next 10 years will need some alternative energy device. "I think the future of the solar energy industry is very, very bright," he says. "The biggest part of the market is in front of us."

Michele Wigginton

FIGURE 14.13
Detail of a flat plate solar collector and pumped solar water heater. (After Farallones Institute.)

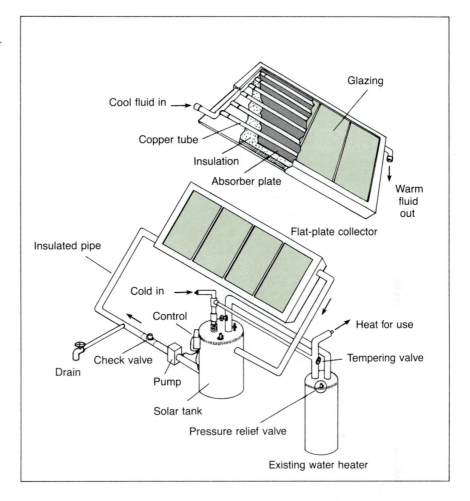

Cool fluid in

Copper tube

Insulation

Absorber plate

Glazing

Warm fluid out

Flat-plate collector

Insulated pipe

Cold in

Control

Heat for use

Tempering valve

Check valve

Drain

Pump

Solar tank

Pressure relief valve

Existing water heater

Solar Cells Another potentially important aspect of direct solar energy involves **solar cells,** or photovoltaics, that convert sunlight directly into electricity. Although such cells might be used in unique situations, electricity produced from them generally costs about 20 times as much as that produced from traditional fossil fuel sources [21]. On the other hand, because the field of solar technology is changing so quickly, low-cost solar cells may become widely available (Fig. 14.14).

Power Towers An interesting type of solar system is the **solar power tower,** shown in Figure 14.15. The system works by collecting solar energy as heat and delivering this energy in the form of steam to turbines that produce electric power. An experimental 10–MW power tower near Barstow, California, is approximately 100 m high and is surrounded by approximately 2000 mirror modules, each with a reflective area of about 40 m^2. The mirrors will adjust continually to reflect as much sunlight into the tower as possible. When excess steam is available, it is stored so that it can be extracted during periods when no sun is available. The Japanese are currently trying to produce 1 MW of electricity from a tower approximately 75 m high. If the Japanese experiment proves successful, they hope to eventually build a 60–MW plant. Al-

FIGURE 14.14

(a) Photovoltaic cells made of silicon (and other materials). When sunlight strikes the silicon atoms it causes electrons to be ejected. Electrons can flow out of the photovoltaic cells through electrical wires where they can do useful work. Electron vacancies are filled as electrons complete circuit. (b) The largest roof-mounted photovoltaic system in the world, consisting of more than 4400 PV modules. Located on the Intercultural Center, Georgetown University, Washington, D.C., the system provides electricity for the university's operation. (a) from Daniel D. Chiras, *Environmental Science: A Framework for Decision Making*, Figure 15–6. © 1985 by the Benjamin/ Cummings Publishing Company, Inc. Used by permission.

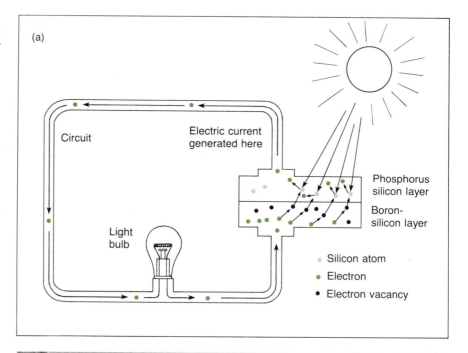

(a)

Circuit

Electric current generated here

Phosphorus silicon layer

Boron-silicon layer

Light bulb

- Silicon atom
- Electron
- Electron vacancy

(b)

though there is certainly room for optimism concerning power towers, the electricity generated is going to be very expensive during the first few years when the technology is being developed. In fact, it is probably safe to state that power towers may prove not to be economically viable in all sites presently being considered. Nevertheless, the research to develop the technology is certainly worthwhile and should continue. A new generation of power towers is also being talked about

FIGURE 14.15
Solar power tower being tested near Barstow, California, in the Mojave Desert. This power plant is expected to produce as much as 10 MW of electricity and is a cooperative effort between the U.S. Department of Energy and the Southern California Edison Company. (Modified after a drawing prepared by Southern California Edison Company.)

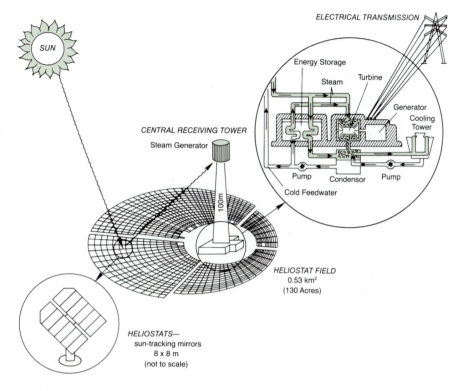

that might involve solar cells that will directly turn sunlight to electricity without the intermediate step of making steam.

Solar Ponds   The use of shallow **solar ponds** to generate relatively low-temperature water of about 68°C (180°F) is an interesting prospect for sources of commercial, industrial, and agricultural heat. Presently two types of ponds are being developed. One type is relatively deep (3 m) and is approximately 20 m long by 10 m wide. The pond is designed to collect heat during the summer, building up to a bottom water temperature of about 68°C in the fall. During the winter, heat may then be extracted from the bottom. The heated water is kept on the bottom by the addition of salt, which makes the bottom water heavier. Circulation is restricted so that the dense bottom water remains on the bottom and does not mix with the water above. Reportedly, the pond works very well, even in areas with a relatively severe winter. For example, up to 25 cm of ice and snow may accumulate on the surface of the pond and the bottom water will still be approximately 38°C (100°F) throughout the winter [21].

The second type of solar pond resembles a large waterbed approximately 3.5 m wide by 60 m long and 5 to 10 cm deep. The top of the "bed" is transparent to solar energy, while the bottom is an energy-absorbing black material. The pond is insulated from below to prevent heat loss to soil and rock. These ponds are essentially very large solar collectors, much like the smaller panels used for heating water in homes. To date, several ponds have been tested and the results are optimistic, especially because the cost is presently competitive with that of burning fossil fuel oil for heat. This type of solar pond would work well in relatively small-scale industrial and agricultural applications [21].

Ocean Thermal Conversion   A last example of direct utilization of solar energy involves using part of the natural oceanic environment as a gigantic solar collector. The surface temperature of ocean water in the tropics is often about 28°C (82°F). However, at the bottom of the ocean, at a depth as shallow as about 600 m, the temperature of the water may be 1°–3°C (35–38°F). Low-efficiency heat engines can be designed to exploit this temperature differential either by directly using the sea water or by employing an appropriate heat exchange system in a closed cycle in which a fluid such as ammonia or propane is vaporized by the warm water. The expanding vapor is then used to propel a turbine and generate electricity. Following generation of electricity, the vapor is cooled and condensed by the cold water. The construction of large-scale ocean thermal plants will depend upon whether they can be built close to potential markets and whether the plants are economically feasible [20]. Because answers to these questions are very uncertain, the future of ocean thermal plants is very speculative at present.

Use of Direct Solar Energy Solar energy has a relatively low impact on the environment. Its major disadvantage is that solar energy is rela-

tively dispersed and a large land area is required to generate a large amount of energy. This problem is negligible when solar collectors can be combined with existing structures, as with the addition of solar hot-water heaters on the roofs of existing houses. Highly centralized and high-technology solar energy units, such as solar power towers, have a greater impact on the land. By locating these centralized systems in areas not used for other purposes and making use of dispersed solar energy collectors on existing structures wherever possible, this impact can be minimized.

The increased development of active solar energy technology may result in the widespread use of exotic materials which may themselves present environmental problems. Passive solar collectors, which use common materials like water and rock, pose negligible pollution problems.

Figure 14.16 shows in a very general way the estimated year-round availability of solar energy in the United States. However, this view of solar energy is analogous to painting a picture with a paint roller. Solar energy is site-specific, and detailed observation in the field is necessary to evaluate the

FIGURE 14.16
Estimated year-round availability of solar energy for the conterminous United States. (Modified after National Wildlife Federation.)

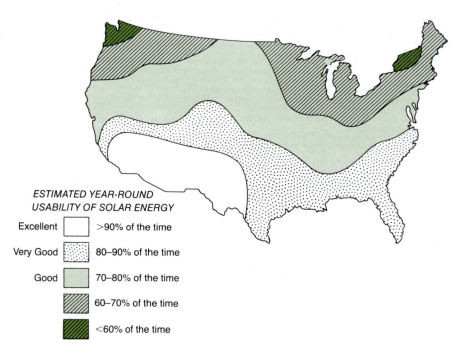

ESTIMATED YEAR-ROUND
USABILITY OF SOLAR ENERGY

Excellent   >90% of the time

Very Good   80–90% of the time

Good   70–80% of the time

   60–70% of the time

   <60% of the time

solar energy potential in a given area. The energy that might be saved by converting to direct solar power is also quite variable. Optimistic people hope that by the year 2000 direct solar energy may supply up to 20% of the total energy demand. Considering how fast the solar energy industry is growing and the short lead time necessary for conversion to some solar energy technology, these hopes may be realistic. On the other hand, the conversions may be much slower if other sources of energy at cheaper prices become available in the next few years. The future of solar energy seems quite secure.

Water Power

Water power, which is really a form of stored solar energy, has been used successfully since at least the time of the Roman Empire. Water wheels that harness water power and convert it to mechanical energy were turning in western Europe in the seventeenth century, and during the eighteenth and nineteenth centuries large water wheels provided energy to power grain mills, sawmills, and other machinery in the United States. Today, hydroelectric power plants provide about 15% of the total electricity produced in the United States.

Small-scale Systems Although the total amount of electrical power produced by running water from large dams will increase somewhat in the coming years in the United States, it is recognized that most of the acceptable good sites are probably already being utilized. On the other hand, small-scale hydropower systems may be much more common in the future (Fig. 14.17a). These are systems designed for individual homes, farms, or small industries. They will typically have power outputs of less than 100 kw and are termed micro-hydropower systems [22]. Micro-hydropower is one of the world's oldest and most common energy sources. Numerous sites in many areas have potential for producing small-scale electrical power. This is particularly true in mountainous areas, where potential energy from stream water is most available. Micro-hydropower development is by its nature very site-specific, depending upon local regulations, economic situation, and hydro-

logic limitations. Of particular importance is the fact that hydropower can be used to generate either electrical power or mechanical power to run machinery. Such plants may help cut the high cost of importing energy and help small operations become more independent of local utility providers [22].

An interesting aspect of hydropower is "pump storage" (Fig. 14.17b and c), the objective of which is to make better use of total electrical energy produced through energy management. The basic idea is that, during times when demand for power is low, electricity from oil, coal, or nuclear plants may be used to pump water up to a storage site or reservoir (high pool). Then, during times when demand for electricity is high, the stored water flows back down to the low pool through generators to supplement the power supply. It is important to keep in mind that pump storage systems are not as efficient as conventional hydroelectric plants. The bottom line is that about three units of energy from an oil, gas, or nuclear power plant are needed to produce two delivered units of energy from a pump storage facility. The advantage lies in the timing of energy production and use: the two units can be drawn during peak demand and the three units are used to pump the water to the high pool when the demand is low.

Tidal Power Another form of water power may be derived from ocean tides in a few places with favorable topography, such as the Bay of Fundy region of the northeastern United States and Canada. The tides in the Bay of Fundy have a maximum rise of about 15 m. A minimum rise of about 8 m is necessary to even consider developing tidal power. To harness tidal power, dams are built across the entrance to a bay, creating a basin on the landward side such that a difference in water level exists between the ocean and the basin. Then, as the water fills or empties the basin, it can be used to run hydraulic turbines, which will produce electricity [23].

Use of Water Power Water power is clean power; it requires no burning of fuel, does not pollute the atmosphere, produces no radioactive or other waste, and is efficient. However, there is an

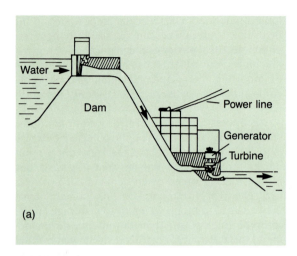

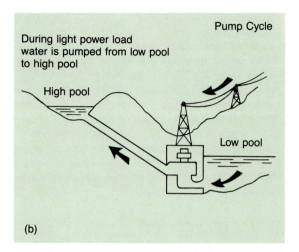

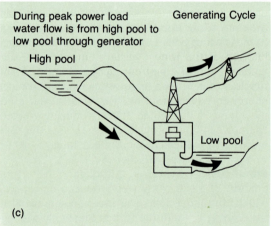

FIGURE 14.17
(a) Basic components of a hydroelectric power station.
(b,c) How a pump storage system works. (Modified from
Council on Environmental Quality, 1975.)

environmental price to pay. Water falling over high dams may pick up nitrogen gas, which enters the blood of fish, expands, and kills them. Nitrogen has killed many migrating game fish in the Pacific Northwest. Furthermore, dams trap sediment that would otherwise reach the sea and replenish the sand on beaches. In addition, for a variety of reasons, many people do not want to turn all of the wild rivers into a series of lakes. For these reasons, and because many good sites for dams are already utilized, the growth of large-scale water power in the future appears limited. On the other hand, there seems to be an increase in interest for micro-hydropower to supply electricity or mechanical energy. Environmental impact of numerous micro-hydropower installations may be considerable in an area. The sites will change the natural stream flow, affecting the stream biota and productivity. Small dams and reservoirs also tend to fill more quickly with sediment, making their potential useful time period much shorter. Because micro-hydropower development can adversely affect stream environment, careful consideration must be given to its development over a wide region. A few such sites may cause little environmental degradation, but if the number becomes excessive, the impact over a wider region may be appreciable. This is a consideration that must be given to many forms of technology that involve small sites. The impact of one single site may be nearly negligible in a broad region, but as the number of sites increases, the total impact may become very significant.

Wind Power

Wind power, like solar power, has evolved over a long period of time, from early Chinese and Persian civilizations to the present. Wind has propelled ships as well as driven windmills used to grind grain or pump water. More recently, wind has been used to generate electricity. Winds are produced when differential heating of Earth's surface creates air masses with differing heat contents and densities. The potential energy that might be eventually derived from the wind is tremendous, and yet there will be problems because winds tend to be highly variable in time, place, and intensity [24].

Wind prospecting will become an important endeavor in the future (see Plate 2c). On a national scale, regions with the greatest potential for development of wind energy are the Pacific Northwest coastal area, the coastal region of the northeastern United States, and a belt extending from northern Texas northward through the Rocky Mountain states and the Dakotas. However, there are many other good sites, such as the mountain areas in North Carolina and the northern Coachella Valley in southern California.

At a particular site the direction, velocity, and duration of the wind may be quite variable, depending on local topography and regional to local magnitude of temperature differences in the atmosphere [24]. For example, wind velocity often increases over hilltops or mountains, or wind may be funneled through a broad mountain pass (Fig. 14.18). The increase in wind velocity over a mountain is due to a vertical convergence of the wind, whereas in a pass the increase is partly due to a horizontal convergence as well. Because the shape of a mountain or a pass is often related to the local or regional geology, prospecting for wind energy is a geologic as well as a geographic and meteorological problem.

Significant improvements in the size of windmills and the amount of power they produce occurred from the late 1800s through approximately 1950, when many European countries and the United States became interested in large-scale generators driven by the wind. In the United States, thousands of small wind-driven generators have been used on farms. Most of the small windmills generated approximately 1 kw of power, which is much too small to be considered for central power generation needs. Interest in wind power declined for several decades prior to the 1970s because of the abundance of cheap fossil fuels, but now there is revived interest in building windmills.

FIGURE 14.18
Some of the ways that the geologic environment may converge wind in the vertical or horizontal direction, thus increasing the speed of the wind.

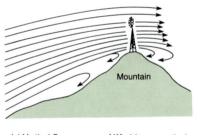

(a) Vertical Convergence of Wind (cross section)

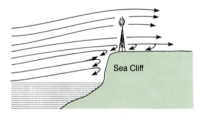

(b) Small Vertical Convergence of Wind with Severe Turbulence (cross section)

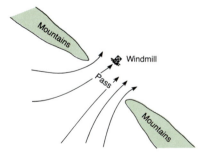

(c) Horizontal Convergence of Wind (plan view)

Small-scale Producers Small-scale power production from windmills in the United States was made more feasible by passage of the U.S. Public Utility Regulatory Policy Act (PURPA) in 1978. This act requires utilities to interconnect with small-scale independent producers of power and pay fair market price for the electricity produced. PURPA initiated an entrepreneurism by providing a market to small-scale power producers. This is nowhere better exemplified than in California, where in the last several years approximately nine thousand windmills, with a generating capacity exceeding 700 MW have been installed. Individual windmills produce from 60 to 75 kw of power and are arranged in wind farms consisting of clusters of windmills located in mountain passes. Electricity produced at these sites is connected to the general utility lines. In 1984 alone these wind farms produced sufficient electricity to supply approximately 70,000 homes, making a significant contribution in the modern utility grid. Tax incentives have helped the wind-power industry become established, and in California it is expected that wind power may be the state's second least expensive source of power by the year 1990, second only to hydropower.

Use of Wind Power The use of wind power will not solve all of our energy problems, but as one more alternative energy source it can be used in particular sites to reduce our dependency on fossil fuel. Wind energy does have a few disadvantages. First, demonstration projects have suggested that vibrations from windmills may produce objectionable noise. Second, windmills may interfere with radio and television broadcasts. Finally, many windmills may degrade an area's scenic resources. Still, everything considered, wind energy has a relatively low environmental impact, and its continued use should be carefully researched and evaluated. In fact, a number of large demonstration units are now being tested.

Energy from Biomass

Biomass fuel is a new name for the oldest human fuel. Biomass is organic matter that can be burned directly as a fuel or converted to a more convenient form and then burned. For example, we can burn wood in a stove or convert it to charcoal and then burn it. Biomass has provided a major source of energy for human beings throughout most of the history of civilization. When North America was first settled, there was more wood fuel than could be used. The forests often were cleared for agriculture by girdling trees (cutting through the bark all the way around the base of a tree) to kill them and then burning the forests.

Until the end of the nineteenth century, wood was the major fuel source in the United States. During the early mid-twentieth century, when coal, oil, and gas were plentiful and high-grade mines in the United States provided abundant cheap energy, burning wood became old-fashioned and quaint; it was something done for pleasure in an open fireplace that conducted more heat up the chimney than it provided for space heating. Now, with other fuels reaching a limit in abundance and production, there is renewed interest in the use of natural organic materials for fuel.

Firewood is the best known and most widely used biomass fuel, but there are many others. In India and other countries, cattle dung is burned for cooking. Peat provides heating and cooking fuel in northern countries like Scotland, where peat is abundant.

On a global scale, over 1 billion people in the world today still use wood as their primary source of energy for heat and cooking. Energy from biomass may take several routes: direct burning of biomass to produce either electricity or heat water and air, and distillation of biomass to produce alcohol for a fuel. Today in the United States, various biomass sources supply nearly 2% of the entire energy consumption (approximately 1.5 exajoules per year), primarily from the use of wood for home heating [25].

Sources of Biomass Fuel There are two primary sources of biomass fuels in North America: forest products and otherwise unused agricultural products. It has been estimated that by the year 2000 energy from biological processes could supply up to 15–20% of the current energy consumption in the United States. However, this estimate is dependent upon a number of factors, including availability of cropland, increased yields, good resource management, and, most importantly, the development of efficient conversion processes. Most of the increase is expected to result from burning a greater amount of wood. Figure 14.19a summarizes energy use in the United States in 1979, and Figure 14.19b shows two possible scenarios for potential bioenergy supplies.

Biomass may also be recycled. Today there are 20 facilities in the United States that process urban

waste to be used to generate electricity or to be used as a fuel. Presently, only about 1% of the nation's municipal solid wastes are being recovered for energy. However, if all the plants were operating at full capacity and if the additional 20 plants or so under construction were completed and operating, then about 10% of the country's waste, or 18 million tons per year, could be used to extract energy. At processing plants such as those in Bal-

FIGURE 14.19
(a) Energy use in the United States for 1979. (b) Two scenarios of potential bioenergy supplies, excluding speculative sources and municipal waste. (From Office of Technology Assessment.)

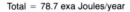

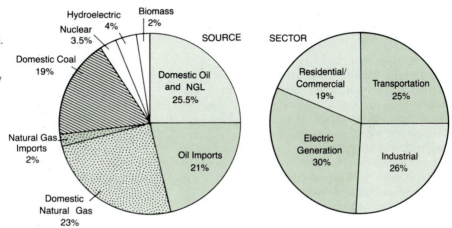

(a) *U.S. ENERGY USE IN 1979*

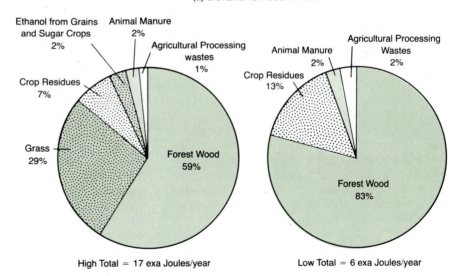

(b) *POTENTIAL BIOENERGY SUPPLIES*

timore County, Maryland; Chicago, Illinois; Milwaukee, Wisconsin; Tacoma, Washington; and Akron, Ohio, municipal waste is burned and the heat energy used to make steam for a variety of purposes, from space heating to industrial generation of electricity. The United States has been slower to utilize urban waste as an energy source than have other countries. For example, in western Europe a number of countries now utilize from one-third to one-half of their municipal waste for energy production. With the end of cheap, available fossil fuels, certainly more and more energy recovery systems utilizing urban waste will be forthcoming [26].

Net Energy Yield   A problem with biomass fuels is their net yield of energy. Because the density of vegetation production is comparatively low, and the density of unused forest and agricultural residues even lower, considerable energy is required to collect the biomass for fuel. Processing the biomass into more convenient fuels also requires energy. Biomass fuels provide the greatest net gain in energy when they are used locally. For example, in the production of sugar from sugar cane, unused parts of the cane can be burned to provide energy for local processing. When fuels are consumed far from their source, and if much conversion is required, there may be no net gain in energy. For example, converting corn stalks to alcohol and then transporting alcohol long distances to be used as a fuel for cars and trucks may produce little or no net gain in energy.

Use of Biomass   The use of biomass fuels can pollute the air and degrade the land. For most of us, the odor of smoke fumes from a single campfire is part of a pleasant outdoor experience, but wood smoke from many chimneys in narrow valleys under certain weather conditions can lead to unpleasant and dangerous air pollution. In recent years, the renewed use of wood stoves in homes has led to reports of such air pollution in Vermont.

The use of biomass as fuels places another pressure on already heavily used resources. The world shortage of firewood is adversely affecting natural areas and endangered species. For example, the need for firewood caused problems in the Gir Forest in India, the last home of the Indian lion. The forest contains other rare species of large mammals who feed on the woody vegetation and were, in the past, food for the lion. Although the forest is set aside as a preserve, the nearby residents are taking badly needed firewood (as well as vegetation for cattle) and slowly destroying the forest trees. If our need for forest products and forest biomass fuel exceeds the productivity of our forests, they will also decrease. Any use of biomass fuel must be part of the general planning for all uses of the land's products.

Biomass in its various forms appears to have a bright future as an energy source. The only questions are the amount of energy it will provide and how quickly the energy will be available. As the price of fossil fuels—particularly oil and gas—rises, these renewable energy sources certainly will become more attractive. Because the transition from fossil fuels to renewable energy sources is now just underway, it is difficult to predict how long and how complete the transition will be.

ENERGY FOR TOMORROW

We established earlier in this chapter that we will have to get used to living with a good deal of uncertainty concerning the availability, cost, and environmental effects of energy use. Furthermore, we can expect that serious shocks will continue to occur, disrupting the flow of energy to various parts of the world.

Supply and demand for energy are difficult to predict because technical, economic, political, and social assumptions underlying projections are constantly changing. Large annual variations in energy consumption must also be considered. Figure 14.20 shows that energy consumption peaks during the winter months, with a secondary peak in the summer. Future changes in population or intensive conservation measures may change this pattern, as might better design of buildings and more reliance on solar energy. One recent prediction holds that energy consumption in the United States in the year 2010 may be as high as 137 exajoules or as low as 63 exajoules; such a wide disparity suggests the great potential for conservation

FIGURE 14.20
Energy consumption by month for the United States. (Data from U.S. Department of Energy.)

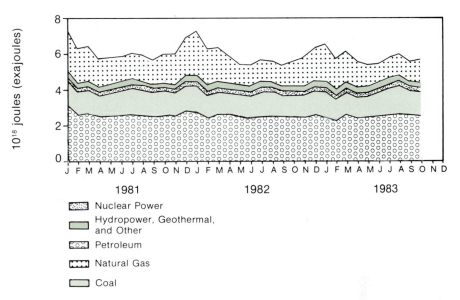

in the emerging energy scenario. (Energy consumption in 1979 was about 78 exajoules.) The high value assumes no change in energy policies, whereas the low value assumes very aggressive energy conservation policies. Figure 14.21 shows the recent energy flow in the United States.

There has been a strong movement to change patterns of energy consumption through measures such as conservation, increased efficiency, and cogeneration. Conservation of energy refers to a moderation of energy use or simply getting by with less demand for energy. In a pragmatic sense this

has to do, then, with adjusting our energy needs and uses to minimize the expenditure of energy necessary to accomplish a given task. Efficiency is related to designing equipment to yield more power from a given amount of energy [2]. Finally, cogeneration refers to a number of processes, the objective of which is to capture waste heat rather than simply release it into the atmosphere or water as thermal pollution.

The three concepts of energy conservation, increased efficiency, and cogeneration are very much interrelated. For example, when electricity is pro-

FIGURE 14.21
Highly generalized flow of energy in the United States. (Modified after Fowler.)

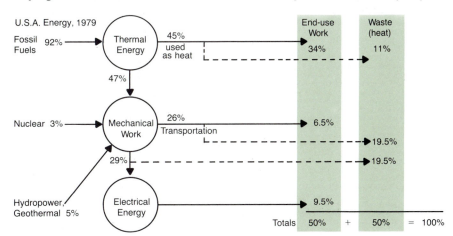

duced at large coal-burning power stations, large amounts of heat may be emitted into the atmosphere. Production of electricity typically burns three units of fuel to produce one unit of electricity. Cogeneration, which involves recycling of that waste heat, can increase the efficiency of a typical power plant from 33% to as high as 75%. Effectively, this reduces losses from 67% to 20% [2]. Cogeneration of electricity also involves the production of electricity as a byproduct from industrial processes that normally produce and use steam as part of their regular operations. Optimistic energy forecasters estimate that we may eventually be able to meet approximately one-half of the electrical power needs of industry through cogeneration [27]. From another source, it has been estimated that, by the year 2000, over 10% of the power capacity of the United States could be provided through cogeneration. Fuel savings through this would amount to as much as two million barrels of oil per day! Such a savings is really talking about conservation as well, showing how these two concepts are interrelated.

Efficiency and Conservation

A simple definition of efficiency is the ratio of the output of work to the input of energy. This definition is sometimes called the first-law efficiency, because it refers only to the amount of energy and does not consider the quality of availability of energy. Another measure is the second-law efficiency, defined as the ratio of the minimum quantity of available work needed to perform a particular task to the actual quantity of available work used to perform that task. Table 14.5 lists some of the first- and second-law efficiencies for selected energy forms and processes. Of particular importance are the low second-law efficiencies because they indicate where potential improvements in energy planning (such as matching supplies to end uses) can be expected.

The first-law efficiency can be expressed also as a thermal efficiency. When working with thermal efficiency, scientists use the Kelvin temperature scale. Absolute zero is 0°K; at atmospheric conditions, water freezes at 273°K and boils at 373°K. It is easy to convert °C to °K by adding 273: °K = °C + 273. Then, the formula for efficiency can be derived:

$$\text{Efficiency} = 1 - \frac{\text{Temperature in °K cold (out)}}{\text{Temperature in °K hot (in)}} \times 100$$

For example, if steam enters a power plant at 800°K (527°C) and exhausts at about 373°K (100°C), then the theoretical upper limit of the ef-

TABLE 14.5
Selected examples of first- and second-law efficiencies.

First-Law Efficiency:

Energy Form	First-Law Efficiency (%)	Waste Heat (%)
Incandescent light bulb	5	95
Fluorescent light	20	80
Automobile	20–25	75–80
Power plants (electric): fossil fuel and nuclear	30–40	60–70
Burning fossil fuels (used directly for heat)	65	35
All energy (USA)	50	50

Second-Law Efficiency:

Energy Form	Second-Law Efficiency (%)	Potential for Savings
Automobile	10	Moderate
Water heating	2	Very high
Space heating and cooling	6	Very high
Power plants (electric)	30	Low to moderate
All energy (USA)	10–15	High

ficiency is about 53%, with an actual efficiency of about 40%. Nuclear reactors operating at an ingoing temperature of approximately 620°K (347°C) and an exhaust of about 373°K (100°C) have a theoretical efficiency of about 40%, with an actual operating efficiency of about 30%. For one final example, an automobile with a combustion temperature of about 3255°K (2982°C) and an output of about 1433°K (1160°C) provides an upper limit efficiency of about 56%, with an actual efficiency of about 25% [28].

The average first-law efficiency of 50% (Table 14.5) emphasizes the "thermal bottleneck." As chemical energy is converted to thermal and mechanical uses, large amounts of energy are lost in producing electricity and in transporting people and goods. New innovations in energy production are likely to unplug part of the "thermal bottleneck." Of particular importance will be energy uses with applications below 100°C because a large portion of the total U.S. energy consumption (for uses below 300°C) is for space heating and water heating (Fig. 14.22).

If we consider where our effort should go for developing more energy-efficient machinery, then we need to look at the total energy-use picture. In the United States, space heating of homes and offices, water heating, industrial processes (to produce steam) and automobiles account for nearly 60% of the total energy use. By comparison, air conditioners and transport by train, bus, and air account for only about 5%. Therefore, if we wish to target certain areas for developing more energy efficiency we need to look at building design, industrial energy use, and automobile design [2].

Building Design For residential buildings there is a spectrum of possible actions concerning energy efficiency and conservation. If we consider new homes, the answer may be something like the "integral urban house" [29], which involves efficient design and construction to minimize utilization of resources necessary to establish the goal of comfortable living. For example, buildings may be designed through better architecture to utilize building sites better, taking advantage of passive solar potential. The totally integral urban house therefore incorporates strong conservation principles for energy, water, and organic materials. Efficiency in planning and self-sufficiency are rated high with this concept. The basic idea of the house is that the entire living area is connected in a unified, holistic way to provide the occupants with a comfortable living system that minimizes utilization of resources, maximizes the utility of the site, and is as efficient as possible [29]. More aspects of the integral urban house are discussed and illustrated in Chapter 19.

Many of our residential buildings were constructed a number of years ago and for these homes the best way to approach conservation is through insulation, caulking, weatherstripping, installation of storm windows, and good maintenance. For these buildings and homes, architectural design for the site is extremely limited because the position of the building is already established. Furthermore, construction cost and modifications are often not cost effective.

A final thought concerning residential buildings is that with everything there is a price to pay. If we construct our buildings very tightly to conserve energy, then there may be a higher possibility for indoor air pollution problems to develop. Furthermore, construction of specific houses on a specific site may be difficult and fees to architects and engineers may be quite expensive. Initial costs may be higher for the features that we might desire in

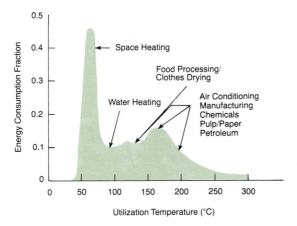

FIGURE 14.22
Spectra of energy use below 300°C in the United States. (From Los Alamos Scientific Laboratory.)

houses that approach the "integral urban house." Nevertheless, moving toward better design of homes and residential buildings to conserve energy is certainly a worthwhile endeavor.

Industrial Energy Use In looking at industrial use of energy in the 1980s it is apparent that the rate of energy utilization is approximately 25% below that of the early 1970s. In spite of this, industrial production is 77% higher! The reason that we have been able to have higher productivity with less energy use is that industries are more commonly using cogeneration and developing more efficient machinery [2, 12].

Automobile Design As a final consideration in our argument concerning conservation and efficiency, consider the automobile. There have been steady improvements in the development of fuel-efficient automobiles during the last fifteen years. In the early 1970s the average American automobile burned approximately one gallon of gas for each fourteen miles traveled. By 1985, the average miles per gallon (mpg) had risen to 27 and it is projected it may reach as high as 45 mpg by the year 2000. The trend that accounts for this better efficiency and resulting conservation of fuel has been the turn to smaller cars with smaller engines and constructed of lighter materials [2].

Furthermore, the engines are designed to be more efficient. Of course, there is a cost to pay for this. The smaller cars are more prone to break on impact, and, at the same time that cars have gotten smaller, large trucks have tended to stay the same size or get even larger! As a result, the number of accidents between cars and trucks seems to be rising and the cars seldom get the lesser impact.

ENERGY POLICY

Hard Path versus Soft Path

Energy policy today is at or near a crossroads. One road leads to development of so-called hard technologies, which involve finding ever greater amounts of fossil fuels and building larger power plants. Following the "hard path" means continu-

ing as we have been for a number of years. In this respect, the hard path is more comfortable. That is, it requires no new thinking or realignment of political, economic, or social conditions. It also involves little anticipation of the inevitable depletion of the fossil fuel resources on which the hard path is built.

Those in favor of the hard path argue that, with the exception of the major oil-producing nations, environmental degradation has resulted because people in less developed countries have had to utilize so much of their local resources, such as wood, for energy rather than, say, for land conservation and erosion control. It is argued that the way to solve the environmental problems in less developed countries is to provide them with cheap energy that utilizes more heavy industrialization and technology, not less. Proponents of this argument point out that the United States and other countries with a sizeable energy resource in coal or petroleum should exploit that resource to make certain that the environmental degradation that is now plaguing other countries of the world will not strike here. In other words, the argument is to let the energy industry develop the available resources—that this freedom will ensure a steady supply of energy and less total environmental damage than if the government regulates the energy industry. Proponents of this view would argue that the present increase in the burning of firewood across the United States is an early indicator of the effects of strong governmental controls on energy supplies. Furthermore, they would argue that this is just the beginning and that the eventual depletion of forest resources will have an appreciably detrimental effect on the environment as it has done in so many less developed countries.

The other road is designated as the "soft path" [30]. One of the champions of this choice has been Amory Lovins, who states that the soft path involves energy alternatives that are renewable, flexible, and environmentally more benign than those of the hard path. As defined by Lovins, these alternatives have several characteristics:

1 They rely heavily on renewable energy resources such as solar, wind, and biomass.
2 They are diverse, tailored for maximum effectiveness under specific circumstances.

3 They are flexible; that is, they are relatively low technologies that are accessible and understandable to many people.

4 They are matched in both geographical distribution and scale to prominent end-use needs (the actual use of energy).

5 There is good agreement or matching between energy quality and end-use.

This last point is of particular importance because, as Lovins points out, people are not particularly interested in having a certain amount of oil, gas, or electricity delivered to their homes; rather, they are interested in having comfortable homes, adequate lighting, food on the table, and energy for transportation [30]. These latter uses are called end-uses, and only about 5% of the end-uses really require high-grade energy like electricity. Nevertheless, a lot of electricity is used to heat homes and water. For some purposes, continual use of electricity is very important; but for others, Lovins shows that there is an imbalance in using nuclear reactions at extremely high temperatures or in burning fossil fuels at high temperatures simply to meet needs where the temperature increase necessary may be only a few tens of degrees. Such large discrepancies are thought wasteful.

The bridge, or transition, from the hard to the soft path will presumably take place through the utilization of present energy sources such as coal and natural gas. Although there is sufficient coal to last hundreds of years, those in favor of the soft path would prefer to use this source as a transition rather than an ultimate long-term source.

Energy in the Future

Assuming that in the future we will be able to get by on a lower rate of energy consumption, it is interesting to speculate on low-energy scenarios. One, published by Lovins (Fig. 14.23), involves a moderate decrease in energy consumption following a maximum consumption of about 100 exajoules in the year 2000. The eventual reduction accompanies the shift from dependence on fossil fuels to the soft technologies (renewable energy resources).

Another recently published low-energy scenario

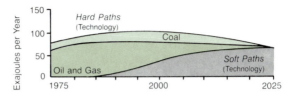

FIGURE 14.23
Low-energy scenario for the future as envisioned by A. B. Lovins. See text for further explanation. (Modified after Lovins.)

for the United States involves a 40% reduction by the year 2020 of total energy used. The authors of this scenario (Fig. 14.24) emphasize, as does Lovins, that such a reduction does not have to be associated with a lower quality of life, but rather with increased conservation of energy and a more energy-efficient distribution of urban populations, agriculture, and industry. These authors offer the following alternatives: new, more energy-efficient settlement patterns that maximize accessibility of services and minimize the need for transportation; new agricultural practices that emphasize locally grown and consumed food and that require less total energy than the energy required to support diets more dependent on beef and pork; and new industrial guidelines that promote energy conservation and minimize production of consumer waste [9]. To some extent these alternatives are already being practiced in some areas; that is, in some instances, highway construction has a lower priority than mass transit systems; agricultural lands near urban centers are preserved; and industry is more receptive to recycling and decreased production of consumer waste (such as unnecessary packaging). This low-energy scenario is different from that of the soft technology because it still relies heavily on fossil fuels, primarily coal. Both scenarios, however, do speculate that nuclear energy will not play an important part in the total energy picture by the year 2020. Both assumptions—the eventual demise of nuclear energy and the increase in coal production—are speculative, as is the notion that we really can obtain most of our energy needs from renewable energy sources in the next 50 years.

From an energy-planning viewpoint, the next 30 years will be crucial to the United States and the

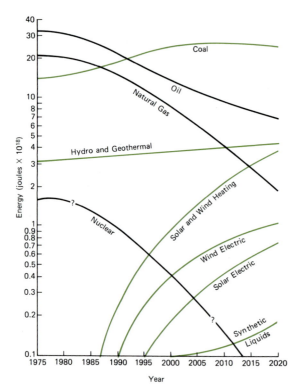

FIGURE 14.24
Energy supply for low-energy scenario of the United States. (Data from Steinhart et al.)

and other sources of energy. Quality of life is not necessarily directly related to greater consumption of energy.

The origin of fossil fuels (coal, oil, and gas) is intimately related to the geologic cycle. These fuels are essentially stored solar energy in the form of organic material that has escaped total destruction by oxidation. The environmental disruption associated with exploration and development of these resources must be weighed against the benefits gained from the energy. However, this development is not an either-or proposition, and good conservation practices combined with pollution control and reclamation can help minimize the environmental disruption associated with fossil fuels.

Because our fossil fuel resources are finite and expensive and may have unacceptable environmental consequences, we must explore a mixture of energy options, including coal, nuclear energy, and renewable energy resources. Of particular importance in the next few years will be the continued growth in use of direct solar energy as well as in recycling of urban waste to produce energy.

Nuclear fission will remain an important source of energy. However, the growth of fission reactors as energy sources in the United States will not be as rapid as projected because of concern for environmental hazards and increasing costs to construct large nuclear power plants. Nuclear fusion, a potential energy source for the future, may eventually supply a tremendous amount of energy from a readily available and nearly inexhaustible fuel supply.

Use of geothermal energy will become much more widespread in the western United States, where natural heat flow from Earth is relatively high. Although the electrical energy produced from this internal heat will probably never exceed 10% of the total electrical power generated, it nevertheless will be significant. However, geothermal energy also has an environmental price; withdrawal of fluids and heat may cause surface subsidence, and injection of hot waste water back into the ground may produce earthquakes.

Renewable sources of energy are dependent upon solar energy and may take a variety of forms: wind power, water power, passive and active solar

rest of the industrialized world. The energy decisions we make in the very near future will greatly affect both our standard of living and quality of life. Optimistically, we have the necessary information and technology to insure a bright, warm, lighted, and moving future—but time is short, and we need action now. We can either continue to take things as they come and live in the year 2000 with the results of our present inaction, or we can build for the future an energy picture that we can be proud of [27].

SUMMARY

The world's ever-increasing population and appetite for energy are staggering. However, industrialized nations must seriously question the need and desirability of an increased demand for electrical energy, and energy from biomass (including recycled biomass from urban waste). Each of these energy sources generally causes little environmental disruption. Because these sources will not be depleted, they are dependable for the long term.

Water power will undoubtedly continue to be an important source of electricity, but large-scale hydropower is not expected to grow much owing to lack of potential sites and environmental considerations.

Use of wind power, solar power, and small-scale hydropower as well as some of the biomass alternatives is somewhat speculative and growth of such use difficult to predict. Nevertheless, we can expect increases in the utilization of these energy sources provided that incentives for research, development, and sales are encouraged by both private and government sectors.

Energy for the future will continue to be trou-

bled by uncertainties. However, what appears to be certain is that we will continue to look more seriously at conservation, energy efficiency, and cogeneration. The most likely targets for energy efficiency and conservation as well as cogeneration are in the area of space heating for homes and offices, water heating, industrial processes that provide heat (mostly steam) for various manufacturing processes, and automobiles. These areas collectively account for approximately 60% of the total energy used in the United States today.

We may be at a crossroads today concerning energy policy. The choice is between the "hard path," characterized by centralized, high-technology energy sources and the "soft path," characterized by decentralized, flexible, renewable energy sources. Perhaps the best path will be a mixture of the old and the new, ensuring a rational, smooth shift from fossil fuels as they become scarce.

STUDY QUESTIONS

1 What evidence supports the notion that our present energy shortage is not the first in human history but may be unique in other ways?

2 Distinguish between *energy, work,* and *power.*

3 Explain the difference between nuclear fission and nuclear fusion. What are the similarities and differences in the potential environmental problems associated with each?

4 Compare and contrast the environmental problems associated with extracting oil and gas and those associated with geothermal energy.

5 Discuss the various solar energy options. Which is preferred? When and why?

6 Which has greater future potential for energy production, wind or water power? Which has more environmental problems?

7 What are some of the problems associated with energy from biomass?

8 What are some of the principal issues associated with reclamation of large coal strip mines?

9 Compare and contrast potential advantages and possible disadvantages of a major shift from "hard path" to "soft path" energy development.

10 Compare and contrast environmental problems associated with nuclear power with the more conventional sources such as oil, gas, and coal.

11 You have just purchased a wooded island in Puget Sound. Your house is uninsulated and built of raw timber. Although the island receives some wind, trees over 40 m tall block most of this wind. You have a diesel gen-

erator for electric power, and hot water is produced by an electric heater run by the diesel generator. Oil and gas can be brought in by ship. Discuss the steps you would take in the next five years to reduce your costs for energy with the least damage to the island.

12 It is the year 2500. Natural oil and gas are rare curiosities that people see in museums. Considering the technologies available to us today, what would seem to be the most sensible fuel for airplanes? How would this fuel be produced to minimize adverse environmental effects?

FURTHER READING

BERG, P., and TUKEL, G. 1980. *Renewable energy and bioregions.* San Francisco: Planet Drum Foundation.

COMMITTEE ON NUCLEAR AND ALTERNATIVE ENERGY SYSTEMS. 1980. *Energy and the fate of ecosystems.* Washington, D.C.: National Academy of Sciences.

DAVIS, W. K. 1974. *U.S. energy prospects: An engineering viewpoint.* Washington D.C.: National Academy of Engineering.

HARRIS, N. C., and THOMAS, I. E. 1985. *Solar energy systems design.* New York: Wiley.

HOYLE, F., and HOYLE, G. 1980. *Common sense in nuclear energy.* San Francisco: W. H. Freeman.

HUBBERT, M. K. 1971. The energy resources of the Earth. *Scientific American* 224: 60–70.

INGLIS, D. R. 1978. *Windpower and other energy options.* Ann Arbor: University of Michigan Press.

KRAUSHAAR, J. J., and RISTINEN, R. A. 1986. *Energy and problems of technical society.* New York: Wiley.

KREIDER, J. F.; KREITH, F.; and ENVIRONMENTAL CONSULTING SERVICES, INC. (Boulder, Colo.). 1975. *Solar heating and cooling: Engineering, practical design, and economics.* New York: McGraw-Hill.

LINDSAY, B. R. 1975. *Energy: Historical development of the concept.* Stroudsburg, Pa.: Dowden, Hutchinson, and Ross.

———. 1977. *The control of energy.* Benchmark Papers on Energy 6. Stroudsburg, Pa.: Dowden, Hutchinson, and Ross.

LOVINS, A. B. 1979. *Soft energy paths: Towards a durable peace.* New York: Harper & Row.

MOROWITZ, H. J. 1978. *Foundation of bioenergetics.* New York: Academic Press.

ROMER, R. H. 1976. *Energy, an introduction to physics.* San Francisco: W. H. Freeman.

RUEDISILI, L. C., and FIREBAUGH, M. W., eds. 1978. *Perspectives on energy.* 2nd ed. New York: Oxford University Press.

STOBOUGH, R., and YERGIN, D. 1979. *Energy future.* New York: Random House.

TELLER, E. 1979. *Energy from heaven and Earth.* San Francisco: W. H. Freeman.

15

Mineral Resources

- [ ] The standard of living in modern society is related to availability of natural resources.
- [ ] Waste products are a major environmental impact of mineral resource utilization.
- [ ] Mineral resources are classified as reserves when they become legally, technologically, and economically extractable.
- [ ] Limited mineral resources and reserves threaten humanity's affluence worldwide.
- [ ] Minerals are not uniformly distributed throughout Earth's crust. Processes responsible for the distribution patterns include plate tectonics, igneous processes, sedimentary processes, biological processes, and weathering processes.
- [ ] Environmental impacts of mineral exploitation depend on mining procedures, local hydrologic conditions, climate, rock types, size of operation, topography, and other interrelated factors.
- [ ] Social impacts of mineral exploitation may result from a rapid influx of workers into areas unprepared for growth.
- [ ] Before recycling can become a widespread practice, improved technologies and more economic incentives are needed.

PALO ALTO GOLDEN SLUDGE

It was recently discovered that ash from the incineration of sewage sludge in Palo Alto, California, contains large concentrations of gold (30 ppm), silver (660 ppm), copper (8000 ppm), and phosphorus (6.6%) Each metric ton of the ash contains approximately 1 troy ounce of gold and 20 ounces of silver. The gold is concentrated above natural abundance by a factor of 7500 times, making the "deposit" double the average grade that is mined today. Silver in the ash has a concentration similar to that of rich ore deposits in Idaho. Copper is concentrated in the ash by a factor of 145, similar to that of a common ore grade. The ash in the Palo Alto dump represents a silver and gold deposit with a 1980 value of about $10 million, and gold and silver worth approximately $2 million are being concentrated and delivered each year [1]. Commercial phosphorus deposits vary from 2% to 16%, so the ash is a phosphorus resource of great value.

The most likely source of the metals in the Palo Alto sewage is the large electronics industry as well as the photographic industry located in the area. Gold in significant amounts has been found in the sewage of only one other city, and silver is usually present in much smaller concentrations than at Palo Alto. Thus Palo Alto's unique urban ore offers an unusual opportunity to study and develop methods to recycle valuable materials concentrated in urban waste [1]. The city has now employed a private company to extract the gold and silver.

THE IMPORTANCE OF MINERALS TO SOCIETY

Modern society depends on the availability of mineral resources [2]. Consider the mineral products found in a typical American home (Table 15.1). Specifically, consider your breakfast this morning. You probably drank from a glass made primarily of sand, ate food from dishes made from clay, flavored your food with salt mined from the earth, ate fruit grown with the aid of fertilizers such as potassium carbonate (potash) and phosphorus, and

TABLE 15.1
Selected examples of mineral products in a typical American home.

Building materials: sand, gravel, stone, brick (clay), cement, steel, aluminum, asphalt, glass
Plumbing and wiring materials: iron and steel, copper, brass, lead, cement, asbestos, glass, tile, plastic
Insulating materials: rock wool, fiberglass, gypsum (plaster and wallboard)
Paint and wallpaper: mineral pigments (such as iron, zinc, and titanium) and fillers (such as talc and asbestos)
Plastic floor tiles, other plastics: mineral fillers and pigments, petroleum products
Appliances: iron, copper, and many rare metals
Furniture: synthetic fibers made from minerals (principally coal and petroleum products); steel springs; wood finished with rottenstone polish and mineral varnish
Clothing: natural fibers grown with mineral fertilizers; synthetic fibers made from minerals (principally coal and petroleum products)
Food: grown with mineral fertilizers; processed and packaged by machines made of metals
Drugs and cosmetics: mineral chemicals
Other items, such as windows, screens, light bulbs, porcelain fixtures, china, utensils, jewelry: all made from mineral products

Source: U.S. Geological Survey, 1975.

used utensils made from stainless steel, which comes from processing iron ore and other minerals.

Minerals are so important to people that, other things being equal, one's standard of living increases with the increased availability of minerals in useful forms. Furthermore, the availability of mineral resources is one measure of the wealth of a society. Those who have been successful in the location, extraction, or importation and use of minerals have grown and prospered. Without mineral resources, modern technological civilization as we know it would not be possible.

UNIQUE CHARACTERISTICS OF MINERALS

Minerals can be considered our nonrenewable heritage from the geologic past. Although new deposits are still forming from present Earth processes, these processes are producing new mineral deposits too slowly to be of use to us today. Locations where mineral deposits are found tend to occupy a small area and tend to be hidden. They must, therefore, be discovered. Unfortunately, most of the easy-to-find deposits have been exploited, and if civilization were to vanish, our descendents would have a much harder time discovering minerals for technological advance than we did. Unlike biological resources, minerals can't be managed to produce a sustained yield—the supply is finite. Recycling and conservation will help, but eventually the supply will be exhausted.

THE ORIGIN AND DISTRIBUTION OF MINERAL RESOURCES

Metals in mineral form are generally extracted from naturally occurring, anomalously high concentrations of earth materials. When metals are concentrated in anomalously high amounts by geologic processes—or by urban processes, such as in Palo Alto—**ore** deposits are formed. Natural ore deposits allowed early peoples to exploit copper, tin, gold, silver, and other metals while slowly developing skills in working with metals.

The origin and distribution of mineral resources is intimately related to the history of the biosphere and to the entire geologic cycle. Nearly all aspects and processes of the geological cycle are involved to some extent in producing local concentrations of useful materials.

Earth's outer layer, or crust, is silica-rich, made up mostly of rock-forming minerals containing silica, oxygen, and a few other elements. The elements are not evenly distributed in the crust: eight elements (oxygen, 46.4%; silicon, 28.2%; aluminum, 8.2%; iron, 5.6%; calcium, 4.2%; sodium, 2.4%; potassium, 2.1%; and titanium, 0.6%) account for over 99% by weight. Remaining elements are found (on the average) in trace concentrations. Fortunately, the geologic cycle occasionally concentrates elements in a local environment to a greater degree than would be found on the average.

The ocean, covering nearly 71% of Earth, is another reservoir for many materials. Most elements in the ocean have been weathered from crustal rocks and transported to the oceans by rivers.

Other elements are transported to the ocean by wind or glaciers. Ocean water contains about 3.5% dissolved solids, most of which is chlorine (55.1% by weight). Each cubic kilometer of ocean water contains about 2.0 metric tons zinc, 2.0 metric tons copper, 0.8 metric ton tin, 0.3 metric ton silver, and 0.01 metric ton gold. These concentrations are low compared with those in the crust, where corresponding values (in metric tons/km^3) are zinc, 170,000; copper, 86,000; tin, 5700; silver, 160; and gold, 5. Thus, if we deplete rich crustal ore deposits, we would be more likely to extract metals from lower grade ore deposits or even common rock rather than from ocean water. On the other hand, if mineral extraction technology becomes more efficient, this prognosis could change.

Why are there local concentrations of minerals? It is now believed by planetary scientists that Earth, like the other planets in the solar system, formed by condensation of matter surrounding the sun. Gravitational attraction brought together matter that was dispersed around the forming sun. As the mass of the proto-Earth increased, the material condensed and was heated by the process. The heat was sufficient to produce a molten liquid core. This core consists primarily of iron and other heavy metals, which sank toward the center. The crust formed of generally lighter elements and is a mixture of many different elements. The crust does not have a uniform distribution of elements because geological processes and some biological processes selectively dissolve, transport, and deposit elements and minerals.

Plate Boundaries

Plate tectonics are responsible for the formation of some mineral deposits. According to the theory of plate tectonics, the continents "float" on the material below them—called tectonic plates—and move slowly across Earth's surface. Metallic ores are thought to be deposited both where the tectonic plates separate, or diverge, and where they come together, or converge (Fig. 15.1). At divergent plate boundaries cold ocean water comes in contact with hot molten rock. The heated water is lighter and more active chemically. It rises through fractured rocks and leaches metals from them. The

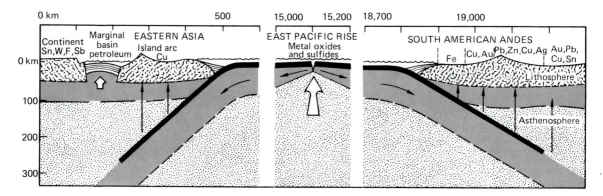

FIGURE 15.1
Relationship between the East Pacific Rise (divergent plate boundary), Pacific margins (convergent plate boundaries), and metallic ore deposits. (After NOAA.)

metals are carried in solution and then deposited as metal sulfides when the water cools and its chemistry changes.

At convergent plate boundaries, rocks saturated with sea water are forced together, heated, and subjected to intense pressure, which causes partial melting. The combination of heat, pressure, and partial melting mobilizes metals in the molten rocks. For example, most major mercury deposits are associated with volcanic regions, which occur close to convergent plate boundaries. Geologists believe that the mercury is distilled out of the tectonic plate as it moves downward and that the mercury moves upward and is deposited as the plate cools.

Igneous Processes

Ore deposits may form when molten rocks cool. As molten rock cools, heavier minerals that crystallize early may slowly sink or settle toward the bottom, while lighter minerals that crystallize later are left at the top. Deposits of an ore of chromium, called chromite, are thought to be formed in this way. When molten rocks containing carbon under very high pressure cool slowly, diamonds may be produced.

Hot waters moving within the crust are perhaps the source of most ore deposits. It is speculated that circulating groundwater is heated and enriched with minerals upon contact with deeply buried molten rocks. This water then moves up or laterally to other, cooler rocks, where the cooled water deposits the dissolved minerals.

Sedimentary Processes

Sedimentary processes are often significant in concentrating economically valuable materials in sufficient amounts for extraction. As sediments are transported, running water and wind help segregate the sediment by size, shape, and density. Thus, the best sand or sand and gravel deposits for construction purposes are those in which the finer materials have been removed by water or wind. Sand dunes, beach deposits, and deposits in stream channels are good examples. The sand and gravel industry amounts to over $1 billion/yr, and by volume mined it is the largest nonfuel mineral industry in the United States. Figure 15.2 shows the production data for sand and gravel compared with those for other construction materials [3].

Stream processes transport and sort all types of materials according to size and density. Therefore, if the bedrock in a river basin contains heavy metals such as gold, streams draining the basin may concentrate heavy metals to form **placer deposits** in areas where there is little water turbulence or velocity, such as in open crevices or fractures at the bottoms of pools, on the inside curves of bends, or on riffles. Placer mining of gold—which was known as a "poor man's method" because a

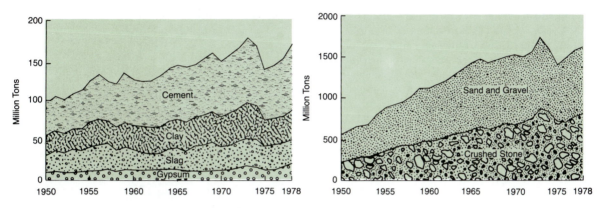

FIGURE 15.2
Supplies of major construction materials in the United States from 1950 to 1978. (U. S. Bureau of Mines, Mining and Mineral Policy, 1979.)

miner needed only a shovel, a pan, and a strong back to work the streamside claim—helped to stimulate settlement of California, Alaska, and other areas of the United States. Furthermore, the gold in California attracted miners who acquired the expertise necessary to locate and develop other resources in the western conterminous United States and Alaska.

Rivers and streams that empty into the oceans and lakes carry tremendous quantities of dissolved material derived from the weathering of rocks. From time to time, geologically speaking, a shallow marine basin may be isolated by tectonic activity that uplifts its boundaries, thereby restricting circulation and facilitating evaporation. In other cases, climatic variations during the ice ages produced large inland lakes with no outlets, which eventually dried up. In either case, as evaporation progresses, the dissolved materials precipitate, forming a wide variety of compounds, minerals, and rocks that have important commercial value. Most of these **evaporite** deposits can be grouped into one of three types: marine evaporites (solids)—potassium and sodium salts, gypsum, and anhydrite; nonmarine evaporites (solids)—sodium and calcium carbonate, sulfate, borate, nitrate, and limited iodine and strontium compounds; and brines (liquids derived from wells, thermal springs, inland salt lakes, and sea waters)—bromine, iodine, calcium chloride, and magnesium [4]. Heavy

metals (such as copper, lead, and zinc) associated with brines and sediments in the Red Sea, Salton Sea, and other areas are important resources that may be exploited in the future.

Evaporite materials are widely used in industrial and agricultural activities, and their annual value is about $1 billion [3]. Fortunately, evaporite and brine resources in the United States are substantial, assuring no shortages for many years.

Biological Processes

Some mineral deposits are formed by biological processes, and many minerals are formed under conditions of the biosphere that have been greatly altered by life. For example, the major iron ore deposits exist in sedimentary rocks that were formed more than 2 billion years ago [5]. There are several types of iron deposits. One important type, called grey beds, contains unoxidized iron. Red beds contain oxidized iron (the red color is the color of iron oxide). The grey beds formed when there was relatively little oxygen in the atmosphere, and the red beds formed when there was relatively more oxygen. Although the processes are not completely understood, it appears that major deposits of iron stopped forming when the atmospheric concentration of oxygen reached its present level. This suggests that early life was important in beginning and ending the ore-forming processes for iron [6].

Organisms are able to form many kinds of minerals, such as the calcium minerals in shells and bones. Some of these minerals cannot be formed inorganically in the biosphere. Thirty-one different biologically produced minerals have been identified. Minerals of biological origin contribute significantly to sedimentary deposits [7].

Weathering Processes

Weathering is responsible for concentrating some materials to the point that they can be extracted with reasonable effort. Insoluble ore deposits such as native gold are generally residual and unless removed by erosion will accumulate in the soil. Accumulation is favored where the parent rock is relatively soluble, such as limestone. Intensive weathering of certain soils derived from aluminum-rich igneous rocks may concentrate oxides of aluminum and iron, while the more soluble elements, such as silica, calcium, and sodium, are selectively removed by soil and biological processes. If sufficiently concentrated, residual aluminum oxide forms an ore of aluminum known as bauxite. Important nickel and cobalt deposits are also found in such soils developed from ferromagnesian-rich igneous rocks.

Weathering is also involved in secondary enrichment processes to produce sulfide ore deposits from low-grade primary ore. Near the surface, primary ore containing minerals such as iron, copper, and silver sulfides is in contact with slightly acid soil water in an oxygen-rich environment. As the sulfides are oxidized, they are dissolved, forming solutions that are rich in sulfuric acid and silver and copper sulfate and that migrate downward, producing a leached zone devoid of ore minerals (Fig. 15.3). Below the leached zone and above the groundwater table, oxidation continues, and sulfate solutions continue their downward migration. Below the water table, if oxygen is no longer available, the solutions are deposited as sulfides, enriching the metal content of the primary ore by as much as ten times. In this way, low-grade primary ore is rendered more valuable, and high-grade primary ore is made even more attractive [8, 9].

Several disseminated copper deposits have become economically successful because of second-

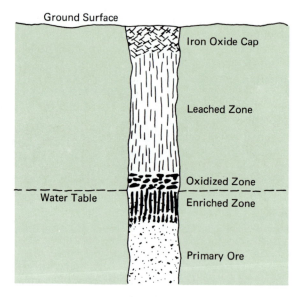

FIGURE 15.3
Typical zones that form during secondary enrichment processes. Sulfide ore minerals in the primary ore vein are oxidized and altered and then are leached from the oxidized zone by descending groundwater and redeposited in the enriched zone. The iron oxide cap is generally a reddish color and may be helpful in locating ore deposits that have been enriched. (After Foster.)

ary enrichment, which concentrates dispersed metals. For example, secondary enrichment of a disseminated copper deposit at Miami, Arizona, increased the grade of the ore from less than 1% copper in the primary ore to as much as 5% in some localized zones of enrichment [8].

Minerals from the Sea

Mineral resources in sea water or on the bottom of the ocean are vast and, in some cases, such as magnesium, are nearly unlimited. In the United States, magnesium was first extracted from sea water in 1940. By 1972, one company in Texas produced 80% of domestic magnesium, utilizing sea water as its raw material source. Companies in Alabama, California, Florida, Mississippi, and New Jersey are also extracting magnesium from sea water.

The deep-ocean floor may be the site of the next

big mineral rush. Two types of deposits have been identified: massive sulfide deposits associated with hydrothermal vents and manganese oxide nodules.

Massive sulfide deposits, containing zinc, copper, iron, and trace amounts of silver, are produced at divergent plate boundaries (oceanic ridges) by the forces of plate tectonics. Pressure created by several thousand meters of water at ridges forces cold sea water deep into numerous rock fractures, where it is heated by upwelling magma and emerges as hot springs. The circulating water leaches the rocks, removing metals that are deposited as hot mineral-rich water is ejected at temperatures up to 350°C into the cold sea. Sulfide minerals precipitate near vents, known as "black smokers" because of the color of the ejected mineral-rich water, forming massive towerlike formations rich in metals. The hot vents are of particular biologic significance because they support a unique assemblage of animals, including giant clams, tube worms, and white crabs (Fig. 15.4). Communities of these animals base their existence on sulfide compounds extruded from black smokers, existing through a process called chemosynthesis as opposed to photosynthesis, which supports all other known ecosystems on Earth.

The extent of sulfide mineral deposits along oceanic ridges is poorly known, and although leases to some possible deposits are being considered, it seems unlikely that such deposits will be extracted at a profit in the near future. Certainly potential environmental degradation, including serious physical and biological impacts associated with water quality and sediment pollution, will have to be carefully evaluated prior to any proposed mining activity in the future.

Manganese oxide nodules, which contain manganese (24%) and iron (14%) with secondary copper (1%), nickel (1%), and cobalt (0.25%), cover vast areas of the deep-ocean floor. The nodules are found in the Atlantic Ocean off Florida, but the richest and most extensive accumulations occur in large areas of the northeastern, central, and southern Pacific, where the nodules cover 20–50% of the ocean floor [10].

The average size of the manganese nodules varies from a few millimeters to a few tens of centimeters in diameter. Composed primarily of concentric layers of manganese in iron oxides mixed with a variety of other materials, each nodule formed around a nucleus of broken nodules, fragments of volcanic rock, and sometimes fossils. The estimated rate of growth is 1–5 mm per million years. The nodules are most abundant in those parts of the ocean where sediment accumulation is at a minimum, generally at depths of 2500–6000 m [11].

The origin of the nodules is not well understood. Most likely, material weathered from the continents and transported by rivers to the oceans is carried by ocean currents to deposition sites in the deep-ocean basins. Both inorganic precipitation and bacteria-induced precipitation are probably important in the formation of nodules.

Expenditures for mining and metallurgical research to recover the nodules have surpassed $190 million, and proposed expenditures through the 1980s are expected to approach $800 million. At least 20 corporations in several countries are examining metallurgical systems to process the nodules. Some would produce cobalt, copper, nickel, and manganese, while others would produce combinations of only copper and nickel [12].

Actual mining involves lifting the nodules off the bottom and up to the mining ship. French and Japanese researchers are experimenting with a system with a continuous-line bucket dredge, in which a continuous rope with buckets attached at prescribed intervals is strung out between two ships. The buckets drag along the bottom as the two ships move, and the nodules are dumped into one of the ships as the rope loop is reeled from one ship to the other. Other methods of recovery being examined are hydraulic lifting and use of airlift in conjunction with hydraulic dredging [12]. It is a fair statement that the whole manganese oxide nodule industry is in its infancy, and considerable change in methods and technology is likely. Nevertheless, from current data it has been determined that mining of the nodules is technologically feasible and potentially profitable. However, prospective interest groups must cooperate in management of the resources and carefully evaluate the environmental impact of the mining on the ecology of the ocean bottom so that the sea bed is not degraded.

FIGURE 15.4

(a) Oceanic ridge hydrothermal environment. (b) Detail of black smokers, where massive sulfide deposits form.

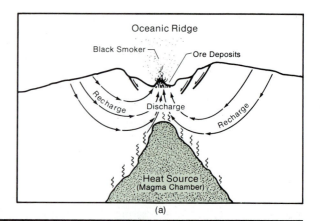

(a)

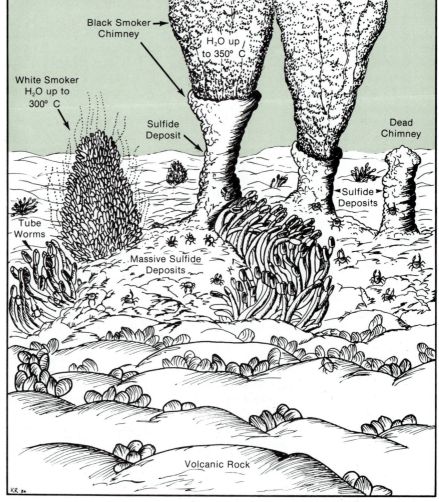

(b)

RESOURCES AND RESERVES

To this point we have casually referred to resources without a specific definition. **Mineral resources** are broadly defined as elements, chemical compounds, minerals, or rocks that are concentrated in a form that can be extracted to obtain a usable commodity. It is also assumed that a resource can be extracted economically or at least has the potential for economical extraction. A **reserve,** on the other hand, is that portion of a resource which is identified and from which usable materials can be legally and economically extracted at the time of evaluation.

The main point about resources and reserves is that resources are not reserves. An analogy from a student's personal finances will help clarify this point. A student's reserves are the liquid assets, such as money in the pocket or bank, whereas the student's resources include the total income the student can expect to earn during his or her lifetime. This distinction is often critical to the student in school because resources are "frozen" assets or next year's income and cannot be used to pay this month's bills [13].

Regardless of potential problems, it is very important for planning to estimate future resources. This requires a continual reassessment of all components of a total resource by considering new technology, probability of geologic discovery, and shifts in economic and political conditions [2].

The example of silver will illustrate some important points about resources and reserves. Earth's crust (to a depth of 1 km) contains almost 2 million million (2×10^{12}) metric tons of silver—an amount much larger than the annual world use, which is approximately 10,000 metric tons. If this silver existed as pure metal concentrated into one large mine, it would represent a supply sufficient for several hundred million years at current levels of use. Most of this silver, however, exists in extremely low concentrations—too low to be extracted economically with current technology. The known reserves of silver, reflecting the amount we could obtain immediately with known techniques, is about 200,000 metric tons, or a 20–year supply at current use levels.

The problem with silver, as with all mineral resources, is not with its total abundance but with its concentration and relative ease of extraction. When an atom of silver is used, it is not destroyed, but remains an atom of silver. It is simply dispersed and may become unavailable. In theory, given enough energy, all mineral resources could be recycled, but this is not possible in practice. Consider lead, which is mined and used in gasolines. This lead is now scattered along highways across the world and deposited in low concentration in forests, fields, and salt marshes close to these highways. Recovery of this lead is, for all practical purposes, impossible.

AVAILABILITY OF MINERAL RESOURCES

Earth's mineral resources can be divided into several broad categories, depending on our use of them: elements for metal production and technology; building materials; minerals for the chemical industry; and minerals for agriculture. Metallic minerals can be classified according to their abundance. The abundant metals include iron, aluminum, chromium, manganese, titanium, and magnesium. Scarce metals include copper, lead, zinc, tin, gold, silver, platinum, uranium, mercury, and molybdenum.

Some mineral resources, such as salt (sodium chloride), are necessary for life. Primitive peoples traveled long distances to obtain salt when it was not locally available. Other mineral resources are desired or considered necessary to maintain a certain level of technology.

The basic issue with mineral resources is not actual exhaustion or extinction, but the cost of maintaining an adequate stock within an economy through mining and recycling. At some point, the costs of mining exceed the worth of material. When the availability of a particular mineral becomes a limitation, there are four possible solutions: find more sources; recycle what has already been obtained; find a substitute; or do without. Which choice or combination of choices is made depends on social, economic, and environmental factors.

The availability of a mineral resource in a certain form, in a certain concentration, and in a certain total amount at that concentration is determined by Earth's history and is a geological issue. What a resource is and when it becomes limited are ultimately social questions. Before metals were discovered, they could not be considered resources. Before smelting was invented, the only metal ores were those in which the metals appeared in their pure form. Originally, gold was obtained as a pure or "native" metal. Now gold mines are deep beneath the surface, and the recovery process involves reducing tons of rock to ounces of gold.

In reality then, mineral resources are limited, which raises important questions. How long will a particular resource last? How much short- or long-term environmental deterioration are we willing to concede to ensure that resources are developed in a particular area? How can we make the best use of available resources? These questions have no easy answers. We are now struggling with ways to estimate better the quality and quantity of resources.

We can use a particular mineral resource in several ways: rapid consumption, consumption with conservation, or consumption and conservation with recycling. Which option is selected depends in part on economic, political, and social criteria. Figure 15.5 shows the hypothetical depletion curves corresponding to these three options. Historically, with the exception of precious metals, rapid con-

sumption has dominated most resource utilization. However, as more resources become in short supply, increased conservation and recycling are expected. Certainly the trend toward recycling is well established for metals such as copper, lead, and aluminum.

We usually think of mineral resources as the metals used in structural materials, but in fact (with the exception of iron) the predominant mineral resources are not of this type. Consider the annual world consumption of a few selected elements. Sodium and iron are used at a rate of approximately 0.1 to 1 billion tons per year. Nitrogen, sulfur, potassium, and calcium are used at a rate of approximately 10–100 million tons/yr. These four elements are used primarily as soil conditioners or fertilizers. Elements such as zinc, copper, aluminum, and lead have annual world consumption rates of about 3–10 million tons, and gold and silver have annual consumption rates of 10,000 tons or less. Of the metallic minerals, iron makes up 95% of all the metals consumed, and nickel, chromium, cobalt, and manganese are used mainly in alloys of iron (as in stainless steel). Therefore, we can conclude that the nonmetallics, with the exception of iron, are consumed at much greater rates than elements used for their metallic properties.

As the world population and the desire for a higher standard of living increase, the demand for mineral resources expands at a faster and faster rate. From a global viewpoint, our limited mineral resources and reserves threaten our affluence. Approximately 9900 kg of new mineral material (excluding energy resources) are required each year for each person in the United States. Predicted world increases in the use of iron, copper, and lead compared with population increases suggest that the rate of production of these metals would have to increase by several times if the world per capita consumption rate were to rise to the U.S. level. Such an increase is very unlikely; affluent countries will have to find substitutes for some minerals or use a smaller proportion of the world annual production.

Domestic supplies of many mineral resources in the United States and many other affluent nations are insufficient for current use and must be supple-

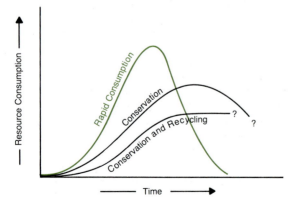

FIGURE 15.5
Several hypothetical depletion curves. See text for further explanation.

TABLE 15.2

Deficiency of U.S. reserves of selected nonfuel minerals. Foreign sources subject to potential interruption by political, economic, or military disruption are shown in lighter print.

	Commodity	Adequacy of U.S. Reserves for Cumulative U.S. Demand 1982–2000 (0 10 20 30 40 50 60 70 80 90 100%)	Major Foreign Source
Essentially No Reserves	Manganese		Gabon, Brazil
	Cobalt		Zaire
	Tantalum		Malaysia, Thailand, **Canada**
	Columbium		Brazil, **Canada**
	Platinum group		South Africa, USSR
	Chromium		USSR, South Africa
	Nickel		**Canada**, New Caledonia
	Aluminum		Jamaica, Australia
	Tin		Malaysia, Bolivia
	Antimony		South Africa, Bolivia
	Fluorine		**Mexico**, South Africa
	Asbestos		**Canada**, South Africa
	Vanadium		South Africa, Chile
Reserve Deficiency	Mercury		
	Silver		**Canada, Mexico**
	Tungsten		**Canada**, Bolivia
	Sulfur		**Canada, Mexico**
	Zinc		**Canada, Mexico**
	Gold		**Canada**, USSR
	Potash		**Canada**, Israel

Source: U.S. Geological Survey, 1984.

mented by imports from other nations. Table 15.2 shows the deficiency of U.S. reserves for selected nonfuel minerals projected to the year 2000. The table also shows major foreign sources for the needed minerals and indicates potentially unstable sources. Of particular concern to industrial countries is the possibility that supply of a much desired or needed mineral may become interrupted by political, economic, or military instability of the supplying nation. For example, the recent civil war in Zaire caused sufficient concern that the spot market in cobalt increased by 800% [14]. Cobalt is a metal used to strengthen steel and thus is in great demand in many industrial countries. Today the United States, along with many other countries, is dependent on a steady supply of imports to meet the mineral demand of industries. Of course the fact that a mineral is imported into a country does not mean that it does not exist in quantities that could be mined within the country. Rather, it suggests that there are economic, political, or envi-

ronmental reasons that make it easier, more practical, or more desirable to import the material.

Our ingenuity allows us to circumvent some problems of resource availability, but it is difficult to maintain a constant average standard of living on a finite resource base when population continues to increase. Thus our resource problem is fundamentally a people problem—too many people chasing after a limited supply of resources. How do we plan for the future? Because estimates of reserves and resources change with new technology and social, political, and economic conditions, a continual reassessment is necessary for long-range planning.

ENVIRONMENTAL IMPACT OF MINERAL DEVELOPMENT

The impact of mineral exploitation on the environment depends upon such factors as mining procedures, local hydrologic conditions, climate, rock types, size of operation, topography, and many more interrelated factors. Furthermore, the impact varies with the stage of development of the resource. For example, the exploration and testing stage involves considerably less impact than the mining and processing stages.

Exploration activities for mineral deposits vary from collecting and analyzing remote-sensing data gathered from airplanes or satellites to field work involving surface mapping, drilling, and gathering of geophysical data. Generally, exploration has a minimal impact on the environment provided care is taken in sensitive areas, such as some arid lands, marshlands, and areas underlain by permafrost. Some arid lands are covered by a thin layer of pebbles over fine silt several centimeters thick. The layer of pebbles, called desert pavement, protects the finer material from wind erosion. When the pavement is disturbed by road building or other activity, the fine silts may be eroded, impairing physical, chemical, and biological properties of the soil in the immediate environment and scarring the

land for many years. In other areas, such as marshlands and the northern tundra, wet organic-rich soils render the land sensitive to even light traffic.

Mining and processing of mineral resources generally have a considerable impact on land, water, air, and biologic resources as well as initiating social impacts because of increased demand for housing and services in mining areas. As it becomes necessary to use lower and lower grade ores, we are faced with the problem of how to minimize mining's negative effects on the environment.

One of the major practical issues is whether surface or subsurface mines should be developed in an area. Surface mining is cheaper but has more direct environmental effects. The trend in recent years has been away from subsurface mining and toward large, open-pit (surface) mines such as the Bingham Canyon copper mine in Utah (Fig. 15.6, Plate 12a) and Liberty Pit near Ruth, Nevada (Fig. 15.7). The Bingham Canyon mine is one of the world's largest artificial excavations, cover-

FIGURE 15.6
The Bingham Canyon copper mine, one of the largest artificial excavations in the world.

FIGURE 15.7
The Liberty Pit surface
mine near Ruth, Nevada.

ing nearly 8 km² to a maximum depth of nearly
800 m.

Surface mines and quarries today cover less
than one-half of 1% of the total area of the United
States. Even though the impact of these operations
is a local phenomenon, numerous local occur-
rences will eventually constitute a larger problem.
Environmental degradation tends to extend beyond the excavation and surface plant areas of
both surface and subsurface mines. Large mining
operations disturb the land by directly removing
material in some areas, thus changing topography,
and by dumping waste in others. At best these actions produce severe aesthetic degradation. Dust at
mines may affect air resources, even though care
is often taken to reduce dust production by sprin-
kling roads and other sites that generate dust.
Water resources are particularly vulnerable to degradation even if drainage is controlled and sediment pollution reduced. Surface drainage is often
altered at mine sites, and runoff from precipitation
(rain or snow) may infiltrate waste material, leaching out trace elements and minerals. Trace elements (cadmium, cobalt, copper, lead, molybdenum, and others), when leached from mining
wastes and concentrated in water, soil, or plants,
may be toxic or may cause diseases in people and

other animals who drink the water, eat the plants,
or use the soil. Specially constructed ponds to collect such runoff help, but cannot be expected to
eliminate all problems.

The white streaks in Figure 15.8 are mineral deposits apparently leached from tailings from a zinc
mine in Colorado. Similar-looking deposits may
cover rocks in rivers for many kilometers downstream from some mining areas. Thus, a potential
problem associated with mineral resource development is the possible release of harmful trace
elements to the environment.

Groundwater may also be polluted by mining
operations when waste comes into contact with
slow-moving subsurface waters. Surface water infiltration or groundwater movement causes leaching of sulfide minerals that may pollute groundwater and eventually seep into streams to pollute
surface water. Groundwater problems are particularly troublesome because reclamation of polluted
groundwater is very difficult and expensive.

Even abandoned mines can cause serious problems. For example, subsurface mining for lead and
zinc in the Tri-State Area (Kansas, Missouri, and
Oklahoma), which started in the late nineteenth
century and ceased in some areas in the 1960s, is
causing serious water pollution problems in the

FIGURE 15.8
Tailings from a zinc mine in Colorado.

tion Agency in 1982 designated it as the nation's No. 1 hazardous waste site.

Physical changes in the land, soil, water, and air associated with mining directly and indirectly affect the biological environment. Direct impacts include deaths of plants or animals caused by mining activity or contact with toxic soil or water from mines. Indirect impacts include changes in nutrient cycling, total biomass, species diversity, and ecosystem stability due to alterations in ground and/or surface water availability or quality. Periodic or accidental discharge of low-grade pollutants through failure of barriers, ponds, or water diversions or through breach of barriers during floods, earthquakes, or volcanic eruptions also damages local ecological systems.

Because the demand for mineral resources is going to increase, we must minimize both on-site and off-site problems by controlling sediment, water, and air pollution through good engineering and conservation practices. Although these actions will raise the cost of mineral commodities and hence the price of all items produced from these materials, they will yield other returns of equal or higher value to future generations. We must realize, however, that even the most careful measures to control environmental disruption associated with mining will occasionally fail.

Social impacts associated with large-scale mining result from a rapid influx of workers into areas unprepared for growth. Stress is placed on local services: water supplies, sewage and solid waste disposal systems, schools, and rental housing. Land use shifts from open range, forest, and agriculture to urban patterns. More people also increase the stress on nearby recreation and wilderness areas, some of which may be in a fragile ecological balance. Construction activity and urbanization affect local streams through sediment pollution, reduced water quality, and increased runoff. Air quality is reduced as a result of more vehicles, dust from construction, and generation of power.

Adverse social impacts also occur when mines are closed, for towns surrounding large mines come to depend on the income of employed miners. Closures of mines produced the well-known

1980s. The mines, extending to depths of 100 m below the water table, were kept dry by pumping when the mines were in production. However, since mining stopped, some have flooded and started to overflow into nearby creeks. The water is very acidic because sulfide minerals in the mine react with oxygen and groundwater to form sulfuric acid, a problem known as "acid mine-drainage." The problem was so severe in the Tar Creek area of Oklahoma that the Environmental Protec-

"ghost towns" in the old American West, and today the price of coal and other minerals directly affects the lives of many small towns. This is especially true in the Appalachian Mountain region of the United States where closures of coal mines are taking their toll. These mine closings are partly the result of lower prices for coal and partly the result of rising mining costs. One of the reasons mining costs are rising is the increased level of environmental regulation of the mining industry. Of course, regulations have also helped make mining safer and have facilitated land reclamation. Some miners, however, believe the regulations are not flexible enough, and there is some truth to their arguments. For example, some areas might be reclaimed for use as farmland following mining, if the original hills have been leveled. Regulations, however, may require the restoration of the land to its original hilly state, even though hills make inferior farmland.

RECYCLING OF RESOURCES

The cycle of mineral resources is idealized in Figure 15.9. Inspection of this diagram reveals that many components of the cycle are connected to waste disposal. In fact, the major environmental impacts of mineral resource utilization are related

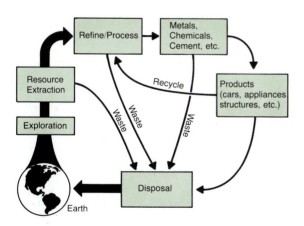

FIGURE 15.9
Flow chart of the resource cycle.

to waste products. Wastes produce pollution that may be toxic to humans, are dangerous to natural ecosystems and the biosphere, and are aesthetically undesirable. They may attack and degrade other resources such as air, water, soil, and living things. Wastes also deplete nonrenewable mineral resources with no offsetting benefits for human society. Recycling of resources is one way to reduce these wastes.

Over 180 million metric tons of household and industrial waste are collected each year in the United States alone. Of this, about 27 million metric tons are incinerated, generating over 6 million metric tons of residue. The tremendous tonnage of waste not incinerated and the residues from burning are usually disposed of at sanitary landfill sites or open dumps. These materials are sometimes referred to as urban ore because they contain many materials that could be recycled and used again to provide energy or useful products [15, 16].

The notion of reusing waste materials is not new, and such metals as iron, aluminum, copper, and lead have been recycled for many years (Fig. 15.10). About 40% of steel is recycled in the United States [13]. Of the millions of automobiles discarded annually, nearly 90% are now dismantled by auto wreckers and scrap processors for metals to be recycled [16]. Recycling metals from discarded automobiles is a sound conservation practice, considering that nearly 90% by weight of the average automobile is metal (Fig. 15.11).

Recycling may be one way to delay or partly alleviate a possible crisis caused by the convergence of a rapidly rising population and a limited resource base. However, recycling the wide variety of materials found in urban waste is not an easy task. Before recycling can become a widespread practice, improved technology and more economic incentives are needed. Figure 15.12 shows a flow chart of equipment necessary to recycle urban refuse. The results of experiments conducted at a pilot plant by the U.S. Bureau of Mines using these techniques have been encouraging, and while refinements are necessary, urban refuse has been successfully separated into concentrates of light-gauge iron, massive metals, glass, paper, plastics, and organic and other combustible wastes [15].

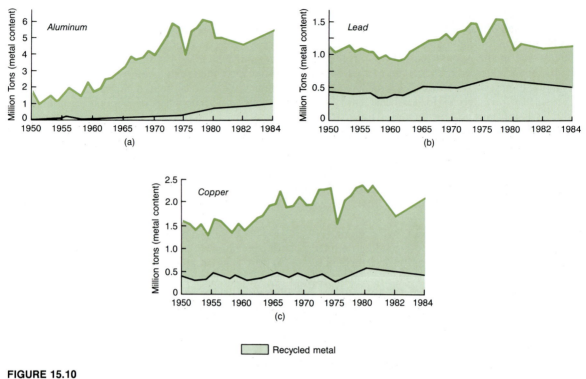

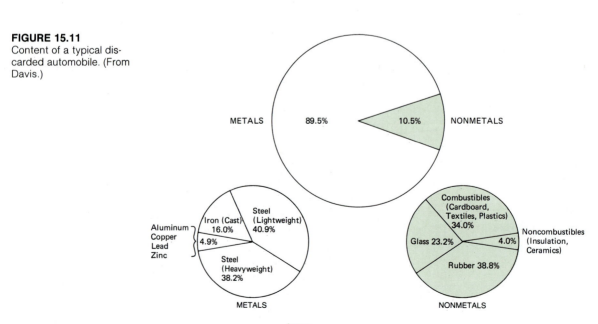

FIGURE 15.10
U.S. consumption and recycling of selected metals. (From U.S. Bureau of Mines, 1984.)

FIGURE 15.11
Content of a typical discarded automobile. (From Davis.)

472

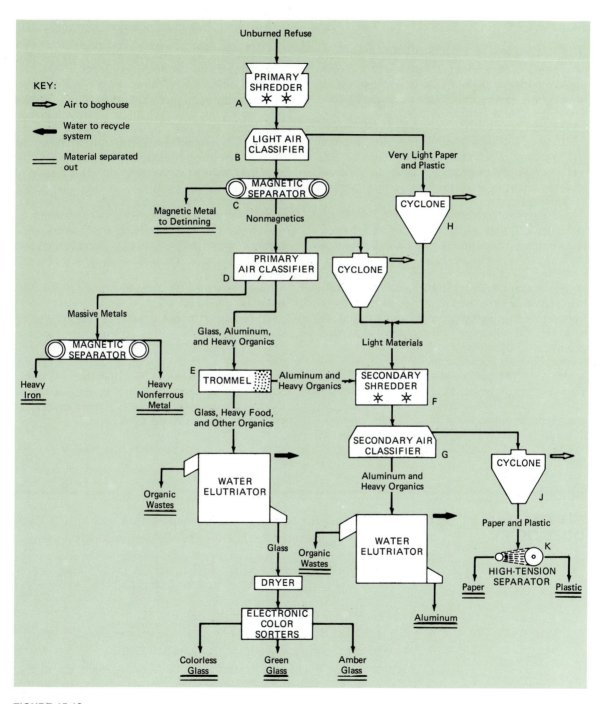

FIGURE 15.12
Flow chart showing how raw refuse may be separated for recycling of resources. (From Sullivan et al.)

473

SUMMARY

Mineral resources are generally extracted from naturally occurring, anomalously high concentrations of earth materials. These natural deposits allowed early peoples to exploit minerals while slowly developing technological skills.

The origin and distribution of mineral resources is intimately related to the history of the biosphere and to the entire geologic cycle. Nearly all aspects and processes of the geological cycle are involved to some extent in producing local concentrations of useful materials.

An important concept in analyzing resources and reserves is that resources are not reserves. Unless discovered and captured, resources cannot be used to solve present shortages.

Availability of mineral resources is one measure of the wealth of a society. In fact, modern technological civilization as we know it would not be possible without exploitation of mineral resources. However, it is important to recognize that mineral deposits are not infinite and that we cannot maintain exponential population growth on a finite resource base. The United States and many other affluent nations have insufficient domestic supplies of many mineral resources for current use and must supplement them by imports from other nations. In the future, as other nations industrialize and develop, such imports may be more difficult to obtain, and affluent countries may have to find substitutes for some minerals or use a smaller portion of the world's annual production.

The environmental impact of mineral exploitation depends upon many factors, including mining procedures, local hydrologic conditions, climate, rock types, size of operation, topography, and many more interrelated factors. In addition, the impact varies with the stage of development of the resource. In general, the mining and processing of mineral resources greatly affect the land, water, air, and biological resources as well as initiate certain social impacts due to increasing demand for housing and services in mining areas. Because the demand for mineral resources is going to increase, we must strive to minimize both on-site and off-site problems by controlling sediment, water, and air pollution through good engineering and conservation practices.

Recycling of mineral resources appears to be one way to delay or partly alleviate a possible crisis caused by the convergence of a rapidly rising population and a limited resource base. However, recycling a wide variety of materials found in urban waste is not an easy task, and innovative refinements in recycling methods will be necessary to ensure that the recycling trend continues.

STUDY QUESTIONS

1   What is the difference between a *resource* and a *reserve?*

2   Under what circumstances might sewage sludge be considered a mineral resource?

3   If surface mines and quarries cover less than one-half of 1% of the land surface of the United States, why is there environmental concern about them?

4   When is recycling of a mineral a viable option?

5   What is the difference between a renewable and a nonrenewable resource?

6   Which biological processes influence mineral deposits?

7   You meet a deep-sea diver who claims that the oceans can provide all of our mineral resources with no negative environmental effects. Do you agree or disagree?

8   What factors determine the availability of a mineral resource?

9 How does plate tectonics affect the nature and occurrence of mineral resources?

10 Making available a mineral resource involves three phases: (a) exploration; (b) recovery; and (c) consumption. Which phase has the greatest environmental effects?

FURTHER READING

AMERICAN CHEMICAL SOCIETY. 1971. *Solid wastes.* Washington, D. C.: American Chemical Society.

BATEMAN, A. M. 1950. *Economic ore deposits.* 2nd ed. New York: Wiley.

————. 1951. *The formation of mineral deposits.* New York: Wiley.

BROOKINS, D. G. 1981. *Earth resources, energy, and the environment.* Columbus, Ohio: Charles E. Merrill.

COMMITTEE ON MINERAL RESOURCES AND THE ENVIRONMENT. 1975. *Mineral resources and the environment.* Washington, D. C.: National Academy of Science.

KESLER, S. E. 1976. *Our finite mineral resources.* New York: McGraw-Hill.

PARK, C. F., Jr., and MacDIARMID, R. A. 1970. *Ore deposits.* 2nd ed. San Francisco: W. H. Freeman.

SKINNER, B. J., ed. 1981. *Use and misuse of Earth's surface.* Los Altos, Calif.: William Kaufmann.

16

Waste Disposal

- The historical "dilute and disperse" concept of waste disposal is no longer adequate; we now seek to "concentrate and contain" or "recycle."
- The conversion of waste to useful material is the ideal, but there are often technological and economic barriers to its achievement. Increasing costs of raw materials, energy, transportation, and land make it more feasible to recycle resources.
- Solid waste disposal is primarily an urban problem. Common methods include on-site disposal, composting, incineration, open dumps, and sanitary landfills.
- Hazardous waste pollutants from a disposal site may enter the environment by volatilization into the air, entering and being held in the soil, entering the groundwater system, entering the surface water network, and entering the food chain through plants.

- Management of hazardous chemical wastes is one of the most serious environmental problems ever to face the United States. Indiscriminate dumping continues to be a serious problem.
- Methods of managing hazardous chemical waste include on-site processing, microbial breakdown, chemical stabilization, high-temperature decomposition, incineration, use of secure landfills, or deep-well injection.
- For low-level radioactive waste, the "dilute and disperse" philosophy is appropriate. Stable bedrock offers the most promise as a disposal repository for high-level radioactive waste.
- Ocean dumping continues to degrade the oceanic environment; population growth in coastal areas is likely to make this problem worse.

LOVE CANAL

In 1976, in a residential area near Niagara Falls, New York, trees and gardens began to die. Children found the rubber on their tennis shoes and on their bicycle tires disintegrating. Dogs sniffing in a landfill area developed sores that would not heal. Puddles of toxic, noxious substances began to ooze to the soil surface; a swimming pool popped its foundations and was found to be floating on a bath of chemicals.

A study revealed that the residential area had been built on the site of a chemical dump. The area had originally been excavated in 1892 as the beginnings of the Love Canal, which was supposed to provide a transportation route between industrial centers. When that plan failed, the ditch was unused for decades and seemed a convenient dump for wastes. From the 1920s to the 1950s, more than 80 different chemicals were dumped there. Finally, in 1953, the company dumping the chemicals donated the land to the city of Niagara Falls for one dollar. Eventually 200 homes and an elementary school were built on and near the site

(Fig. 16.1). Heavy rainfall and heavy snowfall during the winter of 1976–77 set off the events that made Love Canal a household word.

A study of the site identified a number of substances present there—including benzene, dioxin, dichlorethylene, and chloroform—that were suspected of being carcinogens. Although officials readily admitted that very little was known about the impact of these chemicals and others at the site, there was grave concern for the people living in the area. The concern has been well documented now because of the alleged higher-than-average rates of miscarriages, blood and liver abnormalities, birth defects, and chromosome damage. However, a study by the New York health authorities suggests that no chemically caused health effects have been absolutely established [1,2,3].

The cost to clean up the Love Canal site and relocate residents will eventually exceed $100 million. Over $75 million has already been spent in the initial cleanup and relocation efforts. In a recent settlement it was decided that over 1000 former and current residents of the canal would divide $20 million to compensate for past and future

FIGURE 16.1
Former location of Love Canal, between black parallel lines. The white, patchy areas indicate sections where vegetation will not grow.

medical bills and property damage resulting from presumed or possible exposure to toxic chemicals and necessary relocation.

The cleanup of the Love Canal is becoming an important case to demonstrate state-of-the-art technology of hazardous waste treatment. The objective has been to contain and stop the migration of wastes through the groundwater flow system and remove and treat dioxin-contaminated soil and sediment from stream beds and sewers. Hundreds of drums of contaminated soil and sediment are now being stored on the site prior to treatment or disposal [4].

The method being used to minimize further production of contaminated water is to cover the dump site and adjacent contaminated area with a 1 m thick layer of compacted clay and a polyethylene plastic cover to reduce infiltration of surface water. Lateral movement of water is inhibited from entering the site by specially designed impervious walls. These procedures will greatly reduce subsurface seepage of water through the site, and the water that does seep out is collected and treated [1,2,3,4].

What went wrong in Love Canal to produce a suburban ghost town? How can we avoid such disasters in the future? The real tragedy of Love Canal is that it is probably not an isolated incident. That is, there are many hidden "Love Canals" across the country, "time bombs" waiting to explode [1,2].

NECESSITY OF WASTE DISPOSAL

Waste disposal sites are necessary if society is to function smoothly. However, no one wants to live near a waste disposal site, be it a sanitary landfill for municipal waste or a hazardous waste-disposal operation for chemical materials. Perhaps the largest waste disposal site in the world is located on a 1500-ha site on Staten Island, New York. The waste disposal facility known as Fresh Kills accepts approximately 11,000 tons of waste every day of the approximate 24,000 tons of municipal and commercial waste collected in the city of New York. The waste disposal site already has refuse piled several tens of meters above sea level and, with the prospect that the site may eventually accept up to 20,000 tons/day, it is expected that the

refuse pile will eventually reach an elevation of 150–200 m above sea level. This, in fact, is the construction of a large hill or small mountain of urban waste. Unfortunately, the story doesn't end here because the city of New York, like many other large cities, is running out of places to dispose of its waste. As large as the Fresh Kills site is, it will be completely filled, unable to accept further waste, in only 10–15 years. Today, many large cities are seriously considering alternatives to landfills for disposal of urban waste. This is a necessity: the distance from collection to disposal sites has grown longer and there is growing concern for the safety of people living in close proximity to large landfills that may pollute the surrounding environment [5].

Early Concepts of Waste Disposal

The utopian view of waste disposal would consider the technology that is capable of accepting an unlimited amount of waste and safely containing it forever outside the human sphere of life. Although such a waste disposal scheme might some day be possible, it is not likely to arise in the near future. During the first century of the industrial revolution, the volume of waste produced was relatively small and the concept of "dilute and disperse" was adequate. Factories were located near rivers because the water provided easy transport of materials by boat, ease of communication, sufficient water for processing and cooling, and easy disposal of waste into the river. With few factories and sparse population, "dilute and disperse" seemed to remove the waste from the environment [6].

Unfortunately, as industrial and urban areas expanded, the concept of "dilute and disperse" became inadequate and a new concept known as "concentrate and contain" became popular. It has become apparent, however, that containment was and is not always achieved. Containers, natural or artificial, may leak or break and allow waste to escape. As a result, another concept developed—"resource recovery." This philosophy holds that wastes may be converted to useful materials, in which case they are no longer wastes but resources. However, even with our state-of-the-art technology there are large volumes of waste that

Hazardous Waste in My Trashcan?

Hazardous waste isn't just a problem associated with big chemical or oil companies. Among the mountains of trash cities generate every day are hazardous wastes that are disposed of legally but improperly. Even ordinary household trash cans include paint thinners, pesticides, bleaches, PCBs in old TV sets, mercury in spent watch batteries, butane residue in disposable cigarette lighters, lye in oven cleaner cans, and dioxin or DDT in old pesticides.

For regulatory purposes the government classifies such materials as hazardous if they are ignitable, corrosive, dangerously reactive, or toxic; however, "hazard" is further defined by quantity so that "small generators" such as homeowners and small businesses are exempt from regulation. As a result, most municipal landfills are receiving small quantities of a broad range of products that would require disposal in a hazardous waste facility if they came from "big generators." The irony is that, collectively, we small generators may pose one of the biggest health hazards to ourselves: municipal waste is mounting quietly and universally in unlined pits that allow a "witches' brew" of substances to leach into public groundwater supplies.

As the waste mounts, however, grassroots efforts to curb such groundwater pollution are beginning to stir in a number of states: Florida sponsors statewide collections of household wastes and local programs are being developed in Wisconsin, Washington, California, Michigan, and Ohio. But such efforts are slow to get underway, primarily because so few areas have hazardous waste disposal facilities—no one wants such a facility in the backyard. For the few facilities that do exist, some won't accept wastes containing ingredients—PCBs, for example—that would be bad for relations with the surrounding community, even when such items can be disposed of safely. And, as with any new venture on such a broad scale, it is hard for public interest groups to find money to organize collection, identification, and separation and to determine final disposal.

We are slowly learning that everyone who lives in an industrial society generates hazardous waste; however, it is not clear, in the short run, how we can dispose of our household share responsibly. In a universe of disposables, we can't dispose of them. But one thing is clear: If we are to continue to enjoy the benefits and conveniences of high technology, responsible waste management must become an integral part of our lives. It may boil down to taking a lesser risk of siting a hazardous waste facility in our "backyard"—it's our problem now.

Mary Kuhner

Hazardous Wastes Commonly Found in Household Trash

Item	Ignitible	Corrosive	Reactive	Toxic
Batteries		X		X
Shaving cream can			X	
Used motor oil	X			X
Empty spray paint can			X	
Drain cleaner		X		X
Empty insecticide spray can			X	X
Unused matches	X		X	
Used matches	X			
Unused drugs and medications				X
Unused fertilizer	X		X	X
Broken thermometer (silver colored)				X
Rug spot remover				X
Lacquer	X			X
Pet flea collar				X
Newspaper (colored inks)				X
Used spray deodorant can			X	
Hydrochloric acid (from school lab)		X		X

Source: *Environmental Education Program: Hazardous Waste Curriculum*, Missouri Department of Natural Resources, 1984, p. 20.

cannot be economically converted or are essentially indestructible. Therefore we still have waste disposal problems [6].

Modern Trends

Disposal or treatment of liquid and solid waste by federal, state, and municipal agencies costs billions of dollars every year. In fact, it is one of the most costly environmental expenditures of governments, accounting for the majority of total environmental expenditures [7].

All types of societies produce waste, but industrialization and urbanization have caused an ever-increasing effluence that has greatly compounded the problem of waste management. Although tremendous quantities of liquid and solid waste from municipal, industrial, and agricultural sources are being collected and recycled, treated or disposed of, new and innovative programs remain necessary if we are to keep ahead of what might be called a waste crisis. A popular idea is to consider the so-called waste as "resources out of place." Although we will probably never be able to recycle all waste, it seems apparent that the increasing cost of raw materials, energy, transportation, and land will make it financially feasible to recycle more resources as well as to reuse the land where wastes not recycled are buried, creating new land re-sources for development. This concept is known as sequential land use. For example, the city of Denver, Colorado, used abandoned sand and gravel pits for landfill sites that today are sites of a parking lot and the Denver Coliseum (Fig. 16.2). It is emphasized, however, that sequential land uses must be carefully selected. Urban housing, schools, hospitals, and other such construction should not be placed over old waste disposal sites.

Of particular importance is the growing awareness that many of our waste management programs simply involve moving waste from one site to the other and not really properly disposing of it. For example, waste from urban areas may be placed in landfills but eventually these may cause further problems from the production of methane gas or noxious liquids that leak from the site to contaminate the surrounding areas. Disposal sites are also capable of producing significant air pollution problems. Even the sewage treatment plants that have received so much state and federal assistance in construction are now found to be producing air pollutants, some of which are carcinogenic. It is safe to assume that waste management is going to be a public concern for a long time. Of particular importance will be the development of new methods of waste disposal that will not endanger the public health, create a nuisance, or create an environmental time bomb.

(a)

(b)

FIGURE 16.2
Example of sequential land use in Denver, Colorado. (a) Gravel pits were used as a sanitary landfill site as long ago as 1948. (b) Today the Denver Coliseum and parking lots cover the landfill site.

For discussion purposes, it is advantageous to break the management, treatment, and disposal of waste into several categories: solid-waste disposal, hazardous chemical waste management, radioactive waste management, and ocean dumping.

SOLID-WASTE DISPOSAL

Disposal of solid waste is primarily an urban problem. In the United States alone, urban areas produce about 640 million kilograms of solid waste each day. That amount of waste is sufficient to cover more than 1.6 km^2 of land every day to a depth of 3 m [8]. Table 16.1 lists the generalized composition of solid waste likely to end up at a disposal site. It is no surprise that paper is by far the most abundant of these solid wastes; however, we emphasize that this is only an average content, and considerable variation can be expected because such factors as land use, economic base, industrial activity, climate, and season of the year vary. In some areas, infectious wastes from hospitals and clinics can create problems if they are not properly sterilized before disposal (some hospitals have facilities to incinerate such wastes). In large urban areas a large amount of toxic materials may also end up at disposal sites. Some urban landfills are now being considered hazardous waste sites that may require costly cleanup.

The common methods of solid-waste disposal, summarized from a U.S. Geological Survey report,

include on-site disposal, composting, incineration, open dumps, and sanitary landfills [8]. Of these, the physical factors are most significant in siting of sanitary landfills. Without careful consideration of the soils, rocks, and hydrogeology, a landfill program may not function properly.

On-site Disposal

By far the most common on-site disposal method in urban areas is the mechanical grinding of kitchen food waste. Garbage disposal devices are installed in the waste-water pipe system from a kitchen sink, and the garbage is ground and flushed into the sewer system. This effectively reduces the amount of handling and quickly removes food waste, but final disposal is transferred to the sewage treatment plant where solids such as sewage sludge still must be disposed of [8]. Hazardous liquid chemicals may also be inadvertently or deliberately disposed of in sewers, requiring treatment plants to handle toxic materials. Illegal dumping in urban sewers has only recently been identified as a potential major problem.

Another method of on-site disposal is small-scale incineration. This method is common in institutions and apartment houses [8]. It requires constant attention and periodic maintenance to insure proper operation. In addition, the ash and other residue must be removed periodically and transported to a final disposal site.

TABLE 16.1
Generalized composition of solid waste likely to end up at a disposal site.

Type of Waste	Average (%)
Paper products	43.8
Food wastes	18.2
Metals	9.1
Glass and ceramics	9.0
Garden wastes	7.9
Rock, dirt, and ash	3.7
Plastics, rubber, and leather	3.1
Textiles	2.7
Wood	2.5
Total	100.0

Composting

Composting is a biochemical process in which organic materials decompose to a humuslike material. It is rapid, partial decomposition of moist, solid, organic waste by aerobic organisms. The process is generally carried out in the controlled environment of mechanical digesters [7]. Although composting is not common in the United States, it is popular in Europe and Asia, where intense farming creates a demand for the compost [7]. A major drawback of composting is the necessity to separate the organic material from the other waste. Therefore, it is probably economically advantageous only when organic material is collected separately from other waste [9].

Incineration

Incineration is the reduction of combustible waste to inert residue by burning at high temperatures (900°–1000°C). These temperatures are sufficient to consume all combustible material, leaving only ash and noncombustibles. Incineration effectively reduces the volume of waste that must be disposed of by 75–95% [8].

Advantages of incineration at the municipal level are twofold. First, it can effectively convert a large volume of combustible waste to a much smaller volume of ash to be disposed of at a landfill; and second, combustible waste can be used to supplement other fuels in generating electrical power. Disadvantages are that it requires high capital outlay, high maintenance cost, and additional handling to remove materials that do not burn, and it can cause air pollution. Because of the disadvantages, it seems unlikely that incineration will become a common way for urban areas to dispose of wastes [8]. Nevertheless, hundreds of incinerator plants are now operating in the United States, collectively burning over one hundred thousand metric tons of waste per day [8].

Open Dumps

Open dumps (Fig. 16.3) are the oldest and most common way of disposing of solid waste and, although thousands have been closed in recent years, many still are being used. In many cases, they are located wherever land is available, without regard to safety, health hazards, and aesthetic degradation. The waste is often piled as high as equipment allows. In some instances, the refuse is ignited and allowed to burn. In others, the refuse is periodically leveled and compacted [8].

Although well known, the potential for water pollution caused by indiscriminate dumping generally has not been studied sufficiently to determine the long-range effects of dumping or the extent of the pollution. One interesting example was reported from Surrey County, England, where household wastes were dumped into gravel pits, polluting the groundwater [8]. Refuse was dumped directly into 7–m–deep pits with about 4 m of water in the bottom. The maximum rate of dumping over a 6–year period (1954–60) was about

FIGURE 16.3
Open dump. Although still widely used, open dumps are gradually being replaced by sanitary landfills.

90,000 metric tons per year. After the dumping was terminated, observation of water quality revealed that chloride concentrations at the dump were 800 mg/L, over three times the maximum concentration of 250 mg/L considered safe for a public water supply. Adjacent gravel pits revealed chloride concentrations of 290 mg/L, and pits as far as 800 m away had concentrations of 70 ml/L. In addition, bacterial pollution also was detected within 800 m of the disposal site [8].

As a general rule, open dumps tend to create a nuisance by being unsightly, breeding pests, creating a health hazard, polluting the air, and sometimes polluting groundwater and surface water. Fortunately, open dumps are giving way to the better planned and managed sanitary landfills that have nearly taken their place.

Sanitary Landfill

A sanitary landfill as defined by the American Society of Civil Engineering is a method of solid-waste disposal that functions without creating a nuisance or hazard to public health or safety. Engineering principles are used to confine the waste to the smallest practical area, reduce it to the smallest practical volume, and cover it with a layer of compacted soil at the end of each day of operation, or more frequently if necessary. This covering of the waste with compacted soils makes the sanitary landfill "sanitary." The compacted layer effectively denies continued access to the waste by insects, rodents, and other animals. It also isolates the refuse from the air, thus minimizing the amount of surface water entering into and gas escaping from the wastes [9].

The sanitary landfill as we know it today emerged in the late 1930s; by 1960, more than 1400 cities disposed of their solid waste by this method. Two types are used: area landfill on relatively flat sites and depression landfill in natural or artificial gullies or pits. The depths of landfills vary from about 2 to 13 m. Normally, refuse is deposited, compacted, and covered by a minimum of 15 cm of compacted soil at the end of each day. The finishing cover is at least 50 cm of compacted soil designed to minimize infiltration of surface water [8].

Leachate The most significant possible hazard from a sanitary landfill is groundwater or surface-water pollution. If waste buried in a landfill comes into contact with water percolating down from the surface water or with groundwater moving laterally through the refuse, obnoxious, mineralized liquid capable of transporting bacterial pollutants called leachate is produced [10]. For example, two landfills dating from the 1930s and 1940s in Long Island, New York, have produced leachate plumes that are several hundred meters wide and have migrated several kilometers from the disposal site.

The nature and strength of leachate produced at a disposal site depends on the composition of the waste, the length of time that the infiltrated water is in contact with the refuse, and the amount of water that infiltrates or moves through the waste [8]. Compared to raw sewage and slaughterhouse waste, landfill leachate has a much higher concentration of pollutants. Fortunately, however, the amount of leachate produced from urban waste disposal is much less than the amount of raw sewage produced.

Site Selection Factors controlling the feasibility of sanitary landfills include topographic relief, location of the groundwater table, amount of precipitation, type of soil and rock, and the location of the disposal zone in the surface-water and groundwater flow system. The best sites are those in which natural conditions ensure reasonable safety in disposal of solid waste; conditions may be safe because of climatic, hydrologic, or geologic conditions, or combinations of these [11].

The best sites are in arid regions. Disposal conditions are relatively safe there because in a dry environment, regardless of whether the burial material is permeable or impermeable, little leachate is produced. On the other hand, in a humid environment some leachate will always be produced; therefore an acceptable level of leachate production must be established to determine the most favorable sites. What is acceptable varies with local water use, local regulations, and the ability of the natural hydrologic system to disperse, dilute, and otherwise degrade the leachate to a harmless state.

The most desirable site in a humid climate is shown in Figure 16.4. There the waste is buried

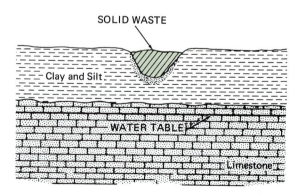

FIGURE 16.4
Most desirable landfill site in a humid environment. Waste is buried above the water table in a relatively impermeable environment. (After Schneider.)

above the water table in relatively impermeable clay and silt soils. Any leachate produced will remain in the vicinity of the site and be degraded by natural filtering action and base exchange of some ions between the clay and the leachate. This would also hold for high water table conditions, as is often the case in humid areas, provided the impermeable material is present. Ideally, a minimum of 10 m of relatively impermeable material is desired between the base of the landfill and the shallowest aquifer. If less than 10 m of relatively impermeable material is present, then the nature of the bedrock must be considered [12].

If the refuse is buried above the water table over a fractured-rock aquifer, as shown in Figure 16.5, the potential for serious pollution is low because the leachate is partly degraded by natural filtering as it moves down to the water table. Furthermore, the dispersion of contaminants is confined to the fracture zones [7]. However, if the water table were higher or the cover material thinner and permeable, then widespread groundwater pollution of the fractured-rock aquifer might result.

If the geologic environment of a landfill site is characterized by an inclined limestone-rock aquifer, overlaid by permeable sand and gravel soils, as shown in Figure 16.6, considerable contamination of the groundwater might result. This happens because the leachate moves quickly through the permeable soil and enters the limestone, where

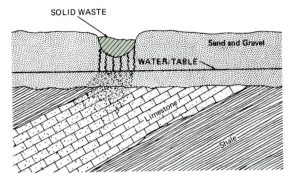

FIGURE 16.6
Solid-waste-disposal site where waste is buried above the water table in permeable material in which leachate can migrate down to fractured bedrock (limestone). The potential for groundwater pollution may be high because of the many open and connected fractures in the rock. (After Schneider.)

open fractures or cavities may transport the pollutants with little degradation other than dispersion and dilution. Of course if the inclined rock is all shale, which is impermeable, little pollution will result.

In summary, the following guidelines [12] should be followed in site selection of sanitary landfills:

- ☐ Limestone or highly fractured rock quarries and most sand and gravel pits make poor landfill sites because these earth materials are good aquifers.
- ☐ Swampy areas, unless properly drained to prevent disposal into standing water, make poor sites.
- ☐ Clay pits, if kept dry, may provide satisfactory sites.
- ☐ Flat upland areas are favorable sites provided an adequate layer of impermeable material such as clay is present above any aquifer.
- ☐ Floodplains likely to be periodically inundated by surface water should not be considered as acceptable sites for refuse disposal.
- ☐ Any permeable material with a high water table is probably an unfavorable site.
- ☐ In rough topography, the best sites are near the heads of gullies where surface water is at a minimum.

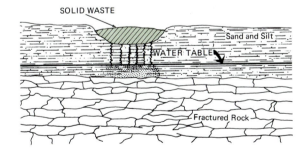

FIGURE 16.5
Waste disposal site where refuse is buried above the water table over a fractured rock aquifer. Potential for serious pollution is low because leachate is partially degraded by natural filtering as it moves down to the water table. (After Schneider.)

We emphasize that, while these guidelines are useful, they are not intended to preclude a hydrogeological investigation including drilling to obtain samples, permeability testing, and other tests to predict the movement of leachate from the buried refuse [9].

Monitoring Pollution   Once a site is chosen for a sanitary landfill, monitoring the movement of groundwater should begin before filling commences. After the operation starts, continued monitoring of the movement of leachate and gases should be continued as long as there is any possibility of pollution. This is particularly important after the site is completely filled and the permanent cover material is in place because a certain amount of settlement always occurs after a landfill is completed, and if small depressions form, then surface water may collect, infiltrate, and produce leachate. Therefore, monitoring and proper maintenance of an abandoned landfill will reduce its pollution potential [9].

Hazardous waste pollutants from a solid-waste-disposal site may enter the environment [13] by as many as six paths (Fig. 16.7):

1   Compounds volatilized in the soil and fill after placement such as methane, ammonia, hydrogen sulfide, and nitrogen gases may enter the atmosphere.
2   Heavy metals such as lead, chromium, and iron are retained in the soil.
3   Soluble material such as chloride, nitrate, and sulfate readily pass through the fill and soil to the groundwater system.
4   Overland runoff may pick up leachate and transport it into the surface-water network.
5   Some crops and cover plants growing in the disposal area may selectively take up heavy metals and other toxic materials to be passed up the food chain as people and animals eat them.
6   If the plant residue left in the field contains toxic substances, it will return these materials to the environment through soil-forming and runoff processes.

A thorough monitoring program will consider all six possible paths by which pollutants enter the environment. Generally, atmospheric pollution by gas from landfills is not a problem, and this trend probably will continue as more and more food wastes are ground and flushed into the sewage system. Many landfills have no surface runoff, and therefore monitoring of surface water is not necessary; however, thorough monitoring is required if overland runoff does occur. Monitoring of soil and plants should include periodic chemical analysis at prescribed sampling locations. A minimum of nine sample sites is recommended. It is advisable to collect plant samples at harvest time or, if plants are left in the field, after they become dormant. Soil sample sites should be analyzed twice a

FIGURE 16.7
Several ways that hazardous waste pollutants from a solid-waste-disposal site may enter the environment.

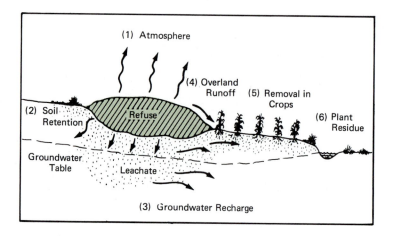

year—in early summer and late fall. The need for monitoring of groundwater quality through observation wells is minimal if the landfill is in relatively impermeable soil overlying dense permeable rock. In this case, leachate and groundwater movement may be less than 30 cm/yr. However, if permeable, water-bearing zones exist in the soil or bedrock, then observation wells to sample the water quality periodically and monitor the movement of the leachate are necessary [13]. It is important also to monitor water in the unsaturated zone above the water table. The purpose is to identify potential pollution problems *before* they reach and contaminate groundwater resources, where correction is very expensive.

HAZARDOUS CHEMICAL WASTE MANAGEMENT

The creation of new chemical compounds has proliferated tremendously in recent years. In the United States alone, approximately 1000 new chemicals are marketed each year and a total of about 50,000 chemicals are currently on the market. Although many of the chemicals have been beneficial to people, approximately 35,000 of the chemicals used in the United States are classified as being either definitely or potentially hazardous to the health of people (Table 16.2). The United States currently is generating several hundred metric tons of hazardous chemical waste per year.

In the recent past, as much as half of the total volume of wastes was being indiscriminately dumped [14].

Uncontrolled Sites

In the United States, there are 32,000–50,000 uncontrolled waste disposal sites, and of these probably 1200–2000 contain sufficient waste to be a serious threat to public health and the environment. For this reason, a number of scientists believe that management of hazardous chemical materials may be the most serious environmental problem ever to face the United States.

Uncontrolled dumping of chemical waste may pollute the soil and groundwater resources in several ways (Fig. 16.8). First, chemical waste may be stored in barrels either on the surface of the ground or buried at a disposal site. Eventually the barrels corrode and leak, with a potential to pollute surface, soil, and groundwater. Second, liquid chemical waste may be dumped in an unlined "lagoon," where the contaminated water may then percolate through the soil and rock and eventually to the groundwater table. Third, liquid chemical waste may be illegally dumped in deserted fields or even along dirt roads.

We must recognize that hazardous landfills and other sites for the disposal of chemical waste are not merely a potential problem. Examples from Nevada, Kentucky, New Jersey, and New York illustrate that they are affecting the lives of an ever-

TABLE 16.2
Examples of products we use and potentially hazardous waste they generate.

Products	Waste
Plastics	Organic chlorine compounds
Pesticides	Organic chlorine compounds, organic phosphate compounds
Medicines	Organic solvents and residues, heavy metals (mercury and zinc, for example)
Paints	Heavy metals, pigments, solvents, organic residues
Oil, gasoline, and other petroleum products	Oil, phenols, and other organic compounds; heavy metals; ammonia salts; acids; caustics
Metals	Heavy metals, fluorides, cyanides, acid and alkaline cleaners, solvents, pigments, abrasives, plating salts, oils, phenols
Leather	Heavy metals, organic solvents
Textiles	Heavy metals, dyes, organic chlorine compounds, solvents

Source: Council on Environmental Quality, 1983.

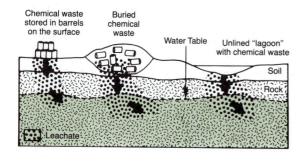

FIGURE 16.8
Ways that uncontrolled dumping of chemical waste may pollute soil and/or groundwater.

growing number of people. Waste generated from production of pesticides and organic solvents at Henderson, Nevada, may be contaminating Lake Mead, the water supply for Las Vegas; and at a location near Louisville, Kentucky, known as the "Valley of the Drums," thousands of leaking drums of waste chemicals stored on the surface or buried are oozing toxic materials.

Located near Elizabeth, New Jersey, are the remains of about 50,000 charred drums, stacked four high in places, next to a brick and steel building once owned by a now-bankrupt chemical corporation. The drums and other containers had been left to corrode for nearly ten years and many had been either improperly labeled or had been burned so that the nature of the chemicals could not be determined simply from outside markings. Leaking barrels allowed unknown waste to seep into an adjacent stream that eventually flows into the Hudson River. The site was so bad that clean-up efforts were very difficult—there is little precedent for what to do with unknown dangerous chemicals. Identification of some of the materials at the site showed that there were two containers of nitroglycerine, numerous barrels of biological agents, cylinders of phosgene and phosphoric gases (which are extremely volatile and ignite when exposed to air), as well as a variety of heavy metals, pesticides, and solvents, some of which are very toxic. It took months of work with a large crew of people to remove most of the material from the New Jersey site. Unfortunately, it is difficult to know if all the waste has been removed; additional

material may be buried at other locations that are more difficult to locate [15].

Responsible Management

In the United States, the federal government moved in 1976 to begin the management of hazardous waste with the passage of the Resource Conservation and Recovery Act, which is intended to provide for "cradle to grave" control of hazardous waste. At the heart of the act is the identification of hazardous wastes and their life cycles. Regulations are included to ensure that stringent record keeping and reporting are done to verify that wastes do not present a public nuisance or a public health problem. The act also identifies wastes considered hazardous in terms of several categories: materials that are highly toxic to people and other living things; wastes that may explode or ignite when exposed to air; wastes that are extremely corrosive; and wastes that are otherwise unstable.

Recognizing that there were a great number of waste disposal sites that presented hazards, Congress in 1980 passed the Environmental Response Compensation and Liability Act, which established a revolving fund (popularly called the Superfund) to clean up several hundred of the worst abandoned hazardous chemical waste disposal sites known to exist around the country. Although the fund has experienced significant management problems and is way behind schedule, a small number of sites have been treated. Unfortunately, the funds available are not sufficient to pay for decontamination of all the targeted sites. That would cost many times more, perhaps as much as one hundred billion dollars. Furthermore, there is concern that the present technology is not sufficiently advanced to treat all of the abandoned waste disposal sites and so the strategy may be to simply try to confine the waste to those sites until better disposal methods are developed. It seems apparent that abandoned disposal sites are likely to persist for some time to come.

Management of hazardous chemical waste includes several options, including recycling, on-site processing to recover byproducts with commercial value, microbial breakdown, chemical stabilization, high-temperature decomposition, incineration, and disposal by secure landfill or deep-well injection. A number of technological advances have been made in the field of toxic waste management, and as land disposal becomes more and more expensive, the trend toward on-site treatment that has recently started is likely to continue. However, on-site treatment will not eliminate all hazardous chemical waste; disposal will remain necessary. Table 16.3 compares hazardous waste reduction technology in terms of treatment and disposal. Notice that all of the technologies available will cause some environmental disruption. There is no one simple solution for all waste management issues.

Secure Landfill

The basic idea of the secure landfill is to confine the waste to a particular location, control the leachate that drains from the waste, and collect and treat the leachate. Figure 16.9 demonstrates these procedures. A dike and liner (made of clay or other impervious material such as plastic) confine the waste, and a system of internal drains concentrates the leachate in a collection basin from which it is pumped out and transported to a waste-water treatment plant. Designs of new facilities today often include multiple barriers consisting of several impermeable layers and filters. The function of impervious liners is to ensure that the leachate

does not contaminate soil and, in particular, groundwater resources. However, this type of waste-disposal procedure must have several monitor wells to alert personnel if and when leachates leak out of the system and present the possibility of contaminating water resources.

It has recently been argued that there is no such thing as a really secure landfill, implying that they all leak to some extent. This is probably true; impervious plastic liners, filters, and clay layers can fail, even with several backups, and drains can become clogged, causing overflow. Yet landfills that are carefully sited and engineered can minimize problems. Preferable sites are those with good natural barriers—thick clay deposits, an arid climate, or a deep water table—to migration of leachate. Nevertheless, land disposal should be used only for specific chemicals compatible and suitable for the method.

Land Application

Application of waste materials to the surface soil horizon is referred to as land application, land spreading, or land farming. Land application of waste may be a desirable method of treatment for certain biodegradable industrial waste. Such waste includes petroleum oily waste and certain organic chemical-plant waste. A good indicator of the usefulness of land application of a particular waste is

FIGURE 16.9
A secure landfill for hazardous chemical waste. The impervious liner and systems of drains are an integral part of the system to ensure that leachate does not escape from the disposal site. Monitoring in the unsaturated zone is important and involves periodic collection of soil water by using a suction device.

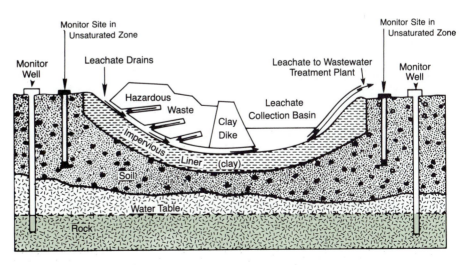

TABLE 16.3
Comparison of hazard reduction technologies.

	Disposal		Treatment		
	Landfills and Impoundments	Injection Wells	Incineration and Other Thermal Destruction	Emerging High-Temperature Decomposition[a]	Chemical Stabilization
Effectiveness: How well it contains or destroys hazardous characteristics	Low for volatiles, questionable for liquids; based on lab and field tests	High, based on theory but limited field data available	High, based on field tests except little data on specific constituents	Very high; commercial scale tests	High for many metals; based on lab tests
Reliability issues	Siting, construction, and operation. Uncertainties: long-term integrity of cells and cover, linear life less than life of toxic waste	Site history and geology, well depth, construction and operation	Monitoring uncertainties with respect to high degree of DRE: surrogate measures, PICs, incinerability[c]	Limited experience. Mobile units, on-site treatment avoids hauling risks. Operational simplicity	Some inorganics still soluble. Uncertain leachate test, surrogate for weathering
Environment media most effected	Surface and ground water	Surface and ground water	Air	Air	Groundwater
Least compatible wastes[b]	Liner reactive, highly toxic, mobile, persistent, and bioaccumulative	Reactive; corrosive; highly toxic, mobile, and persistent	Highly toxic and refractory organics, high heavy metals concentration	Some inorganics	Organics
Costs: Low, Mod., High	L–M	L	M–H (Coincin. = L)	M–H	M
Resource recovery potential	None	None	Energy and some acids	Energy and some metals	Possible building material

Source: Council on Environmental Quality, 1983.

[a]Molten salt, high-temperature fluid well, and plasma arc treatments.

[b]Wastes for which this method may be less effective for reducing exposure, relative to other technologies. Wastes listed do not necessarily denote common usage.

[c]DRE = destruction and removal effeciency. PIC = product of incomplete combustion.

the biopersistence (the measure of how long a material remains in the biosphere) of the materials. The greater or longer the biopersistence, the less suitable the wastes are for land application procedures. Land application is not an effective treatment or disposal method for inorganic substances such as salts and heavy metals [16].

Land application of biodegradable waste works because, when such materials are added to the soil, they are attacked by microflora (bacteria, molds, yeast, and other organisms) that decompose the waste material. The soil may thus be thought of as a microbial farm that constantly recycles organic and inorganic matter by breaking it down into more fundamental forms useful to other living things in the soil. Because the upper soil zone contains the largest microbial populations, land application is restricted to the uppermost 15–20 cm of the soil profile [16].

There are potential advantages to land application of waste. It is both effective and environmentally safe and has a reasonable cost. It is fairly simple and requires no dependence on high maintenance of failure-prone equipment. Finally, the method makes use of natural processes that recycle the waste [16].

Sites where land application of waste may be accomplished must be chosen carefully to ensure that the facility functions as designed. Of particular importance in siting of land application facilities are soil type, depth to groundwater, distance to streams and other surface discharges of water, rate of potential migration of waste, and topography. Because land application of waste produces a storage site in the soil for material such as metals, salts, dusts, and other materials that are not biodegradable, care must be taken to ensure that these materials do not build up to toxic levels. In particular, wastes that are ignitable, reactive, volatile, toxic to life, or incompatible with soil should not be applied. At the present time, approximately half of all petroleum oily wastes and some pharmaceutical and organic chemical wastes are being treated by land application methods [16].

The process of land application involves a microbial conversion that is a public service function of natural ecosystems. In some cases, the microbes do not use the compounds but merely convert them from toxic to nontoxic form. However, care must be taken because the opposite may also occur. That is, microbes may convert a less toxic form to a more toxic one. For example, microbes can convert inorganic mercury to methyl mercury, which is very toxic. Nevertheless, we can and do make use of natural processes when we treat or dispose of waste into streams, marshes, and agricultural or forest soils and when we use microbial activity in sewage treatment. All these methods work as long as the concentrations of the waste do not exceed the capacities of the microbes to utilize, break down, or change the waste.

Surface Impoundment

Natural topographic depressions and excavations by people have been used to hold hazardous liquid waste. These are primarily formed of soil or other surficial materials, but may be lined with manufactured materials such as plastic. The impoundment is designed to hold the waste; examples include aeration pits and lagoons at hazardous waste facilities. Surface impoundments have been criticized because they are especially prone to seepage, resulting in pollution of soil and groundwaters. Evaporation from surface impoundments can also produce an air pollution problem.

Deep-well Disposal

Another method of waste disposal is by injection into deep wells. The term "deep" refers to rock (not soil) that is below and completely isolated from all freshwater aquifers, thereby assuring that injection of waste will not contaminate or pollute existing or potential water supplies. This generally means that the waste is injected into a permeable rock layer several thousand meters below the surface in geologic basins confined above by relatively impervious, fracture-resistant rock, such as shale or salt deposits [6].

Deep-well injection of oil-field brine (salt water) has been important in the control of water pollution in oil fields for many years, and huge quantities of liquid waste (brine) pumped up with oil have been injected back into the rock. Today, more than four billion liters per day are pumped into subsurface rocks [17]. In recent years, the technique has been used more commonly for permanent storage of industrial waste deep underground. By mid-1973, there were several hundred deep-well disposal units pumping industrial waste underground [13]. A typical well is about 700 m deep, and wastes are pumped into a 60–m-thick zone at a rate of about 400 L/min [18].

Deep-well disposal of industrial wastes should not be viewed as a quick and easy solution to industrial waste problems [19]. Even where geologic conditions are favorable for deep-well disposal, there are natural restrictions because there are a limited number of suitable sites, and within these sites there is limited space for disposal of waste.

Problems with Deep-well Disposal Several problems associated with disposal of liquid waste in deep wells have been reported [18, 19]. Perhaps the best known are earthquakes caused by injection of waste from the Rocky Mountain Arsenal near Denver, Colorado. These earthquakes occurred between 1962 and 1965. The injection zone was fractured metamorphic rock at a depth of 3.6 km; the increased fluid pressure evidently initiated movement along the fractures. This is not a unique case. Similar initiations of earthquakes have been reported in oil fields in western Colorado, Texas, and Utah [18]. A similar activation of faults in

southern California caused by injection of fluids into the Inglewood oil field for secondary recovery is thought to have contributed to the failure of the Baldwin Hills Reservoir. In a different sort of incident, in 1968, a disposal well on the shore of Lake Erie in Pennsylvania "blew out," releasing several millions of liters of harmful chemicals from a paper plant into the lake [19]. Regardless of these incidents, most oil-field brine and industrial disposal wells are functioning as designed and are not degrading the near-surface environment.

Monitoring Disposal Wells An essential part of any disposal system is monitoring. It is very important to know exactly where the wastes are going, how stable they are, and how fast they are migrating. It is especially important in deep-well disposal where toxic or otherwise hazardous materials are involved.

Effective monitoring requires that the geology be precisely defined and mapped before initiation of the disposal program. Especially important is the locating of all freshwater-bearing zones and old or abandoned oil or gas wells that might allow the waste to migrate up to freshwater aquifers or to the surface (Fig. 16.10). A system of deep observation wells drilled into the disposal reservoir in the vicinity of the well can monitor the movement of waste, and shallow observation wells

FIGURE 16.10
How liquid waste might enter a freshwater aquifer through abandoned wells. This diagram illustrates why all abandoned wells should be located, and it emphasizes the necessity of monitoring wells. (After Irwin and Morton.)

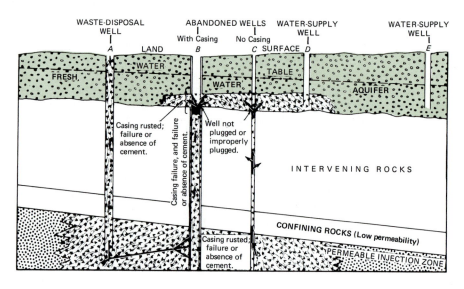

drilled into freshwater zones can monitor the water quality to quickly identify any upward migration of the waste.

Incineration of Hazardous Chemical Waste

Hazardous waste may be destroyed through use of high-temperature incineration. Because incineration produces an ash residue that must be buried in a landfill, it is considered an option of waste treatment. The technology used in incineration and other high-temperature decomposition or destruction is changing rapidly. Figure 16.11 shows a generalized diagram of one type of high-temperature incineration system that may be used to burn toxic waste. Waste—as liquid, solid, or sludge—

may enter the rotating combustion chamber, where it is rolled and burned. Ash from this burning process may be collected in a water tank while remaining gaseous materials move into a secondary combustion chamber, where the process is repeated. Finally, the remaining gas and particulates move through a scrubber system that eliminates surviving particulates and acid-forming components. Carbon dioxide, water, and air then are emitted from the stack. As shown in Figure 16.11, ash particulates and waste water are produced at various parts of the incineration process and these must be either treated or disposed of in a landfill. More advanced types of incineration and thermal decomposition of waste are being developed. One of these utilizes a molten salt bed that should be useful in destroying certain organic materials. Fi-

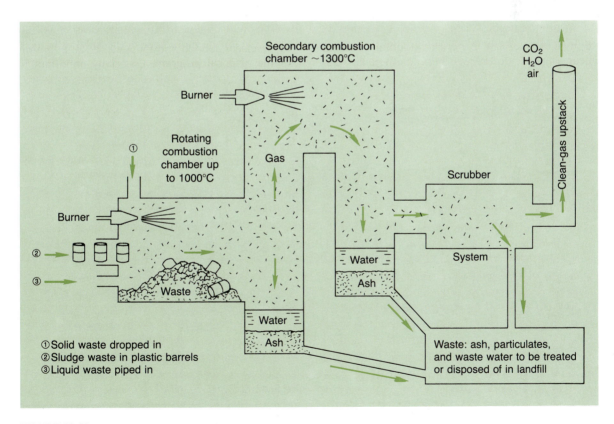

FIGURE 16.11
High-temperature incinerator system to burn toxic waste.

nally, other incineration techniques include liquid-injection incineration on land or sea, fluidized-bed systems, and multiple-hearth furnaces. Which incineration method is used for a particular waste depends upon the nature and composition of the waste and the temperature necessary to destroy the hazardous components. For example, the generalized incineration system shown in Figure 16.11 could be used to destroy PCBs.

Summary of Management Alternatives

Direct land disposal of hazardous waste is often not the best initial alternative. This results because there is a general consensus that even with extensive safeguards and state-of-the-art designs, land disposal alternatives cannot guarantee that the waste is contained and will not cause environmental disruption in the future. This holds true for all land disposal facilities, including landfill, surface

impoundments, land application, and injection wells. Pollution of air, land, surface water, and groundwater may result from failure of a land disposal site to contain hazardous waste. Pollution of groundwater is perhaps the most significant result of failure of a land disposal system because such pollution provides a convenient route for pollutants to reach humans and other living things. Figure 16.12 shows some of the paths that pollutants may take from land disposal sites to contaminate the environment. These paths include initiation of improper landfill procedures that eventually produce leakage and runoff to surface water or groundwater; seepage, runoff, or air emissions from unlined lagoons; percolation and seepage resulting from surface land application of waste to soils; leaks in pipes or other equipment associated with deep-well injection; and leaks from buried drums, tanks, or other containers.

The philosophy of handling hazardous chemical waste should be multifaceted and should include

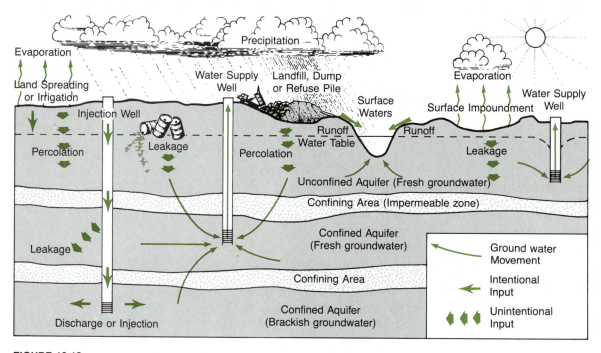

FIGURE 16.12
Examples of how land disposal/treatment methods of managing hazardous wastes may contaminate the environment. (Modified after Cox.)

such processes as source reduction, recycling and resource recovery, treatment, and incineration [20].

Source Reduction   Source reduction has the objective of reducing the amount of hazardous waste that is generated by a manufacturing or other process. For example, changes in the chemical processes involved, equipment used, raw materials used, or maintenance measures may be successfully employed to reduce either the amount or toxicity of the hazardous waste produced [20].

Recycling and Resource Recovery   Hazardous chemical waste may contain materials that can be successfully recovered for future use. For example, acids and solvents collect contaminants when they are used in manufacturing processes. These acids and solvents can be processed to remove the contaminants and can then be reused in the same or different manufacturing processes [20].

Treatment   Hazardous chemical waste may be treated by a variety of processes to change the physical or chemical composition of the waste in such a way as to reduce its toxic or hazardous characteristics. Examples include neutralizing acids, precipitation of heavy metals, and oxidation to break up hazardous chemical compounds [5].

Incineration   Hazardous chemical waste can be successfully destroyed by high-temperature incineration. Incineration is considered to be a waste treatment rather than a disposal method because the process produces an ash residue that can be disposed of in a landfill operation [16].

It has recently been argued that alternatives to land disposal are not being utilized to their full potential. That is, the volume of waste could be reduced and the remaining waste could be recycled or treated in some form prior to land disposal of the residues of the treatment processes [20]. Advantages to source reduction, recycling, treatment, and incineration are

- ☐ The actual waste that must be later disposed of is reduced to a much smaller volume.
- ☐ Useful chemicals may be reclaimed and reused.

- ☐ Treatment of wastes may make them less toxic and therefore less likely to cause problems in landfills.
- ☐ Because less waste is actually disposed of, there is less stress on the dwindling number of acceptable landfill sites.

RADIOACTIVE WASTE MANAGEMENT

Radioactive wastes are byproducts that must be expected as electricity is produced from nuclear reactors or weapons are produced from plutonium. Considering waste disposal procedures, radioactive waste may be grouped into two general categories: low-level waste and high-level waste. In addition, the tailings (materials that are removed by mining activity but which are not processed and which remain at the site) from uranium mines and mills must also be considered very hazardous (Fig. 16.13). The existence in the western United States of more than 20 million tons of abandoned tailings that will produce radiation for at least 100,000 years emphasizes the problem.

Low-level wastes contain sufficiently low concentrations or quantities of radioactivity that they do not present a significant environmental hazard if properly handled. Included here are a wide variety of items such as residuals or solutions from chemical processing; solid or liquid plant waste, sludges, and acids; and slightly contaminated equipment, tools, plastic, glass, wood, fabric, and other materials [21].

The philosophy for management of low-level waste is the previously mentioned "dilute and disperse." Experience suggests that low-level radioactive waste can be buried safely in carefully controlled and monitored near-surface burial areas in which the hydrologic and geologic conditions severely limit the migration of radioactivity [21].

High-level wastes are produced as fuel assemblages in nuclear reactors become contaminated with large quantities of fission products. This spent fuel must periodically be removed and reprocessed or disposed of. Fuel assemblies will probably not be reprocessed in the near future in the United States; therefore the present waste management

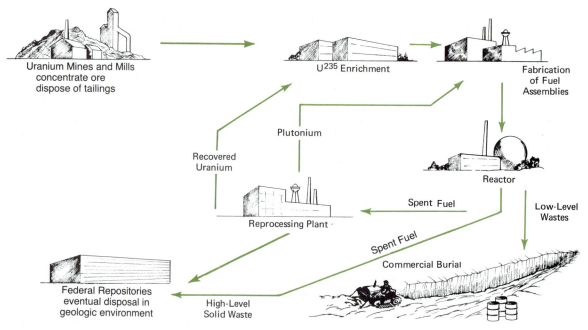

FIGURE 16.13
The nuclear fuel cycle. The United States does not now reprocess spent fuel. Disposal of tailings, which because of their large volume may be more toxic than high-level wastes, has been treated casually.

problems involve removal, transport, storage, and eventual disposal of spent fuel assemblies [22].

Hazardous radioactive materials produced from nuclear reactors include fission products such as krypton-85 (half-life of 10 years), strontium-90 (half-life of 28 years), and cesium-137 (half-life of 30 years). The half-life is the time required for the radioactivity to be reduced to one-half its original level. Generally, at least 10 half-lives (and preferably more) are minimal before a material is no longer considered a health hazard. Therefore, a mixture of the fission products mentioned above will require hundreds of years of confinement from the biosphere. Reactors also produce a small amount of plutonium-239 (half-life of 24,000 years), which is an artificial element. Because plutonium and the fission products must be isolated from the biological environment for very long periods of time (a quarter of a million years or longer) their permanent disposal is a geologic problem.

Scope of Disposal Problem

High-level waste is extremely toxic and a sense of urgency surrounds its disposal as the total volume of spent fuel assemblies slowly accumulates. But there is also conservative optimism that the waste disposal problem will be solved.

It has been projected that, if there is no disposal program, by the year 2000 several hundred thousand spent fuel elements from commercial reactors will be in storage awaiting disposal or eventual reprocessing to recover plutonium and unfissioned uranium. With reprocessing, solid high-level waste would occupy only several thousand cubic meters, a volume that would not even cover a football field to a depth of 1 m [22].

Production of plutonium for weapons also generates high-level waste. At present, several hundred thousand cubic meters of liquid and solid high-level waste are being stored at U.S. Department of Energy repositories at Hanford, Washington; Savannah River, Georgia; and Idaho Falls, Idaho.

Serious problems with radioactive waste have occurred with liquid waste buried in underground tanks. Sixteen leaks involving 1330 m³ were located at Hanford from 1958 to 1973. An incident in 1973 involved a leak of 437 m³ of low-temperature waste. Since then, improvements such as stronger, double-shelled storage tanks, reduction of the volume of liquid waste stored through the solidification program, and increased reserve capacity have been made. It is hoped these improvements will reduce the chance of future incidents [23].

Storage of high-level waste is at best a temporary solution that allows the federal government to meet its commitments for accepting waste. Regardless of how safe any "storage" program is, it requires continuous surveillance and periodic repair or replacement of tanks or vaults. Therefore it is desirable to develop more permanent "disposal" methods in which retrievability may be possible but not absolutely necessary.

Disposal in the Geologic Environment

There is fair agreement that the geologic environment can provide the most certain safe containment of high-level radioactive waste. Because "disposal" of high-level waste is a certain necessity, the federal government is actively pursuing and developing possible alternative methods. Although such concepts as disposal into polar ice caps and sediment in deep ocean basins are being explored, stable bedrock offers the most promise.

A comprehensive geologic disposal development program [22] should have a number of objectives:

☐ To identify sites that meet broad geologic criteria of tectonic stability and slow movement of groundwater with long flow paths to the surface
☐ To conduct intensive subsurface exploration of possible sites to positively determine geologic and hydrologic characteristics
☐ To predict future behavior of potential sites on the basis of present geologic and hydrologic situations and assumptions for future

changes in variables such as climate, groundwater flow, erosion, and tectonics
☐ To evaluate risk associated with various predictions
☐ To make a political decision as to whether the risks are acceptable to society

The Nuclear Waste Policy Act of 1982 initiated a comprehensive federal-state, high-level nuclear waste disposal program. The Department of Energy is responsible for investigating several potential sites. The act originally called for the President to recommend a site by 1987, but now it appears the date will be extended to at least 1990. The act also establishes the right of the host state to object to the site but such an objection can be overridden by agreement of both houses of Congress.

The geologic environment that received early attention for permanent disposal of high-level waste was bedded salt. There are several advantages to disposing of nuclear waste in salt:

☐ Salt is relatively dry and impervious to water.
☐ Fractures that might develop in salt tend to be self-healing.
☐ Salt permits the dissipation of larger quantities of heat than is possible in other rock types.
☐ Salt is approximately equal to concrete in its ability to shield harmful radiation.
☐ Salt has a high compressive strength (when dry) and generally is located in areas of low earthquake activity.
☐ Salt deposits are relatively abundant and use of some for waste disposal will cause a negligible resource loss.

Many scientists have studied the feasibility of salt as a disposal for high-level wastes. The general conclusion is that salt should effectively isolate the waste from the biosphere for hundreds of thousands of years [23]. On the other hand, salt has recently been criticized because it has a relatively low ability to absorb radioactive nuclides from the waste in an insoluble form. Furthermore, pockets of brine (very salty water) have been found in some salt deposits; this would certainly create serious problems and jeopardize waste retrieval if a repository were accidentally flooded. The presence of brine or other groundwater will also decrease the strength of salt. Finally, it is suspected that bedded salt may slowly flow and that even a centimeter of movement could be hazardous [24]. On the positive side again, careful site evaluation might enable identification of areas where brine might cause problems; waste could be wrapped in materials that readily adsorb harmful nuclides from the waste; and areas of potential flowage of salt might be predicted. Figure 16.14 is an idealized diagram of a possible disposal operation.

The potential of tuff (naturally welded volcanic ash) at the Nevada test site and basalt at Hanford, Washington, is also being evaluated for possible disposal of high-lead radioactive wastes. These sites are being evaluated not because these rocks are geologically favorable but because disposal would be on an existing nuclear reservation, minimizing potential social and political opposition. It has been argued that the Washington site is a poor choice because of the proximity of the Columbia River and problems of predicting groundwater

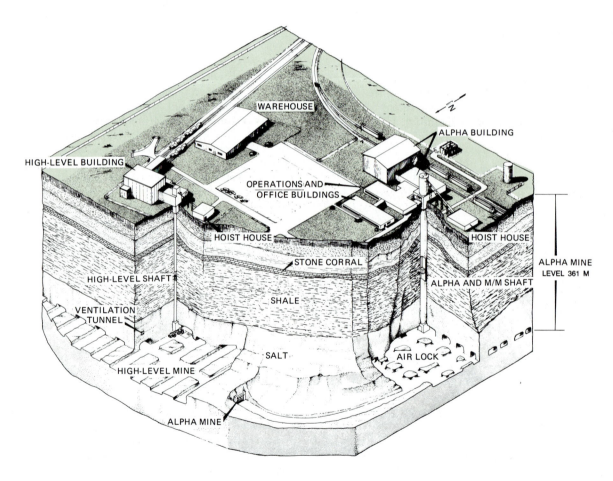

FEDERAL REPOSITORY

FIGURE 16.14
How underground bedded salt may be used as a disposal site for solidified, high-level radioactive wastes. (Courtesy of ERDA.)

movement through basalt. The tuff is a better prospect because of the present arid climate, low rate of groundwater recharge, little chance of surface-water contamination, and location far from population centers [24,25].

Salt domes in Mississippi and Texas are also being considered, but are a poor choice for high-level nuclear waste disposal sites because, in addition to having the same potential problems as bedded salt, they are not nearly as stable as bedded salt, having moved thousands of meters during emplacement of the dome. Furthermore, the salt domes tend to be located in a highly populated, wet-climate part of the country [24].

Long-term Safety

Disposal of radioactive wastes in the geologic environment is not a simple task. No rock or location is likely to be absolutely satisfactory and therefore we will have to choose the lesser evil. Furthermore, considering the long time that high-level wastes are dangerous and the many variables in the disposal process, it is likely that an accident will eventually happen [24]. Therefore it is critical to select a site where accidental contamination will not produce a potentially catastrophic problem.

Repositories for high-level waste currently being planned call for retrievability for 10 to as long as 50 years. This presents problems because it may necessitate a shallower disposal than would otherwise be necessary. There have been suggestions that the waste can be disposed of at shallow depths (up to several hundred meters) either in thick unsaturated zones or in shallow, carefully engineered and monitored tunnels in the arid western United States. Certainly these options also deserve careful consideration [23,26].

A major problem with the disposal of high-level radioactive waste remains: How credible are long-range (thousands to a few million years) geologic predictions [22]? There is no easy answer to this question because geologic processes vary over both time and space. Climates change over long periods of time, as do areas of erosion, deposition, and groundwater activity. For example, large earthquakes hundreds or even thousands of kilometers from a site may permanently change groundwater levels. The seismic record for most of the United States extends back in time for only a few hundred years and, therefore, estimates of future earthquake activity are tenuous at best. The bottom line is that geologists can suggest sites that have been relatively stable in the geologic past, but they cannot absolutely guarantee future stability. Therefore, decision makers (not geologists) need to evaluate the uncertainty of prediction in light of pressing political, economic, and social concerns [22]. These problems do not mean that the geologic environment is not suitable for safe containment of high-level radioactive waste, but care must be taken to ensure that the best possible decisions are made on this very critical and controversial issue.

OCEAN DUMPING*

The oceans of the world, 363 million square km^2 of water, cover more than 70% of Earth. They play a part in maintaining the world's environment by providing the water necessary to maintain the hydrologic cycle, contributing to the maintenance of the oxygen-carbon dioxide balance in the atmosphere and affecting global climate. In addition, the oceans are very valuable to people, providing such necessities as foods and minerals.

It seems reasonable that such an important resource as the ocean would receive preferential treatment, yet in 1968 alone, more than 43 million metric tons of waste were dumped at 246 sites off the coasts of the United States. Federal legislation and regulation by the Environmental Protection Agency in 1972 reduced the number of sites to 188, but ocean dumping continues to degrade the oceanic environment [7]. Furthermore, if population growth in coastal regions continues as expected, increased amounts of waste can be expected to adversely impact the oceans.

The types of wastes [27] that have been dumped in the oceans off the United States include the following: dredge spoils—solid materials such as sand, silt, clay, rock, and pollutants deposited

*Discussion of ocean dumping is summarized in part from *Ocean dumping: a national policy.* (Washington, D.C.: Council on Environmental Quality, 1970, pp. 1–25.)

from industrial and municipal discharges and re-moved from the bottom of water bodies generally to improve navigation; industrial waste—acids, re-finery wastes, paper mill wastes, pesticide wastes, and assorted liquid wastes; sewage sludge—solid material (sludge) that remains after municipal wastewater treatment; construction and demoli-tion debris—cinder block, plaster, excavation dirt, stone, tile, and other materials; solid waste—re-fuse, garbage, or trash; explosives; and radioactive waste.

The 1972 Marine Protection Research and Sanc-tuaries Act prohibits ocean dumping of radiologi-cal, chemical, and biological warfare agents and any high-level radioactive waste. Furthermore, it provides for regulation of all other waste disposal in the oceans off the United States by the Environ-mental Protection Agency or, in the case of dredge spoil, by the U.S. Army Corps of Engineers. In ad-dition to materials prohibited by law from being dumped, the Environmental Protection Agency has prohibited material whose effect on marine eco-systems cannot be determined; persistent inert materials that float or remain suspended, unless they are processed to ensure that they sink and re-main on the bottom; and material containing more than trace concentrations of mercury and mercury compounds, cadmium and cadmium compounds, organohalogen compounds (organic compounds of chlorine, fluorine, and iodine, etc.), and com-pounds that may form from such substances in the oceanic environment; as well as crude oil, fuel oil, heavy diesel oil, lubricating oils, and hydraulic fluids. The Environmental Protection Agency also requires special permits and strictly regulated dumping of arsenic, beryllium, chromium, and lead; low-level nuclear waste; organo-silicon com-pounds; organic chemicals; and petrochemicals. A major objective of the act is to prevent ocean dumping of wastes that, before recent federal laws were enacted, were discharged into rivers and the atmosphere [7].

Ocean Dumping and Pollution

Ocean dumping contributes to the larger problem of ocean pollution, which has seriously damaged the marine environment and caused a health haz-

FIGURE 16.15
Ocean dumping damages the marine environment, pol-lutes beaches and harbors, and poses a hazard to people as well as to marine life.

ard to people in some areas (Fig. 16.15). Shellfish have been found to contain pathogens such as polio virus and hepatitis, and at least 20% of the nation's commercial shellfish beds have been closed because of pollution. Beaches and bays have been closed to recreational uses. Lifeless zones in the marine environment have been cre-ated. Heavy kills of fish and other organisms have occurred and profound changes in marine ecosys-tems have taken place [27].

Major impacts of marine pollution on oceanic life include the following: killing or retarding growth, vitality, and reproductivity of marine or-ganisms by toxic pollutants; reduction of dissolved oxygen necessary for marine life because of in-creased oxygen demand from organic decomposi-tion of wastes; biostimulation by nutrient-rich waste, causing excessive blooms of algae in shallow waters of estuaries, bays, and parts of the continental shelf, resulting in depletion of oxygen and subsequent killing of algae that may wash up and pollute coastal areas; and habitat change caused by waste-disposal practices that subtly or drastically change entire marine ecosystems [27].

Major impacts on people and society caused by marine pollution include the following: production of a public health hazard caused by marine organisms transmitting disease to people; loss of visual and other amenities as beaches and harbors become polluted by solid waste, oil, and other materials; and economic loss. Loss of shellfish from pollution in the United States amounts to many millions of dollars per year. In addition, a great deal of money is being spent cleaning solid waste, liquid waste, and other pollutants in the coastal areas [27].

Ocean Dumping: The Conflict

It is unfortunate that the people interested in ocean dumping and those interested in harvesting marine resources such as shellfish and finned fish both prefer to do their jobs near the shore—the former because of convenience and transportation costs and the latter because of the richness of near-shore fisheries. The city of Los Angeles provides a classic example of the conflict.

For over 30 years, sewage and sewage sludge have been dumped several miles offshore into Santa Monica Bay. The rate of flow in recent years has been about 400 million gallons per day, only about 25% of which receive secondary treatment. Los Angeles successfully fought state and federal regulations for 14 years to avoid having to provide secondary treatment for all sewage.

It is now recognized that the bay is seriously polluted by the sewage and by earlier waste disposal going back to the 1940s, when oil refinery wastes, cyanide, and polychlorinated biphenyls (PCBs) began to be introduced into the marine environment. Concerns over potential health-related issues have convinced local government officials that the sewage should all receive secondary treatment. The Los Angeles City Council's recent decision to spend an additional 172 million dollars for

secondary treatment ends a long environmental battle.

Alternatives to Ocean Dumping

The ultimate solution to the problem of ocean dumping is development of economically feasible and environmentally safe alternatives. To emphasize some of the possibilities, we will discuss some of the alternatives to ocean dumping of dredge spoils and sewage sludge.

Disposal of dredge spoils represents the vast majority of all ocean dumping. Such spoils are removed primarily to improve navigation and are usually redeposited only a few kilometers away. Approximately one-third are seriously polluted with heavy metals such as cadmium, chromium, lead, and nickel, as well as other industrial, municipal, and agricultural wastes. As a result, disposal in the marine environment can be a significant source of pollution [27].

The long-range alternative to disposal of dredge spoils is phasing out ocean disposal of polluted dredge spoils; however, this is not possible at present because of the great volume involved. Until land-base disposal can handle the necessary volume, interim techniques should be developed, such as determining which spoils are polluted before disposal and then hauling the polluted spoils farther from the dredging site to a safe disposal site. The main disadvantage here is the increased cost of longer hauls [27].

Environmental problems from disposal of sewage sludge at sea are important in terms of their volume, toxic and possibly pathogenetic materials involved, and possible effects on marine life. Based on a very conservative estimate of 54 g of sludge generated per person per day, by the year 2000 more than 1.8 million metric tons of sludge will be generated in the coastal regions, representing an increase of 50% in 30 years. Most sewage sludge is currently disposed of on land or is incinerated, but in some areas tremendous quantities are disposed of by ocean dumping [27].

Alternatives to ocean dumping of sewage sludge in coastal regions include various methods of land disposal. Unfortunately, land disposal is considerably more expensive than near-shore marine disposal. However, if the sludge is digested (treated to control odors and pathogens) or barged long distances from shore, the cost becomes comparable, and land disposal may even be cheaper [27].

Perhaps the best long-range alternative to ocean dumping is the use of digested sludge for land reclamation, especially strip-mined land reclamation. Many strip mines in other areas are in great need of reclamation, and the nutrient value and organic material in this sludge can improve lands with undesirable low-productivity soils by improving soil texture, composition, and nutrient levels. Unfortunately, there are limits on how much sludge can be realistically utilized and, as noted, some sludge contains toxic materials.

SUMMARY

The history of waste-disposal practices since the industrial revolution has been from a practice of "dilution and dispersion" to a new concept of "concentrate, contain, and recycle."

The most common method for disposal of urban waste is the sanitary landfill. However, around many large cities, space for landfills is hard to find and few people wish to live near any waste disposal operation. We may be headed toward a disposal crisis if new methods are not developed soon. One trend is toward more incineration of waste—a process that reduces the volume of material sent to a landfill.

Hazardous chemical waste management may be the most serious environmental problem in the United States. Hundreds or even thousands of uncontrolled disposal sites may be time bombs that eventually will cause serious public health problems. Being realistic, we know we are going to continue to produce hazardous chemical wastes. Therefore, it is imperative that safe disposal methods be developed and used. Management of hazardous chemical wastes includes several options, including on-site processing to recover byproducts with commercial value, microbial breakdown, chemical stabilization, incineration and disposal by secure landfill, and deep-well injection.

Radioactive-waste management presents a serious and ever-increasing problem. High-level wastes that remain hazardous for thousands of years and currently are being stored will have to be permanently disposed of eventually. A likely method is disposal in a carefully and continuously monitored appropriate geologic environment, possibly bedded salt. Apparently, low-level waste can be buried safely and carefully controlled and monitored at near-surface sites.

Ocean dumping can be a significant source of marine pollution, and efforts to control indiscriminate dumping are in effect. Alternatives to ocean dumping of materials such as polluted dredge spoils, sewage sludge, and other potentially hazardous materials are being developed, but in many cases such alternatives are not yet practical or economically feasible.

STUDY QUESTIONS

1 Have you ever contributed to the hazardous waste problem through disposal methods practiced in your home, school laboratory, or other location? If so, how big a problem do you think such events are? For example, how bad is it to dump paint thinner down a drain?

2 Discuss why it is so difficult to ensure safe land disposal of hazardous waste.

3 Would you approve the siting of a waste disposal facility in your part of town? If not, why not, and where do you think such facilities should be sited?

4 Discuss why there seems to be a trend toward on-site disposal rather than land disposal of hazardous waste. Consider physical, biological, social, legal, and economic aspects of the question.

5 Is government doing enough about cleaning up abandoned hazardous waste dumps? Do private citizens have a role in choosing where cleanup funds should be allocated?

6 Considering how much waste has been dumped in the near-shore marine environment, how safe is it to swim in bays and estuaries near large cities?

7 What makes radioactive waste so different from other hazardous materials we deal with? Do you think the geologic environment can contain radioactive waste? What are other alternatives?

8 Do you think we should collect household waste and burn it in special incinerators to make electrical energy? What problems do you see with this and what advantages are there over other disposal options?

9 Lots of jobs will be available in the next few years in hazardous waste monitoring and disposal. Would you take such a position? If not, why not? If yes, do you feel secure that your health will not be jeopardized?

10 Should companies that dumped hazardous waste years ago when the problem was not understood or recognized be held liable today for health-related problems their dump may have contributed to?

11 Suppose you found that the home you had been living in for 15 years is located over a buried waste disposal site. What would you personally do, and what kinds of studies could be done to evaluate the potential problem?

FURTHER READING

BREDEHOEFT, J. D.; ENGLAND, A. W; STEWART, D. B.; TRASK, J. J; and WINOGRAD, I. J. 1978. *Geologic disposal of high-level radioactive wastes—Earth science perspectives.* U.S. Geological Survey Circular 779.

ELLIOT, J. 1980. Lessons from Love Canal. *Journal of the American Medical Association* 240: 2033–34, 2040.

HUDDLESTON, R. L. 1979. Solid-waste disposal: Landfarming. *Chemical Engineering* 86(5): 119–124.

MacFADYEN, J. T. 1985. Where will all the garbage go? *The Atlantic* 225 (3): 29–38.

PIPER, A. M. 1970. *Disposal of liquid wastes by injection underground: Neither myth nor millennium.* U.S. Geological Survey Circular 631.

SCHNEIDER, W. J. 1970. *Hydraulic implications of solid-waste disposal.* U.S. Geological Survey Circular 601F.

WALKER, W. H. 1974. Monitoring toxic chemical pollution from land disposal sites in humid regions. *Ground Water* 12: 213–18.

V
The Environmental Process

17
Natural Hazards

- Most "natural hazards" are "natural processes." They become hazards when we interact in a negative way with natural processes.
- The magnitude and frequency of natural hazardous processes depend on climate, geology, vegetation, and other factors. In general, there is an inverse relationship between the magnitude of an event and its frequency; most of the processes active in changing Earth's surface and causing trouble to people are of moderate magnitude and frequency.
- Activities of humans influence many natural processes to produce or intensify hazards—flooding, erosion, earthquakes, fire. Some natural hazards are independent of human activity—volcanic eruptions, hurricanes, tornadoes, expansive soils.
- Prediction of hazards involves identifying locations, determining probability of occurrence, noting precursor events, forecasting, and warning.

- How scientists interact with the media and public in warnings and risk assessment is important in how a hazard is perceived.
- Major adjustments to natural hazards and processes include land-use planning, disaster preparedness, insurance, evacuation, reconstruction, and bearing the loss.
- Natural processes/hazards can yield improvements: flooding may supply nutrients to a floodplain; earthquake faults can dam groundwater, producing a water resource; volcanic ash adds nutrients to soil; earthquakes and related uplift produce scenic mountains; and so on.
- Relatively extreme rare events of high magnitude are significant to long-term ecosystem stability and evolution. Catastrophic events may be triggering mechanisms for ecological succession.
- Ecosystems without disturbance are unnatural; ecosystems continually subject to exteme disturbance cannot persist.

MT. HELGAFELL AND MT. ST. HELENS

People are basically optimistic in their outlook toward natural hazards. This attitude prevails in part because many processes that are hazardous to people occur relatively infrequently, and when a hazardous process does occur, it affects only a few people (relative to the world population).

The experience of about 5000 Icelandic people on the island of Heimaey is a good example of people responding to a serious, destructive hazard. In January of 1973, the dormant volcano Mt. Helgafell came alive, and subsequent eruptions nearly buried the town of Vestmannaeyjar in ash and lava flows (Fig. 17.1). The harbor, a major fishing port, was nearly blocked, and with the exception of about 300 town officials, firefighters, and police, the inhabitants were evacuated. Those people who remained behind to fight the volcano began the

world's most ambitious attempt to stop slow-moving lava flows. The method they used is known as hydraulic chilling—the application of large amounts of water to slowly advancing lava flows. Fortunately, the flow was slow enough and cool enough at its surface that heavy equipment could be driven up and pipes placed at strategic locations. Watering at each location lasted several weeks, or until the steam stopped coming out of the lava in that particular area. In the beginning, watering had little effect, but then that part of the flow began to slow down. Following the outpouring of lava, which stopped in June of 1973, the harbor was still usable. In fact, by fortuitous circumstances, the shape of the harbor was actually improved, because the new rock provided additional protection from the sea (Fig 17.1b) [1,2].

In July 1973, the people returned to the island to survey the damage and to estimate the chances of rebuilding their lives and the town. The situa-

(a)

(b)

FIGURE 17.1
Lava flow from the eruption of Mt. Helgafell on the island of Heimaey, Iceland, in 1973, dramatically altered the contour of the island: (a) 1960; (b) 1973.

tion was grim—ash had drifted up to 4 m thick and covered much of the island and town. Furthermore, molten lava was still steaming near the volcano. The first task the returnees undertook was to dig out their homes and shops, salvaging what they could. They then used the same volcanic debris that had buried their town to pave new roads and an area for an airport that would allow materials to be moved in and distributed. They decided to take advantage of the volcano, and by January of 1974 the first home was heated by heat from the cooling lava [1,2].

Unfortunately, all volcanoes are not as calm as Mt. Helgafell was in 1973. At 8:32 A.M. on May 18, 1980, an earthquake registering 5.0 on the Richter scale was recorded on Mt. St. Helens in the southwest corner of the state of Washington. That earthquake triggered a large landslide-avalanche that involved the entire north flank of the mountain, on which a bulge had been growing at the rate of about 1.5 m/day for a period of several weeks. The avalanche shot down the north flank of the mountain, displacing water in nearby Spirit Lake, struck and overtopped a ridge 8 km to the north, and then made an abrupt turn and moved for a distance of 18 km down the Toutle River. The avalanche released internal pressure, and Mt. St. Helens erupted with a lateral blast directly from the area occupied by the bulge. At nearly the same time, a large vertical cloud quickly rose to an altitude of approximately 19 km (Fig. 17.2). Eruption of the volcano's vertical column continued for more than 9 hours, and large volumes of volcanic ash fell on a wide region of Washington, northern Idaho, and western and central Montana. During the 9 hours of eruption a number of pyroclastic flows (hot mixtures of gas, volcanic ash, and other debris) swept down the northern slope of the volcano.

On the northern slope of the volcano, the upper part of the north fork of the Toutle River basin was devastated as forested slopes were transformed into a gray, hummocky landscape consisting of volcanic ash, rocks, blocks of melting glacial ice, narrow gullies, and hot steaming pits. Several mudflows, consisting of mixtures of water, volcanic ash, rock, and organic debris such as logs, occurred shortly after the start of the eruption. The flows and accompanying flood raced down the valleys of the north and south forks of the Toutle

River at estimated speeds of 29–55 km/hr. Water levels in the river reached at least 4 m above flood stage, and nearly all bridges along the river were destroyed. The hot mud quickly raised the temperature of the Toutle River to as high as 38°C. Mud, logs, and boulders were carried 70 km downstream and deposited into the Cowlitz River, to be eventually deposited 28 km farther downstream in the Columbia River. Nearly 40 million m^3 of material was dumped into the Columbia River, reducing the depth of the shipping channel from a normal 12 m to 4.3 m over a distance of about 6 km [3].

When the volcano could again be viewed following the eruption, it was observed that the maximum altitude of the volcano was reduced by 350–400 m and that the mountain, originally symmetrical, was now a huge, steep-walled amphitheater facing northward. The landslide-avalanche, horizontal blast, pyroclastic flows, and mudflows devastated a large area (nearly 400 km^2), killing 24 persons and leaving 44 others missing and presumed dead. Over 100 homes were destroyed by the flooding, and several billion board feet of timber were flattened by the blast. The total damage is estimated to be several billion dollars, but long-term damage to fisheries and other resources is difficult to estimate [3].

Before the eruption, the slopes of Mt. St. Helens were forested with Douglas fir and western hemlock below 1200 m elevation, mountain hemlock and true firs above. The stands were valuable timber.

Following the eruption, the landscape was devastated and seemed devoid of life, but to the surprise of almost everyone, including ecologists, life returned rapidly. Where the debris was not too thick above the original soil, fireweed and other plants, common in clearcut forest areas, sprouted. Around fallen trees, spring flowers, like trillium, appeared, and trees sprouted in areas protected from the blast and heat. Life was returning, and the process of ecological succession—the establishment of an ecosystem and its ecological community—had begun on the mountain.

As the story of Mt. St. Helens illustrates, ecosystems are subjected to natural hazards and are capable of recovering from them. Indeed, throughout the history of Earth these hazards have been common enough so that some species are adapted

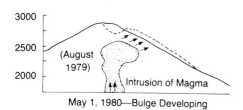

(August 1979)

Intrusion of Magma

May 1, 1980—Bulge Developing

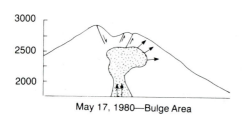

May 17, 1980—Bulge Area

Elevation (m)

May 18, 1980—Avalanche
8:32 Eruption Starts

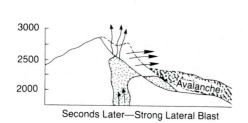

Avalanche

Seconds Later—Strong Lateral Blast

(a)

(b)

(c)

510

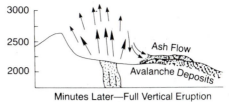

Minutes Later—Full Vertical Eruption

(d)

to them. These early successional species require disturbance to persist.

The two case histories of Mt. St. Helens and Mt. Helgafell are quite different in terms of the magnitude of the volcanic event involved. Certainly, planning for volcanic hazards in Iceland may be quite different than in the Cascades, where more explosive eruptions may be likely. Mt. St. Helens is a valuable example of the kind of problems that can be expected during and after a high-magnitude physical event that disrupts a large area. As such, the experience should help in devising emergency plans for future volcanic eruptions and other hazardous events such as large earthquakes. On the other hand, the Icelandic event is encouraging because it points out the necessity to learn to live with natural processes and hazards, be they floods, earthquakes, or volcanic eruptions. How we live with these natural processes, however, will vary with the expected type of event. Thus evacuation of a very large area is necessary if an explosive eruption is likely. However, if an eruption is likely to be characterized by volcanic ash and slow-moving lava flow, then there may be time to partially control the process advantageously, as was done in Iceland. Throughout the rest of this chapter we will focus on how people and other life forms adjust to natural hazards.

NATURAL HAZARD OR NATURAL PROCESS?

There have always been natural earth processes that are hazardous to people. These natural hazards must be recognized. They must be avoided where possible, and their threat to human life and property must be minimized.

We established from our discussion of uniformitarianism in Chapter 2 that present physical and biological processes have been operating a good deal longer than people have been on Earth. Therefore, people have always had to contend with processes that make their lives difficult. Surprisingly, however, *Homo sapiens* appears to have evolved during recent ice ages—a period of harsh climates and environments.

Many physical processes continue to cause loss of life and property damage, including earth-

quakes, landslides, and flooding of coastal or floodplain areas. In addition, biological processes often mix with physical events to produce hazards. For example, after earthquakes and floods, water may be contaminated by bacteria and the rate of the spread of diseases increased. The magnitude (intensity of energy released) and frequency (recurrence interval) of natural, hazardous processes depend on such factors as the region's climate, geology, and vegetation. In general, there is an inverse relationship between the magnitude of an event and its frequency. That is, the larger the flood, the less frequently it occurs. Studies have demonstrated generally that most of the work in forming Earth's surface is done by processes of moderate magnitude and frequency rather than by processes with low magnitude and high frequency or by extreme events of high magnitude and low frequency. As an analogy to the magnitude-frequency concept, consider the work in logging a forest done by termites, people, and elephants, The termites are small but work quite steadily; the people work less often than termites but are stronger. Given enough time, termites are able to fell most of the trees in the forest and therefore do a great deal of work. Imagine several elephants that rarely visit the forests, but when they do are capable of knocking down many trees. We can see from this analogy that most of the work is done by people, who work at a rather moderate expenditure of energy and time, rather than by the termites' frequent but low expenditure of energy or the elephants' infrequent high expenditure of energy.

Natural hazards are nothing more than natural processes. They become hazards only when people live or work in areas where these processes occur naturally. The naturalness of these hazards is a philosophical barrier that we encounter when we try to minimize their adverse effects. It is the environmental scientist's job, therefore, to identify potentially hazardous processes and make this information available to planners and decision makers so that they can formulate various alternatives to avoid or minimize the threat to human life or property.

Natural processes (hazards) have always influenced all forms of life, and life on Earth has adapted to the occurrence of such events. Some species are especially adapted to taking advantage of the environmental conditions that exist soon after such a natural event. In attempting to conserve such species, we must take their natural adaptations into account.

The Natural Service Function of Hazardous Processes

It is ironic that natural processes or hazards, while taking human life and destroying property, also perform important service functions. For example, flooding supplies nutrients to the floodplains, as in the case of the Mississippi River and the Nile Delta prior to the building of the Aswan Dam. Flooding also causes erosion on mountain slopes, delivering sediment to beaches from rivers and flushing pollutants from estuaries in the coastal environment.

Landslides also may perform some natural service functions, particularly in the formation of lakes. Landslide debris may form dams, making lakes in mountainous areas. These lakes provide valuable water storage and are an important aesthetic resource.

Volcanic eruptions, while having the potential to produce real catastrophes, perform numerous public service functions. New land can be created, as in the Hawaiian Islands, which are completely volcanic in origin. In addition, nutrient-rich volcanic ash may settle on soils and quickly become incorporated in them. Earthquakes also perform a number of natural service functions. For example, groundwater barriers may be created when rocks are pulverized to form a clay zone known as **fault gouge.** There are numerous cases where groundwater has been dammed upslope from a fault, producing a water resource. Earthquakes are also important in mountain building and thus are directly responsible for many of the scenic resources of the western United States.

NATIONAL AND REGIONAL OVERVIEW

Evaluation of mean annual losses in the United States from several natural hazards provides insight into the magnitude of the problem. Table 17.1 summarizes losses from selected natural hazards or processes for the United States. The largest loss of life every year is associated with tornadoes and windstorms, but other processes such as lightning strikes, floods, and hurricanes also take a heavy toll in human life. In terms of cost per year, expansive soils (expansion and contraction of soils due to changing water content) are, surprisingly, the greatest hazard, about twice as costly as floods, landslides, and frost and freeze effects.

TABLE 17.1
Effects of selected natural hazards/processes in the United States.

Hazard	Deaths per Year	Cost per Year (million $)	Occurrence Influenced by Human Use	Catastrophe Potential[b]
Flood	86	1200	Yes	H
Earthquake[a]	50+?	130+?	Yes	H
Landslide	25	1000	Yes	M
Volcano[a]	<1	20	No	H
Coastal erosion	0	330	Yes	L
Expansive soils	0	2200	No	L
Hurricane	55	510	Perhaps	H
Tornado and windstorm	218	550	Perhaps	H
Lightning	120	110	Perhaps	L
Drought	0	792	Perhaps	M
Frost and freeze	0	1300	Yes	L

Source: Modified after White and Haas.
[a]Estimate based on recent or predicted loss over 150-year period. Actual loss of life and/or property could be much greater.
[b]Catastrophe potential: high (H), medium (M), low (L).

An important aspect of all natural hazards and processes is the potential to produce a catastrophe, defined as any situation in which the damages to people, property, or society in general are sufficient that recovery and/or rehabilitation is a long, involved process [4]. Those processes most likely to produce a catastrophe include floods, hurricanes, tornadoes, tsunamis (seismic sea waves), volcanoes, and large fires (Table 17.1). Other processes, such as landslides, generally cover a smaller area and may have only a moderate catastrophe potential. Drought, which may cover a wide area but generally involves plenty of warning time, also has a moderate catastrophe potential. Processes with a low catastrophe potential include coastal erosion, frost, lightning strikes, and expansive soils [4].

Loss of life and property damage in the United

FIGURE 17.3
Loss of life and property damages from four natural processes over a 50-year period. Loss of life has decreased while property damage has increased. The potential for catastrophe has increased because more people live in high-risk areas. (From Council on Environmental Quality, 1981.)

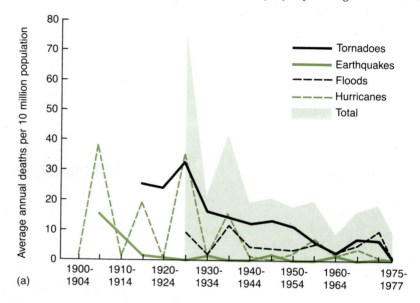

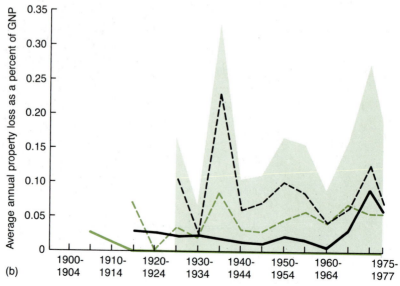

States from natural hazards shift with time because of changes in land-use patterns, which influence people to develop on marginal lands; urbanization, which changes the physical properties of earth materials; and increasing population. Figure 17.3 summarizes in a qualitative way some of these changes. Damage from most hazards in the United States is increasing, but the number of deaths from many are decreasing due to better warning, forecasting, and prediction of some hazards.

HUMAN USE AND HAZARDS

Many natural processes can be influenced by people's activities, as shown in Table 17.1. In this section we will discuss a few specific cases where human activities affect these processes.

Urban Flooding

Flooding in urban areas may be greatly increased by urbanization. Small drainage basins of a few square kilometers are most susceptible to hydrologic changes associated with urbanization. Hydrologically speaking, urbanization means an increase in the area rendered impermeable (covered by parking lots, streets, and roofs), increasing runoff because less water is able to infiltrate the soil. Urban areas also may be drained by storm sewers that quickly deliver water to urban streams. Lag time (time between when most of the rain falls and the greatest runoff occurs) decreases owing to quicker runoff after urbanization, and there is an increase in flood peak after urbanization. It is the increase in flood peak that causes urban flood problems; that is, compared with preurban conditions, urban areas for a given set of storms will flood more often and with higher discharge.

The effects of urbanization are also most pronounced with floods that can be expected to recur in 2–30 years. High-magnitude floods with large recurrence intervals (for example, 50 years) are little changed by urbanization. Because very large floods are produced by large, infrequent storms with rainfall intensities that greatly exceed the infiltration rate of water into a soil, it makes little difference if the land is urbanized or not.

Land Use and Landslides

Urbanization often modifies slopes, leading to an increase in landslides, particularly on steep slopes. Four ways in which a stable slope or cut can be rendered unstable are steepening a slope, increasing the height of a slope by excavation, saturating a slope, and placing fill on top of a slope; all may decrease stability and produce a landslide. Because it may steepen or load a slope, construction of roads and highways may be particularly troublesome (Fig. 17.4).

Removing or changing vegetation may also decrease slope stability and produce landslides. Timber harvesting in conjunction with adverse geologic conditions is often associated with an increase in landslides, usually several years following logging. The lag time between logging and

FIGURE 17.4
Landslide in Rio de Janeiro that demolished several houses and two apartment buildings. More than 132 people died as a result of the slide. The large slide was evidently facilitated by a smaller landslide associated with a highway cut that overloaded the slope.

landslides is thought to be due in part to the slow decay of tree roots. Live tree roots help hold the soil together (increasing soil strength), thus inhibiting landsliding. Following timber harvesting, the roots slowly die and soil strength decreases.

A mixture of human use and adverse geologic conditions resulted in a bizarre landslide in 1960 in Handlova, Czechoslovakia. A large coal-burning power plant in Handlova burned soft coal, emitting a large volume of ash that was deposited downwind. So much ash had accumulated that land used for grazing had to be plowed. Plowing allowed rain water to infiltrate at a greater rate, disturbing a delicate groundwater situation and initiating the slide. A well-organized program to stop the land motion by draining the slide material was successful, but not before 20 million m^3 of earth had moved about 150 m, destroying 150 homes [5]. The Handlova slide is a good example of the fundamental ecological principle that everything affects everything else.

Earthquakes Caused by People

Earthquakes have been caused by several types of human activity, including disposal of liquid waste deep underground, building of large reservoirs, and exploding of nuclear devices underground. Several hundred earthquakes near Denver, Colorado, from 1962 to 1965 were apparently related to deep-well disposal of liquid chemical waste. The earthquakes, while not particularly large, were sufficient to knock bottles off shelves in stores. Correlation between the number of earthquakes and the rate of waste injected (Fig. 17.5) clearly shows that the waste disposal was responsible for the earthquakes.

Numerous small local earthquakes occurred during the first 10 years following the completion of Hoover Dam, on the Colorado River near Las Vegas, Nevada. Most were very small, but one was at least moderate. Earthquakes induced by building large reservoirs can kill people, and one in India killed approximately 200 people. Evidently, fracture zones or faults are activated by the increased load of the water on the land and by the increased water pressure in the rocks below the reservoir.

The problem of induced seismicity associated with large reservoirs is being intensively studied.

Numerous, generally small, earthquakes have also been triggered by nuclear explosions at Nevada test sites. The information from these and other earthquakes produced by human use and interest in the land may eventually be applied to control or predict earthquake activity.

Coastal Erosion and Human Activity

The process of coastal erosion is definitely influenced by human use, particularly when structures are built in the coastal zone. In areas characterized by a sea cliff, urban runoff may increase cliff erosion by delivering large amounts of water to the face of the cliff (see Plate 13b). Careful control of storm water runoff will help to minimize erosion.

Along the eastern coast of the United States, particularly south of New York City and along the Gulf Coast, much of the coastal zone is characterized by barrier islands. **Barrier islands** are long, narrow strings or chains of sand that separate the mainland from the coast. Landward of the islands there is a salt marsh or lagoon (Fig. 17.6), and inlets (openings or breaks in the barrier island) with strong tidal currents allow water from the salt marsh or lagoon to exchange with the ocean. The islands have developed in the last few thousand years in response to a slow rise in sea level and tend to migrate shoreward through a number of processes, one of which is known as overwash. Overwash occurs when the frontal line of sand dunes is broken by waves during storms, and sand and other sediment are washed toward the salt marsh behind the dunes. There has been a continued controversy as to the importance of overwash in the development of barrier islands. Although many kilometers of sand dunes in the past have been protected by artificial means, we now recognize that this program has disrupted the natural environment and may have actually increased erosion.

Construction of breakwaters to form a small boat harbor or of jetties to protect a river mouth has often caused coastal erosion. Erosion occurs because the breakwater or jetty interferes with the

FIGURE 17.5
(a) The Rocky Mountain Arsenal well. (b) Graph showing the relationship between earthquake frequency and rate of liquid waste disposal for five characteristic periods. [Part (b) from Evans.]

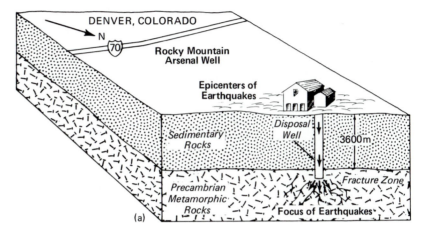

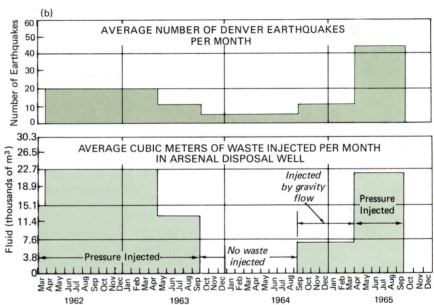

natural flow of sand along a beach. The flow of sand, known as **littoral** drift, is produced by waves as they strike the shore at an angle. Deposition of sand in one area of the coast is encouraged by the positioning of breakwaters and is compensated for by erosion in the downdrift direction. Sand must be dredged where it accumulates and placed back in the littoral drift system downcoast beyond the breakwater or jetty, replenishing beach material and thereby minimizing erosion.

People also increase the rate of coastal erosion by removing the natural vegetation. As was discussed in Chapter 5, ecological succession occurs along beaches and dunes, and certain species of grasses put out a network of underground runners that help anchor the sandy soil and prevent erosion. Removal of these plants, or even severe trampling by walkers or by dune vehicles, can destroy this network of underground runners and increase the rate of erosion. To counter this effect in New

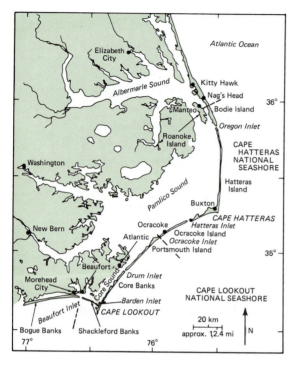

FIGURE 17.6
The prominent barrier island system of the Outer Banks of North Carolina. (From Godfrey and Godfrey.)

Zealand and the United States, local private conservation groups and government agencies have begun planting dune grasses and other plants to restabilize native vegetation in coastal areas.

Fire and People

Fires are a natural hazard that appear to have been part of the landscape ever since land plants first evolved. As was discussed in Chapter 5, species of animals and plants are adapted to the conditions that follow fire, and some kinds of trees like jack pine may tend to increase the chance of fire by naturally producing abundant fuel. Throughout the twentieth century there has been an active policy in the United States to prevent forest fires; it was believed that forest fires were always damaging and to be avoided.

Currently there is considerable controversy concerning strategies to manage natural lands and

fires. Suppression of fires ultimately leads to greater fuel on the ground and a higher potential to produce catastrophic, damaging fires. In contrast, more frequent natural fires may result in less permanent damage and often have beneficial effects. For example, in Yosemite National Park, California, suppression of fire prevented the regeneration of the giant sequoia trees. One management strategy is to introduce controlled burns that limit the intensity of the fires. This clears away dead wood that could lead to catastrophic fires and promotes regeneration of sequoia.

On the other hand, controlled burns may be difficult to confine, and the decision whether to use such fires is particularly difficult near urban areas. Controlled burning has become an accepted method of management of forest and brushlands, although it is still controversial among some groups of people and must be handled very carefully.

PREDICTION OF HAZARDS

Learning how to predict hazards so we can minimize human loss and property damage is an important endeavor. For each particular hazard or process, we have a certain amount of information; in some cases it is sufficient to predict or forecast events accurately. When there is insufficient information to make accurate forecasts or predictions, the best we may be able to do is simply locate areas where hazardous events have occurred and infer where and when similar future events might take place. Thus, reducing effects of hazards involves the following aspects: identified locations where a hazard occurs, probability of occurrence, precursor events, forecast, and warning.

For the most part, we know where a particular hazard is likely to occur. For example, the major zones for earthquakes and volcanic eruptions have been delineated satisfactorily on a global scale by mapping earthquake epicenters and recent volcanic rocks and volcanoes. Most are located along or near major boundaries of tectonic plates. On a regional scale, based on the past record of activity, areas likely to have a significant hazard from a large mudflow or ash eruptions associated with a volcanic eruption have also been delineated for several Cascade volcanoes, including Mt. Rainier. On a local scale, detailed work with soils may easily identify slopes that are likely to fail (landslide) or where expansive soils exist. Certainly we can predict where flooding is likely to occur on the basis of location of the floodplain and evidence from recent floods, such as flood debris and the high-water line.

We can determine the probability of occurrence of a particular event, such as a flood, hurricane, or drought, as part of a hazard prediction. For many rivers we have sufficiently long records of flow to develop probability models that will accurately predict the 25- or 100-year flood. The 25-year flood is a flood that is expected, on the average, every 25 years. However, this probability is similar to the chances of throwing a particular number on a die or drawing to an inside straight in poker; thus it is possible for several 25-year floods to occur in any one year, just as it is possible to throw two straight sixes with a die. Likewise, droughts may be assigned a probability on the basis of past occurrence of rainfall in a particular region. For example, Figure 17.7 shows percent chance (in any one year) of a hurricane occurring along a particular 80-km south Atlantic coastal segment. Notice that there is an 11% chance that a hurricane will strike Cape Hatteras, North Carolina, in a given year and a 2% chance that it will be a great hurricane.

Work with hazards such as earthquakes and volcanic events has not yet advanced to the point that probability of occurrence and short-range prediction may be calculated accurately on a regular basis. Nevertheless, a national earthquake hazard map based on probability has been developed (Fig. 17.8). Although it is not useful for small, site-specific studies, the map is valuable in regional planning. Long-range prediction of earthquakes based on geologic evidence has been more successful. Figure 17.9 shows the relative or approximate probability of future earthquake activity on the San Andreas fault in California (see also Plate 14).

FIGURE 17.7
Probability that a hurricane will strike a particular 80–km south Atlantic coastal segment in a given year. (From Council on Environmental Quality, 1981.)

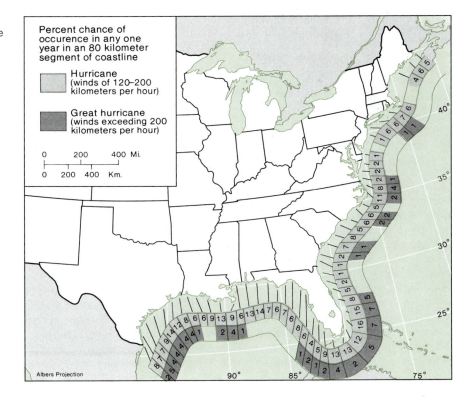

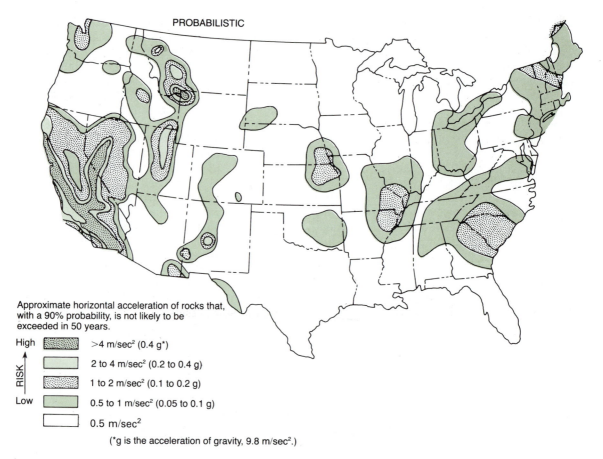

PROBABILISTIC

Approximate horizontal acceleration of rocks that, with a 90% probability, is not likely to be exceeded in 50 years.

High — >4 m/sec² (0.4 g*)

2 to 4 m/sec² (0.2 to 0.4 g)

1 to 2 m/sec² (0.1 to 0.2 g)

Low — 0.5 to 1 m/sec² (0.05 to 0.1 g)

0.5 m/sec²

(*g is the acceleration of gravity, 9.8 m/sec².)

FIGURE 17.8
A probabilistic approach to the seismic hazard in the United States. The darker the area on the map, the greater the hazard. (After Algermissen and Perkins.)

Many hazardous earth processes have precursor events. For example, the surface of the ground may creep or move slowly for a long period prior to an actual landslide. Often the rate of creep has increased up to the final failure and landslide. Volcanoes have been noticed to swell or bulge before an eruption, and there often is a significant increase in local seismic activity in the area surrounding the volcano.

Precursor events associated with earthquakes are not particularly well known nor understood, but increases in emission of radon gas from wells, foreshock activity, unusual tilt or uplift of the land, and perhaps even strange animal activity may be precursor events. Anomalous tilt or uplift may begin months or even years prior to the earthquake (Fig. 17.10), whereas unusual animal activity may occur close to the time of the event (use of anomalous animal behavior is very speculative, but is being studied seriously). Seismic gaps (areas where earthquakes are expected but have not occurred) at both regional and local scales have also been valuable in predicting some earthquakes.

With some natural processes it is possible to accurately forecast when the event will arrive. For example, Mississippi River flooding, which occurs in the spring in response to snow melt or very large regional storm systems, is fairly predictable, and

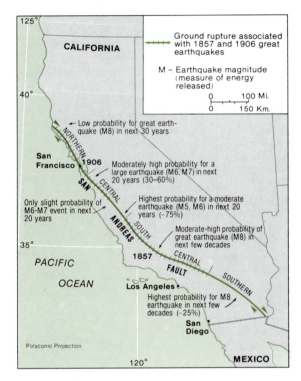

FIGURE 17.9
Approximate probability of future earthquakes along four segments of the San Andreas fault in California.

we can sometimes forecast when the river will reach a particular flood stage. When hurricanes are spotted far out to sea and tracked toward the shore, we can forecast when they will actually strike the land. **Tsunamis,** or seismic sea waves, generated by disturbance of ocean waters by earthquakes or submarine volcanoes, may also be forecast (Fig. 17.11). The tsunami warning system has been fairly successful in the Pacific Basin, and in some instances the time of arrival of the waves has been forecast precisely.

After a prediction for a hazardous event has been made and verified, the public must be warned. The flow of information leading to the warning of a possible hazard such as a large earthquake or flood should move along a path similar to that shown on Figure 17.12. When the public is informed that a prediction or advisory warning has been issued by scientists, that prediction may not

be welcomed with open arms. For example, in 1982, when geologists advised that a volcanic eruption near Mammoth Lakes, California, was quite likely, it caused loss of tourist business and apprehension on the part of the residents. The eruption did not occur and the advisory was eventually lifted. Similarly, in July 1986 scientists issued an advisory that a large earthquake was likely to occur in the Bishop, California, area. The advisory was issued following a series of earthquakes, over a four-day period, that began with an earthquake of magnitude 3 and culminated in an earthquake of magnitude 6.1, which caused significant damage. Local business owners stated that the advisory in their opinion was irresponsible and would chase potential tourists away from the eastern Sierra Nevada during the summer months when tourism is generally high. Scientists justified their advisory by pointing out that they were trying to make a responsible statement concerning the hazard. Some residents stated that they believed that government scientists were simply trying to scare them and that such advisories ought not to be issued. One resident was reported to have stated that if there was going to be a big earthquake, he wished it would just occur and get it over with! Clearly, issuing the advisory was producing anxiety among the local inhabitants north of Bishop, where the larger earthquake was thought likely to occur. Although we are not yet able to accurately predict earthquakes, it does seem that scientists have a responsibility to make informed judgments even if their predictions do not come to pass. An informed public is probably better able to act responsibly than an uninformed public, even if the subject leads to uncomfortable feelings. Captains of ships regularly review weather advisories and warnings, knowing that conditions can change. Weather warnings have proven to be very useful for planning and the careful skipper takes them seriously. Likewise, official warning of hazardous events such as earthquakes, landslides, and floods will also be useful to people who must make decisions concerning where they live, work, and travel. Considering the case of the potential of volcanic eruption and possible loss of life in the Mammoth Lake area, it would have been irresponsible not to issue the advisory. Scientists knew that the

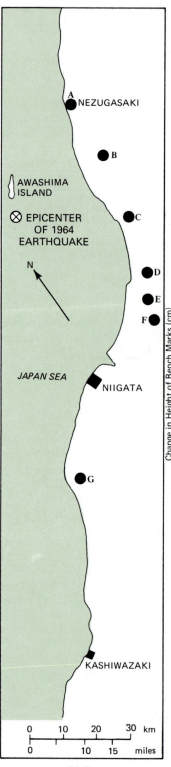

FIGURE 17.10
Anomalous uplift of Earth's crust observed for approximately 10 years before the 7.5 magnitude earthquake that struck Niigata, Japan, in 1964. (From "Earthquake prediction" by F. Press. Copyright © 1975 by Scientific American, Inc. All rights reserved.)

FIGURE 17.11
(a) The tsunami warning system. Map shows reporting stations and tsunami travel times to Honolulu, Hawaii. (From NOAA.) (b) Tsunami striking a pier in the harbor at Hilo, Hawaii. The man at lower left was killed.

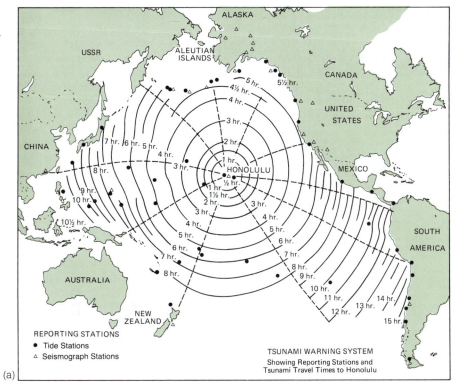

(a)

REPORTING STATIONS
• Tide Stations
△ Seismograph Stations

TSUNAMI WARNING SYSTEM
Showing Reporting Stations and
Tsunami Travel Times to Honolulu

(b)

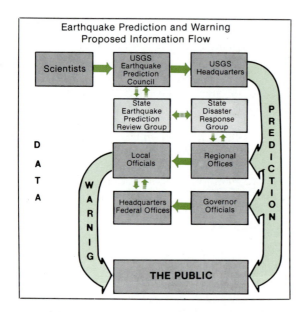

FIGURE 17.12
Possible flow path for issuance of a prediction or warning for natural hazards. (After McKelvey.)

seismic data suggested that molten rock was moving toward the surface. Issuing the advisory, even though the eruption did not occur, led to development of evacuation routes and consideration of disaster preparedness. Furthermore, it is very likely that a volcanic eruption will occur in the Mammoth Lake area in the future. The most recent event occurred only six hundred years ago! Certainly the community is better informed today than it was several years ago concerning the volcanic hazard. When an event does occur, they should be better prepared to handle the situation.

SCIENTISTS, THE MEDIA, AND HAZARDS

People today learn about events happening in the world by watching television, listening to the radio, or reading newspapers and magazines. The people who report for the media are generally more interested in the impact of a particular event on people than in the scientific aspects of an event

[6]. Even major volcanic eruptions or earthquakes in unpopulated areas may receive little media attention, whereas moderate or even small events in populated areas are reported in great detail. Reporters want to sell stories and what sells is spectacular events that impact people and their possessions.

In a perfect world we would like to see good relations between scientists and the news media, but this lofty ideal may be difficult to achieve. This results because, on the one hand, are scientists, who tend to be conservative, critical people afraid of being misquoted by what they perceive to be pushy, aggressive reporters who tend to report only half-truths while seeking out differences of scientific opinion to embellish a story. On the other hand, those doing the gathering of material for stories perceive scientists as speaking a lot of jargon, while being generally uncooperative, aloof, and unappreciative of the deadlines that the reporters face [6].

Recognizing that scientists do have an obligation to provide information to the general public concerning natural hazards, it is a good policy for a research team to pick one spokesperson to talk to the media and public so that the information is consistent with what is known concerning the problem at hand. For example, if scientists are studying a swarm of earthquakes near Los Angeles and there is speculation among them as to what the swarm means (as there usually is), then it is best to report a consensus to the media rather than a variety of opinions—the general public may be led to believe that the scientists don't know what they are talking about. The development of multiple working hypotheses is the general rule for the earth scientist—a group of scientists may talk for long periods of time concerning various possibilities and scenarios for the future. When dealing with the news media, however, on a topic that may be concerned with people, their lives, and their property, it is best to be conservative and provide information with as little jargon as possible. Reporters, on the other hand, should strive to provide their readers or viewers or listeners with factual information that has been verified as correct by the scientists. Embarrassing scientists by misquoting them will only lead to more mistrust and poor communication between scientists and journalists [6]

RISK ASSESSMENT

Before rational people can discuss and consider adjustments to hazards, they must have a good idea of the risk that they face under various scenarios. The field of risk assessment is a rapidly growing one in the analysis of hazards, and its use and application should probably be expanded. The risk of a particular event is defined as the product of the probability of that event occurring times the consequences should it occur [7]. When considering a particular risk-assessment problem, as for example damaging of a nuclear reactor by an earthquake, risks for a variety of different combinations of possible events should be calculated. For example, researchers may wish to know the risk involved with a large versus a small earthquake or perhaps the risk of a moderate event. The large or rare event has a lower probability of occurrence but the consequences may be greater. Consequences could be expressed in a variety of scales. For example, if we are dealing with a power plant, the consequences may be evaluated in terms of radiation released, which then can be related to damages to people and other living things.

The risk that society or people are willing to take depends upon the situation involved. For example, even though driving an automobile is fairly risky, most of us accept that risk as part of living in a modern world. On the other hand, acceptable risk of radiation poisoning from a nuclear power plant is very low because such events are considered unacceptable. The reason there is so much controversy over nuclear power plants today is that many people perceive them as the source of a very high risk. Even though the probability of an accident may be relatively low, the consequences are very high, resulting in a high risk. This was dramatically pointed up during and after the nuclear accident at a power plant near Chernobyl, U.S.S.R. Millions of people were exposed to elevated levels of radioactivity that killed approximately 20 people. The exact toll from the event will not be known for many years until it is determined how many cancers may have been caused by the accident.

One problem with risk analysis today has to do with the reliability of geologic data necessary for the analysis. It is often very difficult to assign probabilities to a series of events. This results because, for many geologic processes such as earthquakes and volcanic eruptions, the known chronology for past events may be very inadequate or short. Thus the probability calculations are limited at best [7]. Similarly, it may be very difficult to determine the consequences of a particular event or series of events. For example, if we are concerned with the release of radiation into the environment, then we need to have a lot of information about the local biology, geology, hydrology, and meterology, some of which may be complex and difficult to understand. In spite of these limitations, risk analysis is a step in the right direction, and as we learn more concerning the calculation of the probability of an event and its consequences, we should be able to provide the better analysis necessary for decision making.

ADJUSTMENTS TO HAZARDS

Major adjustments to natural hazards and processes include land-use planning, construction of structures to control natural processes, insurance, evacuation, disaster preparedness, and bearing the loss. Which option is chosen by an individual depends upon a number of factors, the most important of which is hazard perception.

In recent years a good deal of work has been done to try to understand how people perceive various natural hazards. This is obviously an important endeavor because the success of hazard reduction programs depends on the attitude of the people likely to be affected by the hazard. For example, it has been difficult to develop earthquake hazard reduction programs where strong earthquakes occur only once every few generations. Similarly, it is difficult to tell an individual who has lived many years in a particular home on the floodplain that he is living in a very dangerous area because the floodplain is inundated by water on the average of once every 100 years. Because flooding at a particular site may occur infrequently, the individual may not perceive flooding to be a serious hazard for him. While there may be an adequate perception of hazards at the institutional level, this may not filter down to the general population. This is particularly true for those hazards that occur infrequently.

Proximity to hazards such as volcanoes and coastal erosion seems to be very important. That is, people who live near volcanoes or in the coastal zone are more likely to be aware of the hazard and possibly will take steps needed to minimize potential damages.

People are more aware of hazards such as brush or forest fires, which may occur every few years. There may even be institutionalized as well as local ordinances to control damages resulting from these events. For example, homes built in some areas of southern California have roofs that are constructed with shingles that will not burn readily and may even have sprinkler systems, and the lots are often cleared of brush. Such measures are often noticeable during the rebuilding phase following a fire.

One of the most environmentally sound adjustments to hazards involves land-use planning. That is, people can avoid building on floodplains, in areas where there are active landslides or active fault traces, and in areas where coastal erosion is likely to occur. In many cities, floodplains have been delineated and zoned for a particular land use. Zoning associated with active and potentially active faults is also commonplace in California. With respect to landslides, legal requirements for soils engineering and engineering geology studies at building sites may greatly reduce potential damages. Although it may be possible to control physical processes in specific instances, certainly land-use planning to accommodate natural processes is often preferable to a technological fix that may or may not work.

Insurance is another option that people may exercise in dealing with natural hazards. Flood insurance is relatively common in many areas, and earthquake insurance is also available. However, other than fire insurance or enforced insurance against flood, few people purchase extra policies. Only a small percentage of people in southern California, for example, have earthquake insurance.

Evacuation is an important option or adjustment to the hurricane hazard in the Gulf States and along the eastern coast of the United States. Often there will be sufficient time for people to evacuate provided they heed the predictions and warnings. However, if people do not react quickly and the affected area is a large urban region, then evacuation routes may be blocked by people panicking in the last minute and trying to evacuate. There is concern that a large hurricane in an urban area would cause catastrophic loss of life and property and that people either will not evacuate or will have trouble doing so. A great number of people were able to evacuate prior to hurricane Allen's approach to the Texas coastline in August of 1979, and by fortuitous circumstances the storm struck a relatively uninhabited stretch of coastline and did relatively little damage. If the storm had not stalled offshore for several hours and lost energy, a catastrophe would certainly have resulted if it had struck a large urban area.

Disaster preparedness is an option that individuals, families, cities, states, or even entire nations can implement. Of particular importance here is the training of individuals and institutions to handle large numbers of injured people or people attempting to evacuate an area after a warning is issued.

An option that all too often is chosen is bearing the loss caused by a natural hazard. Many people are optimistic about their chances of making it through any sort of natural hazard and therefore will take little action in their own defense. This is particularly true for those hazards—such as volcanic eruptions and earthquakes—that may occur only rarely in a particular area.

Impact of and Recovery from Disasters

The impact of a disaster upon a population may be either direct or indirect. Direct effects include people killed, injured, dislocated, or otherwise damaged by a particular event; indirect impacts are generally responses to the disaster and include responses of people who are generally bothered or disturbed by the event and of people who donate money or goods, as well as the taxing of people to help pay for emergency services, restoration, and

FIGURE 17.13
(a) Impact of disaster in terms of the continuum of effects; (b) comparison with real data from four disasters. [From White and Haas, 1975. Part (a) adapted from Bowden and Kates.]

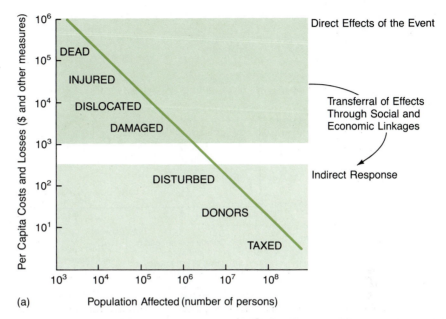

(a)

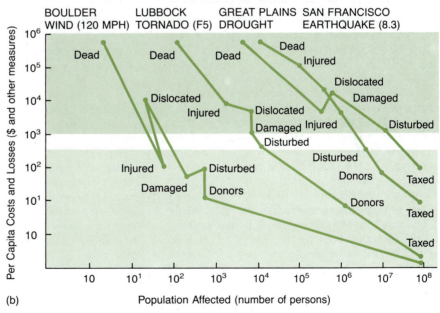

(b)

eventual reconstruction. These concepts are summarized in Figure 17.13a, which shows that direct effects cost more but affect fewer people, while indirect effects cost less but affect more people. Figure 17.13b shows actual data for several types of

natural disasters, thus demonstrating this continuum of effects [8,9].

The stages following a disaster are emergency work, restoration of services and communication lines, and reconstruction. Figure 17.14 shows an

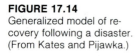

FIGURE 17.14
Generalized model of recovery following a disaster. (From Kates and Pijawka.)

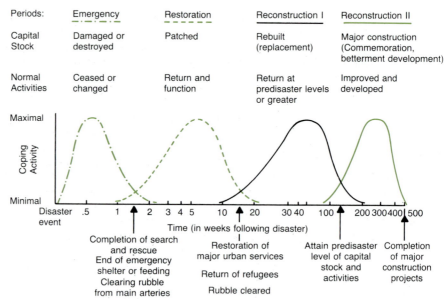

Periods:	Emergency	Restoration	Reconstruction I	Reconstruction II
Capital Stock	Damaged or destroyed	Patched	Rebuilt (replacement)	Major construction (Commemoration, betterment development)
Normal Activities	Ceased or changed	Return and function	Return at predisaster levels or greater	Improved and developed

idealized model of recovery. This model can be compared to actual recovery activities following the 1964 earthquake in Anchorage, Alaska, and the 1972 flash flood in Rapid City, South Dakota. Restoration following the earthquake in Anchorage began almost immediately in response to a tremendous influx of dollars from federal programs, insurance companies, and other sources approximately one month after the earthquake. As a result, reconstruction was a hectic process, with everyone trying to obtain as much of the available funds as possible. In Rapid City, the restoration did not peak until approximately 10 weeks after the flood, and the community took time to carefully think through the best alternatives. As a result, Rapid City today has an entirely different land use on the floodplain, and the flood hazard is much reduced. On the other hand, in Anchorage the rapid restoration and reconstruction were accompanied by little land-use planning. Apartments and other buildings were hurriedly constructed across areas that had suffered ground rupture and were simply filled in and regraded. In ignoring the potential benefits of careful land-use planning, Anchorage is vulnerable to the same type of earthquake that struck in 1964. In Rapid City, the floodplain is now a green belt with golf courses and other such ac-

tivities—a change that has reduced the flood hazard [4,8,9].

ARTIFICIAL CONTROLS OF NATURAL PROCESSES

Attempts to artificially control natural processes such as landslides, floods, and lava flows have had mixed success, and even the best designed structures cannot be expected to always successfully defend against an extreme event.

Retaining walls and other structures to defend slopes from failure by landslide have generally been successful when well designed. Even the casual observer has probably noticed the variety of such structures along highways and urban land in hilly areas. Structures to defend slopes have limited impact on the environment and are necessary where construction demands artificial cuts be excavated or where unstable slopes impinge on human structures.

Two common methods of flood control are construction of dams and channelization. Both of these tend to provide floodplain residents with a false sense of security because neither method can be expected to protect people and their property absolutely from high-magnitude floods.

Dams and Environment

Environmental effects of dams are considerable and include (1) loss of land and biologic resources in the reservoir area; (2) storage behind the dam of sediment that would otherwise move downstream to coastal areas where it supplies sand to beaches; and (3) downstream changes in hydrology and potential to transport sediment that change the entire river environment and the things that live there.

The Grand Canyon of the Colorado River provides a good example of a river adjusting to the impact of a large dam. In 1963 the Glen Canyon Dam was completed upstream from the Grand Canyon. From a hydrologic viewpoint the Colorado River is tamed; the higher flows are reduced and the average flow increased. However, the flow is highly unstable owing to fluctuating needs to generate power. Also, changing the hydrology of the Colorado River in the Grand Canyon has greatly changed the morphology of the river, especially the distribution of sediment and vegetation (Fig. 17.15).

In June of 1983 a record snow melt in the Rocky Mountains forced the release of about 2500 m^3 of water per second, which is about three times that normally released and about the same as an average spring flood prior to the dam. The resulting flood scoured the river bed and banks, releasing stored sediment that replenished the sediment on sand bars, and scoured out or broke off some of the vegetation that had taken root [10,11]. The effects of the large release of water were beneficial to the river environment and emphasize the importance of the larger events (floods) to maintaining the system in a more natural state. Perhaps management of rivers below some dams should call for the periodic release of large flows to help cleanse the system.

(a)

(b)

FIGURE 17.15
Crystal Rapid of the Colorado River in the Grand Canyon (a) before and (b) after the construction of the Glen Canyon Dam. Photograph (a), taken in 1963, shows the rapid essentially as it existed prior to the building of the dam. Photograph (b), taken in 1967, shows the effect of a 1965 flash flood. The debris and rock delivered from Crystal Creek (left) form a fan-shaped deposit in the Colorado River. This deposit has made the rapid more difficult to negotiate, and the debris will remain in the river for a relatively long time as large floods that would normally remove some of the debris are controlled by the dam.

Channelization and Environment

For over 200 years, people in the United States have lived and worked on floodplains. Of course, building houses, factories, public buildings, and farms on the floodplain invites disaster, but floodplain residents have refused to recognize the natural floodway of the river for what it is: part of the natural river system. As a result, flood control and drainage of wetlands have become prime concerns. Historically, people have attempted to control flooding by constructing dams and levees or even by rebuilding the entire stream to more efficiently remove the water from the land. Every new project lures more people to the floodplain in the false hope of controlling all floods.

Channelization of streams consists of straightening, deepening, widening, clearing, or lining existing stream channels (see Plate 11). Basically, it is an engineering technique to control floods, drain wetlands, control erosion, and improve navigation [12]. Of these four objectives, flood control and drainage improvement are cited most often in channel improvement projects.

Thousands of kilometers of streams in the United States have been modified, and thousands more kilometers of channelization are being planned or constructed. Considering that there are approximately 5.6 million km of streams in the United States, and the average yearly rate of channel modification is only a very small fraction of 1% of the total, the impact may appear small. However, many of the alterations occur in flood-sensitive areas, and a change of 1% per year means all U.S. waterways will be altered in one century.

Channelization is not necessarily a bad practice, but its adverse environmental effects are not being adequately addressed. In fact, too little is known about these effects, and too little is being done to evaluate them [12]. Opponents of channelizing natural streams emphasize that the practice inhibits the production of fish and wetland wildlife and degrades the streams' aesthetic qualities.

Examples of channel work projects that have adversely affected the environment are well known. For example, channelization of the Blackwater River in Missouri enlarged the stream channel, reduced biological productivity, and increased downstream flooding [13].

The channelization of the Blackwater River is a good example of trade-offs and unforeseen degradations caused by channelization. The upper reaches benefited from the utilization of more floodplain land. However, this benefit must be weighed against the loss of farmland to erosion, the cost of bridge repair, the loss of biological life in the stream, and downstream flooding. A more reasonable trade-off might have been to straighten the channel less, still providing a measure of flood protection but not causing such rapid environmental degradation. The difficult question is, How much straightening can be done before it causes unacceptable damage to the river system?

Channelization of the Kissimmee River in Florida is another example of potential problems and conflict in river management. Channelization of the river started in 1962 and eventually, after nine years of construction and $24 million spent, the sinuous river was converted into an 83–km-long straight ditch. Unfortunately the channelization did not provide the expected flood protection, degraded valuable wildlife habitat, contributed to water quality problems associated with the land drainage, and caused aesthetic degradation. Now, at a cost that may exceed the original cost of channelization, the river may be returned to its original sinuous path! The restoration of the Kissimmee River may become the most ambitious restoration project ever attempted in the United States. Work will begin on a 16–km experimental stretch of river and, if successful, will be expanded to other parts of the channelized river.

Not all channelization causes serious environmental degradation, and in many cases drainage projects can be beneficial. Such benefits are probably best observed in urban areas subject to flooding and in rural areas where previous land use has caused drainage problems. Other examples can be cited to show where channel modification has improved navigation or reduced flooding and has not disrupted the environment. To end this discussion on another positive point, in recent years more consideration is being given to environmental aspects of channelization, and some projects are being designed to allow modified channels to behave more like natural channels than do straight ditches.

GLOBAL CLIMATE AND HAZARDS

Global and regional climatic change can significantly affect the incidence of hazardous natural processes such as storm damage (floods and erosion), landslides, drought, and fires. This was dramatically illustrated during the 1982–1983 El Niño event, which may have brought with it a tremendous increase in hazards on a global scale by putting an unusual amount of heat energy into the atmosphere. The hazardous events in 1982–83 killed several thousand people while causing over $10 billion in damages to crops, structures, utilities, and so forth. Particularly hard hit were Australia, the Americas, and Africa. Drought struck Australia, where a single brush fire in February 1983 burned over 400,000 ha, killing 74 people and destroying more than 2000 houses [14]. Total damage in Australia was about $3 billion. In normally arid areas of Bolivia, Peru, and Ecuador on the west coast of South America, rainfall over 350 cm fell compared to a normal 10–12 cm, resulting in catastrophic floods and landslides that killed over 600 people while causing damages of about $1 billion (Fig.

17.16). Floods and drought in other parts of South America caused another $3 billion in damages and killed over 150 people. In North America, droughts struck Mexico and Central America, and storms in the United States killed about 100 people and inflicted over $2 billion damages. The Pacific Coast and mountain states were particularly hard hit; coastal erosion destroyed numerous homes and businesses and inland rivers flooded, causing severe damage to crops and structures [15,16].

The impact on Africa, due in part to El Niño, was drought that destroyed crops and resulted in starvation of people. The drought was particularly cruel in Africa because (1) previous drought was already a problem in some areas; (2) political problems and desertification in some areas make planting and harvesting crops difficult in good times; and (3) overpopulation is a growing problem in much of the troubled parts of Africa. Although there is disagreement on how much of the damage and loss of life in 1982–83 due to natural hazards is directly attributable to El Niño—some researchers believe the effects were confined to tropical regions, causing about $2 billion damages [17]—it certainly was a year to remember when it comes to hazardous natural processes.

El Niño lasted a short time. It naturally simulated in a compressed time frame some of the ef-

FIGURE 17.16
Flood damage in Ecuador caused by the 1982–83 El Niño event.

fects of the long-range global warming trend we are likely precipitating by the burning of fossil fuels and other activities. What might be the effect of a more prolonged climatic change on the magnitude and frequency of hazardous earth processes? If this trend continues, climatic patterns will change and coastal erosion will increase. Present food production areas will change as some areas receive more precipitation and others less. Deserts and semiarid areas would likely expand and more northern latitudes would become productive. We may not be able to do anything about El Niño (although some venture that human activity contributes to such events), but we can do a lot about atmospheric CO_2.

ECOSYSTEMS AND EXTREME EVENTS

Many ecosystems have evolved over a long period of time and are adjusted to a variety of natural processes of variable magnitude and frequency. The important principle here is that relatively extreme rare events of high magnitude, such as hurricanes and wildland fires, are probably as significant to long-term ecosystem stability and evolution as lesser magnitude more common events. For example, wildland fires can either maintain, advance, or retard the stage of ecological succession in forest or brushlands. Burning of plants (trees, brush, or grass) releases important nutrients for recycling through new plant growth. Effects of fire and nutrient release can release fire-resistant seeds and therefore reduce competition for specific plants [14]. In the brushlands (chaparral) of southern California, periodic fires have for at least 6000 years been important in maintaining the ecosystem through cycling of plant growth and nutrients. In the redwood forest of northern California, high-magnitude storms are the events that cause tree mortality and litter fall important in nutrient cycling, soil formation, and introduction of new trees in open spots created by fallen trees. Redwood trees that fall on the forest floor or in streams may reside there for centuries, providing significant and variable forest and stream habitat for animals and fish that would otherwise be lacking in the red-

wood forest. In fact, in many old-growth redwood areas, pools in streams are created or enhanced by large, fallen organic debris, and these pools provide summer holding areas for salmon and steelhead trout. Fish productivity in these streams is closely related to the existence of fallen redwood trees that enter the stream as a result of high-magnitude storms and floods.

Equally important to the preceding discussion is the fact that certain species are adapted to environmental conditions that follow catastrophes, as was discussed in Chapter 5 when we considered ecological succession. If we want to preserve these species, we must allow changes to occur in the environment, which means in some cases that we must let natural events such as fires and floods occur.

The discussion of natural hazards reinforces the view of nature as dynamic and changing. Our modern understanding of natural hazards therefore tells us that we cannot view our environment as a snapshot or painting fixed and permanent in time. Rather, the environment and life in the environment are part of a moving picture show. This discussion is important to how we view nature and see ourselves in nature. A landscape without natural hazards would also have less variety; it would be safer but less interesting and probably less aesthetically pleasing. The jury is still out on how much natural hazards should be controlled and how much they should be allowed to occur. This is one of the most important issues in the management of our environment. Ecosystems without disturbance are unnatural, while at the other extreme ecosystems continually subject to extreme disturbance cannot persist. Somewhere in between these extremes lies a more natural rate of disturbance and change that we must learn to live with if we wish to conserve the maximum number of species and maintain life on Earth in the most desirable condition.

POPULATION INCREASE AND NATURAL HAZARDS

Earlier, we have said that population increase is *the* environmental problem. As our population continues to increase, putting greater demands on our land and resources, the need for planning to minimize losses from natural hazards/processes also increases. This is dramatically illustrated by the recent loss of thousands of lives in Mexico and Colombia. In the autumn of 1985, Mexico endured a magnitude 7.8 earthquake that killed about 10,000 people in Mexico City alone (Fig. 17.17). Two months later, mudflows following the eruption of a volcano killed approximately 25,000 people in Colombia (Fig. 17.18).

Mexico City is the center of the world's most populous urban area. Approximately 18 million people are concentrated in an area of about 2300 km^2 and about one-third of the families (which average five in number) live in a single room. The city is built on ancient lake beds, which accentuate earthquake shaking, and parts of the city have been

sinking at the rate of a few centimeters per year owing in part to groundwater withdrawal. The subsidence has not been uniform, so the buildings tilt and are even more vulnerable to the shaking of earthquakes [18].

The Colombian volcano Nevado del Ruiz erupted in February of 1845, producing a mudflow that roared down the east slope of the mountain. The mudflow killed approximately 1000 people in the town of Ambalema, located on the banks of the Lagunilla River 80 km from the volcano's summit. Deposits from that event produced rich soils at a site 32 km up the river valley and an agricultural center developed there. The town that the area supported was known as Armero and, by 1985, had a population of about 22,500 people.

On November 13, 1985, a mudflow buried the

FIGURE 17.17
Thousands of deaths and extensive property damage in Mexico City resulted from the 1985 earthquake.

FIGURE 17.18
(a) Mudflows from a volcanic eruption buried the town of Armero, Colombia, on November 13, 1985. The rectilinear pattern of building foundations shows through the mudflow deposits. (b) A Colombian Red Cross rescue team pulls a victim from the mud at Armero.

(a)

(b)

newer town, leaving about 20,000 people dead or missing. A matter of 140 years multiplied the volcano's mudflow toll twenty times because of population increase over that period. Ironically, the same force that stimulated development and population of the area later decimated it.

The sequence of events that culminated in the 1985 catastrophe started with a tremendous volcanic eruption (heard as far away as 250 km) that blasted ash and other volcanic debris high into the atmosphere, but produced little lava. The heat from the eruption and molten rock within the volcano melted snow and ice at the top of the mountain. The resulting water mixed with ash to produce viscous volcanic mud which, in turn, flowed down river valleys on the flanks of the volcano. In the Lagunilla River Valley, the mudflow—augmented by runoff from three days of rain—reached velocities of over 40 km/hour and depths of 5–15 m [19].

The first signs that the Colombian volcano was returning to activity came in September of 1985, and geologists warned that a catastrophic eruption was likely. The area at the base of the volcano was declared to be a hazardous region. People were designated to monitor the volcano, develop hazard maps, and prepare an emergency plan. Unfortunately, the eruption occurred before the Colombian government could fully respond to the potential for hazard.

The people in the town accepted the volcano and its awakening activity as part of their environment. They were given warnings of what to do if a major eruption occurred, but the eruption—which occurred at night—still caught them unprepared. So, too, do people in earthquake areas accept their geology as a fact of life and sometimes suffer accordingly.

SUMMARY

One of the fundamental principles of environmental studies is that there have always been earth processes that are hazardous to people. The emphasis is on the term "Earth process." That is, most natural hazards are simply natural processes that become a problem when people live close to a potential danger or modify processes in such a way as to increase the hazard.

Many processes will continue to cause loss of life and property damage, including flooding of coastal or floodplain areas, landslides, earthquakes, volcanic activity, wind, expansive soils, drought, fire, and coastal erosion. However, the magnitude and frequency of these processes or events depend on such diverse factors as climate, geology, vegetation, and human use of the land. Once a process has been identified and the potentially hazardous aspects studied, this information must be made available to planners and decision makers so that they may avoid these hazards or processes or minimize their threat to human life and property. Of particular significance are how a warning is issued, how scientists communicate with the media, and how we can calculate risks associated with hazards.

Major adjustments to natural hazards and processes include land-use planning, artifical control, insurance, evacuation, disaster preparedness, and bearing the loss. Which of these options is chosen by an individual or segment of society depends upon a number of factors, the most important of which may be hazard perception.

The impact of a hazardous process (disaster) upon a population may be either direct or indirect. Direct effects include people killed, dislocated, or otherwise damaged by a particular event. Indirect impacts involve people generally bothered or disturbed by the event, people who donate money or goods, and taxing people to help pay for emergency services, restoration, and eventual reconstruction following a disaster. The reconstruction phase following a disaster often takes place through several stages, including emergency work, restoration of services and communication lines, and, finally, rebuilding.

Attempts to artificially control natural processes have had mixed success and usually cannot be expected to defend against extreme events.

Global climatic change, even if it is a short-term event, can affect the incidence of hazardous natural processes. The 1982–83 El Niño event is a good example.

Many ecosystems have evolved with and are dependent upon high-magnitude events such as fires or storms for stability. Examples include fires in the chaparral of southern California and storms in the redwood forests.

As the world's population increases, there will be greater demand on all land resources. This will necessitate better planning at all levels if we are to minimize losses from natural hazards/processes.

STUDY QUESTIONS

1 Why is it sometimes difficult to distinguish between a natural hazard and a natural process?

2 A two-year resident on the floodplain of a small urban stream says that upstream development is responsible for a recent flood that damaged his home. How would you respond to him?

3 If you pave over (with cement) the entire drainage area of the Mississippi River, the floods at New Orleans would not increase in magnitude or frequency. Do you agree or disagree? Why?

4 Discuss some of the ways human activity has caused earthquakes. Could any of these cause a really large earthquake, like the one that destroyed San Francisco in 1906?

5 What are some of the ways that hazardous natural processes are predicted? Which hazards can we predict best? Why?

6 Discuss major adjustment strategies people use in dealing with hazardous processes. Which are best? Why?

7 What are the stages of recovery following a disaster? What factors affect how long recovery takes?

8 How can knowing something about the magnitude and frequency of a particular process help in planning to minimize possible damage?

9 What do you think was learned from the 1980 eruptions of Mt. St. Helens that may help in planning for future high-magnitude (natural hazard) events in the United States?

10 Compare the benefits of stream channelization with its adverse environmental effects.

11 While rafting down a wild river in the wilderness, your guide argues that all channelization is bad. Would you agree or disagree? Why?

FURTHER READING

BASCOMB, W. 1980. *Waves and beaches.* Garden City, N.Y.: Anchor Books.

BOLT, B. A. 1978. *Earthquakes: A primer.* San Francisco: W. H. Freeman.

BURTON, I.; KATES, R. W.; and WHITE, G. F. 1978. *The environment as hazard.* New York: Oxford University Press.

HAAS, J. E.; KATES, R. W.; and BOWDEN, M. J., eds. 1977. *Reconstruction following disaster.* Cambridge, Mass.: The MIT Press.

OAKESHOTT, G. B. 1976. *Volcanoes and earthquakes.* New York: McGraw-Hill.

WHITE, G. F., ed. 1974. *Natural hazards: Local, national, global.* New York: Oxford University Press.

WHITE, G. F., and HAAS, J. E. 1975. *Assessment of research on natural hazards.* Cambridge, Mass.: The MIT Press.

18

Environmental Planning

- Evaluating, planning, and forecasting are all necessary in dealing with the environment. We often do not have all the data needed to make the best choices, but as our ability to alter the environment increases, planning becomes more important.

- In recent years, the need for land near urban areas has led to multiple land use and sequential land use.

- Land-use plans include statements of land-use issues, goals and objectives, a summary of data collection and analysis, a land classification map, and a description of appropriate development for areas of special environmental concern.

- Recently, physiographic determinism has emerged as a philosophy of site evaluation, developing a plan maximizing the natural qualities of the landscape.

- Emergency planning is in response to pressing needs. If it is not well thought-out, it may be inadequate or worse.

- Mitigation measures are at the heart of the environmental impact assessment process, which must be scientifically, technically, and legally defensible.

- The accuracy of computer models currently used in global forecasting and evaluation is debatable, but they force us to recognize the meaning of what we think we know, suggest where knowledge is lacking, and draw attention to current issues.

MESA VERDE VILLAGE

Oliver Wendell Homles wrote, "Every year, if not every day, we have to wager our solution upon some prophecy based upon imperfect knowledge." This statement certainly applies to environmental planning, where we often do not have all the data necessary to make the best possible choices. Even so, remaining buildings from earlier societies suggest that careful attention was paid to the environment. For example, approximately 1000 years ago in Mesa Verde, Arizona, native Americans had some unusual design features in their houses. Set in shallow recesses along the steep sides of mesas, the houses were positioned so that they were shaded from the summer sun by the rocks above but were warmed directly by winter sun (Fig. 18.1). The sun in winter was (and is) at a lower angle in the sky and shone directly on the houses. The summer sun in midday was at a much higher angle in the sky and the houses were shaded by overhanging rocks. Thus, the Mesa Verde Indians' homes took advantage of certain local aspects of the environment (the local rock formations) and certain characteristics of the transmission of the sun's energy [1]. The Mesa Verde Indians built their houses with what we call today a "design with nature" concept [2].

In contrast, many houses built in the United States during the middle of the twentieth century, when central heating and air conditioning were common and fossil fuels cheap, were designed with little concern for their location relative to sunlight. In some tract housing developments, the same design would be repeated on different streets or on different sides of the same street and facing in different compass directions. In like manner, little consideration was given to the physical environment, so many older homes today stand on ancient landslides, active traces of faults, and other unstable areas, such as the sea cliff environment.

Fortunately, this unplanned development is giving way to more modern planning concepts involving consideration of the entire environment. For example, the Franconia area in Fairfax County, Virginia, less than 15 km southwest of the District of Columbia, has integrated the concept of designing with nature into planning for housing development (Fig. 18.2). Such features as topography, geology, hydrology, and hazards analysis are integrated into a land capability map, which is a computer composite showing favorable areas for development. These maps have had a significant impact on decisions to rezone existing land or to allow new development in the Franconia area.

Today we recognize the advantages of careful house siting in relation to nature, as the Mesa Verde Indians practiced long ago. The environment has specific characteristics that we may use to our benefit or to our loss. Some decisions, like the choice of the siting of a house, may affect the future no longer than the lifetime of that house. However, some effects of land use tend to be cumulative and, therefore, we have an obligation to future generations to minimize the negative effects of land use. In other words, we need to plan for the future.

Planning takes place at local, regional (state and national), and global levels. Planning methods are themselves in various stages of development and testing; these methods and techniques are an important component of applied environmental work. Evaluating, planning, and forecasting are all part of the process of dealing with the environment.

Local land-use planning, including site selection, construction, and determination of environmental impact, is now a common practice. At regional, state, and national levels, there is planning for transportation facilities, recreational areas (including national and state parks), wilderness areas, water supply, clean air and rivers, and renewable natural resources.

Global planning today consists primarily of evaluation and forecasting. It involves evaluating the effects of our highly technological civilization on the biosphere (for example, the effects of burning fossil fuel on climate), and forecasting the worldwide changes in the abundance of people and resources, as well as the amount of resources available per individual in the future.

All technology, from the most primitive to the most recent inventions, causes some change in the environment. However, the industrial and scientific revolutions have led to ever more rapid changes in our environment. As our ability to alter the environment increases, planning becomes more and more important.

FIGURE 18.1
(a) Simplified diagram of Mesa Verde houses. (b) The Cliff Palace, largest of Mesa Verde's adobe dwellings, housed at least 200 people.

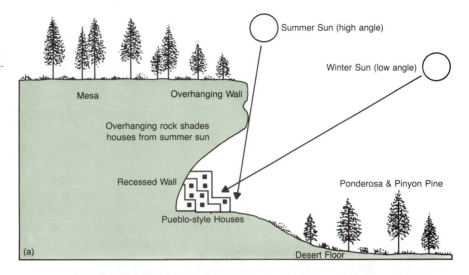

(b)

LAND-USE PLANNING

The use of land in the United States and almost everywhere else in the world has changed during the twentieth century. For example, the amount of land converted from rural to nonrural uses has increased. Although the increase in conversion of rural land to nonagricultural uses appears to be very slow, currently it amounts to about 8100 km^2/ yr—an area more than two and one-half times the

FIGURE 18.2
The modern land-planning process is illustrated by this flow chart, which shows the use of many kinds of information about the environment in land-use planning for the Franconia area of Fairfax County, Virginia. The planning process involves inventory, analysis, and synthesis phases. (Modified from Froelich et al.)

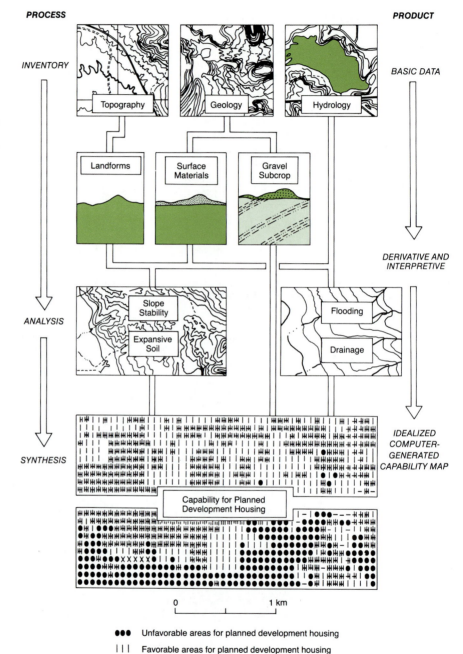

PROCESS

PRODUCT

INVENTORY

Topography

Geology

Hydrology

BASIC DATA

Landforms

Surface Materials

Gravel Subcrop

DERIVATIVE AND INTERPRETIVE

ANALYSIS

Slope Stability

Expansive Soil

Flooding

Drainage

SYNTHESIS

IDEALIZED COMPUTER-GENERATED CAPABILITY MAP

Capability for Planned Development Housing

0   1 km

●●●   Unfavorable areas for planned development housing

| | | Favorable areas for planned development housing

卅 卅   Developed areas

– – –   Potential retention pond site

XXX   Special engineering studies required prior to development

size of Rhode Island. The intensive conversion of rural land to urban development, transportation networks and facilities, and reservoirs is nearly matched by the extensive conversion of rural land to wildlife refuges, parks, and wilderness and recreation areas (Fig. 18.3).

In recent years the need for land near urban areas has led to the concepts of multiple and sequential land use rather than permanent, exclusive use. An example of multiple land use is active subsurface mining below urban land. Multiple use is less common than sequential land use, which involves changing use with time. The basic idea of sequential land use is that after a particular activity (e.g., mining or a sanitary landfill operation) is completed, the land is reclaimed for another purpose.

There are several well-known examples of sequential land use. Sanitary landfill sites are often planned to be used, when filled, for other purposes. Part of J. F. Kennedy International Airport in New York City is built on landfill. Other sanitary landfill sites in California, North Carolina, and other locations are being planned so that when

each site is completely filled in, the land will be used for a golf course. The city of Denver used abandoned sand and gravel pits for sanitary landfill sites, then converted these to a parking lot and the Denver Coliseum. Enormous underground limestone mines in Kansas City, Springfield, and Neosho, Missouri, have been profitably converted to warehousing and cold-storage sites, offices, and manufacturing plants. Other possibilities also exist: for example, abandoned surface mines could be used for parking below shopping centers or for chemical or petroleum storage [3].

The Land-use Plan

There are four basic elements of a land-use plan: (1) a statement of land-use issues, goals, and objectives; (2) a summary of data collection and analysis; (3) a land classification map; and (4) a report that describes appropriate development for areas of special environmental concern [4]. The preparation of a land-use plan is complex and requires a team approach.

The statement of major land-use issues assists

FIGURE 18.3
Approximate annual conversion of rural land in the United States to nonagricultural uses. (After Council on Environmental Quality.)

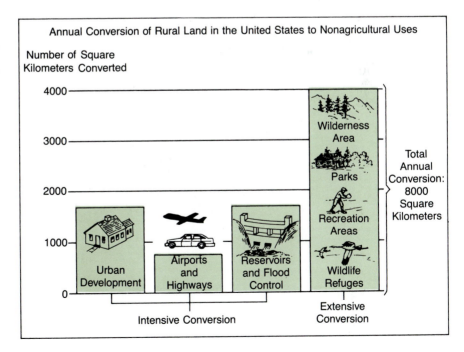

TABLE 18.1
Required and optional data analysis items for the land-use plan.

Element	Required	Optional

1. Present conditions
  a. Population and
    economy
	Brief analysis, utilizing existing information	More detailed analyses relating to human resources (population compositon, migration rates, educational attainment, etc.) and economic development factors (labor force characteristics, market structure, employment mix, etc.)

b. Existing land use	Mapped at generalized categories	Mapped with more detailed categories, including more detailed analyses, building inventory, etc.

c. Current plans, policies,
    and regulations
    1) Plans and policies
	1) Listing and summary	1) Detailed impact analysis of plans and policies upon land-development patterns

2) Local regulations	2) Listing and description of their enforcement mechanism	2) Detailed assessment of adequacy and degree of enforcement
3) Federal and state regulations	3) Listing and summary (to be provided by N. C. Dept. of Natural and Economic Resources)	

2. Constraints
  a. Land potential
    1) Physical limitations
	1) Analysis of following factors (maps if information available):
	—Hazard areas
	—Areas with soil limitations
	—Sources of water supply
	—Steep slopes
		1) Detailed analysis and mapping of required items
		Analysis and mapping of additional factors:
		—Water-quality limited areas
		—Air-quality limited areas
		—Others as appropriate

2) Fragile areas	2) Analysis of following factors (maps if information available): —Wetlands —Frontal dunes —Beaches —Prime wildlife habitats	2) Detailed analysis and mapping of required items Analysis and mapping of additional factors

Source: North Carolina Coastal Resurces Commission.

in planning future development for at least a 10–year period and therefore should be prepared in cooperation with citizens and public agencies. The statement includes information on issues such as impact of economic and population trends; housing and services; conservation of natural resources; and protection of important natural environments and of cultural, historical, and scenic resources [4].

Data collection and analysis include the follow-

TABLE 18.1
continued

Element	Required	Optional
	—Scenic and prominent high points —Unique natural areas —Other surface waters —Fragile areas	
3) Areas with resource potential	3) Analysis of following factors (maps if information available): —Areas well suited for woodland management —Productive and unique agricultural lands —Mineral sites —Publicly owned forests, parks, fish and game lands, and other outdoor recreational lands —Privately owned wildlife sanctuaries	3) Detailed analysis and mapping of required items Analysis and mapping of additional factors: —Areas with potential for commercial wildlife management —Outdoor recreation sites —Scenic and tourist resources
b. Capacity of community facilities	—Identification of existing water and sewer service areas —Design capacity of water-treatment plant, sewage-treatment plant, schools, and primary roads —Percent utilization of the above	Detailed community facilities studies or plans (housing, transportation, recreation, water and sewer, police, fire, etc.)
3. Estimated demand a. Population and economy 1) Population	1) 10-yr estimates based upon Dept. of Administration figures as appropriate	1) Detailed estimate and analysis, adapted to local conditions using Department of Administration model
2) Economy	2) Identification of major trends and factors in the economy	2) Detailed economic studies
b. Future land needs	Gross 10-yr estimate allocated to appropriate land classes	Detailed estimates by specific land-use category (commercial, residential, industrial, etc.)
c. Community facilities demand	Consideration of basic facilities needed to service estimated growth	Estimates of demands and costs for some or all community facilities and services

ing information: analyses of present population, economy, and land use and current plans, policies, and regulations; constraints, such as land potential or the capacity of community facilities (water and sewer service, schools, etc.); and estimated demand from changes in population and economy, future land needs, and demand for facilities. Table 18.1 lists in detail required and optional data-analysis items for land-use plans submitted under the North Carolina Coastal Management Act of 1974.

The land-classification map is the heart of the land-use plan. It serves as a statement of land-use policy and has five aims: (1) to achieve and encourage coordination and consistency between local and state land-use policies; (2) to provide a guide for public investment in land; (3) to provide a useful framework for budgeting and planning construction of facilities, such as schools, roads, and sewer and water systems; (4) to coordinate regulatory policies and decisions; and (5) to help provide guidelines for development of an equitable land tax. An example of a currently used land classification system is shown in Table 18.2.

The report accompanying the land-classification map gives special attention to areas of environmental concern—those areas in which uncontrolled or incompatible development might produce irreparable damage. Examples of such areas include coastal marshland; estuaries; renewable resources (watersheds or aquifers); and fragile, historic, or natural resource areas (in the North Carolina example, the Outer Banks, Barrier Islands, etc.). The report should be precise regarding permissible land uses of these areas [6].

TABLE 18.2
Example of a land classification system.

a. *Developed*—Lands where existing population density is moderate to high and where there are a variety of land uses that have the necessary public services

b. *Transition*—Lands where local government plans to accommodate moderate- to high-density development and basic public services during the following 10-year period will be provided to accommodate that growth

c. *Community*—Lands where low-density development is grouped in existing settlements or will occur in such settlements during the following 10-year period and which will not require extensive public services now or in the future

d. *Rural*—Lands whose highest use is for agriculture, forestry, mining, water supply, etc., on the basis of their natural resource potential; also included are lands for future needs not currently recognized

e. *Conservation*—Fragile, hazardous, and other lands necessary to maintain a healthy natural environment and necessary to provide for the public health, safety, or welfare

Source: North Carolina Coastal Resources Commission.

Site Selection and Evaluation

Site selection is the process of choosing and evaluating a physical environment that will support human activities. It is a task shared by professionals from many aspects of environmental studies, including engineering, landscape architecture, planning, earth sciences, biological sciences, social science, and economics and thus involves a multidimensional approach. The goal of site selection for a particular land use is to ensure that the site development is compatible with both the possibilities and the limitations of the natural environment.

Physiographic Determinism   In recent years, a philosophy of site evaluation known as physiographic determinism has emerged [2]. The basic thrust of this philosophy is "design with nature." Rather than laying down an arbitrary design or plan for an area, the approach is to find a plan that nature has already provided in the topography, soils, vegetation, and climate [5]. Using this method, planners maximize the natural qualities of the landscape while minimizing social and economic expenditures whenever possible [6].

Although the philosophy of working in harmony with nature is obviously advantageous, it is often overlooked. People still purchase land for various activities without considering if the land use they have in mind is compatible with the site they have chosen. There are well-known examples of poor siting resulting in increased expense, limited production, or even abandonment of partially completed construction. Construction of a West Coast nuclear power facility was terminated when fractures in a rock (active faults) were discovered and possible serious foundation problems arose (Fig. 18.4). The productivity of a large chicken farm in the southeastern United States was greatly curtailed because the property was purchased before it was determined if there was sufficient groundwater to meet the projected needs. A housing developer in northern Indiana purchased land and built country homes in one of the few isolated areas where bedrock (shale) was at the surface. Thus, septic-tank systems had to be abandoned and a surface sewage treatment facility built. Furthermore, the rock made it much more expensive

FIGURE 18.4
Nuclear power development was abandoned because of an earthquake hazard at this site at Bodega Bay, California, after expenditure of millions of dollars and years of time in site preparation. This waste of time and money could have been avoided had the data on the fault been available earlier.

to excavate for basements and foundations for the homes.

The concept of "design with nature," coined by Ian McHarg, is illustrated by his analysis of the development of a sandy beach like that on Cape Cod, Massachusetts, or along the New Jersey coast. First, the geological and ecological processes that form and maintain the dunes are considered. In this case, the dunes are formed by windblown sand. The sand is stabilized by vegetation, and the dune in turn protects the leeward side from salt spray and allows thickets and woodland to develop (Fig. 18.5a). In this stage of analysis two points are recognized: (1) the dunes are dynamic—they change over time and depend on an influx of sand, and (2) the vegetation plays an important role in stabilizing the dune, and therefore the vegetation must be protected.

In the second stage of analysis, other factors that are important to the vegetation and the dune are measured (Fig. 18.5b). For example, salt spray is lower on the back dune, allowing vegetation to grow that is not resistant to that spray.

Finally, a land-use scheme is developed (Fig. 18.5c). The previous stages of analysis clarify which parts of the dune system are fragile and

must be protected and which can tolerate heavy use. For example, the primary dune is easily destroyed because it is stabilized by vegetation that exists in a harsh environment and is easily killed by trampling and other human impacts. On the other hand, as long as the primary dune remains intact, the back dune can tolerate considerable use; its vegetation exists in a less harsh environment and grows back after disruption more rapidly. The back dune is also less subject to disturbance from wind and storms. Conclusion: Protect the primary dune and develop the back dune. Design *with* nature.

Landscape Aesthetics Scenery in the United States has been recognized as a natural and national resource at least since 1864, when the first national park, Yosemite Valley in California, was established. At that time, the purpose of establishing a park was to preserve unique scenic landscapes. Since then, the definition of "scenic value" has broadened. Even "everyday" nonurban landscapes are considered to have scenic value that enhances the total resource base of a region. We now accept that there are varying scenic values relating to other, more tangible resources [7].

(a) Analysis of geological and ecological processes

Dune forms on a new sand bar by wind moving sand

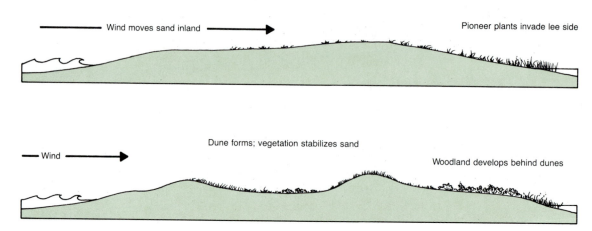

Wind moves sand inland ⟶

Pioneer plants invade lee side

Dune forms; vegetation stabilizes sand

⟶ Wind ⟶

Woodland develops behind dunes

Mature Dune System

Ocean Primary Dune Secondary Dune Woodland develops Bay

(b) The dune system is analyzed for limiting factor

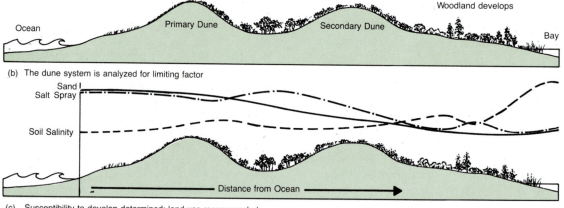

Sand
Salt Spray

Soil Salinity

⟵ Distance from Ocean ⟶

(c) Susceptibility to develop determined; land use recommended

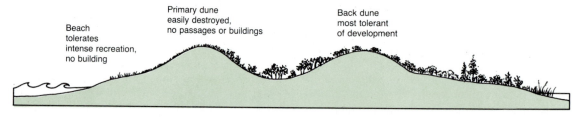

Beach tolerates intense recreation, no building

Primary dune easily destroyed, no passages or buildings

Back dune most tolerant of development

FIGURE 18.5
Designing with nature for a sand dune area. (a) The natural geological and biological processes that maintain the dunes are analyzed first. (b) The important variables are analyzed
to determine which are limiting. (c) A synthesis of information yields a map of the susceptibility to development and the best land use for each part of the dune. (After McHarg.)

Quantitative evaluation of tangible natural resources such as water, forests, or minerals is standard procedure before economic development or management of a particular land area. Water resources for power or other uses may be evaluated by the flow in the rivers and storage in lakes; forest resources may be evaluated by the number, type, and size of the trees and their potential yield of lumber; and mineral resources may be evaluated by estimating the number of tons of economically valuable mineral material (ore) at a particular location. We can make a statement of quality and quantity for each tangible resource compared with some known low quality or quantity. Ideally, we would like to make similar statements about the more intangible resources, such as scenery [8]. Unfortunately, few specific standards are available for comparison. Landscape evaluation of scenic resources as part of land-use planning or assessing environmental impact generally rests on a rather subjective methodology.

Environmental Impact Assessment

The probable effects of human use of the land are generally referred to as **environmental impact.** This term became widely known after passage of the National Environmental Policy Act (NEPA) in 1969. This act requires that all major federal actions that could possibly affect the quality of the human environment be preceded by an evaluation of the project and its impact on the environment. In order to meet both the letter and the spirit of NEPA, the Council on Environmental Quality has prepared guidelines to assist in preparing environmental impact statements. The major components of the council's statement, revised in 1979 [9], are:

1 A statement of purpose and need for the project.
2 A rigorous comparison of the reasonable alternatives.
3 A succinct description of the environment of the area to be affected.
4 A discussion of the environmental consequences of the proposed project and its alternatives. This discussion must include direct and indirect effects; energy requirements and conservation potential; resource requirements; impacts on urban quality and cultural or historical resources; possible conflicts with state or local land-use policies and controls; and mitigation measures. Mitigations are actions taken to reduce adverse environmental impacts. They include repair and restoration of the environment, reduction or elimination of impacts, and compensation to affected parties. The success of mitigation determines the real significance of impacts and the ranking of alternatives.
5 A list of the names and qualifications of the persons primarily responsible for preparation of the environmental impact statement and a list of agencies to which the statement was sent.
6 An index.

For example, consider a plan to develop a new electric power plant on a major river. The site lies in agricultural land within 50 km of a major city. The purpose is the production of electricity, and the description of need would include current and projected electrical usage in the area and current and projected production. The comparison of reasonable alternatives would include the effects of energy conservation and siting the plant elsewhere. The river and land in the areas that would be affected would be part of the description of the environment. The projected future for the site without the proposed project (e.g., the site might be expected to undergo development for residential and commercial use even without the power plant) would be included. The description of the environmental consequences would include the project's effects (e.g., the power plant would remove water from the river for cooling and return it at a higher temperature) and its impacts, both short-term (e.g., fish swim away from the heated water) and long-term (e.g., the reproduction and therefore population size of some fish species are expected to decrease). A mitigation could be a plan to stock the river with young fish grown in state fish hatcheries.

Because mitigations determine the real significance of impacts, the professional environmental planner must place considerable emphasis on this aspect. The environmental impact analysis is intended not only to determine the negative effects, but also to outline what positive steps may be taken to promote wise use. In some cases, such as a plan that would affect the wintering grounds of an endangered bird species like the whooping crane, there may be no mitigating actions. In those cases the recommendation would be for preservation and no development.

The environmental impact statement process was criticized during the first 10 years under NEPA because it initiated a tremendous volume of paperwork by requiring detailed reports that tended to obscure important issues. No one knew exactly what had to be included or what might be attacked, and it seemed safer to include more information rather than less. There was a tendency to produce extremely long documents that listed every possible impact and lacked a focus on crucial issues. Therefore, the revised regulations (1979) introduced two other important changes: scoping and record of decision.

Scoping is the process of identifying important environmental issues that require detailed evaluation early in the planning of a proposed project. The record of decision is a concise statement by the planning agency of the alternatives considered and which alternatives are environmentally preferable. The agency then has the responsibility to monitor the project to ensure its decision is carried out. This is a very significant point. For example, if in an environmental impact statement for a proposal to construct an interstate highway the agency commits itself to specific designs and locations for the right-of-way in order to minimize environmental degradation, then the contracts authorizing the work must be conditional on incorporation of those designs and locations.

There is no accepted method for assessing the environmental impact of a particular project or action. Furthermore, because of the wide variety of actions—from the hunting of migratory birds to the construction of a large reservoir—there is no one methodology of impact assessment appropriate for all situations. What is important is that those responsible for preparing the statement strive to minimize personal bias and maximize objectivity. The analysis must be scientifically, technically, and legally defensible and prepared by highly objective scientific inquiry [10].

Environmental impact analysis for major projects often requires the combined efforts of scientists from different disciplines. It is important to remember that the specific function of the members of the task force is to evaluate; they are not to decide the issues. The task force provides necessary information to those with authority to make just decisions. At this stage in the development of our environmental awareness, we are still trying to determine the kind and amount of information necessary to make good decisions. However, as more and more work is done and decisions are made, the critical elements of environmental information will be better understood, and eventually some will be acknowledged as requirements in the same way as cost and profit data are now required in economic analysis [10].

In keeping with the spirit of NEPA, we must consider environmental consequences of a particular action before it is implemented and identify potential conflicts and problem areas as early as possible. In this way, we can minimize regrettable and expensive environmental deterioration.

Three case histories—the High Dam at Aswan, the Trans-Alaska Pipeline, and Cape Hatteras National Seashore—will illustrate the importance of environmental impact analysis.

CASE HISTORY: THE HIGH DAM AT ASWAN

The High Dam at Aswan and Lake Nasser in Egypt is a dramatic example of what can happen when environmental impacts are ignored or inadequately evaluated. The High Dam project is causing many serious problems, including health problems that could one day be catastrophic, as the following case study will demonstrate [11].

The High Dam at Aswan, completed in 1964, is one of the biggest and most expensive dams in the world. It was designed to store a sufficient amount of the Nile's yearly floodwaters to irrigate existing land, reclaim additional land from the desert, produce electricity, and protect against drought and famine.

Unexpected water loss in the reservoir of the Aswan, which may present problems in dry years, occurs because of two factors: a 50% error in com-

Career Profile: Jean Schumann

"I am a bureaucrat," says Jean Schumann. "I do a lot of paperwork—research and analytical." Schumann is an analyst with a Washington, D.C. consulting firm that does mainly environmental work. She is a member of the firm's Technical Assistance Team (TAT), which currently is contracted to assist EPA's hazardous substance emergency response division.

Schumann says a hazardous substance is any material that is going to pose a threat to public health or the environment. EPA has a Remedial Program which deals with large sites that may take years to clean up. TAT is involved with EPA's Removal Program, which deals with sites that pose imminent danger to the public and need immediate attention. EPA cleans up sites when the responsible parties will not clean them up, Schumann says.

TAT is nationwide, consisting of field personnel at hazardous substance sites throughout the country and personnel in Washington, such as Schumann, involved in administering the cleanup programs.

Schumann describes her job as "a mixed bag of things." Currently, she is also involved in compiling information for EPA on the costs of cleaning up underground storage tanks. EPA wants to develop regulations governing proper use, monitoring, and cleanup of under-

ground tanks storing petroleum, gasoline, diesel fuel, and hazardous substances.

Schumann helped with a National Response Team Survey for EPA. TAT surveyed all of the national EPA offices concerning federal, state, and local preparedness in responding to hazardous substance emergencies. TAT developed and conducted the survey, analyzed the results, and presented a report to EPA.

She has also been involved in analyzing the impact of a Superfund amendment, in terms of budget and personnel requirements for the EPA Removal Program.

Schumann majored in psychology until her junior year of college, when she took a course about the environmental movement, to fulfill a history requirement. She says, "I loved it." Although her interest in psychology continued—during

her last years of college she was a counselor at a halfway house—she says, "I knew I wanted to do something environmental." She completed degrees in both psychology and environmental studies.

After college, she went to Washington and got a job as an assistant environmental analyst with a government environmental agency. After several years with the agency, she answered a classified ad for her present job.

"The hardest thing to learn after the idealism of college," Schumann says, "was that you have to learn to work within systems that are already established." People are needed to fight the system because the system needs to change, but you have to learn the system in order to accomplish goals, she says. "You can't just have sit-ins."

Schumann hopes college students today develop an understanding of people's feelings. "What needs to be done now is to change people's attitudes," she says. Historically, the United States has been the land of abundance; there always seemed to be more of everything. But there are limits and we have to learn to live within the limits. Shortsightedness will do us harm, Schumann says. "We need to start planning now because in the future there will be no alternatives."

Michele Wigginton

puting evaporation loss and tremendous water losses to underground water systems. The error in computation of evaporation loss, which meant an unanticipated loss of 5 billion m³ of water per year, resulted from overlooking the evaporation loss induced by high-velocity winds traveling over the tremendous expanse of water in this very hot, dry region of Earth. A chain of smaller and less expensive dams would have avoided this waste of water resources. However, even this loss is small compared with the water lost underground [11].

It has long been known that, for hundreds of kilometers upriver from Aswan, the Nile cut across an immense sandstone aquifer that fed the river an enormous amount of water. When the first and much smaller Aswan Dam was built in 1902, the flow of groundwater was reversed, the water pressure caused by the reservoir forced the water to move elsewhere through numerous fissures and fractures in the sandstone. That smaller dam remained until 1964, when the High Dam was completed. From 1902 until 1964, the Aswan Reservoir stored about 5 billion m³ of water per year, but lost 12 billion m³/yr through reversed groundwater flow. The amount of water escaping from the modern Lake Nasser behind the new dam is unknown, but because the new reservoir is designed to store 30 times more water than the old Aswan Reservoir, and because seepage tends to vary directly with lake depth, the amount of water being lost must be tremendous [11].

It might be argued that in time the clay settling out from the lake will plug fractures in the rock and the lake will fill. However, if the fractures are very large and numerous, the water could essentially escape forever, and Egypt might well end up with less water than it had before the dam was constructed [11].

Unfortunately, the direct water problems with the High Dam and Lake Nasser are only part of the project's total impact. There are five other major environmental consequences of this project. First, the High Dam lacks sluices to transport sediment through the reservoir, so the reservoir traps 134 million tons of the Nile's sediment per year. Historically, the sediment has produced and replenished the fertile soils along the banks of the Nile. Second, the eastern Mediterranean is deprived of the nutrients in the Nile's sediment, resulting in a one-third reduction of the plankton, which is the food base for sardine, mackerel, lobster, and shrimp. Third, the lake and associated canals are becoming infested with snails that carry the dreaded disease schistosomiasis (snail fever). This disease has always been a problem in Egypt, but the swift currents of the Nile floodwaters flushed out the snails each year. Fourth, there is an increased threat of a killer malaria carried by a particular mosquito often found only 80 km from the southern shores of Lake Nasser. The reservoir might be invaded on a permanent basis by the disease-carrying insects. Fifth, salinity of soils is increasing at rather alarming rates in middle and upper Egypt. Soil salinity has been a long-standing problem on the Nile delta, but was alleviated upstream by the natural flushing of the salt by the floodwaters of the Nile River.

On the positive side, the High Dam and lake have converted 2800 km² from natural floodwater irrigation to canal irrigation and allowed double cropping—but at a tremendous cost. In the future, however, tremendous amounts of money will have to be spent on fertilizers to replenish soil nutrients and to control water- and insect-borne disease [11].

CASE HISTORY: THE TRANS-ALASKA PIPELINE

The Trans-Alaska Pipeline, which was completed in 1977, provides a good example of environmental impact analysis. In 1968, vast subsurface reservoirs of oil and gas were discovered near Prudhoe Bay in Alaska. Because the Arctic Ocean is frozen much of the year, it is impractical to ship the oil by tankers, and thus a 1270–km pipeline from Prudhoe Bay to Port Valdez, where tankers can dock and load oil the entire year, was suggested [10,12].

The general route of the Trans-Alaska Pipeline is shown in Figure 18.6. The corridor for the pipeline traverses rough topography, large rivers, areas with extensive permafrost, and areas with a high earthquake hazard. Over 80% of the pipeline crosses federal lands. Because of the sensitive na-

FIGURE 18.6
Approximate corridor for
the Trans-Alaska Pipeline.
(After Brew.)

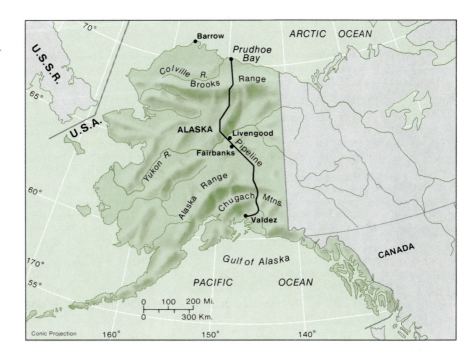

ture of the Arctic environment and the certainty of irreversible environmental degradation, a comprehensive impact analysis was required to evaluate both the negative and the positive aspects of the project [10].

The pipeline crosses three major mountain ranges: the Brooks Range, the Alaska Range, and the tectonically active Chugach Mountains. On the north side of the Alaska Range, the pipeline crosses the Denali fault, an active fault zone that has experienced recent displacement of the ground.

The corridor also traverses a number of large rivers, and it was feared that erosion at meander bends might damage the pipeline. A study to evaluate the river crossings [13] identified areas that might experience excessive bank erosion during the 30–year expected life of the pipeline.

The permafrost (permanently frozen ground) areas crossed by the pipeline presented another potential hazard. Once frozen ground melts, it is extremely unstable. This aspect of the project has been thoroughly engineered, and it is hoped that problems with permafrost will be minimized.

Nevertheless, the many kilometers of a large hot-oil pipeline crossing vast areas of permafrost provide cause for concern.

Analysis of possible physical, biological, and socioeconomic impacts associated with the pipeline established many areas of concern [10]. A list of primary and secondary effects of the Trans-Alaska hot-oil pipeline, gas pipeline, and tanker transport system considered by the task force to evaluate environmental impact is shown in Table 18.3.

In addition to evaluating these effects, possible indirect linkages between the effects had to be evaluated. For example, an oil spill or an unavoidable release of oil in the tanker operation into the marine environment obviously affects marine resources. The extent of the effects, however, is difficult to evaluate.

Based on the environmental analysis, there were three main unavoidable effects: (1) disturbances of terrain; fish and wildlife habitats; and human use of the land during construction, operation, and maintenance of the entire project, including the pipeline itself and access roads, high-

TABLE 18.3
Primary and secondary impacts associated with the Trans-Alaska Pipeline, Arctic gas pipelines, and the proposed tanker system.

A. Primary effects associated with Arctic pipelines:
1. Disturbance of ground
2. Disturbance of water (including treated effluent discharge into water)
3. Disturbance of air (including waste discharged to air and noise)
4. Disturbance of vegetation
5. Solid waste accumulation
6. Commitment of physical space to pipeline system and construction activities
7. Increased employment
8. Increased utilization of invested capital
9. Disturbance of fish and wildlife
10. Barrier effects on fish and wildlife
11. Scenery modification (including erosional effects)
12. Wilderness instrusion
13. Heat transmitted to or from the ground
14. Heat transmitted to or from water
15. Heat transmitted to or from air
16. Heat to or from vegetation
17. Moisture to air
18. Moisture to vegetation
19. Extraction of oil and gas
20. Bypassed sewage to water
21. Human-caused fires
22. Accidents that would amplify unavoidable impact effects
23. Small oil losses to the ground, water, and vegetation
24. Oil spills affecting marine waters
25. Oil spills affecting freshwater lakes and drainages

26. Oil spills affecting ground and vegetation
27. Oil spills affecting any combination of the foregoing

B. Secondary effects associated with Arctic pipelines:
1. Thermokarst development
2. Physical habitat loss for wildlife
3. Restriction of wildlife movements
4. Effects on sports, subsistence, and commercial fisheries
5. Effects on recreational resources
6. Changes in population, economy, and demands on public services in various communities, including native communities, and in native populations and economies
7. Development of ice fog and its effect on transportation
8. Effects on mineral resource exploration

C. Primary effects associated with tanker system:
1. Treated ballast water into Port Valdez
2. Vessel frequency in Port Valdez, Prince William Sound, open ocean, Puget Sound, San Francisco Bay, southern California waters, and other ports
3. Oil spills in any of those places

D. Secondary effects associated with tanker system:
1. Effects on sports and commercial fisheries
2. Effects on recreational resources
3. Effects on population in Valdez and other communities

Source: Brew.

ways, and other support facilities; (2) discharge of effluents and oil into Port Valdez from the tanker transport system; and (3) increased human pressures on services, utilities, and many other areas, including cultural changes of the native population.

The major threatened effect was accidental loss of oil from the oilfield, pipeline, or tanker system. Accidental loss of oil from the pipeline could be caused by slope failure (landslides), differential settlement in permafrost areas, stream bed or bank scour at river crossings, or destructive sea waves causing a leak or rupture in the pipeline. Oil loss from tankers could be caused by shipwreck or accidental loss during transfer operations at Port Valdez.

The pipeline generated great controversy because of the conflicts in balancing the need for resource development and the known or predicted environmental degradation. Although alternative routes were extensively evaluated (Fig. 18.7), the route to Port Valdez was ultimately approved, perhaps because this route led to the most rapid resource development while maintaining national security.

Comparison of alternative routes suggested that a trans-Alaska-Canada route to Edmonton, Canada, was the route that would have caused the least environmental impact. This route would have avoided the marine environment and earthquake zones and would have enabled both an oil and a gas pipeline to be placed in one corridor. It was

FIGURE 18.7
Alternative routes for transporting oil from the North Slope of Alaska. (From Brew.)

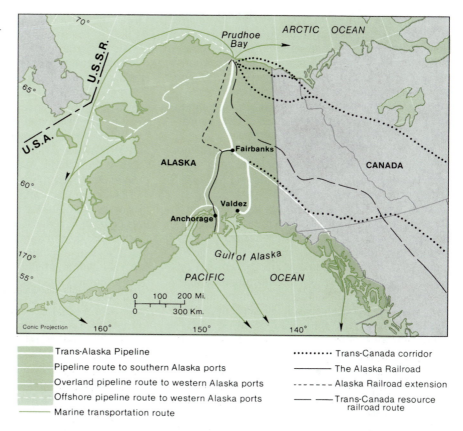

▓ Trans-Alaska Pipeline	⋯⋯ Trans-Canada corridor
── Pipeline route to southern Alaska ports	── The Alaska Railroad
─ ─ Overland pipeline route to western Alaska ports	- - - - Alaska Railroad extension
⋯⋯ Offshore pipeline route to western Alaska ports	── ── Trans-Canada resource railroad route
── Marine transportation route	

nevertheless rejected. Consideration of alternatives shows the scientist's obligation to state an opinion based on sound scientific information, even though this opinion may be either unpopular or likely to be overridden in the final balancing of alternatives. Diverse political maneuvering at all levels can significantly affect which alternative is chosen.

CASE HISTORY: CAPE HATTERAS NATIONAL SEASHORE

The Outer Banks of North Carolina have for generations been inhabited by people living and working in a marine-dominated environment. Until recently, the way of life had depended on raising livestock, fishing, hunting, boat building, and other marine pursuits [14].

The landscape of the Outer Banks characteristically can change in a very short time in response to major storms such as hurricanes and northeasters that periodically strike the islands. Of the two types of storms, the more frequent northeasters probably cause the most erosion. On the other hand, infrequent hurricanes can cause major changes, including extensive overwash and formation of new inlets.

Historically, the people of the Outer Banks have philosophically lived with and adjusted to a changing landscape. In recent times, however, this philosophy has changed because of economic pressure to develop coastal property. A new philosophy of coastal protection has arisen in an attempt to stabilize the coastal environment. Stabilization through erosion control instills the perception of a constant-appearing landscape necessary to encourage commercial development.

Congress approved in 1937 and amended in 1940 an act establishing the Cape Hatteras National Seashore as the first national seashore. The park consists of 115 km^2 along a 120–km portion of the Outer Banks and includes portions of three islands of the more than 240 km of the Barrier Island system. The Barrier Islands essentially bound and protect the largely undeveloped coastal plains lowland of North Carolina [14].

Eight unincorporated villages are bounded by the Cape Hatteras National Seashore and are spaced along nearly the entire length of the seashore. Legislation authorizing the park provided for the continued existence of these villages, including the beach in front of each of them facing the Atlantic Ocean. This legislation has been interpreted by many as an obligation of the federal government to maintain and stabilize beach access and frontage of these villages. Unfortunately, stabilization has been difficult and, in some villages, less than 60 m of beach remains because of recent coastal erosion. This philosophy of protection is contrary to that during the early development of the islands, which was mainly on the sound (inland) side of the islands. With construction of the first dune systems in the 1930s and opening of the road link in the 1950s, however, the basic configuration of the villages began to change as communities began to spread toward the ocean [14].

It was assumed that at one time much of the Outer Banks was heavily forested and that logging and overgrazing had destroyed these forests. Evidence for this is inconclusive. The wooded areas were located in an area protected by a natural dune line, so the logical conclusion was to construct an artificial barrier dune system to help the area return to a natural state by inhibiting beach erosion. Of course, the dune line would also protect the roads and communities. As a result, there is now an artificial dune system along the entire Cape Hatteras National Seashore at an average dune height of 5 m and an average distance of 100 m from the ocean [15]. This artificial erosion-control measure, along with programs to artificially keep sand on the beach, could cost about $1 million per year if continued. The expense of this alternative, along with an essentially geological argument about whether artificial dune lines will jeopardize the fu-

ture of the Barrier Islands, has led to a controversy on how to best manage the park.

The geologic problem and controversy on how dynamic earth processes create and maintain barrier islands are at the philosophical heart of the U.S. Park Service's dilemma in developing a long-range program to maintain the natural environment for the use and enjoyment of present and future generations. Although there are several ideas and known ways that coastal processes can develop barrier islands, there is heated debate on the processes needed to maintain them.

Debate on the nature and extent of geologic processes that maintain the "natural changing" Barrier Islands centers on whether periodic overwash of the frontal dune system by storm waves is essential to maintaining the islands. If the overwash is essential, then building a dune line is contrary to natural processes, and the final result over a period of years may be deterioration of the islands as a natural system. This would be contrary to the Park Service's stated objectives to preserve the islands in a natural state.

Regardless of the historic role of overwash, it is apparent that overwash is a natural process and as such is probably significant in the geologic history of barrier-island migration. This does not mean, however, that it is necessarily always bad to attempt to selectively control rapid coastal erosion by maintaining a protective frontal dune system. Proper placement of dunes and subsequent sound conservation practice in maintaining them remains a feasible alternative to short-range selected coastal erosion problems, particularly near settlements and critical communication lines.

Faced with the problem of selecting a management policy for the Cape Hatteras National Seashore, the Park Service, in 1974, presented five possible alternatives, ranging from essentially no control of natural coastline processes to attempting complete protection. Each alternative was analyzed to determine the entire spectrum of possible impacts. Few people wanted complete protection or complete control of the seashore [14]. The position of the Park Service is to attempt to strike a compromise in which the Barrier Islands for the most part may be preserved in a natural state, while the need to maintain a transportation link with the mainland is recognized. Thus, the communities will have to live with and adjust to the dynamic high-risk environment they choose to live in, much as the people of the Outer Banks historically have. This is contrary to prevailing trends in coastal development that assume a more stable environment and acknowledge that natural processes play a significant role in preserving the natural environment [14].

A general management plan for the Cape Hatteras National Seashore was recently completed after several years of careful environmental impact work and public review. The plan proposes several actions:

☐ Allowing natural seashore processes and dynamics to occur except in instances when life, health, or significant cultural resources on the major transportation link are jeopardized
☐ Controlling use of off-road vehicles
☐ Expanding and allowing easier access to recreation sites on the beach and sound
☐ Controlling the spread of exotic vegetation species
☐ Ensuring that significant natural and cultural resources are preserved and maintained

☐ Cooperating with state and local governments in mutually beneficial planning endeavors [16]

For planning purposes, the national seashore was divided into four environmental resource units (ERUs): ocean/beach, vegetated sand flats, interior dunes/maritime forest, and marsh/sound. Table 18.4 summarizes planning objectives for each ERU, and Figure 18.8 illustrates the principle of management zoning for Hatteras Island.

The major impact of the proposed management program will be threefold. First, the Cape Hatteras National Seashore will be preserved in a natural state. Second, residents of the villages will have to live with and adjust to the effects of natural events to a greater extent. Third, economic development of the villages will change, and even though the road will be maintained, it will be subject to more periodic damage.

COASTAL ZONE MANAGEMENT

Although coastal areas are varied in topography, climate, and vegetation, they are all generally dy-

TABLE 18.4
Planning objectives for Cape Hatteras National Seashore Environmental Resource Units (ERU).

ERU	Characteristics	Planning Objectives
Ocean/beach	Shifting sands, frequent overwash, limited vegetation on dunes	Allow natural processes to continue unhampered; allow for wide range of unstructured recreational activities by visitors; no construction allowed
Vegetated sand flats	Located between dune line and edge of saltwater marsh	Continue use as transportation corridor; allow development necessary to support visitor activities and resource protection
Interior dunes/ maritime forest	Found in relatively few locations; variable topography, remoteness, dense vegetation	Maintain in natural state; allow passive recreation; design any construction to minimize impact on natural processes and systems
Marsh sound	Includes the sound, sound shore, and associated marshes	Maintain in natural state; provide limited access to the sound; allow limited development to support passive recreational activities

Source: National Park Service.

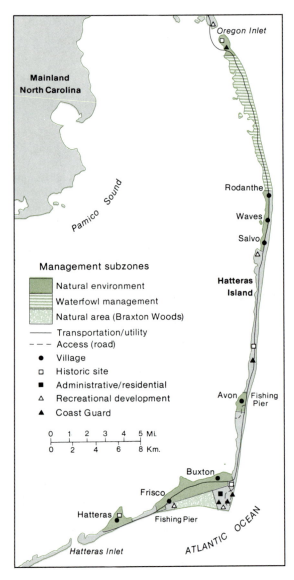

FIGURE 18.8
Proposed management subzones for part of the Cape
Hatteras National Seashore. (After National Park Service.)

located near the coast. This is especially true in the
United States where it is expected that most of the
population will eventually be concentrated along
the nation's 150,000 km of shoreline, including the
Great Lakes. Today, the nation's largest cities lie in
the coastal zone and approximately 75% of the
population lives in coastal states [17]. Because of
existing and potential conflicts in the coastal zone
the U.S. Congress in 1972 passed the Coastal Zone
Management Act, which was amended in 1976.

The purpose of the act was to establish a federal
program to assist states in developing land-use
plans for coastal areas. In particular, the act man-
dated that individual states define the boundaries
of the coastal zone, specify permissible land uses
within the zone, and address issues of particular
public concern. This last category refers to issues
such as public access to the coastal zone and protection of fragile environments or endangered species. All coastal states are now involved to a lesser
or greater degree in coastal zone management. At
about the time the federal act was being passed,
citizens in California concerned about coastal
areas voted to require a permit for any development taking place in a zone extending 900 m from
the sea's high tide to about 5 km seaward. The law
also called for a master plan for coastal development to be prepared and adopted as state policy.
Although the original law has been weakened
somewhat, it has served a valuable function in
coastal zone management, particularly in areas
concerned with development and coastal access.

The people of North Carolina, recognizing the
importance of planning for their fragile coastal environments along barrier islands, passed the
Coastal Area Management Act of 1974. This act
recognizes the people's need for an opportunity to
enjoy the aesthetic, cultural, and recreational
qualities of the natural coastline. One major objective of the act is to provide a management system
that allows preservation of estuaries, barrier islands, sand dunes, and beaches so that their natural productivity and biological, economic, and
aesthetic values are safeguarded. The second objective is to ensure that development in the coast
areas does not exceed the capabilities of the land
and water resources.

The North Carolina Act establishes a cooperative program of coastal management between

namic environments. Continental and oceanic processes converge along coasts to produce a landscape that is characteristically capable of rapid
change. The impact of hazardous coastal processes
is considerable because many populated areas are

local and state government in which local government has the initiative and the planning. The role of state government is to set standards and to review and support local government in the planning program. The planning has three main steps: development of state planning guidelines for coastal areas; development and adoption of a land-use plan for each county in the coastal area; and use of plans with criteria for issuing or denying permits to develop land or water resources within the coastal area.

An interesting case in coastal management occurs in Alaska, where some of the boundaries for the coastal zone are set many kilometers inland at boundaries of watersheds. The rationale is that the streams that flow to the ocean are natural migratory routes for fish such as salmon and as such there is a natural tie between the rivers and the coastal zone. Thus development such as urbanization or timber harvesting within the river basin must pass through the coastal zone management system as well. Although the boundaries in Alaska seem rather remote from the ocean in some instances, the argument is that protection of marine and coastal resources (in this case the fish) is certainly warranted. The program seems to be working.

RECREATION AND ENVIRONMENT

Planning for recreational activities on government lands (including national forests and national parks) is becoming a controversial issue. Some regulation seems necessary if environmental degradation resulting from the recreational activities of people is to be minimized. In some areas such as the popular Yosemite National Park or Grand Canyon this may simply require limiting the number of permits that allow access to trails or to the river. For example, the number of people allowed to raft the Grand Canyon has had to be limited to protect the river environment from overzealous recreational land use. Limiting people in national parks is fairly straightforward and most visitors understand the necessity to protect park lands. In fact, it is a congressional mandate that park environments be maintained for future generations. Concerning national forest lands, however, there is

more controversy concerning controlling land use for recreational purposes. Managers for national forests tend to accommodate various interest groups through a concept known as multiple use. This has had variable success because some uses are basically incompatible. As an example we will consider off-road vehicles.

Off-road Vehicles (ORVs)

The widespread use of off-road vehicles (ORVs) has had significant impact on the environment. There are now more than 12 million ORVs, many of which are invading the deserts, coastal dunes, and forested lands of the United States. Intensive use of ORVs causes soil erosion, changes in hydrology, and damage to plants and animals (see Plate 15). The problem is not insignificant. A single motorcycle need travel only 7.9 km to affect 1000 m^2; a 4-wheel drive vehicle will affect the same area by traveling only 2.4 km. Furthermore, in some desert areas the tracks produce scars that remain part of the landscape for hundreds of years [18,19].

ORVs cause mechanical erosion and facilitate wind and water erosion of materials loosened by their passing. Runoff from ORV sites is as much as eight times greater than that for adjacent unused areas, and sediment yields are comparable to those found on construction sites in urbanizing areas [19]. Figure 18.9 shows an ORV site in the Mojave Desert. Motorcycles and dune buggies nearly destroyed the vegetative cover on the sandy soil, thus contributing to a 1973 dust storm that was visible on satellite. In areas of intensive use, ORVs are often the dominant agents of erosion, turning vegetative hills into eroding wastelands.

Hydrologic changes from ORV activity are primarily the result of soil compaction, which reduces the soil's ability to absorb water, makes the water less available to plants and animals, and changes the variability of soil temperature. Animals are killed or displaced and vegetation is destroyed by intensive ORV activity. The result is a combination of soil erosion, compaction, temperature change, and moisture content change [19].

Environmental planning that encompasses the use of ORVs is a difficult task. There is little doubt that some land must be set aside for ORV use. The

FIGURE 18.9
South end of the Shadow Mountains, Mojave Desert. Dune buggies and motorcycles have destroyed the vegetative cover, allowing the sandy soil to be removed easily by wind and running water. This area contributed sediment to a dust storm recognizable on satellite imagery.

disruption and damage trails less than horses. As long as the number of mountain bikes remains small this may be true. However, bicycles are not nearly as expensive as horses and they don't have to be fed. There is little doubt that if the mountain bike sport continues to grow that intensive use in some areas will be associated with environmental degradation, such as damage to plant life and accelerated erosion.

The management of public lands for recreational activities requires planning at a variety of levels with considerable public input. For example, when a national forest is developing management plans, there is often a series of public meetings in which people are advised of the process by which the plan is developed and asked for ideas and suggestions. Maximizing public input will provide better communication between those managing resources and those using them for recreational purposes. However, government officials and scientists involved in developing use plans are faced with complex land-use problems at a variety of levels. Often the complexity of a problem is such that no easy answers can be found. However, action and inaction today can have serious consequences for tomorrow, so it seems best to have conservative plans to protect and preserve a quality environment for future generations.

Management of Recreational Activities

Management plans for many of the national forest and national park lands in the United States have been, or are being, developed. Developers of these plans tend to consider a spectrum of recreational activities and attempt to balance the desires of several user groups. Certain areas have been set aside for intensive off-road vehicle use and other areas have been closed entirely. Limits in wilderness areas are placed on the number of people admitted, and coastal areas may have regulations limiting activities such as jet skiing and surfing in swimming areas. In regions where endangered species exist, more stringent regulations to govern the activities of people may be present. For example, in Yellowstone National Park in Wyoming and Montana, special consideration is given to grizzly

problems are how much land should be involved and how to minimize environmental damage. The possible effects of airborne soil removal (by wind) must also be evaluated carefully, as must the sacrifice of nonrenewable cultural, biological, and geological resources [18]. Intensive ORV use is incompatible with nearly all other land uses and it is very difficult to restrict ORV damages to a specific site. Material removed by mechanical, water, and wind erosion will always have an impact on other areas and activities [18,19].

In recent years there has been a trend in some areas towards the use of all-terrain bicycles (ATBs, or mountain bicycles) that may be ridden on trails. Controversy is growing concerning how to manage ATBs, particularly in areas frequently used by pedestrians and people on horseback. Riders of ATBs have commented they cause little environmental

bear habitat through controlling where humans may venture.

Other recreational activities that are or may become subject to regulation include hiking, camping, fishing, hunting, boating, skiing, and such recently popularized activities as "treasure hunting," which includes panning for gold on a large scale.

Activities that occur on government lands may be more easily regulated than those occurring elsewhere, but the preservation of a quality environment is a concern common to all regardless of land ownership.

PLANNING FOLLOWING EMERGENCIES

In recent years two types of planning have emerged: projects in which design and environmental impact analysis are integral parts and emergency projects following catastrophic events, such as hurricanes or volcanic eruptions, which cause widespread damage. Emergency planning is always in response to pressing needs and an influx of millions of dollars in emergency money. Too often the work authorized is overzealous—beyond what is necessary—and is not carefully thought out. As a result, the emergency projects may cause further environmental disruptions. While emergency work is desperately needed, care must be taken when emergency money arrives to ensure that it is used for the best purposes possible.

For example, following severe storms and floods that struck Virginia in the aftermath of Hurricane Camille in 1969, emergency federal aid was used to channelize streams in hopes of alleviating future floods. In some instances, local bulldozer operators with little or no instruction or knowledge of streams were contracted to clear and straighten stream channels. Results of this unplanned and unsupervised channel work have been disastrous to many kilometers of streams. Catastrophic storms can seriously damage roads, farms, and homes, in which case emergency channel work is clearly needed, but such emergency work should be confined to stream channels that require immediate attention. Emergency funds should not be considered a license for wholesale

modification of any stream in the damaged area at the request of property owners or others.

The eruption and catastrophic landslide/debris avalanche of Mt. St. Helens in 1980 delivered 2.5 km^3 of debris into the Toutle River. Fearing continued downstream sediment pollution, the U.S. Army Corps of Engineers constructed two emergency catch dams to filter the water through rockfill and gravel barriers, thus maintaining the flow of water in the river while trapping the sediment in the catch dams. Unfortunately, the dams were constructed before reliable estimates could be made of the volume of sediment likely to be delivered to the dams. On the north fork of the Toutle River, the catch dam had a capacity to hold 0.0065 km^3 of debris. The Corps of Engineers estimated that the sediment load would be 0.01–0.02 km^3/yr, so the river would have to be dredged two or three times per year to remain in service. However, after observing the effects of a small August flood, the U.S. Geological Survey estimated that the sediment yield would be closer to 0.3–0.38 km^3/yr, and that the catch dams were about 100 times too small to survive expected winter storms and floods. This prediction was proven true during a storm in late October when the dams failed. Thus, while the idea of catch dams was worthwhile, they were constructed with poor or incomplete planning and were too small.

Even if there is not sufficient time to prepare an environmental impact statement, planning following emergencies should be carefully carried out. Immediate work may be necessary to restore communication and protect property, but those responsible should limit early work to what is absolutely necessary. Other projects should be more carefully evaluated to determine whether they really are necessary and whether they will cause future problems.

REGIONAL PLANNING

Land-use planning occurs at a variety of levels from local to county to state and less frequently at the regional level. Probably one of the earliest examples of regional planning in the United States goes back to 1933 when Franklin D. Roosevelt introduced his "New Deal," which included a number of programs such as the Tennessee Valley Authority. The regional plan for the Tennessee River established a semi-independent authority whose responsibility was to promote economic growth and social well-being for the people of the region. The area included parts of seven states and was in an economically depressed state at the time the authority was established. In particular there had been rampant exploitation of timber and petroleum resources and the people living in the region were some of the poorest in the entire country [20]. Today the Tennessee Valley Authority is reported to be one of the best examples in the world of regional planning (Fig. 18.10). It is characterized by a multidimensional and multilevel planning system to manage land and water resources. In particular the authority is involved in production and regulation of electrical power, flood control, navigation, and outdoor recreation.

As a second example of regional planning, consider the Lake Tahoe area in the Sierra Nevada Mountains of California and Nevada. The lake is located within the Tahoe basin and since the 1960s has undergone rapid change due to the influx of people into the highly attractive area. Lake Tahoe is very deep and is renowned for its incredibly clear water. Planning around the lake was difficult because it involved two states and a number of counties and cities, each with differing regulations and ideas. California and Nevada together formed the Tahoe Regional Planning Agency in 1969 to coordinate concerns in the Tahoe basin. Then in 1980 the Federal Government entered the picture when the Congress passed into law the Tahoe Regional Planning Compact, which gave federal recognition to the regional agency and gave that agency the power to establish "environment threshold carrying capacity" [20]. These thresholds are related to items such as water and air pollution as well as sediment pollution.

Considerable research is ongoing at the present time to establish some of the environmental standards necessary for proper regional planning for the Tahoe area. As the thresholds are developed, they are incorporated into the basin's regional plan. Such plans are the basis for ordinances that will help ensure that the Lake Tahoe region maintains its high-quality environment.

FIGURE 18.10
The once flood-prone Tennessee River has been converted by the Tennessee Valley Authority into a series of lakes confined by nine major dams, including Wheeler Dam (shown), in northwestern Alabama.

NATIONAL PLANNING

As pressures on the land from many uses have increased during the last decades, planning at the national level has developed for certain land uses, particularly those that affect very sensitive areas. Wilderness is one such sensitive area. For example, the National Wilderness Preservation Act of 1964 set aside 3.6 million ha (9 million acres) of wilderness, which has increased since then to include more than 7 million ha (17 million acres) in more than 170 areas. These designated wilderness areas occur in lands with many kinds of jurisdiction. For example, the U.S. Forest Service administers more than 100 wilderness areas, totaling more than 6.7 million ha (16.6 million acres). The National Wild and Scenic Rivers System is another example of national planning to protect sensitive land areas [21].

The National Wilderness Preservation Act required the U.S. Forest Service to study a number of roadless areas to consider whether they should be made part of the wilderness system. Thirty-four areas were studied under a project called RARE I (Roadless Areas Review and Evaluation). As a result, 5.6 million ha (12.3 million acres) out of 25.5 million ha (56 million acres) studied were selected for inclusion in the wilderness system. RARE I was followed by RARE II, which was designed to consider the entire national forest system for planning wilderness areas. The RARE II report is important because it provides maps showing areas in several different kinds of relatively undisturbed stages and suggests new additions to the wilderness system [21].

These national plans are part of the attempt to develop multiple and sequential land use. There are other such planning attempts, some of which, like the project called "Man and the Biosphere," are international.

GLOBAL FORECASTING

The global effects of our modern technological civilization have been discussed in earlier chapters. The burning of fossil fuels is adding a significant amount of carbon dioxide to the atmosphere; lead used in gasoline fuels has spread to the glaciers of Greenland; and DDT and other pesticides and artificial organic compounds are found in marine organisms inhabiting the Antarctic. We can imagine other effects, such as those of a nuclear war or of a large-scale release of a toxic compound. Few have yet tried to plan on a global level. However, in the last decade procedures for global forecasting and evaluation have been developed.

In response to these global concerns, an international group of business executives, intellectuals, and government officials founded the Club of Rome, an organization whose objectives were to promote a better understanding of humanity's predicament; to disseminate information about this predicament; and to stimulate development of new attitudes, policies, and institutions to redress the present situation.

Out of the concerns of this organization came the development of computer simulation models—models of global phenomena such as human population growth, the use of the world's resources, and human impacts on the biosphere. The results of the use of these models were reviewed in *The Limits to Growth* [22]. This book was controversial in many ways. First of all, its forecasts showed some dire consequences of our current activities. Supporters of *The Limits to Growth* hailed it as a new approach that could help save us from ourselves by forcing us to recognize the true limits to our uses of the biosphere. Opponents condemned it as another example of the "GIGO" rule of computer simulation—garbage in, garbage out. They claimed that it said nothing more than had been said by Malthus hundreds of years before.

Since the publication of *The Limits to Growth*, global forecasting has become an important aspect of modern civilization's attempt to deal with its own global effects. The Council on Environmental Quality was directed by the President to conduct a study of the probable changes in the world's population, natural resources, and environment through the end of the century. This study resulted in *The Global 2000 Report to the President* [23]. This report used several methods to assess the status of population resources and environment by the end of the century, including a review of several computer models for global forecasting.

The methods of analysis used in global forecasting are illustrated in a general way in Figure 18.11, which shows the two steps in integrating the environment into the process of analysis. The actual models are more complex, involving many sections or compartments. Figure 18.12 shows the basic diagram of the world model of global forecasting by M. Mesarovic and E. Pestel. Many factors are considered, from population and food de-

FIGURE 18.11
The steps in global fore-
casting consider a number
of environmental factors.
The gray area represents
the analysis prior to inte-
gration with the environ-
mental analysis. (From
Council on Environmental
Quality and the Depart-
ment of State.)

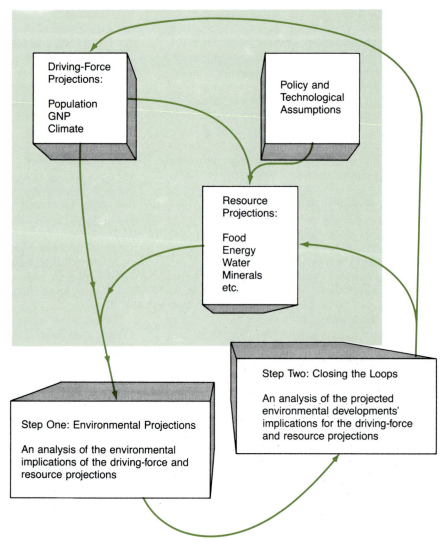

mand to economics, trade, machinery, and education. Such a model can be used to investigate the implications of different assumptions about present and future trends (Fig. 18.13). For example, the projections in Figure 18.13a assume no changes in certain political aspects, while the projections in Figure 18.13b assume isolationist policies. Too many assumptions cloud the meaning of the projections, and we must be careful not to take the projections at face value. Important information for such forecasts will come in the future from global remote-sensing data, which will provide large-scale images necessary for a global perspective. In addition, a better understanding of the history of climate and long-term changes in the distribution and abundance of life on Earth will help us in our attempt to make projections.

Global forecasting remains a controversial activity. It is always difficult, if not impossible, to predict the future. The more we understand about the processes that govern change in the environment, the more likely our forecasts will be helpful. Such

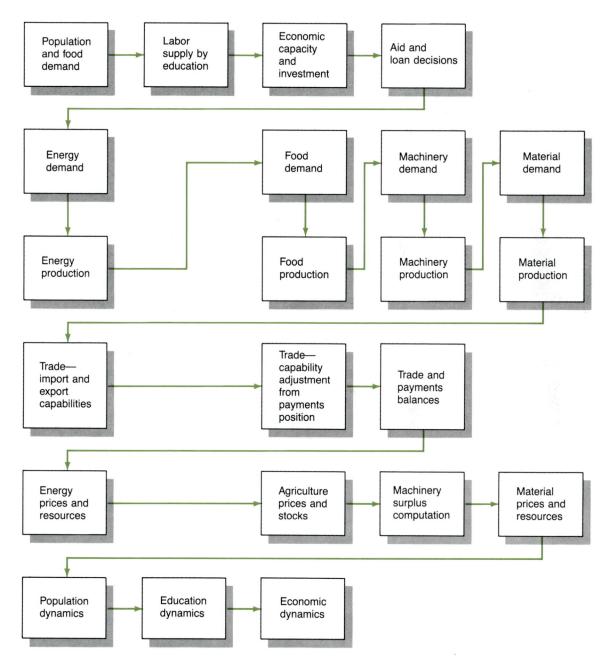

FIGURE 18.12
This flow chart of the Mesarovic-Pestel model for global forecasting shows the sequence in which calculations are made. Other world models involve similar calculations. (From Case Western Reserve University, Systems Research Center, and Council on Environmental Quality and the Department of State.)

FIGURE 18.13
Projections of future trends
from global models are
made under different as-
sumptions or "scenarios."
Here the model diagram in
Figure 18.12 is used to project trends for (a) a "no
change" political policy
and (b) an isolationist political policy. (From Case
Western Reserve Univer-
sity, Systems Research
Center, and Council on Environmental Quality and the
Department of State.)

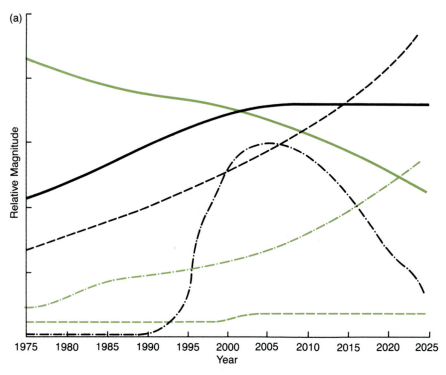

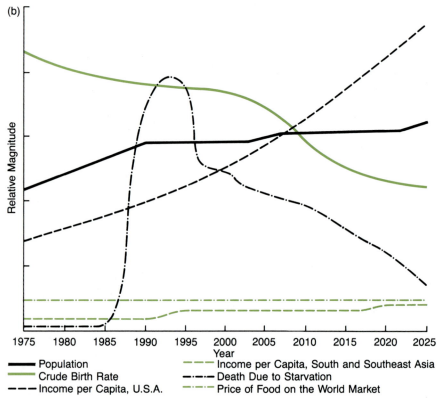

Population — Income per Capita, South and Southeast Asia
Crude Birth Rate — Death Due to Starvation
Income per Capita, U.S.A. — Price of Food on the World Market

forecasts are perhaps most valuable in showing us general effects, or the consequences of what we assume governs these processes. In this way the forecasts force us to recognize the meaning of what we think we know and suggest to us where our knowledge is lacking.

The most important impact of the global forecasts is the public attention they have drawn to the issues. *The Global 2000 Report* is important because it is a projection of the future, concluding with an endorsement of a limit to growth, that has the approval of the President of the United States. In addition, *The Global 2000 Report* provides a useful summary of current trends.

SUMMARY

Landscape evaluation, including land-use planning, site selection, evaluation of landscape intangibles, and environmental impact analysis, is one of the most controversial environmental issues of our times. We are now trying to develop sound methods to ensure that land and water resources are evaluated, used, and conserved in ways consistent with an emerging land ethic.

As our land resources become more limited, it will be necessary to use the same piece of land in a number of ways at the same time, and the uses will change over time. Therefore, future land-use planning will have to emphasize sequential or multiple land use rather than exclusive use.

The basic elements of a land-use plan are a statement of land-use objectives, issues and goals, analysis and summary of pertinent data, a land classification map, and a report discussing appropriate developments.

In the process of site selection and evaluation, the physical environment is evaluated to determine its capability of supporting human activity and, conversely, the possible effects of human activity on the environment. A philosophy of site evaluation based on physiographic determinism,

or "design with nature," serves to balance the traditional economic aspects of site-evaluation issues. Evaluation of scenic resources and other environmental intangibles is becoming more important in landscape evaluation. Because such intangibles are difficult to measure quantitatively, they cannot be easily compared with economic factors.

Evaluation of environmental impact is now required by law for all federal actions that could possibly affect the quality of the human environment; the result of such an evaluation is an environmental impact statement. There is no one method for determining environmental impact for the wide spectrum of possible actions and projects that might affect the environment. The objective of analysis before design and construction is to minimize the possibility of causing extensive environmental degradation. In the past, pollution, loss of resources, or creation of a hazard have accompanied certain projects. These problems have led to unfortunate closings of industries and have forced people to adjust to possible hazards and economic loss.

The High Dam at Aswan, the Trans-Alaska Pipeline, and the Cape Hatteras National Seashore are significant examples of the way possible impacts and alternatives are evaluated. Furthermore, these examples stress the importance of considering the many different environmental aspects of proposed projects.

Environmental planning has expanded in recent years to include coastal zone management, management of recreational activities, planning following emergencies, and regional planning. This expansion of environmental work emphasizes our commitment to future generations.

As our population increases, pressures for many different uses of the land will increase. We will need to continue to plan at larger scales so that the nation and the biosphere can maintain land with all of the variety of uses required by a modern society.

STUDY QUESTIONS

1 Make a map of your neighborhood. Does your neighborhood seem planned with the environment in mind?

2 Make a plan for a solar energy installation on your home. Where would you locate it, and which direction would you have it face?

3 What is meant by "mitigation of an environmental impact"?

4 An expert on impact analysis tells you that "mitigation is the impact. Once you have determined the mitigating factors, you have determined the impact." Explain. Do you agree?

5 What are the major steps that must be taken in the assessment of any environmental impact?

6 Discuss the elements of a land-use plan. Which is likely to be the most controversial? Why?

7 Differentiate between sequential and multiple land use. Provide examples of each.

8 Why is planning immediately following disasters loaded with potential problems?

9 Compare and contrast the "design with nature" method of site selection with benefits-cost evaluation (which tries to compare the benefits of a particular project over some time period with its cost).

10 Do you think scenery is a resource? Why or why not?

11 Discuss the major components of an environmental impact statement. Which are the most necessary? Why?

12 What are the major advantages of the scoping process in environmental impact analysis?

13 Discuss potential conflicts in management of recreational activities.

14 What are the advantages of regional and national planning and what are potential problems?

FURTHER READING

COUNCIL ON ENVIRONMENTAL QUALITY AND THE DEPARTMENT OF STATE. 1980. *The global 2000 report to the President: Entering the twenty-first century.*

FORRESTER, J. W. 1971. *World dynamics.* Cambridge, Mass.: Wright-Allen Press.

McHARG, I. L. 1971. *Design with nature.* Garden City, N.Y.: Doubleday.

MEADOWS, D. L., and MEADOWS, D. H., eds. 1973. *Toward a global equilibrium.* Cambridge, Mass.: Wright-Allen Press.

MESAROVIC, M., and PESTEL, E. 1974. *Mankind at the turning point.* New York: Sutton Press.

RAU, J. G., and WOOTEN, D. C., eds. 1980. *Environmental impact analysis handbook.* New York: McGraw-Hill.

SMITH, N. J. H. 1981. Colonization lessons from a tropical forest. *Science* 214: 755–61.

19

Urban Environments

- [ ] A city influences and is influenced by its environment and is an environment itself; it creates an environment different from its surroundings.
- [ ] A city must provide for a flow of energy and cycling of chemical elements needed for life. There must be a source of energy and material resources and a sink for wastes.
- [ ] The location of cities is strongly influenced by site and situation.
- [ ] A city depends on other cities and rural areas and, because of environmental constraints, can never be self-sustaining.
- [ ] The first cities emerged with the development of agriculture. Later, larger cities were made possible by more efficient transportation. With telecommunications and air travel, cities may become cleaner, more pleasant centers of civilization. However, lack of energy and material resources could make them less livable.
- [ ] A good site includes a good geologic substrate, nearby sources of water, local agricultural land, abundant natural resources, benign local climate, and easily defensible location. Excellent situation can compensate for poor site. Technology can change the characteristics of a site, or alter the situation.
- [ ] Aesthetics has long been a consideration in city and town planning.
- [ ] City residents are subjected to higher concentrations of pollutants than are rural people. Careful design, planning, and development can reduce such exposure.
- [ ] The problem of bringing nature to the city has evolved into several specialized professions.

VENICE SINKING

The city of Venice, Italy, was known to be slowly sinking for a long time, but no one knew the cause or a solution. Famous as the city of canals and architectural beauty, the city was in danger of being destroyed by the very lagoon that had sustained its commerce for more than 1000 years. Then the reason that the city was sinking was discovered: groundwater over a wide area was being removed by means of wells. Once the water was removed, the soil compressed under the weight of material above it. The wells that influenced Venice were located on mainland Italy as well as in the island city, and many of these wells supplied water to nearby industries, as well as for domestic use (Fig. 19.1).

The wells were capped and other sources of water were found; as a result the city has stopped sinking. This is an example of the application of scientific research on the environment to achieve a solution helpful to a major city.

Venice was founded by people escaping from the hordes that pillaged cities at the end of the Roman empire. Its location in the marshes along the Adriatic Sea was easily defended, and the seaside was also a good location for transportation and trade. The location of Venice presented environmental problems that had to be solved so that the city could become a major center—the shifting muds along the flat coast were a poor foundation for buildings. To improve the site, the early Venetians drove poles (made from saplings from surrounding forests on the mainland) into the mud and built on these. Venice still stands on this foundation, begun more than 1000 years ago.

Venice's success as a city depended on its location relative to its surroundings, which were a source of raw materials and resources and a market for its products.

Venice is affected today in many ways by its surroundings. It receives most raw goods and necessities from outside: most food (except fish), fuel, and so forth. Its buildings suffer from acid rain generated by industries nearby on the mainland and from farther away; its waters are high in heavy metals from industrial sources on the mainland. Thus from this example we see that the environment of a city influences its growth, success, and importance and can also be the seeds of its destruction. As with Venice, all cities are so influenced, and those who plan, manage, and live in cities must be aware of all aspects of the urban environment.

The sinking of Venice is known as **subsidence.** This is an important problem for other cities as a result of water removal, oil and gas wells, and mining. The city of Long Beach, California, experienced subsidence as the result of the removal of oil and gas from wells, as well as the removal of

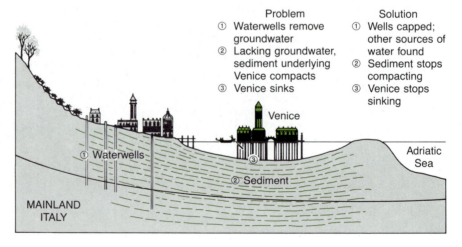

FIGURE 19.1
Why Venice was sinking. (1) Water wells on the mainland and within the city removed ground water. (2) Without the water between the particles of clay, the soil compacted under the weight of the city buildings. (3) The buildings sank as the soil compacted. Once this was recognized, the wells were capped, other sources of water were found, and the city was stopped from sinking further.

Problem
① Waterwells remove groundwater
② Lacking groundwater, sediment underlying Venice compacts
③ Venice sinks

Solution
① Wells capped; other sources of water found
② Sediment stops compacting
③ Venice stops sinking

Venice

Adriatic Sea

① Waterwells

② Sediment

MAINLAND ITALY

groundwater [1]. Mexico City has also suffered from subsidence; removal of groundwater there has led to subsidence of as much as 7 m.

As the people of Venice, Long Beach, and Mexico City learned, cities influence and are influenced by their environment. We can ignore these relationships only at our own peril and expense. As we become aware of city-environment relationships, we can develop and maintain our cities wisely so that they function well, are pleasing, and have bright futures. In the past, the emphasis of most environmental action has concerned wilderness, wildlife, endangered species, and the impact of pollution on natural landscape. Now it is time to increase the emphasis on city environments.

CITY LIFE

In the United States, about 70% of the people live on 3% of the land area (Fig. 19.2) [2]. It is projected that 50% of the people in the world will live in cities by the year 2000.

Economic development leads to urbanization. In the developed countries, almost 80% of the people live in cities, while in the lowest income developing countries only 20% of the people live in cities.

Not only is the human population becoming increasingly urbanized, but there is a rapid growth of huge metropolitan areas with more than 10 million residents; these greatly increase the pressures on urban environments. In 1950 there were only two such areas in the world—New York City and its nearby New Jersey areas (12.2 million residents) and greater London (12.4 million). By 1975 Mexico City, Los Angeles, Tokyo, Shanghai, and São Paulo, Brazil, had joined this list. It is estimated that by the year 2000, 20 more cities and their surrounding areas will have grown to this size, and 25 urban areas will have a total of almost 400 million residents [3]. In the future most people will live in cities, and in most nations, most of the urban residents will live in the single largest city.

The City as a System

Like any life-supporting system, a city must maintain a flow of energy, provide necessary material resources, and have ways of removing wastes. These ecosystem functions are maintained in a city by transportation and communication with outlying areas. A city is not a self-contained ecosystem; it depends on other cities and rural areas. A city takes in raw materials from the surrounding countryside: food, water, wood, energy, mineral ores—

FIGURE 19.2
Computer generated image of the United States at night, showing the locations of major urban areas, which appear as bright areas because of the concentration of electric lighting. This image illustrates how much we have become an urban civilization.

everything that a society uses; the city produces and exports material goods and, if it is a truly great city, exports ideas, innovations, inventions, arts, and the spirit of civilization. A city cannot exist without a countryside to support it. As was said half a century ago, city and country, urban and rural, are one thing, not two things (Fig. 19.3) [4].

Cities also export waste products: polluted water, air, and solids, which the countryside has had to absorb and dispose of. It is no wonder, therefore, that relationships between people in cities and in the countryside have often been strained. Why, a country dweller wants to know, should he have to deal with the wastes of those in the city? Many of our serious environmental problems occur at the interface between urban and rural areas.

It has been estimated that the average city resident in an industrial nation annually uses, directly or indirectly, 208,000 liters of water (207,000 kg), 660 kg of food, and 3146 kg of fossil fuel, and produces 1,660,000 liters of sewage, 660 kg of solid wastes, and 200 kg of air pollutants.

Thus a city can never be free of environmental constraints, even though its human constructions give us a false sense of security. As Lewis Mumford, the historian of cities, has written, "Cities give us the *illusion* of self-sufficiency and independence and of the possibility of physical continuity without conscious renewal," but this is only an illusion [4].

An Environmental History of Cities

With this background in mind, we can now appreciate the importance of the relationships between environment, society, technology, and the history of cities. From this perspective, we can divide the history of cities into roughly four stages.

The Rise of Towns The first cities emerged on the landscape thousands of years ago during the New Stone Age with the development of agriculture, which provided the excess of food resources that is necessary to the maintenance of a city [4]. In this first stage, the density of people per square kilometer is much higher than in the surrounding countryside, but the density is still too low to cause rapid, serious disturbance to the land. In fact, city dwellers and their animals provide waste, which is an important fertilizer for the surrounding farmlands. In this stage, the city's size is restricted by the ability of primitive transportation methods to bring food and necessary resources into the city and to remove wastes. Because of such limitations,

FIGURE 19.3
The city as a system: energy and materials flow. A city must function as part of a city-countryside ecosystem, with an input of energy and materials, internal cycling, and an output of waste heat energy and material wastes. As with any natural ecosystem, recycling of materials can reduce the need for input and the net output of wastes.

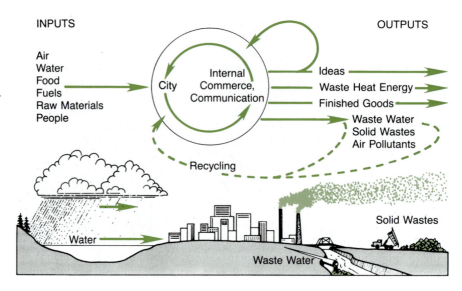

INPUTS

Air
Water
Food
Fuels
Raw Materials
People

City

Internal Commerce, Communication

Recycling

Water

Waste Water

Solid Wastes

OUTPUTS

Ideas
Waste Heat Energy
Finished Goods
Waste Water
Solid Wastes
Air Pollutants

no medieval town served only by land transportation had a population greater than 15,000 [5].

The Urban Center Waterways and roads made possible the first large cities. In the second stage, more efficient transportation made possible the development of much larger urban centers, with a totally urban social core. Boats, barges, canals, and harbor wharfs, and roads, horses, carriages, and carts made possible a city that depended on agriculture far away. Rome, originally dependent on local produce, became a city fed by granaries of Africa and the Near East.

A city in this second stage was limited in size by pedestrian travel. The city could be no larger in area than the distance a worker could walk to work, do a day's work, and walk home. The density of people per square kilometer was limited by architectural techniques and primitive waste disposal. Thus these cities never exceeded a population of one million, and there were few cities of this size, most notably Rome and some cities in China.

Such cities contained the seeds of their own destruction. There was a tendency to transform the city center from natural to artificial and to replace grass and soil with pavement, gravel, house, and temple, creating an impression of the dominance of the environment by civilization. Ironically, the very artificial aspects of the city that make it seem so independent of the rest of the world make it in fact all the more dependent on its rural surroundings for all resources. So although it appears to its inhabitants to be stronger and more independent, the city is actually more fragile [4]. A city in this stage grows at the expense of the surrounding countryside, destroying the surrounding landscape on which it ultimately depends. As the nearby areas are ruined for agriculture and the transportation network extends, the use, misuse, and destruction of the environment increase. In this stage, many of the classic cities of history were built, prospered, and declined.

The Industrial Metropolis The industrial revolution allowed greater modification of the environment and greatly increased the ease and capacity of transportation. Two technological advances that had significant effects on the environment were improved sanitation methods, which led to the control of many diseases, and modern transportation methods, including the improved sailing ship and the steam engine.

In the third stage, rapid transportation led to the development of suburbs, while increased industrialization intensified pollution. These changes increased the urban dwellers' sense of separateness from their "natural" environment. In the climax of the third stage, the city became more concentrated and artificial, with skyscrapers reaching nearly a kilometer upward and surface and underground transit systems moving people long distances to and from work. In this stage the urban park achieved a new importance.

The Center of Civilization We are at the beginning of a fourth stage in the development of cities. With telecommunications (telephones, television, and computers linked by satellite and cable), much can be done by people isolated from one another, at home, or long distances apart. Perhaps, as telecommunications free us from the necessities of certain kinds of commercial travel and related activities, the city can return to a cleaner, more pleasing center of civilization. The airplane has freed us even more from the traditional limitation of situation. We now have urban areas where previously transportation was poor—in the far north (Fairbanks, Alaska) or on islands (Honolulu, Hawaii).

In this stage, the negative effects of urban sprawl are leading many back to the urban centers. The drawbacks of suburban commuting and the destruction of the landscape in suburbs have brought the city center a new appeal.

An optimistic future for cities requires a continued abundance of energy and material resources, which are certainly not guaranteed, and a wise use of these resources. However, if energy resources are rapidly depleted, modern mass transit may fail; fewer people will be able to live in suburbs and the cities will become crowded; reliance on coal and wood will increase air pollution; and the continued destruction of the land within and near cities could compound transportation problems, making local production of food impossible. The future of our cities depends on our ability to plan and to conserve and use our resources wisely.

ENVIRONMENT, LOCALE, AND SUCCESS

Cities are not located at random; their locations are strongly influenced by the environment. In ancient Rome, for example, all important cities were located near waterways. As a more modern example, most major cities of the eastern United States are situated either at major ocean harbors or at the fall line on major rivers (Fig. 19.4). The fall line occurs where there is an abrupt drop in elevation. Because this topographic feature has several advantages, many eastern cities were established near the fall line. The fall line provides good sites for water power, which was an important source of energy in the eighteenth and nineteenth centuries. It is the farthest inland that larger ships could navigate, and just above the fall line was the farthest downstream that the river could be easily bridged. In fact, it was only with the development of steel bridges in the late nineteenth century that the spanning of wider regions of the rivers below the falls became practical [6].

River valleys have other advantages for the location of cities. Valley bottoms and flats have rich water-deposited soils that are good for agriculture. The rivers also provided one simple means of waste disposal.

As in the case of the fall line and harbors, cities often are founded at crucial transportation points, growing up around a market, a river crossing, or a fort. Newcastle, England, and Budapest, Hungary, are located at the lowest bridging points on their rivers; other cities, such as Geneva, Switzerland, are located where a river enters or leaves a major lake. Cities located at crucial defensive locations include those with rock outcrops, such as Edinburgh, Scotland; Athens, Greece; and Salzburg, Austria; or on a peninsula, such as Istanbul, Turkey; and Monaco, Monaco. Other cities are located at the confluence of major rivers. For example, St. Louis, Missouri, lies close to where the Missouri and Mississippi rivers meet. Pittsburgh, Pennsylvania; Koblenz, FRG; and Khartoum, Sudan, are other cities located at the confluence of several rivers. Cities are often founded close to a mineral resource, such as salt (Salzburg); metals (Kalgoorlie, Australia); and medicated waters and thermal springs (Spa in Belgium, Bath in Great Britain, Vichy in France, and Saratoga Springs in New York). A successful city can grow and spread over surrounding terrain so that its original purpose may be obscured to a resident; its original market or fort may have evolved into a minor square or a historical curiosity.

Site and Location

The location of a city is influenced by two factors: site, which is the exact spot where the city is located and all of its environmental features; and situation, which is the location of the city with respect to other areas. A good site includes a good geologic substrate, including a firm rock base and well-drained, dry land for buildings; good nearby supplies of water; local, good agricultural land; abundant timber and other natural resources; benign local climate; and a location that is easily defended.

An ideal location for a city would have both a good site and a good situation, but this does not always occur. Paris is an example of a city with a good site and a good situation. Paris was founded on an island in the Seine River—a site that was easily defended, had ample water, and was relatively easily crossed. There are several advantages to the situation of Paris: it is located near where several tributaries join the Seine, thus connecting the city to rivers from the northeast, east, and southeast; the Seine flows into the English Channel, which made it possible for vessels to travel from the ocean to the island of Paris. The city is also near the center of a large, prosperous farming region. This highly advantageous natural site and situation was improved further by social and technological developments. Canals were dug to improve and extend transportation, thus providing access to the regions of the Loire, the Rhone-Saône, the Lorraine industrial area, and the French-Belgian industrial area.

An excellent situation can sometimes compensate for a poor site, as we learned for Venice, and

FIGURE 19.4
The major cities of the eastern and southern United States lie either at the sites of good harbors or along the fall line, marking locations of waterfalls or rapids on most major rivers in this area (shown as the colored line). The location of cities is thus strongly influenced by the characteristics of the environment. (From *Natural regions of the United States and Canada* by Charles B. Hunt. Copyright © 1974 by W. H. Freeman and Company.)

as is also true for New Orleans, Louisiana. Lying at the mouth of the Mississippi, New Orleans is an important transportation center. However, the city has a poor site. It is located on the low delta of the Mississippi, which floods frequently and which provides a poor substrate for construction. The slow backwaters and swampy areas provide good breeding areas for mosquitoes but offer little as a local resource.

Situation is a product of environmental and social factors. Society can make a situation significant by social, political, or technological means. The decision to locate Washington, D.C., at the approximate north-south center of the original thirteen states was primarily a political effect on situation. The site of Washington, D.C. (low, marshy ground along the Potomac River), which was of little utility originally, was excavated and filled. Once developed, the land became valuable, transportation routes developed, and so forth. Moscow, USSR, and Madrid, Spain, are other examples of cities that owe their location to political factors.

Mecca, Saudi Arabia; Jerusalem, Israel; and Salt Lake City, Utah, have situations created in part by religious and cultural history, which give these cities an importance beyond that of their natural site or situation.

Modern technology can alter situation. For example, Santa Fe, New Mexico, is considered to have an excellent site. When it was bypassed by the transcontinental railroad in the nineteenth century, its importance declined in relation to Albuquerque, where the railroad was located [5].

Site and situation can change over time. For example, towns and cities that have lost their waterways have lost importance. Bruges and Ghent in Belgium, and Ravenna in Italy are cities whose harbors silted; Ghent responded by improving its artificial situation by building a canal [5].

Site Modification

Site begins as something provided by the environment, but technology can change the characteristics of a site. People can improve the site of a city. This has been done when the situation of a city made it important and when the citizens could afford large projects.

In fact, city planning has a long history. Although many cities in history have grown without any conscious plan, formal plans for new cities can be traced in modern history as far back as the fifteenth century. Sometimes cities have been designed for specific social purposes, with little consideration of the environment; in other cases, the environment and its effect on city residents have been major planning considerations.

Among the earliest European planned towns and cities were walled fortress cities, designed for defense (Fig. 19.5). But even in these early plans the aesthetics of the town were considered. In the fifteenth century, one such planner, Leon Battista Alberti, argued that large and important towns should have broad and straight streets; smaller, less fortified towns should have winding streets to

FIGURE 19.5
The city of Vitry-le-Francois, planned in 1545, was designed with an emphasis on fortification.

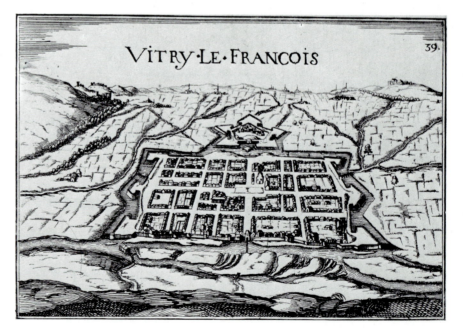

increase their beauty, and he advocated the inclusion of town squares and recreational areas [7].

The usefulness of walled cities essentially ended with the invention of gunpowder, and the Renaissance sparked an interest in the "ideal city." A preference for gardens and parks—emphasizing recreation—developed in the seventeenth and eighteenth centuries, culminating in the plan of Versailles, France, with parks and tree-lined walks.

From the time the earliest towns in North America were established, urban planners have attempted to provide for defense, transportation, access to necessary resources, needs of residential and commercial buildings, and aesthetics. Both fortress town and park town planning influenced the planning of cities in North America. The importance of aesthetic considerations is illustrated in the plan of Washington, D.C., designed by the Frenchman Pierre-Charles L'Enfant. He mixed a traditional rectangular grid pattern of streets with broad avenues set at angles. The intention was to design a city of beauty (Fig. 19.6).

One of the most important events in the development of city parks was the creation of Central Park in New York City by Frederick Law Olmsted. Central Park was the first large public park in the United States. In his plan, Olmsted carefully considered the opportunities and limitations of the topography, geology, hydrology, and vegetation (Fig. 19.7), placing recreational areas in the southern area that included flat meadows; creating depressed roadways that allowed traffic to cross the park without detracting from the vistas as seen by park visitors. Central Park is an example of "design with nature." The design of Central Park influenced other U.S. city parks, and Olmsted remained a major figure in American planning throughout the nineteenth century [8].

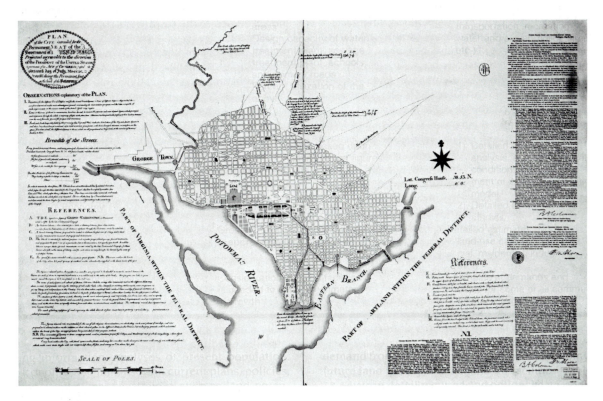

FIGURE 19.6
L'Enfant's 1791 plan for Washington, D.C., showing the emphasis on aesthetics as an important factor in the design.

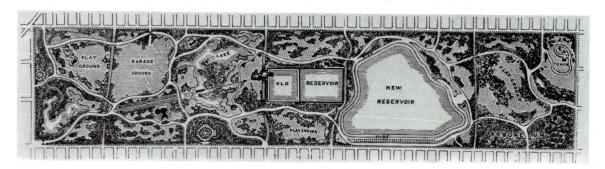

FIGURE 19.7
Frederick Law Olmsted's 1871 plan for Central Park in New York City. This plan had a great impact on subsequent city planning. Variety, the use of natural topography, and the successful designing for multiple uses make this plan a landmark in the history of city planning.

An important related development was the "garden city," a phrase coined in 1902 by Ebenezer Howard. Howard's idea was that city and countryside should be planned together. A garden city would be surrounded by a green belt, and garden cities would be located as a set, forming a series of countryside and urban landscapes.

The garden city idea caught on, and garden cities were planned and developed in Great Britain and the United States. Greenbelt, Maryland, just outside of Washington, D.C., is one of these cities, as is Lecheworth, England. These concepts—of Olmsted's use of the natural landscape in designing city parks and Howard's garden city—still influence city planning today. They are two important approaches to making cities livable.

The history of Boston, Massachusetts, illustrates that modification of a city's environment can make the city more livable. The original site of Boston had certain advantages, including a narrow peninsula with several hills that could be easily defended, a good harbor, and a good water supply. As Boston grew, however, there was increasing demand for more land for building, more area for docking ships, and a better water supply, as well as a need to control the ocean floods and to dispose of solid and liquid wastes. Much of the original tidal flats, which were too wet to build on and too shallow to navigate, have been filled in (Fig. 19.8). Hills were leveled and the marshes filled with soil. The largest project was the filling of Back Bay, which began in 1858 and continued for dec-

ades. Once filled, the area suffered from flooding and water pollution [9]. The solution to these problems was a water control project called "The Fens," a famous example of landscape planning by Frederick Law Olmsted [8].

Olmsted's goal was to "abate existing nuisances," by keeping sewage out of the streams and ponds and providing artifical banks for the streams to prevent flooding, but to do this in a natural-looking way. Depressions dug out of the tidal flats, the fens followed a meandering pattern like a natural stream. There were areas set aside as holding ponds for tidal flooding, and a natural salt marsh was restored, planted with vegetation tolerant of the brackish water. Olmsted made the control of water an aesthetic addition to the city. The blending of several goals made the development of the fens a landmark in city planning—the area appears to the casual stroller to be simply a park for recreation [8].

THE CITY AS AN ENVIRONMENT

A city changes the landscape and therefore the relation between the biological and physical aspects of the environment. Areas that had natural soils and ecosystems, readily absorbing rain water, are converted to water-impervious roadways, walkways, and buildings.

Everything is concentrated in a city; this means

FIGURE 19.8
Boston is an example of a city whose site has been modified over time to improve the environment and provide more building locations. This map shows land filled in Boston to provide new building sites as of 1982. While such landfill allows for expansion of the city, it can also create new environmental problems, which then must be solved. (From *The Granite Garden: Urban Nature and Human Design* by Anne Whiston Spirn. Copyright © 1984 by Anne Whiston Spirn. Reprinted by permission of Basic Books, Inc., publishers.)

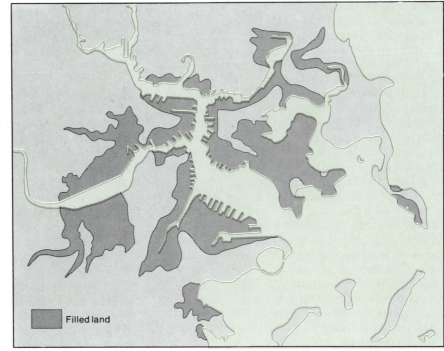

Filled land

that all classes of pollutants are concentrated. City dwellers are exposed to more kinds of toxic chemicals in higher concentrations and to more human-produced noise, heat, and particulates than their rural neighbors.

The environment in cities makes life riskier. The age-adjusted mortality rates for adults in the United States indicate a consistent 13% excess of cancer mortality in metropolitan counties that include central cities as compared with other areas [10]. Deaths from cancer are highest in central cities, intermediate in noncentral city metropolitan counties, and lowest elsewhere. This pattern holds regardless of race or sex [10]. Air pollution is heaviest in the central city, particularly along waterfronts where industries tend to be concentrated. Deaths from cancer are 50% greater for people living in the area of highest air pollution than for those living in the least polluted area. The environment of cities is obviously different from those of lower-density human residential areas and natural areas.

The Urban Atmosphere and Climate

Cities affect the local climate; as the city changes, so does its climate. Cities are in general less windy than nonurban areas because buildings and other structures obstruct the flow of air. City buildings also channel the wind and can make for local wind tunnels with a high wind speed. The actual flow of wind around one building is influenced by nearby buildings, so that the total wind flow through a city is the result of the relationships among all the buildings. In planning a new building, its shape as well as its location among other buildings must be taken into account. In some cases when this has not been done, dangerous winds around tall buildings have resulted in blown-out windows.

Particulates in the atmosphere over cities are often 10 times or more greater than for surrounding areas (see Chapter 12). Although the particulates tend to reduce incoming solar radiation by up to 30% and thus cool the city, the effect of particulates is small relative to the effects of processes that produce heat in the city [11].

Cities are warmer than surrounding areas (see Chapter 12). The observed increase in temperature in urban areas is approximately 1–2°C in the winter and 0.5–1.0°C in the summer for mid-latitude areas. The temperature increase results from increased production of heat energy; the heat emitted from the burning of fossil fuels and other industrial, commercial, and residential sources; and the decreased rate of heat loss, because the dust in the urban air traps and reflects back into the city long-wave (infrared) radiation emitted from the city surface. Concrete, asphalt, and roofs also tend to act as solar collectors and quickly emit heat, helping to increase the sensible heat in cities [12].

Throughout the history of cities, it has been common to make use of solar energy to heat houses. Because of cheap and easily accessible fossil fuel, solar heating was little used in the first half of the twentieth century in cities of industrialized nations. But cities in ancient Greece, Rome, and China were designed so that solar energy was most accessible to each household (see Chapter 14).

During the industrial revolution in eighteenth- and nineteenth-century Europe, most poor working class people lived in dark slums that took no advantage of the sunlight. The lack of adequate sunlight was recognized in the second half of the nineteenth century as a problem for the poor, and new city designs began to include plans for solar heating and exposure. At the beginning of the twentieth century, a French housing officer studied the sun's position at the winter solstice for ten major cities of Europe and North America and determined that houses should be separated by two and one-half times their height so that they would not interfere with each other's collection of sunlight [12]. Today some cities have enacted solar energy ordinances that make it against the law to shade another property owner's building in such a way that he loses solar heating capability.

Water in the Urban Environment

The water budget is changed by the city's heavy water demand, large impervious surfaces, and lack of surface water. There is less exchange (evapora-

tion) of water from the surface to the atmosphere, explaining why mid-latitude cities generally record a lower relative humidity (2% lower in winter to 8% lower in summer) than the surrounding countryside.

Particulates in the dust dome above a city provide particles for condensation of raindrops and thus urban areas experience 5–10% more precipitation and considerably more cloud cover and fog than do surrounding areas. The formation of fog is particularly troublesome in the winter and may impede air traffic into and out of airports. If the pollution dome moves downwind, then increased precipitation may be reported outside of the urban area (see Chapter 12).

The construction of modern cities affects the water cycle greatly; this, in turn, affects soils and, consequently, plants and animals in the city. Paved city streets and city buildings prevent water infiltration; when the rain falls, most of it runs off directly and is channeled into storm sewer systems. The pavement increases the chances of local flooding within the city, and the increased runoff from the city to the countryside can increase the chances of flooding downstream.

Most cities have a single underground sewage system. During times of no rain or light rain, this system handles sewage alone. But during periods of heavy rain, the runoff is mixed with the sewage, and this can exceed the capacity of sewage treatment plants.

Thus, in most cities during heavy rains, sewage is emitted downstream without sufficient treatment. It is too expensive to build a completely new and separate runoff system in an existing city, so other solutions must be found. When a new city is developed, our knowledge of the problems with flooding and water runoff can be used to plan a better flow of water. This has been done in the new town of Woodlands, a suburb of Houston, Texas. That town was designed so that most houses and roads were placed on ridges; the lowlands were left as natural open space. The lowlands provide areas for temporary storage of floodwater and, because the land is unpaved, allow the rain to penetrate the soil and recharge the aquifer for Houston. This has another benefit. In this region of Texas, low-lying wetlands are common and are the habitat of native wildlife such as deer and of large,

Paving the Good Earth: The Urbanization of America's Farmlands

From the grain fields of the Midwest, to the citrus groves of Florida, to the vegetable farms of California, the United States has some of the best agricultural lands to be found anywhere on Earth. Over half the grains in the world export market are produced from the rich, flat or gently rolling expanses of America's farmlands.

But these farmlands, ultimately worth more than the oil reserves of the Middle Eastern countries, are disappearing at an unprecedented rate.

Each day in this nation, 10 km^2 of prime farmland are converted to nonagricultural uses. A cornfield becomes a shopping center; a wheatfield disappears under the asphalt of a highway; an orange orchard is transformed into a residential area.

America's prime farmlands, those that are rain-fed and have flat or gently rolling terrain with fertile soils, are the most productive, yielding bountiful harvests with minimum input of fuel, fertilizers, and labor. They are also the most threatened: In the country's 100 top agricultural counties, development is twice the national rate. The annual loss of prime farmland totals one million acres, the equivalent of a half-mile (nearly a kilometer) strip of land stretching from New York to California. Combined with an additional two million acres (5 million ha) of lesser quality agricultural lands lost to development each year, the total annual loss is the equivalent of 320 acres (791 ha) per hour.

Once farmland is paved over, built on, or otherwise developed, it is, in effect, permanently lost for future food production. As America's best farmlands are converted to nonagricultural uses, other lands less suitable for crop production are planted. Hillsides, poorer soils, and regions that require irrigation all demand more labor and energy inputs, augmenting costs for both farmers and consumers. Environmental problems such as soil erosion and sedimentation increase.

Although present trends point to continued loss of agricultural lands to development, there are ways to stem the tide.

Land-use planning on the local, state, or national level, or a combination thereof, is essential. Restrictions can be made by legislation or by tax reductions to both farmers and developers that encourage them to allow productive agricultural lands to keep producing. Development rights have been purchased from farmers in some regions, either with local government funds or by the American Farmlands Trust, ensuring that their land will remain unspoiled for future production.

We are now at a critical juncture; we can pave farmlands today or save them for future generations. The choice is ours.

David Perry

pleasant trees such as magnolias, which provide food and habitat for birds. It is estimated that a conventional drainage system would have cost $14 million more [9].

The problem with flooding and overtaxing storm sewage systems is made worse in many cities that are built on floodplains. Floodplains are often chosen as sites for cities because the land is flat and easy to build on, and transportation is nearby at the river. This leads to a conflict, because the cities typically are built as if there would never be flooding. Floods damage buildings and other property, cause the loss of lives, and are generally considered a natural catastrophe. Where a city is built on a floodplain, the river has typically been channeled and levees built along the shores. In this way long stretches of major rivers are channelized. This has two negative effects. First, when the river is maintained in an artificial channel, its sediment load is not deposited on the land, and the land's fertility is not renewed. Second, this sediment load passes downriver and is lost at the mouth, where it causes siltation and may fill in important harbors and do damage to cities at the oceanside. As an example, much of the Mississippi River is now channelized and its sediment load is deposited in the Gulf of Mexico.

Water Conservation While too much water is a serious problem on occasion, in general water is a precious resource for cities, and few cities have too much usable, drinkable water. Most city housing in industrialized countries was designed before there was a concern for careful water conservation, and there is much that can be done to reduce the amount of water used in an urban home. In a standard house, water of drinking quality is used for all purposes, including watering the lawn and garden. In a modified house, so called "gray water"— water used for washing, but not for toilets—could be reused for outdoor watering. In addition, a major use of water in a standard house is for flushing a standard toilet; in a modified house, dry toilets could be used [13].

Soils in the City

A modern city has a great impact on soils. Most soil is covered by cement, asphalt, or stone; the soil no longer has its natural cover of vegetation and its natural exchange of gases with the air is greatly reduced. Such soil will slowly lose its organic matter, because this can no longer be replenished from above. The normal soil organisms lack food and oxygen and will die. The process of construction and the weight of the buildings tend to compact the soil, thereby restricting water flow. City soils are therefore more likely to be compacted, water-logged, impervious to water flow, and lacking in organic matter.

Pollution in the City

A resident in a city is subjected to much higher concentrations of most pollutants than his rural neighbor. Some of this pollution comes from motor vehicles, which contribute lead in gasoline, nitrogen oxides, ozone, carbon monoxide, and other air pollutants from exhaust; from stationary power sources and home heating, which contribute particulates, sulfur oxides, nitrogen oxides, and other toxic gases; from industrial production, which contributes a wide variety of chemicals; and from the pollution of water from sewage and industrial activity (see Chapters 13 and 16).

Although it is impossible to eliminate exposure to pollutants in a city, it is possible to reduce the exposure by careful design, planning, and development. For example, exposure to lead is greater near a road than away from it. The exposure to lead can be reduced by placing houses and recreational areas away from roadways and by developing a buffer zone that makes use of trees of species resistant to the pollutant. These trees absorb the pollutants and slow the rate of its spread away from the roadway [9]. In addition, such buffer zones can reduce the amount of noise in residential areas of a city.

BRINGING NATURE TO THE CITY

A practical problem for planners and managers of cities is how to bring nature to the city; that is, how to make plants (especially) and animals a part of a city landscape. This activity has evolved into several specialized professions. One of these is that of an urban forester, more often called a "tree warden;'' another is the landscape architect. Both work along with the city planner and city engineers. Most cities have an urban forester on their payroll. The urban forester determines the best sites to plant trees and chooses the kind of trees to suit the environment, taking into account climate, soils, and the general influences of the urban setting, such as the shading imposed by tall buildings and pollution from motor vehicles.

Vegetation in Cities

Planting of trees, shrubs, and flowers improves the beauty of a city. Plants provide for different needs in different locations. Along city streets, trees provide shade that reduces the need for air conditioning and makes travel in the city much pleasanter in hot weather.

In parks, vegetation provides places for solitude; trees and shrubs can block some of the city sounds, and the complex shapes and structures create the sense of solitude. Plants also provide habitat for wildlife such as birds and squirrels, which are considered pleasant additions to a city by many urban residents.

The use of trees in cities has grown since the time of the European Renaissance. In earlier times, trees and shrubs were set apart in gardens, to be viewed as scenery, but not experienced as part of ordinary activities. Street trees were first used in Europe in the eighteenth century; among the first such tree-lined streets were the Rue de Rivoli in Paris and Bloomsbury Square in London. In many cities trees are now considered an essential element of the urban visual scene. As an indication of the importance of trees, major cities have large tree planting programs. For example, in New York City 11,000 trees are planted each year and Vancouver, British Columbia, plants 4,000 [14].

Vegetation in cities is under special kinds of stress. Trees along city streets are often surrounded by cement, which prevents normal access to water and air. The root systems, therefore, are more likely to experience extremes of dryness and soil saturation (immediately following or during a rain storm). Because city soils tend to be compacted and do not drain well, trees planted in a city sidewalk tend to be overwatered and the roots die from lack of oxygen. A solution, as suggested by

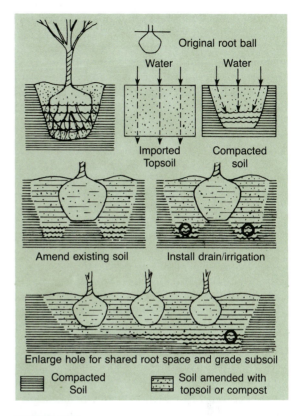

FIGURE 19.9
The problem: the ''teacup'' syndrome (top), common cause of death in newly planted urban trees. In wet seasons, accumulated water sits in tree pits, unable to drain, and tree roots rot. In drought, roots cannot penetrate compacted soil to reach groundwater. The solution: planting techniques that permit air and water to move through the soil and provide room to grow will increase both lifespan and size of urban trees. (From *The Granite Garden: Urban Nature and Human Design* by Anne Whiston Spirn. Copyright © 1984 by Anne Whiston Spirn. Reprinted by permission of Basic Books, Inc., publishers.)

the landscape architect Anne Spirn, is to connect the plantings of a series of trees so that a larger volume of soil is available to each of them and water can drain between them (Fig. 19.9) [9].

Many species of trees and plants are very sensitive to air pollution. For example, Eastern white pine of North America is extremely sensitive to ozone pollution and does not do well in cities with heavy motor vehicle traffic or along highways. Dust can interfere with the exchange of oxygen and carbon dioxide, necessary for photosynthesis and respiration of the trees. City trees also suffer direct damage from physical impact from bicycles, cars, and trucks; they suffer from vandalism. Trees subject to such stress are more susceptible to attacks by fungus diseases and insects, and the lifetime of trees in a city is generally shorter than in their natural woodland habitats unless the trees are given considerable care. Some species of trees are more useful and successful in cities than others. An ideal urban tree would be resistant to all forms of urban stress; have a beautiful form and foliage; and produce no messy fruit, flowers, or leaf litter that requires cleaning.

Wild plants that do particularly well in cities are those characteristic of disturbed areas and of early stages in ecological succession. City roadsides in Europe and North America have wild mustards, asters, and other early successional plants. Disturbances in cities promote the occurrence of certain kinds of plants. Curiously, during World War II, many species of wildflowers not recorded previously were found near bombed (and therefore cleared) areas in London. In addition, 342 species of plants were recorded where fewer than 100 had been recorded before. For example, bracken fern, rare in an English city, became common during that war and persisted afterward in London [15].

Wildlife in Cities

With the exception of some birds and small, docile mammals such as squirrels, most forms of wildlife in cities are considered pests. But there is much more wildlife in cities, much of it unnoticed. We can divide city wildlife into the following categories: (1) those species that cannot persist in an urban environment and disappear; (2) those that tolerate an urban environment, but do better elsewhere; (3) those that have adapted to urban environments, are abundant there, and are either neutral or beneficial to human beings; and (4) those that are so successful that they are pests.

The City as Wildlife Habitat Peregrine falcons once hunted pigeons above the streets of Manhattan. Unknown to most New Yorkers, the falcons

nested on the ledges of skyscrapers and dived on their prey in an impressive display of predation. The falcons disappeared when DDT and other organic pollutants caused a thinning of their eggshells and a failure in reproduction, but they have been reintroduced recently into the city. In New York City's Central Park approximately 260 species of birds have been observed—100 in a single day. Foxes live in London, feeding on garbage and road kills (animals run over by motor vehicles); shy and nocturnal, they are seen by few Londoners [15].

We do not associate wildlife with cities, but, as these examples show, cities provide homes to many forms of life. Cities are a habitat, albeit artificial. They can provide all the needs—physical structures and necessary material resources (food, minerals, water)—for many plants and animals. We can identify ecological food chains in cities (Fig. 19.10).

For some species, the city's artificial structures are sufficiently like their original habitat to be a home. For example, chimney swifts originally lived in hollow trees but are now common in factory chimneys and other vertical shafts. Their nests are glued to the walls with saliva. A city can easily have more chimneys per square kilometer than a forest has hollow trees.

Cities include natural habitats in parks and preserves. Modern parks provide some of the world's best wildlife habitats, and the importance of parks will increase as the truly wild areas are reduced in extent. Jamaica Bay, a park in New York City, was recovered from natural marshes and wetlands. Until the 1960s, the area had been polluted by sewage and had become a wasteland, supporting only a few species. After restoration, it now includes 7000 ha (15,000 acres) with a diverse population of birds. During the spring and fall migration, many bird watchers from New York visit the bay to see avocets, dowitchers, sandpipers, and godwits, among others [15]. Jamaica Bay is unusual in that it was planned as a natural park, emphasizing native vegetation and habitats, and has succeeded in attracting native species of animals.

Cities that are major harbors often have many species of marine wildlife at their doorsteps. New York City's waters include sharks, bluefish, mackerel, tuna, shad, striped bass, and nearly 250 other

FIGURE 19.10
(a) An urban food chain based on plants of disturbed places and insect herbivores. (b) An urban food chain based on road kills.

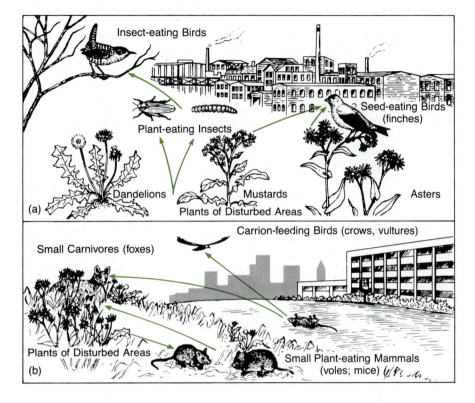

species of fish [15]. Small ponds contain freshwater fish and frogs.

Animal Pests and Their Control   Pests are familiar to almost every urban dweller. These include cockroaches, fleas, termites, mice, rats, and pigeons, but there are many more, especially species of insects. In gardens and parks, pests include insects, birds, and mammals that feed on fruit and vegetables and destroy foliage of shade trees and decorative plants. Pests compete with people for food and spread diseases. Before modern sanitation and medicine, such diseases played a major role in limiting the human population density in cities. Although cities are still less healthy than rural areas in terms of the effects of pollutants on human health, the control of these diseases has been an important improvement.

Those species that survive best in cities have certain common characteristics. In general, urban pest animals are generalists in their food choice,

so that they can share their diet with people. These pests also generally have a very high growth rate and therefore a short average lifetime (these tend to go together).

An animal is a pest when it is in the wrong place at the wrong time doing the wrong thing. For example, a termite in a woodland helps in the natural regeneration of wood by hastening decay and speeding the return of chemical elements to the soil so that they are available to living plants. But termites in a house are pests because they can threaten the physical structure where one is living.

We can best control pests by recognizing how they fit into their natural ecosystem and identifying their natural controlling factors. It is often assumed that the best way, and the only way, to control and get rid of animal pests is to use poisons, but there are limitations to this approach. The earlier poisons used in pest control were generally toxic to people and to nonpests. Another problem with the dependence on a single toxic compound is that, through evolution, a species gradually can develop resistance. This can lead to "rebound." If a pesticide is spread widely but at a single time, then it will greatly reduce the population of the pest. However, when the pesticide's effectiveness is lost, then the population can increase rapidly as long as the habitat is suitable and food plentiful. This happened in an attempt to control the Norway rat in Baltimore. The problem in this case was that the habitat remained good, with plenty of waste food for the rats to eat and an abundance of areas in which to breed, hide, and travel.

The best way to control rats in the long run is to make the city a bad habitat for them by reducing the amount of garbage that is open for them to feed on, by restricting their travel, and by eliminating areas where they can hide and nest. Common access areas used by rats are openings in buildings where pipes and cables enter and between walls. Houses can be constructed to restrict these entrances and the places that rats can travel within walls. In older buildings, areas of access can be sealed.

In addition to changing the habitat (a practice referred to as sanitation of the habitat), the most successful approach is that of **integrated pest management.** In this approach, a variety of methods are used, including some applications of pesticides, sanitation of the habitat, and the introduction of natural enemies, including diseases and predators. (See Chapter 10 for more information on integrated pest management.)

URBAN ECOLOGY

In the development of the modern environmental movement in the 1960s and 1970s, it was fashionable to consider everything about cities bad and everything about wilderness good. Cities were thought of simply as polluted, lacking in wildlife and native plants, dirty, and artificial—and therefore bad. Wilderness was thought of as unpolluted, clean, full of wildlife and native plants, and natural—and therefore good. But while it was fashionable to disdain cities, most people lived in them and in their environments and suffered directly from declining urban environments.

There have been only a small number of people concerned with urban ecology. As a result, many urban people have felt themselves to be outside of environmental issues. In fact, they are in the center of some of the most important. Today there is a rebirth of interest in urban environments and in the development of urban ecology. We seem to have realized that we cannot hike in the wilderness while our Romes burn from sulfur dioxide pollution.

Although it is common to think of cities as unpleasant environments, cities have been centers of civilization and have often created an environment believed beautiful by the inhabitants. For example, a writer earlier in the twentieth century remembered earlier days in a city with great nostalgia. "The clicking of the hoofs upon the hard macadam, the rhythmical creaking of the harness, the merry rattle of the lead bars," he wrote, "are delectable sounds" [16].

In a sense, cities are one of the ways that human society is able to pass beyond the direct limitations the environment imposes on nonhuman species. We have built cities north of the Arctic Circle; for example, Tromsö, Norway, which lies at latitude 69°40′N. We have also built cities in deserts or near deserts; Los Angeles, for example, is located in a region where local rainfall is too low to support a huge urban population and water is supplied from far away.

In planning for our future, it is useful to consider the relationships between a city and the environment. How will a city change as the environment changes? Is a city's environment healthy or unhealthy? How can we plan a city to make it more livable?

The goals of urban environmental management are (1) to make the internal environment as pleasant, beautiful, and healthy as possible; (2) to provide residents with access to parks and other contact with plants and animals; (3) to sustain the urban life-support system, minimizing the use of natural resources; and (4) to minimize the negative environmental effects of the city on the countryside.

In recent years there has been a growing development of self-help programs and the establishment of private groups to improve city environments and to develop better methods for people to

Career Profile: Marian Cobb

I didn't have a strong interest in environmental affairs in college," says Marian Cobb. Now she is an urban planner with the Atlanta, Georgia, Bureau of Planning. "I consider the environmental consequences of any action that the city is going to undertake," she says.

With a B.S. in English, she began working for the city of Atlanta as a librarian in an environmental assessment section within the Department of Community and Human Development. While setting up an environmental record review file, she became interested in community development and environmental assessment. She says the city was "in a crunch once," so she volunteered to do an environmental assessment. She did not want the city to do a project without considering the effects—human and otherwise.

She continued to do environmental assessments and several years later when the city government was reorganized, she was transferred to the Bureau of Planning. Later she became an urban planner. While on the job, she has done further study toward a master's degree in urban planning at Georgia Tech University.

Other planners on the bureau staff are concerned mainly with transportation, housing, land use, urban design, economic development, recreation, or historic preservation. Cobb's

main area of concern is environment.

The various planners work together to prepare an annual comprehensive development plan for the city of Atlanta. Cobb describes the comprehensive plan as a progress report showing where the city is and where it is going. As an environmental planner, part of Cobb's responsibility is to get community input about environmental concerns that need to be included in the comprehensive plan. She also works closely with the Atlanta Regional Planning Commission, monitoring issues that the city needs to be concerned with.

Her main responsibility with the Atlanta Bureau of Planning is preparing environmental assessments for community development grant projects. She says she takes into account anything that is going to affect

quality of life in the city, such as air pollution, noise, and public safety.

The environmental assessments that Cobb prepares include descriptions of a project, the present condition of the proposed site, and what would happen if the project were *not* implemented. She has a 62–item checklist of various impacts that she analyzes to determine how the project will affect the environment at the site.

The assessment goes on public review for 30 days. Then, money may be released from the funding agency if the project has environmental clearance.

Cobb says, "I don't remember any time that environmental objections were ignored." If there is potential for environmental "overtones," she says a project may be redesigned.

"I think being involved in this [environmental assessment] process has made me acutely aware of how important it is to safeguard our environment," Cobb says. "I think all of us need to be strongly aware of the fact that, as time goes by, our living space dwindles and that makes it ever more important to safeguard the space we're going to have to live in. We have to look at everything we do to our environment as a potentially life-prolonging or life-shortening factor."

Michele Wigginton

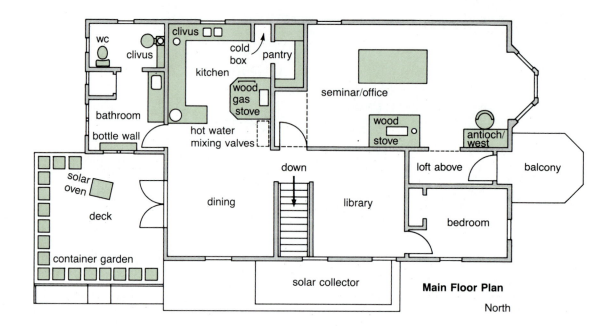

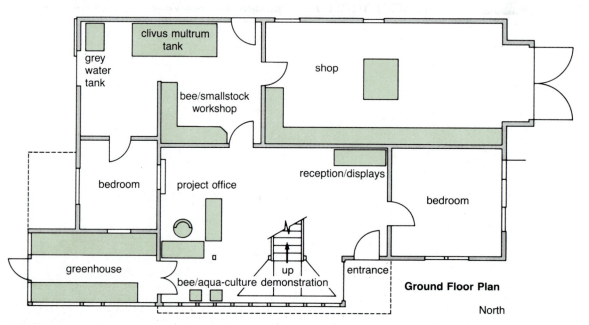

FIGURE 19.11

Integral urban house: (a) floor plan; (b) diagram of functions in the experimental house in Berkeley. (From *The Integral Urban House: Self-Reliant Living in the City* by Helga Olkowski, Bill Olkowski, Tom Javits, and the Farallones Institute staff. Copyright © 1979 by Sierra Club Books. Reprinted with permission of Sierra Club Books.)

SOLAR COLLECTORS capture the sun's radiant energy for heating household water. A flat-plate collector on the southern roof daily heats 120 gallons of water to temperatures above 140°. A small electric water heater provides a back-up on cloudy days.

A "BOTTLE WALL" in the southern window of the bathroom employs the principle of "thermal lag" to store the sun's energy to moderate internal temperatures.

A SOLAR OVEN warms and cooks food produced in the vegetable garden, in the animal yard, and breads from the kitchen.

SOLAR ENERGY

FOOD RAISING

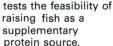

DOMESTICATED BEES produce honey and pollinate vegetable crops and fruit trees. An observation hive provides an inside view of the honey bee's life.

A VEGETABLE GARDEN, based on labor saving and environmentally sound techniques of food raising, yields produce enough for the family of four.

AN AQUACULTURE POND tests the feasibility of raising fish as a supplementary protein source.

A ROOFTOP GARDEN utilizes otherwise nonproductive space for raising vegetables in lightweight planters.

A GREENHOUSE provides a warm protective environment for germinating seeds and raising tomatoes and cucumbers in the winter.

RABBITS AND CHICKENS, housed in sanitary pens on the cool north side of the house, provide a dependable source of high quality protein. Much of their diet is raised on the premises, and their wastes are recycled to the soil.

A KITCHEN PANTRY provides storage for garden surpluses preserved by canning, pickling, and drying.

ORNAMENTAL CROPS demonstrate how food can be produced by planting a landscape of dwarf fruit trees, herbs, and edible flowering foliage.

INSECTS are controlled using biological and cultural methods of pest management. No synthetic pesticides are used.

WASTE RECYCLING

HUMANS

SOLID WASTES, such as glass, aluminum, tin, and newspaper, are sorted into bins and delivered to neighborhood recycling centers.

HOUSEHOLD WASTE WATER from wash basins and the shower is filtered, mixed with human urine, and reused as a garden irrigation water in rich nutrients.

THE CLIVUS MULTRUM waterless toilet converts human excrement into a pathogenically safe soil conditioner for use on fruit trees and ornamental crops. The process conserves water and recycles nutrients.

COMPOSTING wastes and returning their nutrients to the soil is a central theme in the Integral House. A variety of biological systems transform garden, animal, and kitchen wastes into a valuable soil amendment.

live in harmony with their environment in the city. These activities range from comparatively informal urban gardening programs to incorporated activities such as the Community Environmental Council of Santa Barbara, California.

An outstanding example of such activity is the integral urban house project of Berkeley, California. This was begun in the early 1970s when architects, engineers, and biologists began to meet to discuss ways that their knowledge and skills could be combined to make use of principles of ecology and to improve urban life. The group began to develop an experimental house to attempt to minimize fuel energy, minimize the use of water, and minimize the creation of pollution. This house makes use of solar energy for heating, hot water, and cooking; includes an urban garden to supplement food; and incorporates techniques to reduce water use, such as use of a dry toilet (Fig. 19.11) [13].

While the integral urban house focuses on the individual home, the Community Environmental Council of Santa Barbara, California, is a private organization that attempts to deal with a city's problem of waste disposal and promotes recycling. The Community Environmental Council runs the recycling of paper and metals in the city, using the profits from this operation to fund research on recycling and other aspects of the urban environment.

These organizations represent a new trend: the development of private organizations that apply principles of environmental studies to the city to improve urban life and to reduce waste of resources.

SUMMARY

As an urban society, we must recognize the city's relation to the environment. A city influences and is influenced by its environment and is an environment itself.

Like any life-supporting system, a city must provide for a flow of energy and a cycling of chemical elements necessary for life. Not being self-sufficient, a city must have a source of energy and material resources and must have a sink for waste disposal. These in turn require a transportation network.

Because cities depend on outside resources, they could appear only when human ingenuity resulted in an excess of production. The history of cities can be divided into four stages: (1) the rise of towns; (2) the era of classic urban centers, (3) the industrial metropolises; and (4) the age of mass telecommunication, computers, and new forms of travel.

The locations of cities are strongly influenced by the environment. It is clear that cities are not located at random, but in places of particular importance and environmental advantage, such as near ocean harbors, at the fall line, near mineral resources, or at crucial transportation points. Location is a consequence of site and situation. The site is the exact location where the city is built and the characteristics of that location. The situation is the relationship to other areas. A good site includes firm, solid geological foundations for construction; well-drained soil with abundant water; defensibility; and a moderate climate. A good situation includes good, natural transportation, such as a place where a river is most easily crossed or a transfer point between two modes of transportation. Most of the great cities of history are located at good sites and important situations. However, one can compensate for another. In particular, an important situation can compensate for a poor site.

A city creates an environment that is different from that of its surrounding areas. Cities change the local climate and are commonly cloudier, warmer, rainier, and less humid than their surroundings. In general, life in a city is riskier because of higher concentrations of pollutants and pollutant-related diseases. Although pollution levels have improved in cities in recent decades, the trend is expected to worsen in the future. Because there are so many factors that affect a city's potential for air pollution, careful planning is needed to improve air quality.

Because cities are ecological islands, they favor certain kinds of animals and plants. Natural habitats in city parks and preserves will become more important as true wilderness decreases. Trees in a city have become an important part of urban environments. The urban environment, however, creates many stresses on trees, and special attention must be paid to the condition of urban soils and the supply of water for trees, as well as to the physical stress to which trees are subjected.

The control of pests such as rats, termites, fleas, and cockroaches is an important urban problem. From the principles of environmental studies we understand that the key to this control is the habitat: reducing the food supply and the areas in which pests can breed and hide is essential to long-term control. Pesticides alone provide only temporary solutions without management of the urban habitats; integrated pest management provides the best overall approach.

STUDY QUESTIONS

1 How does the environment influence the location of cities?

2 What types of cities are most likely to become ghost towns in the next 30 years? In answering this question, make use of your knowledge of changes in resources, transportation, and communication.

3 Some futurists picture a world that is one giant biospheric city. Is this possible? Under what conditions?

4 Among ancient Greeks it was said that a city should have no more people than the number that can hear the sound of a single voice. Would you apply this rule today? If not, how would you decide how to plan the size of a city?

5 Standing on top of the Sears Tower in Chicago, Illinois, you overhear someone say, "Planning never works. The most interesting cities just grow. Planned cities are always dull and sterile." He points to large, low-income housing developments far in the distance. How would you respond?

6 You are the manager of Central Park in New York City and receive the following requests. Which would you approve? Explain your reasons.
 (a) A gift of $1 million to plant trees from all of the eastern states.
 (b) A gift of $1 million to set aside half the park to be forever untouched, thus producing an urban wilderness.
 (c) A gift of the construction of an asphalt jogging track and a gym for physical fitness. The donor says that lack of physical fitness is a major urban health problem.
 (d) A request to install an ice skating rink with artificially made ice. Facilities include an elegant restaurant with many views of the park.

7 Your state asks you to locate and plan a new town. The purpose of the town is to house people who will work at a "wind farm"—a large area of many windmills, all linked to produce electricity. You must locate the site for the wind farm first, then plan the town. Describe how you would proceed and what factors you would take into account.

8 Visit your town center. What changes, if any, would make better use of the environmental location? How could the area be made more livable?

9 In what ways does air travel alter the location of cities? The value of land within a city?

10 You are put in charge of ridding your city's parks of slugs, which eat up the vegetable gardens rented to residents. Describe how you would approach controlling this pest.

FURTHER READING

BURTON, J. A. 1977. *Worlds apart: Nature in the city*. Garden City, N.Y.: Doubleday.

BUTTI, K., and PERLIN, J. 1980. *The golden thread: 2500 years of solar architecture and technology*. New York: Cheshire.

DE BLIJ, H. J. 1977. *Human geography: Culture, society and space*. New York: Wiley.

FARALLONES INSTITUTE. 1979. *The integral urban house: Self-reliant living in the city*. San Francisco: Sierra Club Books.

LEGGETT, R. F. 1973. *Cities and geology*. New York: McGraw-Hill.

MUMFORD, L. 1961. *The city in history*. New York: Harcourt, Brace and World.

NADEL, I. B.; OBERLANDER, C. H.; and BOHM, L. R. 1977. *Trees in the city*. New York: Pergamon Press.

REPS, J. W. 1965. *The making of urban America*. 2nd ed. Princeton, N.J.: Princeton University Press.

SMITH, D. 1983. *Urban ecology*. London: George Allen & Unwin.

WHYTE, W. H. 1968. *The last landscape*. Garden City, N.Y.: Doubleday.

20

Environmental Economics

- ☐ The individual's profit motive does not always act in the best interest of the environment.
- ☐ Externalities, not normally accounted for in benefit-cost analysis, often include environmental factors.
- ☐ How to deal with the discount factor in an economic analysis of environmental issues is an unresolved problem. Conservationists argue that the future environment is not to be valued less than the present.
- ☐ The level of acceptable risk is a social-economic-environmental tradeoff that changes over time in society. Novel or new risks appear to be less acceptable than long established or natural risks. Acceptability of risk involves ethical and psychological attitudes of individuals and society.

- ☐ Environmental intangibles are difficult to evaluate quantitatively.
- ☐ The judgment of what is displeasing is more universal than is the determination of what is aesthetically pleasing.
- ☐ The marginal cost of reducing pollutants increases rapidly as percentage reduction increases.
- ☐ Knowledge and understanding of specific resources, economics, and the characteristics of ecosystems are necessary to choose the best methods of using a desirable resource and of reducing undesirable effects. Environmental economics provides methods to analyze and understand these issues.

VICUÑA HARVEST

The vicuña, a relative of the South American llama, lives in the Andes of Ecuador, Peru, and Bolivia at extremely high elevations, from 4000 m to 6000 m. It is said to have the finest wool fleece of any animal, which makes the vicuña extremely valuable. As a result, the animals have been overhunted to the extent that the species has become endangered (Fig. 20.1).

Today approximately 80% of the world's population of vicuña lives in a single preserve, the Reserva Nacional de Vicuñas de Pampa Galeras (the National Vicuña Reserve of the Pampa Galeras),

FIGURE 20.1
A young vicuña.

which lies at an altitude of 4000 m and more, about 500 km south of Lima, Peru [1].

The preserve was originally set up to protect the vicuña from extinction, and this effort has been successful. There were only 1200 vicuña in the preserve in 1967, and the number has increased to around 10,000 (the estimates are difficult to obtain in the high-altitude habitat and vary considerably) [1].

The population increased to such an extent that a plan was proposed to begin harvesting the vicuña for their wool. The arguments in favor of this project included (1) the vicuña were locally overabundant and needed to be controlled; (2) they were extremely valuable and would provide a highly beneficial economic resource; and (3) if the vicuña were economically valuable, the inhabitants would take more interest in their preservation. The West German government entered into a cooperative agreement with the Peruvian governnment to begin planning for this harvest.

Those concerned with the protection of the vicuña argued against this plan on the grounds that (1) there were still too few animals in the park to allow any hunting; (2) the hunting was unlikely to be economically profitable; (3) the growth rate of the vicuña was not sufficient for a sustained economic harvest; and (4) the conservation of the wild vicuña was more important (that is, more valuable) than the economic return from their harvest.

The conflicts over the vicuña illustrate some of the important issues in environmental economics. These include: (1) Could the vicuña provide a long-term sustained yield that would be economically useful? (2) How do we determine whether the population can sustain an economically valuable harvest? (3) If we allow hunting, how are we to choose who should do it, and what is a fair way to distribute the allowable harvest? And finally, (4) How can we compare intangible values—like the value of a wild population of vicuña in a preserve—with tangible and easily quantifiable values like the price of vicuña wool? In this chapter we will discuss the basic concepts of environmental economics; these provide insight into why people do not always act to conserve our environment and how we might best modify our policies so that conservation becomes integrated into economic development.

Environmental decision making often involves analysis of both economic factors and intangibles such as aesthetic factors. Of the two, the intangibles are more complicated to deal with because they are hard to measure and it is difficult to determine their value. In spite of these problems, evaluation of the intangibles is becoming more important in local, regional, and national land-use planning and environmental analysis. Therefore we must develop a method of aesthetic evaluation that is easy to understand and is quantitatively credible and predictive.

Other significant questions in environmental decision making are, How do we turn our choices into decisions, and how do we ensure that individuals and society will act in a way to accomplish environmental goals? What are the options open to society? To attempt to answer some of these questions, we will discuss selected aspects of environmental economics, risk-benefit analysis, and environmental intangibles.

The management of biological resources involves several major economic and social issues. Two of these issues are, How can we increase the production of biological resources without endangering their long-term survival or other aspects of the environment? and, What is the upper limit of world production of each of these resources?

THE ENVIRONMENT AS A "COMMONS"

A society has a number of social mechanisms to achieve its environmental goals. Laws and legal regulation are one method; use of resources can be limited by setting quotas or by selling a limited number of licenses (as with sport fishing). Or a society might rely on individual motivation, on the assumption that what an individual finds best for himself will also be best for society. This approach leaves the individual complete freedom of action.

One of the first questions often asked about managing the environment is, Why don't individuals want to act in a way that always protects the environment and maintains biological resources in a renewable state? One way to answer this question is provided by economic analysis. Economic analysis shows us that the individual's profit motive alone will not always act in the best interest of the environment. This is illustrated in the following examples.

Some biological resources, such as much of the U.S. forests, are situated on privately owned lands. Other resources, such as 38% of our nation's forests, are on nationally owned lands. Resources in international regions are not controlled by any single nation. Many of the world's fisheries are in this last category.

When biological resources occur in international or national areas with open access, the resources are threatened by what Garrett Hardin has called the "tragedy of the commons" [2]. The commons were parts of old English and New England towns where every farmer could graze his cattle. This practice works as long as the number of cattle is low. Hardin points out that each herdsman in such a situation is trying to maximize his gain and must ask himself periodically whether he should add more cattle. The addition has both a positive and negative utility. The positive utility is the benefit the herdsman receives when he sells the cattle; the negative one is the overgrazing caused by the addition of any one animal. Hardin argues that because the benefit to the individual of selling a cow is greater than his individual loss in the degradation of the commons, freedom of action in a commons inevitably brings ruin to all. He says that, without some management or control, all natural resources treated like commons will be inevitably destroyed. The overcrowding of national parks and the pollution of the atmosphere are given as examples of this tragedy [2].

As another example, many have argued for a reduction or elimination of commercial whaling in the interest of conserving the great whales. A question that naturally arises about whaling is, If whalers profit by harvesting whales, why do they not act to protect the resource on which their livelihood depends? Ranchers, after all, do not intentionally kill all their cattle just because they can make

Career Profile: Allen Kneese

I work primarily in water resources and environmental economics," says Allen Kneese. He is a Senior Fellow in Quality of the Environment Division at Resources for the Future (RFF) in Washington, D.C. He graduated from Indiana University with a Ph.D. in economics in 1956.

RFF was established by the Ford Foundation in the mid-1950s. Kneese began working at RFF in 1960 as an economic researcher in the water resources division. "The area of study then was resources with an economics and futurist orientation," Kneese says. His task was to develop a program of research on water quality. He went on to direct the Water Resources Program and Quality of the Environment Division.

"RFF has been in transition recently," Kneese says. Originally all of the funding was private. For 25 years, it operated with Ford Foundation grants. Now about 60% of the funding comes from outside contracts, mainly from the federal government. An endowment provides the remainder of the funding from private sources. As a result, Kneese has participated in studies for a variety of organizations.

Kneese traces his interest in the environment to early origins. "I grew up on a farm and was concerned with the natural ways. Economics seemed like a good way of linking my interest in natural ways to policy questions." He feels the environmental field is inherently interdisciplinary. "I have worked extensively with scientists and engineers," he says.

Kneese believes the field of environmental economics requires specialized economic training as well as study in the physical and natural sciences as applicable. He points out, "Courses in environmental economics are taught at almost all major universities today." At various times since 1960, Kneese has taken leave from RFF to teach at Stanford University, the University of New Mexico, and the University of California. Currently he is an adjunct professor at the University of New Mexico.

Kneese feels the role of economics in the use of resources and minimization of pollution is central in the sense that the United States relies on market transactions as the main form of control. Nonmarket mechanisms for controlling these things are not used much in the United States. Other countries make greater use of nonmarket mechanisms, such as requiring payment for effluent discharges.

Kneese says that environmental costs are more straightforward than environmental benefits. For example, sewage treatment plants and electrostatic precipitators are items of market interest. Estimating environmental benefits is harder. He mentions that surveys are used a lot recently to place a value on the environment. Things such as the benefits of air and water are difficult to determine.

Kneese is the author of numerous books and articles in the field of environmental economics. Most recently he has edited two volumes of handbooks concerning resources and energy in an economic series. "Environmental economics has become a field within a broader field of economics. It has become a product of the present generation of economists," Kneese says.

Michele Wigginton

money by selling cattle. However, whalers have brought species of the great whales to the brink of extinction. The blue whale was reduced to only an estimated few hundred before harvesting was stopped in the 1960s (Fig. 20.2). (See Chapter 8 for more information about whaling.)

Hardin's analysis shows that a fundamental issue in whaling and fishing is the lack of property rights. Ranchers refrain from killing off entire herds because the benefits of maintaining the herds (and the yet unborn) are reaped by them in the future. Fishermen or whalers, however, cannot be assured that they will reap those benefits. The offspring of the fish or whales they do not kill today are not theirs to harvest in the future.

From the example of whaling, one might argue in favor of private ownership of what have been the commons. On the other hand, some argue that private ownership of public goods, like fisheries and forests, is undemocratic and unfair. The issue of resource regulation and ownership has been raised by the "Sagebrush Rebellion"—a political movement of western ranchers who want more local control and access to public lands for private cattle grazing. As the human population grows and resources remain constant or decline, greater and greater competition will occur for their use, and any decisions about political and economic control will be more hotly contested.

Another reason that individuals will tend to overexploit natural resources held in common, according to mathematician Colin Clark, has to do with what economists call economic rent [3]. To understand this concept, consider the whales in the ocean and whale oil, which is a marketable product, as the capital investment of the industry. Whalers have a variety of policies that they might adopt toward harvesting whales. A policy is a set of rules to determine which actions will lead to a certain goal. How can whalers get the best return on their "capital"? (Here we need to remind ourselves that the whales, as a biological population, increase only if there are more births than deaths.) Let's examine two extreme policies. If the whalers adopt a conservative policy, they will harvest only the net biological productivity each year and maintain the total abundance of whales at its current level; that is, they will stay in the whaling business indefinitely. If they adopt the maximum immediate profit policy, they will harvest all the whales now, sell the oil, get out of the whaling business, and invest the profits.

Suppose they adopt the first policy. What is the maximum gain they can expect? Whales, like other large, long-lived creatures, reproduce slowly; a calf born every 3 or 4 years per female is typical. The total net growth of a whale population is unlikely to be more than 5%/yr. If all the oil in the whales in the ocean today represented a value of $10 million, then the most the whalers could expect to take in each year would be 5% of this, or $500,000.

If they adopt the second policy and harvest all the whales, then they could invest the money from

FIGURE 20.2
Annual blue whale catch from 1925 to 1965. After 1965, the whales were protected. (From Clark, 1973.)

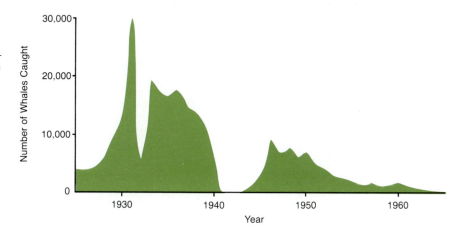

the oil. Although investment income varies, even a conservative investment of $10 million would very likely yield more than 5%, particularly because this income could be received without the cost of paying a crew, maintaining the ships, buying fuel, marketing the oil, and so on.

Thus, it is quite reasonable—and in fact quite practical, if one considers only direct profit—to adopt the second policy: Harvest all the whales, invest the money, and relax. Whales just are not a highly profitable long-term investment. It is no wonder that there are fewer and fewer whaling companies and countries and no wonder that countries leave the whaling business when their ships become old and inefficient.

The problems of the commons and of economic rent point out several important things. First of all, if we want to conserve whales, we must think beyond the immediate, direct economic advantages of whaling. Second, policies that seem ethically good to us may not be the most profitable for an individual. In the example of whaling, the economic analysis clarifies how an environmental resource is used. An economist would say that we must be concerned with externalities in whaling. An externality is an effect not normally accounted for in the cost-revenue analysis of producers [3]. In this case, externalities include the loss of revenue to tourist boats used to view whales and the loss of an ecological role played by whales in marine ecosystems.

Other factors to consider in resource use are the relative scarcity of a necessary resource and its price. For example, if a whaler lived on a desert island and whales were the only food he could obtain, then he would have to consider his interest in staying alive for a while as well as his short-term profit. Of course, even a whale-eating whaler might choose a policy somewhere in between the two extremes. He might decide that his own life expectancy was only 10 years, and he would try to harvest the whales so that they and he would go extinct at the same time. "You can't take it with you" would be his attitude. This would not happen necessarily if ocean property rights existed. A whaler could then sell his rights to future whalers, or mortgage against them, and thus reap the benefits of whales to be caught after his death.

THE DISCOUNT FACTOR

The preceding example reminds us of the old saying, "A bird in hand is worth two in the bush." That is, a profit now is worth much more than a profit in the future. This economic concept—the future value compared with the present value—is another important one for environmental studies. Economists refer to this concept as the discount factor. The discount factor is how much something is worth in the future compared with what it is worth now. Economists observe that the market determines a discount rate that is often, but not always, less than 1. (A discount factor less than 1 means that something promised in the future has less value than something given today.) The market-determined discount factor is the result of the interaction of the consumer's preferences for present and future consumption and of the technology for transferring present consumption into future consumption.

As an example, suppose you were dying of thirst on a desert and met two people; one offered to sell you a glass of water now, and the other offered to sell you a glass of water if you could be at the well tomorrow. How much is each glass worth? If you believed you would die today without water, the glass of water today would be worth all of your money and the glass tomorrow would be worth nothing. This is an extreme example of a discount factor.

In real life, things are rarely so simple and distinct. But we all know we are mortal, so we tend to value personal wealth and goods more if they are available now than in the future. This evaluation is made more complex, however, because we are accustomed to think of the future—to plan for retirement or a nest egg for our children.

Modern concerns with the environment have placed a novel emphasis on the discount factor. Conservationists often argue that we have a debt to future generations and must leave the environment in at least as good a condition as we found it. Such conservationists would argue that the future environment is not to be valued less than the present. In economic terms, this means that the discount factor is 1 (the environment in the future is just as valuable as the environment today) or greater than 1 (the environment in the future is worth more than the environment today).

For example, suppose you are the manager of the whooping cranes and are paid in relation to your success in keeping that species from extinction. The assurance that whooping cranes would be alive 10 years from now would seem to have more value to you than the assurance that they would be alive tomorrow. These different attitudes toward the discount factor pose a dilemma for environmental studies.

First of all, economists would argue that it is difficult, if not impossible, to make a sound economic analysis when the discount factor is greater than 1. Suppose we agree that a whooping crane alive next year is worth twice a live one today, and so on. In 2 years, the whooping crane is 4 times as valuable, and in 3 years, 8 times as valuable. If your salary is proportional to that value, your salary will very quickly become larger than all the material resources of the universe. Clearly, this is not a feasible approach.

Second, many would argue that, rhetoric to the contrary, everybody really does place a higher value on a possession in hand today rather than promised tomorrow. In other words, you would really rather have whooping cranes today while you are alive to enjoy them than whooping cranes tomorrow when you might be dead. This situation would be subject to the technological devices that affect the transfer of present consumption into future consumption.

How to deal with the discount factor in an economic analysis of environmental issues is an unsolved problem. The concept of the discount factor is, however, very important as we seek the environment we desire.

From the preceding discussion we see that effective management of the environment requires a clear understanding of the reasons for overexploit-ing our resources. That is, we need to know about the problems of the commons and the concepts of the discount factor, economic rent, and externalities.

RISK/BENEFIT ANALYSIS

Our discussion of the economics of whaling and the discount factor illustrates that the riskiness of the future influences the value we place on things now. Another important concept used in environmental economics is that of risk/benefit analysis. All of life, including populations, resources, ecosystems, and the biosphere, involves risk. Consider, for example, the effects of pollutants on life. How can we deal with these? How much are we willing to pay to reduce or eliminate a pollutant? The answers depend on the risks involved.

Pollutants have effects on human health, commercially important or essential products such as food crops, wildlife, natural ecosystems, and the biosphere. The ecosystem and biospheric effects may in turn have indirect negative effects on human beings. Pollutants can cause annoyance, injury, or death. Like natural hazards, they can be dangerous to human beings; but unlike natural hazards, they often act in subtle and slow, sometimes almost imperceptible, ways. How do we know if something is indeed dangerous or toxic?

Death is the fate of all individuals, and every activity in life involves risk of injury or death. What then does it mean to save a life by reducing the level of a pollutant?

With some activities, the relative risk is clear. It is much more dangerous to stand in the middle of a busy highway than to stand on the sidewalk. Hang gliding has a much higher mortality rate than hiking. Table 20.1 gives the risk associated with a variety of activities. The effects of pollutants, however, are often more subtle. Populations subject to high levels of certain pollutants have a lower average life expectancy or a high incidence of certain diseases. But even in such a population any one of us might live a "normal" lifespan, or even longer.

The degree of risk is important in our legal processes. For example, the Toxic Substances Control Act states that no one may manufacture a new chemical substance or process a chemical substance for a new use without obtaining a clearance from the U.S. Environmental Protection Agency (EPA). The act establishes procedures to estimate the hazard to the environment and to human health of any new chemical before it becomes widespread. The EPA examines the data provided and judges the degree of risk associated with all aspects of the production of the new chemical or the new process, including extraction of raw materials, manufacturing, distribution, processing, use, and disposal. The chemical can be banned or restricted in either manufacturing or use if the evidence suggests that it will pose an unreasonable risk of injury to human health or to the environment. But what is "unreasonable" [4]?

The preceding discussion indicates that pollutants increase the risk of injury or death to individuals and the risk of damage to the environment. It is commonly believed that future discoveries will help to decrease the risk, eventually allowing us to attain a zero-risk environment. But the more likely case is that any given society has a socially, psychologically, and ethically acceptable level of risk for any cause of death or injury. While ideally one would like to eliminate all pollutants from the environment, detailed analyses reveal that complete elimination in many cases is either technologically

impossible or too expensive. Figure 20.3 shows that the total cost of pollution is the sum of the costs to control pollution and the loss from pollution damages. These two factors have opposite trends in terms of economic cost and their intersection point forms a minimum total cost as shown by point A in Figure 20.3. If the minimum total cost involves a pollution level that is too high a risk, then additional control may add considerable expense. The level of acceptable pollution (and thus risk) is then a social-economic-environmental tradeoff. The level of acceptable risk changes over time in society, depending on the risks from other causes, the expense of decreasing the risk, and the social and psychological acceptability of the risk.

Therefore, we must ask several questions. What risk from a particular pollutant is acceptable? How much is a certain reduction in risk from that pollutant worth to us? How much will each of us, as individuals or collectively as a society, be willing to pay for a certain reduction in that risk?

Novel or new risks appear to be less acceptable than long established or "natural" risks. Thus our society tends to pay more to reduce novel risks than to reduce natural or long-established ones. For example, in France approximately $1 million is spent to reduce the likelihood of one air traffic death, but only $30,000 is spent for the same reduction in automobile deaths [5]. Some argue that

FIGURE 20.3
The total cost of pollution is the sum of the costs to control pollution and the loss from pollution damages. These two factors have opposite trends in terms of economic cost and their intersection point forms a minimum total cost as shown by point A. If the minimum total cost involves a pollution level that is too high a risk, then additional control may add considerable expense. The level of acceptable pollution (and thus risk) is then a social-economic-environmental tradeoff.

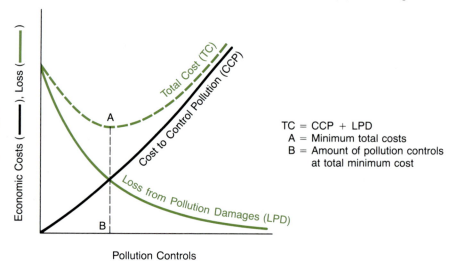

$$TC = CCP + LPD$$
A = Minimum total costs
B = Amount of pollution controls at total minimum cost

the greater safety of commercial air travel compared with automobile travel is in part a function of the relatively novel fear of flying compared with the more ordinary fear of death from a road accident.

While in an ethical sense it is impossible to put a value on a human life, it is possible to find out how much people are willing to pay for a certain reduction in risk or a certain probability of an increase in longevity. For example, a study by the Rand Corporation considered measures, such as increasing ambulance services and initiating pretreatment screening programs, that would save the lives of heart attack victims. According to the study, which identified the likely cost per life saved and the willingness of people to pay, people were willing to pay approximately $32,000 per life saved or $1,600 per year of longevity [5].

The willingness to pay would vary with the essentialness and desirability of an activity. For example, many people accept much higher than average risks for sports or recreational activities than they would for risks associated with transportation or employment (Table 20.1).

Although information is very incomplete, it is possible to estimate the cost of extending lives in

TABLE 20.1
The risk of death for various activities*

Activity	Risk/year
Sports	
Auto racing	1.2 chances in 1,000
Football	4 chances in 100,000
Water sports	1.9 chances in 100,000
Biking	1 chance in 100,000
Travel	
Motor vehicles	2.2 chances in 10,000
Air travel (one transcontinental trip across U.S.)	3 chances in one million
Natural hazards	
Lightning	4 chances in 10 million
Hurricanes	4 chances in 10 million
Tornadoes	5 chances in 10 million
Pollution	
Air pollution	1.5 chances in 10,000

*Given as the chance of death per year; only selected examples are shown.

Source: Wilson, R. 1980. Risk/benefit analysis for toxic chemical. *Ecotoxicology and Environmental Safety.* 4:370–383.

terms of the dollars per person per year for various actions (Fig. 20.4). For example, on the basis of direct effects on human health, it costs more to in-

FIGURE 20.4
One way to rank the effectiveness of various efforts to reduce pollutants is to estimate the cost of extending a life in dollars per year. This graph shows that reducing sulfur emissions from power plants to the Clean Air Act level (A) would extend a human life 1 year at a cost of about $10,000. Similar restrictions applied to automobile emissions (B, C) would increase lifetimes by 1 day. More stringent automobile controls would be much more expensive (D), while mobile units and screening programs for heart problems would be much cheaper (E). (After Wilson.)

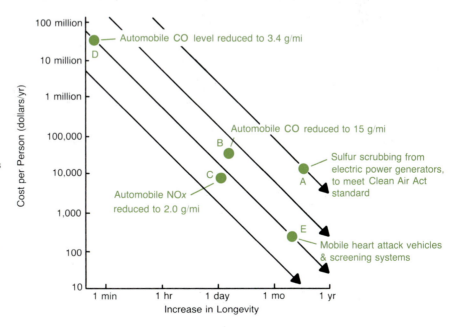

crease longevity by a reduction in air pollution than it would to directly reduce deaths by the addition of a coronary ambulance system. Such a comparison is useful as a basis for decision making. Clearly, when a society chooses to reduce air pollution, many factors beyond the direct measurable health benefits are considered. We might want to choose a slightly higher risk of death in a pleasanter environment (spend money to clean up the air instead of on increased ambulance services) than increase the chances of living longer in a poor environment. Whether we like it or not, we cannot avoid making choices of this kind. The issue boils down to whether we should improve the quality of life for the living or extend life expectancy regardless of the quality of life [6].

Although pollution control may involve many dollars, the cost per family in the United States, in terms of reduced purchasing power for other things, has been estimated to be between $30 and $60 per year for a family with a median income. On the other hand, federal air quality standards are estimated to reduce the risk of asthma 3%, and the risk to locally exposed adults of chronic bronchitis and emphysema 10–15%. Air pollution contributes to inflation by reducing the number of productive work days, reducing work efficiency, adding to direct expenditures on health treatments, and incurring costs of restoration of nonhuman environmental damage. Estimates of the total cost of the direct and indirect effects on human health from stationary sources of air pollution are $250 per family per year. On this basis, air pollution control appears not to be inflationary; in fact, it has economic benefits [8].

In summary, the risk associated with a pollutant can be determined by the present levels of exposure and predicted future trends. These trends depend on the production and origin of the pollutant, the pathways it follows through the environment, and the changes it undergoes along these pathways. Dose-response curves establish the risk to a population from a particular level of a pollutant (see Chapter 11). The relative risks of different pollutants can be determined by comparing the current levels and their dose-response curves.

So far we have described scientific and technological steps to estimate risk, but an acceptable risk is much more than a scientific or technical issue. Once the risk is established, it is then possible to estimate the cost of reducing that risk. The acceptability of a risk involves ethical and psychological attitudes of individuals and of society. Risks that are voluntary appear to be more acceptable than those that are not voluntary. Risks that affect a small portion of a population (such as all employees at nuclear power plants) are usually more acceptable than those that involve all of a society (such as the risk from radioactive fallout). Finally, familiar, long-established risks seem to be more acceptable than novel ones.

ENVIRONMENTAL INTANGIBLES

Environmental intangibles such as the visual or other sensual pleasures of experiences, whether in the natural or urban environment, are extremely difficult to evaluate. A nature photographer about to find an elusive subject on a lonely mountain top; a hunter in the blind on a crisp autumn morning; a beachcomber searching coastal tidal pools on a misty morning; picnickers relaxing in an urban park; or a motorist out for a Sunday drive in the country—all perceive to a lesser or greater extent various aspects of the environment and react to it with various types of behavior. Their experiences and memories cannot be readily assigned an economic value, but they may be priceless to each individual.

One of the perplexing problems associated with aesthetic evaluation is personal preference. For example, one person may appreciate a high mountain meadow far removed from civilization while a second prefers, as an outdoor experience, visiting with others on a patio at a trailhead lodge. A third person may prefer to visit a city park. If we are going to consider aesthetic factors in environmental analysis we must develop a method of aesthetic evaluation that allows for individual differences.

Basic criteria necessary to judge aesthetic qualities include unity, vividness, and variety [8]. Unity refers to the quality or wholeness of the perceived landscape, not as an assemblage but as a single harmonious unit. Vividness refers to that quality of landscape that reflects a visually striking scene and is nearly synonymous with intensity, novelty, or clarity. Variety refers to how different one landscape is from another. Variety includes ideas of diversity and uniqueness. However, it is not always the case that the greater diversity, the greater the aesthetic value.

Intangible resources are difficult to evaluate quantitatively. In contrast, quantitative evaluation of tangible natural resources such as air, water, forests, or minerals prior to development or management of a particular area is standard procedure. Water resources for power or other uses may be evaluated by the amount of flow of the rivers and the quantity of water storage in rivers and lakes; forest resources may be evaluated by the number, type, and sizes of trees and their subsequent yield of lumber; and mineral resources may be evaluated by estimating the number of tons of economically valuable mineral material at a particular location. We can make a statement of the quality and quantity of each tangible resource compared to some known quality or quantity. Ideally we would like to make similiar statements about the more intangible resources, such as scenery. That is, we would like to compare scenery to specific standards and one scene with another [8]. Unfortunately, this is a very difficult task for which few standards are available.

Scenic resources may be defined as the visual portion of an aesthetic experience. Scenic resources produce visual "amenities." Areas with recognized visual amenities are of particular public concern and may be subject to protection.

The general philosophical framework used to evaluate scenic resources includes the following concepts: First, scenic resources are visual amenities that can be evaluated in terms of an aesthetic judgment. Second, scenic resources like soil and other resources vary in quality from place to place. Third, topographic relief, presence of water, and diversity of form and color are significant positive characteristics of scenic quality, whereas artificial change is generally a negative characteristic. Fourth, landscape that is unique is more significant to society than common landscape. Fifth, although the determination of what is aesthetically pleasing varies from person to person, the judgment of what is really displeasing is more universal [9].

Virtually all schemes to evaluate scenic resources involve measuring or observing specifically selected factors. Such observation is admittedly subjective but is not necessarily a bad practice as long as relevent factors based upon sound judgments are chosen. Furthermore, a completely objective method of analyzing scenic resources based on our present knowledge of how people perceive the landscape is probably not possible and certainly not practical. Examination of present methods to evaluate scenic resources suggests that three general categories of factors are appropriate. The first is landform characterization, which assumes that, as terrain becomes steeper, more diverse, and has greater altitudinal differences (relief), the scenic quality increases. The second is natural characterization, which assumes that scenic quality increases as (1) the percentage of an area in natural surfaces (water, forest, marshland, or mountains) increases and (2) the diversity of natural surface types increases. The third is artificial characterization, assuming that as the amount of area covered by artificial features increases, scenic quality decreases.

Using these concepts, several different methods have been developed to quantify landscape aesthetics. A study of several river valleys in Indiana evaluated uniqueness and scenic quality in terms of the Wild and Scenic River Act, public law 90–542 of 1968. The study involved observation, measurement, and analysis of variables that describe the physical, biological, and human use of the landscape to determine uniqueness and scenic quality [10]. Figure 20.5 shows a summary for five Indiana streams and rivers in terms of their uniqueness and scenic quality as compared to the "ideal" scenic river, defined as a unique stream or river that is clear running, unpolluted, and unlittered. Numerical summaries were made in terms of physical, biologic and water quality, and human use and interest factors to illustrate what part of the total uniqueness or scenic quality is due to those groups of factors. This method allows us to compare and contrast several valleys in a region and make generalized statements concerning their individual scenic resources.

Quantifying scenic resources is valuable because the results can be displayed visually and dif-

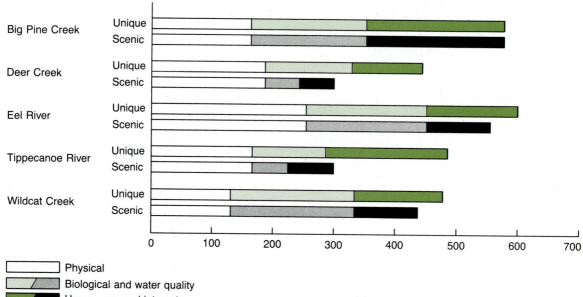

Physical

Biological and water quality

Human use and interest

FIGURE 20.5
Bar graph of uniqueness and scenic river indices for five Indiana streams. Units are on a scale of 1000. (From Melhorn et al.)

ferent landscapes ranked hierarchically. Quantification is basically another tool to help in decision making for land-use planning and environmental analysis. It tends to separate facts from emotion while finding a way to balance the intangibles with the more readily evaluated tangible aspects of landscape evaluation.

WHO PAYS AND HOW?

How does a society achieve an environmental goal? For our purposes in this section we will distinguish two such goals: (1) the use of a desirable resource (catching fish, hiking in the wilderness, obtaining wood or fuel, and so on) and (2) the reduction of an undesirable product (minimizing the release of a pollutant).

Any society has several methods to achieve these goals: persuasion, regulation (establishing laws, regulatory agencies, and so forth), taxation and subsidies, and licenses (Tables 20.2 and 20.3). Society has various policy instruments, which are

means to accomplish goals (Table 20.2). These include moral suasion (which politicians call "jawboning"—persuading people by talk, publicity, and social pressure); direct controls, which include regulations; market processes, which affect the price of goods and processes and include taxation of various kinds; subsidies; licenses; and deposits. Society also has administrative mechanisms to make sure that the policy instruments chosen actually function.

Studies of the uses of different policy instruments for environmental matters has led to some ability to evaluate their relative success (Table 20.3). For example, moral suasion is reliable but not very permanent in its effect. Sale of licenses or permits has been found to be among the more successful recourses. In every environmental matter there is a desire on the one hand to maintain individual freedom of choice and on the other to achieve a specific social goal. In ocean fishing, for example, how does a society allow every individual to choose whether or not to fish and yet prevent everyone from fishing at the same time so as to

TABLE 20.2
Approaches to environmental policy.

POLICY INSTRUMENTS

1. Moral Suasion (publicity, social pressure, etc.)
2. Direct Controls
   a. Regulations limiting the permissible levels of emissions
   b. Specification of mandatory processes or equipment
3. Market Processes[a]
   a. Taxation of environmental damage
      1) Tax rates based on evaluation of social damage
      2) Tax rates designed to achieve preset standards of environmental quality
   b. Subsidies
      1) Specified payments per unit of reduction of waste emissions
      2) Subsidies to defray costs of damage-control equipment
   c. Issue of limited quantities of pollution ''licenses''
      1) Sale of licenses to the highest bidders
      2) Equal distribution of licenses with legalized resale
   d. Refundable deposits against environmental damage
   e. Allocation of property rights to give individuals a proprietary interest in improved environmental quality

4. Government Investment
   a. Damage prevention facilities (e.g., municipal treatment plants)
   b. Regenerative activities (e.g., reforestation, slum clearance)
   c. Dissemination of information (e.g., pollution-control techniques, opportunities for profitable recycling)
   d. Research
   e. Education
      1) Of the general public
      2) Of professsional specialists (ecologists, urban planners, etc.)

ADMINISTRATIVE MECHANISMS

1. Administering Unit
   a. National agency
   b. Local agency
2. Financing
   a. Payment by those who cause the damage
   b. Payment by those who benefit from improvements
   c. General revenues
3. Enforcement mechanism
   a. Regulatory organization or police
   b. Citizen suits (with or without sharing of fines)

Source: From Baumol and Oates.

[a]Subsidies and taxes can also be distinguished by using a property-rights framework. Per unit subsidies implicitly confer ownership of the right to pollute on the polluter, and these rights are then purchased by the government via the subsidy. Taxes essentially say that there is public ownership of usage rights which can be purchased from the public through its agent, the government, by private parties upon payment of the tax (price).

cause extinction of the fish? This interplay between private good and public good is at the heart of environmental issues. Some argue that the market itself will provide the proper control. For example, it can be argued that people will stop fishing when there is no longer a profit to be made. We have already seen, however, that two factors interfere with this argument: (1) The level of fishing that results in no economic gain may still be a level that causes biological extinction. (2) Even when one may not make a profit today, there may be an advantage in harvesting the entire resource and getting out of the business.

Use of Resources

Desirable resources can be privately owned or controlled by a single user (as are many mineral mines or some forests) or can be common property. The ocean fish resources provide an example of the use of different policy instruments. The oceans are common property, as are the fish and mammals who live in them. What is common property may change over time. The move by many nations to define international waters as beginning 200 miles (325 k) from the coast has turned some fisheries from completely open common property to national property open only to domestic fishermen.

In fisheries there are four main management options:

1 Establish total catch quotas for the entire fishery.
2 Issue a restricted number of licenses, but allow each licensed fisherman to catch many fish.
3 Tax the catch (the fish brought in) or the effort (the cost of ships, fuel, and other essential items).
4 Allocate fishing rights [11].

TABLE 20.3
Performance of various policy instruments by specified criteria.

Policy Instrument	Reliability	Permanence	Adaptability to Growth	Resistance to Inflation
Moral suasion	Good[a]	Poor	Good*	Good*
Direct controls				
a. By quota	Fair	Poor	Fair	Excellent
b. By specification of technique	Fair	Poor	Good*	Good*
Fees	Excellent	Excellent	Fair	Fair
Sale of permits or licenses	Excellent	Excellent	Excellent	Excellent
Subsidies				
a. Per unit reduction	Fair[d]	Good	Fair	Fair
b. For equipment purchase	Fair	Good	Fair	Fair
Government investment	Good	?	?	?

Source: From Baumol and Oates.

*Baumol and Oates's judgment.

[a]For short periods of time when urgency of appeal is made very clear.

[b]Induces contributions from decision makers who are most cooperative, not necessarily from those able to do the job most effectively (most inexpensively).

[c]Tends to allocate reduction "quotas" among firms in cost-minimizing manner, but if the number of emissions permits is too small it will force the community to devote an excessive quantity of resources to environmental protection.

[d]Tends to allocate reduction quotas among firms in cost-minimizing manner, but introduces inefficiency into the environmental protection process by attracting more polluting firms into the subsidized industry, so that aggregate response is questionable.

When total catch quotas are established, the fishery is closed when the catch quota is reached. Whales, Pacific halibut, tropical tuna, and anchovies have been regulated in this way. Although regulating the total catch might be done in a way that helps the fish, it tends to increase the number of fishermen and the capacity of vessels, and the end result is a hardship on fishermen.

Recent economic analysis suggests that taxes which take into account the cost of externalities can work to the best advantage of fishermen and fish. Another technique with similar results is a transferable and salable quota allocated to each fisherman.

Which of these social methods achieves the best use of a desirable environmental resource is not simple to answer. The answer will vary with the specific attributes of both the resource and the users. However, we can use the tools of economics to determine the methods that will work best within a given social framework.

The Control of Pollutants

In discussing the control of pollutants, the concept of the marginal cost is useful. Marginal cost is the cost to reduce a unit of pollutant. It is generally true that the marginal cost increases rapidly as the percentage reduction increases. For example, the marginal cost of reducing the biological oxygen demand in waste water from petroleum refining increases exponentially. When 20% of the pollutants have been removed, the cost of removing an additional kilogram is 5 cents. When 80% of the pollutants have been removed, it costs 49 cents to remove an additional kilogram. Extrapolating from this, it would cost an infinite amount to remove all the pollution.

There are two types of direct controls of pollution: (1) setting maximum levels of pollution emission and (2) requiring specific procedures and processes that reduce pollution. In the first case, a political body could set a maximum level for the

TABLE 20.3
(*continued*)

Incentive for Improved Effort	Economy	Feasibility without Metering	Noninterference in Private Decisions	Political Attraction	
				Actual	Potential
Fair	Poor[b]	Excellent	Excellent	Excellent	—
Poor	Poor	Poor	Poor	Excellent	—
Poor	Poor	Excellent	Poor	Excellent	—
Excellent	Excellent	Poor	Excellent	Poor	Good
Excellent	Excellent[c]	Poor	Excellent	Poor	Good
Excellent	Good	Poor	Excellent	Good	—
Good	Poor	Excellent	Excellent	Good	—
—	?	Excellent	—	Good	—

amount of sulfur emitted from the smokestack of an industry. In the second, it could restrict the kind of fuel. In fact, many areas have chosen the latter method by prohibiting the burning of high-sulfur coal. The problem with the first approach—controlling emissions—is that careful monitoring is required indefinitely to make certain the allowable levels are not exceeded. Such monitoring is costly and may be difficult to carry out. The disadvantages of the second approach are that the required methodology may impose a financial burden on the producer of the pollutant, restrict the kinds of production methods open to an industry, and become technologically obsolete.

Although the United States has emphasized the use of direct regulation to control pollution, other countries have been successful in controlling pollution by charging effluent fees. For example, charges for effluents into the Ruhr River in West Germany are assessed on the basis of both the quality (concentration of pollutant) and total quantity (total amount of polluted water) emitted into the river. As a result of this practice, plants have introduced water recirculation and internal treatment in order to reduce emissions [12].

In recent years the U.S. government has spent considerable amounts of money in environmentally related programs. Protection and enhancement (rehabilitation of sites, protection of unique natural areas, and other measures) cost more than

$1 billion per year. Pollution control and abatement cost almost $2 billion per year. Programs for observing and predicting weather, ocean conditions, and environmental disturbances such as earthquakes cost more than $1 billion per year [12].

Another problem in environmental economics is placing a value on a public good. A "public good," such as clean air, cannot be sold by private sellers. For example, suppose an individual went into the business of cleaning up the air. Anyone can use the clean air, so people will not voluntarily pay a charge for it. Natural ecosystems provide this service to some extent. Forests may absorb particulates, salt marshes may convert toxic compounds to nontoxic forms, and sewage put into streams can be removed by biological activity. We all profit from these public service functions of natural ecosystems, but we have no simple way to put a value on them or even to estimate the amount of pollution removal that takes place (Fig. 20.6).

To summarize, knowledge of the specific resource and an understanding of economics as well as the characteristics of ecosystems and of the entire biosphere are necessary to choose the best methods of using a desirable resource and of reducing undesirable pollutants. In all such practices there is a desire to maintain individual freedom of action while ensuring a public good. Environmental economics, an important and developing field,

FIGURE 20.6
How much is a quality environment worth? The amount to prevent its spoilage? The amount to clean it up once spoiled? The amount of economic activity lost by not developing an area? What other economically intangible considerations come to mind?

provides methods to analyze and understand these issues.

SUMMARY

Once we develop a set of values about nature, we attempt to achieve or maintain a desirable condition for the environment while maintaining human activities, freedom of individual action, and a high standard of living. Economics provides a basic framework for analysis of the policies that will achieve these social goals for the environment. The principles of economics can help us achieve effective use of resources and regulation of pollutants and help explain why we exploit and threaten our natural resources. A clear understanding of the basic reasons for overexploitation is a prerequisite for effective regulation.

Two major issues are important for society: (1) the use of a desirable resource (fish in the ocean, oil in the ground, forests on the land) and (2) the minimization of undesirable pollution. Resources may be common property, or they may be privately controlled. The kind of ownership affects the methods available to achieve an environmental goal. From the example of whaling, we learned that there is a tendency to overexploit a common property resource and to harvest to extinction nonessential resources whose innate growth rate is low. The discount factor can be an important determinant of the level of exploitation. The relation between risk and benefit affects our willingness to pay for an environmental good.

Evaluation of environmental intangibles such as landscape aesthetics and scenic resources is becoming more common in environmental analysis. When quantitative, such evaluation balances the more traditional economic evaluation while helping separate facts from emotion in complex environmental problems.

Societal methods to achieve an environmental goal include persuasion, direct regulation, taxation and subsidies, licensing, and establishment of quotas. All five kinds of controls have been applied to the use of desirable resources. In the United States, regulation and licensing have been commonly used to control the use of desired resources; regulation has been the common method to control pollution. Taxation and the establishment of salable quotas can be shown to be most effective in fisheries management.

The field known as environmental economics provides principles, guidelines, and methods to help us make the transition from knowing what we want for our environment to developing policies and taking action to achieve our goals.

STUDY QUESTIONS

1   What is meant by the phrase "the tragedy of the commons"? Which of the following are the result of this "tragedy": (a) the California condor, (b) the right whale, (c) the high price of walnut wood used in furniture?

2   Explain what is meant by "risk assessment."

3   You are invited by a friend to invest in a walnut plantation. She tells you that walnut is an extremely valuable wood and the price can only go higher as the tree becomes more scarce. You investigate further and discover that walnut is one of the longer-lived trees of eastern North America. Would you join your friend's investment? Why or why not?

4   Cherry and walnut are valuable woods used to make fine furniture. Using the information below, which would you invest in: (a) a cherry plantation; (b) a walnut plantation; (c) a mixed stand of both species; or (d) an unmanaged woodland where you see some cherry and walnut growing?

Species	Longevity	Maximum Size	Maximum Value
walnut	400 years	1 m	$15,000 per tree
cherry	100 years	1 m	$10,000 per tree

5   Flying over Los Angeles, you see smog below you. Your neighbor in the next seat says, "That smog looks bad, but eliminating it would save only a few lives. Doing that isn't worth the cost. We should spend the money on other things, like new hospitals." Do you agree or disagree? Give your reasons.

6   Which of the following are intangible resources? Which are tangible? (a) the view of Mt. Wilson in California; (b) owning property with a view of Mt. Wilson; (c) porpoises in the ocean; (d) tuna fish in the ocean; (e) clean air; (f) owning property outside the smog area of Los Angeles.

7   Explain why an economist would say that a discount factor must be less than 1. What does it mean to say that the discount factor for a blue whale is less than 1? greater than 1?

8   Discuss ways that one might put a monetary value on the conservation of vicuña in the preserve discussed at the beginning of this chapter.

9   The statement "Extinction is forever" implies what kind of discount value for a species? Discuss how we might approach providing an economic analysis for extinction.

10   Which of the following can be thought of as "commons" in the sense discussed by Garrett Hardin in "The Tragedy of the Commons"? Explain.
    (a)   Tuna fisheries in the open ocean
    (b)   Catfish grown in artifical freshwater ponds

    (c)   Grizzly bears in Yellowstone National Park
    (d)   A view of Central Park in New York City
    (e)   Air over Central Park in New York City

FURTHER READING

ABELSON, P. 1979. *Cost benefit analysis and environmental problems.* New York: Saxon House.

BAUMOL, W. J., and OATES, W. E. 1979. *Economics, environmental policy, and the quality of life.* Englewood Cliffs, N. J.: Prentice-Hall.

CLARK, C. 1976. *Mathematical bioeconomics: The optimal management of renewable resources.* New York: Wiley.

HARDIN, G. 1968. The tragedy of the commons. *Science* 162: 1243–48.

KNEESE, A. V., and BOWER, B. T. 1972. *Environmental quality analysis: Theory and method in the social sciences.* Baltimore: Johns Hopkins University Press.

NIJKAMP, P. 1977. *Theory and application of environmental economics.* New York: North Holland.

PAGE, T. 1977. *Conservation and economic efficiency.* Baltimore: Johns Hopkins University Press.

PEARCE, D. W., and WALTER, I. 1977. *Resource conservation: Social and economic dimensions of recycling.* New York: New York University Press.

SCHNAIBERG, A. 1980. *The environment: From surplus to scarcity.* New York: Oxford University Press.

21

Citizens, Laws, and Agencies

- [ ] The U.S. legal system has historically focused on the protection of the individual from society. Early U.S. history did not emphasize the public trust concept, but that concept has received more attention of late.

- [ ] Early federal legislation dealing with the environment was directed toward resource conservation. Legislation directed toward pollution and waste disposal did not become prominent until the late 1960s. Since the 1960s, some earlier legislation has been reinterpreted by the courts to emphasize environmental quality concerns.

- [ ] Administrative agencies devise and implement specific procedures to carry out general directions in legislation. The Environmental Protection Agency was created to centralize administration of environmental quality regulation.

- [ ] When resolution of issues is delegated to administrative agencies, they use the rule-making process to flesh out the skeleton provided by the legislation. Once in place, the final rule has the full force of law.

- [ ] The National Environmental Policy Act has been interpreted by the courts to encourage greater foresight and prevent thoughtless environmental damage from large federal projects.

- [ ] Environmental groups working through the courts are a powerful force in shaping the course of environmental quality control.

- [ ] Environmental mediation is an alternative to the courts; it can save time and money.

- [ ] All states have their own laws dealing with environmental quality.

- [ ] Some areas of environmental concern such as land use are traditionally controlled at local levels of government.

MONO LAKE

Mono Lake, located in the Mono basin at the foot of the Sierra Nevada east of Yosemite National Park in California, is the focus of recent controversy, which centers around the very existence of the lake. From the lake's watershed, approximately 100,000 acre feet of water per year is diverted south to the city of Los Angeles. Mono Lake is large, measuring approximately 21 by 13 km, with an average depth of about 17 m. These dimensions make it the largest lake by volume contained entirely within the state of California.

During the last million years, a number of important geologic events associated with active uplift of the Sierra Nevada, volcanic activity, and glaciation have affected the lake and consequently there is now no natural outlet from the lake. The lake is fed by a number of streams from the Sierra Nevada and some groundwater flow as well. Because there is no natural outlet, the lake is salty, having a salinity approximately three times that of sea water.

Mark Twain, who wrote about Mono Lake, is said to have once stated, "Half a dozen little mountain brooks flow into Mono Lake but not a stream of any kind flows out of it. What it does with its surplus water is a dark and bloody mystery" [1]. What happens to the water, of course, is that it evaporates. In fact, approximately 22 cm/yr evaporate from the surface of Mono Lake. Under natural conditions this loss would be matched from streams that feed the lake system [1].

Mono Lake and the basin it is in have a long and interesting history going back at least to 1853, when Yosemite Indians were pursued by the military to the shores of the lake. About that time, gold was discovered in the area, initiating a small gold rush that lasted until approximately 1889. Then in 1913 the city of Los Angeles considered importing water into the growing urban area, and by 1930 funds had been approved for the construction of dams, reservoirs, and a tunnel to divert water from the eastern Sierra and Mono Lake area. In 1941 diversion of water from the Mono basin began in earnest and by 1981 the lake level had dropped approximately 15 m. This decreased the volume of the lake by approximately one-half and resulted in increasing the salinity by 100%.

Brine shrimp grow in great abundance in the lake and provide the major food source for the migrating birds. If the salinity were to become too high, the brine shrimp would die and the birds would have no food during a crucial stage in their migration.

The lowering of the lake level also exposed nearly 9000 ha of highly alkaline lake bed. During windy periods alkali may rise into the atmosphere several thousand feet and be transported both around the basin and out of the basin, causing air pollution [1].

More significantly, lowering of the lake formed a land bridge to several volcanic islands in the lake that are major breeding grounds for California gulls. In 1979, after the land bridge had formed, coyotes entered the nesting area and routed all 34,000 nesting birds [1]. Extremely wet years in 1983 and 1984 caused the lake level to rise a bit but it was still much lower than the 1941 level. Figure 21.1 shows the 1980 situation with inflow and a diversion of waters.

People interested in the preservation of Mono Lake and its ecosystem would like to see the lake level stabilized approximately 3 m above that necessary to support the healthy ecosystem. They advocate a wet year/dry year plan that would limit diversion to the dry years when the city of Los Angeles really needs the water. They further advocate a statewide program to conserve urban and agricultural water.

No one disagrees with the advocacy of water conservation. The city of Los Angeles, however, which receives approximately 17% of its water supply from the Mono basin, would like to see diversions continue at a rate greater than that advocated by the people who would like to see the lake preserved. The people in favor of continued diversion point out that the project produces a good deal of energy (approximately 300 million kwh/yr, which saves approximately half a million barrels of oil per year). They would like to see the diversions continued and the lake level eventually stabilized at about 15 m below the 1981 level. One of their arguments is that the city of Los Angeles

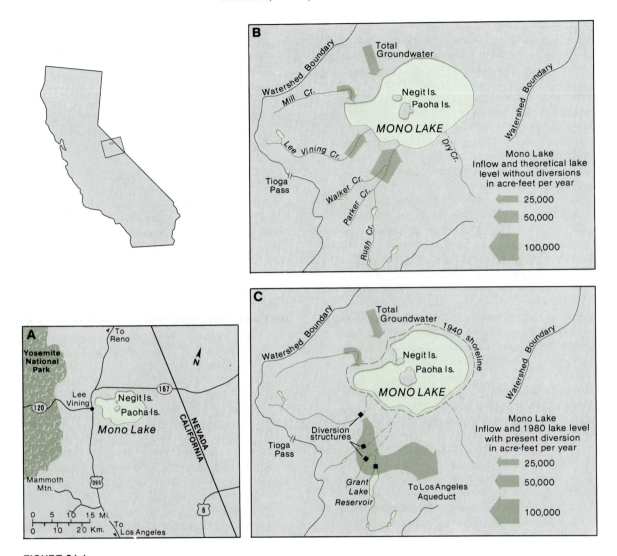

FIGURE 21.1
(a) Location of Mono Lake. (b) Situation without water diversion, and (c) with water diversion.
(From Mono Lake Committee.)

has invested more than $100,000,000 in the area since the 1930s and it really needs the water.

The Mono Lake story is an important one in environmental law because in 1983 the California Supreme Court reaffirmed the public interest in protecting natural resources through what is known as the Public Trust Doctrine. The 1983 decision states that it is the duty of the state to protect the people's common heritage, including streams, lakes, marshlands and tidelands. In essence the court decided that public trust obligates the State of California to protect lakes such as Mono as much as possible, even if this means reexamining past water allocations [1].

The case of Mono Lake has not yet come to trial but eventually the courts may have to weigh the public trust values at Mono Lake against the water needs of the people of Los Angeles. Ideally, the resolution will reflect a balance between concern for environmental issues and the water needs of urban people. The case brings into the forefront the Trust Doctrine, which is a theory of law closely related to constitutional issues involving people's right to a quality environment.

Although nowhere in the Constitution is this right stated, students of law agree that such a right can be inferred from the Ninth Amendment of the Constitution, which recognizes that the presence of a list of specific rights in the Bill of Rights does not deny the existence of other unlisted rights. That is, many rights may not be specifically listed but are always held by the people [2]. It is argued under the Ninth Amendment that people have a right to clean air, clean water, and the resources necessary to ensure a quality environment. In the case of Mono Lake, this includes the right of future generations to observe and enjoy places like Mono Lake.

THE DEVELOPMENT OF ENVIRONMENTAL LAW

Actions that affect the environment are controlled by an elaborate network of legislation and regulation at federal, state, and local levels. The sheer volume and the intricacies of what we now call environmental law suggest that decades must have been necessary to construct a structure of such complexity. In fact, before 1970, government actions to protect the environment were so widely scattered and so modest that the term environmental law did not exist. This explosion of government action was a response to public perception of an environmental crisis and was in part a continuation of an evolution that had been occurring more gradually for many years in the system of law. An understanding of this development provides a useful setting for an examination of our present system of environmental regulation. The great variations in legal processes around the world are beyond the scope of this book. This

chapter describes environmental law in the United States, as an example of social and legal processes in a democracy.

Origins in Common Law

The legal system of the United States has historic origins in the English system, and while there are important differences, they are outweighed by the similarities. When our legal system was formed, English law was intended more for the protection of the individual from society than the reverse, a tendency that was strengthened in laws as adopted here by the circumstances preceding the American Revolution. Individual freedom and nearly unlimited discretion to use property as the owner pleased were given high priority, and powers of the federal government were strictly limited. Natural resources seemed limitless and little need to control their development or exploitation was apparent. However, when behavior was so egregious that it interfered with the enjoyment of property by its owner, the common law (i.e., law derived from custom, judgment, and decrees of the courts, as distinguished from legislation) provided protection by doctrines prohibiting trespass and nuisance. Thus damage from erosion or flooding from improper management of adjacent land or smoke from fires could be controlled by use of the law if an individual suffered special damage. If the harm was more widely spread to the community, then only the government had the authority to limit certain air and water pollution to abate a public nuisance.

The common law provides another doctrine, that of public trust, which both grants and limits authority of government over certain natural areas of special character. Beginning with Roman law, navigable and tidal waters were entrusted to the government to hold in trust for public use. More generally, "the Public Trust Doctrine makes the government the public guardian of those valuable natural resources which are not capable of self-regeneration and for which substitutes cannot be made by man" [3]. For such resources, the government is under the strong duties of the trustee to provide protection and is not able to transfer such properties into private ownership. This doctrine

Career Profile: David Knotts

David Knotts says his concern for the environment is a product of his own interest and the trends of society. He has had an environmental awareness since childhood, attributable to family outings and Boy Scouting in his home state of North Carolina. In college, that environmental awareness "took off," Knotts says.

In the early 1970s at Indiana University, he was a history and environmental studies major. It was a time of much societal concern about the consequences of environmental pollution.

Knotts began working summers at Yellowstone National Park in Wyoming. At first he worked for park concessions rather than the National Park Service (NPS). He trained bus tour guides who were what he terms "free enterprise naturalists." Later, he applied for a seasonal naturalist position at Yellowstone with NPS and was hired.

As a ranger-naturalist Knotts roved the park, on patrol. He was also involved in interpretive programs, such as leading nature hikes. "It was a wonderful job," he says, "very rewarding in terms of the response I got from people."

Knotts says the major problem facing NPS is exploitation of resources around the parks. For example, Yellowstone is

threatened by proposed geothermal drilling outside the park. Air pollution, mining, and grazing are also threatening the parks. Budgets, law enforcement, and maintenance of facilities are additional ongoing problems. Overcrowding continues to be a problem in some parks, although most visitors use only a small percentage of the area in a park. "The park service may have to take measures to keep the parks from being loved to death, so to speak," says Knotts.

As a ranger, Knotts was involved in law enforcement training. During one session, someone said, "You ought to go to law school." Nine months later, that is what Knotts was doing. He had thought about law school before, but he says his interest in environmental law would not have been as keen if he had gone to law

school without his naturalist experience.

"Ultimately, it's really people's attitudes that determine how things end up," he explains. As a naturalist, he felt he influenced people's attitudes about environmental issues indirectly. As an attorney, he felt his influence would be more direct and immediate.

As voters, civic leaders, and politicians, people from diverse backgrounds—whether science-oriented or not—will have their say about environmental matters. Knotts says, "The more they know, the better off everyone will be. You don't have to be a scientist to care about environmental quality or do something about it."

After completing his law degree at the University of Oregon, Knotts is working in Boise, Idaho, not far from Yellowstone. As a judicial clerk for a judge on the Idaho Supreme Court, he is involved in a variety of cases, some of which are natural resources related. Knotts points out that a judge's responsibility is to decide questions of law according to what the law requires, not from a particular doctrine. However, he feels a judge may take a responsible approach to natural resources, considering environmental impacts as well as other concerns.

Michele Wigginton

was considerably weakened by the exaltation of private property rights and strong development pressures in this country, but in more recent times has shown increased vitality, especially in preservation of coastal areas.

Thus, while the common law provides a few examples of environmental protection possibilities, the vast majority of the activities we regulate today in the name of the environment would proceed unrestricted by common law. These needs have been filled by legislation enacted at all levels of government.

Early Environmental Legislation

Early federal legislation with environmental consequences was largely directed toward conservation of natural resources; acts established Yellowstone (Fig. 21.2) as the first national park (in 1872) and authorized the formation of national forests (the Forest Reserve Act of 1891). Although the latter act protected forests largely for utilitarian purposes—"for the purpose of securing favorable

conditions of water flow, and to furnish a continuous supply of timber for the use and necessities of citizens of the United States" [4]—the final section of the act quietly accomplished what early conservationists had for years failed to achieve. By granting to the President the authority to declare specified areas of federal lands as forest reserves, Presidents Harrison, Cleveland, and especially Theodore Roosevelt were able to preserve more than 200 million acres of national forests.

In the areas of legislation we now think of as the core of environmental policy—control of air and water pollution and toxic waste disposal—there was virtually no federal involvement until the 1960s. Some states, and even some cities, adopted limited regulations, such as smoke control ordinances, but there were strong economic pressures that prevented effective results. If asked to spend to reduce the effluents they discharged, polluting industries could threaten to (and did) move to more hospitable locations. In a few cases, legislation already on the books was reexamined and found to contain powers for environmental

FIGURE 21.2
Yellowstone Lake, in Yellowstone National Park, the first national park.

control that certainly had not been foreseen when these acts were adopted. A good example is the Rivers and Harbors Act of 1899 (commonly called the Refuse Act), which for sixty years was thought to have jurisdiction only over discharge of materials that would interfere with navigation. Growth of industry and commerce over the next half-century led to problems that were much more severe than discarded floating trash (Fig. 21.3), and the Refuse Act was found to provide federal authority to address these critical issues. Two Supreme Court cases (1960 and 1966) held that the Refuse Act applied to discharge of industrial wastes. These decisions authorized the requirement of permits for those discharging pollutants, a program that in 1972 was strengthened by the Federal Water Pollution Control Act. This evolution of authority from legislation to encompass issues not envisioned by the drafters is an important but controversial route for the growth of the law.

Development of Administrative Agencies

Although Congress did not give environmental matters much attention in the first half of the twentieth century, other legislative areas were ex-

panding rapidly to deal with the increasing complexities of technological development and the interactions of growing populations. Naturally enough, complex issues led to complicated legislation, which was well beyond the capabilities of Congress to oversee directly, and Congress turned to the formation of the administrative agency. Agencies could be given general directions and statements of purpose through legislation and then left to devise and to carry out the specifics of implementation. As regulation became more intricate, greater specialization and expertise were required for these tasks, and Congress was forced more and more to delegate authority to the agencies. Growth of administrative agencies reached a peak during the New Deal in the 1930s and has moderated thereafter. State governments, for very similar reasons, also developed administrative agencies. Most of these agencies, at both state and federal levels, report to the executive branch, and their chief officers are appointed by the President or Governor.

At the time that public demand for improved environmental quality began to grow rapidly in the late 1960s, federal authority to meet this demand was scattered among a number of agencies, including the Department of Health, Education, and Welfare, the Department of the Interior, and the

FIGURE 21.3
Direct discharge of industrial wastes into rivers and harbors has caused serious pollution problems.

Department of Agriculture. An executive reorganization, authorized by President Nixon in 1970, centralized these functions in a new agency, the Environmental Protection Agency (EPA). The EPA is headed by an administrator who reports to the President and who is responsible for implementing most major federal environmental legislation, except for management of federal lands (Fig. 21.4). Federal administrators and directors are chosen with care to reflect the political philosophy of the President, but once in office they have a great deal of autonomy on all but the largest issues.

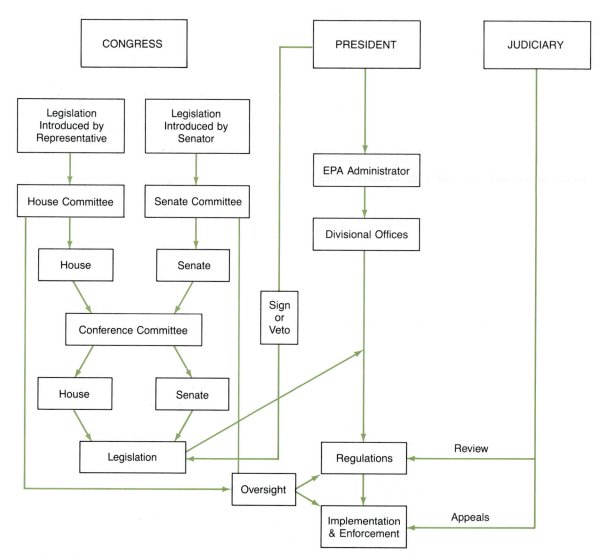

FIGURE 21.4
Interaction of branches of the federal government involved in environmental regulation.

RECENT FEDERAL ENVIRONMENTAL LEGISLATION

Public perception of a rapidly deteriorating environment reached crisis levels at the end of the 1960s, and Congress responded in the early seventies with significant federal environmental legislation (Fig. 21.5).

National Environmental Policy Act

The first and the most general legislation was the National Environmental Policy Act (NEPA), signed into law by Richard Nixon on New Year's Day, 1970 [5]. This act recognized as national policy the "profound impact of man's activity on the interrelations of all components of the natural environment" that already had reached the national consciousness and instructed all branches of the federal government to "fulfill the responsibilities of each generation as trustee of the environment for succeeding generations." This directive, along with others of similarly high tone, doubtless would have had very little effect, but for Section 102(2)(C), often called the "action forcing" section of the legislation. This section requires that proposals for "major federal actions significantly affecting the quality of the human environment" shall include what has come to be called an **environmental impact statement (EIS).** This statement describes the environmental effect, any unavoidable adverse effects, alternatives to the action (including taking no action), relations between short-term use of the environment and long-term productivity and irreversible and irretrievable commitments. This instruction extended the scope of issues a federal agency needed to consider well beyond what prior practice had established. Agencies that provided funds for highways and dams had been concerned about adequate engineering and cost containment but had given very little thought to the effect of these projects on the natural environment. Agency officials now were instructed to adopt a much broader view and to consider environmental protection as an important goal of their projects. Indeed the environmental impact statement requirement was a bold attempt

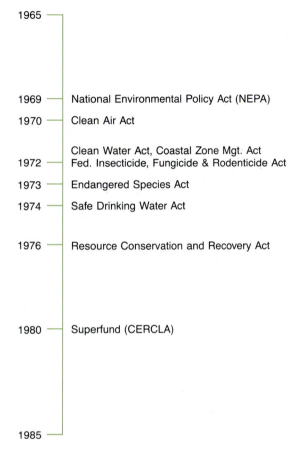

1965	
1969	National Environmental Policy Act (NEPA)
1970	Clean Air Act
1972	Clean Water Act, Coastal Zone Mgt. Act Fed. Insecticide, Fungicide & Rodenticide Act
1973	Endangered Species Act
1974	Safe Drinking Water Act
1976	Resource Conservation and Recovery Act
1980	Superfund (CERCLA)
1985	

FIGURE 21.5
Major federal environmental legislation and the year enacted. Most important environmental legislation was adopted from 1969 to 1976. Some laws were enacted earlier in a much less comprehensive form (e.g., the Clean Air Act in 1963) and most have been amended subsequently. The year shown here is when the legislation was first put in its current general form.

to incorporate the holistic understanding of ecology into the thinking of administrative agency personnel.

Despite its high purpose and broad scope, NEPA is very brief, and there is much that is not said. No mention is made, for example, of what sanctions might be applied if an agency neglects to prepare an EIS or, as later occurred, if an EIS did not attempt seriously to address the specified issues. As we will see in later sections of this chapter, the courts, environmental groups, and individual citizens cooperated to devise remedies that made NEPA a powerful force to encourage greater foresight and prevent thoughtless damage from large federal projects. Because "federal action" was interpreted broadly to include granting of federal permits, licenses, or funds, as federal authority over the environment increased, NEPA's authority extended to large private projects whose potential for environmental impact brought them under a federal environmental statute.

Clean Air Act

The next major piece of federal environmental legislation, also passed in 1970, was the Clean Air Act [6]. Strictly speaking, this act was an amendment to earlier air pollution control legislation adopted in 1965 and revised in 1967, but the earlier acts were so ineffective and the changes made in 1970 so sweeping that the effect was that of new, and indeed of a new *kind* of legislation. In sharp contrast to the broad scope and general language of NEPA, the Clean Air Act (CAA) was lengthy (more than 100 pages) and very specific in its instructions to the EPA. The level of detail was well beyond what had been the practice in environmental legislation (or in federal legislation in other areas, save perhaps in the tax code), even to the point of specifying which pollutants were to be controlled and on what time schedule. For example, automobiles were viewed as a particularly challenging pollution problem. U.S. automakers had not compromised their opposition to any automobile pollution control so the act called for specific reductions in emissions (e.g., 90% reductions in carbon monoxide and hydrocarbon emissions) and set a schedule (within five years, barring extensions) by which the reductions should be achieved. Because technologies did not exist to reach these reduction levels, these sections of the CAA were labeled as "technology-forcing." The specificity of instruction to EPA in this and other sections of the act were quite unusual and resulted from the resolve of Congress, bolstered by strong public concern, to tolerate no delay in bringing air pollution under control.

Much of the work of drafting the CAA was done in the Senate Committee on Public Works, under the direction of Senator Edmund S. Muskie. He was at that time actively exploring a run for the Presidency and adopted environmental protection as his primary legislative initiative. Extensive hearings were held on the several bills on air pollution control that eventually surfaced in the Senate and by the House Committee on Interstate and Foreign Commerce on related bills in the House. A conference committee reconciled the differences between the bills eventually passed by the House and the Senate. In addition to testimony given in the formal hearings, intense lobbying occurred on both sides of the issue, with industry attempting to contain costs for pollution control and environmental groups pressing for stringent controls.

INFLUENCING LEGISLATION

Generally, lobbyists working with the staff of the relevant House or Senate committee and occasionally with legislators are able to influence important details of the language in proposed legislation. Individuals, unless they have the opportunity to testify before a committee, usually are not in a position to suggest specific language. Of course, collections of individuals, by writing or telephoning their congressional representatives, may exert significant influence on whether or not the bill is approved by a committee or survives a floor vote. While this opportunity and responsibility is presented to the point of tedium in elementary and high school discussions of government, most congressional offices report surprisingly limited public comment on most bills. As a result, as few as fifty letters and calls can be taken by a legislative representative as a sign of significant constituent sentiment. This public lassitude has allowed groups such as the Sierra Club, by organizing members to write to targeted legislators on critical issues, to be effective well beyond the numbers they represent directly. An individual can influence legislation in a more general manner by voting in favor of legislators with strong environmental records and opposing incumbents who have not demonstrated an environmental commitment. The League of Conservation Voters issues an annual "grading" of members of Congress on their voting records on environmental and energy legislation. This can provide a guide at election time.

The published hearings and records of debates in the committees and on the floor of Congress provide the "legislative history" of an act. It is to these reports that individuals and courts may turn to attempt to understand the intent of the legislators who wrote sections of the act that may be unclear. Careful examination of these reports can provide a helpful illumination of the legislative process. Often the vagueness in the actual language of an act will be found to have resulted not from oversight or incompetent drafting, but from a legislative compromise between two positions that could not otherwise be reconciled. In such cases, Congress, in order to gather the votes necessary for committee approval, may decide to delegate the resolution of the issue to the agency that must implement the act. The agency then must use the rule-making process to provide the specificity that the legislature could not achieve.

THE ADMINISTRATIVE RULE-MAKING PROCESS

Even legislation that is written in such unusual detail as the Clean Air Act cannot provide the full range of information necessary to implement a regulatory process, and so agencies authorized to oversee these acts are given the responsibility to write regulations or rules (for our purposes, these words can be used interchangeably) to "flesh out" the skeleton provided by the legislation (Fig. 21.6).

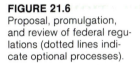

FIGURE 21.6
Proposal, promulgation, and review of federal regulations (dotted lines indicate optional processes).

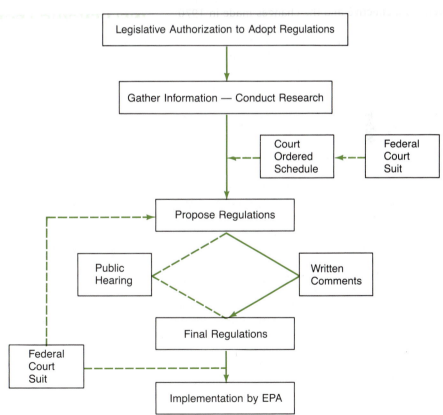

Because an agency specializes in a particular subject matter area, it is in a better position to articulate the plan to implement the purposes of the legislation than are legislators and their staff, who by definition must be generalists. In many cases, after providing the general regulatory framework, the agency is left to set its own schedule for writing regulations. In the two main regulatory environmental laws passed in the early 1970s, however, the sense of national urgency led Congress to set strict deadlines by which the agency was to complete the rule-making process. Often, Congress underestimated the technical and political complexities of setting regulations, and agencies missed deadlines by months and years.

In such cases, national environmental groups, such as the Natural Resources Defense Council (NRDC) and the Environmental Defense Fund (EDF) turned to the courts to enforce the congressional schedule. Thus, in the mid-seventies, NRDC and EDF brought a series of legal actions to "force EPA into more rapid and comprehensive action under various provisions of the Federal Water Pollution Control Act" (FWPCA, later called the Clean Water Act) [7]. Under Section 307(a)(1) of the FWPCA, EPA was required to compile a list of water pollutants toxic to "any organism" and of concern because of biopersistence. The importance of the threatened organism was also to be indicated. For each pollutant so listed, EPA was required to establish effluent limitations or to prohibit the discharge of that pollutant. In the first two years the FWPCA was in force, EPA listed only a few pollutants under this section, so NRDC sought orders requiring EPA to expand its published list, and EDF sued to require EPA to establish effluent standards for toxic pollutants that already had been listed. The EPA and the environmental groups reached a compromise and signed a settlement agreement (consent decree) that established "a detailed comprehensive regulatory program for implementation by EPA of the toxic pollutant control and pretreatment objectives of the Act." Subsequently, NRDC had to go to court again, to force EPA to comply with the agreed implementation schedule. Eventually, many of the elements of the settlement agreement were ratified by congressional action and incorporated into the 1977 amendments of the act.

Depending on the level of knowledge in a particular area at the time legislation is enacted, Congress may instruct the agency to complete a study on which rule-making can be based. If some study already has been done, the agency may be given a shorter time to compile information and take action on it. For example, when the Clean Air Act went into effect, some information was available on the health effects of five pollutants, and EPA was given only 30 days to set standards adequate to protect the public health. Generally more time is allowed, because of the complexity of the rule-making process.

The process begins with gathering information. Agencies rely on staff, paid consultants, and voluntary advisory boards. The EPA, for example, has its own research laboratories and regularly contracts with consultants in the private sector to compile the information on which regulations will be based. Researchers at a hospital might study the effect of varying levels of ozone on asthmatics or on the performance of athletes. An engineering firm might measure the efficiency with which a biological treatment system purifies wastewater. Occasionally the agency will announce to the public that it is studying a particular problem and ask for submission of information and opinion, often in response to rather precise questions.

The approach taken by EPA in revising standards for the allowable concentration of fluoride in drinking water, under the authority of the Safe Drinking Water Act, provides examples of the information-gathering process and a judicially enforced schedule for issuing regulations. The Department of Health and Environmental Control of South Carolina petitioned EPA in 1981 to revoke an interim standard, contending that (1) fluoride is not a public health hazard and (2) the cost of reducing fluoride concentrations is prohibitively high and is not justified by its benefits. EPA replied that it would issue revised regulations "as soon as current epidemiology studies are completed, reported and evaluated." In 1984 South Carolina sued EPA, seeking faster action on its request. EPA complied with the court-approved agreement that settled the suit (a consent decree) by proposing new standards in May 1985. In considering revisions, EPA requested opinions from the Surgeon General and the National Drinking Water Advisory Council. EPA published the results of these studies, guidelines set by other agencies, including the World Health Organization, and its regulatory options in the *Federal Register* [8]. This publication included a request for comments on specific points, including whether discoloration of teeth from fluoride exposure (dental fluorosis) should be considered a cosmetic effect or an adverse health effect, a choice that influenced the level at which the fluoride standard will be set.

Agencies communicate with the public through a newspaper called the *Federal Register,* issued each working day. Because the *Federal Register* serves all federal agencies and commissions, it is quite voluminous, and while it is available in most libraries, regularly scanning each issue (which may run hundreds of pages) requires unusual dedication. To ease this chore, specialized services, such as the *Environment Reporter* published by the Bureau of National Affairs (BNA), issue weekly summaries of *Federal Register* items of environmental concern.

When the agency has enough information to form a tentative opinion, it will publish proposed regulations in the *Federal Register.* Depending on the agency's confidence in its position, the degree of controversy the proposal is likely to generate, and the urgency with which the matter must be dealt, the proposal can be preliminary (a kind of trial balloon) or final. Sometimes, when an agency is unable to reach a consensus, it will issue preliminary proposals and ask for comment on which idea the public prefers. In addition to the proposed regulation, the *Federal Register* publication will provide background information and will explain how the agency decided to make this particular proposal. Given the complicated nature of most environmental issues, not all information on which the agency relies can be published, and so this information is compiled in a docket that is open to public inspection in Washington. While obviously not many average citizens will be able to take advantage of this opportunity, organizations

with strong interests in the regulatory process will find it worthwhile to maintain offices in Washington, in part to have ready access to this information.

After the proposed regulation appears in the *Federal Register,* comments are received from the public, usually for a period of between 30 and 90 days, with a minimum comment period set by the Administrative Procedures Act or by the enabling legislation. For especially important regulations, EPA sometimes holds hearings in Washington or at various locations around the country to take testimony on the proposed regulation. Notices of these hearings also appear in the *Federal Register.* While anyone is free to write comments or offer testimony, comment most commonly is offered by those with economic interests in the activity to be regulated and by national environmental groups. Thus regulations on air emissions from coal-burning electrical generating plants are certain to be commented on by the utility industry and the coal industry as well as NRDC. All comments and testimony are added to the docket and so are available for review and rebuttal.

If the comments generally support the agency's proposal and no political opposition has arisen, the agency will publish a final rule in the *Federal Register,* along with commentary that gives its response to the comments received. Usually some changes are made as a result of the comments and further reflection by the agency. If the original proposal is unpopular or controversial, the agency may decide to study the matter further and, if a significant revision in the first proposal seems appropriate, then the revised proposal may be presented for further comment. This process of reconsideration and reproposal may take years before a final rule is enacted (promulgated).

Once it is in place, the final rule has the full force of the law, and violations of its standards or requirements carry the penalties set by the enabling statute. For ease in locating relevant regulations, final rules are republished and grouped by subject matter areas (codified) in the *Code of Federal Regulations* (CFR), which is available in law libraries and larger public libraries. Copies of these regulations also can be obtained by request from the issuing agency (e.g., EPA) and most regulations of significance are reprinted in the *Environment Reporter*.

Because of the significant economic and environmental impact such regulations can have, all parties involved often know in advance that the final regulations will be challenged in court in an attempt to delay their implementation or to either strengthen or reduce the level of environmental control that they require. With this in mind, potential litigants will take particular care to put before the agency and into the "record" all of the data upon which a later challenge can be based.

ENVIRONMENTAL LITIGATION

Environmental groups working through the courts have been a powerful force in shaping the direction of environmental quality control since the early 1970s. This is in part because the courts, appearing to respond to the national sense of environmental crisis of that time, took a more activist stance and were less willing to defer to the judgment of agencies. At the same time, citizens were granted an unprecedented access to the courts and through them to environmental policy.

Standing

Traditionally, courts limited the right to initiate a legal action (a right called "standing") to those who were directly and specially affected by the outcome of that action. (For a broader view of the standing issue, see the discussion of "Should Trees Have Standing" in Chapter 1.) This limit arises from a basic tenet of the adversary system: the court must rely on the parties before it to bring in all of the relevant facts and to present them persuasively. A litigant who was not much affected by the outcome of a case was thought to lack the incentive to bring to the court all of the information necessary to ensure a carefully considered judicial decision, thus risking injustice to someone with a stronger interest in the matter who was not before the court. Also, preventing those without a strong

interest in a case from filing a legal action will tend to reduce the load of cases that a judge must manage.

The difficulty in applying restrictive standing requirements to environmental quality issues is that, while the effect of an environmentally intrusive activity may be very significant, it often is spread across a wide area and a large population. As a result, a small number of individuals cannot show that they have been particularly affected. Similarly, while an industry whose activities are to be controlled by a regulation always has the standing to challenge it in court, citizens who might benefit from the required control often could not, under the old, restrictive standards for standing, show special benefits and were denied the right of judicial review.

The major regulatory environmental laws recognize the drawback of a restrictive standing requirement and specifically authorize legal actions by citizens to enforce the provisions of the acts. This liberalization of standing provides both a backup for and a check on agency actions. Should an agency fail to take an enforcement action against a polluter, for example, a neighbor can sue to stop the illegal activity. Or, if an agency misses a legislatively imposed deadline, any citizen can bring an action seeking a court order to accelerate the process.

Citizen Suits

Even without specific legislative authorization for citizen's suits, courts, as part of a trend to liberalize standing requirements, have allowed citizen actions in environmental cases. The most significant and one of the earliest examples was the willingness of the courts to entertain suits to enforce NEPA. The statute itself and its legislative history do not mention either judicial review or standing, and the courts were left to decide whether a judicial remedy should be applied. Without such a remedy, and in the face of very substantial reluctance on the part of administrative agencies to change their habitual ways of doing business, it is very unlikely that the EIS requirement would ever have had significant influence on agency actions. Because NEPA did not provide a mechanism to ensure implementation and because agency compliance was required "to the fullest extent possible," courts reasoned that a remedy should be created and made available to an individual, even if the harm that person suffered was shared equally by the public at large. Consequently, almost from the first NEPA cases, courts were willing to order agencies to halt (i.e., to enjoin) work on projects for which environmental impact statements had not been prepared. Thus, judges were asked to decide which projects represented "major federal actions" and had the potential to affect the human environment "significantly"; the terms were somewhat amorphous in the legislation. Once a project had been found to pass these threshold tests, an injunction to halt the project was logical: to allow the project to continue in the absence of the EIS would have made its preparation futile.

Another early issue that courts had to face was whether an agency could prepare an EIS and then ignore its content in implementing a major project; that is, was NEPA to be seen as purely procedural, or was it to have some substantive effect? A challenge to the use the Atomic Energy Commission made of an EIS in the licensing of an atomic power plant [9] set the standard for subsequent reviews. Judge J. Skelly Wright concluded that "NEPA mandates a particular sort of careful and informed decision-making process and creates judicially enforceable duties. The reviewing courts probably cannot reverse a substantive decision on its merits . . . unless it be shown that the actual balance of costs and benefits that was struck was arbitrary or clearly gave insufficient weight to environmental values. But if the decision was reached procedurally without individualized consideration and balancing of environmental factors—conducted fully and in good faith—it is the responsibility of the courts to reverse." In NEPA cases and in environmental cases generally, a very important judicial trend in the 1970s was to require thoughtful consideration of environmental issues and a careful explanation of actions taken. No longer were administrators able to take an action without explaining the reasoning that led them to conclude that the action was desirable. This development occurred in a general climate of suspicion of government, arising out of protests against U.S. military involvement in Vietnam and from the political scandals of Watergate.

The first legislatively authorized citizen's suit provision was in the Clean Air Act, and the ten major environmental statutes enacted since that time (1970) all contain citizen's suit provisions. Each of these requires that a citizen file notice with the person or agency that will be sued and with the agency responsible for implementing the act under which the suit will be brought. No further action can be taken in the 60 day period following this notice. This provides an opportunity for the agency to take action itself—to correct its own behavior or to bring its own enforcement action against a violator. If the agency does take action, the citizen's suit is blocked, although it may be possible to intervene in the agency enforcement action. The purpose of the citizen's suit was both to assist enforcement agencies that were short of resources and to prevent agencies from becoming lax in carrying out their nondiscretionary duties.

A case reported by Yannacone, Cohen, and Davison [10] in Colorado further emphasizes the power of citizen groups to use the law. The conflict surrounded the use of 7.3 km^2 of land near Colorado Springs. The land is part of the Florissant Fossil Beds, where insect bodies, seeds, leaves, and plants were deposited in an ancient lake bed about 30 million years ago. Today, they are remarkably preserved in thin layers of volcanic shale (Fig. 21.7). Unfortunately, the fossils are delicate and, unless protected, tend to disintegrate when exposed. Many people consider the fossils unique and irreplaceable. At the time of the controversy, a bill had been introduced into Congress to establish a Florissant Fossil Beds National Monument. The bill had passed the Senate, but the House of Representatives had not yet acted on it.

While the House of Representatives was deliberating the bill, a land development company that had contracted to purchase and develop recreational homesites on 7.3 km^2 of the ancient lake bed announced that it was going to bulldoze a road through a portion of the proposed national monument site to gain access to the property it wished to develop. A citizens' group formed to fight the development until the House acted on the bill. The group tried to obtain a temporary restraining

FIGURE 21.7
Fossil preserved in volcanic shale at Florissant Fossil Beds National Monument, Colorado.

The court order prohibiting destruction of the fossil beds may have deprived a landowner of making the most profitable use of the property, but it does not prohibit all uses consistent with protecting the fossils. For instance, the property owners are free to develop the land for tourism or scientific research. While this might not result in the largest possible return on the property owner's investment, it probably would return a reasonable profit.

Agency Review

During the 1970s, more citizen's suits were brought against agencies than against alleged polluters. Environmental groups brought many actions, both to challenge the interpretation given by an agency to a legislative command and in an attempt to obtain more stringent environmental controls. Regulated industries brought challenges with the opposite purpose, to reduce the degree of control that would be required. Often the same agency decision was challenged by both groups, one claiming the agency had been too demanding and the other that the agency had been too lenient. Because certain federal courts seemed generally to favor one philosophy or the other, there sometimes was a race to file a challenge to a regulation, with each side trying to file first in a forum that would favor its position and block the suit filed by opponents in courts that tended to favor a different view. At one point, it became EPA practice to issue regulations near mid-day, so that courts across the nation would be open and available for the "race."

order, which was first denied because there was no law preventing the owner of the property from using that land in any way he wished provided that existing laws were upheld. The conservationists then went before an appeals court and argued that even though there was no law protecting the fossils, they were subject to protection under the Trust Doctrine and the Ninth Amendment. The argument was that protection of an irreplaceable, unique fossil resource was an unwritten right retained by the people under the Ninth Amendment, and that furthermore, because the property had tremendous public interest, it was also protected by the Trust Doctrine. An analogy used by the plaintiffs was that if a property owner were to find the Constitution of the United States buried on the land and wanted to use it to mop the floor, certainly that person would be restrained. After several more hearings on the case, the court issued a restraining order to halt development; shortly thereafter, the bill to establish a national monument was passed by Congress and signed by the President [10].

While challenges of this kind have proven to be a powerful influence on the scope and the stringency of environmental laws, the process is slow, often taking years to reach the desired result. A good example is provided by the protracted battle over the use of very high smokestacks ("tall stacks") to disperse pollutants. In the initial implementation of the Clean Air Act, EPA allowed industries to use tall stacks and other dispersant techniques in place of emission control devices and process changes that would have reduced the amount of pollutant discharged instead of merely dispersing it over a wider area. Because in many cases tall stacks were a less expensive alternative, they proved to be a popular option for industry but were criticized by environmental groups ("dilution is not the solution to pollution").

In 1974 the NRDC challenged EPA's approval of tall stacks as a method to meet ambient air quality standards, and the Fourth Circuit Court of Appeals agreed that tall stacks and other dispersion techniques could be used only after "the maximum degree of emission limitations" had been achieved by other means [11]. EPA did not respond to this decision until 1976, when it issued guidelines limiting tall stack use, but still allowing use where other technologies would be "economically unreasonable or technologically unsound."

At the time of Clean Air Act reauthorization in 1977, Congress rejected this exception, in large part because of the growing realization that dispersion techniques were contributing to the formation of acid rain, and instructed EPA to adopt new regulations limiting tall stacks no later than six months after the amendments were enacted, in August of 1977. EPA, however, did not even propose regulations until January 1979, seventeen months after the amendments were in place, and in February 1982 the Sierra Club had to obtain a court-ordered timetable to force the promulgation of the final regulations. And when the regulations were issued, they continued to allow tall stacks, under the rubric of "good engineering practice." NRDC and Sierra Club once again returned to court, this time to the D.C. Circuit Court of Appeals, for a judicial instruction to EPA to limit tall stack use. Here, in October 1983, they received a favorable judgment [12], which the Supreme Court allowed to stand by refusing to review the case (denying a petition for *certiori*) in July 1984 [13]. Not only does this decision apply prospectively, but industries (mostly utilities) that built very tall stacks, well beyond the height dictated by the "good engineering practice" standard, will be forced to add pollution controls. These controls promise to bring a substantial reduction in acid deposition in the Northeast. So, while it now appears that incentives to use tall stacks have been sharply reduced, more than ten years of efforts in the courts and the Congress were required to reach that result.

Citizen Enforcement

In recent years a higher proportion of cases has been brought directly against alleged polluters. This appears to have resulted from a sharp decline in enforcement actions brought directly by EPA shortly after Ronald Reagan became President. Both national and regional environmental groups stepped into this vacuum and began to file enforcement actions in substantial numbers under the Clean Water Act. For evidence, these suits relied mainly on information the defendant had supplied to EPA on the concentration of pollutants in discharges regulated by the National Pollution Discharge Elimination System (NPDES). Where these concentrations were above those allowed by the NPDES permits and when EPA had taken no enforcement action, a citizen's enforcement action was especially attractive because the polluter had admitted a legal violation. Nearly two hundred notices to sue under the Clean Water Act were given and 88 suits filed in the sixteen months beginning in January 1983. Only 41 notices were given and 19 suits filed under the Clean Water Act in the preceding five years [14]. This surge of actions under the Clean Water Act was not accompanied by a similar increase in activity under the other environmental statutes, probably because only the Clean Water Act provides financial penalties if the suit is successful. These penalties go to the government, but if the suit is settled before trial, the group bringing the action may be able to receive payment and, through a consent decree, also obtain an agreement from the polluter to refrain from further pollution.

The entry level court in the federal system (the trial court) generally is the federal district court, and citizen's enforcement actions brought under federal environmental laws must be filed in these courts. These cases necessarily are civil cases and with rare exceptions are nonjury trials in which the judge hears the evidence and renders a judgment. In enforcement actions brought by an administrative agency or an attorney general, if there is reason to believe that violation of the law was deliberate, criminal charges may be filed, and the defendant is entitled to a jury trial. The standard of proof in the two cases is quite different. In the criminal case, guilt must be established "beyond a reasonable doubt" to reduce the probability of imposing a penalty as severe as imprisonment on an innocent person. The standard in a civil case is less demanding, and usually the prevailing party must establish only a "preponderance of the evidence."

Appeals from district court decisions are taken to Federal Circuit Courts of Appeal, which, with one exception (the District of Columbia Circuit) serve a number of states. To reduce the time required for the review, certain challenges to environmental regulations and standards are allowed by statute to be filed directly with the Circuit Court. Appeals from Circuit Court decisions take the form of petitions for *certiori* to the U.S. Supreme Court, which is able to approve only a very limited number of these requests. The Supreme Court is more likely to accept a case, however, when Circuit Court opinions on similar cases seem to be applying different standards. This process of reconciliation provides some limit to the benefit that can be gained by winning the race to a favored court. A recent example of such reconciliation is the Supreme Court's review of EPA policy on granting variances from uniform standards for treating discharges to public wastewater treatment plants [15]. The Third Circuit Court of Appeals decided that EPA exceeded its authority in granting such variances, while the Fourth Circuit agreed with the EPA position. The Supreme Court, in a five to four vote, upheld the Fourth Circuit's decision.

Costs of Litigation

While it is possible for an individual to file a citizen's suit without legal representation (to file "pro-se") the complexity of environmental legislation makes this a rare and relatively unproductive practice. Industries with a financial stake in the outcome of litigation can, of course, use corporate counsel or retain a law firm as a cost of doing business. Those who seek more stringent environmental regulation, on the other hand, rarely derive a financial benefit even if they are successful in their suit because citizen suit provisions in environmental legislation do not provide for the award of financial damages to a successful plaintiff. However, in order to encourage such cit-

izen actions, a suit that is brought in good faith and judged to be a substantial contribution to the goals of the statute can lead to the award of attorney's fees, even if the individual or group seeking the fees did not prevail in all aspects of the case. These fees provide substantial assistance to the more litigious environmental groups, although they by no means meet most of their costs. Without this attorney-fee provision, it is doubtful that many suits would be brought. The average cost of bringing an action under the Clean Water Act was between $35,000 and $40,000 and ranged up to a high of $200,000 [14]. In some cases, local attorneys may be persuaded to represent citizens at no fee ("pro bono") in circumstances where their interests might otherwise not be represented.

Another use of citizen's suits is to seek expansion of the scope of an environmental law beyond that seen by the EPA. A good example of this type of action was the judicial interpretation of the statement in the first section of the Clean Air Act that the purpose of the act was to "protect and enhance the quality of the Nation's air." The Sierra Club brought an action in federal district court [16] seeking an interpretation that this phrase meant that air of higher quality than demanded for protection of human health and welfare (i.e., air in compliance with air quality standards) could not be diminished in quality—a nondeterioration policy. Read strictly, this policy would have allowed little or no new development that emitted air pollutants (absent a matching decrease of pollutants from an existing source) and so was seen as a severe limitation on economic growth. Despite the total absence of support for this policy in any of the detailed sections of the act, the court upheld the Sierra Club petition, a decision that was allowed to stand by a Circuit Court and the Supreme Court. After some modification, this policy is now in force, in the form of regulations for the Prevention of Significant Deterioration.

Mediation

The expense and delay of litigation have led to a search for other methods to resolve disputes. An alternative that has received considerable recent attention in environmental conflicts is a negotiation process between the adversaries, guided by a neutral facilitator (environmental mediation). The task of the mediator is to clarify the issues in contention, help each party to understand the position and the needs of other parties, and attempt to arrive at a conclusion where each party gains enough from a compromise to prefer an agreed settlement to the risk and costs of litigation. Often citizen's suits or the possibility that a suit might be filed gives an environmental group a "place at the table" in such a mediation. Litigation, which may delay a project for years, becomes something that can be bargained away in order to gain concessions of decreased environmental impact (mitigation) from a developer. Mediation has had some success where bargaining positions are approximately equal and where participants who truly represent the conflicting interests can be identified and persuaded to devote the considerable effort that the process demands. In some states, mediation is required by legislation as an alternative or a precedent to litigation in the highly contentious siting of waste treatment facilities. For example, in Rhode Island a developer who wishes to construct a hazardous waste treatment facility must negotiate with representatives of the host community and submit to arbitration issues not resolved by negotiation. Costs of the negotiation process are borne by the developer.

There is another class of litigation which, while it is not usually described as environmental, has a significant impact on actions affecting the environment. Individuals who believe that they have been harmed by some environmental contamination can sue the polluter to recover payment in recompense for that harm (a tort action). Thus, a homeowner whose well is contaminated by leakage from a nearby petroleum storage tank can sue for the costs of providing an alternative water supply and for any damage to health that might have occurred, although proof of the cause of the latter type of injury is difficult to establish.

A new field of law, called "toxic torts" is developing as the special problems of linking cause to a health effect that occurs decades later becomes better appreciated. Obviously, if these suits are successful, they will discourage the harmful activity. Somewhat paradoxically, if the injury from an irresponsible action is sufficiently widespread and appears to be so serious that many successful damage suits will be brought, bankruptcy law may provide an escape for the offending corporation. The Johns Manville Corporation, faced with hundreds of potential suits for injury from exposure to the asbestos they manufacture, has protected its assets by declaring bankruptcy, even though the corporation continues as a highly profitable business.

STATE ENVIRONMENTAL PROGRAMS

All states have their own body of law that governs control of environmental quality within their boundaries. Where this law deals with the same subject matter as federal law, the Supremacy Clause of the U.S. Constitution requires that federal law take precedence in areas of conflict. In some cases, the federal legislation in a particular area is so extensive that state legislation is preempted. In other cases, federal law specifically allows states to set environmental standards that are more stringent than the federal standards. Several of the major federal regulatory statutes (e.g., the Clean Water Act and the Resource Conservation and Recovery Act) allow for delegation of federal regulatory authority to the states if the states can show that they will meet minimum federal standards. In contrast, the Clean Air Act assigns primary authority for planning and implementing air quality control plans to the states and allows the EPA to assume this authority only if the state defaults.

In some areas where there is little federal regulation, state regulation has been encouraged by federal grants that have been made available to states whose programs meet federal standards. The major impact of the Coastal Zone Management Act has been to encourage the formation of coastal management programs by the states through federal funding. Substantial federal funds have been available to assist state programs in air, water, and toxic waste control. The funds structure these programs through the application of grant guidelines.

The federal "carrot" has often been as effective as the "stick."

In still other environmental areas, such as land use, there is virtually no federal legislation, and a few states (Vermont, Oregon, and Hawaii) have developed statewide regulation in an attempt to limit development to the level the environment can tolerate (i.e., to the carrying capacity of the land). Some states also have developed the state equivalent of NEPA, which requires environmental impact statements for state projects of potential significant environmental effect. These statements provide for study and public information on projects that lack federal involvement and would thereby not fall under NEPA jurisdiction.

Litigation also can be brought in state courts to clarify and to implement state environmental legislation and regulations. Because the jurisdiction of such suits is limited to state boundaries, the financial impact is much less than for federal suits, and national trade organizations are much less likely to be involved. Similarly, national environmental organizations are rarely involved, unless there is reason to believe that decisions in the case might influence courts in other states (provide a precedent) when they decide related issues. Consequently, litigation in state courts is more likely to involve disputes over the application of legislation and regulation than to be a challenge to the regulations directly. Also, state environmental legislation less frequently includes provisions for citizen suits and a direct interest in the outcome of the case may be necessary to establish standing.

LOCAL ENVIRONMENTAL PROGRAMS

Certain areas of the environment traditionally are controlled by smaller units of government that derive their power from the state. Thus, municipal governments usually are granted zoning authority and other land-use responsibilities and can exert powerful influences on the physical environment. Zoning ordinances can be used to restrict the density of development to that suitable for the treatment of wastewater by individual sewage disposal systems, which leach treated water into the ground, and avoid the necessity of centralized plants. Local governments and special districts can restrict rate of growth on the basis of availability of potable water and thus reduce the need to create new supplies or to import water from other watersheds—actions that often result in considerable adverse environmental impact. Zoning authority also can be used to protect open space, to provide recreation, and to preserve natural habitats. Because zoning ordinances are adopted at the local level (albeit necessarily in compliance with state enabling legislation), they can be tailored to meet the needs of the community. This feature has been used as an argument against transferring land-use authority to higher levels of government.

When land is especially fragile and unsuitable for development, zoning can be used to restrict land use severely, as in the case of prohibitions on construction on barrier beaches or in wetlands. The federal Constitution (as well as state constitutions) sets some limits on this power, however. The Fifth Amendment prevents the federal government from taking private land for public use without just compensation. If the local government authority is perceived as being invoked to prevent harm to the public—to prevent flood damage, for example (Fig. 21.8)—then development restrictions are likely to be found by a court to be constitutional. If, however, the restrictions are viewed as providing a public benefit, such as recreational space, then the courts may find that the public should recompense the private owner for the damage suffered by loss of profit from development.

Review of land-use restrictions is especially severe when most of the probable uses of the land are prevented and the owner is left with "no beneficial use" for the property. A few state court cases have held that zoning can take strict regard of the fragility of natural systems. In 1967, Marinette County, Wisconsin, adopted a shoreland zoning ordinance that sharply limited the rights of land owners to drain, dredge, or fill wetlands. In 1961, a family named Just had purchased 36 acres of land in this county. Part of this land was a lakeshore wetland, which, six months after the wetlands ordinance was in place, Ronald Just attempted to fill. The Wisconsin court chose this case to examine a very important and general

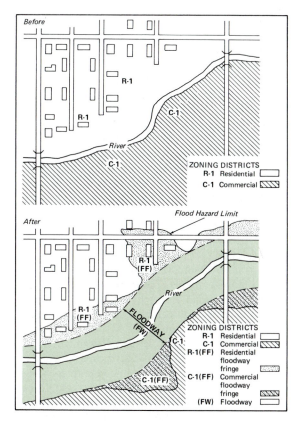

FIGURE 21.8
Typical zoning map before and after the addition of local floodplain regulations. (From Water Resources Council.)

question: "Is the ownership of a parcel of land so absolute that man can change its nature to suit any of his purposes?" The court concluded that "an owner of land has no absolute and unlimited right to change the essential natural character of his land so as to use it for a purpose for which it was unsuited in its natural state and which injures the rights of others" and so the court held: "The changing of wetlands and swamps to the damage of the general public by upsetting the natural environment and the natural relationship is not a reasonable use of that land which is protected from . . . regulation" [17]. Not all state courts have taken such a pro-environment position, and the constitutional restriction on "taking" is an ever-

present concern in devising environmental protection policies.

Local land-use control authority is understandably popular, because it provides a community and the individuals in it with greater control over their own destiny. Thus, although local authority is granted by the state and theoretically could be taken away by the state, there is powerful public resistance to such a change. This political reality recently has paralyzed developments that generally are agreed to be necessary to solve urgent environmental problems. These problems are most severe in the case of waste treatment and disposal. Following the media attention given to Love Canal, virtually no communities nationwide have been willing to accept construction of new facilities that are intended to manage hazardous waste materials, even if evidence is presented that risks from the facility would be no greater than those usually tolerated by our industrialized society. And a similar public distaste seems to be developing toward resource recovery incinerators, which burn solid waste to recover energy and thus reduce the need for landfills. We are presented with the paradox of developments nearly everyone agrees are seriously needed for the public good, but which no community will allow to occur within its boundaries. In the face of this dilemma, state governments have attempted to recapture authority for the siting of such controversial but necessary facilities but have encountered vigorous political resistance from local communities. A typical pattern is to form a state siting commission to select the "best" site for a waste treatment facility. The commission often can develop siting criteria with little controversy, as long as these criteria are not particularly site specific, but as soon as application of the criteria results in nomination of a desirable site, residents of that community descend on their legislature and force a veto of that option. Political will has not yet been sufficiently strong to resist this force.

Local control almost guarantees substantial diversity, of course, and political factions, which often are pro-development, can have significant influence in their own communities. In cases where this diversity is undesirable, as in building codes, for example, state standards may be set, to be enforced by local authority. Thus implementation of building energy standards, of water conservation devices, or of wastewater treatment restrictions may depend on local government interest and efficacy.

Individuals also have proportionately greater influence in their own communities and have the opportunity to testify at zoning variance hearings on the probable environmental effects of proposed changes. Local citizen groups have been effective in keeping environmental issues visible but often find that they have a continuing need to educate local zoning boards on these issues. Sustained interest and sufficient numbers of interested individuals attending hearings can be effective and place a premium on strong community organization.

INTERNATIONAL ENVIRONMENTAL LAW

International law is different in basic concept from domestic laws and thus is well beyond the scope of this chapter. Because there is no world government with enforcement authority over nations, international ''law'' must depend on agreement of the parties concerned to bind themselves to behavior that many residents of a particular nation may oppose. Certain issues of multinational concern are addressed by a collection of policies, agreements, and treaties that are loosely called international environmental law. Recalcitrant nations can be moved to change their positions on environmental issues by the pressure of world opinion and by the possibility of economic sanctions. Thus Japan and the Soviet Union have to some extent yielded to pressures to limit their whaling industries. When political power is unequal, however, agreement is less likely, as in the failure of the United States to respond to Canadian pleas for reduction in emissions in the United States that cause acid deposition within Canadian boundaries.

SUMMARY

The legal and administrative structure for environmental management is complex, often expensive, and time consuming. Yet it provides an unusual opportunity for public involvement directly in policy decisions if the individual or interest group is willing to devote the effort to becoming well informed on issues and can sustain the efforts and assemble personal and economic resources. There are numerous examples nationwide of single individuals whose determination and persuasion have been a powerful positive force to improve the quality of the environment.

STUDY QUESTIONS

1   Do rocks have rights?

2   You are asked to negotiate between tuna fishing fleets and a conservation group trying to save porpoises. Porpoises are caught in the tuna nets and die accidentally. What information do you need? What would you suggest?

3   Should our laws lead us to a risk-free society?

4   In general, why are water pollution laws easier to enforce than air pollution laws?

5   Air pollution laws have led industries to build taller stacks and to reduce the emission of dark smoke. What are the benefits of these changes? What are the drawbacks of these changes?

6   Wild horses roam parts of the American West. What protection are these animals afforded by the U.S. Endangered Species Act?

7   What is the Trust Doctrine, and why is it important in environmental law?

8 Are we more likely to achieve cleaner air by legally requiring pollution abatement equipment or by charging a fee according to the amount of pollution emitted?

FURTHER READING

BUREAU OF NATIONAL AFFAIRS. *Environment Reporter,* issued weekly, Washington, D.C.

DAWSON, A. D. 1982. *Land-use planning and the law.* New York: Garland STPM Press.

DEUTSCH, S. L. ed., *Land use and environmental law review,* issued annually, New York: Clark Boardman Co.

ENVIRONMENTAL LAW INSTITUTE. 1974. *Federal environmental law.* St. Paul, Minn.: West Publishing Co.

STONE, C. D. 1974. *Should trees have standing? Towards legal rights for natural objects.* Los Altos, Calif.: William Kaufmann.

Appendixes

APPENDIX A:
THE KINDS OF LIVING THINGS

The millions of species on Earth are classified into five major groups called **kingdoms.** These kingdoms form a family tree of species with similar characteristics. The five kingdoms are (1) **prokaryotes,** which include bacteria and blue-green algae; (2) the **protists,** which are primarily single-celled organisms; (3) **fungi;** (4) **plants;** and (5) **animals.** Table A.1 lists the major characteristics of each kingdom. The prokaryotes are generally believed to be the most ancient because their cells lack a **nucleus** and other features of the other kingdoms. The appearance of prokaryoticlike forms in the oldest fossils also suggests that the prokaryotes are more primitive than the other kingdoms. Prokaryotes, however, carry out certain chemical transformations, such as the fixation of nitrogen, which are not carried out by organisms in the other kingdoms. The protists include some single-celled organisms that are autotrophs (make their own food) and others that are heterotrophs, such as amoebae.

Biologists believe that the species within a kingdom are more closely related to each other than to species in other kingdoms. According to the theory of evolution, species have evolved from others through the process of **natural selection.** Individuals in a population differ from one another in inherited, or **genetic,** traits. If individuals with one kind of trait have more offspring than others, then natural selection is said to occur with regard to that trait. As a consequence, this trait becomes more and more common in the genetic material, or the **gene pool.** Changes in the environment can change which genetic traits are favored and thus lead to natural selection. Genetic changes can also occur by **mutation,** a change that occurs in the chemical characteristics of the genetic material. Mutations may occur at random or may be caused by the effects of ionizing radiation. Certain chemicals seem to increase the rate of mutation. When a chemical substance or form of radiation causes mutations, it is said to be **mutagenic** or is referred to as a **mutagen.** If two populations become isolated from breeding with one another for a long enough time, they can undergo genetic changes that make interbreeding no longer possible. The two populations therefore can no longer exchange genetic material and are by definition said to be different species. By this process, it is believed that the five kingdoms evolved over Earth's history. The family tree of connections is shown in Figure A.1.

TABLE A.1
The five kingdoms.

Kingdom	Cell Nucleus	Chlorophyll	Cell Specialization	Nervous System	Nutrition	Oxygen Requirement	Examples
Prokaryotes	None	Some kinds, but not in chloroplasts	Rare	None	Autotrophs and heterotrophs	Some kinds require oxygen	Bacteria; blue-green algae
Protists	All	Some kinds, in chloroplasts	In a few kinds	Primitive	Autotrophs and heterotrophs	All	Amoebae; dino-flagellates; euglena
Fungi	All	None	In most, but limited	None	Heterotrophs	Most	Mushrooms; molds; yeasts
Plants	All	Almost all; in chloroplasts	All	None	Autotrophs	All	Water lilies; redwoods; moss; wheat
Animals	All	None	All	All	Heterotrophs	All	Crabs; termites; goldfish; elephants; human beings

Source: Modified from Margulis and Schwartz, 1982.

FIGURE A.1
The family tree of the five kingdoms.

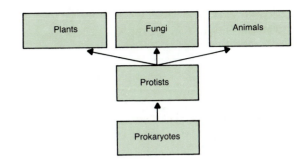

APPENDIX B:
COMMON CONVERSION FACTORS

Length

1 yard = 3 ft, 1 fathom = 6 ft

	in.	ft	mi	cm	m	km
1 inch (in.) =	1	0.083	1.58×10^{-5}	2.54	0.0254	2.54×10^{-5}
1 foot (ft) =	12	1	1.89×10^{-4}	30.48	0.3048	—
1 mile (mi) =	63,360	5,280	1	160,934	1,609	1.609
1 centimeter (cm) =	0.394	0.0328	6.2×10^{-6}	1	0.01	1.0×10^{-5}
1 meter (m) =	39.37	3.281	6.2×10^{-4}	100	1	0.001
1 kilometer (km) =	39,370	3,281	0.6214	100,000	1,000	1

Area

1 square mi = 640 acres, 1 acre = 43,560 ft^2 = 4046.86 m^2 = 0.4047 ha
1 ha = 10,000 m^2 = 2.471 acres

	in.^{2}	ft^2	mi^2	cm^2	m^2	km^2
1 in.^{2} =	1	—	—	6.4516	—	—
1 ft^2 =	144	1	—	929	0.0929	—
1 mi^2 =	—	27,878,400	1	—	—	2.590
1 cm^2 =	0.155	—	—	1	—	—
1 m^2 =	1,550	10.764	—	10,000	1	—
1 km^2 =	—	—	0.3861	—	1,000,000	1

Volume

	in.³	ft³	yd³	m³	qt	liter	barrel	gal (U.S.)
1 in.³ =	1	—	—	—	—	0.02	—	—
1 ft³ =	1,728	1	—	0.0283	—	28.3	—	7.480
1 yd³ =	—	27	1	0.76	—	—	—	—
1 m³ =	61,020	35.315	1.307	1	—	1,000	—	—
1 quart (qt) =	—	—	—	—	1	0.95	—	0.25
1 liter (l) =	61.02	—	—	—	1.06	1	—	0.2642
1 barrel (oil) =	—	—	—	—	168	159.6	1	42
1 gallon (U.S.) =	231	0.13	—	—	4	3.785	0.02	1

Mass and Weight

1 pound = 453.6 grams = 0.4536 kilogram = 16 ounces
1 gram = 0.0353 ounce = 0.0022 pound
1 short ton = 2000 pounds = 907.2 kilograms
1 long ton = 2240 pounds = 1008 kilograms
1 metric ton = 2205 pounds = 1000 kilograms
1 kilogram = 2.205 pounds

Energy and Power

1 kilowatt-hour = 3413 Btus = 860,421 calories
1 Btu = 0.000293 kilowatt-hour = 252 calories = 1055 joules
1 watt = 3.413 Btu/hr = 14.34 calorie/min
1 calorie = the amount of heat necessary to raise the temperature of 1 gram (1 cm³) of water 1 degree Celsius
1 quadrillion Btu = (approximately) 1 exajoule
1 horsepower = 7.457×10^2 watts
1 joule = 9.481×10^{-4} Btu = 0.2389 cal = 2.778×10^{-7} kilowatt-hour

Temperature

$$F = \tfrac{9}{5}C + 32$$

F is degrees Fahrenheit.
C is degrees Celsius (centigrade).

Fahrenheit		Celsius
32	Freezing of H_2O (Atmospheric Pressure)	0
50	————	10
68	————	20
86	————	30
104	————	40
122	————	50
140	————	60
158	————	70
176	————	80
194	————	90
212	Boiling of H_2O (Atmospheric Pressure)	100

Other Conversion Factors

1 ft^3/sec = 0.0283 m^3/sec = 7.48 gal/sec = 28.32 liter/sec
1 acre-foot = 43,560 ft^3 = 1233 m^3 = 325,829 gal
1 m^3/sec = 35.32 ft^3/sec
1 ft^3/sec for one day = 1.98 acre-feet
1 m/sec = 3.6 km/hr = 2.24 mi/hr
1 ft/sec = 0.682 mi/hr = 1.097 km/hr
1 atmosphere = 14.7 lb(in.$^{-2}$) = 2116 lb(ft^{-2}) = 1.013 × 10^5 N(m^{-2})

APPENDIX C:
GEOLOGIC TIME SCALE AND BIOLOGIC EVOLUTION

Era	Approx. Age in Millions of Years Before Present	Period	Epoch	Life Form
	Less than 0.01	Quaternary	Recent (Holocene)	Humans
	0.01–2	Quaternary	Pleistocene	Humans
	2			
Cenozoic	2–5		Pliocene	
	5–24		Miocene	
	24–38	Tertiary	Oligocene	
	38–55		Eocene	Mammals
	55–63		Paleocene	
	63			
Mesozoic	63–138	Cretaceous		
	138–205	Jurassic		Flying reptiles, birds
	205–240	Triassic		Dinosaurs
	240			
Paleozoic	240–290	Permian		Reptiles
	290–360	Carboniferous		Insects
	360–410	Devonian		Amphibians
	410–435	Silurian		Land plants
	435–500	Ordovician		Fish
	500–570	Cambrian		
	570			
	700			Multicelled organisms
	3,400			One-celled organisms
Precambrian	4,000	Approximate age of oldest rocks discovered on earth		
	4,500	Approximate age of the earth and meteorites		

References

CHAPTER 1

1   UDALL, S. L. 1963. *The quiet crisis.* New York: Avon.
2   SEARS, P. 1935. *Deserts on the march.* Norman: University of Oklahoma Press.
3   CARSON, R. 1962. *Silent spring.* Boston: Houghton Mifflin.
4   GLACKEN, C. J. 1967. *Traces on the Rhodian shore: Nature and culture in Western thought from ancient times to the end of the eighteenth century.* Berkeley: University of California Press.
5   McLUHAN, T. C. 1971. *Touch the Earth: A self-portrait of Indian existence.* New York: Promontory.
6   KLAEBER, F., ed. 1950. *Beowulf and the fight at Finnsburg.* Boston: D. C. Heath.
7   LECLERC, G. L. (Count de Buffon). 1812. *Natural history, general and particular.* (Translated by W. Smellie.) London: C. Wood.
8   EGERTON, F. N. 1975. Aristotole's population biology. *Arethusa* 8: 307–30.
9   CICERO, M. T. 1972. *The nature of the gods.* (Translated by H. C. P. McGregor.) Aylesbury, England: Penguin Press.
10 LUCRETIUS (Titus Lucretius Carus). 1968. *De rerum natura.* (Translated by R. Humphries.) Bloomington: Indiana University Press.
11 NASH, R. 1967. *Wilderness and the American mind.* New Haven, Conn.: Yale University Press.
12 NASH, R. 1979. Wilderness is all in your mind. *Backpacker* 31: 39.
13 NICOLSON, M. H. 1959. *Mountain gloom and mountain glory.* Ithaca, N. Y.: Cornell University Press.
14 SHELLEY, P. B. "Mont Blanc." Lines 127, 96–97, 139–41.
15 SANDBURG, C. 1970. "The People, Yes." In *The complete poems of Carl Sandburg,* pp. 439–617. New York: Harcourt, Brace, Jovanovich.
16 BOTKIN, B. A. 1944. *A treasury of American folklore.* New York: Crown Publishers.
17 MARSH, G. P. 1967. *Man and nature.* Cambridge, Mass.: Belknap Press. (Originally published in 1864, ed. D. Lowenthal, by Charles Scribner's Sons, New York.)

18 RUNTE, A. 1979. *National parks: The American experience.* Lincoln: University of Nebraska Press.

19 STONE, C. D. 1972. Should trees have standing? Toward legal rights for natural objects. *California Legal Review* 45: p. 450,ff.

20 WOOD, W. 1634. *New England's prospect.* Prince Society (eds.), Boston, 1865.

21 DAY, G. M. 1953. The Indian as an ecological factor in the northeastern forest. *Ecology* 34: 329–346.

22 KALM, P. 1750. *Travels in North America.* Reprinted in 1963 by Dover Books, New York, from the 1770 English version (A. B. Benson, translator), (2 volumes).

23 HEIZER, R. F. 1955. Primitive Man as an ecological factor. *Anthropological Society Papers* 13: 1–31.

24 MARTIN, P. S. 1973. The discovery of North America. *Science* 179: 969–74.

25 IVERSON, J. 1956. Forest clearing in the Stone Age. *Scientific American* 194: 36–41.

26 COLLINS, D. 1969. Cultural traditions and environments of early man. *Current Anthropology* 10: 267–316.

27 CARROLL, C. F. 1970. The forest civilization of New England. Ph.D. dissertation, Brown University.

28 LEOPOLD, A. 1949. *A Sand County almanac.* New York: Oxford University Press.

29 STRONG; D. H., and ROSENFIELD, E. S. 1976. Ethics or expediency: An environmental question. *Environmental Affairs* 5: 255–270.

30 SHADER-FRECHETTE, K. S., ed. 1981. *Environmental ethics.* Pacific Grove, Calif.: Boxwood Press.

31 PARTRIDGE, E. 1981. *Responsibilies to future generations: Environmental ethics.* Buffalo, N.Y.: Prometheus Books.

32 LOVELOCK, J. E., and MARGULIS, L. 1973. Atmospheric homeostasis by and for the biosphere: The Gaia hypothesis. *Tellus* 26: 1–9.

CHAPTER 2

1 WESTERN, D., and VAN PRAT, C. 1973. Cyclical changes in habitat and climate of an East African ecosystem. *Nature* 241 (549): 104–06.

2 DUNNE, T., and LEOPOLD, L. B. 1978. *Water in environmental planning.* San Francisco: W. H. Freeman.

3 HUTCHINSON, G. E. 1950. Survey of contemporary knowledge of biochemistry. 3. The biogeochemistry of vertebrate excretion. *Bulletin of the American Museum of Natural History* 96: 481–82.

4 BARTLETT, A. A. 1980. Forgotten fundamentals of the energy crisis. *Journal of Geological Education* 28: 4–35.

5 GATES, D. M. 1980. *Biophysical ecology.* New York: Springer-Verlag.

6 MARSH, W. M., and DOZIER, J. 1981. *Landscape.* Reading, Mass.: Addison-Wesley.

7 ANONYMOUS. 1980. Phosphate: Debate over an essential resource. *Science* 209: 372.

8 PESTRONG, R. 1974. *Slope stability.* New York: McGraw-Hill.

9 KRYNINE, D. P., and JUDD, W. R. 1957. *Principles of engineering geology and geotechnics.* New York: McGraw-Hill.

10 MATHEWSON, C. C.; CASTLEBERRY, J. P., II; and LYTTON, R. L. 1975. Analysis and modeling of the performance of home foundations on expansive soils in central Texas. *Bulletin of the Association of Engineering Geolgists* 17: 275–302.

11 ANONYMOUS. 1979. *Environmentally sound small scale agricultural projects.* Mt. Rainier, Md.: Mohonk Trust, Vita Publications.

12 OLSON, G. W. 1981. *Soils and the environment.* New York: Chapman-Hall.

CHAPTER 3

1 SHEFFER, V. B. 1951. The rise and fall of a reindeer herd. *Scientific Monthly* 73: 356–62.

2 HANNA, G. D. 1922. The reindeer herds of the Pribilof Islands. *Scientific Monthly* 15: 181–86.

3 Le BOEUF, B. J. 1981. The elephant seal. In *Problems in the management of locally abundant wild mammals,* eds. P. A. Jewel, S. J. Holt, and D. Hart, pp. 291–301. New York: Academic Press.

4 EGERTON, F. N. 1975. Aristotle's population biology. *Arethusa* 8: 307–30.

5   LOTKA, A. J. 1956. *Elements of mathematical biology*. New York: Dover.

6   CAUGHLEY, G. 1970. Eruption of ungulate populations, with emphasis on Himalayan thar in New Zealand. *Ecology* 51: 53–72.

7   ELTON, C. 1942. *Voles, mice, and lemmings. Problems in population dynamics*. Oxford: Clarendon. Hudson's Bay Company, unpublished data, 1978 (personal communication).

8   PETERSON, R. O.; PAGE, R. E.; and DODGE, R. M. 1984. Wolves, moose and the allometry of population cycles. *Science* 224 1350–52.

9   WU, L. S. and BOTKIN, D. B. 1980. Of elephants and man. *American Naturalist* 116: 831–849.

10 JORDAN, P. A.; BOTKIN, D. B.; and WOLF, M. I. 1971. Biomass dynamics in a moose population. *Ecology* 52: 147–52.

11 EISENBERG, R. M. 1966. The regulation of density in a natural population of the pond snail *Lymnaea elodes. Ecology* 47: 889–906.

12 GRUBB, P. 1974. Population dynamics of the Soay sheep. In *Island survivors: The ecology of Soay sheep of St. Kilda*, eds. P. A. Jewel, C. Milner, and J. M. Boyd. London: Athlone Press.

13 FOWLER, C. W.; BUNDERSON, W. T.; CHERRY, M. R.; RYEL, R. J.; and STEELE, B. B. 1980. *Comparative population dynamics of large mammals: A search for management criteria*. National Technical Information Service Publication No. PB80-178627. Washington, D.C.: U.S. Department of Commerce.

14 BOTKIN, D. B. 1984. The garden of the unicorn: The ecosystem context for the management of endangered species. In *Conservation of threatened habitats*, ed. A. V. Hall. Council for Scientific and Industrial Research, Cooperative Scientific Programs, *Pretoria* 92: 66–81.

15 TALBOT, L. 1984. An international perspective on applied ecology. *Applied Ecology Newsletter* 13: 1–3.

16 COLWELL, R. K. 1979. The geographic ecology of hummingbird flower mites in relation to their host plants and carriers. *Recent Advances in Acarology* II: 461–468.

17 COLWELL, R. K. 1981. Group selection is implicated in the evolution of female-biased sex ratios. *Nature* 290: 401–404.

18 BOTKIN, D. B. 1985. The need for a science of the biosphere. *Interdisciplinary Science Reviews*.

19 MOORE, R. M., ed. 1970. *Australian Grasslands*. Canberra: Australian National University.

20 SCHOENER, T. W. 1983. Field experiments in interspecific competition. *American Naturalist* 122: 240–285.

21 GAUSE, G. F. 1934. *The struggle for existence*. Baltimore, Md.: Williams and Wilkins.

22 MURDOCK, W. W.; REEVE, J. D.; HUFFAKER, C. B.; and KENNETT, C. E. 1984. Biological control of olive scale and its relevance to ecological theory. *American Naturalist* 123: 371–392.

23 LUCK, R. F. 1984. Integrated pest management in California citrus. *Proceedings of the International Society of Citriculture* 2: 630–635.

24 PU, CHE-LUNG. 1976. Biological control of insect pests in China. *Acta Entomologica Sinica* 19: 247–252.

25 FEDER, H. M. 1966. Cleaning symbiosis in the marine environment. In *Symbiosis*, ed. S. M. Henry, pp. 327–380. New York: Academic Press.

26 LIMBAUGH, C. 1961. Cleaning symbiosis. *Scientific American* 205: 42–49.

CHAPTER 4

1   HUTCHINSON, G. E., ed. 1970. Ianula: An account of the history and development of the Lago di Monterosi, Latium, Italy. *Transactions of the American Philosophical Society* 60:1–178.

2   MAUGH, T. H. 1979. Restoring damaged lakes. *Science* 203: 425–27.

3   LEHMAN, J. T. 1986. Control of eutrophication in Lake Washington. In *Application of ecological knowledge to environmental problems*, ed. G. H. Orians, Chap. 20. Committee on the Applications of Ecology Theory to Environmental Problems, Commission on Life Sciences. Washington D. C.: National Academy of Science.

4 EDMONDSON, W. T., and LEHMAN, J. T., 1981. The effect of changes in the nutrient income on the condition of Lake Washington. *Limnology and Oceanography* 26: 1–29.

5 SCHINDLER, D. W.; KLING, H.; SCHMIDT, R. V.; PROKOWICH, J.; FROST, V. E.; REID, R. A.; and CAPEL, M. 1973. Eutrophication of lake 227 by addition of phosphate and nitrate: The second, third, and fourth years of enrichment, 1970, 1971, and 1972. *Journal of the Fisheries Research Board of Canada* 30: 1415–40.

6 RISSER, P. G. 1985. Toward a holistic management perspective. *BioScience* 35: 414–418.

7 MOROWITZ, H. J. 1979. *Energy flow in biology.* Woodbridge, Conn.: Oxbow Press.

8 LAVIGNE, D. M.; BARCHARD, W.; INNES, S.; and ORITSLAND, N. A. 1976. *Pinniped bioenergetics.* ACMRR/MM/SC/112. Rome: United Nations Food and Agriculture Organization.

9 SCHRODINGER, E. 1942. *What is life?* Cambridge, England: Cambridge University Press.

10 CORLISS, J. B.; DYMOND, J.; GORDON, L. I.; EDMOND, J. M.; VON HERZEN, R. P.; BALLARD, R. D.; GREEN, K.; WILLIAMS, D.; BAINBRIDGE, A.; CRANE, K.; and VAN ANDEL, T. H. 1979. Submarine thermal springs on the Galapagos Rift. *Science* 203: 1073–1082.

11 SLOBODKIN, L. B. 1960. Ecological energy relations at the population level. *American Naturalist.* 95: 213–236.

12 JORDAN, J. D.; BOTKIN, D. B.; and WOLF, M. I. 1971. Biomass dynamics in a moose population. *Ecology* 52: 147–152.

13 LIKENS, G. E.; BORMANN, F. H.; PIERCE, R. S.; EATON, J. S.; and JOHNSON, N. M. 1977. *Biochemistry of a forested ecosystem.* New York: Springer-Verlag.

CHAPTER 5

1 ESTES, J. A., and PALMISANO, J. F., 1974. Sea otters: Their role in structuring nearshore communities. *Science* 185: 1058–60.

2 KENYON, K. W. 1969. *The sea otter in the eastern Pacific Ocean.* North American Fauna No. 68. Washington, D.C.: Bureau of Sport Fisheries and Wildlife, U.S. Department of the Interior.

3 DUGGINS, D. O. 1980. Kelp beds and sea otters: An experimental approach. *Ecology* 61: 447–53.

4 VALENTINE, J. W. 1969. Patterns of taxonomic and ecological structure of the shelf benthos during Phanerozoic time. *Palaeontology* 12: 684–708.

5 WEST, D. C.; SHUGART, H. H.; and BOTKIN, D. B., eds. 1981. *Forest succession: Concepts and applications.* New York: Springer-Verlag.

6 MARSH, G. P. 1967. *Man and nature* (Originally published in 1864, reprinted and edited by D. Lowenthal.) Cambridge, Mass.: Belknap Press.

7 ODUM, E. P. 1969. The strategy of ecosystem development. *Science* 164: 262–70.

8 WALKER, J.; THOMPSON, C. H.; FERGUS, I. F.; and TUNSTALL, B. R. 1981. Plant succession and soil development in coastal sand dunes of subtropical eastern Australia. In *Forest succession: Concepts and applications,* eds. D. West, H. H. Shugart, and D. B. Botkin, pp. 107–31. New York: Springer-Verlag.

9 GORHAM, E.; VITOUSEK, P. M.; and REINERS, W. A. 1979. The regulation of chemical budgets over the course of terrestrial ecosystem succession. *Annual Review of Ecology and Systematics* 10: 53–84.

10 BOTKIN, D. B. 1979. A grandfather clock down the staircase: Stability and disturbance in natural ecosystems. *Forests: Fresh perspectives from ecosystem analysis,* ed. R. H. Waring, pp. 1–10. Proceedings of the 40th Annual Biology Colloquium. Corvallis: Oregon State University Press.

11 HEINSELMAN, M. L. 1970. Landscape evolution, peatland types, and the environment in the Lake Agassiz Peatlands Natural Area, Minnesota. *Ecological Monographs* 40: 235–61.

12 BOTKIN, D. B., and SOBEL, M. J. 1975. Stability in time varying ecosystems. *American Naturalist* 109: 625–46.

13 PIMM, S. L. 1984. The complexity and stability of ecosystems. *Nature* 307: 321–26.

14 HOLLING, C. S. 1985. Resilience of ecosystems: Local surprise and global change. In *Global Change,* T. F. Malone and J. G. Roederer, eds. pp. 228–69. Cambridge, England: Cambridge University Press.

CHAPTER 6

1 BOTKIN, D. B., and MILLER, R. S. 1974. Complex ecosystems: Models and predictions. *American Scientist* 62: 448–53.

2 ANAGNOSTAKIS, S. A. 1982. Biological control of chestnut blight. *Science* 215: 446–471.

3 WILSON, E. O. 1985. The biological diversity crisis. *BioScience* 35: 700–706.

4 WALLACE, A. R. 1876. *The geographical distribution of animals.* Vol. 1. (Reprinted 1962 by Hafner, New York.)

5 VALENTINE, J. W. 1973. Plates and provinces, a theoretical history of environmental discontinuity. In *Organisms and continents through time,* ed. N. F. Hughes, pp. 79–92. Special Papers in Paleontology 12.

6 BOTKIN, D. B. 1977. The vegetation of the west. In *The reader's encyclopedia of the American West,* ed. H. R. Lamar, pp. 1216–1224. New York: Thomas Y. Crowell.

7 DAVIS, M. B. 1981. Quarternary history and the stability of forest communities. In *Forest succession: Concepts and applications,* eds. D. C. West, H. H. Shugart, and D. B. Botkin, pp. 132–153. New York: Springer-Verlag.

8 HUTCHINSON, G. E. 1958. Concluding remarks, Cold Spring Harbor Symposium in Quantitative Biology 22: 415–427.

9 KNOLL, A. H. 1984. Patterns of extinction in the fossil record of vascular plants. In *Extinctions,* ed. M. H. Nitecki, pp. 21–68. Chicago: University of Chicago Press.

10 CONNELL, J. H. 1978. Diversity in tropical rain forests and coral reefs. *Science* 199: 1302–1310.

11 DARWIN, C. R. 1859. *The Origin of species by means of natural selection or the preservation of favored races in the struggle for life.* London: Murray.

12 COX, C. B.; HEALEY, I. N.; and MOORE, P. D. 1973. *Biogeography.* New York: Halsted.

13 MacARTHUR, R. H., and WILSON, E. O. 1967. *The theory of island biogeography.* Princeton, N.J.: Princeton University Press.

14 LOVEJOY, T.; BIERREGAARD, R. O.; RANKIN, J.; and SCHUBART, H. O. R. 1983. Ecological dynamics of tropical forest fragments. In *Tropical rain forest: Ecology and management,* eds. S. L. Sutton, T. C. Whitmore, and A. C. Chadwick, pp. 377–384. Oxford, England: Blackwell.

15 BOTKIN, D. B. 1977, Strategies for the reintroduction of species into damaged ecosystems. In *Recovery and restoration of damaged ecosystems,* ed. J. Cairns, pp. 241–260. Charlottesville, Va.: University of Virginia Press.

16 SOULE, M. E. 1985. What is conservation biology? *BioScience* 35: 727–734.

17 SOULE, M. E. 1980. Thresholds for survival: Maintaining fitness and evolutionary potential. In *Conservation biology,* eds. M. E. Soule and B. A. Wilcox, pp. 151–69. Sunderland, Mass.: Sinauer.

18 COUES, E., ed. 1979. *The history of the Lewis and Clark Expedition.* Vol. 1. New York: Dover.

19 WORLD BANK. 1984. *World development report.* Oxford, England: Oxford University Press.

20 SINCLAIR, A. R. E. 1977. *The African buffalos.* Chicago: University of Chicago Press.

Tropical Rain Forests: Nature at Its Finest
BATES, M. 1960. *The forest and the sea.* New York: Random House.
MYERS, N. 1978. Deforestation in the tropics: Who gains, who loses? In *Where have all the flowers gone? Deforestation in the Third World,* eds. Sutlive et al. Williamsburg, Va.: College of William and Mary.
PRANCE, G. T. 1982. The Amazon: Earth's most dazzling rain forest. *Garden,* January/February.
RICHARDS, P. W. 1981. *The tropical rain forest.* 8th ed. Cambridge, England: Cambridge University Press.

Ethnobotany: Linking the Past to the Future
ALLEN, R. 1980. *How to save the world—Strategy for world conservation.* Totowa, N. J.: Barnes & Noble.
BLOOM, B. 1985. Advocacy botany for the neotropics. *Garden,* May/June.

MEYERS, N. 1979. *The sinking ark: A new look at the problem of disappearing species.* Oxford: Pergamon Press.

MORAN, E. F. 1978. Strategies for survival: Resource use along the Transamazon Highway. In *Changing agricultural systems in Latin America,* eds. Sutlive et al. Williamsburg, Va.: Department of Anthropology, College of William and Mary.

OLDFIELD, M. L. 1979. Tropical deforestation and genetic resources conservation. In *Blowing in the wind: Deforestation and long-range implications,* eds. Sutlive et al. Williamsburg, Va.: Department of Anthropology, College of William and Mary.

TREACY, J. 1982. Bora Indian agroforestry: An alternative to deforestation. *Cultural Survival Quarterly,* Spring.

CHAPTER 7

1   EVERETT, G.D. 1961. One man's family. *Population Bulletin* 17: 153–69.
2   MALTHUS, T.R. 1798. *An essay on the principle of population.* London: Murray.
3   HAUB, C. 1981. *1981 world population data sheet.* Washington, D.C.: Population Reference Bureau.
4   GRAUNT, J. 1662. *Natural and political observations made upon the bill of mortality.* London: Roycraft. (Reprinted in 1973 by Gregg International Publishers, Ltd., Germany.)
5   HAUPT, A., and KANE, T. T., 1978. *The Population Reference Bureau's Population Handbook.* Washington, D.C.: Population Reference Bureau.
6   WELLER, R.H., and BOUVIER, L. F. 1981. *Population: Demography and policy.* New York: St. Martin's Press.
7   WORLD BANK. 1984. *World Development Report 1984.* Oxford, England: Oxford University press.
8   DUMOND, D. E. 1975. The limitation of human population: A natural history. *Science* 187: 713–721.
9   DESMOND, A. 1962. How many people have ever lived on Earth? *Population Bulletin* 18: 1–19.
10 THOMLINSON, R. 1965. *Population dynamics: Causes and consequences of world demographic change.* New York: Random House.
11 DEEVY, E. S., JR. 1960. The human population. *Scientific American* 203: 194–204.
12 BORRIE, W. D. 1970. *The growth and control of the world's population.* London: Weidenfield and Nicolson.
13 MATRAS, J. 1973. *Populations and societies.* Englewood Cliffs, N.J.: Prentice-Hall.
14 LE ROY LADURIE, E. 1971. *Times of feast, times of famine: A history of climate since the year 1000.* Garden City, N.Y.: Doubleday.
15 WESTING, A. H. 1981. A note on how many people that have ever lived. *BioScience* 31: 523–524.
16 COUNCIL ON ENVIRONMENTAL QUALITY. 1983. *Environmental Quality.* 14th Annual Report. Washington, D.C.
17 SAI, F. T. 1984. The population factor in Africa's development dilemma. *Science* 226: 801–810.
18 BROWN, L. R. 1979. *Resource trends and population policy: A time for reassessment.* Worldwatch Papers 29. Washington, D.C.: Worldwatch Institute.
19 U. S. BUREAU OF THE CENSUS. 1979. *Illustrative projections of world populations to the twenty-first century.* Current Population Reports. Ser. P-23, No. 79. Washington, D.C.: U.S. Government Printing Office.
20 FREJKA, T. 1973. The prospects for a stationary world population. *Scientific American* 228: 15–23.
21 WU, L. S., and BOTKIN, D. B. 1980. Of elephants and men. *American Naturalist* 116: 831–849.

CHAPTER 8

1   MILLER, R. S., and BOTKIN, D. B. 1974. Endangered species: Models and predictions. *American Scientist* 62: 172–81.
2   WILBUR, S. R. 1978. *The California condor, 1966–1976: A look at its past and future.* U. S. Fish and Wildlife Service, North American Fauna No. 72. Washington, D. C.: U. S. Department of the Interior.

3 WALLACE, A. R. 1876. *The geographical distribution of animals.* New York: Hafner. (Reissued in 1962 in 2 vols.)

4 LEOPOLD, A. 1947. *Game management.* New York: Scribners and Sons.

5 BROKAW, H. P. 1978. *Wildlife and America.* Washington, D. C.: Council on Environmental Quality.

6 U. S. FISH AND WILDLIFE SERVICE. 1981. *Federal aid in fish and wildlife restoration.* 1980 Washington D. C.: U.S. Department of the Interior.

7 MYERS, N. 1979. *The sinking ark.* Oxford, England: Pergamon Press.

8 BLACK, J. D. 1954. *Biological conservation.* New York: McGraw–Hill.

9 TALBOT, L. E.; PAYNE, W. J. A.; LEDGER, H. P.; VERDCOURT, L. D. and TALBOT, M. H. 1965. *The meat production potential of wild animals in Africa.* Technical Communication 16. Farnham Royal, Bucks, England: Commonwealth Agricultural Bureau.

10 MARES, M. A., and OJEDA, R. A. 1984. Faunal commercialization and conservation in South America. *BioScience* 34: 580–84.

11 EHRLICH, P., and EHRLICH, A. 1981. *Extinction: The causes and consequences of the disappearance of species.* New York: Random House.

12 MYERS, N. 1983. *A wealth of wild species.* Boulder, Colo: Westview Press.

13 LEVIN, R. 1970. Extinction. In *Some mathematical questions in biology*, ed. M. Gerstenhaber, Vol. II, pp. 77–107. Providence, R. I.: American Mathematical Society.

14 SOULE, M. E. 1980. Thresholds for survival: Maintaining fitness and evolutionary potential. In *Conservation Biology*, eds. M. E. Soule and B. A. Wilcox, pp. 151–69. Sunderland, Mass.: Sinauer.

15 FISHER, J.; SIMON, H.; and VINCENT, V. 1969. *Wildlife in danger.* New York: Viking Press.

16 EHRENFELD, D. W. 1972. *Conserving life on earth.* New York: Oxford University Press.

17 COUNCIL ON ENVIRONMENTAL QUALITY AND THE DEPARTMENT OF STATE. 1980. *The global 2000 report to the President: Entering the twenty-first century.*

18 BELL, F. W. 1978. *Food from the sea: The economics and politics of ocean fisheries.* Boulder, Colo.: Westview Press.

19 CUSHING, D. 1975. *Fisheries resources of the sea and their management.* London: Oxford University Press.

20 AUSTRALIA, INQUIRY INTO WHALES AND WHALING. 1979. *The whaling question: The inquiry by Sir Sidney Frost of Australia.* San Francisco: Friends of the Earth.

21 U. N. FOOD AND AGRICULTURE ORGANIZATION. 1978. *Mammals in the seas.* Report of the FAO Advisory Committee on Marine Resources Research, Working Party on Marine Mammals. FAO Fisheries Series 5, Vol. 1. Rome: U. N. Food and Agriculture Organization.

22 BOCKSTOCE, J. R., and BOTKIN, D. B. 1980. *The historical status and reduction of the western Arctic bowhead whale* (Balaena mysticetus) *population by the pelagic whaling industry, 1848–1914.* New Bedford, Conn.: Old Dartmouth Historical Society.

CHAPTER 9

1 BERWICK, S. 1976. The Gir Forest: An endangered ecosystem, *American Scientist* 64: 28–40.

2 WOOD, W. 1634. *New England's prospect.* Prince Society (eds.), Boston, 1865.

3 SPURR, S. H., and BARNES, B. V. 1973. *Forest ecology.* New York: Ronald Press.

4 SMIL, V. 1984. *The bad Earth: Environmental degradation in China.* Armonk, N.Y.: M.E. Sharpe.

5 U.S. FOREST SERVICE. 1980. *An assessment of the forest and rangeland situation in the United States.*

6 COUNCIL ON ENVIRONMENTAL QUALITY AND THE DEPARTMENT OF STATE. 1980. *The global 2000 report to the President: Entering the twenty-first century.*

7 BUSCHBACHER, R. J. 1986. Tropical deforestation and pasture development. *BioScience* 36: 3–4

8 WOOLRIDGE. 1984. IUCN Bulletin 3: 3–4.

9 OFFICE OF TECHNOLOGY ASSESSMENT. 1983. *Technologies to sustain tropical forest resources.* Washington, D. C.: Congress of the United States.

10 MORGAN, W. B., and ROSS, R. P. 1981. *Fuelwood and rural energy production and supply in the humid tropics.* Dublin: United Nations University, Tycooly International Publications.

11 ECKHOLM, ERIC. 1975. The other energy crisis: Firewood. *Worldwatch Paper* 1. Washington, D. C.: Worldwatch Institute.

12 WORLD RESOURCES INSTITUTE. 1986. *Tropical forests: A call to action.* Washington, D. C.: World Resources Institute.

13 LIKENS, G. E.; BORMAN, F. H.; PIERCE, R. S.; EATON, J. S.; and JOHNSON, N. M. 1977. *The biogeochemistry of a forested ecosystem.* New York: Springer-Verlag.

14 SWANSON, F. J., and DYRNESS, C. T. 1975. Impact of clearcutting and road construction on soil erosion by landslides in the western Cascade Range, Oregon. *Geology* 3: 393–396.

15 FREDRIKSEN, R. L. 1971. Comparative chemical water quality—natural and disturbed streams following logging and slash burning. In *Forest land uses and stream environment,* pp. 125–137. Corvallis: Oregon State University.

16 ABER, J. D.; BOTKIN, D. B.; and MELILLO, J. M. 1979. Predicting the effects of different harvesting regimes on productivity and yield in northern hardwoods. *Canadian Journal of Forest Research* 9: 10–14.

17 RICHTER, D. D.; RALSTON, C. W.; and HARMES, W. R. 1982. Prescribed fire: Effects on water quality and forest nutrient cycling. *Science* 215: 661–663.

18 RUNTE, A. 1979. *National parks, The American experience.* Lincoln: University of Nebraska.

19 BOTKIN, D. B. 1977. Strategies for the reintroduction of species into damaged ecosystems. In *Recovery and restoration of damaged ecosystems,* ed. J. Cairns. Charlottesville, Va.: University of Virginia Press.

20 ANONYMOUS. 1984. Parks: How big is big enough? *Science* 225: 611–612.

21 NASH, R. 1978. International concepts of wilderness preservation. In *Wilderness Management,* eds. Hendee, J. C., Stankey, G. H., and Lucas, R. C. pp. 43–59. U.S. Forest Service Misc. Pub. No. 1365.

22 HENDEE, J. C.; STANKEY, G. H.; and LUCAS, R. C. 1978. *Wilderness Management,* U.S. Forest Service Misc. Pub. No. 1365.

Agroforestry: Production and Protection for the Tropics

DE LAS SALAS, G., ed. *Workshop, agroforestry systems in Latin America.* Turrialba, Costa Rica: CATIE 1979.

CHAPTER 10

1 SHEPARD, J. 1984. Africa: Drought of the century. *Atlantic Monthly* 253 (4): 36–42

2 GRAINGER, A. 1982. *Desertification: How people make deserts, how people can stop and why they don't.* Earthscan Books, 2nd ed. London: Russell Press, Ltd., Nottingham.

3 McDOWELL, E. 1984. Brazil: Famine in the backlands. *Atlantic Monthly* 253 (3): 22–9.

4 WITTWER, S. H. 1983. The new agriculture: A view from the 21st century. In *Agriculture in the 21st century.* Richmond, Va.: Phillip Morris Operations Complex.

5 PIMENTEL, D.; TERHUNE, E. C.; DYSON-HUDSON, R.; ROCHEREAU, S.; SAMIS, R.; SMITH, E. A.; DENMAN, D.; REIFSCHNEIDER, D., and SHEPARD, M. 1976. Land degradation: Effects on food and energy resources. *Science* 194: 149–155.

6 JOHNSON, G. L., and WITTWER, S. H. 1984. *Agricultural technology until 2030: Prospects, priorities, and policies.* Michigan State University Agricultural Experiment Station, Special Report 12.

7 FLANNERY, K. V. 1965. The ecology of early food production in Mesopotamia. *Science* 147: 1247–56.

8 HANSEN, M.; BUSCH, L.; BURKHARDT, J.; LACY, W. B.; and LACY, L. R. 1986. Plant breeding and biotechnology. *BioScience* 36: 29–45.

9 BORLAUG, N. E. 1983. Contributions of conventional plant breeding to food production. *Science* 219: 689–93.

10 HINMAN, W. 1984. New crops for arid lands. *Science* 225: 1445–48.

11 BARDARCH, J. E. 1968. Aquaculture. *Science* 161: 1098–1106.

12 SMIL, V. 1984. *The bad Earth: Environmental degradation in China.* Armonk, N. Y.: M. E. Sharpe.

13 RILEY, B. Personal communication.

14 LASHOF, J. C., ed. 1979. Pest management strategies in crop protection. Vol I. Washington, D. C.: Office of Technology Assessment, U.S. Congress.

15 BALDWIN, F. L., and SANTELMANN, P. W. 1980. Weed science in integrated pest management. *BioScience* 30: 675–78.

16 MAY, R. M. 1985. Evolution of pesticide resistance. *Nature* 315: 12–13.

17 BARFIELD, C. S., and STIMAC, J. L. 1980. Pest management: An entomological perspective. *BioScience* 30: 683–88.

18 VITOUSEK, Personal communication.

19 U.S. FOREST SERVICE. 1980. An assessment of the forest and range land situation in the United States. U.S. Department of Agriculture Publication. (FS-345; 631pp.)

20 BUSCHBACHER, R. J. 1986. Tropical deforestation and pasture development. *BioScience* 36: 22–28

21 UNITED NATIONS. 1978. *United Nations Conference on Desertification: Roundup, Plan of Action and Resolutions.* New York: United Nations.

22 CURREY, B., and HUGO, G. 1984. *Famine as a geographical phenomenon.* Boston: D. Reidel.

23 SHERIDAN, D. 1981. *Desertification of the United States.* Washington, D. C.: Council on Environmental Quality.

24 MURDOCK, W. M. 1980. *The poverty of nations: The political economy of hunger and population.* Baltimore: Johns Hopkins University Press.

25 JENSEN, N. F. 1978. Limits to growth in world food production. *Science* 201: 317–24.

Vanishing Genetic Resources
ALLEN, R. 1980 *How to save the world. Strategy for world conservation.* Totowa, N.J.: Barnes & Noble.

COUNCIL ON ENVIRONMENTAL QUALITY and THE DEPARTMENT OF STATE. 1982. *The global 2000 report to the president.* Vol. 1.

MEYERS, N. 1979. *The sinking ark: A new look at the problem of disappearing species.* Oxford: Pergamon Press.

CHAPTER 11

1 EHRLICH, P. R.; EHRLICH, A. H.; and HOLDREN, J. P. 1970. *Ecoscience: Population, resources, environment.* San Francisco: W. H. Freeman.

2 WALDBOTT, G. L. 1978. *Health effects of environmental pollutants.* 2nd ed. St. Louis: C. V. Mosby.

3 WARREN, H. V., and DeLAVAULT, R. E. 1967. A geologist looks at pollution: Mineral variety. *Western Mines* 40: 23–32.

4 van KOEVERING, T. E., and SELL, N. J. 1986. *Energy: A conceptual approach.* Englewood Cliffs, N.J.: Prentice Hall.

5 UNIVERSITY OF MAINE AND MAINE DEPARTMENT OF HUMAN SERVICES. 1983. Radon in water and air. *Resource Highlights,* February.

6 HANSON, W. G. 1967. Cesium-137 in Alaskan lichens, caribou, and Eskimos. *Health Physics* 13: 383–89.

7 MacLEOD, G. K. 1981. Some public health lessons from Three Mile Island: A case study in chaos. *Ambio* 10: 18–23.

8 GREENWALD, J. 1986. *Time* 27(19): 39–52.

9 PERRY, J. J. 1980. Oil in the biosphere. In *Introduction to environmental toxicology,* eds. F. E. Guthrie and J. J. Perry, pp. 198–209. New York: Elsevier.

10 OFFICE OF TECHNOLOGICAL ASSESSMENT. 1979. *Pest management strategies in crop protection.* Vol. 1.

11 WHITE, G. F. 1980. Environment. *Science* 209: 183–90.

12 BROWN, A. W. A. 1978. *Ecology of pesticides.* New York: Wiley.

13 CARSON, R. 1962. *Silent Spring.* Boston: Houghton Mifflin.

14 STICKEL, W. H. 1975. Some effects of pollutants in terrestrial ecosystems. In *Ecological research: Effects of heavy metals and organo- halogen compounds*, eds. A. D. McIntyre and C. F. Mills, pp. 25–74. New York: Plenum Press.

15 CLESCERI, L. S. 1980. PCBs in the Hudson River. In *Introduction to environmental toxi- cology*, eds. F. E. Guthrie and J. J. Perry, pp. 227–35. New York: Elsevier.

16 MAIN, J. 1983. Dow vs. the dioxin monster. *Fortune:* May 30: 83–90.

17 CARLSON, E. A. 1983. International sympo- sium on herbicides in the Vietman War: An appraisal. *BioScience* 33: 507–12.

18 GRADY, D. 1983. The dioxin dilemma. *Dis- cover*, May: 78–83.

19 CHANLETT, E. T. 1979. *Environmental protec- tion.* 2nd ed. New York: McGraw-Hill.

20 HAMRICK, M. H.; ANSPAUGH, D. J; and EZELL, G. 1986. *Health.* Columbus, Ohio: Charles E. Merrill.

21 PIER, S. M. 1975. The role of heavy metals in human health. *Teax Reports on Biology and Medicine* 31: 85–106.

22 WOODWELL, G. M., and REDBUCK, A. L. 1967. Effects of chronic gamma radiation on the structure and diversity of an oak-pine for- est. *Ecological Monographs* 37: 53–69.

23 TURCO, R. P.; TOON, O. B.; ACKERMAN, T. P.; POLLACK, J. B.; and SAGAN, C. 1983. Nuclear winter: Global consequences of multiple nu- clear explosions. *Science* 222: 1203–92.

24 EHRLICH, P. R.; HARTE, J.; HARWELL, M. A.; RAVEN, P. H.; SAGAN, C.; WOODWELL, G. M.; AYENSU, E. S.; EHRLICH, A. H.; EISNER, T.; GOULD, S. J.; GROVER, H. D.; HERRERA, R.; MAY, R. M.; MAYR, E.; McKAY, C. P.; MOONEY, H. A.; MYERS, N.; PIMENTAL, D.; and TEAL, J. M. 1983. Long-term biological consequences of nuclear war. *Science* 222: 1293–1300.

25 GROVER, H. D. and HARWELL, M. A. 1985. Biological effects of nuclear war II: Impact on the biosphere. *BioScience*, 35: 576–83.

26 STEPHENS, S. L. and BIRKS, J. W. 1985. After nuclear war: Perturbations in atmospheric chemistry. *BioScience* 35: 557–62.

27 GROVER, H. D., and WHITE, G. F. 1985. To- ward understanding the effects of nuclear war. *BioScience* 35: 552–56.

The Trashing of Low Earth Orbit

DRAGO, V. J.; EDGECOMBE, D. S.; WELLER, A. E. 1972. *An analysis of meteorite impact cas- ualty hazards using current space debris reen- try hazard estimation techniques.* Battelle Technical Memorandum. Columbus, Ohio: Battelle.

COLUMBUS DISPATCH, 1985. *Orbiting junk poses threat to space ships.* April 28.

EDGECOMBE, D. S. 1985. *Orbital debris policy is- sues/Battelle involvement and some personal observations.* Orbital Debris, NASA Confer- ence Publication 2360, pp. 402–9.

FISHER, N. Section Manager, Space Systems and Transportation, Battelle Columbus Laborato- ries. Personal communication.

WOLFE, M. G. 1985. *Space debris: An AIAA position paper.* Orbital Debris, NASA Conference Pub- lication 2360, pp. 365–71.

CHAPTER 12

1 MARSH, W. M., and DOZIER, J. 1981. *Land- scape.* New York: Wiley.

2 NATIONAL PARK SERVICE. 1984. Air re- sources management manual.

3 PITTOCK, A. B.; FRAKES, L. A.; JENSSEN, D.; PETERSON, J. A.; and ZILLMAN, J. W., eds. 1978. *Climatic change and variability: A southern perspective.* (Based on a conference at Monash University, Australia, 7–12 Decem- ber, 1975.) New York: Cambridge University Press.

4 ANTHES, R. A.; CAHIR, J. J.; FRASER, A. B.; and PANOFSKY, H. A. 1981. *The atmosphere.* 3rd ed. Columbus, Ohio: Charles E. Merrill.

5 DETWYLER, T. R., and MARCUS, M. G., eds. 1972. *Urbanization and the environment.* North Scituate, Mass.: Duxbury Press.

6 GATES, D. M. 1972. *Man and his environment: Climate.* New York: Harper & Row.

7 LYNN, D. A. 1976. *Air pollution—Threat and response.* Reading, Mass.: Addison-Wesley.

8 COUNCIL ON ENVIRONMENTAL QUALITY AND THE DEPARTMENT OF STATE. 1980. *The global 2000 report to the President: Entering the twenty-first century.*

9   ZIMMERMAN, M. R. 1985. Pathology in Alaskan mummies. *American Scientist* 73: 20–5.

10 OFFICE OF TECHNOLOGY ASSESSMENT. 1984. Balancing the risks. *Weatherwise* 37: 241–9.

11 CANADIAN DEPARTMENT OF ENVIRONMENT. 1984. *The acid rain story.*

12 LIPPMANN, M., and SCHLESINGER, R. B. 1979. *Chemical contamination in the human environment.* New York: Oxford University Press.

13 U.S. ENVIRONMENTAL PROTECTION AGENCY. 1980. *Acid rain.*

14 CRANDALL, R. W. 1983. *Controlling industrial pollution.* Washington, D.C.: The Brookings Institution.

15 EKDAHL, C. A., and KEELING, C. D. 1973. Atmospheric carbon dioxide and radiocarbon in the natural carbon cycle: 1. Quantitative deductions from records at Mauna Loa Observatory and at the South Pole. In *Carbon and the biosphere.* eds. G. M. Woodwell and E. V. Pecan, pp. 51–85. Brookhaven National Laboratory Symposium No. 24. Oak Ridge, Tenn.: Technical Information Service.

16 RAMPINO, M. R., and SELF, S. 1984. The atmospheric effects of El Chicón. *Scientific American* 250: 48–57.

17 STOKER, H. S., and SEAGER, S. L. 1976. *Environmental chemistry: Air and water pollution.* 2nd ed. Glenview, Ill.: Scott, Foresman.

18 STERN, A. C.; BOUBEL, R. T.; TURNER, D. B.; and FOX, D. L. 1984. *Fundamentals of air pollution.* 2nd ed. Orlando: Academic Press.

19 ANONYMOUS. 1981. How many more lakes have to die? *Canada Today* 12 (2): 1–11.

Acid Rain

THE NATIONAL CLEAN AIR COALITION. Acid rain. In *The Clean Air Act: A briefing book for members of Congress*, Washington, D.C. pp. 105–36.

MASSACHUSETTS DEPARTMENT OF ENVIRONMENTAL QUALITY ENGINEERING, DIVISION OF AIR QUALITY CONTROL. 1984. *Acid rain and related air pollutant damage: A national and international call for action.*

SWEDISH MINISTRY OF AGRICULTURE. 1983. *Acidification: A boundless threat to our environment.*

LOWE, J. 1985. Ruined history. *National Parks*, March/April, pp. 11–13.

PETERSON, R. 1983. The Audubon view: The acid test. *Audubon*, March, p. 4.

WAXMAN, H. A. 1985. Acid rain: We know the costs. We need the cure. *National Parks*, March/April, pp. 14–15.

CHAPTER 13

1   COUNCIL ON ENVIRONMENTAL QUALITY and THE DEPARTMENT OF STATE. 1980. *The global 2000 report to the president: Entering the twenty-first century.* Vol. 2.

2   WATER RESOURCES COUNCIL. 1978. *The nation's water resources, 1975–2000.* Vol. 1.

3   HENDERSON, L. J. 1913. *The fitness of the environment: An inquiry into the biological significance of the properties of matter.* New York: Macmillan.

4   LIKENS, G. E.; BORMANN, F. H.; PIERCE, R. S.; EATON, J. S.; and JOHNSON, N. M. 1977. *The biogeochemistry of a forested ecosystem.* New York: Springer-Verlag.

5   SOLLEY, W. B.; CHASE, E. B.; and MANN, W. B., IV. 1983. *Estimated use of water in the United States in 1980.* U.S. Geological Survey Circular 1001.

6   ALEXANDER, G. 1984. Making do with less. *National Wildlife*, Special Report February/March: 11–13.

7   LEOPOLD, L. B. 1977. A reverence for rivers. *Geology* 5: 429–30.

8   ROBINSON, A. R. 1973. Sediment, our greatest pollutant? In *Focus on environmental geology*, ed. R. W. Tank, pp. 186–92. New York: Oxford University Press.

9   BOTKIN, B. A. 1944. *A treasury of American folklore.* New York: Crown.

10 YORKE, T. H. 1975. Effects of sediment control on sediment transport in the northwest branch, Anacostia River Basin, Montgomery County, Maryland. *Journal of Research* 3: 487–94.

11 COUNCIL ON ENVIRONMENTAL QUALITY. 1979. *Environmental quality.*

12 ANONYMOUS. 1982. *U. S. Geological Survey*

Activities, Fiscal Year 1982. U. S. Geological Survey Circular 875: 90–93.

13 GEISER, K. and WANECK, G. 1983. PCB's and Warren County. Science for the people.

14 WEIR, D., and SCHAPICO, M. 1980. The circle of poison. *The Nation*, November 15.

15 CAREY, J. 1984. Is it safe to drink? *National Wildlife.* Special Report, February/March: 19–21.

16 PYE, U. I., and PATRICK, R. 1983. Ground water contamination in the United States. *Science* 221: 713–718.

17 FOXWORTHY, G. L. 1978. Nassau County, Long Island, New York—Water problems in humid country. In *Nature to be commanded,* eds. G. D. Robinson and A. M. Spieker, pp. 55–68. U.S. Geological Survey Professional Paper 950.

18 PARIZEK, R. R., and MYERS, E. A. 1968. *Recharge of groundwater from renovated sewage effluent by spray irrigation.* Proceedings of the Fourth American Water Resources Conference, pp. 425–43.

19 HEPHER, B., and SCHROEDER, G. L. 1977. Waste water utilization in Israel aquaculture. In *Wastewater renovation and reuse,* ed. F. M. D'Itri, pp. 529–59. New York: Marcel Dekker.

20 ALLEN, G. H., and CARPENTER, R. L. 1977. The cultivation of fish with emphasis on salmonids in municipal wastewater lagoons as an available protein source for human beings. In *Wastewater renovation and reuse,* ed. F. M. D'Itri, pp. 479–528. New York: Marcel Dekker.

21 KASPERSON, R. E. 1977. Water re-use: Need prospect. In *Water re-use and the cities,* eds. R. E. Kasperson and J. X. Kasperson, pp. 3–25. Hanover, N. H.: University Press of New England.

22 COUNCIL ON ENVIRONMENTAL QUALITY. 1981. *Environmental trends.* Washington, D. C.: U.S. Government Printing Office.

23 LEVINSON, M. 1984. Nurseries of life. *National Wildlife.* Special Report, February/March: 18–21.

24 CANFIELD, C. 1985. *In the rainforest.* New York: Alfred A. Knopf.

Irrigating the Desert: A Temporary Eden?
COUNCIL ON ENVIRONMENTAL QUALITY and THE DEPARTMENT OF STATE. 1980. *The global 2000 report to the president.* Vol. 1.

POSTEL, S. 1985. Shocking glimpses of famished drought victims dramatize water's crucial role. *Natural History,* April.

SCHWARZ, J. 1981. Salty solution from the sea: Irrigating the desert with seawater. *Oceans,* July/August.

SHERIDAN, D. 1975. *Underexploited tropical plants with promising economic value.* Washington, D. C.: National Academy of Sciences.

SHERIDAN, D. 1981. Desert blooms—at a price. *Environment,* April.

CHAPTER 14

1 BUTTLI, K., and PERLIN, J. 1980. *A golden thread.* Palo Alto, Calif.: Cheshire Books.

2 DARMSTADTER, J.; LANDSBERG, H. H.; MORTON, H. C.; with CODA, M. J. 1983. *Energy today and tomorrow.* Englewood Cliffs, N.J.; Prentice-Hall.

3 BREW, D. A. 1974. *Environmental impact analysis: The example of the proposed trans-Alaska pipeline.* U.S. Geological Survey Circular 695.

4 U.S. ENVIRONMENTAL PROTECTION AGENCY. 1973. *Processes, procedures and methods to control pollution from mining activities.* EPA-430/9-73-001.

5 COUNCIL ON ENVIRONMENTAL QUALITY. 1978. *Progress in environmental quality.*

6 COMMITTEE ON ENVIRONMENTAL AND PUBLIC PLANNING. 1974. Environmental impact on conversion from gas or oil to coal for fuel. *The Geologist,* Newsletter of the Geological Society of America, supplement to vol. 9, no. 4.

7 DUNCAN, D. C., and SWANSON, V. E. 1965. *Organic-rich shale of the United States and world land areas.* U.S. Geological Survey Circular 523.

8 COMMITTEE ON ENVIRONMENTAL AND PUBLIC PLANNING. 1974. Development of oil shale in the Green River Formation. *The Geologist,* Newsletter of the Geological Society of America, supplement to vol. 9, no. 4.

9 OFFICE OF TECHNOLOGY ASSESSMENT.

1980. *An assessment of oil shale technologies.* OTA-M-118.

10 FINCH, W. I., et al. 1973. Nuclear fuels. In *United States mineral resources,* eds. D. A. Brobst and W. P. Pratt, pp. 455–76. U.S. Geological Survey Professional Paper 820.

11 DUDERSTADT, J. J. 1978. Nuclear power generation. In *Perspectives on energy,* 2nd ed., eds. L. C. Ruedisili and M. W. Firebaugh, pp. 249–73. New York: Oxford University Press.

12 FLAVIN, C. 1984. *Electricity's future: The shift to efficiency and small-scale power.* Worldwatch Paper 61. Washington D.C.: Worldwatch Institute.

13 U.S. DEPARTMENT OF ENERGY. 1980. *Magnetic fusion energy.* DOE/ER-0059.

14 U.S. DEPARTMENT OF ENERGY. 1979. *Environmental development plan for magnetic fusion.* DOE/EDP-0052.

15 U.S. DEPARTMENT OF ENERGY. 1978. *The United States magnetic fusion energy program.* DOE/ET-0072.

16 SMITH, R. L., and SHAW, H. R. 1975. Igneous-related geothermal systems. In *Assessment of geothermal resources of the United States—1975,* eds. D. F. White and D. L. Williams, pp. 58–83. U.S. Geological Survey Circular 726.

17 WHITE, D. F., and WILLIAMS, D. L. 1975. Introduction. In *Assessment of geothermal resources of the United States—1975,* eds. D. F. White and D. L. Williams, pp. 1–4. U.S. Geological Survey Circular 726.

18 MUFFLER, L. J. P. 1973. Geothermal resources. In *United States mineral resources,* eds. D. A. Brobst and W. P. Pratt, pp. 251–61. U.S. Geological Survey Professional Paper 820.

19 WORTHINGTON, J. D. 1975. *Geothermal development.* Status Report—Energy Resources and Technology, a report of the Ad-Hoc Committee on Energy Resources and Technology, Atomic Industrial Form, Incorporated.

20 EATON, W. W. 1978. Solar energy. In *Perspectives on energy,* 2nd ed., eds. L. C. Ruedisili and M. W. Firebaugh, pp. 418–36. New York: Oxford University Press.

21 RALOFF, J. 1978. Catch the sun. *Science News* 113: 16.

22 ALWARD, R.; EISENBART, S.; and VOLKMAN, J. 1979. *Micro-hydro power: Reviewing an old concept.* National Center for Appropriate Technology. U.S. Department of Energy.

23 COMMITTEE ON RESOURCES AND MAN, NATIONAL ACADEMY OF SCIENCES. 1969. *Resources and man.* San Francisco: W. H. Freeman.

24 NOVA SCOTIA DEPARTMENT OF MINES AND ENERGY. 1981. *Wind power.*

25 OFFICE OF TECHNOLOGY ASSESSMENT. 1980. *Energy from biological processes.* OTA-E-124.

26 COUNCIL ON ENVIRONMENTAL QUALITY. 1979. *Environmental quality.*

27 STEINHART, J. S.; HANSON, M. E.; GATES, R. W.; DEWINKEL, C. C.; BRIODY, K.; THORNSJO, M.; and KAMBALA, S. 1978. A low energy scenario for the United States: 1975–2000. In *Perspectives on energy,* 2nd ed., eds. L. C. Ruedisili and M. W. Firebaugh, pp. 553–80. New York: Oxford University Press.

28 FOWLER, J. M. 1978. Energy and the environment. In *Perspectives on energy,* 2nd ed., eds. L. C. Ruedisili and M. W. Firebaugh, pp. 11–28. New York: Oxford University Press.

29 FARALLONES INSTITUTE. 1979. *The integral urban house.* San Francisco, Calif.: Sierra Club Books.

30 LOVINS, A. B. 1979. *Soft energy paths: Towards a durable peace.* New York: Harper & Row.

CHAPTER 15

1 GULBRANDSEN, R. A.; RAIT, N.; DRIES, D. J.; BAEDECKER, P. A.; and CHILDRESS, A. 1978. *Gold, silver, and other resources in the ash of incinerated sewage sludge at Palo Alto, California—A preliminary report.* U. S. Geological Survey Circular 784.

2 McKELVEY, V. E. 1973. Mineral resource estimates and public policy. In *United States mineral resources,* eds. D. A. Brobst and W. P. Pratt, pp. 9–19. U. S. Geological Survey Professional Paper 820.

3 YEEND, W. 1973. Sand and gravel. In *United*

States mineral resources, eds. D. A. Brobst and W. P. Pratt, pp. 561–65. U. S. Geological Survey Professional Paper 820.

4 SMITH, G. I.; JONES, C. L.; CULBERTSON, W. C.; ERICKSON, G. E.; and DYNI, J. R. 1973. Evaporites and brines. In *United States mineral resources,* eds. D. A. Brobst and W. P. Pratt, pp. 197–216. U. S. Geological Survey Professional Paper 820.

5 AWRAMIK, S. A. 1981. The pre-Phanerozoic biosphere—Three billion years of crises and opportunities. In *Biotic crises in ecological and evolutionary time,* ed. M. H. Nitecki, pp. 83–102. New York: Academic Press.

6 MARGULIS, L., and LOVELOCK, J. E. 1974. Biological modulation of the Earth's atmosphere. *Icarus* 21: 471–89.

7 LOWENSTAM, H. A. 1981. Minerals formed by organisms. *Science* 211: 1126–30.

8 BATEMAN, A. M. 1950. *Economic ore deposits.* 2nd ed. New York: Wiley.

9 PARK, C. F., Jr., and MacDIARMID, R. A. 1970. *Ore deposits.* 2nd ed. San Francisco: W. H. Freeman.

10 CORNWALL, H. R. 1973. Nickel. In *United States mineral resources,* eds. D. A. Brobst and W. P. Pratt, pp. 437–42. U. S. Geological Survey Professional Paper 820.

11 VAN, N.; DORR, J.; CRITTENDEN, M. D.; and WORL, R. G. 1973. Manganese. In *United States mineral resources,* eds. D. A. Brobst and W. P. Pratt, pp. 385–99. U. S. Geological Survey Professional Paper 820.

12 SECRETARY OF THE INTERIOR. 1975. *Mining and mineral policy, 1975.*

13 BROBST, D. A.; PRATT, W. P; and McKELVEY, V. E. 1973. *Summary of United States mineral resources.* U. S. Geological Survey Circular 682.

14 ANONYMOUS. 1984. *Yearbook, Fiscal Year 1983.* U. S. Geological Survey.

15 SULLIVAN, P. M.; STANCZYK, M. H.; and SPENDBUE, M. J. 1973. *Resource recovery from raw urban refuse.* U. S. Bureau of Mines Report of Investigations 7760.

16 DAVIS, F. F. 1972. Urban ore. *California Geology,* May 1972: 99–112.

CHAPTER 16

1 ELLIOT, J. 1980. Lessons from Love Canal. *Journal of the American Medical Assoiation* 240: 2033–34, 2040.

2 KUFS, C., and TWEDWELL, C. 1980. Cleaning up hazardous landfills. *Geotimes* 25: 18–19.

3 ALBESON, P. H. 1983. Waste management. *Science* 220: 1003.

4 ESCH, M. 1985. Love Canal waste leaves ghost town. *Santa Barbara News Press.* Jan. 27.

5 MacFADYEN, J. T. 1985. Where will all the garbage go? *The Atlantic* 225, (3): 29–38.

6 GALLEY, J. E. 1968. Economic and industrial potential of geologic basins and reservoir strata. In *Subsurface disposal in geologic basins: A study of reservoir strata,* ed. J. E. Galley, pp. 1–19. American Association of Petroleum Geologists Memoir 10.

7 COUNCIL ON ENVIRONMENTAL QUALITY. 1973. *Environmental quality—1973.* Washington, D.C.: U.S. Government Printing Office.

8 SCHNEIDER, W. J. 1970. *Hydraulic implications of solid-waste disposal.* U.S. Geological Survey Circular 601F.

9 TURK, L. J. 1970. Disposal of solid wastes—Acceptable practice or geological nightmare? In *Environmental geology,* pp. 1–42. Washington, D.C.: American Geological Institute Short Course, American Geological Institute.

10 HUGHES, G. M. 1972. *Hydrologic considerations in the siting and design of landfills.* Environmental Geology Notes, No. 51. Illinois State Geological Survey.

11 BERGSTROM, R. E. 1968. *Disposal of wastes: Scientific and administrative considerations.* Environmental Geology Notes, No. 20, Illinois State Geological Survey.

12 CARTWRIGHT, K., and SHERMAN, F. B. 1969. *Evaluating sanitary landfill sites in Illinois.* Environmental Geology Notes, No. 27. Illinois State Geological Survey.

13 WALKER, W. H. 1974. Monitoring toxic chemical pollution from land disposal sites in humid regions. *Ground Water* 12: 213–18.

14 ENVIRONMENTAL PROTECTION AGENCY.

1980. *Everybody's problem: Hazardous waste.* SW-826.

15 MAGNUSON, E. 1980. The poisoning of America. *Time* 116(12): 58–69.

16 HUDDLESTON, R. L. 1979. Solid-waste disposal: Landfarming. *Chemical Engineering* 86(5): 119–124.

17 McKENZIE, G. D., and PETTYJOHN, W. A. 1975. Subsurface waste management. In *Man and his physical environment,* eds. G. D. McKenzie and R. O. Utgard, pp. 150–56. Minneapolis: Burgess Publishing.

18 PIPER, A. M. 1970. *Disposal of liquid wastes by injection underground: Neither myth nor millennium.* U.S. Geological Survey Circular 631.

19 COMMITTEE OF GEOLOGICAL SCIENCES. 1972. *The earth and human affairs.* San Francisco: Canfield Press.

20 CECELIA, C. 1985. *The Buried Threat.* California Senate Office of Research. No. 115–5.

21 OFFICE OF INDUSTRY RELATIONS. 1974. *The nuclear industry, 1974.* Washington, D.C.: U.S. Government Printing Office.

22 BREDEHOEFT, J. D.; ENGLAND, A. W.; STEWART, D. B.; TRASK, J. J.; and WINOGRAD, I. J. 1978. *Geologic disposal of high-level radioactive wastes—Earth science perspectives.* U.S. Geological Survey Circular 779.

23 MICKLIN, P. P. 1974. Environmental hazards of nuclear wastes. *Science and Public Affairs* 30: 36–42.

24 HUNT, C. B. 1983. How safe are nuclear waste sites? *Geotimes* 28(7): 21–22.

25 HEIKEN, G. 1979. Pyroclastic flow deposits. *American Scientist* 67: 564–571.

26 HAMMON, R. P. 1979. Nuclear wastes and public acceptance. *American Scientist:* 146–150.

27 COUNCIL ON ENVIRONMENTAL QUALITY. 1970. *Ocean dumping: A national policy.* Washington, D.C.: U.S. Government Printing Office.

Hazaradous Waste in My Trashcan?

CENTRAL STATES EDUCATION CENTER. 1984. Hazardous waste: An introduction. Champaign, Ill.

MISSOURI DEPARTMENT OF NATURAL RESOURCES. 1984. Environmental education program: Hazardous waste curriculum.

National Geographic 167 (3): 318–51.

SASSON, T. Ohio Environmental Protection Agency. Personal communication.

U.S. OFFICE OF TECHNOLOGY ASSESSMENT. 1983. Technologies and management strategies for hazardous waste management.

CHAPTER 17

1 WILLIAMS, R. S. Jr., and MOORE, J. G. 1973. Iceland chills a lava flow. *Geotimes* 18: 14–18.

2 CORNELL, J., ed. 1974. *It happened last year—Earth events—1973.* New York: Macmillan.

3 HAMMOND, P. E. 1980. Mt. St. Helens blasts 400 meters off its peak. *Geotimes* 25: 14–15.

4 WHITE, G. F., and HAAS, J. E. 1975. *Assessment of research on natural hazards.* Cambridge, Mass.: The MIT Press.

5 LEGGETT, R. F. 1973. *Cities and geology.* New York: McGraw-Hill.

6 PETERSON, D. W. 1986. Volcanoes—Tectonic setting and impact on society. In *Studies in Geophysics: Active tectonics,* pp. 231–46. Washington, D. C.: National Academy Press.

7 CROWE, B. W. 1986. Volcanic hazard assessment for disposal of high-level radioactive waste. In *Studies in geophysics: Active tectonics,* pp. 247–60. Washington, D. C.: National Academy Press.

8 KATES, R. W., and PIJAWKA, D. 1977. Reconstruction following disaster. In *From rubble to monument: The pace of reconstruction,* eds. J. E. Haas, R. W. Kates, and M. J. Bowden. Cambridge, Mass.: The MIT Press.

9 COSTA, J. E., and BAKER, V. R. 1981. *Surficial geology.* New York: Wiley.

10 DOLAN, R.; HOWARD, A.; and GALLENSON, A. 1974. Man's impact on the Colorado River and the Grand Canyon. *American Scientist,* 62: 392–401.

11 LAVENDER, D. 1984. Great news from the Grand Canyon. *Arizona Highways,* January: 33–38.

12 U.S. CONGRESS, HOUSE; 1973. *Stream channelization: What federally financed draglines and bulldozers do to our nation's streams.* House Report 93-530.

13 EMERSON, J. W. 1971. Channelization: A case study. *Science* 173: 325–26.

14 ALBINI, F. A. 1984. Wildland Fires. *American Scientist* 72: 590–597.

15 SIEGEL, B. 1983. El Niño: The world turns topsy-turvy: *Los Angeles Times,* Aug. 17.

16 CANBY, T. Y. 1984. El Niño's ill winds. *National Geographic* 165: 144–181.

17 DENNIS, R. E. 1984. A revised assessment of worldwide economic impacts, 1982–1984 El Niño/Southern Oscillation Event. *EOS,* Transactions of the American Geophysical Union 65(45): 910.

18 MAGNUSON, E. 1985. A noise like thunder. *Time* 126(13): 35–43.

19 RUSSELL, G. 1985. Colombia's mortal agony. *Time* 126(21): 46–52.

CHAPTER 18

1 KNOWLES, R. L. 1974. *Energy and form.* Cambridge, Mass.: The MIT Press.

2 McHARG, I. L. 1971. *Design with nature.* Garden City, N.Y.: Doubleday.

3 HAYES, W. C., and VINEYARD, J. D. 1969. *Environmental geology in town and country.* Missouri Geological Survey and Water Resources, Educational Series No. 2.

4 NORTH CAROLINA COASTAL RESOURCES COMMISSION. 1975. *State guidelines for local planning in the coastal area under the Coastal Area Management Act of 1974.* Raleigh, N. C.

5 WHYTE, W. H. 1968. *The last landscape.* Garden City, N.Y.: Doubleday.

6 FLAWN, P. T. 1970. *Environmental geology.* New York: Harper & Row.

7 ZUBE, E. H. 1973. Scenery as a natural resource. *Landscape Architecture* 63: 126–32.

8 LINTON, D. L. 1968. The assessment of scenery as a natural resource. *Scottish Geographical Magazine* 84: 219–38.

9 COUNCIL ON ENVIRONMENTAL QUALITY. 1979. *Environmental quality.*

10 BREW, D. A. 1974. *Environmental impact analysis: The example of the proposed Trans-Alaska Pipeline.* U.S. Geological Survey Circular 695.

11 STERLING, C. 1971. The Aswan disaster. *National Parks and Conservation Magazine* 45: 10–13.

12 NATIONAL RESEARCH COUNCIL, COMMITTEE ON GEOLOGICAL SCIENCES. 1972. *The Earth and human affairs.* San Francisco: Canfield Press.

13 BRICE, J. 1971. *Measurements of lateral erosion at proposed river crossing sites of the Alaskan Pipeline.* U.S. Geological Survey, Water Resources Division, Alaska District.

14 NATIONAL PARK SERVICE. 1974. *Cape Hatteras Shoreline Erosion Policy Statement.* U.S. Department of Interior.

15 NATIONAL RESEARCH COUNCIL. 1972. *The earth and human affairs.* San Francisco: Canfield Press.

16 NATIONAL PARK SERVICE. 1984. *General management plan, development concept plan, and amended environmental assessment, Cape Hatteras National Seashore.*

17 COATS, D. R., ed. 1973. *Coastal geomorphology.* Binghamton, N. Y.: Publications in Geomorphology, State University of New York.

18 WILSHIRE, H. G., and NAKATA, J. K. 1976. Off-road vehicle effects on California's Mojave Desert. *California Geology* 29: 123–32.

19 WILSHIRE, H. G., et al. 1977. *Impacts and management of off-road vehicles.* Geological Society of America. Report to the Committee on Environment and Public Policy.

20 STEINER, F. 1983. Regional planning: Historic and contemporary examples. *Landscape Planning* 10: 297–315.

21 U.S. FOREST SERVICE. 1978. *RARE II. Draft environmental statement roadless area review and evaluation.*

22 MEADOWS, D. H.; MEADOWS, D. L.; RANDERS, J.; and BEHRENS, W. W., III. 1972. *The limits to growth: A report for the Club of Rome's Project on the Predicament of Mankind.* New York: Universe Books (Potomac Associates).

23 COUNCIL ON ENVIRONMENTAL QUALITY AND THE DEPARTMENT OF STATE. 1980. *The* *global 2000 report to the President: Entering the twenty- first century.*

CHAPTER 19

1 POLAND, J. F., and DAVIS, G. H. 1969. Land subsidence due to withdrawal of fluids. In *Reviews in engineering geology,* eds. D. J. Varnes and G. Kiersch, pp. 187–269. Boulder, Colo.: The Geological Society of America.

2 COUNCIL ON ENVIRONMENTAL QUALITY AND THE DEPARTMENT OF STATE. 1980. *The global 2000 report to the President: Entering the twenty-first century.*

3 WORLD BANK. 1984. *World development report.* Oxford: Oxford University Press.

4 MUMFORD, L. 1972. The natural history of urbanization. In *The ecology of man: An ecosystem approach,* ed. R. L. Smith, pp. 140–52. New York: Harper & Row.

5 LEIBBRAND, K. 1970. *Transportation and town planning.* (Translated by N. Seymer.) Cambridge, Mass.: The MIT Press.

6 HUNT, C. B. 1974. *Natural regions of the United States and Canada.* San Francisco: W. H. Freeman.

7 REPS, J. W. 1965. *The making of urban America.* 2nd ed. Princeton, N.J.: Princeton University Press.

8 McLAUGHLIN, C. C., ed. 1977. *The papers of Frederick Law Olmsted.* Vol. 1: *The formative years 1822–1852.* Baltimore: Johns Hopkins University Press.

9 SPIRN, A. W. 1984. *The granite garden: Urban nature and human design.* New York: Basic Books.

10 FORD, A. B., and BIALIK, O. 1980. Air pollution and urban factors in relation to cancer mortality. *Archives of Environmental Health* 35: 350–59.

11 DETWYLER, T. R., and MARCUS, M. G., eds. 1972. *Urbanization and the environment.* North Scituate, Mass.: Duxbury Press.

12 BUTTI, K., and PERLIN, J. 1980. *The golden thread: 2500 years of solar architecture and technology.* New York: Cheshire.

13 FARALLONES INSTITUTE. 1979. *The integral urban house: Self-reliant living in the city.* San Francisco: Sierra Club Books.

14 NADEL, I. B.; OBERLANDER, C. H.; and BOHM, L. R. 1977. *Trees in the city.* New York: Pergamon Press.

15 BURTON, J. A. 1977. *Worlds apart: Nature in the city.* Garden City, N.Y.: Doubleday.

16 BOTKIN, B. A., ed. 1954. *Sidewalks of America.* (Reprinted in 1976.) Westwood, Conn.: Greenwood Press.

Paving the Good Earth: The Urbanization of America's Farmlands

BROWN, L. R. 1978. *The worldwide loss of cropland.* Worldwatch Paper No. 24. Washington, D.C., October 1978.

COLE, J. N. 1982. We're losing our precious farmland! *National Wildlife,* August/September 1982.

FIELDS, S. F. 1980. Where have all the farmlands gone? Washington, D.C.: National Agricultural Lands Study.

COUNCIL ON ENVIRONMENTAL QUALITY and THE DEPARTMENT OF STATE. 1980. *The global 2000 report to the President: Entering the twenty-first century.*

SHEETS, K. R. 1981. Is the U.S. paving over too much farmland? *U.S. News and World Report,* February 2.

CHAPTER 20

1 HOFMANN, R., and OTTE, K.-C. 1977. *Utilization of vicuñas in Peru.* German Agency for Technical Cooperation, Ltd. Bruchwiesenweg, Germany: TZ-Verlagesgesellschaft MbH Pub.

2 HARDIN, G. 1968. The tragedy of the commons. *Science* 162: 1243–48.

3 CLARK, C. W. 1973. The economics of overexploitation. *Science* 181: 630–34.

4 CAIRNS, J., Jr. 1980. Estimating hazard. *BioScience* 20: 101–7.

5 SCHWING, R. C. 1979. Longevity and benefits and costs of reducing various risks. *Technological Forecasting and Social Change* 13: 333–45.

6 GORI, G. B. 1980. The regulation of carcinogenic hazards. *Science* 208: 256–61.

7 OSTRO, B. D. 1980. Air pollution, public health, and inflation. *Environmental Health Perspectives* 345: 185–89.

8 LITTON, R. B. 1973. Aesthetic dimensions of the landscape. In *Natural environments* ed. J. V. Kantilla. Baltimore: Johns Hopkins University Press.

9 LINTON, D. L. 1968. The assessment of scenery as a natural resource. *Scottish Geographical Magazine* 84: 219–238.

10 MELHORN, W. N.; KELLER, E. A.; and McBANE, R. A. 1975. *Landscape aesthetics numerically defined (land system): Application to fluvial environments.* Water Resources Research Center Technical Report No. 37; West Lafayette, Ind.: Purdue University.

11 CLARK, C. W. 1981. Economics of fishery management. In *Renewable resource management: Lecture notes in biomathematics,* eds. T. L. Vincent and J. M. Skowronski, pp. 95–111. New York: Springer-Verlag.

12 BAUMOL, W. J., and OATES, W. E. 1979. *Economics, environmental policy, and the quality of life.* Englewood Cliffs, N.J.: Prentice-Hall.

CHAPTER 21

1 MONO LAKE COMMITTEE. 1985. *Mono Lake: Endangered oasis.* Lee Vining, California, 45 pp.

2 LANDAN, N. J., and RAGINGOLD, P. D. 1971. *The environmental law handbook.* New York: Ballentine.

3 COHEN, B. S. 1970. The Constitution, the Public Trust Doctrine and the environment. *Utah Law Review* 388.

4 16 U.S.C. Section 475 (1970).

5 42 U.S.C.A. Section 4321.

6 42 U.S.C. Section 1857 et. seq.

7 *NRDC* v. *Costle,* 12 ERC 1833.

8 EPA Proposal to set a recommended contaminant level for fluoride in drinking water under the Safe Drinking Water Act, 50 FR 20164, 14 May 1985.

9 *Calvert Cliffs' Coordinating Committee* v. *AEC,* 449 F.2d 1109.

10 YANNACONE, V. J., Jr.; COHEN, B. S.; and DAVIDSON, S. G. *Environmental rights and remedies.* Rochester, N.Y.: Lawyers Co-operative Pub. 1972, pp. 39–46.

11 *NRDC* v. *EPA,* 489 F. 2d 390.

12 *Sierra Club* v. *EPA,* 19 ERC 1897.

13 *Alabama Power* v. *Sierra,* 21 ERC 1336.

14 *Citizen suits: An analysis of enforcement actions under EPA administered statutes,* Environmental Law Institute, 1984.

15 *Chemical Manufacturers Assoc.* v. *NRDC,* 22 ERC 1305.

16 *Sierra Club* v. *Ruckelshaus,* 344 F. Supp 253.

17 *Just* v. *Marinette County,* 4 ERC 1841.

Glossary

Acid rain   Rain made artificially acid by pollutants, particularly oxides of sulfur and nitrogen. (Natural rainwater is slightly acid owing to the effect of carbon dioxide dissolved in the water.)

Active solar energy systems   Direct use of solar energy which requires mechanical power; usually consists of pumps and other machinery to circulate air, water, or other fluids from solar collectors to a heat sink where the heat may be stored.

Adaptive radiation   The process that occurs when a species enters a new habitat that has unoccupied niches and evolves into a group of new species, each adapted to one of these niches.

Aerobic   Characterized by the presence of free oxygen.

Age dependency ratio   The ratio of dependent-age people (those unable to work) to working-age people. It is customary to define working-age people as those aged 15 to 65.

Age structure (of a population)   Structure of a population divided into groups by age. Sometimes the groups represent the actual number of each age in the population; sometimes the group represents the percentage or proportion of the population of each age.

Anaerobic   Characterized by the absence of free oxygen.

Aquaculture   Production of food from aquatic habitats.

Atmosphere   Layer of gases surrounding Earth.

Atmospheric inversion   A condition in which warmer air is found above cooler air, restricting air circulation; often associated in urban areas with a pollution event.

Autotroph   An organism that produces its own food from inorganic compounds and a source of energy. There are photoautotrophs (photosynthetic plants) and chemical autotrophs.

Barrier island   Island separated from the mainland by a salt marsh. It generally consists of a multiple system of beach ridges and is separated from other barrier islands by inlets that allow the exchange of seawater with lagoon water.

Biogeochemical cycle   The cycling of a chemical element through the biosphere; its pathways, storage locations, and chemical forms in

657

the atmosphere, oceans, sediments, and lithosphere.

Biochemical oxygen demand (BOD) A measure of the amount of oxygen necessary to decompose organic materials in a unit volume of water. As the amount of organic waste in water increases, more oxygen is used, resulting in a higher BOD.

Biogeography The geography of living things; the study of the distribution of living things and their history, origin, migrations, and the causes of these.

Biomagnification Also called *biological concentration*. The tendency for some substances to concentrate with each trophic level. Organisms preferentially store certain chemicals and excrete others. When this occurs consistently among organisms, the stored chemicals increase as a percentage of the body weight as the material is transferred along a food chain or trophic level. For example, the concentration of DDT is greater in the herbivores than in plants and greater in plants than in the nonliving environment.

Biomass The amount of living material; or the amount of organic material contained in living organisms, both as live and dead material, as in the leaves (live) and stemwood (dead) of trees.

Biome A kind of ecosystem. The rain forest is an example of a biome; rain forests occur in many parts of the world, but are not all connected with each other.

Biosphere That part of a planet where life exists. On Earth it extends from the depths of the oceans to the summit of mountains, but most life exists within a few meters of the surface.

Biota A general term for all the organisms of all species living in an area or region up to and including the biosphere, as in "the biota of the Mojave Desert" or "the biota in that aquarium."

Biotic province A region inhabited by organisms sharing a related ancestry, bound by barriers that prevent their spread and the immigration of foreign species.

Birth rate The rate at which births occur in a population, measured either as the number of individuals born per unit of time or the percentage of births per unit of time compared to the total population.

Body burden The amount of concentration of a toxic chemical, especially radionuclides, in an individual.

Capillary action The rise of water along narrow passages, facilitated and caused by surface tension.

Carcinogen Any material that is known to produce cancer in humans or other animals.

Carrying capacity The maximum population size that can exist in a habitat or ecosystem without detrimental effects to either that population or to the habitat or ecosystem.

Chaparral A dense scrubland found in areas with Mediterranean climate (a long warm dry season and a cooler rainy season).

Chemosynthesis Synthesis of organic compounds by energy derived from chemical reactions.

Clay May refer to a mineral family or to a very fine-grained sediment. It is associated with many environmental problems, such as shrinking and swelling of soils and sediment pollution.

Climate The representative or characteristic conditions of the atmosphere at particular places on Earth. *Climate* is the average or expected conditions over long periods; *weather* is the particular conditions at one time in one place.

Climax stage (of ecological succession) The final stage of ecological succession and therefore an ecological community that continues to reproduce itself over time; or a stage in ecological succession during which an ecological community achieves the greatest biomass or diversity. (The first definition is the classical definition.)

Closed-canopy forest Forests in which the leaves of adjacent trees overlap or touch, so that the trees form essentially continuous shade.

Cohort All the individuals in a population born during the same time period. Thus, all the people born during the year 1980 represent the world human cohort for that year.

Commensalism A relationship between two kinds of organisms in which one benefits from the relationship and the other is neither helped nor hurt.

Community, ecological A group of populations of different species living in the same local area and interacting with one another. A *community* is the living portion of an ecosystem.

Competition The situation that exists when different individuals, populations, or species both compete for the same resource(s), and the presence of one has a detrimental effect on the other. Sheep and cows eating grass in the same field are competitors.

Competitive exclusion principle The idea that two populations of different species with exactly the same requirements cannot persist indefinitely in the same habitat—one will always win out and the other will go extinct. Which one wins depends on the exact environmental conditions. Referred to as a "principle," the idea has some basis in observation and experimentation.

Cone of depression A cone-shaped depression in the water table caused by withdrawal of water at rates greater than the rates at which the water can be replenished by natural groundwater flow.

Contamination Presence of undesirable material that makes something unfit for a particular use.

Continental drift The movement of continents in response to sea-floor spreading. The most recent episode of continental drift supposedly started about 200 million years ago with the breakup of the supercontinent Pangaea.

Continental shelf Relatively shallow ocean area between the shoreline and the continental slope that extends to approximately a 600–ft water depth surrounding a continent.

Convection The transfer of heat involving the movement of particles; for example, the boiling of water in which hot water rises to the surface and displaces cooler water, which moves toward the bottom.

Convergent evolution See *Evolution, convergent.*

Convergent plate boundary Boundary between two lithospheric plates in which one plate descends below the other (subduction).

Death rate The rate at which deaths occur in a population, measured either as the number of individuals dying per unit time, or the percentage of a population dying per unit time.

Decomposer An organism that obtains its energy and nutritional requirements by feeding on dead organisms; or, a feeder on dead organisms.

Demographic transition The pattern of change in birth and death rates as a country is transformed from undeveloped to developed. There are three stages: (1) in an undeveloped country, birth and death rates are high, and the growth rate low; (2) the death rate decreases, but the birth rate remains high, and the growth rate is high; (3) the birth rate drops toward the death rate, and the growth rate therefore also decreases.

Demography The study of populations, especially their patterns in space and time.

Denitrification The conversion of nitrate to molecular nitrogen by the action of bacteria—an important step in the nitrogen cycle.

Density-dependent population effects Factors whose effects on a population change with population density. The term is usually restricted to apply to population growth, reproduction, and mortality. For example, during a famine the mortality rate increases. In this case the food supply can be said to have a density-dependent population effect.

Density-independent population effects Changes in the size of a population due to factors that are independent of the population size. For example, certain climatic factors, which are not affected by the size of a specific population, can affect the entire population. A storm which will knock down all trees in a forest, no matter how few or how many there are, is a density-independent population effect.

Desertification The process of creating a desert where there was not one before. Farming in marginal grasslands, which destroys the soil and prevents the future recovery of natural vegetation, would be an example of desertification.

Divergent evolution Change that occurs when a population is separated, usually by geographic barriers; the separated subpopulations evolve separately into new species but retain some common characteristics.

Divergent plate boundary Boundary between lithospheric plates characterized by the production of new lithosphere. Found along oceanic ridges.

Dominant species Generally, the species that are most abundant in an area, ecological community, or ecosystem.

Dose dependency Dependence upon the dose or concentration of a substance for its effects on a particular organism.

Drainage basin The area that contributes surface water to a particular stream network.

Ecological gradient A change in the relative abundance of a species or group of species along a line or over an area.

Ecological succession The process of the development of an ecological community or ecosystem, usually viewed as a series of stages: early, middle, late, mature (or climax), and sometimes post-climax. Primary succession is an original establishment; secondary succession is a reestablishment.

Ecology The science of the study of the relationships between living things and their environment.

Ecosystem An ecological community and its local nonliving environment.

Efficiency The ratio of output to input. With machines, usually the ratio of work or power produced to the energy or power used to operate or fuel them. With living things, efficiency may be defined as either the useful work done or the energy stored in a useful form compared with the energy taken in.

Effluent Any material that flows outward from something. Examples include waste water from hydroelectric plants and water discharged into streams from waste-disposal sites.

Effluent stream Type of stream where flow is maintained during the dry season by groundwater seepage into the channel.

Electromagnetic spectrum All the possible wavelengths of electromagnetic energy, considered as a continuous range. The spectrum includes long wavelength (used in radio transmission), infrared, visible, ultraviolet, X-rays, and gamma rays.

Endemic Referring to all of the factors confined to a given region, such as an island or a country. The whooping crane is endemic to North America.

Energy An abstract concept referring to the ability or capacity to do work.

Entropy A measure in a system of the amount of energy that is unavailable for useful work. As the disorder of a system increases, the entropy in a system also increases.

Environment All of the factors (living and nonliving) that actually affect an individual organism or population at any point in the life cycle. *Environment* is also sometimes used to denote a certain set of circumstances surrounding a particular occurrence (environments of deposition, for example).

Environmental ethics A school, or theory, in philosophy that deals with the ethical value of the environment, including especially the rights of nonhuman objects and systems in the environment; for example, trees and ecosystems.

Environmental geology The application of geologic information to environmental problems.

Environmental impact The effects of some action on the environment, particularly by human beings.

Environmental impact statement A written statement that assesses and explores possible impacts, associated with a particular project, that may affect the human environment. The statement is required in the U.S. by the National Environmental Policy Act of 1969.

Environmentalism A social, political, and ethical movement concerned with protecting the environment and using its resources wisely.

Environmental law A field of law concerning the conservation and use of natural resources and the control of pollution.

Equilibrium A point of rest. A system that does not tend to undergo any change of its own accord, but remains in a single, fixed condition, is said to be in *equilibrium*. Compare with *steady state*.

Eukaryote Organism whose cells have nuclei and certain other characteristics that separate it from the *prokaryotes*. The eukaryotes include flowering plants, animals, and many single-celled organisms.

Eutrophic Referring to bodies of water having an abundance of the chemical elements required for life.

Evolution, convergent Evolution in which unrelated, isolated kinds of organisms evolve under similar environments to have similar adaptations, as in their morphology and physiology. For example, cactus in the New World and Euphorbia in Africa both have green stems and reduced leaves, which are adaptations to desert climate.

Exotic species Species introduced into a new area by human action.

Exponential growth Growth in which the rate of increase is a constant percentage of the current size. Also called *geometric growth*. The graph of exponential growth is sometimes referred to as the J-curve.

Extinction Disappearance of a life form from existence; usually applied to a species.

Fission The splitting of an atom into smaller fragments with the release of energy.

Floodplain Flat topography adjacent to a stream in a river valley that has been produced by the combination of overbank flow and lateral migration of meander bends.

Food chain The chain of who eats whom, beginning with autotrophs.

Food web A network of who feeds on whom or a diagram showing who feeds on whom.

Force A push or pull that affects motion.

Fusion, nuclear Combining of light elements to form heavier elements with the release of energy.

Genetic drift Random changes in the gene complex of a population due to chance preservation or extinction of particular genes.

Geochemical cycle The pathways of chemical elements in geological processes, including the chemistry of the lithosphere, atmosphere, and hydrosphere.

Geologic cycle The formation and destruction of earth materials and the processes responsible for these events. The geologic cycle includes the following subcycles: *hydrologic*, *tectonic*, *rock*, and *geochemical*.

Geometric growth See *Exponential growth*.

Geothermal energy The useful conversion of natural heat from the interior of Earth.

Gravel Unconsolidated, generally rounded fragments of rocks and minerals greater than 2 mm in diameter.

Gross production (biology) Production before respiration losses are subtracted.

Groundwater Water found beneath Earth's surface within the zone of saturation.

Growth rate The net increase in some factor per unit time. In ecology, the growth rate of a population is sometimes measured as the increase in numbers of individuals or biomass per unit time, and sometimes as a percentage increase in numbers or biomass per unit time.

Habitat (a) The place where an organism, population, or species lives or can live; (b) the place and its specific environmental characteristics where an organism, population, or species lives or can live.

Half-life The time required for half of a substance to disappear; the average time required for one half of a radioisotope to be transformed to some other isotope; the time required for one-half of a toxic chemical to be converted to some other forms.

Heat energy Energy of the random motion of atoms and molecules.

Heterotroph An organism that feeds on other organisms.

Hydrologic cycle Circulation of water from the oceans to the atmosphere and back to the oceans by way of evaporation, runoff from streams and rivers, and groundwater flow.

Hydrology   The study of surface and subsurface water.

Igneous rocks   Rocks formed from the solidification of magma. They are *extrusive* if they crystallize on the surface of Earth and *intrusive* if they crystallize beneath the surface.

Influent stream   Type of stream that is everywhere above the groundwater table and flows in direct response to precipitation. Water from the channel moves down to the water table, forming a recharge mound.

Integrated pest management (IPM)   The coordinated use of several techniques of pest control done in an ecologically and economically sound manner to achieve a stable crop production. A goal of IPM is to maintain pest damage below an economically significant level while minimizing hazards to people, other living things, and the abiotic environment.

Island arc   A curved group of volcanic islands associated with a deep-oceanic trench and subduction zone (convergent plate boundary).

Kinetic energy   The energy of motion. For example, the energy in a moving car due to the mass of the car traveling at a particular velocity.

Land ethic   A set of ethical principles that affirm the right of all resources, including plants, animals, and earth materials, to continued existence and, at least in some locations, to continued existence in a natural state.

Land-use planning   Complex process involving development of a land-use plan to include a statement of land-use issues, goals, and objectives; a summary of data collection and analysis; a land-classification map; and a report that describes and indicates appropriate development in areas of special environmental concern.

Law of the Minimum (Liebeg's Law of the Minimum)   The concept that the growth or survival of a population is directly related to the life requirement that is in least supply and not to a combination of factors.

LD-50   The lethal dose for 50 percent of a population. The dose of a toxin which causes death in 50 percent of a population or which can be expected on the average to cause death in 50 percent of the population.

Liebeg's Law of the Minimum   See *Law of the Minimum.*

Life expectancy   The estimated average number of years (or other time period used as a measure) an individual of a specific age can expect to live.

Lithosphere   Outer layer of Earth, approximately 100 km thick, of which the plates that contain the ocean basins and the continents are composed.

Littoral drift   Movement caused by wave motion in nearshore and beach environments.

Logistic equation   The equation that results in a logistic growth curve, i.e., the growth rate $dN/dt = rN[(K - N)/N]$, where r is the intrinsic rate of increase, K is the carrying capacity, and N is the population size.

Logistic growth   The S-shaped growth curve that is generated by the logistic growth equation. In the logistic, a small population grows rapidly, but the growth rate slows down, and the population eventually reaches a constant size.

Macronutrients   Chemical elements required in large amounts by all forms of life.

Magma   A naturally occurring silica melt, a good deal of which is in a liquid state.

Mariculture   Production of food from marine habitats.

Maximum sustainable yield (MSY)   The maximum usable production of a biological resource that can be obtained in a specified time period. The MSY level is the population size that results in maximum sustainable yield.

Microclimate   The climate of a very small, local area. For example, the climate under a tree, near the ground within a forest, or near the surface of streets in a city.

Micronutrients   Chemical elements required in very small amounts by at least some forms of life. Boron, copper, and molybdenum are examples of micronutrients.

Mineral   Naturally occurring inorganic material with a definite internal structure and physical and chemical properties that vary within prescribed limits.

Mutualism   See *symbiosis*.

Net production (biology)   The production that remains after utilization. In a population, net production is sometimes measured as the net change in the numbers of individuals. It is also measured as the net change in biomass or in stored energy. In terms of energy, it is equal to the gross production minus the energy used in respiration.

Niche   (1) The "profession," or role, of an organism or species; or (2) all of the environmental conditions under which the individual or species can persist. The *fundamental niche* is all the conditions under which a species can persist in the absence of competition; the *realized niche* is the set of conditions as they occur in the real world with competitors.

Nonrenewable resource   A resource that is cycled so slowly by natural Earth processes that once used, it is essentially not going to be made available in any useful time framework.

Oligotrophic   Referring to bodies of waters having a low concentration of the chemical elements required for life.

Open woodlands   Areas in which trees are a dominant vegetation form, but the leaves of adjacent trees generally do not touch or overlap, so that there are gaps in the canopy. Typically, grasses or shrubs grow in these gaps.

Optimum sustainable population (OSP)   The population level that results in an optimum sustainable yield; or the population level that is in some way "best" for that population, its ecological community, its ecosystem, or the biosphere.

Optimum sustainable yield (OSY)   The largest yield of a renewable resource achievable over a long time period without decreasing the ability of the population or its environment to support the continuation of this level of yield.

Organic compound   A compound of carbon; originally used to refer to the compounds found in and formed by living things.

Passive solar energy system   Direct use of solar energy through architectural design to enhance or take advantage of natural changes in solar energy that occur throughout the year without requiring mechanical power.

Pebble   A rock fragment between 4 and 64 mm in diameter.

Pedology   The study of soils.

Permafrost   Permanently frozen ground.

Photosynthesis   Synthesis of sugars from carbon dioxide and water by living organisms using light as energy. Oxygen is given off as a byproduct.

Physiographic province   A region characterized by a particular assemblage of landforms, climate, and geomorphic history.

Pioneer species   Species found in early stages of succession.

Placer deposit   A type of ore deposit found in material transported and deposited by agents such as running water, ice, or wind; for example, gold and diamonds found in stream deposits.

Plate tectonics   A model of global tectonics which suggests that the outer layer of Earth, known as the *lithosphere*, is composed of several large plates that move relative to one another. Continents and ocean basins are passive riders on these plates.

Pollutant   In most general terms, any factor that has a harmful effect on living things or their environment.

Pollution   The process by which something becomes impure, defiled, dirty, or otherwise unclean.

Pool (geology)   Common bed form produced by scour in meandering and straight channels.

Population   A group of individuals of the same species living in the same area or interbreeding and sharing genetic information.

Population dynamics   The study of changes in population sizes and the causes of these changes.

Population regulation   See *Density-dependent population effects* and *Density-independent population effects*.

Potential energy   Energy that is stored. Examples include the gravitational energy of water behind a dam; chemical energy in coal, fuel oil, and gasoline; and nuclear energy (in the forces that hold atoms together).

Power   The time rate of doing work.

Primary treatment (of waste water) Removal of large particles and organic materials from waste water through screening.

Production, ecological The amount of increase in organic matter, usually measured per unit area of land surface or unit volume of water, as in grams per square meter (g/m^2). Production is divided into *primary* (that of autotrophs) and *secondary* (that of heterotrophs). It is also divided into *net* (that which remains stored after use) and *gross* (that added before any use).

Production, primary The production by autotrophs.

Production, secondary The production by heterotrophs.

Productivity, ecological The *rate* of production; that is, the amount of increase in organic matter per unit time (for example, grams per meter squared *per year*). See *production, ecological*.

Prokaryote A kind of organism that lacks a true cell nucleus and has other cellular characteristics that distinguish it from the *eukaryotes*. Bacteria and blue-green algae are prokaryotes.

Protocooperation A symbiotic relationship that is beneficial, but not obligatory, to both species.

Radioactive waste Type of waste produced in the nuclear fuel cycle; generally classified as high-level or low-level.

Radioisotope Any isotope that is radioactive; examples are uranium-235 or carbon-14.

Renewable resource A resource such as timber, water, or air that is naturally recycled or recycled by artificial processes within a time framework useful for people.

Replacement level fertility Fertility rate required for the population to remain a constant size.

Reserves Known and identified deposits of earth materials from which useful materials can be extracted profitably with existing technology and under present economic and legal conditions.

Resources Reserves plus other deposits of useful earth materials that may eventually become available.

Respiration The complex series of chemical reactions in organisms that makes energy available for use. Water, carbon dioxide, and energy are the products of respiration.

Riffle A section of stream channel characterized at low flow by fast, shallow flow. Generally contains relatively coarse bedload particles.

Rock (engineering) Any earth material that has to be blasted in order to be removed.

Rock (geologic) An aggregate of a mineral or minerals.

Rock cycle A group of processes that produce igneous, metamorphic, and sedimentary rocks.

Sand Grains of sediment having a size between 1/16 and 2 mm in diameter; often sediment composed of quartz particles of the above size.

Sand dune A ridge or hill of sand formed by wind action.

Savannah An area with trees scattered widely among dense grasses.

Secondary enrichment A weathering process of sulfide ore deposits that may concentrate the desired minerals.

Secondary treatment (of waste water) Use of biologic processes to degrade waste water in a treatment facility.

Seismic Referring to vibrations in Earth produced by earthquakes.

Silicate minerals The most important group of rock-forming minerals.

Silt Sediment between 1/16 and 1/256 mm in diameter.

Sinkhole A surface depression formed by the solution of limestone or the collapse over a subterranean void such as a cave.

Soil The top layer of a land surface where the rocks have been weathered to small particles. Soils are made up of inorganic particles of many sizes, from small clay particles to large sand grains. Many soils also include dead organic material.

Soil (in engineering) Earth material that can be removed without blasting.

Soil (in soil science) Earth material modified by biological, chemical, and physical processes such that the material will support rooted plants.

Soil horizon Layer in soil (A, B, C) that differs from another layer in chemical, physical, and biological properties.

Solar cell (photovoltaic) Device that directly converts light into electricity.

Solar collector Device for collecting and storing solar energy. For example, home water heating is done by flat panels consisting of a glass cover plate over a black background upon which water is circulated through tubes. Short-wave solar radiation enters the glass and is absorbed by the black background. As long-wave radiation is emitted from the black material, it cannot escape through the glass, so the water in the circulating tubes is heated up, typically to temperatures of 38° to 93°C.

Solar energy Collecting and using energy from the sun directly.

Solar pond Shallow pond filled with water and used to generate relatively low-temperature water.

Solar power tower A system of collecting solar energy that delivers the energy to a central location where the energy is used to produce electric power.

Species A group of individuals capable of interbreeding.

Stable equilibrium A condition in which a system will remain if undisturbed and to which it will return when displaced.

Steady state When input equals output in a system, there is no net change and the system is said to be in a steady state. A bathtub with water flowing in and out at the same rate maintains the same water level and is in steady state. Compare with *equilibrium*.

Stress Force per unit area. May be compression, tension, or shear.

Subduction A process in which one lithospheric plate descends beneath another.

Subsidence A sinking, settling, or otherwise lowering of parts of the crust of Earth.

Symbiosis A living together of individuals of two different species that is beneficial to both. Obligatory symbiosis is called *mutualism;* non-obligatory symbiosis is called *protocooperation*.

Synergism Cooperative action of different substances such that the combined effect is greater than the sum of the effects taken separately.

Tectonic cycle The processes that change Earth's crust, producing external forms such as ocean basins, continents, and mountains.

Tertiary treatment (of waste water) Advanced form of waste-water treatment involving chemical treatment or advanced filtration. An example is chlorination of water.

Thermal (heat) energy) The energy of the random motion of atoms and molecules.

Thermodynamics, First Law of A law that states that energy is always conserved. That is, energy is never created or destroyed but only changes form.

Thermodynamics, Second Law of A law that states that, in any real process, energy always tends to go from a more usable form to a less usable form. That is, as energy transformations take place, the system goes from a state that is relatively ordered to one that is relatively disordered, or more random, and in which less of the energy is available for useful work.

Toxic Harmful, deadly, or poisonous.

Trophic level In an ecological community, all the organisms that are the same number of food chain steps from the primary source of energy. For example, in a grassland, the green grasses are on the first trophic level; grasshoppers on the second, birds that feed on grasshoppers on the third; and so forth.

Tundra The treeless land area in alpine and arctic areas, characterized by plants of low stature and including bare areas without any plants and covered areas with lichens, mosses, grasses, sedges, and small flowering plants, including low shrubs.

Unified soil classification system A classification of soils, widely used in engineering practice, based upon the amount of coarse particles, fine particles, or organic material.

Uniformitarianism The principle that processes that operate today operated in the past. Therefore, observations of processes today can explain events that occurred in the past and leave evidence, for example, in the fossil record or in geologic formations.

Water budget Inputs and outputs of water for a particular system (a drainage basin, region, continent, or the entire Earth).

Watershed An area of land that forms the drainage of a stream or river. If a drop of rain falls anywhere within a watershed, it can flow out only through the same stream.

Water table The surface that divides the zone of aeration from the zone of saturation. The surface below which all the pore space in rocks is saturated with water.

Weathering Changes that take place in rocks and minerals at or near the surface of Earth in response to physical, chemical, and biological changes. The physical, chemical, and biological breakdown of rocks and minerals.

Wilderness An area unaffected now or in the past by human activities, and without noticeable presence of human beings.

Work (physics) Force times the distance through which it acts.

Zone of aeration The zone or layer above the water table in which some water may be suspended or moving in a downward migration toward the water table or laterally toward a discharge point.

Zone of saturation Zone or layer below the water table in which all the pore space of rock or soil is saturated.

Acknowledgments

ALGERMISSEN, S. T., and PERKINS, D. M. 1976. U.S. Geological Survey Open File Report 76–416.

AMERICAN CHEMICAL SOCIETY, SUBCOMMITTEE ON ENVIRONMENTAL IMPROVEMENT, in *Cleaning our environment—The chemical basis for action*. Washington, D.C.: American Chemical Society, 1969, p. 107.

AMERICAN NUCLEAR SOCIETY. 1976. *Nuclear power and the environment: Questions and answers*. Hinsdale, Ill.: American Nuclear Society.

ANTHES, R. A.; CAHIR, J. J.; FRASER, A. B.; and PANOFSKY, H. A. 1981. *The atmosphere*. 3rd ed. Columbus, Ohio: Charles E. Merrill.

AUSTRALIA, INQUIRY INTO WHALES AND WHALING. 1979. *The whaling question: The inquiry by Sir Sidney Frost of Australia*. San Francisco: Friends of the Earth.

AWRAMIK, S. M. 1981. The pre-Phanerozoic biosphere—three billion years of crises and opportunities. In *Biotic crises in ecological and evolutionary time*, ed. M. H. Nitecki, pp. 83–102. New York: Academic Press.

BAKER, V. R. 1976. Hydrogeomorphic methods for the regional evaluation of flood hazards. *Environmental Geology* 1: 261–81.

BARR, T. N. 1981. The world food situation and global grain prospects. *Science* 214: 1087.

BAUMOL, W. J., and OATES, W. E. 1979. *Economics, environmental policy, and the quality of life*. Englewood Cliffs, N.J.: Prentice-Hall.

BELL, F. W. 1978. *Food from the sea: The economics and politics of ocean fisheries*. Boulder, Colo.: Westview Press.

BILLINGS, W. D. 1970. *Plants, man, and the ecosystem*. 2nd ed. Belmont, Calif.: Wadsworth.

BOCKSTOCE, J. R., and BOTKIN, D. B. 1980. *The historical status and reduction of the western Arctic bowhead whale* (Balaena mysticetus) *population by the pelagic whaling industry, 1848–1914*. New Bedford, Conn.: Dartmouth Historical Society.

BOLIN, B.; DEGENS, E. T.; KEMPE, S.; and KETNER, P., eds. 1979. *The global carbon cycle*. New York: Wiley.

BORNE, A. G. 1964. Birth of an island. *Discovery* 25: 16.

BORRIE, W. D. 1970. *The growth and control of*

world population. London: Weidenfeld and Nicolson.

BOWEN, H. J. M. 1966. *Trace elements in biochemistry.* New York: Academic Press.

BREW, D. A. 1974. *Environmental impact analysis: The example of the proposed Trans-Alaska Pipeline.* U.S. Geological Survey Circular 695.

BROBST, D. A., and PRATT, W. P., eds. 1973. *United States mineral resources.* U.S. Geological Survey Professional Paper 820.

BUDYKO, M. I. 1974. *Climate and life.* (English edition edited by D. H. Miller.) New York: Academic Press.

BURCHFIEL, B. C.; FOSTER, R. J.; KELLER, E. A.; MELHORN, W. N.; BROOKINS, D. G.; MINTZ, L. W.; and THURMAN, H. V.. 1982. *Physical geology: The structures and processes of the Earth.* Columbus, Ohio: Charles E. Merrill.

CALIFORNIA ENERGY COMMISSION. 1980. *Comparative evaluation of nontraditional energy resources.* Sacramento: California Energy Commission.

CANADA TODAY. 1981. *How many more lakes have to die?* Vol. 2, No. 2.

CHAIKEN, E. I.; POLONCSIK, S.; and WILSON, C. D. 1973. Muskegon sprays sewage effluents on land. *Civil Engineering* 43: 49–53.

CHANLETT, E. T. 1979. *Environmental protection.* 2nd ed. New York: McGraw-Hill.

CLARK, C. W. 1967. *Population growth and land use.* New York: Macmillan, St. Martin's Press.

————.1973. The economics of overexploitation. *Science* 181: 630–34.

COMMITTEE FOR THE GLOBAL ATMOSPHERIC RESEARCH PROGRAM. 1975. *Understanding climatic change: A program for action.* Washington, D.C.: National Academy of Sciences.

CORNING, R. V. 1975. *Virginia Wildlife,* February, pp. 6–8.

COUNCIL OF STATE GOVERNMENTS, TASK FORCE ON NATURAL RESOURCES AND LAND USE INFORMATION AND TECHNOLOGY. 1976. *Land use policy and program analysis.* Lexington, Ky.: Council of State Governments.

COUNCIL ON ENVIRONMENTAL QUALITY. 1970. *Ocean dumping: A national policy.*

————.1973. *Environmental quality.*

————.1978. *Progress in environmental quality.*

————.1979. *Environmental quality.*

————.1983. *Environmental quality—1983.*

COUNCIL ON ENVIRONMENTAL QUALITY. 1975. *Energy alternatives: A comparative analysis.* Prepared by the Science and Public Policy Program, University of Oklahoma, Norman.

COUNCIL ON ENVIRONMENTAL QUALITY and THE DEPARTMENT OF STATE. 1980. *The global 2000 report to the President: Entering the twenty-first century.* Vols. 1 and 2.

COX, C. B. 1985. *The buried threat.* California Senate Office of Research, No. 115–5.

COX, C. B.; HEALEY, I. N.; and MOORE, P. D. 1973. *Biogeography.* New York: Halsted Press.

CRANDELL, D. R., and MULLINEAUX, D. R. 1975. Techniques and rationale of volcanic hazards. *Environmental Geology* 1: 23–32.

CRANDELL, D. R., and WALDRON, H. H. 1969. Volcanic hazards in the Cascade Range. In *Geologic hazards and public problems, conference proceedings,* eds. R. Olsen and M. Wallace, pp. 5–18. Office of Emergency Preparedness, Region 7.

CUSHING, D. 1975 *Fisheries resources of the sea and their management.* New York: Oxford University Press.

DAVIS, F. F. 1972. Urban ore. *California Geology,* May, pp. 99–112.

DAVIS, M. B. 1981. Quaternary history and the stability of forest communities. In *Forest succession: Concepts and applications,* eds. D. C. West; H. H. Shugart; and D. B. Botkin, pp. 132–53. New York: Springer-Verlag.

DELWICHE, C. C., and LIKENS, G. E. 1977. Biological response to fossil fuel combustion products. In *Global chemical cycles and their alterations by man,* ed. W. Stumm, pp. 73–88. Berlin: Abakon Verlagsgesellschaft.

DESMOND, A. 1962. How many people have ever lived on Earth? *Population Bulletin* 18: 1–19.

DESSENS, J. 1962. Man-made tornadoes. *Nature* 193: 13.

————.1964. Man-made thunderstorms. *Discovery* 25: 40.

DEWEY, J. F. 1972. Plate tectonics. *Scientific American* 22: 56–58. Copyright © 1972 by Scientific American, Inc. All rights reserved.

DRAKE, C. L. 1972. Future considerations concerning geodynamics. *American Association of Petroleum Geologists Bulletin* 56: 260–68.

DUNCAN, D. C., and SWANSON, V. E. 1965. *Organic-rich shale of the United States and world land areas.* U.S. Geological Survey Circular 523.

DUNN, T., and LEOPOLD, L. B. 1978. *Water in environmental planning.* San Francisco: W. H. Freeman.

EDMONSON, W. T. 1975. Fresh water pollution. In *Environment: Resources, pollution, and society,* ed. W. M. Murdoch, pp. 250–71. Sunderland, Mass.: Sinauer.

EHRLICH, P. R.; EHRLICH, A. H.; and HOLDREN, J. P. 1977. *Ecoscience: Population, resources, environment.* 3rd ed. San Francisco: W. H. Freeman.

EISENBERG, R. M. 1966. The regulation of density in a natural population of the pond snail *Lymnaea elodes. Ecology* 47: 889–906.

EKDAHL, C. A., and KEELING, C. D. 1973. Atmospheric carbon dioxide and radiocarbon in the natural carbon cycle: 1. Quantitative deductions from records at Mauna Loa Observatory and at the South Pole. In *Carbon and the biosphere,* eds. G. M. Woodwell and E. V. Pecan, pp. 51–85. Brookhaven National Laboratory Symposium No. 24. Oak Ridge, Tenn.: Technical Information Service.

ESTES, J. A., and PALMISANO, J. F. 1974. Sea otters: Their role in structuring nearshore communities. *Science* 185: 1058–60.

EVANS, D. M. 1966. Man-made earthquakes in Denver. *Geotimes* 10: 11–18.

FARALLONES INSTITUTE. 1979. *The integral urban house.* San Francisco: Sierra Club.

FERRIANS, O. J., Jr.; KACHADOORIAN, R.; and GREENE, G. W. 1969. *Permafrost and related engineering problems in Alaska.* U.S. Geological Survey Paper 678.

FISKE, R. S., and KOYANAGI, R. Y. 1968. *The December 1965 eruption of Kilauea Volcano, Hawaii.* U.S. Geological Survey Professional Paper 607.

FOOD AND AGRICULTURE ORGANIZATION OF THE UNITED NATIONS. 1978. *Mammals in the seas.* Report of the FAO Advisory Committee on Marine Resources Research, Working Party on Marine Mammals. FAO Fisheries Series 5, vol. 1. Rome: FAO.

FOSTER, R. J. 1983. *Physical geology.* 4th ed. Columbus, Ohio: Charles E. Merrill.

FOWLER, C. W.; BUNDERSON, W. T.; CHERRY, M. R.; RYEL, R. J.; and STEELE, B. B. 1980. *Comparative population dynamics of large mammals: A search for management criteria.* National Technical Information Service Publication PB80–178627. Washington, D.C.: U.S. Department of Commerce.

FOWLER, J. M. 1978. Energy and the environment. In *Perspectives on energy,* 2nd ed., eds. L. C. Ruedisili and M. W. Firebaugh, pp. 11–28. New York: Oxford University Press.

FOXWORTHY, G. L. 1978. Nassau County, Long Island, New York—Water problems in humid country. In *Nature to be commanded,* eds. G. D. Robinson and A. M. Spieker, pp. 55–68. U.S. Geological Survey Professional Paper 950.

FREDRIKSEN, R. L. 1971. Comparative chemical water quality—Natural and disturbed streams following logging and slash burning. In *Forest land use and stream environment,* pp. 125–37. Corvallis: Oregon State University.

FREED, V. H.; CHIOU, C. T.; and HAGUE, R. 1977. Chemodynamics: Transport and behavior of chemicals in the environment—A problem in environmental health. *Environmental Health Perspectives* 20: 55–77.

FROELICH, A. J.; GARNAAS, A. D.; and VAN DRIEL, J. N. 1978. Franconia area, Fairfax County, Virginia: Planning a new community in an urban setting—Lehigh. In *Nature to be commanded,* eds. G. D. Robinson and A. M. Spieker, pp. 69–89. U.S. Geological Survey Professional Paper 950.

GARRELS, R. M.; MacKENZIE, F. T.; and HUNT, C. 1975. *Chemical cycles and the global environment.* Los Altos, Calif.: William Kaufmann.

GARRITY, T. A., and NITZSCHKE, E. T. 1968. *Water law atlas: A water law primer.* Circular 95. Socorro, N.M.: State Bureau of Mines and Mineral Resources.

GATES, D. M. 1965. Heat, radiant and sensible. *Meteorological Monographs* 6: 1–26.

—————.1980. *Biophysical ecology.* New York: Springer-Verlag.

GIDDINGS, J. C. 1973. *Chemistry, man, and environmental change: An integrated approach.* San Francisco: Canfield Press.

GODFREY, P. J., and GODFREY, M. M. 1973. Comparison of ecological and geomorphic interactions between altered and unaltered barrier island systems in North Carolina. In *Coastal geomorphology,* ed. D. R. Coates, pp. 239–58. Binghamton: State University of New York.

GRAHAM, H. D. 1955. Fire whirlwinds. *Bulletin of the American Meteorological Society* 36: 99.

GRAUNT, J. 1662. *Natural and political observations made upon the bills of mortality.* London: Roycraft. (Reprinted in 1973 with introduction by P. Laslett by Gregg International Publishers, Ltd., Germany.)

HANSON, W. G. 1967. Cesium-137 in Alaskan lichens, caribou, and Eskimos. *Health Physics* 13: 383–89.

HAUB, C. 1981. *1981 world population data sheet.* Washington, D.C.: Population Reference Bureau.

HAUPT, A., and KANE, T. T. 1978. *The Population Reference Bureau's population handbook.* Washington, D.C.: Population Reference Bureau.

HERSEY, J. R. 1946. *Hiroshima.* New York: Knopf.

HIDY, G. M., and BROCK, J. R. 1971. *Topics in current aerosol research.* New York: Pergamon Press.

HUBBERT, M. K. 1962. *Energy resources.* Report to the Committee on Natural Resources of the National Academy of Sciences—National Research Council. Washington, D.C.: National Academy of Sciences—National Research Council.

HUNT, C. B., 1967. *Physiognomy of the United States.* San Francisco: W. H. Freeman.

———.1974. *Natural regions of the United States and Canada.* San Francisco: W. H. Freeman.

HUTCHINSON, G. E. 1950. Survey of contemporary knowledge of biogeochemistry. 3. The biogeochemistry of vertebrate excretion. *Bulletin of the American Museum of Natural History* 96: 481–82.

———, ed. 1970. Ianula: An account of the history and development of the Lago di Monterosi, Latium, Italy. *Transactions of the American Philosophical Society* 60: 1–178.

———. 1973. Eutrophication. *American Scientist* 61: 269–79.

———. 1978. *An introduction to population ecology.* New Haven, Conn.: Yale University Press.

INDIANA STATE BOARD OF HEALTH.

IRWIN, J. H., and MORTON, R. B. 1969. *Hydrogeologic information on the Glorieta Sandstone and the Ogallala Formation in the Oklahoma Panhandle and adjoining areas as related to underground waste disposal.* U.S. Geological Survey Circular 630.

JANERICK, D. T.; BURNETT, W. S.; FECK, G.; HOFF, M.; NASCA, P.; POLEDNAK, A. P.; GREENWALD, P.; and VIANNA, N. 1981. Cancer incidence in the Love Canal area. *Science* 212: 1404–7.

JENSEN, W. A., and SALISBURY, F. B. 1972. *Botany: An ecological approach.* Belmont, Calif.: Wadsworth.

JORDAN, P. A.; BOTKIN, D. B.; and WOLF, M. I. 1971. Biomass dynamics in a moose population. *Ecology* 52: 147–52.

KASPERSON, R. E. 1977. Water re-use: Need prospect. In *Water re-use and the cities,* eds. R. E. Kasperson and J. X. Kasperson, pp. 3–25, Hanover, N.H.: University Press of New England.

KATES, R. W., and PIJAWKA, D. 1977. Reconstruction following disaster. In *From rubble to monument: The pace of reconstruction,* eds. J. E. Haas; R. W. Kates, and M. J. Bowden. Cambridge, Mass.: MIT Press.

LANDSBERG, H. 1947. Fire storms resulting from bombing conflagrations. *Bulletin of the American Meteorological Society* 28: 72.

LANGER, W. L. 1964. The Black Death. *Scientific American* 210: 114–21.

LAVIGNE, D. M.; BARCHARD, W.; INNES, S.; and ORITSLAND, N. A. 1976. *Pinniped bioenergetics.* ACMRR/MM/SC/112. Rome: Food and Agriculture Organization of the United Nations (FAO).

LAWS, R. M.; PARKER, I. S. C.; and JOHNSTONE, R. C. B. 1975. *Elephants and their habitats.* Oxford, England: Clarendon Press.

LECLERC, G. L. (Count de Buffon). 1812. *Natural history, general and particular.* (Translated by W. Smellie.) London: C. Wood.

LEOPOLD, L. B. 1968. *Hydrology for urban land planning.* U.S. Geological Survey Circular 559.

LIKENS, G. E.; BORMANN, F. H.; PIERCE, R. S.;

EATON, J. S.; and JOHNSON, N. M. 1977. *The biogeochemistry of a forested ecosystem.* New York: Springer-Verlag.

LINDORFF, D. E. 1979. Ground-water pollution: A status report. *Ground Water* 17(1): 9–17.

LINDORFF, D. E., and CARTWRIGHT, K. 1977. *Ground-water contamination problems and remedial action.* Illinois State Geological Survey Environmental Geology Notes, No. 81.

LINSLEY, R. K., JR.; KOHLER, M. A.; and PAULHUS, J. L. H. 1975. *Hydrology for engineers.* 2nd ed. New York: McGraw-Hill.

LIPPMANN, M., and SCHLESINGER, R. B. 1979. *Chemical contamination in the human environment.* New York: Oxford University Press.

LOS ALAMOS SCIENTIFIC LABORATORY. 1978. LASL 78–24.

LOTKA, A. J. 1956. *Elements of mathematical biology.* New York: Dover.

LOVINS, A. B. 1979. *Soft energy paths: Towards a durable peace.* New York: Harper & Row.

MacARTHUR, R. H. 1958. Population ecology of some warblers of northeastern coniferous forests. *Ecology* 39: 599–619.

MacARTHUR, R. H., and CONNELL, J. H. 1966. *The biology of populations.* New York: Wiley.

MacARTHUR, R. H., and WILSON, E. O. 1963. An equilibrium theory of insular zoogeography. *Evolution* 17: 373–87.

MACKINTOSH, N. A. 1965. *The stocks of whales.* London: Fishing News Books, Ltd.

MADER, G. G.; SPANGLE, W. E.; BLAIR, M. L.; MEEHAN, R. L.; and BILODEAU, S. W. 1980. *Land-use planning after earthquakes.* Portola Valley, Calif.: William Spangle and Associates.

MARGULIS, L., and LOVELOCK, J. E. 1974. Biological modulation of the Earth's atmosphere. *Icarus* 21: 471–89.

MARGULIS, L., and SCHWARTZ, K. V. 1982. *The five kingdoms.* San Francisco: W. H. Freeman.

MARSH, W. M., and DOZIER, J. 1981. *Landscape.* New York: Wiley.

MARTIN, P. S. 1973. The discovery of America. *Science* 179: 969–74.

MARUYAMA, M. 1963. The second cybernetics: Deviation-amplifying mutual causal processes. *American Scientist* 51: 164–79.

MATTHEWS, W. H., et al., eds. 1971. *Man's impact on the climate.* Cambridge, Mass.: MIT Press.

MATHEWSON, C. C., and CASTLEBERRY, J. P., II. (undated). *Expansive soils: Their engineering geology.* College Station: Texas A & M University.

MATRAS, J. 1973. *Populations and societies.* Englewood Cliffs, N.J.: Prentice-Hall.

McHARG, I. L. 1971. *Design with nature.* Garden City, N.Y.: Doubleday.

McKELVEY, V. E. 1976. *Earthquake prediction—Opportunity to avert disaster.* U.S. Geological Survey Circular 729.

MELHORN, W. N.; KELLER, E. A.; and McBANE, R. A. 1975 *Landscape aesthetics defined (land system): Application to fluvial environments.* Water Resources Research Center Technical Report No. 37. Lafayette, Ind.: Purdue University.

MILLER, G. T., JR. 1985. *Living in the environment: An introduction to environmental science.* 4th ed. Belmont, Calif.: Wadsworth.

MILLER, P. C.; BRADBURY, D. E.; HAJEK, E.; LA MARCHE, V.; and THROWER, N. J. W. 1977. Past and present environment. In *Convergent evolution in Chile and California,* ed. H. A. Mooney, pp. 27–72. Stroudsburg, Pa.: Dowden, Hutchinson & Ross.

MUNIZ, I. P.; LEIVESTAD, H.; GJESSING, E.; JORANGER, E.; and SVALASTOG, D. 1976. *Acid precipitation: Effects on forest and fish.* SNSF Project. IR 13/75. As, Norway: Government of Norway.

MUROZIMI, M.; CHOW, T. J.; and PATTERSON, C. 1969. Chemical concentration of pollutant lead aerosol; terrestrial dusts; and sea salts in Greenland and Antarctic snow strata. *Geochimica et Cosmochimica Acta* 33: 1247–94.

MURPHY, J. E. 1966. *Sulfur content of United States coals.* U.S. Bureau of Mines Information Circular 8312.

NASH, R. 1977. Do rocks have rights? *The Center Magazine* 10: 2–12.

NATIONAL OCEANIC AND ATMOSPHERIC ADMINISTRATION (NOAA). 1977. Earth's crustal plate boundaries: Energy and mineral resources. *California Geology* 30: 108–9.

NATIONAL PARK SERVICE. 1984. *General management plan, Cape Hatteras National Seashore.*

NATIONAL RESEARCH COUNCIL, ADVISORY COMMITTEE ON THE BIOLOGICAL EFFECTS OF IONIZING RADIATIONS. 1972a. *The effects on pop-*

ulations of exposure to low levels of ionizing radiation. Washington, D.C.: National Academy of Sciences—National Research Council.

NATIONAL RESEARCH COUNCIL, COMMITTEE ON GEOLOGICAL SCIENCES. 1972b. *The Earth and human affairs.* San Francisco: Canfield Press.

NEIBURGER, M.; EDINGER, J. G.; and BONNER, W. D. 1973. *Understanding our atmospheric environment.* San Francisco: W. H. Freeman.

NEWMAN, J. R. 1980. *Effects of air emissions on wildlife resources.* U.S. Fish and Wildlife Service, Biological Services Program, National Power Plant Team. FWS/OBS-80/40. Washington, D.C.: U.S. Fish and Wildlife Service.

NICHOLS, D. R., and BUCHANAN-BANKS, J. M. 1974. *Seismic hazards and land-use planning.* U.S. Geological Survey Circular 690.

NOBLE, E. R., and NOBLE, G. A. 1976. *Parasitology: The biology of animal parasites.* 4th ed. Philadelphia: Lea & Febiger.

NORTH CAROLINA COASTAL RESOURCES COMMISSION. 1975. *State guidelines for local planning in the coastal area under the Coastal Area Management Act of 1974.* Raleigh, North Carolina.

ODÉN, S. 1976. The acidity problem—An outline of concepts. *Water, Air, and Soil Pollution.* 6: 137–66.

OFFICE OF INDUSTRY RELATIONS. 1974. *The nuclear industry: 1974.*

OFFICE OF TECHNOLOGY ASSESSMENT. 1980. *Energy from biological processes.* OTA-E-124.

————. 1984. Balancing the risks. *Weatherwise* 37: 241–9.

PARIZEK, R. R., and MYERS, E. A. 1968. Recharge of groundwater from renovated sewage effluent by spray irrigation. *Proceedings of the Fourth American Water Resources Conference,* pp. 425–43.

PARK, C. F., Jr., 1968. *Affluence in jeopardy: Minerals and the political economy.* San Francisco: Freeman, Cooper, and Co.

PARK, T. 1948. Experimental studies of interspecies competition. 1. Competition between populations of the flour beetles, *Tribolium confusum* Duval and *Tribolium castaneum* Herbst. *Ecological Monographs* 18: 265–308.

PATRICK, C. H. 1977. Trace substances and electric power generation: The need for epidemiological studies to determine health problems. In *Conference on trace substances in environmental health,* pp. 63–69. Columbia, Mo.: Conference on Trace Substances in Environmental Health.

PAYNE, R. 1968. Among wild whales. *The New York Zoological Society Newsletter.*

PEARL, R. 1932. The influence of density of population upon egg production in *Drosophila melanogaster. Journal of Experimental Zoology* 63: 57–84.

PERSSON, R. 1974. *World forest resources.* Stockholm: Royal College of Forestry of Sweden.

PIERROU, U. 1976. The global phosphorus cycle. In *Nitrogen, phosphorus, and sulfur—Global cycles,* eds. B. H. Svensson and R. Soderlund, pp. 75–88. Stockholm: Ecological Bulletin.

PIMENTEL, D.; TERHUNE, E. C.; DYSON-HUDSON, R.; ROCHEREAU, S.; SAMIS, R.; SMITH, E. A., DENMAN, D.; REIFSCHNEIDER, D.; and SHEPARD, M. 1976. Land degradation: Effects on food and energy resources. *Science* 194: 149–55.

PRESS, F. 1975. Earthquake prediction. *Scientific American* 232: 14–23.

RICHARDS, J. L., AND ASSOCIATES LTD., and LABRECQUE, VERINA AND ASSOCIATES. 1973. *Snow disposal study for the National Capital Area technical discussion.* Report for the Committee on Snow Disposal, Ottawa, Ontario, Canada.

ROTTY, R. M. 1976. *Energy and the climate.* Institute for Energy Analysis. Oak Ridge Associated Universities, Oak Ridge, Tennessee.

RUGG, D. S. 1979. *Spatial foundations of urbanization.* 2nd ed. Dubuque, Iowa: William C. Brown.

SCHLÜTER, O. 1952. *Die Siedlungsräume Mitteleuropas in frühgeschichtlicher Zeit,* Part I. Hamburg, Germany.

SCHNEIDER, W. J. 1970. *Hydraulic implications of solid-waste disposal.* U.S. Geological Survey Circular 601F.

SHEFFER, V. B. 1951. The rise and fall of the reindeer herd. *Scientific Monthly* 73: 356–62.

————. 1976. Exploring the lives of whales. *National Geographic* 150: 752–66.

SKINNER, S. P.; GENTRY, J. B.; and GIESY, J. P., Jr. 1976. Cadmium dynamics in terrestrial food webs of a coal ash basin. In *Environmental chemistry and cycling processes symposium,* sponsored by U.S. Energy Research and Development Administration and the University of Georgia, 28 April—May 1976, Augusta, Georgia.

SLOBODKIN, L. B. 1980. *Growth and regulation of animal populations.* New York: Dover Press. (First published in 1961 by Holt, Rinehart and Winston, New York.)

SLOSSON, J. E., and KROHN, J. P. 1977. Effective building codes. *California Geology* 30: 136–319.

SNEKVIK, E. 1970. *Norwegian directorate for game and freshwater fish.* Unpublished report.

SOIL CONSERVATION SERVICE, SOIL SURVEY STAFF. 1975. *Soil taxonomy.* Agricultural Handbook No. 436.

SOLLEY, W. B.; CHASE, E. B.; and MANN, W. B., IV. 1983. *Estimated use of water in the United States in 1980.* U.S. Geological Survey Circular 1001.

SPIRN, A. W. 1984. *The granite garden: Urban nature and human design.* New York: Basic Books.

STEINHART, J. S.; HANSON, M. E.; GATES, R. W.; DEWINKEL, C. C.; BRIODY, K.; THORNSJO, M.; and KAMBALA, S. 1978. A low-energy scenario for the United States: 1975–2000. In *Perspectives on energy,* 2nd ed., eds. L. C. Ruedisili and M. W. Firebaugh, pp. 553–80. New York: Oxford University Press.

STODDARD, C. H. 1978. *Essentials of forestry practice.* 3rd ed. New York: Wiley.

STRAHLER, A. N. 1973. *Introduction to physical geography.* 3rd ed. New York: Wiley.

SULLIVAN. P. M.; STANCZYK, M. H.; and SPENDBUE, M. J. 1973. *Resource recovery from raw urban refuse.* U.S. Bureau of Mines Report of Investigations 7760.

SWEENEY, J. G. 1977. *Themes in American painting.* Grand Rapids, Mich.: Grand Rapids Art Museum.

SYMONS, G. E. 1968. Water re-use: What do we mean? *Water and Waste Engineering* 5: 40–41.

TARBUCK, E. J., and LUTGENS, F. K.. 1985. *Earth Science.* Columbus, Ohio: Charles E. Merrill.

TAYLOR, R. J., et al. 1973. Convective activity above a large-scale brush fire. *Journal of Applied Meteorology* 12: 1144.

THOMAS, W. L., Jr., ed. 1974. *Man's role in changing the face of the Earth.* 9th ed. Chicago: The University of Chicago Press.

THORARINSSON, S., and VONNEGUT, B. 1964. Whirlwinds produced by the eruption of Surtsey volcano. *Bulletin of the American Meteorological Society* 45: 440.

TRIMBLE, S. W. 1969. Culturally accelerated sedimentation on the middle Georgia Piedmont. Master's thesis, University of Georgia, Athens, Georgia.

UNIVERSITY OF MAINE and MAINE DEPARTMENT OF HUMAN SERVICES. 1983. Radon in water and air. *Resource Highlights,* February.

U.S. BUREAU OF THE CENSUS. 1979. *Statistical abstract of the United States.* 100th ed. Washington, D.C.: U.S. Department of Commerce.

————. 1980. *1980 Census of population.*

U.S. BUREAU OF MINES. 1971. *Strippable reserves of bituminous coal and lignite in the United States.* U.S. Bureau of Mines Information Circular 8531.

————. 1979. *Mining and mineral policy 1979.*

U.S. DEPARTMENT OF COMMERCE. 1970. *Some devastating North Atlantic hurricanes of the 20th century.*

U.S. DEPARTMENT OF ENERGY. 1978. *The United States magnetic fusion energy program.* DOE/ET-0072.

————. 1979a. *Annual report to Congress.*

————. 1979b. *Environmental development plan for magnetic fusion.* DOE/EDP-0052.

————. 1980. *Magnetic fusion energy.* DOE/ER-0059.

U.S. ENERGY AND RESEARCH DEVELOPMENT ADMINISTRATION. 1976. *Advance nuclear reactors: An introduction.* ERDA-76–107.

————. 1980. *Guidelines for public reporting of daily air quality—Pollutant Standard Index.*

U.S. ENVIRONMENTAL PROTECTION AGENCY. 1980. *Acid rain.*

U.S. FOREST SERVICE. 1980. *An assessment of the forest and range land situation in the United States.*

U.S. GEOLOGICAL SURVEY. 1975. *Mineral resource perspectives 1975.* Professional Paper 940.

————. 1984. *Yearbook, fiscal year 1983.*

U.S. SECRETARY OF THE INTERIOR. 1975. *Mining and mineral policy, 1975.*

————. 1979. *Mining and mineral policy, 1979.*

————. 1980a. *Principles of a resource/reserve classification for minerals.* U.S. Geological Survey Circular 831.

————. 1980b. *Mining and mineral policy, 1980.*

VAN DER TAK, J.; HAUB, C.; and MURPHY, E. 1979. Our population predicament: A new look. *Population Bulletin* 34: 1–8.

WAGNER, A. A. 1957. *The use of the Unified Soil Classification System by the Bureau of Reclamation.* London: International Conference on Soil Mechanics and Foundation Engineering.

WALDBOTT, G. L. 1978. *Health effects of environmental pollutants.* 2nd ed. St. Louis: C. V. Mosby.

WALLACE, A. R. 1876. *The geographical distribution of animals.* New York: Hafner. (Reissued in 1962 in two volumes.)

WALLACE, R. E. 1974. *Goals, strategies and tasks of the earthquake hazard reduction program.* U.S. Geological Survey Circular 701.

WALTER, H. 1973. *The vegetation of the Earth.* New York: Springer-Verlag.

WATER RESOURCES COUNCIL. 1971. *Regulation of flood hazard areas to reduce flood losses.*

————. 1978. *The nation's water resources, 1975–2000.*

WAY, D. S. 1978. *Terrain analysis.* 2nd ed. Stroudsburg, Pa.: Dowden, Hutchinson & Ross.

WHITE, D. F., and WILLIAMS, D. L. 1975. Introduction. In *Assessment of geothermal resources of the United States—1975,* eds. D. F. White and D. L. Williams, pp. 1–4. U.S. Geological Survey Circular 726.

WHITE, G. F. 1980. Environment. *Science* 209: 183–90.

WHITE, G. F., and HAAS, J. E. 1975. *Assessment of research on natural hazards.* Cambridge, Mass.: The MIT Press.

WHITTAKER, R. H. 1970 . *Communities and ecosystems.* New York: Macmillan.

WHITTAKER, R. H., and LIKENS, G. E. 1973. Carbon in the biota. In *Carbon and the biosphere,* eds. G. M. Woodwell and E. V. Pecan, pp. 281–302. Brookhaven National Laboratory Symposium No. 24. Oak Ridge, Tenn.: Technical Information Service.

WHITTLE, K. J.; HARDY, R.; HOLDEN, A. V.; JOHNSTON, R.; and PRENTREATH, R. J. 1977. Occurrence and fate of organic and inorganic contaminants in marine animals. *Annals of the New York Academy of Science* 298: 47–79.

WILCOX, B. A. 1980. Insular ecology and conservation. In *Conservation biology,* eds. M. E. Soulé and B. A. Wilcox, pp. 95–117. Sunderland, Mass.: Sinauer.

WILLIAMSON, S. J. 1973. *Fundamentals of air pollution.* Reading, Mass.: Addison-Wesley.

WILSON, R. 1980. Risk/benefit analysis for toxic chemicals. *Ecotoxicology and Environmental Safety* 4: 370–83.

WOLMAN, M. G. 1967. A circle of sedimentation and erosion. *Geografiska Annaler* 49A: 386.

WOODWELL, G. M., and REBUCK, A. L. 1967. Effects of chronic gamma radiation on the structure and diversity of an oak-pine forest. *Ecological Monographs* 37: 53–69.

WORLD BANK. 1985. *Population change and economic development.* Oxford: Oxford University Press.

WRIGHT, R. F.; DALE, T.; GJESSING, E. G.; HENDREY, G. R.; HENRIKSEN, A.; JOHANNESSEN, M.; and MUNIZ, I. P. 1976. Impact of acid precipitation on freshwater ecosystems in Norway. *Water, Air, and Soil Pollution* 6: 438–99.

ZISWILER, V. 1967. *Extinct and vanishing species.* New York: Springer-Verlag.

PHOTO CREDITS

All photos copyrighted by the individuals or companies listed.

Rod Allin/Tom Stack and Associates, p. 87.

AP Laserphoto, photograph by Carlos Gonzalez, p. 534(b).

AP/Wide World Photos, p. 346(a, b).

Argonaut Press, "U.S.A. at Night," p. 569.

Daniel B. Botkin, Plate 2a, b, c; Plate 3a, b, c; Plate 4c; Plate 6a, b; Plate 8a, b; Plate 9 b, c; pp. 24, 77, 133, 139(c), 157(b, c), 166 (6.13c, 6.14).

Daniel S. Brody/Art Resource, pp. 483, 615.

Brookhaven National Laboratory, Plate 9a.

Canadian Embassy, p. 354.

CARE photo by Ron Burkard, p. 533.

Cheshire Books, p. 419.

Columbus Zoo, p. 147(c, e, f, g, h).

Steve Delaney/EPA, p. 314.

Environmental Science Services Administration, p. 62.

ERTS, Plate 14.

Florida State Department of Natural Resources, p. 157(d).

Food and Agriculture Organization, photographs by F. Botts, p. 261(a); C. Fornari, p. 263; F. Mattioli, p. 274(b); I. Velez, p. 277.

Jeff Foott/Foott Prints, pp. 215(a, b, c), 310.

C. H. Greenewalt, p. 84.

E. Hanumantharao/Tom Stack and Associates, p. 234.

Hawaii Volcanos National Park, Plate 7a.

Icelandic Geodetic Survey, p. 508(b).

International Society for Educational Information, Inc., p. 203.

Japan Information Center, Consulate General of Japan, New York, N.Y., p. 266.

John Deere Company, p. 284.

Edward A. Keller, Plate 10a, b; Plate 11a, b; Plate 15a, b; Plate 16; p. 470.

Kennecott Copper Corporation, pp. 468, 469.

Stephen Krasemann/DRK Photo, Plate 7c.

Library of Congress, pp. 574, 575.

Loeb Memorial Library, Harvard Graduate School of Design, p. 576.

Los Angeles Zoo, pp. 167(a, b, c), 207(a), 592.

L. Margulis, Plate 6c.

Michigan Department of Natural Resources, pp. 139(a), 312.

Gary Milburn/Tom Stack and Associates, p. 505.

Missouri Geological Society, photographs by J. D. Vineyard, p. 428(a, b).

Missouri Geological Survey, p. 481(a, b).

NASA Goddard Space Flight Center, Plate 5a, b.

New Hampshire, State of, p. 9 (1.2).

New York State Department of Commerce, p. 606.

New York State Department of Environmental Conservation, photograph by John George, p. 478.

NOAA/NESDIS, p. 523.

Orlando Sentinel Star, photograph by George Remaine, Plate 13a.

David Perry, pp. 160, 161, 254, 531, 579.

Rick Prebeg, pp. 128 (5.3), 147(d), 210.

Keith Ronnholm, Geophysics Program, University of Washington, p. 510(a, b, c).

Santa Barbara Natural History Museum, Plate 7b.

D. W. Schindler, p. 102.

Spencer Swanger/Tom Stack and Associates, p. 1.

Swiss National Tourist Office, p. 9 (1.1).

Herb Taylor/EPA Newsphoto/Art Resource, p. 500.

Tennessee Valley Authority, pp. 388, 560.

Shirley Valencia, p. 157(e).

Don Weaver, Plate 13b.

Westland National Park, New Zealand, Plate 4a, b.

Rex Weyler, Greenpeace Media, p. 227(b).

World Health Organization, photograph by W. Cutting, p. 261(b).

Wyoming Travel Commission, p. 248(b).

U.S. Air Force, p. 508(a).

U.S. Department of Agriculture: pp. 59, 375(a, b, c), photograph by R. S. Branstead, p. 394 (13.17); Forest Service, pp. 128 (5.4), 166(a, b); National Agricultural Library, U.S. Forest Service Photo Collection, pp. 139 (5.10b), 145(a, b); Soil Conservation Service, pp. 243, 282; photographs by R. W. Hufnagle, p. 274(a); E. W. Cole, p. 283(a); H. E. Alexander, 283(b); Tim McCabe, p. 287; Frank M. Roadman, p. 394 (13.18); W. B. Parker, p. 406.

U.S. Department of Energy, pp. 433, 440.

U.S. Fish and Wildlife Service, photograph by John Sarurs, p. 67.

U.S. Department of the Interior: Bureau of Reclamation photographs by Lyle C. Axthelm, p. 389; A. E. Turner, p. 529(a); Mel Davis, p. 529(b); Bureau of Sport Fisheries and Wildlife, 207(b); National Park Service, pp. 10, 248(a), 614; photographs by Jack Boucher, p. 539; Mike Patty, p. 624.

U.S. Geological Survey, pp. 534(a), 545; photographs by F. C. Whitmore, Jr., p. 384; Robert Frimmel, p. 511; F. O. Jones, p. 515; H. G. Wilshire, p. 558.

U.S. Windpower, Inc., photograph by Ed Linton, p. 295.

Index

WE VALUE YOUR OPINION—PLEASE SHARE IT WITH US

Merrill Publishing and our authors are most interested in your reactions to this textbook. Did it serve you well in the course? If it did, what aspects of the text were most helpful? If not, what didn't you like about it? Your comments will help us to write and develop better textbooks. We value your opinions and thank you for your help.

Text Title _____ Edition _____

Author(s) _____

Your Name (optional) _____

Address _____

City _____ State _____ Zip _____

School _____

Course Title _____

Instructor's Name _____

Your Major _____

Your Class Rank _____ Freshman _____ Sophomore _____ Junior _____ Senior

_____ Graduate Student

Were you required to take this course? _____ Required _____ Elective

Length of Course? _____ Quarter _____ Semester

1. Overall, how does this text compare to other texts you've used?

_____ Superior _____ Better Than Most _____ Average _____ Poor

2. Please rate the text in the following areas:

	Superior	Better Than Most	Average	Poor
Author's Writing Style	_____	_____	_____	_____
Readability	_____	_____	_____	_____
Organization	_____	_____	_____	_____
Accuracy	_____	_____	_____	_____
Layout and Design	_____	_____	_____	_____
Illustrations/Photos/Tables	_____	_____	_____	_____
Examples	_____	_____	_____	_____
Problems/Exercises	_____	_____	_____	_____
Topic Selection	_____	_____	_____	_____
Currentness of Coverage	_____	_____	_____	_____
Explanation of Difficult Concepts	_____	_____	_____	_____
Match-up with Course Coverage	_____	_____	_____	_____
Applications to Real Life	_____	_____	_____	_____

3. Circle those chapters you especially liked:
   1   2   3   4   5   6   7   8   9   10   11   12   13   14   15   16   17   18   19   20
   What was your favorite chapter? _____
   Comments:

4. Circle those chapters you liked least:
   1   2   3   4   5   6   7   8   9   10   11   12   13   14   15   16   17   18   19   20
   What was your least favorite chapter? _____
   Comments:

5. List any chapters your instructor did not assign. _____

6. What topics did your instructor discuss that were not covered in the text?_____

   _____

7. Were you required to buy this book? _____ Yes _____ No

   Did you buy this book new or used? _____ New _____ Used

   If used, how much did you pay? _____

   Do you plan to keep or sell this book? _____ Keep _____ Sell

   If you plan to sell the book, how much do you expect to receive? _____

   Should the instructor continue to assign this book? _____ Yes _____ No

8. Please list any other learning materials you purchased to help you in this course (e.g., study guide, lab manual).

   _____

9. What did you like most about this text? _____

   _____

10. What did you like least about this text? _____

    _____

11. General comments:

    May we quote you in our advertising? _____ Yes _____ No

    Please mail to: Boyd Lane
                      College Division, Research Department
                      Box 508
                      1300 Alum Creek Drive
                      Columbus, Ohio 43216

    Thank you!